$631 \div 6 = n$, $n = 105$ r1; 235

$408 \div 4 = n$, $n = 102$; 6.07×1

$6.07 \times 17 = n$, $n = 103.19$; 26

$\div 4 = n$, $n = 102$;

$n = 105$ r1; $235 \div 4$

$6.07 \times 17 = n$, $n =$

Math

ADVANTAGE

HARCOURT BRACE

Orlando • Atlanta • Austin • Boston • San Francisco • Chicago • Dallas • New York • Toronto • London

http://www.hbschool.com

Printed in the United States of America

ISBN 0-15-311438-X

4 5 6 7 8 9 10 048 2000 99

Senior Authors

Grace M. Burton
Chair, Department of Curricular Studies
Professor, School of Education
University of North Carolina at Wilmington
Wilmington, North Carolina

Evan M. Maletsky
Professor of Mathematics
Montclair State University
Upper Montclair, New Jersey

Authors

George W. Bright
Professor of Mathematics Education
The University of North Carolina at Greensboro
Greensboro, North Carolina

Sonia M. Helton
Professor of Childhood Education
Coordinator, College of Education
University of South Florida
St. Petersburg, Florida

Loye Y. (Mickey) Hollis
Professor of Mathematics Education
Director of Teacher Education and Undergraduate Programs
University of Houston
Houston, Texas

Howard C. Johnson
Dean of the Graduate School
Associate Vice Chancellor for Academic Affairs
Professor, Mathematics and Mathematics Education
Syracuse University
Syracuse, New York

Joyce C. McLeod
Visiting Professor
Rollins College
Winter Park, Florida

Evelyn M. Neufeld
Professor, College of Education
San Jose State University
San Jose, California

Vicki Newman
Classroom Teacher
McGaugh Elementary School
Los Alamitos Unified School District
Seal Beach, California

Terence H. Perciante
Professor of Mathematics
Wheaton College
Wheaton, Illinois

Karen A. Schultz
Associate Dean and Director of Graduate Studies and Research
Research Professor, Mathematics Education
College of Education
Georgia State University
Atlanta, Georgia

Muriel Burger Thatcher
Independent Mathematics Consultant
Mathematical Encounters
Pine Knoll Shores, North Carolina

Advisors

Anne R. Biggins
Speech-Language Pathologist
Fairfax County Public Schools
Fairfax, Virginia

Carolyn Gambrel
Learning Disabilities Teacher
Fairfax County Public Schools
Fairfax, Virginia

Lois Harrison-Jones
Education Consultant
Dallas, Texas

Asa G. Hilliard, III
Fuller E. Callaway Professor of Urban Education
Georgia State University
Atlanta, Georgia

Marsha W. Lilly
Secondary Mathematics Coordinator
Alief Independent School District
Alief, Texas

Judith Mayne Wallis
Elementary Language Arts/ Social Studies/Gifted Coordinator
Alief Independent School District
Houston, Texas

CONTENTS

USING WHOLE NUMBERS AND DECIMALS CHAPTERS 1–4

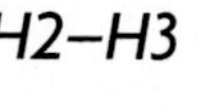

* **Algebra Readiness**

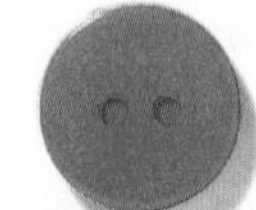

* **Algebra Readiness**

CHAPTER 5 Multiplying by One-Digit Numbers . . 72

Troubleshooting Lesson
Multiplying by One Digit
H8–H9

CHAPTER 6 Multiplying Larger Numbers 90

Troubleshooting Lesson
Estimating Products
H10–H11

* **Algebra Readiness**

CHAPTER 7 Dividing by One-Digit Numbers 108

Troubleshooting Lesson
Recording Division H12–H13

CHAPTER 8 Dividing by Two-Digit Numbers 126

Extension Lesson
Using the Calculator to Divide H34–H35

Chapters 5–8 ✓Checkpoint

* **Algebra Readiness**

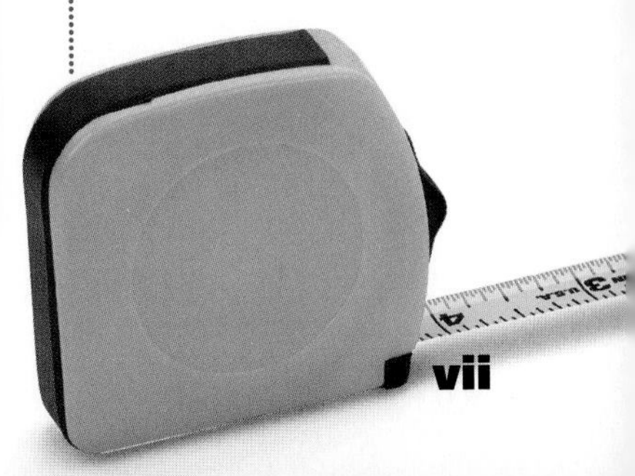

CHAPTER 9 Analyzing and Graphing Data 152

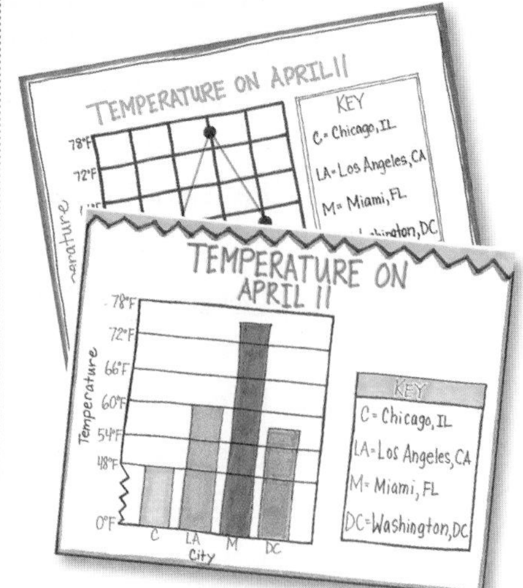

Extension Lesson
Interpreting Histograms
H36–H37

CHAPTER 10 Circle, Bar, and Line Graphs 170

Troubleshooting Lesson
Fractions: Parts of a Whole
H14–H15

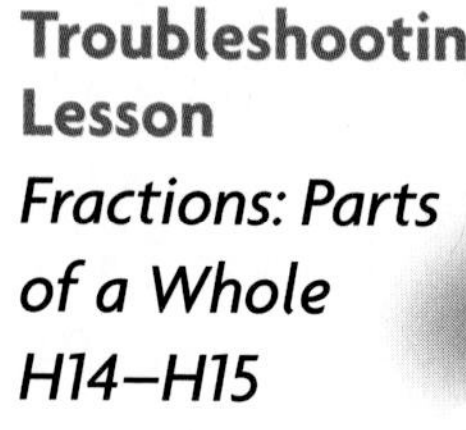

* **Algebra Readiness**

CHAPTER 11 Probability 186

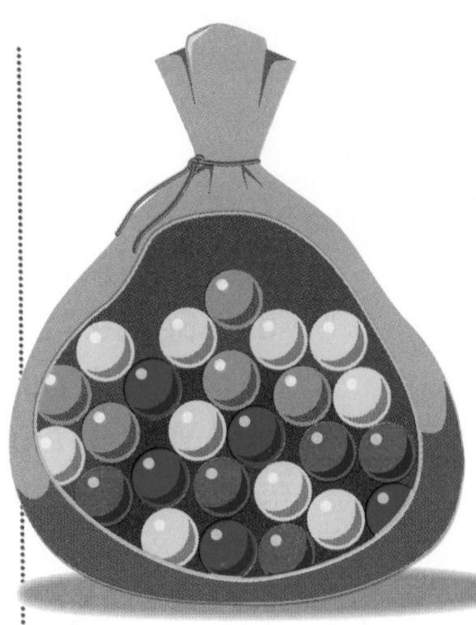

Extension Lesson
Conduct a Simulation
H38–H39

Chapters 9–11 ✓Checkpoint

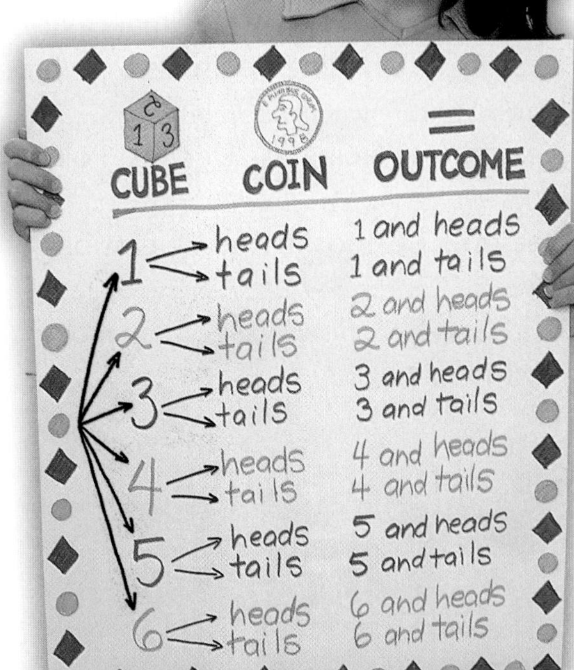

* **Algebra Readiness**

CHAPTER 12 Multiplying Decimals 208

CHAPTER 13 Dividing Decimals 228

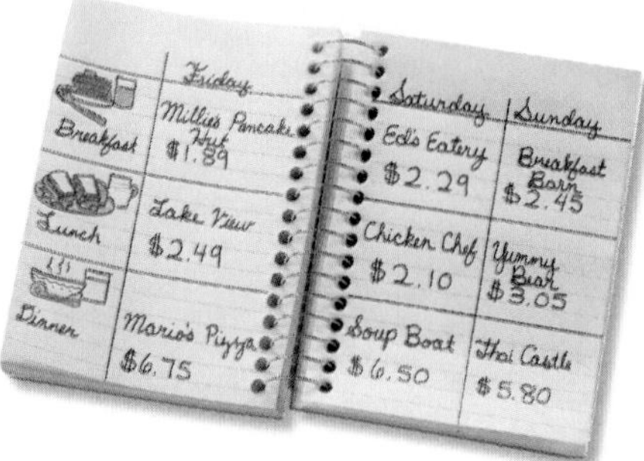

* **Algebra Readiness**

CHAPTER 14 Measurement: Metric Units 246

Troubleshooting Lesson

Chapters 12–14 ✓Checkpoint

* Algebra Readiness

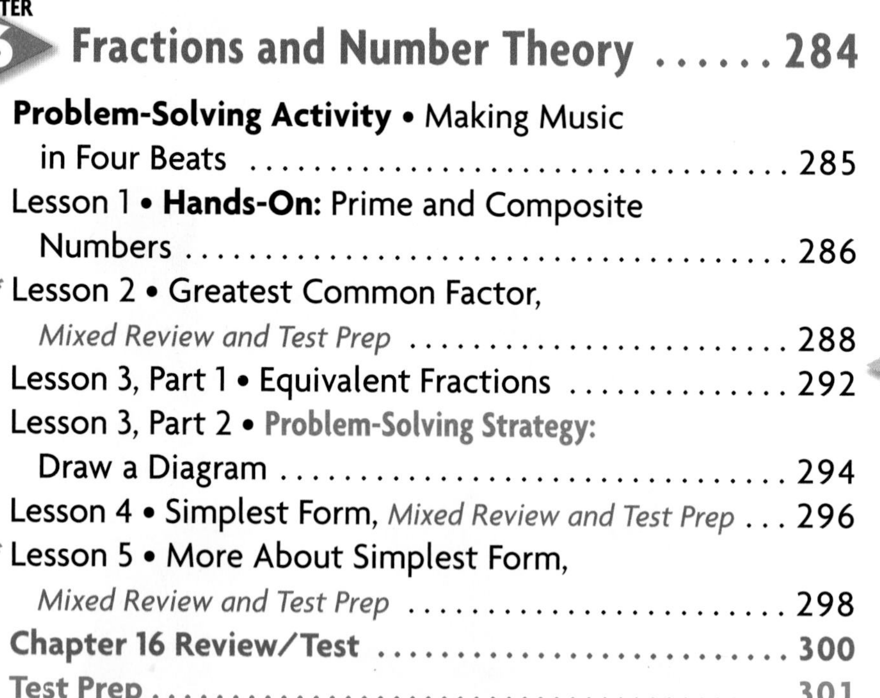

* **Algebra Readiness**

CHAPTER 17 Modeling Addition of Fractions 302

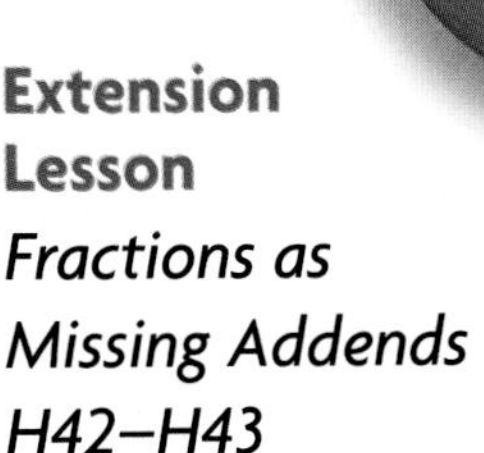

Extension Lesson
Fractions as Missing Addends
H42–H43

CHAPTER 18 Modeling Subtraction of Fractions 316

Extension Lesson
Using Fraction Circles to Subtract
H44–H45

Chapters 15–18 ✓Checkpoint

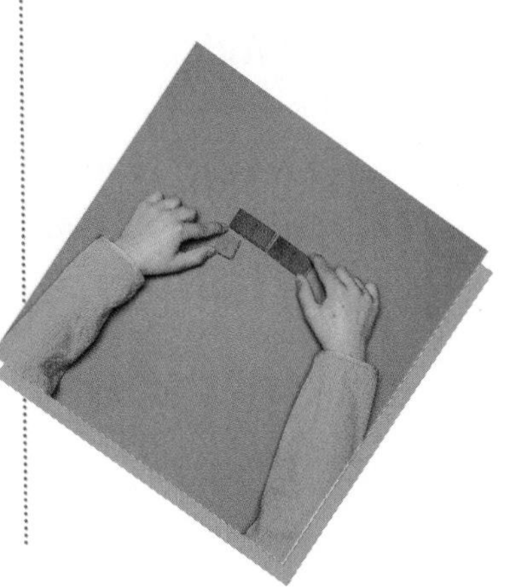

* Algebra Readiness

CHAPTER 19 Adding and Subtracting Fractions . . . 336

CHAPTER 20 Adding and Subtracting Mixed Numbers . . . 352

* **Algebra Readiness**

CHAPTER 21 Measurement: Customary Units ... 366

CHAPTER 22 Multiplying Fractions 386

Chapters 19–22 ✓Checkpoint

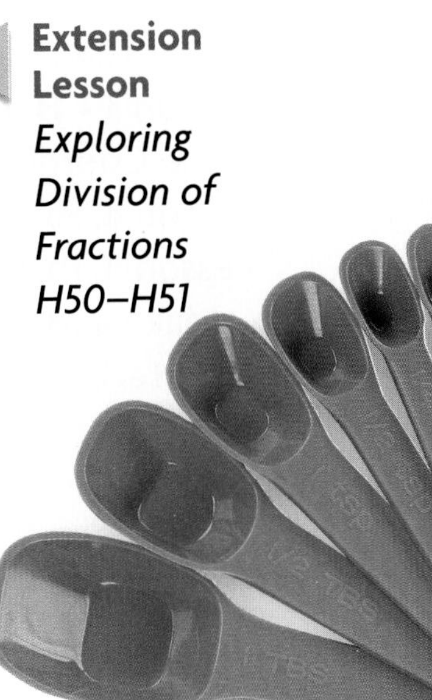

* **Algebra Readiness**

CHAPTER 23 Plane Figures and Polygons 406

CHAPTER 24 Transformations, Congruence, and Symmetry 424

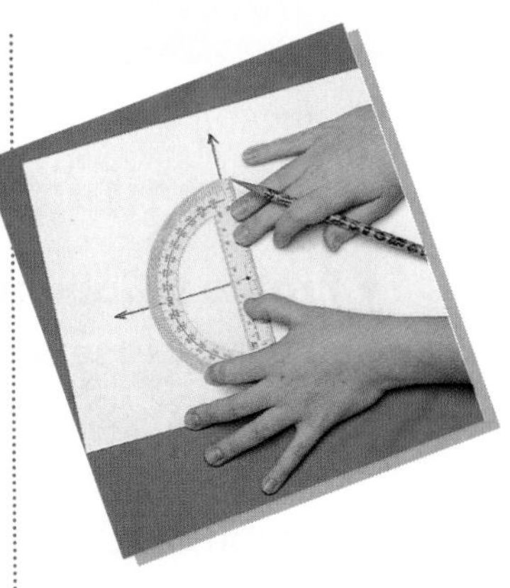

Chapters 23–26 ✓Checkpoint

* **Algebra Readiness**

CHAPTER 27

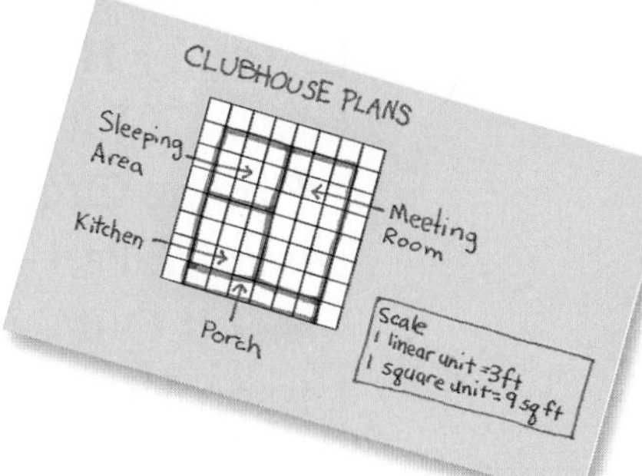

CHAPTER 28

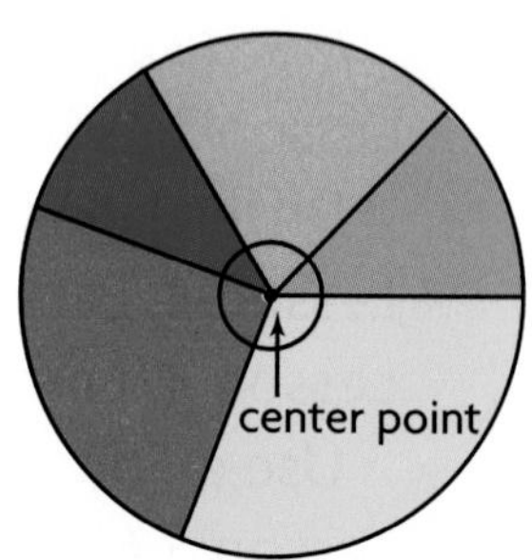

* **Algebra Readiness**

Chapters 27–28 ✓Checkpoint

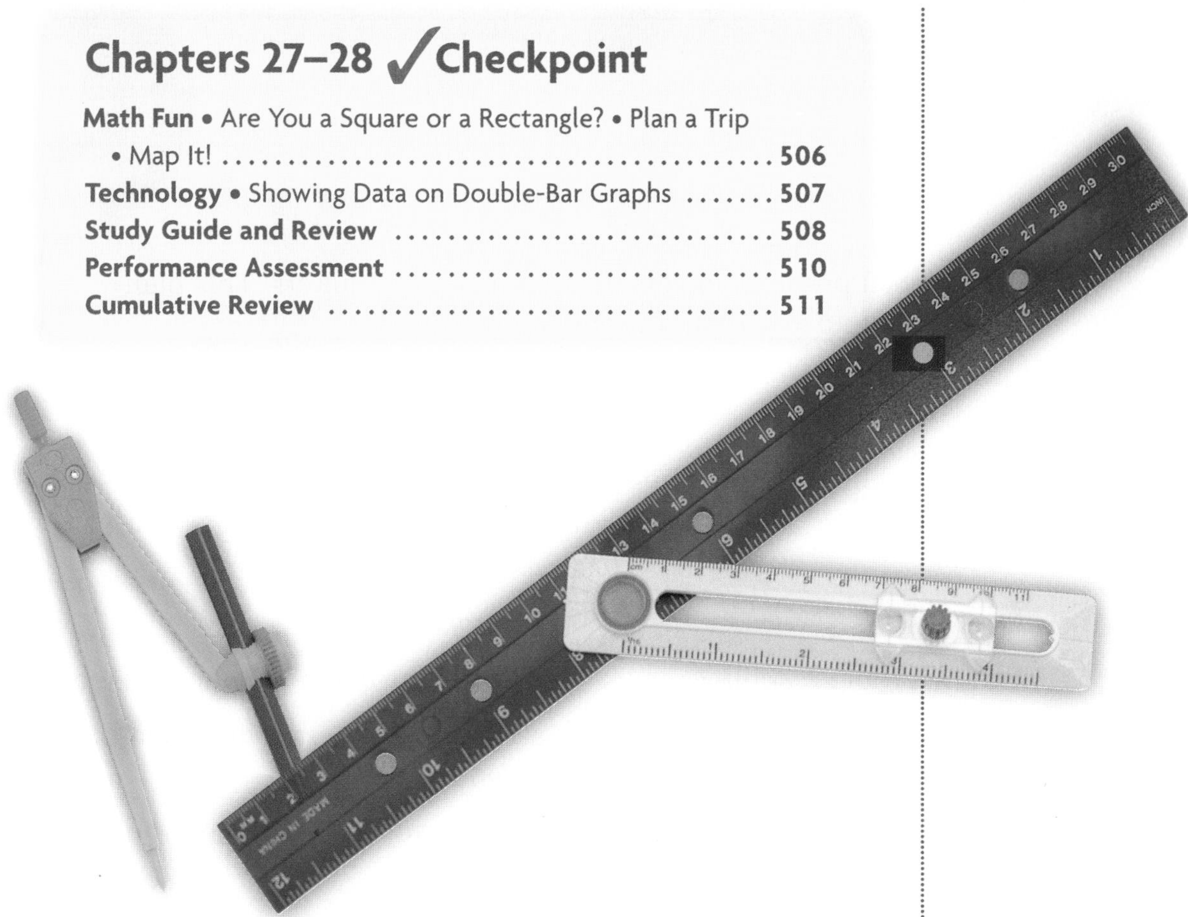

STUDENT HANDBOOK

BE A GOOD PROBLEM SOLVER

Good problem solvers need to be good thinkers. This plan can help you think through a problem.

UNDERSTAND the problem

Ask yourself...	Then try this.
• What is the problem about?	Retell the problem in your own words.
• What is the question?	Say the question as a fill-in-the-blank sentence.
• What information is given?	List the information given in the problem.

PLAN how to solve it

Ask yourself...	Then try this.
• What strategies might I use?	List some strategies you can use.
• About what will the answer be?	Predict what your answer will be. Make an estimate if it will help.

SOLVE it

Ask yourself...	Then try this.
• How can I solve the problem?	Follow your plan and show your solution.
• How can I write my answer?	Write your answer in a complete sentence.

LOOK BACK and check your answer

Ask yourself...	Then try this.
• How can I tell if my answer is reasonable?	Compare your answer to your estimate. Check your answer by redoing your work. Match your answer to the question.
• How else might I have solved the problem?	Try using another strategy to solve the problem.

You can be a good problem solver!
Remember these important words—

Ask yourself questions as you think through the problem. Then be proud of your success!

GOOD PROBLEM SOLVERS USE STRATEGIES

Good problem solvers need to know and use these strategies.

- Draw a Diagram
- Act It Out
- Make a Model
- Use a Formula
- Work Backward
- Find a Pattern
- Guess and Check
- Solve a Simpler Problem
- Make or Use a Table
- Make or Use a Graph
- Write a Number Sentence
- Make an Organized List

Think about how strategies were used to solve these problems:

Megan is designing a quilt square. The square will have 4 congruent triangles. She will make $\frac{1}{2}$ of the square red and $\frac{1}{2}$ blue. What are two ways that Megan can make her square?

Make a model to show two ways that Megan can make her square.

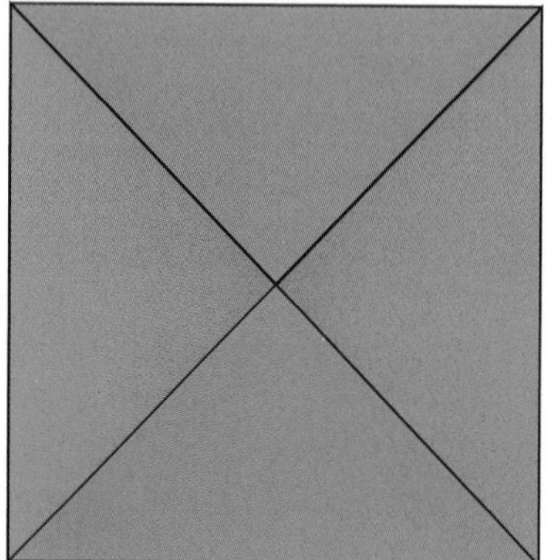

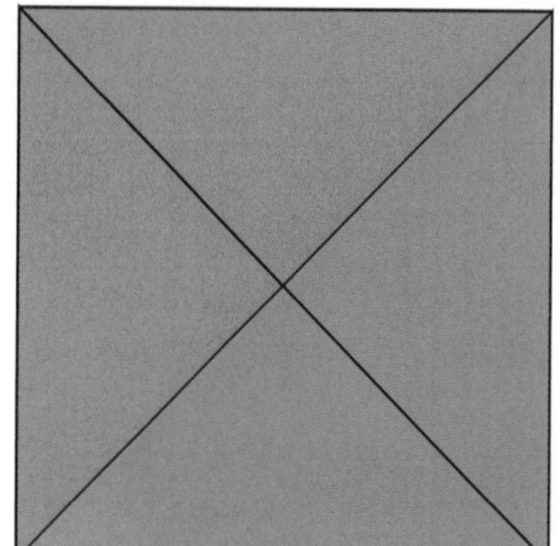

So, Megan can make a quilt square that can be colored in two different ways.

Matthew had \$12.57 in his piggy bank. He spent \$6.79 on an airplane model. He put the \$3.75 he earned for sweeping his neighbor's sidewalk in his bank. How much money is in his bank now?

Write number sentences to find out how much money Matthew has in his bank.

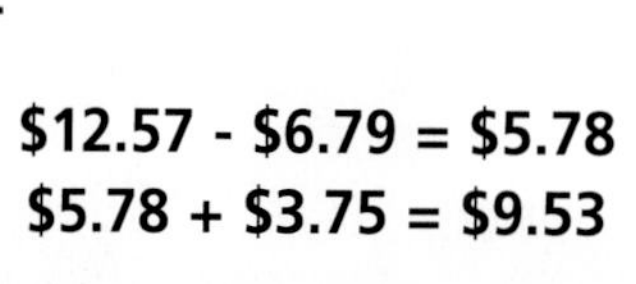

\$12.57 - \$6.79 = \$5.78
\$5.78 + \$3.75 = \$9.53

So, Matthew has \$9.53 in his piggy bank.

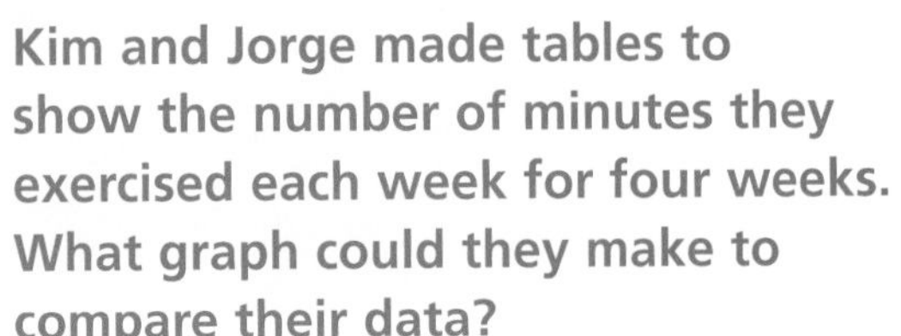

Kim and Jorge made tables to show the number of minutes they exercised each week for four weeks. What graph could they make to compare their data?

Kim's Record

Weeks	Minutes Exercised
1	150
2	145
3	105
4	180

Jorge's Record

Weeks	Minutes Exercised
1	165
2	105
3	155
4	150

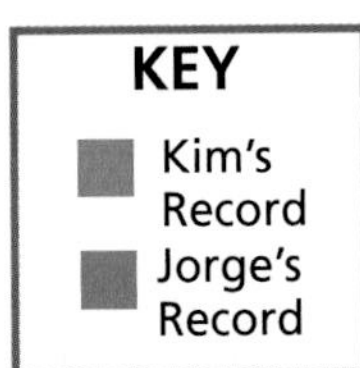

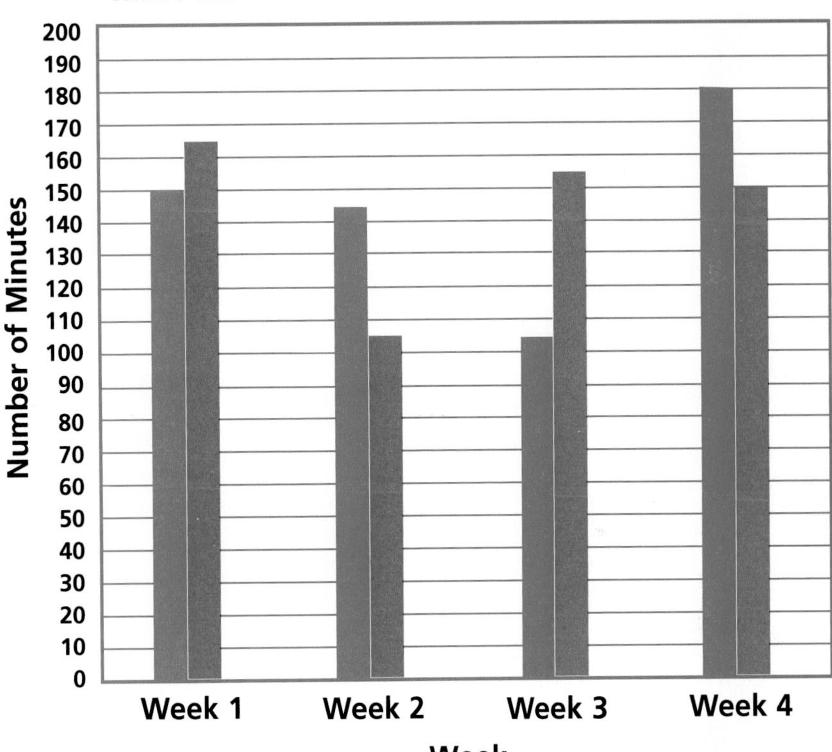

So, Kim and Jorge can make a double-bar graph to compare the number of minutes each one exercised.

Talk About It

How does using strategies help you become a good problem solver?

1 PLACE VALUE OF WHOLE NUMBERS

SCIENCE **LINK**

The El Segundo butterfly lives in dunes near the Los Angeles International Airport. This lovely butterfly has a wing span of about 2.5 cm and a life span of 4-6 days.

Problem-Solving Activity

Seven Special Numbers

Numbers are all around you—if you look in the right places. Search for 7 special numbers. Look for numbers in books, magazines, newspapers, on the Internet, and during interviews with people.

Make a list of all the numbers you find. Then look for a theme that connects seven of the numbers.

YOU WILL NEED: books, magazines, tagboard

- Make a list of theme numbers and choose 7: a 1-digit number, a 2-digit number, and so forth up to a 7-digit number.
- Explain each number's unit such as miles, feet, or gallons, and tell where you found the number.
- Make a chart.

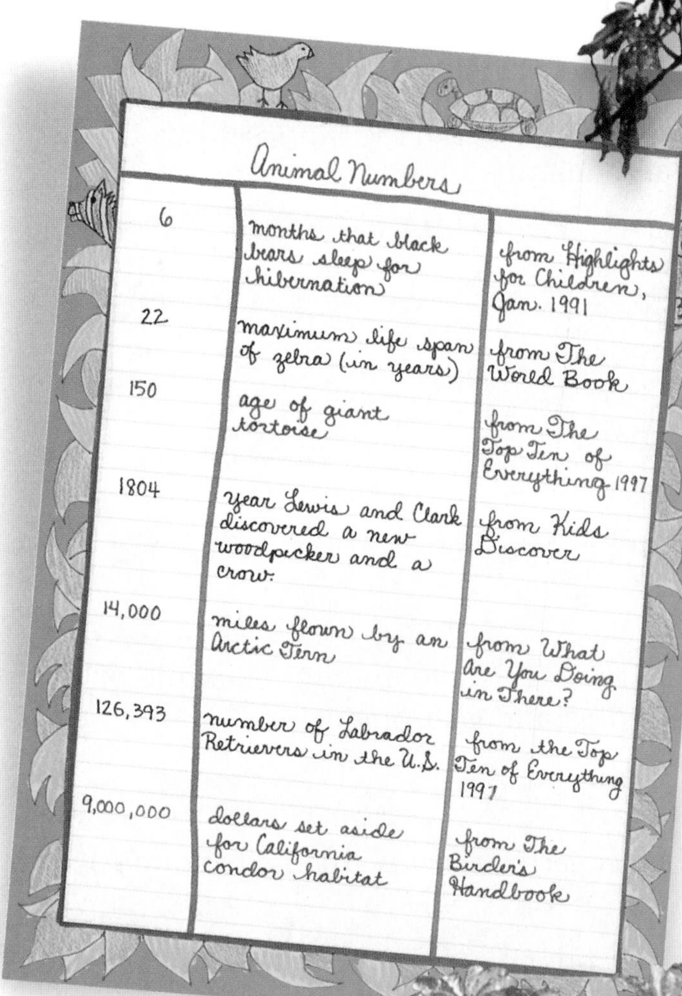

Animal Numbers

6	months that black bears sleep for hibernation	from Highlights for Children, Jan. 1991
22	maximum life span of zebra (in years)	from The World Book
150	age of giant tortoise	from The Top Ten of Everything 1997
1804	year Lewis and Clark discovered a new woodpecker and a crow.	from Kids Discover
14,000	miles flown by an Arctic Tern	from What Are You Doing in There?
126,393	number of Labrador Retrievers in the U.S.	from the Top Ten of Everything 1997
9,000,000	dollars set aside for California condor habitat	from The Birder's Handbook

DID YOU

- ✓ choose 7 special numbers related to a theme?
- ✓ explain the numbers and tell where you found them?
- ✓ make a chart?

LESSON 1

Using Numbers

Why learn this? You can recognize different ways numbers are used every day, such as in your telephone number or your age.

VOCABULARY
cardinal
ordinal
nominal

Numbers can be expressed in different ways. **Cardinal** numbers tell how many. **Ordinal** numbers tell position or order. **Nominal** numbers name things. Look at how numbers are used in this poster.

- Which numbers in the poster are cardinal numbers? ordinal numbers? nominal numbers?

____

WELCOME TO THE 3RD ANNUAL
West Oaks Festival
When:
Saturday, September 5, 1998
12:00 noon - 8:30 P.M.
Where:
West Oaks School
567 East Fifth Avenue
Asbury, TX 65778
(4 miles east of Route 287)
Admission: $3.50
Call 555-2907
for more information.
15 Rides for $12.50
150 T-Shirt Designs
Food
Crafts Booth
Sports Events
25
8

Cardinal numbers can be expressed as measurements.

A. Measure temperature in degrees.

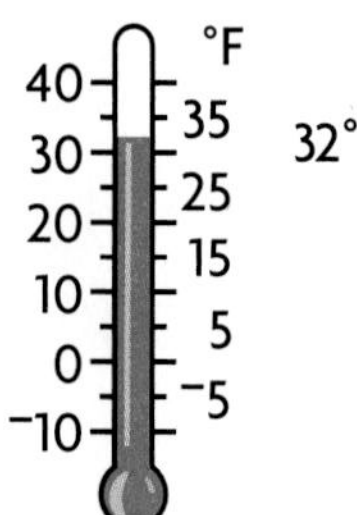

B. Measure length in inches.

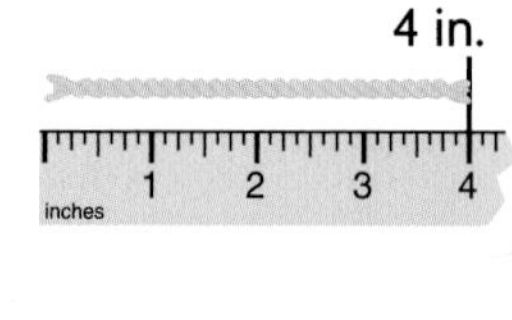

C. Measure capacity in cups.

D. Measure weight in pounds.

CRITICAL THINKING Name another example of a number expressed as a measurement.

▶ CHECK

Tell whether each number is expressed as *cardinal, ordinal,* or *nominal.*

1. Sandy's phone number is (407) 555-3809.

2. Jason is 15th in line.

3. Mary put 2 cups of flour in the bowl.

4. Tim placed first in the sack race.

5. There were 5 puppies in the basket.

6. The number on Joe's football jersey is 72.

7. 72nd

8. twenty-six

9. 35 mm

10. 3295 Oak St.

▶ PRACTICE

Tell whether the number in each picture is expressed as *cardinal, ordinal,* or *nominal.*

11. 

12. 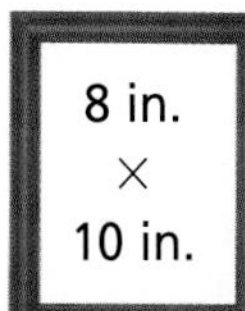

13. 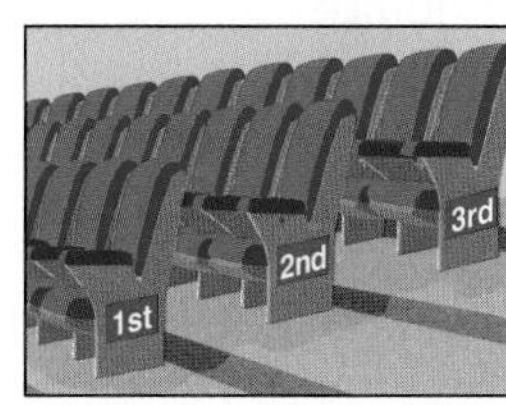

14. 

Tell whether each number is expressed as *cardinal, ordinal,* or *nominal.*

15. My phone number is (914) 555-2030.

16. Susan is tenth in line to use the computer.

17. It is 78°F outside today.

18. Bob lives at 319 Oak St.

19. Lee got 93 answers correct on the test.

20. Sofia won 2nd place in the essay contest.

21. A 10-lb box of paper was delivered to the class.

22. There are 25 students in our classroom.

Problem Solving • Mixed Applications

Using Data For Problems 23–26, use the table.

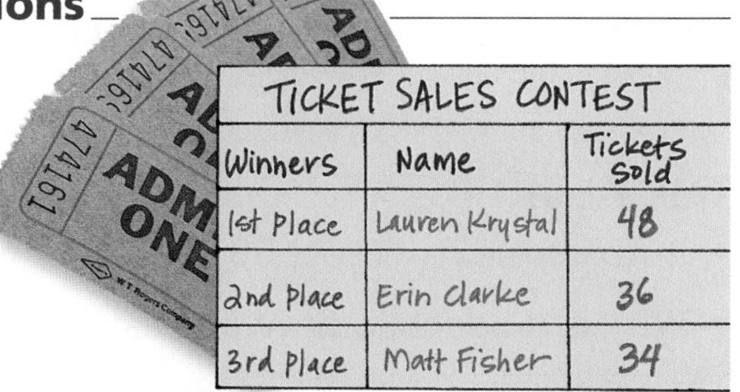

TICKET SALES CONTEST

Winners	Name	Tickets Sold
1st Place	Lauren Krystal	48
2nd Place	Erin Clarke	36
3rd Place	Matt Fisher	34

23. What is the total number of tickets sold by the 3 winners?

24. **Money** If each ticket sold for $2, did Lauren make more than or less than $100?

25. If the second-place winner sold the same number of tickets on each of 4 days, how many tickets did she sell each day?

26. **Write a problem** using the table.

Mixed Review and Test Prep

Write the letter of the unit used to measure the elapsed time. **(taught in 4th grade)**

a. days	b. hours	c. minutes

27. to be at school

28. to eat lunch

29. to travel from home to school

30. to be on vacation out of town

Choose the letter that tells how many tens. **(taught in 4th grade)**

31. 237 **A** 2 tens **B** 3 tens **C** 4 tens **D** 7 tens

32. 1,463 **F** 3 tens **G** 4 tens **H** 1 ten **J** 6 tens

MORE PRACTICE page H70

LESSON 2

Benchmark Numbers

VOCABULARY
benchmark

Why learn this? You can estimate the number of beans in a jar by comparing them to a familiar number of beans, such as 10.

A **benchmark** is a point of reference. Benchmark numbers such as 5, 10, 25, 100, or 1,000 can help you determine whether an estimate is reasonable without counting.

EXAMPLES

A Which estimate of the slices of bread in the tray is most reasonable, 50, 150, or 1,500?

Benchmark: 1 loaf has about **15** slices.

So, the most reasonable estimate of slices of bread in the tray is 150.

B Which estimate of the nickels in the full jar is most reasonable, 60, 300, or 3,000?

Benchmark: **50** nickels

So, the most reasonable estimate of the nickels in the full jar is 300.

Talk About It

- In Example A, why is 50 not a reasonable estimate?
- Why is a benchmark of 50 easier to use than 15?

CRITICAL THINKING What benchmark numbers would you use to estimate the number of students in your school?

▶ CHECK

Use the benchmark number to choose the more reasonable estimate.

1. pennies in the jar

100 or 1,000

2. pretzels in the bag

15 or 75

3. windows on the building

60 or 600

▶ PRACTICE

Use the benchmark number to choose the more reasonable estimate.

4. seats in the audience

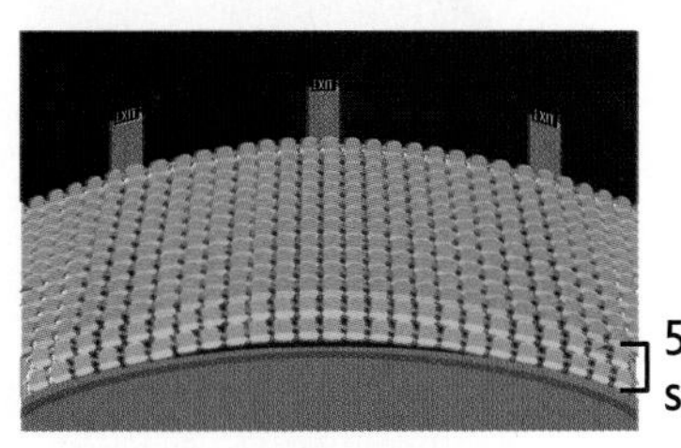

500 or 5,000

5. soccer balls

10 or 100

6. paper clips

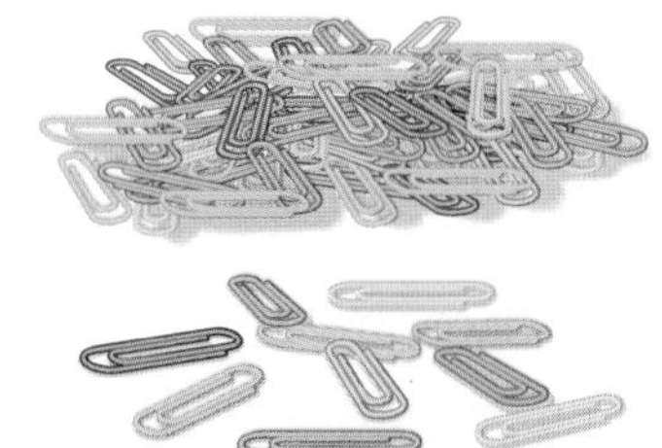

25 or 100

Write *yes* or *no* to tell whether the estimate is reasonable. Explain.

7. • 10 pans of cupcakes
• Each pan holds 12 cupcakes.
Estimate: There are about 25 cupcakes in the bakery.

8. • 20 sections in the gymnasium
• Each section seats 50 people.
Estimate: There are about 100 seats in the gymnasium.

9. • 19 packages of paper on the shelf
• 100 sheets of paper per package
Estimate: There are about 2,000 sheets of paper on the shelf.

10. • 8 pencils in a box
• 40 boxes at the school store
Estimate: There are about 100 pencils in the school store.

Problem Solving • Mixed Applications

11. Estimation A group of students signed up to play basketball. There will be about 10 students on each team. About 20 teams will be formed. Did more than or less than 100 students sign up?

12. Reasoning Angelo guessed there were 260 jelly beans in the jar. Ben guessed there were 325 jelly beans. There were actually 293 jelly beans. Whose guess was closer?

13. Money Julia can hold 20 nickels in her hand at one time. She has enough nickels for 5 handfuls. About how much money does Julia have in nickels?

14. Write About It Explain when you would use a benchmark number.

Mixed Review and Test Prep

Write the number that is 1,000 more. (taught in 4th grade)

15. 3,046 **16.** 14,189 **17.** 29,504 **18.** 99,897

Use mental math to complete the equation. (taught in 4th grade)

19. $\underline{?} \times 10 = 8 \times 5$ **A** 5 **B** 40 **C** 2 **D** 4

20. $70 + 5 = 25 + \underline{?}$ **F** 50 **G** 10 **H** 3 **J** 40

MORE PRACTICE page H70

LESSON 3

Place Value to Hundred Thousands

Why learn this? You can read and write large numbers, such as the distance from Earth to the moon.

Use the chart to see the value of 4 in each place-value position for the number 444,444.

THOUSANDS			ONES				
Hundreds	Tens	Ones ,	Hundreds	Tens	Ones		
					4 × 1	=	4
				4 × 10		=	40
			4 × 100			=	400
		4 × 1,000				=	4,000
	4 × 10,000					=	40,000
4 × 100,000						=	400,000
							444,444

Talk About It

- How does the value of the 4 change as it moves from right to left?
- How does the expanded form of 444,444 show a pattern of zeros?

CRITICAL THINKING How can you find the value of a digit when you know its place-value position?

REMEMBER:

Expanded form is a way to write numbers by showing the sum of the value of each digit.

567 = 500 + 60 + 7

▶ CHECK

Write the value of the digit 8 in each number.

1. 1,486 **2.** 38,042

3. 854,369 **4.** 781,203

Write the value of the blue digit.

5. 560 **6.** 4,086

7. 13,859 **8.** 618,097

9. 47,092 **10.** 302,561

11. 712,583 **12.** 609,532

13. 507,146 **14.** 168,290

SCIENCE LINK

The average distance from Earth to the moon is 238,857 mi. What is the value of the digit in the greatest place-value position of that number?

▶ PRACTICE

Write the value of the blue digit.

15. 475,902 **16.** 695,337 **17.** 980,765 **18.** 871,253

19. 301,584 **20.** 820,426 **21.** 713,225 **22.** 214,607

Complete.

23. 765,910 = (_?_ × 100,000) + (_?_ × 10,000) + (_?_ × 1,000) + (_?_ × 100) + (_?_ × 10) + (_?_ × 1)

24. 802,054 = (_?_ × 100,000) + (_?_ × 10,000) + (_?_ × 1,000) + (_?_ × 100) + (_?_ × 10) + (_?_ × 1)

25. 642,703 = (6 × _?_) + (4 × _?_) + (2 × _?_) + (7 × _?_) + (_?_ × 10) + (3 × _?_)

Write the expanded numbers in standard form.

26. 200,000 + 50,000 + 6,000 + 900 + 80 + 3

27. 400,000 + 90,000 + 1,000 + 700 + 20 + 3

28. 700,000 + 0 + 4,000 + 200 + 30 + 5

29. 900,000 + 90,000 + 0 + 900 + 0 + 9

200,000
50,000
6,000
900
80
3
???,???

Problem Solving • Mixed Applications

30. Science The Earth's equator measures 24,902 mi. Write the value of the digit 4 in this number.

31. Reasoning I am a number greater than 149,998 but less than 150,000. What number am I?

32. Money The Butlers bought a house for $149,950. Two years later they sold it for $155,275. How much more did their house sell for?

33. Write About It Explain how you know the value of the digit 7 in the number 742,126.

Mixed Review and Test Prep

Write *true* or *false* for each statement. **(taught in 4th grade)**

34. There are 100 pennies in $10. **35.** There are 1,000 pennies in $10.

36. There are 10 dimes in $1. **37.** There are 10 dimes in $10.

38. There are 100 dimes in $10. **39.** There are 100 $1-bills in $10.

Choose the letter of the greatest place-value position in which the digits differ. **(taught in 4th grade)**

40. 145 and 147 **A** tens **B** ones **C** hundreds **D** Not Here

41. 694 and 964 **F** hundreds **G** ones **H** tens **J** Not Here

MORE PRACTICE page H71

Place Value of Larger Numbers

VOCABULARY
million
billion

Why learn this? You can recognize and interpret large numbers, such as the distances between the planets and the sun.

What kinds of movies are most popular? If you look at the data, you will find that animated cartoons and movies about outer space are among the favorites. In the year it was released, the film *Apollo 13* earned about $334,100,000.

Look at the number on the place-value chart. One **million** is 1,000 thousands.

MILLIONS			THOUSANDS			ONES		
Hundreds	Tens	Ones	Hundreds	Tens	Ones	Hundreds	Tens	Ones
3	3	4,	1	0	0,	0	0	0

Each period in a large number contains three place-value positions. Commas separate the periods and help you read the number.

Standard Form: 334,100,000

Expanded Form: 300,000,000 + 30,000,000 + 4,000,000 + 100,000 + 0 + 0 + 0 + 0 + 0

Word Form: three hundred thirty-four *million*, one hundred *thousand*

Each group of three numbers in a large number is called a *period*.

PERIODS

Millions	Thousands	Ones
5 6 7,	2 3 6,	4 5 1

Talk About It

- Why is a comma used to separate periods when writing large numbers?
- What is alike about the periods?
- How do you use periods to help you read a number?

CRITICAL THINKING How many 1,000's are in 1,000,000?

SCIENCE LINK

Astronauts first landed on the moon in 1969. Americans landed on the moon five more times after that. Unmanned spacecraft have gone as far as Neptune and Uranus. From Earth to Uranus is about 1 billion, 7 hundred million miles. How would you write that number in standard form?

Calculator Activities page H58

By October 1997, the two films *Jurassic Park* and *The Lost World: Jurassic Park* together had earned more than $1,096,599,010.

- How many hundred millions are in one billion?

Look at the number on the place-value chart. One **billion** is 1,000 millions.

BILLIONS			MILLIONS			THOUSANDS			ONES		
Hundreds	Tens	Ones	Hundreds	Tens	Ones	Hundreds	Tens	Ones	Hundreds	Tens	Ones
		1,	0	9	6,	5	9	9,	0	1	0

Standard Form: 1,096,599,010

Expanded Form: 1,000,000,000 + 0 + 90,000,000 + 6,000,000 + 500,000 + 90,000 + 9,000 + 0 + 10 + 0

Word Form: one *billion*, ninety-six *million*, five hundred ninety-nine *thousand*, ten

- How do you find the value of a digit?

CRITICAL THINKING How many 1,000's are in 1,000,000,000?

▶ CHECK

Write the value of the blue digit.

1. 46,785,039 **2.** 39,806,527 **3.** 5,148,713,002

4. 268,432,116 **5.** 4,956,630,210 **6.** 780,904,652

Write each number in standard form.

7. five million, three hundred two thousand, fourteen

8. twelve billion, six hundred eleven thousand, one hundred seven

Use the number 4,302,698,051 to answer Exercises 9–12.

9. Write the number in expanded form.

10. Write the number in word form.

11. Write the name of the period that has the digits 698.

12. Write the place-value position of the digit 4.

▶ PRACTICE

Write each number in standard form.

13. two million, three hundred six thousand, fifteen

14. thirty billion, two hundred nine thousand, five hundred eight

15. three hundred forty-five billion, eight hundred seventy million, two hundred ninety thousand, four hundred ninety-two

16. twenty-two billion, eight hundred sixty-three million, four hundred ten thousand, thirty

Write two other forms for each number.

17. 65,200,108

18. 207,910,036

19. 1,480,200,965

20. 500,000,000 + 80,000,000 + 0 + 400,000 + 0 + 1,000 + 200 + 0 + 9

21. sixteen billion, forty-two million, seven hundred eleven thousand, one

22. 1,000,000,000 + 300,000,000 + 0 + 1,000,000 + 500,000 + 60,000 + 0 + 800 + 0 + 1

23. seven hundred thirty million, eight hundred ninety-five thousand, fifteen

Movie	1st Year's Earnings
The Lion King	$670,900,000
Pocahontas	$342,600,000
Apollo 13	$334,100,000

Problem Solving • Mixed Applications

Using Data For Problems 25–28, use the table.

24. Money Another movie hit, *Aladdin*, earned about four hundred ninety million dollars. How would you write that amount in standard form?

25. Write the earnings of *The Lion King* in word form.

26. Money What was the sum in earnings of *The Lion King* and *Pocahontas* in standard form?

27. Money Write the sum in earnings of *The Lion King* and *Pocahontas* in word form.

28. **Write About It** Explain how you know the place value of the digit 9 in the earnings for *The Lion King*.

Technology Link

In ***Mighty Math Number Heroes,*** the game *Quizzo* challenges you to read numbers to solve problems. Use Grow Slide Level G.

29. Reasoning Write the greatest 10-digit number possible without repeating a digit. What is the value of the digit 6?

SCIENCE CONNECTION

HOW FAR TO THE SUN?	
Planet in the Solar System	Approximate Average Distance From the Sun (In Miles)
Mercury	35,960,000
Earth	92,900,000
Neptune	2,793,000,000
Pluto	3,664,000,000

30. Collecting Data Look up the average distance from the Sun of the other five planets. Then make your own table, listing all nine planets' distances in standard form.

31. Compare How much farther from the Sun is Earth than Mercury?

32. CRITICAL THINKING Does writing large numbers in standard form make them easier to compare? Explain.

SCIENCE LINK

The Sun is the center of our solar system. Compared to other stars in the universe, the Sun is average-sized. All living things on Earth depend on the Sun's heat and light for energy. The temperature at the Sun's core is about 27 million degrees Fahrenheit. How would you write that number in standard form?

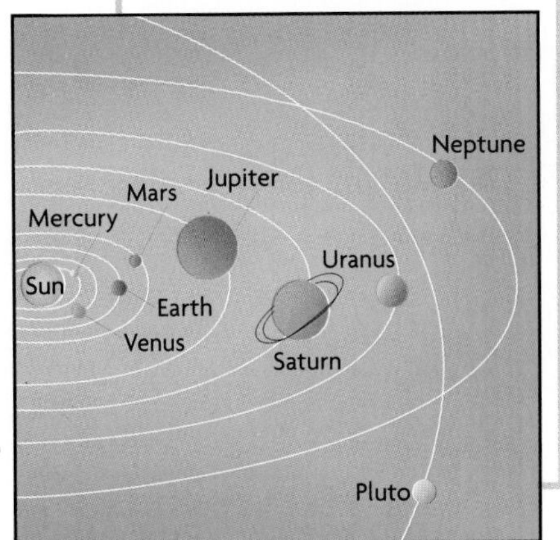

Mixed Review and Test Prep

Write the number as you would say it with period names. (taught in 4th grade)

33. 5,147,216 5 __?__ ,147 __?__ ,216

34. 2,306,114,067 2 __?__ ,306 __?__ ,114,067

35. 4,875,309 4 __?__ ,875 __?__ ,309

36. 1,637,293,405 1 __?__ ,637,293 __?__ ,405

Choose the letter of the next three numbers in the pattern. (taught in 4th grade)

37. 6, 9, 12, 15 **A** 16, 17, 18 **B** 18, 21, 24 **C** 20, 25, 30

38. 1, 2, 4, 7, 11 **F** 16, 22, 29 **G** 13, 15, 17 **H** 15, 19, 23

39. 40, 35, 30, 25 **A** 30, 40, 50 **B** 30, 35, 40 **C** 20, 15, 10

40. 4, 8, 12, 16 **F** 20, 24, 28 **G** 24, 32, 40 **H** 18, 20, 22

41. 32, 28, 24, 20 **A** 21, 14, 7 **B** 16, 14, 10 **C** 16, 12, 8

42. 6, 8, 11, 15 **F** 18, 24, 30 **G** 20, 28, 35 **H** 20, 26, 33

MORE PRACTICE page H71

Comparing and Ordering

Why learn this? You can compare distances, such as the distance from home to school and to the store.

The Pacific Ocean and the Indian Ocean are two of the deepest on Earth. The average depth of the Indian Ocean is 12,598 ft. The average depth of the Pacific Ocean is 12,925 ft. Compare these two numbers to find which ocean has the greater average depth.

Compare numbers by comparing the digits in each place-value position. Start at the left. Check each place until the digits are different.

MODEL

Step 1

Compare the ten thousands.

12,598
↓ same number of ten thousands
12,925

Step 2

Compare the thousands.

12,598
↓ same number of thousands
12,925

Step 3

Compare the hundreds.

12,598
↓ $9 > 5$
12,925

So, $12,925 > 12,598$.

Since $12,925 > 12,598$, the Pacific Ocean has the greater average depth.

REMEMBER:

As you move to the right on a *number line*, the number gets larger. When you move to the left, the number gets smaller.

25 ↓ 85 ↓
0 10 20 30 40 50 60 70 80 90 100

Read: $25 < 85$ or $85 > 25$

Order numbers by comparing them in the same way. Order these numbers from greatest to least: 24,785; 25,864; 22,678.

MODEL

Step 1

Compare the ten thousands.

24,785
↓
25,864 same number of ten thousands
↓
22,678

Step 2

Compare the thousands. Order the digits.

24,785
↓
25,864 $5 > 4 > 2$
↓
22,678

Step 3

Order the numbers.

So, $25,864 > 24,785 > 22,678$.

CRITICAL THINKING How would you order the numbers from least to greatest?

▶ CHECK

Start at the left. Name the first place-value position where the numbers differ.

1. 1,733; 1,418 **2.** 25,670; 25,680 **3.** 178,452; 179,452

4. 9,678; 12,768 **5.** 807; 870 **6.** 205,769; 205,796

▶ PRACTICE

Write <, >, or = for each ●.

7. 489 ● 498 **8.** 5,650 ● 5,650

9. 7,890 ● 8,790 **10.** 187,418 ● 187,418

11. 2,450,000 ● 2,500,000

12. 6,158,000,000 ● 6,160,000,000

Order from *greatest* to *least*.

13. 397; 379; 739 **14.** 5,217; 5,721; 7,521

15. 16,295; 16,925; 19,625 **16.** 418,652; 481,562; 418,562

17. 3,050,000; 3,500,000; 5,300,000

Order from *least* to *greatest*.

18. 895; 590; 859 **19.** 4,210; 2,410; 4,120

20. 49,086; 49,680; 48,690 **21.** 235,289; 236,287; 236,178

22. 1,800,000,000; 1,600,000,000; 1,900,000,000

GEOGRAPHY LINK

Two of the highest mountains in the world are Aconcagua in South America at 22,834 ft and Mt. Everest in Asia at 29,028 ft. Which mountain is higher?

Problem Solving • Mixed Applications

Using Data For Problems 23–28, use the table.

23. Which of these national parks covers the most acres?

24. Which national park is larger, Mammoth Cave or Mesa Verde?

25. Geography How much larger is Kings Canyon National Park than Mount Rainier National Park?

UNITED STATES NATIONAL PARKS		
Name	Location	Acres
Mammoth Cave	Kentucky	52,419
Bryce Canyon	Utah	35,835
Mesa Verde	Colorado	52,122
Kings Canyon	California	461,901
Mount Rainier	Washington	235,612

26. Geography What is the difference in the number of acres in the largest park and the number of acres in the smallest park?

27. Social Studies List the national parks in order from the park with the fewest acres to the park with the most acres.

28. **Write a problem** using the information in the table.

LESSON CONTINUES

MORE PRACTICE page H71

Problem-Solving Strategy: Use a Table

▶ **THE PROBLEM** Tammy's class will take a 6-day field trip during Spring Break. The planning committee has recommended five trips. The principal asked the committee to narrow down the choices to the three trips with the least traveling distances. The parents asked the class to choose, from those three trips, the one that costs the least. Which trip will the class take?

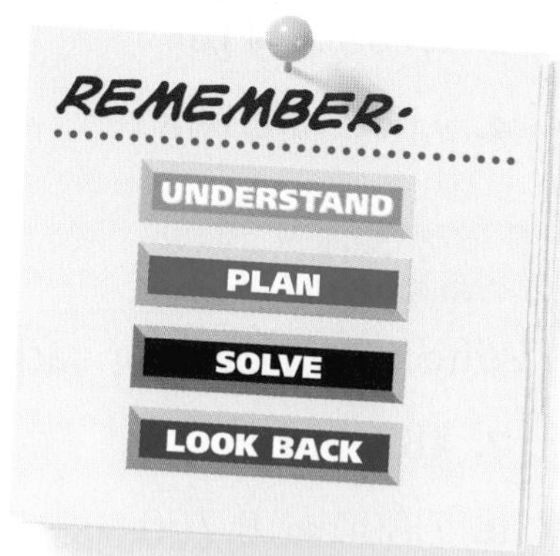

UNDERSTAND

- What are you asked to do?
- What information will you use?
- Is there information you will not use? If so, what?

PLAN

- What strategy can you use to solve the problem?

  You can *use a table* to analyze the data.

SOLVE

- How can a table help you solve this problem?

  The table organizes the data. Compare the distances. Find the 3 trips with the least distances. Then choose from those three, the one that costs the least.

	Trip 1	Trip 2	Trip 3	Trip 4	Trip 5
Place	New York City	Washington, D.C. area camp out	Kennedy Space Center	Dude Ranch	Mountain Camping
Points of Interest	Museums Famous Landmarks	National Landmarks Smithsonian	Space Shuttle & Museum Space Camp	Horseback Riding Hikes	Hiking Rafting Canoeing
Traveling Distance	1,456 mi	1,198 mi	1,748 mi	1,308 mi	1,099 mi
Cost (per student)	$1,375	$325	$1,067	$410	$351

The three trips with least distances are: Trips 5, 2, and 4. So, the least costly of those three trips is Trip 2 to Washington, D.C. at $325 per student.

LOOK BACK

- How does the table help you find the answer?
- What other strategy could you use?

▶ PRACTICE

Use a table to solve.

1. This table shows some capital cities in the United States and their populations. Which of these cities has the greatest population? the least population?

CAPITAL CITIES		
City	State	Population
Atlanta	Georgia	394,017
Juneau	Alaska	26,751
Phoenix	Arizona	983,392
Montpelier	Vermont	8,247
Santa Fe	New Mexico	55,859

2. This table shows five states in the United States and their areas in square miles. Which of these states has the greatest area? the least area?

U.S. STATES	
Name	Area (square miles)
New Jersey	8,215
Michigan	96,705
California	158,869
Delaware	2,396
Nevada	110,567

Mixed Applications

Solve.

CHOOSE a strategy and a tool.

- Act It Out
- Use a Table
- Guess and Check
- Work Backward
- Make an Organized List

Paper/Pencil

Calculator

Hands-On

Mental Math

3. The highest waterfall in the world is Angel Falls in Venezuela. How much higher is Angel Falls than Yosemite Upper Falls?

WATERFALLS	
Falls	Height (in ft)
Angel	3,212
Yosemite Upper	1,430

4. The Browns drove a total of 540 mi in 2 days. They drove twice as far on Tuesday as they did on Monday. How many miles did they drive on Monday? on Tuesday?

5. Elena's family is planning a trip. They can go to either the beach or the mountains. They can drive, fly, or take the train to their destination. Make a list of their choices.

6. Carmen spent $18 on a ticket to a theme park. She spent $6 for food during the day, and she bought a gift for $5. Carmen had $6 when she got home. How much money did she have when she left home?

7. The clock shows the time Melba arrived in Atlanta. Her airplane flight took 1 hour. She was at the airport for 45 minutes before her flight left. It took her 30 minutes to drive to the airport from her house. At what time did she leave her house?

MORE PRACTICE page H72

CHAPTER 1 Review/Test

▶ CHECK Understanding

VOCABULARY

1. Numbers that tell how many are __?__ numbers.
Numbers that tell position or order are __?__ numbers.
Numbers that name things are __?__ numbers. (page 2)

2. A __?__ number is a point of reference. (page 4)

Tell whether each number is expressed as *cardinal, ordinal,* or *nominal.* (pages 2–3)

3. 23,968 **4.** (215) 555-9807 **5.** fifty-sixth **6.** 35 ft

Use the benchmark number to choose the best estimate. (pages 4–5)

7. beans in the bag

30 or 300

8. cookies in a jar

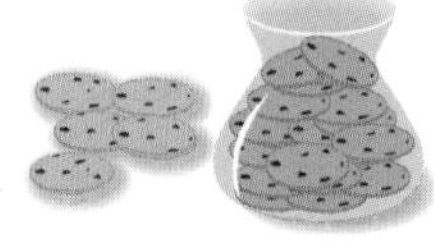

48 or 480

9. people in a stadium

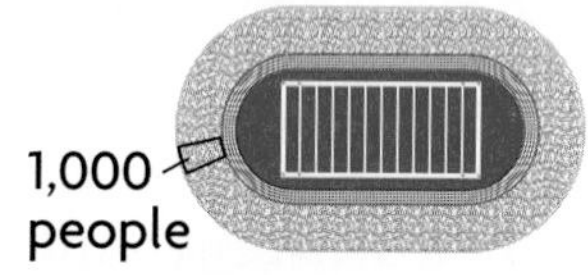

5,000 or 50,000

▶ CHECK Skills

Write two other forms for each number. (pages 6–11)

10. 13,092 **11.** 40,000 + 0 + 500 + 60 + 3

Write the value of the blue digit. (pages 6–11)

12. 406,213,893 **13.** 42,067 **14.** 973,536 **15.** 211,356,841

Write $<$, $>$, or $=$ for each ●. (pages 12–13)

16. 489 ● 498 **17.** 5,650 ● 5,650 **18.** 7,890,000 ● 8,790,000

▶ CHECK Problem Solving

Solve. (pages 14–15)

CHOOSE a strategy and a tool.

- Work Backward
- Draw a Diagram
- Use a Table

Paper/Pencil

Calculator

Hands-On

Mental Math

19. Each 1 of 4 walls in a room is 40 ft long. If stereo speakers are placed every 20 ft, how many speakers are in the room?

20. List the lakes from the least area to the greatest area.

Lakes	Area (sq mi)
Michigan	22,300
Erie	9,910
Superior	31,700
Huron	23,000

Test Prep

Choose the best answer.

1. Which number is expressed as ordinal?

   A 555-6209 **B** 2,067
   C 12 feet **D** 16th

2. There were 467 people attending the football game. How is the number 467 expressed?

   F nominal
   G ordinal
   H cardinal
   J Not Here

3. Which group of numbers is in order from *least* to *greatest*?

   A 751; 898; 1,382; 981
   B 898; 923; 967; 1,099
   C 1,382; 890; 945; 937
   D 1,001; 954; 945; 924

4. Use the benchmark number to choose the most reasonable estimate.

5 tacks

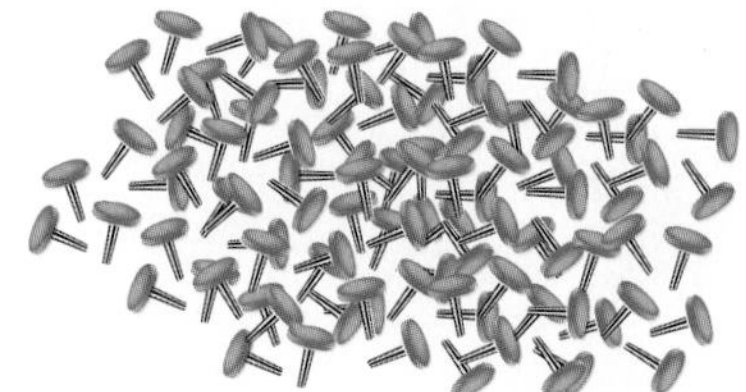

   F 100
   G 10
   H 1,000
   J 10,000
   K Not Here

5. For the number 3,506,782, in which place-value position is the digit 5?

   A thousands
   B hundred thousands
   C millions
   D ten thousands

6. Which number is 3,000,000 + 0 + 60,000 + 7,000 + 400 + 10 + 0 in standard form?

   F 367,410 **G** 3,067,410
   H 36,007,401 **J** 3,607,410

7. What is the value of 6 in 3,967,402?

   A 6 thousands
   B 6 ten thousands
   C 6 hundred thousands
   D 6 millions

8. In the numbers 15,086 and 15,860, name the first place-value position where the numbers differ. Start at the left.

   F thousands
   G ten thousands
   H tens
   J hundreds

9. What is the value of 3 in 3,789,516?

   A 3 ten millions
   B 3 millions
   C 3 thousands
   D 3 hundred thousands

2 ADDING AND SUBTRACTING WHOLE NUMBERS

DATA LINK

In 1994 about 98 out of 100 homes in the United States had television sets while only 94 out of 100 homes had telephone service! That represents about 211 million television sets, with an average of a little more than 2 sets per home.

Tube Tracking

Have you ever wondered who watches more TV—fifth graders or adults? Your class will find out by doing a 3-day survey. As a class, you can decide on dates to track and whether to count hours, half-hours, or minutes.

YOU WILL NEED: paper, pencils, calculators

Design and use a tracking sheet to record the time spent watching TV for 3 days.

- Interview one adult whom you will track.
- Record the times spent watching television by the adult and by yourself for 3 days.
- Add viewing time in two categories: fifth graders and adults.
- Write a report that compares adult TV viewing time with that of fifth graders.

Hours Spent Watching TV

	Monday	Tuesday	Wednesday	Total
Julia	2	2	3	7
Julia's Mom	2	1	0	3
Kyle	1	2	2	5
Kyle's Dad	1	1	2	
Jamal	3	4	2	
Jamal's Dad	0	2	1	

DID YOU

- ✓ design a tracking sheet and conduct an interview?
- ✓ record TV-watching times daily?
- ✓ write a report that compares TV-watching habits of adults and fifth graders?

LESSON 1

Adding and Subtracting with Data

VOCABULARY
inverse

Why learn this? You can add numbers such as scores in a game or how many hours you spend watching television.

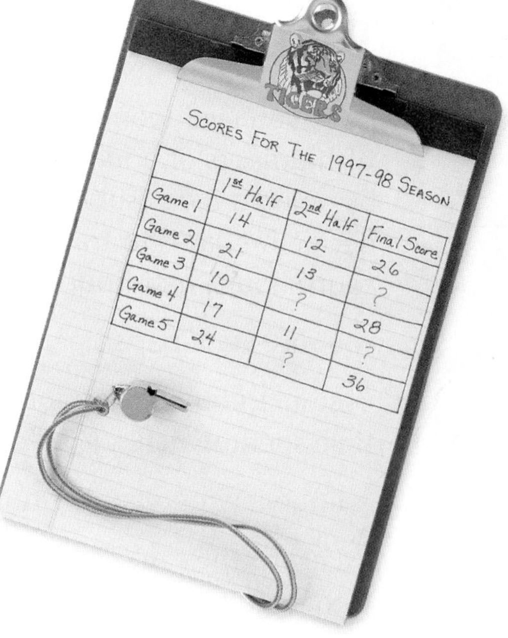

The football coach keeps a table of the scoring statistics for the games played each season. Help him complete the table.

Add to find the final score for Game 2.

You can use *n* instead of ? for a missing number.

$21 + 13 = n$, or

$$\begin{array}{r} 21 \\ +13 \\ \hline 34 \end{array}$$

So, the final score for Game 2 is 34.

Subtract to find the missing addend for the 2nd-half score in Game 3.

$10 + n = 28$, or

$$\begin{array}{r} 28 \\ -10 \\ \hline 18 \end{array}$$

So, the 2nd-half score for Game 3 is 18.

- Explain how to complete the table for Games 4 and 5.

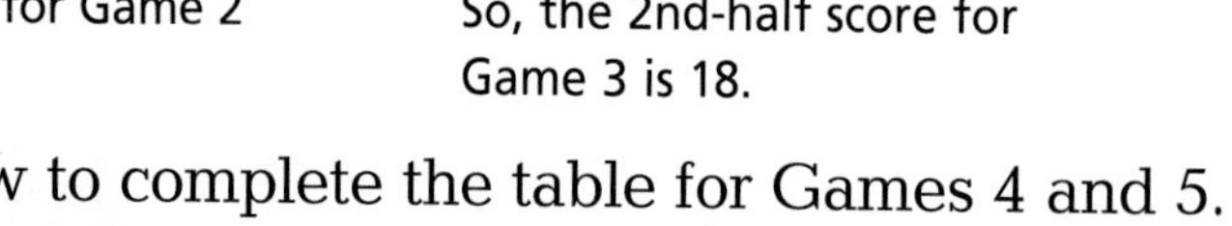

Addition and subtraction are **inverse** operations. This means that one operation undoes the other operation. This inverse relationship allows you to check an addition problem by using subtraction. It also lets you check a subtraction problem by using addition.

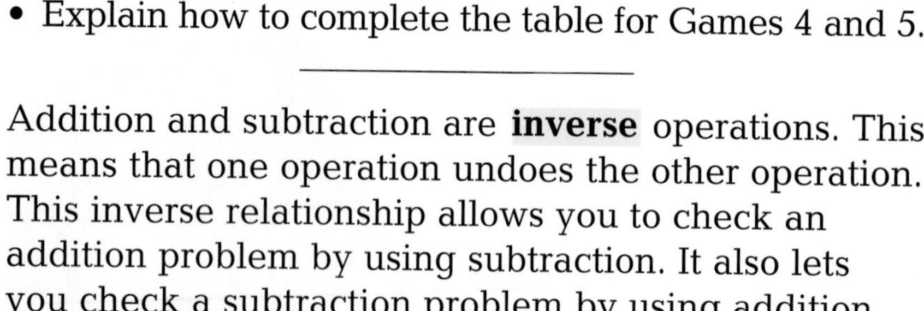

EXAMPLES

A Problem / Check

$$\begin{array}{r} 12 \\ +15 \\ \hline 27 \end{array} \qquad \begin{array}{r} 27 \\ -15 \\ \hline 12 \end{array}$$

B Problem / Check

$$\begin{array}{r} 538 \\ -415 \\ \hline 123 \end{array} \qquad \begin{array}{r} 123 \\ +415 \\ \hline 538 \end{array}$$

CRITICAL THINKING What number sentences can you write with the numbers 21, 63, and 84? How are the number sentences related?

▶ CHECK

Solve. Use the inverse operation to check each problem.

1. $\begin{array}{r} 24 \\ +83 \\ \hline \end{array}$ **2.** $\begin{array}{r} 56 \\ -14 \\ \hline \end{array}$ **3.** $\begin{array}{r} 235 \\ +162 \\ \hline \end{array}$ **4.** $\begin{array}{r} 837 \\ -506 \\ \hline \end{array}$

SOCIAL STUDIES LINK

In 1928, the first regularly scheduled television programs were broadcast on station WGY in Schenectady, N.Y. For how many years have television programs been on the air?

▶ PRACTICE

For Problems 5–8, use the data in the table.

GIRLS' BASKETBALL GAME SCORES 1998–99	
Game	Score
1	55
2	69
3	48
4	73
5	75

School Basketball Champs

5. How many total points were scored by the end of Game 3?
6. How many more points were scored in Game 5 than in Game 1?
7. How many points in all were scored during the 1998–99 season?
8. How many more points were scored in the 1998–99 season than the 279 points scored in the 1997–98 season?

Write the related number sentence. Find the sum or difference.

9. $85 - 32 = n$ **10.** $125 - 78 = n$ **11.** $140 - 96 = n$ **12.** $36 + n = 52$

13. $49 + n = 83$ **14.** $75 + n = 142$ **15.** $251 - 89 = n$ **16.** $n + 55 = 94$

Solve. Use the inverse operation to check each problem.

17. $\begin{array}{r} 16 \\ +25 \\ \hline \end{array}$ **18.** $\begin{array}{r} 49 \\ -32 \\ \hline \end{array}$ **19.** $\begin{array}{r} 37 \\ +26 \\ \hline \end{array}$ **20.** $\begin{array}{r} 125 \\ -\ 94 \\ \hline \end{array}$ **21.** $\begin{array}{r} 704 \\ -395 \\ \hline \end{array}$

Problem Solving • Mixed Applications

22. **Sports** Heather scored 28 points in the basketball game. She scored 16 points in the first half of the game. How many points did she score in the second half?
23. **Measurement** Antonio ran 118 yards in the first half of the football game. He ran 96 yards in the second half. How many yards did he run in the football game?
24. A professional basketball team played 82 games one year. They won 51 games. How many games did they lose?
25. **Write a problem** using the numbers 14 and 25.

Mixed Review and Test Prep

Tell whether each number is expressed as *cardinal, ordinal,* or *nominal.* (pages 2–3)

26. 6 feet **27.** 2nd **28.** 118 **29.** (904) 555-1842

Choose <, >, or = for each ●. (pages 12–13)

30. 375 ● 357 **A** < **B** > **C** =

31. 4,536 ● 4,563 **F** < **G** > **H** =

32. 7,061 ● 7,061 **A** < **B** > **C** =

33. 16,496 ● 16,469 **F** < **G** > **H** =

MORE PRACTICE page H72

More About Subtracting

You will investigate how to use counters to model subtraction of whole numbers.

Jon and his family are going to the beach on vacation. They must travel 532 miles to get there. On Saturday they traveled 346 miles. How many miles are left to travel?

Use subtraction to find how many miles are left to travel. Use color counters to model the subtraction.

MATERIALS: blue, red, green, and yellow counters; place-value mat

MODEL

Let ● = 1,000; ● = 100; ● = 10; ● = 1

Step 1

Model the problem. Start by placing 5 red counters, 3 green counters, and 2 yellow counters on the place-value mat.

$$\begin{array}{r} 532 \\ -346 \\ \hline \end{array}$$

Hundreds	Tens	Ones

Step 2

Look at the ones. Decide whether to regroup. Since 6 > 2, regroup 3 tens 2 ones as 2 tens 12 ones.

To subtract, take away 6 ones.

$$\begin{array}{r} \scriptstyle 2\,12 \\ 5\,\cancel{3}\,\cancel{2} \\ -3\,4\,6 \\ \hline 6 \end{array}$$

Hundreds	Tens	Ones

Step 3

Look at the tens. Since 4 > 2, regroup 5 hundreds 2 tens as 4 hundreds 12 tens. To subtract, take away 4 tens.

$$\begin{array}{r} \scriptstyle 12 \\ \scriptstyle 4\,\cancel{2}\,12 \\ \cancel{5}\,\cancel{3}\,\cancel{2} \\ -3\,4\,6 \\ \hline 8\,6 \end{array}$$

Hundreds	Tens	Ones

Step 4

Look at the hundreds. 3 < 4

To subtract, take away 3 hundreds.

$$\begin{array}{r} \scriptstyle 12 \\ \scriptstyle 4\,\cancel{2}\,12 \\ \cancel{5}\,\cancel{3}\,\cancel{2} \\ -3\,4\,6 \\ \hline 1\,8\,6 \end{array}$$

Hundreds	Tens	Ones

Record

Explain how to use counters to find a difference.

▶ TRY THIS

1. Find the difference of 3,031 and 1,456. Make a model and record the subtraction for the model.
2. How is regrouping with counters different from regrouping with place-value blocks?
3. **Write About It** Write a problem in which you take away to subtract. Explain how to solve the problem.

Technology Link

You can use a regrouping model to subtract large numbers by using E-Lab, Activity 2. Available on CD-ROM and on the Internet at **www.hbschool.com/elab**

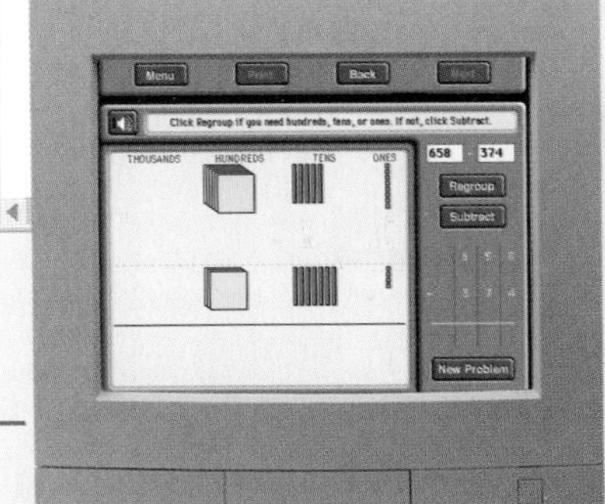

▶ PRACTICE

Draw the counters after regrouping. Find the difference.

4.

```
  1 13
 4 2̸ 3̸
−2 1 5
```

Hundreds	Tens	Ones

5.

```
  4 11
 7 5̸ 1̸
−5 3 9
```

Hundreds	Tens	Ones

Find the difference. You may use counters.

6. 274 − 165
7. 398 − 159
8. 415 − 231
9. 563 − 356
10. 628 − 147
11. 324 − 163
12. 495 − 276
13. 718 − 325
14. 1,825 − 752
15. 4,395 − 1,787
16. 6,211 − 4,523
17. 9,532 − 5,986

Problem Solving • Mixed Applications

Using Data For Problems 18–20, use the map.

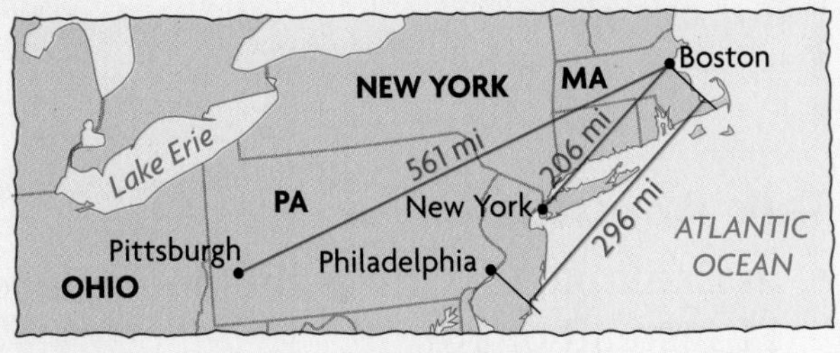

18. **Geography** How many more miles is it from Boston to Pittsburgh than from Boston to Philadelphia?
19. **Geography** How many more miles is it from Boston to Pittsburgh than from Boston to New York City and back to Boston?
20. **Measurement** If you drove round-trip from Boston to each of these cities, how many total miles would you travel?
21. Jerome's book has 238 pages. He has read 165 pages. How many more pages does he have to read?
22. **Write About It** Explain how to regroup to subtract 186 from 325.

MORE PRACTICE page H72

LESSON 3

Subtracting Across Zeros

Why learn this? You can find how far you have to go to reach a goal, such as selling a large number of tickets.

The band members are selling tickets for the homecoming football game. Their goal is to sell 3,000 tickets. They have sold 1,740 tickets. How many more tickets must they sell to reach their goal?

MODEL

Step 1	Step 2	Step 3
Subtract. $3{,}000 - 1{,}740 = n$ Subtract the ones. Look at the tens. Since $4 > 0$, regroup. There are 0 hundreds, so regroup 3 thousands as 2 thousands 10 hundreds.	Regroup 10 hundreds 0 tens as 9 hundreds 10 tens. Subtract the tens.	Subtract the hundreds and thousands.
2 10 ~~3~~,~~0~~00 −1,740 0	9 2 ~~10~~10 ~~3~~,~~0~~~~0~~0 −1,740 60	9 2 ~~10~~10 ~~3~~,~~0~~~~0~~0 −1,740 1,260

So, the band members must sell 1,260 more tickets to reach their goal.

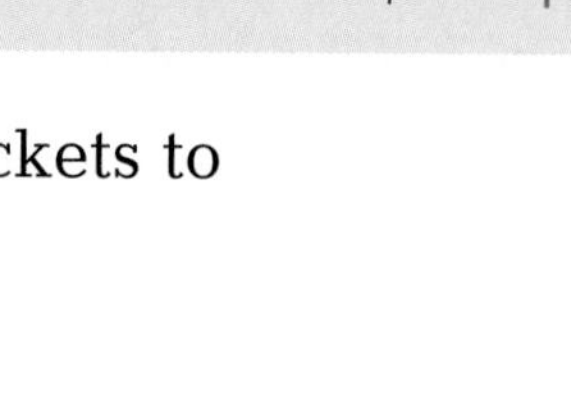

You can show regrouping in different ways.

EXAMPLES

A

3 9 910
~~4,000~~
−1, 8 6 3
2, 1 3 7

Regroup 400 tens as 399 tens 10 ones.

B

5 910
~~600~~
−4 7 2
1 2 8

C

2 9 911
1 ~~3,001~~
−1 2, 5 6 7
4 3 4

D

5 9 9 910
~~60,000~~
−3 9, 6 8 3
2 0, 3 1 7

Talk About It

- In Example C, why is the ones place regrouped to 11 instead of 10?
- How would you regroup 5,000 to subtract 16?

▶ CHECK

Show how you regrouped for each problem. Solve.

1. 300 − 147
2. 506 − 284
3. 8,004 − 3,567
4. 12,000 − 9,326
5. 30,005 − 18,690

▶ PRACTICE

Show how you regrouped for each problem. Solve.

6. $400 - 216$ **7.** $2,005 - 1,376$ **8.** $6,000 - 3,489$ **9.** $14,000 - 8,713$ **10.** $20,004 - 12,562$

Find the difference.

11. $300 - 197$ **12.** $800 - 76$ **13.** $4,000 - 362$ **14.** $1,002 - 543$ **15.** $7,000 - 2,895$

16. $8,000 - 2,560$ **17.** $12,000 - 9,962$ **18.** $18,000 - 4,021$ **19.** $30,000 - 23,918$ **20.** $70,000 - 55,739$

21. $6,000 - 4,773$ **22.** $24,000 - 7,888$ **23.** $13,000 - 7,095$ **24.** $50,000 - 27,688$ **25.** $37,000 - 19,408$

Problem Solving • Mixed Applications

26. The student council's goal is to sell 500 tickets to the dance. They sold 215 tickets during the week at school, and they sold 256 tickets at the door. How many more tickets do they need to sell to meet their goal?

27. Music There are 300 students in the marching band at Lakemont High School. Edgewater High School has 238 members in its band. How many more students are in the Lakemont band?

28. Sports During one professional football season, a leading player rushed 1,002 yards. His teammate rushed 875 yards. How many more yards did the leading player rush than his teammate?

29. **Write a problem** about a football stadium that seats 63,000 people. Use subtraction.

Technology Link

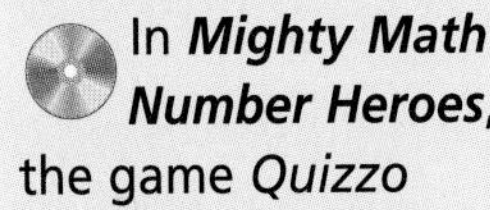

In *Mighty Math Number Heroes,* the game *Quizzo* challenges you to subtract large numbers to win a game. Use Grow Slide Level L.

Mixed Review and Test Prep

Find the sum. **(taught in 4th grade)**

30. $24 + 56 = n$ **31.** $216 + 37 = n$ **32.** $421 + 378 = n$

Choose the letter that tells the value of the blue digit. **(pages 6–11)**

33. 18,970,654 **A** 8 tens **B** 8 hundreds **C** 8 millions **D** 8 thousands

34. 48,065,129 **F** 6 ones **G** 6 millions **H** 6 hundreds **J** 6 ten thousands

LESSON 4

Choosing Addition or Subtraction

Why learn this? You will know whether to add or subtract to solve problems such as comparing the costs of two items.

You can analyze a problem to decide which operation to use.

A. Jeff has 837 U.S. stamps and 296 foreign stamps in his stamp collection. How many stamps does Jeff have altogether?

Add if the problem asks you to *join groups.*

$$\begin{array}{r} {\scriptstyle 1\,1} \\ 837 \\ +\,296 \\ \hline 1{,}133 \end{array}$$

So, Jeff has 1,133 stamps.

B. Elissa has 304 U.S. coins and 165 foreign coins in her coin collection. How many more U.S. coins than foreign coins does Elissa have?

Subtract if the problem asks you to *take away* part of the group or to *compare* two groups.

$$\begin{array}{r} {\scriptstyle 2\;9\;14} \\ \not{3}\,\not{0}\,\not{4} \\ -\,1\,6\,5 \\ \hline 1\,3\,9 \end{array}$$

So, Elissa has 139 more U.S. coins than foreign coins.

C. Use a calculator to add and subtract.

Add. $764 + 549 = n$

Press:

Subtract. $403 - 289 = n$

Press: 4 0 3 − 2 8 9 = | = 114.

CRITICAL THINKING How is the relationship between the numbers in the problem and the answer different for addition and subtraction?

▶ CHECK

Choose and name the operation. Solve.

1. Erica has 23 red ribbons and 12 green ribbons. How many ribbons does she have in all?

2. The store had 4,020 baseball cards and 1,839 were sold. How many does the store have left?

3. Jason has 56 antique cars and 123 new cars in his mini-car collection. How many more new cars are there?

4. Sue's class collected 337 shells. Bill's class collected 295 shells. How many shells were collected by the two classes?

Calculator Activities page H59

▶ PRACTICE

Choose and name the operation. Solve.

5. Felipe scored 124 points in a bowling game, and Robert scored 98 points. How many more points did Felipe score?

6. Caroline bought a bicycle for $118 and a helmet for $24. How much did she spend for the two items?

7. Leslie collected 1,256 cards, and Robert collected 864 cards. What is the total number of cards the two friends collected?

8. There were 12,890 people at a gymnastics event on Friday. On Saturday 9,965 people attended. How many more people were there on Friday?

Problem Solving • Mixed Applications

Using Data For Problems 9–10 and 13, use the table.

DAILY NEWS

SPORTS EXTRA

1996 OLYMPIC GAMES MEDALS TALLY

COUNTRY	GOLD	SILVER	BRONZE	TOTAL
U.S.A.	44	32	25	101
RUSSIA	26	21	16	63
GERMANY	20	18	27	65
CHINA	16	22	12	50

9. How many more total medals did the United States win than Russia?

10. Which country won 5 more silver medals than bronze medals?

11. History The first modern Olympic Games in 1896 had athletes competing in 9 events. In 1996, athletes competed in 271 events. How many more events were there in 1996?

12. Sports In the 1976 Olympics in Montreal, there were 1,247 women competitors. In 1996 in Atlanta 3,700 women competed in the Olympics. How many more women competed in 1996 than in 1976?

13. **Write a problem** using the information in the table.

Mixed Review and Test Prep

Order from least to greatest. (pages 12–13)

14. 9,230; 9,203; 9,300

15. 12,486; 12,864; 12,468

Use the number 569,302,481 to answer Exercise 16. (pages 8–11)

16. What is the name of the period that has the digits 302?

A Ones **B** Thousands

C Millions **D** Not Here

CULTURAL LINK

One of the first United States coins was called a *fugio*, or Franklin cent, named after Benjamin Franklin. It was made in 1787. How long ago was the Franklin cent made?

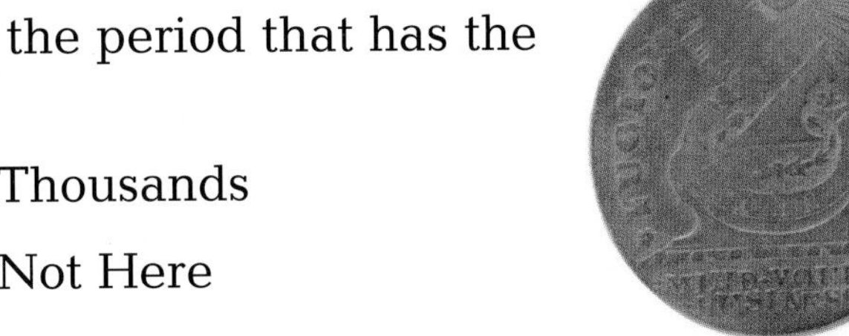

Estimation and Column Addition

VOCABULARY
compatible numbers

Why learn this? You can estimate the cost of several items to be sure you have enough money to buy them.

The fifth-grade classes have been collecting books for their school library. The table below shows the number of books they have collected. About how many books have they collected so far?

Estimate the sum of 323, 408, 289, and 391.

Estimate by rounding to the greatest place-value position.

323 → 300
408 → 400
289 → 300
+391 → 400
1,400

So, to the nearest hundred, about 1,400 books have been collected so far.

- How does rounding to the greatest place-value position make estimating easier?

REMEMBER:

Rounding Rules

- Decide which digit is to be rounded.
- If the digit to its right is less than 5, the digit being rounded stays the same.
- If the digit to its right is 5 or more, the digit being rounded is increased by 1.

Estimate another way by using **compatible numbers**. These are numbers that are easy to compute mentally.

Estimate. $48 + 51 + 85 + 16 = n$

48, 51 → $48 + 51 \approx$ 100

85, +16 → $85 + 16 \approx$ +100

200

$\approx$ is the sign for "is approximately equal to."

So, the sum of $48 + 51 + 85 + 16$ is about 200.

Books Collected

Book	Number
Science	323
Fiction	408
History	289
Hobbies	391

▶ CHECK

Choose a method and estimate each sum.

1.	2.	3.	4.	5.
45	73	287	152	695
63	30	164	348	301
10	53	339	220	210
+88	+46	+592	+181	+799

▶ PRACTICE

Show how you estimated each problem. Solve.

6.	7.	8.	9.	10.
18	23	34	179	318
27	78	92	226	295
32	85	47	481	187
+47	+11	+12	+243	+206

Choose a method and estimate each sum.

11.	12.	13.	14.	15.
13	52	479	809	940
25	65	618	659	768
82	73	735	458	832
+91	+95	+321	+575	+995

16.	17.	18.	19.	20.
905	711	299	450	1,006
642	788	103	289	2,972
756	702	111	649	3,112
+596	+704	+692	+198	+4,989

Problem Solving • Mixed Applications

Using Data For Problems 21–24, use the table.

OAK RIDGE SCHOOL MAGAZINE SUBSCRIPTION SALES	
Grade	Number Sold
2nd	98
3rd	135
4th	196
5th	264

21. **Estimation** About how many magazine subscriptions were sold by all four grades?

22. **Estimation** The school's goal is to sell 1,000 subscriptions. About how many more subscriptions do they need to sell?

23. **Compare** How many more subscriptions did the fifth grade sell than the fourth grade? the third grade sell than the second grade?

24. The school set a new goal for sales next year. The new goal is to sell 1,500 subscriptions. What might be the new goals for each grade?

25. **Logic** Corey sold more subscriptions than Sandy but fewer than Sol. Christine sold the fewest subscriptions. Who sold the most?

26. **Money** Steve spent $4.89 for car wax, $1.98 for a sponge, and $3.59 for window cleaner. How much did he spend?

27. **Write a problem** that uses estimation and this data: Alana buys four items priced $9, $12, $25, and $18.

MORE PRACTICE page H73

Problem–Solving: Estimate or Exact Answer?

▶ **THE PROBLEM** Suppose you go to a pet store to buy supplies for your kitten. You take a $10.00 bill with you. You want to buy litter for $1.98, a collar for $3.89, and treats for $2.79. Do you have enough money to pay for all three items? How much will you pay at the register? How much change will you receive?

UNDERSTAND

- What are you asked to do?
- What information will you use?
- Is there information you will not use? If so, what?

PLAN

- How can you solve the problem?

  Estimate first. Then, find the exact amount of the items and the amount of change received.

SOLVE

- Sometimes you need an exact answer to a problem. Sometimes an estimate will do.

Question 1

Will you have enough money to pay for all 3 items?

To answer this question, you can estimate. Round to the next higher dollar.

$$\begin{array}{rcr} \$1.98 & \longrightarrow & \$2.00 \\ 3.89 & \longrightarrow & 4.00 \\ +\ 2.79 & \longrightarrow & 3.00 \\ \hline & & \$9.00 \end{array}$$

9 < 10, so $10.00 should be enough to pay for the three items.

Question 2

How much will you pay at the cash register, and how much change will you receive?

To answer these questions, you need exact answers. Add to find the exact amount to pay at the cash register. Subtract that sum from $10.00 to find the amount of change you will receive.

$$\begin{array}{r} \$1.98 \\ 3.89 \\ +\ 2.79 \\ \hline \$8.66 \end{array} \qquad \begin{array}{r} \$10.00 \\ -\ \ 8.66 \\ \hline \$\ 1.34 \end{array} \text{ change}$$

The exact cost of all three items is $8.66. You will receive $1.34 in change.

LOOK BACK

- How can you decide if your answer is reasonable?
- What other method could you use?

▶ PRACTICE

Decide whether you need to estimate, find the exact answer, or both. Solve.

1. Mrs. Dunn has $10.00 with her at the grocery store. She chooses a roast for $5.89, potatoes for $1.79, and broccoli for $0.98. Does she have enough money to pay for all three items? How much will she pay at the cash register? How much change will she receive?

2. Michael received $40.00 for his birthday. He wants to buy headphones for $12.98, a microphone for $11.99, and a compact disc for $12.95. Does he have enough money to pay for all three items? How much will he pay? How much change will he receive?

3. Chet took $20.00 to spend at the theme park. He paid $8.95 for admission and $5.25 for lunch. Will he be able to spend $10.00 at the gift shop?

4. Ronnetta wants to buy a pattern for $3.95, material for $8.99, and buttons for $5.75. She has $20.00. How much will she spend on the items? How much change will she receive?

Mixed Applications

Solve.

CHOOSE a strategy and a tool.

- Use a Table
- Write a Number Sentence
- Guess and Check
- Work Backward

Paper/Pencil

Calculator

Hands-On

Mental Math

5. The table shows four Olympic winners in the Decathlon. Which of these winners earned the most points? Which earned the least points?

DECATHLON WINNERS		
Year	Name	Points
1984	Daley Thompson	8,798
1988	Christian Schenk	8,488
1992	Robert Zmelik	8,611
1996	Dan O'Brien	8,824

6. Pedro signed up for karate with a special offer. He paid $44.95 for two half-hour lessons and a uniform. The regular price for a half-hour lesson is $24.95, and a uniform is $9.95. Which is the better buy? If Pedro chose the better buy, how much did he save?

7. The Dunns arrived home at 10:30. It had taken them 30 minutes to get home from the football game, which lasted 2 hours and 30 minutes. It took 15 minutes for them to drive from their home to the stadium. At what time did the Dunns leave their house?

8. The softball coach has 42 students trying out for her team, and the swimming coach has 26. The track coach has 12 more students trying out than the swimming coach. If no student is on more than one team, how many students try out in all?

MORE PRACTICE page H74

CHAPTER 2 Review/Test

CHECK Understanding

VOCABULARY

1. When one operation undoes the other operation, they are _?_ operations. (page 20)

2. Numbers that are easy to compute mentally are _?_ numbers. (page 28)

Draw the counters after regrouping. Find the difference. (pages 22–23)

3.
```
  3 11
 3 4 1
−2 1 3
```

Hundreds	Tens	Ones
●●●	●●●●	●

4.
```
  3 13
 8 4 3
−5 2 8
```

Hundreds	Tens	Ones
●●●●●●●●	●●●●	●●●

CHECK Skills

Solve. Use the inverse operation to check each problem. (pages 20–21)

5. 23 + 54

6. 48 − 15

7. 317 + 152

8. 956 − 435

Find the difference. (pages 24–25)

9. 4,000 − 1,230

10. 13,000 − 8,943

Choose a method and estimate each sum. (pages 28–29)

11. 289 + 156 + 392 + 235

12. 519 + 284 + 304 + 489

13. 199 + 418 + 526 + 311

Choose and name the operation. Solve. (pages 26–27)

14. Mary had $154 in savings. She spent $29 for a birthday gift. How much does Mary have left?

15. Jerry has 129 U.S. stamps and 317 foreign stamps. How many stamps does he have?

CHECK Problem Solving

Solve. (pages 30–31)

CHOOSE a strategy and a tool.

- Write a Number Sentence
- Act It Out
- Guess and Check

Paper/Pencil

Calculator

Hands-On

Mental Math

16. Stan ordered a T-shirt for $9.98, a belt for $5.25, and a cap for $6.79. He has $20.00. Does Stan have enough money for the 3 items?

17. A pencil costs $0.98 and a package of paper costs $1.97. Kelly spent $9.82. How many pencils and packages of paper did she buy?

Test Prep

CUMULATIVE
CHAPTERS 1–2

Choose the best answer.

1. $24 - 5 = 9 + \underline{\ ?\ }$

A 5 **B** 6

C 9 **D** 10

For Problems 2–3, use the graph.

The graph shows girls' basketball scores for 4 quarters of a game.

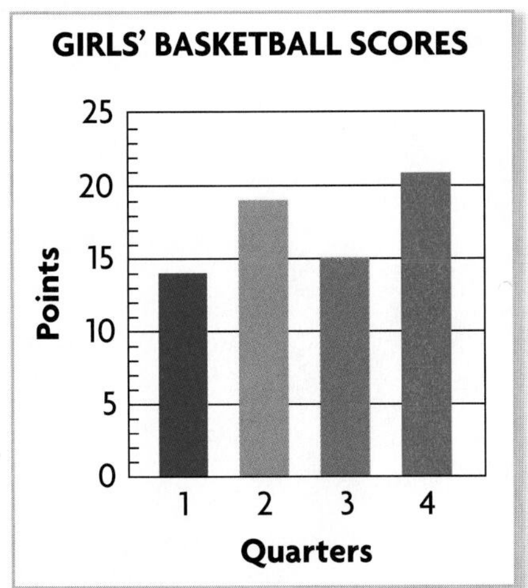

2. How many more points were scored in the 4th quarter than in the 2nd quarter?

F 3 **G** 5

H 2 **J** 20

3. In which quarters was the score more than 15 points?

A Quarters 1 and 2

B Quarters 2 and 3

C Quarters 1 and 4

D Quarters 2 and 4

E Not Here

4. 4,394 − 1,657 =

F 2,737 **G** 2,747

H 3,739 **J** 3,747

5. Akela's family traveled 445 miles on Thursday, 572 miles on Friday, and 257 miles on Saturday. How many miles did they travel in these 3 days?

A 1,264 mi **B** 1,274 mi

C 1,364 mi **D** 1,384 mi

6. Paul planted carrots in 4 rows. He planted 43 carrots in row one, 59 in row two, 32 in row three, and 41 in row four. Which is the best estimate of the number of carrots he planted?

F About 120 **G** About 170

H About 190 **J** About 200

7. Jake bought some grapes for $1.44. He gave the clerk $2.00. How much change should he receive?

A $1.56 **B** $1.44

C $0.56 **D** $0.44

8. What is the value of 7 in 5,017,643,216?

F 7 billion

G 7 million

H 7 thousand

J 7 hundred million

K Not Here

9. 13 + 38 ● 60 − 8

A >

B <

C =

D Not Here

3 PLACE VALUE OF DECIMALS

HEALTH **LINK**

Tasty, crunchy salad sprouts can be grown from many different grains or beans. The sprouts used in Chinese cooking come from mung beans, which are available in health food stores.

Problem-Solving Activity

Speedy Sprouters

True or false? By the end of the week you can be eating salad sprouts you grew yourself. You will track the sprouting of the seeds. At the end of the week, you will compare two types of seeds to see which is the speedier sprouter.

YOU WILL NEED: 200 seeds (100 of each kind), 2 paper towels, 2 closeable plastic bags, 2 plates

- Follow the steps to grow sprouts from each type of seed.
- Record the number of each kind of seed that sprouts on each day for one week.
- Make a decimal model that represents the number of seeds that sprouted out of each 100.
- Report your results.

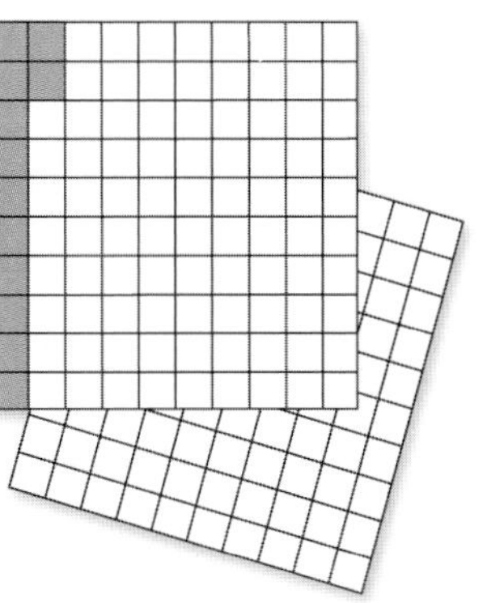

STEPS TO GROWING SPROUTS

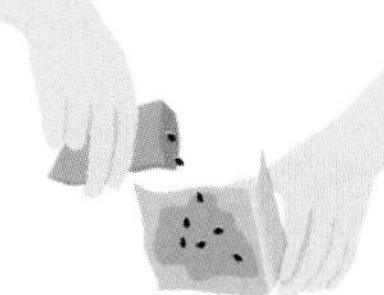

Place seeds in moist paper towel.

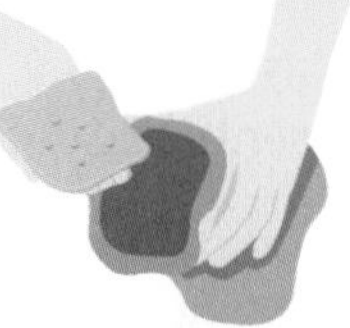

Put the folded paper towel in a labeled plastic bag. Store in a warm, dark place.

Transfer sprouted seeds to a moist paper towel in a dish. Move them to a well-lit place. Change the towel daily.

DID YOU

- ✓ follow the steps for growing the sprouts?
- ✓ make a recording sheet for each day of the week and record the number of seeds that sprouted?
- ✓ make a model to represent how many seeds sprouted out of each 100 seeds?

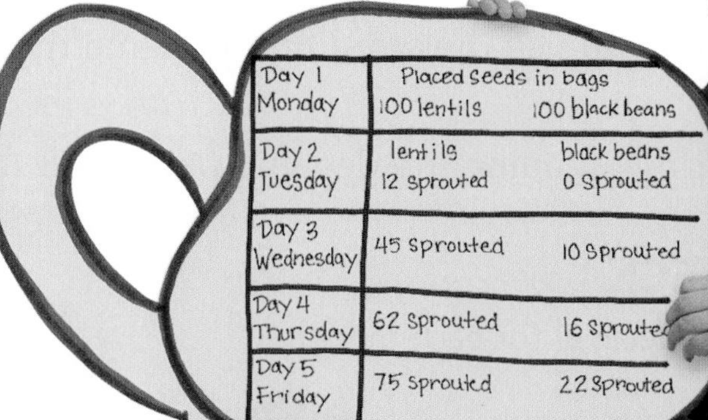

LESSON 1

Using Tenths and Hundredths

VOCABULARY
tenth
hundredth

Why learn this? You can identify the value of each decimal place when you are measuring the height of a plant to the nearest decimeter or centimeter.

Use base-ten blocks to model decimals.

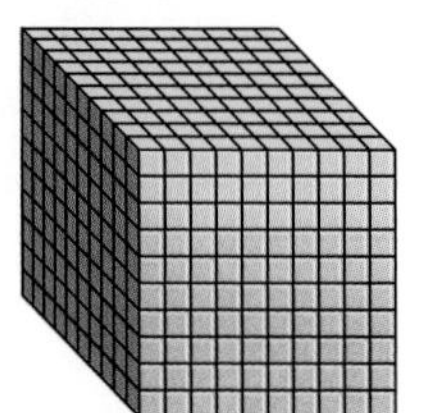	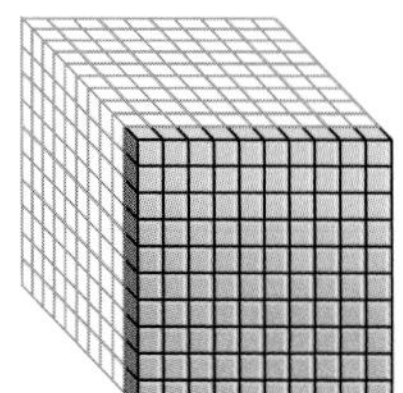	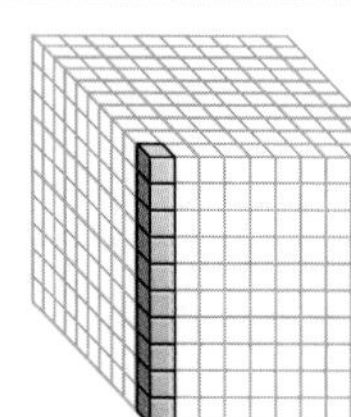
Let this model represent one whole, or 1.	The whole is divided into 10 equal parts. Each part is $\frac{1}{10}$.	The whole is divided into 100 equal parts. Each part is $\frac{1}{100}$.
Read: one	**Read:** one **tenth**	**Read:** one **hundredth**
Write: 1, or 1.0	**Write:** $\frac{1}{10}$, or 0.1	**Write:** $\frac{1}{100}$, or 0.01

SCIENCE LINK

Scientists use decimals when measuring plant growth. In the metric system, the decimeter is one *tenth* of a meter and the centimeter is one *hundredth* of a meter. One plant is 24 cm tall. How can you use a decimal to express this measurement in meters?

CRITICAL THINKING In the models, what are the relationships of tenths and hundredths to the whole?

____

Use a place-value chart to find the value of each digit. Show 1.45 on the place-value chart.

Ones	Tenths	Hundredths
1 •	4	5
$1 \times 1 = 1.0$	$4 \times 0.1 = 0.4$	$5 \times 0.01 = 0.05$

Standard Form: 1.45
Expanded Form: $1 + 0.4 + 0.05$
Written Form: one and forty-five hundredths

Talk About It

- Why do you use the word *and* to name the decimal point?
- How do you name the decimal part?

▶ CHECK

Write the decimal for each model.

1. 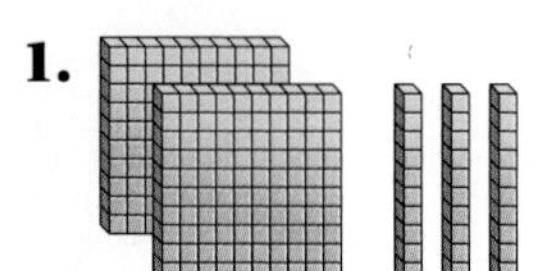

2. 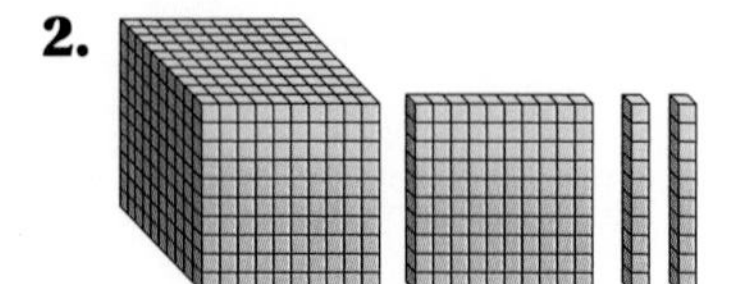

3. 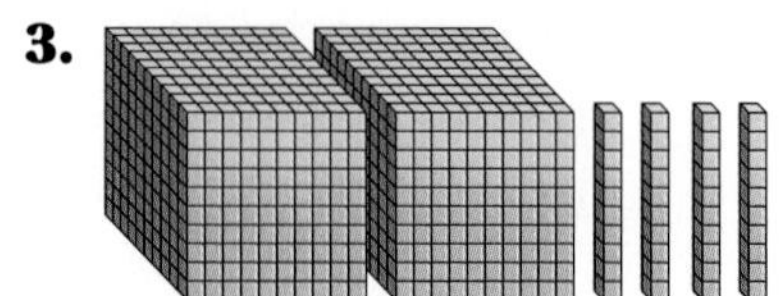

▶ PRACTICE

Write the letter of the decimal that matches each model.

a. 1.21 **b.** 2.22 **c.** 2.12 **d.** 2.21

4. 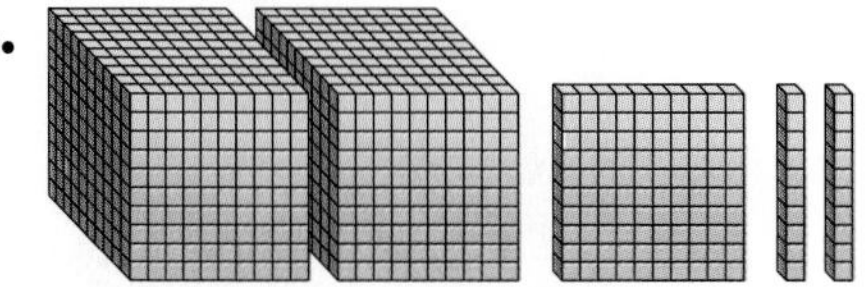

5. 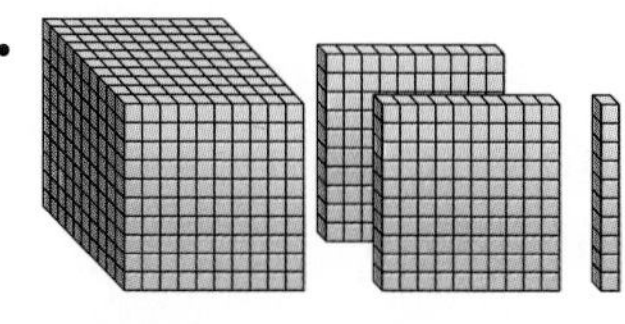

6. 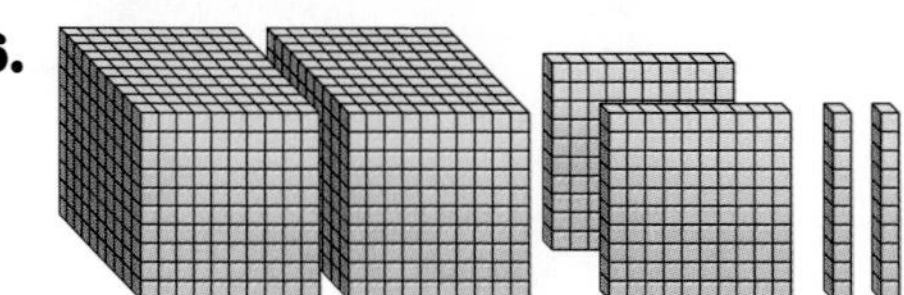

7. 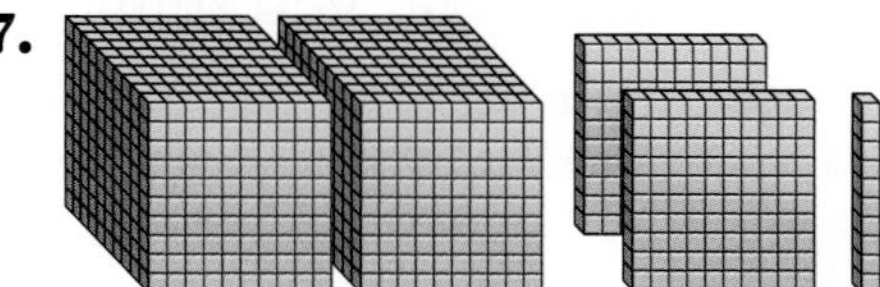

Write the decimal and fraction for each.

8. three and six tenths
9. eighteen hundredths
10. one and six hundredths
11. one and six tenths
12. four and eight hundredths
13. forty–five hundredths

Problem Solving • Mixed Applications

Using Data For Problems 14–16, use the gymnast's score.

14. What is the value of the 5 in the gymnast's score?

15. Write the gymnast's score in written form.

16. **Write a problem** about the gymnast's score.

17. Sports Mary is an Olympic gymnast. She practices gymnastics for 4 hours every day after school. On Saturday and Sunday she practices 6 hours each day. How many hours does Mary practice each week?

18. Time Brad left school at 3:20. He has practice at 4:30. It takes him 20 minutes to ride home, 15 minutes to eat a snack and get ready, and 25 minutes to ride to practice. What time will he arrive at practice?

Mixed Review and Test Prep

Order from greatest to least. (pages 12–13)

19. 5,479; 5,974; 4,597

20. 18,768; 18,678; 18,687

Choose the letter that tells the value of the blue digit. (pages 6–7)

21. 123,985 **A** 3 tens **B** 3 hundreds **C** 3 ten-thousands **D** 3 thousands

22. 475,932 **F** 9 ones **G** 9 tens **H** 9 hundreds **J** 9 thousands

MORE PRACTICE page H74

Thousandths

VOCABULARY
thousandths

You will investigate decimal numbers to the thousandths.

Working in the science lab

Scientists sometimes use liters and milliliters to measure the volume of liquids. One milliliter equals one thousandth of a liter.

Base-ten blocks can help you think about **thousandths**.

Ones	Tenths	Hundredths	Thousandths
one 1.0, or 1	one tenth 0.1, or $\frac{1}{10}$	one hundredth 0.01, or $\frac{1}{100}$	one thousandth 0.001, or $\frac{1}{1,000}$

- What part of a ones block is a thousandths block? What part of a liter is a milliliter?

▶ EXPLORE

Use base-ten blocks to show 7 milliliters.

MATERIALS: base-ten blocks

Record

Draw a picture of the base-ten blocks, and record the decimal number on a place-value chart. Write a number sentence to solve the problem.

Ones	Tenths	Hundredths	Thousandths
? •	?	?	?

Standard Form: ?
Expanded Form: ?
Written Form: ?

▶ TRY THIS

1. Use base-ten blocks to model 1.342. Record by drawing the model and writing the decimal on a place-value chart.
2. How many places to the right of the decimal point do you place the thousandths digit?

Calculator Activities page H69

3. **Write About It** Explain how you know that the thousandths block is $\frac{1}{1{,}000}$ of the ones block.

▶ PRACTICE

Use base-ten blocks to model each number. Record the number in a place-value chart.

4. 0.005 **5.** 2.134 **6.** 1.045 **7.** 3.003

8. 1.067 **9.** 0.123 **10.** 2.065 **11.** 3.206

Write in standard form.

12. eight thousandths **13.** three and six thousandths

14. fifty-four thousandths **15.** two and ninety-five thousandths

16. one hundred thirty-two thousandths **17.** eight and one hundred five thousandths

Write in expanded form.

18. 0.456 **19.** 0.037 **20.** 0.105 **21.** 0.068

Write in written form.

22. 0.002 **23.** 0.023 **24.** 0.405 **25.** 1.016

Problem Solving • Mixed Applications

For Problems 26–27, use the calculator display.

26. Express the number in written form.

27. In what place-value position is the digit 3?

28. Measurement Talia needs 1,000 mL of water for an experiment. There were 530 mL of water in a beaker. She added 380 mL of water. Does she have enough water for the experiment?

29. Using Data Maria surveyed 1,000 people before an election. The most popular candidate received 638 votes. How many of the people surveyed did not choose the most popular candidate? Express the number as a decimal.

Technology Link

In ***Mighty Math Calculating Crew***, the game *Nautical Number Line* challenges you to identify decimals on the number line. Use Grow Slide Level O.

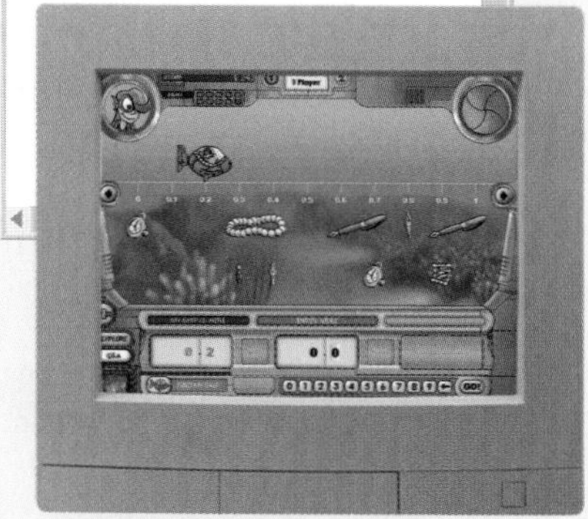

Technology Link

You can estimate decimals by using E-Lab, Activity 3. Available on CD-ROM and on the Internet at **www.hbschool.com/elab**

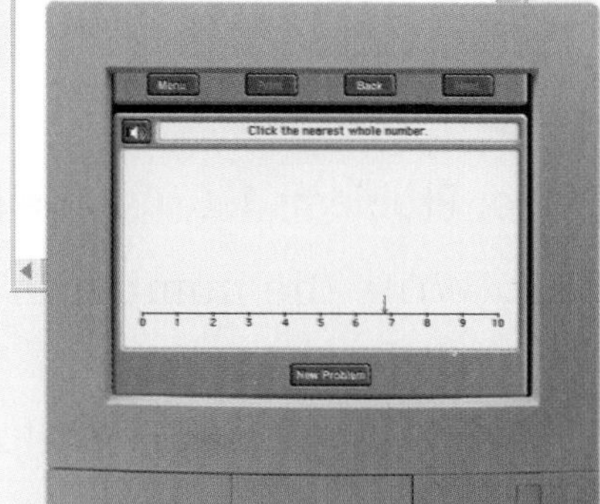

MORE PRACTICE page H74

LESSON 3

Place Value

Why learn this? You can read decimal numbers such as a measure of the distance an airplane can travel in one hour.

A science magazine reported that the Concorde, an airplane built by the English and the French, can travel 2,125.348 kilometers per hour.

Use a place-value chart to show the value of each digit in 2,125.348.

Thousands	Hundreds	Tens	Ones	Tenths	Hundredths	Thousandths
2 ,	1	2	5 .	3	4	8
2 × 1,000 = 2,000	1 × 100 = 100	2 × 10 = 20	5 × 1 = 5	3 × 0.1 = 0.3	4 × 0.01 = 0.04	8 × 0.001 = 0.008

Standard Form: 2,125.348
Expanded Form: 2,000 + 100 + 20 + 5 + 0.3 + 0.04 + 0.008
Written Form: two thousand, one hundred twenty-five and three hundred forty-eight thousandths

REMEMBER:

A *mixed decimal* is a number that is made up of a whole number and a decimal.

2.4

Talk About It

- Which part of the number is the whole-number part?
- Which part of the number is the decimal part?
- What is used to separate the whole-number part from the decimal part of the number?

CRITICAL THINKING What part of a mixed decimal names a number greater than 1 and what part names a number less than 1?

▶ CHECK

For Problems 1–6, use the number 4,605.271.

1. Write the number in expanded form.
2. Write the value of the digit 7.
3. Name the place-value position of the 5.
4. Write the written form of the number.
5. Write the value of the digit 2.
6. Name the place-value position of the digit 1.

▶ PRACTICE

Write in standard form.

7. 4,000 + 200 + 50 + 6 + 0.1 + 0.03 + 0.005

8. one thousand, two hundred five and three hundred six thousandths

9. 2,000 + 500 + 0 + 8 + 0.3 + 0.07 + 0.009

10. three thousand, seventeen and one hundred fifteen thousandths

One last lap to go!

Write the value of the digit 3 in each number.

11. 2,467.138 12. 3,108.657

13. 1,942.673 14. 4,508.305

Problem Solving • Mixed Applications

Using Data For Problems 15–18, use the table.

AUTO RACING ONE-MILE SPEED RECORD		
Driver	Year	Miles per hour
Milon	1920	155.046
Campbell	1933	272.109
Breedlove	1965	600.601
Noble	1983	633.468

15. Write the speed record for 1965 in written form.

16. Write the speed record for 1983 in expanded form.

17. Name the place-value position of the digit 9 in the 1933 speed record.

18. **Reasoning** How many years after 1920 did the speed record increase more than 475 miles per hour?

19. What number has 5 in the thousands and thousandths place, 6 in the hundreds and hundredths place, 7 in the tens and tenths place, and 9 in the ones place?

20. **Write a problem** using a number from thousands to thousandths.

Mixed Review and Test Prep

Write the expanded numbers in standard form. (pages 6–7)

21. 300,000 + 20,000 + 8,000 + 0 + 60 + 5

22. 700,000 + 0 + 0 + 500 + 30 + 2

23. 400,000 + 0 + 4,000 + 400 + 40 + 4

24. 80,000 + 3,000 + 0 + 40 + 3

Choose the related number sentence. (pages 20–21)

25. $45 + n = 82$ **A** 82 + 45 = 127 **B** 82 − 45 = 37 **C** 45 − 26 = 19

26. $97 - 68 = n$ **F** 97 − 39 = 58 **G** 97 + 29 = 126 **H** 68 + 29 = 97

MORE PRACTICE page H75

LESSON 4

Equivalent Decimals

VOCABULARY
equivalent decimal

Why learn this? You can use equivalent decimals when you are measuring heights or making change.

Numbers can have many names.

Here are some ways you can express the number 35.

3 tens 5 ones	35 ones	thirty-five	30 + 5
5×7	$40 - 5$	$70 \div 2$	35.00

Equivalent decimals are different names for the same number or amount.

Use base-ten blocks to model equivalent decimals.

EXAMPLES

A Equivalent Decimals — 0.3, 0.30

B Not Equivalent Decimals — 0.02, 0.002

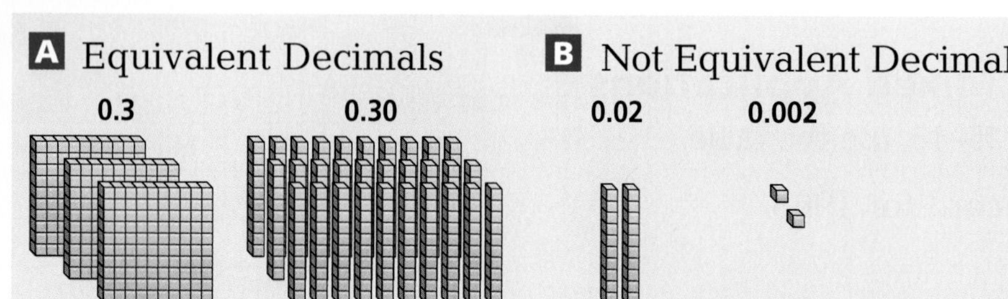

Talk About It

- In Example A, how do the blocks show that 0.3 and 0.30 are equivalent?
- In Example B, what happens to the size of the blocks when an additional zero is placed to the *left* of the digit?

CRITICAL THINKING Are 0.4 and 0.40 equivalent decimals? Explain how you know.

SCIENCE LINK

Giraffes are the tallest animals living in Africa. Newborn giraffes are about 1.8 m tall, and adult giraffes are from 4.25 m to 5.5 m tall.

Write an equivalent decimal for 1.8 and 5.5.

▶ CHECK

Write *equivalent* or *not equivalent* to describe each set of decimals.

1. 0.04 and 0.004

2. 1.2 and 1.20

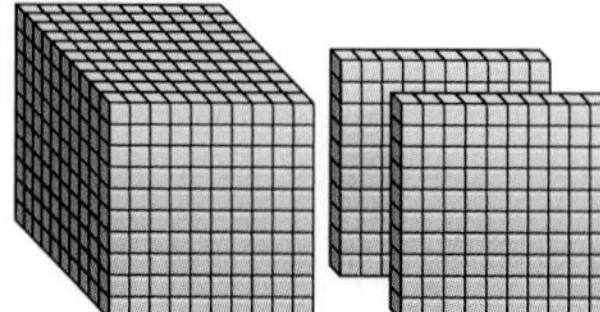

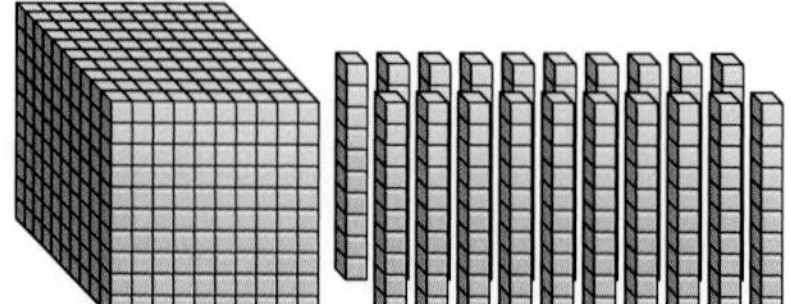

▶ PRACTICE

Write *equivalent* or *not equivalent* to describe each set of decimals.

3. 0.06 and 0.006

4. 1.3 and 1.30

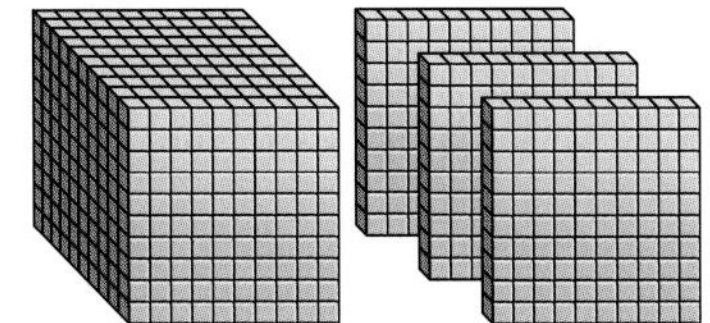

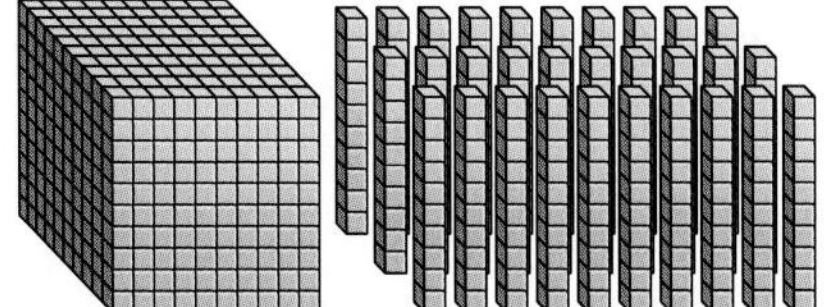

5. 1.052 and 1.025

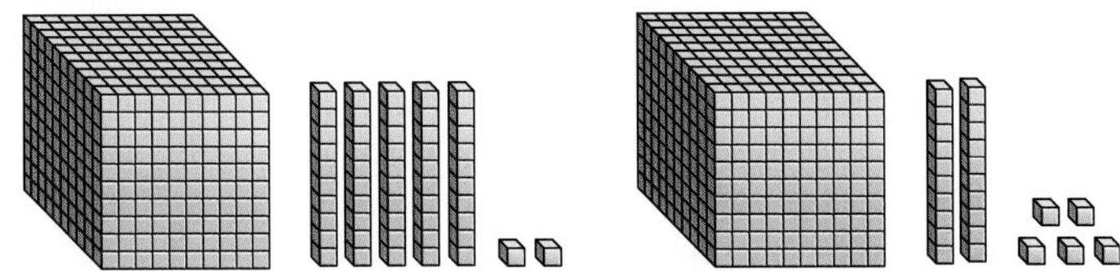

Write an equivalent decimal for each.

6. 0.01	**7.** 0.4	**8.** 0.53	**9.** 1.3	**10.** 0.600
11. 2.45	**12.** 0.070	**13.** 4.20	**14.** 3.300	**15.** 5.550

Problem Solving • Mixed Applications

16. Measurement At a long-jump competition, Phoebe jumped 96.2 inches. Write an equivalent decimal for the length of Phoebe's jump.

17. Consumer Danny stopped at the gas station to buy gas. Write an equivalent decimal for the number of gallons Danny bought.

18. **Write a problem** about the change Danny receives from a $10 bill when he buys gasoline.

Mixed Review and Test Prep

Find the difference. (pages 24–25)

19. 800 − 267	**20.** 4,000 − 1,976	**21.** 15,000 − 7,542	**22.** 40,000 − 32,618

Choose the letter of the best estimate. (pages 28–29)

23. 34 + 15 + 19 + 28
A 70 **B** 100 **C** 110 **D** 130

24. 259 + 140 + 209 + 391
F 800 **G** 900 **H** 1,000 **J** 1,200

25. 2,109 + 4,873 + 1,003 + 6,901
A 1,500 **B** 12,000 **C** 15,000 **D** 20,000

MORE PRACTICE page H75

Comparing and Ordering

Why learn this? You can compare scores at a sports event.

At the gymnastics meet, Melanie scored 8.69 on the balance beam, and Cindy scored 8.85. Whose score was higher?

Use a number line to compare decimals.

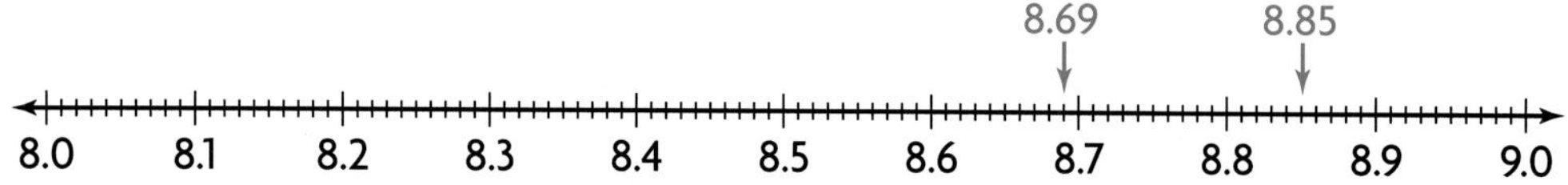

The number 8.85 is to the right of 8.69. This means that 8.85 is greater than 8.69. So, since 8.85 > 8.69, or 8.69 < 8.85, Cindy's score was higher.

Compare 3.452 and 3.456. Look for the first place where the digits are different.

Step 1	Step 2	Step 3	Step 4
Begin at the left. Compare the ones.	Compare the tenths.	Compare the hundredths.	Compare the thousandths.
3.452 ↓ 3.456 same number of ones	3.452 ↓ 3.456 same number of tenths	3.452 ↓ 3.456 same number of hundredths	3.452 ↓ 3.456 6 > 2, or 2 < 6

So, 3.456 > 3.452, or 3.452 < 3.456.

Order numbers by comparing them in the same way.
Order these numbers from least to greatest: 4.37, 4.42, 4.21

MODEL

Step 1	Step 2	Step 3	Step 4
Begin at the left. Compare the ones.	Compare the tenths.	Order the digits.	Order the numbers.
4.37 ↓ 4.42 ↓ 4.21 same number of ones	4.37 ↓ 4.42 ↓ 4.21	2 < 3 < 4	4.21 < 4.37 < 4.42

- How can you order the numbers from greatest to least?

▶ CHECK

Use the number line to compare the decimals. Write <, >, or = for each ●.

6.0 6.1 6.2 6.3 6.4 6.5 6.6 6.7 6.8 6.9 7.0

1. 6.52 ● 6.25 **2.** 6.4 ● 6.39 **3.** 6.02 ● 6.10

4. 6.09 ● 6.90 **5.** 6.60 ● 6.6 **6.** 6.76 ● 6.67

▶ PRACTICE

Write <, >, or = for each ●.

7. 0.65 ● 0.63 **8.** 4.25 ● 4.52 **9.** 35.83 ● 35.85

10. 1.04 ● 1.040 **11.** 132.94 ● 132.49 **12.** 156.938 ● 156.839

13. 229.035 ● 229.305 **14.** 12.7 ● 12.700 **15.** 999.989 ● 999.998

16. 13.07 ● 13.707 **17.** 210.946 ● 210.946 **18.** 435.691 ● 435.961

Order from least to greatest.

19. 4.13, 4.05, 4.09 **20.** 15.49, 15.36, 15.63 **21.** 8.010, 8.001, 8.100

22. 21.025, 20.250, 20.052 **23.** 6.783, 6.387, 6.873, 6.837

Problem Solving • Mixed Applications

Using Data For Problems 24–28, use the menu.

24. Write the salads in order from the least expensive to the most expensive.

25. Money Which soup costs more than tomato soup?

26. Money Which item costs more than fruit salad but less than yogurt?

27. Money Which two items each cost more than yogurt but less than onion soup?

28. Write the soups in order from the most expensive to the least expensive.

29. Sports The soccer team earned $300 to purchase new equipment. They spent $237 at the sports store. How much money do they have left?

30. Write About It Explain how you know that 1.26 is greater than 1.06.

LESSON CONTINUES

Problem–Solving Strategy: Make a Table

▶ **THE PROBLEM** Kendra's science fair project was to compare Fertilizers A, B, and C to see which one would produce the tallest plant. She planted 3 identical plants and used a different fertilizer on each plant. After four weeks, the plants measured 0.27 meter, 0.38 meter, and 0.31 meter. Which fertilizer produced the tallest plant?

REMEMBER:

UNDERSTAND

PLAN

SOLVE

LOOK BACK

UNDERSTAND

- What are you asked to do?
- What information will you use?
- Is there information you will not use? If so, what?

PLAN

- What strategy can you use to solve the problem?

You can *make a table* to analyze the data.

Math and science work together.

SOLVE

- How can a table help you solve this problem?

You can make a table to record the measurements of the plants after they had grown for four weeks. Then you can compare the three decimal numbers to determine which fertilizer produced the tallest plant.

PLANT GROWTH AFTER FOUR WEEKS

Fertilizer	Height
A	0.27 meter
B	0.38 meter
C	0.31 meter

$0.38 > 0.31 > 0.27$

So, Fertilizer B produced the tallest plant after four weeks of growth.

Technology Link

You can use ***Graph Links Plus*** computer software to make a data table.

LOOK BACK

- How did the table help you find the answer?
- What other strategy could you use?

▶ PRACTICE

Make a table to solve.

1. Sara, Tara, and Tom were at the doctor's office. Sara's temperature was 98.9°F, Tara's was 99.8°F, and Tom's was 98.7°F. Who had the highest temperature?

2. Four friends are measuring their heights. Sharon is shorter than Bobby. Jenny is taller than Bobby but shorter than Sammy. Who is the tallest?

3. Three students were in the long-jump competition. Sam jumped 6.25 meters, Ron jumped 6.32 meters, and Vicki jumped 6.20 meters. Who made the longest jump?

4. At the gymnastics competition, Brandi scored 9.925 on the vault, Wendy scored 9.950 on the vault, and Susie scored 9.910 on the vault. Which gymnast had the highest score?

Mixed Applications

Solve.

CHOOSE a strategy and a tool.

- Draw a Diagram
- Work Backward
- Write a Number Sentence
- Make a Table
- Guess and Check

Paper/Pencil  Calculator  Hands-On  Mental Math

5. The map shows five countries in Europe and their areas in square miles. Which of these European countries has the greatest area? the least area?

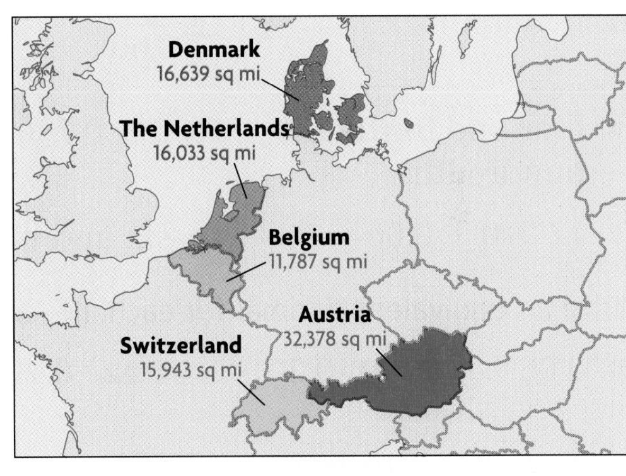

6. In the month of December, it rained 3.3 inches in Tampa, 2.4 inches in Miami, and 2.8 inches in Jacksonville. Which city had the greatest amount of rainfall in December?

7. Jack now has $435 in a savings account. He deposited $125 after his birthday in March. In August he deposited the $230 he earned over the summer. How much money did Jack have before the two deposits?

8. The Millers bought a new car for $14,589. If they paid a total of $17,438, including $925 for tax and tag, $819 for shipping, and payment for accessories, how much were the accessories?

9. Two numbers have a sum of 18 and a product of 56. What are the two numbers?

10. Jane's car gets 28 miles to a gallon of gasoline. Its tank holds 12 gallons of gasoline. How far can Jane drive on one tank of gas?

MORE PRACTICE page H75

CHAPTER 3 Review/Test

CHECK Understanding

VOCABULARY

1. The base-ten block that this model represents is one __?__. (page 38)

2. __?__ decimals are different names for the same number or amount. (page 42)

Write the decimal for each model. (pages 36–39)

3. 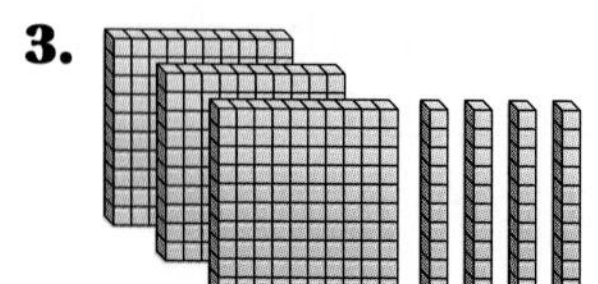

4. 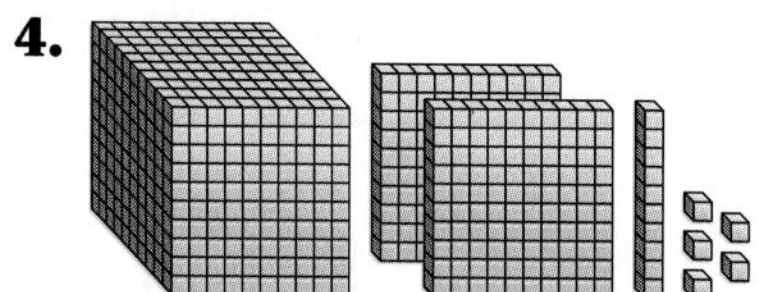

5. 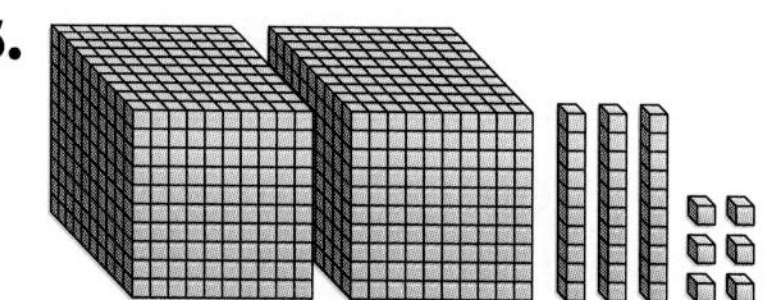

CHECK Skills

Write the value of each underlined digit as a decimal and as a fraction. (pages 36–41)

6. 0.<u>2</u>1
7. 4.8<u>3</u>
8. <u>5</u>.904
9. 1.90<u>2</u>
10. 2.7<u>1</u>2

Write the decimal for each. (pages 36–41)

11. five tenths
12. $\frac{26}{100}$
13. one and two hundredths
14. four and thirteen hundredths
15. $5 + 0.7 + 0 + 0.002$
16. $\frac{3}{1,000}$
17. $12 + 0 + 0.06$
18. six and nine thousandths
19. $7\frac{46}{100}$

Write an equivalent decimal for each. (pages 42–43)

20. 0.06
21. 0.30
22. 0.720
23. 1.60
24. 0.900

CHECK Problem Solving

Solve. (pages 46–47)

CHOOSE a strategy and a tool.

- Work Backward
- Make a Table
- Act It Out
- Draw a Diagram

Paper/Pencil

Calculator

Hands-On

Mental Math

25. Roxanne knitted three scarves. The blue one is 0.75 meter, the red one is 0.85 meter, and the green one is 0.80 meter. Which scarf is the shortest?

26. What number has 8 in the thousands and thousandths places, 6 in the hundreds and hundredths places, 3 in the tens and tenths places, and 0 in the ones place?

Test Prep

Choose the best answer.

1. Masud practiced drums for 15 minutes on Monday, 21 minutes on Tuesday, 27 minutes on Wednesday, and 33 minutes on Thursday. How many minutes did Masud practice on those four days?

A 95 min

B 94 min

C 96 min

D 92 min

E Not Here

2.
$$\begin{array}{r} 50{,}000 \\ -23{,}918 \\ \hline \end{array}$$

F 26,082

G 26,092

H 26,182

J 36,082

3. If Mrs. Ray pays for her new television in cash, it will cost \$190. If she makes monthly payments, it will cost \$250. How much will she save if she pays for the television in cash?

A \$50 **B** \$60

C \$75 **D** \$100

4. What is the value of 8 in 8,756,091?

F 8 thousands **G** 80 thousands

H 8 hundreds **J** 8 millions

5. How is 4 and 2 thousandths written in standard form?

A 4.002 **B** 4.02

C 4.2 **D** 42.2

6. Which of the following is an equivalent decimal for 3.4?

F 3.04 **G** 3.004

H 3.40 **J** 34

7. This table shows four states in the United States and their areas in square miles.

U.S. STATES	
Name	**Area (square miles)**
New Jersey	8,215
Michigan	96,705
California	158,869
Delaware	2,396

What is the difference in area between the state with the greatest area and the state with the least area?

A 94,216

B 96,705

C 156,473

D 163,707

8.
$$\begin{array}{r} 346 \\ 108 \\ +953 \\ \hline \end{array}$$

F 1,407

G 1,508

H 1,307

J 2,407

K Not Here

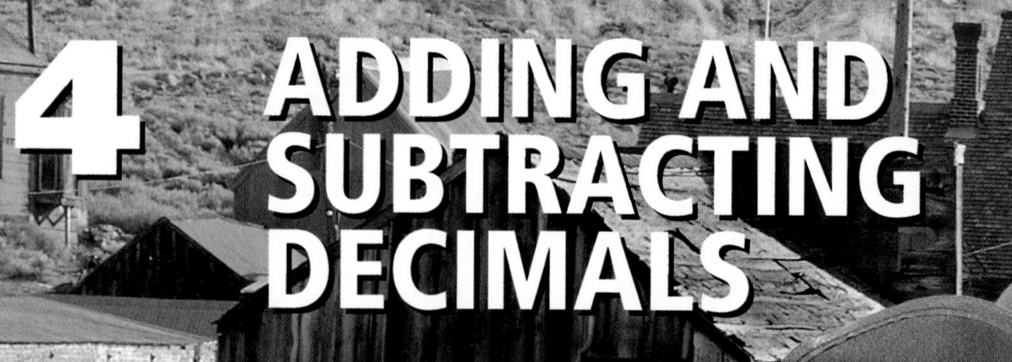

4 ADDING AND SUBTRACTING DECIMALS

HISTORY LINK

People went to California from 1848 to 1850 to mine gold. With so many people competing for supplies, prices rose dramatically. A pair of boots that cost $2.50 back home might cost from $12 to $16 in the mining towns.

Problem-Solving Activity

Try Your Luck at Mining

Suppose it is mid-March in 1850. You have just arrived in California and plan to pan for gold. The miner's store will give you credit to buy food and supplies.

You will start on April 1 and will try 8 weeks of panning for gold. On May 27, you will decide if you want to go on.

YOU WILL NEED: The Miner's Shopping List, calculators, number cubes

- Make a shopping list of 100 pounds of food and the Miner's Tool Pack. Show the total cost.
- "Pan for gold" with number cubes.
- Make a chart showing how much you spent and earned.
- Decide whether to continue to mine gold.

Miner's Shopping List

Food prices per pound:

ham	\$0.45
beans	\$0.07
lard	\$0.30
cheese	\$0.35
cornmeal	\$0.10
rice	\$0.12
beef jerky	\$0.75
dried apples	\$0.62
coffee	\$0.12
tea	\$1.00
brown sugar	\$0.12
molasses	\$1.50 per gallon
flour	\$8.00/hundred pounds

Miner's Tool Pack \$145.95

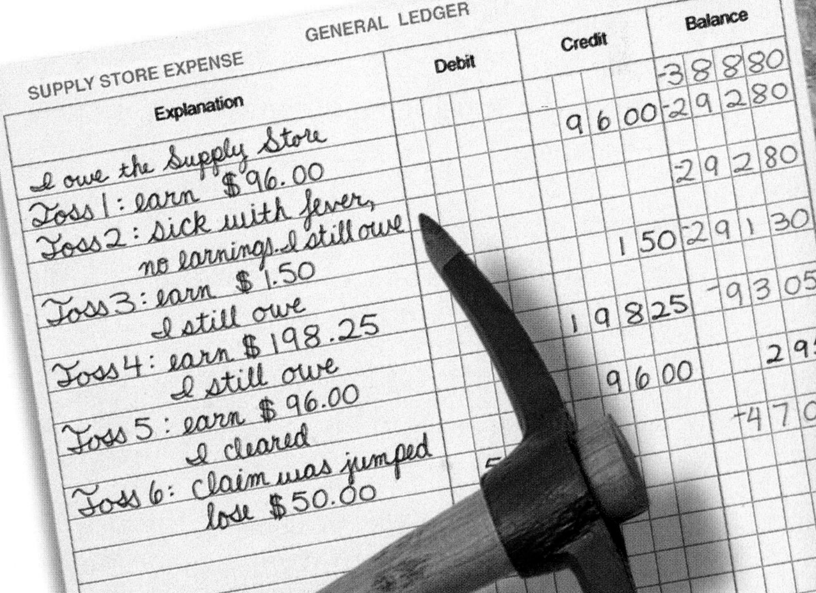

DID YOU

- ✓ make a shopping list and calculate the amount you owe the store?
- ✓ play Panning for Gold?
- ✓ make a chart to track your spending and earning?
- ✓ decide whether to continue?

Adding Decimals

VOCABULARY
decimal point

You will investigate adding decimals in tenths, hundredths, and thousandths.

Use base-ten blocks to find decimal sums.

▶ EXPLORE

Find $1.62 + 0.53 = n$.

MATERIALS: base-ten blocks

MODEL

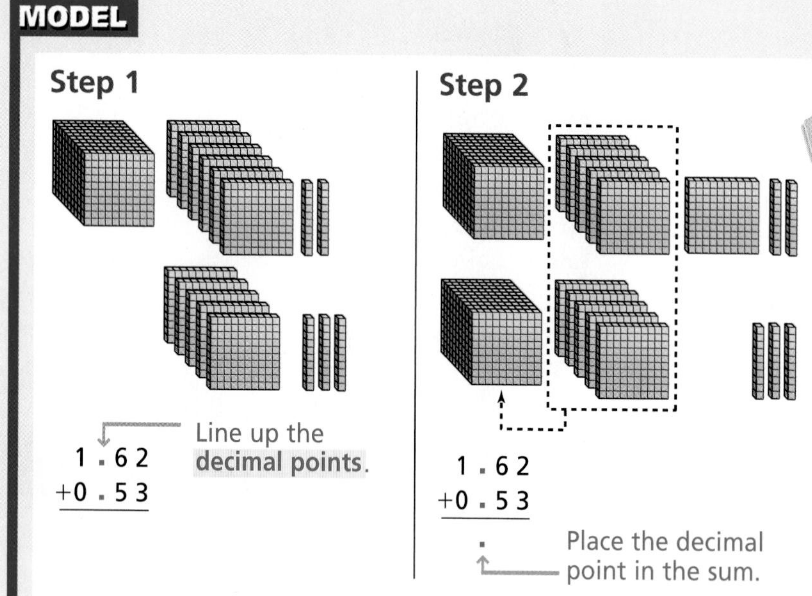

- When adding decimals, how do you know when to regroup?

Record

Use a place-value chart to record the problem and the answer. Explain how you found the sum.

Now, investigate adding decimals to thousandths.

▶ TRY THIS

1. Find $0.582 + 1.431 = n$. Model the problem with base-ten blocks. Record on a place-value chart.
2. How does the Order or Commutative Property apply to adding decimals?

REMEMBER:

The addition properties for whole numbers apply to decimals.

Order or Commutative Property Addends can be added in any order. The sum is always the same.

$2.67 + 1.32 = 3.99$ or
$1.32 + 2.67 = 3.99$

Zero Property When zero is added to any addend, the sum is the other addend.

$3.45 + 0 = 3.45$ or
$0 + 3.45 = 3.45$

Grouping or Associative Property Addends can be grouped differently. The sum is always the same.

$(1.2 + 3.6) + 2.0 = 6.8$ or
$1.2 + (3.6 + 2.0) = 6.8$

3. **Write About It** How is adding decimals like adding whole numbers?

▶ PRACTICE

Use base-ten blocks to model. Record the sum on a place-value chart.

4. $\begin{array}{r} 0.1 \\ +0.7 \\ \hline \end{array}$ 5. $\begin{array}{r} 0.3 \\ +0.9 \\ \hline \end{array}$ 6. $\begin{array}{r} 1.15 \\ +0.62 \\ \hline \end{array}$

7. $\begin{array}{r} 0.57 \\ +1.07 \\ \hline \end{array}$ 8. $\begin{array}{r} 1.525 \\ +0.795 \\ \hline \end{array}$ 9. $\begin{array}{r} 1.032 \\ +0.451 \\ \hline \end{array}$

Find the sum.

10. $\begin{array}{r} 2.1 \\ +1.7 \\ \hline \end{array}$ 11. $\begin{array}{r} 3.6 \\ +4.3 \\ \hline \end{array}$ 12. $\begin{array}{r} 2.45 \\ +0.63 \\ \hline \end{array}$ 13. $\begin{array}{r} 5.08 \\ +4.18 \\ \hline \end{array}$ 14. $\begin{array}{r} 1.21 \\ +1.73 \\ \hline \end{array}$

15. $\begin{array}{r} 3.41 \\ +2.54 \\ \hline \end{array}$ 16. $\begin{array}{r} 1.746 \\ +0.243 \\ \hline \end{array}$ 17. $\begin{array}{r} 6.037 \\ +1.547 \\ \hline \end{array}$ 18. $\begin{array}{r} 3.985 \\ +1.125 \\ \hline \end{array}$ 19. $\begin{array}{r} 2.505 \\ +1.449 \\ \hline \end{array}$

20. $\begin{array}{r} 12.3 \\ +\ 9.7 \\ \hline \end{array}$ 21. $\begin{array}{r} 3.53 \\ +1.68 \\ \hline \end{array}$ 22. $\begin{array}{r} 0.509 \\ +0.684 \\ \hline \end{array}$ 23. $\begin{array}{r} 4.185 \\ +8.906 \\ \hline \end{array}$ 24. $\begin{array}{r} 1.506 \\ +3.937 \\ \hline \end{array}$

25. $2.3 + 1.2 = n$ 26. $3.95 + 2.19 = n$ 27. $5.31 + 2.24 = n$

28. $1.84 + 1.92 = n$ 29. $1.347 + 4.616 = n$ 30. $2.095 + 1.294 = n$

31. $8.67 + 7.55 = n$ 32. $6.224 + 2.478 = n$ 33. $9.007 + 4.773 = n$

Problem Solving • Mixed Applications

34. At Pacific High School's stadium, there were 293 fans in the upper seats and 332 fans in the lower seats. Atlantic High School's stadium had 221 fans in each of the upper and lower seats. Which school had more fans?

35. **Science** The weather forecaster says the temperature will drop 20 degrees by Monday. Sunday's temperature is 76.8°F. What is the temperature expected to be on Monday?

36. **Money** Steven went to the soccer game. He paid $9.45 for a ticket and $3.75 for snacks. How much money did Steven spend?

37. **Write a problem** about a temperature of 76.8°F that uses subtraction.

Technology Link

You can add and subtract decimals by using E-Lab, Activity 4. Available on CD-ROM and on the Internet at **www.hbschool.com/elab**

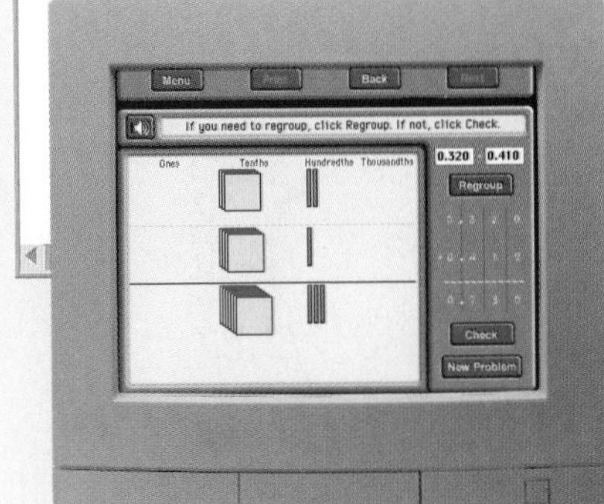

MORE PRACTICE page H76

More About Adding Decimals

Why learn this? You can add the costs of two items with different prices, such as $10.00 and $15.69.

Suppose you wanted to add decimal amounts with different place values?

Use equivalent decimals to write addition problems.

Find the sum of 25.8 and 56.75.

$$\begin{array}{r} 25.8 \\ +56.75 \\ \hline \end{array} \rightarrow \begin{array}{r} {}^{1\,1} \\ 25.80 \\ +56.75 \\ \hline 82.55 \end{array}$$

Line up the decimal points.
Place a zero to show equivalent decimals.
Place the decimal point in the sum.

So, the sum of 25.8 and 56.75 is 82.55.

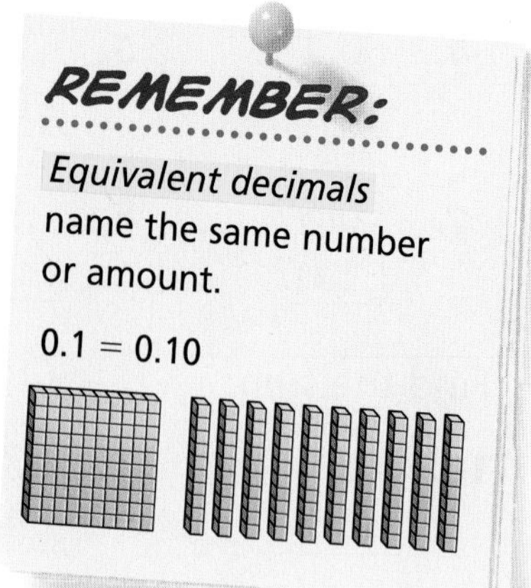

EXAMPLES

A

$$\begin{array}{r} 0.27 \\ +1.893 \\ \hline \end{array} \rightarrow \begin{array}{r} 0.270 \\ +1.893 \\ \hline 2.163 \end{array}$$

B

$$\begin{array}{r} 31.37 \\ +42.8 \\ \hline \end{array} \rightarrow \begin{array}{r} 31.37 \\ +42.80 \\ \hline 74.17 \end{array}$$

C

$$\begin{array}{r} 4 \\ +2.089 \\ \hline \end{array} \rightarrow \begin{array}{r} 4.000 \\ +2.089 \\ \hline 6.089 \end{array}$$

D

$$\begin{array}{r} \$5 \\ +\ 2.98 \\ \hline \end{array} \rightarrow \begin{array}{r} \$5.00 \\ +\ 2.98 \\ \hline \$7.98 \end{array}$$

Talk About It CRITICAL THINKING

- Why is it helpful to show equivalent decimals when adding?
- In Example A, how do you know that 0.27 = 0.270?
- Explain how the Zero Property is used in Example C.

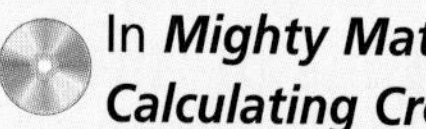

Technology Link

In ***Mighty Math Calculating Crew***, the game *Superhero Superstore* challenges you to add and subtract decimals. Use Grow Slide Levels K and M.

▶ CHECK

Find the sum.

1. $1.08 + 0.236 = n$
2. $7.355 + 9.2 = n$
3. $0.286 + 2.27 = n$
4. $3.54 + 1.2 = n$
5. $2.06 + 1.179 = n$
6. $9.153 + 7.368 = n$
7. $3.7 + 2.014 = n$
8. $5.602 + 2 = n$

▶ PRACTICE

Use an equivalent decimal to find the sum.

9. $2.16 + 0.289 = n$

10. $1.603 + 5.1 = n$

11. $1.35 + 4.767 = n$

12. $4.69 + 7 = n$

13. $23.9 + 18.289 = n$

14. $41.69 + 5.897 = n$

15. $4 + 0.5$

16. $3.8 + 2.37$

17. $2.05 + 0.975$

18. $5 + 9.18$

19. $5.255 + 0.44$

20. $2.8 + 3.54$

21. $6.74 + 0.846$

22. $9.6 + 7.457$

23. $8.359 + 1.2$

24. $12.1 + 9.01$

Problem Solving • Mixed Applications

25. Sports Carlos ran 0.75 mile on his first day of training camp, 0.95 mile on the second day, and 1.25 miles on the third day. How many total miles did he run at training camp?

26. Consumer Mrs. Hall used 35.350 gallons of gas in August, 21.098 gallons in September, and 29.567 gallons in October. How much gas did she use in the three months?

27. Money Bob bought a tennis racket cover for \$9.98, 2 cans of balls for \$2.98 each, and wristbands for \$1.89. How much did Bob spend for all of his purchases?

28. Write About It Explain how writing equivalent decimals helps you find sums.

Mixed Review and Test Prep

Solve. Use the inverse operation to check each problem. (pages 20–21)

29. $20 - 13$

30. $46 + 37$

31. $96 - 75$

32. $87 + 58$

Choose the letter of the correct difference. (pages 24–25)

33. $200 - 134 = n$ **A** 66 **B** 56 **C** 76 **D** 65

34. $8{,}000 - 6{,}982 = n$ **F** 1,019 **G** 1,118 **H** 2,982 **J** Not Here

35. $90{,}000 - 73{,}248 = n$ **A** 17,652 **B** 15,762 **C** 16,753 **D** 16,752

MORE PRACTICE page H76

LESSON 3

Subtracting Decimals

Why learn this? You can compare two distances to find how much farther you have to go.

Arsenio's mom is driving him to baseball practice. They live 1.252 miles from the baseball field. They stopped to pick up a teammate who lives 1.135 miles from Arsenio. How much farther do they have to drive to get to the baseball field?

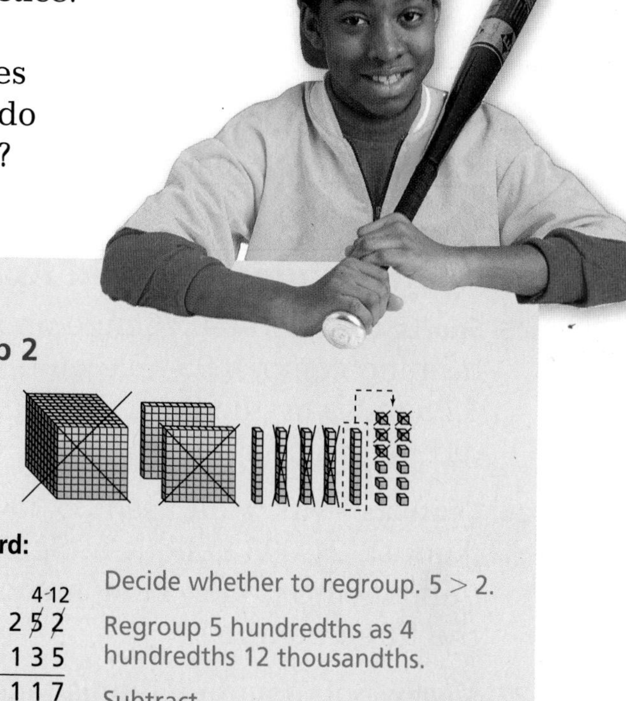

MODEL

Find $1.252 - 1.135 = n$.

Step 1

Record:

Line up the decimal points.

$$\begin{array}{r} 1.252 \\ -1.135 \\ \hline \end{array}$$

Step 2

Record:

$$\begin{array}{r} \scriptstyle 4\,12 \\ 1.2\not{5}\not{2} \\ -1.135 \\ \hline 0.117 \end{array}$$

Decide whether to regroup. 5 > 2.

Regroup 5 hundredths as 4 hundredths 12 thousandths.

Subtract.

Place a decimal point in the difference.

So, they have 0.117 mile farther to drive to the baseball field.

- How can you find how much more 3.0 is than 1.987?

EXAMPLES

A

$$\begin{array}{r} \scriptstyle 8\,10 \\ 2.\not{9}\not{0} \\ -0.74 \\ \hline 2.16 \end{array}$$

B

$$\begin{array}{r} \scriptstyle 5\,10 \\ 1.\not{6}\not{0}3 \\ -0.342 \\ \hline 1.261 \end{array}$$

C

$$\begin{array}{r} \scriptstyle 9\quad 14 \\ \not{1}\not{0}.\not{4}78 \\ -\ 9.531 \\ \hline 0.947 \end{array}$$

D

$$\begin{array}{r} \scriptstyle 5\,10 \\ 0.1\not{6}\not{0} \\ -0.047 \\ \hline 0.113 \end{array}$$

CRITICAL THINKING In Example C, why is it necessary to regroup in the tens place?

▶ CHECK

Find the difference.

1. $3.25 - 0.856 = n$ **2.** $5.1 - 4.932 = n$ **3.** $0.6 - 0.099 = n$

4. $\begin{array}{r} 2.08 \\ -0.79 \\ \hline \end{array}$ **5.** $\begin{array}{r} 4.2 \\ -2.148 \\ \hline \end{array}$ **6.** $\begin{array}{r} 12.311 \\ -\ 9.635 \\ \hline \end{array}$ **7.** $\begin{array}{r} 3.17 \\ -0.456 \\ \hline \end{array}$

▶ PRACTICE

Find the difference.

8. $\begin{array}{r} 1.3 \\ -0.7 \\ \hline \end{array}$ **9.** $\begin{array}{r} 2.6 \\ -2.3 \\ \hline \end{array}$ **10.** $\begin{array}{r} 3.05 \\ -2.6 \\ \hline \end{array}$ **11.** $\begin{array}{r} 5.7 \\ -4.8 \\ \hline \end{array}$ **12.** $\begin{array}{r} 4.2 \\ -1.02 \\ \hline \end{array}$

13. $\begin{array}{r} 4.43 \\ -2.12 \\ \hline \end{array}$ **14.** $\begin{array}{r} 2.5 \\ -1.646 \\ \hline \end{array}$ **15.** $\begin{array}{r} 6.832 \\ -3.98 \\ \hline \end{array}$ **16.** $\begin{array}{r} 11.537 \\ -\ 9.125 \\ \hline \end{array}$ **17.** $\begin{array}{r} 18.349 \\ -10.24 \\ \hline \end{array}$

18. $2.45 - 1.39 = n$ **19.** $1.4 - 0.422 = n$ **20.** $2.1 - 1.2 = n$

21. $5.95 - 1.994 = n$ **22.** $4.7 - 1.616 = n$ **23.** $5.31 - 2.264 = n$

Problem Solving • Mixed Applications

Using Data For Problems 24–26, use the table.

24. Sports Tim and William ran the 50-meter dash. Which boy won the race? How much faster was his time?

50-Meter Dash	
Tim	9.345 seconds
Tonya	8.483 seconds
William	8.300 seconds
Jennifer	10.293 seconds

The 50-meter dash

25. Time Tonya and Jennifer ran the same race as Tim and William. How much slower was Jennifer's time than Tonya's time?

26. Time How much faster was the fastest runner's time than the slowest runner's time?

27. Health Mary walked 0.85 mile the first day, 1.25 miles the second day, and 2.90 miles the third day. How many miles did Mary walk in all?

28. Write a problem using subtraction and the following information: Jeff is 1.325 meters tall, and Maria is 1.245 meters tall.

Mixed Review and Test Prep

Order from least to greatest. (pages 12–13)

29. 245, 524, 452 **30.** 1,539; 1,935; 1,395

31. 798, 987, 789 **32.** 2,634; 4,326; 2,364

Choose the related number sentence. (pages 20–21)

33. $23 + n = 42$ **A** $42 + 19 = 61$ **B** $42 - 23 = 19$ **C** $42 - 31 = 11$ **D** Not Here

34. $132 - 56 = n$ **F** $132 - 39 = 93$ **G** $56 + 76 = 132$ **H** $56 + 75 = 131$ **J** Not Here

35. $95 - n = 74$ **A** $74 + 21 = 95$ **B** $21 + 29 = 50$ **C** $76 + 19 = 95$ **D** Not Here

MORE PRACTICE page H76

LESSON 4

Estimating Sums and Differences

Why learn this? You can round to estimate times in a race.

Kim ran the race in 35.71 seconds. Ashley ran it in 33.59 seconds. To the nearest tenth of a second, how much faster was Ashley's time?

Estimate by rounding to the nearest tenth.

$$\begin{array}{r} 35.71 \rightarrow 35.7 \\ -33.59 \rightarrow 33.6 \\ \hline 2.1 \end{array}$$

- Line up the decimal points.
- If the digit in the hundredths place is 5 or more, round to the next higher tenths digit.
- If the digit in the hundredths place is less than 5, the tenths digit stays the same.

So, Ashley's time was about 2.1 seconds faster.

- Rounded to the nearest whole second, how much faster was Ashley's time?

____

At the gymnastics meet, Kathy scored 7.872 on uneven parallel bars, 8.747 on floor exercise, 8.645 on balance beam, and 9.020 on vault. To the nearest hundredth, what was her total score for the meet?

Estimate by rounding to the nearest hundredth.

$$\begin{array}{r} 7.872 \rightarrow 7.87 \\ 8.747 \rightarrow 8.75 \\ 8.645 \rightarrow 8.65 \\ +9.020 \rightarrow 9.02 \\ \hline 34.29 \end{array}$$

- Line up the decimal points.
- If the digit in the thousandths place is 5 or more, round to the next-higher hundredths digit.
- If the digit in the thousandths place is less than 5, the hundredths digit stays the same.

So, to the nearest hundredth, Kathy's score for the meet was 34.29.

SPORTS LINK

Each event in gymnastics is based on a perfect score of 10.000. Deductions are made for various errors in the routine. To the nearest hundredth, what would a score be if the deductions equaled 1.255?

▶ CHECK

Estimate the sum to the nearest tenth.

1. $\begin{array}{r} 0.41 \\ +1.79 \\ \hline \end{array}$

2. $\begin{array}{r} 3.62 \\ +5.25 \\ \hline \end{array}$

Estimate the difference to the nearest hundredth.

3. $\begin{array}{r} 1.649 \\ -0.233 \\ \hline \end{array}$

4. $\begin{array}{r} 2.026 \\ -1.163 \\ \hline \end{array}$

▶ PRACTICE

Estimate the sum or difference to the nearest tenth.

5. 5.59 − 1.73

6. 6.61 − 2.34

7. 9.87 + 4.63

8. 25.08 + 14.85

9. 39.25 − 11.02

Estimate the sum or difference to the nearest hundredth.

10. 1.345 + 0.744

11. 4.651 + 9.349

12. 3.050 − 2.363

13. 5.751 − 3.845

14. 2.645 + 0.244

Estimate the sum or difference and compare. Write < or > for each ●.

15. 8.14 − 4.89 ● 7.45 − 2.37

16. 3.82 + 5.46 ● 6.45 + 2.09

17. 7.925 + 5.392 ● 6.401 + 7.396

18. 22.45 − 12.57 ● 42.45 − 31.59

19. 35.24 + 24.76 ● 45.54 + 13.99

20. 68.98 + 46.97 ● 54.29 + 58.09

21. 8.075 − 6.395 ● 2.450 − 1.392

22. 9.269 − 1.423 ● 5.857 − 2.419

Problem Solving • Mixed Applications

23. Consumer Leslie bought a CD for $9.99. One week later the same CD was on sale for $6.89. How much money would Leslie have saved if she had bought the CD on sale?

24. Time Mike watched two movies. The first movie was 115 minutes long. The second movie was 127 minutes long. Write the length of each as hours and minutes.

25. Time Sandy skated the first lap in 25.19 seconds. She skated the second lap in 24.89 seconds. She estimates her total time to be about 50 seconds. Is this a good estimate?

26. Write About It How is estimating decimals like estimating whole numbers?

Mixed Review and Test Prep

Write the value of the digit 8 in each number. (pages 6–7)

27. 2,398 **28.** 3,830 **29.** 8,309 **30.** 380,254

Choose <, >, or = for each ●. (pages 12–13)

31. 433 ● 343 **A** < **B** > **C** = **D** Not Here

32. 8,006 ● 8,060 **F** < **G** > **H** = **J** Not Here

33. 19,782 ● 19,872 **A** < **B** > **C** = **D** Not Here

MORE PRACTICE pages H76–H77

Choosing Addition or Subtraction

Why learn this? You will know whether to add or subtract to solve problems, such as comparing the costs of two items.

Analyze a problem to decide which operation to use.

A. Mario bought a CD for $12.69 and a video game for $23.50. How much did Mario spend?

$$\begin{array}{r} \scriptstyle 1 \\ \$12.69 \\ +\ 23.50 \\ \hline \$36.19 \end{array}$$

Add if the problem asks you to *join groups.*

So, Mario spent $36.19.

B. Sara ran the race in 47.09 seconds. Mandy ran it in 39.15 seconds. How much faster was Mandy's time?

$$\begin{array}{r} \scriptstyle 3\ 16\ \ 10 \\ \not{4}\not{7}.\not{0}9 \\ -39.15 \\ \hline 7.94 \end{array}$$

Subtract if the problem asks you to *take away* part of the group or to *compare* two groups.

So, Mandy's time was 7.94 seconds faster.

- What would happen if you didn't line up the decimal points to subtract?

____

Use a calculator to add and subtract decimals.

Add. 17.643 + 2.5 = *n*

Press: 1 7 . 6 4 3 + 2 . 5 = [= 20.143]

Subtract. 71.3 − 68.755 = *n*

Press: 7 1 . 3 − 6 8 . 7 5 5 = [= 2.545]

CRITICAL THINKING Do you need to place zeros to show equivalent decimals when you use a calculator? Explain.

▶ CHECK

Choose and name the operation. Solve.

1. Jerry had $10. He bought a CD for $8.98. How much does he have left?

2. Ann drove 126.75 miles on Monday and 95.25 miles on Tuesday. How far did she drive in the two days?

▶ PRACTICE

Choose and name the operation. Solve.

3. Eduardo ran 0.52 mile the first day, 0.75 mile the second day, and 1.25 miles the third day. How many total miles did Eduardo run?

4. Scott paid $25.89 for a new video movie at Best Movies. John paid $27.75 for the same movie at another store. How much more did John pay for the movie?

5. Latoya is driving 94.2 miles to see her uncle. She has already traveled 58.7 miles. How many miles does Latoya have left to go?

6. Jose timed a race car doing laps around a race track. The times for three laps were 45.675, 46.849, and 43.439 seconds. How many seconds did it take for all three laps?

For Problems 7–10 and 14, use the items shown below.

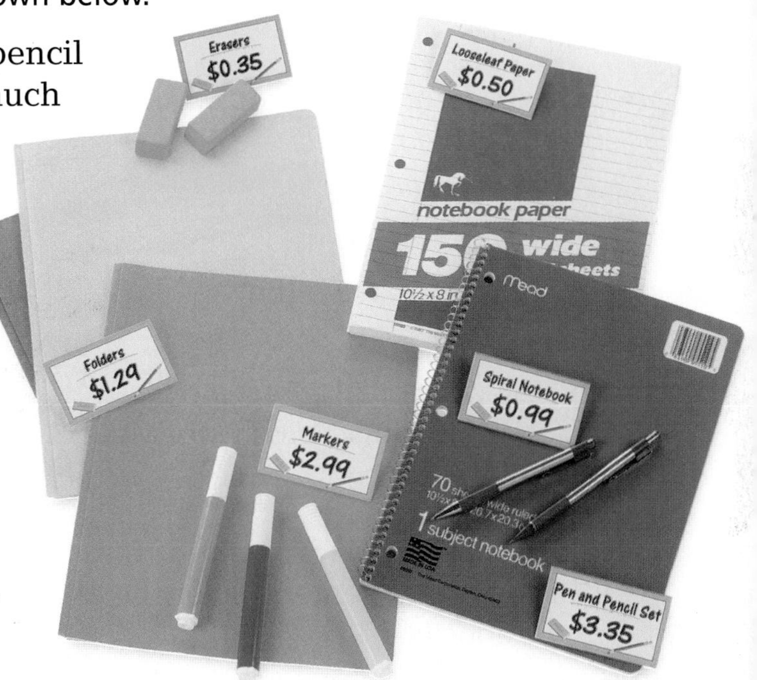

7. James bought 1 folder, 1 pen and pencil set, and 2 spiral notebooks. How much money did James spend in all?

8. Money James paid for these school supplies with a $10 bill. How much change did he receive?

9. Consumer The bookstore held a sale on school supplies. Markers were on sale for $0.50 off. What was the sale price of the markers?

10. Money Cindy received $3.71 in change from the bookstore. She bought 1 folder. How much money did Cindy have to start with?

Problem Solving • Mixed Applications

11. Jill counted 245 flowers on a nature walk. Tracy counted 442 flowers. How many more flowers did Tracy count?

12. Time Side A of Jason's new tape played for 21.5 minutes. Side B played for 19.8 minutes. How much longer did Side A play?

13. Geometry Carl is enclosing a rectangular field with fencing. The field is 120 feet long and 50 feet wide. How much fencing does he need to enclose the field?

14. **Write a problem** that requires addition or subtraction. Use items from the picture above.

Problem–Solving Strategy: Write a Number Sentence

▶ THE PROBLEM Mrs. McKay wants to write a check for $74.97 to the electric company. The bank charges a fee if a customer writes checks for more money than is in the account. Does she have enough money in her checking account to write the check to the electric company?

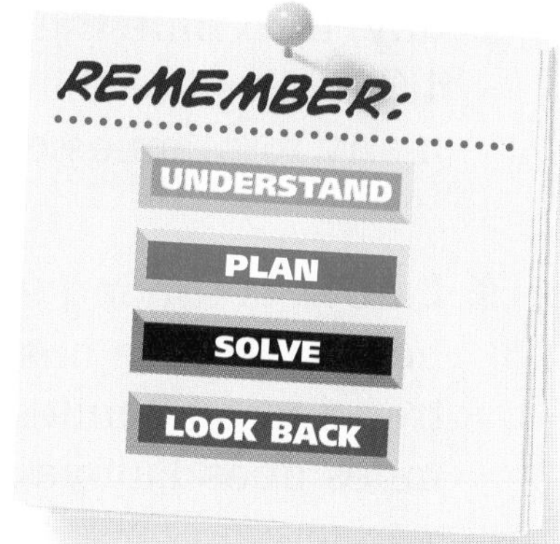

UNDERSTAND

- What are you asked to do?
- What information will you use?
- Is there information you will not use? If so, what?

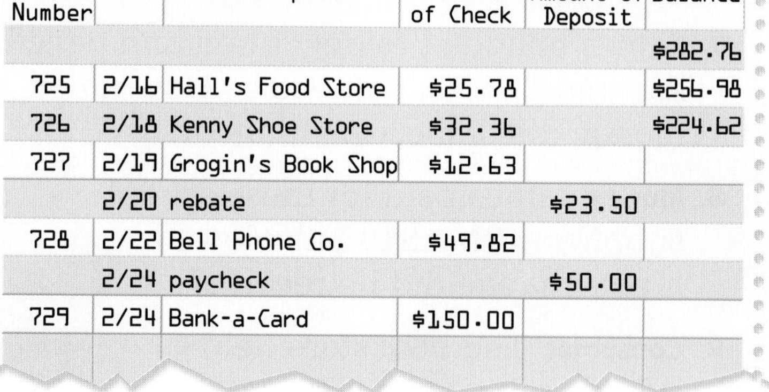

Check Number	Date	Description	Amount of Check	Amount of Deposit	Balance
					$282.76
725	2/16	Hall's Food Store	$25.78		$256.98
726	2/18	Kenny Shoe Store	$32.36		$224.62
727	2/19	Grogin's Book Shop	$12.63		
	2/20	rebate		$23.50	
728	2/22	Bell Phone Co.	$49.82		
	2/24	paycheck		$50.00	
729	2/24	Bank-a-Card	$150.00		

PLAN

- How can you solve the problem?

You can *write number sentences* to show the transactions in Mrs. McKay's checkbook.

SOLVE

- Write number sentences for the checks and deposits.

Begin each number sentence with the previous balance. Subtract the amount of each check, and add the amount of each deposit as it is made. You may wish to use a calculator.

So, Mrs. McKay has $85.67 in her account. This is enough to write the check for $74.97.

LOOK BACK

- How does writing a number sentence help you find the answer?
- What other strategy could you use?

▶ PRACTICE

Write a number sentence to solve.

1. Sara's checking account had a starting balance of $98.29. She wrote checks for $23.84, $52.39, and $14.45. She made deposits of $25.50 and $95.00. What is her balance? Does Sara have enough to write a check for $112.93?

2. Paul received his bank statement in the mail. He had a starting balance of $45.96. The statement shows deposits of $59.90 and $199.28. He wrote checks for $54.29 and $89.48. What is Paul's current balance?

3. At baseball practice, Justin caught 36 fly balls. Brad caught 41 fly balls. Kevin caught 10 fewer than Justin and Brad combined. How many fly balls did Kevin catch?

4. The four girls on the 400-meter relay team each ran 100 meters. Their times were 15.2 seconds, 14.7 seconds, 14.4 seconds, and 15.5 seconds. What was their combined time?

Mixed Applications

Solve.

CHOOSE a strategy and a tool.

- Draw a Diagram
- Write a Number Sentence
- Use a Table
- Work Backward

Paper/Pencil

Calculator

Hands-On

Mental Math

5. Janine's car can get 210 miles to a tank of gas. About how many tanks of gas does she need to drive from Chicago to Boston?

Road Mileage from Chicago	
Boston	963
Atlanta	674
New York	802
Denver	996

6. Sandy drove from Chicago to Atlanta, back to Chicago, and then to Denver. How many miles did she drive in all?

7. Candace wants 2 pairs of running shoes that cost $39.98 a pair. When she buys them, she gets $8 off the price of the second pair. What will Candace pay for the 2 pairs of shoes?

8. The soccer coach had 24 students try out for his team, and the tennis coach had 18 students try out. The basketball coach had 8 more students try out than for soccer and tennis combined. How many students tried out for the basketball team?

Technology Link

You can use ***Data ToolKit*** computer software to display data in a spreadsheet.

MORE PRACTICE page H77

CHAPTER 4 Review/Test

CHECK Understanding

Find the sum or difference. You may use base-ten blocks. (pages 52–53)

1. $\begin{array}{r} 1.3 \\ +0.5 \\ \hline \end{array}$ **2.** $\begin{array}{r} 3.7 \\ +2.8 \\ \hline \end{array}$ **3.** $\begin{array}{r} 5.15 \\ -0.97 \\ \hline \end{array}$ **4.** $\begin{array}{r} 4.09 \\ +6.13 \\ \hline \end{array}$ **5.** $\begin{array}{r} 9.736 \\ -7.524 \\ \hline \end{array}$

Use an equivalent decimal to find the sum or difference. (pages 54–57)

6. $2.32 + 0.287 = n$ **7.** $1.03 - 0.987 = n$ **8.** $0.286 + 2.27 = n$

9. $11.754 - 8.6 = n$ **10.** $5.384 + 8.1 = n$ **11.** $3.1 - 0.985 = n$

CHECK Skills

Find the sum or difference. (pages 52–57)

12. $\begin{array}{r} 2.4 \\ -1.9 \\ \hline \end{array}$ **13.** $\begin{array}{r} 1.76 \\ +4.02 \\ \hline \end{array}$ **14.** $\begin{array}{r} 2.905 \\ +1.973 \\ \hline \end{array}$ **15.** $\begin{array}{r} 6.011 \\ -4.842 \\ \hline \end{array}$ **16.** $\begin{array}{r} 8.254 \\ -6.087 \\ \hline \end{array}$

17. $6.27 + 3.098 = n$ **18.** $4.748 - 2.01 = n$ **19.** $8.009 + 2.91 = n$

Estimate the sum to the nearest tenth. (pages 58–59)

20. $\begin{array}{r} 1.52 \\ +0.24 \\ \hline \end{array}$ **21.** $\begin{array}{r} 4.03 \\ +1.26 \\ \hline \end{array}$

Estimate the difference to the nearest hundredth. (pages 58–59)

22. $\begin{array}{r} 2.753 \\ -0.627 \\ \hline \end{array}$ **23.** $\begin{array}{r} 6.074 \\ -4.255 \\ \hline \end{array}$

Choose and name the operation. Solve. (pages 60–61)

24. Jodie had \$39 in savings. She bought a CD for \$14.69. How much does she have left?

25. Ted rode his bicycle 1.5 miles to school and then returned. Later he rode 0.8 mile to the store and then returned. How far did Ted ride?

CHECK Problem Solving

Solve. (pages 62–63)

CHOOSE a strategy and a tool.

- Write a Number Sentence
- Guess and Check
- Act It Out
- Work Backward

Paper/Pencil

Calculator

Hands-On

Mental Math

26. Ken had \$49.61 in his bank account. He deposited \$52.50 and wrote checks for \$12.89 and \$29.99. How much is left in his account?

27. Jenna won 2 tennis matches more than Shandra. Ann won 1 match more than Shandra. Ann won 4 matches. Who won the most matches?

Test Prep

CUMULATIVE
CHAPTERS 1–4

Choose the best answer.

1. How is the number in the following sentence expressed?

Kate is sixth in line to buy lunch.

A cardinal

B ordinal

C nominal

D Not Here

2. The fifth-grade class collected 345 bottles the first week, 654 bottles the next week, 201 bottles the third week, and 589 bottles the fourth week. Which of the following is a reasonable estimate for the number of bottles the fifth-grade class collected?

F 1,500 **G** 1,800

H 2,000 **J** 2,400

3. Which group of numbers is in order from *least* to *greatest*?

A 7.86, 7.89, 7.8, 7.94

B 7.8, 7.86, 7.89, 7.94

C 7.8, 7.94, 7.89, 7.86

D 7.94, 7.89, 7.86, 7.8

E Not Here

4. For the number 12,432,108,576, in which place-value position is the digit 3?

F billions

G hundred millions

H ten millions

J ten thousands

5. Which of the following is an equivalent decimal for 0.45?

A 0.450 **B** 0.451

C 4.50 **D** 4.5

6. Choose the decimal that matches the model.

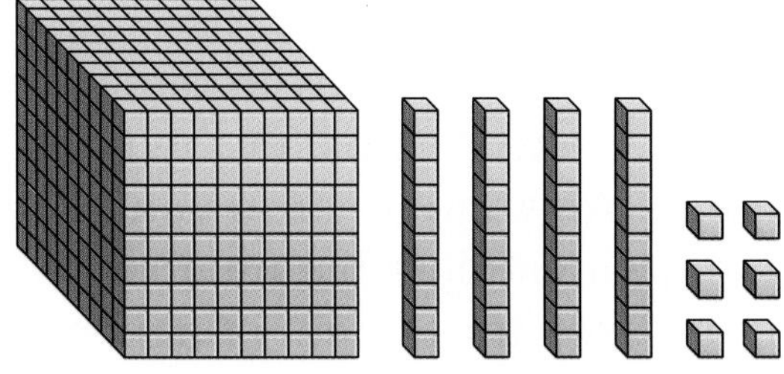

F 1.46 **G** 1.046

H 10.04 **J** 1.406

7. Natalie bought a shirt for $15.79. She saw the same shirt at another store for $13.99. Which number sentence could be used to find the difference in the two prices?

A $13.99 + $15.79 = $29.78

B $15.79 − $15.79 = $0

C $15.79 − $13.99 = $1.80

D $13.99 × $2.00 = $27.98

8. $\begin{array}{r} 13.075 \\ +\ 0.780 \\ \hline \end{array}$

F 12.855

G 12.745

H 13.755

J 13.855

9. $\begin{array}{r} 3.402 \\ -1.679 \\ \hline \end{array}$

A 1.723

B 1.733

C 1.833

D 2.833

CHAPTERS 1–4

Biggest and Smallest Game

PURPOSE To make greatest and least possible numbers, using number cards

YOU WILL NEED 10 index cards, markers

Number each card with digits from 0 to 9. Take 3 cards for the first game. Arrange them so you have the greatest possible number. Write it on a separate sheet of paper.

Then rearrange the cards to create the least number. (You cannot start your number with zero.) Write the least number on your paper. Play by using 4 cards, 5 cards, up to 10 cards.

7 4 2

Greatest	Least
742	

How Many Blues?

PURPOSE To model hundredths of a sample

YOU WILL NEED 100 M&M® candies

Did you know that when your parents were your age, there were no blue M&Ms? Use math to find out what part of your sample is blue.

Count the number of each color in your sample of 100 M&Ms.

Write each as a decimal and compare them.

Which color represents the greatest decimal?

How Many Blues?

28 blue = $\frac{28}{100}$ = 0.28

16 red = $\frac{16}{100}$ = 0.16

YOUR RADIO BAND

PURPOSE To compare and order decimals

YOU WILL NEED crayons, markers, or colored pencils

You will make a chart of favorite radio stations.

Make a list of the radio stations (AM or FM) and their frequencies (the number on the dial).

Ask people to choose their favorite station, and record their choices.

Place all the stations on a chart organized with the lower frequencies on the left and higher ones on the right, like a number line. Use frequency intervals of one tenth.

Ask family members what radio stations they listen to.

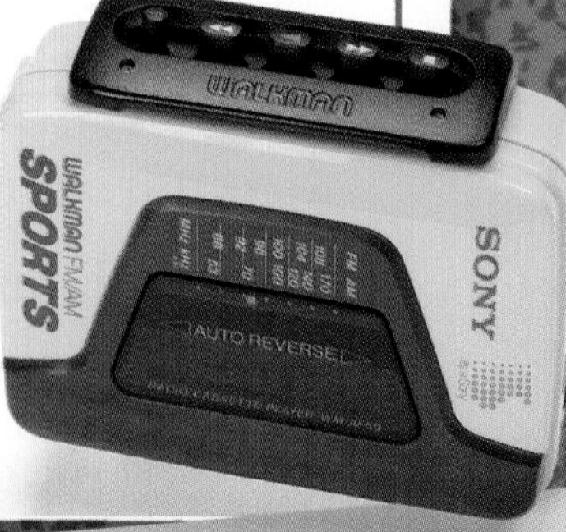

92.1 96.4 100.5 102.7 104.9

Ordering Numbers

VOCABULARY

Ascending means from least to greatest.

Descending means from greatest to least.

MATERIALS *Data ToolKit* or other spreadsheet software

Stan keeps track of the products sold in a hardware store. He recorded 586 rakes, 1,098 paintbrushes, 21,709 one-inch nails, 29 lawn mowers, and 12,069 screwdrivers. List the products in order from least to greatest.

You can order numbers by using a spreadsheet tool. Enter each item into column A and each number into column B. Highlight both columns. Click and hold on the word "spreadsheet" in the menu bar. Then highlight "sort." In the sort window, you can choose **ascending** to order from least to greatest or **descending** to order from greatest to least. Choose ascending. Click "sort."

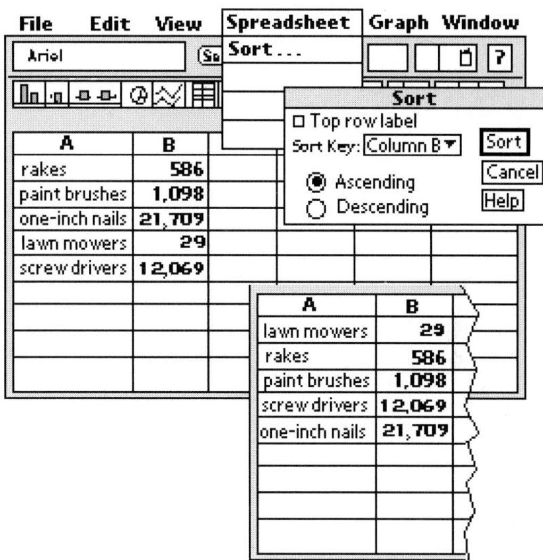

▶ PRACTICE

Order the numbers in each table from least to greatest.

1.

Game Attendance	
Sep	12,079
Oct	10,975
Nov	12,957
Dec	12,759

2.

Populations (1996)	
Texas	19,128,261
Florida	14,399,985
New York	18,184,774

3.

Books Ordered	
Reading	203,876
Math	208,397
Science	230,907
Spelling	197,032

Using the Computer Solve.

4. Toy Mart sold 2,309 bean-bag toys, 1,456 books, 987 dolls, and 1,965 games. List the items in descending order.

5. The Citrus Company packed 19,203,466 oranges, 7,960,327 grapefruits, and 16,094,380 lemons in December. List the fruits in ascending order.

CHAPTERS 1–4

Study Guide and Review

Vocabulary Check

Choose a term from the box to complete each sentence.

VOCABULARY
benchmark
equivalent
inverse

1. A _?_ is a point of reference. (page 4)
2. When one operation undoes another, they are _?_ operations. (page 20)
3. Decimals that are different names for the same number or amount are _?_. (page 42)

Study and Solve

CHAPTER 1

EXAMPLE

Write the value of the underlined digit.

<u>5</u>16,214,890

500,000,000, or
5 hundred millions

The 5 is in the hundred millions place.

Tell whether each number is expressed as *cardinal, ordinal,* or *nominal.* (pages 2–3)

4. 621 Lynn St. **5.** 260,898

6. ninety-fifth **7.** 65 mi

Write the value of the underlined digit. (pages 6–11)

8. 5<u>6</u>,784,091 **9.** 541,0<u>9</u>6,327

10. 1<u>1</u>,537,800,370

Write two other forms for each number. (pages 8–11)

11. 6,453,211 **12.** 5,425,300,670

13. three hundred one million, twenty-four thousand, six hundred fifteen

14. 6,000,000,000 + 0 + 0 + 3,000,000 + 400,000 + 80,000 + 0 + 0 + 79

Write < , > , or = for each ●. (pages 12–13)

15. 5,478 ● 5,480

16. 8,203 ● 8,032

17. 11,000 ● 10,998

18. 14,405 ● 14,405

For Problems 19–20, use the table. (pages 14–15)

1990 POPULATIONS OF OHIO CITIES	
City	**Population**
Cincinnati	364,114
Columbus	632,945
Cleveland	505,616

19. List the cities from the one with the least population to the one with the greatest population.

20. How many more people live in Columbus than in Cincinnati?

CHAPTER 2

EXAMPLE

Find the difference.

```
  3 9 9 10
  4,000
 −2,482
  1,518
```

Regroup 400 tens as 399 tens 10 ones.
Subtract from right to left.

Show how you regrouped for each problem. Solve. (pages 24–25)

21. 3,000 − 1,321

22. 19,000 − 7,942

Choose and name the operation. Solve. (pages 26–27)

23. Lia spent \$68. She gave the clerk \$100. What is Lia's change?

Estimate each sum. (pages 28–29)

24. 289 + 111 + 395 + 205

25. 298 + 184 + 305 + 413

CHAPTER 3

EXAMPLE

Write a decimal and a fraction.

two and five hundredths

decimal: 2.05 fraction: $2\frac{5}{100}$

Write each as a decimal. (pages 36–41)

26. ten and five tenths

27. $2 + 0 + 0.04$

28. six and one thousandth

29. $8\frac{33}{100}$

Write the value of the underlined digit as a decimal and as a fraction. (pages 36–41)

30. 0.$\underline{3}$2

31. 6.50$\underline{6}$

Write an equivalent decimal for each. (pages 42–43)

32. 0.80

33. 1.83

CHAPTER 4

EXAMPLE

Find the sum.

```
  1 1 1
  3.765
 +2.347
  6.112
```

Line up the decimal points.
Add as with whole numbers.
Place the decimal point in the sum.

Find the sum or difference. (pages 52–57)

34. 3.846 + 1.404

35. 6.015 − 3.766

Estimate the sum or difference to the nearest hundredth. (pages 58–59)

36. 2.561 + 4.675

37. 3.458 − 2.379

Choose and name the operation. Solve. (pages 60–61)

38. Blake had \$49.50. He earned \$15.75 more. How much money does he have in all?

CHAPTERS 1–4

Performance Assessment

Tasks: Show What You Know

1. Explain how to use place value to order 5,608, 5,860, 5,806 from the least to the greatest. Then write the numbers in order. (pages 12–15)

2. Show and explain each step as you find the difference. (pages 24–25)

$$\begin{array}{r} 6{,}080 \\ -1{,}245 \\ \hline \end{array}$$

3. Write an equivalent decimal for each. Explain how you know the decimals are equivalent. (pages 42–43)

   0.5; 0.360; 1.22

4. Show and explain each step as you solve the problem. (pages 54–57)

   $2.51 + 6.208 = n$

   $8.5 - 3.19 = n$

Problem Solving

Solve. Explain your method.

CHOOSE a strategy and a tool.

- Use a Table
- Make a Model
- Write a Number Sentence
- Act It Out
- Make a Table

Paper/Pencil

Calculator

Hands-On

Mental Math

5. How many computers were sold in 1995? What conclusion can you draw from this data? (pages 14–15)

Year	Computers Sold
1993	5,085,000
1994	6,725,000
1995	8,225,000
1996	9,525,000

6. A class is buying books for \$49.95, computer software for \$28.89, and science equipment for \$41.25. They have about \$125.00. Estimate. Do they have enough money? (pages 30–31)

7. In the Daytona 500 car race, average winning speeds in 3 different years were 160.627 mph for Driver A; 160.875 mph for Driver B; and 159.730 mph for Driver C. Show the speeds from fastest to slowest. (pages 46–47)

8. Jon's allowance is \$15.00 a week. His lunches cost \$9.45 a week. He earned \$8.75 raking leaves, but he spent \$6.50 for a movie and \$4.30 for a book. Does he have enough money for another movie? (pages 62–63)

Cumulative Review

CHAPTERS 1–4

Solve the problem. Then choose the correct answer.

1. *Seventy-eighth* is a(n) _?_ number.

A. cardinal **B.** measurement
C. nominal **D.** ordinal

(pages 2–3)

2. What is the value of the underlined digit? (pages 8–11)
$3\underline{4}2,461,980$

A. 400,000, or 4 hundred thousands
B. 4,000,000, or 4 millions
C. 40,000,000, or 4 ten millions
D. 400,000,000, or 4 hundred millions

3. What is the standard form for four hundred two million, three hundred sixty thousand, nineteen? (pages 8–11)

A. 402,360,190 **B.** 402,360,019
C. 402,036,019 **D.** 42,360,019

4. Compare. 109,989 ● 110,000

A. $+$ **B.** $=$
C. $>$ **D.** $<$

(pages 12–13)

5. Find the difference.

$$\begin{array}{r} 4,000 \\ -2,436 \\ \hline \end{array}$$

A. 1,564
B. 2,436
C. 2,674
D. 6,436

(pages 24–25)

6. Estimate the sum.

$$\begin{array}{r} 288 \\ 112 \\ +396 \\ \hline \end{array}$$

A. 1,100 **B.** 800
C. 900 **D.** 700

(pages 28–29)

7. Which fraction has the same value as the underlined digit?
$5.73\underline{2}$

A. $\frac{2}{1}$ **B.** $\frac{2}{10}$

C. $\frac{2}{100}$ **D.** $\frac{2}{1,000}$

(pages 36–39)

8. What is the standard form for ten and six thousandths?

A. 10.006 **B.** 10.06
C. 10.6 **D.** 6,010

(pages 36–39)

9. Which decimal is equivalent to 1.070?

A. 1.007 **B.** 1.07
C. 1.7 **D.** 1.70

(pages 42–43)

10. $4.25 + 3.078 = n$

A. 1.172 **B.** 3.503
C. 7.228 **D.** 7.328

(pages 52–55)

11. $7.008 - 3.04 = n$

A. 3.968 **B.** 4.048
C. 6.704 **D.** 10.048

(pages 56–57)

12. Decide whether to estimate or to find the exact answer. Solve.

Alex had $100 to spend on clothes. He paid $34.99 for a sweater and $29.95 for a pair of jeans. Will he be able to buy a pair of shoes for $49.75?

A. exact answer; no
B. exact answer; yes
C. estimate; no
D. estimate; yes

(pages 30–31)

5 MULTIPLYING BY ONE-DIGIT NUMBERS

HEARTBEATS PER MINUTE	
Mouse	650
Newborn baby	120
Child	90
Woman	75
Man	70
Olympic swimmer	40
Marathon runner	35
Hibernating groundhog	3

SCIENCE LINK

Small creatures that are not hibernating have faster heartbeats than large creatures.

Problem-Solving Activity

Feel the Beat

Have you ever wondered how much your heart speeds up with exercise?

Take 1-minute pulse readings at rest, after you have walked, and after you have done the exercise of your choice. Then decide which exercise makes your pulse beat fastest.

YOU WILL NEED: stopwatch, or clock with a second hand

- Record your pulse at rest.
- Go for a 2-minute walk, and record your pulse immediately afterward.
- Do a 2-minute workout such as running in place, jumping rope, or doing jumping jacks. Record your pulse again.
- Make a chart showing your pulse rate at rest, after walking, and after a workout.

CHECK YOUR PULSE

Wherever an artery is just below the skin, you can feel it pulse. Using three fingers, and a little patience, feel the beat in these spots. Be sure not to press hard!

WHERE THE CHIN MEETS THE NECK, ABOUT AN INCH BELOW THE EAR

ON THE UNDERSIDE OF THE WRIST

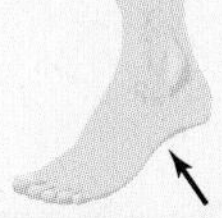

INSTEP OF THE FOOT

Count the number of pulses in 20 seconds; multiply by 3. That's your pulse rate. Take it at rest, walking and exercising.

Hanna's Pulse Rates

	Measurement ×3	Pulse Rate	
Resting	29	87	29 × 3 = 87
After walking 2 minutes	30	90	30 × 3 = 90
After jump rope for 2 minutes	52	156	52 × 3 = 156

DID YOU

- ✓ measure and record your pulse at rest, after walking, and after a workout?
- ✓ make a chart?

LESSON 1

Using Multiplication Properties

Why learn this? Multiplication properties and basic facts are useful when you compute mentally before buying items like CDs.

VOCABULARY

Commutative Property of Multiplication

Associative Property of Multiplication

Property of One for Multiplication

Zero Property for Multiplication

Stacy has 8 shelves. She has 5 CDs on each shelf. Bjorn has 5 shelves. He has 8 CDs on each shelf. Who has more CDs?

COMMUTATIVE PROPERTY OF MULTIPLICATION

You can multiply numbers in any order. The product is always the same.

Example $8 \times 5 = 40$ (factors: 8, 5; product: 40) $5 \times 8 = 40$ (factors: 5, 8; product: 40)

So, Stacy and Bjorn have the same number of CDs.

More Properties

ASSOCIATIVE PROPERTY OF MULTIPLICATION

You can group factors differently. The product is always the same.

Example

$$(4 \times 4) \times 2 = 4 \times (4 \times 2)$$
$$16 \times 2 = 4 \times 8$$
$$32 = 32$$

PROPERTY OF ONE FOR MULTIPLICATION

When one of the factors is 1, the product equals the other number.

Example $8 \times 1 = 8$ $1 \times 8 = 8$

ZERO PROPERTY FOR MULTIPLICATION

When one factor is 0, the product is 0.

Example $6 \times 0 = 0$ $0 \times 6 = 0$

- How is the Commutative Property different from the Associative Property?

Calculator Activities page H61

▶ CHECK

Write the name of the multiplication property used in each number sentence.

1. $2 \times (4 \times 3) = (2 \times 4) \times 3$ **2.** $5 \times 4 = 4 \times 5$ **3.** $6 \times 1 = 6$

4. $8 \times 6 = 6 \times 8$ **5.** $0 \times 7 = 0$ **6.** $(7 \times 3) \times 8 = 7 \times (3 \times 8)$

▶ PRACTICE

Copy and complete the equation. Identify the property used.

7. $5 \times \blacksquare = 5$ **8.** $4 \times (8 \times 3) = (\blacksquare \times 8) \times 3$ **9.** $9 \times 0 = \blacksquare$

10. $4 \times 6 = 6 \times \blacksquare$ **11.** $(8 \times 2) \times 5 = 8 \times (\blacksquare \times 5)$ **12.** $\blacksquare \times 7 = 7 \times 4$

13. $1 \times 3 = \blacksquare$ **14.** $8 \times \blacksquare = 0$ **15.** $5 \times (4 \times 6) = (5 \times \blacksquare) \times 6$

Show two ways to group by using parentheses. Find the product.

16. $3 \times 2 \times 4 = n$ **17.** $2 \times 6 \times 3 = n$ **18.** $7 \times 2 \times 4 = n$

19. $6 \times 3 \times 5 = n$ **20.** $7 \times 5 \times 6 = n$ **21.** $8 \times 4 \times 9 = n$

Problem Solving • Mixed Applications

22. Money Karl has 4 dimes in each of 2 rows. Sue has 3 dimes in each of 3 rows. Who has more money?

24. Measurement Mr. Lee drove 232.5 miles last week and 147.8 miles this week. How far did Mr. Lee drive in the two weeks?

23. Health Tracy took her pulse for 20 seconds. She counted 29 heartbeats. How many beats per minute is that?

25. **Write a problem** in which you multiply three numbers. Write the steps you would follow to solve the problem using the Associative Property of Multiplication.

Mixed Review and Test Prep

Order from least to greatest. (pages 44–45)

26. 3.52, 3.25, 2.35 **27.** 9.64, 6.94, 9.46 **28.** 17.001, 17.107, 17.11

Choose the letter that tells the value of the blue digit. (pages 6–7)

29. 506,923
- **A** 5 tens
- **B** 5 ones
- **C** 5 ten thousands
- **D** 5 hundred thousands

30. 842,042
- **F** 4 ones
- **G** 4 tens
- **H** 4 ten thousands
- **J** 4 hundred thousands

LESSON 2

Recording Multiplication

Why learn this? You can model multiplication problems, such as the total distance traveled on a trip.

Mr. Ruiz drives 215 miles each week. How many miles does he drive in 5 weeks?

Use four colors of counters to make a model.

Let ● = 1,000, ● = 100, ● = 10, and ○ = 1.

MODEL

How can you use colored counters to model this problem?

Step 1

Model the problem by making 5 groups of 215.

$$\begin{array}{r} 215 \\ \times\ 5 \\ \hline \end{array}$$

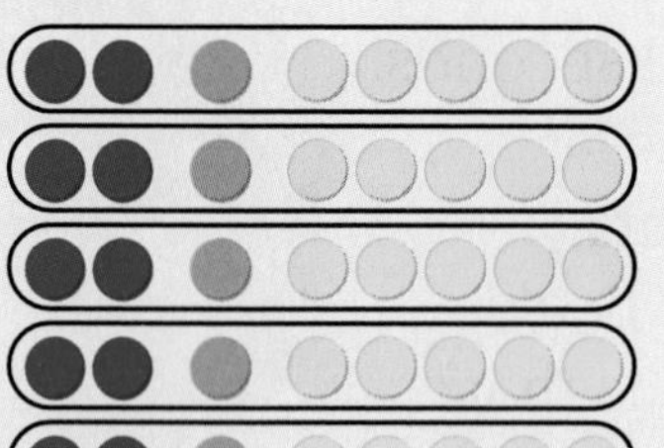

Step 2

Group all counters by color or place value.

$$\begin{array}{rl} 215 & \\ \times\ 5 & \\ \hline 25 & \leftarrow 5 \times 5 \\ 50 & \leftarrow 5 \times 10 \\ 1{,}000 & \leftarrow 5 \times 200 \end{array}$$

Hundreds

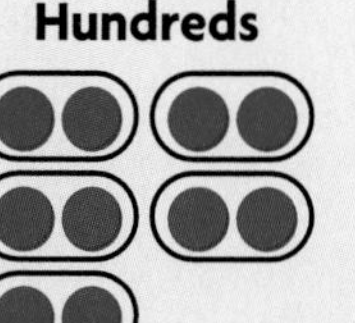

5 groups of 2 hundreds, or 10 hundreds

Tens

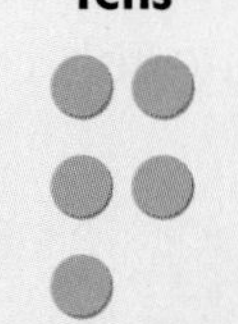

5 groups of 1 ten, or 5 tens

Ones

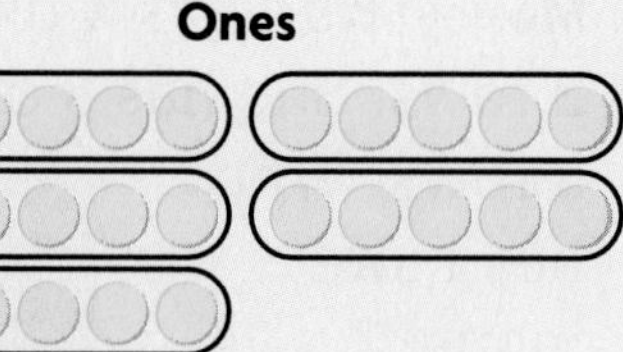

5 groups of 5 ones, or 25 ones

Step 3

Regroup. Start with the ones. Record.

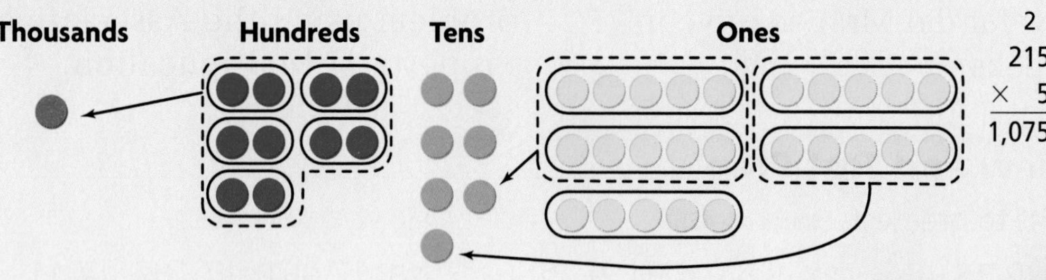

$$\begin{array}{r} {}^{2} \\ 215 \\ \times\ 5 \\ \hline 1{,}075 \end{array}$$

So, Mr. Ruiz drives 1,075 miles in 5 weeks.

- How were the counters representing ones and hundreds regrouped?

▶ CHECK

Explain how you would model with colored counters.

1. 400×3 **2.** 285×5 **3.** 593×6 **4.** 602×7

▶ PRACTICE

Solve by using colored counters.

5. 134×2 **6.** 360×4 **7.** 728×3 **8.** 501×5

9. $6 \times 199 = n$ **10.** $7 \times 263 = n$ **11.** $4 \times 672 = n$ **12.** $6 \times 390 = n$

13. $3 \times 270 = n$ **14.** $5 \times 432 = n$ **15.** $7 \times 391 = n$ **16.** $2 \times 512 = n$

Problem Solving • Mixed Applications

Using Data For Problems 20–21, use the table.

17. Number Sense There are 463,000 people living in Elm City and 657,000 people in Limon. There are 1,200,000 people living in Oakville. Which has more people—Oakville, or Elm City and Limon combined?

18. Time Paulo arrived at soccer practice at 10:00 A.M. and stayed for 2 hours. It took him 20 minutes to get home, 10 minutes to shower, and 30 minutes to eat lunch. What time was it when he finished lunch?

19. Measurement Mrs. Roger drove 25 miles each day for 5 days. Mrs. Blake drove 21 miles each day for 6 days. Who drove a greater distance? How many more miles did she drive?

20. Money Sabrina and Donald went to the movies 2 Friday nights in a row. They each bought a ticket, a popcorn, and a drink both nights. How much did they spend in all?

21. **Write a problem** using the information from the table.

Movie Prices	
Tickets	$ 5.00
Popcorn	$ 2.25
Cold Drink	$ 1.75
Candy	$ 1.50

Mixed Review and Test Prep

Write <, >, or = for each ●. (pages 12–13)

22. 475 ● 457 **23.** 6,120 ● 6,210 **24.** 8,093 ● 8,093 **25.** 9,907 ● 9,709

Choose the letter of the correct decimal. (pages 40–41)

26. 1 + 0.7 + 0.03 **A** 1.73 **B** 0.173 **C** 2.73 **D** 1.37

27. seven and two hundredths **F** 7.2 **G** 7.002 **H** 7.02 **J** 0.702

LESSON 3

Multiplication and Area

Why learn this? You can find out how many items you need, such as tiles for a hallway, without counting or adding.

Mr. Rodrigo is installing new tiles in the school hallways. He bought 7 crates of tiles. Each crate holds 350 tiles. How many tiles did he buy?

Use base-ten blocks or colored counters to find the number of tiles Mr. Rodrigo bought.

Maria used base-ten blocks to make a model.

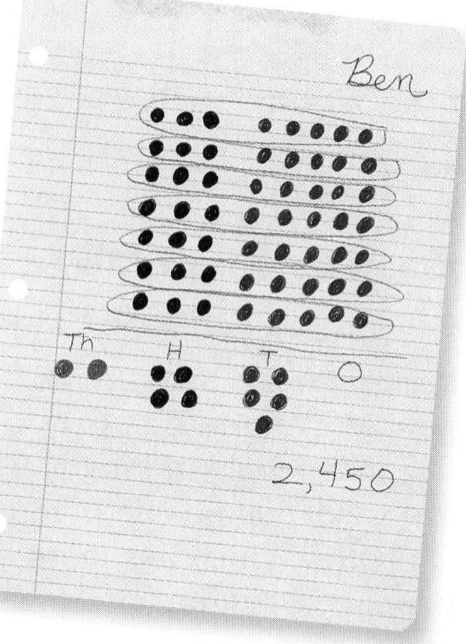

Ben used colored counters to make a model.

You can multiply without using base-ten blocks or counters.

MODEL

What is 7 × 350?

Step 1	**Step 2**	**Step 3**
Multiply the ones. 7 × 0 ones = 0 ones	Multiply the tens. 7 × 5 tens = 35 tens Regroup.	Multiply the hundreds. 7 × 3 hundreds = 21 hundreds. Add the regrouped hundreds.
$\begin{array}{r} 350 \\ \times\ 7 \\ \hline 0 \end{array}$	$\begin{array}{r} {}^{3} \\ 350 \\ \times\ 7 \\ \hline 50 \end{array}$	$\begin{array}{r} {}^{3} \\ 350 \\ \times\ 7 \\ \hline 2{,}450 \end{array}$

So, Mr. Rodrigo has 2,450 tiles.

Calculator Activities page H60

Talk About It

- Why should you multiply in the ones place first?
- Why are there 0 ones in the product?

The tiles Mr. Rodrigo is using for the fifth grade hallway are 1 foot by 1 foot tiles. The length of the hallway is 104 feet and the width is 6 feet. How many tiles does he need for this hallway?

To find out how many tiles are needed, find the area of the hallway by using multiplication.

Multiply the length times the width.

$$\begin{array}{r} {}^{2} \\ 104 \\ \times\ \ 6 \\ \hline 624 \end{array}$$

- Multiply the ones. 6 × 4 ones. Regroup.
- Multiply the tens. 6 × 0 tens. Add the regrouped tens.
- Multiply the hundreds. 6 × 1 hundred.

So, Mr. Rodrigo needs 624 tiles for the fifth grade hallway.

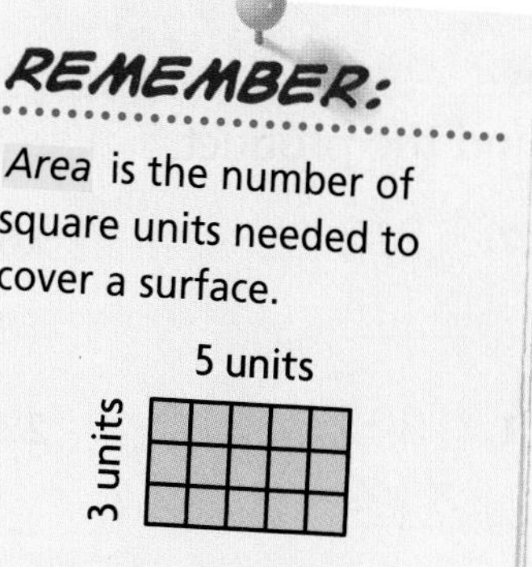

EXAMPLES

A

$$\begin{array}{r} {}^{1} \\ 203 \\ \times\ \ 4 \\ \hline 812 \end{array}$$

B

$$\begin{array}{r} {}^{1} \\ 380 \\ \times\ \ 2 \\ \hline 760 \end{array}$$

C

$$\begin{array}{r} {}^{3\,2} \\ 576 \\ \times\ \ 4 \\ \hline 2{,}304 \end{array}$$

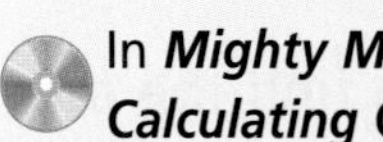

Technology Link

In *Mighty Math Calculating Crew,* the game *Intergalactic Trader* challenges you to multiply by one-digit numbers. Use Grow Slide Level L.

▶ CHECK

Tell which place-value position must be regrouped. Find the product.

1. $\begin{array}{r} 307 \\ \times\ \ 3 \\ \hline \end{array}$ **2.** $\begin{array}{r} 219 \\ \times\ \ 4 \\ \hline \end{array}$ **3.** $\begin{array}{r} 126 \\ \times\ \ 7 \\ \hline \end{array}$ **4.** $\begin{array}{r} 137 \\ \times\ \ 9 \\ \hline \end{array}$

Find the product.

5. $526 \times 6 = n$ **6.** $322 \times 8 = n$ **7.** $624 \times 5 = n$ **8.** $810 \times 3 = n$

Multiply to find the area.

9. length: 304 ft
width: 4 ft

10. length: 260 yd
width: 6 yd

11. length: 110 in.
width: 8 in.

12. length: 483 mi
width: 7 mi

13. length: 175 ft
width: 5 ft

14. length: 306 mi
width: 2 mi

15. length: 420 in.
width: 9 in.

16. length: 509 yd
width: 3 yd

▶ PRACTICE

Find the product.

17. $\begin{array}{r} 212 \\ \times\ 4 \\ \hline \end{array}$ **18.** $\begin{array}{r} 246 \\ \times\ 5 \\ \hline \end{array}$ **19.** $\begin{array}{r} 293 \\ \times\ 7 \\ \hline \end{array}$ **20.** $\begin{array}{r} 250 \\ \times\ 9 \\ \hline \end{array}$

21. $\begin{array}{r} 303 \\ \times\ 2 \\ \hline \end{array}$ **22.** $\begin{array}{r} 324 \\ \times\ 4 \\ \hline \end{array}$ **23.** $\begin{array}{r} 351 \\ \times\ 6 \\ \hline \end{array}$ **24.** $\begin{array}{r} 390 \\ \times\ 6 \\ \hline \end{array}$

25. $\begin{array}{r} 419 \\ \times\ 7 \\ \hline \end{array}$ **26.** $\begin{array}{r} 725 \\ \times\ 3 \\ \hline \end{array}$ **27.** $\begin{array}{r} 506 \\ \times\ 6 \\ \hline \end{array}$ **28.** $\begin{array}{r} 331 \\ \times\ 9 \\ \hline \end{array}$

29. $368 \times 7 = n$ **30.** $452 \times 5 = n$ **31.** $501 \times 8 = n$ **32.** $562 \times 8 = n$

33. $528 \times 6 = n$ **34.** $536 \times 7 = n$ **35.** $572 \times 8 = n$ **36.** $579 \times 9 = n$

37. $190 \times 9 = n$ **38.** $303 \times 4 = n$ **39.** $241 \times 8 = n$ **40.** $953 \times 2 = n$

Multiply to find the area.

41. length: 296 ft
width: 6 ft

42. length: 407 yd
width: 8 yd

43. length: 590 in.
width: 9 in.

44. length: 507 yd
width: 8 yd

45. length: 117 in.
width: 4 in.

46. length: 680 ft
width: 7 ft

Problem Solving • Mixed Applications

47. Estimation Monique sees lightning, counts 5 seconds, and then hears thunder. She knows that sound travels at about 350 meters per second. About how far away is the lightning from Monique?

48. Money Navin collects baseball cards. He had $11.00 at the beginning of the day. He bought 3 cards for $3.50 each. He sold 2 cards for $4.00 each and 4 for $1.25 each. How much money did Navin have at the end of the day?

49. Using Data Jake has 520 points. He earned these scores on his first five tests: 86, 79, 99, 92, and 83 points. What score did he earn on his sixth test?

50. Geometry The third grade hallway was 6 feet by 120 feet, and the fourth grade hallway was 7 feet by 102 feet. Which hallway needed more tiles?

51. Write About It Explain the steps you follow to multiply by a one-digit number.

LANGUAGE ARTS CONNECTION

In the game Scrabble™, players score points by using a set of seven letters to make a word. Each letter has a value, and the player's score is the sum of the values of the letters used.

- If a player's word covers a pink double-word square, the player's score is multiplied by 2.
- If a player's word covers a red triple-word square, the player's score is multiplied by 3.

Values of Letters in Scrabble	
A – 1	N – 1
B – 3	O – 1
C – 3	P – 3
D – 2	Q – 10
E – 1	R – 1
F – 4	S – 1
G – 2	T – 1
H – 4	U – 1
I – 1	V – 4
J – 8	W – 4
K – 5	X – 8
L – 1	Y – 4
M – 3	Z – 10

52. If you make the word *QUICK* and place it over a double-word square, what is your score?

53. If you make the word *WAXES* and place it over a triple-word square, what is your score?

54. Rearrange the letters *U*, *I*, *Q*, *E*, and *T* to form a word that would score 42 points if it covered a triple-word square.

55. Use any six letters and make the highest-scoring word you can. Find its value if it covers a triple-word square.

HISTORY LINK

Scrabble was invented in 1931 by Alfred M. Butts. The average score for a player in one game is about 300 points. An Australian player holds the world record, with a score of 725 points in one game. How much greater is the world record score than the average score?

Mixed Review and Test Prep

Find the difference. (pages 24–25)

56. $200 - 126$

57. $700 - 357$

58. $2{,}000 - 579$

59. $7{,}000 - 6{,}451$

60. $15{,}000 - 9{,}630$

Choose the letter of the equivalent decimal. (pages 42–43)

61. 0.02
- **A** 2.02
- **B** 0.020
- **C** 0.20
- **D** 0.002
- **E** Not Here

62. 0.065
- **F** 0.65
- **G** 0.0065
- **H** 65.00
- **J** 6.05
- **K** Not Here

63. 2.9
- **A** 0.29
- **B** 29.0
- **C** 2.90
- **D** 0.029
- **E** Not Here

64. 0.800
- **F** 0.8
- **G** 8.00
- **H** 0.008
- **J** 0.08
- **K** Not Here

LESSON 4 • HANDS-ON LESSON

Finding Volume

You will investigate finding volumes of rectangular prisms.

VOCABULARY
area
volume
cubic units

Area is the number of square units needed to cover a surface. Area is measured in square units. **Volume** is the measure of the space a solid figure occupies. Volume is measured in **cubic units**.

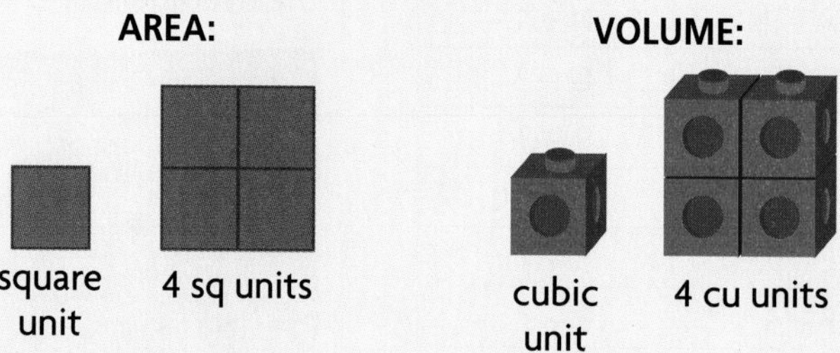

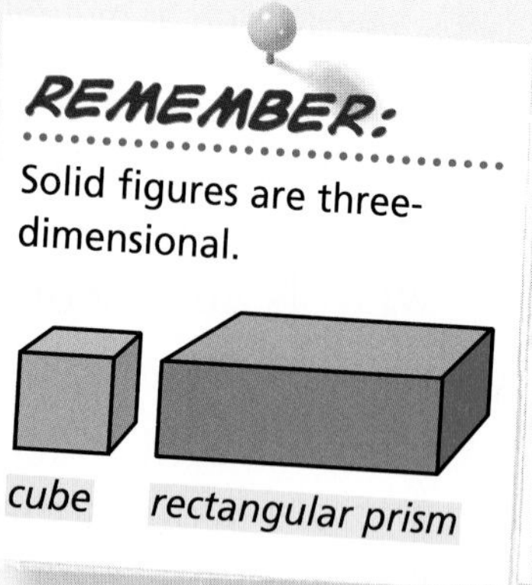

Use unit cubes to build a rectangular prism. Each layer of the prism is 3 cubes long and 2 cubes wide. There are 2 layers in the prism. What is the volume of this rectangular prism?

▶ EXPLORE

MATERIALS: unit cubes

Build a different rectangular prism that has the same volume. Let each unit cube represent 1 cubic unit. Find how many different rectangular prisms you can make with the same volume.

Talk About It Is a $2 \times 1 \times 2$ rectangular prism the same as a $2 \times 2 \times 1$ rectangular prism? Explain.

Record

Record the volume of the rectangular prism in the cubic units.

Record the number of prisms you can make with the same volume. Write the measurements and volume for each prism.

Now, investigate finding the volumes for different rectangular prisms.

▶ TRY THIS

Use unit cubes to build each prism. Copy and complete the table.

	Length of Base	Width of Base	Height (number of layers)	Volume (cubic units)
1.	8 cubes	4 cubes	4 cubes	?
2.	9 cubes	8 cubes	3 cubes	?
3.	7 cubes	5 cubes	4 cubes	?
4.	6 cubes	6 cubes	5 cubes	?

5. **Write About It** What operation can you use to find the volume of a rectangular prism? How do you use the operation to compute volume?

▶ PRACTICE

Use unit cubes to build each rectangular prism. Find the volume.

6. 6 cubes long
3 cubes wide
3 layers high

7. 5 cubes long
3 cubes wide
2 layers high

8. 4 cubes long
5 cubes wide
3 layers high

9. 6 cubes long
4 cubes wide
4 layers high

10. 7 cubes long
2 cubes wide
5 layers high

11. 8 cubes long
4 cubes wide
6 layers high

Technology Link

You can find the volume of a rectangular prism by using E-Lab, Activity 5. Available on CD-ROM and on the Internet at **www.hbschool.com/elab**

Use unit cubes to build each prism. Copy and complete the table.

	Length of Base	Width of Base	Height	Volume
12.	8 cubes	3 cubes	4 cubes	?
13.	5 cubes	?	3 cubes	45 cu units
14.	6 cubes	2 cubes	?	60 cu units
15.	?	4 cubes	2 cubes	64 cu units

Problem Solving • Mixed Applications

16. **Geometry** Matt has the two rectangular prisms shown. He wants to use the prism with the larger volume. Which prism should Matt choose?

A.

B.

17. **Reasoning** How many ways can you build a rectangular prism with a volume of 6 cubic units? What are they?

18. **Money** Daniel's mom gives him $2.75 for every room he cleans and $1.25 for every bush he trims. If he cleans 3 rooms and trims 5 bushes, how much money will he earn?

MORE PRACTICE pages H78–H79

Finding Area and Volume

VOCABULARY
formula

Why learn this? You use area and volume when you build things.

Will wants to build a dog pen. Which pen has the greater area?

Use a formula to find the area of each dog pen. A **formula** is a set of symbols that expresses a mathematical rule. Here is the formula for area.

Area = length × width, or $A = l \times w$

Use the formula to find the area of each dog pen.

A	B
$A = l \times w$ $A = 10 \times 10$ $A = 100$ sq ft	$A = l \times w$ $A = 32 \times 4$ $A = 128$ sq ft

So, Dog Pen B has the greater area.

Will wants to build a dog house. Which dog house has the greater volume?

Here is the formula for volume.

Volume = length × width × height, or $V = l \times w \times h$

Use the formula to find the volume of each dog house.

A	B
$V = l \times w \times h$ $V = 4 \times 5 \times 4$ $V = 80$ cu ft	$V = l \times w \times h$ $V = 6 \times 3 \times 4$ $V = 72$ cu ft

So, Dog House A has the greater volume.

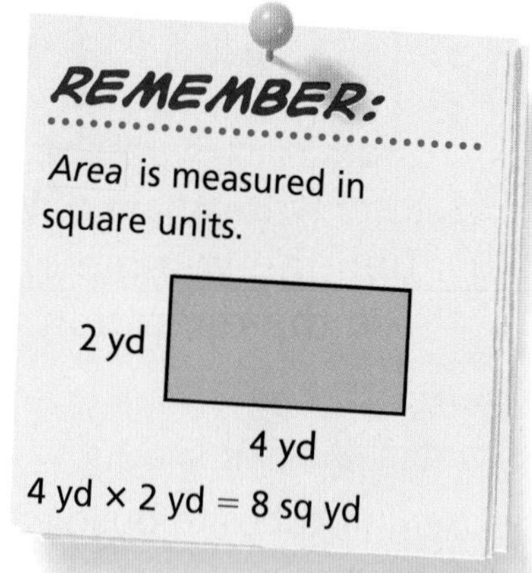

Max and Will

CRITICAL THINKING Which multiplication property can help you compute volume? Explain.

▶ CHECK

Find the area or volume.

1. 8 in. 12 in.

2. 5 yd 23 yd

3. 7 in. 8 in. 4 in.

4.

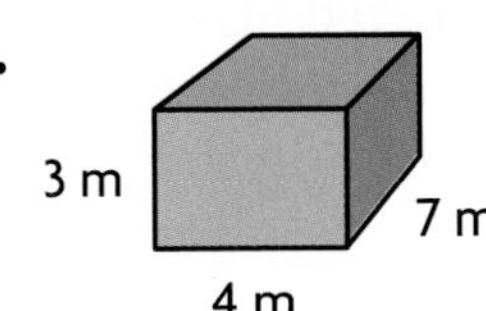

5. $l = 14$ cm
$w = 4$ cm
$A = ▮$ sq cm

6. $l = 35$ in.
$w = 3$ in.
$A = ▮$ sq in.

7. $l = 3$ cm
$w = 6$ cm
$h = 7$ cm
$V = ▮$ cu cm

8. $l = 8$ in.
$w = 5$ in.
$h = 4$ in.
$V = ▮$ cu in.

▶ PRACTICE

Find the area or volume.

9. 6 yd 27 yd

10. 7 in. 18 in.

11.

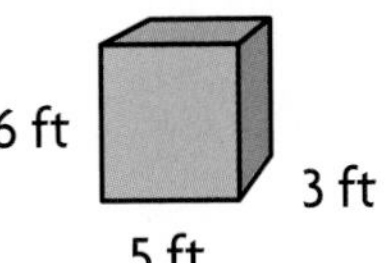

12.

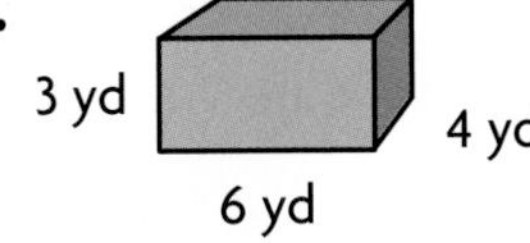

13. $l = 27$ ft
$w = 4$ ft
$A = ▮$ sq ft

14. $l = 38$ m
$w = 5$ m
$A = ▮$ sq m

15. $l = 3$ m
$w = 6$ m
$h = 6$ m
$V = ▮$ cu m

16. $l = 9$ ft
$w = 4$ ft
$h = 4$ ft
$V = ▮$ cu ft

Problem Solving • Mixed Applications

17. Measurement Francesca's dresser is 8 feet long, 2 feet wide, and 4 feet high. Duncan's dresser is 6 feet long, 2 feet wide, and 5 feet high. Who has the dresser with the larger volume? Explain.

18. The fifth grade is going on a field trip. Each class has 22 students, 2 parent chaperones, and 1 teacher. There are 6 classes in the fifth grade. How many people are going on the field trip?

19. Consumer Mr. Schneider's new car runs 23 miles on a gallon of gasoline. The gas tank in the car holds 9 gallons. How far can Mr. Schneider drive with 1 tank of gas?

20. Write About It Suppose you have two rectangular prisms. The area of the base of the first prism is less than the area of the base of the second prism. The volume of the first prism is greater than the volume of the second prism. How is this possible?

LESSON CONTINUES

MORE PRACTICE page H79

LESSON 5 • PART 2

Problem-Solving Strategy: Use a Formula

▶ **THE PROBLEM** Eduardo is buying an aquarium. He has narrowed his choices to two aquariums with the same features. One measures 6 ft × 2 ft × 3 ft and costs $285. The other measures 4 ft × 3 ft × 3 ft and costs $345. Which aquarium is the better buy?

REMEMBER:

UNDERSTAND

PLAN

SOLVE

LOOK BACK

UNDERSTAND

- What are you asked to find?
- What information will you use?
- Is there information you will not use? If so, what?

PLAN

- What strategy can you use to solve the problem?

You can *use a formula* to find the volumes.

SOLVE

- How can you use the strategy to solve the problem?

Use the formula $V = l \times w \times h$ to find the volume of each aquarium. Compare each volume to each price to determine the better buy.

$285 Aquarium	$345 Aquarium
$V = l \times w \times h$ $V = 6 \times 2 \times 3$ $V = 36$ cu ft	$V = l \times w \times h$ $V = 4 \times 3 \times 3$ $V = 36$ cu ft

The two aquariums have the same volume. So, the $285 aquarium is the better buy.

LOOK BACK

- How can you determine if your answer is reasonable?
- What other strategy could you use?

▶ PRACTICE

Use a formula to solve.

1. Marty has narrowed his choices to two aquariums with the same features. One measures 4 ft × 3 ft × 4 ft and costs $243. The other measures 6 ft × 4 ft × 2 ft and costs $212. Which aquarium is the better buy?

2. Jimet can buy a cage for her pet rabbits that measures 5 ft × 4 ft × 3 ft, or she can buy a cage that measures 4 ft × 4 ft × 5 ft. Jimet wants to get the cage with the larger volume. Which cage should she buy?

3. Tony is going to put a new carpet in his room. The floor in his room is 12 feet long and 9 feet wide. How many square feet of carpet should he buy?

4. LaPorsha is decorating the sidewalk with chalk drawings. The sidewalk is 9 feet long and 8 feet wide. What is the area of the sidewalk she is decorating?

Mixed Applications

Solve.

CHOOSE a strategy and a tool.

- Draw a Diagram
- Use a Table
- Use a Formula
- Write a Number Sentence
- Make a Model

Paper/Pencil

Calculator

Hands-On

Mental Math

5. Brittany and her classmates are painting scenery for a play. They need to cover a board that is 9 feet tall and 32 feet wide. What is the area of the board they are painting?

6. Kyle counted the light bulbs around a movie-theater sign that was 12 feet wide and 6 feet tall. The light bulbs were 1 foot apart. How many light bulbs were there?

7. Ms. Enriquez drinks 1 cup of coffee with breakfast. She has 2 glasses of iced tea with lunch, 1 glass of cola with dinner, and 1 cup of hot cocoa before bed. How much caffeine does she consume in one day?

AMOUNTS OF CAFFEINE	
Drink	**Amount (milligrams)**
Coffee	175
Cola	40
Hot Cocoa	10
Iced Tea	25

8. Ray is making a quilt for the arts festival. Each quilt square is divided into 4 equal parts. Each of the 4 parts is a triangle. The quilt is 2 squares long and 2 squares wide. What does it look like?

9. Paul has $20.00 to buy supplies for a project. He buys wood for $4.89 and nails for $2.79. Paint costs $5.63 per bucket. How many buckets of paint can Paul buy? How much money will he have left?

MORE PRACTICE page H79

CHAPTER 5 Review/Test

▶ CHECK Understanding

VOCABULARY

1. The __?__ states that when one of the factors is 1, the product equals the other number. (page 74)
2. The __?__ states that you can group factors differently. The product is always the same. (page 74)
3. The __?__ states that when one factor is 0, the product is 0. (page 74)
4. The __?__ states that you can multiply numbers in any order. The product is always the same. (page 74)
5. __?__ is the measure of the space a solid figure occupies. (page 82)
6. Volume is measured in __?__ units. (page 82)

Tell which place-value position must be regrouped. Find the product. (pages 78–81)

7. 425×7
8. 608×6
9. 900×5
10. 532×3

▶ CHECK Skills

Find the product. (pages 78–81)

11. $43 \times 4 = n$
12. $856 \times 2 = n$
13. $710 \times 3 = n$
14. $604 \times 5 = n$

Find the area. (pages 84–85)

15. $l = 13$ ft, $w = 8$ ft, $A = ■$ sq ft
16. $l = 42$ in., $w = 5$ in., $A = ■$ sq in.

Find the volume. (pages 84–85)

17. $l = 9$ cm, $w = 5$ cm, $h = 3$ cm, $V = ■$ cu cm
18. $l = 6$ m, $w = 4$ m, $h = 7$ m, $V = ■$ cu m

▶ CHECK Problem Solving

Solve. (pages 86–87)

CHOOSE a strategy and a tool.

- Draw a Diagram
- Make a Model
- Use a Formula

Paper/Pencil

Calculator

Hands-On

Mental Math

19. Jacob can buy one of two toolboxes with the same features. Both cost $15. One measures 12 in. × 6 in. × 6 in. The other measures 10 in. × 8 in. × 6 in. Which is the better buy?
20. Hannah glues gold stars around a picture frame that is 8 inches wide and 10 inches tall. She places the stars 2 inches apart. How many stars does she use?

Test Prep

Choose the best answer.

1. Your phone number is a(n) __?__ number.

   A cardinal **B** measurement
   C nominal **D** ordinal

2. Which of the following is a reasonable estimate for 5,432 − 3,980?

   F 0 **G** 500
   H 1,000 **J** 2,500

3. Which fraction has the same value as the underlined digit?

   9.82<u>5</u>

   A $\frac{5}{1}$ **B** $\frac{5}{10}$
   C $\frac{5}{100}$ **D** $\frac{5}{1,000}$

4. Amir asked all the fifth graders which kind of fruit they liked best—bananas, apples, or peaches. The results showed that 25 chose bananas, 16 chose apples, and 47 chose peaches. How many fifth graders answered Amir's survey?

   F 72 **G** 78
   H 82 **J** 88

5. $4.361 + 6.88 = n$

   A 4.049
   B 6.241
   C 11.24
   D 10.241
   E Not Here

6. $7.36 - n = 2.5$

   F 4.8 **G** 4.086
   H 4.86 **J** 4.0

7. Lizzie needs one piece of wood that is 11.5 cm long, one that is 12.6 cm long, and one that is 9 cm long. Which of the following is a reasonable estimate for how much wood she should buy?

   A 30 cm **B** 34 cm
   C 40 cm **D** 75 cm

8. Hannah has 6 pages of photos. Each page has 8 photos. Which number sentence should be used to find the number of photos she has in all?

   F $6 + 8 = \square$ **G** $8 - 6 = \square$
   H $6 \times 8 = \square$ **J** $8 \div 6 = \square$

9. Which expression has the same value as $5 \times (3 \times 8)$?

   A $(5 \times 3) \times 8$
   B 5×3
   C 5×8
   D $(5 \times 3) \times 7$
   E Not Here

10. $8 \times 10 = 10 \times 8$ shows the __?__ of Multiplication.

    F Zero Property
    G Commutative Property
    H Associative Property
    J Property

6 MULTIPLYING LARGER NUMBERS

CONSUMER LINK

A vegetable garden should be located in a spot that gets at least 6 hours of sunlight each day.

Your Critter-Proof Budget Garden

You have $100.00 to create a garden. Plan a fence around your garden to keep critters out. Make a plan to figure out costs.

YOU WILL NEED: 1-inch grid paper, colored pencils or markers, scissors, paper for a diagram

- Design a garden plot. Draw it on 1-inch grid paper, making 1 square inch equal 1 square foot.
- Cut out your garden plot. Combine plots to make any pattern you like.
- Find out how many feet of fencing and how much soil you need.
- Figure out how much money you spent. If you spent more than $100.00, redesign your plot and try again.

COSTS

FENCING................$1.59 per ft
SOIL........................ $0.52 per sq ft

DID YOU

- ✓ draw a garden plot on 1-inch grid paper?
- ✓ put the plots together to make a garden?
- ✓ figure out how many feet of fencing and how much soil the whole garden needs?
- ✓ figure out the total cost of your garden?

Using the Distributive Property

VOCABULARY
Distributive Property

You will investigate using the Distributive Property of Multiplication.

The **Distributive Property** states that multiplying a sum by a number is the same as multiplying each addend by the number and then adding the products.

MODEL

How can you use the Distributive Property to multiply 10×15?

Step 1

On grid paper, outline a rectangle that is 10 units high and 15 units wide. Think of the area as the product of 10×15.

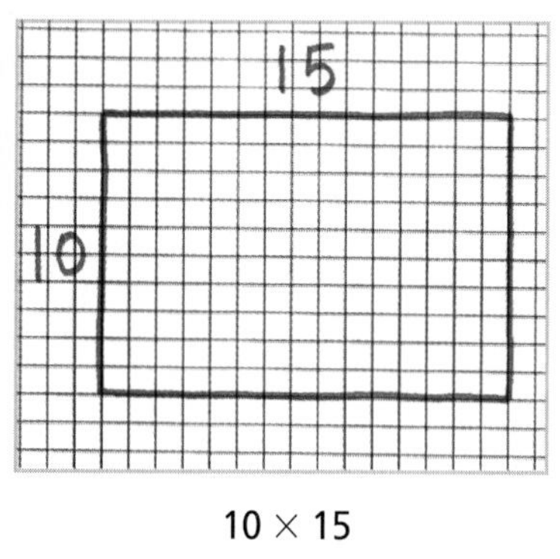

10×15

Step 2

Count over 10 units from the left, and draw a line to break apart the rectangle.

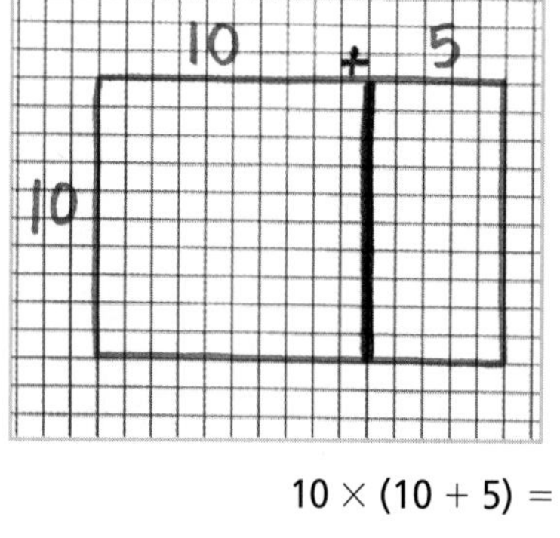

$10 \times (10 + 5) =$

Step 3

Use the Distributive Property to restate the problem as a sum of two products. Multiply what is in parentheses first. Add the products.

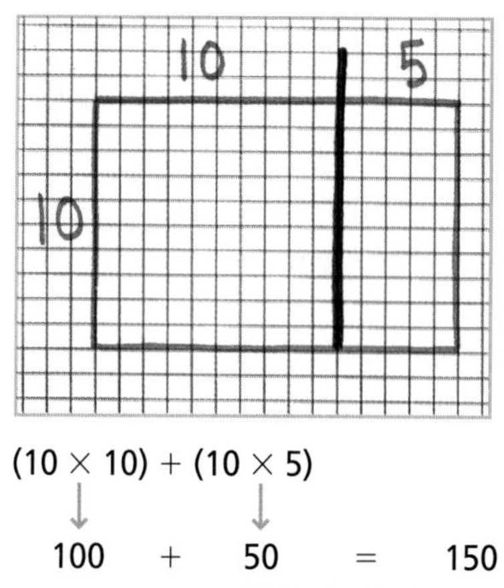

$(10 \times 10) + (10 \times 5)$

$100 + 50 = 150$

So, $10 \times 15 = 150$.

Talk About It

- How was place value used to break apart the rectangle in Step 2 of the model?
- Why was 15 broken into $10 + 5$?

Write About It Explain how the rectangle in Step 1 was broken apart in Step 3.

▶ EXPLORE

MATERIALS: grid paper

Use grid paper to find $20 \times 17 = n$.

On grid paper, outline a rectangle that is 20 units high and 17 units wide.

$20 \times 17 = n$

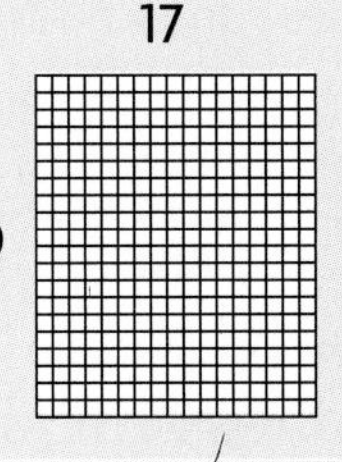

Record

Draw your model and record the steps you used to break apart 20×17. Record the product.

- In what other way can you break apart the factors so they are easy to multiply?

Now, investigate making your own model for the Distributive Property.

Technology Link

You can model the Distributive Property by using E-Lab, Activity 6. Available on CD-ROM and on the Internet at **www.hbschool.com/elab**

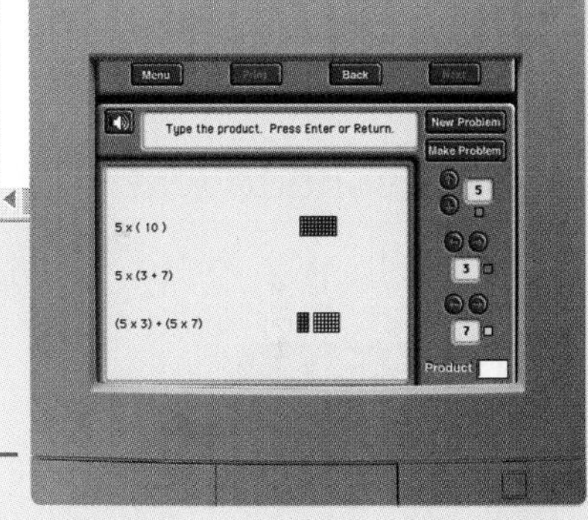

▶ TRY THIS

1. Use grid paper to model $25 \times 14 = n$. Draw your model and record your method and the product.
2. **Write About It** Why does breaking apart the numbers make it easy to compute products?

▶ PRACTICE

Use grid paper to model. Find the product.

3. $20 \times 19 = n$
4. $20 \times 28 = n$
5. $30 \times 29 = n$
6. $30 \times 15 = n$

Use the Distributive Property to rewrite each equation. Find the product.

7. $14 \times 16 = n$
8. $20 \times 27 = n$
9. $30 \times 39 = n$
10. $40 \times 15 = n$
11. $10 \times 23 = n$
12. $20 \times 34 = n$
13. $30 \times 18 = n$
14. $40 \times 29 = n$

Problem Solving • Mixed Applications

15. Darrell bought 24 cookies for each class. There are 4 fifth-grade classes. How many cookies did Darrell buy?
16. Eric grows carrots in his garden. He eats 5 carrot sticks each day. How many carrot sticks does he eat in 14 days?

MORE PRACTICE page H80

LESSON 2

Multiplying by Two-Digit Numbers

Why learn this? You can find the total number of miles run in a race.

Jeanette is training for the Boalsburg Marathon. The marathon is 27 days away. On each of the 27 days, Jeanette will walk 19 miles. How many miles will she walk in all?

MODEL

What is 19×27?

Step 1	Step 2	Step 3
Multiply by the ones.	Multiply by the tens.	Add the products.
$\begin{array}{r} {}^{6}\\ 27 \\ \times 19 \\ \hline 243 \end{array} \leftarrow 9 \times 27$	$\begin{array}{r} 27 \\ \times 19 \\ \hline 243 \\ 270 \\ \hline \end{array} \leftarrow 10 \times 27$ ↑ The zero shows there are 27 tens.	$\begin{array}{r} 27 \\ \times 19 \\ \hline 243 \\ +270 \\ \hline 513 \end{array}$

So, Jeanette will walk 513 miles in all.

- In Step 2, why is it important to show the zero?

EXAMPLES

A

$$\begin{array}{rl} {}^{1} & \\ 34 & \\ \times 24 & \\ \hline 136 & \leftarrow 4 \times 34 \\ +680 & \leftarrow 20 \times 34 \\ \hline 816 & \end{array}$$

B

$$\begin{array}{rl} 60 & \\ \times 35 & \\ \hline 300 & \leftarrow 5 \times 60 \\ +1{,}800 & \leftarrow 30 \times 60 \\ \hline 2{,}100 & \end{array}$$

C

$$\begin{array}{rl} {}^{2} & \\ 105 & \\ \times 15 & \\ \hline 525 & \leftarrow 5 \times 105 \\ +1{,}050 & \leftarrow 10 \times 105 \\ \hline 1{,}575 & \end{array}$$

▶ CHECK

1. Why should you multiply by the ones before multiplying by the tens?
2. In Example C, what happens to the regrouped digit when there is a zero in the factor?
3. How could you use the Distributive Property to find 35×54?

▶ PRACTICE

Find the product.

4. $\begin{array}{r} 15 \\ \times 14 \\ \hline \end{array}$ 5. $\begin{array}{r} 17 \\ \times 13 \\ \hline \end{array}$ 6. $\begin{array}{r} 18 \\ \times 16 \\ \hline \end{array}$ 7. $\begin{array}{r} 19 \\ \times 15 \\ \hline \end{array}$

8. $\begin{array}{r} 21 \\ \times 12 \\ \hline \end{array}$ 9. $\begin{array}{r} 23 \\ \times 14 \\ \hline \end{array}$ 10. $\begin{array}{r} 26 \\ \times 17 \\ \hline \end{array}$ 11. $\begin{array}{r} 34 \\ \times 19 \\ \hline \end{array}$

12. $\begin{array}{r} 60 \\ \times 25 \\ \hline \end{array}$ 13. $\begin{array}{r} 70 \\ \times 45 \\ \hline \end{array}$ 14. $\begin{array}{r} 105 \\ \times \ 20 \\ \hline \end{array}$ 15. $\begin{array}{r} 110 \\ \times \ 35 \\ \hline \end{array}$

16. $81 \times 56 = n$ 17. $102 \times 36 = n$ 18. $117 \times 48 = n$

19. $110 \times 45 = n$ 20. $124 \times 37 = n$ 21. $131 \times 45 = n$

SPORTS LINK

The first Boston Marathon was held on April 19, 1897, to honor Paul Revere's famous ride in 1775. Of the 15 runners who started the race, 8 finished. Some marathon runners run 15 to 20 miles each day. How many miles do they run in 7 days?

Problem Solving • Mixed Applications

22. One restaurant has 27 servers. Each server can wait on 15 people at the same time. How many people can they serve in all?

23. A roller-coaster car can take 32 people on every ride. You waited for 8 rides for your turn. How many people rode the roller coaster ahead of you?

24. **Money** Kristina had $45.00. She paid $15.75 for a ticket to a football game. She bought a drink for $3.50, a shirt for $12.95, and a hat for $10.55. How much does she have left?

25. **Number Sense** Mr. Fanning has 120 tickets to a baseball game. There are 32 students in his class. Each student wants 4 tickets. How many more tickets does Mr. Fanning need?

26. **Measurement** Carlos wants to buy new carpet for his bedroom. His bedroom floor is 17 feet by 12 feet. What is the area of the floor?

27. **Write About It** How would you multiply a two-digit number by a two-digit number?

Mixed Review and Test Prep

Write $<$, $>$, or $=$ for each ●. (pages 44–45)

28. 3.46 ● 3.64 29. 74.76 ● 74.760 30. 124.98 ● 124.89

Choose the letter of the correct sum. (pages 54–55)

31. $4.21 + 0.773 = n$ **A** 4.983 **B** 11.94 **C** 1.194 **D** 0.4983

32. $3.05 + 5.197 = n$ **F** 55.02 **G** 5.502 **H** 8.247 **J** 0.8247

MORE PRACTICE page H80

LESSON 3

Estimating Products

Why learn this? You can decide how much clay to buy based on your estimate.

Ms. Russo, the art teacher, is ordering supplies for the year. She teaches 153 fifth-grade students. Each student will use about 12 slabs of clay. About how many slabs of clay should Ms. Russo order?

When you see the word "about" in a question, you can estimate the product.

MODEL

How can you estimate 12 × 153?

Step 1	**Step 2**
Round each factor to its greatest place-value position.	Multiply the rounded factors.
153 → 200 × 12 → × 10	200 × 10 2,000

So, Ms. Russo should order about 2,000 slabs of clay.

- To which place-value position was 153 rounded? 12?

EXAMPLES

A 329 → 300; × 55 → × 60; 18,000

B 461 → 500; × 42 → × 40; 20,000

REMEMBER:

To *round* a number:

- Find the digit in the place to be rounded.
- Look at the digit to its right.
- If that digit is *less than* 5, the digit being rounded remains the same.
- If the digit is *5 or greater*, the digit being rounded increases by 1.

Talk About It CRITICAL THINKING

- Which basic multiplication facts helped you find the products in Examples A and B?
- Look for a pattern of zeros in the factors and products. How can you tell how many zeros to add at the end of the product for the basic fact?
- How does estimation help you determine if your answer is reasonable?

CULTURAL LINK

Native people of the southwestern United States have been making pottery from the clays of the area for more than 2,000 years. If a Navajo potter used about 8 slabs of clay to make a pot, about how many slabs of clay would be needed to make 210 pots?

▶ CHECK

Round each number to its greatest place-value position.

1. 495 **2.** 51 **3.** 74 **4.** 649

▶ PRACTICE

Estimate the product by rounding each factor to its greatest place-value position.

5. 103×21

6. 110×35

7. 143×68

8. 519×25

9. 157×38

10. 232×73

11. 298×81

12. 428×49

13. 376×79

14. 423×93

15. 592×72

16. 650×34

17. $48 \times 602 = n$

18. $88 \times 746 = n$

19. $94 \times 864 = n$

20. $12 \times 365 = n$

21. $43 \times 421 = n$

22. $83 \times 682 = n$

23. $26 \times 883 = n$

24. $63 \times 943 = n$

25. $89 \times 896 = n$

Problem Solving • Mixed Applications

Using Data For Problems 26 and 28, use the table.

FOOTBALL CARD COLLECTIONS

	Have Cards	Do Not Have Cards
Boys	345	672
Girls	196	853

26. Estimation Suppose that every student who collects football cards has 14 cards. Estimate the number of cards in all.

27. Art The students in Mrs. Ling's class wanted to help decorate the school. Mrs. Ling's class has 15 girls and 14 boys. Each student made 15 decorations. How many decorations did Mrs. Ling's class make in all?

28. **Write a problem** using the information in the Football Card Collections table.

Mixed Review and Test Prep

Copy and complete the equation. Identify the property used. (pages 74–75)

29. $\blacksquare \times 4 = 4 \times 9$

30. $6 \times 0 = \blacksquare$

31. $3 \times (7 \times 8) = (3 \times \blacksquare) \times 8$

32. $8 \times \blacksquare = 8$

33. $5 \times 7 = 7 \times \blacksquare$

34. $2 \times \blacksquare = 0$

Choose the standard form for each decimal number. (pages 38–39)

35. one and five thousandths **A** 1.500 **B** 1.05 **C** 1.005 **D** 0.105

36. six and thirty-three thousandths **F** 6.330 **G** 6.0033 **H** 0.6330 **J** 6.033

37. two and forty thousandths **A** 2.040 **B** 2.40 **C** 24.0 **D** 0.240

LESSON 4

Multiplying by Three-Digit Numbers

Why learn this? You can figure out how many people fly on airplanes each day.

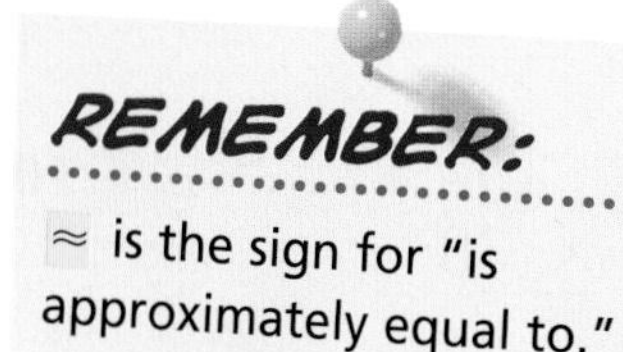

One kind of jet seats 462 passengers. Suppose 135 of these jets leave an airport on one day. If each jet is full, how many passengers will leave on these jets?

Multiply. $135 \times 462 = n$

Estimate. $100 \times 500 = 50{,}000$
So, $n \approx 50{,}000$.

$$\begin{array}{r} 462 \\ \times 135 \\ \hline 2{,}310 \\ 13{,}860 \\ +46{,}200 \\ \hline 62{,}370 \end{array} \quad \begin{array}{l} \\ \\ \leftarrow 5 \times 462 \\ \leftarrow 30 \times 462 \\ \leftarrow 100 \times 462 \\ \\ \end{array}$$

So, 62,370 passengers will leave on the jets.

EXAMPLES

A Multiply. $305 \times 281 = n$

Estimate. $300 \times 300 = 90{,}000$
So, $n \approx 90{,}000$.

$$\begin{array}{r} 281 \\ \times 305 \\ \hline 1{,}405 \\ 0{,}000 \\ +84{,}300 \\ \hline 85{,}705 \end{array} \quad \begin{array}{l} \\ \\ \leftarrow 5 \times 281 \\ \leftarrow 0 \times 281 \\ \leftarrow 300 \times 281 \\ \\ \end{array}$$

B Multiply. $114 \times 4{,}179 = n$

Estimate. $100 \times 4{,}000 = 400{,}000$
So, $n \approx 400{,}000$.

$$\begin{array}{r} 4{,}179 \\ \times \quad 114 \\ \hline 16{,}716 \\ 41{,}790 \\ +417{,}900 \\ \hline 476{,}406 \end{array} \quad \begin{array}{l} \\ \\ \leftarrow 4 \times 4{,}179 \\ \leftarrow 10 \times 4{,}179 \\ \leftarrow 100 \times 4{,}179 \\ \\ \end{array}$$

Talk About It

- In Example A, what property was used to multiply the tens?
- In Example B, what method was used to estimate the factors?

CRITICAL THINKING How does estimating help you determine whether the product is reasonable?

You can use a calculator to multiply large numbers.

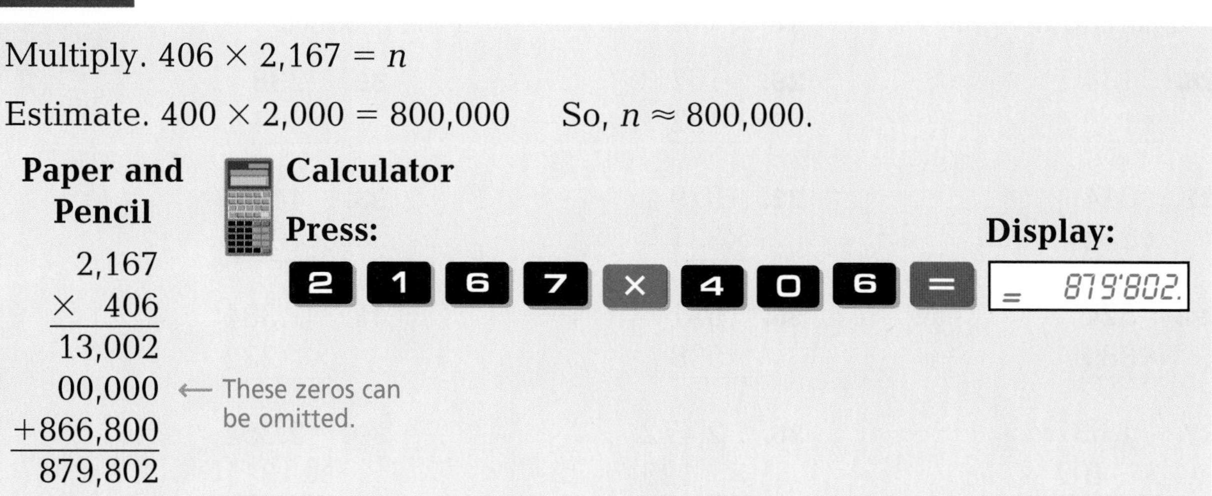

EXAMPLE

Multiply. $406 \times 2{,}167 = n$

Estimate. $400 \times 2{,}000 = 800{,}000$ So, $n \approx 800{,}000$.

Paper and Pencil

$$\begin{array}{r} 2{,}167 \\ \times \quad 406 \\ \hline 13{,}002 \\ 00{,}000 \\ +866{,}800 \\ \hline 879{,}802 \end{array}$$

← These zeros can be omitted.

Calculator

Press: 2 1 6 7 × 4 0 6 =

Display: 879'802.

- In the example, what does 13,002 represent? 866,800?

▶ CHECK

Look for a pattern of zeros. Find the product.

1. $500 \times 100 = n$
2. $300 \times 200 = n$
3. $130 \times 100 = n$
4. $150 \times 200 = n$
5. $190 \times 200 = n$
6. $210 \times 200 = n$
7. $400 \times 200 = n$
8. $600 \times 600 = n$

Estimate to the greatest place-value position. Then find the product.

9. $\begin{array}{r} 257 \\ \times\ 107 \\ \hline \end{array}$
10. $\begin{array}{r} 489 \\ \times\ 213 \\ \hline \end{array}$
11. $\begin{array}{r} 610 \\ \times\ 392 \\ \hline \end{array}$

Estimate. Then find the product.

12. $243 \times 496 = n$
13. $578 \times 132 = n$
14. $650 \times 809 = n$
15. $420 \times 379 = n$
16. $367 \times 284 = n$
17. $521 \times 333 = n$
18. $789 \times 529 = n$
19. $817 \times 247 = n$
20. $315 \times 184 = n$
21. $174 \times 821 = n$
22. $430 \times 718 = n$
23. $289 \times 301 = n$

Technology Link

In ***Mighty Math Number Heroes***, the game *Quizzo* challenges you to multiply three-digit numbers. Use Grow Slide Level S.

▶ PRACTICE

Look for a pattern of zeros. Find the product.

24. $200 \times 500 = n$ **25.** $300 \times 700 = n$ **26.** $250 \times 300 = n$ **27.** $600 \times 400 = n$

Estimate to the greatest place-value position. Then find the product.

28. 134×115

29. 167×122

30. 238×203

31. 314×246

32. 379×331

33. 448×401

34. 524×389

35. 631×538

36. $1{,}384 \times 232$

37. $1{,}637 \times 402$

38. $2{,}472 \times 125$

39. $2{,}354 \times 311$

Estimate. Then find the product.

40. $332 \times 479 = n$ **41.** $528 \times 625 = n$ **42.** $624 \times 883 = n$

43. $501 \times 158 = n$ **44.** $644 \times 197 = n$ **45.** $789 \times 105 = n$

46. $808 \times 301 = n$ **47.** $864 \times 421 = n$ **48.** $998 \times 210 = n$

Problem Solving • Mixed Applications

49. Health For the past 12 years, Alfredo has brushed his teeth 3 times a day. About how many times has he brushed his teeth?

50. Money Noah worked for 18 hours. He earned \$5.00 each hour. He bought a helmet for \$15.95 and a skateboard for twice that amount. How much money did Noah have left?

51. Career Mr. Thompson sells sheets of stamps at the post office. There are 100 stamps on each sheet. Last week he sold 192 sheets. About how many stamps did he sell in all?

52. Last week 15 schools went to the Health Fair. From each school, 210 students and 6 teachers attended. How many people attended the fair?

53. **Write About It** Why should you estimate the product before multiplying three- and four-digit numbers?

SCIENCE CONNECTION

Have you ever wished that you could fly like a bird? The first successful human flight, in 1783, was aboard a hot-air balloon. Balloons are filled with hydrogen or helium (light gases); so, they become light enough to float in air. In 1903, Wilbur and Orville Wright figured out how to fly a machine that weighed more than the air. Airplanes can fly if they move forward with more energy than the force of gravity.

PASSENGER FLYING MACHINES		
Type	Passenger Capacity	Speed (miles per hour)
Hot-air balloon	3	3
Boeing 747	490	584
Concorde	130	1,330

Some ideas take a long time to become useful. One of the earliest designers of a flying machine was Leonardo da Vinci, the famous Italian artist who painted the *Mona Lisa*. His designs date from about 1500. About how many years did it take for scientists to create an airplane?

Use the table to solve Problems 54–56.

54. Time It would take about 1 hour to fly from New York to Houston on the Concorde. If the hot-air balloon could make the trip, how long would it take?

55. A major airline has 106 Boeing 747's. How many passengers can the airline carry at one time? Estimate and then find the product.

56. Reasoning The Virginia Flyer's Club is planning a field trip to the Computer Museum in Boston, Massachusetts. The 320 members want to fly. Which aircraft should they take? Why?

Mixed Review and Test Prep

Choose a method and estimate each sum. (pages 28–29)

57. 23 + 35 + 19 + 41

58. 56 + 53 + 47 + 38

59. 189 + 501 + 250 + 422

60. 854 + 408 + 119 + 221

61. 901 + 249 + 385 + 267

Choose the letter for the correct difference. (pages 56–57)

62. $2.72 - 1.58 = n$ **A** 0.114 **B** 1.14 **C** 114 **D** 11.40

63. $4.09 - 3.632 = n$ **F** 0.458 **G** 4.58 **H** 45.80 **J** 458

64. $5.78 - 3.803 = n$ **A** 19.77 **B** 0.1977 **C** 1.977 **D** 1.98

MORE PRACTICE page H80

Multiplying to Find Perimeter and Area

Why learn this? You can find the perimeter and area of a rectangular object, such as a bulletin board.

It is your turn to cover and trim the class bulletin board. Work in a group to find out how much construction paper and trim you will need. Estimate first. Then measure to find the perimeter and area.

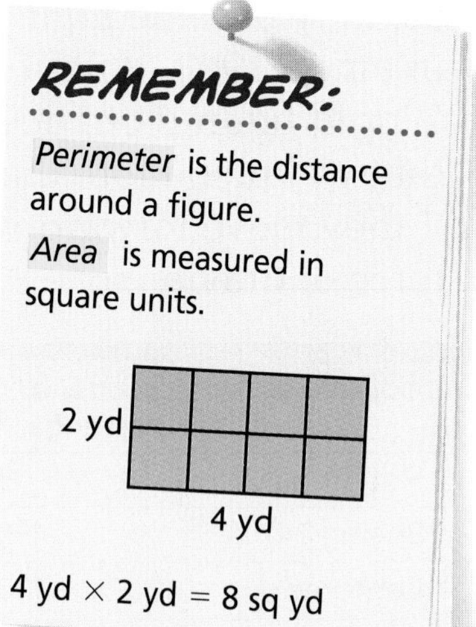

Talk About It

- What is the shape of the bulletin board?
- What parts of the bulletin board do you need to measure to find both the perimeter and area?

Multiply and add to find the perimeter of a rectangle.

Perimeter = (2 × length) + (2 × width)

$P = (2 \times l) + (2 \times w)$

Multiply length times width to find the area in square units.

$A = (l \times w)$

EXAMPLES

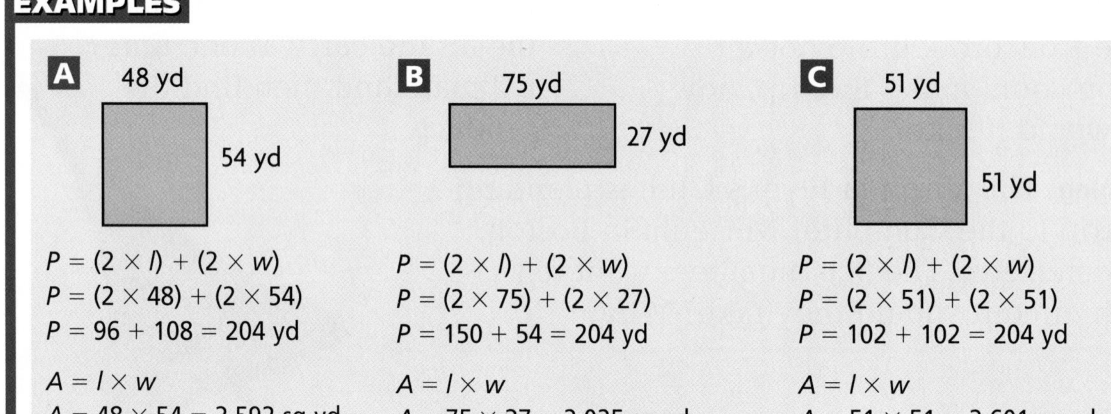

A

$P = (2 \times l) + (2 \times w)$
$P = (2 \times 48) + (2 \times 54)$
$P = 96 + 108 = 204$ yd

$A = l \times w$
$A = 48 \times 54 = 2{,}592$ sq yd

B

$P = (2 \times l) + (2 \times w)$
$P = (2 \times 75) + (2 \times 27)$
$P = 150 + 54 = 204$ yd

$A = l \times w$
$A = 75 \times 27 = 2{,}025$ sq yd

C

$P = (2 \times l) + (2 \times w)$
$P = (2 \times 51) + (2 \times 51)$
$P = 102 + 102 = 204$ yd

$A = l \times w$
$A = 51 \times 51 = 2{,}601$ sq yd

CRITICAL THINKING Is there a shorter number sentence that can be used to find the perimeter for Example C? Explain.

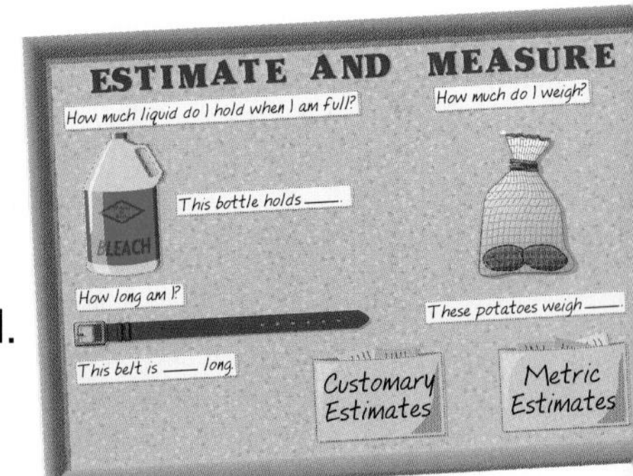

▶ CHECK

Find the perimeter and area for each. Explain the method you used.

1. **2.** **3.**

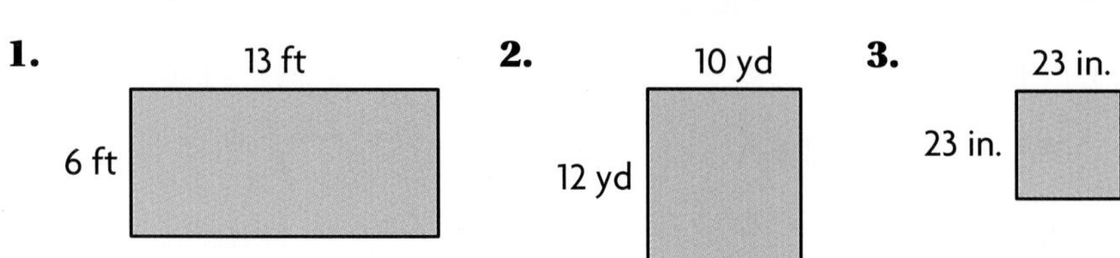

▶ PRACTICE

Find the perimeter and area for each figure.

4. 150 in., 75 in.

5. 147 yd, 118 yd

6. 188 m, 282 m

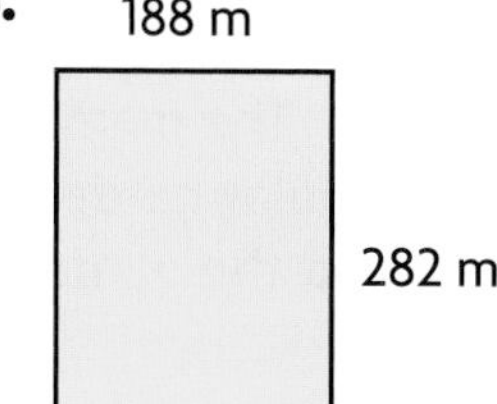

7. 136 cm, 213 cm

8. 202 ft, 104 ft

9. 286 yd, 355 yd

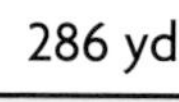

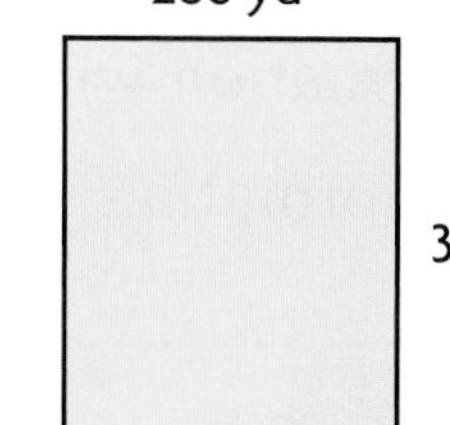

10. 202 cm, 85 cm

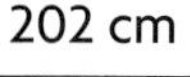

11. 191 ft, 147 ft

12. 253 in., 425 in.

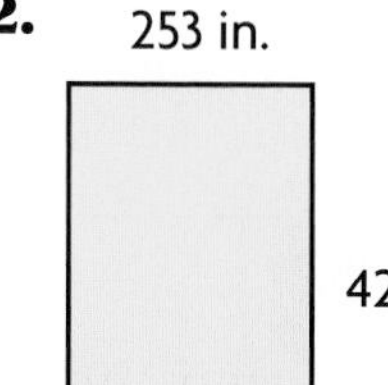

Problem Solving • Mixed Applications

13. Measurement Mason's yard is 107 feet by 238 feet. What are the perimeter and area of Mason's yard?

14. A factory produces 864 cars every week. How many cars does the factory produce in one year? (HINT: 1 year = 52 weeks)

15. Measurement Jerome traveled 17 miles round trip to soccer practice. He practiced 4 days. He traveled 19 miles round trip to his grandma's house on Saturday and again on Sunday. How many miles did he travel in all?

16. Reasoning Ariana, Cari, and Hannah play on the school basketball team. In one year, Ariana scored 562 points. Cari scored 26 fewer points. Hannah scored 12 fewer points than Cari. How many points did Cari and Hannah score?

17. Estimation The fuel tank in Mr. Roja's car holds 18 gallons, and the car travels 14 miles for each gallon of gasoline. About how far can Mr. Roja expect to drive on one tank of gas?

18. **Write a problem** about a playground, using perimeter and area.

MORE PRACTICE page H81

Problem–Solving Strategy: Draw a Diagram

▶ THE PROBLEM The members of the Science Club want to fence in a rectangular garden. They have 68 feet of fencing. What dimensions should the garden be so that it has the greatest area?

REMEMBER:

UNDERSTAND

PLAN

SOLVE

LOOK BACK

UNDERSTAND

- What are you asked to find?
- What information will you use?
- Is there information you will not use? If so, what?

PLAN

- What strategy can you use to solve the problem?

You can *draw a diagram*.

SOLVE

- How can you use the strategy to solve the problem?

You can draw diagrams of different rectangles with a perimeter of 68 feet. Then multiply to find the rectangle with the greatest area.

25 ft × 9 ft	20 ft × 14 ft	19 ft × 15 ft	18 ft × 16 ft	17 ft × 17 ft
Perimeter = 68 ft	Perimeter = 68 ft	Perimeter = 68 ft	Perimeter = 68 ft	Perimeter = 68 ft
$A = l \times w$	$A = l \times w$	$A = l \times w$	$A = l \times w$	$A = l \times w$
$A = 25 \times 9$	$A = 20 \times 14$	$A = 19 \times 15$	$A = 18 \times 16$	$A = 17 \times 17$
$A = 225$ sq ft	$A = 280$ sq ft	$A = 285$ sq ft	$A = 288$ sq ft	$A = 289$ sq ft

So, the garden should be 17 feet long by 17 feet wide to have the greatest area.

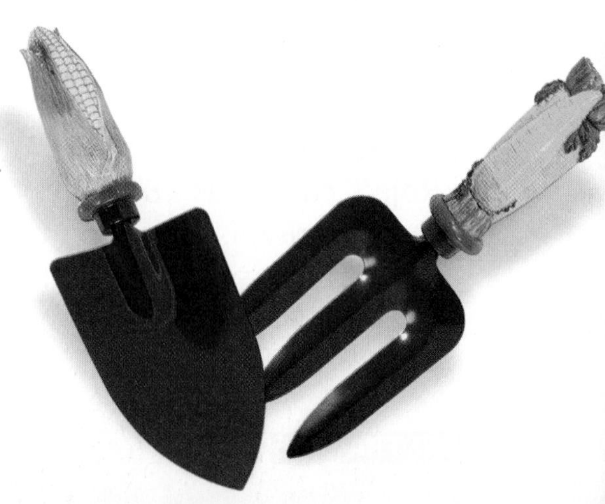

LOOK BACK

- How can you determine if your answer is reasonable?
- What other strategy could you use?

▶ PRACTICE

Draw a diagram to solve.

1. The Rileys want to fence in a rectangular section of their yard. They have 60 yards of fence to use. What dimensions will give the greatest possible area?

2. A school has 72 meters of wood to use to border a rectangular play area. The school wants the area to have the greatest possible area. What dimensions should it have?

3. A bulletin board is 36 inches by 36 inches square. Michael decorates the border by putting a star every 6 inches along the edge, including one in each corner. How many stars are on the bulletin board?

4. Julie uses chalk to write the numbers from 0 to 50, in order, on the sidewalk. She starts at 0 and moves forward 34 numbers, back 29, back 3, and forward 15. On what number does Julie end?

Mixed Applications

Solve.

CHOOSE a strategy and a tool.

- Draw a Diagram
- Use a Formula
- Write a Number Sentence
- Make a Table
- Guess and Check

Paper/Pencil

Calculator

Hands-On

Mental Math

5. It takes Tracy 5 minutes to plant one flower in her garden. How long will it take her to plant 16 flowers in her garden?

6. Jordan's room is 12 feet by 11 feet. Carly's room is 13 feet by 10 feet. Whose room has the greater area?

7. Ms. McKenzie has 144 feet of wire to surround a flower bed. What dimensions should the flower bed have so that it has the greatest area?

8. The Browns' home is 250 square feet larger than the Jacksons' home. The total area of both homes is 4,450 sq ft. How many square feet are in each home?

9. Jerry has baseball, football, and basketball cards. He has twice as many football as baseball cards and 3 times as many basketball as baseball cards. He has 150 cards in all. How many of each kind of card does he have?

10. There are four high schools in the district. Lincoln has 2,285 students. Oakland has 2,187, and Evans has 2,852. Orange has 1,987. Which school has the fewest students? the most students?

11. Ms. Humphrey has the two plastic containers shown. She wants to store food in the container with the greater volume. Which container should she use?

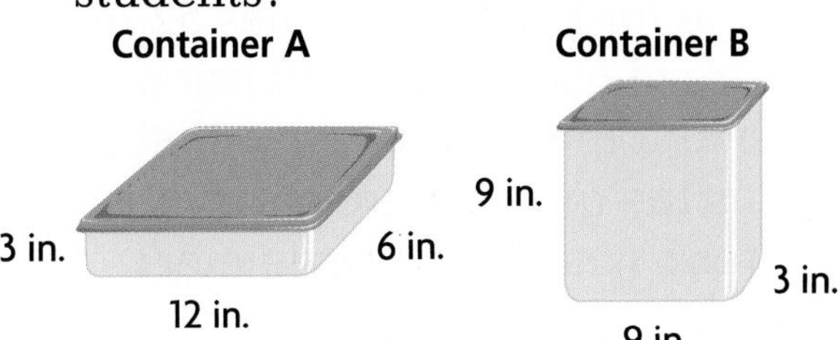

CHAPTER 6 Review/Test

CHECK Understanding

VOCABULARY

1. The __?__ states that multiplying a sum by a number is the same as multiplying each addend by the number and then adding the products. (page 92)

Estimate the product by rounding each factor to its greatest place-value position. (pages 96–97)

2. 526×29
3. 285×41
4. 943×72
5. 836×93

CHECK Skills

Find the product. (pages 94–95, 98–101)

6. 27×24
7. 35×90
8. 96×53
9. 394×33
10. 184×37
11. 603×11
12. 836×497
13. 501×420
14. 315×641
15. $1{,}320 \times 191$
16. $3{,}109 \times 226$
17. $6{,}543 \times 123$

Find the perimeter and area for each figure. (pages 102–103)

18. 94 ft

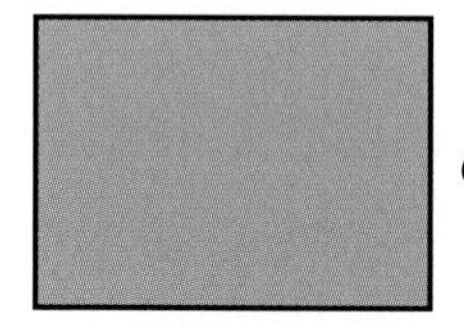

66 ft

19. 58 yd

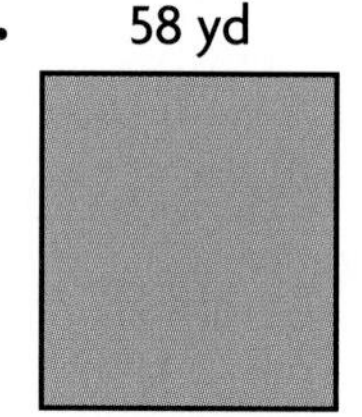

63 yd

20. 121 cm

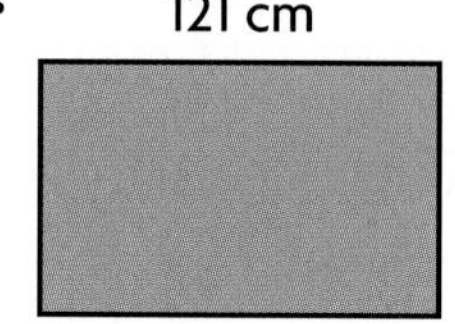

74 cm

CHECK Problem Solving

Solve. (pages 104–105)

CHOOSE a strategy and a tool.

- Draw a Diagram
- Use a Formula
- Write a Number Sentence
- Use a Table

Paper/Pencil

Calculator

Hands-On

Mental Math

21. Kasey is building a rectangular cage for her pet. She has 52 in. of wire to use. What dimensions should the cage have so that it has the greatest area? What is the area? What is the perimeter?

22. There are 73 players on hockey teams. There are twice as many players on basketball teams, and 10 more players on softball teams than on hockey. No player is on more than one team. How many players are there in all?

Test Prep

CUMULATIVE
CHAPTERS 1–6

Choose the best answer.

1. There are 18 loaves of bread. Each loaf has about 20 slices. Which of the following is a reasonable estimate for the total number of bread slices?

A 15 **B** 150

C 200 **D** 400

2. Which of the number sentences below is related to $125 - 62 = n$?

F $62 + n = 125$ **G** $125 + n = 62$

H $62 \times n = 125$ **J** $62 - n = 125$

3. Which group of decimals is in order from *least* to *greatest*?

A 5.387; 5.373; 5.874; 5.840

B 5.373; 5.387; 5.840; 5.874

C 5.840; 5.874; 5.387; 5.373

D 5.373; 5.387; 5.874; 5.840

4. Irene ran the race in 43.08 seconds. Bobbie ran it in 42.31 seconds. Which number sentence could be used to find how much faster Bobbie's time was?

F $43.08 + 42.31 = \square$

G $43.08 - 42.31 = \square$

H $43.08 \times 42.31 = \square$

J $43.08 \div 42.31 = \square$

5. Find the area.

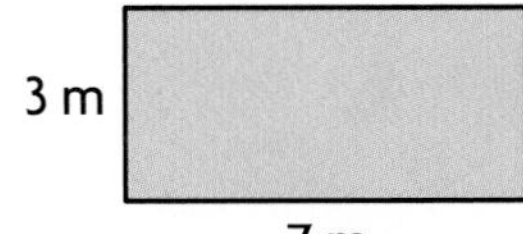

A 10 sq m

B 17 sq m

C 20 sq m

D 21 sq m

E Not Here

6. Find the volume.

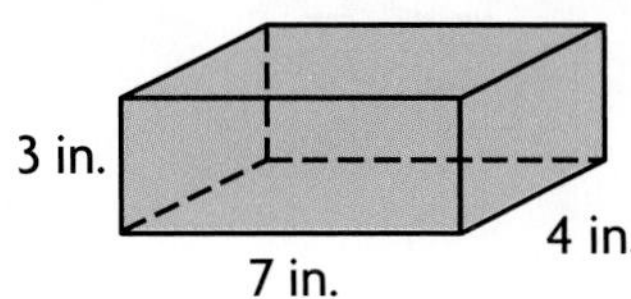

F 12 cu in.

G 24 cu in.

H 84 cu in.

J 96 cu in.

K Not Here

7. Ms. Milham's class has 26 students. Each student has taken 32 quizzes. Which of the following is a reasonable estimate for the number of quizzes Ms. Milham has graded in all?

A 400 **B** 600

C 900 **D** 1,100

8. $\begin{array}{r} 173 \\ \times 122 \\ \hline \end{array}$

F 21,006

G 22,106

H 210,105

J 201,106

K Not Here

9. $216 \times 197 =$

A 45,250

B 42,552

C 4,255

D 42,152

7 DIVIDING BY ONE-DIGIT NUMBERS

MEASUREMENT **LINK**

There are actually about $365\frac{1}{4}$ days in a year. That's why we have a "leap year" once every 4 years.

The extra day in a leap year is February 29. If a year is divisible by 4 or 100, then it is a leap year.

Problem-Solving Activity

Leapin' Leap Years!

Do you know anyone whose birthday is February 29? Leap year birthdays happen only once every 4 years. Suppose your birthday came around only once every 3 years or only once every 6 years.

Find which years are divisible by 3, 4, 5, 6, or 9.

YOU WILL NEED: 1-inch grid paper, calculator, pencil, paper, markers

- Make a chart that shows the next 40 years.
- Identify all the leap years.
- Invent names for years that come every 3 years, 4 years, 5 years, 6 years, or 9 years. For example, "POM" years could happen every 3 years, and "ROCKET" years could happen every 6 years.
- Mark each type of year on your chart with a different symbol. Make a key showing the symbols.
- Describe the patterns on your chart.

WHAT IS DIVISIBILITY?

A number is *divisible* by another number if there is no remainder.

DID YOU

- ✓ make a chart that shows the next 40 years?
- ✓ find which years are divisible by 3, 4, 5, 6, or 9?
- ✓ mark each type of year on your chart with a different symbol?
- ✓ describe the patterns on your chart?

Divisibility

VOCABULARY
divisible

You will investigate the rules of divisibility.

A number is **divisible** by another number if the quotient is a whole number and there is a zero remainder. For example, 32 is divisible by 4 because the quotient is 8 and the remainder is zero.

Some numbers have a *rule of divisibility*. If you know the rule, you can quickly tell whether a number is divisible by that number.

Look at these examples to help you recall the rules of divisibility for 2, 5, and 10.

Numbers divisible by 2: 12, 34, 72, 84, 96, 108, 120
Numbers divisible by 5: 10, 35, 60, 110, 145, 180, 230
Numbers divisible by 10: 20, 40, 70, 100, 140, 190, 250

- What is the rule of divisibility for 2? 5? 10?

▶ EXPLORE

Use a calculator to discover more rules of divisibility.

MATERIALS:  calculator

Step 1	Step 2	Step 3
Use mental math and a calculator. Test the numbers in the second column of the chart to see if they are divisible by 3. Record the numbers that pass the divisibility test.	Read the hint. With your partner, write the rule of divisibility for 3. Then give three other examples of numbers that pass the divisibility test.	Repeat Steps 1 and 2 to discover the rule of divisibility for 9.

Number	Numbers to Test	HINT: Look at
3	15, 20, 36, 70, 105, 141	. . . the sum of the digits of the numbers.
9	63, 95, 138, 216, 531, 882	. . . the sum of the digits of the numbers.

Record

Make a table to record the divisibility rules for 3 and 9 and examples of numbers that are divisible by each.

Now, investigate finding the rules of divisibility for 4 and 6.

▶ TRY THIS

Use a calculator and the hint to test the numbers given. Add them to your table.

	Number	Numbers to Test	HINT: Look at
1.	4	20, 36, 75, 104, 148, 210	. . . the last two digits in the numbers.
2.	6	35, 42, 56, 128, 132, 216	. . . whether the numbers are divisible by both 2 and 3.

3. If a number is divisible by 10, is it also divisible by 2? Explain.

4. If a number is divisible by 5, is it also divisible by 2? Explain.

5. If a number is divisible by 4, is it also divisible by 2? Explain.

6. **Write About It** What is the least number that is divisible by 2, 3, 5, and 10? Explain.

Technology Link

You can use the rules for divisibility by using E-Lab, Activity 7. Available on CD-ROM and on the Internet at **www.hbschool.com/elab**

▶ PRACTICE

Use mental math and a calculator. Test each number for divisibility by 2, 3, 4, 5, 6, 9, and 10. List the numbers that work.

7. 24 **8.** 45 **9.** 72 **10.** 130 **11.** 185 **12.** 308

13. 297 **14.** 519 **15.** 728 **16.** 2,604 **17.** 3,750 **18.** 3,765

19. 605 **20.** 1,896 **21.** 4,420 **22.** 9,951 **23.** 12,035 **24.** 36,390

Mr. Allen wants to divide his science class of 36 students into equal groups for an experiment.

25. What are all the possible equal-sized groups into which he could divide them?

Problem Solving • Mixed Applications

26. **Number Sense** I am a number between 50 and 60. I am divisible by 2, 3, and 9. What number am I?

27. **Mental Math** If 5 friends share 37 marbles equally, how many marbles does each person have? How many are left over?

MORE PRACTICE page H81

LESSON 2

Placing the First Digit

VOCABULARY
compatible numbers

Why learn this? You can find the number of pages filled in a photo album.

Felicia bought a new photograph album. She has 142 photos. Each page of the album holds 6 photos. How many pages can she fill?

Divide. $142 \div 6 = n$ $\quad 6\overline{)142}$

First, estimate.

To estimate a quotient, use compatible numbers.

Compatible numbers are numbers close to the actual numbers and can be divided evenly. Compatible numbers for 6 are numbers divisible by 6, such as 12, 18, or 24.

Look at Felicia's, Tim's, and Anne's estimates.

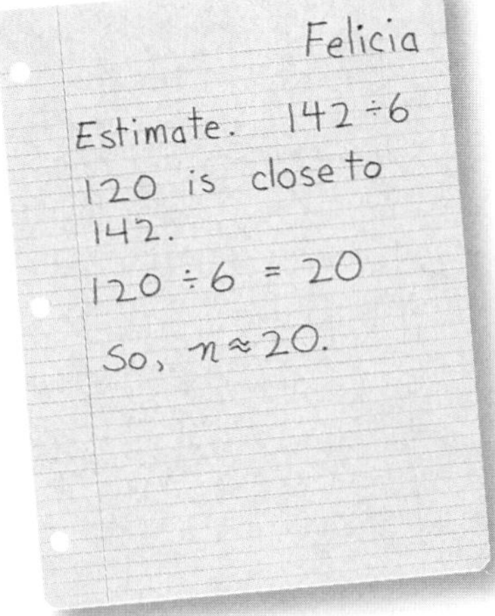
Felicia
Estimate. 142 ÷ 6
120 is close to 142.
120 ÷ 6 = 20
So, n ≈ 20.

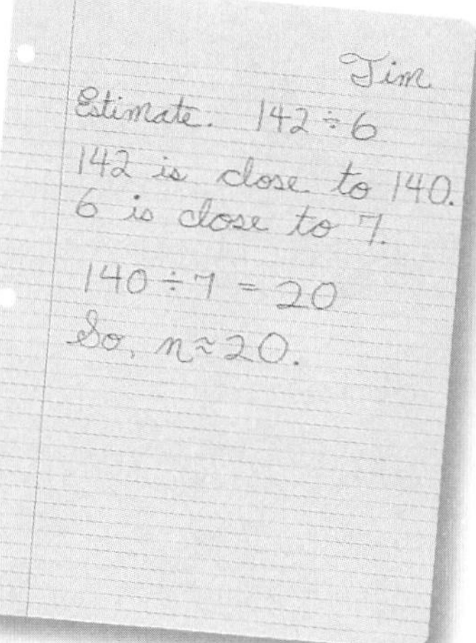
Tim
Estimate. 142 ÷ 6
142 is close to 140.
6 is close to 7.
140 ÷ 7 = 20
So, n ≈ 20.

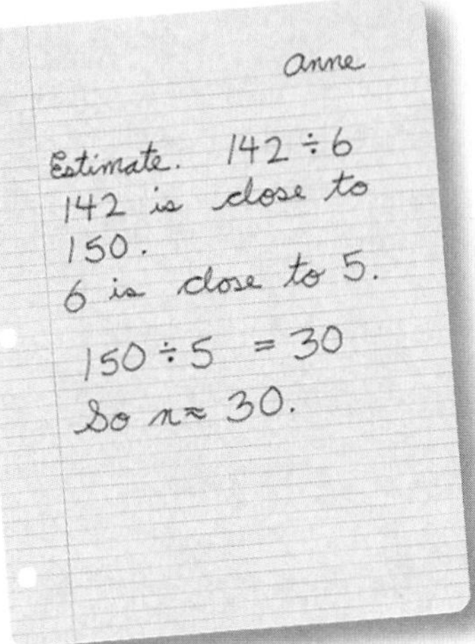
Anne
Estimate. 142 ÷ 6
142 is close to 150.
6 is close to 5.
150 ÷ 5 = 30
So n ≈ 30.

So, both 20 and 30 are good estimates.

Talk About It CRITICAL THINKING

- How do compatible numbers help you estimate mentally?
- How do you know how many digits will be in the quotient?

Use your estimate to divide.

MODEL

What is $142 \div 6$?

Step 1

Decide where to place the first digit in the quotient.

$6\overline{)142}$ with x over the 1: $1 < 6$. There are not enough hundreds.

$6\overline{)142}$ with x over the 4: $14 > 6$. Use 14 tens. Place the first digit in the tens place.

Step 2

Divide the tens. $6\overline{)14}$

Think: $6 \times n = 12$

$$\begin{array}{r} 2 \\ 6\overline{)142} \\ -12 \\ \hline 2 \end{array}$$

Multiply. 6×2

Subtract. $14 - 12$

Compare. $2 < 6$

Step 3

Bring down the ones.

Divide. $6\overline{)22}$

Think: $6 \times n = 18$

$$\begin{array}{r} 23 \text{ r}4 \\ 6\overline{)142} \\ -12 \\ \hline 22 \\ -18 \\ \hline 4 \end{array}$$

Multiply. 6×3

Subtract. $22 - 18$

Compare. $4 < 6$

Since $n = 23$ r4, Felicia will fill 23 pages. The twenty-fourth page will have only 4 photos.

So, the actual quotient is between 20 and 30.

EXAMPLE

What is $431 \div 5$?

Think: $400 \div 5 = 80$

or $450 \div 5 = 90$

So, $431 \div 5 \approx 80$ or 90.

$$\begin{array}{r} 86 \text{ r}1 \\ 5\overline{)431} \\ -40 \\ \hline 31 \\ -30 \\ \hline 1 \end{array}$$

Since 43 tens can be divided by 5, the first digit of the quotient is in the tens place.

▶ CHECK

Write two pairs of compatible numbers for each. Give two possible estimates.

1. $153 \div 34 \approx n$ **2.** $640 \div 87 \approx n$ **3.** $153 \div 18 \approx n$

4. $275 \div 32 \approx n$ **5.** $369 \div 41 \approx n$ **6.** $203 \div 58 \approx n$

Copy each problem. Draw a box where the first digit in the quotient should be placed.

7. $5\overline{)519}$ **8.** $3\overline{)256}$ **9.** $4\overline{)745}$ **10.** $6\overline{)829}$

11. $5\overline{)457}$ **12.** $4\overline{)523}$ **13.** $3\overline{)310}$ **14.** $6\overline{)468}$

15. $8\overline{)742}$ **16.** $9\overline{)195}$ **17.** $7\overline{)804}$ **18.** $2\overline{)173}$

▶ PRACTICE

Estimate the quotient.

19. $145 \div 3 \approx n$ **20.** $298 \div 9 \approx n$ **21.** $501 \div 5 \approx n$ **22.** $375 \div 6 \approx n$

23. $623 \div 3 \approx n$ **24.** $337 \div 4 \approx n$ **25.** $295 \div 7 \approx n$ **26.** $641 \div 3 \approx n$

Copy each problem. Draw a box where the first digit in the quotient should be placed.

27. $6\overline{)325}$ **28.** $4\overline{)714}$ **29.** $5\overline{)318}$ **30.** $2\overline{)931}$ **31.** $6\overline{)519}$

32. $3\overline{)598}$ **33.** $4\overline{)409}$ **34.** $7\overline{)143}$ **35.** $9\overline{)114}$ **36.** $6\overline{)544}$

37. $7\overline{)485}$ **38.** $8\overline{)282}$ **39.** $3\overline{)513}$ **40.** $2\overline{)193}$ **41.** $5\overline{)833}$

Find the quotient.

42. $6\overline{)138}$ **43.** $7\overline{)642}$ **44.** $9\overline{)700}$ **45.** $4\overline{)832}$ **46.** $2\overline{)785}$

47. $5\overline{)277}$ **48.** $3\overline{)343}$ **49.** $7\overline{)615}$ **50.** $9\overline{)569}$ **51.** $8\overline{)941}$

52. $3\overline{)822}$ **53.** $5\overline{)724}$ **54.** $2\overline{)837}$ **55.** $8\overline{)111}$ **56.** $6\overline{)238}$

57. $7\overline{)460}$ **58.** $2\overline{)303}$ **59.** $4\overline{)287}$ **60.** $5\overline{)779}$ **61.** $9\overline{)356}$

Problem Solving • Mixed Applications

62. Measurement Linda bought a 132-ounce jug of shampoo. She was able to completely refill a smaller bottle with the shampoo 8 times. How many ounces did the smaller bottle hold? How many ounces were left over?

63. Each cup of yogurt contains 225 calories. How many calories are in 4 cups of yogurt?

64. Money Rachel saved \$282 from baby-sitting during a 6-month period. She saved the same amount of money each month. How much did she save each month?

65. Mental Math Dan has to wait 56 days until his birthday. How many weeks are there until his birthday?

66. Write About It Explain why it is important to place the first digit correctly when you divide.

GEOGRAPHY CONNECTION

Some of the most spectacular landscapes in the U.S. have become national parks. They are used for hiking, boating, camping, sightseeing, and even hang gliding.

67. A group of 128 Boy Scouts visit Yellowstone. They plan to sleep 4 to a tent. How many tents will they need?

68. Four friends plan to hike a 102-mile section of the Appalachian Trail. They have 9 days for their hike. About how many miles will they have to hike per day?

69. A group of 35 people are going canoeing at Voyageurs National Park. How many canoes will they need if each canoe holds 2 people?

70. Reasoning When I am divided by 4, the quotient has 2 digits. When I am divided by 6, the quotient has 1 digit. My ones digit is 8. Who am I?

HISTORY LINK

Yellowstone National Park is the oldest national park in the world. It became a national park in 1872. In addition to Old Faithful, it has 2,000 other active geysers. Yellowstone also has over 200 species of birds, about 20,000 elk, and about 2,000 bison. There are now 52 national parks in all. If you could visit 2 parks each year, how long would it take to visit all 52?

Mixed Review and Test Prep

Write the value of the blue digit. (pages 8–11)

71. 2,354 **72.** 54,697 **73.** 424,576 **74.** 901,627

75. 29,723 **76.** 2,678,035 **77.** 3,560,217 **78.** 6,078,392,541

Choose the letter of the correct sum. (pages 54–55)

79. $3.12 + 0.683 = n$

A 0.3803
B 3.803
C 38.03
D 9.950

80. $1.492 + 7.5 = n$

F 8.992
G 1.567
H 0.8992
J 0.1567

81. $14.69 + 1.249 = n$

A 27.18
B 15.93
C 15.939
D 0.2718

LESSON 3

Zeros in Division

Why learn this? You can find the number of items divided into equal groups, such as supplies for a group of stores.

Mr. Baxter owns 4 music stores. He is ordering 408 portable stereos for his stores. He wants each store to have the same number of portable stereos. How many will each store receive?

Divide. $408 \div 4 = n$ $\quad 4\overline{)408}$

Estimate. **Think:** $400 \div 4 = 100$ So, $n \approx 100$.

What is $408 \div 4$?

Step 1

Since 4 hundreds can be divided by 4, the first digit in the quotient will be in the hundreds place. Divide the 4 hundreds.

Think: $4 \times n = 4$

$$\begin{array}{r} 1 \\ 4\overline{)408} \\ -4 \\ \hline 0 \end{array}$$

Multiply. 4×1

Subtract. $4 - 4$

Compare. $0 < 4$

Step 2

Bring down the tens.
Divide the 0 tens.
Think: Since $4 > 0$, write 0 in the quotient.

$$\begin{array}{r} 10 \\ 4\overline{)408} \\ -4 \\ \hline 00 \\ -0 \\ \hline 0 \end{array}$$

$0 \div 4 = 0$

$4 \times 0 = 0$

Step 3

Bring down the ones.
Divide the 8 ones.
Think: $4 \times n = 8$

$$\begin{array}{r} 102 \\ 4\overline{)408} \\ -4 \\ \hline 00 \\ -0 \\ \hline 08 \\ -8 \\ \hline 0 \end{array}$$

Multiply. 4×2

Subtract. $8 - 8$

Compare. $0 < 4$

Since 102 is close to the estimate of 100, the answer is reasonable. So, each store will receive 102 stereos.

Talk About It CRITICAL THINKING

- What does the zero indicate in the quotient in the problem above?
- When do you write a zero in the quotient?
- How can you use a rule of divisibility to check if the answer is reasonable?

Technology Link

In ***Mighty Math Calculating Crew***, the game *Intergalactic Trader* challenges you to divide by one-digit numbers. Use Grow Slide Levels P and Q.

▶ CHECK

Estimate the quotient.

1. $5\overline{)250}$ **2.** $7\overline{)734}$ **3.** $4\overline{)824}$ **4.** $6\overline{)305}$ **5.** $3\overline{)927}$

▶ PRACTICE

Estimate the quotient.

6. $3\overline{)310}$ **7.** $7\overline{)440}$ **8.** $4\overline{)340}$ **9.** $2\overline{)419}$ **10.** $9\overline{)873}$

Find the quotient.

11. $4\overline{)816}$ **12.** $3\overline{)908}$ **13.** $6\overline{)612}$ **14.** $5\overline{)525}$ **15.** $6\overline{)624}$

16. $7\overline{)745}$ **17.** $9\overline{)980}$ **18.** $2\overline{)121}$ **19.** $5\overline{)544}$ **20.** $2\overline{)801}$

21. $3\overline{)961}$ **22.** $8\overline{)887}$ **23.** $5\overline{)454}$ **24.** $7\overline{)763}$ **25.** $3\overline{)613}$

26. $122 \div 4 = n$ **27.** $504 \div 5 = n$ **28.** $824 \div 8 = n$ **29.** $631 \div 6 = n$

30. $340 \div 5 = n$ **31.** $130 \div 2 = n$ **32.** $907 \div 7 = n$ **33.** $400 \div 3 = n$

Problem Solving • Mixed Applications

34. On Saturday and Sunday a total of 414 people visited a local beach. If the same number of people came each day, how many visited the beach on Saturday?

35. Elapsed Time Bailey and his family went on a 108-mile hiking trip in the mountains. They hiked 9 miles each day. For how many days did they hike?

36. Money Adult tickets for the school play cost $8. Student tickets cost $5. Lisa sold 20 tickets for $136. How many adult tickets did she sell?

37. Money Ken saved $328 from mowing lawns over an 8-month period. He saved the same amount of money each month. How much did he save each month?

38. The tri-county math fair begins in one week. Each school will have its own display table. The tables will be placed in 15 rows of 15 tables each. How many schools are participating?

39. Write About It Choose one of Exercises 11–33 in which there is no remainder. Explain how you could use a rule of divisibility to determine before dividing that there would be no remainder.

Mixed Review and Test Prep

Find the difference. (pages 24–25)

40. $100 - 57$ **41.** $500 - 176$ **42.** $2{,}000 - 786$ **43.** $5{,}000 - 3{,}067$ **44.** $12{,}000 - 9{,}886$

Choose the letter of an equivalent decimal for each. (pages 42–43)

45. 0.04 **A** 4.0 **B** 0.040 **C** 0.004 **D** 0.40

46. 3.20 **F** 3.200 **G** 0.320 **H** 0.0320 **J** 32.0

MORE PRACTICE page H82

Practicing Division

Why learn this? You can find out how much less something weighs on the moon than on Earth.

Earth's gravity causes things to weigh 6 times as much on Earth as they weigh on the moon. Suppose rocks taken from the moon weighed 108 pounds on Earth. How much did those rocks weigh on the moon?

Divide. $108 \div 6 = n$ $\quad 6\overline{)108}$

Estimate. **Think:** $100 \div 5 = 20$ So, $n \approx 20$.

Predict. **Think:** 108 is divisible by 6 because it is divisible by 2 and by 3.

MODEL

What is $108 \div 6$?

Step 1

Decide where to place the first digit in the quotient.

$$\begin{array}{r} x \\ 6\overline{)108} \end{array}$$

$1 < 6$ There are not enough hundreds.

$$\begin{array}{r} x\blacksquare \\ 6\overline{)108} \end{array}$$

$10 > 6$ Use 10 tens. Place the first digit in the tens place.

Step 2

Divide the tens. $6\overline{)10}$

Think: $6 \times n = 6$

$$\begin{array}{r} 1 \\ 6\overline{)108} \\ \underline{-6} \\ 4 \end{array}$$

Multiply. 6×1

Subtract. $10 - 6$

Compare. $4 < 6$

Step 3

Bring down the ones.

Divide. $6\overline{)48}$

Think: $6 \times n = 48$

$$\begin{array}{r} 18 \\ 6\overline{)108} \\ \underline{-6}\downarrow \\ 48 \\ \underline{-48} \\ 0 \end{array}$$

Multiply. 6×8

Subtract. $48 - 48$

Compare. $0 < 6$

Since $n = 18$, the rocks weighed 18 pounds on the moon.

Check your quotient. Multiply the divisor by the quotient. If there is a remainder, add it to the product.

$$\begin{array}{r} 18 \\ \times\ 6 \\ \hline 108 \end{array} \checkmark$$

EXAMPLES

A

$$\begin{array}{r} 123\text{ r}3 \\ 5\overline{)618} \\ \underline{-5} \\ 11 \\ \underline{-10} \\ 18 \\ \underline{-15} \\ 3 \end{array}$$

Since 6 hundreds can be divided by 5, the first digit of the quotient is in the hundreds place.

Check:

$$\begin{array}{r} 123 \\ \times\ \ 5 \\ \hline 615 \end{array} \qquad \begin{array}{r} 615 \\ +\ \ 3 \\ \hline 618 \end{array}$$

B

$$\begin{array}{r} 330 \\ 3\overline{)990} \\ \underline{-9} \\ 09 \\ \underline{-9} \\ 00 \\ \underline{-\ 0} \\ 0 \end{array}$$

Check:

$$\begin{array}{r} 330 \\ \times\ \ 3 \\ \hline 990 \end{array}$$

▶ CHECK

Use divisibility rules to predict if there will be a remainder.

1. $9\overline{)117}$ **2.** $5\overline{)213}$ **3.** $7\overline{)481}$ **4.** $9\overline{)855}$ **5.** $3\overline{)247}$

Find the quotient. Check by multiplying.

6. $4\overline{)312}$ **7.** $6\overline{)489}$ **8.** $4\overline{)143}$ **9.** $7\overline{)297}$ **10.** $9\overline{)526}$

▶ PRACTICE

Use divisibility rules to predict if there will be a remainder.

11. $9\overline{)493}$ **12.** $3\overline{)472}$ **13.** $5\overline{)515}$ **14.** $4\overline{)374}$ **15.** $6\overline{)204}$

16. $2\overline{)221}$ **17.** $9\overline{)657}$ **18.** $4\overline{)932}$ **19.** $3\overline{)294}$ **20.** $6\overline{)188}$

Find the quotient. Check by multiplying.

21. $3\overline{)635}$ **22.** $7\overline{)698}$ **23.** $3\overline{)457}$ **24.** $2\overline{)164}$ **25.** $4\overline{)978}$

26. $6\overline{)104}$ **27.** $8\overline{)246}$ **28.** $9\overline{)288}$ **29.** $4\overline{)844}$ **30.** $5\overline{)376}$

31. $348 \div 8 = n$ **32.** $807 \div 9 = n$ **33.** $124 \div 6 = n$ **34.** $414 \div 2 = n$

35. $338 \div 7 = n$ **36.** $232 \div 4 = n$ **37.** $472 \div 5 = n$ **38.** $694 \div 3 = n$

Problem Solving • Mixed Applications

39. Money Carl had $20.00 to spend at the book fair. He bought one book for $3.95 and another for $12.95. Posters cost $1.50. How many posters can Carl buy? How much change will he get?

41. What number has 6 in the thousands and tens places, 1 in the hundreds place, 9 in the ones and thousandths places, and 0 in the tenths and hundredths places?

40. History George Washington lived from 1732 to 1799. Abraham Lincoln lived from 1809 to 1865. Who lived longer? How many years longer did he live?

42. **Write a problem** about Doug's stamp collection, using division. He has 458 stamps and 5 stamp albums.

Mixed Review and Test Prep

Find the sum. (pages 52–53)

43. $1.0 + 5.7 = n$ **44.** $2.35 + 7.86 = n$ **45.** $5.982 + 3.067 = n$

Choose the letter of the standard form for each decimal. (pages 38–39)

46. one and four thousandths **A** 1.04 **B** 1.004 **C** 1.0004 **D** 1.040

47. sixty-five thousandths **F** 0.065 **G** 0.0065 **H** 6.50 **J** 0.0650

MORE PRACTICE page H82

Interpreting the Remainder

Why learn this? You can decide what to do with an amount left over when solving a division problem.

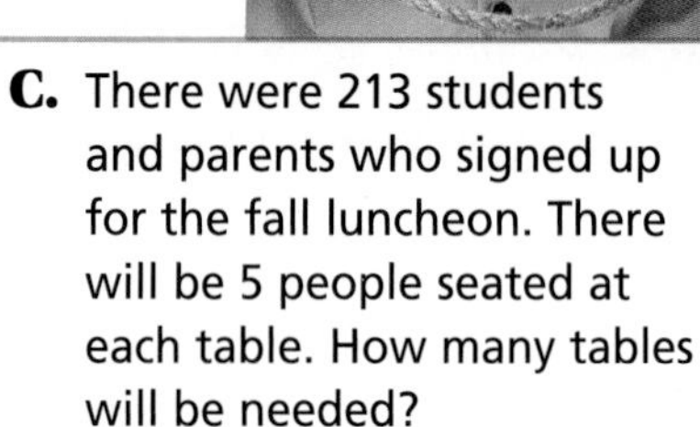

When there is a remainder in a division problem, look at the question. You may need to drop the remainder, round the quotient to the next greater number, or use the remainder as part of your answer.

Determine how the remainder was used to solve each of the following problems.

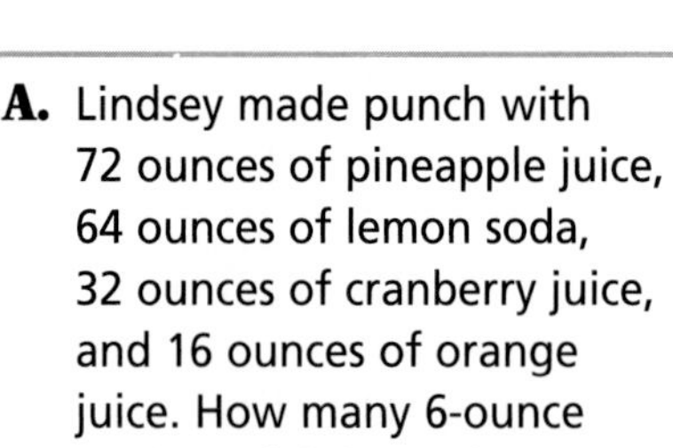

A. Lindsey made punch with 72 ounces of pineapple juice, 64 ounces of lemon soda, 32 ounces of cranberry juice, and 16 ounces of orange juice. How many 6-ounce servings did she make?

```
   30 r4
6)184
 -18
  04
  -0
   4
```

She made 30 six-ounce servings. The 4 ounces left over are not enough for another 6-ounce serving.

B. Mr. Webb brought in a 118-foot rope for the Boy Scouts to practice tying knots. He divided the rope into 3 pieces of equal length. How long was each piece of rope?

$$3\overline{)118} = 39\tfrac{1}{3}$$

```
   39 1/3
3)118
  -9
   28
  -27
    1
```

To write the remainder as a fraction, use the remainder as the numerator and the divisor as the denominator.

When the 1-foot length is divided by 3, each part is $\frac{1}{3}$ foot. So, each piece of rope was $39\frac{1}{3}$ feet long.

C. There were 213 students and parents who signed up for the fall luncheon. There will be 5 people seated at each table. How many tables will be needed?

```
   42 r3
5)213
 -20
  13
 -10
   3
```

Since 42 tables will not be enough to seat everyone, 43 tables will be needed.

You can use a calculator to divide.
Find the quotient $975 \div 9 = n$.

Press:

Display:

- What do Q and R in the display mean?

CRITICAL THINKING Why is the remainder added to the product when checking the quotient?

Calculator Activities page H62

▶ CHECK

1. Explain how the remainder was used to answer problems A–C on page 120.
2. In Problem B, what does the remainder represent?
3. Explain why a fractional remainder was appropriate for Problem B but not for Problems A and C.

▶ PRACTICE

Solve. Explain how you interpreted the remainder.

4. A group of 106 students showed up for ski lessons. There are 9 ski instructors. How many students will be in most of the groups?
5. The track for Brian's model train is 3 times as long as Mario's track. Brian's track is 245 inches long. How long is Mario's track?
6. Mrs. Pfeiffer's flower shop is running a special on roses. She is selling an arrangement of 24 roses for $19.95. She has 146 roses on hand. Can she fill 6 orders for the special?
7. The bleachers in the school gym have 148 seats. There are 8 rows with the same number of seats in all the rows except one. How many seats are in the row with the greatest number of seats?

Problem Solving • Mixed Applications

8. Jake has 170 books to put on shelves in the store. There are 5 shelves for the books. If Jake puts an equal number of books on each shelf, how many books will be on each shelf? How many books will be left over?
9. The Future Leaders Club has 200 tickets to sell for the school dance. Each club member has 8 tickets to sell. How many members are in the club?
10. **Patterns** Penny practiced free throws for a week. She scored 5 on the first day, 10 on the second day, 16 on the third day, and 23 on the fourth day. If this pattern continued, what was her score on day six?
11. **Art** For a crafts project, 9 students divide 537 toothpicks. How many toothpicks does each student get? How many toothpicks are left over?
12. **Write a problem** in which you divide and must interpret the remainder in order to answer the question. Explain how the remainder helps answer the question.

MORE PRACTICE page H82

Problem-Solving Strategy: Guess and Check

▶ THE PROBLEM There were 174 paintings and drawings entered in the self-portrait contest. The portraits were placed in equal groups on walls throughout the school. After the portraits were placed, 6 were left over and were placed on a wall in the main office. How many groups were formed? How many portraits were in each group?

UNDERSTAND

- What are you asked to find?
- What information will you use?
- Is there information you will not use? If so, what?

PLAN

- What strategy can you use to solve the problem?

You can *guess and check.*

SOLVE

- How can you use the strategy?

You can guess an answer and then check to see if your guess is correct.

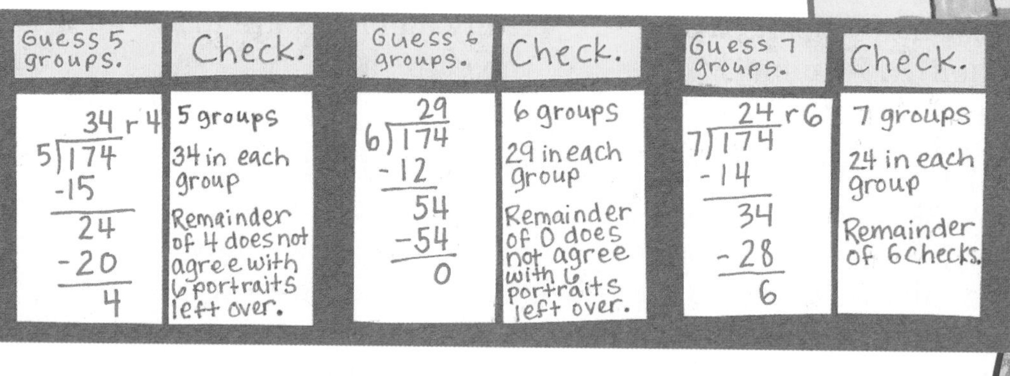

So, one possible answer is that there were 7 groups, with 24 portraits in each group. There were 6 portraits left over.

LOOK BACK

- How can you decide if your answer is reasonable?
- What other strategy could you use?

▶ PRACTICE

Guess and check to solve.

1. Mrs. Hewett has 217 recipe cards. She has them stored in equal groups in boxes, and has started a new box with 2 recipe cards in it. How many boxes of recipe cards does she have? How many are in each box?

2. A bridge toll is $0.50 for cars and $0.75 for trucks. In one hour, $33.50 is collected from 53 vehicles. How many cars and trucks pay the toll?

3. Spencer is 4 years old. His uncle Ralph is 6 times as old. How old will Spencer be when he is half as old as his uncle?

4. The sum of two numbers is 36. Their product is 320. What are the two numbers?

Mixed Applications

Solve.

CHOOSE a strategy and a tool.

- Use a Formula
- Make a Table
- Write a Number Sentence
- Guess and Check

Paper/Pencil

Calculator

Hands-On

Mental Math

5. What is the volume of this box?

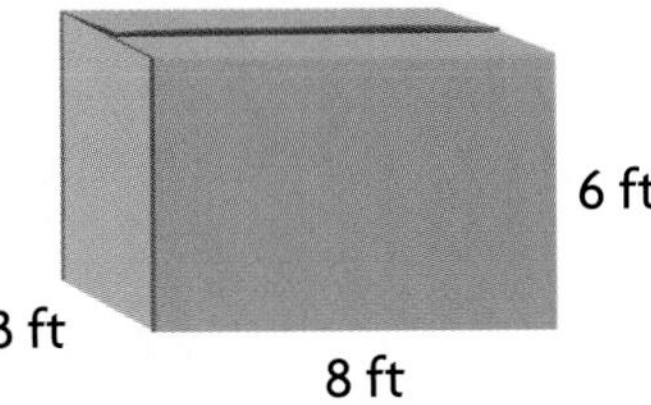

6. Travel Time mailed surveys to find out where people would most like to visit. Of the people who responded, 32,589 said the beach, 32,598 said the mountains, and 32,958 said a city. What are the answers from greatest to least?

7. Becky and Ellen washed 9 cars one afternoon. They earned $4.25 for each car they washed. How much money did they earn?

8. A book is 38 centimeters long and 22 centimeters wide. What is the perimeter of the book? What is the area of its cover?

9. There were 412 men, women, and children on a train. There were 3 times as many men as children. There were 74 children. How many women were on the train?

10. In Glenn's city, it rained 3.2 inches in January, 2.9 inches in February, and 3.1 inches in March. In which month was there the greatest amount of rainfall?

11. For the basketball game, 468 seats were filled. For the wrestling match, 279 seats were filled. How many more seats were filled for the basketball game?

12. A cube has a volume of 125 cubic inches. What is the length of each side? What is the area of each face?

MORE PRACTICE page H82

CHAPTER 7 Review/Test

▶ CHECK Understanding

VOCABULARY

1. A number is __?__ by another number if the quotient is a whole number and there is a zero remainder. (page 110)

2. __?__ are helpful when estimating because they are close to the actual numbers and can be divided evenly. (page 112)

Copy each problem. Draw a box where the first digit in the quotient should be placed. (pages 112–115)

3. $4\overline{)639}$ **4.** $6\overline{)410}$ **5.** $3\overline{)115}$ **6.** $7\overline{)959}$ **7.** $5\overline{)517}$

Estimate the quotient. (pages 112–115)

8. $3\overline{)245}$ **9.** $6\overline{)551}$ **10.** $8\overline{)825}$ **11.** $2\overline{)608}$ **12.** $4\overline{)132}$

▶ CHECK Skills

Test each number for divisibility by 2, 3, 4, 5, 6, 9, and 10. List the numbers that work. (pages 110–111)

13. 38 **14.** 64 **15.** 150 **16.** 489 **17.** 1,012

Find the quotient. Check by multiplying. (pages 112–113)

18. $4\overline{)624}$ **19.** $7\overline{)201}$ **20.** $3\overline{)513}$ **21.** $8\overline{)711}$ **22.** $5\overline{)476}$

23. $2\overline{)836}$ **24.** $6\overline{)940}$ **25.** $5\overline{)728}$ **26.** $7\overline{)342}$ **27.** $3\overline{)907}$

28. $815 \div 3 = n$ **29.** $642 \div 5 = n$ **30.** $706 \div 4 = n$ **31.** $514 \div 7 = n$

▶ CHECK Problem Solving

Solve. (pages 122–123)

CHOOSE a strategy and a tool.

- Use a Formula
- Make a Table
- Write a Number Sentence
- Guess and Check

Paper/Pencil

Calculator

Hands-On

Mental Math

32. Mr. Lehman is shopping for suitcases. He finds one that is 30 in. × 24 in. × 12 in. and another that is 27 in. × 27 in. × 12 in. Which suitcase will hold more?

33. Perry has 122 stickers. He puts an equal number of stickers on each folder. He has started a new folder with 3 stickers. How many other folders have stickers on them? How many stickers are on each?

Test Prep

Choose the best answer.

1. What is the value of 5 in 1,537,092?

   A 5

   B 5 hundreds

   C 5 thousands

   D 5 hundred thousands

   E Not Here

2. $\begin{array}{r} 7{,}000 \\ -\ 3{,}289 \\ \hline \end{array}$

   F 3,711

   G 3,721

   H 3,821

   J 4,821

   K Not Here

3. How is the number seven and sixty-four hundredths written?

   A 764

   B 76.4

   C 7.64

   D 0.764

4. Which of the following is true?

   F $8.49 + 3.02 > 7.89 + 1.04$

   G $8.49 + 3.02 < 7.89 + 1.04$

   H $8.49 + 3.02 = 7.89 + 1.04$

5. $3 \times (4 \times 6) =$

   A 24

   B 27

   C 48

   D 70

   E Not Here

6. Jarrod walked around the *perimeter* of a yard. The yard measures 40 feet by 90 feet. How far did Jarrod walk?

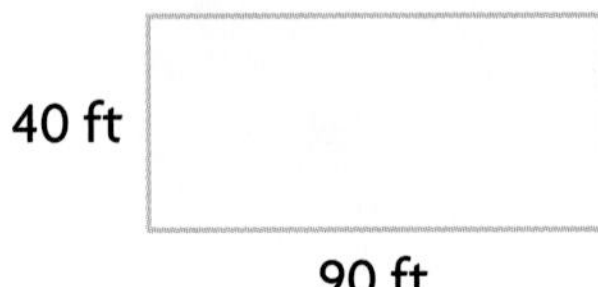

   F 260 ft **G** 360 ft

   H 3,000 ft **J** 3,600 ft

7. Find the volume.

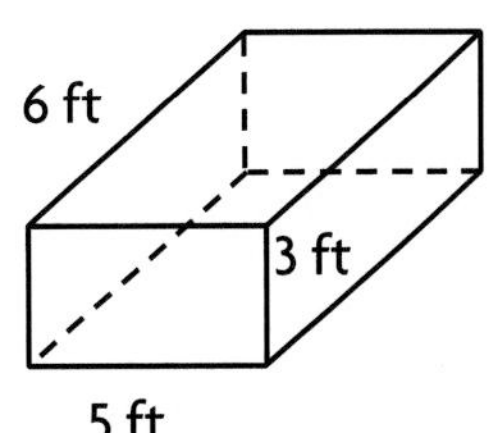

   A 30 cu ft **B** 75 cu ft

   C 90 cu ft **D** 100 cu ft

8. Shelby is 6 years old. Her sister is 3 times as old. How old will Shelby be when she is half as old as her sister?

   F 8 yr old

   G 11 yr old

   H 12 yr old

   J 24 yr old

   K Not Here

9. $4\overline{)344}$

   A 84 **B** 86

   C 96 **D** 860

8 DIVIDING BY TWO-DIGIT NUMBERS

LANGUAGE **LINK**

There are many contests such as Spelling Bees and Geography Bees, held each year for students of all ages.

Problem-Solving Activity

Dividing Contest Prizes

Have you ever wished there was a contest for something that you really like? Plan some kind of contest. Decide what the first prize will be. Then figure out how much each student would earn if your class won first place.

YOU WILL NEED: chart paper, markers

- Brainstorm contest ideas.
- Decide what first prize will be.
- Find out what each person's share of the prize would be if your class won first prize.
- Make a poster that describes your contest, the first prize, and how you would share it with your class.

DID YOU

- ✓ plan a contest and choose a first prize?
- ✓ explain how to share first prize with your class?
- ✓ make a poster showing your contest and ways you would share first prize?

LESSON 1

Division Patterns to Estimate

Why learn this? You can estimate to determine a car's gas mileage.

On vacation, Lindsey's family traveled 412 miles by car during two days. They used 23 gallons of gasoline. About how many miles per gallon did they average?

Estimate.

miles driven		gallons of gasoline used		miles per gallon
412	$\div$	23	$=$	n
↓		↓		↓
400	$\div$	20	$=$	20

So, they averaged about 20 miles per gallon.

- What basic fact was used to find $400 \div 20$? What basic fact would you use to find $600 \div 30$? $4{,}200 \div 70$?

Look at these examples of division patterns.

A.
$80 \div 20 = 4$
$800 \div 20 = 40$
$8{,}000 \div 20 = 400$
$80{,}000 \div 20 = 4{,}000$

B.
$120 \div 60 = 2$
$1{,}200 \div 60 = 20$
$12{,}000 \div 60 = 200$
$120{,}000 \div 60 = 2{,}000$

C.
$350 \div 70 = 5$
$3{,}500 \div 70 = 50$
$35{,}000 \div 70 = 500$
$350{,}000 \div 70 = 5{,}000$

Talk About It CRITICAL THINKING

- How does the pattern of zeros in the divisor and the dividend affect the quotient in the three examples?
- How many zeros will be in the quotient of $10{,}000 \div 10$? How could you check your answer?
- How many zeros will be in the quotient of $30{,}000 \div 60$? Why is this different from the pattern?

CONSUMER LINK

The average American car got about 18 miles per gallon in 1976 and about 28 miles per gallon in 1996. About how many gallons were needed in 1976 for a 450-mile trip? in 1996?

▶ CHECK

Complete the pattern.

1.
$60 \div 20 = 3$
$600 \div 20 = 30$
$6{,}000 \div 20 = n$

2.
$700 \div 70 = 10$
$7{,}000 \div 70 = n$
$70{,}000 \div 70 = 1{,}000$

3.
$400 \div 50 = n$
$4{,}000 \div 50 = 80$
$40{,}000 \div 50 = 800$

▶ PRACTICE

Complete the pattern.

4. $90 \div 30 = n$
$900 \div 30 = 30$
$9{,}000 \div 30 = 300$

5. $100 \div 50 = 2$
$1{,}000 \div 50 = 20$
$10{,}000 \div 50 = n$

6. $450 \div 90 = 5$
$4{,}500 \div 90 = n$
$45{,}000 \div 90 = 500$

7. $420 \div 60 = 7$
$4{,}200 \div 60 = 70$
$42{,}000 \div 60 = n$

8. $240 \div 30 = 8$
$2{,}400 \div 30 = n$
$24{,}000 \div 30 = 800$

9. $150 \div 50 = n$
$1{,}500 \div 50 = 30$
$15{,}000 \div 50 = 300$

Find the quotient.

10. $90 \div 30 = n$ **11.** $40 \div 20 = n$ **12.** $160 \div 40 = n$ **13.** $360 \div 40 = n$

14. $540 \div 90 = n$ **15.** $630 \div 70 = n$ **16.** $450 \div 50 = n$ **17.** $270 \div 90 = n$

18. $60 \div 30 = n$ **19.** $80 \div 40 = n$ **20.** $180 \div 60 = n$ **21.** $250 \div 50 = n$

22. $140 \div 20 = n$ **23.** $210 \div 70 = n$ **24.** $150 \div 30 = n$ **25.** $240 \div 80 = n$

26. $280 \div 40 = n$ **27.** $3{,}000 \div 60 = n$ **28.** $1{,}000 \div 20 = n$ **29.** $3{,}500 \div 50 = n$

30. $7{,}200 \div 90 = n$ **31.** $18{,}000 \div 30 = n$ **32.** $5{,}600 \div 70 = n$ **33.** $36{,}000 \div 90 = n$

Problem Solving • Mixed Applications

34. Measurement In a 30-day month, a bus traveled a total of 6,000 miles. The bus traveled the same number of miles each day. How many miles a day did it travel?

35. Sports Jan was in a jump-rope contest. She made 45 jumps each minute for 5 minutes. How many jumps did Jan make?

36. The seats in an auditorium are arranged in sections of 40. There are 6 sections of seats. How many seats are there in all?

37. **Write About It** Explain how to determine the number of zeros in a quotient.

Mixed Review and Test Prep

Write the name of the multiplication property used in each number sentence. (pages 74–75)

38. $2 \times (3 \times 5) = (2 \times 3) \times 5$ **39.** $3 \times 7 = 7 \times 3$ **40.** $8 \times 1 = 8$

41. $4 \times 0 = 0$ **42.** $(9 \times 4) \times 6 = 9 \times (4 \times 6)$ **43.** $4 \times 5 = 5 \times 4$

Choose the letter of the quotient. (pages 112–115)

44. $5\overline{)265}$ **A** 5 r3 **B** 53 **C** 530 **D** 54

45. $9\overline{)296}$ **F** 32 **G** 328 **H** 32 r8 **J** 3 r28

MORE PRACTICE page H83

LESSON 2

Estimating Quotients

Why learn this? You can compare your estimate with the actual quotient when you divide, such as with money amounts.

On opening night of the play, the box office took in \$1,575. The tickets cost \$9 each. About how many people attended the play?

Estimate. $1{,}575 \div 9$

$\downarrow \quad \downarrow$

$1{,}600 \div 10 = n$

So, $n = 160$. **Think:** $\begin{array}{r} 160 \\ 10\overline{)1{,}600} \end{array}$

So, about 160 people attended the play.

Another method you can use to estimate a quotient is to think of two sets of compatible numbers. Finding more than one estimate will give you two possible quotients.

EXAMPLE

Estimate. $52\overline{)3{,}481}$ **Think:** $50\overline{)3{,}000}$ or $50\overline{)3{,}500}$

3,000 and 3,500 are divisible by 50 because they end with 0 or 5.

Talk About It

- What are the quotients for the two estimates?
- Are both estimates for $52\overline{)3{,}481}$ good estimates? Explain why or why not.
- Based on the estimates, where should the first digit be placed in $52\overline{)3{,}481}$? Why?
- CRITICAL THINKING How does finding two sets of compatible numbers help you divide?

▶ CHECK

Write two pairs of compatible numbers.

1. $276 \div 42 \approx n$ **2.** $524 \div 68 \approx n$ **3.** $1{,}247 \div 34 \approx n$

4. $329 \div 26 \approx n$ **5.** $171 \div 34 \approx n$ **6.** $201 \div 41 \approx n$

CULTURAL LINK

William Shakespeare is one of the most famous playwrights of all time. His theater, the Globe Theater, in England, was built in 1599. The theater seated about 1,500 people. It had a ground area and three tiers, or seating levels. If an equal number of people watched from the ground area and each tier, about how many people would be in each?

REMEMBER:

Compatible numbers are numbers that are close to the actual numbers and can be divided evenly.

Example

$2{,}500 \div 5 = 500$

▶ PRACTICE

Write two pairs of compatible numbers for each. Give two possible estimates.

7. $186 \div 62 \approx n$ **8.** $523 \div 88 \approx n$ **9.** $1{,}275 \div 47 \approx n$

10. $3{,}149 \div 36 \approx n$ **11.** $2{,}548 \div 65 \approx n$ **12.** $6{,}324 \div 76 \approx n$

Estimate the quotient.

13. $12\overline{)914}$ **14.** $42\overline{)528}$ **15.** $29\overline{)364}$ **16.** $34\overline{)279}$ **17.** $53\overline{)485}$

18. $64\overline{)532}$ **19.** $37\overline{)849}$ **20.** $73\overline{)620}$ **21.** $61\overline{)115}$ **22.** $86\overline{)743}$

23. $23\overline{)1{,}260}$ **24.** $47\overline{)3{,}524}$ **25.** $59\overline{)4{,}636}$ **26.** $77\overline{)8{,}199}$ **27.** $31\overline{)6{,}468}$

28. $64\overline{)4{,}275}$ **29.** $81\overline{)2{,}417}$ **30.** $36\overline{)3{,}384}$ **31.** $45\overline{)1{,}407}$ **32.** $92\overline{)5{,}583}$

33. $652 \div 18 \approx n$ **34.** $423 \div 27 \approx n$ **35.** $252 \div 64 \approx n$ **36.** $386 \div 48 \approx n$

37. $2{,}993 \div 75 \approx n$ **38.** $3{,}764 \div 38 \approx n$ **39.** $6{,}520 \div 68 \approx n$ **40.** $9{,}733 \div 89 \approx n$

Problem Solving • Mixed Applications

41. **Consumer** A produce truck delivered 21 crates of oranges to three stores. There were 1,128 oranges in the delivery. About how many oranges were in each crate?

42. Carla is reading a book with 316 pages. Marilyn is reading a book that has 67 more pages. How many pages are in the book Marilyn is reading?

43. **Money** Lars bought a CD for \$16.95. He had only \$5 bills. How many bills did he give the clerk? How much change did he get back?

44. **Measurement** Eva lives 28.7 miles from the airport. Jonas lives two-tenths mile farther away. How far does Jonas live from the airport?

45. Mrs. Lehr had a 34-page booklet copied. She was charged for 850 pages. About how many copies of the booklet did she have made?

46. **Write About It** Explain why using compatible numbers is a helpful way to estimate quotients.

Mixed Review and Test Prep

Find the quotient. Check by multiplying. (pages 118–119)

47. $256 \div 6 = n$ **48.** $734 \div 5 = n$ **49.** $659 \div 7 = n$ **50.** $875 \div 4 = n$

Choose the best answer. (pages 98–101)

51. $325 \times 382 \approx n$ **A** 9,000 **B** 12,000 **C** 120,000 **D** 90,000

52. $684 \times 608 \approx n$ **F** 420,000 **G** 360,000 **H** 35,000 **J** 42,000

LESSON 3

Placing the First Digit

Why learn this? You will know how many digits should be in the quotient when you divide large numbers, such as the number of people in an audience.

During the two weeks the Renaissance Ensemble was in Anna's city, 1,935 people attended the performances. There were 16 performances. At each performance except for the last, the same number of people attended. How many people attended each performance?

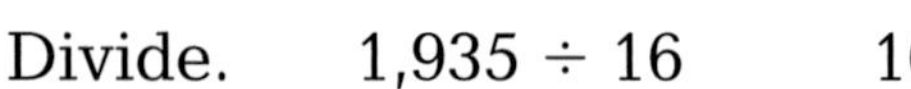

Divide. $1{,}935 \div 16$ $\quad 16\overline{)1{,}935}$

Estimate. $1{,}935 \div 16 \approx n$ **Think:** $20\overline{)2{,}000}$ = 100

So, $n = 90$ or 100.

MODEL

What is $1{,}935 \div 16$?

Step 1

Decide where to place the first digit in the quotient.

x over $16\overline{)1{,}935}$ — no — You *cannot* divide 1 by 16. There are not enough thousands.

x ■ over $16\overline{)1{,}935}$ — yes — You *can* divide 19 by 16. There are enough hundreds.

So, place the first digit in the hundreds place.

Step 2

Divide the hundreds. $16\overline{)19}$ **Think:** $16 \times n = 16$

Write a 1 in the hundreds place in the quotient.

```
     1
16)1,935    Multiply. 16 × 1
  −16       Subtract. 19 − 16
     3      Compare. 3 < 16
```

Step 3

Divide the tens. $16\overline{)33}$ **Think:** $16 \times n = 32$

Write a 2 in the tens place.

```
     12
16)1,935    Multiply. 16 × 2
  −16↓      Subtract. 33 − 32
    33
   −32
     1      Compare. 1 < 16
```

Step 4

Divide the ones. $16\overline{)15}$

Think: Since 16 > 15, write a zero in the ones place in the quotient.

```
     120 r15
16)1,935    Multiply. 16 × 0
  −16       Subtract. 15 − 0
    33
   −32↓
     15
    − 0
     15     Compare. 15 < 16
```

So, 120 people attended each performance, with 15 more people, or 135 people, attending on the last day.

- How does the actual quotient compare to the estimate?

▶ CHECK

Estimate the quotient.

1. $3{,}152 \div 47 \approx n$ **2.** $2{,}816 \div 56 \approx n$ **3.** $3{,}974 \div 23 \approx n$ **4.** $1{,}263 \div 35 \approx n$

5. $3{,}285 \div 54 \approx n$ **6.** $5{,}690 \div 78 \approx n$ **7.** $8{,}149 \div 41 \approx n$ **8.** $1{,}067 \div 11 \approx n$

▶ PRACTICE

Copy each problem. Draw a box where the first digit in the quotient should be placed.

9. $14\overline{)1{,}624}$ **10.** $25\overline{)3{,}205}$ **11.** $63\overline{)1{,}824}$ **12.** $47\overline{)7{,}395}$ **13.** $68\overline{)5{,}430}$

14. $53\overline{)2{,}369}$ **15.** $71\overline{)9{,}546}$ **16.** $89\overline{)3{,}659}$ **17.** $34\overline{)3{,}525}$ **18.** $42\overline{)4{,}178}$

Find the quotient.

19. $37\overline{)4{,}801}$ **20.** $19\overline{)1{,}875}$ **21.** $62\overline{)4{,}500}$ **22.** $43\overline{)3{,}967}$ **23.** $85\overline{)1{,}056}$

24. $58\overline{)9{,}286}$ **25.** $73\overline{)5{,}841}$ **26.** $29\overline{)3{,}180}$ **27.** $26\overline{)5{,}330}$ **28.** $37\overline{)3{,}363}$

Problem Solving • Mixed Applications

29. Time Each episode of *Kids in a Rocket Ship* is 26 minutes long. There are 48 episodes of the show. About how many hours is this? (HINT: Divide the total number of minutes by 60.)

30. There are 1,024 people at the Sweet Corn Festival. Each group of servers can serve 64 people at one time. How many groups of servers are needed to serve all 1,024 people?

31. A passenger train has 12 cars, each seating 44 people. How many people can be seated on the train?

32. **Write a problem** about a bird flying 1,105 miles from Washington, D.C., to Miami. Use division in the problem.

Mixed Review and Test Prep

Estimate the sum or difference to the nearest tenth. (pages 58–59)

33. $4.75 - 1.29$ **34.** $5.34 + 2.29$ **35.** $24.18 - 16.09$ **36.** $16.82 - 7.48$

Estimate the product by rounding each factor to the greatest place-value position. (pages 96–97)

37. $75 \times 291 \approx n$ **A** 24,000 **B** 3,000 **C** 20,400 **D** 20,000

38. $25 \times 608 \approx n$ **F** 1,800 **G** 18,000 **H** 1,200 **J** 12,000

MORE PRACTICE page H83

LESSON 4

Correcting Quotients

Why learn this? You will know how many albums you need for your sports cards.

Greg collects sports cards. He has 245 cards in his collection. The cards are organized in albums that hold 32 cards each. How many sports-card albums does Greg have?

Divide. $245 \div 32$ $32\overline{)245}$

Estimate. $245 \div 32 \approx n$ **Think:** $\begin{array}{r} 7 \\ 30\overline{)210} \end{array}$ or $\begin{array}{r} 8 \\ 30\overline{)240} \end{array}$

So, $n = 7$ or 8.

Try 8.

$$\begin{array}{r} 8 \\ 32\overline{)245} \\ -256 \\ \hline \end{array}$$

Think: Since 256 > 245, this estimate is too high.

Try 7.

$$\begin{array}{r} 7 \text{ r}21 \\ 32\overline{)245} \\ -224 \\ \hline 21 \end{array}$$

So, Greg has 7 full albums and one album with only 21 cards in it. He has a total of 8 sports-card albums.

EXAMPLE

Divide. $376 \div 53$ $53\overline{)376}$

Estimate. $376 \div 53 \approx n$ **Think:** $\begin{array}{r} 6 \\ 50\overline{)300} \end{array}$ or $\begin{array}{r} 7 \\ 50\overline{)350} \end{array}$

So, $n = 6$ or 7.

Try 6.

$$\begin{array}{r} 6 \\ 53\overline{)376} \\ -318 \\ \hline 58 \end{array}$$

Think: Since 58 > 53, this estimate is too low.

Try 7.

$$\begin{array}{r} 7 \text{ r}5 \\ 53\overline{)376} \\ -371 \\ \hline 5 \end{array}$$

Talk About It CRITICAL THINKING

- How do you know when an estimated quotient is too high? too low?
- If you use $40\overline{)280}$ to estimate the quotient $36\overline{)295}$, will your estimate be greater than or less than the quotient? Explain.

▶ CHECK

Write *too high, too low,* or *just right* for each estimate.

1. $\begin{array}{r}4\\25\overline{)83}\end{array}$ **2.** $\begin{array}{r}1\\32\overline{)61}\end{array}$ **3.** $\begin{array}{r}8\\42\overline{)321}\end{array}$ **4.** $\begin{array}{r}3\\57\overline{)239}\end{array}$ **5.** $\begin{array}{r}8\\64\overline{)519}\end{array}$

6. $\begin{array}{r}8\\35\overline{)320}\end{array}$ **7.** $\begin{array}{r}6\\71\overline{)403}\end{array}$ **8.** $\begin{array}{r}2\\45\overline{)122}\end{array}$ **9.** $\begin{array}{r}7\\29\overline{)182}\end{array}$ **10.** $\begin{array}{r}2\\88\overline{)326}\end{array}$

▶ PRACTICE

Choose the better estimate to use for the quotient. Write *a* or *b*.

11. $19\overline{)84}$ **a.** 3 **b.** 4

12. $34\overline{)276}$ **a.** 8 **b.** 9

13. $24\overline{)158}$ **a.** 6 **b.** 7

14. $46\overline{)463}$ **a.** 9 **b.** 10

15. $59\overline{)283}$ **a.** 3 **b.** 4

16. $28\overline{)249}$ **a.** 8 **b.** 9

17. $73\overline{)564}$ **a.** 6 **b.** 7

18. $62\overline{)506}$ **a.** 8 **b.** 9

Find the quotient.

19. $32\overline{)154}$ **20.** $25\overline{)278}$ **21.** $64\overline{)335}$ **22.** $15\overline{)341}$ **23.** $51\overline{)485}$

24. $74\overline{)525}$ **25.** $62\overline{)782}$ **26.** $35\overline{)866}$ **27.** $49\overline{)243}$ **28.** $27\overline{)487}$

Problem Solving • Mixed Applications

29. Sports A total of 126 students are in the relay race. Each relay team has 14 students. Each team needs 1 baton. Will 8 batons be enough?

30. Write About It Explain how to correct an estimated quotient that is too high or too low.

Mixed Review and Test Prep

Estimate the sum or difference and compare. Write $<$ or $>$ for each ●. (pages 58–59)

31. 7.24 − 2.18 ● 6.75 − 1.44

32. 2.95 + 4.21 ● 1.85 + 4.49

Choose the letter of the area. (pages 84–85)

33. $l = 12$ cm
$w = 5$ cm
$A = ■$

A 17 sq cm
B 60 sq cm
C 34 sq cm
D 30 sq cm

34. $l = 25$ in.
$w = 5$ in.
$A = ■$

F 125 sq in.
G 60 sq in.
H 30 sq in.
J 250 sq in.

35. $l = 54$ m
$w = 31$ m
$A = ■$

A 16,740 sq m
B 1,674 sq m
C 270 sq m
D 170 sq m

36. $l = 81$ ft
$w = 25$ ft
$A = ■$

F 2,025 sq ft
G 225 sq ft
H 567 sq ft
J 2,125 sq ft

MORE PRACTICE pages H83–H84

LESSON 5

Using Division

Why learn this? You can find out how a number of items, such as pies, can be shared fairly.

Grandma's Oven, a pie-manufacturing company, made 2,578 pies. The company distributed the pies to 42 food stores. Each store received the same number of pies. How many pies did each store receive?

Divide. $2,578 \div 42$ $\quad 42\overline{)2,578}$

Estimate. $2,578 \div 42 \approx n$ **Think:** $\begin{array}{r}60\\40\overline{)2,400}\end{array}$ or $\begin{array}{r}70\\40\overline{)2,800}\end{array}$

So, $n = 60$ or 70.

MODEL

What is $2,578 \div 42$?

Step 1

Since the estimate is a two-digit number, divide the 257 tens.

$$\begin{array}{r}6\\42\overline{)2,578}\\-252\\5\end{array}$$

Multiply.
Subtract.
Compare. 5 < 42

Step 2

Divide the 58 ones.

$$\begin{array}{r}61\text{ r}16\\42\overline{)2,578}\\-252\\58\\-42\\16\end{array}$$

Multiply.
Subtract.
Compare. 16 < 42

So, each store received 61 pies. There were 16 pies left over.

Suppose Grandma's Oven sells 12 pies for \$28.20. How much would each pie cost?

Divide. $12\overline{)\$28.20}$ **Think:** $\begin{array}{r}\$2\\12\overline{)\$24}\end{array}$ or $\begin{array}{r}\$3\\10\overline{)\$30}\end{array}$

$$\begin{array}{r}\$2.35\\12\overline{)\$28.20}\\-24\\42\\-36\\60\\-60\\0\end{array}$$

- Divide amounts of money the same as you would divide whole numbers.
- Write the quotient with a dollar sign and a decimal point.

So, each pie costs \$2.35.

EXAMPLES

A Divide. 35)843

Think: 40)800 = 20 or 30)900 = 30

```
   24 r3
35)843
  -70
   143
  -140
     3
```

Check by multiplying.

```
   24
  ×35
  120
 +720
  840
```

Add the remainder.
840 + 3 = 843

B Divide. 28)7,120

Think: 30)6,000 = 200 or 25)7,500 = 300

```
   254 r8
28)7,120
  -56
   152
  -140
    120
   -112
      8
```

Check by multiplying.

```
   254
 ×  28
 2,032
+5,080
 7,112
```

Add the remainder.
7,112 + 8 = 7,120

C Divide. 43)$21.93

Think: 40)$20.00 = $0.50 or 50)$20.00 = $0.40

```
   $0.51
43)$21.93
  -215
     43
    -43
      0
```

Check by multiplying.

```
 $0.51
 × 43
  153
+2040
$21.93
```

Write the product with a dollar sign and a decimal point.

Talk About It

- How can you tell where to place the first digit in the quotient?
- How can you tell if each digit in the quotient is large enough?
- How is dividing money different from dividing whole numbers?

Technology Link

In ***Mighty Math Number Heroes***, the game *Quizzo* challenges you to divide by two-digit numbers. Use Grow Slide Level U.

▶ CHECK

Estimate the quotient.

1. 61)3,108 **2.** 43)23,992 **3.** 69)2,118

4. 32)27,717 **5.** 91)5,396 **6.** 48)24,916

Write whether the quotient is *less than* or *greater than* $1.00.

7. 23)$15.83 **8.** 45)$67.14 **9.** 19)$8.47

10. 28)$65.10 **11.** 53)$15.27 **12.** 28)$19.98

Find the quotient. Check by multiplying.

13. 29)1,073 **14.** 39)278 **15.** 17)410

16. 48)1,242 **17.** 19)4,164 **18.** 37)4,591

19. 42)383 **20.** 27)8,754 **21.** 51)4,095

▶ PRACTICE

Estimate the quotient.

22. 49)2,487 **23.** 61)36,182 **24.** 18)4,105 **25.** 42)23,911

26. 73)50,611 **27.** 79)6,416 **28.** 69)2,109 **29.** 29)25,782

Divide. Check by multiplying.

30. 14)93 **31.** 32)79 **32.** 21)57 **33.** 53)98 **34.** 44)89

35. 54)182 **36.** 36)274 **37.** 41)619 **38.** 28)736 **39.** 65)402

40. 26)917 **41.** 50)643 **42.** 18)377 **43.** 45)232 **44.** 56)380

45. 72)463 **46.** 59)285 **47.** 34)125 **48.** 86)342 **49.** 64)875

50. 37)\$85.84 **51.** 14)\$28.56 **52.** 35)\$15.75 **53.** 52)\$41.60 **54.** 85)\$38.25

55. 12)\$67.68 **56.** 28)\$31.92 **57.** 25)\$75.50 **58.** 63)\$11.97 **59.** 11)\$59.51

Find the quotient.

60. $2{,}896 \div 46 = n$ **61.** $1{,}877 \div 33 = n$ **62.** $3{,}591 \div 60 = n$ **63.** $7{,}171 \div 71 = n$

64. $2{,}347 \div 58 = n$ **65.** $9{,}107 \div 85 = n$ **66.** $2{,}054 \div 48 = n$ **67.** $4{,}985 \div 73 = n$

Problem Solving • Mixed Applications

68. The students at Rogers Middle School sold 1,700 tickets to the school carnival. Each student sold 4 tickets. How many students sold tickets?

69. Measurement Mr. Snyder used 45.593 gallons of gas in his car in May, 43.236 gallons of gas in June, and 49.521 gallons in July. How many gallons did he use in the three months combined?

70. Time There are about 52 weeks in a year. Bob sleeps about 56 hours each week. About how many hours does he sleep in a year?

71. Money Miss Mullen wants to buy 24 notebooks for her class journals. A box of 24 notebooks costs \$37.20. One notebook costs \$1.69. How much will Miss Mullen save on each notebook if she buys a box?

72. **Write a problem** about 1,273 baseball cards. Use division in your problem.

SPORTS CONNECTION

In major league baseball, a pitcher who wins 300 games during an entire career is a star. Here is a list of the pitchers who have won the most games, and the number of years, or seasons that each pitched.

Player	Seasons Pitched	Games Won
Cy Young	22	511
Walter Johnson	21	416
Christy Mathewson	17	373
Grover Alexander	20	373
Warren Spahn	21	363

73. Estimate how many games per year Grover Alexander had to win, to win 373 games.

74. Estimation In an average year, about how many games did Cy Young win?

75. Career Suppose that a pitcher is able to pitch for 20 seasons in the major leagues. About how many games would he need to win each year, to win a total of 300 games?

76. Suppose that a pitcher only pitches for 15 seasons. About how many games per year would he need to win, to win a total of 300 games?

HISTORY LINK

In the early days of baseball, before 1910, the baseball was "dead" — it didn't travel far when it was hit. Pitchers threw fewer fastballs, and their arms tired less. As a result, pitchers such as Cy Young often pitched 40 or even 50 games in one season! Today, even the best starting pitchers pitch in only about 30 games per season. A professional baseball team has an average of 10 pitchers and plays about 160 games a year. If all the pitchers played in the same number of games, about how many times would each pitcher pitch?

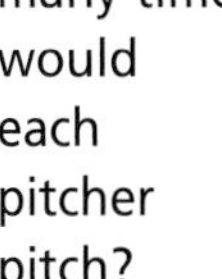

Mixed Review and Test Prep

Find the volume. (pages 84–85)

77. $l = 12$ in.
$w = 6$ in.
$h = 6$ in.
$V = \blacksquare$ cu in.

78. $l = 24$ cm
$w = 15$ cm
$h = 9$ cm
$V = \blacksquare$ cu cm

79. $l = 30$ ft
$w = 21$ ft
$h = 11$ ft
$V = \blacksquare$ cu ft

80. $l = 43$ m
$w = 22$ m
$h = 8$ m
$V = \blacksquare$ cu m

Choose the equation that shows the property. (pages 74–75)

81. Commutative Property of Multiplication

A $8 \times 0 = 0$

B $2 \times (7 \times 3) = (2 \times 7) \times 3$

C $6 \times 1 = 6$

D $10 \times 7 = 7 \times 10$

82. Associative Property of Multiplication

F $9 \times 12 = 12 \times 9$

G $(4 \times 2) \times 3 = 4 \times (2 \times 3)$

H $0 \times 100 = 0$

J $1 \times 37 = 37$

MORE PRACTICE page H84

Choosing the Operation

Why learn this? You will need to choose the correct operation when you solve real-life problems, such as when you're on vacation.

Before you can solve a problem, you must decide what operation to use. The chart shows situations for using each of the four operations.

Operation	Situation
Addition	• Joining groups
Subtraction	• Taking away part of a group • Comparing groups
Multiplication	• Combining equal-size groups
Division	• Separating into equal-size groups • Finding how many groups or how many in each group

Read each problem. Decide which operation should be used to solve.

A. Jeremy and his family plan to drive the 1,143 miles from Baltimore to Miami. They have traveled 659 miles. How much farther do they have to drive before reaching Miami?

B. Melanie has a kit for making beaded jewelry. The kit has 250 beads of each color. There are 12 colors. How many beads are in the kit?

C. There are 120 hot dogs to be shared equally by the 48 members of the East Side Boys Club. How many hot dogs will each boy get?

D. Ed has a stamp collection. He has 1,294 United States stamps and 2,003 foreign stamps. How many stamps does he have?

Talk About It

- What operations did you determine should be used to solve Problems A–D? Explain your reasoning for each.
- Give the solution to each problem.

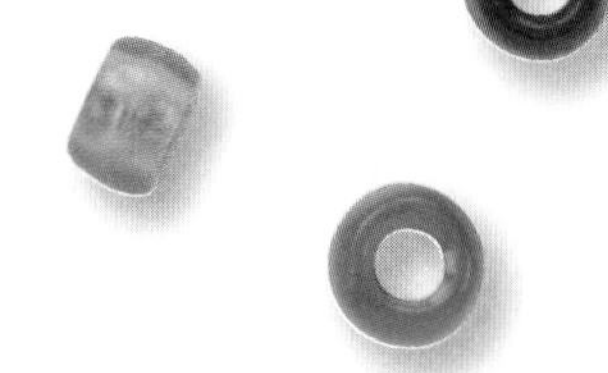

▶ PRACTICE

Tell what operation should be used to solve each problem. Then solve.

1. On the first day of school, every student will get 25 star stickers. How many star stickers are needed for a school with 864 students?

2. A building is 432 feet high and has 36 stories. How high is each story of the building?

3. Three Girl Scout troops collected postage stamps. Elena's troop collected 423 stamps. Marta's troop collected 378 stamps. Lee's troop collected 457 stamps. How many stamps did all three troops collect?

4. Carlos earns $3,480 a month. José earns $2,975 a month. How much more money per month does Carlos earn than José?

Problem Solving • Mixed Applications

WORLD RIVERS	
River	**Length (miles)**
Amazon	4,000
Colorado	1,450
Rio Grande	1,900
Yenisey	2,543

White-water rafting on the Colorado River

5. **Geography** Which is the longest river listed in the table? Which is the shortest? What is the difference in length between the two rivers?

6. **Money** Mr. Stiles took his wife and three children to the movies. The cost of an adult ticket was $6.00 and the cost of a child's ticket was $3.00. How much did all the tickets cost?

7. **Science** Lightning can be as hot as 50,000°F. The surface of the sun is about 11,000°F. How much hotter can lightning be than the surface of the sun?

8. **Consumer** A toy company manufactured 4,644 dolls. The dolls were distributed evenly among 54 stores. How many dolls were sent to each store?

9. **Consumer** Bill bought a basketball for $19.78. Joe bought the same kind of basketball a week later when it went on sale for $13.88. How much more did Bill pay for his basketball?

10. Dominic needs 5 boards that are 36 inches long and 2 boards that are 63 inches long in order to make a bookcase. How many feet of lumber does he need? (HINT: Divide the total number of inches by 12.)

11. **Write a problem** using the information in the table for Problem 5. At least one of the four operations must be used to solve the problem.

MORE PRACTICE page H84

Problem–Solving Strategy: Write a Number Sentence

▶ **THE PROBLEM** Patricia's family bought furniture for their new apartment. The total cost of the furniture was $2,640. The furniture store offers a payment plan in which you may make 24 equal monthly payments. How much will Patricia's family pay per month for the furniture?

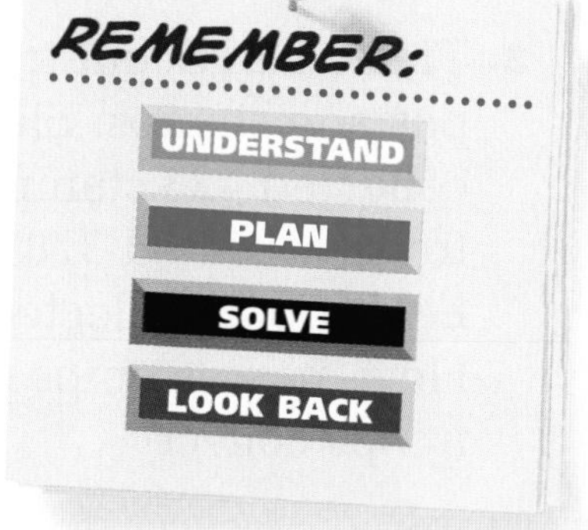

UNDERSTAND

- What are you asked to find?
- What information will you use?
- Is there information you will not use? If so, what?

PLAN

- What strategy can you use to solve the problem?

  You can *write a number sentence* to find the monthly payment amount.

SOLVE

- What number sentence can you write to solve the problem?

  Since you are separating an amount into 24 equal-size groups, divide to find the monthly payment.

Divide. $2,640 ÷ 24

Estimate. $2,000 ÷ 20 = n

So, n = 100.

So, the monthly payment will be $110.

```
    110
24)2,640
  -24
    24
   -24
    00
```

LOOK BACK

- How can you decide if your answer is reasonable?
- What other strategy could you use?

CONSUMER LINK

Frank Lloyd Wright was a famous architect who also designed furniture. His furniture was often designed with geometric shapes. A cube chair and a chair with a hexagon, square, and triangle are examples.

Suppose furniture costs $1,500 and is paid for in 10 monthly payments. What number sentence can you write to find out how much each payment would be?

▶ PRACTICE

Write a number sentence to solve.

1. Alice's mother bought a used car for $6,300. She will pay monthly payments for 36 months. What will each monthly payment be?

2. Steve had 1,158 pennies in a large jar. He put them into rolls, with 50 pennies in each roll. How many rolls of pennies did he have?

3. Kim scored 12,743 on a computer game the first time she played it. She improved her score by 3,879 points the second time she played. What was her score the second time?

4. Sports Place has 22 skateboards in stock. The price of 10 of the skateboards is $13 each, and 12 of them sell for $25 each. How much money will all the skateboards sell for?

Mixed Applications

Solve.

CHOOSE a strategy and a tool.

- Use a Table
- Act It Out
- Guess and Check
- Solve a Simpler Problem
- Write a Number Sentence

Paper/Pencil

Calculator

Hands-On

Mental Math

5. Lynn, Freddie, Eileen, Susan, and Nancy swim in a relay race. Susan swims before Nancy. Freddie swims before Susan but after Eileen. Lynn swims before everyone but Eileen. Who swims third?

6. A subscription to *Up and Coming* magazine is $19 a year. The magazine has 5,489 subscribers. How much money per year does the magazine get from its subscriptions?

7. There are 90 men, women, and children in the movie theater. There are twice as many women as men. There are three times as many children as men. How many of each are there?

8. Rodney's parents bought a car for $15,299. Three years later they sold it for $8,700. How much less was the selling price than the price they paid for the car?

9. Max spent $7 playing video games at the mall. He spent $4 for lunch, and bought a gift for $8. He had $9 when he got home. How much money did he have when he left for the mall?

10. The Hanging Gardens of Babylon were laid out in a square that measures 400 feet on one side. What is the perimeter? the area?

11. How much deeper is the ocean that has the greatest depth than the ocean that has the least depth?

Ocean	Average Depth (ft)
Pacific Ocean	12,925
Atlantic Ocean	11,730
Indian Ocean	12,598
Arctic Ocean	3,407

CHAPTER 8 Review/Test

▶ CHECK Understanding

Write two pairs of compatible numbers for each. Give two possible estimates. (pages 130–131)

1. $811 \div 24 \approx n$ **2.** $352 \div 58 \approx n$ **3.** $1{,}472 \div 26 \approx n$

4. $6{,}265 \div 86 \approx n$ **5.** $2{,}952 \div 41 \approx n$ **6.** $5{,}284 \div 63 \approx n$

Copy each problem. Draw a box where the first digit in the quotient should be placed. (pages 132–133)

7. 32)1,098 **8.** 56)3,374 **9.** 28)4,915 **10.** 45)2,658 **11.** 73)7,420

▶ CHECK Skills

Find the quotient. (pages 128–129, 132–133)

12. $90 \div 30 = n$ **13.** $280 \div 70 = n$ **14.** $4{,}000 \div 40 = n$ **15.** $48{,}000 \div 60 = n$

16. 29)87 **17.** 46)235 **18.** 51)7,866 **19.** 38)1,467 **20.** 74)2,812

Divide. Check by multiplying. (pages 136–139)

21. 57)74 **22.** 26)90 **23.** 38)710 **24.** 40)908 **25.** 61)$7.93

26. 19)2,282 **27.** 39)3,140 **28.** 76)$77.52 **29.** 64)9,072 **30.** 85)3,453

▶ CHECK Problem Solving

Solve. (pages 142–143)

CHOOSE a strategy and a tool.

- Make a Table
- Write a Number Sentence
- Draw a Diagram
- Work Backward
- Solve a Simpler Problem

Paper/Pencil

Calculator

Hands-On

Mental Math

31. Mr. Campbell bought a home computer system for $3,330. He will make monthly payments for 18 months. How much will each monthly payment be?

32. John played 12 computer games in 60 minutes. He scored about 260 points per game. About how many points did he earn per minute?

33. Monica spent $14 to get her hair cut. Then she spent $5 on lunch. After lunch, she bought a purse for $9. She had $16 when she got home. How much money did she have before she went to get her hair cut?

34. Erica saved 1,045 nickels. She put them into rolls, with 40 nickels in each roll. How many full rolls of nickels did she have? How many nickels were left over?

Test Prep

Choose the best answer.

1. Which group of numbers is in order from *greatest* to *least*?

A 798,321 798,325 798,478

B 798,478 789,321 778,325

C 790,478 789,325 798,475

D 798,475 778,324 789,325

2. Which of the following number sentences is related to $39 + n = 102$?

F $63 + n = 102$ **G** $102 - n = 39$

H $102 - 63 = n$ **J** $63 - 39 = n$

3. At the zoo, Nell bought a mug for $4.99 and a cap for $12.25. Which of the following is a reasonable estimate of what Nell spent?

A $15 **B** $17

C $20 **D** $22

4. Point *P* best represents what number?

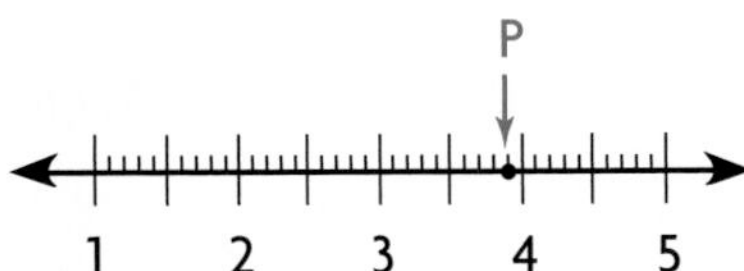

F 3.2

G 3.5

H 3.9

J 4.0

K Not Here

5. $3,000 - 978 =$

A 1,022 **B** 2,018

C 2,978 **D** 2,022

6. Find the volume.

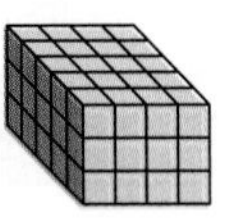

F 12 cu units

G 20 cu units

H 48 cu units

J 60 cu units

7. $72 \div 8 = \square$

A 7 **B** 8

C 8 R1 **D** 9

8. Complete the pattern.

$350 \div 50 = 7$

$3,500 \div 50 = n$

$35,000 \div 50 = 700$

F 7 **G** 70

H 700 **J** 7,000

9. $14\overline{)83}$

A 5

B 5 R13

C 6

D 6 R3

E Not Here

10. $6 \times 0 =$

F 0 **G** 1

H 6 **J** 60

11. $6 \times (3 \times 7) =$

A 86 **B** 125

C 126 **D** 131

CHAPTERS 5–8

MATH FUN!

Domino Snake

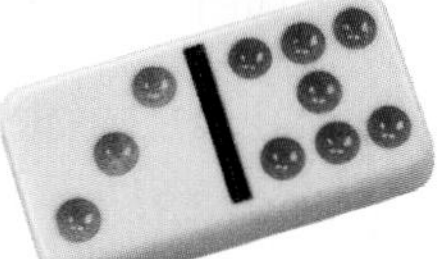

$3 \times 7 = 21$

PURPOSE To practice multiplication facts

YOU WILL NEED dominoes, calculator

Playing Domino Snake will help you practice the basic multiplication facts. Place tiles face down. Say the product of the two numbers shown on the tile. If you don't know the product, let your partner tell it to you. Stand the tiles in a long row, or snake. If neither of you knows the product, find it with a calculator and place the tile back in the pile. The last person to place a tile gets to topple the snake.

Your Moon Weight

PURPOSE To divide and check quotients

YOU WILL NEED pencil and paper, bathroom scale

Find what your weight would be on the moon. Weigh objects around the classroom. Find the moon weight for five objects, people, or animals. Each time, check your answer by using multiplication.

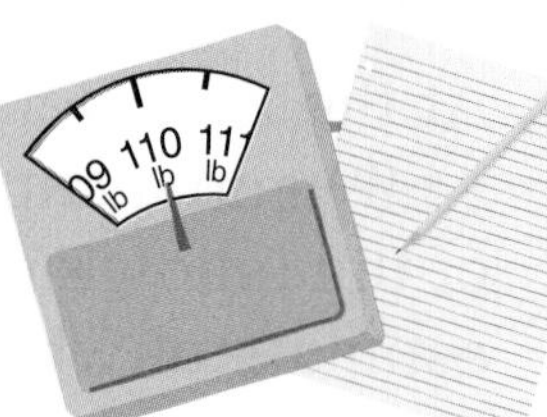

Use this formula:

moon weight = Earth weight $\div$ 6

Nick's Room

PURPOSE To practice finding area

YOU WILL NEED paper and pencil, centimeter grid paper, centimeter ruler

Nick's room is 10 feet square. His mom is helping him choose furniture for his room. Nick finds carpeting for $5 a square foot. His mom will buy him a carpet that costs $150 or less.

Draw a 10-by-10 grid like the one shown. Cut out rectangles to show Nick's furniture. Arrange the furniture and plan two rugs that will cost $150 or less.

Furniture for Nick's Room

Bed	3 squares × 6 squares
Desk	3 squares × 2 squares
Chair	2 squares × 1 square
Dresser	2 squares × 4 squares

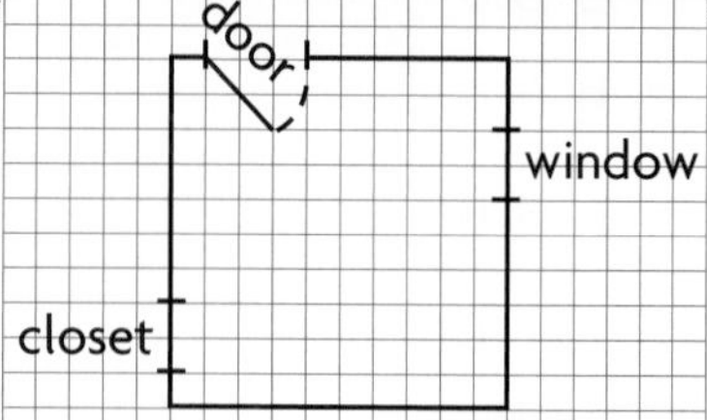

HOME NOTE On a grid, draw a room at home. What is the area of the room?

Order of Operations

You can name a number by using an **expression**.

VOCABULARY

An **expression** is a mathematical phrase that combines operations, and numerals to name a number.

EXAMPLES

A $3 + 4$ is an expression for 7.

B $6 \div 2$ is an expression for 3.

When more than one operation is used in an expression, you need to follow the **rules for the order of operations**.

C $18 \div (2 + 4)$ is an expression for 3.

Solution: $2 + 4 = 6$; $18 \div 6 = 3$

D $2 + 3 \times 5$ is an expression for 17.

Solution: $3 \times 5 = 15$; $2 + 15 = 17$

Order of Operations Rules

1. First, do the operations **in parentheses**.
2. Next, **multiply and divide** from left to right.
3. Then, **add and subtract** from left to right.

- Which rules for the order of operations did you use for Examples C and D?

Using a calculator can help you find the value of an expression. Some calculators follow the order of operations. Test your calculator to see if it follows the order of operations.

Find the value of $4 + 6 \div 2$.

This calculator followed the order of operations.

This calculator did not follow the order of operations.

If you do not have a calculator that follows the order of operations, you can enter the numbers and operations yourself in the correct order.

▶ PRACTICE

Name the operations in the correct order for finding the value of each expression. Then find the value of each expression.

1. $15 + 4 \div 2$

2. $16 \div (2 + 2) \times 3$

3. $6 \times (9 \div 3)$

Using the Calculator Find the value of each expression.

4. $45 - 15 \div 3$

5. $4 \times (9 \div 3)$

6. $2 \times 9 - 1$

7. $18 + 6 \div 2$

8. $(36 - 3) \div 3 + 45 \div 9$

9. $6 \times (7 - 2) \div 5$

Study Guide and Review

Vocabulary Check

Choose a term from the box to complete each sentence.

VOCABULARY
Associative Property of Multiplication
divisible
cubic
Distributive Property

1. You can group factors differently. The product is always the same. The _?_ states this. (page 74)
2. Volume is measured in _?_ units. (page 82)
3. The _?_ states that multiplying a sum by a number is the same as multiplying each addend by the number and then adding the products. (page 92)
4. If you divide 6 by 2, the quotient is a whole number and there is a zero remainder. This means that 6 is _?_ by 2. (page 110)

Study and Solve

CHAPTER 5

EXAMPLE

$$\begin{array}{r} {}^{1\,1} \\ 654 \\ \times\ \ 3 \\ \hline 1{,}962 \end{array}$$

Multiply the ones. Regroup. Multiply the tens. Add the 1 ten you got by regrouping the ones. Regroup. Multiply the hundreds. Add the 1 hundred you got by regrouping the tens.

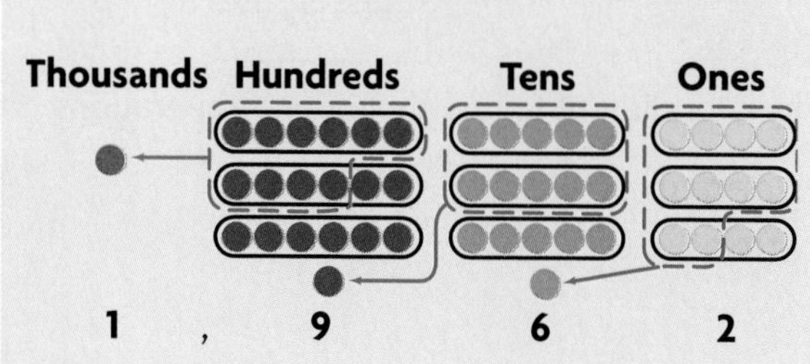

Find the product. (pages 76–81)

5. $65 \times 4 = n$
6. $328 \times 5 = n$
7. $\begin{array}{r} 806 \\ \times\ \ 2 \\ \hline \end{array}$
8. $\begin{array}{r} 17 \\ \times\ 6 \\ \hline \end{array}$

Find the area. (pages 84–85)

9. l = 15 in.
   w = 7 in.
   A = _?_ sq in.
10. l = 33 cm
    w = 8 cm
    A = _?_ sq cm

Find the volume. (pages 84–85)

11. l = 5 m
    w = 6 m
    h = 4 m
    V = _?_ cu m
12. l = 5 ft
    w = 2 ft
    h = 7 ft
    V = _?_ cu ft

Choose a strategy and solve. (pages 86–87)

13. One rug measures 10 feet by 6 feet and costs $120. Another rug measures 12 feet by 5 feet and costs $126. Which is the better buy?

CHAPTER 6

EXAMPLE

432	
×263	
1,296	Multiply. 3 × 432
25,920	Multiply. 60 × 432
+86,400	Multiply. 200 × 432
113,616	Add the products.

Estimate the product by rounding each factor to its greatest place-value position. (pages 96–97)

14. $\begin{array}{r} 626 \\ \times\ 28 \\ \hline \end{array}$

15. $\begin{array}{r} 386 \\ \times\ 51 \\ \hline \end{array}$

Find the product. (pages 94–95, 98–101)

16. $\begin{array}{r} 36 \\ \times 84 \\ \hline \end{array}$

17. $\begin{array}{r} 425 \\ \times\ 62 \\ \hline \end{array}$

18. $\begin{array}{r} 403 \\ \times 262 \\ \hline \end{array}$

19. $\begin{array}{r} 1{,}423 \\ \times\ 310 \\ \hline \end{array}$

Find the perimeter and area for the figure. (pages 102–103)

20.

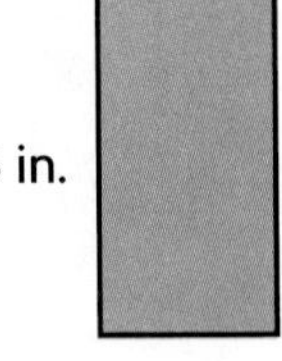

65 in.

44 in.

21.

71 cm

120 cm

Choose a strategy and solve. (pages 104–105)

22. Ms. Raymer has 600 feet of fencing to surround a garden. What dimensions should the garden have so that it has the greatest area?

CHAPTER 7

EXAMPLE

Estimate the quotient.

$148 \div 5 = n$ 150 and 5 are compatible: 150 is divisible by 5 because it has a zero in the ones place.

Think: $150 \div 5 = 30$, so $n \approx 30$.

Estimate the quotient. (pages 112–117)

23. $4\overline{)420}$ **24.** $3\overline{)271}$

25. $5\overline{)403}$ **26.** $7\overline{)1430}$

Find the quotient. Check by multiplying. (pages 112–119)

27. $2\overline{)346}$ **28.** $6\overline{)462}$

29. $415 \div 8 = n$ **30.** $525 \div 5 = n$

Choose a strategy and solve. (pages 122–123)

31. Concert tickets cost $6 each. Sellers raised $918. How many tickets did they sell?

CHAPTER 8

EXAMPLE

$$\begin{array}{r} 38 \text{ r}20 \\ 38\overline{)1{,}464} \\ -114 \\ \hline 324 \\ -304 \\ \hline 20 \end{array}$$

Divide the 146 tens by 38.
Estimate. $120 \div 40 = 3$
Multiply. $3 \times 38 = 114$
Subtract. $146 - 114 = 32$
Bring down the ones.
Repeat the steps.
Write 20 as the remainder.

Divide. Check by multiplying. (pages 136–139)

32. $36\overline{)144}$ **33.** $64\overline{)86}$

34. $8{,}145 \div 62 = n$ **35.** $4{,}104 \div 76 = n$

36. $9{,}200 \div 72 = n$ **37.** $5{,}306 \div 42 = n$

Choose a strategy and solve. (pages 142–143)

38. Ann borrowed $5,592 from her mother. She will pay it back in 24 months. What will her monthly payment be?

CHAPTERS 5–8

Performance Assessment

Tasks: Show What You Know

1. Show and explain each step as you find the product 6×418. (pages 78–79)
2. Show and explain each step as you find the perimeter and area of a sandbox that is 8 feet by 10 feet. (pages 102–103)
3. Show and explain each step as you find the quotient $812 \div 4$. (pages 116–119)
4. Explain how you can use mental math and a pattern of zeros to find the quotient $6{,}000 \div 20 = n$. (pages 128–129)

Problem Solving

Solve. Explain your method.

CHOOSE a strategy and a tool.

- Use a Formula
- Guess and Check
- Solve a Simpler Problem
- Draw a Diagram
- Write a Number Sentence

Paper/Pencil

Calculator

Hands-On

Mental Math

5. Alice is buying a cage for her pet hamster. One cage measures 2 ft by 4 ft by 3 ft. The other measures 3 ft by 3 ft by 2 ft. They each cost $20.00. Which cage has the greater volume ($V = l \times w \times h$)? (pages 86–87)
6. Mr. Foster is building a sandbox for his daughter. He has 24 feet of wood to use as a border. He wants to build the sandbox to have the greatest area. What dimensions should he use? (pages 104–105)
7. Carrie took 138 pictures on her vacation. She put them in an album with an equal number on each page. The last page had only 2 pictures on it. How many pages did she use? How many pictures were on each page? (pages 122–123)
8. Scout troop 555 has set a goal to sell 1,500 boxes of cookies. There are 12 Scouts in the troop. How many boxes should each Scout sell to meet the troop's goal? (pages 142–143)

Cumulative Review

CHAPTERS 1–8

Solve the problem. Then write the letter of the correct answer.

1. What is standard form for three hundred four million, two hundred fifty thousand, six? (pages 8–11)

A. 34,250,006 **B.** 304,025,006
C. 304,250,006 **D.** 304,250,600

---

2. $\begin{array}{r} 534 \\ +477 \\ \hline \end{array}$

A. 901
B. 911
C. 1,001
D. 1,011 (pages 20–21)

---

3. What is the value of the underlined digit?

3.0<u>5</u>6

A. 0.005 **B.** 0.05
C. 0.5 **D.** 5 (pages 36–41)

---

4. $5.012 - 3.365 = n$

A. $n = 1.647$ **B.** $n = 1.746$
C. $n = 4.188$ **D.** $n = 8.377$

(pages 56–57)

---

5. Estimate the sum to the nearest tenth.

$\begin{array}{r} 3.59 \\ +3.73 \\ \hline \end{array}$

A. 6.9
B. 7.1
C. 7.3
D. 7.5 (pages 58–59)

---

6. Here is an example of the __?__ Property of Multiplication:
$3 \times (4 \times 2) = (3 \times 4) \times 2$

A. Commutative **B.** Associative
C. Distributive **D.** Zero

(pages 74–75)

---

7. $\begin{array}{r} 432 \\ \times \quad 9 \\ \hline \end{array}$

A. 288
B. 4,416
C. 3,888
D. 38,880 (pages 78–79)

---

8. Find the volume. (pages 84–85)

$l = 6$ cm, $w = 7$ cm, $h = 3$ cm

A. 16 cu cm **B.** 42 cu cm
C. 126 cu m **D.** 126 cu cm

---

9. Estimate the product by rounding each factor to its greatest place-value position.

$\begin{array}{r} 592 \\ \times \ 43 \\ \hline \end{array}$

A. 20,000
B. 23,600
C. 24,000
D. 30,000 (pages 96–97)

---

10. Find the area. (pages 102–103)

A. 144 sq m **B.** 532 sq m
C. 1,435 sq m **D.** 12,505 sq m

---

11. $4\overline{)634}$

A. 58 r2 **B.** 158
C. 158 r2 **D.** 2,536 (pages 118–119)

---

12. $4{,}050 \div 54 = n$

A. $n = 75$
B. $n = 76$ r46
C. $n = 79$ r14
D. $n = 218{,}700$ (pages 136–139)

9 ANALYZING AND GRAPHING DATA

Miami, Florida Temperature °F				
	highest recorded	average daily max.	average daily min.	lowest recorded
Jan	85°	74°	61°	29°
Feb	88°	75°	61°	27°
Mar	92°	78°	64°	34°
Apr	93°	80°	67°	45°
May	94°	84°	71°	50°
Jun	94°	86°	74°	61°

Chicago, Illinois Temperature °F				
	highest recorded	average daily max.	average daily min.	lowest recorded
Jan	65°	32°	18°	-20°
Feb	68°	34°	20°	-21°
Mar	62°	43°	29°	-12°
Apr	91°	55°	40°	17°
May	98°	65°	50°	27°
Jun	102°	75°	60°	35°

Barrow, Alaska Temperature °F				
	highest recorded	average daily max.	average daily min.	lowest recorded
Jan	33°	-9°	-22°	-53°
Feb	31°	-12°	-25°	-56°
Mar	36°	-8°	-22°	-52°
Apr	42°	7°	-8°	-42°
May	45°	24°	13°	-18°
Jun	70°	39°	29°	8°

SCIENCE LINK

The national record for highest temperature is 134°F. It was recorded in 1913 in Death Valley, California. The record for lowest temperature in the United States is ⁻79.8°F. It was recorded in the Endicott Mountains of Northern Alaska.

Problem-Solving Activity

The Worried Weather Forecaster

Suppose you are a weather forecaster. Your task is to record the high and low temperatures each day. Your supervisor tells you not to worry as long as the daily temperatures don't break any records, and their mean is close to the average temperature for the month.

Make up daily temperature data that will fit the supervisor's comments.

YOU WILL NEED: poster board, calculator, markers or crayons

- Choose a city and a month.
- Make a five-day chart of high and low temperatures that fit the supervisor's comments.
- Calculate the mean for the five high and the five low temperatures.
- Make a graph showing the five high temperatures and the five low temperatures.

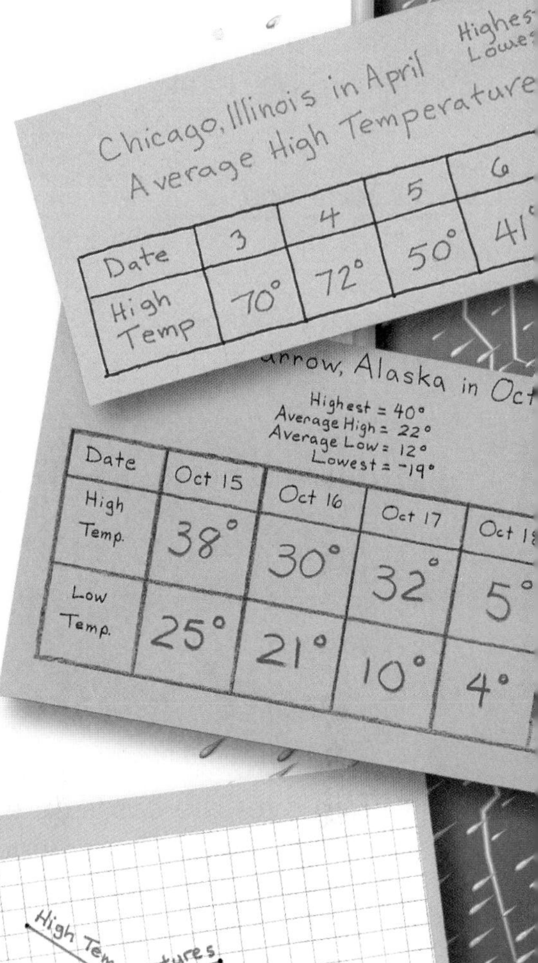

DID YOU

- ✓ make a chart showing high and low temperatures?
- ✓ calculate the mean for the high and the low temperatures and check your calculations?
- ✓ graph the data?

Finding the Median and Mode

VOCABULARY
median
mode

You will investigate finding the median and mode of a set of data.

The coach of the Coyotes basketball team recorded the team's scores in the first 13 games. He organized these data in the table below.

COYOTES' BASKETBALL SCORES													
Game	1	2	3	4	5	6	7	8	9	10	11	12	13
Score	104	95	100	103	99	100	93	104	99	102	93	104	104

EXPLORE

Write each score on a different index card. Use the index cards to find the median and mode.

MATERIALS: index cards

A. To find the *median*, order the scores on the cards from least to greatest.

93 93 95 99 99

Flip over the cards on each end. Keep doing this, moving toward the middle, until one card is left. The score on that card is the median.

B. To find the *mode*, sort the cards by numbers. Find the score that occurred most often.

Record

Write your own definitions for *median* and *mode*. Name the median and mode for the Coyotes' basketball scores.

CRITICAL THINKING How does this activity help you find the difference between median and mode?

Now, investigate finding the median and mode for another set of data. The **median** is the middle number in an ordered series of numbers. The **mode** is the number that occurs most often.

Technology Link

You can find the median of a data set by using E-Lab, Activity 9. Available on CD-ROM and on the Internet at **www.hbschool.com/elab**

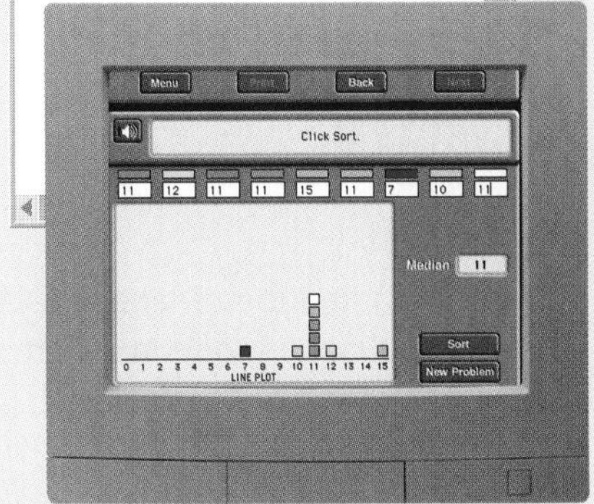

▶ TRY THIS

1. Write each temperature on a different index card. Use the cards to find the median and mode for the temperatures. Record your answers.

AUGUST TEMPERATURES													
DATE	1	2	3	4	5	6	7	8	9	10	11	12	13
TEMP	96°	88°	87°	101°	94°	93°	87°	74°	91°	82°	87°	88°	73°

2. **Write About It** For one season, the median score for one team is 88, and the mode is 87. The median score for another team is 100, and the mode is 104. Which team do you think is better? Explain.

▶ PRACTICE

Use index cards to find the median and mode for each set of data.

3.

KATIE'S TEST SCORES									
Test	1	2	3	4	5	6	7	8	9
Score	94	93	95	87	94	78	85	89	99

4.

STUDENTS' WEIGHTS					
Name	Meg	Ruth	Sara	Jon	Keith
Pounds	84	75	89	103	84

5.

BASEBALL CARD COLLECTION					
Name	Tony	Kara	Ray	Sue	Jay
Number	240	200	200	265	285

6.

PLAY TICKETS SOLD							
Week	1	2	3	4	5	6	7
Number	175	150	225	175	230	190	165

7.

MONEY SAVED IN ONE YEAR					
Initials	L.L.	S.E.	B.S.	M.D.	D.V.
Amount	$125	$150	$175	$125	$180

8.

CANS RECYCLED					
Day	Mon	Tue	Wed	Thu	Fri
Number	68	93	68	75	120

Problem Solving • Mixed Applications

9. **Health** On each of 2 days Tony did 50 sit-ups. On each of the next 2 days he did 75. On the last 3 days he did 100 each day. What are the median and mode for the number of sit-ups Tony did?

10. **Number Sense** There are 36 students on each of 2 buses. There are 43 students on each of 3 buses. What is the total number of students on the 5 buses?

MORE PRACTICE page H85

LESSON 2

Finding the Mean

VOCABULARY
mean

Why learn this? You can describe data, such as the average number of tickets sold.

TICKETS SOLD

Day	Number
Mon	6
Tue	5
Wed	9
Thu	2
Fri	3
Sat	5

The **mean**, or average, is one way to find a number that represents all the numbers in a set of data. What is the mean for the number of tickets sold?

MODEL

Step 1
Use unit cubes. Make 6 stacks of cubes to model the number of tickets sold each day.

Mon | Tue | Wed | Thu | Fri | Sat

Step 2
Arrange the stacks in order from the shortest to the tallest.

Step 3
To find the mean, move the cubes so the 6 stacks are equal in height. The number of cubes in each stack is the mean.

So, the mean is 5 tickets.

Talk About It CRITICAL THINKING

- What operation are you modeling by making 6 equal stacks?
- What information does the mean give you that the median and mode do not?

REMEMBER:

A *stem-and-leaf plot* shows data organized by place value.

Stem	Leaves
1	2 4 4 7
2	1 1 1 9 9
3	0 3 5

The tens digit is called the *stem*. The ones digits are called *leaves*.

You can read data from a stem-and-leaf plot. What is the mean for these data?

Stem	Leaves
4	6 7 8 9 9
5	0 0 1 2 4 4 4 5 5 6 7 7 7 7 8
6	1 1 4 5 8

Ages of First 25 Presidents When Sworn into Office

To compute the *mean*, add the ages of the presidents. Divide the sum by the number of presidents.

1,375 ÷ 25 = 55, so the mean is 55 years.

- What are the median and mode for these data?

▶ CHECK

When you are finding the mean of a set of data, what number is the

1. dividend? **2.** divisor? **3.** quotient?

▶ PRACTICE

For Problems 4–5, use the stem-and-leaf plot.

Stem	Leaves
7	1 3 6
8	4 7
9	5 5 6 7

Angela's Bowling Scores

4. Write the mean for Angela's bowling scores.

5. Write the median and mode.

For Problems 6–7, use the table.

FAIRVIEW ELEMENTARY SCHOOL	
Grade	**Number of Students**
First	120
Second	105
Third	120
Fourth	108
Fifth	112

6. What is the mean for the number of students in each grade at the school?

7. Write the median and the mode for these data.

Find the mean, median, and mode for each set of data.

8. 3, 9, 7, 7, 4 **9.** 20, 30, 25, 40, 20 **10.** 147, 116, 148, 128, 116

Problem Solving • Mixed Applications

11. Using Data There are 5 fifth-grade classes at Duncan's school. In each of 3 classes there are 27 students. One class has 29 students, and one class has 30 students. What are the mean, median, and mode for these data?

12. Heather helped her teacher pack boxes. She packed 146 books into 8 equal-size boxes. Did she pack the same number of books into each box? Explain.

13. Reasoning There are 4 children in Gloria's family. Gloria is 14 years old. Gloria's 3 brothers are 7, 9, and 18 years old. What is the mean for the 4 children's ages?

14. Write About It What do the mean, median, and mode tell you about a set of data?

Mixed Review and Test Prep

Write in written form. (pages 38–39)

15. 0.001 **16.** 0.025 **17.** 0.306 **18.** 5.004

Choose the letter for the correct sum. (pages 52–53)

19. $6.2 + 3.5 = n$ **A** 9.7 **B** 0.97 **C** 97.0 **D** 0.097

20. $2.45 + 4.16 = n$ **F** 0.661 **G** 66.1 **H** 6.601 **J** 6.61

21. $7.904 + 2.616 = n$ **A** 1.052 **B** 10.520 **C** 9.52 **D** 10.51

MORE PRACTICE page H85

LESSON 3

Choosing a Reasonable Scale

VOCABULARY
scale
interval

Why learn this? You can choose a scale that fits your data, such as the number of magazines your class sold.

The fifth-grade students are selling magazines. They sold 35 subscriptions in Week 1, 40 in Week 2, 31 in Week 3, and 25 in Week 4. These data were organized in two different line graphs that show the same information.

Graph A

A line graph uses a line to show how something changes over a period of time.

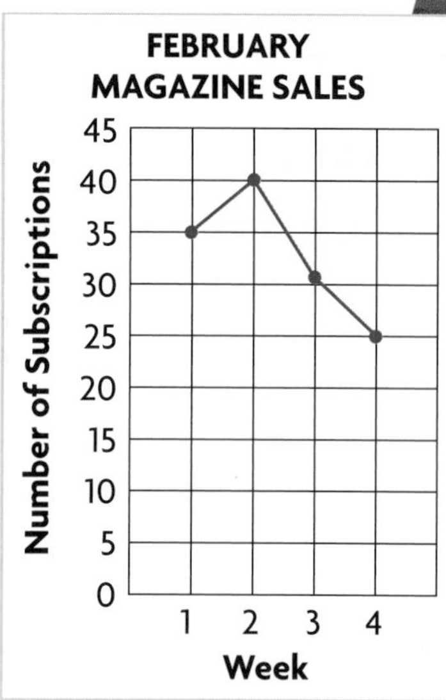

The **scale** is the series of numbers placed at fixed distances. A *reasonable scale* is one for which most data fall on scale lines. The **interval** is the distance between the numbers on the scale.

Notice that

- Graphs A and B have different scales.
- the scales have different intervals.
- both graphs show an increase from Week 1 to Week 2 and a decrease from Week 2 to Week 4.

Talk About It

- What is the interval and the scale in Graph A? in Graph B?
- Would an interval of 20 make a good scale for these data? Explain.

CRITICAL THINKING In which graph do the intervals in the scale make the graph easier to read? Explain.

On a bar graph, the scale that you choose can run vertically or horizontally.

The students at Westhill School voted for a school mascot. The two bar graphs show the election results in different ways.

In *bar* and *double-bar graphs*, the lengths of the bars are related to the numbers in the scale.

Graph C

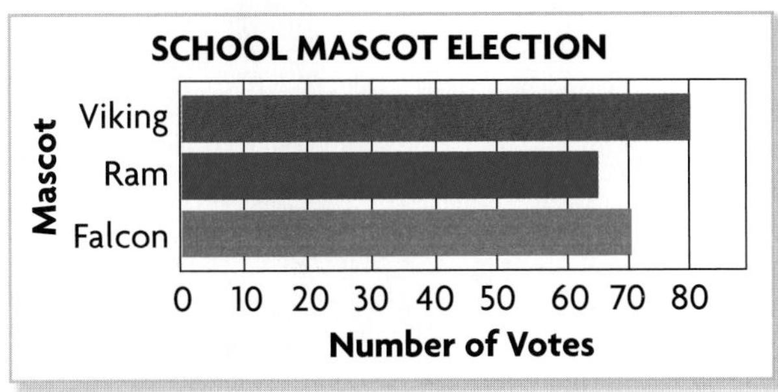

Graph D

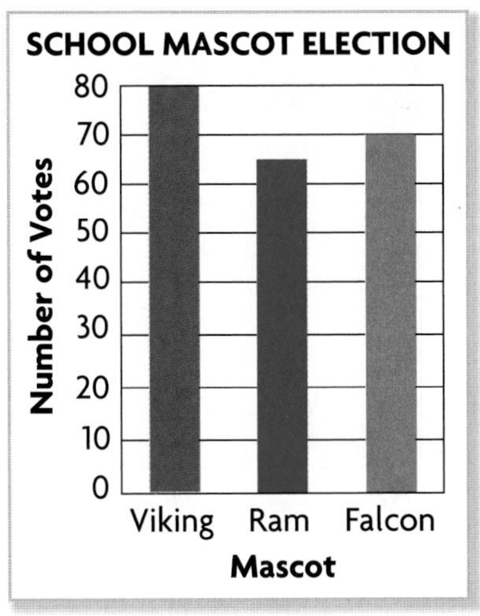

Notice that

- Graphs C and D have the same interval.
- both graphs show that "Viking" was the most popular mascot and that it received 80 votes.

- What happens to the lengths of the bars when the scale numbers are less? are greater?

CHECK

Choose the most reasonable interval for each set of data.

a. 100	**b.** 50	**c.** 25	**d.** 10

1. 10, 62, 18, 21, 31

2. 105, 200, 990, 800, 620

3. 45, 100, 95, 50, 150

4. 20, 31, 40, 78, 85

Choose the most reasonable scale for each set of data.

5.

MATH GAME SCORES	
Game	**Score**
1	30
2	15
3	22
4	46

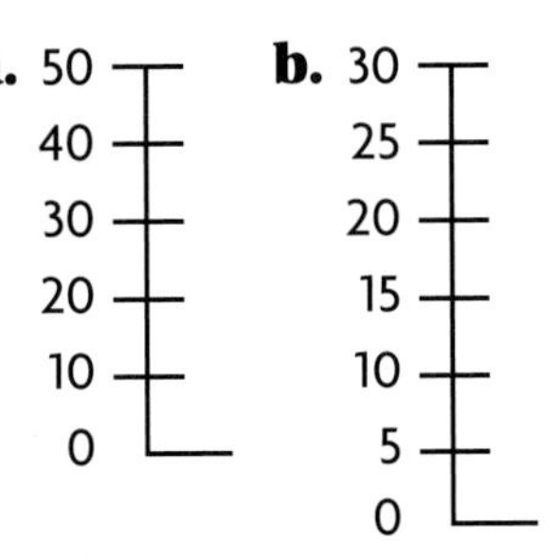

6.

FAVORITE TRIP	
Place	**Votes**
Zoo	6
Beach	4
Fun Park	11
Museum	5

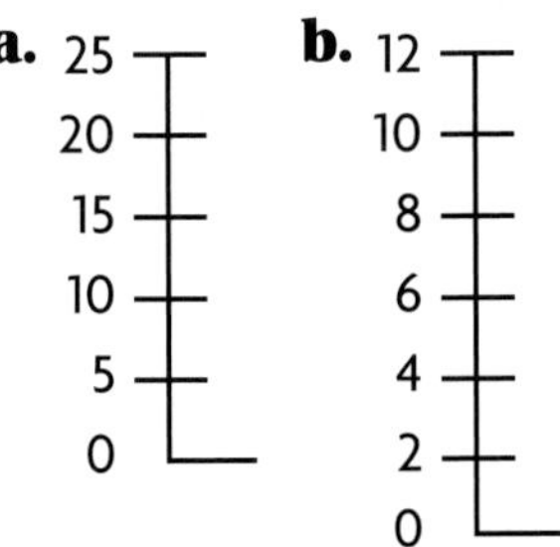

LESSON CONTINUES

▶ PRACTICE

Choose the most reasonable interval for each set of data.

a. 25 **b.** 5 **c.** 10 **d.** 1

7. 2, 5, 6, 3, 1, 4, 7

8. 10, 35, 40, 20, 30

9. 75, 25, 50, 100, 110

10. 10, 5, 20, 15, 17, 25

11. 27, 24, 50, 74, 101

12. 6, 3, 3, 5, 4

Choose the more reasonable scale for the set of data.

13.

FIFTH-GRADE SURVEY	
Favorite Sport	Number of Students
Football	20
Basketball	18
Baseball	15
Soccer	25
Other	5

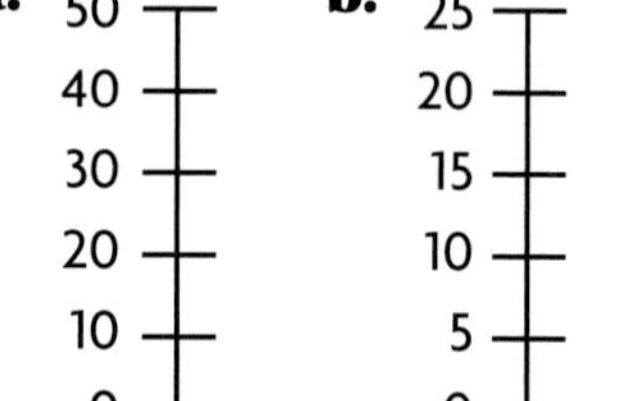

14.

PLANT SALE	
Week	Number Sold
1	20
2	15
3	40
4	30
5	10

a. 50, 40, 30, 20, 10, 0

b. 75, 60, 45, 30, 15, 0

15.

PETS OWNED IN MS. FLOWER'S CLASS	
Pet	Number of Students
Dog	9
Cat	10
Fish	6
Gerbils	4

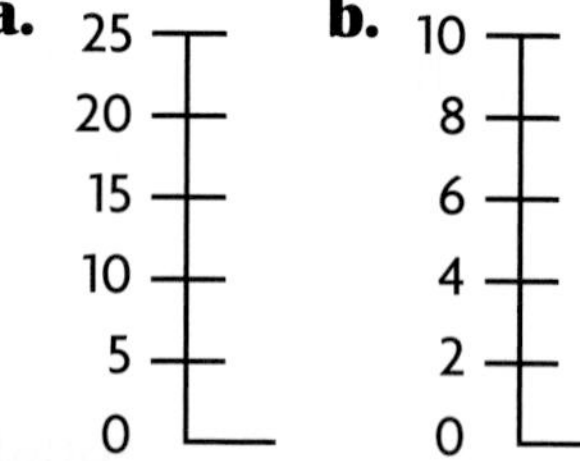

16.

FAVORITE ZOO ANIMALS	
Animal	Number
Bear	7
Lion	12
Elk	6
Zebra	4

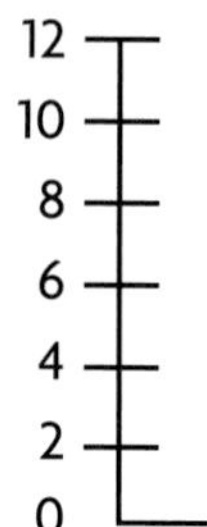

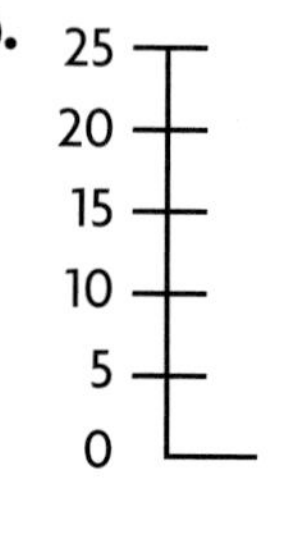

Problem Solving • Mixed Applications

Using Data For Problems 17–21, use the table.

TELEVISION SURVEY	
Favorite Type of Show	Number
Comedy	25
Drama	16
Sports	15
News	5

17. Analyzing Data What would be an appropriate scale for these data?

18. How many students were surveyed?

19. Reasoning Would an interval of 10 make a good scale for these data? Explain.

20. Visual Thinking What type of graph would best show these data, a line graph or a bar graph? Explain.

21. **Write a problem** using the information in the table.

CONSUMER CONNECTION

How do video stores know which videos are most popular? One way is to keep track of how many times a week each copy of a video is rented.

Use the table to answer Problems 22–24.

TOWNE VIDEO MOST POPULAR VIDEOS/WEEK OF DECEMBER 7		
Title	**Rentals per Copy**	**Total Rentals**
The Lost World: Jurassic Park	6	90
Jingle All the Way	3	45
Free Willy 3: The Rescue	2	30
Liar Liar	2	30
Home Alone	4	60

22. What scale would you use to show the number of rentals per copy?

23. What scale would you use to show the total number of rentals for each movie?

24. How would a graph look if you showed both sets of data using one scale?

HISTORY LINK

It may surprise you to know that there were more movies being made and released 70 years ago than there are today! Here are the years in which the most movies were released in the United States.

Year	Made in U.S.	Imported
1928	641	193
1921	854	0
1918	841	0
1920	769	0
1937	538	240

How many films were released in the United States in 1928?

25. If a graph is to show the number of pets owned by students in a class of 30, do you think the scale should be in intervals of one, ten, or fifty? Explain.

Mixed Review and Test Prep

Choose the letter of the correct product. (pages 78–81)

26. 124×5

A 720
B 620
C 520
D 420

27. 219×2

F 348
G 369
H 418
J 438

28. 918×3

A 2,754
B 2,554
C 2,954
D 2,945

29. 367×4

F 1,468
G 1,478
H 1,488
J 1,498

30. 511×9

A 4,511
B 4,799
C 4,699
D 4,599

Use divisibility rules to predict if there will be a remainder. (pages 118–119)

31. $9\overline{)542}$ **32.** $4\overline{)348}$ **33.** $3\overline{)129}$ **34.** $5\overline{)436}$ **35.** $6\overline{)618}$

MORE PRACTICE page H85

LESSON 4

Making Line Graphs

VOCABULARY
range

Why learn this? You can make graphs that show how temperatures change over a period of time.

The table below shows average monthly temperatures for San Juan, Puerto Rico. You can use the table to find the **range**, or difference between the greatest and the least numbers in the set of data.

SAN JUAN AVERAGE MONTHLY TEMPERATURES						
Month	Jun	Jul	Aug	Sep	Oct	Nov
Temperature	82°F	83°F	83°F	82°F	82°F	80°F

The greatest temperature is 83°F. The least temperature is 80°F. Since 83 − 80 = 3, the range is 3.

MODEL

How can you make a line graph to show these data?

Step 1

Decide on the interval and the numbers in the scale. Since the range is 3, it makes sense to use an interval of 1. The scale must be at least from 80°F to 83°F.

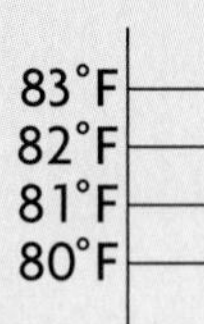

Step 2

Scales on graphs always start at zero. Since there are no data between 0°F and 80°F, you can *break the scale* to save room. Write the temperatures along the left side of the graph.

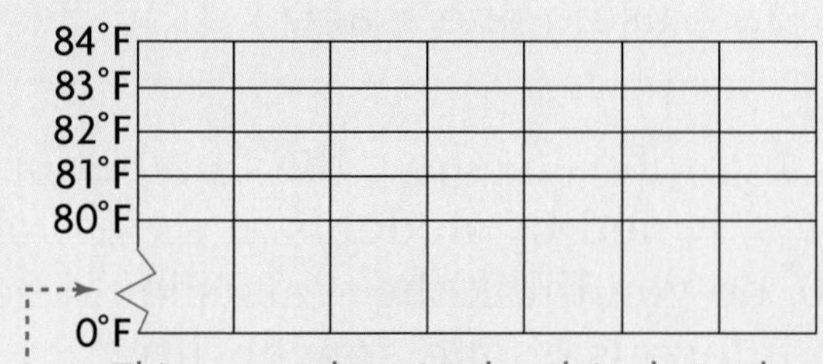

Step 3

Write the names of the months along the bottom of the graph. Label the months, and then label the temperatures along the left side of the graph. Write a title for the graph.

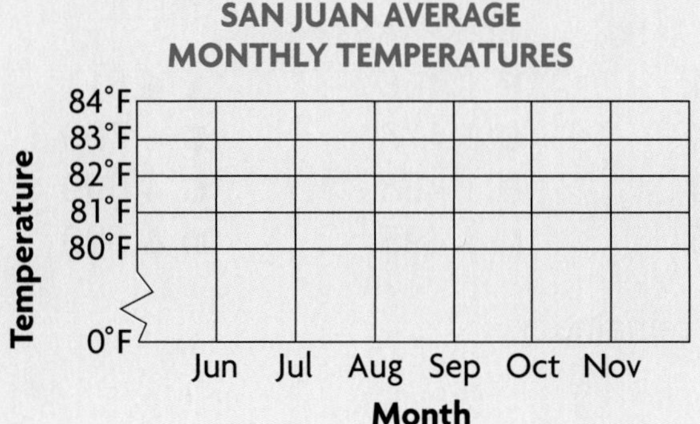

Step 4

Plot the points for the data. Connect the points to show change over time.

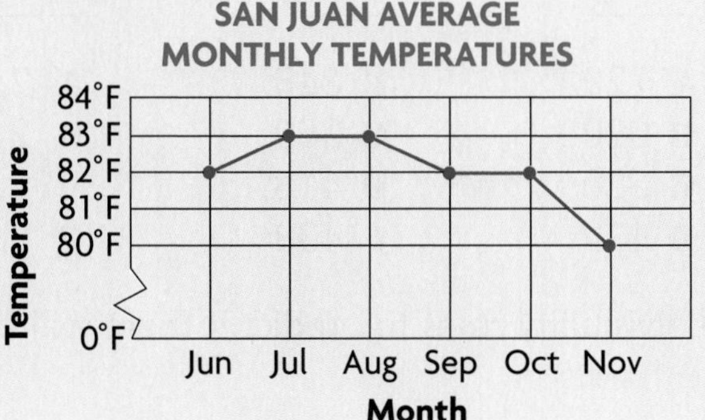

▶ CHECK

1. What does the graph tell you about how the temperature in San Juan changes over time?

2. CRITICAL THINKING Would it make sense to use an interval of 1 for a set of data with a range of 50? Explain.

▶ PRACTICE

Make a line graph for each set of data.

3.

SKATING RINK ATTENDANCE					
Week	1	2	3	4	5
People	150	155	165	180	185

4.

INCHES OF RAINFALL				
Month	Jun	Jul	Aug	Sep
Inches	3	5	6	4

Problem Solving • Mixed Applications

Using Data For Problems 5–7, use the table.

TIME MARIA SPENDS ON HOMEWORK					
Day	Mon	Tue	Wed	Thu	Fri
Time	20 min	45 min	60 min	75 min	0 min

5. What would be an appropriate scale for a line graph displaying these data?

6. What would the label for the scale be?

7. **Reasoning** Describe how the data changed each day.

8. Maria read 20 pages on Monday. On Tuesday she read twice as many pages as she did on Monday. On Friday she read 3 times as many pages as she did on Monday. What is the mean for the number of pages Maria read those 3 days?

9. **Write About It** Explain when a line graph might be a better choice to use than a bar graph.

CULTURAL LINK

Puerto Rico, located on an island in the West Indies, is an independent commonwealth of the United States. *Puerto Rico* is Spanish for "rich harbor." Sea currents keep the temperature in Puerto Rico mild year-round. The island's average high and low temperatures are 89°F and 66°F. What temperature in Puerto Rico is the mean?

Mixed Review and Test Prep

Divide. Check by multiplying. (pages 136–137)

10. $19\overline{)616}$ 11. $42\overline{)275}$ 12. $31\overline{)139}$

Choose the letter for the correct product. (pages 94–95)

13. $34 \times 15 = n$

A 3,570 **B** 184
C 490 **D** 510

14. $187 \times 16 = n$

F 2,992 **G** 2,952
H 2,477 **J** 1,309

MORE PRACTICE page H86

Choosing the Appropriate Graph

Why learn this? You can use graphs to present data about cities in different ways.

Some students used the table at the right to make graphs and plots. Whose graph or plot best displays these data?

MEAN TEMPERATURE ON APRIL 11	
City	**Temperature**
Chicago, IL	48°F
Los Angeles, CA	60°F
Miami, FL	75°F
Washington, DC	57°F

Fernando's Line Plot

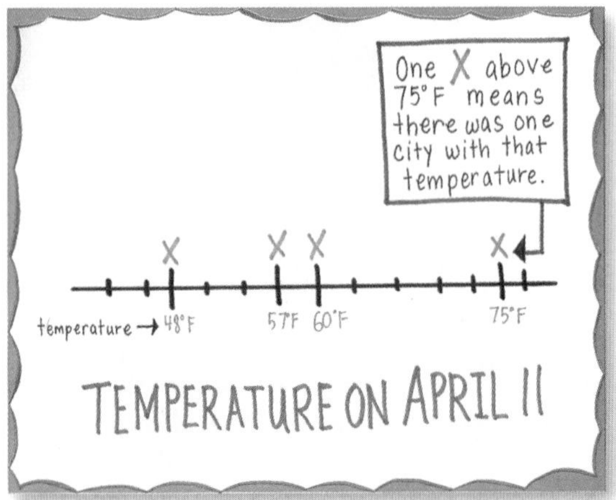

A *line plot* is used to keep track of data as they are collected. The city names are not shown. This is not the best way to display these data.

Joshua's Line Graph

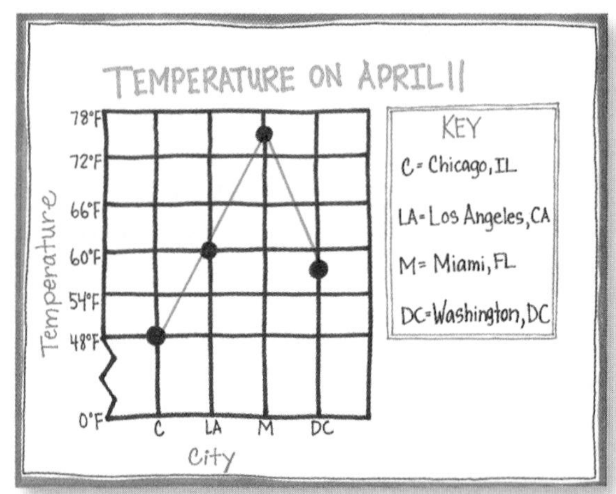

A *line graph* is used to show changes over time. So, this is not an appropriate graph to use.

Tamara's Bar Graph

A *bar graph* is used to compare facts about groups. So, this is an appropriate graph to use.

▶ CHECK

1. Why is Tamara's graph the best for displaying these data?
2. Would a stem-and-leaf plot be appropriate for displaying these data? Explain.
3. Why is a line graph appropriate for displaying the data in the previous lesson but not in this lesson?

▶ PRACTICE

For Problems 4–7, choose a type of graph or plot. Explain your choice.

4. scores for a math test

5. yearbook sales over a four-week period

6. number of students in four schools

7. money a business earned from January to June

Draw the graph or plot that best displays each set of data.

8.

CLASS SURVEY NUMBER OF FAMILY MEMBERS					
Number of Family Members	2	3	4	5	6
Frequency	9	7	4	2	1

9.

DISTANCE HEATHER TRAVELED ON A TRIP						
Day	1	2	3	4	5	6
Miles	250	100	0	50	100	250

10.

FAVORITE RADIO STATIONS					
Station	WRDL	WLRF	WSRS	WEMD	WWEB
Boys	24	16	12	28	20
Girls	36	22	20	4	18

SOCIAL STUDIES LINK

Graphs are often used in magazines and in newspapers. The line graph below shows the population of the world. What does the graph show you about how the population of the world has changed over time?

TOTAL WORLD POPULATION

Billions of People: 0 1 2 3 4 5 6 7

1996

Year: 1800 1850 1900 1950 2000

Problem Solving • Mixed Applications

Using Data For Problems 11–15, use the table.

TEMPERATURE IN ORLANDO ON DECEMBER 31						
Time	6:30 A.M.	9:30 A.M.	12:30 P.M.	3:30 P.M.	6:30 P.M.	9:30 P.M.
Temperature	45°F	55°F	68°F	72°F	65°F	58°F

11. **Analyzing Data** What type of graph would you use to display these data? Explain.

12. **Reasoning** Would it be reasonable to use a scale of 1°? Explain.

13. When did the least change in temperature occur?

14. **Time** Did the temperature change more between 6:30 A.M. and 9:30 A.M. or between 9:30 A.M. and 12:30 P.M.?

15. **Write a problem** using the data in the table.

Technology Link

You can use ***Graph Links Plus*** computer software to make graphs.

MORE PRACTICE page H86

Problem-Solving Strategy: Make a Graph

▶ **THE PROBLEM** Carolyn surveyed the students in her class to find out what type of fund-raiser they want to have. She organized the data in the table below. What graph or plot should she use to display these data?

FUND-RAISER CHOICES			
	Car Wash	Bake Sale	Raffle
Girls	7	3	5
Boys	10	1	4

REMEMBER:

Double-bar graphs are used to compare two sets of data in the same graph.

UNDERSTAND

- What are you asked to find?
- What information will you use?
- Is there information you will not use? If so, what?

PLAN

- What strategy can you use to solve the problem?

You can *make a graph or plot* to organize and clearly display these data.

SOLVE

- Which graph or plot can you make?

You can make a double-bar graph to compare the girls' and boys' responses.

This double-bar graph shows that the greatest number of girls and the greatest number of boys want to have a car wash for the fund-raiser.

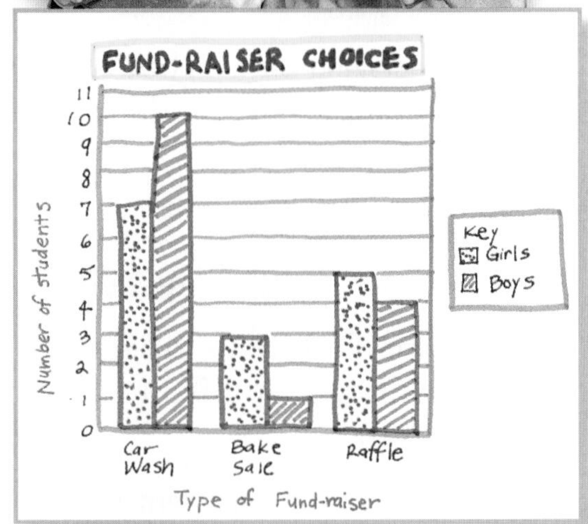

LOOK BACK

- How do you know if this is the best graph or plot to display these data?
- What other strategy could you use?

▶ PRACTICE

Make a graph to solve.

1. Mrs. Cook, the librarian, is getting ready to order new books. She surveyed students to find out what types of books they wanted. She organized the data in the table. What graph or plot should she use to display these data? Make the graph or plot.

NEW BOOKS FOR THE LIBRARY			
	Fiction	Biography	Reference
Boys	18	14	8
Girls	20	13	7

2. Mrs. Mantel surveyed some students. She wanted to find ideas for the end-of-school party. She organized the data in the table. What graph or plot should she use to display these data? Make the graph or plot.

End-of-School Party Ideas			
	Carnival	Games	Sports
Number of Students	30	32	58

Mixed Applications

Solve.

CHOOSE a strategy and a tool.

- Make a Table
- Guess and Check
- Make a Graph
- Write a Number Sentence

Paper/Pencil

Calculator

Hands-On

Mental Math

3. Darien High School had five home football games. On September 13 they sold 1,018 tickets for the game. One week later they sold 650 tickets. The next week they sold 835 tickets. On October 18 they sold 1,186 tickets, and on October 25 they sold 946 tickets. What is the mean for the number of tickets sold?

4. There were 113 fifth graders at the zoo on Friday. Of the 113 students, 3 did not tour the reptile exhibit. The other students toured the reptile exhibit in equal groups. There were 5 groups of students. How many students were in each group?

5. The money shown at the right was in Celeste's wallet. She bought 2 cassettes for $8.99 each and a CD for $12.95. A package of batteries costs $2.29. How many packages of batteries can Celeste buy?

6. The fifth-graders voted on what to buy for the spring cookout. The results are in the table. Which food choice was most popular?

SPRING COOKOUT FOOD CHOICES				
	Burgers	Hot Dogs	Chicken	Ribs
Number of Students	100	105	40	10

MORE PRACTICE pages H86–H87

CHAPTER 9 Review/Test

CHECK Understanding

VOCABULARY

1. The _?_ is the middle number in an ordered series of numbers. (page 155)

2. The _?_ is the series of numbers placed at fixed distances in a graph. (page 158)

3. The _?_ is the number that occurs most often in a set of data. (page 155)

4. The _?_ is the distance between the numbers on the scale. (page 158)

5. The _?_, or average, is a number that represents all the numbers in a set of data. (page 156)

6. The _?_ is the difference between the greatest and the least numbers in a set of data. (page 162)

Choose a type of graph or plot. Explain your choice. (pages 164–165)

7. favorite school subject

8. ages of students' grandparents

CHECK Skills

Find the mean, median, and mode for each set of data. (pages 154–157)

9. 24, 14, 11, 11, 15

10. 14, 29, 36, 18, 14, 14, 36

Choose the more reasonable scale for the set of data. (pages 158–161)

11.

AREAS OF STATES	
State	Area (rounded to nearest 10,000 sq mi)
Florida	60,000
Kansas	80,000
Maine	30,000
Oregon	100,000

a.

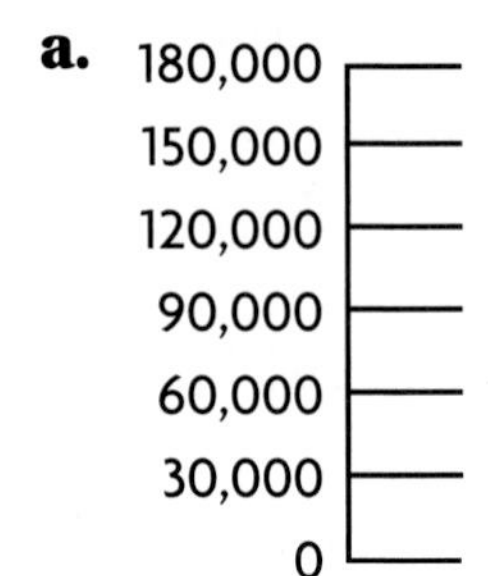

b.

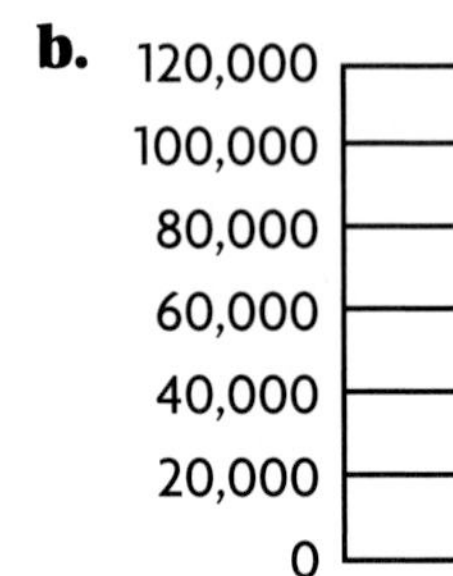

CHECK Problem Solving

Solve. (pages 166–167)

CHOOSE a strategy and a tool.

- Make a Graph
- Guess and Check
- Make a Table
- Write a Number Sentence

Paper/Pencil

Calculator

Hands-On

Mental Math

12. In April Carrie spent $100. In May she spent $120. In June she spent $80, and in July she spent $60. Between which two months did her spending change the most?

13. Mr. Dow is taking a trip. Each day, he drives 75 miles. How many miles will he travel in 14 days? How many days must he drive to complete a 1,500-mile trip?

Test Prep

1. Which of the following numbers is greater than 129,998, but less than 130,000?

   A 128,999 **B** 129,997

   C 129,999 **D** 130,001

2. $$\begin{array}{r} 50{,}000 \\ -\ 37{,}032 \\ \hline \end{array}$$

   F 12,068

   G 12,968

   H 12,978

   J 22,078

   K Not Here

3. 129 × 15 =

   A 1,835 **B** 1,895

   C 1,930 **D** 1,935

4. What is the *area* of the figure?

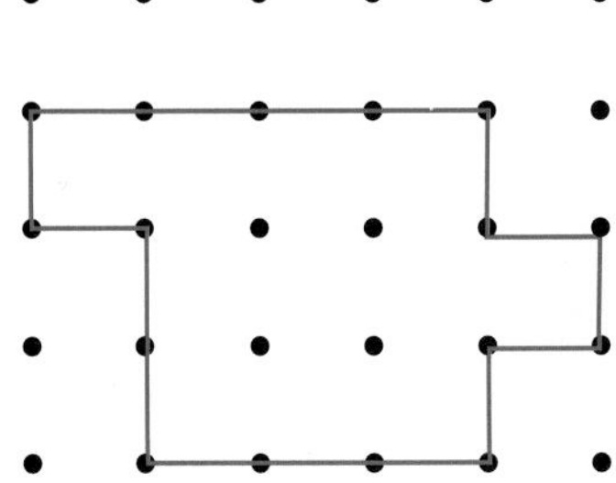

   F 10 sq units **G** 11 sq units

   H 19 sq units **J** 25 sq units

5. 769 ÷ 8 =

   A 96

   B 96 R1

   C 96 R3

   D 97 R1

   E Not Here

6. Find the mean, median, and mode for the following data.

   2, 10, 7, 4, 7

   F mean: 6; median: 7; mode: 7

   G mean: 6; median: 4; mode: 7

   H mean: 5; median: 7; mode: 7

   J mean: 5; median: 7; mode: 10

7. Which of the following is a reasonable estimate for 2,421 divided by 82?

   A 3 **B** 30

   C 40 **D** 300

8. The chart shows the pizzas sold by each member of the soccer team.

TEAM PIZZA SALES	
Team Member	**Number**
Sam	15 pizzas
Jane	5 pizzas
Sal	20 pizzas
Claire	35 pizzas
Len	30 pizzas

   Which of the following is a reasonable interval to graph these data?

   F 1 **G** 5

   H 15 **J** 25

9. Karen has seven dollars and eighty-three cents. How is this amount written?

   A \$7.08 **B** \$7.38

   C \$7.83 **D** \$78.80

10 CIRCLE, BAR, AND LINE GRAPHS

CONSUMER **LINK**

The average person eats 60 slices of pizza a year. The most popular topping is pepperoni. The least popular topping is anchovies.

Problem-Solving Activity

Picture Your Favorites

You are going to conduct your own market survey. You can ask your classmates to name their favorite pizza topping, ice-cream flavor, sport, or whatever else you can think of.

YOU WILL NEED: paper and pencil, copies of class list, 1-inch grid paper, markers or crayons, scissors, tape, ruler, posterboard

Decide on a survey topic.

- Choose a topic different from those chosen by your classmates.
- Make a survey with five choices, including *other*. Survey your classmates.
- Color a 1-inch square for each response.
- Tape or paste the squares into one long strip that you will form into a circle graph.

DID YOU

- ✓ make a survey with five choices, including *other*?
- ✓ survey everyone in your class?
- ✓ make a circle graph and label each section?

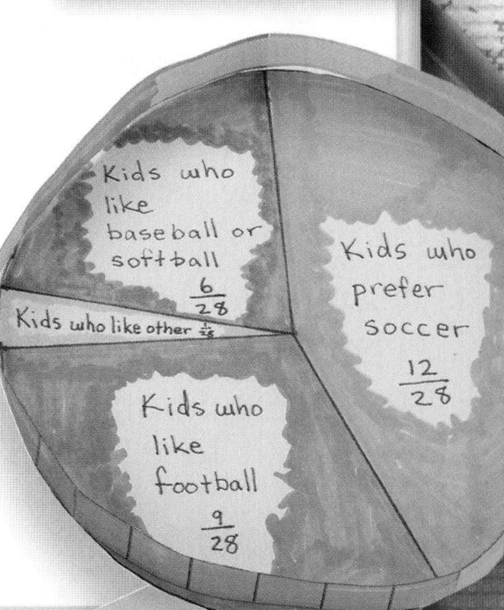

LESSON 1

Reading Circle Graphs

VOCABULARY
circle graph

Why learn this? You can compare data that represent parts of a whole, such as the cost of a field trip.

Driving to the museum

Miss Vier's class is taking a field trip to a museum. Of the $600 collected for the trip, $300 is for the bus, $100 is for food, and $200 is for tickets to the museum. A **circle graph** shows data as parts of a whole circle.

Notice that

- the circle represents the whole. In this circle graph, the whole is the total amount of money collected, or $600.
- one-half of the money, or $300, is for the bus.
- one-sixth of the money, or $100, is for food, and two-sixths of the money, or $200, is for tickets.

Talk About It CRITICAL THINKING

- How does the circle graph show how the parts are related to one another?
- How would the graph change if $300 was for the bus, $300 was for tickets, and no money was collected for food?

▶ CHECK

For Problems 1–4, use the circle graph.

1. What does the whole circle represent?
2. How are the parts in the graph related to one another?
3. What fraction of the exhibit rooms are for dinosaurs? for ancient Egypt? for artifacts?
4. How would the graph change if 4 exhibit rooms were for dinosaurs and 1 was for artifacts?

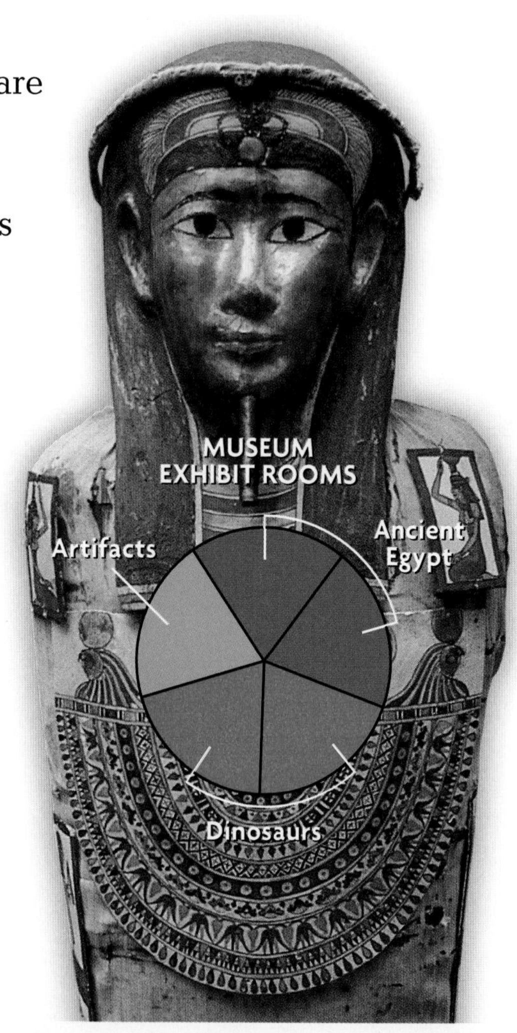

▶ PRACTICE

For Problems 5–7, use the circle graph.

5. What does the whole circle represent?
6. What fraction of the time did Paul spend finding sports scores?
7. How many minutes did Paul spend playing games and sending e-mail?

Describe how the circle graph above would change for the data.

8. Paul spends 30 minutes playing games and 30 minutes sending e-mail.
9. Paul spends 20 minutes playing games, 20 minutes sending e-mail, and 20 minutes finding sports scores.

Problem Solving • Mixed Applications

Using Data For Problems 11–12, use the circle graph.

10. **Time** Lucinda practiced the trumpet from 3:30 to 4:10. That night she practiced from 7:45 to 8:25. How many minutes in all did she spend practicing?
11. **Music** What fraction of the music played in band class is review? warm-up? new songs?
12. **Write About It** How would the graph change if no time was spent on review, the same amount of time was spent on warm-up, and the rest of the time was spent on new songs?

Mixed Review and Test Prep

Make a line graph for each set of data. (pages 162–163)

13.

INCHES OF SNOWFALL				
Month	Nov	Dec	Jan	Feb
Inches	2	3	5	2

14.

LINDA'S SUMMER EARNINGS			
Month	Jun	Jul	Aug
Amount	$25	$45	$30

Choose the set of data that the mean, median, and mode describe. (pages 156–157)

15. mean: 9; median: 8; mode: 5

A 5, 10, 15, 13, 5 **B** 5, 8, 5, 13, 14

C 9, 5, 8, 10, 5 **D** 5, 8, 9, 8, 7

16. mean: 39; median: 45; mode: 45

F 25, 45, 50, 45, 30 **G** 30, 35, 40, 35, 25

H 20, 55, 50, 50, 20 **J** 39, 40, 45, 45, 30

MORE PRACTICE page H87

Making Circle Graphs

You will investigate making circle graphs.

A circle graph can display data that are parts of a whole.

▶ EXPLORE

Fraction-circle pieces can be put together to show a whole circle. Use fraction-circle pieces to make a circle graph for the data in the table below.

MATERIALS: fraction-circle pieces, markers or crayons

32 COMMUNITY CLUB PROJECTS		
Project	Number	Fraction of All Projects
Cleanup	16	$\frac{1}{2}$
Planting	8	$\frac{1}{4}$
Posters	4	$\frac{1}{8}$
Painting	4	$\frac{1}{8}$

Record

Draw the circle graph by tracing each fraction-circle piece. Color each section of the graph a different color. Title the graph and label each section.

CRITICAL THINKING What does the whole circle represent? On what project does the Community Club spend the most time?

Now, investigate using fraction-circle pieces to make another circle graph.

▶ TRY THIS

Use fraction-circle pieces to make a circle graph for the data in this table. Draw the circle graph.

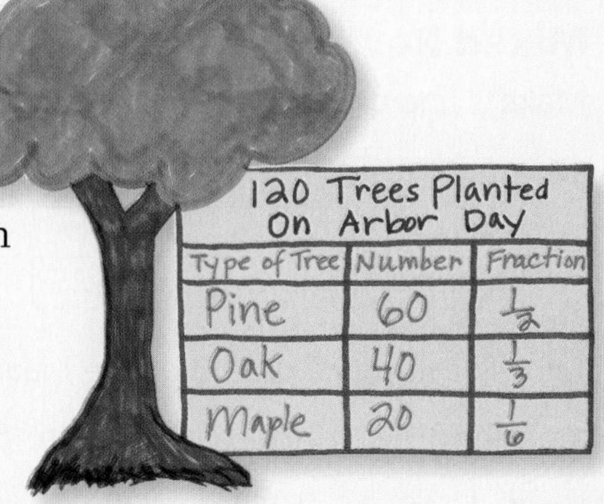

120 Trees Planted On Arbor Day		
Type of Tree	Number	Fraction
Pine	60	$\frac{1}{2}$
Oak	40	$\frac{1}{3}$
Maple	20	$\frac{1}{6}$

1. What does the whole circle represent?
2. **Write About It** Were any trees other than pine, oak, and maple planted? How do you know?

3. **CRITICAL THINKING** A recipe for fruit salad includes $\frac{1}{2}$ qt cherries, $\frac{1}{3}$ qt blueberries, and $\frac{1}{4}$ qt grapes. Can these ingredients be used as data in a circle graph? Explain.

▶ PRACTICE

Use fraction-circle pieces to make a circle graph. Then draw the circle graph.

4.

TONY'S 80 CD-ROMS	
Type of CD-ROM	Fraction of All CD-ROMS
40 Games	$\frac{1}{2}$
10 Reference	$\frac{1}{8}$
30 Educational	$\frac{3}{8}$

5.

24 PICTURES JEREMY TOOK AT THE ZOO		
Animals	Number	Fraction of All Pictures
Monkeys	6	$\frac{1}{4}$
Elephants	6	$\frac{1}{4}$
Lions	6	$\frac{1}{4}$
Birds	6	$\frac{1}{4}$

6.

HOW TONY SPENT 10 HOURS AT THE THEME PARK	
Activity	Fraction of Total Time
5 hours: Rides	$\frac{1}{2}$
2 hours: Eating	$\frac{1}{5}$
3 hours: Walking	$\frac{3}{10}$

7.

LAURA'S SUMMER EARNINGS	
How Money Was Used	Fraction of Total Earnings
Savings $100	$\frac{1}{3}$
New Clothes $100	$\frac{1}{3}$
Entertainment $100	$\frac{1}{3}$

Problem Solving • Mixed Applications

8. **Career** The newspaper staff printed 325 copies of the newspaper on Monday. They printed 150 copies on Tuesday. There are 3 pages in each newspaper. How many pages in all did they copy?

9. **Geometry** Nicole needs 16 small triangles and 12 small squares for each large square in her quilt. There are 30 large squares in her quilt. How many small triangles and small squares does Nicole need in all?

10. **Money** Brandi earned $130 baby-sitting during the summer. She earned twice as much in August as in June. She earned $40 in July. How much did she earn in June and August?

Technology Link

You can draw and analyze circle graphs by using E-Lab, Activity 10. Available on CD-ROM and on the Internet at **www.hbschool.com/elab**

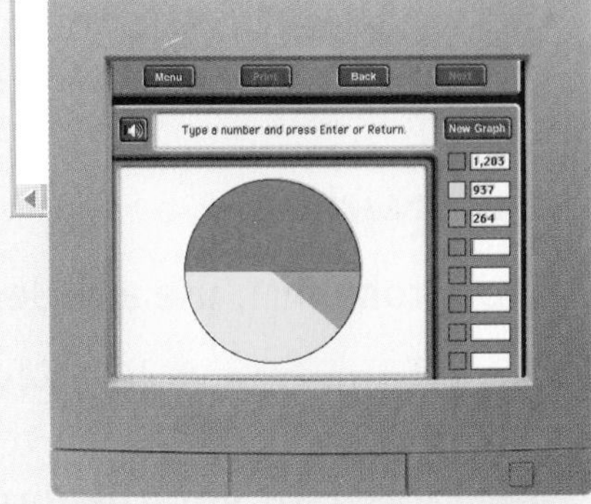

MORE PRACTICE page H87

LESSON 3

Decimals in Circle Graphs

Why learn this? You can interpret amounts in circle graphs, such as money, as fractions or decimals.

Since every fraction can be named as a decimal, all circle-graph data can be represented using decimals. Jenna has ten pencils in her desk at school. The ten pencils represent 1 whole in a circle graph. Of the whole, 0.3 are orange pencils, 0.5 are purple pencils, and 0.2 are blue pencils.

MODEL

How can you display these data in a circle graph?

Step 1

Use a circle divided into 10 equal parts to represent tenths.

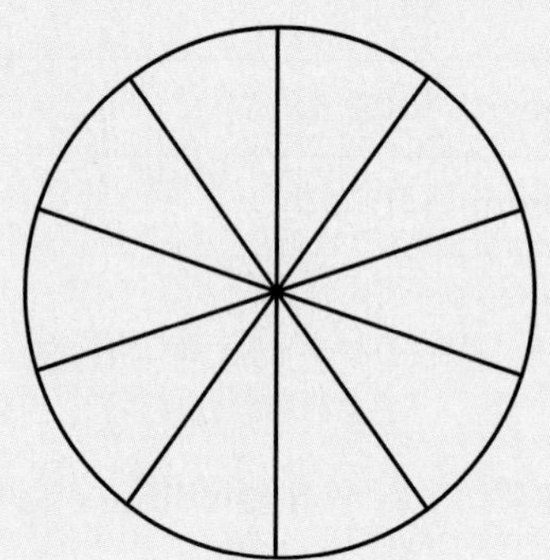

Step 2

Shade 0.3 of the parts to represent the orange pencils. Shade 0.5 of the parts to represent the purple pencils. Shade 0.2 of the parts to represent the blue pencils.

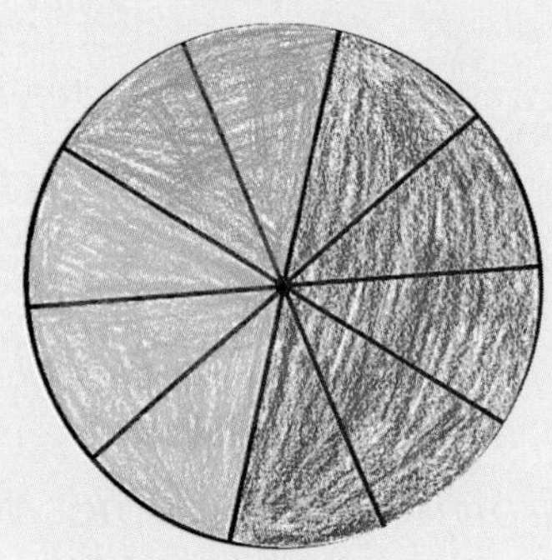

Step 3

Label each part.
Write a title for the graph.

10 PENCILS IN JENNA'S DESK

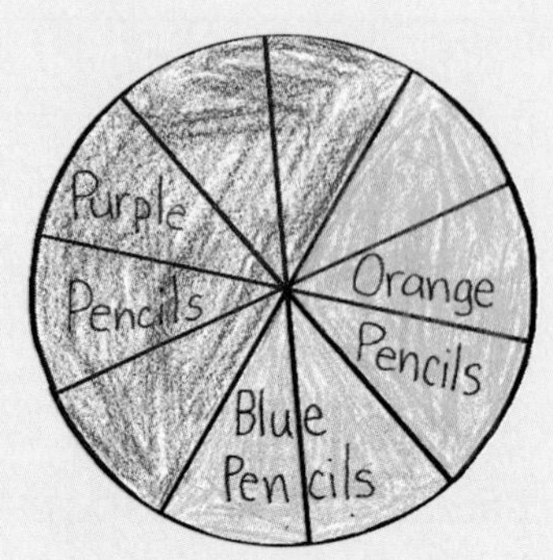

CRITICAL THINKING How do you know that 3 of the 10 parts should be shaded to represent the orange pencils in Jenna's desk?

- What is the sum of the decimals that represent the whole, or the 10 pencils in Jenna's desk?

REMEMBER:

Decimals can be written as fractions.

$0.1 = \frac{1}{10}$

$0.6 = \frac{6}{10}$

Decimals can also be used to express money amounts. There are 10 dimes in $1.00. So, 1 dime is 0.1 of $1.00.

▶ CHECK

For Problem 1, use a circle divided into 10 equal parts.

1. Of the one dollar Mika spent, 0.2 was for an eraser, 0.3 was for a pencil, and 0.5 was for a ruler. How can you display these data?

▶ PRACTICE

For Problems 2–4, use the circle graph.

2. Sue Ann spent $1.00 at the school cafeteria. What part of $1.00 did she spend for a banana and ice cream?

3. What fraction represents the part of the $1.00 Sue Ann spent for a banana? milk? ice cream?

4. How would the circle graph change if the banana cost $0.30, the milk cost $0.30, and the ice cream cost $0.40?

Make a circle graph for the data in the table.

5.

$1.00 SPENT AT A GARAGE SALE		
Item	Amount Spent	Decimal Part
baseball cards	$ 0.40	0.4
pen	$ 0.20	0.2
comic book	$ 0.10	0.1
toy	$ 0.30	0.3

Problem Solving • Mixed Applications

Using Data For Problems 6–9, use the circle graph.

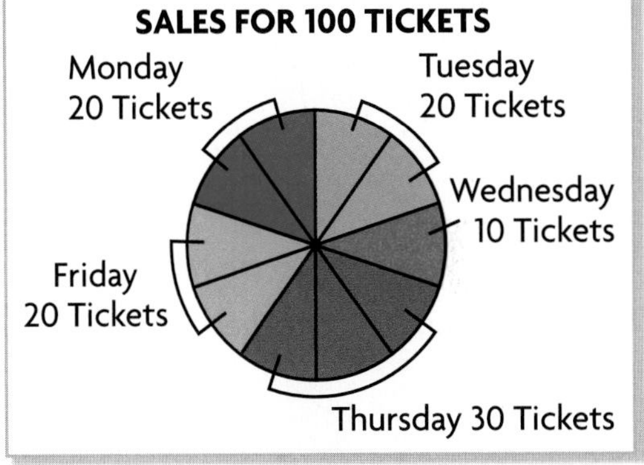

6. Write a decimal to represent the part of the 100 tickets sold on Wednesday.

7. Write a fraction to represent the part of the 100 tickets sold on Monday.

8. **Reasoning** What combination of days represents 0.5, or $\frac{1}{2}$, of the tickets sold?

9. **Write a problem** about the circle graph.

Technology Link

You can use ***Data ToolKit*** computer software to display data in a circle graph.

Mixed Review and Test Prep

Find the quotient. **(pages 128–129)**

10. $20\overline{)80}$ **11.** $40\overline{)240}$ **12.** $70\overline{)210}$

13. $50\overline{)250}$ **14.** $80\overline{)320}$ **15.** $90\overline{)270}$

Choose the letter for the correct product. **(pages 94–95)**

16. 14 × 239 **A** 3,216 **B** 1,165 **C** 3,346 **D** 24,826

17. 26 × 391 **F** 2,948 **G** 9,686 **H** 1,066 **J** 10,166

MORE PRACTICE page H88

LESSON 4

Analyzing Graphs

Why learn this? You can judge whether a graph correctly shows the data about your favorite meals.

When you make a graph, it is important to check your work carefully. Study the graphs below. Does each one correctly show the given data?

Line Graph

KWAN'S ABSENCES DURING ONE SCHOOL YEAR	
Marking Period	**Number of Absences**
First	4
Second	2
Third	2
Fourth	1

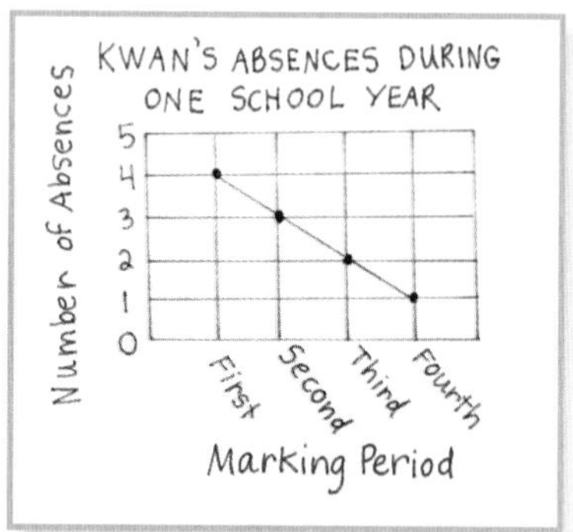

This graph is not correct. Check the plotting of each point.

Bar Graph

FAVORITE MEALS IN CLAUDIA'S CLASS	
Meal	**Number of Students**
Chicken	6
Ham	3
Hamburgers	6
Turkey	12

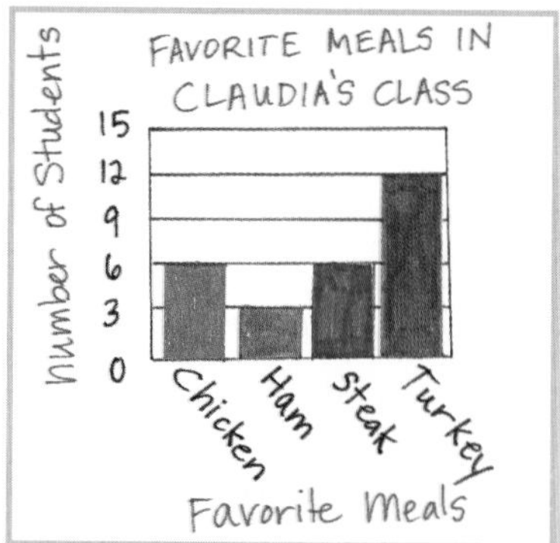

This graph is not correct. Check the labels and the title.

Circle Graph

MONEY JOE SPENT WHILE SHOPPING	
Item Bought	**Decimal Part**
Sunglasses	0.4
Socks	0.3
Lunch	0.2
Drink	0.1

MONEY JOE SPENT WHILE SHOPPING

0.3 Socks, 0.1 Drink, 0.4 Sunglasses, 0.2 Lunch

This graph is not correct. Check how each piece of data is shown.

So, none of these graphs correctly shows the given data.

▶ CHECK

1. Why isn't the line graph correct?
2. Why isn't the bar graph correct?
3. Why isn't the circle graph correct?

▶ PRACTICE

Explain why each graph does *not* correctly show the data.

4.

GRETA'S CD COLLECTION	
Classical	0.5
Popular	0.1
Musicals	0.1
Country	0.3

5.

GRETA'S CD COLLECTION	
Rock	4 CDs
Musicals	1 CD
Classical	2 CDs
Country	3 CDs

6.

GROWTH OF GRETA'S CD COLLECTION	
Jan	1 CD
Feb	2 CDs
Mar	5 CDs
Apr	10 CDs

GRETA'S CD COLLECTION

Classical

Rock

Country

Musicals

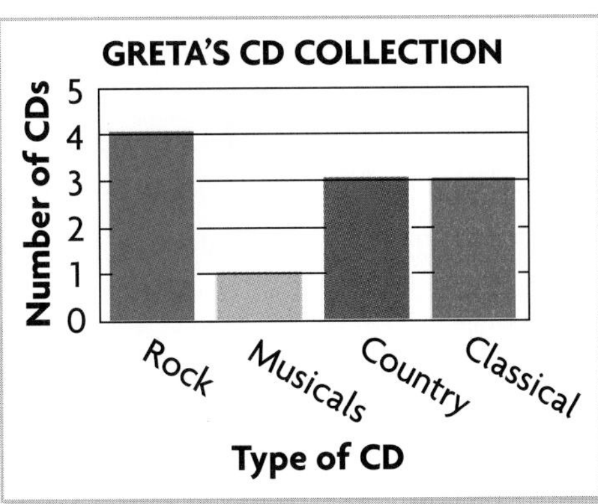

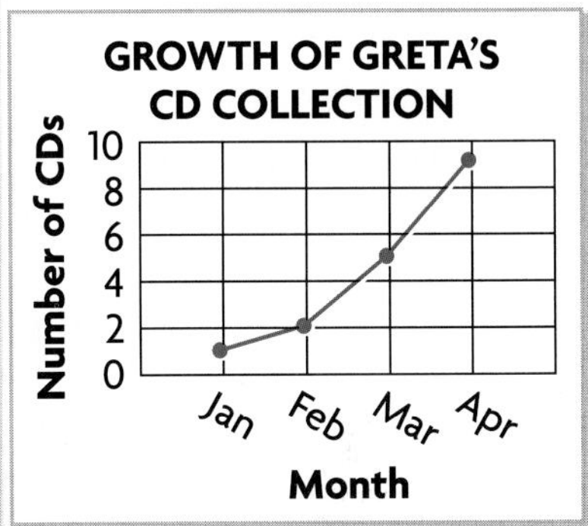

Problem Solving • Mixed Applications

Using Data For Problems 7–9, use the circle graph.

7. **Consumer** What decimal represents the part of the $100 Andrew spent on a bowling ball?

8. What fraction represents the part of the $100 Andrew spent on lessons?

9. **Write About It** Andrew spends an equal part of his savings on a bowling ball, a bag, lessons, shoes, and a membership fee. Explain how the graph and parts would change.

Mixed Review and Test Prep

Find the product. (pages 78–79)

10. $8 \times 149 = n$ 11. $3 \times 298 = n$ 12. $5 \times 732 = n$

Choose the letter for the correct quotient. (pages 116–117)

13. $237 \div 7 = n$ **A** 34 **B** 32 r3 **C** 33 **D** 33 r6

14. $542 \div 4 = n$ **F** 130 r2 **G** 136 **H** 135 r2 **J** 110 r2

15. $486 \div 3 = n$ **A** 162 **B** 128 r2 **C** 163 **D** 122

MORE PRACTICE pages H88–H89

Comparing Graphs

VOCABULARY
bar graph
line graph

Why learn this? You can choose the best kind of graph for the data you want to display, such as data about exercising.

Graphs are effective for presenting facts quickly and easily. It is often easier to interpret a graph than it is to read a written description of something.

Compare the 3 kinds of graphs shown below.

Bar graphs are used with data that can be counted. Bar graphs allow you to compare facts about groups.

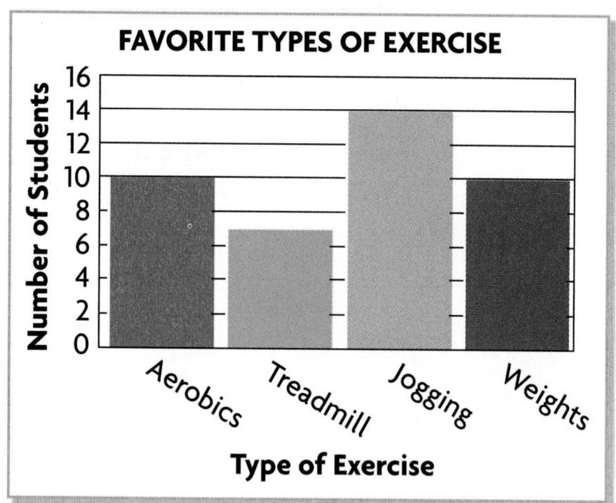

Line graphs are used to show change, or increases and decreases, over a period of time.

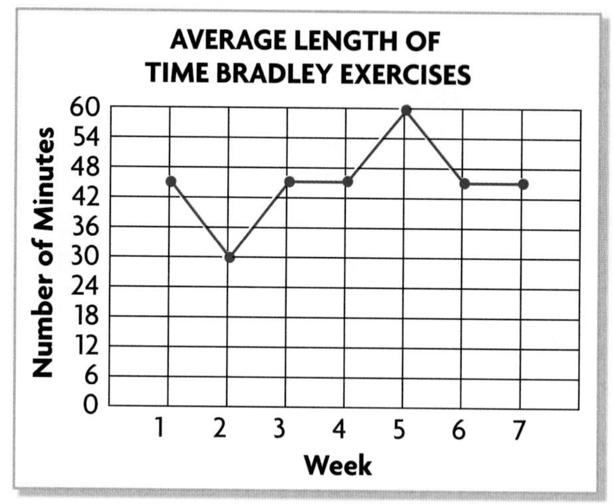

Circle graphs are used to compare parts of a group to the whole group.

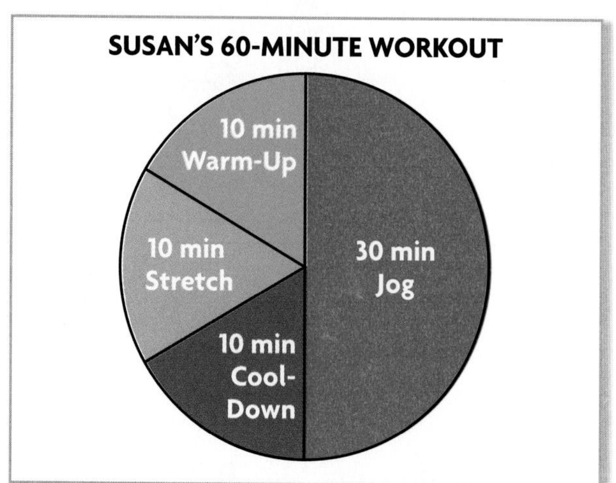

CRITICAL THINKING Explain why each graph on this page is good for displaying its given data.

▶ CHECK

1. Which kind of graph would you use to compare students' shoe sizes?
2. Which kind of graph would you use to show how you spend your time during the day?
3. Which kind of graph would you use to keep track of attendance at after-school clubs for one month?

▶ PRACTICE

Choose the best kind of graph to display the data. Explain your choice.

4. how you spend your allowance each week

5. high temperature each day for a month in your city

6. how you spend the hours in the day

7. the number of types of sports cards that you have

8.

STUDENTS PARTICIPATING IN MATH TOURNAMENT	
Class	Number of Students
Ms. Tucker	16
Mr. Rice	14
Ms. Lee	9
Ms. King	12

9.

CHANGES IN COOKIE SALES	
Week 1	$175
Week 2	$150
Week 3	$135
Week 4	$140

10.

HOW ADAM SPENT $10.00		
Item	Amount	Decimal Part
Lunch	$3.00	0.3
Movies	$4.00	0.4
Popcorn	$1.00	0.1
Drink	$2.00	0.2

11.

ALANA'S DANCE CLASSES EACH WEEK	
Type of Class	Number of Classes
Modern	2
Ballet	3
Jazz	2
Tap	1

Problem Solving • Mixed Applications

Using Data For Problems 12–14 and 18, use the table.

MILES DRIVEN IN JUNE	
Family	Miles
Carter	1,850
Watson	1,865
Price	1,875
Morgan	1,890

12. What kind of graph would best display these data? Explain.

13. **Reasoning** How many more miles did the Morgan family drive than the Carter family?

14. **Number Sense** List the families in order from the one who drove the greatest number of miles in June to the one who drove the least number of miles.

15. **Estimation** Leona rounds a number to the nearest hundred thousand. She gets 500,000. What is the least possible number that she rounded? the greatest?

16. Mr. Janota's minivan can hold 15 passengers. He drives 75 boys to summer camp. How many trips does he need to make?

17. **Measurement** Denise feeds her dog 3 cups of food each day. How many cups does she feed it in 1 week? in 1 year? (HINT: 1 year = 365 days)

LESSON CONTINUES

18. **Write a problem** using the information in the table.

MORE PRACTICE page H89

Problem-Solving Strategy: Make a Graph

▶ **THE PROBLEM** The fifth-grade students collected newspaper, glass, aluminum, and plastic. Of the 500 pounds collected, 0.2 is newspaper, 0.5 is glass, 0.2 is aluminum, and 0.1 is plastic. What graph could you make to display these data? What is the greatest part of the items collected?

REMEMBER:
UNDERSTAND
PLAN
SOLVE
LOOK BACK

UNDERSTAND

- What are you asked to do?
- What information will you use?
- Is there any information you will not use? If so, what?

PLAN

- What strategy can you use to solve the problem?

You can *make a graph* that best shows how the parts are related to the whole.

SOLVE

- How can you use the strategy to solve the problem?

Use a circle divided into 10 equal parts to make a circle graph. Shade 2 parts to represent newspaper. Shade 5 parts to represent glass, 2 parts to represent aluminum, and 1 part to represent plastic. Label each shaded portion and title the graph.

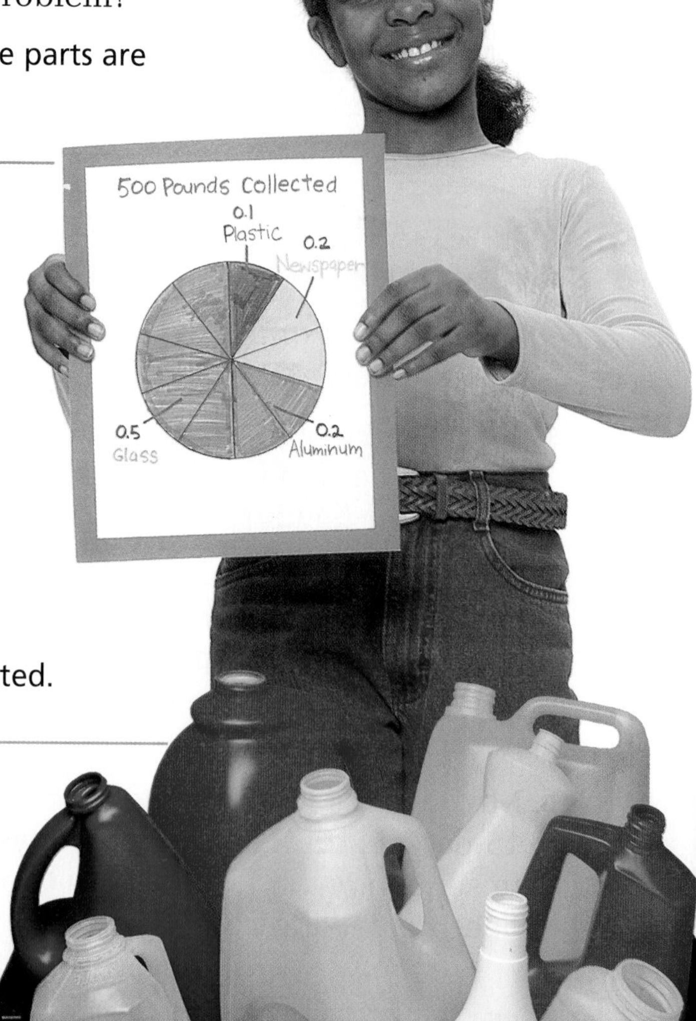

The largest portion of the circle graph is *Glass*. So, glass is the greatest part of the items collected.

LOOK BACK

- How do you know this is the best graph to display these data?
- What other strategy could you use?

▶ PRACTICE

Choose the best kind of graph to display the data. Then make the graph.

1. Riverside Elementary School collected items to donate to charities. Of the items they donated, 0.4 was food, 0.3 was clothing, 0.2 was toys, and 0.1 was household items. What graph could you use to display these data?

2. The fifth graders are presenting a talent show. In the talent show, 30 students act, another 45 sing, and another 25 dance. What graph could you use to display these data?

3. The Gomez family kept track of how their electric bills changed during a six-month period. They organized the data in a table. What graph could they use to display these data?

GOMEZ FAMILY ELECTRIC BILLS					
Jan	Feb	Mar	Apr	May	Jun
\$212	\$198	\$185	\$160	\$165	\$174

Mixed Applications

Solve.

CHOOSE a strategy and a tool.

- Guess and Check
- Make a Graph
- Draw a Diagram
- Act It Out
- Work Backward

Paper/Pencil

Calculator
Hands-On

Mental Math

4. Emily surveyed 50 people to find out their favorite hobbies. Of those surveyed, 22 said they liked reading, 9 liked skating, 15 liked playing computer games, and 4 liked gardening. How many more people liked reading and skating than liked playing computer games and gardening?

5. Ashley's family has a vegetable garden. Of the 32 plants in the garden, $\frac{2}{8}$ are tomatoes and $\frac{2}{8}$ are beans. In the remaining $\frac{1}{2}$ of the garden, there are 4 lettuce plants and 12 squash plants. How does the number of lettuce plants compare with the number of tomato plants?

6. Sam had \$4.96 when he returned home from the store. He had bought garden tools for \$6.25 and garden plants for \$14.79. How much money did he have when he left the house?

7. Bernard began working in his garden at 10:15. He worked for 1 hour and 30 minutes and then took a 45-minute break. He continued to work for 2 hours and 15 minutes. At what time did Bernard finish working?

MORE PRACTICE page H89

CHAPTER 10 Review/Test

▶ CHECK Understanding

VOCABULARY

1. A _?_ shows data as parts of a whole circle. (page 172)

For Problems 2–4, use the circle graph. (pages 172–173, 176–177)

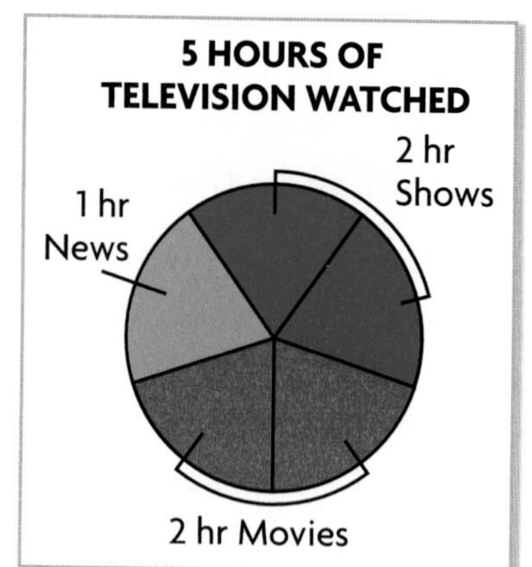

2. What does the whole circle represent?
3. What fraction of the time is spent watching movies?
4. How would the graph change if 2 hours was spent watching news, 3 hours was spent watching movies, and no time was spent watching shows?

▶ CHECK Skills

Make a circle graph for the data in the table. (pages 174–177)

5.

FAVORITE PETS OF 10 STUDENTS	
Cat	4 students
Dog	4 students
Gerbil	1 student
Fish	1 student

6.

BARB'S 10 HOURS AT WORK	
Return messages	1 hr
Work on projects	6 hr
Lunch	1 hr
Meet with clients	2 hr

Choose the best kind of graph to display the data. Explain your choice. (pages 180–181)

7. store earnings during a month
8. flavors of doughnuts in a dozen
9. number of pull-ups done in 1 minute

▶ CHECK Problem Solving

Solve. (pages 182–183)

CHOOSE a strategy and a tool.

- Work Backward
- Make a Graph
- Guess and Check
- Draw a Diagram

Paper/Pencil

Calculator

Hands-On

Mental Math

10. Pizza Land made 100 pizzas. Of the pizzas, 60 had onions, 30 were plain, and 10 had meat. How does the part of the pizzas that had onions compare with the part of the pizzas that were plain?

11. Todd needs \$100 to buy skates. He earned \$5.25 an hour cleaning houses, and worked 16 hours. How much money did Todd earn? How much more money does he need to buy the skates?

Test Prep

Choose the best answer.

1. There are 23 pounds of potatoes. Each pound is about $2\frac{1}{2}$ potatoes. Which of the following is a reasonable estimate for the total number of potatoes?

A 25 **B** 30
C 60 **D** 80

2. Estimate the sum.

$$\begin{array}{r} 119 \\ 229 \\ +485 \\ \hline \end{array}$$

F 700 **G** 800
H 900 **J** 1,100

3. Which fraction has the same value as the underlined digit?

4.<u>8</u>7

A $\frac{8}{1}$ **B** $\frac{8}{10}$
C $\frac{8}{100}$ **D** $\frac{8}{1,000}$

4. $5.08 - 3.12 =$

F 1.86
G 1.906
H 1.97
J 2.96
K Not Here

5. The following is an example of the __?__ Property of Multiplication:

$8 \times 5 = 5 \times 8$

A Associative **B** Commutative
C Distributive **D** Zero

6. Anoki was paid the following amounts for raking leaves:

Week 1: \$10	Week 2: \$7
Week 3: \$9	Week 4: \$10

What amount shows the mean he made per week?

F \$7 **G** \$8
H \$9 **J** \$10

7. Estimate the product by rounding each factor to its greatest place-value position.

$$\begin{array}{r} 445 \\ \times\ 39 \\ \hline \end{array}$$

A 16,000
B 20,000
C 24,000
D 30,000

8. The graph shows how the money for a school dance will be spent.

What fraction of the money will be spent on decorations?

F $\frac{1}{8}$ **G** $\frac{1}{6}$
H $\frac{1}{4}$ **J** $\frac{1}{8}$

11 PROBABILITY

CULTURAL **LINK**

The game Go was invented about 4,300 years ago in China. Today it is considered the most popular board game in Japan. Some games, like chess and Go, depend on strategy. Other games depend on luck.

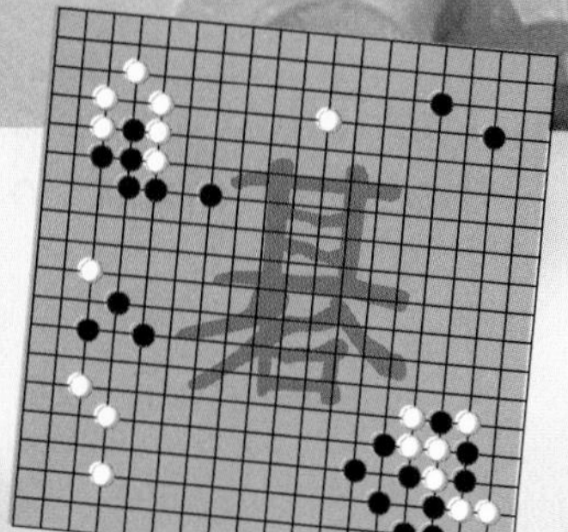

A Go Gameboard

Problem-Solving Activity

A Fair Chance of Winning?

If you like to play games, you know that sometimes winning depends on luck and sometimes it depends on skill and strategy. Try a game of Odd-Even to see if it is fair. Then design a game that depends on luck.

YOU WILL NEED: paper and pencil; markers; supplies for your game, such as spinners, coins, dominoes, or number cubes

Play Odd-Even and make a chart showing who wins for 20 rounds.

- Decide if Odd-Even is a fair game and why.
- Design your own fair game.
- Play several times to test if the game is fair.
- Change the game rules.
- Play several times to test if the game is fair or unfair.

ODD-EVEN
A GAME FOR TWO PLAYERS

One player represents the *Odd* numbers and the other player represents the *Even* numbers. They toss the cubes and add the numbers. Since 5+2=7, and 7 is an odd number, Odd wins this round.

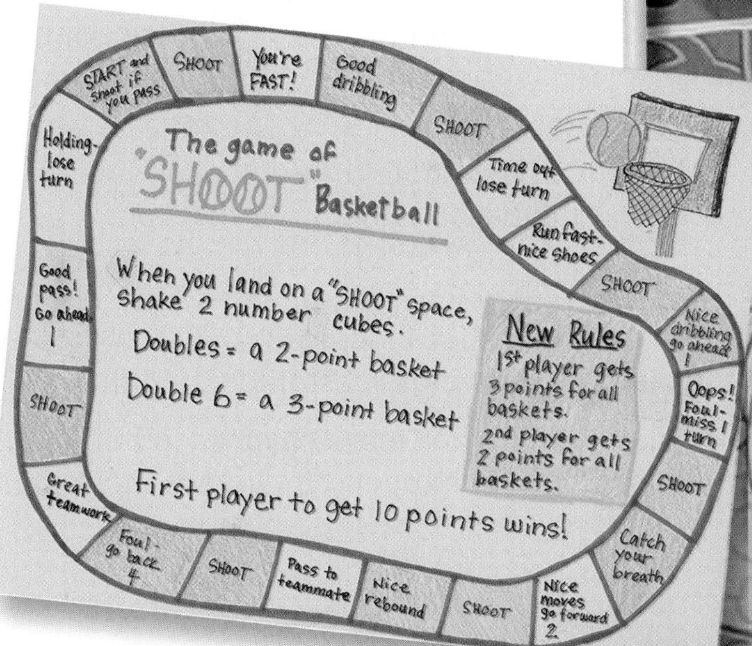

DID YOU

- ✓ play Odd-Even and decide if it was fair?
- ✓ design and play your own fair game?
- ✓ write new rules?
- ✓ play the game again several times to test if it is fair or unfair?

LESSON 1

Certain, Impossible, Likely

Why learn this? You can predict what is likely to happen when you conduct an experiment.

VOCABULARY
certain
impossible
likely

Jerome has six tiles numbered 1–6 in a bag. He reaches in and pulls out a tile. Is it certain or impossible that Jerome will pull a one-digit number? a two-digit number?

An event is **certain** if it will always happen. An event is **impossible** if it will never happen.

So, it is *certain* that Jerome will pull a one-digit number. It is *impossible* that Jerome will pull a two-digit number.

- In the example above, what is another event that is certain? impossible?

REMEMBER:
An *event* is something that happens in an experiment that results in an outcome.

EXAMPLES

A It is certain that December has 31 days.

It is impossible that June has 31 days.

B It is certain that you live on Earth.

It is impossible that you live on the moon.

C It is certain that you are a mammal.

It is impossible that you are an amphibian.

Inga has 20 yellow, 5 red, and 3 blue buttons in a bag. She reaches in and pulls out a button. What color button is Inga most likely to pull?

An event that has more chances to happen is more **likely** to happen. So, Inga is more likely to pull a yellow button.

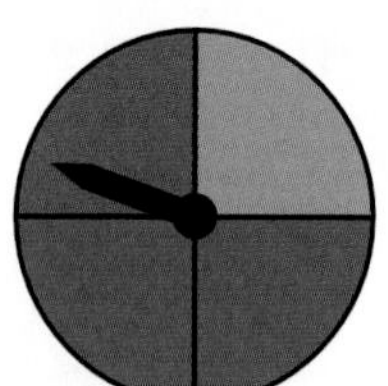

It is likely that the pointer will land on purple when it is spun.

It is unlikely that the pointer will land on green when it is spun.

CRITICAL THINKING Why is it likely that the pointer will land on purple when it is spun?

CULTURAL LINK
The game Parcheesi® is based on a game developed in India in the year 600 or earlier. Before each turn players toss 2 number cubes to determine the total number of spaces to move. What is something that is certain to happen when you play Parcheesi®?

▶ CHECK

Write *certain* or *impossible* for each event.

1. spinning an odd number on a spinner labeled 1, 3, 5, and 7
2. pulling a red counter from a bag containing only blue counters
3. rolling two cubes numbered 1–6 and getting a sum less than 1
4. pulling a vowel from a bag of tiles labeled **A**, **E**, **I**, **O**, and **U**

▶ PRACTICE

Write whether each event is *likely* or *unlikely*.

5. snow falling in July in Texas
6. being tired after running in a race
7. pulling a yellow marble from a bag of nine yellow and two green marbles
8. spinning green on a spinner with one green and eight red sections, all equal sizes
9. tossing a coin 50 times and getting all heads
10. spinning an odd number on a spinner that is numbered 1, 3, 5, 6, 7, and 9

Problem Solving • Mixed Applications

11. **Probability** Susan and her friends were bobbing for apples. Is it certain or likely that Susan will get a red apple?
12. The grocer unpacked 35 boxes of apples. There were 105 apples in each box. How many apples are there in all?
13. **Write About It** Make a list of events that are certain, impossible, and likely.

Mixed Review and Test Prep

Find the quotient. (pages 128–129)

14. $80 \div 20 = n$ 15. $240 \div 30 = n$ 16. $360 \div 90 = n$ 17. $350 \div 50 = n$

Choose the mean, median, and mode for each set of data. (pages 156–157)

18. 2, 4, 8, 2, 14, 2, 10

A mean = 2; median = 6; mode = 4

B mean = 2; median = 4; mode = 6

C mean = 6; median = 4; mode = 2

D mean = 4; median = 2; mode = 6

19. 30, 20, 80, 80, 10

F mean = 30; median = 44; mode = 80

G mean = 40; median = 80; mode = 80

H mean = 44; median = 20; mode = 80

J mean = 44; median = 30; mode = 80

Probability Experiments

VOCABULARY
possible outcomes

You will investigate and identify possible outcomes.

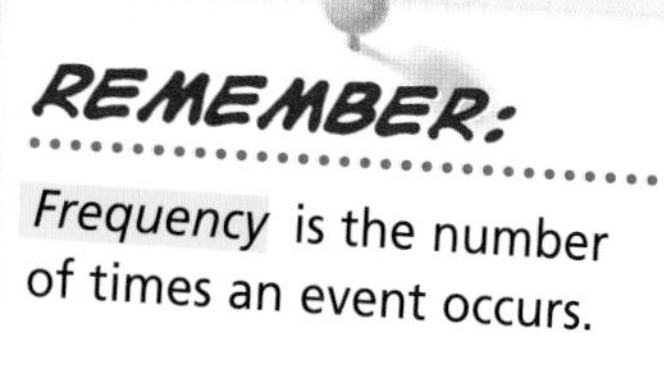

Melanie conducted an experiment by pulling color tiles from a bag of 4 yellow, 4 blue, 8 red, and 4 green tiles. She made a table of **possible outcomes**, or results that could occur. Included in her table are rows for predicted and actual frequencies.

COLOR-TILE EXPERIMENT				
Possible Outcomes	Yellow	Blue	Red	Green
Predicted Frequency				
Actual Frequency				

There are four possible outcomes for this experiment:

- pulling a yellow tile
- pulling a blue tile
- pulling a red tile
- pulling a green tile

Talk About It Which outcome is most likely to occur? Why?

▶ EXPLORE

MATERIALS: color tiles, bag, marbles

Copy the table above. Predict the number of times each outcome will occur if you pull from the bag 10 times, replacing the tile each time before you pull again. Then test your prediction by pulling from the bag, without looking, 10 times.

Record

Use tally marks to record in your table the results for 10 pulls.

- How did your predictions compare with the results for 10 pulls?

Now, investigate pulling from the bag 50 times.

▶ TRY THIS

Make a new table like the one on page 190. Predict and then use tally marks to record in your table the results for 50 pulls.

1. How did your predictions compare with the results for 50 pulls?
2. **Write About It** Explain why the outcomes that are most likely to occur may not occur most often when you conduct a probability experiment.

Technology Link

You can conduct probability experiments by using E-Lab, Activity 11. Available on CD-ROM and on the Internet at **www.hbschool.com/elab**

▶ PRACTICE

For Problems 3–5, use a bag of marbles like the one shown.

3. Make a table of possible outcomes.
4. Predict and record the number of times you think each outcome will occur if you pull 10 times from the bag and replace before you pull again.
5. Pull from the bag 10 times, replacing the marble after each time. Record the results in the table.

For Problems 6–7, use the table.

MARBLE EXPERIMENT				
Outcome	Blue	Green	Red	Yellow
Frequency	卌 卌 ||	|||	|||	||

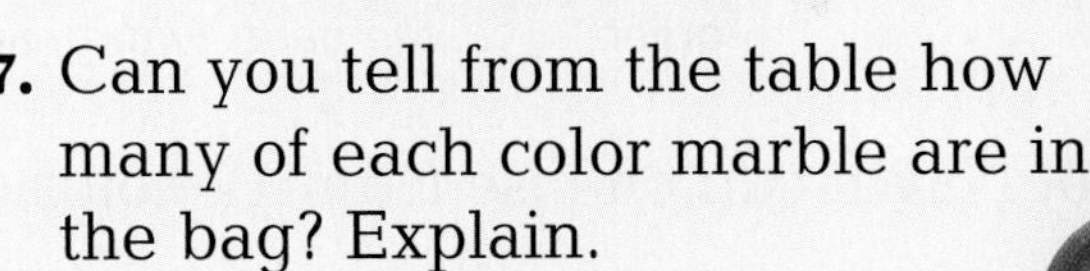

6. Why do you think a blue marble was pulled so often?
7. Can you tell from the table how many of each color marble are in the bag? Explain.

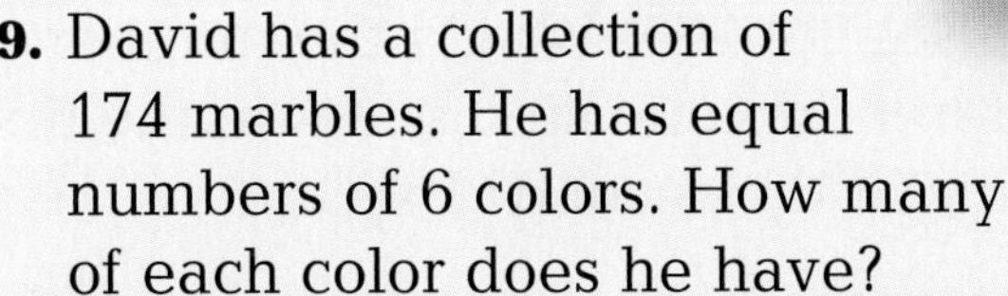

Problem Solving • Mixed Applications

8. **Data** Chris tossed a nickel 10 times. He recorded his outcomes in a table. What are the possible outcomes of this experiment?
9. David has a collection of 174 marbles. He has equal numbers of 6 colors. How many of each color does he have?
10. **Money** Samantha is counting the change in her bank. If she had 4 more nickels, she would have $4.00 in nickels. How many nickels does she have?
11. **Prediction** Felicia has a spinner divided into three equal sections. There are red, blue, and green sections. What would be an impossible event to happen?
12. **Write a problem** about a probability experiment with 24 marbles.

MORE PRACTICE page H90

Recording Outcomes in Tree Diagrams

VOCABULARY
tree diagram

Why learn this? You can use a tree diagram as an organized list of choices, such as what clothes to wear.

Navin needs to choose a pair of pants and a shirt to wear to school. He can choose from blue, black, and tan pants. He can choose from red, white, blue, and green shirts. From how many different color combinations can Navin choose?

How many choices do I have?

You can use a **tree diagram** to show all the possible outcomes of an event.

Pants	Shirts	Choices
blue	red	*blue pants with red shirt*
	white	*blue pants with white shirt*
	blue	*blue pants with blue shirt*
	green	*blue pants with green shirt*
black	red	*black pants with red shirt*
	white	*black pants with white shirt*
	blue	*black pants with blue shirt*
	green	*black pants with green shirt*
tan	red	*tan pants with red shirt*
	white	*tan pants with white shirt*
	blue	*tan pants with blue shirt*
	green	*tan pants with green shirt*

So, Navin can choose from 12 color combinations.

Talk About It

Would the number of choices be different if you listed shirts in the first column and pants in the second? Explain.

- How many choices would Navin have if he could choose from only 3 colors of shirts?

▶ CHECK

Find the number of choices by making a tree diagram.

1. **Peanut Butter and Jelly Sandwiches**
   Peanut Butter: chunky or smooth
   Jelly: grape, strawberry, or blackberry

▶ PRACTICE

Copy and complete the tree diagram. Tell the number of choices.

2. 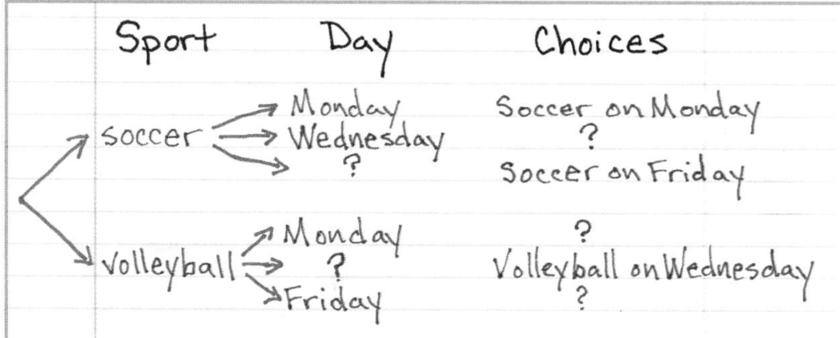

Find the number of choices by making a tree diagram.

3. **Summer School Classes**
   Class: Foreign Language, Computer, Math, or Physical Education
   Session: first or second

4. **Room Decorating Choices**
   Paint: white, yellow, or blue
   Window: curtains or blinds

5. **Garden Choices**
   Type: flower, vegetable, or herb
   Location: front yard, back yard, or side yard

6. **New Car Choices**
   Size: compact, midsize, or minivan
   Color: white, silver, blue, or green

SOCIAL STUDIES LINK

A family tree is a tree diagram that shows an individual's parents, grandparents, great-grandparents, and so on. If George Washington's family tree showed his great-grandparents, how many would there be?

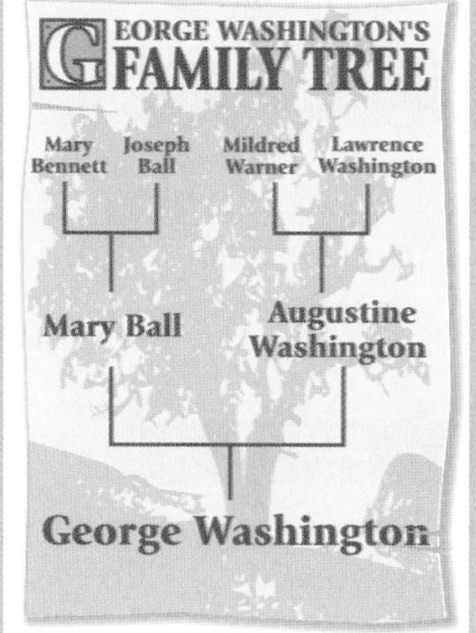

Problem Solving • Mixed Applications

Using Data For Problems 8–10, use the table.

Camera Accessories	
Neck Strap	$ 4.29
Lens Cleaner	$ 3.95
Camera Bag	$14.99
Photo Album	$ 6.99

7. **Consumer** Dana wants to buy a new camera. She can buy an instant camera or a 35-mm camera. She can buy one with or without a zoom lens. List her choices.

8. **Money** Kyle has $25.00. List two combinations of three accessories he has enough money to buy.

9. Jamie wants to buy one of each camera accessory. How much will she spend?

10. **Write a problem** that can be answered by using the information in the table.

LESSON CONTINUES

Problem-Solving Strategy: Make an Organized List

▶ **THE PROBLEM** Kai is conducting a probability experiment. She will toss one number cube and one coin. The number cube has a different number, from 1 through 6, on each face. The coin has heads on one side and tails on the other. How many possible outcomes are there for this experiment? What are the possible outcomes?

UNDERSTAND

- What are you asked to do?
- What information will you use?
- Is there any information you will not use? If so, what?

PLAN

- What strategy can you use to solve the problem?

  You can *make an organized list* of all the possible outcomes.

SOLVE

- How can you use the strategy to solve the problem?

  You can make a tree diagram to organize the possible outcomes.

  So, there are 12 possible outcomes for Kai's experiment. The possible outcomes are shown on the poster.

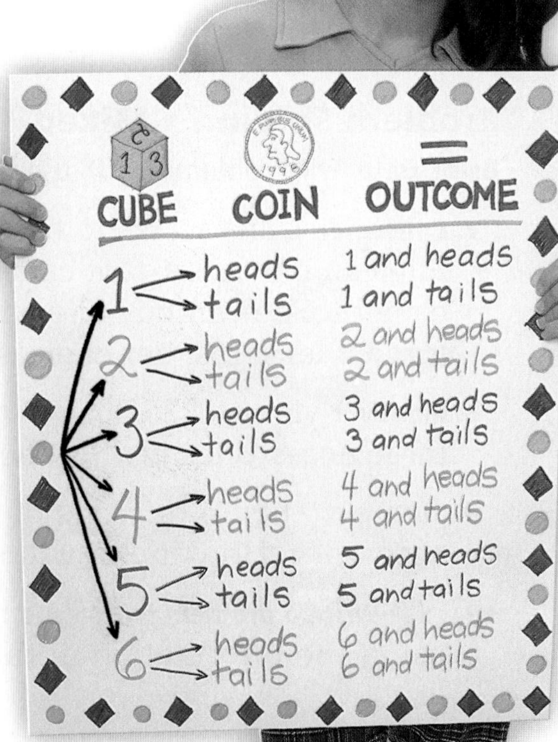

LOOK BACK

- How can you determine if your answer is reasonable?
- What other strategy could you use?

▶ PRACTICE

Make an organized list to solve.

1. Diana is conducting a probability experiment with a spinner and a coin. The spinner is divided into 5 equal sections. Each section is labeled with a different number from 1 through 5. How many possible outcomes are there for this experiment? What are they?

2. Lindsey is conducting a probability experiment by flipping a coin and taking a marble from a bag. There is 1 red, 1 blue, 1 yellow, and 1 green marble in the bag. She will replace the marble after each turn. How many possible outcomes are there for this experiment? What are they?

3. Marshall has 15¢. How many different combinations of coins could he have? What are they?

4. Use the digits 1, 2, and 4. List all the two-digit numbers you can make without repeating any digits in the same number.

Mixed Applications

Solve.

CHOOSE a strategy and a tool.

- Make an Organized List
- Use a Table
- Guess and Check
- Work Backward
- Act It Out

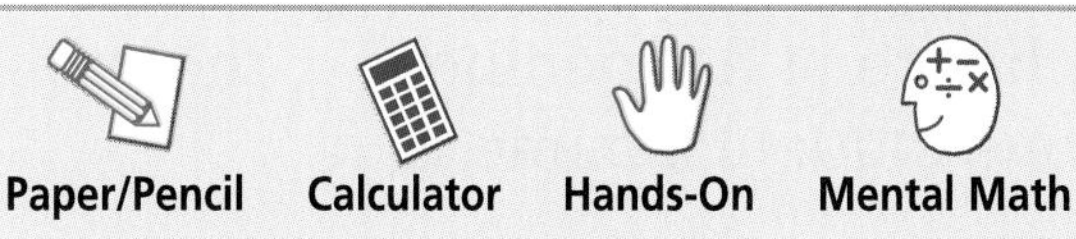

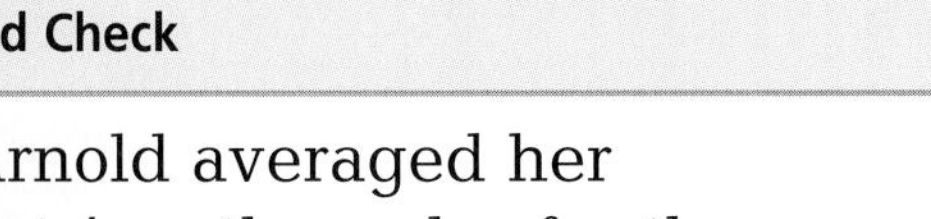

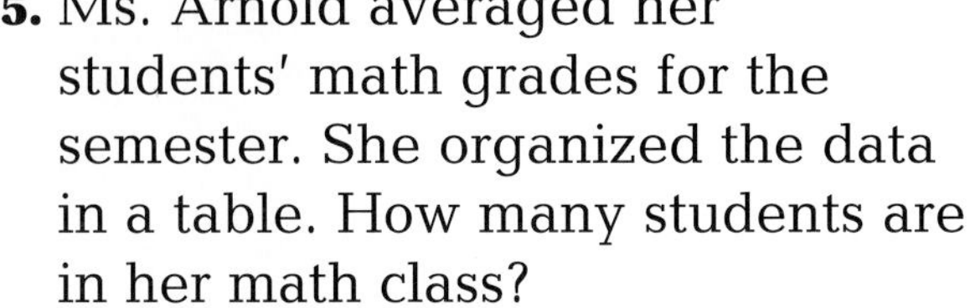

5. Ms. Arnold averaged her students' math grades for the semester. She organized the data in a table. How many students are in her math class?

Math Grades

Number of Students	15	10	4	1
Grade Average	A	B	C	below C

6. Nicole has 6 coins that are dimes and quarters. She has a total of $1.05. What combination of coins does she have?

7. Alexandra has $0.30 more than Barbara. Together they have $4.50. How much money does each girl have?

8. Li was home at 5:15. It took him 35 minutes to ride his bike home from the library. He was at the library for 2 hours 10 minutes. It took him 10 minutes to get from school to the library. At what time did Li leave school?

9. Josh can drink orange juice or grapefruit juice for breakfast. He can eat eggs, cereal, or waffles. From how many different combinations can Josh choose? What are his choices?

10. There are 12 ounces in each can of orange juice. How many ounces are in a case of 24 cans?

MORE PRACTICE page H91

LESSON 4

Finding Probability

Why learn this? You can use probability to predict whether your name will be pulled from a bag containing the names of all the students in your class.

VOCABULARY
probability
equally likely

Mr. Arnaud chooses 1 new student each week to be class secretary. He writes each student's name on an index card, places the cards in a bag, and, without looking, pulls 1 name. Halley wants to be class secretary. There are 25 students in Mr. Arnaud's class. What is the probability that Halley's name will be pulled?

Probability is the chance that an event will happen.

$$\text{Probability} = \frac{\text{number of ways the event occurs}}{\text{number of ways all events can occur}} = \frac{1}{25}$$

So, the probability that Halley's name will be pulled is $\frac{1}{25}$.

Each outcome is **equally likely**, or has the same chance of happening. So, the probability of pulling any one student's name is $\frac{1}{25}$.

The probability of an event occurring can always be expressed as 0, 1, or a fraction between 0 and 1.

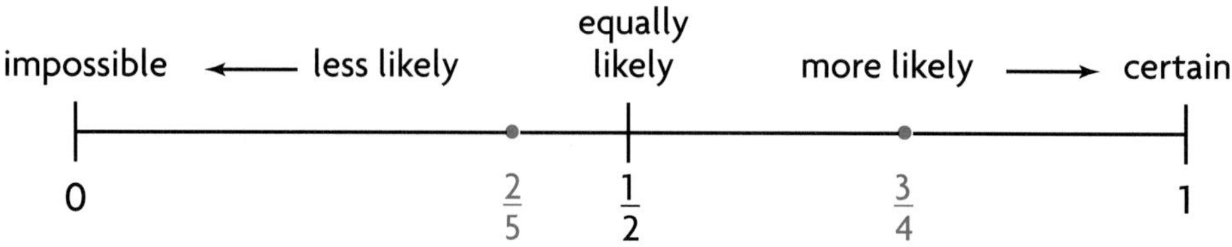

CRITICAL THINKING Which outcome is more likely to occur, that Halley's name will be pulled or that a name other than Halley's will be pulled?

▶ CHECK

1. Which is more likely to occur, an event with a probability of $\frac{2}{5}$ or an event with a probability of $\frac{3}{4}$? Why?
2. Name two equally likely events, using the picture.

▶ PRACTICE

Write a fraction for the probability of spinning each color.

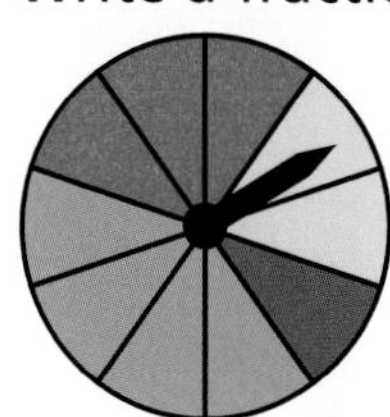

3. red **4.** yellow **5.** green

6. blue **7.** red or yellow **8.** orange

Write the probability of spinning yellow.

9. 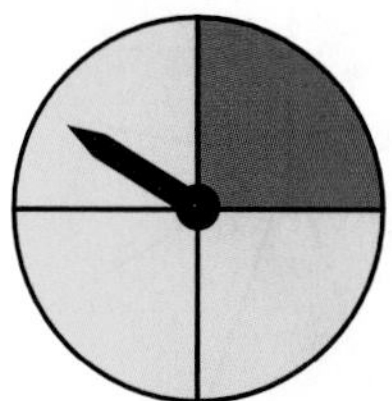 **10.** 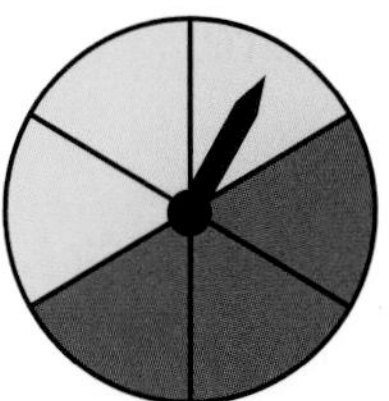 **11.**  **12.** 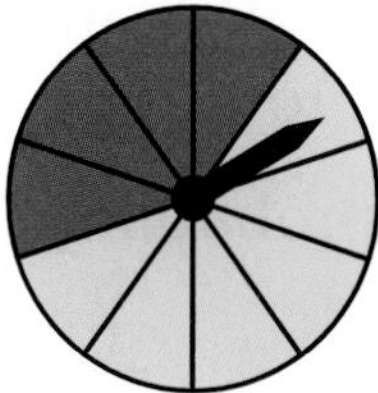

13. On which of the spinners in Exercises 9–12 is yellow most likely to occur?

14. On which of the spinners in Exercises 9–12 is yellow least likely to occur? Why?

Problem Solving • Mixed Applications

15. Sports There are 12 students on Ms. Taylor's basketball team. There are 8 students on Mr. Wang's team. During a game, 5 students on each team play. On which team would you have a better chance of playing?

16. Ben is one of 5 students chosen to read the morning news next week. Each day of the week a different student will have a turn. What is the probability that Ben will read the news on Monday?

17. Money Angelo now has \$4.75. He bought a basketball ticket for \$2.75. He bought a drink for \$0.75 and a taco for \$1.75. How much did he have when he left his house?

18. Write a problem about a spinner with 12 sections and 3 colors.

Mixed Review and Test Prep

Estimate the quotient. (pages 130–131)

19. $17\overline{)163}$ **20.** $58\overline{)305}$ **21.** $27\overline{)219}$ **22.** $49\overline{)389}$ **23.** $76\overline{)560}$

Choose the graph or plot that best displays each set of data. (pages 164–167)

24. class scores on a quiz

A stem-and-leaf plot **B** line graph

C double-bar graph **D** line plot

25. growth of a plant over 6 months

F stem-and-leaf plot **G** line graph

H double-bar graph **J** line plot

MORE PRACTICE page H91

LESSON 5

Comparing Probabilities

Why learn this? You can make decisions based on which events are more likely.

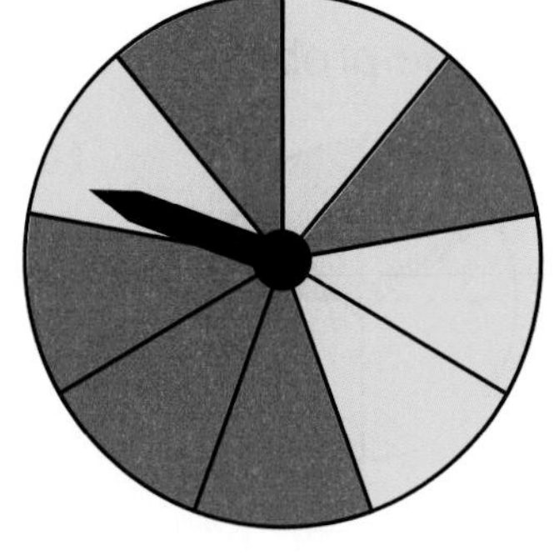

Irene and Mohammed are playing a game, using the spinner at the right. Irene earns a point when the pointer lands on red. Mohammed earns a point when the pointer lands on yellow. Which player is more likely to win the game?

The probability that the pointer will land on red is

$$\frac{\text{number of red sections}}{\text{total number of sections}}, \text{ or } \frac{5}{9}.$$

The probability that the pointer will land on yellow is

$$\frac{\text{number of yellow sections}}{\text{total number of sections}}, \text{ or } \frac{4}{9}.$$

Since $\frac{5}{9} > \frac{4}{9}$, Irene is more likely to win the game.

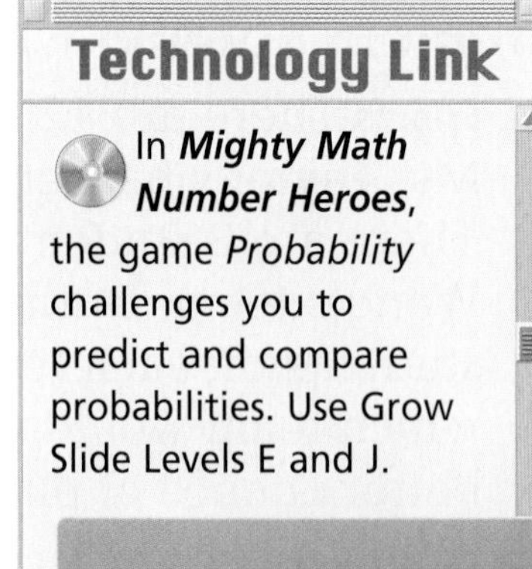

Technology Link

In ***Mighty Math Number Heroes,*** the game *Probability* challenges you to predict and compare probabilities. Use Grow Slide Levels E and J.

Talk About It

Is it certain that Irene will win the game? Explain.

- What is the probability that the pointer will land on blue?
- What is the probability that the pointer will land on either red or yellow?

▶ CHECK

For Problems 1–4, use the spinner. Write each probability as a fraction. Tell which outcome is more likely.

1. The pointer will land on blue; the pointer will land on red.

2. The pointer will land on either blue or green; the pointer will land on either red or yellow.

3. The pointer will land on green; the pointer will land on yellow.

4. The pointer will land on either green or yellow; the pointer will land on either blue or red.

▶ PRACTICE

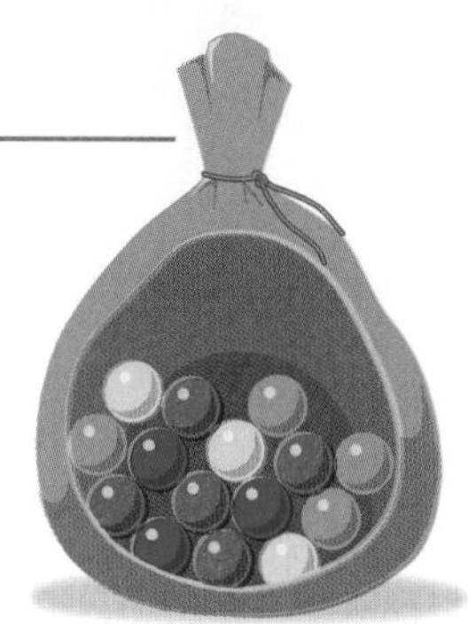

For Problems 5–10, use the bag of marbles. Write each probability as a fraction. Tell which outcome is more likely.

5. You pull a red marble; you pull a blue marble.

6. You pull a yellow marble; you pull a green marble.

7. You pull either a red or blue marble; you pull either a green or yellow marble.

8. You pull a yellow marble; you pull a purple marble.

9. You pull a marble that is not red; you pull a marble that is not yellow.

10. You pull a marble that is not blue; you pull a marble that is not green.

Problem Solving • Mixed Applications

Using Data For Problems 11–14, use the table.

VIDEO GAME SCORES			
Game Number	1	2	3
Player 1	3,076	3,878	2,985
Player 2	2,059	2,880	2,873

11. How many more points in all were scored by Player 1 than by Player 2?

12. Order the scores for Player 2 from the game with the most points to the game with the fewest points.

13. **Reasoning** In which game was Player 1's score greater than 1,000 more points than Player 2?

14. **Write a problem** using the video game scores.

Mixed Review and Test Prep

Divide. Check by multiplying. (pages 136–137)

15. $16\overline{)80}$ **16.** $12\overline{)79}$ **17.** $13\overline{)97}$ **18.** $42\overline{)88}$ **19.** $32\overline{)66}$

20. $21\overline{)531}$ **21.** $19\overline{)610}$ **22.** $39\overline{)822}$ **23.** $18\overline{)757}$ **24.** $41\overline{)965}$

Choose the letter for the correct product. (pages 94–95)

25. $262 \times 32 = n$ **A** 8,384 **B** 7,284 **C** 1,310 **D** 7,384

26. $173 \times 13 = n$ **F** 8,384 **G** 2,249 **H** 1,310 **J** 7,384

27. $203 \times 14 = n$ **A** 2,815 **B** 2,832 **C** 1,015 **D** 2,842

28. $426 \times 32 = n$ **F** 12,532 **G** 13,522 **H** 13,632 **J** 2,120

29. $522 \times 19 = n$ **A** 9,918 **B** 9,908 **C** 9,928 **D** 4,120

MORE PRACTICE page H92

CHAPTER 11 Review/Test

▶ CHECK Understanding

VOCABULARY

1. An event is _?_ if it will always happen. (page 188)

2. An event is _?_ if it will never happen. (page 188)

3. _?_ are results that can occur in an experiment. (page 190)

4. _?_ is the chance that an event will happen. (page 196)

5. You can use a _?_ to show all the possible outcomes of an event. (page 192)

6. Events that are _?_ have the same chance of happening. (page 196)

Write *certain* or *impossible* for each event. (pages 188–189)

7. You are either a boy or a girl.

8. A dog gives birth to kittens.

Write whether each event is *likely* or *unlikely*. (pages 188–189)

9. winning a million dollars

10. having a sunny day in Florida

▶ CHECK Skills

Find the number of choices by making a tree diagram. (pages 192–193)

11. Pizza Choices
Crust: stuffed or plain
Toppings: cheese, meat, veggie, or combo

Write each probability as a fraction. Tell which outcome is more likely. (pages 196–199)

12. You pull a yellow cube; you pull a green cube.

13. You pull a green cube; you pull a blue cube.

▶ CHECK Problem Solving

Solve. (pages 194–195)

CHOOSE a strategy and a tool.

- Make an Organized List
- Guess and Check
- Work Backward
- Act It Out

Paper/Pencil

Calculator

Hands-On

Mental Math

14. Regina is writing a letter. She can write on white, beige, or gray paper. She can use red, blue, or black ink. How many choices does Regina have? What are they?

15. Desmond has 18 more baseball cards than Monty. Together they have 100 baseball cards. How many baseball cards does each boy have?

Test Prep

CUMULATIVE
CHAPTERS 1–11

Choose the best answer.

The graph shows the temperatures recorded for a bowl of ice. Use the graph to answer Questions 1–2.

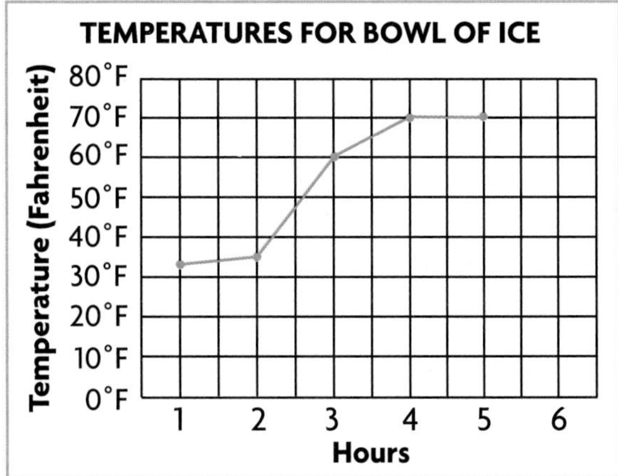

1. What was the difference between the highest and the lowest temperatures?

A 30°

B 35°

C 38°

D 70°

E Not Here

2. Why is a line graph a good choice to display changes in temperature?

F It shows changes over time.

G It compares facts about temperatures.

H It displays fractions of temperatures.

J It compares parts of temperatures to the whole group.

3. Which of the number sentences below is related to $210 - n = 64$?

A $64 + n = 210$ **B** $210 + n = 64$

C $210 - 62 = n$ **D** $210 + 64 = n$

4. Which of the following is a reasonable estimate for the product of 392 and 40?

F 160 **G** 1,500

H 1,600 **J** 16,000

5. What is the area of the figure?

12 cm

135 cm

A 294 sq cm **B** 1,520 sq cm

C 1,620 sq cm **D** 16,200 sq cm

6. Which decimal is equivalent to 3.4?

F 3.1 **G** 3.04

H 3.40 **J** 34.0

7. $72 \div 9 =$

A 7 **B** 8

C 9 **D** 10

8. The cards shown are placed face down.

If you pick 1 card, it is most likely to be a __?__.

F number greater than 20

G 1-digit number

H 2-digit number

J number less than 15

CHAPTERS 9–11

Three M's Game

PURPOSE To practice finding mean, mode, and median

YOU WILL NEED index cards, pencil, calculator

Label two index cards with the same number (the mode). Label the other three cards with different numbers. Find the mean and median of the numbers on your cards. Choose numbers so that the mean, median, and mode are all different. Tell a partner the mean, median, and mode for your set of numbers. Ask your partner to guess the numbers on your cards. Switch roles and play again.

Milk Math

PURPOSE To make a graph

YOU WILL NEED grid paper, pencil

If you were a child in pioneer days, milking a cow would probably be one of your daily chores. Pioneers were lucky to get 21 quarts of milk from a cow each *week*. Today, farmers get about 11 quarts from a cow each *day*.

Make a graph that shows the difference between pioneer days and now.

Figure out how much milk you drink in 1 week. If you were a pioneer, would one cow give you enough milk?

MOMI'S WILD SOCKS

PURPOSE To make an organized list

YOU WILL NEED paper and pencil

Momi has a wild-sock collection. This morning she wanted to pick out a pair of socks to wear to school. Keeping her eyes closed, she picked out 4 socks and said, "I know I have a matching pair." Is she right?

Use the picture. Make an organized list showing all the possible combinations of 4 socks that Momi could have picked out.

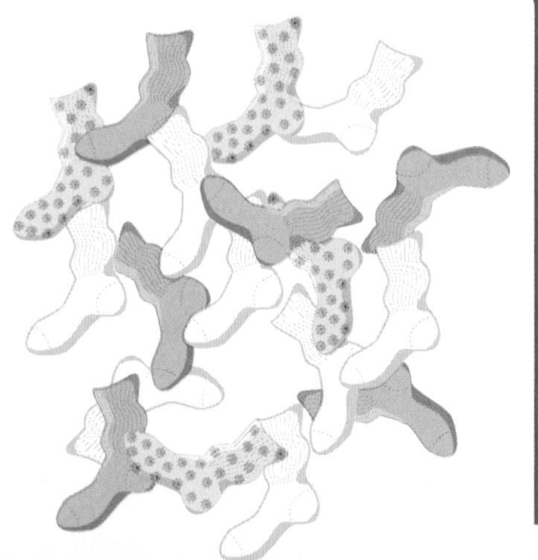

CHAPTERS 9–11

Choosing the Appropriate Graph

VOCABULARY
Data is the information that is displayed in the graph.

What type of graph would best compare the numbers of fourth and fifth graders in each music club activity?

Analyze the **data** to help you decide which type of graph to choose.

MATERIALS: *Graph Links* or other graphing software

Pictographs use pictures to show and compare data.	**Bar and double-bar graphs** use bars to show and compare data.
Line and double-line graphs show changes over time.	**Circle graphs** show how the parts make up the whole.

Data Table

THE 4TH AND 5TH GRADE MUSIC CLUB		
Activities	4th Graders	5th Graders
Singing	5	4
Piano	2	3
Tuba	1	0
Flute	1	1
Guitar	3	4

You can use a graphing program to make a double-bar graph of this data. By using different colors and a key, a double-bar graph helps you compare two sets of data. Begin by entering the data into a table or data center in your graph program. Select all rows to make a double-bar graph.

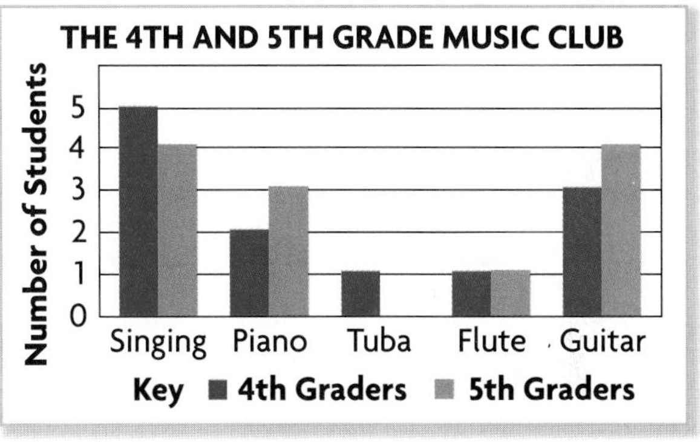

▶ PRACTICE

1. What type of graph would best show membership in the music club over the last 5 years?

2. What type of graph would best show the fraction of fourth graders who play guitar?

Use the table for Problem 3.

3. The number of flute and tuba players in the music club changes each year. Make a graph to show these changes.

FLUTE AND TUBA PLAYERS: 1992–1996					
Instrument	1992	1993	1994	1995	1996
Flute	1	3	4	3	2
Tuba	5	6	4	3	1

4. **Using the Computer** Of the students in the math club, 4 girls and 1 boy play piano, 1 girl and 1 boy play flute, and 2 girls and 5 boys play guitar. Make a graph to show the data.

CHAPTERS 9–11

Study Guide and Review

Vocabulary Check

Choose a term from the box to complete each sentence.

VOCABULARY
interval
mean
median
possible outcomes
probability

1. The middle number in an ordered series of numbers is called the ? . (page 155)
2. One number that represents all the numbers in a set of data is that set's ? , or average. (page 156)
3. The distance between the numbers on the scale of a graph is called the ? . (page 158)
4. Results that could occur in an experiment are called ? . (page 190)
5. The chance that an event will happen is that event's ? . (page 196)

Study and Solve

CHAPTER 9

EXAMPLE

Find the mean of the set of data.

75, 82, 85, 90 — Add the numbers.
The sum is 332. — Divide this sum by the number of data in the set.
$332 \div 4 = 83$
The mean is 83.

Find the mean, median, mode, and range for the set of data. (pages 154–157, 162)

6. 34, 24, 21, 21, 25
7. 19, 26, 8, 4, 4, 20, 10

On a line-graph scale, what is the best interval for each set of data? (pages 158–161)

a. 2 **b.** 10 **c.** 25 **d.** 5

8. 50, 25, 100, 75
9. 8, 12, 6, 10, 16

Choose a graph or plot to display the set of data. Explain your choice. (pages 164–165)

10. ages of your classmates' parents
11. temperatures in several cities

Choose a graph or plot to display the data. Explain your choice. Solve. (pages 166–167)

12. Gas prices per gallon were $1.19 in May, $1.24 in June, $1.25 in July, and $1.27 in August. Tell what happened to the price of gas during these months.
13. Nadia surveyed the fifth grade to find out what food to have at the school dance. Of the students, 75 said pizza, 30 said chicken, and 45 said hamburgers. How many more students said pizza than hamburgers?

CHAPTER 10

EXAMPLE

Use the circle graph to answer the question.

What does the whole circle represent?

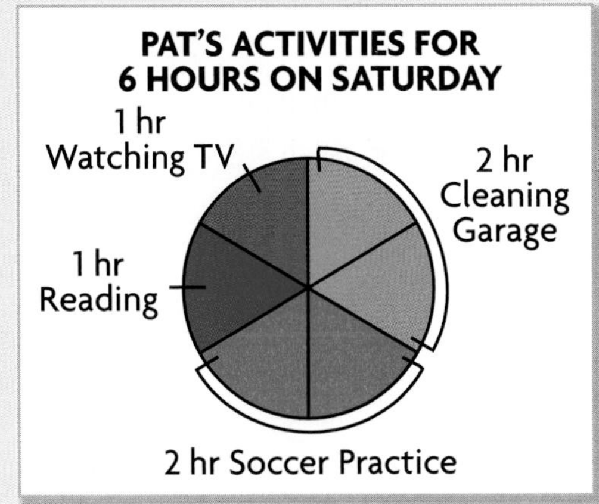

Study the graph and read its title.

The graph shows Pat's activities for 6 hours on Saturday.

For Problems 14–16, use the circle graph above. (pages 172–173)

14. What fraction of her time did Pat spend at soccer practice?

15. Compare the amount of time Pat spent playing soccer to the time she spent reading.

16. How would the graph look if Pat spent 2 hours reading and did not watch TV?

Make a circle graph for the data in the table. (pages 174–177)

17.

$10 SPENT AT THE FAIR	
Rides	$4
Food	$3
Souvenirs	$2
Games	$1

Explain why the circle graph is not accurate. (pages 178–179)

18.

FAVORITE SUBJECTS OF 10 STUDENTS		
Subject	Number of Students	Decimal Part
Math	5	0.5
Science	3	0.3
History	2	0.2

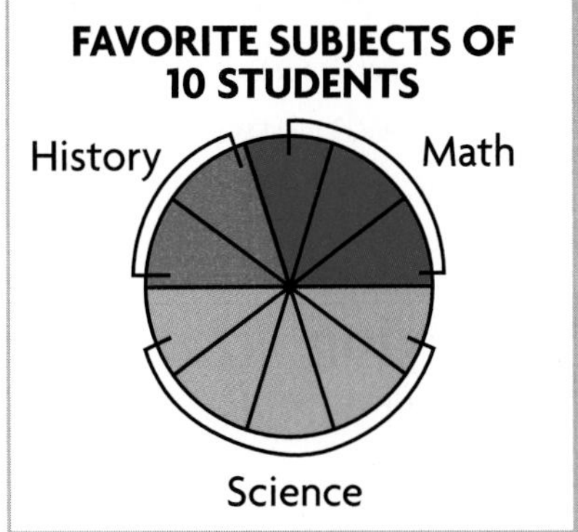

CHAPTER 11

EXAMPLE

Use the spinner.
Write the probability as a fraction.

You will spin yellow.

Only 1 of 10 sections is yellow.

The probability is $\frac{1}{10}$.

Use the spinner above. Write each probability as a fraction. Tell which outcome is more likely. (pages 196–199)

19. You spin green; you spin blue.

Make an organized list to solve. (pages 194–195)

20. Yasmin has green and blue shoes. She has red, pink, and orange socks. How many combinations of shoes and socks can she make?

CHAPTERS 9–11

Performance Assessment

Tasks: Show What You Know

1. Use connecting cubes to help you find the mean for this set of data: 3, 8, 4, 5, 5. Explain each step. (pages 156–157)

2. Explain why the graph is not accurate and how you would change the graph to make it accurate. (pages 178–179)

Beth's Trophy Collection	
Soccer	4
Softball	2
Basketball	1
Swimming	3

3. Explain each step as you make a tree diagram to show the number of different color combinations Megan has if she can choose from blue, brown, and green shorts and from white, yellow, red, and black tops. (pages 192–193)

Problem Solving

Solve. Explain your method.

CHOOSE a strategy and a tool.

- Make an Organized List
- Make a Model
- Make a Graph
- Write a Number Sentence

Paper/Pencil

Calculator

Hands-On

Mental Math

4. Walter surveyed 50 boys and 50 girls to find out their favorite sports. He organized his data in the table. How can you display Walter's data? Explain. (pages 166–167)

FAVORITE SPORTS OF BOYS AND GIRLS			
	Basketball	Gymnastics	Soccer
Boys	25	10	15
Girls	10	25	15

5. Claudia surveyed 40 students about their favorite types of music. Twenty students chose rock music, 10 chose country, 5 chose jazz, and 5 chose classical. What fraction chose country? Make a graph that displays the results of the survey. (pages 182–183)

6. Ruth wants to buy a drink from a vending machine for $0.55. The machine accepts exact change only (no pennies). How many different combinations of coins could she use to buy her drink? (pages 194–195)

Cumulative Review

CHAPTERS 1–11

Solve the problem. Then write the letter of the correct answer.

1. Which is another name for twenty and five hundredths?

   A. 20.005 B. 20.05
   C. 20.5 D. 20,500

   (pages 36–41)

2. 563×72

   A. 1,126
   B. 4,536
   C. 39,410
   D. 40,536

   (pages 94–95)

3. Estimate the quotient. (pages 112–117)

   $9\overline{)449}$

   A. 45 B. 49 r8
   C. 50 D. 60

4. $6{,}000 \div 50 = n$

   A. $n = 12$ B. $n = 100$ r10
   C. $n = 120$ D. $n = 300{,}000$

   (pages 128–129)

5. Find the mean. (pages 156–157)

   44, 34, 31, 31, 35

   A. 13 B. 31
   C. 34 D. 35

For Problems 6–7, use the circle graph.
(pages 172–173)

6. What fraction of the money was spent on books?

   A. $\frac{1}{8}$ B. $\frac{2}{8}$, or $\frac{1}{4}$
   C. $\frac{2}{4}$, or $\frac{1}{2}$ D. 4

   (pages 172–173)

7. What does each $\frac{1}{4}$ of the graph represent?

   A. $1 spent B. $2 spent
   C. $4 spent D. $8 spent

   (pages 172–173)

For Problems 8–10, use the spinner.
(pages 188–189, 196–199)

8. What is the probability of spinning 6?

   A. $\frac{1}{10}$ B. $\frac{2}{10}$, or $\frac{1}{5}$
   C. $\frac{5}{10}$, or $\frac{1}{2}$ D. $\frac{6}{10}$, or $\frac{3}{5}$

9. It is __?__ that you will spin an even number.

   A. certain B. impossible
   C. likely D. unlikely

   (pages 188–189)

10. The probability of spinning 4 is __?__ the probability of spinning 5.

    A. equal to
    B. more likely than
    C. less likely than
    D. impossible, and so is

    (pages 198–199)

12 MULTIPLYING DECIMALS

SPORTS LINK

Some sports equipment has changed over the years. Basketball was invented in 1891. Players shot the ball into a closed-bottom peach basket, which gave the new sport its name.

A Matter of Dollars and Sense

Suppose your fifth-grade class has been given $100 to buy new sports equipment, such as basketballs, a stopwatch, and badminton sets.

Plan a budget. Make a chart showing your budget. Tell how you decided what your class should buy.

- List the sports your class likes to play.
- List the equipment needed for each.
- Decide how many of each item you need and the total cost.
- Keep your choice of equipment within the budget limit of $100.

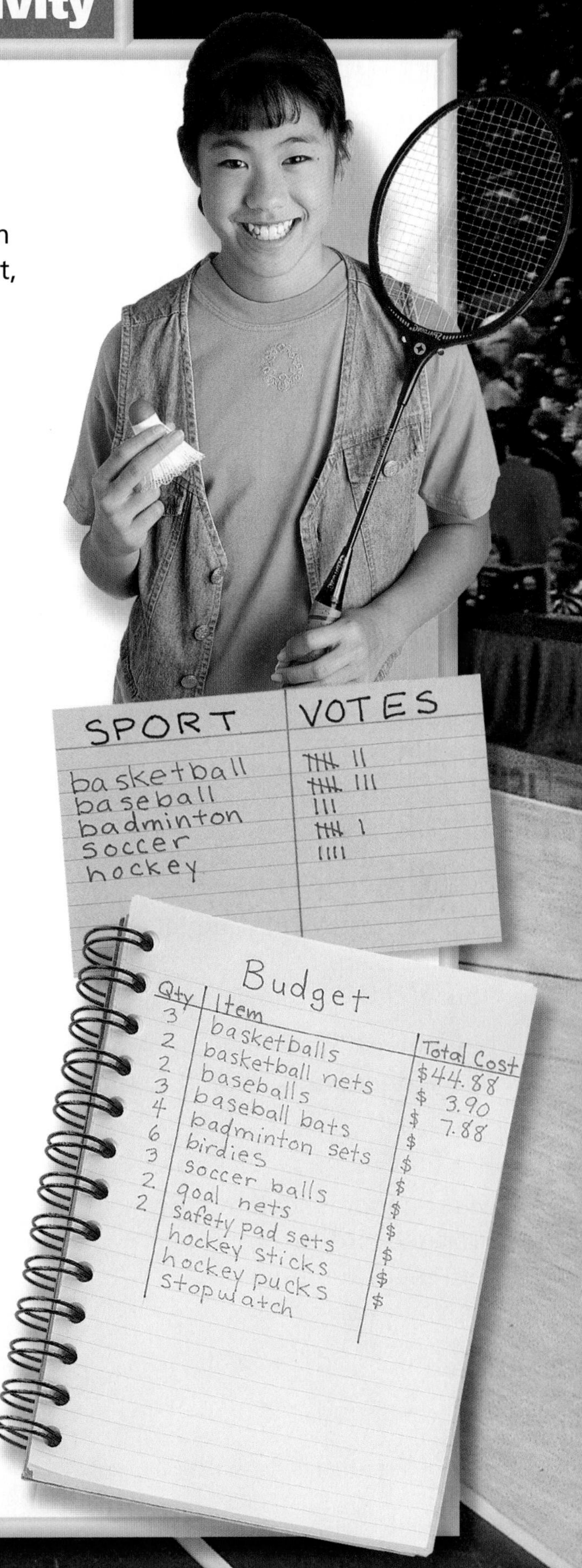

DID YOU

- ✓ list your class's favorite sports?
- ✓ decide what equipment and how many of each item your class needs?
- ✓ find the total cost of the purchases?
- ✓ make choices based on the budget limit of $100?

LESSON 1 • HANDS-ON LESSON

Multiplying Decimals and Whole Numbers

You will investigate how the factors and the product are related when you multiply a decimal and a whole number.

▶ EXPLORE

Make models that show how to multiply 2 × 0.9 and 2 × 0.09.

MATERIALS: tenths and hundredths decimal models, markers, scissors, and tape or paste

MODEL

What is 2 × 0.9?

Step 1

Shade 0.9 of each of the two models.

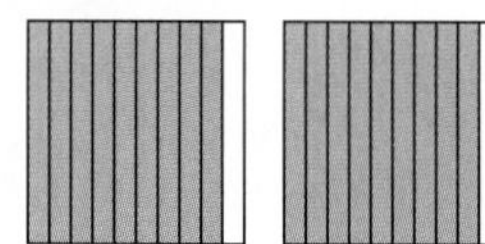

Step 2

Combine the shaded areas of the two models.

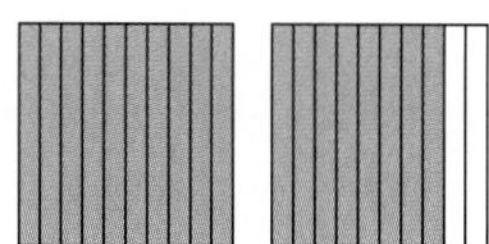

REMEMBER:

This model represents a whole divided into *tenths*. Each part is $\frac{1}{10}$, or 0.1.

This model represents a whole divided into *hundredths*. Each part is $\frac{1}{100}$, or 0.01.

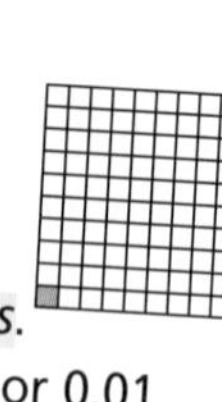

Record

Tape or paste your models to a piece of paper. Record a multiplication number sentence for each of your models.

Now investigate how the product of a whole number and a decimal is related to the whole number factor.

▶ TRY THIS

Make models to show the products. Record number sentences for each of your models.

1. 2 × 0.3 and 2 × 0.30

2. 3 × 0.5 and 3 × 0.50

3. 4 × 0.4 and 4 × 0.40

4. Look at your models and products. How does the product of a decimal less than one and a whole number relate to the whole number factor?

5. **Write About It** Explain how to draw a model to find the product 6×0.35.

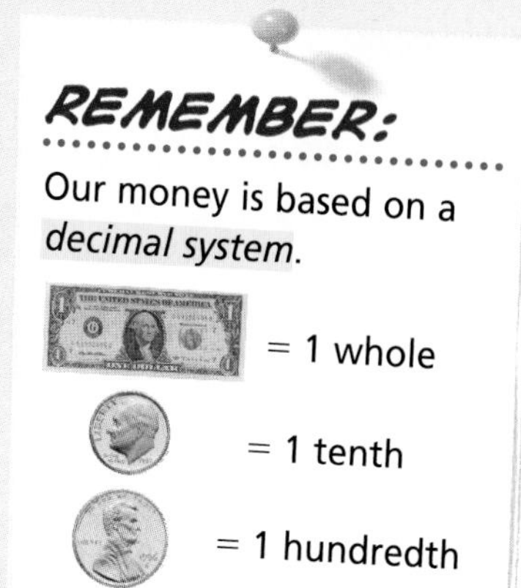

▶ PRACTICE

Make a model to find each product.

6. $2 \times 0.7 = n$ 7. $5 \times 0.5 = n$ 8. $4 \times 0.26 = n$

9. $3 \times 0.23 = n$ 10. $2 \times 0.7 = n$ 11. $5 \times 0.16 = n$

Marcia is shopping at the school store.
For Problems 12–18, use the picture.

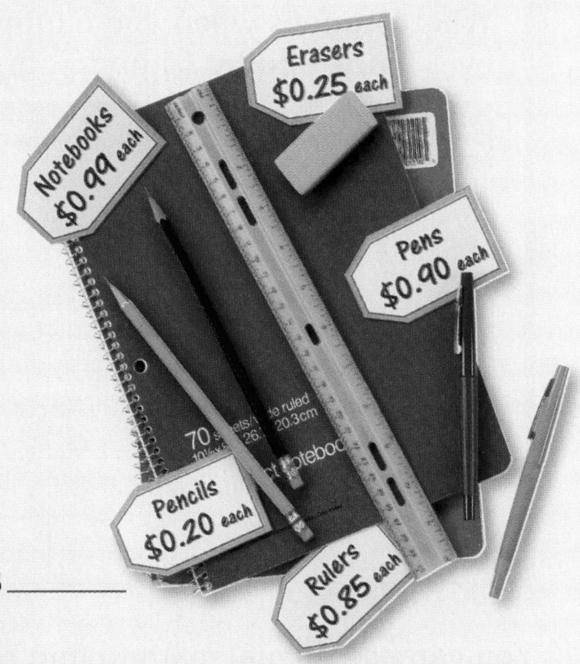

12. 3 pencils, 1 eraser
13. 2 erasers, 2 pens
14. 3 notebooks
15. 1 pencil, 4 erasers, 2 rulers
16. 8 erasers, 2 notebooks, 3 pencils
17. 3 pens, 1 notebook
18. 5 notebooks, 5 pens, 5 rulers

Problem Solving • Mixed Applications

Using Data For Problems 19–20, use the picture.

19. **Consumer** Laura is shopping at the school store. Which costs more—3 pens, or 2 pens and a notebook? 3 rulers, or 2 notebooks and a pen?

20. **Reasoning** Nat spent $2.48 to buy four items from the school store. Which items did he buy?

21. **Number Sense** Jason has $13.00. He is ordering a cheese pizza for $9.99. Additional toppings cost $0.55 each. Does Jason have enough money to order 3 extra toppings on the pizza? If so, how much change will Jason receive?

22. **Money** Carol has $0.75. She has 5 coins. What are the coins?

23. **Reasoning** Suppose Babs wants to buy 3 pens for $0.90 each. She has $3.00. Does she have enough to make the purchase? Explain.

Technology Link

You can multiply decimals by using E-Lab, Activity 12. Available on CD-ROM and on the Internet at **www.hbschool.com/elab**

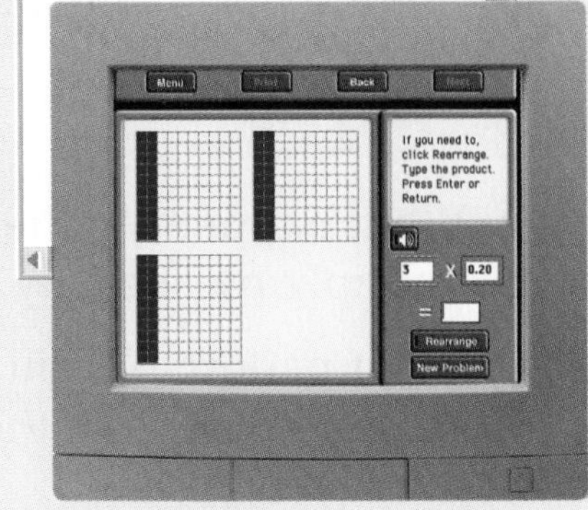

MORE PRACTICE page H92

LESSON 2

Patterns in Decimal Factors and Products

Why learn this? You can figure out how dollars relate to dimes and pennies.

Another way to find products is to look for patterns.

MODEL

What happens when you multiply 2 by 1, by 1 tenth, and by 1 hundredth?

Ones	Tenths	Hundredths	Record
(2 ones blocks)			2 × 1 = 2
	(2 tenths blocks)		2 × 0.1 = 0.2
		(2 hundredths blocks)	2 × 0.01 = 0.02

REMEMBER:

When using base-ten blocks to model decimals, let [cube] equal one whole, or 1.

You can use mental math to find patterns in products. Look for patterns in the placement of the decimal point.

10 × 1 = 10	20 × 1 = 20	1 × 25 = 25
10 × 0.1 = 1.0	20 × 0.1 = 2.0	0.1 × 25 = 2.5
10 × 0.01 = 0.10	20 × 0.01 = 0.20	0.01 × 25 = 0.25

CRITICAL THINKING How can you use the pattern to place the decimal point in the product?

SCIENCE LINK

Numerous patterns can be found in nature. The chambered nautilus, for example, has a pattern that decreases in size. How is that pattern similar to the pattern shown in the model?

▶ CHECK

1. What happens to the size of the block as you multiply by ones, by tenths, and by hundredths?
2. What pattern do you notice in the placement of the decimal point and the number of zeros in the products?

▶ PRACTICE

Record the decimal multiplication sentences for each.

3.

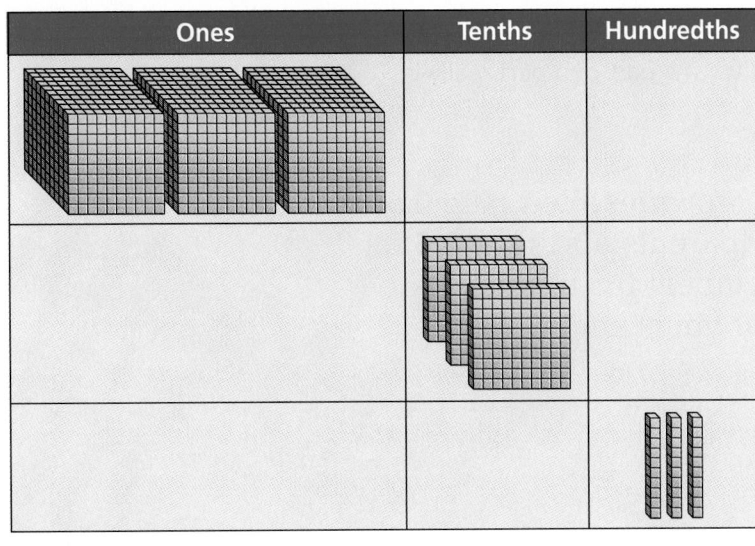

Record

? × ? = ?

? × ? = ?

? × ? = ?

Draw models to find each product.

4. $1 \times 5 = n$
$0.1 \times 5 = n$
$0.01 \times 5 = n$

5. $2 \times 3 = n$
$2 \times 0.3 = n$
$2 \times 0.03 = n$

6. $4 \times 2 = n$
$4 \times 0.2 = n$
$4 \times 0.02 = n$

7. $3 \times 3 = n$
$3 \times 0.3 = n$
$3 \times 0.03 = n$

Use mental math to complete the pattern.

8. $1 \times 8 = 8$
$0.1 \times 8 = 0.8$
$0.01 \times 8 = n$

9. $1 \times 40 = 40$
$0.1 \times 40 = n$
$0.01 \times 40 = 0.4$

10. $1 \times 85 = 85$
$0.1 \times 85 = n$
$0.01 \times 85 = n$

11. $18 \times 1 = 18$
$18 \times 0.1 = n$
$18 \times 0.01 = n$

12. $19 \times 1 = n$
$19 \times 0.1 = n$
$19 \times 0.01 = n$

13. $50 \times 1 = n$
$50 \times 0.1 = n$
$50 \times 0.01 = n$

14. $102 \times 1 = n$
$102 \times 0.1 = n$
$102 \times 0.01 = n$

15. $210 \times 1 = n$
$210 \times 0.1 = n$
$210 \times 0.01 = n$

Problem Solving • Mixed Applications

16. Patterns A penny is 0.01 of a dollar. How much is a roll of 50 pennies? 2 rolls of 50 pennies?

17. A dime is 0.10 and a nickel is 0.05 of a dollar. How much is a roll of 50 dimes? a roll of 40 nickels?

Mixed Review and Test Prep

Write <, >, or = for each ●. (pages 44–45)

18. 5.00 ● 5.05 **19.** 0.07 ● 0.007 **20.** 6.72 ● 6.27 **21.** 1.20 ● 1.2

Choose the letter of the correct sum. (pages 52–53)

22. $\begin{array}{r} 2.3 \\ +3.2 \\ \hline \end{array}$ **A** 0.55 **B** 5.5 **C** 55.0 **D** 0.055

23. $\begin{array}{r} 0.795 \\ +4.073 \\ \hline \end{array}$ **F** 4.768 **G** 4.868 **H** 5.565 **J** 12.023

Multiplying a Decimal by a Decimal

Why learn this? You can understand what a part of a part really is, such as a part of some leftover brownies.

Suppose you baked a pan of brownies. You give 0.5 of the brownies to your grandparents and save 0.5 for you and your own family. If you eat 0.5 of the saved brownies, how much is left for your family?

MODEL

What is 0.5 of 0.5?

Step 1

Divide the square into 10 equal columns. Shade **5 of the columns, or 0.5.**

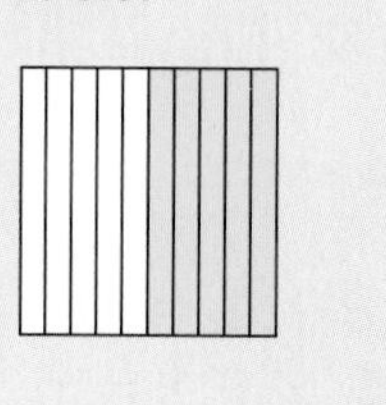

Step 2

Divide the square into 10 equal rows, or 100 equal parts. Shade **5 of the rows, or 0.5.**

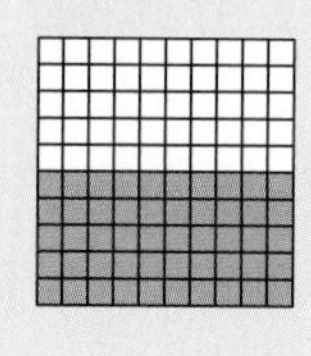

Step 3

The area in which the shading overlaps shows the product, or 0.5 of 0.5.

Record: **0.5 × 0.5 = 0.25,** or 25 hundredths.

So, 0.25, or $\frac{1}{4}$ of the brownies, are left for your family.

▶ CHECK

1. Jill and Jon made models to show 0.6×0.8. How are their models different? How are they alike?

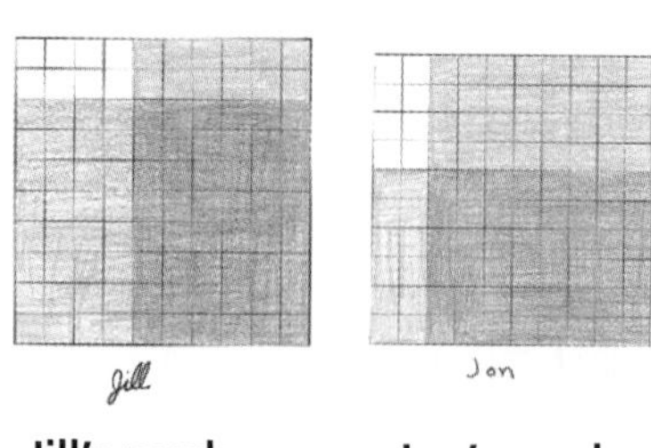

Jill's work Jon's work

2. Make a table like the one below. Make up three other decimal multiplication problems with factors less than 1.

factors less than 1	Product	Is the product less than 1?	Is the product less than each factor?
0.6×0.8	0.48	yes	yes

3. What relationship between the decimal factors and the products do you see?

▶ PRACTICE

Complete the multiplication number sentence for each drawing.

4. 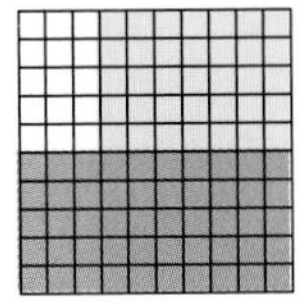

$0.5 \times 0.7 = n$

5. 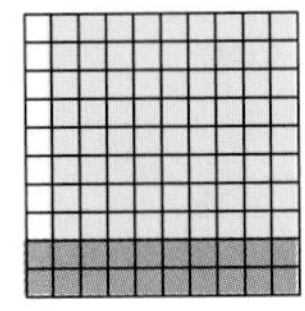

$n \times 0.9 = 0.18$

6. 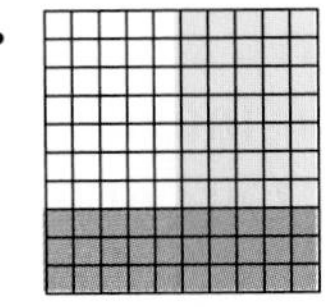

$0.3 \times 0.5 = n$

7.

$n \times 0.8 = 0.24$

8. 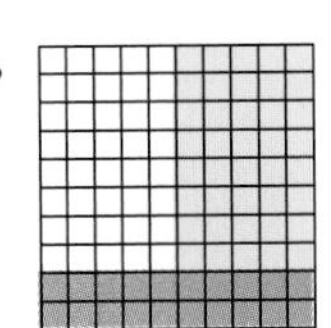

$0.2 \times n = 0.10$

9. 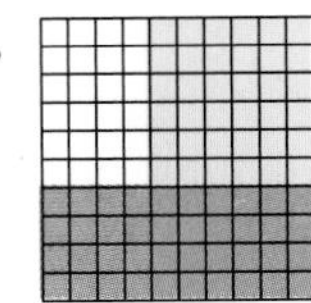

$0.4 \times 0.6 = n$

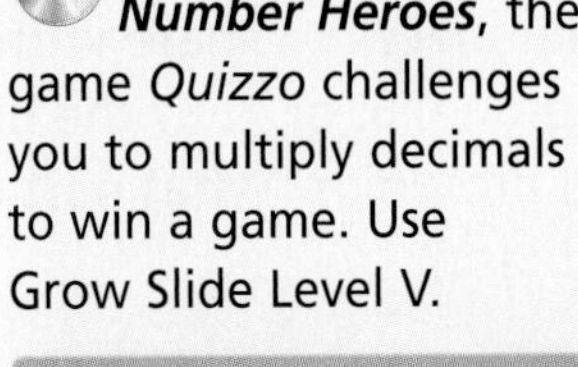

Technology Link

In ***Mighty Math Number Heroes***, the game *Quizzo* challenges you to multiply decimals to win a game. Use Grow Slide Level V.

Multiply. Write each product.

10. $0.7 \times 0.2 = n$ **11.** $0.8 \times 0.8 = n$ **12.** $0.9 \times 0.5 = n$

13. $0.6 \times 0.7 = n$ **14.** $0.5 \times 0.8 = n$ **15.** $0.3 \times 0.9 = n$

16. $0.1 \times 0.3 = n$ **17.** $0.4 \times 0.6 = n$ **18.** $0.6 \times 0.5 = n$

19. $0.4 \times 0.8 = n$ **20.** $0.9 \times 0.8 = n$ **21.** $0.8 \times 0.7 = n$

22. **Write About It** When you multiply tenths times tenths, why does the model show the product as hundredths?

Problem Solving • Mixed Applications

23. **Consumer** Suppose you order a ten-slice pizza. You want 0.5 of the pizza with olives and 0.5 with mushrooms. If 0.8 of the mushroom part includes pepperoni, what part of the pizza has pepperoni and mushrooms?

24. Suppose you may eat 0.4 of the 0.5 brownies that are left. How much can you eat?

25. **Money** Teresa earns $18.75 each day at her job. How much does she earn in 10 days?

26. **Measurement** Mrs. Sander's new car can travel 34.6 miles on a gallon of gas. How far can the car travel on 9 gallons?

27. **Money** Felipe likes to collect postcards. He pays $1.00 for each set of 4 postcards and $0.30 for each additional postcard. How much will Felipe pay for 15 postcards?

Problem-Solving Strategy: Make a Model

▶ THE PROBLEM Suppose you cut a pan of brownies into ten equal pieces to share with 4 of your friends. You put chocolate icing on 0.5, or $\frac{1}{2}$, of the brownies. You put pecans on 0.2 of the iced brownies. What part of the brownies have icing and pecans on them?

REMEMBER:

UNDERSTAND

PLAN

SOLVE

LOOK BACK

UNDERSTAND

- What are you asked to find?
- What information did you use?
- Was there information you did not use? If so, what?

PLAN

- What strategy can you use to solve the problem?

  You can *make a model* to find the part of the brownies that has icing and pecans on them.

SOLVE

- How can you solve the problem?

  You can make a model to find 0.2×0.5.

  Shade 0.5 ($\frac{5}{10}$), or $\frac{1}{2}$, of the columns.

  Then shade 0.2 ($\frac{2}{10}$), or $\frac{1}{5}$, of the rows.

  The product, 0.10, or $\frac{10}{100}$ ($\frac{1}{10}$), is represented by the overlap.

  So, 0.10, or $\frac{1}{10}$, of the brownies have icing and pecans on them.

LOOK BACK

- How did you determine if your answer is reasonable?
- What other strategy could you use?

▶ PRACTICE

Make a model to solve.

1. Suppose you cut a loaf of bread into 10 slices. You put jelly on 0.8 of the slices and peanut butter on 0.5 of the jelly slices. What part of the loaf has peanut butter and jelly?

2. Lee sold school newspapers. She collected $2.50 in coins. If she had 3 nickels, twice as many dimes as nickels, and the rest in quarters, how many of each coin did she have?

3. If 2 people can be seated on each side of a square table, how many people can be seated at 12 square tables that are pushed together end to end to form a rectangle?

4. The five planets closest to the sun are Earth, Venus, Mars, Mercury, and Jupiter. Earth is between Venus and Mars. Mercury is between Venus and the sun. Which of these planets is next to Jupiter?

Mixed Applications

Solve.

CHOOSE a strategy and a tool.

- Work Backward
- Make a Table
- Find a Pattern
- Make a Model
- Write a Number Sentence

Paper/Pencil

Calculator

Hands-On

Mental Math

5. Marta iced 0.6 of the cake with vanilla icing. She put sprinkles on 0.5 of the iced cake. What part of the cake has sprinkles on the icing?

6. Gina feeds each of her 3 cats 0.35 pound of cat food a day. How many pounds of cat food does Gina need for a week?

7. Sammy has 140 papers to deliver. If he can deliver 10 papers in 5 minutes, how long will it take him to deliver all the papers?

8. Ralph buys a package of meat that weighs 4 pounds and costs $2.65 per pound. How much change will he receive from $20.00?

9. Look at the diagram. Each cube is equal to the product of the two cubes directly below it. What are the values for yellow, purple, and orange?

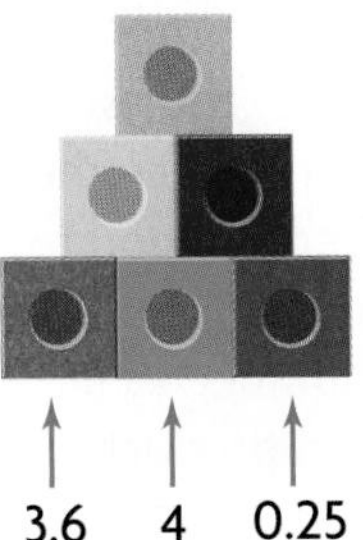

10. Paco recorded money spent for meals on his weekend trip. On Friday, he spent $5.35, $5.89, and $6.75. On Saturday, he spent $2.98, $6.27, and $7.94. On Sunday, he spent $3.00, $4.58, and $7.75. On which day did he spend the most for meals?

11. Pearl earned $38.50 per week for 3 weeks. She put $22.00 a week in her savings account. How much did she keep to spend?

MORE PRACTICE page H93

LESSON 4 • PART 1

Placing the Decimal Point

Why learn this? You can decide whether your answers make sense when you are measuring the mass of an object, such as a pumpkin.

Suppose you have a pumpkin that has a mass of 4.8 kg. You know that almost 0.9 of its mass is water. How much of the pumpkin's mass is water?

You can estimate the product of 4.8×0.9 to decide about how much of the pumpkin's mass is water.

Estimate. $5 \times 1 = 5$

Is it reasonable that the mass of water in a pumpkin is 4.32 kg?

Talk About It

- How can estimation help you solve the problem?
- Is the mass of water in the pumpkin 4.32 kg or 43.2 kg? How do you know?
- What strategy did you use to determine where to place the decimal point?

Estimation or patterns can help you place the decimal point in a product.

MODEL

Use estimation to find 0.6×26.

Step 1

Estimate the product.

Think: 0.6 is close to $\frac{1}{2}$.

$$0.6 \times 26$$
$$\downarrow \quad\quad \downarrow$$
$$\frac{1}{2} \times 26 = 13$$

Step 2

Multiply as with whole numbers.

$$\begin{array}{r} {}^{3} \\ 26 \\ \times 0.6 \\ \hline 156 \end{array}$$

Step 3

Use the estimate to place the decimal point in the product.

$$\begin{array}{r} {}^{3} \\ 26 \\ \times 0.6 \\ \hline 15.6 \end{array}$$

Since the estimate is 13, place the decimal point so there is a whole number 15 in the product.

REMEMBER:

A *number line* can help you estimate by rounding to 0, $\frac{1}{2}$, or 1.

Example:

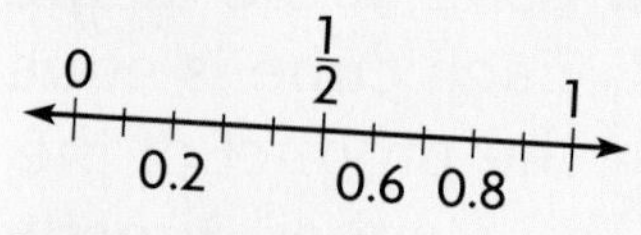

0.2 rounds to 0.

0.6 rounds to $\frac{1}{2}$.

0.8 rounds to 1.

CRITICAL THINKING How does the estimate help you place the decimal point in the product?

EXAMPLES

A Find $65 \times \$0.90$.

Estimate. $65 \times \$1 = \$65$

$$\begin{array}{r} \$0.90 \\ \times \quad 65 \\ \hline 450 \\ +5400 \\ \hline \$58.50 \end{array}$$

Since the estimate is 65, place the decimal point so there is a whole number 58.

B Find 21×0.48.

Estimate. $20 \times 0.5 = 10$

$$\begin{array}{r} 0.48 \\ \times \quad 21 \\ \hline 48 \\ +960 \\ \hline 10.08 \end{array}$$

Since the estimate is 10, place the decimal point so there is a whole number 10.

Look for a pattern in the placement of the decimal point in each product. A decimal such as 0.0001 is called one ten-thousandth. It is $\frac{1}{10}$ of one thousandth.

Number Sentence	Factors	Product
$0.6 \times 0.3 = 0.18$	tenths × tenths	hundredths
$0.6 \times 0.03 = 0.018$	tenths × hundredths	thousandths
$0.06 \times 0.03 = 0.0018$	hundredths × hundredths	ten-thousandths
$0.6 \times 0.003 = 0.0018$	tenths × thousandths	ten-thousandths

CHECK

Choose the best estimate. Write *a* or *b*.

1. $19 \times 0.3 \approx n$ **a.** 6 **b.** 60

2. $41 \times 0.5 \approx n$ **a.** 2 **b.** 20

3. $\$0.10 \times 7 \approx n$ **a.** \$0.07 **b.** \$0.70

Estimate.

4. $29 \times 0.2 \approx n$ **5.** $0.7 \times 18 \approx n$ **6.** $37 \times 0.8 \approx n$

7. $16 \times 0.8 \approx n$ **8.** $0.6 \times 24 \approx n$ **9.** $0.4 \times 42 \approx n$

Use estimation and patterns to place the decimal point in each product.

10. $3.8 \times 6 = 228$ **11.** $0.38 \times 6 = 228$ **12.** $38 \times 6 = 228$ **13.** $38 \times 0.06 = 228$

14. $38 \times 0.6 = 228$ **15.** $3.8 \times 0.6 = 228$ **16.** $0.38 \times 0.6 = 228$ **17.** $3.8 \times 0.06 = 228$

18. **Write About It** In the chart above, what relationship do you see between the number of decimal places in the product and the total number of decimal places in the factors?

HEALTH LINK

Did you know that you should drink about 64 ounces of water a day? You get some of the water you need from fruits and vegetables. How many 8-ounce glasses of water would you need to drink to get 64 ounces?

▶ PRACTICE

Choose the best estimate. Write *a*, *b*, or *c*.

19. $21 \times 0.2 \approx n$ **a.** 4 **b.** 40 **c.** 45

20. $48 \times 0.5 \approx n$ **a.** 5 **b.** 25 **c.** 50

21. $\$0.92 \times 9 \approx n$ **a.** \$0.90 **b.** \$9.00 **c.** \$90.00

22. $0.6 \times 32 \approx n$ **a.** 18 **b.** 1.8 **c.** 0.18

23. $0.3 \times 18 \approx n$ **a.** 6 **b.** 50 **c.** 60

24. $0.5 \times \$0.52 \approx n$ **a.** \$2.60 **b.** \$26.00 **c.** \$0.26

Estimate.

25. $\$0.51 \times 5 \approx n$ **26.** $32 \times 0.2 \approx n$ **27.** $0.1 \times 19 \approx n$

28. $9 \times \$0.21 \approx n$ **29.** $51 \times 0.6 \approx n$ **30.** $0.8 \times 27 \approx n$

Use estimation and patterns to place the decimal point in each product.

31. $2.7 \times 6 = 162$ **32.** $0.27 \times 6 = 162$ **33.** $27 \times 6 = 162$ **34.** $27 \times 0.06 = 162$

35. $27 \times 0.6 = 162$ **36.** $2.7 \times 0.6 = 162$ **37.** $0.27 \times 0.6 = 162$ **38.** $2.7 \times 0.06 = 162$

39. $4.9 \times 3 = 147$ **40.** $49 \times 3 = 147$ **41.** $4.9 \times 0.3 = 147$ **42.** $49 \times 0.3 = 147$

43. $0.49 \times 0.3 = 147$ **44.** $49 \times 0.03 = 147$ **45.** $0.49 \times 3 = 147$ **46.** $4.9 \times 0.03 = 147$

47. $8.1 \times 0.05 = 405$ **48.** $0.81 \times 0.5 = 405$ **49.** $8.1 \times 0.5 = 405$ **50.** $81 \times 0.5 = 405$

51. $81 \times 0.05 = 405$ **52.** $81 \times 5 = 405$ **53.** $0.81 \times 5 = 405$ **54.** $8.1 \times 5 = 405$

Problem Solving • Mixed Applications

55. Estimation George earns \$23.50 a week delivering papers. About how much money does he earn in 12 weeks?

56. Consumer Isabel wants to buy 3 tapes that cost \$4.39 each. If she earns \$2.25 an hour, about how many hours will it take her to have enough to make the purchase?

57. Estimation Steve runs 3.8 miles each day. About how many miles does he run in 5 days?

58. Measurement Steve decided to increase the length of his run by 1.5 miles a day. Exactly how much farther will he run over a 5-day period?

CONSUMER CONNECTION

Mr. Hamilton's fifth-grade class spent a week learning about electricity. The students made a table to show how much it costs to run various appliances in their home. Use the table to answer questions 59-61.

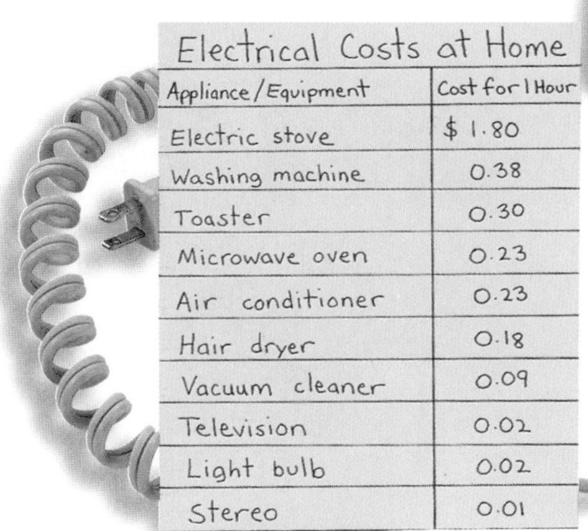

Electrical Costs at Home

Appliance/Equipment	Cost for 1 Hour
Electric stove	$1.80
Washing machine	0.38
Toaster	0.30
Microwave oven	0.23
Air conditioner	0.23
Hair dryer	0.18
Vacuum cleaner	0.09
Television	0.02
Light bulb	0.02
Stereo	0.01

59. Mr. Hamilton ran his washing machine for 3 hours. How much did the electricity cost?

60. The air conditioner in the school office runs all day long (8 hours). How much does the electricity cost each day?

61. If you left a lamp, with one bulb, on for 3 days, what would the electricity cost?

SCIENCE LINK

Electricity is measured in a small unit of power called a watt. The electric company measures electricity in kilowatt hours. A kilowatt is 1,000 watts. A kilowatt hour is 1,000 watts of power running for one hour.

Consumers pay about $0.15 for every kilowatt hour of electricity that is used. How many kilowatts does a 100-watt bulb use in 10 hours?

Mixed Review and Test Prep

Find the product. (pages 76–77)

62. 345×6

63. 239×7

64. 410×2

65. 306×4

Choose the letter of the correct quotient. (pages 128–129)

66. $150 \div 30 = n$
- **A** 4
- **B** 5
- **C** 6
- **D** 7

67. $450 \div 50 = n$
- **F** 9
- **G** 8
- **H** 7
- **J** 6

68. $140 \div 20 = n$
- **A** 5
- **B** 6
- **C** 7
- **D** 8

69. $160 \div 40 = n$
- **F** 4
- **G** 5
- **H** 6
- **J** 7

More About Placing the Decimal Point

Sometimes when you multiply with decimals, there are zeros in the product.

A. Find 0.005 × 16.

$$\begin{array}{r} 16 \\ \times 0.005 \\ \hline 0.080 \end{array}$$

Since 3 decimal places are needed in the product, write a zero for this place.

B. Find 0.06 × $0.90.

$$\begin{array}{r} \$0.90 \\ \times\ 0.06 \\ \hline \$0.0540 \end{array}$$

Since 4 decimal places are needed, write a zero in this place.

Talk About It

- In Example A, how do you know how many decimal places are needed in the product?
- In Example B, what is the product to the nearest cent?

When you use a calculator to multiply decimals, there can be a surprising result.

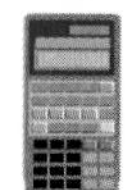

Use a calculator to check the written solutions. Record each calculator answer.

REMEMBER:

Equivalent decimals name the same number.

0.6 = 0.60

A calculator ignores zeros that do not change the value.

0.50 = 0.5

Paper and pencil computation | **Calculator keys**

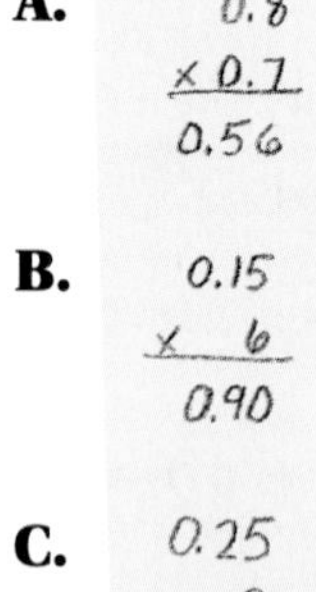

A. 0.8 × 0.7 = 0.56

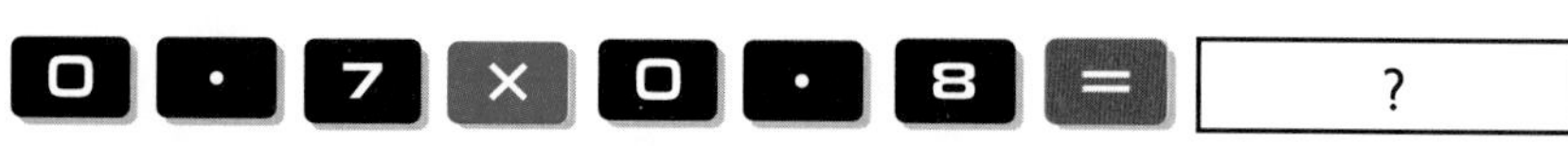

0 . 7 × 0 . 8 = ?

B. 0.15 × 6 = 0.90

6 × 0 . 1 5 = ?

C. 0.25 × 2 = 0.50

2 × 0 . 2 5 = ?

CRITICAL THINKING Compare the paper and pencil answer to the calculator answer for each problem. How are they alike? How are they different?

Calculator Activities page H68

▶ CHECK

Estimate each product.

1. 8×0.18
2. 9×0.3
3. 0.94×61
4. 84×0.6
5. 0.76×12
6. 29×0.02
7. 0.16×98
8. 56×0.3

▶ PRACTICE

Copy and complete the table.

	Number Sentence	Factors	Product
9.	0.5 × 0.8 = 0.40	tenths × tenths	?
10.	0.5 × ? = 0.040	tenths × ?	?
11.	0.05 × ? = 0.0040	?	?
12.	0.5 × 0.008 = ?	?	?

Estimate to place the decimal point. Then find the product.

13. $\$5.25 \times 4 = n$
14. $1.6 \times 12 = n$
15. $0.9 \times 8.9 = n$
16. $2.68 \times 57 = n$
17. $\$5.40 \times 3$
18. 0.75×0.06
19. 0.54×16
20. 1.74×43
21. $\$82.19 \times 7$
22. 0.09×0.7
23. 0.29×1.8
24. 6.07×17

Problem Solving • Mixed Applications

25. **Consumer** If Evan bought 2 dozen eggs at $0.79 a dozen and a loaf of bread at $0.99, about how much did he spend?

26. **Measurement** Suppose you have a watermelon that has a mass of 6.5 kg. If 0.92 of its mass is water, how much of its mass is water? How much is not water?

27. **Money** Which costs more—grapefruit at $0.89 each, or 3 for $2.50? 4 melons for $3.00, or melons for $0.85 each?

28. **Write a problem** including this information: The mass of a whole, unpeeled apple is 0.55 kg, and 0.84 of its mass is water.

Mixed Review and Test Prep

Write <, > or = for each ●. (pages 44–45)

29. 0.6 ● 0.600
30. 0.72 ● 0.072
31. 5.86 ● 5.68
32. 69.34 ● 69.54
33. 4.083 ● 4.308
34. 12.05 ● 12.50
35. 72.601 ● 72.610
36. 1.26 ● 12.6

Choose the letter for the correct product. (pages 94–95)

37. $19 \times 23 = n$ **A** 427 **B** 417 **C** 437 **D** 480

38. $403 \times 61 = n$ **F** 24,583 **G** 2,623 **H** 24,483 **J** 2,821

MORE PRACTICE page H93

LESSON 5

Multiplying Mixed Decimals

VOCABULARY
mixed decimal

Why learn this? When you are shopping, it helps you to decide if you are being charged a reasonable amount.

A **mixed decimal** has a whole number part and a decimal part in the number.

You can find mixed decimal products without making models.

MODEL

What is the product of 1.4×2.3?
Multiply. $1.4 \times 2.3 = n$ Estimate. $1.5 \times 2 = 3.0$

Step 1

Multiply by the tenths.

$$\begin{array}{r} {}^{1} \\ 2.3 \\ \times 1.4 \\ \hline 92 \end{array}$$

Think: 0.4×2.3

Step 2

Multiply by the ones. Add.

$$\begin{array}{r} {}^{1} \\ 2.3 \\ \times 1.4 \\ \hline 92 \\ +230 \\ \hline \end{array}$$

Think: 1.0×2.3

Remember to place a zero here. (← +230)

Step 3

Use the estimate of 3.0 to place the decimal point in the product.

$$\begin{array}{r} {}^{1} \\ 2.3 \\ \times 1.4 \\ \hline 92 \\ +230 \\ \hline 3.22 \end{array}$$

- How does the product compare to the estimate?

EXAMPLES

A Use estimation to find 3.4×1.7.

Estimate: $3 \times 2 = 6$

$$\begin{array}{r} 3.4 \\ \times 1.7 \\ \hline 238 \\ +340 \\ \hline 5.78 \end{array}$$

Since the estimate is 6, place the decimal point so there is a whole number 5.

B Use estimation or count the number of decimal places to place the decimal point in the product. Find 5.8×0.40.

Estimate: $6 \times 0.40 = 2.40$.

$$\begin{array}{rl} 0.40 & \leftarrow \text{2 decimal places} \\ \times\ 5.8 & \text{— 1 decimal place} \\ \hline 320 & \\ +2000 & \\ \hline 2.320 & \leftarrow \text{3 decimal places} \end{array}$$

▶ CHECK

1. In Examples A and B, what relationship do you see between the number of decimal places in the product and the total number of decimal places in the factors?
2. How does using estimation help you place the decimal point?

▶ PRACTICE

Find the product.

3. $\begin{array}{r} 7.89 \\ \times\ 4.2 \\ \hline \end{array}$
4. $\begin{array}{r} 32.5 \\ \times 0.95 \\ \hline \end{array}$
5. $\begin{array}{r} \$87.68 \\ \times\ \ \ 4.8 \\ \hline \end{array}$
6. $\begin{array}{r} 856.4 \\ \times\ 0.84 \\ \hline \end{array}$
7. $\begin{array}{r} 602.74 \\ \times\ \ \ 2.7 \\ \hline \end{array}$

8. $\begin{array}{r} 46.2 \\ \times 9.07 \\ \hline \end{array}$
9. $\begin{array}{r} 29.9 \\ \times\ 7.6 \\ \hline \end{array}$
10. $\begin{array}{r} \$14.34 \\ \times\ \ \ 5.2 \\ \hline \end{array}$
11. $\begin{array}{r} 37.3 \\ \times 4.06 \\ \hline \end{array}$
12. $\begin{array}{r} 1.008 \\ \times\ \ 5.5 \\ \hline \end{array}$

13. $2.4 \times 1.3 = n$ 14. $1.9 \times 1.8 = n$ 15. $3.2 \times 4.3 = n$ 16. $3.7 \times 2.6 = n$

Solve. Use the table for Exercises 17–19.

17. How much are 3 tapes at The Music Store?

18. What is the total cost of 2 CDs at Music Town, including a sales tax of $0.06 on each dollar?

19. **Write About It** If you buy both tapes and CDs, at which store should you shop? Explain.

MUSIC STORE PRICES

Store	Tape	Compact Disc
The Music Store	$8.99	$14.99
Music Town	$8.49	$11.99
Discount Music	$7.90	$12.98
Record City	$10.49	$15.99

Problem Solving • Mixed Applications

20. **Consumer** Paula bought a record cleaner for $0.69. If she paid a sales tax of $0.06 on each dollar, what did she spend on the record cleaner?

21. **Money** Bill made a phone call that cost $2.00 for the first minute and $0.45 for each additional minute. If he was on the phone for 5 minutes, what was the cost of the phone call?

When you are shopping, you are using decimals to solve problems.

Mixed Review and Test Prep

Write the decimal and fraction for each. (pages 36–37)

22. four and two tenths 23. sixteen hundredths 24. one and five hundredths

Choose the letter of the correct product. (pages 94–95)

25. $\begin{array}{r} 15 \\ \times 13 \\ \hline \end{array}$ **A** 60 **B** 85 **C** 185 **D** 195

26. $\begin{array}{r} 116 \\ \times\ 82 \\ \hline \end{array}$ **F** 9,512 **G** 9,102 **H** 1,160 **J** 15,032

MORE PRACTICE page H93

CHAPTER 12 Review/Test

CHECK Understanding

VOCABULARY

1. A _?_ has a whole number and a decimal part in the number. (page 224)

Use mental math to complete the pattern. (pages 212–213)

2. $14 \times 1 = n$
$14 \times 0.1 = n$
$14 \times 0.01 = n$

3. $85 \times 1 = n$
$85 \times 0.1 = n$
$85 \times 0.01 = n$

4. $205 \times 1 = n$
$205 \times 0.1 = n$
$205 \times 0.01 = n$

CHECK Skills

Find the product. (pages 214–225)

5. 0.7×6

6. 0.15×8

7. 0.9×0.4

8. 0.3×0.7

9. $\$8.29 \times 5$

10. 1.8×4

11. 6.94×7

12. 4.52×3

13. 3.67×0.5

14. 7.62×8

15. 2.58×0.6

16. 5.99×0.12

17. 0.7×0.9

18. 1.6×0.2

19. 0.83×0.9

20. $\$2.95 \times 0.6$

21. $\$4.56 \times 0.7$

22. 17.6×0.4

CHECK Problem Solving

Solve. (pages 216–217)

CHOOSE a strategy and a tool.

- Find a Pattern
- Write a Number Sentence
- Solve a Simpler Problem
- Work Backward
- Make a Model
- Guess and Check

Paper/Pencil

Calculator

Hands-On

Mental Math

23. Comic books are \$1.59 each and you want 7 of them. You have \$15.00. Is that enough? How much will you pay?

24. Tami is paid \$0.82 a pound for the strawberries she picks. How much could she receive for 50.5 pounds of strawberries?

25. Tom collected \$3.10 in coins to buy a gift for his teacher. If he had 8 dimes, twice as many nickels as dimes, and the rest in quarters, how many of each coin did he have?

26. Tom colored 0.8 of his book cover blue. He put stickers on 0.5 of the blue part. What part of the book cover has stickers on the blue background?

Test Prep

CUMULATIVE
CHAPTERS 1–12

Choose the best answer.

1. Which fraction has the same value as the underlined digit?

   3.8<u>9</u>

   A $\frac{9}{1}$ **B** $\frac{9}{10}$

   C $\frac{9}{100}$ **D** $\frac{9}{1,000}$

2. April biked 18 miles on Thursday, 15 miles on Friday, and 24 miles on Saturday. What was the mean of the distances biked per day?

   F 15 mi

   G 18 mi

   H 19 mi

   J 57 mi

3. Which product is equal to 56?

   A $2 \times 2 \times 3 \times 7$

   B $2 \times 2 \times 2 \times 7$

   C $2 \times 2 \times 2 \times 2 \times 7$

   D $2 \times 2 \times 2 \times 3 \times 3 \times 7$

   E Not Here

4. Lauren has \$79.82 in her bank account. She writes a check for \$29.05. Which expression can be used to find the new balance?

   F \$79.82 + \$29.05

   G \$79.82 − \$29.05

   H \$29.05 × \$79.82

   J \$79.82 ÷ \$29.05

   K Not Here

5. A truck delivered 34 cartons of berries to a store. There were 585 berries in the delivery. About how many berries were in each carton?

   A about 10

   B about 20

   C about 50

   D about 200

6. Jennifer bought 4 pumpkins. One weighed 7.1 kg, one weighed 8.5 kg, one weighed 3.4 kg, and one weighed 6.9 kg. Which of the following is a reasonable estimate for the total weight of the pumpkins?

   F about 22 kg

   G about 26 kg

   H about 28 kg

   J about 30 kg

7. If a coin is flipped 10 times, what is the probability that it will land with heads up?

   A $\frac{2}{10}$ or $\frac{1}{5}$ **B** $\frac{4}{10}$ or $\frac{2}{5}$

   C $\frac{5}{10}$ or $\frac{1}{2}$ **D** $\frac{7}{10}$

8. Which number completes the pattern?

   $201 \times 1 = 201$

   $201 \times 0.1 = 20.1$

   $201 \times 0.01 = n$

   F 2.01 **G** 20.01

   H 20.10 **J** 200.1

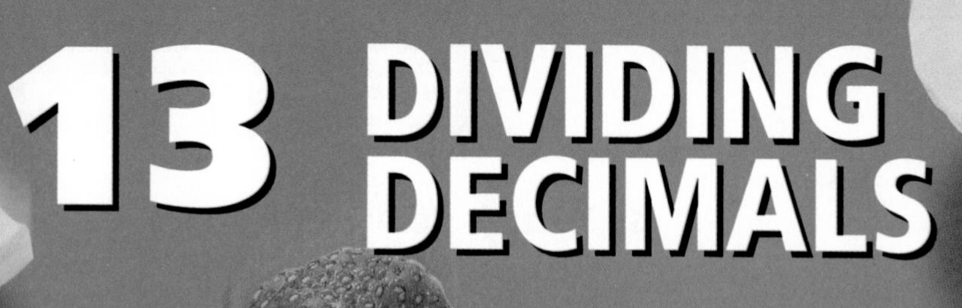

13 DIVIDING DECIMALS

SMOOTHIE INGREDIENTS

Frozen Fruits (sold in bags only)		
Strawberries	$ 4	3-pound bag
Raspberries	$ 6	2-pound bag
Blueberries	$ 7	3-pound bag
Fresh Fruits (you can buy these by the pound)		
Bananas	$ 0.50	1-pound
Honeydew	$ 1	1-pound
Juices (sold in jugs)		
Apple juice	$ 4	8-pound jug
Orange juice	$ 3	6-pound jug

HEALTH LINK

Blueberries, raspberries, and strawberries provide Vitamin C, iron, and fiber. That's why berries make a "berry" good snack.

Problem-Solving Activity

Smoothie Fundraiser

Suppose your class is having a smoothie fundraiser. You have $20 to spend on ingredients. Create and name your smoothie recipe. Then decide how many people it will serve, what to charge for the drinks, and how much profit you will make.

To make a yummy smoothie, you take frozen fruit, fresh fruit, and fruit juice and mix them up!

YOU WILL NEED: recipe ingredients, calculator

Make up a smoothie recipe.

- Figure out how many people you can serve.
- Decide how much to charge for one smoothie.
- Predict how much profit you will make.
- Present your calculations in an easy-to-read report.

Our Sensational Strawberry Smoothie

Ingredients		
$8	strawberries	6 lbs. (two 3 lb. bags)
$4	apple juice	8 lbs.
$5	bananas	10 lbs.
$3	honeydew melon	3 lbs.
$20	TOTAL	27 lbs.

How many people can we serve? Allow 1 pound drink per person (A pint is a pound.) 27 people

How much does it cost for 1 smoothie? $\frac{\$20}{27}$ $0.74 (74 cents)

How much will we charge for it? We will charge about twice the cost of ingredients, but we will round the number. $1.50 per smoothie

If our recipe is chosen as the Smoothie fundraiser, we will charge $1.50 per smoothie. We will sell 27 smoothies. 27 × $1.50 = $40.50. We will pay $20 for ingredients, so our profi[t] will be $20.50.

DID YOU

- ✓ make a recipe and calculate how many people it will serve?
- ✓ decide how much to charge and figure your profit?
- ✓ write a report explaining your calculations?

Patterns in Decimal Division

Why learn this? You can find quotients by seeing patterns and using mental math.

One way to find quotients is to look for patterns. You can use the patterns from quotients you know to find quotients you do not know.

Look for the pattern in these quotients to find $1 \div 5$.

$1{,}000 \div 5 = 200$
$100 \div 5 = 20$
$10 \div 5 = 2$
$1 \div 5 = 0.2$

Notice that

➪ $1 \div 5$ results in a quotient that is a decimal.

REMEMBER:

Use a place-value chart to place the decimal point.

Tens	Ones	Tenths
2	0 •	0
	2 •	0
	0 •	2

EXAMPLES

A
$1{,}000 \div 2 = 500$
$100 \div 2 = 50$
$10 \div 2 = 5$
$1 \div 2 = 0.5$

B
$10{,}000 \div 4 = 2{,}500$
$1{,}000 \div 4 = 250$
$100 \div 4 = 25$
$10 \div 4 = 2.5$

Talk About It

- How does the number of zeros in the dividend change in each example?
- What happens to the position of the decimal point in the quotient in each example?

CRITICAL THINKING How does the pattern in each example above show that $1 \div 5$, $1 \div 2$, and $10 \div 4$ have quotients that are decimals?

ART LINK

M.C. Escher was a Dutch artist. He is famous for his drawings of repeating patterns. In *Ascending and Descending*, which means "up and down," people are walking up stairs and down stairs, but each person will end up in the same place he or she started. What patterns can you find in the picture?

M.C. Escher's "Ascending and Descending"

▶ CHECK

Copy and complete each pattern.

1. $1{,}000 \div 2 = n$
$100 \div 2 = n$
$10 \div 2 = n$
$1 \div 2 = n$

2. $4{,}000 \div 8 = n$
$400 \div 8 = n$
$40 \div 8 = n$
$4 \div 8 = n$

3. $5{,}000 \div 2 = n$
$500 \div 2 = n$
$50 \div 2 = n$
$5 \div 2 = n$

▶ PRACTICE

Copy and complete each pattern.

4. $3{,}000 \div 5 = n$
$300 \div 5 = n$
$30 \div 5 = n$
$3 \div 5 = n$

5. $2{,}000 \div 4 = n$
$200 \div 4 = n$
$20 \div 4 = n$
$2 \div 4 = n$

6. $15{,}000 \div 6 = n$
$1{,}500 \div 6 = n$
$150 \div 6 = n$
$15 \div 6 = n$

7. $2{,}000 \div 5 = n$
$200 \div 5 = n$
$20 \div 5 = n$
$2 \div 5 = n$

8. $20{,}000 \div 8 = n$
$2{,}000 \div 8 = n$
$200 \div 8 = n$
$20 \div 8 = n$

9. $7{,}000 \div 4 = n$
$700 \div 4 = n$
$70 \div 4 = n$
$7 \div 4 = n$

10. $10{,}000 \div 8 = n$
$1{,}000 \div 8 = n$
$100 \div 8 = n$
$10 \div 8 = n$

11. $6{,}000 \div 5 = n$
$600 \div 5 = n$
$60 \div 5 = n$
$6 \div 5 = n$

12. $4{,}000 \div 5 = n$
$400 \div 5 = n$
$40 \div 5 = n$
$4 \div 5 = n$

Problem Solving • Mixed Applications

13. Time Sammy has a newspaper route. He has 140 papers to deliver. He can deliver 7 papers in 5 minutes. How long will it take him to deliver all the papers?

14. Jamie's group used a recipe that makes 68 ounces of smoothies. If each serving is 8 ounces, how many servings can they make?

15. Money Albert has collected 1,372 pennies. How much money does he have in dollars and cents?

16. Money Mr. Fox makes $80 a week. He works 4 hours each week. How much does he make per hour?

Using Data For Problems 17–19, use the information at the right.

17. Paco recorded the amount of money he spent on each meal during his vacation. On which day did he spend the most?

18. On which day did Paco spend the least?

19. Compare How much more did Paco spend for meals on Friday than he did on Saturday?

20. Write About It Explain how a pattern beginning with $300 \div 6 = 50$ leads to a decimal quotient of 0.5.

LESSON CONTINUES

Problem-Solving Strategy: Write a Number Sentence

▶ **THE PROBLEM** Rick wants to buy a stereo system that is on sale for $400. He has 8 weeks to save up for it. If he wants to save an equal amount of money per week, how much should he save each week?

REMEMBER:

UNDERSTAND

PLAN

SOLVE

LOOK BACK

UNDERSTAND

- What are you asked to find?
- What information will you use?
- Is there information you will not use? If so, what?

PLAN

- What strategy can you use to solve the problem?

  You can *write a number sentence* to find the amount Rick should save each week.

SOLVE

- What number sentence can you write to solve the problem?

  Divide to find the amount he should save.

  Use mental math to find the quotient.

  $$\$400 \div 8 = \$50$$

  So, Rick should save $50 each week.

- How can you determine if your answer is reasonable?
- What other strategy can you use?

CONSUMER LINK

In 1897 a guitar cost about $16, and a ten-hole harmonica cost $0.45. Today a beginner's guitar costs about $200. A ten-hole harmonica costs about $20.

About how many guitars could you have bought for $200 in 1897? About how many harmonicas could you have bought for $20 in 1897?

▶ PRACTICE

Write a number sentence to solve.

1. Joan and 3 classmates bought some food to share. The bill was $40.00. They shared the bill equally. How much did each owe?

2. James has deposited $555 in his savings account. He made 5 equal deposits. How much was each deposit?

3. Each week Nina saves $9.75 from her allowance. In 12 weeks, how much money will she have saved?

4. Samuel and Adam worked together on a school project. Adam spent $4.60 on supplies. Samuel spent $3.90. How much did they spend together?

Mixed Applications

Solve.

CHOOSE **a strategy and a tool.**

- Make a Table
- Solve a Simpler Problem
- Write a Number Sentence
- Guess and Check

Paper/Pencil Calculator  Hands-On  Mental Math

5. Dennis wants to buy 2 new baseballs. At Joe's Sports Store, he saw a baseball for $3.95, a bat for $5.95, and a glove for $32.95. At Max's Sports Store, he saw a package of 2 baseballs for $7.95. At which store will he get a better buy on baseballs?

6. Sara Ann wants to buy 2 new video games. At a store 4.5 miles from her house, she can buy 2 games for $39.98. At a store 2 miles from her house, the games are $21.95 each. What is the difference in the cost for one video game?

7. Jared and his brother have been saving baseball cards for 4 years. Jared has 1,123 cards, and his brother has 792 cards. If they continue to save at the same rate during the next 4 years, about how many cards will they have together?

8. Nancy made a phone call that cost $2.00 for the first minute and $0.45 for each additional minute. She was on the phone for 5 minutes. What was the cost of the phone call?

9. Laura needs $130 to buy a coat. She has $45. If she saves $5 each week, how many weeks will it take her to save enough money to buy the coat?

10. Ralph bought this salad. How much change will he receive from $5.00?

11. What is the smallest 4-digit number that can be divided by 50 with a remainder of 17?

MORE PRACTICE page H94

Decimal Division

You will investigate how to divide decimals by using decimal models.

▶ EXPLORE

Make models to show how to divide 1.5 by 3.

MATERIALS: tenths and hundredths decimal models, markers, scissors, and tape or paste

MODEL

Step 1

Show 1.5 by shading two decimal models.

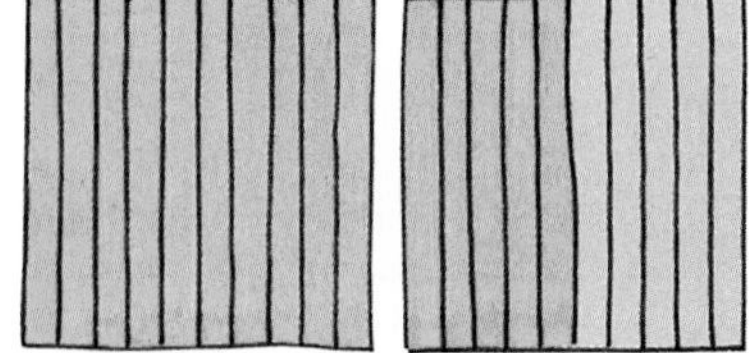

Step 2

Cut each model to show the tenths.

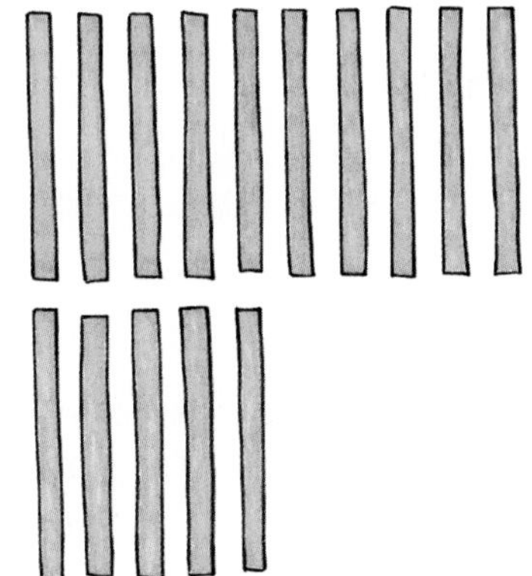

REMEMBER:

Division is separating into equal groups.

This model represents a whole divided into tenths. Each part is $\frac{1}{10}$, or 0.1.

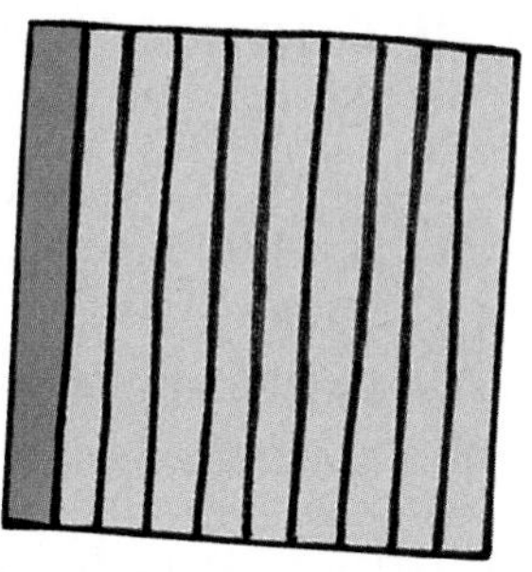

Record

Divide the tenths into three groups of the same size. Tape or paste your model on a piece of paper. Record a division number sentence for your model.

Talk About It

- Look at your model and quotient. What happened to the 1 whole?
- How can you use the pattern below to show that your quotient is correct?

  $150 \div 3 = 50$
  $15 \div 3 = 5$
  $1.5 \div 3 = \underline{\ ?\ }$

Now, investigate dividing hundredths by a whole number.

Technology Link

You can divide decimals by using E-Lab, Activity 13. Available on CD-ROM and on the Internet at **www.hbschool.com/elab**

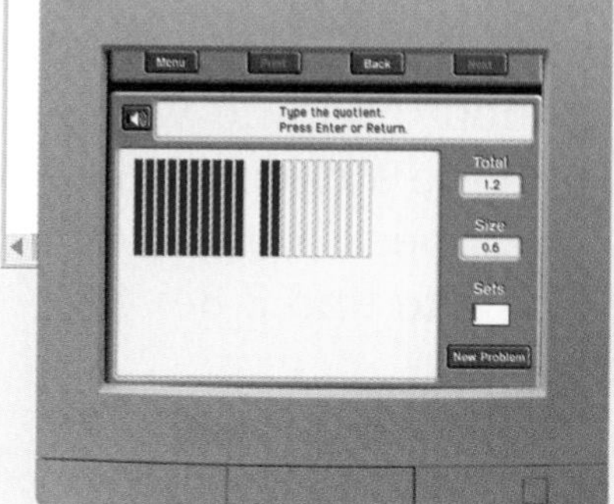

▶ TRY THIS

Make models to show decimal division. Record number sentences for each of your models.

1. 0.09 ÷ 3 = ?　　**2.** 0.24 ÷ 2 = ?

▶ PRACTICE

Make a model and find the quotient.

3. 1.2 ÷ 4 = ?　　**4.** 0.12 ÷ 4 = ?

5. 3.5 ÷ 5 = ?　　**6.** 6.4 ÷ 8 = ?

7. 0.64 ÷ 8 = ?　　**8.** 0.69 ÷ 3 = ?

9. 0.44 ÷ 2 = ?　　**10.** 0.18 ÷ 9 = ?

11. 5.4 ÷ 6 = ?　　**12.** 1.12 ÷ 7 = ?

Use the model to complete the number sentence.

13.

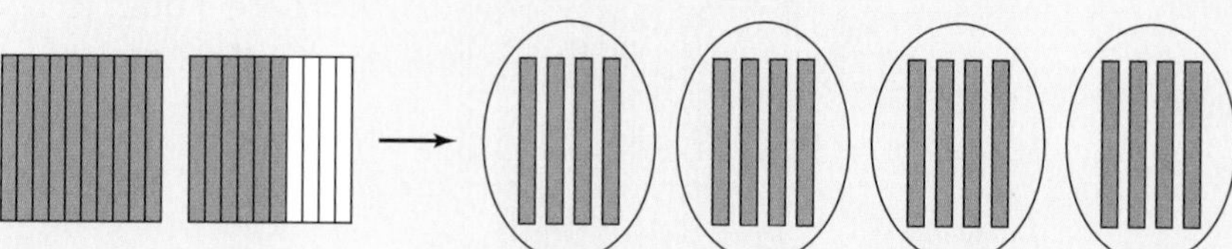

1.6 ÷ 4 = ?

14.

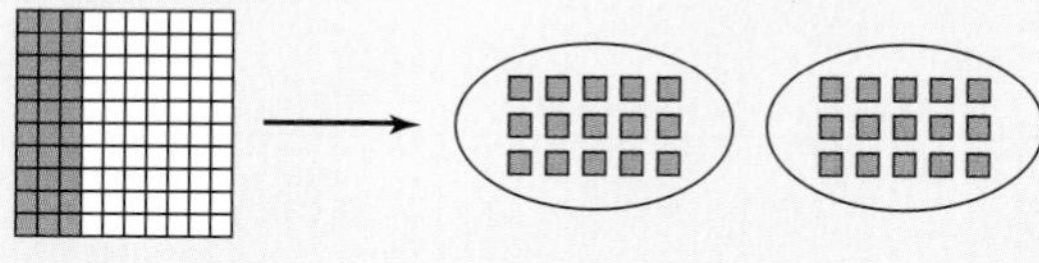

0.30 ÷ 2 = ?

15.

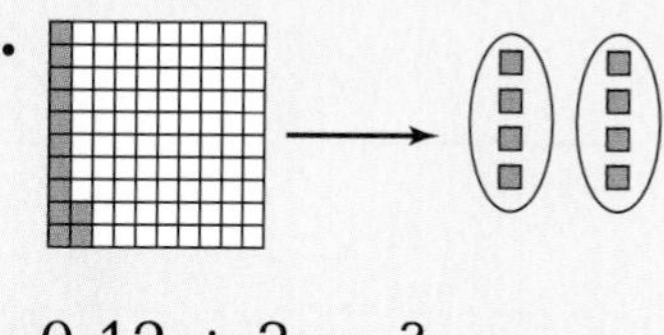

0.12 ÷ 3= ?

Problem Solving • Mixed Applications

16. Consumer Mark is building a doll house for his little sister. For the trim around the roof, he bought 4 pieces of wood for a total of $7.16. If the pieces all cost the same, how much was each piece of wood?

17. Measurement Mr. Wu is organizing a field day for his class. He wants to make 3 award ribbons for each of 3 events. He has a ribbon that is 1.8 meters long. How long can each award ribbon be?

18. Money Four friends are playing a game. They have $39.52 in play money. If each player gets the same amount to begin the game, how much will each player get?

19. Write About It Explain how to draw a model to find the quotient 0.10 ÷ 5.

MORE PRACTICE page H94

LESSON 3

Dividing Decimals by Whole Numbers

Why learn this? You can find equal parts of a decimal so you can share a money amount equally.

Use models and what you know about dividing whole numbers to divide a decimal by a whole number. The model below shows how to find 3.8 ÷ 2.

MODEL

Find 3.8 ÷ 2.

Step 1

Show 3.8.

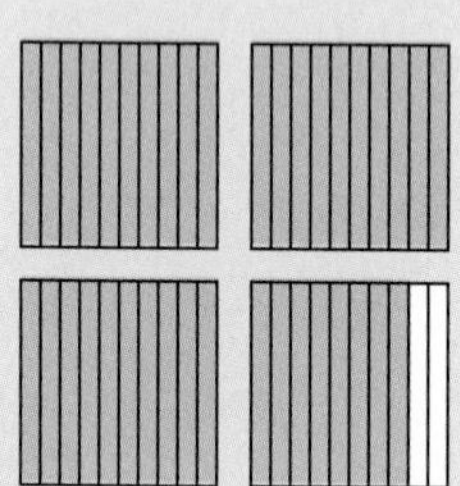

$2\overline{)3.8}$

Step 2

Divide as with whole numbers. Begin with the whole number.

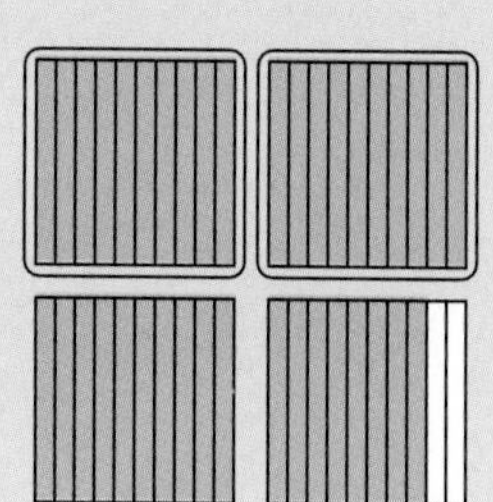

There are 3 ones to divide into 2 groups.

$$\begin{array}{r} 1 \\ 2\overline{)3.8} \\ -2 \\ \hline 1 \end{array}$$

3 ÷ 2 = 1 with 1 whole left over.

Step 3

Rename the 1 whole that is left over as 10 tenths. There are 18 tenths to divide into 2 groups.

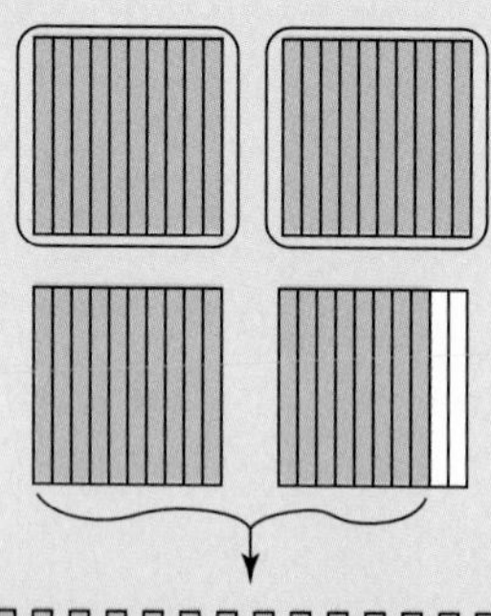

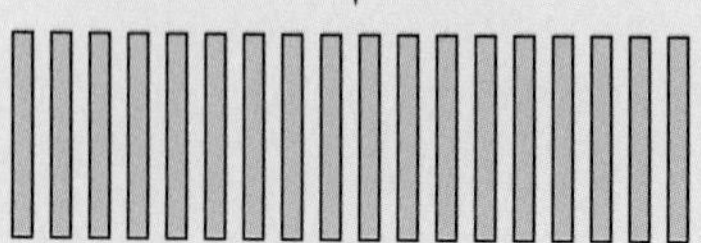

$$\begin{array}{r} 1 \\ 2\overline{)3.8} \\ -2\downarrow \\ \hline 18 \end{array}$$

Step 4

Divide the tenths.

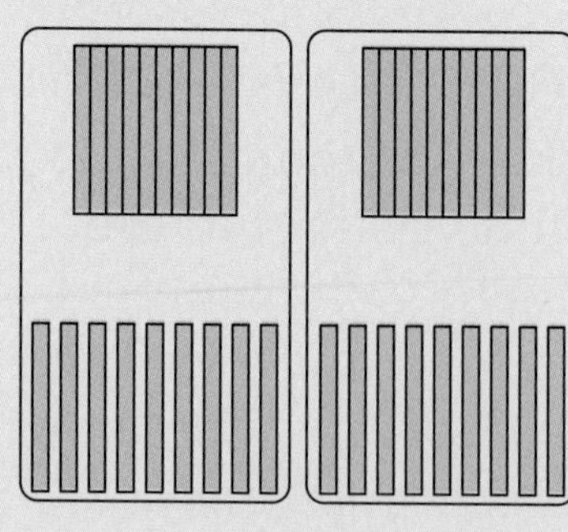

$$\begin{array}{r} 1.9 \\ 2\overline{)3.8} \\ -2\downarrow \\ \hline 18 \\ -18 \\ \hline 0 \end{array}$$

18 ÷ 2 = 9 with 0 left over.

Place a decimal point between the whole and the tenths.

So, 3.8 ÷ 2 = 1.9.

EXAMPLES

A Find 5.40 ÷ 4.

$$\begin{array}{r} 1.35 \\ 4\overline{)5.40} \\ -4 \\ \hline 14 \\ -12 \\ \hline 20 \\ -20 \\ \hline 0 \end{array}$$

Divide the whole number 5 by 4.

Divide 14 tenths by 4.

Divide 20 hundredths by 4.

Check:

$$\begin{array}{r} 1.35 \\ \times \quad 4 \\ \hline 5.40 \end{array}$$

B Find 21.5 ÷ 5.

$$\begin{array}{r} 4.3 \\ 5\overline{)21.5} \\ -20 \\ \hline 15 \\ -15 \\ \hline 0 \end{array}$$

Check:

$$\begin{array}{r} 4.3 \\ \times \quad 5 \\ \hline 21.5 \end{array}$$

Talk About It

- Where do you place the decimal point in the quotient?
- How can a pattern help you decide if the answer in Example B is reasonable?

CRITICAL THINKING How is division with decimals like division with whole numbers? How is it different?

▶ CHECK

Draw a picture to show the quotient.

1. 1.26 ÷ 3 = ?

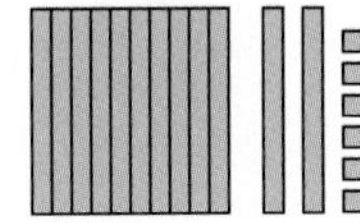

2. 2.38 ÷ 7 = ?

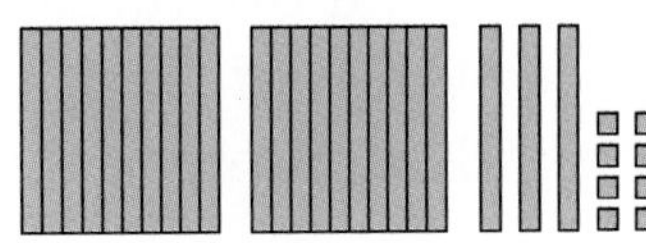

Place the decimal point in the quotient.

3. $\overset{053}{2\overline{)1.06}}$ **4.** $\overset{0009}{5\overline{)0.045}}$ **5.** $\overset{70}{7\overline{)49.0}}$ **6.** $\overset{815}{4\overline{)32.60}}$

7. $\overset{071}{6\overline{)4.26}}$ **8.** $\overset{0122}{3\overline{)0.366}}$ **9.** $\overset{34}{8\overline{)27.2}}$ **10.** $\overset{003}{9\overline{)0.27}}$

Find the quotient. Check by multiplying.

11. $6\overline{)4.8}$ **12.** $3\overline{)9.09}$ **13.** $4\overline{)12.00}$ **14.** $2\overline{)1.04}$

15. $9\overline{)56.7}$ **16.** $7\overline{)21.7}$ **17.** $8\overline{)88.8}$ **18.** $5\overline{)26.5}$

19. $2\overline{)0.48}$ **20.** $5\overline{)0.80}$ **21.** $7\overline{)9.17}$ **22.** $4\overline{)0.16}$

23. $35.7 \div 7 = n$ **24.** $3.57 \div 7 = n$ **25.** $0.54 \div 6 = n$

26. $4.35 \div 5 = n$ **27.** $5.04 \div 8 = n$ **28.** $0.72 \div 8 = n$

LESSON CONTINUES

▶ PRACTICE

Find the quotient. Check by multiplying.

29. $7\overline{)6.3}$ **30.** $4\overline{)8.08}$ **31.** $8\overline{)6.00}$ **32.** $5\overline{)4.05}$

33. $8\overline{)74.4}$ **34.** $3\overline{)27.9}$ **35.** $5\overline{)55.5}$ **36.** $2\overline{)19.6}$

37. $24.6 \div 6 = \underline{?}$ **38.** $2.46 \div 6 = \underline{?}$ **39.** $0.93 \div 3 = \underline{?}$

Place the decimal point in the quotient.

40. $8.05 \div 7 = 115$ **41.** $80.5 \div 7 = 115$ **42.** $85.4 \div 7 = 122$

43. $37.6 \div 8 = 47$ **44.** $3.76 \div 8 = 047$ **45.** $4.24 \div 8 = 053$

46. $0.95 \div 5 = 019$ **47.** $9.3 \div 3 = 31$ **48.** $93.0 \div 3 = 310$

49. $4\overline{)25.6}$ **50.** $5\overline{)14.0}$ **51.** $7\overline{)30.8}$ **52.** $9\overline{)48.6}$

53. $8\overline{)16.8}$ **54.** $2\overline{)36.8}$ **55.** $4\overline{)21.6}$ **56.** $3\overline{)4.2}$

57. $3\overline{)41.1}$ **58.** $5\overline{)23.5}$ **59.** $6\overline{)25.8}$ **60.** $7\overline{)49.7}$

61. $18.5 \div 5 = n$ **62.** $48.3 \div 7 = n$ **63.** $36.8 \div 8 = n$

Problem Solving • Mixed Applications

64. Consumer At Marie's Market, strawberries cost $4.98 for 2 pounds. How much does 1 pound cost?

65. Money Kevin is building a doghouse. He bought 4 pieces of wood for the roof. The 4 pieces cost $6.52. How much did each piece cost?

66. Money Eric earned $17.25 raking leaves for 5 hours. How much did he earn in one hour?

67. Measurement Jean drives a school bus to and from school each day. The round trip is 8.92 miles. What is the distance one way?

68. Consumer Tennis balls sell for $4.79 for a can of three balls or $9.00 for a half dozen balls. Which is the better buy?

69. Logical Reasoning The difference between the prices of two bikes is $16. The sum of their prices is $232. How much is the more expensive bike?

70. **Write a problem** about sharing $5.91 equally with 2 friends.

CONSUMER CONNECTION

Richard saw a pair of in-line skates in a catalog. He decided to save the money to buy them. The catalog price of the skates is $49.98. The charge for shipping and handling is $7.50.

71. **Money** What is the total price of the in-line skates?

72. **Estimation** Estimate how much Richard has to save each month to buy the skates in 6 months.

73. Find out how much Richard has to save each month to buy the skates in 4 months.

74. CRITICAL THINKING Why is it important to place the decimal point correctly when dividing money?

HISTORY LINK

In-line skates were introduced in the United States in the late 1970's. They had the quiet, smooth rolling polyurethane wheels that were first created for skateboards. Polyurethane wheels roll twice as fast as rubber or metal wheels. The original roller skates were invented about 1760. About how many more years passed before in-line skates were invented?

Mixed Review and Test Prep

Write the decimal for each model. (pages 36–37)

75. 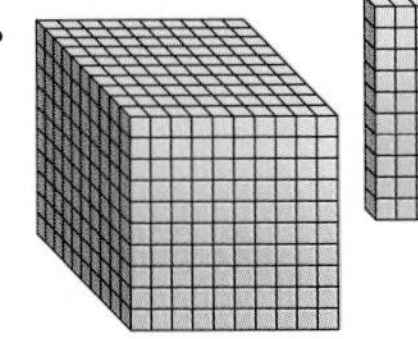

76. 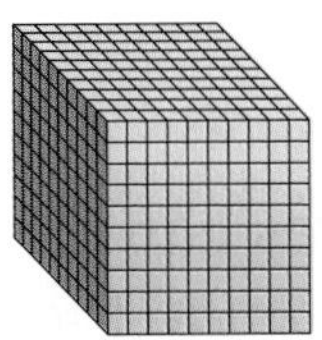 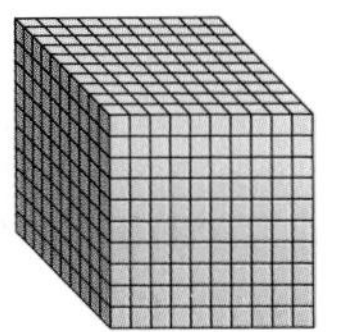 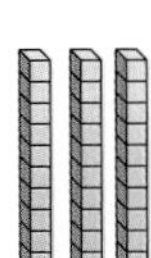

Choose the equivalent decimal for each number. (pages 42–43)

77. 0.03
- **A** 0.003
- **B** 0.30
- **C** 0.030
- **D** 0.3

78. 5.20
- **F** 520.0
- **G** 0.520
- **H** 0.52
- **J** 5.2

79. 0.500
- **A** 0.5
- **B** 0.05
- **C** 5.0
- **D** 0.0500

80. 3.75
- **F** 0.375
- **G** 37.5
- **H** 3.750
- **J** 375.0

LESSON 4

Placing the Decimal Point

Why learn this? The position of the decimal point determines the value of the number, for example, 4.00 miles is less than 40.0 miles.

Natalia walked 3 miles in 4 days. What average distance did she walk each day?

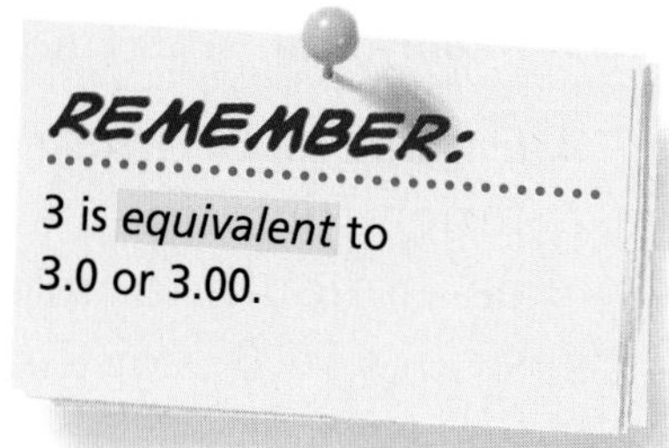

Estimate 3 ÷ 4 to help solve the problem.

Since 3 ÷ 4 is less than 1, add a decimal point and zeros to divide.

$4\overline{)3}$ can be written as $4\overline{)3.0}$ or $4\overline{)3.00}$.

MODEL

Step 1

Since 3 ÷ 4 is less than 1, place a 0 in the ones place. Then place a decimal point.

$$\begin{array}{r} 0. \\ 4\overline{)3.00} \end{array}$$

Step 2

Divide as with whole numbers.

$$\begin{array}{r} 0.75 \\ 4\overline{)3.00} \\ -28 \\ \hline 20 \\ -20 \\ \hline 0 \end{array}$$

Step 3

Check by multiplying.

$$\begin{array}{r} 0.75 \\ \times \quad 4 \\ \hline 3.00 \end{array}$$

Notice that

➩ the decimal point in the quotient goes directly above the decimal point in the dividend.

So, Natalia walked an average of 0.75 mile each day.

Since 0.75 is less than 1, the quotient is reasonable.

- In Step 1, how many zeros can you write after the decimal point and not change the value of the 3?

EXAMPLES

A

$$\begin{array}{r} 60.5 \\ 7\overline{)423.5} \\ -42 \\ \hline 03 \\ -00 \\ \hline 35 \\ -35 \\ \hline 0 \end{array}$$

Use estimation to place the decimal point.

420 ÷ 7 = 60

So, place the decimal point so there is a whole number 60 in the quotient.

B

$$\begin{array}{r} 0.73 \\ 2\overline{)1.46} \\ -14 \\ \hline 06 \\ -6 \\ \hline 0 \end{array}$$

Use estimation and a pattern to place the decimal point.

140 ÷ 2 = 70
14 ÷ 2 = 7
1.4 ÷ 2 = 0.7

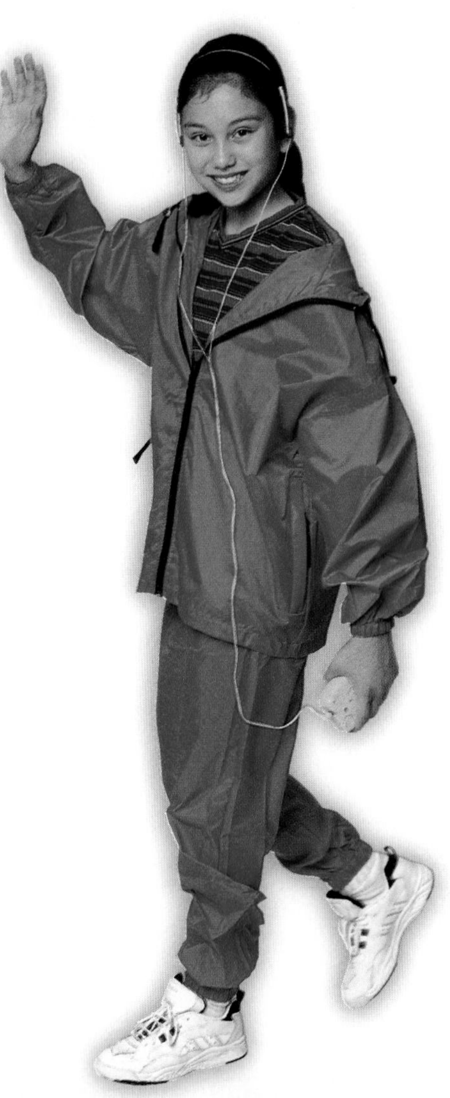

▶ CHECK

1. In Example A, why is the quotient 60.5, not 6.05?
2. How can you use the pattern below to help place the decimal point?

   $300 \div 4 = 75$
   $30 \div 4 = 7.5$
   $3 \div 4 = n$

3. What basic division facts did you use to solve the problem?

Technology Link

In ***Mighty Math Calculating Crew***, the game *Superhero Superstore* challenges you to make purchases by dividing money amounts. Use Grow Slide Levels J and T.

▶ PRACTICE

Use estimation or patterns to place the decimal point. Then find the quotient.

4. $3\overline{)1.8}$ **5.** $4\overline{)2.0}$ **6.** $6\overline{)0.24}$ **7.** $5\overline{)3.5}$

8. $7\overline{)1.47}$ **9.** $3\overline{)3.69}$ **10.** $9\overline{)83.7}$ **11.** $4\overline{)44.8}$

12. $8\overline{)56.8}$ **13.** $6\overline{)54.48}$ **14.** $2\overline{)19.62}$ **15.** $5\overline{)19.75}$

Problem Solving • Mixed Applications

Using Data For Problems 16–19, use the price list.

16. Estimate the cost of 1 pound of potatoes.
17. **Money** Evan bought a dozen eggs and 2 loaves of bread. How much did he spend?
18. **Logic** Suppose you need to buy 1 gallon of milk. Would you buy 2 half-gallon containers of milk or 1 one-gallon container of milk? Why?
19. **Write a problem** that can be solved by dividing. Use the price list.

Price List

5-pound bag potatoes	$2.39
half-gallon milk	$1.35
gallon milk	$2.39
dozen eggs	$0.99
bread	$1.19

Mixed Review and Test Prep

Use an equivalent decimal to find the sum. (pages 54–55)

20. $1.25 + 0.786 = n$ **21.** $2.30 + 8.604 = n$ **22.** $12.35 + 1.459 = n$

Choose the letter of the best estimate. (pages 116–117)

23. $58 \div 6$
A 1 B 15 C 10 D 8

24. $430 \div 6$
F 70 G 90 H 60 J 50

25. $209 \div 7$
A 300 B 30 C 20 D 200

26. $355 \div 6$
F 6 G 7 H 60 J 70

MORE PRACTICE page H94

LESSON 5

Choosing the Operation

Why learn this? You can decide which operation you should use to solve a problem, such as how to share an item equally with several people.

Mr. Regan shared the seafood that he bought at the market with 3 of his neighbors. His purchases are listed in the table at the right. If they shared each kind of seafood equally, how many pounds of salmon was each person's share?

The table shows that Mr. Regan bought 16.8 pounds of salmon. Since he and his 3 neighbors are sharing equally, you can divide 16.8 by 4 to find the answer.

$$\begin{array}{r} 4.2 \\ 4\overline{)16.8} \\ -16 \\ \hline 0\,8 \\ -8 \\ \hline 0 \end{array}$$

So, each person's share was 4.2 pounds of salmon.

SEAFOOD PURCHASES	
Type of Seafood	**Amount (in pounds)**
Salmon	16.8
Haddock	12.0
Shrimp	9.6

Suppose Mr. Fu bought 22.8 pounds of seafood 5 weeks in a row for his restaurant. How many pounds of seafood did he buy in all?

Since he bought the same amount 5 weeks in a row, you need to multiply to find the answer.

$$\begin{array}{r} 22.8 \\ \times \quad 5 \\ \hline 114.0 \end{array}$$

So, Mr. Fu bought 114 pounds of seafood.

Talk About It CRITICAL THINKING

- How do you know when to divide?
- How do you know when to multiply?

▶ CHECK

Choose the operation and solve.

1. Sam, Joe, and Bob share 14.4 pounds of shrimp equally. How much is Bob's share?
2. If Bob buys the same amount of shrimp for 4 weeks in a row, how much shrimp will he buy in all?

SCIENCE LINK

Chinook salmon live along the Pacific coast. They spend from one to five years in the ocean and then return to lay eggs in the stream of their origin. Large female salmon usually lay between 2,000 and 3,000 eggs. How many salmon from one female survive if 0.10 of her eggs survive and grow? if 0.01 of her eggs survive and grow?

▶ PRACTICE

For Problems 3–6, use the table on page 242. Choose the operation and solve.

3. How much haddock did Mr. Regan have after sharing with his neighbors?

4. How much shrimp did Mr. Regan and each of his neighbors get?

5. Mr. Regan bought the same amount of shrimp 4 weeks in a row. How many pounds of shrimp did he buy?

6. Mr. Regan bought the same amount of salmon 3 weeks in a row. How many pounds of salmon did he buy?

7. Carl receives an allowance of $3.75 a week. If Carl saves all his allowance, how much will he have in 4 weeks?

8. Lola wants to buy a touring bike for $599.94. She agrees to pay off the total cost of the bike in 9 months. How much does she have to pay each month?

Problem Solving • Mixed Applications

9. Consumer Amy is comparing breakfast cereals. A box of Brand A weighs 13 ounces and sells for $2.08. A box of Brand B weighs 14 ounces and sells for $2.10. Which cereal costs less per ounce?

10. Estimation Janell bought 2 shirts for $11.98 each, a sweater for $18.95, and 3 pairs of socks for $3.05 a pair. About how much did these items cost?

11. Money Each week for 6 weeks, Harry deposited his check of $74.28 into his bank account. During that time he also deposited $25.00 he received as a gift. How much did he deposit during the 6 weeks?

12. Write a problem that can be solved by dividing a decimal.

Mixed Review and Test Prep

Find the area. (pages 84–85)

13. l = 12 ft
w = 4 ft
A = ▒ sq ft

14. l = 23 ft
w = 3 ft
A = ▒ sq ft

15. l = 48 ft
w = 7 ft
A = ▒ sq ft

16. l = 18 ft
w = 5 ft
A = ▒ sq ft

Choose the letter of the correct quotient. (pages 136–137)

17. 1,089 ÷ 37 **A** 32 r5 **B** 29 r16 **C** 28 r4 **D** 20 r15

18. 6,156 ÷ 18 **F** 341 r1 **G** 342 **H** 34 r7 **J** 340 r2

19. 5,172 ÷ 25 **A** 206 **B** 206 r22 **C** 205 r37 **D** 205 r22

MORE PRACTICE page H95

CHAPTER 13 Review/Test

▶ CHECK Understanding

Copy and complete each pattern. (pages 230–231)

1. $3{,}000 \div 6 = n$
$300 \div 6 = n$
$30 \div 6 = n$
$3 \div 6 = n$

2. $8{,}000 \div 5 = n$
$800 \div 5 = n$
$80 \div 5 = n$
$8 \div 5 = n$

3. $7{,}000 \div 2 = n$
$700 \div 2 = n$
$70 \div 2 = n$
$7 \div 2 = n$

4. $9{,}000 \div 5 = n$
$900 \div 5 = n$
$90 \div 5 = n$
$9 \div 5 = n$

Use the model to complete the number sentence. (pages 234–235)

5. 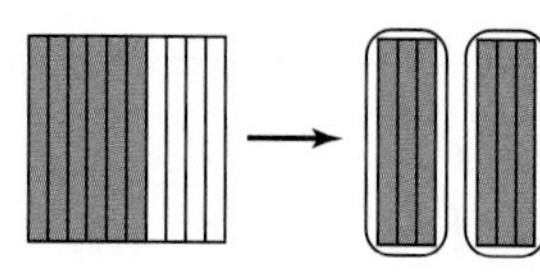

$0.6 \div 2 = \underline{?}$

6. 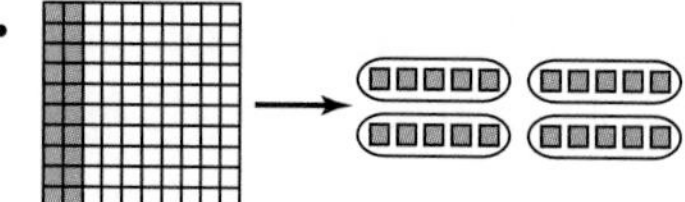

$0.20 \div 4 = \underline{?}$

Use estimation or patterns to place the decimal point.
Then find the quotient. (pages 240–241)

7. $2\overline{)18.2}$ **8.** $5\overline{)9.5}$ **9.** $4\overline{)0.24}$ **10.** $4\overline{)2.4}$

▶ CHECK Skills

Find the quotient. Check by multiplying. (pages 236–239)

11. $9\overline{)1.8}$ **12.** $5\overline{)2.5}$ **13.** $6\overline{)0.42}$ **14.** $8\overline{)3.2}$

15. $6\overline{)28.8}$ **16.** $3\overline{)2.13}$ **17.** $2\overline{)2.44}$ **18.** $6\overline{)37.2}$

Choose the operation and solve. (pages 242–243)

19. Bobbie bought 2 cans of tennis balls at $3.95 for each can. How much did the tennis balls cost?

20. Jared paid $150 to attend 8 computer classes. How much did he pay per class?

▶ CHECK Problem Solving

Solve. (pages 232–233)

CHOOSE a strategy and a tool.

- Make a Table
- Guess and Check
- Write a Number Sentence

Paper/Pencil

Calculator

Hands-On

Mental Math

21. Ed bought 4 magazines for $3.00 each. He paid a sales tax of $0.06 on each dollar of his purchase. How much sales tax did he pay?

22. From Monday through Friday, Hillary drove 4.8 miles to and from work each day. How many miles did she drive for the week?

Test Prep

Choose the best answer.

1. $7\overline{)407}$

A 57

B 58

C 58 R1

D 58 R6

E Not Here

2. Jerry runs four days a week. This week he ran 4.2 mi on Monday, 5.5 mi on Wednesday, 4.8 mi on Friday, and 7.1 mi on Saturday. Which of the following is a reasonable estimate for the total distance he ran this week?

F about 32 mi **G** about 22 mi

H about 10 mi **J** about 40 mi

3. $21 \times 0.5 =$

A 1.5 **B** 10.5

C 100.5 **D** 105

4. Nita was paid the following amounts for babysitting.

BABYSITTING EARNINGS	
Days	**Amount**
Monday	$12
Tuesday	$ 7
Wednesday	$ 9
Thursday	$10
Friday	$12

What is the average amount she made per day?

F $7 **G** $9

H $10 **J** $12

5. Dave is ordering a snack and a drink. For the snack, he can choose from a muffin, pretzels, or an apple. For a drink, his choices are orange juice or lemonade. How many different combinations could he have?

A 3 **B** 5

C 6 **D** 9

6. Rick has 2 pennies, 3 quarters, and 1 nickel in his pocket. He takes 1 coin from his pocket. What is the chance it will be a penny?

F $\frac{1}{5}$ **G** $\frac{1}{6}$

H $\frac{2}{6}$, or $\frac{1}{3}$ **J** $\frac{3}{6}$, or $\frac{1}{2}$

7. A writer bought 3 packs of paper. Each pack of paper contained 500 sheets. How many sheets of paper did the writer buy in all?

A 500

B 800

C 1,000

D 1,500

8. Which number completes the pattern?

$1{,}200 \div 4 = 300$
$120 \div 4 = 30$
$12 \div 4 = 3$
$1.2 \div 4 = \square$

F 300 **G** 30

H 3 **J** 0.3

14 MEASUREMENT: METRIC UNITS

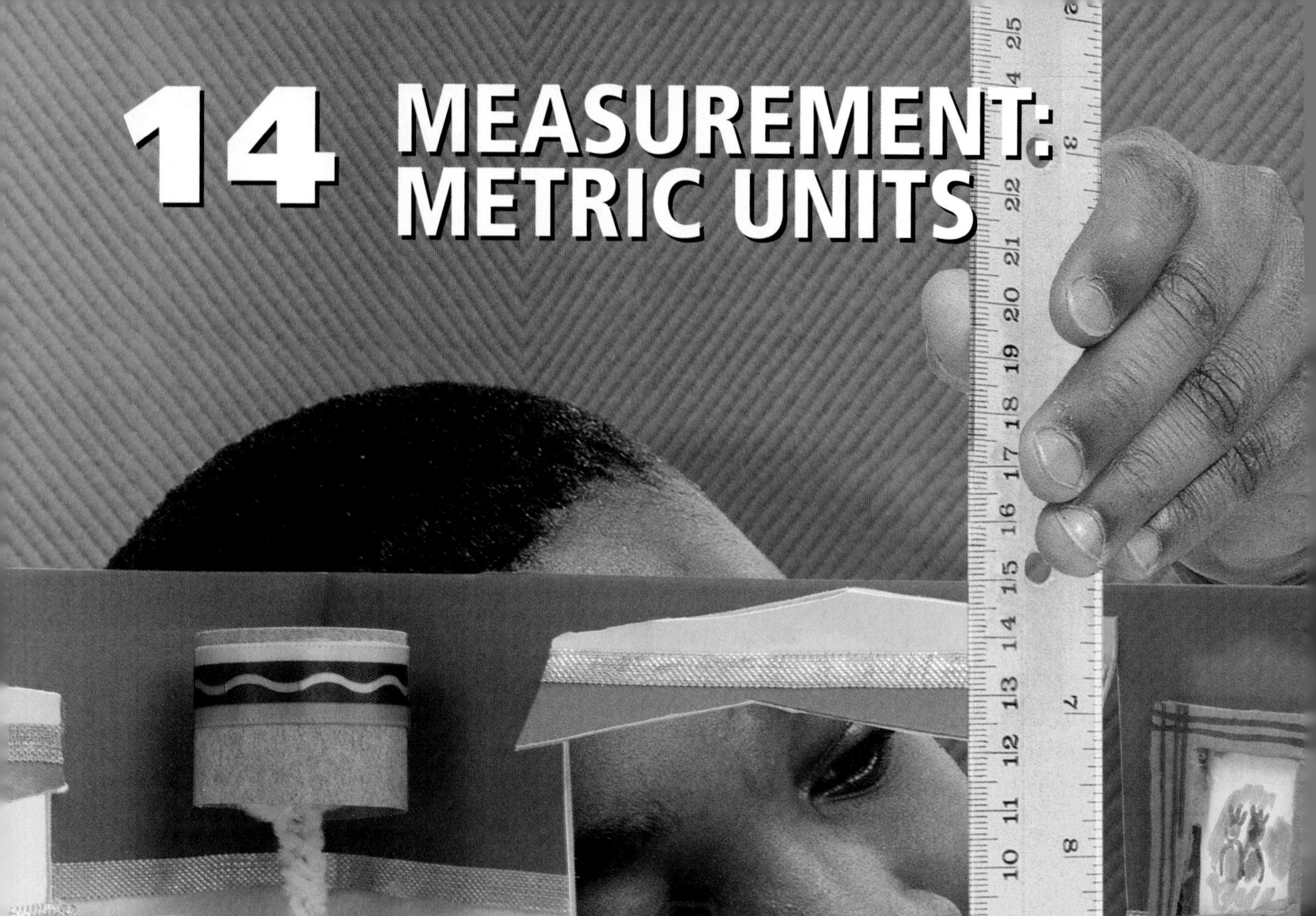

MEASUREMENT **LINK**

Although the U.S. has not officially adopted the metric system, all U.S. automobiles have been designed to metric specifications since 1990.

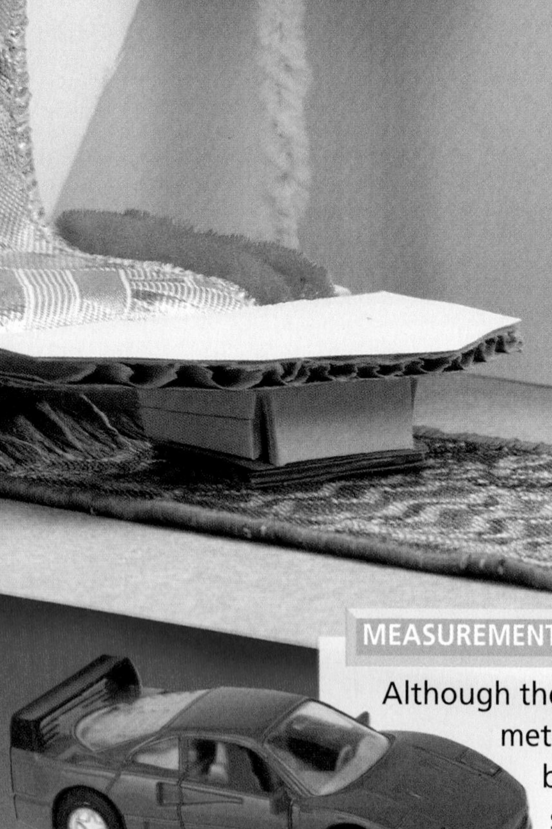

Problem-Solving Activity

Make a Miniature Metric Room

Tiny action figures need places to live, too.

Create a unique environment for the action figure of your choice. When you and your classmates' rooms are finished, present them in a mini-metric room tour.

YOU WILL NEED: an action figure, a cardboard box, paper and fabric scraps, small boxes, spools and so on, scissors, glue, and a cm ruler

- Measure an action figure and a box.
- Divide the tasks of making and measuring furniture, doors, windows, rugs, or any other furnishings.
- Make a chart with the dimensions of the room and each item in it.
- Present your room at a mini-metric room tour.

DID YOU

- ✓ measure the action figure, the box, and all the furnishings in centimeters?
- ✓ make a chart with all measurements?
- ✓ present your room at a mini-metric room tour?

LESSON 1

Linear Units

Why learn this? You can choose which metric units to use to measure objects, such as a door or a toy car.

VOCABULARY
centimeter (cm)
meter (m)
millimeter (mm)

The objects shown below will help you understand some metric units that are used to measure length.

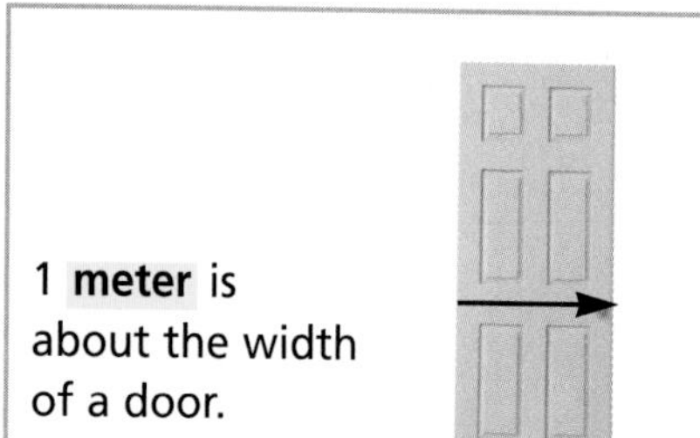 1 **meter** is about the width of a door.	 1 **centimeter** is about the width of a large paper clip.	 1 **millimeter** is about the thickness of a dime.

Kara and Luke want to use metric units to measure the length of the action figure's car. They made the list at the right to help them decide which unit to use.

Units of Length

1,000 millimeters (mm) = 1 meter (m)
100 centimeters (cm) = 1 meter (m)
10 decimeters (dm) = 1 meter (m)
1 kilometer (km) = 1,000 meters (m)

The length of the car is shorter than a meter. A centimeter is shorter than a meter. So, Kara and Luke decided to use centimeters to measure the action figure's car.

CRITICAL THINKING Is an object with a length of 10 centimeters longer than an object with a length of 2 meters? Explain how you know.

CHECK

1. Which units are shorter than a meter? longer than a meter?
2. Which unit would you use to measure the height of your desk? Explain why your choice is reasonable.
3. What objects in your classroom would you measure in meters? Explain why your choices are reasonable.
4. Would it be reasonable to measure a baseball bat in kilometers? Why or why not?

The action figure's car is 17 cm long.

▶ PRACTICE

Choose the most reasonable unit of measure. Write *mm, cm, dm, m,* or *km*.

5. thickness of paper

6. distance to the next state

7. length of a bulletin board

8. thickness of a dime

9. height of a chalkboard

10. distance around a baseball field

11. distance from Earth to the moon

12. length of a pencil

13. length of a truck

14. distance from your home to school

Write the measurements in order from shortest to longest.

15. 10 m, 10 km, 10 dm

16. 8 mm, 8 dm, 8 cm

17. 4 km, 4 m, 4 cm

18. 12 m, 12 mm, 12 cm

Problem Solving • Mixed Applications

19. Lani's house is 2 km from the library. How many meters is Lani's house from the library?

20. Compare Fran has a piece of ribbon 14 cm long. Ken has a piece of ribbon 2 dm long. Whose ribbon is longer? How much longer?

21. Greg and Malita measured the length of the chalkboard. Greg said it measured 3 dm long. Malita said it measured 3 m long. Whose measurement is more reasonable?

22. Science Mary used 3 pieces of string for her science project. They were 9.5 cm, 12.7 cm, and 5.3 cm in length. How many cm of string did Mary use?

23. Career Cameron drives 10.7 km to get to the office where he works. Jon drives twice as far to work. How far does Jon drive?

24. **Write a problem** about using m, dm, or cm to measure something in your house.

Mixed Review and Test Prep

Use mental math to complete the pattern. (pages 212–213)

25. $1 \times 5 = 5$
$0.1 \times 5 = 0.5$
$0.01 \times 5 = n$

26. $1 \times 3 = 3$
$0.1 \times 3 = n$
$0.01 \times 3 = 0.03$

27. $16 \times 1 = 16$
$16 \times 0.1 = 1.6$
$16 \times 0.01 = n$

28. $84 \times 1 = 84$
$84 \times 0.1 = n$
$84 \times 0.01 = n$

Choose the letter for the correct product. (pages 214–215)

29. $0.8 \times 0.3 = n$ **A** $n = 2.4$ **B** $n = 0.024$ **C** $n = 24$ **D** $n = 0.24$

30. $0.2 \times 0.9 = n$ **F** $n = 18$ **G** $n = 0.018$ **H** $n = 0.18$ **J** $n = 1.8$

31. $0.4 \times 0.4 = n$ **A** $n = 1.6$ **B** $n = 0.16$ **C** $n = 16$ **D** $n = 0.016$

32. $0.5 \times 0.7 = n$ **F** $n = 0.35$ **G** $n = 0.035$ **H** $n = 3.5$ **J** $n = 35$

MORE PRACTICE page H95

LESSON 2

Units of Mass

Why learn this? You can choose which metric unit to use to find the mass of an object, such as a book.

VOCABULARY
gram (g)
kilogram (kg)
milligram (mg)

Marti wants to use metric units to find the mass of a quarter and a book. She knows that the mass of a large paper clip is about 1 gram. She can estimate the mass of each object by comparing it with the mass of a paper clip.

Units of Mass

1,000 milligrams (mg) = 1 gram (g)

1,000 grams (g) = 1 kilogram (kg)

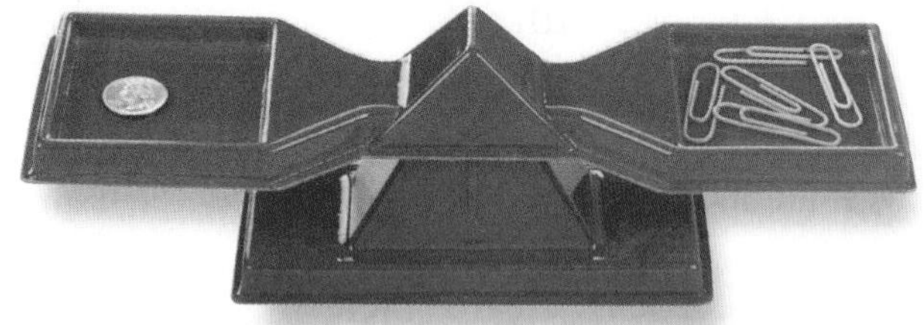

It takes about 5 large paper clips to balance a quarter. So, a quarter has a mass of about 5 grams.

It takes about 1,000 paper clips to balance this book. So, this book has a mass of about 1,000 grams, or 1 kilogram.

Talk About It

- Which unit is less than a gram? more than a gram?
- Which objects in your classroom would you measure the mass of in kilograms? in grams? Explain how to put these items in order from the least mass to the greatest mass.

CRITICAL THINKING You know the mass of a pencil and you have a box of pencils. How can you use the pencils to find the mass of another object?

▶ CHECK

Choose the most reasonable unit. Write *kg, g,* or *mg.*

1. a computer
2. a loaf of bread
3. a grain of rice
4. a full box of cereal
5. a bicycle

▶ PRACTICE

Choose the most reasonable unit. Write *kg, g,* or *mg.*

6. a stamp

7. a large dog

8. a bagel

9. a snowflake

10. a bag of apples

11. a full suitcase

Choose the more reasonable measurement.

12. 

225 g or 225 kg

13. 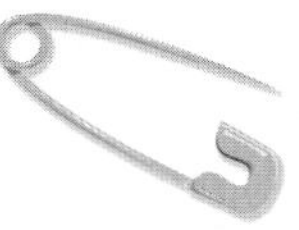

175 mg or 175 g

14. 

5 g or 5 kg

15. 

450 mg or 450 kg

16. 

30 g or 30 kg

17. 

4 mg or 4 g

18. 

15 g or 15 kg

19. 

35 mg or 35 g

Problem Solving • Mixed Applications

20. Compare One cereal bar has a mass of 37 g. What is the mass of 6 cereal bars? Is that more than or less than 1 kg?

21. Career Mr. Sigman, the gardener, needs 1 kg of potting soil for his plants. He has 750 g. How much more soil does he need?

22. Wanda needs to move 110 kg of rocks. She can carry 10 kg each trip. How many trips must she make?

23. Sports Brian ran a 100-meter dash in 10.45 seconds. Chris ran the race in 9.98 seconds. How much faster was Brian's time?

24. Logic Fran is using a recipe that makes 1 dozen cookies. Would the mass of the cookies be greater than or less than a kilogram?

25. **Write a problem** about the mass of an item in your kitchen.

Mixed Review and Test Prep

Copy and complete each pattern. **(pages 230–231)**

26. $200 \div 5 = n$
$20 \div 5 = n$
$2 \div 5 = n$

27. $300 \div 6 = n$
$30 \div 6 = n$
$3 \div 6 = n$

28. $100 \div 4 = n$
$10 \div 4 = n$
$1 \div 4 = n$

29. $600 \div 5 = n$
$60 \div 5 = n$
$6 \div 5 = n$

Choose the letter for the correct product. **(pages 218–219)**

30. $1.6 \times 4 = n$ **A** 64 **B** 6.4 **C** 0.64 **D** 0.064

31. $1.6 \times 0.04 = n$ **F** 0.064 **G** 0.64 **H** 64 **J** 0.0064

32. $0.16 \times 4 = n$ **A** 64 **B** 6.4 **C** 0.64 **D** 0.604

MORE PRACTICE page H95

Units of Capacity and Volume

You will investigate estimating and measuring with metric units of capacity.

VOCABULARY
capacity
kiloliter (kL)
liter (L)
milliliter (mL)

The **capacity** of a container measures the amount the container will hold. The metric units of capacity are listed at the right.

In the metric system, volume and capacity are related. A volume of 1 cubic centimeter (cc) can hold 1 milliliter (mL) of water.

Units of Capacity
1,000 milliliters (mL) = 1 liter (L)
1,000 liters (L) = 1 kiloliter (kL)
1 metric cup = 250 milliliters (mL)
4 metric cups = 1 liter (L)
1mL
1 cm
1 cm

REMEMBER:
Volume is measured by length × width × height. It is expressed in cubic units.

▶ EXPLORE

MATERIALS: 5 empty containers of different sizes, water, metric measuring cup marked with mL and cc units

- Label each container with a different letter from *A* to *E*.
- Use metric units of capacity to estimate how much liquid each container can hold.
- Fill each container with water. Pour the water from the container into the measuring cup to find the capacity and volume of each container.

Record

Copy the table and use it to record your measurements.

CRITICAL THINKING A gardener mixed 500 mL of liquid plant food with 2,500 mL of water. How many liters is the combined mixture?

Container	A	B	C	D	E
Estimated Capacity					
Measured Capacity (mL)					
Volume (cc)					

Talk About It

- How can the shape of a container make estimating its capacity difficult?
- How did you find the volume of the container once you knew its capacity?
- How would you determine which unusual shape container has the greatest capacity?

Now, investigate the capacity of objects in your classroom or school.

HEALTH LINK

Water plays an important role in good health. It helps keep our temperature constant. Young people need to drink about 1 to $1\frac{1}{2}$ liters of water each day. About how many milliliters of water do you need to drink each day to keep healthy?

▶ TRY THIS

1. Choose two containers, such as a paper cup and a coffee can. Estimate the capacity of each. Then use a metric measuring cup to find the capacity and volume of each container.
2. **Write About It** What do you notice about the size of each object and its capacity?

▶ PRACTICE

Choose the reasonable unit. Write *mL, L,* or *kL.*

3. 

4. 

5. 

Choose the more reasonable measurement.

6. 

250 mL or 250 L

7. 

4 mL or 4 L

8. 
50 mL or 50 L

Technology Link

You can convert units of measure by using E-Lab, Activity 14. Available on CD-ROM and on the Internet at **www.hbschool.com/elab**

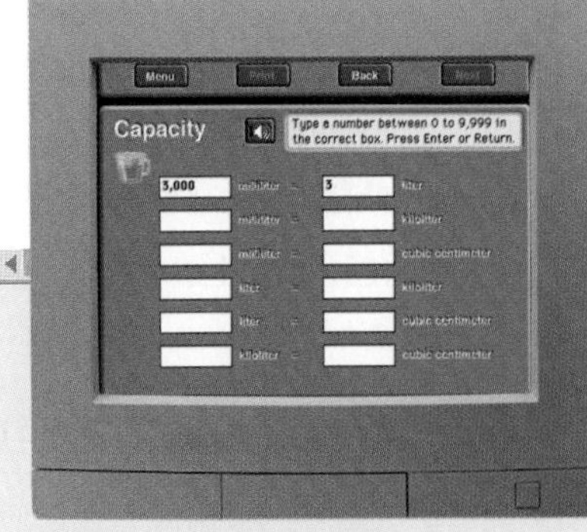

Problem Solving • Mixed Applications

9. **Number Sense** Travis found an old recipe for pancakes. He cannot read some of it. The recipe makes 12 to 14 pancakes. Would the amount of milk be 300 mL or 30 L?

10. **Write a problem** using this information. A carton holds 1 L of orange juice.

MORE PRACTICE page H96

LESSON 4

Relating Metric Units

Why learn this? You can understand the prefixes and know which units are very small, such as those used to measure medicine, and which are very large, such as those used to measure great distances.

You have seen how metric units can be used to measure length, capacity, and mass. Metric units use a *prefix* and a *base unit.*

Length	Capacity	Mass
millimeter	milliliter	milligram
centimeter		
decimeter		
meter	liter	gram
kilometer	kiloliter	kilogram

Metric units are related to place value. The prefix determines the value of the unit.

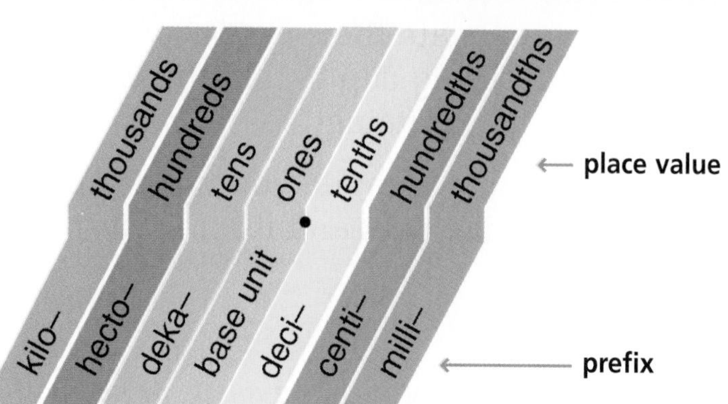

You can write measurements by using the base unit.

7 kilograms = ? grams	3 milliliters = ? liter
Think: 1 kilogram = 1,000 grams	Think: 1 milliliter = 0.001 liter
$7 \times 1{,}000 = 7{,}000$	$3 \times 0.001 = 0.003$
7 kilograms = 7,000 grams	3 milliliters = 0.003 liter

Talk About It CRITICAL THINKING

- Which prefixes indicate units smaller than the base units?
- Which prefix indicates a unit 1,000 times as great as the base unit?

▶ CHECK

Write the equivalent measurement.

1. 4 centimeters = ? meter

2. 5 milligrams = ? gram

3. 2 milliliters = ? liters

4. 3 kilograms = ? grams

▶ PRACTICE

Choose the smaller unit of measure. Write *a* or *b*. Use the prefix to help you.

5. a. kilometer
b. meter

6. a. milliliter
b. liter

7. a. gram
b. milligram

Choose the larger unit of measure. Write *a* or *b*. Use the prefix to help you.

8. a. kiloliter
b. liter

9. a. gram
b. kilogram

10. a. decimeter
b. centimeter

Write the equivalent measurement.

11. 5 decimeters = __?__ meter

12. 4 milliliters = __?__ liter

13. 8 grams = __?__ milligrams

14. 9 milligrams = __?__ gram

15. 2 milliliters = __?__ liter

16. 6 kilograms = __?__ grams

17. 4 centimeters = __?__ meter

18. 12 milligrams = __?__ gram

Problem Solving • Mixed Applications

19. Science In science class, Carl has an object with a mass of 1 kg. Mark has an object with a mass of 1 mg. Who has the object with a smaller mass?

20. Art Rita is painting a mural in her classroom. She needs 1.5 L of paint to complete the mural. She has only 0.25 L of paint. How much more paint does she need?

21. Art Conner and Kelly need string for their art projects. Conner needs 3.5 m of string, and Kelly needs 4.2 m of string. How much string do they need in all?

22. Number Sense Dustin used a piece of wire that was 4.5 m long. He cut the wire into 5 equal pieces. Was each piece of wire greater than or less than 1 m?

23. Compare Suzanne has a piece of ribbon 2.2 dm long. Joel has a piece of ribbon 22 cm long. Whose ribbon is longer?

24. Write About It Explain how to decide if the capacity of a container should be measured in milliliters or liters.

Mixed Review and Test Prep

Find the quotient. Check by multiplying. (pages 236–239)

25. $9\overline{)3.6}$ **26.** $7\overline{)4.9}$ **27.** $9\overline{)8.1}$ **28.** $3\overline{)3.3}$ **29.** $2\overline{)4.04}$

Choose the letter for the correct product. (pages 224–225)

30. $2.5 \times 1.8 = n$ **A** 4.5 **B** 0.45 **C** 45 **D** 0.045

31. $3.9 \times 4.6 = n$ **F** 179.4 **G** 17.94 **H** 1.794 **J** 0.1794

32. $2.05 \times 9.9 = n$ **A** 202.95 **B** 20.295 **C** 2.295 **D** 0.295

MORE PRACTICE page H96

Changing Units

Why learn this? You can change units of measure to make them more reasonable, such as naming the length of a room as 6.5 meters instead of 650 centimeters.

Changing units in the metric system is like moving from one place-value position to another.

×10 →	×10 →	×10 →	×10 →	×10 →	×10 →	
kilo- **thousands**	**hecto-** **hundreds**	**deka-** **tens**	**base** **ones**	**deci-** **tenths**	**centi-** **hundredths**	**milli-** **thousandths**
← ÷10	← ÷10	← ÷10	← ÷10	← ÷10	← ÷10	

A. To change units to smaller units, multiply.
5 m = __?__ cm

Hint: Meters are longer than centimeters.

To change base unit meter to centimeters, move two places to the right.

Multiply by 10 × 10, or 100.

5 × 100 = 500

×10 →	×10 →	
m **ones**	**dm** **tenths**	**cm** **hundredths**

So, 5 m = 500 cm.

B. To change units to larger units, divide.
4,000 L = __?__ kL

Hint: Liters are less than kiloliters.

To change base unit liters to kiloliters, move three places to the left.

Divide by 10 × 10 × 10, or 1,000.

4,000 ÷ 1,000 = 4

kL **thousands**	**hL** **hundreds**	**daL** **tens**	**L** **ones**
← ÷10	← ÷10	← ÷10	

So, 4,000 L = 4 kL.

CRITICAL THINKING If you get fewer units when you change from one unit to another, did you start with a larger or smaller unit?

▶ CHECK

1. If you change 7 meters to centimeters, does the number become larger or smaller? Explain how you know.
2. Why do you multiply to change 7 kilograms to grams?
3. Why do you divide to change 8 mL to liters?

▶ PRACTICE

Write the missing unit.

4. 4 kg = 4,000 __?__
5. 60 km = 60,000 __?__
6. 9 m = 900 __?__
7. 8.136 L = 8,136 __?__
8. 9.373 kg = 9,373 __?__
9. 800 mm = 80 __?__
10. 5.9 m = 590 __?__
11. 5,560 mm = 5.56 __?__
12. 2,000 mL = 2 __?__
13. 30 m = 300 __?__
14. 6,800 g = 6.8 __?__
15. 7 kg = 7,000 __?__

Write *multiply* or *divide*. Then write the equivalent measurement.

16. 2.5 cm = __?__ mm
17. 70 mm = __?__ cm
18. 5 cm = __?__ dm
19. 12 L = __?__ mL
20. 8,000 mg = __?__ g
21. 6,000 g = __?__ kg
22. 34,000 mL = __?__ L
23. 6.25 g = __?__ mg
24. 8.8 L = __?__ mL
25. 3.75 m = __?__ cm
26. 50 mm = __?__ dm
27. 1,600 mL = __?__ L
28. 0.005 m = __?__ mm
29. 7,700 mg = __?__ g
30. 9 g = __?__ kg

Problem Solving • Mixed Applications

31. **Science** Tara poured 0.5 L of water into a beaker. During an experiment, she added 200 mL of water. How much water was in the beaker at the end of the experiment?

32. **Science** While he was doing a science experiment, Todd learned that weather balloons burst at an altitude of 27 km. What is this altitude in meters?

33. **Art** Janis had a piece of string for her string-art project that was 2.7 m long. She cut the string into 3 equal pieces. Was each piece of string longer than or shorter than 1 m?

34. **Write About It** Explain how to decide when to multiply and when to divide when changing units.

LESSON CONTINUES

Problem-Solving Strategy: Draw a Diagram

▶ **THE PROBLEM** Sammy, Jamal, and Enrique skate 6 days each week. They skate 2.3 km each day. How many meters do they skate each day?

UNDERSTAND

- What are you asked to find?
- What information will you use?
- Is there information you will not use? If so, what?

PLAN

- What strategy can you use to solve this problem?

  You can *draw a diagram* to find how many meters Sammy, Jamal, and Enrique skate.

SOLVE

- What diagram can you draw to solve the problem?

  You can use the diagram shown below.

  2.3 km = __?__ m Multiply by 10 × 10 × 10, or 1,000.

  2.3 km = 2,300 m 2.3 x 1,000 = 2,300

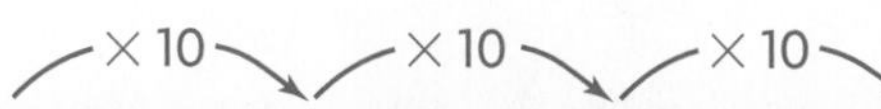

kilo-	hecto-	deka-	base
thousands	hundreds	tens	ones
2.3 km	23 hm	230 dam	2,300 m

So, Sammy, Jamal, and Enrique each skate 2,300 m each day.

LOOK BACK

- How can you decide if your answer is reasonable?
- What other strategy can you use?

▶ PRACTICE

Draw a diagram to solve.

1. Darla found that her Spanish book has a mass of 0.650 kg. What is the mass of Darla's Spanish book in grams?

2. Gary's height is 1.5 m. Rick is 1 dm taller than Gary. How tall is Rick in meters?

3. Derrick poured 0.4 L of milk into a pitcher. Then his dad poured 0.23 L of milk into the pitcher. How many milliliters of milk are in the pitcher?

4. A dog run will be 6 yd long and 3 yd wide. One side that is 6 yd long will be formed by a garage. The other three sides will be made of fencing. How much fencing is needed?

Mixed Applications

Solve.

CHOOSE a strategy and a tool.

- Work Backward
- Draw a Diagram
- Write a Number Sentence
- Find a Pattern
- Make an Organized List

Paper/Pencil

Calculator

Hands-On

Mental Math

5. Ken will do a science project on either electricity, sea life, space, or weather. He can work on the project either alone or with a partner. What are the choices Ken has for doing the science project?

6. During a rainstorm, a rain barrel contained 1.5 in. of water at 4:00 P.M. By 5:00 P.M. it held 3 in. of water. At 6:00 P.M. there were 4.5 in. of water. If rain continues to fall at this rate, how many inches of water will the barrel contain at 9:00 P.M.?

7. Nicki can juggle up to 5 pounds of juggling balls, regardless of the number of balls. If she wants to juggle 10 balls of equal weight, what is the most each ball can weigh?

8. Sara poured 0.2 L of orange juice into each of 3 glasses. How many milliliters of orange juice did Sara use?

9. Christa spent half her weekly allowance on materials for her art project. Then she spent half of what was left on colored pencils. Part of her receipt is shown at the right. How much is her weekly allowance?

MORE PRACTICE page H97

CHAPTER 14 Review/Test

CHECK Understanding

VOCABULARY

1. The __?__ of a container measures the amount the container can hold. (page 252)
2. The width of a large paper clip is about 1 __?__ . (page 248)
3. The width of a doorway is about 1 __?__. (page 248)
4. The thickness of a dime is about 1 __?__. (page 248)
5. A __?__ is equivalent to 1,000 mg. (page 250)
6. A unit of mass that is 1,000 times as much as a gram is a __?__. (page 250)
7. A capacity of 1,000 mL is equivalent to 1 __?__. (page 252)
8. A __?__ is equivalent to 1,000 L. (page 252)

Choose the more reasonable measurement. (pages 248–253)

9. 

17 cm or 17 dm

10. 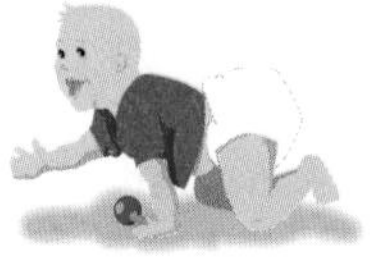

10 kg or 10 g

11. 

200 g or 200 mg

12. 

2 L or 2 mL

CHECK Skills

Write the equivalent measurement. (pages 254–257)

13. 6 m = __?__ mm
14. 2,000 mg = __?__ g
15. 4 L = __?__ kL
16. 77 cm = __?__ dm
17. 4.2 g = __?__ mg
18. 35 mL = __?__ L
19. 5 kg = __?__ g
20. 0.008 L = __?__ mL
21. 0.7 m = __?__ dm

CHECK Problem Solving

Solve. (pages 258–259)

CHOOSE a strategy and a tool.

- Find a Pattern
- Make an Organized List
- Draw a Diagram

Paper/Pencil

Calculator

Hands-On

Mental Math

22. Jason can buy either a blue, red, green, or black bike. It can be either a 10-speed or a 12-speed bike. What choices does Jason have?
23. Jackie and each of her 3 friends had a glass of juice at their picnic. There were 300 mL of juice in each glass. How many liters of juice did Jackie and her friends drink?

Test Prep

CUMULATIVE
CHAPTERS 1–14

Choose the best answer.

1. May worked in a community project planting trees. The graph shows the number of trees planted for each of 5 weeks.

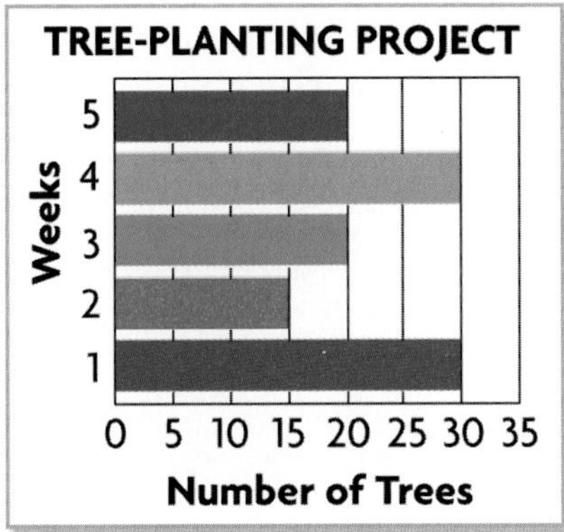

What is the difference between the greatest number of trees planted and the least number of trees planted?

A 15 **B** 20

C 25 **D** 30

2. Taylor bought 5 baseball cards. The lowest-priced card cost $1.25, and the highest-priced card cost $2.75. What is a reasonable total for the cost of the 5 cards?

F Less than $3

G Between $3 and $5

H Between $5 and $15

J Between $15 and $20

3. Michelle's garden measures 5 feet by 12 feet. What is her garden's area?

A 17 sq ft **B** 34 sq ft

C 48 sq ft **D** 60 sq ft

4. Jim needs 1 kilogram of salt for an experiment. He has 800 grams. How much more salt does he need?

F 2 g

G 20 g

H 200 g

J 2 kg

K Not Here

5. Ms. Willis paid Clinton $120 to walk her 3 dogs over the summer. How much was Clinton paid per dog?

A $4 **B** $40

C $80 **D** $120

6. Which number completes the pattern?

$$2{,}000 \div 5 = 400$$
$$200 \div 5 = 40$$
$$20 \div 5 = 4$$
$$2 \div 5 = n$$

F 40 **G** 4

H 0.4 **J** 0.04

7. $950 \div 50 =$

A 19 **B** 20

C 190 **D** 200

8. Mike bought a computer for $942. He is paying for it in 6 equal payments. How much is each payment?

F $57 **G** $257

H $147 **J** $157

CHAPTERS 12–14

PURPOSE To see patterns in dividing 10.00

YOU WILL NEED calculator

Your kitten is missing, and your family is offering a $10 reward if someone finds it. Great news! You hear that your kitten has been found—by more than one person.

How will you divide the reward between 2 people? 3 people? up to 10 people? Make a chart of the amount per person. Which numbers will not come out evenly?

Number of People	Amount per Person
1	$10.00
2	
3	

ON TARGET?

PURPOSE To estimate whether a quotient is more or less than one

YOU WILL NEED calculator

Write a division problem in which the dividend (number to be divided) is a decimal.

Your partner will estimate whether the quotient (answer) will be more or less than one or equal to one.

Check the division with a calculator. Is the estimate on target?

Switch. Play at least three rounds with large and small numbers.

2)9.9

5)0.85

You Can Raise Money by Washing Cars

PURPOSE To use multiplication and division to solve problems

YOU WILL NEED calculator

You can choose the goal and be the brains behind your class project.

Figure out how much to charge and state a goal in dollars.

Calculate how many cars you would need to wash to meet your goal.

Do you think your class could reasonably wash that many cars in 4 weekends? Why or why not?

Weekend Car Wash

Help pay for the 5th Grade Class Trip!

Type of Car	Price of Wash
Compact:	$ 2.00
Sedan:	$ 2.75
Van:	$ 3.50

Look in the yellow pages of your phone book for car-washing services. Call one or two of them to find out what they charge.

Multiplying Three Factors

MATERIALS:
Casio fx-55, or another calculator

Emilio wants to know how many kilometers he bikes to work each week. He rides 5.25 miles each day for 5 days. He knows that 1 mile = 1.61 kilometers.

Using a calculator is sometimes easier than using paper and pencil. Emilio uses his calculator to multiply 1.61 × 5.25 × 5.

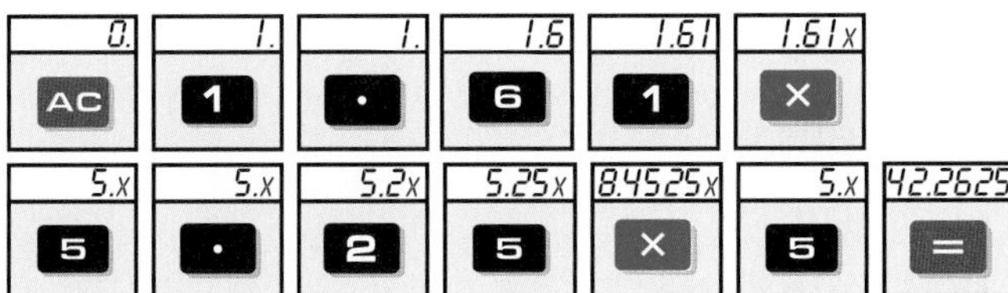

REMEMBER:
You can multiply the factors in any order and get the same product.
Example: 3 x 4 x 7 = 84
4 x 3 x 7 = 84

Emilio rounds his answer to the nearest kilometer.

42.2625 rounds to 42. So, Emilio bikes about 42 kilometers to work each week.

EXAMPLE

Multiply. 2.65 × 1.2 × 3

First, estimate. 2.65 → 3
1.21 → 1
3 → 3 So, 3 × 1 × 3 = 9.

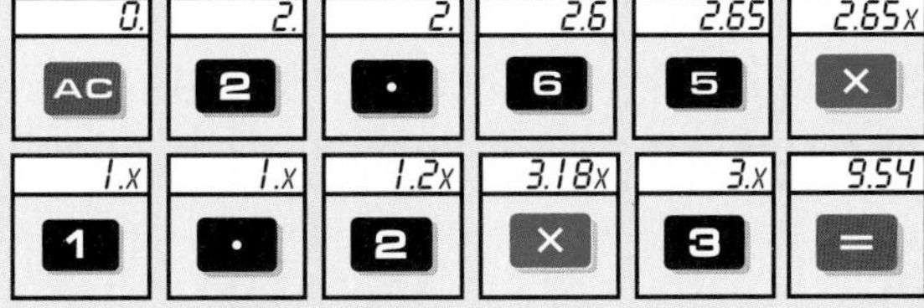

9 is close to 9.54. So, 9.54 is reasonable.

▶ PRACTICE

1. Emilio's friend in Japan rode her bike 9.75 kilometers a day for 8 days. One km = 0.62 mile. How many miles did she ride in 8 days?

2. Kelly's mother cut 2 strips of molding. Each strip is 2.5 meters long. One meter = 39.37 inches. How many inches of molding does she have?

Using the Calculator Find the product. Estimate first to see if your answer is reasonable.

3. 6.3 × 4.82 × 4
4. 8 × 5.34 × 1.75
5. 7.8 × 5 × 3.92

CHAPTERS 12–14

Study Guide and Review

Vocabulary Check

Choose a term from the box to complete each sentence.

VOCABULARY
gram
centi-
liter
meter
mixed decimal
capacity

1. A number with a whole number part and a decimal part is a _?_. (page 224)
2. There are 100 centimeters (cm) in 1 _?_. (page 248)
3. A container's _?_ measures the amount it can hold. (page 252)
4. A mass of 1,000 milligrams (mg) is equivalent to 1 _?_. (page 250)
5. A capacity of 1 _?_ is equivalent to 1,000 milliliters (mL). (page 252)
6. The prefix _?_ indicates a metric unit that is $\frac{1}{100}$ of the base unit. (page 254)

Study and Solve

CHAPTER 12

EXAMPLE

Estimate to place the decimal point. Find the product.

$$\begin{array}{r} {}^{3\,4} \\ 2.57 \\ \times\ 0.6 \\ \hline 1.542 \end{array}$$

Multiply as with whole numbers. Use estimation to place the decimal point.

Think: 0.6 × 2.57 is about 0.5 × 3, or about half of 3, which is 1.5.

Use mental math to complete the pattern. (pages 212–213)

7. $64 \times 1 = n$
   $64 \times 0.1 = n$
   $64 \times 0.01 = n$
8. $302 \times 1 = n$
   $302 \times 0.1 = n$
   $302 \times 0.01 = n$
9. $33 \times 1 = n$
   $33 \times 0.1 = n$
   $33 \times 0.01 = n$
10. $430 \times 1 = n$
    $430 \times 0.1 = n$
    $430 \times 0.01 = n$

Find the product. (pages 210–225)

11. 0.8×9
12. 0.37×4
13. 0.7×0.5
14. $\$6.14 \times 6$
15. 1.9×3
16. 5.63×7
17. 3.42×0.8
18. 2.31×0.4
19. $\$2.98 \times 0.5 = n$
20. $0.76 \times 2.2 = n$
21. $4.07 \times 3.6 = n$
22. $7.25 \times 1.6 = n$

Choose a strategy and solve. (pages 216–217)

23. After a party, 0.4 of a pizza was left. Al ate 0.5 of the leftover pizza. How much of a whole pizza did he eat?

CHAPTER 13

EXAMPLE

Find the quotient.

$$3\overline{)27.9}\quad 9.3$$

Divide as with whole numbers. Place the decimal point in the quotient above the decimal point in the dividend, between the ones place and the tenths place.

Copy and complete each pattern. (pages 230–231)

24. $4{,}000 \div 5 = n$
$400 \div 5 = n$
$40 \div 5 = n$
$4 \div 5 = n$

25. $9{,}000 \div 4 = n$
$900 \div 4 = n$
$90 \div 4 = n$
$9 \div 4 = n$

26. $6{,}000 \div 8 = n$
$600 \div 8 = n$
$60 \div 8 = n$
$6 \div 8 = n$

27. $3{,}000 \div 6 = n$
$300 \div 6 = n$
$30 \div 6 = n$
$3 \div 6 = n$

Find the quotient. Check by multiplying. (pages 236–241)

28. $7\overline{)3.5}$ **29.** $5\overline{)4.5}$

30. $6\overline{)0.36}$ **31.** $8\overline{)5.68}$

32. $3\overline{)3.69}$ **33.** $4\overline{)7.2}$

34. $2\overline{)6.08}$ **35.** $9\overline{)82.8}$

Choose a strategy and solve.

36. Vicky and Raúl went to lunch. Their bill was $23.88. They decided to split the cost. How much did each pay? (pages 232–233)

37. The market is selling chicken at $2.25 per pound. How much do 3 pounds cost? (pages 242–243)

CHAPTER 14

EXAMPLE

Write the equivalent measurement.

66 cm = __?__ dm Since 1 dm = 10 cm, multiply by 0.1.

66 cm = 6.6 dm $66 \times 0.1 = 6.6$

Write the equivalent measurement. (pages 254–257)

38. 5 m = __?__ cm

39. __?__ mm = 8 m

40. 4,000 g = __?__ kg

41. 3.5 g = __?__ mg

42. 9 L = __?__ kL

43. __?__ L = 55 mL

Choose the more reasonable measurement. (pages 248–253)

44. 15 cm or 15 m

45. 8 g or 8 kg

46. 

40 g or 40 kg

47. 

2 mL or 2 L

Choose a strategy and solve. (pages 258–259)

48. Karla is 150 cm tall. Pablo is 1 dm shorter than Karla. How tall is Pablo in centimeters? in meters?

CHAPTERS 12–14

Performance Assessment

Tasks: Show What You Know

1. Explain the pattern you see in the problems. Then explain how to use mental math to find the products and name the products. (pages 212–213)

$45 \times 1 = n$
$45 \times 0.1 = n$
$45 \times 0.01 = n$

2. Show and explain each step as you use patterns or estimation to place the decimal point and then find the quotient. (pages 236–241)

$8\overline{)32.8}$

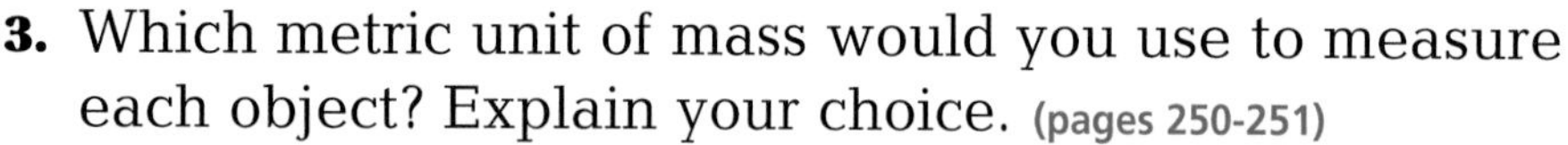

3. Which metric unit of mass would you use to measure each object? Explain your choice. (pages 250-251)

- a bag of potatoes
- a stamp
- a quarter

Problem Solving

Solve. Explain your method.

CHOOSE a strategy and a tool.

- Find a Pattern
- Make a Model
- Write a Number Sentence
- Act It Out
- Make a Table

Paper/Pencil

Calculator

Hands-On

Mental Math

4. Suppose you collect 10 pounds of paper. Of the paper, 0.5 is newspaper and 0.5 is computer paper. If 0.8 of the newspaper is colored pages, how much of the paper collected is colored? (pages 216–217)

5. Pens cost \$0.59 each when purchased separately, or 5 pens for \$1.99 when purchased in packages. Write a number sentence to find out which is the better buy. Explain your answer. (pages 232–233)

6. Hector is 1.5 m tall. His dog, Pepper, is 5 dm shorter than he is. Rosa, his sister, is 3 dm taller than Pepper. How tall are Rosa and Pepper, in meters? (pages 258–259)

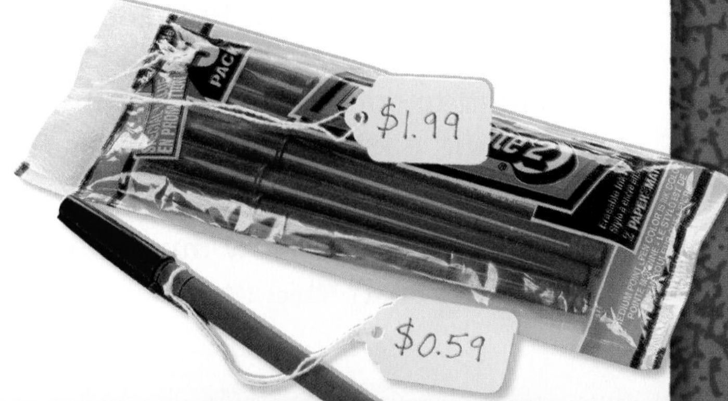

Cumulative Review

CHAPTERS 1–14

Solve the problem. Then write the letter of the correct answer.

1. What is the value of the blue digit?

203,462,851

A. 2
B. 200,000
C. 2,000,000
D. 200,000,000

(pages 6–11)

---

2. Dan has $15.00 with him at the bookstore. He chooses a book for $8.95, a greeting card for $2.25, and a magazine for $1.95. Does he have enough for all three items if the sales tax is about $1.00? Estimate what he will pay at the cash register, including tax.

A. yes; about $12.00
B. yes; about $14.00
C. no; about $15.50
D. no; about $16.00

(pages 30–31)

---

3. $228 \times 4 = n$

A. $n = 57$
B. $n = 232$
C. $n = 912$
D. $n = 9{,}120$

(pages 78–81)

---

4. By which numbers is 884 divisible?

A. 2, 3
B. 2, 3, 4
C. 2, 3, 5
D. 2, 4

(pages 110–111)

---

5. Which number is divisible by 2, 3, and 9?

A. 12
B. 63
C. 54
D. 27

(pages 110–111)

---

6. Find the mode.

105, 110, 115, 105, 130

A. 25
B. 105
C. 110
D. 113

(pages 154–155)

---

7. $3.54 \times 0.6 = n$

A. $n = 2.124$
B. $n = 4.14$
C. $n = 21.24$
D. $n = 212.4$

(pages 214–223)

---

8. $4\overline{)6.84}$

A. 1.71
B. 17.1
C. 171
D. 27.36

(pages 236–241)

---

9. A dime is about 1 __?__ thick.

A. centimeter
B. kiloliter
C. milligram
D. millimeter

(pages 248–253)

---

10. Choose the most reasonable measurement.

A. 25 mm
B. 25 cm
C. 25 m
D. 25 km

(pages 248–249)

---

11. 5 kg = __?__ g

A. 0.005
B. 0.5
C. 500
D. 5,000

(pages 250–251, 254–255)

15 UNDERSTANDING FRACTIONS

CULTURAL **LINK**

In the early 1800's, people all over the world enjoyed a Chinese puzzle called a tangram. How can you arrange the seven pieces of the tangram to make a picture?

Problem-Solving Activity

Fraction Time with Tangrams

You have probably made tangram puzzles by arranging the seven pieces in different ways. But have you ever thought about why the pieces fit together?

Analyze tangram pieces as fractions of one whole. Then make a poster showing designs that add up to $\frac{1}{2}$.

YOU WILL NEED: tangram pattern, scissors, poster board, markers

- Figure out which pieces make $\frac{1}{4}$, which pieces make $\frac{1}{8}$, and which pieces make $\frac{1}{16}$ of the whole square.
- Write the fractions on each piece.
- Use the tangram pieces to make designs that cover $\frac{1}{2}$ of the whole square.
- Make a poster showing your designs.
- Share your tangram poster with the class.

RULES FOR MAKING TANGRAMS THAT ADD UP TO $\frac{1}{2}$

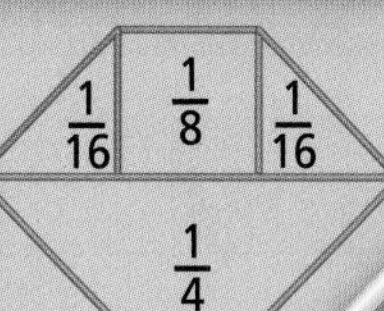

- Pieces must add up to $\frac{1}{2}$.
- Write the fraction on each piece.
- It is all right to flip pieces over.
- It is all right to use small pieces from more than one tangram.

DID YOU

- ✓ figure out the fraction for each tangram piece?
- ✓ make designs that add up to $\frac{1}{2}$?
- ✓ make a poster of your designs?
- ✓ share your poster with the class?

LESSON 1

Understanding Fractions

Why learn this? You can use fractions to describe a number of groups within your class.

Lita's class is making tangram designs. Of the students, $\frac{1}{2}$ make people, $\frac{1}{3}$ make animals, and $\frac{1}{4}$ make flowers. Which group is largest?

You can use fraction strips and number lines to show fractions. The fraction strips and number lines below show the fractions $\frac{1}{1}$, $\frac{1}{2}$, $\frac{1}{3}$, and $\frac{1}{4}$.

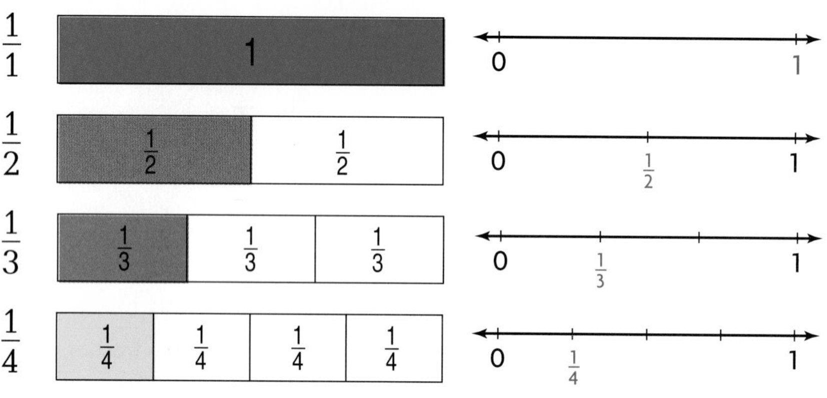

So, the group that makes people is largest.

- If the denominator increases and the numerator stays the same, what happens to the size of the part of the whole?

____

The fraction strips and number lines below show the fractions $\frac{1}{4}$, $\frac{2}{4}$, $\frac{3}{4}$, and $\frac{4}{4}$.

Fraction	Fraction strip	Number line
$\frac{1}{4}$	$\frac{1}{4}$ $\frac{1}{4}$ $\frac{1}{4}$ $\frac{1}{4}$	0, $\frac{1}{4}$, 1
$\frac{2}{4}$	$\frac{1}{4}$ $\frac{1}{4}$ $\frac{1}{4}$ $\frac{1}{4}$	0, $\frac{2}{4}$, 1
$\frac{3}{4}$	$\frac{1}{4}$ $\frac{1}{4}$ $\frac{1}{4}$ $\frac{1}{4}$	0, $\frac{3}{4}$, 1
$\frac{4}{4}$	$\frac{1}{4}$ $\frac{1}{4}$ $\frac{1}{4}$ $\frac{1}{4}$	0, 1

- If the denominator stays the same and the numerator increases, what happens to the size of the part of the whole?

CHECK

Write the fraction shown.

1. | $\frac{1}{3}$ | $\frac{1}{3}$ | $\frac{1}{3}$ |
|---|---|---|

2. | $\frac{1}{5}$ | $\frac{1}{5}$ | $\frac{1}{5}$ | $\frac{1}{5}$ | $\frac{1}{5}$ |
|---|---|---|---|---|

3. **Write About It** Why do the parts of the whole get smaller when the denominator increases and larger when the numerator increases?

PRACTICE

Write the fraction shown.

4. | $\frac{1}{5}$ | $\frac{1}{5}$ | $\frac{1}{5}$ | $\frac{1}{5}$ | $\frac{1}{5}$ |
|---|---|---|---|---|

5. | $\frac{1}{6}$ | $\frac{1}{6}$ | $\frac{1}{6}$ | $\frac{1}{6}$ | $\frac{1}{6}$ | $\frac{1}{6}$ |
|---|---|---|---|---|---|

6. | $\frac{1}{8}$ | $\frac{1}{8}$ | $\frac{1}{8}$ | $\frac{1}{8}$ | $\frac{1}{8}$ | $\frac{1}{8}$ | $\frac{1}{8}$ | $\frac{1}{8}$ |
|---|---|---|---|---|---|---|---|

7. | $\frac{1}{10}$ | $\frac{1}{10}$ | $\frac{1}{10}$ | $\frac{1}{10}$ | $\frac{1}{10}$ | $\frac{1}{10}$ | $\frac{1}{10}$ | $\frac{1}{10}$ | $\frac{1}{10}$ | $\frac{1}{10}$ |
|---|---|---|---|---|---|---|---|---|---|

Shade a fraction strip to show the fraction.

8. $\frac{2}{3}$ **9.** $\frac{1}{6}$ **10.** $\frac{5}{8}$ **11.** $\frac{9}{10}$ **12.** $\frac{3}{4}$

13. $\frac{2}{9}$ **14.** $\frac{7}{12}$ **15.** $\frac{3}{5}$ **16.** $\frac{1}{3}$ **17.** $\frac{5}{6}$

Draw a number line. Locate the fraction.

18. $\frac{4}{5}$ **19.** $\frac{3}{6}$ **20.** $\frac{3}{10}$ **21.** $\frac{2}{3}$ **22.** $\frac{5}{6}$

Problem Solving • Mixed Applications

23. Science Gina is planting 8 rows of vegetables in her garden. Today she planted 3 rows. What fraction of her garden does she have left to plant?

24. Write a problem about a family sharing a pie. Use fractions in your problem.

Mixed Review and Test Prep

Solve. Use the inverse operation to check each problem. (pages 20–21)

25. $11 + 25$ **26.** $37 - 14$ **27.** $44 + 17$ **28.** $132 - 91$

Choose the number that has the given value of the digit 4. (pages 40–41)

29. 4 thousand **A** 3,512.046 **B** 5,423.681 **C** 2,138.054 **D** 4,325.062

30. 4 tenths **F** 5,640.315 **G** 5,117.462 **H** 1,318.042 **J** 6,250.004

31. 4 hundredths **A** 3,406.002 **B** 6,926.482 **C** 3,523.704 **D** 1,525.147

MORE PRACTICE page H97

LESSON 2

Mixed Numbers

VOCABULARY
mixed number

Why learn this? You can use mixed numbers to name amounts made up of wholes and parts, such as a whole pizza and slices.

The fifth-grade soccer team had a pizza party. They ordered two rectangular pizzas that were cut into eighths. The team ate one whole pizza and three slices from the other pizza.

A **mixed number** is made up of a whole number and a fraction. Look at the fraction bars that represent the pizza the soccer team ate.

Read: one and three eighths

Write: $1\frac{3}{8}$

- How many eighths are represented by the fraction bar for 1? How many eighths are shown in all? What fraction does this name?

CRITICAL THINKING Are all mixed numbers greater than 1? Why or why not?

EXAMPLES

A one and two fifths

$1\frac{2}{5}$

B two and one fourth

$2\frac{1}{4}$

C three and five sixths

$3\frac{5}{6}$

When a fraction is greater than 1, it can be renamed as a mixed number.

EXAMPLE

Rename $\frac{5}{4}$ as a mixed number.

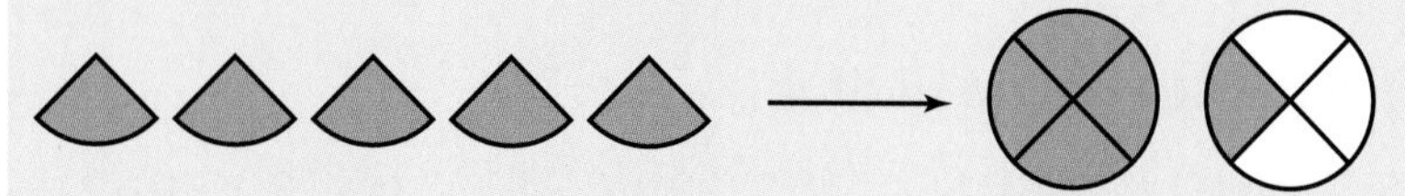

- How can you tell if a fraction is greater than 1?

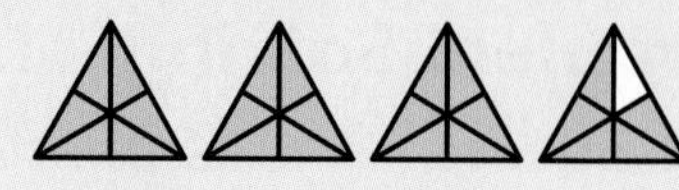

In *Mighty Math Calculating Crew*, the game *Nautical Number Line* challenges you to identify mixed numbers. Use Grow Slide Level K.

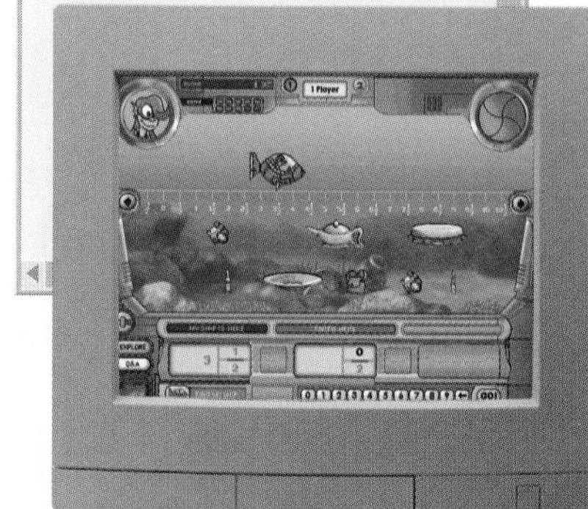

Calculator Activities page H64

You can also use a calculator to change a fraction to a mixed number.

Press: 6   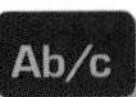

Display: 

▶ CHECK

For Problems 1–4, use the figures at the right.

1. How many whole figures are shaded?

2. Into how many parts is each figure divided?

3. How many parts of the fourth figure are shaded?

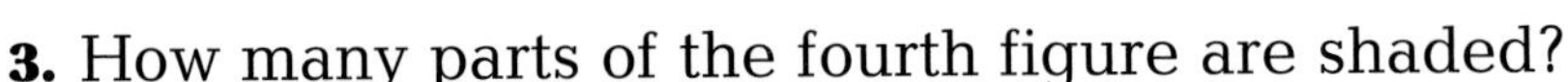

4. Write a fraction and a mixed number for the picture.

▶ PRACTICE

Rename each fraction as a mixed number.

5. $\frac{21}{8}$ **6.** $\frac{9}{2}$ **7.** $\frac{7}{6}$ **8.** $\frac{13}{5}$ **9.** $\frac{15}{4}$

Rename each mixed number as a fraction.

10. $2\frac{1}{2}$ **11.** $3\frac{1}{4}$ **12.** $7\frac{2}{3}$ **13.** $1\frac{3}{4}$ **14.** $2\frac{4}{5}$

Problem Solving • Mixed Applications

15. Tina found a page from her great-grandmother's old math book. Tina wants to rename all the fractions as mixed numbers. Rename the fractions for her.

FRACTIONS 139

Change each fraction to a mixed number.

1. $\frac{3}{2}$ 2. $\frac{5}{2}$ 3. $\frac{5}{4}$ 4. $\frac{9}{4}$ 5. $\frac{15}{8}$

16. For every 3 hours Mike works, he earns $15.75. How much will he earn in 9 hours?

17. **Write About It** Explain how to rename a mixed number as a fraction.

Mixed Review and Test Prep

Write in standard form. (pages 40–41)

18. four thousand, two hundred fifty and sixty-one thousandths

19. six thousand, one hundred and two hundred four thousandths

Choose the letter for the correct sum. (pages 54–55)

20. $5 + 0.8 = n$ **A** 6.8 **B** 5.8 **C** 5.080 **D** 4.81

21. $4.7 + 2.96 = n$ **F** 3.43 **G** 7.66 **H** 7.6 **J** 6.66

22. $8.53 + 0.491 = n$ **A** 13.44 **B** 9.021 **C** 8.921 **D** 12.44

MORE PRACTICE page H97

Multiples and Least Common Multiples

You will investigate finding the least common multiple of two numbers.

VOCABULARY
- multiple
- common multiples
- least common multiple (LCM)

A **multiple** is the product of two or more numbers.

Multiples of one number that are also multiples of another number are called **common multiples**. The least number that is a common multiple is called the **least common multiple**, or **LCM**.

EXPLORE

MATERIALS: red and yellow counters

Use counters to find the least common multiple of 3 and 4.

MODEL

Step 1

Place 3 red counters in a row. Place 4 yellow counters in a row directly below.

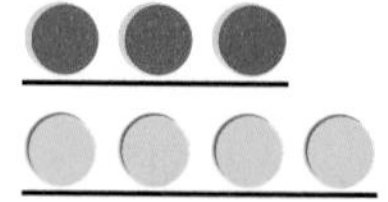

Step 2

Continue placing groups of 3 red and 4 yellow counters until both rows have the same number of counters. At that point, the number of counters in each row is the least common multiple, or LCM, of 3 and 4.

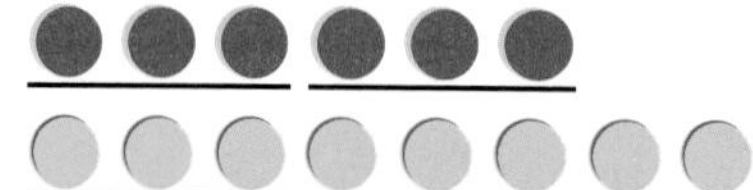

Complete the steps to find the least common multiple of 3 and 4. Use the same method to find the least common multiple of 4 and 5.

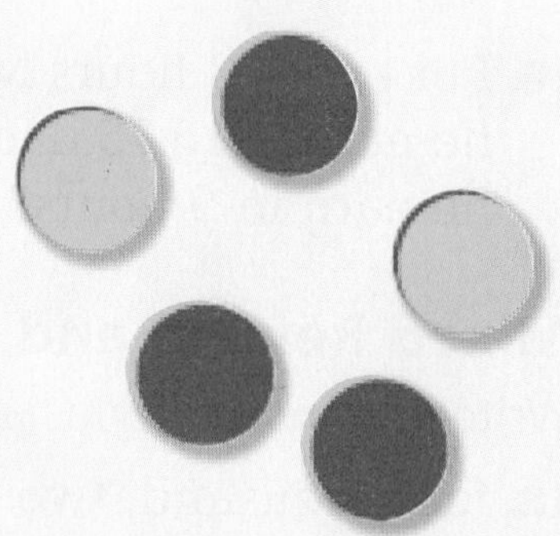

Record

Write the least common multiple of 3 and 4 and the least common multiple of 4 and 5. Explain how you know.

Talk About It Can two numbers have more than one common multiple? Explain.

CRITICAL THINKING How could you make a drawing to find the LCM for two numbers?

You can also find the LCM of two or more numbers by making a list or using a number line.

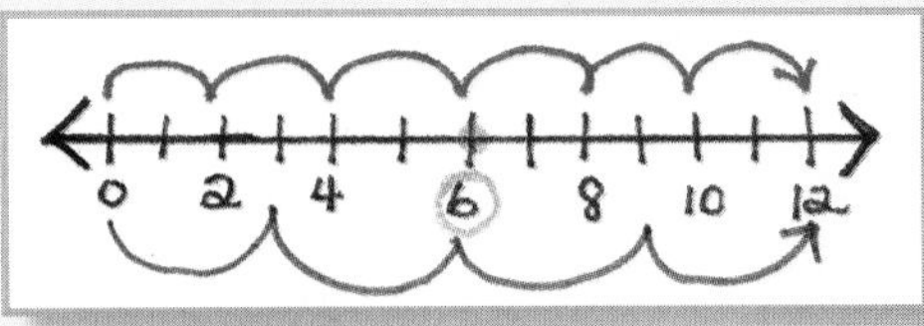

Multiples of 2: 2, 4, 6, 8, 10, 12
Multiples of 3: 3, 6, 9, 12, 15, 18

So, the least common multiple, or LCM, is 6.

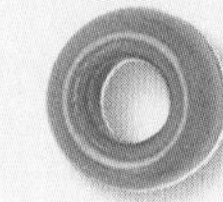

▶ TRY THIS

You can use the least common multiple, or LCM, to rename fractions with unlike denominators as fractions with like denominators.

EXAMPLE

Rename $\frac{1}{2}$ and $\frac{2}{3}$ so they have the same denominator.

Use the least common multiple, or LCM, of the denominators as the new denominator. The LCM of 2 and 3 is 6.

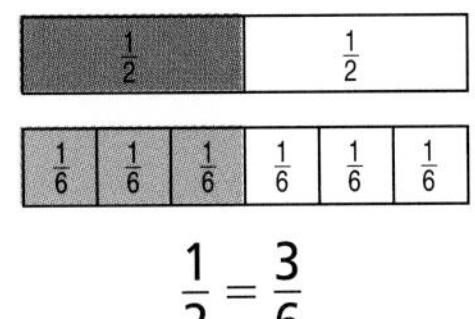

$\frac{1}{2} = \frac{3}{6}$

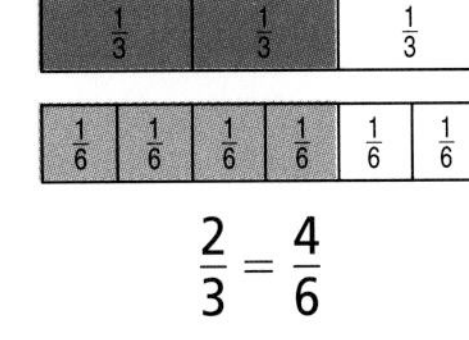

$\frac{2}{3} = \frac{4}{6}$

Technology Link

You can find the least common multiple by using E-Lab, Activity 15. Available on CD-ROM and on the Internet at **www.hbschool.com/elab**

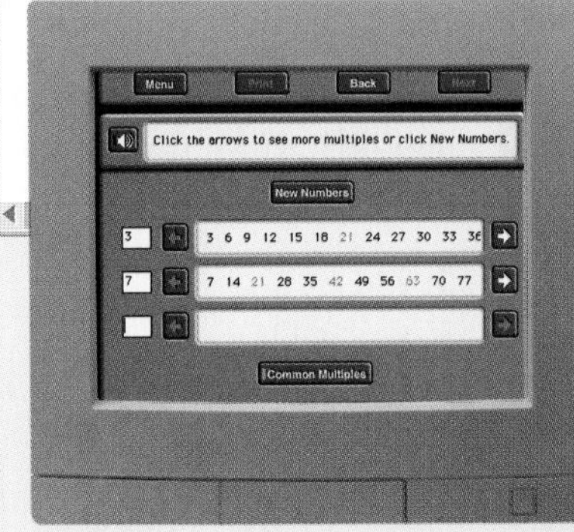

1. Use fraction strips and the LCM to rename $\frac{3}{4}$ and $\frac{2}{3}$ so they have the same denominator. Write the new pair of fractions.

2. **Write About It** How is the LCM used to rename fractions?

▶ PRACTICE

Use counters to name the least common multiple for each.

3. 2 and 4 **4.** 2 and 5 **5.** 4 and 6 **6.** 9 and 3 **7.** 4 and 8

Rename each pair of fractions so they have the same denominator. Use fraction strips and the LCMs from Exercises 3–7.

8. $\frac{1}{2}$ and $\frac{1}{4}$ **9.** $\frac{1}{2}$ and $\frac{2}{5}$ **10.** $\frac{1}{4}$ and $\frac{5}{6}$ **11.** $\frac{5}{9}$ and $\frac{2}{3}$ **12.** $\frac{3}{4}$ and $\frac{5}{8}$

Problem Solving • Mixed Applications

13. Measurement Ethan rides his bike $\frac{3}{4}$ mile every day. Brad rides his bike $\frac{4}{6}$ mile. How can you rename the distances Ethan and Brad ride so that they have the same denominators?

14. Reasoning Nita will use all the ceramic and glass beads she buys. Ceramic beads come 5 to a pack, and glass beads come 3 to a pack. She uses the same number of each bead. What is the least number of beads she will buy?

MORE PRACTICE pages H97–H98

LESSON 4

Comparing

Why learn this? You can compare fractional amounts when cooking.

To compare fractions with unlike denominators, you can use fraction strips.

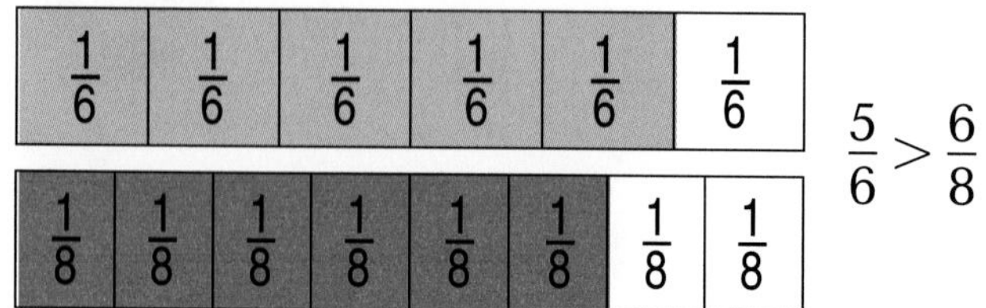

$\frac{5}{6} > \frac{6}{8}$

To compare fractions with *like denominators*, compare the *numerators*.

Since $3 > 1$, $\frac{3}{4} > \frac{1}{4}$.

You can also rename fractions with unlike denominators, such as $\frac{1}{2}$ and $\frac{2}{3}$, so they have like denominators.

MODEL

Step 1

Find the least common multiple, or LCM, of the denominators.

2: 2, 4, 6, 8
3: 3, 6, 9, 12

So, the LCM is 6.

Step 2

Use 6 as a denominator. Find the missing factor to rename each denominator as 6.

$\frac{1 \times \blacksquare}{2 \times \blacksquare} = \frac{}{6}$ The missing factor is 3.

$\frac{2 \times \blacksquare}{3 \times \blacksquare} = \frac{}{6}$ The missing factor is 2.

Step 3

Multiply the numerator and the denominator by the missing factor from Step 2. Compare the numerators of the renamed fractions.

$\frac{1 \times 3}{2 \times 3} = \frac{3}{6}$

$\frac{2 \times 2}{3 \times 2} = \frac{4}{6}$ Since $3 < 4$, $\frac{3}{6} < \frac{4}{6}$.

So, $\frac{1}{2} < \frac{2}{3}$.

EXAMPLE

Use the LCM to compare $\frac{3}{5}$ and $\frac{7}{10}$.

Find the LCM of the denominators.

5: 5, 10, 15, 20
10: 10, 20, 30, 40

Rename the fractions.

$\frac{3 \times 2}{5 \times 2} = \frac{6}{10}$

$\frac{7 \times 1}{10 \times 1} = \frac{7}{10}$

Compare.

Since $6 < 7$, $\frac{6}{10} < \frac{7}{10}$.

So, $\frac{3}{5} < \frac{7}{10}$.

- Can the least common multiple of two numbers be one of the numbers? Explain.

CRITICAL THINKING Which pair of fractions is easier to compare, $\frac{2}{3}$ and $\frac{5}{9}$ or $\frac{2}{3}$ and $\frac{5}{7}$? Explain.

▶ CHECK

Compare the fractions. Write $<$, $>$, or $=$ for each ●.

1. $\frac{2}{3}$ ● $\frac{3}{4}$

$\frac{1}{3}$	$\frac{1}{3}$	$\frac{1}{3}$	
$\frac{1}{4}$	$\frac{1}{4}$	$\frac{1}{4}$	$\frac{1}{4}$

2. $\frac{3}{8}$ ● $\frac{1}{4}$

$\frac{1}{8}$	$\frac{1}{8}$	$\frac{1}{8}$	$\frac{1}{8}$	$\frac{1}{8}$	$\frac{1}{8}$	$\frac{1}{8}$	$\frac{1}{8}$
$\frac{1}{4}$		$\frac{1}{4}$		$\frac{1}{4}$		$\frac{1}{4}$	

▶ PRACTICE

Rename, using the least common multiple, and compare.
Write $<$, $>$, or $=$ for each ●.

3. $\frac{5}{21}$ ● $\frac{3}{7}$ **4.** $\frac{4}{6}$ ● $\frac{2}{3}$ **5.** $\frac{2}{9}$ ● $\frac{3}{18}$ **6.** $\frac{11}{15}$ ● $\frac{4}{5}$

7. $\frac{3}{8}$ ● $\frac{5}{16}$ **8.** $\frac{4}{12}$ ● $\frac{1}{3}$ **9.** $\frac{2}{3}$ ● $\frac{25}{27}$ **10.** $\frac{13}{20}$ ● $\frac{3}{5}$

11. $\frac{5}{6}$ ● $\frac{3}{4}$ **12.** $\frac{5}{6}$ ● $\frac{3}{8}$ **13.** $\frac{1}{2}$ ● $\frac{4}{7}$ **14.** $\frac{2}{3}$ ● $\frac{4}{5}$

15. $\frac{3}{10}$ ● $\frac{1}{4}$ **16.** $\frac{2}{5}$ ● $\frac{3}{4}$ **17.** $\frac{4}{9}$ ● $\frac{2}{6}$ **18.** $\frac{1}{3}$ ● $\frac{3}{8}$

Problem Solving • Mixed Applications

19. Jan used $\frac{2}{3}$ cup flour to make cookies. She used $\frac{3}{4}$ cup flour to make brownies. For which did she use more flour?

20. Consumer The Grocery Store sells 4 bags of rice for $16.20. The Warehouse Market sells 1 bag of rice for $4.10. The Country Store sells 6 bags of rice for $25.00. In which store is the price the least?

21. Patterns Park rangers moved 2 alligators from one lake to another this month. For the next 5 months, they will move 3 more than the month before. How many alligators will they move in all?

22. Write About It When renaming fractions, why do you multiply the numerator by the same number by which you multiply the denominator?

Mixed Review and Test Prep

Order from least to greatest. (pages 44–45)

23. 3.34, 3.61, 3.01 **24.** 9.400, 9.004, 9.040 **25.** 14.43, 14.29, 14.91

Choose the letter for the correct difference. (pages 56–57)

26. $2.6 - 0.9 = n$ **A** 1.7 **B** 2.3 **C** 2.7 **D** 17

27. $5.04 - 0.7 = n$ **F** 43.4 **G** 4.34 **H** 0.434 **J** 434

MORE PRACTICE page H98

Ordering

Why learn this? You will be able to compare more than two fractional amounts, such as several different ice cream toppings.

ICE CREAM DREAM SHOP	
$\frac{5}{6}$ pound peanut butter chips	$0.40
$\frac{1}{2}$ pound chocolate chips	$0.30
$\frac{1}{4}$ pound granola	$0.50

Mr. Scott bought some supplies for the Ice Cream Dream Shop. Which item was the heaviest? Which was the lightest?

You can use fraction strips to order fractions from least to greatest.

1					
$\frac{1}{6}$	$\frac{1}{6}$	$\frac{1}{6}$	$\frac{1}{6}$	$\frac{1}{6}$	$\frac{1}{6}$
$\frac{1}{2}$	$\frac{1}{2}$				
$\frac{1}{4}$	$\frac{1}{4}$	$\frac{1}{4}$	$\frac{1}{4}$		

The fraction strips show that $\frac{1}{4} < \frac{1}{2} < \frac{5}{6}$. So, the peanut butter chips were the heaviest and the granola was the lightest.

You can also rename the fractions so they have like denominators and then put them in order.

MODEL

Step 1

Find the least common multiple, or LCM, of 2, 4, and 6.

2: 2, 4, 6, 8, 10, 12
4: 4, 8, 12
6: 6, 12

Step 2

Rename the fractions so that the LCM is the denominator.

$\frac{1 \times 3}{4 \times 3} = \frac{3}{12}$

$\frac{1 \times 6}{2 \times 6} = \frac{6}{12}$

$\frac{5 \times 2}{6 \times 2} = \frac{10}{12}$

Step 3

Compare the numerators. Put them in order from least to greatest.

Since 3 < 6 < 10,

$\frac{3}{12} < \frac{6}{12} < \frac{10}{12}$.

So, $\frac{1}{4} < \frac{1}{2} < \frac{5}{6}$.

Talk About It

- How would you order the fractions above from greatest to least?
- Explain how to place $\frac{1}{2}$, $\frac{2}{3}$, $\frac{1}{4}$, and $\frac{5}{6}$ in order from least to greatest.

CRITICAL THINKING Can you compare fractions with *like* numerators and *unlike* denominators, like $\frac{2}{5}$ and $\frac{2}{3}$, without renaming or using fraction strips? Explain.

▶ CHECK

Rename the fractions, using the LCM as the denominator.

1. $\frac{1}{2}, \frac{1}{4}, \frac{1}{5}$ **2.** $\frac{1}{8}, \frac{3}{4}, \frac{1}{2}$ **3.** $\frac{2}{3}, \frac{2}{5}, \frac{4}{5}$

4. $\frac{1}{6}, \frac{1}{4}, \frac{1}{8}$ **5.** $\frac{7}{12}, \frac{3}{4}, \frac{7}{8}$ **6.** $\frac{5}{6}, \frac{7}{9}, \frac{2}{3}$

▶ PRACTICE

Write in order from least to greatest.

7. $\frac{7}{12}, \frac{3}{4}, \frac{1}{2}$ **8.** $\frac{3}{5}, \frac{1}{3}, \frac{4}{15}$ **9.** $\frac{5}{8}, \frac{3}{4}, \frac{1}{2}$

10. $\frac{1}{10}, \frac{3}{5}, \frac{1}{2}$ **11.** $\frac{2}{3}, \frac{3}{4}, \frac{7}{12}$ **12.** $\frac{9}{14}, \frac{1}{2}, \frac{5}{7}$

Write in order from greatest to least.

13. $\frac{7}{15}, \frac{1}{5}, \frac{2}{3}$ **14.** $\frac{4}{5}, \frac{1}{2}, \frac{9}{10}$ **15.** $\frac{11}{16}, \frac{3}{4}, \frac{7}{8}$

16. $\frac{5}{6}, \frac{2}{3}, \frac{7}{9}$ **17.** $\frac{2}{5}, \frac{1}{2}, \frac{3}{4}$ **18.** $\frac{1}{2}, \frac{2}{3}, \frac{5}{9}$

Problem Solving • Mixed Applications

19. Money It will cost Heath \$27.50 to get into the amusement park. He wants to buy a shirt that costs \$12.99. Heath earns \$7.00 each week mowing lawns. How long will it take him to earn enough money to go to the amusement park and buy the shirt?

20. Reasoning Aaron has already bought $\frac{1}{2}$ pound trail mix for \$2.89, $\frac{1}{3}$ pound cashew nuts for \$1.25, and $\frac{1}{4}$ pound raisins for \$1.00. He can spend \$10.00 in all. Does he have enough money to buy 1 more pound of trail mix? Explain.

21. Consumer Tara paid \$2.25 for $\frac{1}{3}$ pound yogurt-covered pretzels and \$2.00 for $\frac{1}{4}$ pound chocolate-covered pretzels. Which cost more per pound?

22. There are 1,200 students at South Middle School. There are the same number of students in each grade from sixth through eighth. How many students are in each grade?

23. Bernard scored 97, 88, 89, 93, and 83 on 5 spelling tests. What is his mean score?

24. Money Each week, Remy saves \$15.95. How much money will he save in 4 weeks?

25. Measurement Lea is making punch. She uses $\frac{1}{2}$ gallon orange juice, $\frac{2}{3}$ gallon ginger ale, and $\frac{3}{4}$ gallon apple juice. List the ingredients in order from greatest to least.

26. **Write a problem** using the fractions $\frac{1}{2}$, $\frac{3}{4}$, and $\frac{1}{3}$.

Problem–Solving Strategy: Draw a Diagram

▶ THE PROBLEM Mr. Lucas is making a fruit salad. He adds $\frac{1}{4}$ cup strawberries, $\frac{2}{3}$ cup peaches, and $\frac{1}{2}$ cup pineapple. What is the order of the fruit Mr. Lucas used from least to greatest?

REMEMBER:
UNDERSTAND
PLAN
SOLVE
LOOK BACK

UNDERSTAND

- What are you asked to find?
- What information will you use?
- Is there information you will not use? If so, what?

PLAN

- What strategy can you use to solve the problem?

You can *draw a diagram* of a number line.

SOLVE

- How can you solve the problem?

First, find the LCM and rename the fractions.

Multiples of 4: 4, 8, 12, 16, 20, 24 $\frac{1 \times 3}{4 \times 3} = \frac{3}{12}$ cup strawberries

Multiples of 3: 3, 6, 9, 12, 15, 18 $\frac{2 \times 4}{3 \times 4} = \frac{8}{12}$ cup peaches

Multiples of 2: 2, 4, 6, 8, 10, 12 $\frac{1 \times 6}{2 \times 6} = \frac{6}{12}$ cup pineapple

Next, make a number line divided into twelfths. Plot each fraction on the number line.

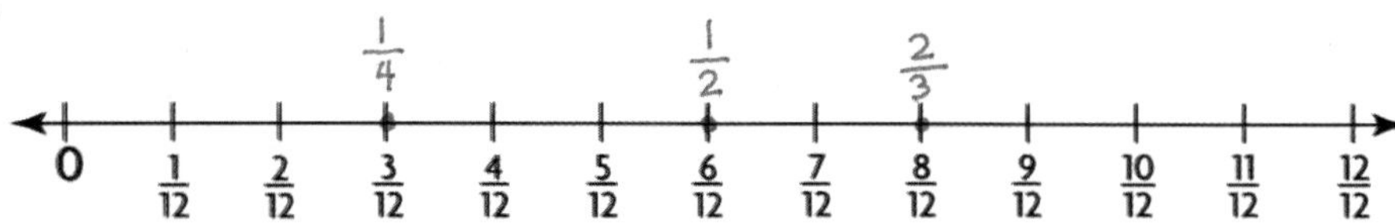

So, the order of the fruit from least to greatest is strawberries, pineapple, peaches.

LOOK BACK

- How can you decide if your answer is reasonable?
- What other strategy could you use?

▶ PRACTICE

Draw a diagram to solve.

1. Mr. Lucas is making a dinner salad. He adds $\frac{7}{8}$ cup lettuce, $\frac{1}{4}$ cup carrots, and $\frac{1}{2}$ cup tomatoes. What is the order of the ingredients Mr. Lucas uses from least to greatest?

2. Niki has red, green, and blue balloons. She has a total of 12 balloons. If $\frac{1}{3}$ of her balloons are red and $\frac{1}{4}$ are green, how many blue balloons does she have?

3. Carla used a recipe calling for $\frac{3}{4}$ cup raisins, $\frac{2}{3}$ cup water, $\frac{1}{2}$ cup honey, and $\frac{1}{3}$ cup flour. List the ingredients in order from the greatest amount to the least amount.

4. A spinner has 10 equal sections. $\frac{1}{5}$ of the spinner is green, $\frac{1}{10}$ is yellow, $\frac{1}{2}$ is blue, and $\frac{1}{5}$ is red. How many sections make up each color?

Mixed Applications

Solve.

CHOOSE a strategy and a tool.

- Draw a Diagram
- Write a Number Sentence
- Work Backward
- Find a Pattern

Paper/Pencil

Calculator

Hands-On

Mental Math

5. Roxie spent 20 minutes in her garden on Monday, 30 minutes on Tuesday, 45 minutes on Wednesday, and 65 minutes on Thursday. If the pattern continues, how much time will she spend in her garden on Friday? on Saturday?

6. Greg is making a wood frame for a poster of his favorite music group. The poster is 72 cm long and 48 cm wide. How many centimeters of wood does Greg need to buy?

7. There are 15 bushes around a circular sidewalk. Julie picks a flower from every fourth bush. How many times will she have to walk around the sidewalk in order to pick one flower from each bush?

8. Blake has $5.40 left after going to the mall. He spent $4.95 on lunch, $3.50 on a book, and $15.95 on a CD. How much did he have when he left for the mall?

9. Mrs. Green's class asked 40 students in their school to name their favorite vegetable. The table at the right shows the results as fractions of the students surveyed. What is the most popular vegetable? the least popular vegetable?

Favorite Vegetables

Vegetable	Students
Broccoli	$\frac{1}{10}$
Peas	$\frac{1}{8}$
Corn	$\frac{3}{8}$
Green Beans	$\frac{2}{5}$

MORE PRACTICE page H98

CHAPTER 15 Review/Test

▶ CHECK Understanding

VOCABULARY

1. A __?__ is made up of a whole number and a fraction. (page 272)

2. A __?__ is the product of two or more numbers. (page 274)

3. Multiples of one number that are also multiples of another number are called __?__. (page 274)

4. The least number that is a common multiple of two or more numbers is called the __?__. (page 274)

Write the fraction shown. (pages 270–271)

5.

$\frac{1}{5}$ (shaded)	$\frac{1}{5}$	$\frac{1}{5}$	$\frac{1}{5}$	$\frac{1}{5}$

6.

$\frac{1}{4}$ (shaded)	$\frac{1}{4}$ (shaded)	$\frac{1}{4}$ (shaded)	$\frac{1}{4}$

7.

$\frac{1}{8}$ (shaded)	$\frac{1}{8}$ (shaded)	$\frac{1}{8}$ (shaded)	$\frac{1}{8}$	$\frac{1}{8}$	$\frac{1}{8}$	$\frac{1}{8}$	$\frac{1}{8}$

8.

$\frac{1}{10}$ (shaded)	$\frac{1}{10}$ (shaded)	$\frac{1}{10}$ (shaded)	$\frac{1}{10}$ (shaded)	$\frac{1}{10}$ (shaded)	$\frac{1}{10}$ (shaded)	$\frac{1}{10}$ (shaded)	$\frac{1}{10}$ (shaded)	$\frac{1}{10}$ (shaded)	$\frac{1}{10}$

▶ CHECK Skills

Rename each fraction as a mixed number. (pages 272–273)

9. $\frac{5}{3}$ **10.** $\frac{7}{2}$ **11.** $\frac{11}{6}$ **12.** $\frac{9}{5}$ **13.** $\frac{19}{4}$

Rename, using the least common multiple, and compare.
Write $<$, $>$, or $=$ for each ●. (pages 276–277)

14. $\frac{2}{5}$ ● $\frac{7}{15}$ **15.** $\frac{3}{8}$ ● $\frac{9}{16}$ **16.** $\frac{6}{7}$ ● $\frac{1}{2}$ **17.** $\frac{4}{5}$ ● $\frac{4}{8}$

Write in order from least to greatest. (pages 278–279)

18. $\frac{2}{3}, \frac{3}{4}, \frac{1}{5}$ **19.** $\frac{3}{8}, \frac{1}{4}, \frac{5}{8}$ **20.** $\frac{1}{3}, \frac{4}{5}, \frac{1}{2}$

▶ CHECK Problem Solving

Solve. (pages 280–281)

CHOOSE a strategy and a tool.

- Make an Organized List
- Draw a Diagram
- Find a Pattern

Paper/Pencil

Calculator

Hands-On

Mental Math

21. Mandy mixed $\frac{1}{3}$ cup bananas, $\frac{1}{4}$ cup pineapple juice, $\frac{1}{2}$ cup milk, and $\frac{5}{6}$ cup ice in a blender. What is the order of the ingredients she used from least to greatest?

22. Ken ran $\frac{1}{2}$ mile on Monday, 1 mile on Tuesday, 2 miles on Wednesday, and 4 miles on Thursday. If this pattern continues, how many miles will he run on Friday?

Test Prep

Choose the best answer.

1. The Akashi Kaikyo Bridge in Japan is one of the world's longest bridges at 3,910 meters long. What is this number rounded to the nearest hundred?

A 3,200 **B** 3,900
C 3,000 **D** 4,000

2. Which of the following is an equivalent decimal for 0.2?

F 0.002
G 0.020
H 0.200
J 2.00
K Not Here

3. Find the volume of the box.

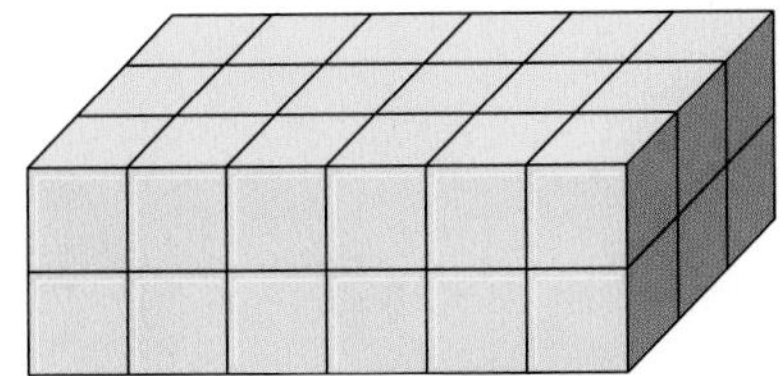

A 30 cu units
B 48 cu units
C 24 cu units
D 36 cu units

4. Renee picked 50 flowers. She plans to give an equal number of flowers to 6 friends. About how many flowers can she give each friend?

F 6 **G** 7
H 8 **J** 48

5. Zachary ran the following mileage over a 4-week period.

MILES RUN	
Week	**Miles**
1	11 miles
2	14 miles
3	18 miles
4	21 miles

What was the average distance he ran per week?

A 16 mi **B** 18 mi
C 20 mi **D** 64 mi

6. Which number completes the pattern?

$2 \times 4 = 8$

$2 \times 0.4 = n$

$2 \times 0.04 = 0.08$

$2 \times 0.004 = 0.008$

F 80 **G** 8
H 0.8 **J** 0.08

7. Jim needs a string that is 80 mm long. How many centimeters is that?

A 0.8 cm **B** 8 cm
C 80 cm **D** 800 cm

8. Which of the following fractions is greater than $\frac{1}{6}$?

F $\frac{1}{3}$ **G** $\frac{1}{12}$
H $\frac{2}{12}$ **J** $\frac{4}{24}$

16 FRACTIONS AND NUMBER THEORY

MUSIC **LINK**

A time signature tells how many beats there are in a measure. The time signature $\frac{4}{4}$ means there are 4 whole beats in a measure and a quarter note gets 1 beat.

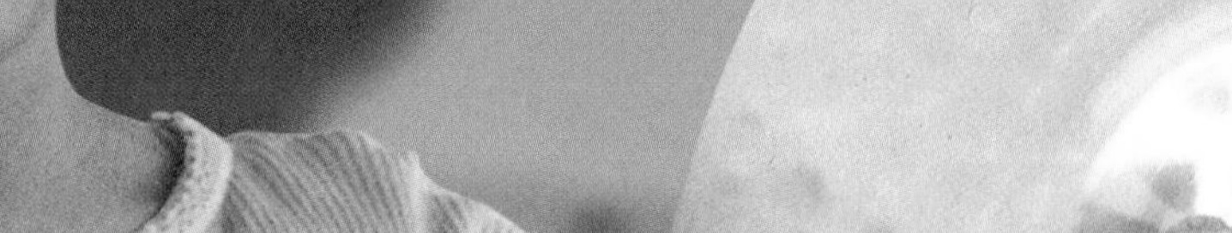

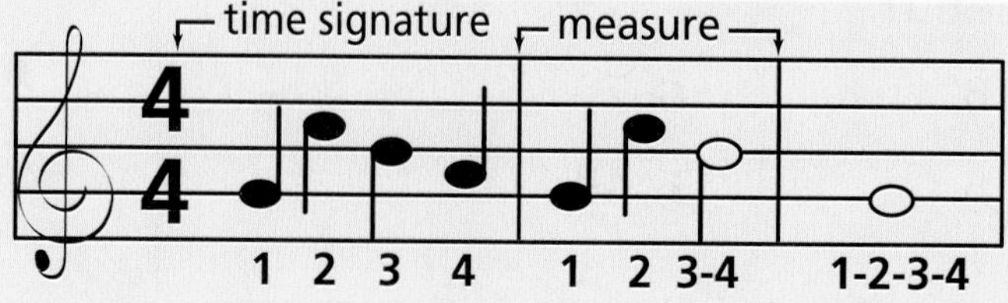

Problem-Solving Activity

Making Music in Four Beats

Music is written in measures, or sections, just like words are written in sentences. When we say that music is in $\frac{4}{4}$ time, that means there are 4 beats to a measure. We count it like this: "1, 2, 3, 4."

Write measures of music by combining at least 16 notes in different ways.

- Use at least 16 notes to write some music in $\frac{4}{4}$ time.
- Use each kind of note at least twice. Some kinds of notes are whole notes, half notes, quarter notes, and eighth notes.
- Divide your notes so that there are four beats per measure.
- Below each note, write it as a fraction.
- Share your music with the class.

CHART OF NOTE VALUES

	In $\frac{4}{4}$ time
whole note	4 beats
half ($\frac{1}{2}$) note	2 beats
quarter ($\frac{1}{4}$) note	1 beat
eighth ($\frac{1}{8}$) note	$\frac{1}{2}$ beat

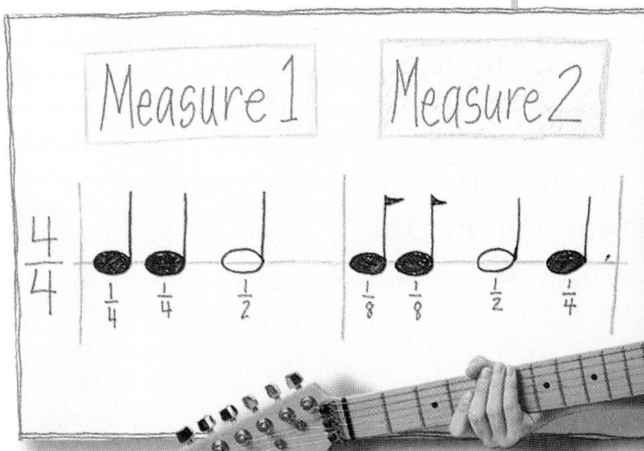

DID YOU

- ✓ write at least 16 musical notes?
- ✓ divide your notes into measures of $\frac{4}{4}$ time?
- ✓ write each note as a fraction?
- ✓ share your music with the class?

LESSON 1 • HANDS-ON LESSON

Prime and Composite Numbers

You will investigate finding factors of numbers to determine if they are prime or composite.

VOCABULARY
- **square number**
- **prime number**
- **composite number**

▶ EXPLORE

How are prime and composite numbers different?

MATERIALS: 16 square tiles

Use 16 square tiles. Show all the ways the tiles can be arranged in a rectangular array.

REMEMBER:

Factors are numbers multiplied together to find a product.

2	×	4	=	8
factor		*factor*		*product*

The *Property of One for Multiplication* says the product of any number and 1 is the number.

6 × 1 = 6

Record

Draw a picture of each rectangle. Record the length and the width. The length and width are also factors.

- How many different factors were used to show the lengths and widths?
- What do you notice about the shape of the array when two factors are the same?

When both factors are the same, the product is called a **square number**.

- Name another square number. Explain.

Now, investigate prime and composite numbers.

Prime numbers have exactly two factors, 1 and the number itself. **Composite numbers** have more than two factors. The number 1 is neither prime nor composite.

▶ TRY THIS

Use tiles to find out which numbers are prime or composite.

1. Is 6 prime or composite? Explain.
2. Is 7 prime or composite? Explain.
3. Is 9 prime or composite? Explain.

4–14. Use tiles to show all the ways the numbers 2–12 can be arranged to form a rectangle. Copy and complete the table below.

Models

Numbers	2	3	4
Length and Width	1 x 2 2 x 1	1 x 3 3 x 1	1 x 4 ? ?
Factors	1, 2	1, 3	?

15. Which numbers on your table are square numbers?

16. **Write About It** The prime factors of 12 are 2, 2, and 3. What are the prime factors of 15? Explain how you know.

▶ PRACTICE

Use square tiles to show all the arrays. Record the length and the width of each array.

17. 13 **18.** 11 **19.** 15 **20.** 14 **21.** 16

Write *prime* or *composite* for each number. Identify the square numbers.

22. 13 **23.** 19 **24.** 14 **25.** 21 **26.** 25

27. 23 **28.** 15 **29.** 36 **30.** 18 **31.** 33

32. 20 **33.** 41 **34.** 32 **35.** 37 **36.** 49

Technology Link

You can find prime and composite numbers by using E-Lab, Activity 16. Available on CD-ROM and on the Internet at **www.hbschool.com/elab**

Problem Solving • Mixed Applications

37. Reasoning Why is 2 the only even prime number? Explain.

38. Estimation Is 17 a reasonable quotient for 311 ÷ 3? Explain.

39. Visual Thinking Five students sit in the same row in math class. Nick sits in front of Carla, and Pat sits four seats behind Jordan. Carla sits in front of Tony. Who sits directly behind Jordan?

40. **Write About It** You and your friend are the same age. Your age is a prime number. Your friend says that his age is a composite number. Is this possible? Explain.

LESSON 2

Greatest Common Factor

VOCABULARY
common factors
greatest common factor (GCF)

Why learn this? You can pack items such as two different kinds of candies in the same-sized boxes.

John and Stacey made 12 peanut butter candies and 18 chocolate candies to give as gifts. They want to pack the candies in the largest box possible with only one kind of candy in each box. How many candies will each box hold?

To find out how many candies each box will hold, find all the factors of 12 and 18.

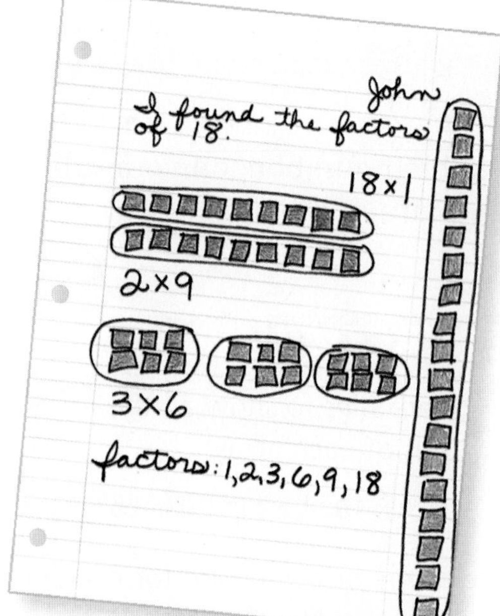

John drew arrays and listed the factors.

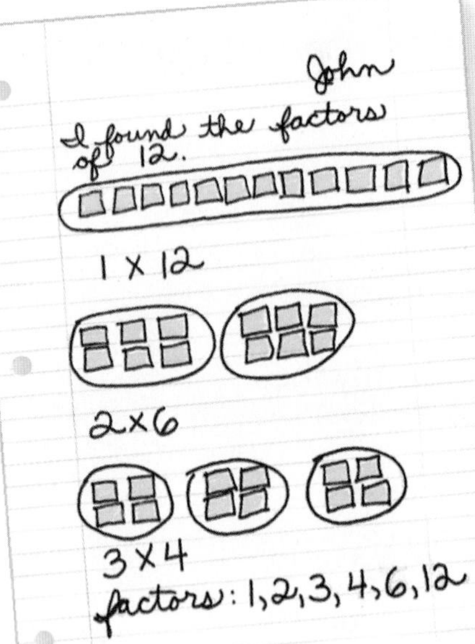

Stacey made a Venn diagram.

Factors of 12: 1, 2, 3, 4, 6, 12

Factors of 18: 1, 2, 3, 6, 9, 18

Both 12 and 18 have the factors 1, 2, 3, and 6. They are called **common factors** because each is a factor of two or more numbers.

The **greatest common factor** or **GCF**, is the greatest number that is a factor of each of two or more numbers. The greatest common factor is 6.

So, the number of candies each box will hold is 6, the GCF of 12 and 18.

CRITICAL THINKING How do you know if a number is a factor of another number?

▶ CHECK

List the factors for each number.

1. 4 1 × 4, 2 × 2

2. 6 1 × 6, 2 × 3

3. 9 **4.** 10 **5.** 7 **6.** 15 **7.** 21

List the factors for each number. Write the common factor for each pair of numbers.

8. 6 and 12 **9.** 3 and 15 **10.** 8 and 16 **11.** 9 and 18

12. 5 and 10 **13.** 10 and 20 **14.** 15 and 45 **15.** 18 and 22

List the factors for each number and identify the common factors. Write the greatest common factor for each pair of numbers.

16. 4 and 12 **17.** 5 and 25 **18.** 14 and 21 **19.** 12 and 28

20. 8 and 24 **21.** 3 and 18 **22.** 6 and 9 **23.** 15 and 35

24. 3 and 12 **25.** 12 and 30 **26.** 14 and 35 **27.** 12 and 27

28. If two numbers are even numbers, what factors will they always have in common?

▶ PRACTICE

List the factors of each number.

29. 14 **30.** 16 **31.** 20 **32.** 23 **33.** 24

34. 28 **35.** 30 **36.** 35 **37.** 36 **38.** 42

39. 47 **40.** 22 **41.** 32 **42.** 45 **43.** 40

List the factors of each number. Write the common factors for each pair of numbers.

44. 2 and 14 **45.** 5 and 20 **46.** 11 and 15 **47.** 18 and 21

48. 8 and 12 **49.** 15 and 45 **50.** 9 and 27 **51.** 30 and 50

52. 13 and 26 **53.** 6 and 30 **54.** 35 and 45 **55.** 28 and 49

List the factors of each number and identify the common factors. Write the greatest common factor for each pair of numbers.

56. 4 and 8 **57.** 12 and 21 **58.** 6 and 15 **59.** 7 and 14

60. 12 and 20 **61.** 7 and 35 **62.** 18 and 45 **63.** 30 and 50

64. 9 and 15 **65.** 24 and 16 **66.** 16 and 28 **67.** 32 and 24

68. 12 and 36 **69.** 16 and 24 **70.** 42 and 49 **71.** 50 and 60

Problem Solving • Mixed Applications

Using Data For Problems 72–73, use the table at the right.

72. The members of the Garden Club are selling boxes of marigold and petunia plants. They want to pack the plants in boxes that hold the same number. Each box will have the same kind of plants. What is the greatest number of plants each box will hold?

Plant	Number of Plants
Marigold	18
Tomato	24
Garlic	12
Pepper	36
Petunia	30

73. Reasoning The Garden Club buys empty boxes in packages of 5. How many boxes in all are needed to pack all the plants? How many packages of boxes are needed?

74. Write About It Explain how to find the greatest common factor of three numbers.

75. Reasoning I am thinking of two numbers. Each number is between 20 and 30. The GCF of the numbers is 4. What are the numbers?

76. Estimation Juan's new car can travel 52.6 miles for each gallon of gas. Estimate how far he can travel on 6 gallons of gas.

HISTORY LINK

The first Hershey Chocolate factory opened for business in 1905. In 1906, the village where it was located was renamed Hershey, PA. Today about 80 million chocolate Kisses are produced daily. To celebrate its 90th anniversary, Hershey built the Kissmobile,® which tours the nation, giving away chocolate Kisses and raising funds for charity. In what year did Hershey celebrate its 90th anniversary?

CONSUMER CONNECTION

The band is selling Hershey's® treats to raise money for new uniforms. Each member puts the treats into boxes. Use the table to answer Problems 77 and 78.

HERSHEY'S® TREATS	
Treats	**Number per box**
Hershey's Kisses®	64
Gummy Bears	56
Reese's Pieces®	32
Twizzlers®	48

77. Using Data What are the possible equal-sized groups that you could make with each treat?

78. Each box will have the same kind of treat and will hold the same number. How many treats will each box hold?

Mixed Review and Test Prep

Find the quotient. Check by multiplying. (pages 236–237)

79. $9\overline{)3.6}$ **80.** $8\overline{)6.4}$ **81.** $5\overline{)25.5}$ **82.** $7\overline{)21.07}$ **83.** $4\overline{)86.6}$

Write the measurements in order from shortest to longest. (pages 248–249)

84. 7 km, 7 m, 7 cm **85.** 16 dm, 16 mm, 16 km **86.** 18 dm, 18 cm, 18 mm

Choose the most reasonable unit of measure. (pages 248–249)

87. length of a pen

A km
B cm
C mm
D m
E Not Here

88. distance from New York to Boston

F dm
G km
H m
J mm
K Not Here

89. thickness of a page in a book

A mm
B m
C dm
D cm
E Not Here

Equivalent Fractions

VOCABULARY
equivalent fractions

Why learn this? It will help you know how to read and play music.

Mary and Mark remember from music lessons that a half note has the same number of beats as two quarter notes. So, $\frac{1}{2}$ and $\frac{2}{4}$ name the same amount. You can write $\frac{1}{2} = \frac{2}{4}$.

$\frac{1}{4}$ $\frac{1}{4}$ $\frac{1}{2}$

Look at the number lines that show $\frac{1}{2}$ and $\frac{2}{4}$. Fractions that name the same amount are called **equivalent fractions**.

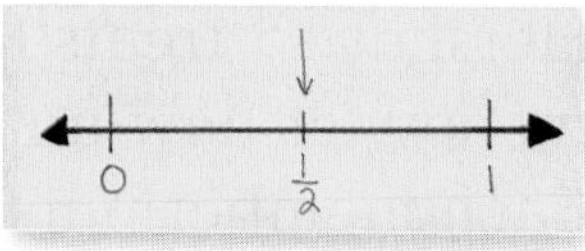

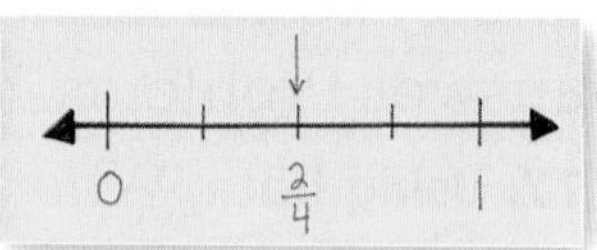

Use these two methods to find equivalent fractions.

EXAMPLES

A *Multiply* the numerator and the denominator by any number.

$$\frac{2}{3} = \frac{2 \times 2}{3 \times 2} = \frac{4}{6}$$

B *Divide* the numerator and the denominator by a common factor.

$$\frac{8}{12} = \frac{8 \div 4}{12 \div 4} = \frac{2}{3}$$

Technology Link

In ***Calculating Crew***, the game *Nautical Number Line* challenges you to find equivalent fractions on a number line. Use Grow Slide Level L.

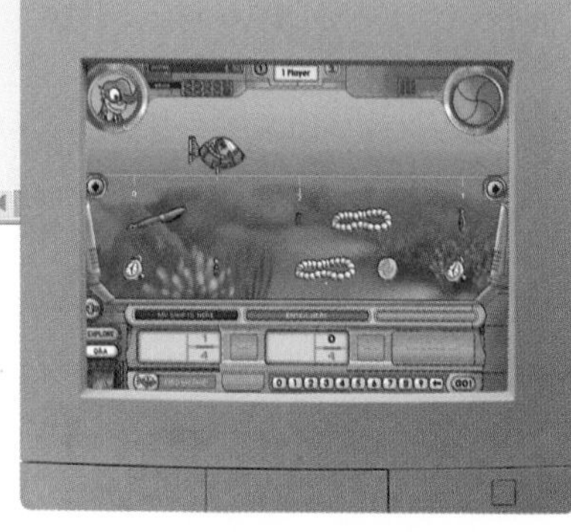

Talk About It CRITICAL THINKING

- How is using multiplication to find equivalent fractions different from using division?
- How can you use a number line to show that the fractions in Examples A and B are equivalent?

▶ CHECK

Use the number lines to name an equivalent fraction for each.

1. $\frac{3}{4}$ **2.** $\frac{2}{8}$ **3.** $\frac{2}{4}$ **4.** $\frac{6}{8}$

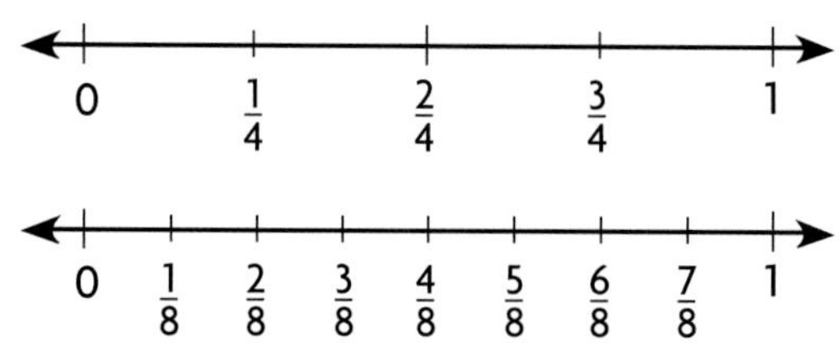

5. Draw number lines to show that $\frac{4}{16}$ is equivalent to $\frac{1}{4}$.

▶ PRACTICE

Use the number lines to name an equivalent fraction for each.

6. $\frac{1}{2}$ **7.** $\frac{2}{6}$ **8.** $\frac{2}{3}$ **9.** $\frac{1}{3}$

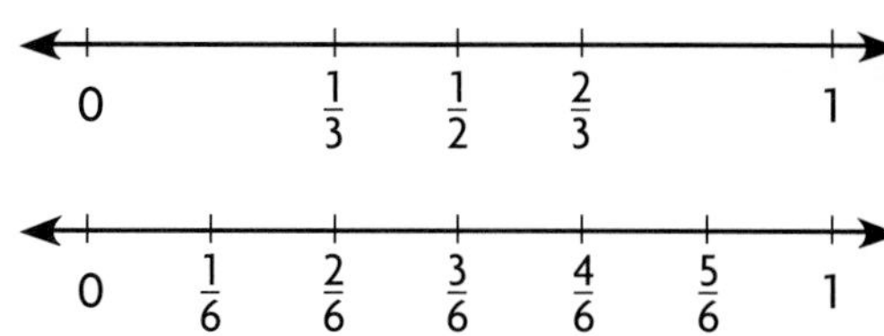

Find an equivalent fraction. Use multiplication or division.

10. $\frac{1}{4}$ **11.** $\frac{2}{16}$ **12.** $\frac{2}{5}$ **13.** $\frac{9}{12}$ **14.** $\frac{1}{3}$ **15.** $\frac{5}{6}$

16. $\frac{4}{11}$ **17.** $\frac{5}{25}$ **18.** $\frac{7}{10}$ **19.** $\frac{3}{15}$ **20.** $\frac{7}{21}$ **21.** $\frac{7}{8}$

Which fraction is *not* equivalent to the given fraction?
Write *a*, *b*, or *c*.

22. $\frac{3}{4}$ **a.** $\frac{15}{20}$ **b.** $\frac{12}{16}$ **c.** $\frac{6}{12}$

23. $\frac{4}{6}$ **a.** $\frac{2}{3}$ **b.** $\frac{1}{2}$ **c.** $\frac{8}{12}$

24. $\frac{1}{2}$ **a.** $\frac{6}{12}$ **b.** $\frac{3}{7}$ **c.** $\frac{4}{8}$

25. $\frac{4}{12}$ **a.** $\frac{2}{3}$ **b.** $\frac{1}{3}$ **c.** $\frac{5}{15}$

Problem Solving • Mixed Applications

26. Number Sense Nick and 5 friends decide to share some pizza. Each pizza is cut into 10 pieces. How many pizzas will they have to buy in order for everyone to get 3 pieces? How many pieces will be left over?

27. Nick ordered a large pizza with 12 slices. Suppose he ate 4 pieces of pizza. Write two equivalent fractions to represent the part of the pizza Nick ate.

28. Money Lanni has $10.50 to spend on seeds from the garden catalog. She wants to buy 2 packages of zinnia seeds. Does she have enough to also buy at least one package of each of the other types of seeds? If not, how much more does she need?

Type of Seed	Price per Package
Zinnia	$1.85
Marigold	$1.50
Ageratum	$1.90
Pansy	$1.66
Petunia	$1.98
Salvia	$2.10

29. Dave and Selena each have some leftover pansy seeds. Dave has $\frac{3}{4}$ package left and Selena has $\frac{2}{3}$ left. Who has more pansy seeds left?

30. Write About It Explain how to use multiplication or division to find equivalent fractions.

LESSON CONTINUES

Problem-Solving Strategy: Draw a Diagram

▶ **THE PROBLEM** Wanda is having a party. She is making a vegetable dip. The recipe calls for $\frac{1}{4}$ cup of yogurt, $\frac{2}{8}$ cup of grated carrots, $\frac{3}{12}$ cup of sour cream, and $\frac{4}{16}$ cup of chopped spinach. Which ingredient in the dip is there more of?

REMEMBER:

UNDERSTAND

PLAN

SOLVE

LOOK BACK

UNDERSTAND

- What are you asked to find?
- What information will you use?
- Is there information you will not use? If so, what?

PLAN

- What strategy can you use to solve the problem?

You can *draw a diagram,* using number lines, to compare.

SOLVE

- How can you use the strategy to solve the problem?

Draw a number line for each fraction. Mark its location on each of the number lines.

$\frac{1}{4}, \frac{2}{8}, \frac{3}{12},$ and $\frac{4}{16}$ are equivalent fractions.

So, Wanda used equal amounts of each ingredient to make the dip.

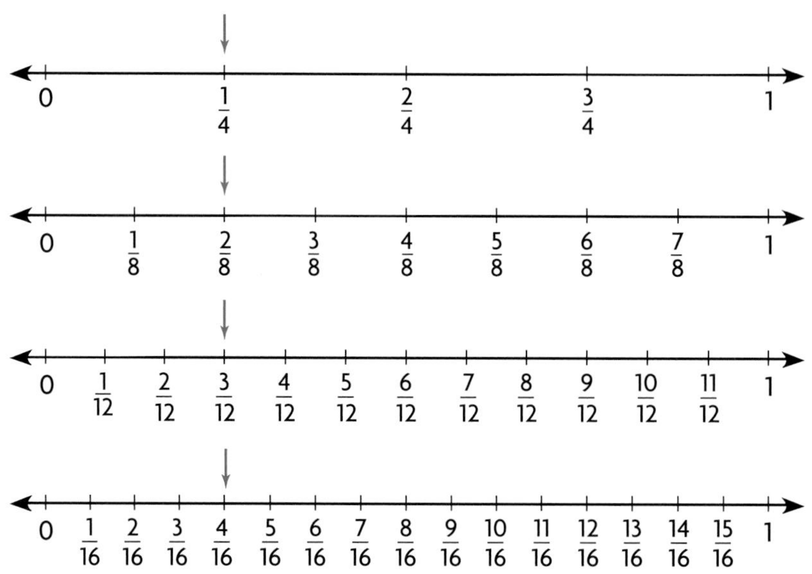

LOOK BACK

- How can you decide if your answer is reasonable?
- What other strategy could you use?

▶ PRACTICE

Draw a diagram to solve.

1. For the party, Kevin spends $\frac{2}{16}$ of his money on favors and $\frac{3}{8}$ on food. On which item is he spending more money? Explain how you know.

2. Shari bought 18 dishes, 8 of which are plates. Ned said that $\frac{4}{9}$ of the dishes she bought are plates. Is Ned right? Explain.

3. Mr. Frank had a package containing 10 cans of juice. He gave 3 cans to Greg and 5 to Margaret. Write two equivalent fractions to describe the fraction of the package of juice that is left.

4. Tori has equal numbers of red, yellow, and green apples. She has a total of 21 apples. To describe the fraction of the apples that are red, write two equivalent fractions.

Mixed Applications

Solve.

CHOOSE a strategy and a tool.

- Draw a Diagram
- Make a Model
- Guess and Check
- Write a Number Sentence

Paper/Pencil

Calculator

Hands-On

Mental Math

5. Anita had 16 rosebushes to sell. She sold 12 rosebushes. What fraction of the rosebushes did she sell?

6. Corey ran $\frac{4}{5}$ of a mile on Monday, and $\frac{8}{10}$ of a mile on Tuesday. Which day did Corey run farther?

7. There were 53 people in the hotel. Today 8 people checked out and 4 times that number checked in. How many people are in the hotel now?

8. A garden store sells 3 packs of seeds for $5.25. A catalog sells each pack for $1.49. What is the difference in the price per pack between the stores?

9. Casey's garden has 5 rows of strawberry plants, with 10 plants in each row. She picks about 10 strawberries from each plant. About how many strawberries does she pick?

10. Josh, Leslie, and Rob saved $57 to buy flowers for their mother for Mother's Day. Josh saved $17, and Leslie saved $8 less than Rob. How much money did Rob save?

11. Sara bought in-line skates for $69. You buy a $115 pair of in-line skates for $87. How much more do you pay than Sara?

12. **Write a problem** that uses fractions.

MORE PRACTICE page H100

Simplest Form

VOCABULARY
simplest form

Why learn this? You use simplest form when reading measuring tools like cups.

Cooks find the simplest forms of fractions every day. A fraction is in **simplest form** when it matches the largest fraction bar possible.

What is $\frac{6}{12}$ in simplest form?

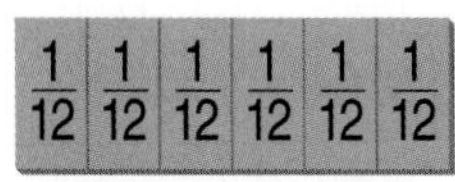

Show $\frac{6}{12}$.

Line up fraction bars equivalent to $\frac{6}{12}$.

Find the largest fraction bar possible.

So, $\frac{6}{12}$ in simplest form is $\frac{1}{2}$.

CRITICAL THINKING How do you know when you have found the simplest form of a fraction?

EXAMPLES

A $\frac{3}{6}$

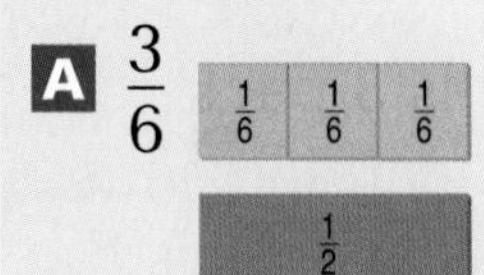

$\frac{3}{6}$ in simplest form is $\frac{1}{2}$.

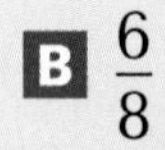

B $\frac{6}{8}$

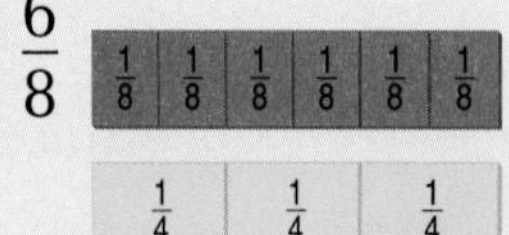

$\frac{6}{8}$ in simplest form is $\frac{3}{4}$.

C $\frac{3}{5}$

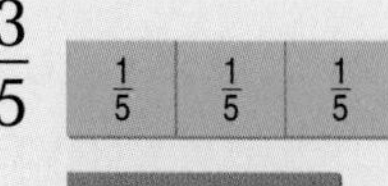

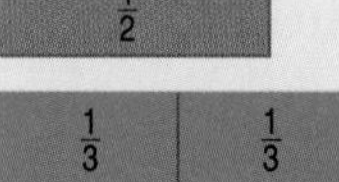

Since no other fraction bars line up with $\frac{3}{5}$, it is in simplest form.

▶ CHECK

Use fraction bars. Write each fraction in simplest form.

1. $\frac{4}{8}$

2. $\frac{3}{12}$

3. $\frac{2}{6}$

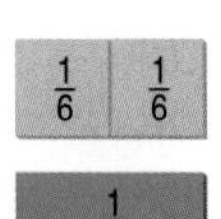

4. $\frac{4}{10}$

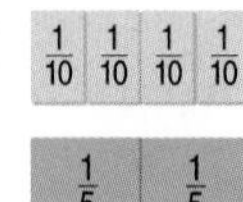

5. $\frac{4}{12}$ **6.** $\frac{3}{6}$ **7.** $\frac{3}{4}$ **8.** $\frac{3}{12}$ **9.** $\frac{8}{10}$ **10.** $\frac{6}{8}$ **11.** $\frac{6}{12}$

Calculator Activities page H63

▶ PRACTICE

Is the fraction in simplest form? Write *yes* or *no*.

12. $\frac{2}{3}$ **13.** $\frac{4}{8}$ **14.** $\frac{6}{12}$ **15.** $\frac{3}{8}$ **16.** $\frac{6}{9}$

Use fraction bars. Write the fraction in simplest form.

17. $\frac{2}{10}$ ($\frac{1}{10}$ $\frac{1}{10}$ = $\frac{1}{5}$)

18. $\frac{8}{12}$ ($\frac{1}{12}$ $\frac{1}{12}$ $\frac{1}{12}$ $\frac{1}{12}$ $\frac{1}{12}$ $\frac{1}{12}$ $\frac{1}{12}$ $\frac{1}{12}$ = $\frac{1}{3}$ $\frac{1}{3}$)

19. $\frac{5}{6}$ ($\frac{1}{6}$ $\frac{1}{6}$ $\frac{1}{6}$ $\frac{1}{6}$ $\frac{1}{6}$ = ?)

Write each fraction in simplest form.

20. $\frac{1}{2}$ **21.** $\frac{3}{12}$ **22.** $\frac{9}{12}$ **23.** $\frac{5}{10}$ **24.** $\frac{7}{8}$

25. $\frac{9}{15}$ **26.** $\frac{4}{5}$ **27.** $\frac{4}{12}$ **28.** $\frac{6}{10}$ **29.** $\frac{5}{15}$

30. $\frac{10}{12}$ **31.** $\frac{3}{21}$ **32.** $\frac{4}{16}$ **33.** $\frac{6}{18}$ **34.** $\frac{7}{14}$

Problem Solving • Mixed Applications

35. Analyzing Data Hannah used $\frac{1}{2}$ cup sugar, $\frac{2}{3}$ cup cornmeal, and $\frac{3}{4}$ cup flour in her corn muffin recipe. Of these ingredients, which is the greatest amount? How do you know?

36. Logical Reasoning Victor had 12 pencils. He gives 2 pencils to his friends, accidentally breaks 3 times that many, and trades 1 pencil for a marker with his teacher. How many pencils does Victor have now?

37. Write a problem using fractions about Andrea and Joey dividing the lemon cake their mom baked for them.

CONSUMER LINK

Measuring cups used for cooking are often in sets of 1, $\frac{3}{4}$, $\frac{2}{3}$, $\frac{1}{2}$, $\frac{1}{3}$, and $\frac{1}{4}$ cup. When baking a cake, why is it important to know how to convert fractions to their simplest form?

Mixed Review and Test Prep

Copy and complete each pattern. (pages 230–231)

38. $800 \div 4 = n$
$80 \div 4 = n$
$8 \div 4 = n$

39. $2{,}500 \div 5 = n$
$250 \div 5 = n$
$25 \div 5 = n$

40. $1{,}200 \div 3 = n$
$120 \div 3 = n$
$12 \div 3 = n$

Use estimation or patterns to place the decimal point. Then choose the letter of the correct quotient. (pages 240–241)

41. $7\overline{)3.5}$ **A** 0.05 **B** 5.0 **C** 0.5 **D** Not Here

42. $3\overline{)2.37}$ **F** 0.79 **G** 79 **H** 7.90 **J** 0.97

More About Simplest Form

VOCABULARY
simplest form

Why learn this? Items such as fruit or nuts are sold by weight and often priced by using fractions in simplest form.

Farmer's Market
$5.99
per $\frac{1}{4}$ lb

A fraction is in **simplest form** when the greatest common factor, or GCF, of the numerator and denominator is 1. Since the GCF of the numerator and denominator of $\frac{18}{24}$ is not 1, the fraction is not in simplest form.

Use the GCF to write $\frac{18}{24}$ in simplest form.

MODEL

Step 1

Use a Venn diagram to find the greatest common factor of 18 and 24.

Factors of 18: 1, 2, 3, 6, 9, 18

Factors of 24: 1, 2, 3, 4, 6, 8, 12, 24

The GCF is 6.

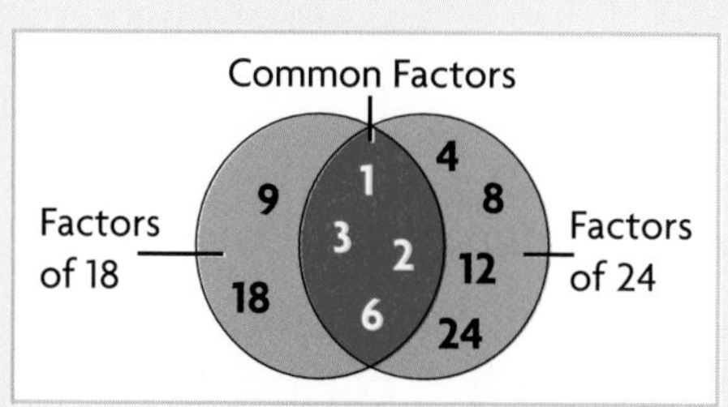

Step 2

Divide the numerator and the denominator by the GCF.

$$\frac{18 \div 6}{24 \div 6} = \frac{3}{4}$$

Since the GCF of 3 and 4 is 1, $\frac{3}{4}$ is in simplest form.

So, $\frac{18}{24}$ in simplest form is $\frac{3}{4}$.

Divide the numerator and denominator by any common factor until the GCF of the numerator and denominator is 1.

$$\frac{18}{24} = \frac{18 \div 2}{24 \div 2} = \frac{9 \div 3}{12 \div 3} = \frac{3}{4}$$

Notice that the product of the common factors, 2 and 3, is 6, the greatest common factor.

So, the simplest form of $\frac{18}{24}$ is $\frac{3}{4}$.

Talk About It

- How are the two methods different?
- Why are all fractions with a numerator of 1 already in simplest form?

CRITICAL THINKING If a fraction is not in simplest form, can the greatest common factor of the numerator and denominator be 1? Explain.

Calculator Activities page H66

▶ CHECK

Find the simplest form by using the GCF and any common factor.

1. $\frac{2}{6}$ **2.** $\frac{2}{10}$ **3.** $\frac{8}{12}$ **4.** $\frac{4}{8}$ **5.** $\frac{3}{18}$ **6.** $\frac{9}{15}$ **7.** $\frac{6}{20}$

▶ PRACTICE

Is the fraction in simplest form? Write *yes* or *no*. If it isn't, write it in simplest form.

8. $\frac{4}{12}$ **9.** $\frac{4}{5}$ **10.** $\frac{9}{12}$ **11.** $\frac{2}{8}$ **12.** $\frac{5}{14}$ **13.** $\frac{5}{10}$

Write each fraction in simplest form.

14. $\frac{3}{15}$ **15.** $\frac{3}{4}$ **16.** $\frac{12}{36}$ **17.** $\frac{15}{25}$ **18.** $\frac{15}{18}$ **19.** $\frac{3}{12}$

20. $\frac{14}{21}$ **21.** $\frac{18}{30}$ **22.** $\frac{15}{40}$ **23.** $\frac{6}{16}$ **24.** $\frac{18}{45}$ **25.** $\frac{20}{25}$

Problem Solving • Mixed Applications

26. Money Sasha receives $12 a week for baby-sitting. She puts $8 of that money in her savings account. Write in simplest form the fraction of her earnings that Sasha saves.

27. Science Stan's class is doing a science project. He brought 8 plants to school for this project. His class brought 36 plants in all. Write in simplest form the fraction of plants Stan brought.

28. Patterns Chris works 10 minutes in her garden on Monday, 20 minutes on Tuesday, 35 minutes on Wednesday, and 55 minutes on Thursday. If the pattern continues, how long will she work in the garden on Saturday?

29. Write About It Explain how you know that a fraction such as $\frac{3}{4}$ is in simplest form.

Mixed Review and Test Prep

Choose the letter of the smallest unit of measure. Use the prefix to help you. (pages 254–255)

30. A kilometer
B decimeter
C meter

31. A liter
B milliliter
C kiloliter

32. A milligram
B kilogram
C gram

Write the missing unit. (pages 256–257)

33. 4 L = 4,000 ___?___ **34.** 500 mm = 50 ___?___ **35.** 60 g = 60,000 ___?___

MORE PRACTICE page H100

CHAPTER 16 Review/Test

CHECK Understanding

VOCABULARY

1. Fractions that name the same amount are called _?_. (page 292)

2. The greatest number that is a factor of each of two or more numbers is called the _?_. (page 289)

3. Numbers that have exactly two factors, 1 and the number itself, are called _?_. (page 286)

4. A fraction is in _?_ when the GCF of the numerator and denominator is 1. (page 298)

5. Numbers that have more than two factors are called _?_. (page 286)

6. When both factors are the same, the product is called a _?_. (page 286)

Write *prime* or *composite* for each number. Identify the square numbers. (pages 286–287)

7. 15 **8.** 2 **9.** 9 **10.** 50

CHECK Skills

Find an equivalent fraction. Use multiplication or division. (pages 292–293)

11. $\frac{6}{18}$ **12.** $\frac{2}{7}$ **13.** $\frac{1}{6}$ **14.** $\frac{7}{15}$ **15.** $\frac{8}{18}$

List the factors of each number. Write the greatest common factor for each pair of numbers. (pages 288–291)

16. 6, 8 **17.** 7, 14 **18.** 8, 12 **19.** 6, 15 **20.** 12, 16

Write each fraction in simplest form. (pages 296–299)

21. $\frac{2}{8}$ **22.** $\frac{9}{15}$ **23.** $\frac{18}{20}$ **24.** $\frac{15}{35}$ **25.** $\frac{10}{12}$

CHECK Problem Solving

Solve. (pages 294–295)

CHOOSE a strategy and a tool.

- Make a Model
- Draw a Diagram
- Find a Pattern

Paper/Pencil

Calculator

Hands-On

Mental Math

26. Jane made 24 oatmeal cookies and 36 raisin cookies. She wants to put the cookies in bags that contain the same number of one kind of cookie. What is the greatest number she can put into each bag?

27. Carla cut $\frac{1}{2}$ yard of blue fabric, $\frac{3}{4}$ yard of red fabric, and $\frac{4}{12}$ yard of green fabric. Of which color fabric does she have the least?

Test Prep

CUMULATIVE
CHAPTERS 1–16

Choose the best answer.

1. Josh had 8 math problems to solve. He solved 2 of the problems in school. Which fraction shows how many of the problems he solved in school?

   A $\frac{1}{8}$ B $\frac{1}{4}$

   C $\frac{2}{3}$ D $\frac{3}{4}$

2. Maria sorted nails into groups according to size and has arranged the nails from longest to shortest. In what order has Maria placed the nails?

   F $\frac{5}{8}$ in., $\frac{1}{2}$ in., $\frac{3}{4}$ in.

   G $\frac{1}{2}$ in., $\frac{5}{8}$ in., $\frac{3}{4}$ in.

   H $\frac{3}{4}$ in., $\frac{5}{8}$ in., $\frac{1}{2}$ in.

   J $\frac{3}{4}$ in., $\frac{1}{2}$ in., $\frac{5}{8}$ in.

3. In a total of 10 spins, which color will the spinner probably point to the least number of times?

   A red

   B blue

   C yellow

   D green

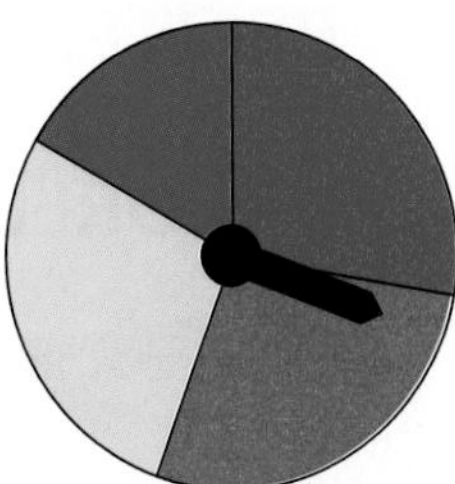

4. $7\overline{)406}$

   F 57

   G 48

   H 59

   J 58

5. Roy paid $12.95 for a CD and $15.95 for a video. Sara paid $9.99 for the same CD at another store. How much more did Roy pay for the CD?

   A $12.95 B $3.94

   C $3.04 D $2.96

6. 250 × 9

   F 1,850

   G 1,859

   H 2,250

   J 2,259

   K Not Here

7. Saul's yard measures 50 feet by 200 feet. How many feet are in the perimeter of his yard?

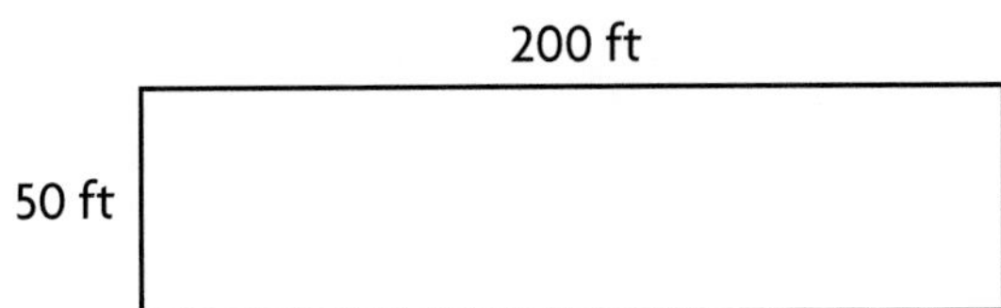

   A 100 ft B 250 ft

   C 400 ft D 500 ft

8. Barb, Gail, Sally, and Tara play baseball, golf, soccer, and tennis. No girl plays a game which begins with the same letter as her name. Which of the following is a reasonable conclusion?

   F Sally plays soccer.

   G Gail does not play baseball.

   H Tara does not play tennis.

   J Barb does not play golf.

17 MODELING ADDITION OF FRACTIONS

Poetry City Auditorium

CENTRAL SCHOOL

LIVE

REPORTINGLIVE
FROMPOETRYCITY
AUDITORIUMSITEOF
THEANNUALSCHOOL
POETRYPRESENTATIONS
WHERESTUDENTSFROM
ALLOVERTHESTATE
RECITEPOEMSTO
AUDIENCES
WORLDWIDE

LANGUAGE **LINK**

An announcer says about 104 words each minute during a news broadcast.

Problem-Solving Activity

Your Poetry Presentation

Do you ever have trouble understanding someone who talks too fast?

See how fast you talk. Plan a poetry reading and time yourself.

YOU WILL NEED: clock or timer, poem books, construction paper, ruler, scissors, glue

- Choose 3 poems to read.
- Time your reading of each poem to the nearest $\frac{1}{4}$ minute. (HINT: There are 60 seconds in 1 minute. $\frac{1}{4} = \frac{?}{60}$)
- Write a $\frac{1}{4}$-minute introduction.
- Make a different colored strip to show how long it will take to read each poem.
- Make a chart that lists each title and time.
- Add your reading times to find out how long your presentation will last.

HOW TO FOLD PAPER TO SHOW $\frac{1}{4}$ MINUTE

1 2 3 4 5 6
inches

Cut a paper strip that is 6 inches long. This represents 1 minute.

Fold the paper in half. Each section represents $\frac{1}{2}$ minute.

Fold the paper in half again. Each section represents $\frac{1}{4}$ minute.

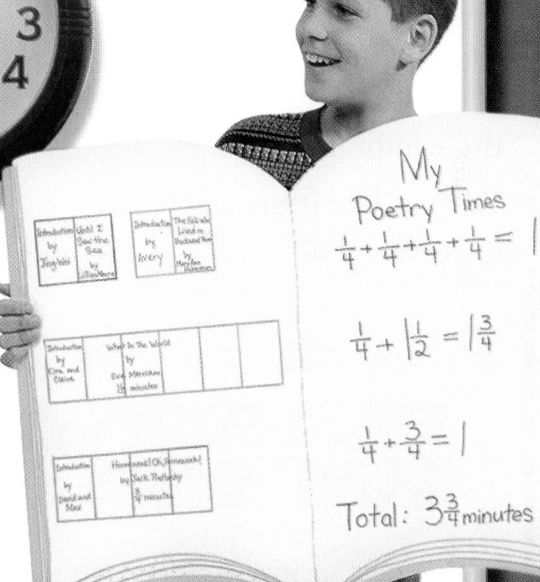

DID YOU

- ✓ time the reading of each poem to the nearest $\frac{1}{4}$ minute?
- ✓ write a $\frac{1}{4}$-minute introduction?
- ✓ make a strip to show how long it will take to read the poems?
- ✓ make a chart?
- ✓ find out how long your presentation will last?

LESSON 1

Adding Like Fractions

Why learn this? You can solve problems that involve finding the sum of parts, such as the parts of a pizza eaten.

Max and Gayle shared a small pizza. Max ate $\frac{3}{8}$ of the pizza. Gayle ate $\frac{1}{8}$ of the pizza. What part of the pizza did they eat together?

You can use fraction bars to show the part of the pizza each person ate.

Max ate $\frac{3}{8}$ of the pizza.

Gayle ate $\frac{1}{8}$ of the pizza.

Together, they ate $\frac{3}{8} + \frac{1}{8} = \frac{4}{8}$, or $\frac{1}{2}$ of the pizza.

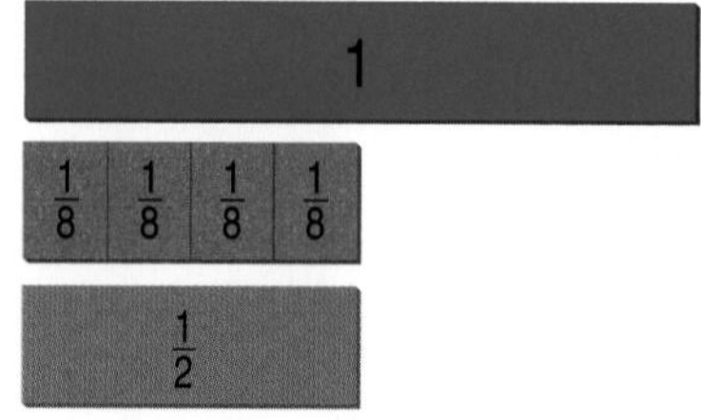

REMEMBER:

Like fractions are fractions that have the same denominators.

Example $\frac{1}{8}$ and $\frac{3}{8}$

SCIENCE LINK

Time is often expressed as a fraction of an hour. For example, 15 minutes equals $\frac{1}{4}$ hour and 30 minutes equals $\frac{1}{2}$ hour. How many minutes equal $\frac{3}{4}$ hour?

Talk About It

- How do you know that the sum is $\frac{4}{8}$?
- What do you notice about the numerator of the sum of the two like fractions? What do you notice about the denominator?
- Why is $\frac{4}{8}$ written as $\frac{1}{2}$?

EXAMPLES

A Find the sum of $\frac{2}{3}$ and $\frac{2}{3}$.

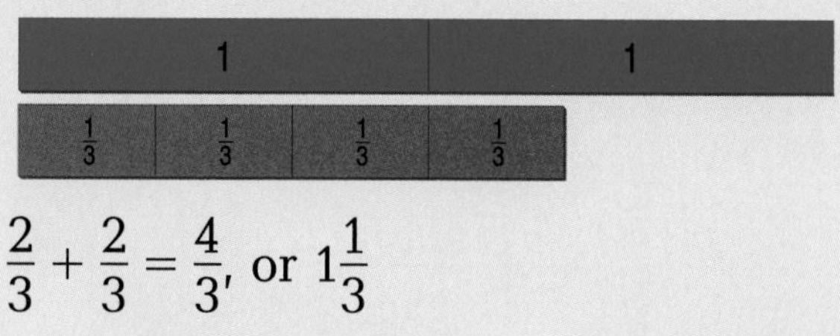

$$\frac{2}{3} + \frac{2}{3} = \frac{4}{3}, \text{ or } 1\frac{1}{3}$$

B Find the sum of $\frac{3}{10}$ and $\frac{5}{10}$.

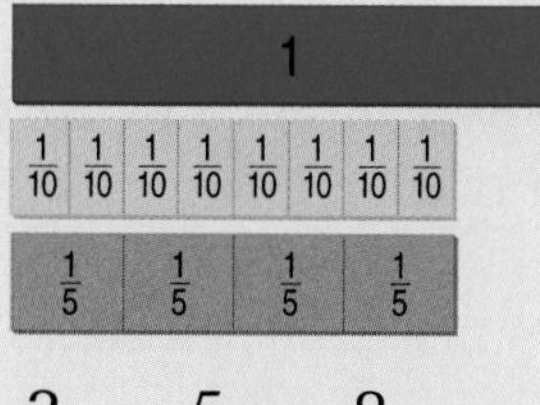

$$\frac{3}{10} + \frac{5}{10} = \frac{8}{10}$$

$$\frac{8}{10} = \frac{4}{5}$$ ← Remember to write the answer in simplest form.

CRITICAL THINKING How do you know if the sum of two fractions is greater than 1?

▶ CHECK

Write an addition sentence for each drawing.

1. 

2. 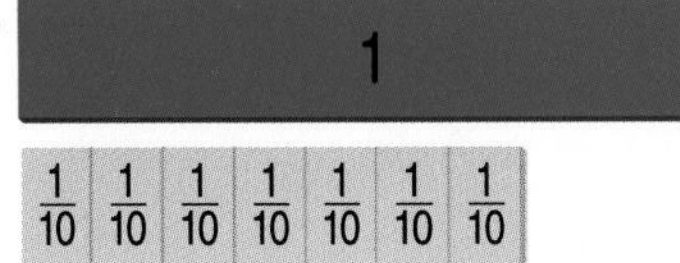

3. 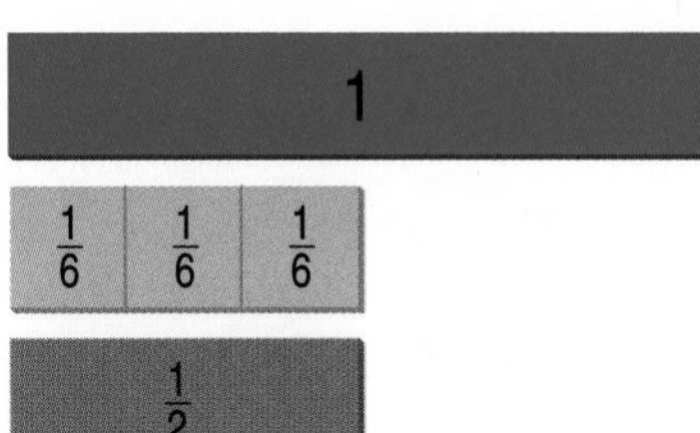

4. 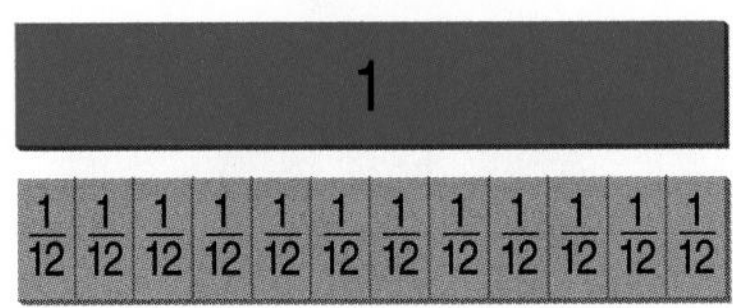

5. 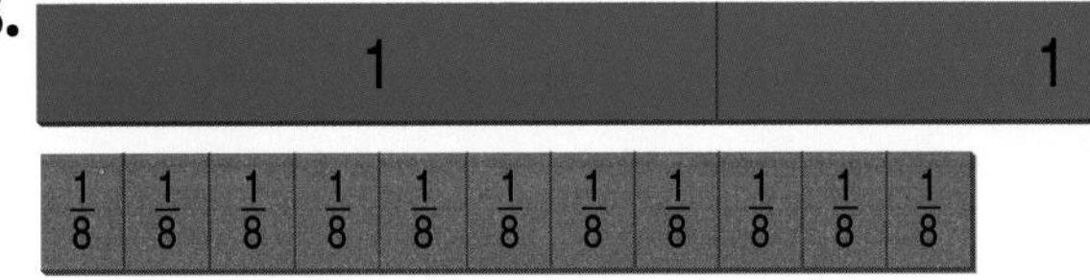

6. What rule can you write for adding fractions with like denominators?

▶ PRACTICE

Use fraction strips to find the sum. Write the answer in simplest form.

7. $\frac{1}{3} + \frac{1}{3} = n$ **8.** $\frac{2}{4} + \frac{3}{4} = n$ **9.** $\frac{2}{5} + \frac{4}{5} = n$ **10.** $\frac{1}{9} + \frac{2}{9} = n$

11. $\frac{1}{6} + \frac{3}{6} = n$ **12.** $\frac{5}{7} + \frac{4}{7} = n$ **13.** $\frac{3}{8} + \frac{5}{8} = n$ **14.** $\frac{1}{6} + \frac{5}{6} = n$

15. $\frac{3}{5} + \frac{4}{5} = n$ **16.** $\frac{4}{9} + \frac{2}{9} = n$ **17.** $\frac{2}{4} + \frac{3}{4} = n$ **18.** $\frac{2}{12} + \frac{4}{12} = n$

Problem Solving • Mixed Applications

19. Carmen used $\frac{4}{8}$ of a package of paper. Her friend used $\frac{3}{8}$ of the paper. How much of the package did they use?

20. Money Jason was making a sign. He bought a package of 8 markers for $3.76. How much did each marker cost?

21. Mark's family walks together three times a week. They walk $\frac{1}{5}$ mile, $\frac{3}{5}$ mile, and $\frac{2}{5}$ mile. How far does Mark's family walk in all?

22. **Write a problem** about three friends eating apple pie, using like fractions.

Mixed Review and Test Prep

Write *certain* or *impossible* for each event. (pages 188–189)

23. Money will grow in your garden.

24. The Earth will heat the sun.

Choose the letter for the missing unit. (pages 256–257)

25. 700 mm = 70 __?__ **A** km **B** dm **C** m **D** cm

26. 6,043 mm = 6.043 __?__ **F** m **G** cm **H** dm **J** km

LESSON 2 • HANDS-ON LESSON

Adding Unlike Fractions

You will investigate using fraction bars to add fractions with unlike denominators.

Joyce and Renee baked two kinds of muffins for the bake sale. They used $\frac{1}{8}$ cup sugar for one kind. They used $\frac{1}{2}$ cup sugar for the other kind. How much sugar did they use in all?

▶ EXPLORE

Use fraction bars to add fractions with unlike denominators.

MATERIALS: fraction bars

MODEL

What is $\frac{1}{8} + \frac{1}{2}$?

Step 1

Model with fraction bars.

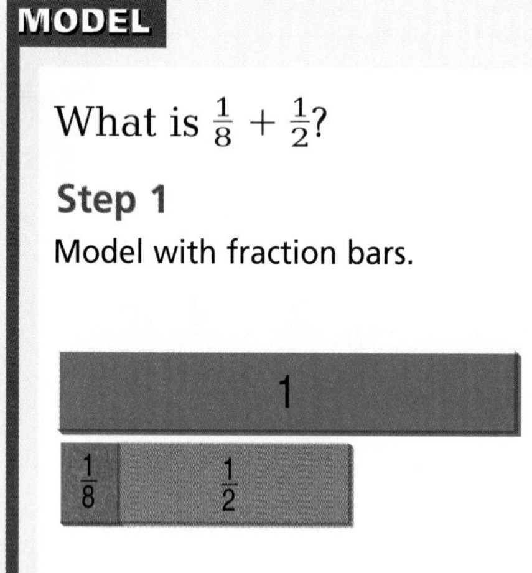

Step 2

Find the like fraction bars that are equivalent to $\frac{1}{8} + \frac{1}{2}$ in length.

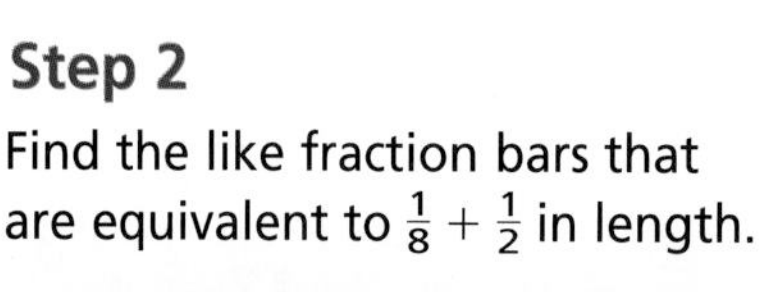

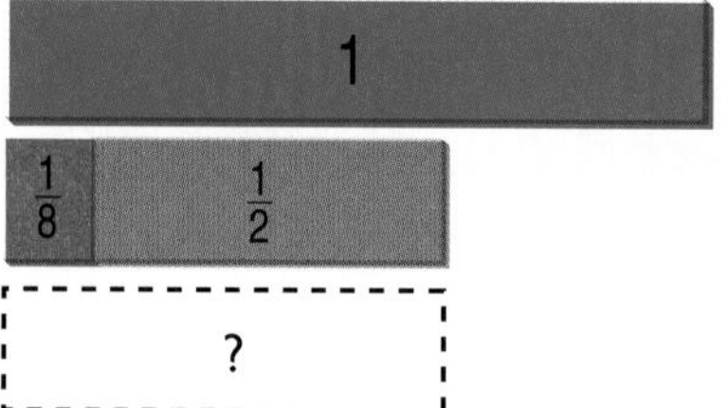

Record

Write a fraction for the amount of sugar Joyce and Renee used in all. Record an addition sentence for the model. Explain how you used the fraction bars to find the sum.

Now, investigate adding different unlike fractions.

▶ TRY THIS

1. Use fraction bars to find the sum of $\frac{1}{2}$ and $\frac{2}{3}$. Record by writing a number sentence.

2. What is the least common multiple of 2 and 3? What do you notice about the LCM and the sum of $\frac{1}{2}$ and $\frac{2}{3}$?

3. **Write About It** Explain how to add fractions with unlike denominators.

Technology Link

You can add unlike fractions by using E-Lab, Activity 17. Available on CD-ROM and on the Internet at **www.hbschool.com/elab**

▶ PRACTICE

Use fraction bars to find the sum.

4. 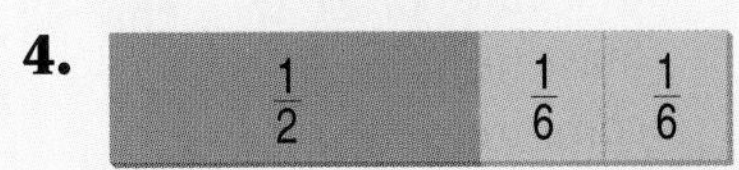

5. 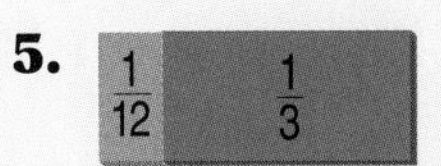

6. 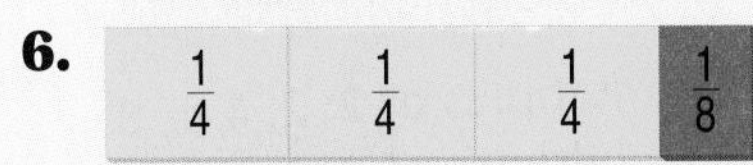

7. 

8. $\frac{1}{3}$ $\frac{1}{2}$

9. $\frac{1}{2}$ $\frac{1}{5}$ $\frac{1}{5}$

10. $\frac{1}{3}$ $\frac{1}{4}$

11. $\frac{1}{3}$ $\frac{1}{6}$

12. $\frac{1}{4}$ $\frac{1}{8}$

13. 

Use fraction bars to find the sum.

14. $\frac{1}{4} + \frac{1}{6} = n$

15. $\frac{1}{5} + \frac{3}{10} = n$

16. $\frac{3}{4} + \frac{5}{6} = n$

17. $\frac{2}{5} + \frac{1}{2} = n$

18. $\frac{5}{6} + \frac{1}{12} = n$

19. $\frac{1}{4} + \frac{1}{3} = n$

20. $\frac{3}{10} + \frac{1}{2} = n$

21. $\frac{1}{2} + \frac{5}{6} = n$

22. $\frac{4}{10} + \frac{1}{2} = n$

Problem Solving • Mixed Applications

23. Consumer Maria and Kevin have \$25.00. They bought 3 cans of paint for \$3.99 each and 2 paint brushes for \$2.89 each. Posterboard costs \$1.75 per sheet. How many sheets of posterboard can they buy? How much change will they get?

24. Measurement Frank is baking muffins for a school bake sale. He used $\frac{1}{3}$ cup brown sugar and $\frac{3}{4}$ cup white sugar. How much sugar did he use in all?

25. Reasoning John needs one board that is $\frac{1}{2}$ foot long and one that is $\frac{1}{4}$ foot long. He has a board that is $\frac{7}{8}$ foot long. Can John cut the shorter boards from the longer board? Explain.

26. Measurement Roy has $\frac{1}{4}$ yard of ribbon. He needs $\frac{3}{8}$ yard more for the costume he is making. How much ribbon does he need in all?

MORE PRACTICE page H101

LESSON 3

Using the Least Common Denominator to Add Fractions

VOCABULARY
least common denominator (LCD)

Why learn this? You can add unlike fractions, such as fractions of a pound.

REMEMBER:
The *least common multiple*, or *LCM*, is the least number that is a common multiple of two or more numbers.

Multiples of 2: 2, 4, 6, 8
Multiples of 3: 3, 6, 9, 12
LCM: 6

Shawna used $\frac{1}{6}$ pound of tuna fish to make a sandwich. Preston used $\frac{1}{4}$ pound. How many pounds of tuna fish did they use in all?

To find the sum of unlike fractions, you need to rename them as like fractions. The least common multiple of two or more denominators is used to find the **least common denominator**, or **LCD**.

MODEL

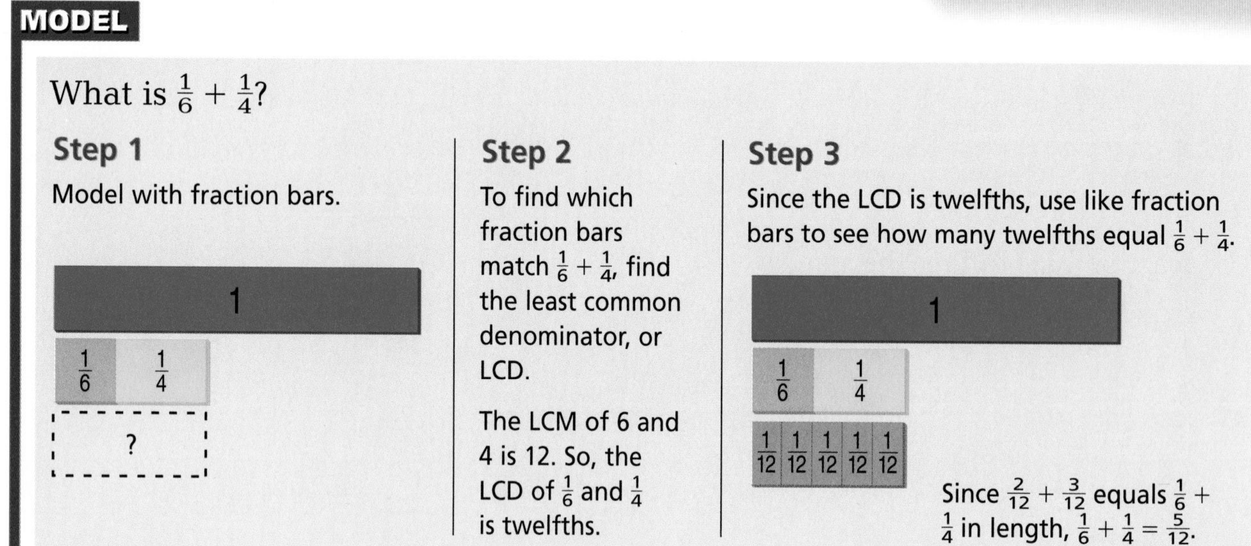

What is $\frac{1}{6} + \frac{1}{4}$?

Step 1
Model with fraction bars.

Step 2
To find which fraction bars match $\frac{1}{6} + \frac{1}{4}$, find the least common denominator, or LCD.

The LCM of 6 and 4 is 12. So, the LCD of $\frac{1}{6}$ and $\frac{1}{4}$ is twelfths.

Step 3
Since the LCD is twelfths, use like fraction bars to see how many twelfths equal $\frac{1}{6} + \frac{1}{4}$.

Since $\frac{2}{12} + \frac{3}{12}$ equals $\frac{1}{6} + \frac{1}{4}$ in length, $\frac{1}{6} + \frac{1}{4} = \frac{5}{12}$.

So, Shawna and Preston used $\frac{5}{12}$ pound of tuna fish in all.

CRITICAL THINKING What fraction bars would you use to find the sum of $\frac{1}{6}$ and $\frac{1}{3}$? Explain.

▶ CHECK

1. How does knowing the least common multiple help you find the least common denominator?
2. How does knowing the LCD help you find the sum?

Technology Link

In ***Mighty Math Number Heroes***, the game *Fraction Fireworks* challenges you to add fractions with unlike denominators. Use Grow Slide Level T.

▶ PRACTICE

Use the LCM to name the least common denominator, or LCD, for each pair of fractions.

3. $\frac{1}{5}$ and $\frac{1}{10}$ **4.** $\frac{1}{4}$ and $\frac{1}{3}$ **5.** $\frac{1}{4}$ and $\frac{1}{8}$ **6.** $\frac{1}{3}$ and $\frac{1}{9}$

7. $\frac{1}{3}$ and $\frac{1}{2}$ **8.** $\frac{1}{4}$ and $\frac{1}{2}$ **9.** $\frac{1}{6}$ and $\frac{1}{4}$ **10.** $\frac{1}{5}$ and $\frac{1}{2}$

Use fraction strips to find the sum. Write the answer in simplest form.

11. $\frac{1}{8} + \frac{3}{4} = n$ **12.** $\frac{1}{2} + \frac{4}{5} = n$ **13.** $\frac{1}{10} + \frac{4}{5} = n$ **14.** $\frac{1}{2} + \frac{1}{12} = n$

15. $\frac{2}{3} + \frac{1}{6} = n$ **16.** $\frac{1}{4} + \frac{2}{3} = n$ **17.** $\frac{9}{10} + \frac{2}{5} = n$ **18.** $\frac{3}{8} + \frac{3}{4} = n$

19. $\frac{2}{4} + \frac{2}{3} = n$ **20.** $\frac{1}{4} + \frac{2}{8} = n$ **21.** $\frac{5}{6} + \frac{2}{3} = n$ **22.** $\frac{3}{9} + \frac{1}{3} = n$

Problem Solving • Mixed Applications

23. Money Morey earns $3.25 an hour at his job. He wants to buy a puppy for his sister. A puppy costs $25.00, a collar costs $8.99, a leash costs $12.99, and a food bowl costs $1.77. How many hours will Morey have to work until he has enough money?

24. Consumer A grocery store is having a sale on apples and oranges. Which is cheaper, apples at $0.45 cents each or 3 for $1.25? Oranges for $0.36 each or 8 oranges for $3.00?

25. Music Of the 11 members in Jose's band, 8 members do not play guitar. What fraction of the members play guitar?

26. **Write a problem** in which you have to add unlike fractions.

Mixed Review and Test Prep

Find the quotient. Check by multiplying. **(pages 236–237)**

27. 18.9 ÷ 9 = ? **28.** 5.34 ÷ 6 = ? **29.** 0.94 ÷ 2 = ?

30. 52.4 ÷ 4 = ? **31.** 3.93 ÷ 3 = ? **32.** 5.88 ÷ 7 = ?

Choose the letter of the measurements that are in order. **(pages 248–249)**

33. From shortest to longest

A 2 cm, 2 km, 2 m

B 2 cm, 2 m, 2 km

C 2 km, 2 m, 2 cm

D 2 m, 2 cm, 2 km

34. From longest to shortest

F 9 m, 9 cm, 9 mm

G 9 mm, 9 m, 9 cm

H 9 mm, 9 cm, 9 m

J 9 cm, 9 mm, 9 m

MORE PRACTICE page H101

Adding Three Fractions

Why learn this? You can analyze survey results that involve three fractions with unlike denominators.

Miss Fox surveyed her students to find their favorite activities. Of the students, $\frac{1}{3}$ said playing sports, $\frac{1}{4}$ said reading, and $\frac{1}{6}$ said playing musical instruments. The rest of the students didn't have a preference. What fraction of Miss Fox's students have a favorite activity?

Add 3 fractions the same way you add 2 fractions.

MODEL

What is $\frac{1}{3} + \frac{1}{4} + \frac{1}{6}$?

Step 1

Model with fraction bars.

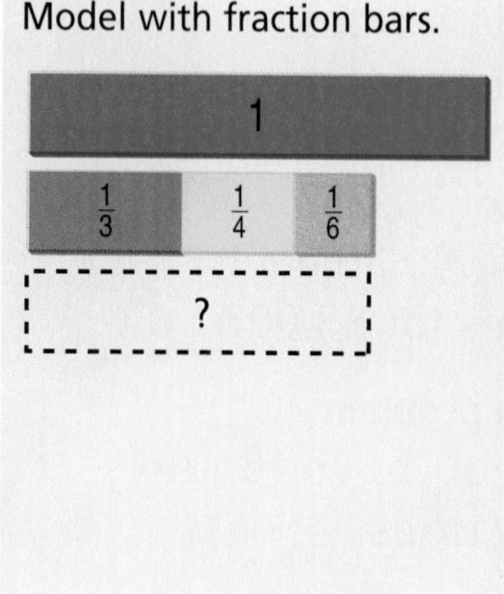

Step 2

To find which fraction bars match $\frac{1}{3} + \frac{1}{4} + \frac{1}{6}$, find the least common denominator, or LCD.

The LCM of 3, 4, and 6 is 12. So, the LCD of $\frac{1}{3}$, $\frac{1}{4}$, and $\frac{1}{6}$ is twelfths.

Step 3

Since the LCD is twelfths, use like fraction bars to see how many twelfths equal $\frac{1}{3} + \frac{1}{4} + \frac{1}{6}$.

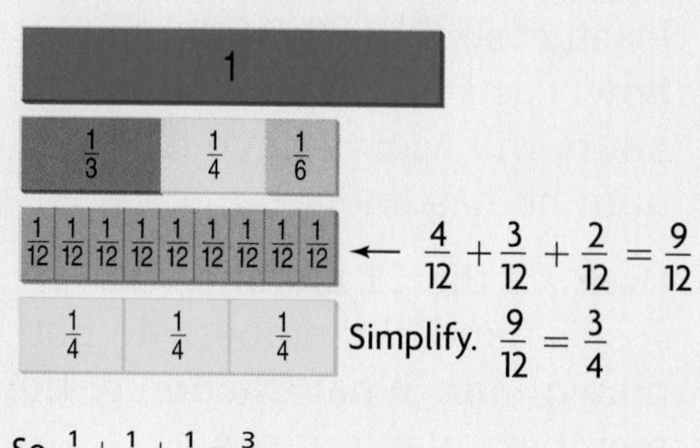

$\leftarrow \frac{4}{12} + \frac{3}{12} + \frac{2}{12} = \frac{9}{12}$

Simplify. $\frac{9}{12} = \frac{3}{4}$

So, $\frac{1}{3} + \frac{1}{4} + \frac{1}{6} = \frac{3}{4}$.

So, $\frac{3}{4}$ of the students have a favorite activity.

- In Step 3, why are the 3 bars for $\frac{1}{4}$ shown?

EXAMPLES

A Find $\frac{1}{4} + \frac{1}{2} + \frac{3}{8}$.

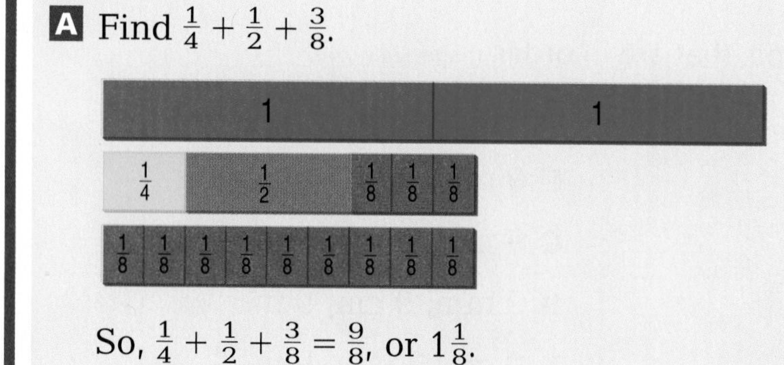

So, $\frac{1}{4} + \frac{1}{2} + \frac{3}{8} = \frac{9}{8}$, or $1\frac{1}{8}$.

B Find $\frac{1}{2} + \frac{1}{3} + \frac{1}{6}$.

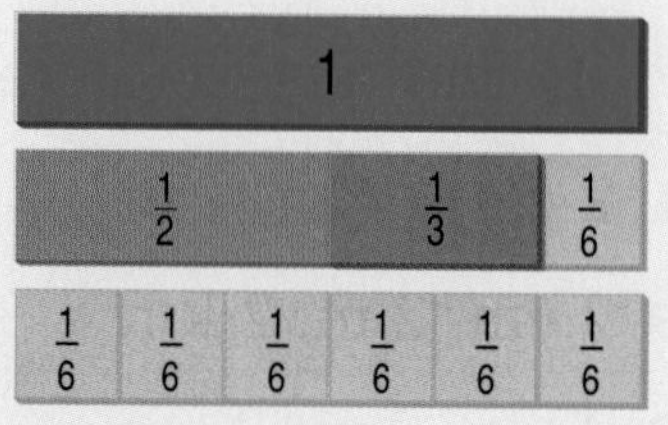

So, $\frac{1}{2} + \frac{1}{3} + \frac{1}{6} = \frac{6}{6}$, or 1.

Calculator Activities page H63

▶ CHECK

1. Why is it important to compare to the fraction bar for 1?

2. You can use a calculator to add $\frac{1}{3} + \frac{1}{4} + \frac{1}{8}$. What is the LCM of the 3 fractions, according to this calculator display?

Press: 1 / 3 + 1 / 4 + 1 / 8 = **Display:** 17/24

▶ PRACTICE

Use the LCM to name the least common denominator, or LCD, for each group of fractions.

3. $\frac{1}{5}, \frac{1}{10},$ and $\frac{1}{2}$ **4.** $\frac{1}{2}, \frac{1}{4},$ and $\frac{1}{6}$ **5.** $\frac{1}{2}, \frac{1}{3},$ and $\frac{1}{12}$

6. $\frac{1}{2}, \frac{1}{4},$ and $\frac{1}{3}$ **7.** $\frac{1}{6}, \frac{1}{2},$ and $\frac{1}{3}$ **8.** $\frac{1}{12}, \frac{1}{6},$ and $\frac{1}{3}$

Use fraction strips to find the sum. Write the answer in simplest form.

9. $\frac{3}{4} + \frac{1}{2} + \frac{1}{4} = n$ **10.** $\frac{1}{6} + \frac{1}{2} + \frac{1}{3} = n$ **11.** $\frac{1}{5} + \frac{2}{5} + \frac{7}{10} = n$

12. $\frac{1}{5} + \frac{3}{10} + \frac{1}{2} = n$ **13.** $\frac{1}{4} + \frac{2}{3} + \frac{1}{6} = n$ **14.** $\frac{1}{4} + \frac{1}{3} + \frac{1}{12} = n$

15. $\frac{1}{8} + \frac{3}{8} + \frac{1}{4} = n$ **16.** $\frac{5}{6} + \frac{1}{3} + \frac{1}{4} = n$ **17.** $\frac{7}{8} + \frac{3}{4} + \frac{1}{2} = n$

Problem Solving • Mixed Applications

18. Patterns Mountain National Park rangers wanted to relocate 60 wolves. The first month, they relocated 4 wolves. Each month after that, they relocated twice as many wolves as the month before. How many months did it take?

An adult timber wolf can measure up to $6\frac{1}{2}$ feet long.

19. Brianna brought 140 cookies for the fifth grade. There are 6 classes, and each class has the same number of people. How many cookies did she give to each class? Did she have any cookies left over?

20. Reasoning Ray has two equal-size cans of nuts. One can is $\frac{1}{3}$ full and one is $\frac{1}{9}$ full. He puts the nuts from both cans into one can. How full is the combined can?

21. **Write About It** How does adding three fractions with unlike denominators differ from adding two fractions with unlike denominators?

MORE PRACTICE pages H101–H102

Problem-Solving Strategy: Make a Model

▶ **THE PROBLEM** Tara bought a tomato plant for \$0.75. On Monday it had grown $\frac{1}{8}$ inch. On Wednesday it had grown another $\frac{1}{4}$ inch, and on Friday it had grown $\frac{1}{2}$ inch more. How much did the tomato plant grow that week?

UNDERSTAND

- What are you asked to find?
- What information will you use?
- Is there information you will not use? If so, what?

PLAN

- What strategy can you use to solve this problem?

You can *make a model* with fraction strips.

SOLVE

- What model can you make?

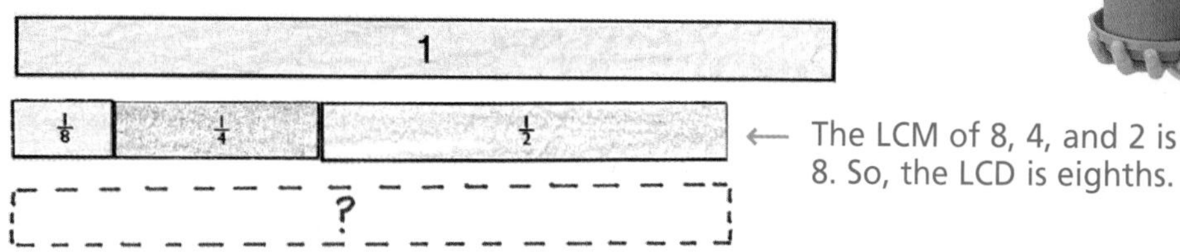

← The LCM of 8, 4, and 2 is 8. So, the LCD is eighths.

Since the LCD is eighths, use like fraction bars to see how many eighths equal $\frac{1}{8} + \frac{1}{4} + \frac{1}{2}$.

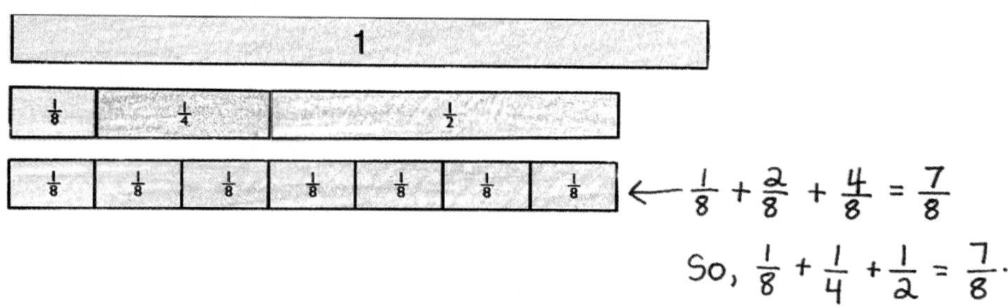

So, the tomato plant grew $\frac{7}{8}$ inch that week.

LOOK BACK

- How can you decide if your answer is reasonable?
- What other strategy can you use?

▶ PRACTICE

Make a model to solve.

1. Jan planted vegetables in $\frac{2}{3}$ of her garden, flowers in $\frac{1}{6}$ of her garden, and herbs in $\frac{1}{6}$ of her garden. How much of Jan's garden was planted?

2. Every day that Jerry walks home from school, he walks $\frac{1}{2}$ mile. He walked home from school 3 days in a row. How far did he walk?

3. Anita made a 3 × 3 square design with 1 white, 4 red, 2 blue, and 2 yellow squares. She glued a red square in each corner. She glued the white square in the middle, a blue square above and below the white square, and a yellow square in the two remaining spaces. What does Anita's design look like?

4. At Jones Elementary School, $\frac{1}{3}$ of the students have one pet, $\frac{1}{4}$ have two pets, and $\frac{1}{6}$ have three or more pets. The rest of the students do not have any pets. What part of the school has pets?

Mixed Applications

Solve.

CHOOSE a strategy and a tool.

- Make an Organized List
- Guess and Check
- Make a Model
- Work Backward
- Use a Table

Paper/Pencil

Calculator

Hands-On

Mental Math

5. Cara had 40 pencils. She gave some of her pencils to Ed and Sarah. She gave twice as many pencils to Ed as she gave to Sarah. Cara has 22 pencils left. How many pencils did she give to Ed? to Sarah?

6. Brett is playing a game. On his last turn he earned 12 points, lost 5 points, and earned 3 more points. Now he has 32 points. How many points did Brett have before his last turn?

7. Maya can wear a red or orange shirt. She can wear black, blue, or white pants. How many choices does she have? What are they?

8. Rita, Kyle, and Kira shared a pizza. Rita ate $\frac{1}{3}$ of the pizza, Kyle ate $\frac{1}{3}$, and Kira ate $\frac{1}{4}$. What part of the pizza did they eat?

9. George and Kerry are allowed to go to a movie if they clean their rooms for more than 2 hours each week. The table shows how long they cleaned every day. Will George be allowed to go to the movie? Will Kerry? Explain.

MINUTES SPENT CLEANING

	Mon	Tue	Wed	Thu	Fri
George	20 min	20 min	40 min	30 min	30 min
Kerry	50 min	50 min	15 min	15 min	5 min

MORE PRACTICE page H102

CHAPTER 17 Review/Test

▶ CHECK Understanding

VOCABULARY

1. The least common multiple of two or more denominators is used to find the __?__. (page 308)

Use the LCM to name the least common denominator, or LCD, for each group of fractions. (pages 308–311)

2. $\frac{2}{3}$ and $\frac{2}{9}$

3. $\frac{1}{2}$ and $\frac{1}{3}$

4. $\frac{3}{10}$ and $\frac{2}{5}$

5. $\frac{1}{3}$, $\frac{3}{4}$, and $\frac{2}{3}$

6. $\frac{1}{8}$, $\frac{1}{4}$, and $\frac{1}{2}$

7. $\frac{2}{3}$, $\frac{1}{2}$, and $\frac{5}{6}$

▶ CHECK Skills

Use fraction strips to find the sum. Write the answer in simplest form. (pages 306–311)

8. $\frac{3}{10} + \frac{3}{5} = n$

9. $\frac{1}{4} + \frac{4}{8} = n$

10. $\frac{5}{6} + \frac{1}{3} = n$

11. $\frac{4}{5} + \frac{2}{10} = n$

12. $\frac{2}{3} + \frac{5}{9} = n$

13. $\frac{2}{8} + \frac{1}{2} = n$

14. $\frac{1}{3} + \frac{1}{4} + \frac{2}{3} = n$

15. $\frac{3}{8} + \frac{3}{4} + \frac{1}{2} = n$

16. $\frac{1}{5} + \frac{1}{10} + \frac{1}{2} = n$

▶ CHECK Problem Solving

Solve. (pages 312–313)

CHOOSE a strategy and a tool.

- Work Backward
- Write a Number Sentence
- Make a Model
- Act It Out

Paper/Pencil

Calculator

Hands-On

Mental Math

17. Brent harvested $\frac{1}{4}$ of his garden in September, $\frac{3}{8}$ in October, and $\frac{1}{8}$ in November. What part of his garden did Brent harvest in those three months?

18. Kalin has 216 photos in an album with 36 pages. The album is full, and each page has an equal number of photos. How many photos are on each page?

19. Devon has 11 quarters. She has twice as many dimes as quarters and 5 fewer nickels than dimes. She has the same number of pennies as the other coins combined. How many of each coin does Devon have? How much money is that?

20. Trevor just came home from the mall. He has $17.04. While he was at the mall, he bought a T-shirt for $9.95 and lunch for $3.01. Then his sister gave him $5.00. How much money did Trevor begin with?

Test Prep

Choose the best answer.

1. Which of these numbers is 650 when rounded to the nearest ten and 700 when rounded to the nearest hundred?

A 605

B 645

C 656

D 675

E Not Here

2. Which of the following is an example of the Associative Property of Multiplication?

F $89 \times 1 = 89$

G $(2 \times 4) \times 3 = 2 \times (4 \times 3)$

H $15 \times 0 = 0$

J $8 \times 5 = 5 \times 8$

3. At a concert, the box office took in $780. Tickets cost $8 each. Which of the following is a reasonable estimate for the number of people who attended the concert?

A 50 **B** 65

C 100 **D** 200

4. Which number completes the pattern?

$6 \times 35 = 210$
$6 \times 3.5 = 21$
$6 \times 0.35 = \square$
$6 \times 0.035 = 0.21$

F 0.21 **G** 2.1

H 21 **J** 210

5. The graph shows ticket sales for a school play. Who sold the most tickets?

A Jane

B Kelly

C Kim

D Tina

6. Which of the following group of fractions is in order from greatest to least?

F $\frac{7}{10}, \frac{3}{10}, \frac{3}{5}$

G $\frac{3}{5}, \frac{6}{10}, \frac{1}{2}$

H $\frac{7}{10}, \frac{3}{5}, \frac{2}{5}$

J $\frac{2}{5}, \frac{3}{5}, \frac{9}{10}$

K Not Here

7. Which of the following fractions is in simplest form?

A $\frac{2}{5}$ **B** $\frac{2}{4}$

C $\frac{4}{8}$ **D** $\frac{3}{12}$

8. $\frac{1}{5} + \frac{2}{5} =$

$\frac{1}{5}$	$\frac{1}{5}$	$\frac{1}{5}$

F $\frac{1}{5}$ **G** $\frac{2}{5}$

H $\frac{3}{5}$ **J** $1\frac{2}{5}$

18 MODELING SUBTRACTION OF FRACTIONS

CONSUMER LINK

To make house frames, builders use "two by fours," or boards that measure 2 in. by 4 in. These boards shrink when the wood dries. A "two by four" actually measures only $1\frac{1}{2}$ in. by $3\frac{1}{2}$ in.

Problem-Solving Activity

Designing Fraction Bars

Design a fraction-bar kit that includes halves, thirds, fourths, sixths, and eighths. Then compare and measure the fraction bars.

YOU WILL NEED: construction paper in five colors, scissors, ruler, pencil, calculator

- Choose the length that will represent 1 whole. All of the bars you start with to make your kit will have to be the same length.
- Make bars for each denominator.
- Compare and measure the different pieces. What is the difference in their lengths?
- Make a poster to display your results.

FRACTION BARS COLOR KEY

$\frac{1}{2}$ tan

$\frac{1}{3}$ green

$\frac{1}{4}$ yellow

$\frac{1}{6}$ gold

$\frac{1}{8}$ red

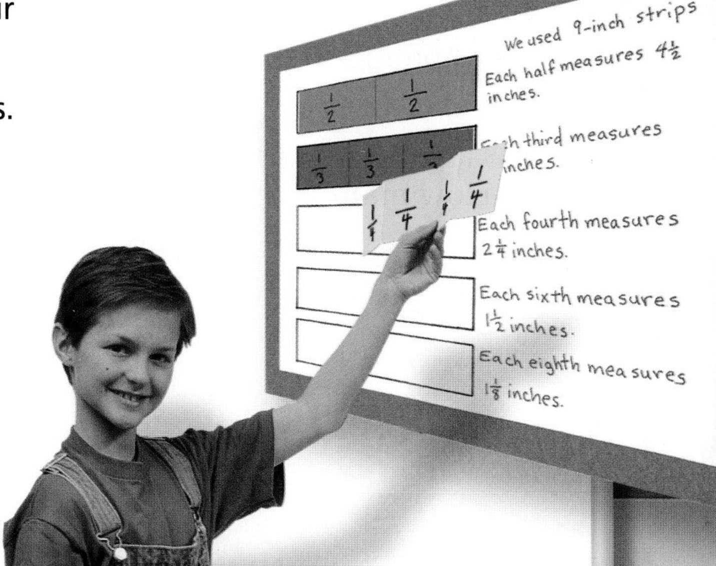

DID YOU

- ✓ choose the length to represent 1 whole?
- ✓ make fraction bars for each denominator?
- ✓ compare and measure the pieces?
- ✓ make a poster to display your results?
- ✓ report your results?

LESSON 1

Subtracting Like Fractions

Why learn this? You can find the fraction that is left over when you use part of a part, such as a part of some leftover food.

Mona had $\frac{5}{8}$ pound of ground beef. She used $\frac{2}{8}$ pound to make a hamburger. How much meat is left?

One way to use fraction bars to subtract like fractions is to take away bars.

MODEL

TAKE AWAY: What is $\frac{5}{8} - \frac{2}{8}$?

Step 1

Model $\frac{5}{8}$ with fraction bars.

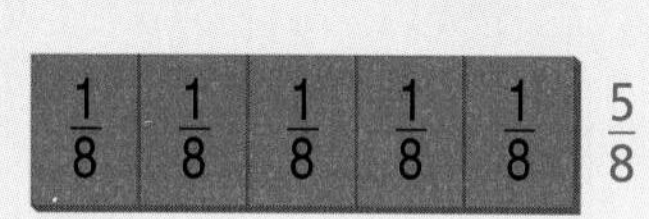

Step 2

Take away 2 bars, or $\frac{2}{8}$.

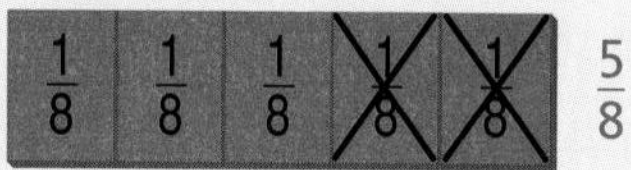

Step 3

Count the bars left.

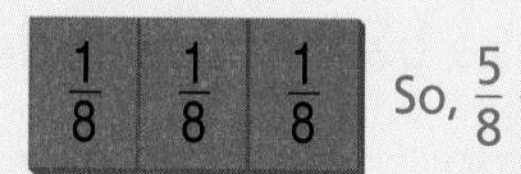

So, $\frac{5}{8} - \frac{2}{8} = \frac{3}{8}$.

So, there is $\frac{3}{8}$ pound of ground beef left.

Franco has $\frac{3}{6}$ yard of gift wrap. James has $\frac{1}{6}$ yard of gift wrap. How many more yards does Franco have?

Another way to use fraction bars to subtract like fractions is to compare bars.

REMEMBER:

A fraction is in *simplest form* when the greatest common factor, or GCF, of the numerator and denominator is 1.

MODEL

COMPARISON: What is $\frac{3}{6} - \frac{1}{6}$?

Step 1

Model $\frac{3}{6}$ and $\frac{1}{6}$ with fraction bars.

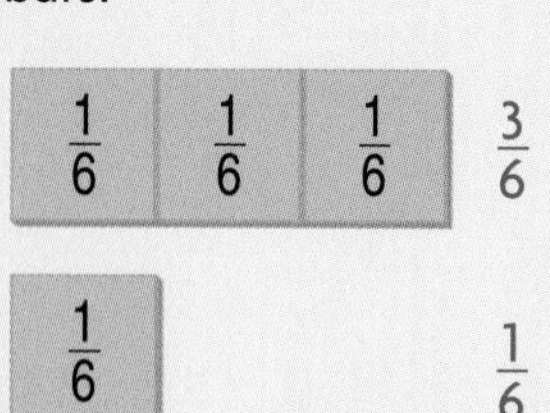

Step 2

Compare the bars for $\frac{3}{6}$ with the bar for $\frac{1}{6}$. Find the difference.

$\frac{1}{6}$ $\frac{1}{6}$ $\frac{1}{6}$

$\frac{1}{6}$? $\frac{2}{6}$

Step 3

Find the largest bar or bars of the same length to write the answer in simplest form.

$\frac{1}{6}$ $\frac{1}{6}$ $\frac{2}{6} = \frac{1}{3}$

$\frac{1}{3}$ So, $\frac{3}{6} - \frac{1}{6} = \frac{1}{3}$.

So, Franco has $\frac{1}{3}$ yard more.

CRITICAL THINKING How are the two models alike? How are they different?

▶ CHECK

Use fraction strips to find the difference.

1. $\frac{4}{5} - \frac{3}{5} = n$ **2.** $\frac{7}{10} - \frac{4}{10} = n$ **3.** $\frac{8}{9} - \frac{4}{9} = n$ **4.** $\frac{7}{12} - \frac{1}{12} = n$

5. What rule can you write for subtracting like fractions with fraction bars?

▶ PRACTICE

Use fraction strips to find the difference.

6. $\frac{4}{8} - \frac{3}{8} = n$ **7.** $\frac{4}{6} - \frac{3}{6} = n$ **8.** $\frac{9}{10} - \frac{3}{10} = n$ **9.** $\frac{7}{12} - \frac{1}{12} = n$

Use fraction strips to find the difference. Write the answer in simplest form.

10. $\frac{5}{12} - \frac{1}{12} = n$ **11.** $\frac{3}{4} - \frac{1}{4} = n$ **12.** $\frac{5}{10} - \frac{3}{10} = n$

13. $\frac{5}{6} - \frac{3}{6} = n$ **14.** $\frac{5}{6} - \frac{1}{6} = n$ **15.** $\frac{10}{12} - \frac{7}{12} = n$

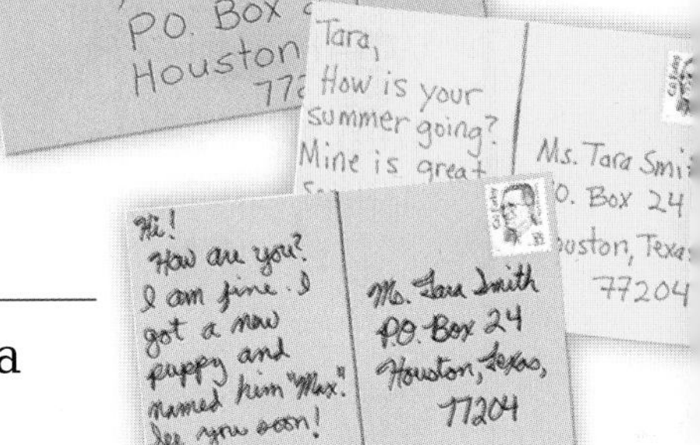

Problem Solving • Mixed Applications

16. Probability Rich pulls a marble from a bag of 10 black, 5 red, 4 blue, and 2 green marbles. Which outcome is most likely? least likely?

17. Reasoning Tara got 5 letters in the mail on Monday. Of the letters, 3 were from friends. What fraction of the letters was *not* from friends?

18. When Max arrived, there was $\frac{7}{8}$ of a pizza left. He ate $\frac{4}{8}$ of the pizza. How much of the pizza was left after Max ate?

19. Write About It How can you use the comparison model to show $\frac{7}{8} - \frac{3}{8}$?

Mixed Review and Test Prep

Find the number of choices by making a tree diagram. (pages 192–193)

20. Breakfast Choices
Food: cereal or eggs
Drink: orange juice, milk, tomato juice, or apple juice

Choose the letter of the most reasonable unit of measure.
(pages 248–249)

21. length of large paper clip **A** mm **B** cm **C** dm **D** m

22. height of the room **F** mm **G** dm **H** m **J** km

Subtracting Unlike Fractions

You will investigate using fraction bars to subtract fractions with unlike denominators.

Use the comparison model to subtract fractions with unlike denominators.

EXPLORE

Use fraction bars to subtract fractions with unlike denominators.

MATERIALS: fraction bars

MODEL

What is $\frac{2}{3} - \frac{1}{6}$?

Step 1

Model $\frac{2}{3}$ and $\frac{1}{6}$ with fraction bars.

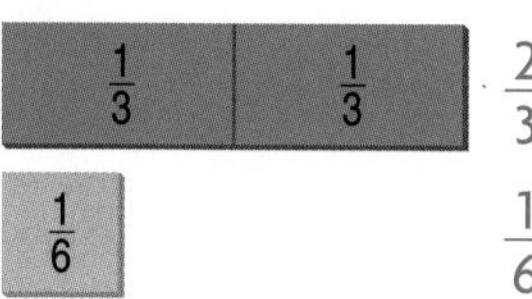

$\frac{2}{3}$

$\frac{1}{6}$

Step 2

Compare the bars. Find the like fraction bars that fit exactly across. This is the difference.

$\frac{1}{3}$ $\frac{1}{3}$

$\frac{1}{6}$?

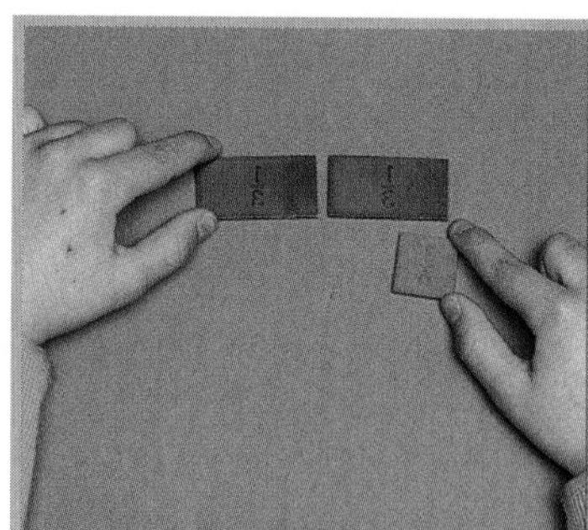

Record

Record a subtraction sentence for the model. Describe how you found the missing part.

Talk About It How did you decide what fraction bars to try? Did more than one size fit? Why?

Now investigate finding the difference of other unlike fractions.

TRY THIS

1. Find $\frac{3}{4} - \frac{1}{2}$. Explain how you used fraction bars to find the difference. Record a number sentence.
2. How is finding the difference with like fractions different from finding the difference with unlike fractions?

3. **Write About It** Explain how to subtract fractions with unlike denominators.

Technology Link

You can subtract unlike fractions by using E-Lab, Activity 18. Available on CD-ROM and on the Internet at **www.hbschool.com/elab**

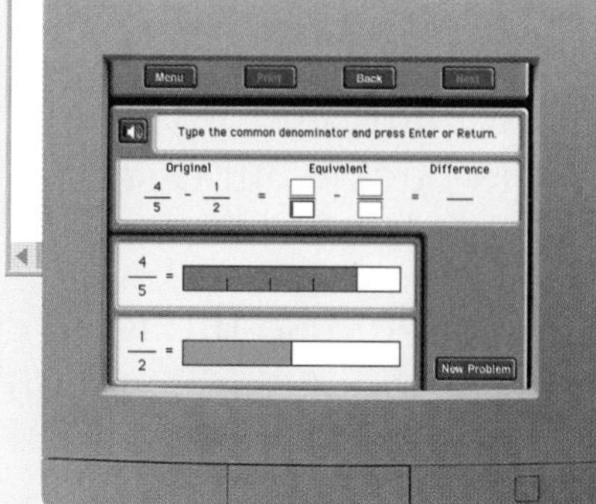

▶ PRACTICE

Use fraction bars to find the difference.

4. 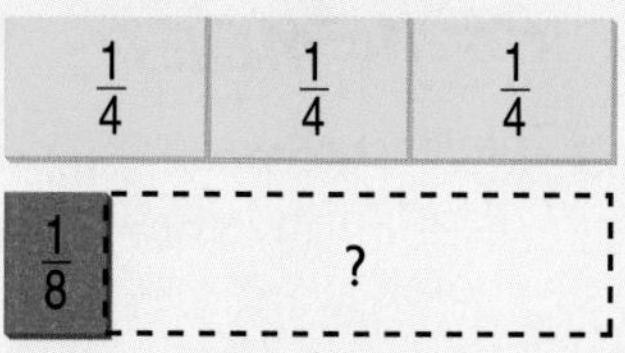

5. 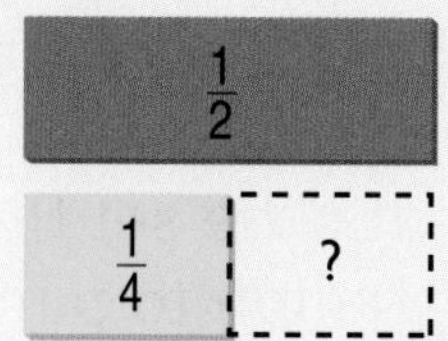

6. 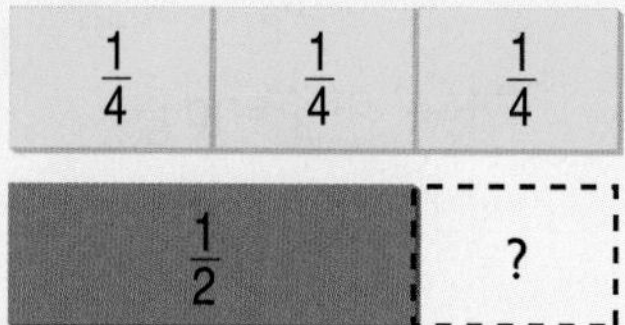

7. $\frac{1}{5}$ $\frac{1}{5}$ $\frac{1}{5}$

$\frac{1}{10}$ $\frac{1}{10}$ $\frac{1}{10}$?

8. $\frac{1}{4}$ $\frac{1}{4}$ $\frac{1}{4}$

$\frac{1}{12}$ $\frac{1}{12}$ $\frac{1}{12}$ $\frac{1}{12}$ $\frac{1}{12}$ $\frac{1}{12}$ $\frac{1}{12}$?

9. 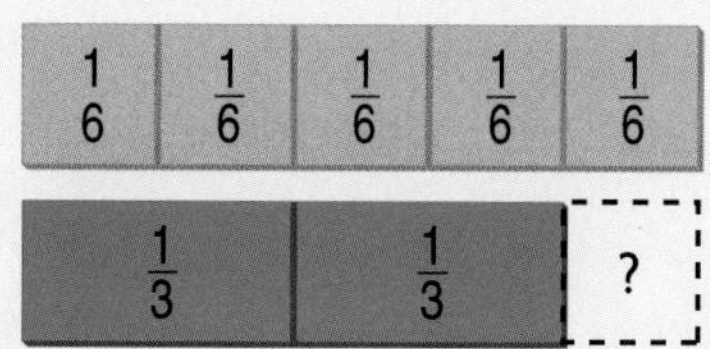

10. $\frac{3}{4} - \frac{3}{8} = n$

11. $\frac{5}{6} - \frac{1}{12} = n$

12. $\frac{4}{6} - \frac{1}{3} = n$

13. $\frac{7}{10} - \frac{1}{2} = n$

14. $\frac{6}{8} - \frac{1}{4} = n$

15. $\frac{5}{6} - \frac{1}{3} = n$

16. $\frac{1}{2} - \frac{1}{10} = n$

17. $\frac{7}{8} - \frac{3}{4} = n$

18. $\frac{2}{3} - \frac{1}{12} = n$

Problem Solving • Mixed Applications

19. **Time** There are 60 seconds in a minute. Pam can run 1 lap around the track in 45 seconds. How many seconds will it take Pam to run 12 laps around the track at that speed? How many minutes is that?

20. **Number Sense** Doug and Lisa invited 25 friends to a cookout. Doug, Lisa, and each friend will eat 2 hot dogs. Hot dogs come 8 to a pack. How many packs should Doug and Lisa buy?

21. **Measurement** The Wegners drove from Akron to Indianapolis. They drove for 5 hours and traveled 292.5 miles in all. They did not make any stops. How fast did they drive?

22. **Time** Carl worked outside for $\frac{5}{6}$ hour. He tilled his garden for $\frac{1}{2}$ hour, planted seeds for $\frac{1}{6}$ hour, and watered for the rest of the time. For what part of an hour did he water?

MORE PRACTICE page H102

LESSON 3

Using the Least Common Denominator to Subtract Fractions

Why learn this? You can subtract fractions, such as parts of a gallon of paint, to find the amount left over.

> **REMEMBER:**
>
> The least common multiple, or LCM, of two or more denominators is used to find the *least common denominator*, or *LCD*.
>
> The LCD of $\frac{1}{3}$ and $\frac{1}{6}$ is sixths.

Lloyd and Kishi had $\frac{3}{4}$ gallon of paint for the set they are making for the play. They used $\frac{1}{3}$ gallon to paint the background scenery. How much paint do they have left?

You can use the least common denominator, or LCD, to help you subtract unlike fractions.

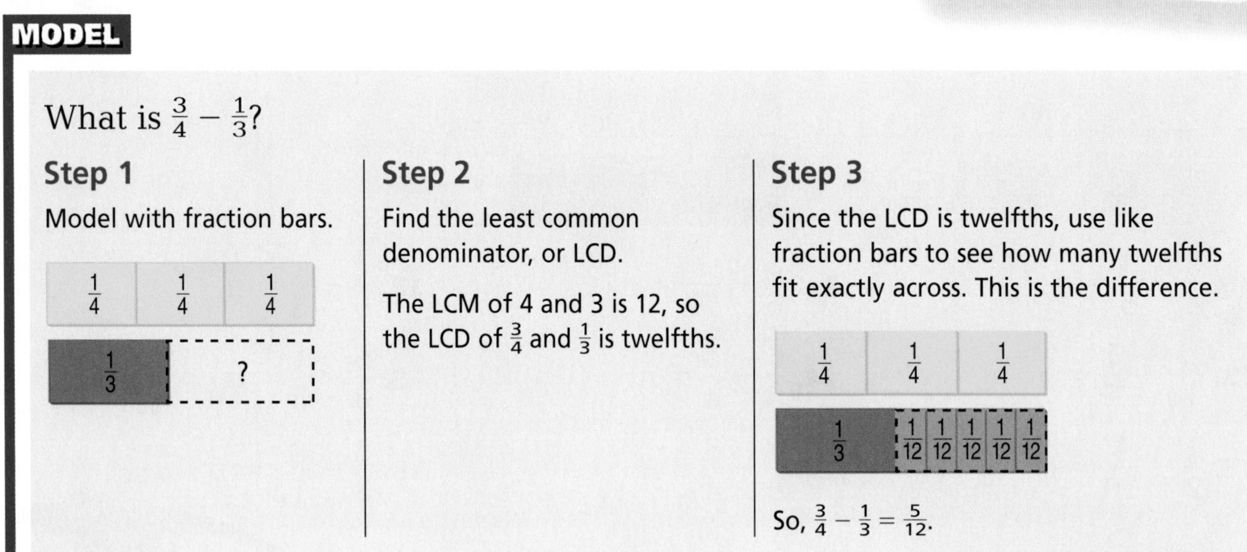

MODEL

What is $\frac{3}{4} - \frac{1}{3}$?

Step 1

Model with fraction bars.

Step 2

Find the least common denominator, or LCD.

The LCM of 4 and 3 is 12, so the LCD of $\frac{3}{4}$ and $\frac{1}{3}$ is twelfths.

Step 3

Since the LCD is twelfths, use like fraction bars to see how many twelfths fit exactly across. This is the difference.

So, $\frac{3}{4} - \frac{1}{3} = \frac{5}{12}$.

So, Lloyd and Kishi have $\frac{5}{12}$ gallon of paint left.

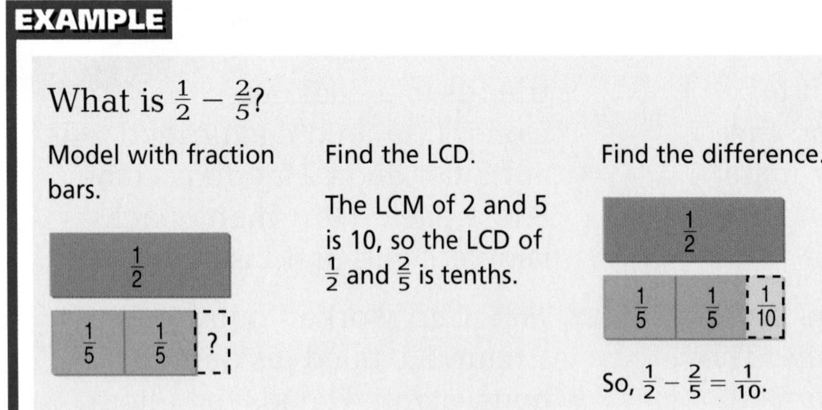

EXAMPLE

What is $\frac{1}{2} - \frac{2}{5}$?

Model with fraction bars.

Find the LCD.

The LCM of 2 and 5 is 10, so the LCD of $\frac{1}{2}$ and $\frac{2}{5}$ is tenths.

Find the difference.

So, $\frac{1}{2} - \frac{2}{5} = \frac{1}{10}$.

- How does using the LCD help you model this problem?

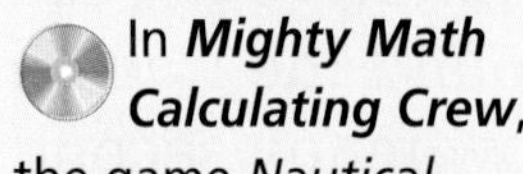

Technology Link

In ***Mighty Math Calculating Crew***, the game *Nautical Number Line* challenges you to subtract fractions. Use Grow Slide Level M.

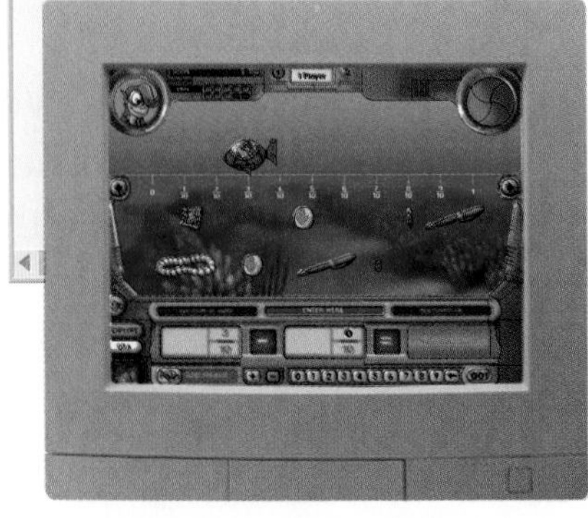

▶ CHECK

Name the least common denominator, or LCD.
Use fraction strips to find the difference.

1. $\frac{1}{2} - \frac{1}{3} = n$ **2.** $\frac{3}{5} - \frac{1}{3} = n$ **3.** $\frac{1}{3} - \frac{1}{4} = n$

▶ PRACTICE

Name the least common denominator, or LCD, for each pair of fractions.

4. $\frac{1}{9}$ and $\frac{1}{3}$ **5.** $\frac{1}{4}$ and $\frac{1}{8}$ **6.** $\frac{1}{2}$ and $\frac{1}{4}$ **7.** $\frac{1}{6}$ and $\frac{1}{4}$

Use fraction strips to find the difference. Write the answer in simplest form.

8. $\frac{5}{6} - \frac{3}{4} = n$ **9.** $\frac{3}{5} - \frac{1}{2} = n$ **10.** $\frac{7}{8} - \frac{3}{4} = n$ **11.** $\frac{9}{10} - \frac{1}{5} = n$

12. $\frac{2}{3} - \frac{1}{9} = n$ **13.** $\frac{7}{8} - \frac{1}{2} = n$ **14.** $\frac{11}{12} - \frac{1}{6} = n$ **15.** $\frac{7}{12} - \frac{1}{3} = n$

16. $\frac{5}{6} - \frac{1}{2} = n$ **17.** $\frac{11}{12} - \frac{2}{3} = n$ **18.** $\frac{4}{5} - \frac{3}{10} = n$ **19.** $\frac{5}{8} - \frac{1}{4} = n$

Problem Solving • Mixed Applications

20. Number Sense Dan wrote a report for history. He found $\frac{1}{8}$ of the information for the report on the Internet and $\frac{1}{2}$ at the library. How much information did he get from sources other than the Internet and the library?

21. Consumer Ms. Aquil bought a box of 144 pencils. She gave an equal number of pencils to each of her 24 students. How many pencils did each student get?

22. Time Mandy spent $\frac{7}{8}$ of the weekend practicing for the school play. Linda spent $\frac{1}{2}$ of the weekend practicing. How much longer did Mandy practice?

23. **Write a problem** in which you subtract unlike fractions.

Mixed Review and Test Prep

Find the quotient. Check by multiplying. (pages 236–241)

24. $6\overline{)1.08}$ **25.** $9\overline{)2.25}$ **26.** $4\overline{)3.92}$ **27.** $7\overline{)3.78}$ **28.** $8\overline{)5.84}$

Choose the letter of the correct product. (pages 214–215)

29. $0.7 \times 0.9 = n$ **A** 6.3 **B** 0.63 **C** 63 **D** 63.0

30. $0.8 \times 0.6 = n$ **F** 4.8 **G** 48.0 **H** 0.48 **J** 480

LESSON 4 • PART 1

Subtracting Fractions Using a Ruler

Why learn this? You can compare measurements that are less than an inch, such as plant growth.

On Monday a bean plant was $\frac{1}{2}$ inch tall. On Friday the plant was $\frac{5}{8}$ inch tall. How much did the plant grow from Monday to Friday?

You can compare and subtract unlike fractions on a ruler the same way you compare and subtract unlike fractions with fraction bars.

What is $\frac{5}{8} - \frac{1}{2}$?

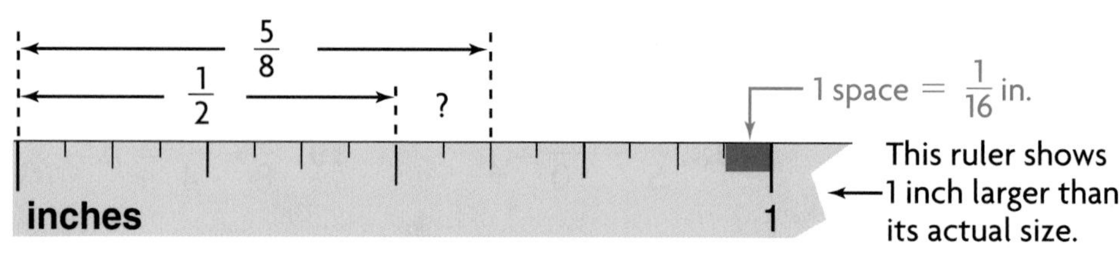

This ruler shows 1 inch larger than its actual size.

On this ruler, each space equals $\frac{1}{16}$ inch. Every 2 spaces equals $\frac{1}{8}$ inch, every 4 spaces equals $\frac{1}{4}$ inch, and every 8 spaces equals $\frac{1}{2}$ inch. The difference between $\frac{5}{8}$ inch and $\frac{1}{2}$ inch is 2 spaces, or $\frac{1}{8}$ inch.

So, the plant grew $\frac{1}{8}$ inch from Monday to Friday.

Talk About It CRITICAL THINKING

- How is subtracting unlike fractions on a ruler like using fraction bars to subtract?
- How is subtracting unlike fractions on a ruler different from using fraction bars?

SOCIAL STUDIES LINK

The common bean is grown in all parts of the world. It is an important source of protein in the diets of more than 50 million people. Some families get about $\frac{2}{3}$ of the protein they need from beans and the rest from beef and milk. What fraction of their protein comes from beef and milk?

▶ CHECK

Use the ruler to find the difference.

1. $\frac{1}{4}$ in. $-$ $\frac{3}{16}$ in. $=$?

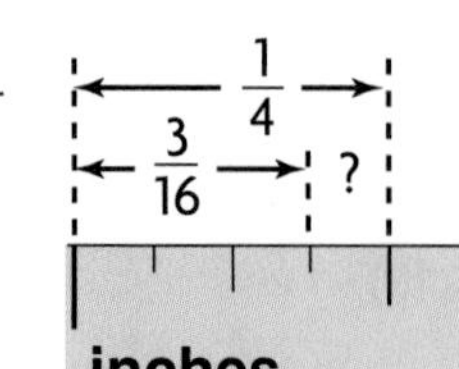

inches 1

▶ PRACTICE

Use the ruler to find the difference.

2. $\frac{15}{16}$ in. − $\frac{7}{16}$ in. = ?

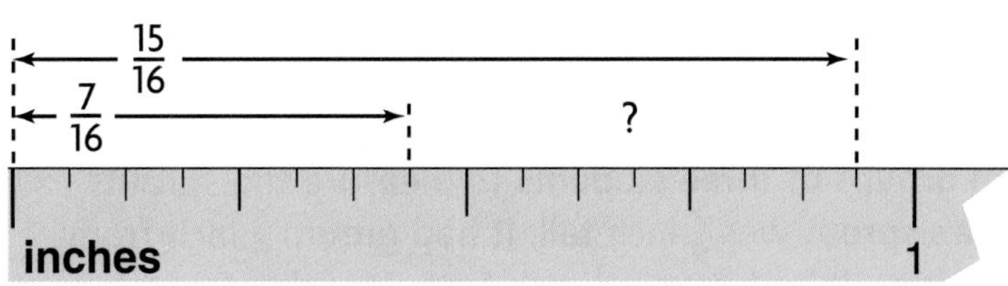

3. $\frac{1}{2}$ in. − $\frac{3}{8}$ in. = ?

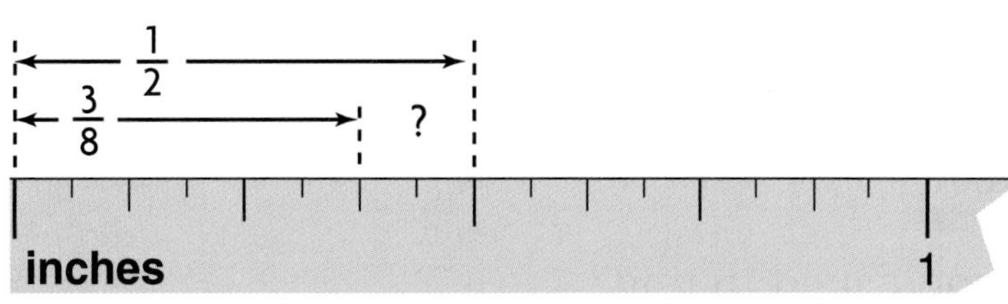

4. $\frac{3}{4}$ in. − $\frac{1}{8}$ in. = ?

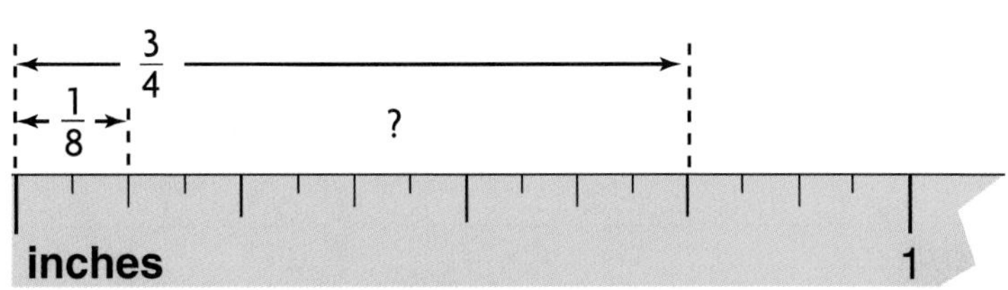

5. $\frac{1}{2}$ in. − $\frac{3}{16}$ in. = ?

6. $\frac{7}{8}$ in. − $\frac{1}{2}$ in. = ?

7. $\frac{7}{16}$ in. − $\frac{3}{8}$ in. = ?

8. $\frac{5}{8}$ in. − $\frac{1}{4}$ in. = ?

9. $\frac{11}{16}$ in. − $\frac{1}{2}$ in. = ?

10. 1 in. − $\frac{1}{4}$ in. = ?

Problem Solving • Mixed Applications

For Problems 11–14, use a ruler to solve.

11. Measurement Rudy's longest fingernail is $\frac{5}{8}$ inch long. Her shortest fingernail is $\frac{5}{16}$ inch long. What is the difference in length between the two fingernails?

12. Logic Terry is $\frac{1}{2}$ inch taller than Lisa. Rodelin is $\frac{3}{4}$ inch taller than Lisa. How much taller is Rodelin than Terry?

13. Measurement On Monday, a potato plant was $\frac{1}{4}$ inch tall. On Friday, it was $\frac{7}{16}$ inch tall. How much did the potato plant grow from Monday to Friday?

14. Reasoning Dawn is sewing a shirt. She makes a buttonhole that is 1 inch wide to fit a button that is $\frac{5}{8}$ inch wide. How much wider is the buttonhole than the button?

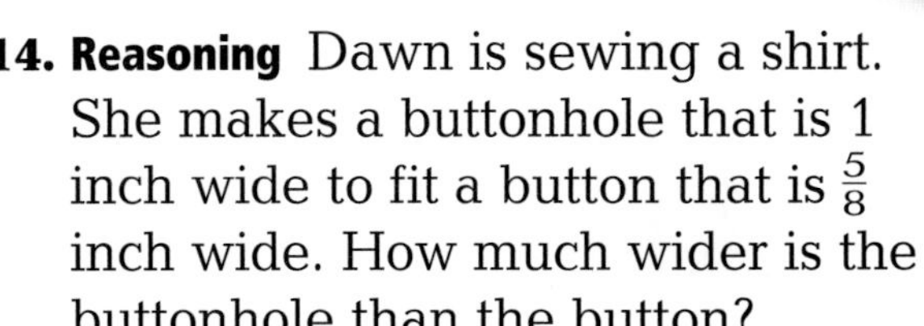

15. Measurement Bernie, a fifth-grade student, is 1.5 meters tall. He grew 5 cm during his fourth-grade year. He grew 8 cm during his third-grade year. How tall was Bernie at the beginning of third grade? (HINT: 1 cm = 0.01 m)

16. **Write a problem** that you could solve by subtracting fractions on a ruler.

MORE PRACTICE page H103

Problem–Solving Strategy: Work Backward

▶ **THE PROBLEM** The students in Alana's class planted seeds. They worked in groups of three students to measure the sprouts. On Friday, Alana's sprout was $\frac{7}{8}$ inch tall. It had grown $\frac{1}{4}$ inch from Wednesday to Friday. It had grown $\frac{1}{2}$ inch from Monday to Wednesday. How tall was Alana's sprout on Monday?

UNDERSTAND

- What are you asked to find?
- What information will you use?
- Is there information you will not use? If so, what?

PLAN

- What strategy can you use to solve this problem?

  You can *work backward* to find out how tall the sprout was on Monday.

SOLVE

- How can you work backward to solve?

  Use a ruler. Start at $\frac{7}{8}$ inch. Subtract the $\frac{1}{4}$ inch the sprout grew from Wednesday to Friday. Then subtract the $\frac{1}{2}$ inch the sprout grew from Monday to Wednesday. The answer is the height the sprout was on Monday.

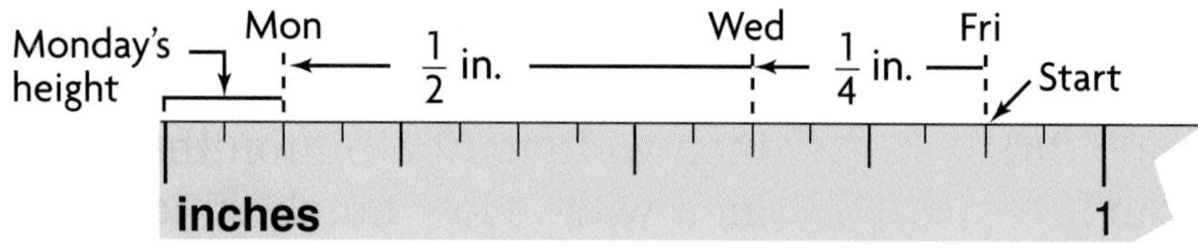

So, Alana's sprout was $\frac{1}{8}$ inch tall on Monday.

LOOK BACK

- How can you determine if your answer is reasonable?
- What other strategy can you use?

▶ PRACTICE

Work backward to solve.

1. Len is in Alana's class. On Friday his sprout was $\frac{3}{4}$ inch tall. It had grown $\frac{1}{8}$ inch from Wednesday to Friday. It had grown $\frac{3}{8}$ inch from Monday to Wednesday. How tall was Len's sprout on Monday?

2. Maria planted a marigold seed. On Friday the marigold sprout was $\frac{5}{8}$ inch tall. It had grown $\frac{1}{4}$ inch from Wednesday to Friday. It had grown $\frac{1}{4}$ inch from Monday to Wednesday. How tall was Maria's marigold on Monday?

3. Brian came home from a baseball game with $7.26. At the game he spent $7.50 for a ticket, $2.25 for lunch, and $3.99 for a souvenir. Then he won $1.00 because he was sitting in the prize seat. How much money did Brian have before the game?

4. Faye's puppy is 8 months old. It is 0.31 meters tall. The puppy grew 4 cm from when it was 7 months to 8 months old. It grew 2 cm from when it was 6 months to 7 months old. How tall was Faye's puppy when it was 6 months old?

Mixed Applications

Solve.

CHOOSE a strategy and a tool.

- Work Backward
- Guess and Check
- Write a Number Sentence
- Make an Organized List

Paper/Pencil

Calculator

Hands-On

Mental Math

5. Micah's school has assemblies on Mondays and Fridays. Monday assemblies last 1 hour. Friday assemblies last 2 hours. How many hours of assemblies are there in 4 weeks?

6. Charity gave 12 baseball cards to Rhonda and 18 to James. Then she traded 5 of her cards for 3 of Andy's cards. Charity now has 48 cards. How many cards did she have to begin with?

7. Carlotta bought 9 packages of lemonade for $1.10 each and 2 packages of cups for $1.09 each. She sold 23 cups of lemonade every hour for 4 hours at $0.40 per cup. How much more money did Carlotta earn than she spent on supplies?

8. Sherwood earned $35 last week. He earned twice as much for baby-sitting as he did for cleaning the bathrooms. He earned twice as much for cleaning the bathrooms as he did for mowing the lawn. How much did Sherwood earn for each job?

9. Leon goes to Camp Jewell. How many combinations of food can he eat at dinner? What are they?

MORE PRACTICE page H103

CHAPTER 18 Review/Test

CHECK Understanding

Use fraction strips to find the difference. (pages 320–321)

1. $\frac{1}{12}$ $\frac{1}{12}$ $\frac{1}{12}$ $\frac{1}{12}$ $\frac{1}{12}$ $\frac{1}{12}$ $\frac{1}{12}$
$\frac{1}{6}$?

2. 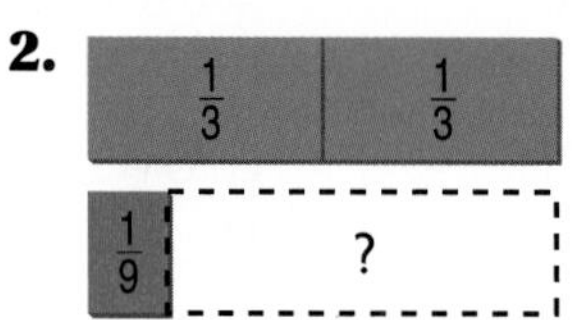

3. 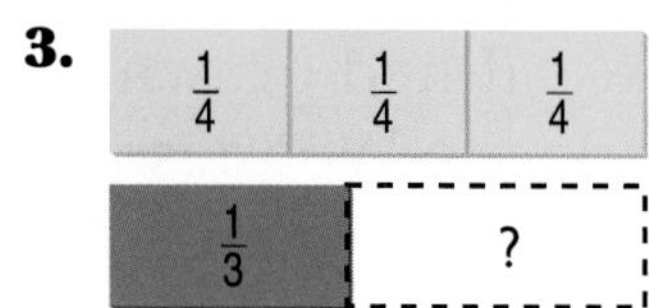

Name the least common denominator, or LCD, for each pair of fractions. (pages 322–323)

4. $\frac{2}{3}$ and $\frac{1}{6}$
5. $\frac{3}{4}$ and $\frac{3}{8}$
6. $\frac{2}{3}$ and $\frac{1}{4}$
7. $\frac{3}{4}$ and $\frac{1}{2}$
8. $\frac{3}{10}$ and $\frac{1}{5}$
9. $\frac{7}{9}$ and $\frac{2}{3}$

CHECK Skills

Use fraction strips to find the difference. Write the answer in simplest form. (pages 318–319, 322–323)

10. $\frac{5}{8} - \frac{3}{8} = n$
11. $\frac{11}{12} - \frac{5}{12} = n$
12. $\frac{8}{9} - \frac{5}{9} = n$
13. $\frac{3}{4} - \frac{1}{2} = n$
14. $\frac{5}{8} - \frac{1}{2} = n$
15. $\frac{1}{3} - \frac{1}{12} = n$
16. $\frac{7}{10} - \frac{1}{2} = n$
17. $\frac{4}{5} - \frac{2}{10} = n$
18. $\frac{3}{4} - \frac{3}{8} = n$
19. $\frac{3}{4} - \frac{2}{3} = n$
20. $\frac{5}{8} - \frac{1}{4} = n$
21. $\frac{2}{3} - \frac{1}{6} = n$

CHECK Problem Solving

Solve. (pages 326–327)

CHOOSE a strategy and a tool.

- Work Backward
- Guess and Check
- Write a Number Sentence

Paper/Pencil

Calculator

Hands-On

Mental Math

22. Art planted a lima bean. On Friday the sprout was $\frac{7}{8}$ inch tall. It had grown $\frac{3}{8}$ inch from Wednesday to Friday. It had grown $\frac{1}{4}$ inch from Monday to Wednesday. How tall was the sprout on Monday?

23. Brenda gave away 21 stickers. She gave half as many stickers to her brother as she gave to her teacher. She gave twice as many to her best friend as she gave to her teacher. How many stickers did Brenda give to each person?

Test Prep

CUMULATIVE CHAPTERS 1–18

Choose the best answer.

1. Which of the following groups of decimals is in order from *least* to *greatest*?

A 2.01, 3.42, 2.1, 3.22

B 2.01, 2.1, 3.22, 3.42

C 3.42, 3.22, 2.01, 2.1

D 2.1, 2.01, 3.22, 3.42

2. Which number is the greatest common factor of 7 and 18?

F 1 **G** 6

H 7 **J** 18

3. The math club sold magazines for one month. The table shows the money raised each week.

MATH CLUB SALES	
Week	Amount
1	$100
2	$125
3	$200
4	$175

What was the average amount raised per week?

A $100 **B** $125

C $150 **D** $600

4. Which number completes the pattern?

$3{,}500 \div 1$
$350 \div 1$
$35 \div 1$
$3.5 \div 1$
$\underline{?} \div 1$

F 0.0035

G 3.50

H 0.35

J 0.035

5. The sum of two numbers is 18. Their product is 72. What are the two numbers?

A 1 and 17

B 3 and 15

C 4 and 16

D 6 and 12

E Not Here

6. To raise money for a field trip, 65 students made caramel apples. Each student made 12 apples. How many caramel apples were made in all?

F 77 **G** 770

H 780 **J** 885

7. $\frac{1}{6} + \frac{5}{6} = \square$

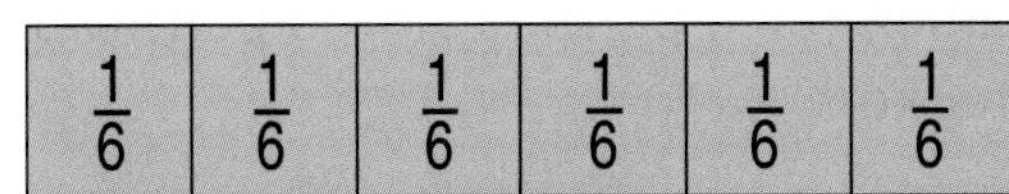

A $\frac{1}{6}$ **B** $\frac{4}{6}$, or $\frac{2}{3}$

C $\frac{5}{6}$ **D** $\frac{6}{6}$, or 1

8. Use the ruler to find $\frac{1}{2}$ inch $-$ $\frac{1}{4}$ inch = $\underline{?}$.

F $\frac{1}{2}$ in. **G** $\frac{1}{4}$ in.

H $\frac{1}{8}$ in. **J** $\frac{1}{16}$ in.

CHAPTERS 15–18

MATH FUN!

EGYPTIAN FRACTIONS

PURPOSE To practice adding unlike fractions

YOU WILL NEED pencil and paper, fraction strips

The ancient Egyptians wrote all fractions as sums of unit fractions with different denominators. Unit fractions have 1 as the numerator. For example, to show $\frac{3}{4}$, they wrote $\frac{1}{2} + \frac{1}{4}$.

$\frac{1}{2}$ $\frac{1}{4}$ $\frac{1}{8}$ $\frac{1}{16}$

Write each of the following fractions as the sum of unit fractions: $\frac{3}{8}$, $\frac{5}{8}$, $\frac{3}{16}$, and $\frac{11}{16}$. Make up two other fractions and write them as the sum of unit fractions.

Teach a family member how to write Egyptian fractions.

Fraction Flags

PURPOSE To add unlike fractions

YOU WILL NEED centimeter grid paper, ruler, pencil, colored pencils or markers

Design 2 flags, using one main color.

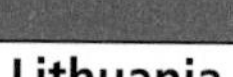

Indonesia Mexico Lithuania

Make one flag $\frac{1}{4}$, $\frac{1}{2}$, or $\frac{3}{4}$ the main color. Make the other flag $\frac{1}{3}$ or $\frac{2}{3}$ the main color.

Which of the flags above are about $\frac{1}{3}$ red?

PLAN THE PAN

PURPOSE To model fractions

YOU WILL NEED paper and pencil, crayons

You have made a pan of brownies. Before you cut them, the phone rings. Your teammates are coming over! You want to give each visitor a brownie.

Draw a rectangular pan for each of the three situations given. Color one brownie. Write the fraction it shows.

Three Situations

Your basketball team calls. You will need brownies for 6.

Your baseball team visits. You will need brownies for 10.

Your soccer team is coming over. You will need brownies for 12.

Make up your own situation. Use any number you like.

Situation: My whole class is coming over! With Mom, that makes 25.

Technology

CHAPTERS 15–18

Venn Diagrams and Greatest Common Factor

MATERIALS
Claris Draw, or other drawing program

Venn diagrams show how sets of numbers are related. Make a Venn diagram that shows the common factors of 42, 56, and 105 in overlapping circles. What is the greatest common factor (GCF) of 42, 56, and 105?

First find the factors of each number.

42: 1 × 42, 2 × 21, 3 × 14, 6 × 7

56: 1 × 56, 2 × 28, 4 × 14, 7 × 8

105: 1 × 105, 3 × 35, 5 × 21, 7 × 15

Make three circles that overlap. Leave enough room where the circles overlap to write in the common factors. Remember to label each circle.

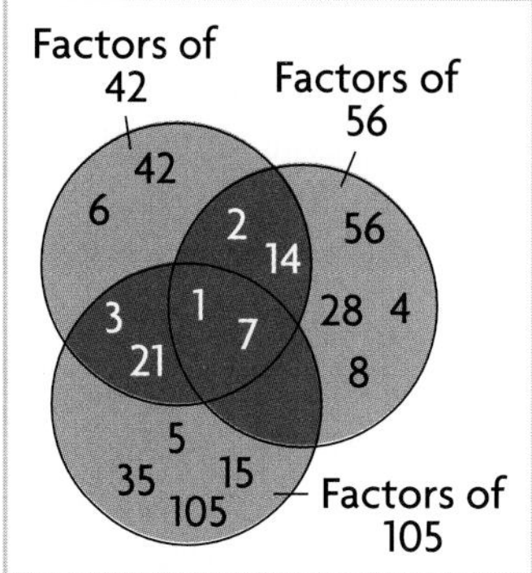

1 and 7 are factors of all three sets of numbers. The GCF is 7.

EXAMPLES

Anna's garden has 48 tulips, 24 roses, and 36 daisies. She wants to make the largest bouquets possible with only one type of flower in each bouquet. Use a Venn diagram to show the largest number, or GCF, for each type of flower she can include.

The GCF is 12. So, Anna can put 12 of each type of flower in each bouquet.

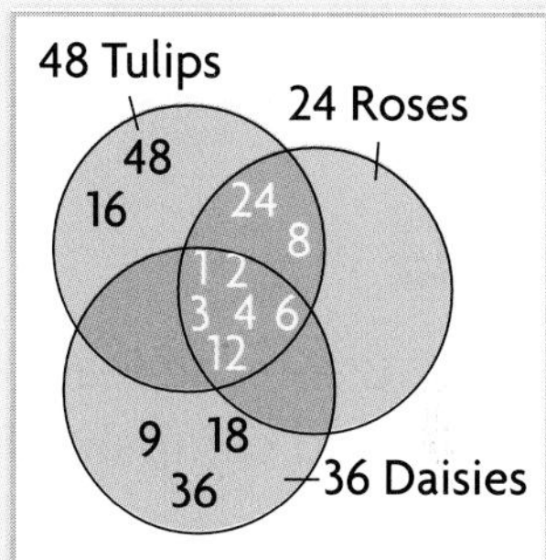

▶ PRACTICE

1. Make a Venn diagram to find the GCF of 10, 25, and 50.

2. Make a Venn diagram to find the GCF of 20, 76, and 91.

3. Use this Venn diagram to name the GCF of 35 and 28.

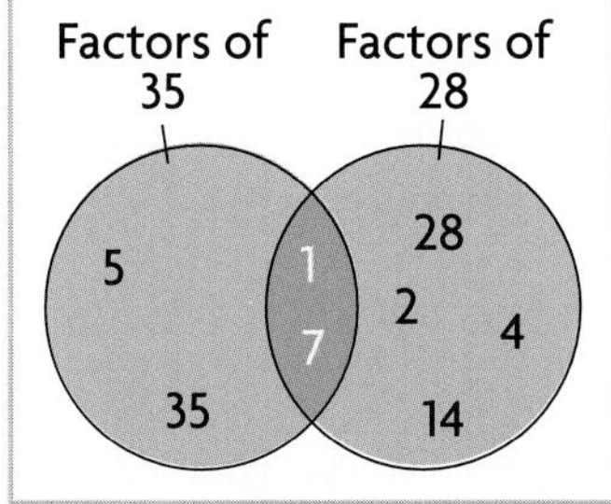

4. **Using the Computer** Erica is making bead necklaces. She has 45 blue beads, 27 red beads, and 63 white beads. She wants to make necklaces with the same number of each color bead. Use a Venn diagram to help you find the greatest number of beads of each color to put in each necklace.

CHAPTERS 15–18

Study Guide and Review

Vocabulary Check

Choose a term from the box to complete each sentence.

VOCABULARY
prime
equivalent
least common denominator, or LCD
least common multiple, or LCM
mixed number
simplest form

1. A number that is made up of a whole number and a fraction is called a __?__. (page 272)
2. The least number that is a common multiple of two or more numbers is called the __?__. (page 274)
3. A number that has exactly two factors, 1 and the number itself, is called a __?__ number. (page 286)
4. Fractions that name the same amount are __?__. (page 292)
5. When the greatest common factor of a fraction's numerator and denominator is 1, that fraction is in __?__. (page 298)
6. The least common multiple of two or more denominators is used to find the __?__. (page 308)

Study and Solve

CHAPTER 15

EXAMPLE

Rename, using the least common multiple, and compare. Write <, >, or = for the ●.

$\frac{2}{3}$ ● $\frac{3}{4}$ — The LCM of 3 and 4 is 12.

$\frac{2}{3} \times \frac{4}{4} = \frac{8}{12}$

$\frac{3}{4} \times \frac{3}{3} = \frac{9}{12}$

Multiply each fraction so that the renamed fractions both have denominators of 12.

$\frac{8}{12}$ ● $\frac{9}{12}$

$\frac{8}{12} < \frac{9}{12}$

Compare the numerators. Since $8 < 9$, $\frac{8}{12} < \frac{9}{12}$. So, $\frac{2}{3} < \frac{3}{4}$.

Rename each fraction as a mixed number. (pages 272–273)

7. $\frac{9}{7}$
8. $\frac{19}{5}$

Rename, using the least common multiple, and compare. Write <, >, or = for each ●. (pages 276–277)

9. $\frac{6}{12}$ ● $\frac{1}{2}$
10. $\frac{5}{8}$ ● $\frac{4}{5}$

Write in order from least to greatest. (pages 278–279)

11. $\frac{2}{3}, \frac{1}{2}, \frac{3}{4}$
12. $\frac{7}{8}, \frac{1}{4}, \frac{5}{16}$

Choose a strategy and solve. (pages 280–281)

13. Julie swam $\frac{1}{4}$ mile on Monday, $\frac{1}{2}$ mile on Tuesday, and $\frac{6}{8}$ mile on Wednesday. If this pattern continues, how far will she swim on Thursday?
14. Pedro owns 24 books. If $\frac{1}{3}$ are science fiction and $\frac{1}{4}$ are history books, how many of his books are about other topics?

CHAPTER 16

EXAMPLE

Write in simplest form.

$\frac{15}{20}$ Find the GCF of 15 and 20.
Factors of 15: 1, 3, 5, 15
Factors of 20: 1, 2, 4, 5, 10, 20

$\frac{15}{20} \div \frac{5}{5} = \frac{3}{4}$ The GCF is 5. Divide the numerator and the denominator by 5.
So, $\frac{15}{20}$ in simplest form is $\frac{3}{4}$.

Write the greatest common factor for each pair of numbers. (pages 288–291)

15. 6, 9 **16.** 4, 16

Find an equivalent fraction. Use multiplication or division. (pages 292–293)

17. $\frac{3}{8}$ **18.** $\frac{4}{12}$

Write each fraction in simplest form. (pages 296–297)

19. $\frac{3}{9}$ **20.** $\frac{16}{20}$

21. $\frac{12}{15}$ **22.** $\frac{8}{24}$

Choose a strategy and solve. (pages 294–295)

23. Quentin ate 3 slices of a pizza that was cut into sixths. Lynn said he had eaten $\frac{1}{2}$ of the pizza. Was she right? Explain.

CHAPTER 17

EXAMPLE

Use fraction strips to find the sum.

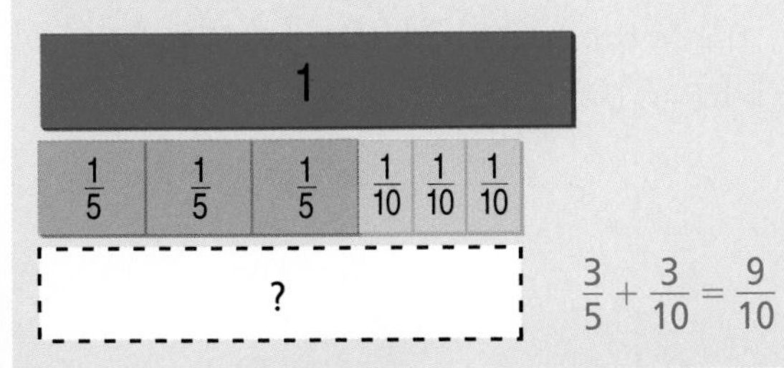

Use fraction strips to find the sum. Write the answer in simplest form. (pages 304–311)

24. $\frac{1}{8} + \frac{3}{8} = n$ **25.** $\frac{3}{5} + \frac{7}{10} = n$

Name the least common denominator for each group of fractions. (pages 308–311)

26. $\frac{2}{3}$ and $\frac{1}{2}$ **27.** $\frac{1}{2}$, $\frac{3}{4}$, and $\frac{5}{6}$

Choose a strategy and solve. (pages 312–313)

28. Danny used $\frac{1}{2}$ cup of flour, $\frac{1}{3}$ cup of cornmeal, and $\frac{1}{4}$ cup of sugar in a muffin recipe. How many cups of ingredients was this?

CHAPTER 18

EXAMPLE

Use fraction strips to find the difference.

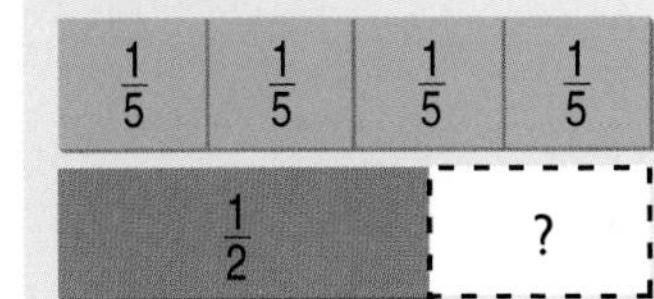

Use fraction strips to find the difference. Write the answer in simplest form. (pages 318–323)

29. $\frac{5}{6} - \frac{1}{3} = n$ **30.** $\frac{3}{4} - \frac{2}{3} = n$

Choose a strategy and solve. (pages 326–327)

31. Lupe used $\frac{3}{4}$ inch of ribbon. She had $\frac{2}{8}$ inch left. How much ribbon did she have to start with?

32. Sandy walked $\frac{1}{2}$ mile to the park. Then she walked $\frac{2}{3}$ mile to her aunt's house. How far did Sandy walk?

CHAPTERS 15–18

Performance Assessment

Tasks: Show What You Know

1. Explain how you would name a fraction and a mixed number for the shaded part. (pages 272–273)

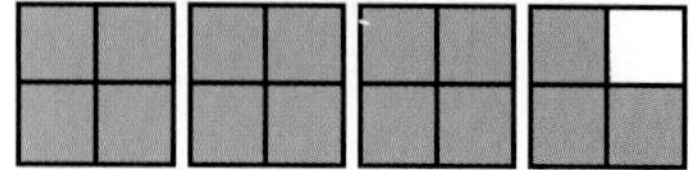

2. Explain how to use fraction bars to help you write $\frac{8}{12}$ in simplest form. (pages 296–299)

$\frac{1}{12}$	$\frac{1}{12}$	$\frac{1}{12}$	$\frac{1}{12}$	$\frac{1}{12}$	$\frac{1}{12}$	$\frac{1}{12}$	$\frac{1}{12}$

3. Show and explain each step as you use fraction strips and the least common denominator to find the sum $\frac{1}{2} + \frac{2}{5} + \frac{3}{10}$. Write the sum in simplest form. Draw a picture of what you did. (pages 308–311)

4. Show and explain each step as you use a ruler to find the difference: $\frac{1}{2}$ in. $- \frac{1}{8}$ in. $= n$. Draw a picture to show what you did. (pages 324–325)

Problem Solving

Solve. Explain your method.

CHOOSE a strategy and a tool.

- Work Backward
- Draw a Diagram
- Make a Model
- Write a Number Sentence

Paper/Pencil

Calculator

Hands-On

Mental Math

5. Sara is putting together a gift box of 12 decorated eggs. She wants $\frac{1}{3}$ of the eggs to be blue, $\frac{1}{4}$ to be yellow, and $\frac{5}{12}$ to be green. How many eggs will she have for each color? Show the order from least to greatest. (pages 280–281)

6. Cam spent $\frac{4}{12}$ of her allowance on clothes, $\frac{1}{4}$ on books, and $\frac{3}{6}$ on a software program. What did she spend most of her money on? (pages 294–295)

7. In Thelma's class, $\frac{1}{4}$ of the students watch TV after school, $\frac{1}{2}$ do homework, $\frac{1}{6}$ play outside, and the rest eat a snack. What part of the class eats a snack? (pages 312–313)

8. Anna was $52\frac{1}{8}$ in. tall in July. She had grown $\frac{1}{2}$ in. since June. From May to June she grew $\frac{1}{4}$ in. How tall was Anna at the beginning of May? (pages 326–327)

Cumulative Review

CHAPTERS 1–18

Solve the problem. Then write the letter of the correct answer.

1. Robyn had $205.16 in her bank account. She deposited $56.47 and wrote checks for $120.08 and $113.99. How much was left in her account?

A. $27.56 **B.** $141.55
C. $261.63 **D.** $382.76 (pages 62–63)

2. Find the perimeter.

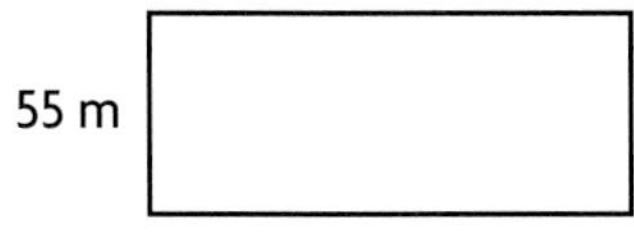

A. 192 m **B.** 247 m
C. 384 m **D.** 7,535 m
(pages 102–103)

3. What would be the best type of graph or plot to display data on students' and teachers' favorite colors?

A. double-bar graph
B. circle graph
C. line graph
D. stem-and-leaf plot (pages 164–165)

4. It is __?__ that you will see a live dinosaur.

A. certain **B.** impossible
C. likely **D.** unlikely
(pages 188–189)

5. $\begin{array}{r} 0.35 \\ \times\ 0.7 \\ \hline \end{array}$

A. 0.215
B. 0.245
C. 0.5
D. 24.5 (pages 214–223)

6. $7\overline{)0.49}$

A. 0.07 **B.** 0.7
C. 3.43 **D.** 7 (pages 236–241)

7. A doorway is about 1 __?__ wide.

A. centimeter
B. gram
C. liter
D. meter (pages 248–253)

8. Rename, using the least common multiple, and compare.

$\frac{2}{3}$ ● $\frac{3}{7}$ **A.** < **B.** >
C. = **D.** +
(pages 276–277)

9. What is the greatest common factor for 9 and 12?

A. 3 **B.** 6
C. 12 **D.** 108 (pages 288–291)

For Problems 10–11, use fraction strips to solve. Choose the correct answer that is in simplest form. (pages 306–311, 318–319)

10. $\frac{3}{4} + \frac{2}{3} = n$

A. $n = \frac{5}{12}$ **B.** $n = \frac{5}{7}$
C. $n = \frac{4}{3}$ **D.** $n = 1\frac{5}{12}$

11. $\frac{7}{8} - \frac{5}{8} = n$

A. $n = 2$ **B.** $n = \frac{12}{16}$
C. $n = \frac{1}{4}$ **D.** $n = \frac{2}{8}$

19 ADDING AND SUBTRACTING FRACTIONS

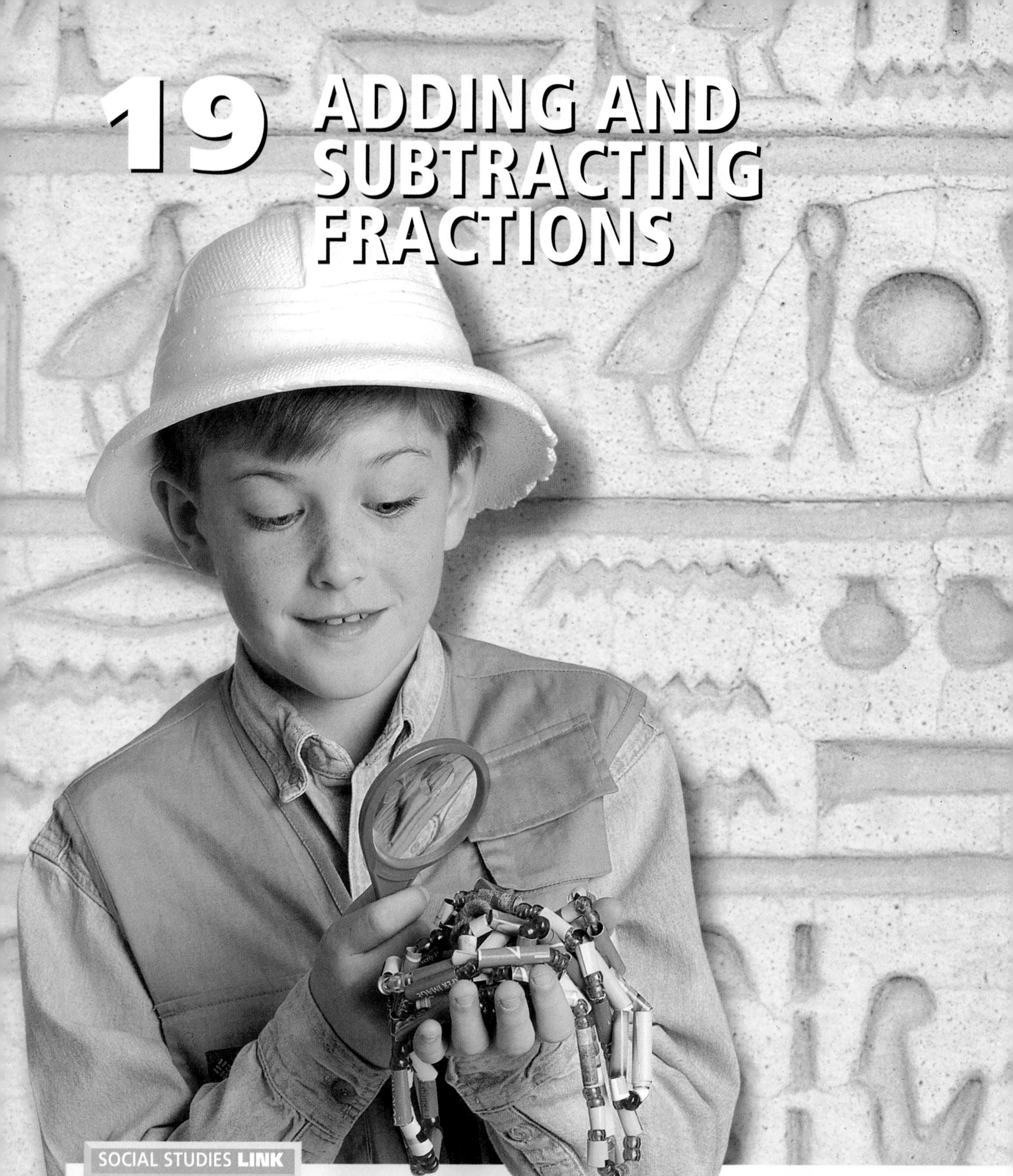

SOCIAL STUDIES **LINK**

Beads have been used since ancient times to decorate clothing. Beads are made from materials such as shells, seeds, and minerals. Archaeologists have found evidence of beads that date back as far as 1,600 B.C. If you were making a bead necklace or bracelet, what measurement would you need?

Problem-Solving Activity

Bead Fractions

Have you ever wanted to go on a dig? Archaeologists find beads and necklaces that are thousands of years old.

Make your own modern-day beads from colorful paper.

YOU WILL NEED: colorful magazine pages, scissors, paint brushes, white glue, yarn

- Choose paper in three colors or tones (dark, medium, light).
- Follow the steps for How to Make a Bead.
- Create a necklace in a pattern that uses 24 paper beads in at least three different colors.
- Draw a diagram of your necklace, and find out what fraction of your necklace is in each color.
- Write a fraction equation to describe your necklace.

HOW TO MAKE A BEAD

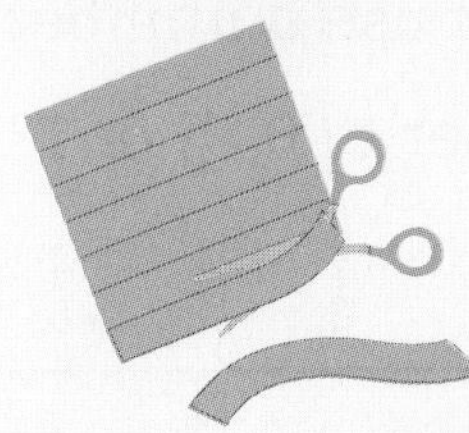

Cut a strip of magazine paper.

Roll the strip over a small paint brush or pencil.

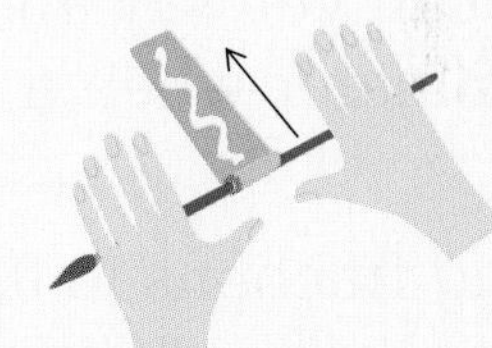

Add glue; then roll over the glued surface. Remove pencil.

Set aside to dry.

DID YOU

- ✓ make a necklace in a pattern that uses at least 24 paper beads in different colors?
- ✓ draw a diagram of your necklace?
- ✓ find out what fraction of your necklace is in each color?
- ✓ write an equation with fractions to describe your necklace?

LESSON 1

Estimating Sums and Differences

Why learn this? You can estimate when an exact answer is not needed or check that your answer is reasonable.

You can use a number line to estimate fractions.

Is $\frac{3}{8}$ closer to 0, $\frac{1}{2}$, or 1?

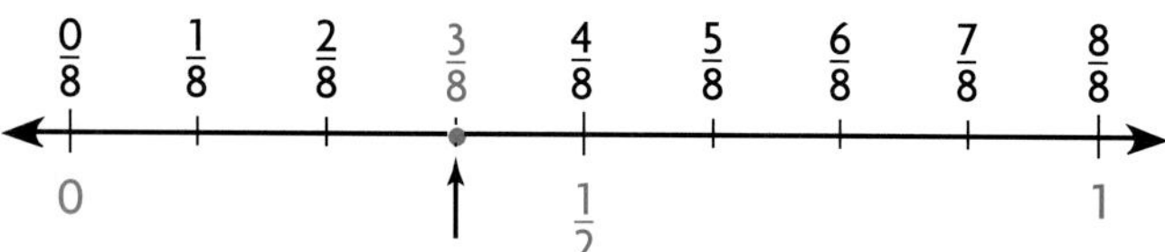

So, $\frac{3}{8}$ is closer to $\frac{1}{2}$.

Talk About It

- How do you know when a fraction is close to zero?
- What can you say about the numerator and denominator when a fraction is close to $\frac{1}{2}$? to 1?

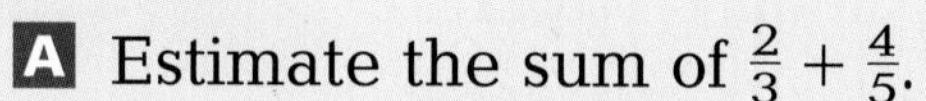

Rounding fractions to 0, $\frac{1}{2}$, or 1 on a number line can help you estimate sums and differences.

EXAMPLES

A Estimate the sum of $\frac{2}{3} + \frac{4}{5}$.

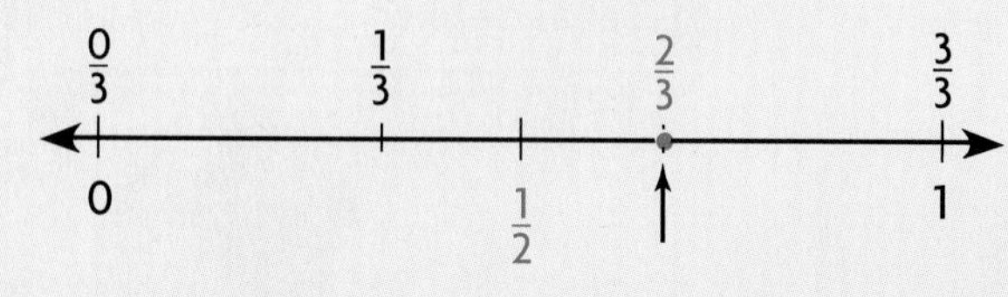

$\frac{2}{3}$ is close to $\frac{1}{2}$.

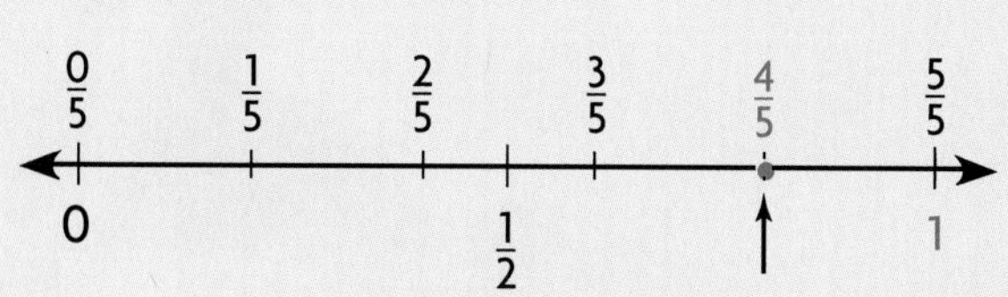

$\frac{4}{5}$ is close to 1. $\frac{1}{2} + 1 = 1\frac{1}{2}$

So, $\frac{2}{3} + \frac{4}{5}$ is about $1\frac{1}{2}$.

B Estimate the difference of $\frac{5}{8} - \frac{1}{6}$.

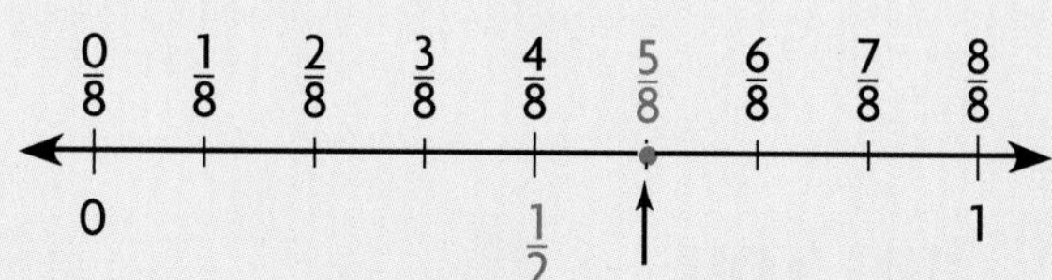

$\frac{5}{8}$ is close to $\frac{1}{2}$.

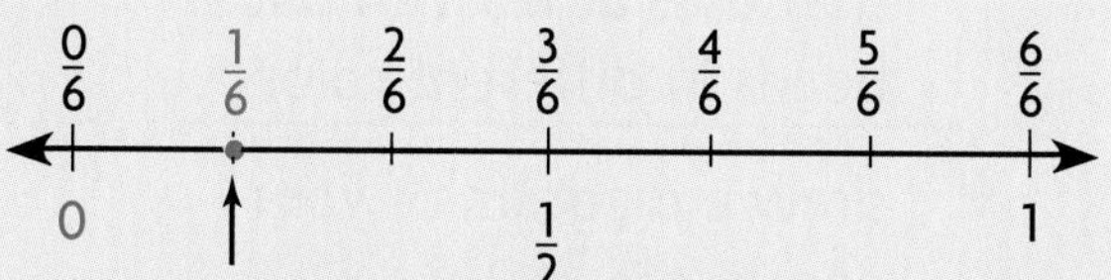

$\frac{1}{6}$ is close to 0. $\frac{1}{2} - 0 = \frac{1}{2}$

So, $\frac{5}{8} - \frac{1}{6}$ is about $\frac{1}{2}$.

CRITICAL THINKING If the estimated sum of two fractions is close to $\frac{1}{2}$, what do you know about the addends?

CHECK

Use the number lines to estimate if the fraction is closer to 0, $\frac{1}{2}$, or 1.

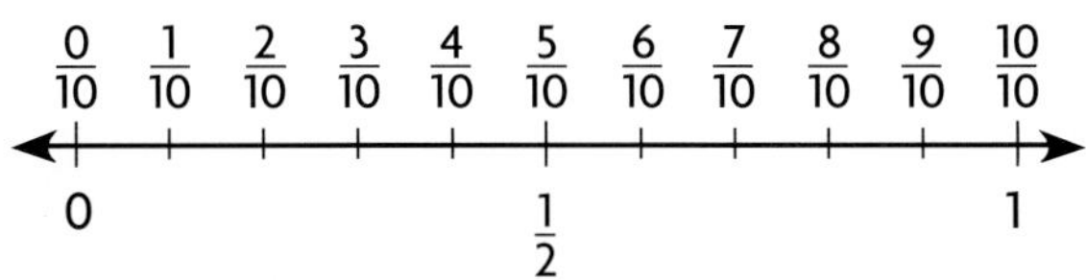

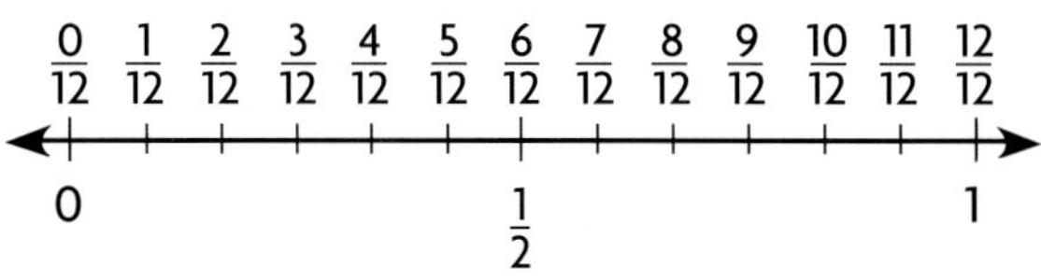

1. $\frac{7}{10}$ **2.** $\frac{1}{12}$ **3.** $\frac{3}{10}$ **4.** $\frac{5}{12}$ **5.** $\frac{9}{10}$ **6.** $\frac{2}{12}$

PRACTICE

Write whether the fraction is closer to 0, $\frac{1}{2}$, or 1.

7. $\frac{8}{9}$ **8.** $\frac{1}{3}$ **9.** $\frac{4}{5}$ **10.** $\frac{4}{7}$ **11.** $\frac{2}{9}$ **12.** $\frac{3}{11}$

Estimate each sum or difference.

13. $\frac{1}{9}+\frac{5}{6}$ **14.** $\frac{2}{3}+\frac{5}{6}$ **15.** $\frac{3}{8}-\frac{1}{5}$ **16.** $\frac{9}{10}-\frac{3}{8}$ **17.** $\frac{7}{12}+\frac{1}{7}$

18. $\frac{7}{10}-\frac{2}{3}$ **19.** $\frac{6}{7}+\frac{1}{5}$ **20.** $\frac{14}{15}-\frac{2}{3}$ **21.** $\frac{7}{8}+\frac{2}{3}$ **22.** $\frac{4}{9}+\frac{1}{5}$

23. $\frac{4}{9}-\frac{1}{8}$ **24.** $\frac{3}{5}+\frac{8}{9}$ **25.** $\frac{5}{6}+\frac{1}{10}$ **26.** $\frac{5}{8}-\frac{3}{15}$ **27.** $\frac{6}{11}+\frac{5}{12}$

Problem Solving • Mixed Applications

28. Estimation Art practiced playing the piano for about $\frac{9}{10}$ hour on Monday, about $\frac{4}{5}$ hour on Tuesday, and about $\frac{5}{6}$ hour on Wednesday. About how long did he practice during those three days?

29. Art Maria used 12 beads to make a necklace. She used 3 white beads, 2 blue beads, and 7 red beads. Which color beads make up about $\frac{1}{2}$ of the necklace?

30. Reasoning Karla and 11 of her friends formed a computer club. There are 8 boys in the club. What fraction of the club is girls?

31. Write About It Describe how to round $\frac{3}{5}$ and $\frac{1}{10}$ so you can estimate the sum.

Mixed Review and Test Prep

Write *prime* or *composite* for each number. Identify *square* numbers. (pages 286–287)

32. 25 **33.** 61 **34.** 76 **35.** 43

Choose the correct list of factors of each number. (pages 288–289)

36. 6 **A** 6, 12, 18, 24 **B** 2, 3, 6 **C** 1, 2, 3, 6 **D** 2, 3

37. 15 **F** 1, 3, 5, 15 **G** 3, 5 **H** 1, 3, 5 **J** 5, 15, 30

MORE PRACTICE page H103

LESSON 2

Adding and Subtracting Like Fractions

Why learn this? You can find the total amount of time spent on an activity, such as practicing a favorite sport.

Christa practiced playing basketball for $\frac{3}{8}$ hour on Monday and $\frac{5}{8}$ hour on Tuesday. How long did Christa practice on Monday and Tuesday?

Add. $\frac{3}{8} + \frac{5}{8} = n$ Estimate. $\frac{1}{2} + \frac{1}{2} = 1$ So, $n \approx 1$.

MODEL

Step 1	**Step 2**	**Step 3**
Compare the denominators. They are the same.	Add the numerators.	Write the sum over the denominator. Write the sum in simplest form.
$\frac{3}{8}$ $+\frac{5}{8}$	$\frac{3}{8}$ ← 3 eighths $+\frac{5}{8}$ ← 5 eighths **Think:** $3 + 5 = 8$	$\frac{3}{8}$ $+\frac{5}{8}$ $\frac{8}{8} = 1$ So, $n = 1$.

So, Christa practiced for 1 hour on Monday and Tuesday.

How much longer did Christa practice on Tuesday than on Monday?

Subtract. $\frac{5}{8} - \frac{3}{8} = n$ Estimate. $\frac{1}{2} - \frac{1}{2} = 0$ So, $n \approx 0$.

MODEL

Step 1	**Step 2**	**Step 3**
Compare the denominators. They are the same.	Subtract the numerators.	Write the difference over the denominator. Write the difference in simplest form.
$\frac{5}{8}$ $-\frac{3}{8}$	$\frac{5}{8}$ ← 5 eighths $-\frac{3}{8}$ ← 3 eighths **Think:** $5 - 3 = 2$	$\frac{5}{8}$ $-\frac{3}{8}$ $\frac{2}{8} = \frac{1}{4}$ So, $n = \frac{1}{4}$.

So, Christa practiced $\frac{1}{4}$ hour longer on Tuesday than on Monday.

CRITICAL THINKING What is the *difference* between adding and subtracting like fractions? What is the *same*?

▶ CHECK

Find the sum or difference. Write the answer in simplest form.

1. $\frac{2}{3} + \frac{1}{3} = n$ **2.** $\frac{1}{4} + \frac{2}{4} = n$ **3.** $\frac{5}{10} + \frac{2}{10} = n$

4. $\frac{2}{3} - \frac{1}{3} = n$ **5.** $\frac{7}{8} - \frac{1}{8} = n$ **6.** $\frac{5}{6} - \frac{2}{6} = n$

SPORTS LINK

Basketball games are played in four quarters, each lasting $\frac{1}{5}$ hour, or 12 minutes. What part of an hour does the actual playing time of a basketball game take up?

▶ PRACTICE

Find the sum. Write the answer in simplest form.

7. $\frac{1}{6} + \frac{3}{6} = n$ **8.** $\frac{5}{7} + \frac{1}{7} = n$ **9.** $\frac{5}{8} + \frac{7}{8} = n$

10. $\frac{4}{5} + \frac{1}{5} = n$ **11.** $\frac{7}{12} + \frac{1}{12} = n$ **12.** $\frac{4}{9} + \frac{1}{9} = n$

13. $\frac{2}{11} + \frac{7}{11} = n$ **14.** $\frac{3}{8} + \frac{1}{8} = n$ **15.** $\frac{4}{6} + \frac{2}{6} = n$

Find the difference. Write the answer in simplest form.

16. $\frac{3}{10} - \frac{1}{10} = n$ **17.** $\frac{5}{7} - \frac{1}{7} = n$ **18.** $\frac{5}{10} - \frac{4}{10} = n$

19. $\frac{7}{8} - \frac{2}{8} = n$ **20.** $\frac{8}{9} - \frac{2}{9} = n$ **21.** $\frac{10}{12} - \frac{6}{12} = n$

22. $\frac{3}{4} - \frac{1}{4} = n$ **23.** $\frac{8}{12} - \frac{6}{12} = n$ **24.** $\frac{4}{5} - \frac{3}{5} = n$

Problem Solving • Mixed Applications

25. Time Rick read for $\frac{5}{6}$ hour on Saturday and $\frac{2}{6}$ hour on Sunday. How much longer did he read on Saturday than on Sunday?

26. Number Sense Fran has $\frac{3}{5}$ of her stamp collection in a special album. What part of her collection is not in the album?

27. Measurement Don can ride his bike 10 times as fast as he can walk. He can walk 2.7 km an hour. How far can he ride his bike in that time?

28. Write About It When you add or subtract two like fractions, when is the answer a fraction with a different denominator?

Mixed Review and Test Prep

Find an equivalent fraction. Use multiplication or division. (pages 292–293)

29. $\frac{3}{8}$ **30.** $\frac{4}{7}$ **31.** $\frac{2}{12}$ **32.** $\frac{1}{2}$ **33.** $\frac{3}{4}$ **34.** $\frac{5}{15}$

Choose the letter of the least common denominator, or LCD. (pages 308–309)

35. $\frac{1}{3}$ and $\frac{1}{2}$ **A** thirds **B** fourths **C** sixths **D** twelfths

36. $\frac{1}{4}$ and $\frac{1}{2}$ **F** fourths **G** eighths **H** sixths **J** twelfths

MORE PRACTICE page H103

Adding and Subtracting Unlike Fractions

Why learn this? You can solve problems such as finding the total number of yards of material needed to make a costume.

Lisa and Tim were making costumes for the play. For each costume, they needed $\frac{1}{2}$ yard of brown fabric and $\frac{1}{6}$ yard of yellow fabric. How much fabric is needed for the costume?

Add. $\frac{1}{6} + \frac{1}{2} = n$ Estimate. $0 + \frac{1}{2} = \frac{1}{2}$ So, $n \approx \frac{1}{2}$.

REMEMBER:

The *least common denominator (LCD)* is the least common multiple (LCM) of the denominators.

Example

$\frac{1}{2}$ and $\frac{3}{8}$

The least common multiple of 2 and 8 is 8. So, the LCD is eighths.

MODEL

Step 1

The LCM of 6 and 2 is 6. So, the LCD of $\frac{1}{6}$ and $\frac{1}{2}$ is sixths. Use the LCD to change the fractions to like fractions.

$$\frac{1}{6} = \frac{1}{6}$$
$$+\frac{1}{2} = \frac{1 \times 3}{2 \times 3} = \frac{3}{6}$$

Step 2

Add the fractions. Write the answer in simplest form.

$$\frac{1}{6} + \frac{3}{6} = \frac{4}{6}, \text{ or } \frac{2}{3}$$

So, $n = \frac{2}{3}$.

So, $\frac{2}{3}$ yard of fabric is needed for the costume.

- Why didn't $\frac{1}{6}$ change?

Subtract. $\frac{3}{4} - \frac{1}{6} = n$ Estimate. $\frac{1}{2} - 0 \approx \frac{1}{2}$

MODEL

Step 1

The LCM of 4 and 6 is 12. So, the LCD of $\frac{3}{4}$ and $\frac{1}{6}$ is twelfths. Use the LCD to change the fractions to like fractions.

$$\frac{3}{4} = \frac{3 \times 3}{4 \times 3} = \frac{9}{12}$$
$$-\frac{1}{6} = \frac{1 \times 2}{6 \times 2} = \frac{2}{12}$$

Step 2

Subtract the fractions. Write the answer in simplest form.

$$\frac{9}{12} - \frac{2}{12} = \frac{7}{12}$$

$\frac{7}{12}$ is in simplest form. So, $n = \frac{7}{12}$.

Talk About It

- Why was 3 used to change $\frac{3}{4}$ to $\frac{9}{12}$?
- How do you know $\frac{7}{12}$ is in simplest form?

CHECK

Write the sum or difference in simplest form.

1. $\frac{6}{12} - \frac{1}{4} = \frac{3}{12}$ 2. $\frac{4}{5} + \frac{1}{2} = \frac{13}{10}$ 3. $\frac{5}{7} + \frac{1}{2} = \frac{17}{14}$

Technology Link

In ***Mighty Math Number Heroes***, the game *Fraction Fireworks* challenges you to add and subtract unlike fractions. Use Grow Slide Levels T and U.

PRACTICE

Write the sum or difference in simplest form.

4. $\frac{2}{3} + \frac{1}{4} = n$ 5. $\frac{1}{5} + \frac{1}{2} = n$ 6. $\frac{7}{10} - \frac{2}{5} = n$

7. $\frac{2}{3} - \frac{1}{2} = n$ 8. $\frac{5}{6} + \frac{1}{3} = n$ 9. $\frac{5}{9} - \frac{1}{6} = n$

10. $\frac{5}{12} - \frac{1}{6} = n$ 11. $\frac{1}{2} - \frac{3}{20} = n$ 12. $\frac{3}{4} - \frac{1}{12} = n$

13. $\frac{7}{8} - \frac{1}{2} = n$ 14. $\frac{4}{5} + \frac{3}{10} = n$ 15. $\frac{5}{6} - \frac{7}{12} = n$

Problem Solving • Mixed Applications

16. **Reasoning** John and Jack both made a book shelf from the same board. John said he used $\frac{3}{8}$ of the board. Jack said he used $\frac{3}{4}$ of the board. Is this possible? Explain.

17. **Measurement** Eve rode her bike $\frac{1}{2}$ mile to school. After school she went to a friend's house $\frac{1}{4}$ mile away and then rode $\frac{3}{4}$ mile home. How far did Eve ride her bike in all?

18. **Probability** To decide which day students will present a book report, each student draws the name of a school day from a hat. What is the probability of drawing a day that begins with T?

19. **Write About It** Explain how to add or subtract unlike fractions.

Mixed Review and Test Prep

Is the fraction in simplest form? Write *yes* or *no*. (pages 296–297)

20. $\frac{2}{3}$ 21. $\frac{3}{9}$ 22. $\frac{2}{12}$ 23. $\frac{4}{16}$ 24. $\frac{7}{8}$

Choose the letter of the equivalent unit. (pages 256–257)

25. 3 kg = ▮ **A** 3,000 g **B** 3,000 mg **C** 300 g **D** 30,000 g

26. 10 km = ▮ **F** 1,000 m **G** 100 m **H** 10,000 mm **J** 10,000 m

MORE PRACTICE page H104

LESSON 4

Practicing Addition and Subtraction

Why learn this? You can add or subtract fractions to find how many of an item, such as tickets, were sold and the fraction that was left.

The Student Council is selling tickets to the school play. The students sold $\frac{1}{8}$ of the tickets at the PTA meeting and $\frac{3}{4}$ of them at Open House. How many of the tickets have been sold so far?

James, Leslie, and Drew are each solving the problem.

EXAMPLES

James uses fraction bars. Leslie uses a ruler. Drew uses paper and pencil.

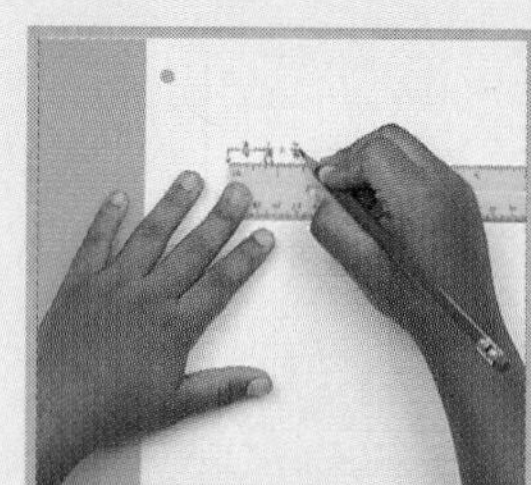

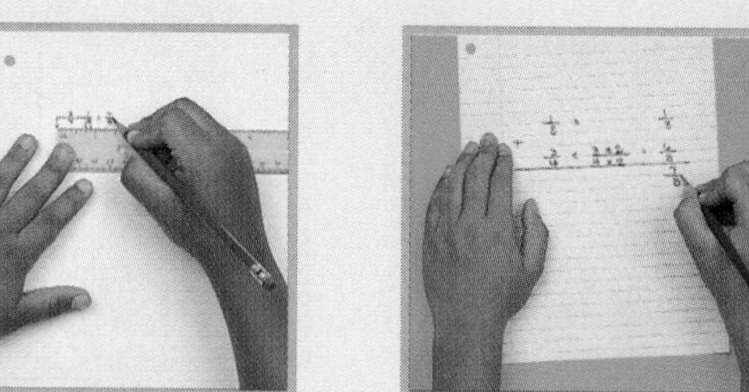

Find $\frac{1}{8} + \frac{3}{4}$.

The LCM of 8 and 4 is 8.

So, the LCD of $\frac{1}{8}$ and $\frac{3}{4}$ is eighths. Use the LCD of eighths to write like fractions. Then add.

$$\frac{1}{8} = \frac{1}{8}$$

$$+\frac{3}{4} = \frac{3 \times 2}{4 \times 2} = \frac{6}{8}$$

$$\frac{7}{8}$$

So, $\frac{7}{8}$ of the tickets have been sold so far.

Talk About It CRITICAL THINKING

- How do the bars and the ruler help you find the sum?
- Which method would you use to solve the problem? Why?

▶ CHECK

Add or subtract. Write the answer in simplest form.

1. 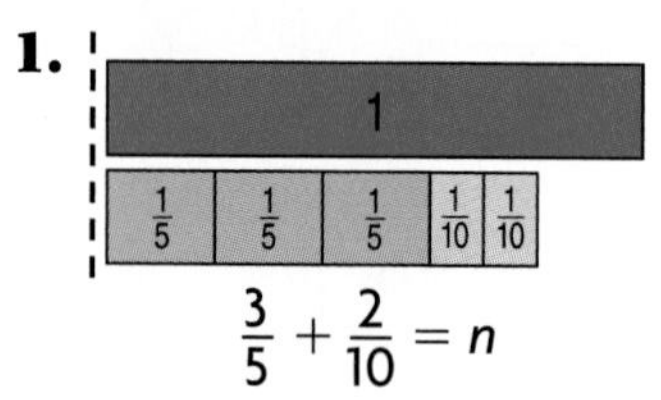

$\frac{3}{5} + \frac{2}{10} = n$

2. $\frac{1}{2}$ $\frac{1}{4}$ $= \frac{?}{?}$

$\frac{1}{2} + \frac{1}{4} = n$

3. 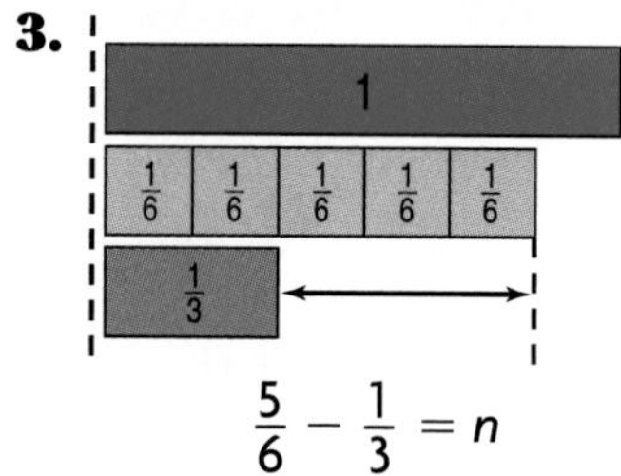

$\frac{5}{6} - \frac{1}{3} = n$

4. $\frac{4}{5} - \frac{1}{5} = n$

5. $\frac{7}{10} + \frac{1}{10} = n$

6. $\frac{5}{6} + \frac{1}{6} = n$

7. $\frac{7}{12} - \frac{5}{12} = n$

PRACTICE

Find the sum or difference. Write each answer in simplest form.

8. $\frac{1}{3} + \frac{2}{3} = n$ **9.** $\frac{1}{3} + \frac{1}{6} = n$ **10.** $\frac{5}{6} - \frac{1}{6} = n$

11. $\frac{5}{6} + \frac{1}{2} = n$ **12.** $\frac{3}{7} - \frac{1}{4} = n$ **13.** $\frac{7}{8} - \frac{1}{8} = n$

14. $\frac{2}{3} + \frac{3}{4} = n$ **15.** $\frac{3}{10} - \frac{1}{10} = n$ **16.** $\frac{7}{15} + \frac{1}{3} = n$

17. $\frac{9}{10} - \frac{3}{10} = n$ **18.** $\frac{3}{4} - \frac{1}{5} = n$ **19.** $\frac{6}{7} + \frac{1}{4} = n$

Problem Solving • Mixed Applications

20. Consumer Tami used $\frac{2}{3}$ of her stamps to mail letters to friends and $\frac{1}{6}$ of her stamps to mail letters to relatives. What fraction of her stamps did she use?

21. Sarah invited 20 friends to her party on Saturday. Then 4 of the friends she invited could not come. What fraction of the friends Sarah invited came to her party?

22. David had $\frac{3}{8}$ package of notebook paper left. He gave $\frac{1}{8}$ package to his sister. What part of the package is left?

23. Consumer Patrick had $\frac{3}{4}$ box of candles to sell. He sold $\frac{1}{3}$ to his neighbors. What fraction of the box of candles does he have left?

24. Reasoning A Girl Scout troop had 6 more 11-year-old girls than 12-year-old girls. There were 24 girls in the troop. How many of the girls were 12 years old?

25. Number Sense The cast included 10 students. If there were 4 boys in the cast, what fraction of the cast were girls?

26. Jane mailed 198 flyers on Monday, 356 on Tuesday, and 219 on Wednesday. By the end of the week, Jane must mail 1,000 flyers. How many flyers are left to be mailed?

27. **Write a problem** in which you have to add and subtract unlike fractions.

Mixed Review and Test Prep

Rename each fraction as a mixed number. (pages 272–273)

28. $\frac{9}{2}$ **29.** $\frac{14}{5}$ **30.** $\frac{13}{3}$ **31.** $\frac{20}{3}$ **32.** $\frac{19}{4}$

Choose the letter for the correct difference. (pages 56–57)

33. $3.59 - 1.27 = n$ **A** 0.232 **B** 2.32 **C** 23.2 **D** 4.86

34. $12.15 - 9.79 = n$ **F** 2.36 **G** 2.46 **H** 3.46 **J** 23.6

35. $40.08 - 25.19 = n$ **A** 14.89 **B** 25.89 **C** 25.99 **D** 14.99

MORE PRACTICE page H104

LESSON 5 • PART 1

Choosing Addition or Subtraction

Why learn this? You will know whether to add or subtract when comparing two fractional amounts, such as fractions of a mile.

You can use addition when you are joining groups. You can use subtraction when you are comparing groups or finding how many are left in a group.

Decide whether to add or subtract the fractions to solve these problems.

A. Julio rode $\frac{1}{3}$ mile to school, $\frac{5}{12}$ mile to the store, and then $\frac{3}{4}$ mile home. How far did Julio ride?

B. Evelyn has $\frac{3}{8}$ yard of material. She needs $\frac{3}{4}$ yard to make a costume for her class play. How much more material does she need for the costume?

C. Mrs. Chen had $\frac{5}{6}$ of a box of pancake mix. She used $\frac{1}{3}$ of the box to make pancakes for breakfast. How much of the box of pancake mix was left?

D. Jason completed $\frac{1}{4}$ of his homework before soccer practice, and $\frac{1}{3}$ after practice. How much of his homework did Jason complete?

Talk About It CRITICAL THINKING

- In which examples might you add to solve the problem? Why?
- In which examples might you subtract to solve the problem? Why?
- In each problem, what helped you decide whether to add or subtract?

Good pass!

▶ CHECK

Tell whether you would add or subtract to solve the problem. Solve.

1. Julianne uses $\frac{1}{4}$ cup of pecans to make nut bread and $\frac{3}{8}$ cup to make muffins. How many cups of pecans does she use in all?

2. Alex had $\frac{3}{4}$ pitcher of orange juice. He drank $\frac{1}{3}$ of the juice. How much orange juice was left?

3. Will collected 28 baseball cards, and 79 basketball cards. How many cards does will have?

4. Debbie had $\frac{7}{8}$ of the pizza left. She gave $\frac{1}{2}$ to her sister. How much pizza did Debbie keep?

▶ PRACTICE

Tell whether you would add or subtract to solve the problem. Solve.

5. Mark wrote $\frac{1}{2}$ of his science report on Monday and $\frac{2}{5}$ of it on Tuesday. What part of his science report did he write on Monday and Tuesday?

6. Carla had $\frac{2}{3}$ cup of flour. She used $\frac{1}{2}$ cup to make biscuits. How much flour does she have left?

7. Raul lives $\frac{1}{2}$ mile from Luke. Tonya lives $\frac{3}{4}$ mile from Raul. Raul lives between Luke and Tonya. How far does Luke live from Tonya?

8. Jason practiced piano for $\frac{7}{8}$ hour on Thursday and $\frac{1}{2}$ hour on Friday. How much longer did he practice on Thursday?

Problem Solving • Mixed Applications

9. **Drama** Corey memorized $\frac{1}{6}$ of his lines for the play on Monday and $\frac{1}{4}$ of his lines on Tuesday. What part of his lines did he memorize on Monday and Tuesday?

10. The cast for the school play includes actors and dancers. There are 6 dancers and 24 actors in the play. What part of the cast for the play are the dancers?

11. **Music** Ms. Wright teaches a music class of 3rd, 4th, and 5th grade students. The 4th graders make up $\frac{1}{4}$ of the class and the 5th graders make up $\frac{1}{3}$ of the class. What part of the class are 3rd graders?

12. **Money** The students at Bay School collected 3,240 pennies for the Lucky Penny Club. They had already collected $47.89. How much did the students give to the Lucky Penny Club?

13. **Consumer** Ted took $\frac{3}{4}$ of his allowance to the amusement park. He spent $\frac{1}{6}$ on food and $\frac{1}{4}$ on souvenirs. How much of his allowance did Ted have left after he bought food and souvenirs?

14. **Measurement** A blueberry-nut muffin recipe calls for $\frac{3}{4}$ cup of whole-wheat flour. If Tyra has $\frac{1}{2}$ cup whole-wheat flour, how much more does she need?

15. Brady is making her costume for the play. She needs $\frac{1}{3}$ yd of red fabric, $\frac{1}{2}$ yd of blue fabric, and $\frac{3}{4}$ yd of white fabric. How much fabric does Brady need?

16. **Estimation** Amal mixed together $3\frac{2}{5}$ gallons of white paint and $4\frac{9}{10}$ gallons of red paint. About how many gallons of paint did Amal mix?

17. **Write a problem** that you would solve by subtracting two unlike fractions.

MORE PRACTICE page H104

Problem-Solving Strategy: Draw a Diagram

▶ **THE PROBLEM** The fifth graders can enroll in after-school programs. They can enroll in the music program, the athletics program, or the acting program. Of the fifth graders enrolled in these programs, $\frac{1}{3}$ are in music, $\frac{1}{2}$ are in athletics, and $\frac{1}{6}$ are in acting. There are 4 fifth graders in the acting program. How many students are enrolled in each of the other programs? How many are enrolled in the three programs?

UNDERSTAND

- What are you asked to find?
- What information will you use?
- Is there information you will not use? If so, what?

Tryouts for the school play.

PLAN

- What strategy can you use to solve this problem?

You can *draw a diagram* to find out how many fifth graders are enrolled in music and athletics.

SOLVE

- How can you draw a diagram to solve?

Use a number line to model the problem. The whole number line represents the total number of students.

$\frac{1}{6}$ $\frac{1}{3}$ $\frac{1}{2}$

0 $\frac{1}{6}$ $\frac{2}{6}$ $\frac{3}{6}$ $\frac{4}{6}$ $\frac{5}{6}$ 1

$\frac{1}{6} = 4$ students in acting

$\frac{1}{3}$, or $\frac{2}{6} = 2 \times 4$, or 8. So, there are 8 students in music.

$\frac{1}{2}$, or $\frac{3}{6} = 3 \times 4$, or 12. So, there are 12 students in athletics.

$4 + 8 + 12 = 24$. So, there are 24 fifth graders enrolled in the after-school programs.

LOOK BACK

- How can you determine if your answer is reasonable?
- What other strategy can you use?

▶ PRACTICE

Draw a diagram to solve.

1. Students at three schools are giving a concert. Of the students participating, $\frac{1}{4}$ are from Rhodes Elementary School, $\frac{1}{2}$ are from South Elementary School, and $\frac{1}{4}$ are from West Elementary School. There are 36 students from Rhodes. How many students are participating in the concert?

2. Ms. Smith asked the students in her class whether they prefer to watch movies, television, or plays. Of her students, $\frac{5}{8}$ chose movies, $\frac{1}{4}$ chose television, and $\frac{1}{8}$ chose plays. There were 3 students who chose plays. How many students are in Ms. Smith's class?

3. Andrea walks a certain number of miles every week. She walks $\frac{1}{3}$ the total weekly distance on Monday, $\frac{2}{5}$ on Wednesday, and $\frac{4}{15}$ on Friday. She walks 5 miles on Monday. How many miles does Andrea walk every week?

4. Nina, Debbie, and Peter are comparing their heights. At 54 inches, Nina is 6 inches taller than Peter. Peter is 3 inches shorter than Debbie. How tall is Debbie?

Mixed Applications

Solve.

CHOOSE a strategy and a tool.

- **Draw a Diagram**
- **Write a Number Sentence**
- **Use a Table**
- **Guess and Check**

Paper/Pencil

Calculator

Hands-On

Mental Math

5. The 5th grade class is going to see a play. There are 150 5th graders. How many buses will be needed if each bus can hold 40 students?

6. Eric is 5 years old. His Uncle Tim is 7 times as old. How old will Eric be when he is one third as old as his uncle?

7. Lee counted 50 instruments in the orchestra. What fraction of the orchestra is percussion?

ORCHESTRA	
Section	**Number**
Woodwinds	12
Percussion	5
Strings	25
Brass	8

8. The members of the choir had a practice for their concert. The vote showed that $\frac{2}{3}$ of the members preferred Monday evening. There were 20 members who voted for Monday evening. How many students are in the choir?

9. A bridge toll is \$0.75 for a car and \$1.25 for a truck. In 30 minutes, \$26.25 was collected from 27 vehicles. How many cars and trucks paid the toll?

10. One store sells 6 cans of juice for \$3.90. Another store sells each can for \$0.69. What is the difference in price per can at the two stores?

MORE PRACTICE page H104

CHAPTER 19 Review/Test

CHECK Understanding

Estimate the sum or difference. (pages 338–339)

1. $\frac{2}{3} + \frac{1}{6}$
2. $\frac{3}{8} - \frac{1}{10}$
3. $\frac{1}{6} + \frac{1}{10}$
4. $\frac{9}{10} - \frac{3}{5}$
5. $\frac{7}{9} - \frac{3}{5}$
6. $\frac{7}{8} + \frac{4}{5}$
7. $\frac{8}{9} - \frac{1}{6}$
8. $\frac{2}{5} + \frac{7}{12}$

CHECK Skills

Find the sum or difference. Write the answer in simplest form. (pages 340–345)

9. $\frac{3}{4} + \frac{1}{4} = n$
10. $\frac{3}{4} - \frac{1}{4} = n$
11. $\frac{5}{7} + \frac{1}{7} = n$
12. $\frac{11}{12} - \frac{3}{4} = n$
13. $\frac{1}{2} + \frac{1}{8} = n$
14. $\frac{4}{5} - \frac{1}{2} = n$
15. $\frac{4}{5} + \frac{1}{3} = n$
16. $\frac{1}{4} + \frac{7}{8} = n$
17. $\frac{7}{10} - \frac{2}{5} = n$
18. $\frac{5}{6} + \frac{1}{3} = n$
19. $\frac{3}{4} - \frac{1}{6} = n$
20. $\frac{3}{8} + \frac{5}{12} = n$
21. $\frac{5}{8} - \frac{1}{4} = n$
22. $\frac{9}{10} + \frac{2}{5} = n$
23. $\frac{5}{6} - \frac{1}{3} = n$
24. $\frac{1}{3} + \frac{2}{9} = n$

Tell whether you would add or subtract to solve the problem. Solve. (pages 346–347)

25. Valeska made two cakes for her party. She used $\frac{3}{4}$ cup flour for one cake and $\frac{2}{3}$ cup flour for the other cake. How much flour did she use for both cakes?

26. Mr. Danko spent $\frac{3}{4}$ hour shopping and $\frac{1}{2}$ hour cooking. How much more time did he spend shopping than cooking?

CHECK Problem Solving

Solve. (pages 348–349)

CHOOSE a strategy and a tool.

- Draw a Diagram
- Guess and Check
- Act It Out
- Work Backward

Paper/Pencil

Calculator

Hands-On

Mental Math

27. Tickets to the concert sold for \$10, \$12, and \$15. Of the tickets sold, $\frac{1}{10}$ were \$15 tickets, $\frac{1}{5}$ were \$12 tickets, and $\frac{7}{10}$ were \$10 tickets. There were one hundred \$15 tickets sold. How many tickets were sold to the concert?

28. Ashley had 60 calendars to sell. She sold 20 calendars to friends and 25 calendars to neighbors. What fraction of the calendars does she have left to sell?

Test Prep

CUMULATIVE
CHAPTERS 1–19

Choose the best answer.

1. Kaya has a picture that is $2\frac{3}{4}$ inches wide. She wants to fit it into a picture frame that is $2\frac{1}{2}$ inches wide. How much should she trim off the picture?

   A $\frac{1}{8}$ in. **B** $\frac{1}{4}$ in.

   C $\frac{1}{2}$ in. **D** 1 in.

2. How is the number fifteen and twenty-three hundredths written in standard form?

   F 1,523

   G 152.3

   H 15.23

   J 1.523

   K Not Here

3. Maria plans to build a fence around the perimeter of her yard. How much fencing does Maria need?

   35 ft | Maria's Yard | 60 ft

   A 95 ft **B** 190 ft

   C 315 ft **D** 3,150 ft

4. Ed said he ran a 5 kilometer race. How far did Ed run in meters?

   F 5 m **G** 50 m

   H 500 m **J** 5,000 m

5. Which number is the greatest common factor of 12 and 18?

   A 1 **B** 2

   C 3 **D** 6

6. The cards shown are placed face down.

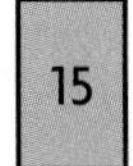

   If you pull 1 card, which one is most likely to be chosen?

   F Number less than 15

   G One-digit number

   H Two-digit number

   J Number greater than 20

7. Alano had \$20.00. He bought a T-shirt for \$9.95 and a cap for \$6.95. About how much change did he receive?

   A About \$3

   B About \$5

   C About \$9

   D About \$11

8. About how much is $\frac{1}{10}$?

   F About 0

   G About $\frac{1}{2}$

   H About $\frac{3}{4}$

   J About 1

20 ADDING AND SUBTRACTING MIXED NUMBERS

CULTURAL **LINK**

An English game of Bowls involves rolling a ball closest to the target ball known as the jack and represented by a dot. Look at the score card. About how much closer to the dot is Jenna?

Score Card

Bill - $8\frac{1}{2}$ in. from the dot

Jenna - $4\frac{1}{4}$ in. from the dot

Problem-Solving Activity

Try a Game of Bowls

Play the game of Bowls. This game is usually played outside. Use subtraction to compare distances between rolls.

YOU WILL NEED: one tennis ball per group, a dot, tape, a yardstick

Play three rounds of Bowls.

- Measure and record your distances.
- Find the difference between your best roll and your worst.
- Share results and game strategies.

HOW TO PLAY BOWLS

- Each player kneels behind the starter's tape and gently rolls the ball, trying to get it to stop as near to the dot as possible.
- Any ball that stops more than three feet away from the dot can be rolled again.
- A teammate measures the distance from the ball to the dot.
- Record distance to the nearest $\frac{1}{4}$ of an inch.
- After three rolls, each player finds the difference between his or her best roll and worst roll.

TO MEASURE A DISTANCE

- Place a piece of tape where your ball touches the floor. Then measure between the tape and the dot.

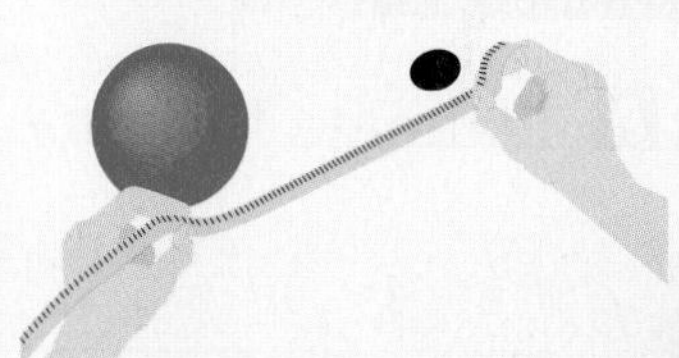

DID YOU

- ✓ play three rounds of Bowls?
- ✓ measure the distance for each roll?
- ✓ find the difference between your best roll and your worst?
- ✓ share your results with the class?

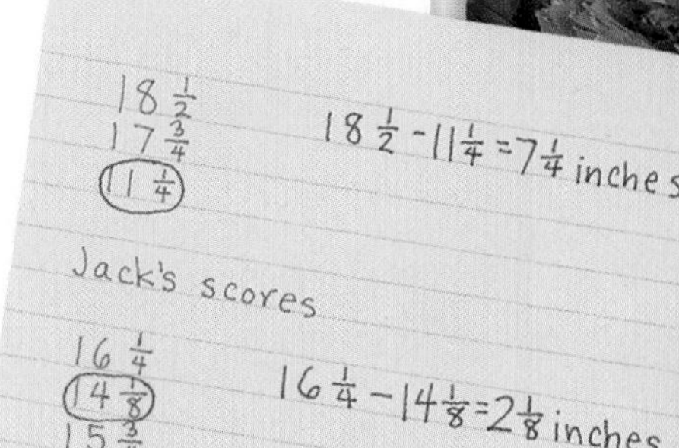

LESSON 1

Estimating Sums and Differences

Why learn this? You can estimate distances when playing a game.

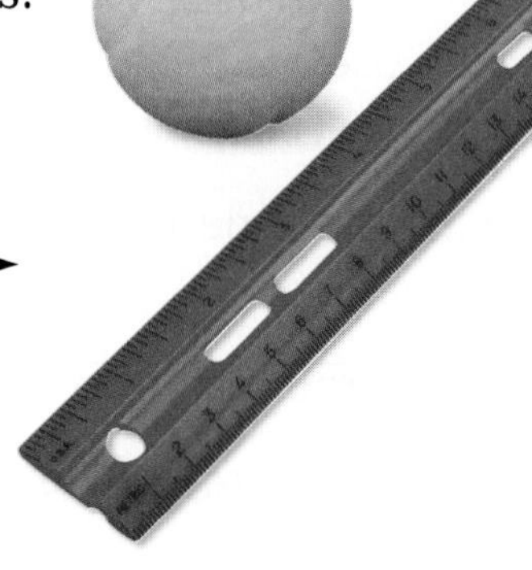

You can use a number line to estimate mixed numbers.

Is $2\frac{1}{8}$ closer to $1\frac{1}{2}$, 2, or $2\frac{1}{2}$?

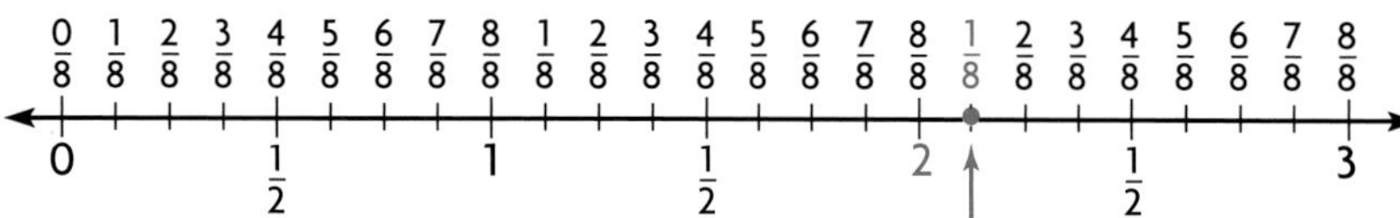

So, $2\frac{1}{8}$ is closer to 2.

Talk About It

- What can you say about the mixed number when the numerator and denominator of the fraction are about the same?
- Is $1\frac{5}{8}$ closer to $1\frac{1}{2}$, 2, or $2\frac{1}{2}$? Explain how you know.

Rounding mixed numbers to the nearest whole number or one half on a number line can help you estimate sums and differences of mixed numbers.

REMEMBER:

You can *round* fractions to the nearest 0, $\frac{1}{2}$, or 1.

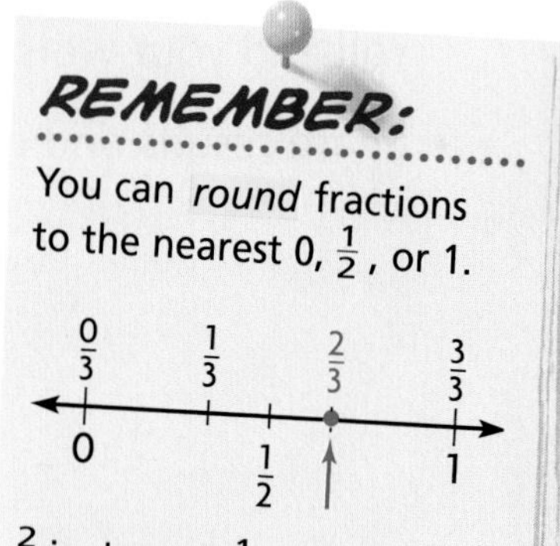

$\frac{2}{3}$ is close to $\frac{1}{2}$.

EXAMPLES

A Estimate the sum of $2\frac{2}{3} + 1\frac{1}{6}$.

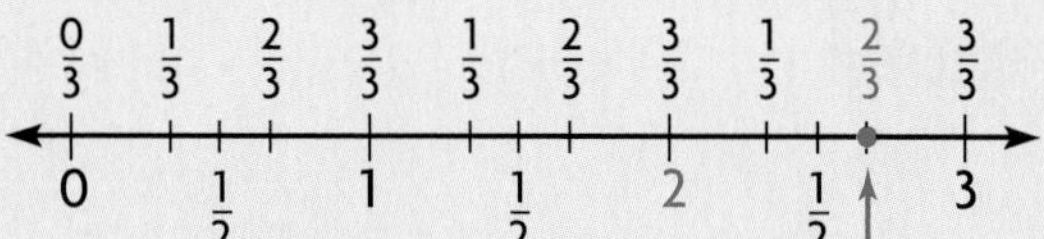

$2\frac{2}{3}$ is close to $2\frac{1}{2}$.

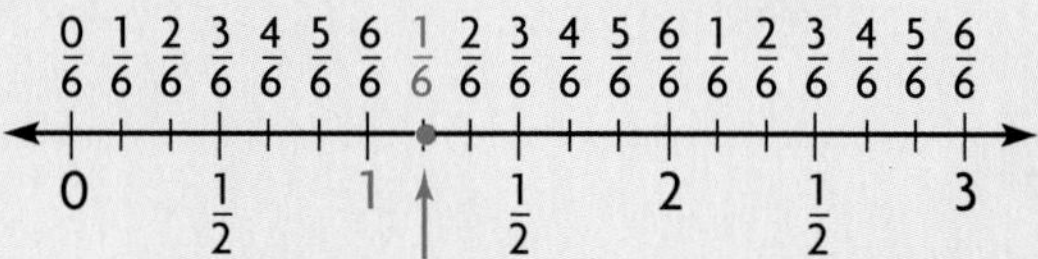

$1\frac{1}{6}$ is close to 1. $2\frac{1}{2} + 1 = 3\frac{1}{2}$

So, $2\frac{2}{3} + 1\frac{1}{6}$ is about $3\frac{1}{2}$.

B Estimate the difference of $2 - 1\frac{3}{5}$.

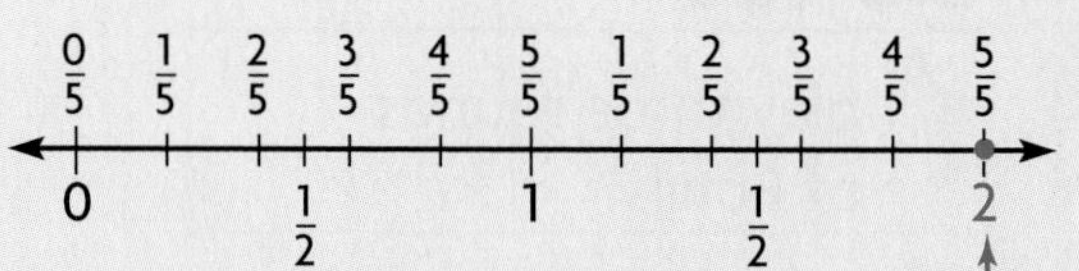

2 is equal to 2.

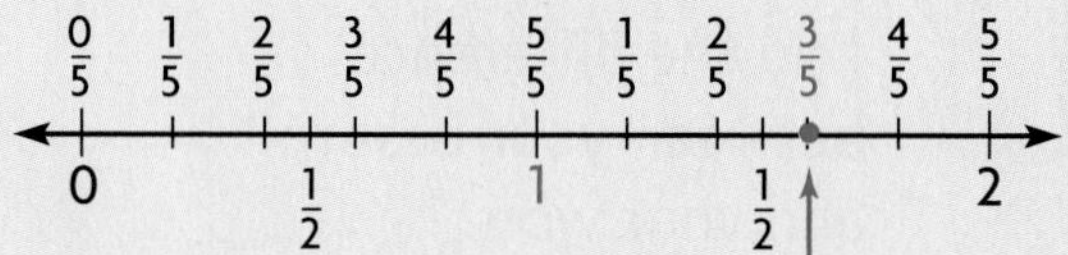

$1\frac{3}{5}$ is close to $1\frac{1}{2}$. $2 - 1\frac{1}{2} = \frac{1}{2}$

So, $2 - 1\frac{3}{5}$ is about $\frac{1}{2}$.

CRITICAL THINKING How could you use a ruler to estimate the sum of $1\frac{1}{8}$ in. and $2\frac{3}{16}$ in.?

▶ CHECK

Round the mixed number to the nearest $\frac{1}{2}$ or whole number.

1. $4\frac{7}{8}$ **2.** $2\frac{5}{6}$ **3.** $1\frac{7}{8}$ **4.** $3\frac{3}{5}$ **5.** $6\frac{1}{12}$ **6.** $8\frac{4}{9}$

▶ PRACTICE

Round the mixed number to the nearest $\frac{1}{2}$ or whole number.

7. $1\frac{1}{8}$ **8.** $9\frac{6}{8}$ **9.** $3\frac{1}{4}$ **10.** $7\frac{1}{16}$ **11.** $4\frac{7}{12}$ **12.** $6\frac{2}{3}$

Estimate the sum or difference.

13. $2\frac{1}{8} + 4\frac{15}{16}$ **14.** $3\frac{7}{8} - 2\frac{1}{2}$ **15.** $1\frac{9}{16} + 1\frac{5}{8}$ **16.** $6\frac{9}{10} - 4\frac{4}{5}$

17. $9\frac{1}{8} + 1\frac{10}{12}$ **18.** $6\frac{4}{9} + 7\frac{1}{5}$ **19.** $9\frac{4}{9} - 6\frac{1}{8}$ **20.** $9\frac{5}{8} - 3\frac{14}{16}$

21. $7\frac{5}{12} + 1\frac{5}{6}$ **22.** $2\frac{3}{5} + 5\frac{7}{8}$ **23.** $4\frac{3}{8} - 1\frac{1}{8}$ **24.** $3\frac{1}{6} - 2\frac{5}{8}$

Problem Solving • Mixed Applications

25. Time Janis read her book for $\frac{3}{4}$ hour in the morning. After school she read for another $\frac{1}{4}$ hour. She read for $\frac{1}{3}$ hour before bedtime. What is the total amount of time she spent reading?

26. Measurement Seth needs $6\frac{3}{4}$ yards of wallpaper border for his kitchen. He needs $10\frac{3}{8}$ yards for his hallway. About how many yards of wallpaper border does he need?

27. Estimation Kelli used $2\frac{7}{8}$ yards of fabric for her dress. She started with $4\frac{1}{8}$ yards. About how much fabric does she have left?

28. Write About It How is estimating the sum or difference of mixed numbers like estimating the sum or difference of fractions?

Mixed Review and Test Prep

Draw a number line. Locate the fraction. (pages 270–271)

29. $\frac{3}{5}$ **30.** $\frac{2}{6}$ **31.** $\frac{5}{10}$ **32.** $\frac{7}{8}$ **33.** $\frac{1}{3}$

34. $\frac{1}{4}$ **35.** $\frac{3}{8}$ **36.** $\frac{5}{12}$ **37.** $\frac{2}{3}$ **38.** $\frac{1}{5}$

Choose the letter of the least common denominator, or LCD, for each pair of fractions. (pages 308–309)

39. $\frac{1}{2} + \frac{1}{6}$ **A** thirds **B** sixths **C** twelfths **D** eighths

40. $\frac{1}{4} + \frac{1}{3}$ **F** ninths **G** sixteenths **H** twelfths **J** eighths

LESSON 2

Adding Mixed Numbers

Why learn this? You can find the sum of two amounts, such as two measurements.

The Boy Scouts are having their annual Pinewood Derby. Juwan is making a banner for the finish line. He needs $2\frac{1}{8}$ yards of black fabric and $1\frac{1}{4}$ yards of white fabric to make the checkered banner. How many yards of fabric does Juwan need for the banner?

MODEL

Add $2\frac{1}{8}$ and $1\frac{1}{4}$. Estimate. $2 + 1 = 3$

Step 1

The fractions are unlike. Use the LCD to change the fractions to like fractions. Add the fractions.

$$2\frac{1}{8} = 2\frac{1}{8}$$
$$+1\frac{1}{4} = 1\frac{2}{8}$$
$$\frac{3}{8}$$

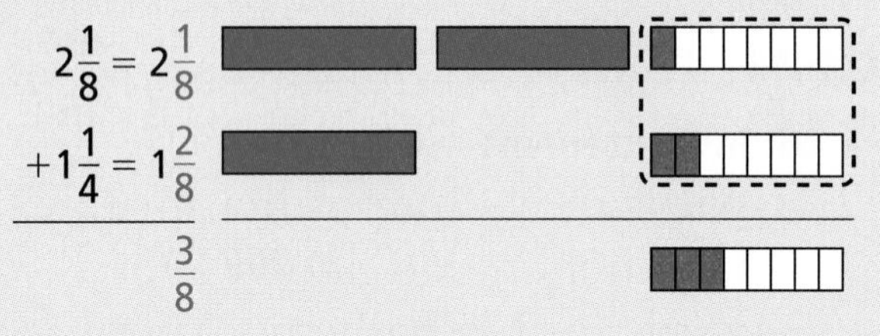

Step 2

Then add the whole numbers.

$$2\frac{1}{8} = 2\frac{1}{8}$$
$$+1\frac{1}{4} = 1\frac{2}{8}$$
$$3\frac{3}{8}$$

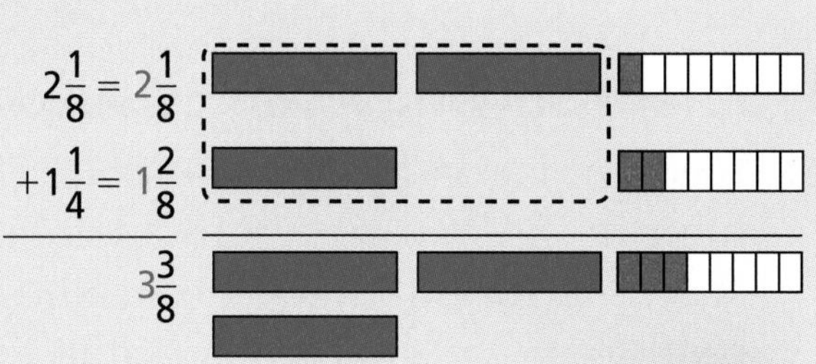

So, Juwan needs $3\frac{3}{8}$ yards of fabric for the banner.

Talk About It CRITICAL THINKING

- How did you add the fractions?
- How did you add the whole numbers?
- How does your solution compare to your estimate?

EXAMPLES

A

$$1\frac{1}{3} = 1\frac{2}{6}$$
$$+3\frac{4}{6} = 3\frac{4}{6}$$
$$4\frac{6}{6}, \text{ or } 5$$

B

$$2\frac{5}{8} = 2\frac{5}{8}$$
$$+2\frac{1}{2} = 2\frac{4}{8}$$
$$4\frac{9}{8}, \text{ or } 5\frac{1}{8}$$

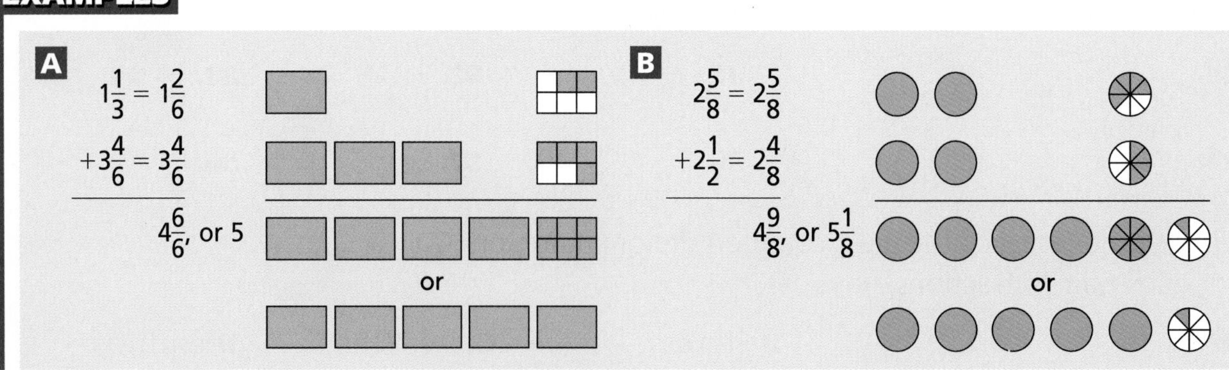

- How are Examples A and B different from the model?

▶ CHECK

Find the sum. You may wish to draw a picture. Write the answer in simplest form.

1. $1\frac{1}{4} + 2\frac{1}{2}$
2. $1\frac{1}{5} + 3\frac{2}{5}$
3. $5\frac{1}{3} + 2\frac{1}{6}$
4. $2\frac{5}{6} + 1\frac{1}{3}$

SCIENCE LINK

The Pinewood Derby is a Boy Scout event. Each Scout makes a small car out of a block of wood and plastic wheels. The cars race by gravity down an inclined track that is 32 ft long. If one car used $3\frac{1}{4}$ in. of decal tape and a second car used $4\frac{1}{2}$ in. of tape, how much tape would be needed in all?

▶ PRACTICE

Find the sum. Write the answer in simplest form.

5. $4\frac{2}{3} + 2\frac{4}{9}$
6. $5\frac{2}{5} + 1\frac{4}{10}$
7. $4\frac{5}{8} + 2\frac{1}{4}$
8. $4\frac{3}{4} + 3\frac{3}{12}$

9. $4\frac{3}{4} + 2\frac{3}{8} = n$
10. $3\frac{3}{4} + 1\frac{1}{8} = n$
11. $3\frac{1}{2} + 5\frac{3}{4} = n$
12. $3\frac{1}{10} + 2\frac{3}{5} = n$
13. $3\frac{2}{3} + 4\frac{1}{6} = n$
14. $3\frac{5}{6} + \frac{2}{3} = n$

Problem Solving • Mixed Applications

15. **Music** The dancers will form 5 equal rows for the finale of the recital. There are 65 dancers. How many will be in each row?

16. **Time** Kendall recorded music for $1\frac{5}{6}$ hours on Monday and $2\frac{1}{3}$ hours on Tuesday. How much time did he spend recording the music?

17. **Measurement** Jill and Lee are making hair ribbons. Jill has $4\frac{1}{2}$ yards of pink ribbon. Lee has $3\frac{1}{3}$ yards of white ribbon. How much ribbon do they have in all?

18. **Write About It** Explain how adding mixed numbers is the same as adding fractions.

Mixed Review and Test Prep

Find the sum. Write the answer in simplest form. (pages 342–343)

19. $\frac{7}{8} + \frac{1}{4} = n$
20. $\frac{5}{6} + \frac{7}{12} = n$
21. $\frac{2}{3} + \frac{1}{4} = n$
22. $\frac{2}{3} + \frac{2}{9} = n$

Choose the letter of the equivalent fraction. Use multiplication or division. (pages 292–293)

23. $\frac{4}{16} = \underline{?}$ **A** $\frac{2}{4}$ **B** $\frac{1}{4}$ **C** $\frac{8}{16}$ **D** $\frac{4}{8}$

24. $\frac{1}{5} = \underline{?}$ **F** $\frac{1}{10}$ **G** $\frac{15}{20}$ **H** $\frac{3}{15}$ **J** $\frac{5}{20}$

MORE PRACTICE page H105

LESSON 3 • PART 1

Subtracting Mixed Numbers

Why learn this? You can find how much is left, such as how much paper is left after part of a package is used.

Louis had $2\frac{3}{4}$ packages of paper for his computer printer. He placed $1\frac{1}{2}$ packages into the printer. How much paper was left?

MODEL

Subtract $2\frac{3}{4}$ and $1\frac{1}{2}$. Estimate. $3 - 1\frac{1}{2} = 1\frac{1}{2}$

Step 1

The fractions are unlike. Use the LCD to change the fractions to like fractions. Subtract the fractions.

$$\begin{array}{r} 2\frac{3}{4} = 2\frac{3}{4} \\ -1\frac{1}{2} = 1\frac{2}{4} \\ \hline \frac{1}{4} \end{array}$$

Step 2

Then subtract the whole numbers.

$$\begin{array}{r} 2\frac{3}{4} = 2\frac{3}{4} \\ -1\frac{1}{2} = 1\frac{2}{4} \\ \hline 1\frac{1}{4} \end{array}$$

So, Louis has $1\frac{1}{4}$ packages of paper left.

Talk About It

- How does subtraction of mixed numbers compare to addition of mixed numbers?
- How can you check your subtraction?

EXAMPLES

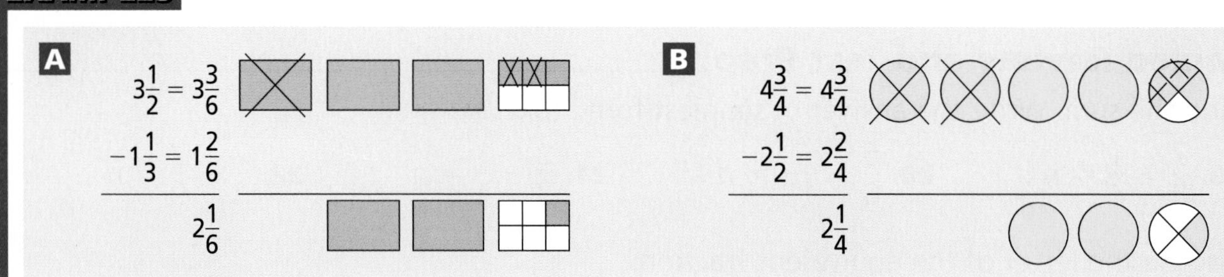

CRITICAL THINKING How do you know you must rename the fractions when you subtract two mixed numbers?

Calculator Activities page H65

▶ CHECK

Subtract. Write the answer in simplest form.

1. $\begin{array}{r} 4\frac{2}{3} = 4\frac{4}{6} \\ -1\frac{1}{6} = 1\frac{1}{6} \\ \hline \end{array}$

2. $\begin{array}{r} 4\frac{5}{6} = 4\frac{5}{6} \\ -2\frac{2}{3} = 2\frac{4}{6} \\ \hline \end{array}$

3. $\begin{array}{r} 9\frac{1}{2} = 9\frac{4}{8} \\ -8\frac{1}{4} = 8\frac{2}{8} \\ \hline \end{array}$

▶ PRACTICE

Subtract. Write the answer in simplest form.

4. $\begin{array}{r} 9\frac{4}{5} = 9\frac{8}{10} \\ -2\frac{3}{10} = 2\frac{3}{10} \\ \hline \end{array}$

5. $\begin{array}{r} 3\frac{1}{2} = 3\frac{2}{4} \\ -1\frac{1}{4} = 1\frac{1}{4} \\ \hline \end{array}$

6. $\begin{array}{r} 5\frac{7}{9} = 5\frac{7}{9} \\ -3\frac{1}{3} = 3\frac{3}{9} \\ \hline \end{array}$

7. $\begin{array}{r} 7\frac{3}{4} = 7\frac{9}{12} \\ -4\frac{7}{12} = 4\frac{7}{12} \\ \hline \end{array}$

8. $\begin{array}{r} 5\frac{5}{8} = 5\frac{5}{8} \\ -2\frac{1}{4} = 2\frac{2}{8} \\ \hline \end{array}$

9. $\begin{array}{r} 6\frac{1}{3} = 6\frac{4}{12} \\ -3\frac{3}{12} = 3\frac{3}{12} \\ \hline \end{array}$

10. $5\frac{11}{12} - 2\frac{1}{4} = n$

11. $8\frac{5}{6} - 3\frac{1}{3} = n$

12. $4\frac{8}{10} - 1\frac{2}{5} = n$

13. $6\frac{7}{8} - 2\frac{1}{2} = n$

14. $9\frac{4}{5} - 1\frac{3}{10} = n$

15. $2\frac{7}{12} - \frac{2}{6} = n$

Problem Solving • Mixed Applications

Using Data For Problems 16–17, use the table.

16. Career Amanda made the table to keep track of the gift-wrapping paper in stock. Copy and complete the table for her.

Color of Paper	Yards Started with	Yards Used	Yards Left
Red	$16\frac{3}{4}$	$3\frac{1}{2}$	?
White	$20\frac{3}{4}$	?	$10\frac{1}{3}$
Blue	?	$5\frac{7}{12}$	$10\frac{1}{12}$
Yellow	$21\frac{2}{3}$	$14\frac{7}{12}$	?

17. Measurement Amanda decided to reorder the same amount of red and white paper that she started with. How many yards of paper should she reorder?

18. Time Arlo worked $2\frac{1}{4}$ hours on Monday and $3\frac{2}{3}$ hours on Tuesday. How many hours did he work?

19. Write a problem that can be solved by adding or subtracting mixed numbers. Use the information in the table.

LESSON CONTINUES

MORE PRACTICE page H105

Problem-Solving Strategy: Work Backward

▶ **THE PROBLEM** Mrs. Miller drives a school bus. She leaves the garage and drives to the first bus stop. Then she drives $3\frac{1}{10}$ miles to the second bus stop, $1\frac{3}{10}$ miles to the third bus stop, $2\frac{2}{10}$ miles to the fourth bus stop, and then $2\frac{3}{10}$ miles to the school. If Mrs. Miller drives a total of 10 miles, what is the distance from the bus garage to the first bus stop?

UNDERSTAND

- What are you asked to find?
- What information will you use?
- Is there information you will not use? If so, what?

PLAN

- What strategy can you use to solve this problem?

  You can *work backward* to find the distance from the bus garage to the first bus stop.

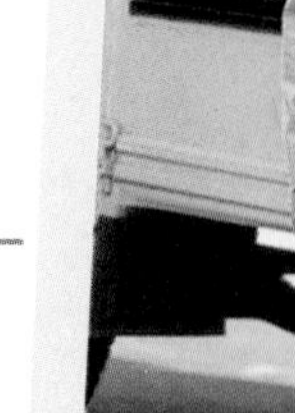

SOLVE

- How can you work backward to solve the problem?

  First, show what you know and what you need to find.

Miles to the first stop	Miles from the first stop to the second stop	Miles from the second stop to the third stop	Miles from the third stop to the fourth stop	Miles from the fourth stop to the school	Total miles
? →	$+3\frac{1}{10}$ →	$+1\frac{3}{10}$ →	$+2\frac{2}{10}$ →	$+2\frac{3}{10}$ →	10 →
? =	← $-3\frac{1}{10}$	← $-1\frac{3}{10}$	← $-2\frac{2}{10}$	← $-2\frac{3}{10}$	← 10
$1\frac{1}{10}$	$1\frac{1}{10}$	$4\frac{2}{10}$	$5\frac{5}{10}$	$7\frac{7}{10}$	10

So, the distance from the bus garage to the first bus stop is $1\frac{1}{10}$ miles.

LOOK BACK

- How can you determine if your answer is reasonable?
- What other strategy can you use?

▶ PRACTICE

Work backward to solve.

1. Terri used ribbon to decorate a hat. She used $2\frac{3}{8}$ yards of ribbon to decorate a T-shirt, and $3\frac{1}{8}$ yards of ribbon to make a costume. She had 3 yards of ribbon left. How much ribbon did she have to start with?

2. Mr. Wills returned home after running errands for $2\frac{1}{2}$ hours. During that time he spent $\frac{3}{4}$ hour at the mall, $\frac{1}{2}$ hour at the grocery store, and the rest of the time driving. How much time did Mr. Wills spend driving?

3. Cindy and Jake played a number game. Cindy told Jake to choose a number. Then she told him to multiply it by 4, add 6, divide by 2, and subtract 5. When Jake said his number was 6, Cindy told him what number he chose to begin with. What was Jake's starting number?

4. Dana went shopping for birthday gifts. He spent \$16 on his brother's gift and \$12 on his sister's gift. He returned an item to the sports store and got a refund of \$5. He had \$13 left. How much did he have to start with?

Mixed Applications

Solve.

CHOOSE a strategy and a tool.

- Work Backward
- Act It Out
- Draw a Diagram
- Write a Number Sentence

Paper/Pencil

Calculator

Hands-On

Mental Math

5. When Gail paid for groceries, she received \$8.88 in change. She bought items that cost \$1.89, \$5.70, \$3.39, and \$0.89. She turned in a coupon worth \$0.75. How much did Gail give the clerk to pay for the groceries?

6. Theo spent $\frac{1}{4}$ of his free time on Saturday playing basketball at the park. He spent $\frac{1}{2}$ of his free time watching a movie. If he played basketball for 1 hour, how much free time did he have on Saturday?

7. Lucia's parents bought new carpet for her bedroom. Her bedroom is 10 feet wide and 12 feet long. They had 10 square feet of carpet left over after carpeting her bedroom. How many square feet of carpeting did they buy?

8. Randy is looking at his sports cards. Of the cards, $\frac{1}{3}$ are baseball cards, $\frac{1}{2}$ are football cards, and $\frac{1}{6}$ are basketball cards. If he has 10 baseball cards, how many total cards does he have?

9. Christopher saved \$4.50 of his allowance each week for 7 weeks. Which computer program does he have enough money to buy?

MORE PRACTICE page H106

More About Subtracting Mixed Numbers

You will investigate renaming to subtract mixed numbers.

You can use the fraction bars to rename mixed numbers so you can subtract.

▶ EXPLORE

Use fraction bars to model the problem and to rename the mixed number so you can subtract.

MATERIALS: fraction bars

What is $1\frac{1}{6} - \frac{2}{3}$?

Step 1

Model $1\frac{1}{6}$ with fraction bars.

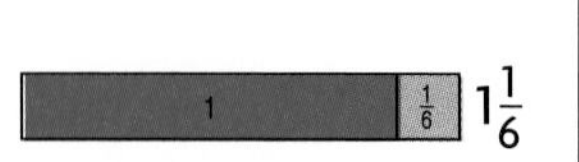

Step 2

Subtract $\frac{2}{3}$ from $1\frac{1}{6}$. Since the LCD is sixths, change $\frac{2}{3}$ to sixths.

Think: $\frac{2}{3} = \frac{4}{6}$

Step 3

Before you can take $\frac{4}{6}$ away from $1\frac{1}{6}$, you have to rename $1\frac{1}{6}$.

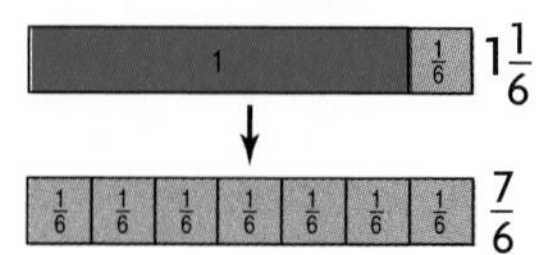

Step 4

Now, take $\frac{4}{6}$ away from $\frac{7}{6}$. Write the answer in simplest form.

Record

Record a subtraction sentence for the model. Explain how you can take away fraction bars to subtract mixed numbers.

Now, investigate subtracting other mixed numbers.

▶ TRY THIS

1. Find the difference of $2\frac{1}{2} - 1\frac{3}{4}$. Make a model and record by writing a number sentence.
2. How did you rename $2\frac{1}{2}$ so you could subtract?
3. **Write About It** How do you know when to rename one of the whole numbers to fractions?

Technology Link

In ***Mighty Math Calculating Crew***, the game *Nautical Number Line* challenges you to add and subtract mixed numbers. Use Grow Slide Level N.

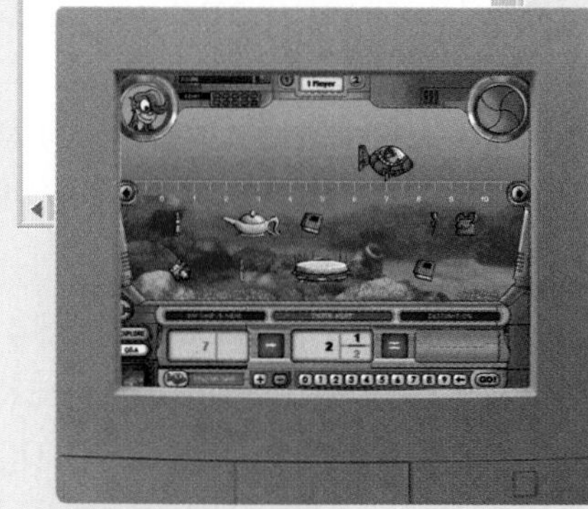

▶ PRACTICE

Match the mixed number with the fraction bars.

4. $2\frac{2}{5}$ **a.** 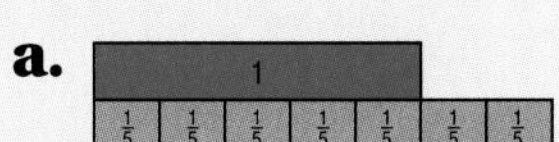

b. 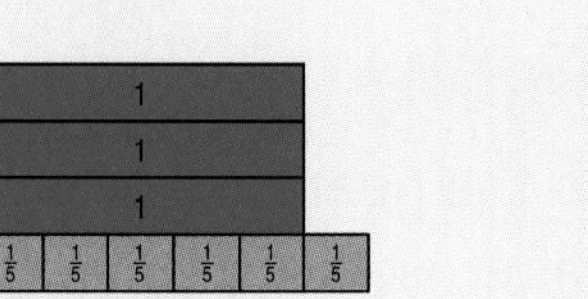

5. $3\frac{2}{3}$

6. $4\frac{1}{5}$ **c.** 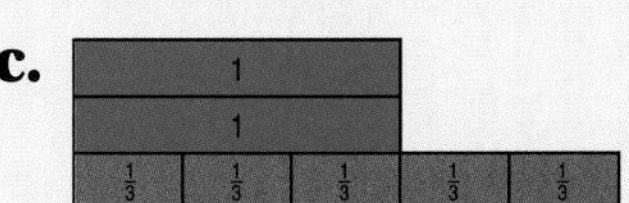

Technology Link

You can subtract mixed numbers by using E-Lab, Activity 20. Available on CD-ROM and on the Internet at **www.hbschool.com/elab**

Use fraction bars to find the difference.

7. $2\frac{3}{4} - \frac{1}{2}$

8. $6\frac{3}{5} - 4\frac{9}{10}$

9. $5\frac{3}{4} - 2\frac{7}{8}$

10. $8\frac{1}{6} - 2\frac{2}{3}$

11. $7\frac{1}{8} - 1\frac{3}{4}$

12. $9\frac{1}{3} - 4\frac{1}{2}$

13. $6\frac{3}{4} - 4\frac{7}{8}$

14. $10\frac{1}{6} - 3\frac{2}{3}$

15. $8\frac{7}{10} - 4\frac{1}{2} = n$

16. $6\frac{1}{2} - 2\frac{7}{8} = n$

17. $8\frac{1}{3} - 4\frac{5}{6} = n$

18. $6\frac{1}{2} - 1\frac{7}{10} = n$

19. $9\frac{1}{4} - 4\frac{5}{8} = n$

20. $6\frac{1}{3} - 5\frac{5}{12} = n$

Problem Solving • Mixed Applications

21. Measurement Sean bought $2\frac{1}{2}$ gallons of orange juice for his party. He had $\frac{1}{4}$ gallon left after the party. How much orange juice did Sean serve at his party?

22. Time Tara spent $1\frac{3}{4}$ hours exercising on Saturday. She spent $\frac{1}{2}$ hour exercising on Sunday. How many hours did she exercise this weekend?

23. Money On Saturday Ms. Rowe spent \$4 on lunch and \$15 on dinner. This is half the amount of money she started with. How much money did Ms. Rowe have to start with?

24. Career Alonzo teaches an exercise class for $1\frac{2}{3}$ hour each on Mondays, Wednesdays, and Fridays. How much time does Alonzo spend teaching his classes each week?

25. **Write a problem** about subtracting two mixed numbers.

MORE PRACTICE page H106

CHAPTER 20 Review/Test

▶ CHECK Understanding

Round the mixed number to the nearest $\frac{1}{2}$ or whole number. You may use a number line or a ruler. (pages 354–355)

1. $2\frac{7}{8}$ **2.** $1\frac{1}{6}$ **3.** $4\frac{3}{8}$ **4.** $5\frac{4}{5}$ **5.** $7\frac{1}{10}$ **6.** $3\frac{5}{9}$

Match the mixed number with the fraction bars. (pages 362–363)

7. $3\frac{2}{5}$

8. $2\frac{1}{6}$

9. $5\frac{3}{5}$

a. 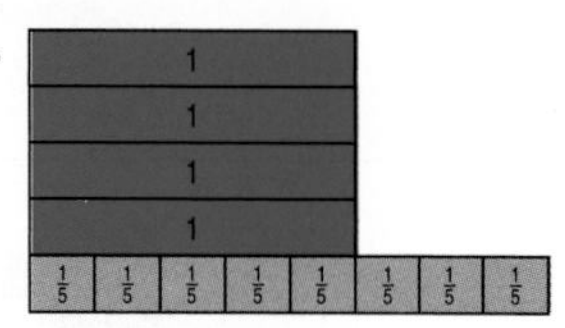

b. 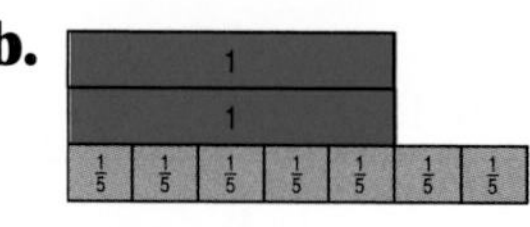

c. 

▶ CHECK Skills

Estimate the sum or difference. (pages 354–355)

10. $1\frac{3}{8} + 3\frac{11}{12}$ **11.** $4\frac{1}{8} - 2\frac{3}{4}$ **12.** $2\frac{8}{9} + 1\frac{1}{3}$

Find the sum. (pages 356–357)

13. $1\frac{1}{4} + 4\frac{1}{2} = n$ **14.** $3\frac{1}{3} + 1\frac{1}{6} = n$ **15.** $2\frac{5}{8} + 1\frac{3}{4} = n$

Find the difference. (pages 358–359)

16. $8\frac{3}{4} - 4\frac{1}{2} = n$ **17.** $5\frac{2}{3} - 4\frac{1}{6} = n$ **18.** $6\frac{5}{8} - 2\frac{1}{2} = n$

Add or subtract. Write the answer in simplest form. (pages 356–363)

19. $6\frac{2}{3} + 1\frac{5}{6} = n$ **20.** $8\frac{2}{5} - 4\frac{3}{10} = n$ **21.** $6\frac{1}{4} + 2\frac{7}{8} = n$

▶ CHECK Problem Solving

Solve. (pages 360–361)

CHOOSE a strategy and a tool.

- Work Backward
- Act It Out
- Draw a Diagram
- Write a Number Sentence

Paper/Pencil

Calculator

Hands-On

Mental Math

22. Kim used $9\frac{1}{2}$ in. of lace for a white dress and $6\frac{1}{2}$ in. for a blue dress. She had 8 in. of lace left. How much lace did Kim have to start with?

23. Last week Ned ran 1 mile on Monday, 2 miles on Tuesday, 5 miles on Wednesday, and 3 miles on Thursday. He ran a total of 15 miles by Friday. How many miles did he run on Friday?

Test Prep

Choose the best answer.

1. Mason has \$20. He wants to buy 3 books that cost \$5.95 each. Which of the following is a reasonable estimate of the change Mason will receive?

   A \$0 **B** \$2
   C \$4 **D** \$6

2. What is the volume of the figure below?

   F 35 cu units **G** 70 cu units
   H 90 cu units **J** 105 cu units

3. For the school craft project, 7 students collected a total of 224 cereal boxes. Each student collected exactly the same number of boxes. How many boxes did each student collect?

   A 32
   B 35
   C 231
   D 1,568

4. The cross-country team ran 7 miles Monday, 11 miles Tuesday, 6 miles Wednesday, 10 miles Thursday, and 11 miles on Friday. What is the mean of the distances they ran each day?

   F 5 mi **G** 9 mi
   H 10 mi **J** 45 mi

5. Mu Lan went shopping at the mall. She came home with \$2.40. She spent \$10.50 on a pair of shorts and \$7.35 on a poster. Lunch cost \$4.75. How much money did Mu Lan have before she went to the mall?

   A \$20.00 **B** \$20.25
   C \$22.60 **D** \$25.00

6. What symbol makes the following number sentence true?

   $\frac{3}{6} \bullet \frac{1}{2}$

   F $<$ **G** $>$
   H $=$ **J** $+$

7. $\frac{5}{8} - \frac{3}{8} =$

   A $\frac{1}{8}$ **B** $\frac{2}{8}$, or $\frac{1}{4}$
   C $\frac{3}{8}$ **D** $\frac{8}{8}$, or 1

8. What is $5\frac{7}{8}$ rounded to the nearest whole number?

   F 5 **G** 6
   H 7 **J** 8

9. Sara swam 3,000 meters during swim team practice. How far did she swim in kilometers?

   A 3 km
   B 30 km
   C 300 km
   D 3,000 km
   E Not Here

21 MEASUREMENT: CUSTOMARY UNITS

SCIENCE LINK

Very, very small objects cannot be measured with a ruler. A tool called a micrometer caliper can measure the thickness of objects to $\frac{1}{1,000}$ of an inch.

Problem-Solving Activity

Your Closest Call

How precisely can you measure with a ruler? How many teaspoons are in a cup? You can experiment to see how precise your measurements will be.

YOU WILL NEED: ruler, 3 objects to measure, salt, teaspoon, tablespoon, a measuring cup

Choose three objects to measure with a ruler.

- Measure the length, width, and height of each object and record your measurements.
- Fill a cup by using tablespoons and then by using teaspoons. Record your findings.
- Compare your most precise measurements with your classmates' measurements.

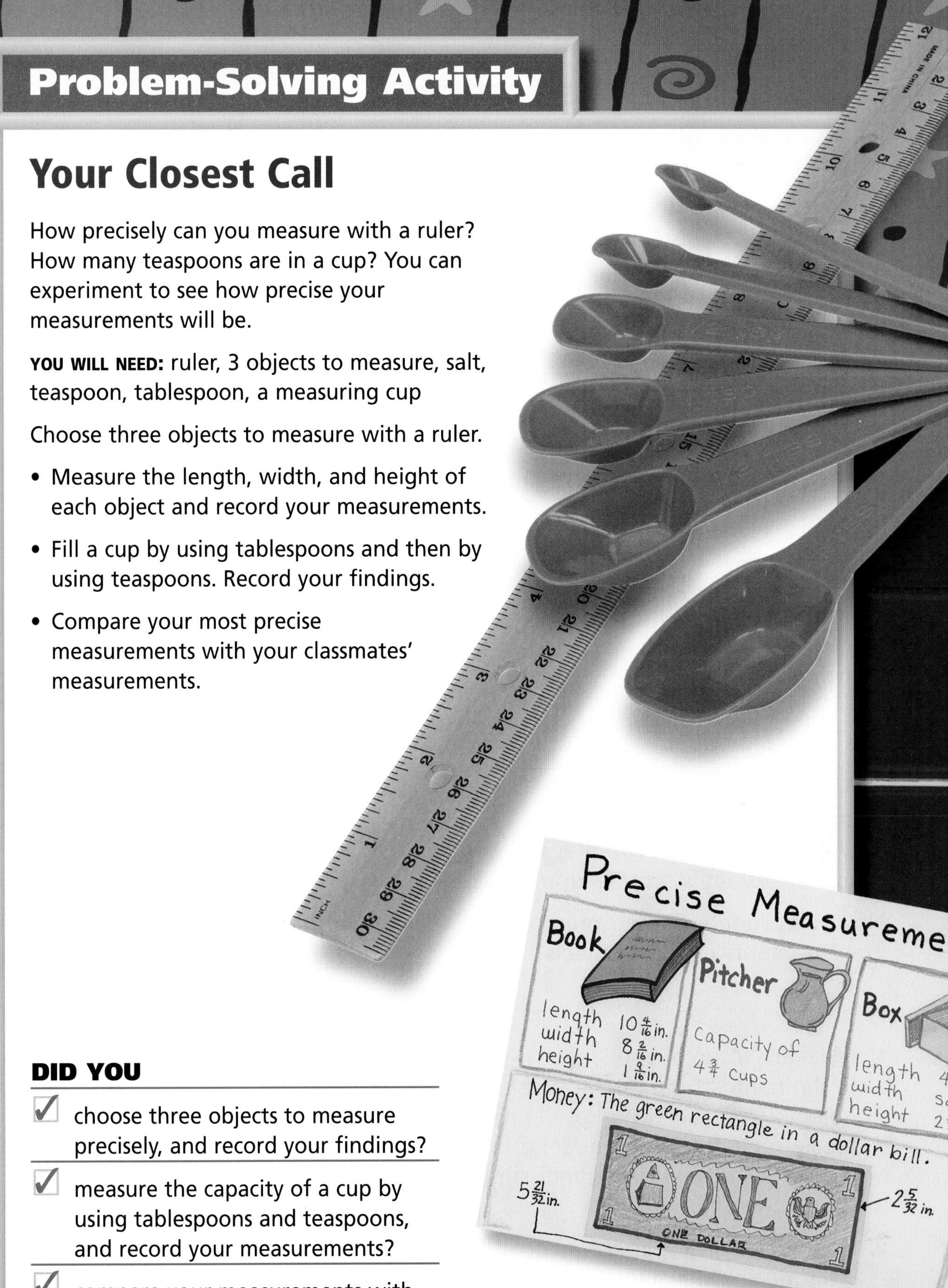

DID YOU

- ✓ choose three objects to measure precisely, and record your findings?
- ✓ measure the capacity of a cup by using tablespoons and teaspoons, and record your measurements?
- ✓ compare your measurements with those of your classmates?

Precise Measurements

VOCABULARY
precise

You will investigate how to use a ruler to measure length to the nearest $\frac{1}{16}$ of an inch.

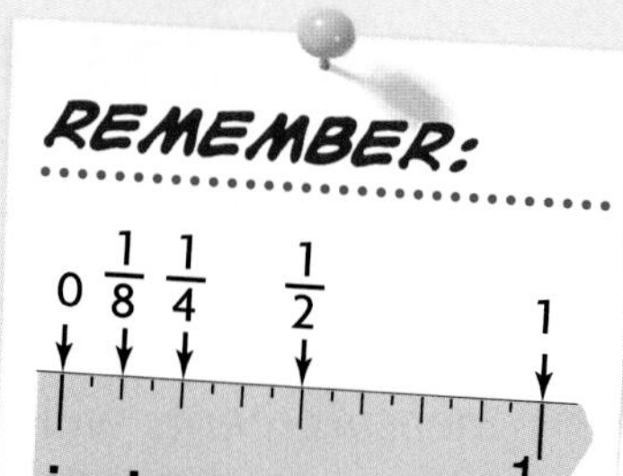

You can measure to a *half* inch, a *quarter* inch, or an *eighth* inch.

Sometimes you need a more precise measurement. **Precise** means finding a unit that measures nearest to the actual length of an object. The smaller the unit, the more precise the measurement will be.

▶ EXPLORE

Jeremy wants his new pen to fit inside his school-supply box, which is $5\frac{1}{4}$ inches long. Use a customary ruler to measure the pen to the nearest $\frac{1}{16}$ inch.

MATERIALS: customary ruler with $\frac{1}{16}$ in. marks

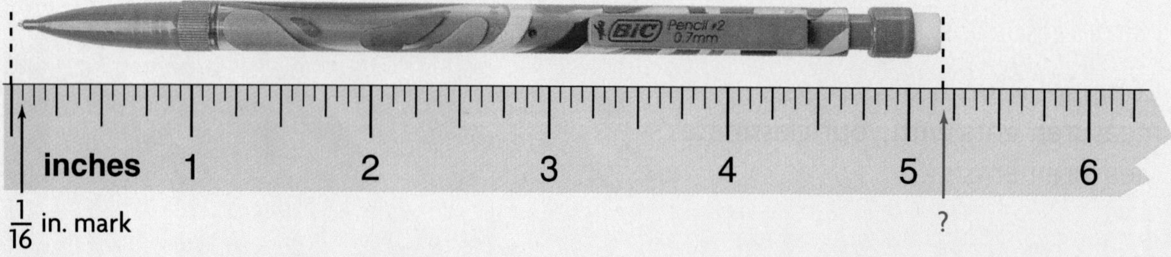

Record

Write the measurement of the pen. Explain how you determined whether the pen would fit inside Jeremy's school-supply box.

Now, investigate finding precise measurements of other objects.

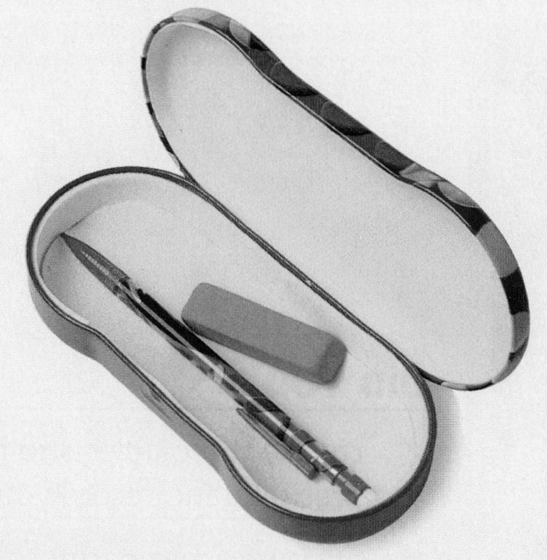

▶ TRY THIS

1. Measure three of your pens, pencils, or crayons to the nearest $\frac{1}{16}$ inch. Be sure to line up the object with the left end of the ruler. Record the measurements. Draw the length of each item. Describe the smallest school-supply box that they all will fit into.
2. How is measuring to the nearest inch different from measuring to the nearest $\frac{1}{16}$ inch?
3. **Write About It** Choose an object and explain how you would measure it to the nearest $\frac{1}{16}$ inch.

▶ PRACTICE

For Problems 4–7, use a customary ruler.

4. Measure the length of the paper clip to the nearest $\frac{1}{4}$ inch.

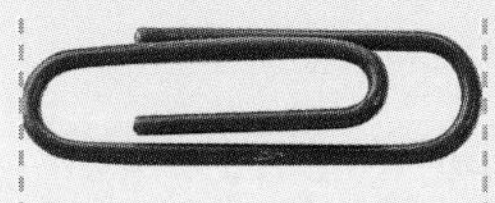

5. Measure the length of the chalk to the nearest $\frac{1}{16}$ inch.

6. Measure the length of the eraser to the nearest $\frac{1}{8}$ inch.

7. Measure the length of the sticker to the nearest $\frac{1}{16}$ inch.

Draw a line segment to the given length.

8. $2\frac{1}{4}$ inch **9.** $3\frac{3}{16}$ inch **10.** $4\frac{7}{16}$ inch

11. $1\frac{3}{8}$ inch **12.** $2\frac{11}{16}$ inch **13.** $5\frac{5}{8}$ inch

14. $3\frac{1}{2}$ inch **15.** $4\frac{7}{8}$ inch **16.** $2\frac{7}{16}$ inch

Use a ruler to compare the measurements. Write <, >, or = for each ●.

17. $3\frac{1}{16}$ in. ● $2\frac{11}{16}$ in. **18.** $1\frac{3}{16}$ in. ● $1\frac{5}{16}$ in.

19. $5\frac{1}{4}$ in. ● $5\frac{2}{8}$ in. **20.** $6\frac{3}{4}$ in. ● $6\frac{3}{16}$ in.

21. $7\frac{1}{2}$ in. ● $7\frac{5}{8}$ in. **22.** $4\frac{1}{8}$ in. ● $4\frac{2}{16}$ in.

Technology Link

You can measure objects by using E-Lab, Activity 21. Available on CD-ROM and on the Internet at **www.hbschool.com/elab**

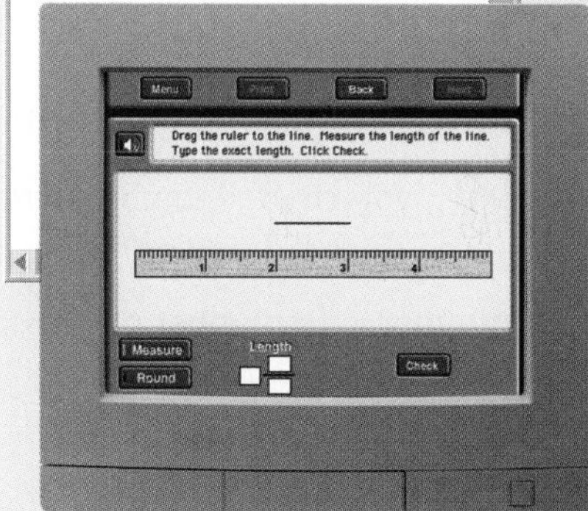

Problem Solving • Mixed Applications

23. Compare Measure the two leaves. How much longer is the yellow leaf than the green leaf?

24. LaToya wants to sew two ribbons together to make one long ribbon. Her seam will reduce the length of each ribbon by $\frac{1}{4}$ inch. One ribbon is $5\frac{1}{4}$ inches long. The other is $6\frac{3}{4}$ inches long. How long will her finished ribbon be?

25. **Write a problem** about the lengths of two objects that are between 5 and 6 inches long.

MORE PRACTICE page H106

Changing Customary Units

Why learn this? You may need to change small units of measure to large units, or large units to small units, when you compare measurements such as feet and yards of fabric.

Customary Units for Linear Measure
12 inches (in.) = 1 foot (ft)
3 feet = 1 yard (yd)
5,280 feet = 1 mile (mi)
1,760 yards = 1 mile

The fifth-grade class is making costumes for the school play. Each costume requires 5 feet of fabric. A local store has donated 25 yards of fabric for the costumes. How many feet of fabric do the students have?

When you change larger units to smaller units, you multiply. Since you are changing yards to feet, multiply by 3.

number of yards		number of feet in 1 yard		total feet
25	$\times$	3	=	?

Since $25 \times 3 = 75$, the students have 75 ft of fabric.

- How can you find the number of costumes the students can make?

The students made a green banner to stretch across the stage. It was 360 inches long. How many feet long was the banner?

You can use a calculator when changing units.

When you change smaller units to larger units, you divide. Since you are changing inches to feet, divide by 12.

number of inches		number of inches in 1 foot		total feet
360	$\div$	12	=	?

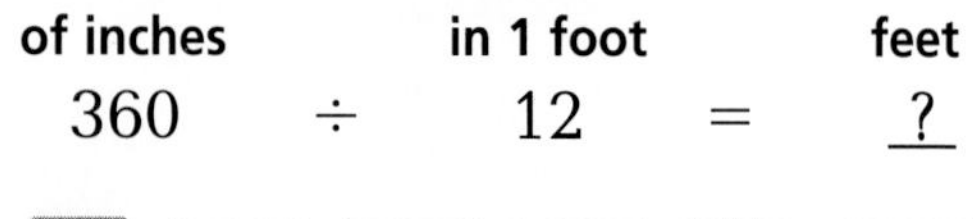

Since $360 \div 12 = 30$, the banner is 30 feet long.

Talk About It CRITICAL THINKING

- When a change is made from feet to inches, will there be more inches or fewer inches? Explain.
- When a change is made from feet to yards, will there be more yards or fewer yards?

▶ CHECK

Write *multiply* or *divide* to tell how to change the unit.

1. yards to feet **2.** yards to miles **3.** inches to feet **4.** miles to feet

Change the unit. You may use a calculator.

5. 12 ft = __?__ yd **6.** 48 in. = __?__ ft **7.** 50 yd = __?__ ft

8. 2 mi = __?__ ft **9.** 6 ft = __?__ in. **10.** 30 ft = __?__ yd

▶ PRACTICE

Write *more* or *fewer*.

11. When I change miles to feet, I expect to have __?__ feet.

12. When I change feet to yards, I expect to have __?__ yards.

Write *multiply* or *divide*. Solve.

13. How many feet are in 120 inches?

14. How many feet are in 3 miles?

Change the unit. You may use a calculator.

15. 60 yd = __?__ ft **16.** 5 ft = __?__ in. **17.** 1,760 yd = __?__ mi

18. 33 ft = __?__ yd **19.** 300 ft = __?__ yd **20.** 2,640 ft = __?__ mi

Problem Solving • Mixed Applications

Using Data For Problems 21–22, use the picture.

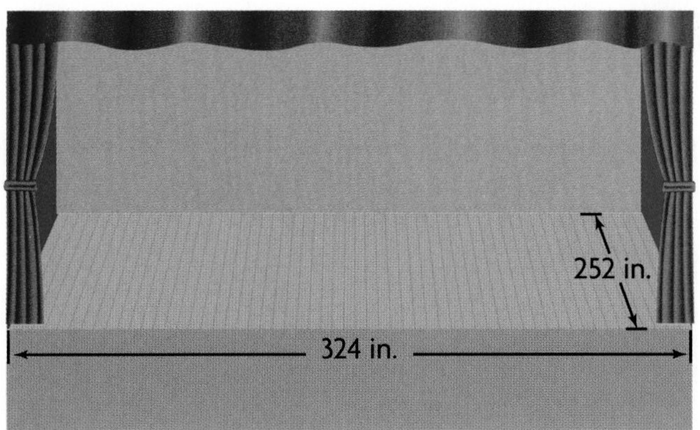

21. Drama The Theater Club is getting ready for the fifth-grade talent show. They are measuring the width of the stage. How many feet wide is the stage?

22. Reasoning The club needs an extension cord that will reach across the stage. Extension cords come in 10-ft, 25-ft, or 50-ft lengths. Which one should they choose?

23. Money James needs 16 sheets of plywood to make the sets. Each sheet costs $12.69. How much will he pay for the plywood?

24. Write About It Explain when to multiply and when to divide in order to change linear units.

LESSON CONTINUES

MORE PRACTICE pages H106–H107

LESSON 2 • PART 2

Computing Customary Units

Alison works at the school publishing center. She makes book covers for books the students have written. She had 2 feet 10 inches of ribbon to use as a border on the book covers. The teacher gave her 3 feet 9 inches more ribbon. How much ribbon does Alison have?

You may need to change units when adding or subtracting measurements.

MODEL

Add 2 ft 10 in. and 3 ft 9 in.

Step 1

Add each kind of unit.

$$\begin{array}{r} 2\text{ ft } 10\text{ in.} \\ +3\text{ ft } \ \ 9\text{ in.} \\ \hline 5\text{ ft } 19\text{ in.} \end{array}$$

Step 2

Since 19 in. is more than 1 ft, rename 19 in. as 1 ft 7 in.

Think: 12 in. = 1 ft

$$\begin{array}{l} \ \ 2\text{ ft } 10\text{ in.} \\ +3\text{ ft } \ \ 9\text{ in.} \\ \hline \ \ 5\text{ ft } 19\text{ in.} = \\ \ \ 5\text{ ft} + (1\text{ ft} + 7\text{ in.}) \end{array}$$

Step 3

Combine like units.

$$\begin{array}{l} \ \ 2\text{ ft } 10\text{ in.} \\ +3\text{ ft } \ \ 9\text{ in.} \\ \hline \ \ 5\text{ ft } 19\text{ in.} = \\ \ \ (5\text{ ft} + 1\text{ ft}) + 7\text{ in.} = 6\text{ ft } 7\text{ in.} \end{array}$$

So, Alison has 6 ft 7 in. of ribbon.

Alison used 1 foot 9 inches of ribbon on the first book she covered. How much ribbon does she have left?

Subtract 1 foot 9 inches from 6 feet 7 inches.

MODEL

Step 1

Decide whether to rename. Since 9 in. > 7 in., rename 6 ft 7 in.

$$\begin{array}{r} 5\text{ ft } 19\text{ in.} \\ \not{6}\text{ ft } \ \ \not{7}\text{ in.} \\ -1\text{ ft } \ \ 9\text{ in.} \\ \hline \end{array}$$

Think: 1 ft = 12 in.
5 ft + 12 in. + 7 in.

Step 2

Subtract the inches. Subtract the feet.

$$\begin{array}{r} 5\text{ ft } 19\text{ in.} \\ \not{6}\text{ ft } \ \ \not{7}\text{ in.} \\ -1\text{ ft } \ \ 9\text{ in.} \\ \hline 4\text{ ft } 10\text{ in.} \end{array}$$

So, Alison has 4 ft 10 in. of ribbon left.

CRITICAL THINKING When must you rename units to add measurements? When must you rename units to subtract measurements?

▶ CHECK

Rename the measurements.

1. 30 in. = _?_ ft _?_ in.
2. 10 ft = _?_ yd _?_ ft
3. 27 in. = _?_ ft _?_ in.
4. 4 ft 5 in. = 3 ft _?_ in.
5. 3 ft 16 in. = 4 ft _?_ in.
6. 5 ft 6 in. = 4 ft _?_ in.
7. 12 yd 1 ft = 11 yd _?_ ft
8. 14 yd = 13 yd _?_ ft
9. 20 yd 2 ft = 19 yd _?_ ft

▶ PRACTICE

Find the sum or difference.

10. 8 ft 4 in. + 2 ft 10 in.
11. 6 ft 3 in. − 1 ft 8 in.
12. 5 yd 2 ft + 2 yd 2 ft
13. 9 yd 1 ft − 7 yd 2 ft
14. 7 yd 4 ft − 3 yd 5 ft
15. 11 yd 9 ft + 10 yd 2 ft
16. 12 ft − 10 ft 8 in.
17. 20 ft 11 in. + 17 ft 10 in.
18. 18 ft 6 in. + 17 ft 9 in.
19. 23 ft 5 in. + 29 ft 11 in.
20. 26 yd 7 ft + 19 yd 6 ft
21. 13 yd − 10 yd 2 ft

Problem Solving • Mixed Applications

Using Data For Problems 25–28, use the picture.

22. Reasoning Brenda is buying lace to trim the perimeter of a tablecloth that is 80 inches long and 40 inches wide. Will she need to buy more or less than 6 yards of lace? Explain.

23. Money Brooke spent $7.75 on fabric, $2.98 for a pattern, and $3.79 for buttons. Does she have enough money left over from $15.00 to buy thread for $0.79?

24. Number Sense Mary has 4 ceramic cats in her collection. Their heights are 10.2 in., 8.4 in., 7.9 in., and 8.3 in. What is the average height of the cats in her collection?

25. Compare How much taller is Sara than Michael?

26. Compare If Kristen grows 6 inches by the time she is in tenth grade, how tall will she be?

27. Michael's older sister is 5 ft 5 in. tall. How much taller is she than Michael?

28. **Write a problem** using the information in the picture.

MORE PRACTICE page H107

Capacity

Why learn this? You can decide whether to buy ice cream by the pint or by the half gallon.

Maria made punch for the party. The recipe makes enough punch to fill a 2-gallon punch bowl. Maria wants to make sure she has enough to give a cup to each of her 24 guests. Does she have enough?

Maria needs to find out the number of cups in 2 gallons.

MODEL

Step 1

First, find how many quarts are in 2 gallons.

number of gallons		number of quarts in 1 gallon		total quarts
2	×	4	=	8

So, 2 gallons equals 8 quarts.

Step 2

Now find how many cups are in 8 quarts.

number of quarts		number of cups in 1 quart		total cups
8	×	4	=	32

So, Maria has 32 cups of punch, more than enough for her 24 guests.

Customary Units of Capacity
8 fluid ounces (fl oz) = 1 cup (c)
2 cups = 1 pint (pt)
2 pints = 1 quart (qt)
4 cups = 1 quart
4 quarts = 1 gallon (gal)

Talk About It CRITICAL THINKING

- Why did you multiply in Step 2?
- How can you find how many fluid ounces are equal to 1 pint? Explain.
- How can you find how many gallons are equal to 16 pints? Explain.

LANGUAGE LINK

Some people think the word *pint* comes from the same Latin root as the word *paint*. An old English meaning for *pint* is "a container of paint." How many pints of paint make a gallon?

▶ CHECK

Write *multiply* or *divide*. Change the unit.

1. 1 qt = ? c **2.** 20 qt = ? gal **3.** 1 gal = ? fl oz **4.** 5 c = ? fl oz

5. 4 c = ? pt **6.** 8 pt = ? qt **7.** 3 qt = ? c **8.** 2 pt = ? fl oz

▶ PRACTICE

Change the unit.

9. 8 c = ? pt **10.** 1 gal = ? pt **11.** 8 c = ? qt **12.** 1 pt = ? fl oz

13. 3 gal = ? qt **14.** 12 pt = ? qt **15.** 5 pt = ? c **16.** 10 c = ? fl oz

For Exercises 17–20, use the picture.

17. How many cups of yogurt?

18. How many quarts of milk?

19. How many fluid ounces of juice?

20. How many fluid ounces of milk?

Write <, >, or = for each ●.

21. 4 c ● 1 gal **22.** 3 pt ● 1 qt **23.** 16 c ● 1 gal **24.** 36 fl oz ● 1 qt

25. 4 qt ● 8 pt **26.** 2 gal ● 10 qt **27.** 7 pt ● 110 oz **28.** 32 fl oz ● 4 c

29. 2 gal ● 7 pt **30.** 2 c ● 16 fl oz **31.** 5 qt ● 1 gal **32.** 48 fl oz ● 4 pt

Problem Solving • Mixed Applications

33. Career Barry works in a pet store. He is filling a 10-gallon fish tank with water. He plans to use 9 gallons to leave a space at the top. His pitcher holds 1 quart. How many pitchers of water does he need?

34. Reasoning Yolanda is painting her room. After she finishes the 3rd wall, she has enough paint left to cover 350 square feet. The 4th wall is 8 ft by 12 ft. How many more square feet will Yolanda be able to paint after she finishes the 4th wall?

35. Consumer George is helping his mom shop. His little sister wants him to buy a 6-pack of box drinks, each with 6 fl oz, for \$2.16. A 48-oz bottle of juice costs \$2.20. Which is the better buy?

36. Write About It Explain how to find out how many pints are in 2 gallons.

Mixed Review and Test Prep

Write the missing unit. (pages 256–257)

37. 5.6 m = 560 ? **38.** 4,700 g = 4.7 ? **39.** 8 kg = 8,000 ?

Choose the letter of the correct quotient. (pages 236–237)

40. $7.2 \div 8 = n$ **A** 9 **B** 0.09 **C** 0.9 **D** 0.009

41. $88.4 \div 4 = n$ **F** 0.221 **G** 2.21 **H** 221 **J** 22.1

LESSON 4

Weight

Why learn this? You can compare products, such as bags of dog food, by their unit price to get the better buy.

Barry bought a 50-lb bag of dog food for his dog, Max. Max eats 10 oz of food each day. How many days will the bag of dog food last?

Think about the units of weight in the customary system.

Customary Units for Measuring Weight
16 ounce (oz) = 1 pound (lb)
2,000 lb = 1 ton (T)

EXAMPLES

1 ounce

1 pound

1 ton

Now, find how many ounces are in 50 pounds.

When you change larger units to smaller units, you multiply. Since you are changing pounds to ounces, multiply by 16. You may use a calculator.

number of pounds		number of ounces in 1 pound		total ounces
50	×	16	=	800

Press:

So, the 50-lb bag of dog food holds 800 oz.

Since Max eats 10 oz a day, you can divide to find the number of days the food will last. $800 \div 10 = n$

Press:

$n = 80$.

So, Max has enough food for 80 days.

- How can you use a calculator to find the number of pounds equal to 144 ounces?

SPORTS LINK

Hitting a fast-moving baseball with a bat is very difficult. Ball players have discovered that lighter bats that weigh 28 ounces or less allow them to hit with greater speed. Babe Ruth used a heavy 42-ounce bat. How does a lighter bat weighing 28 ounces compare to Babe Ruth's bat?

Calculator Activities page H60

▶ CHECK

What unit would you use to describe the weight of these objects? Write *tons, pounds,* or *ounces*.

1. a bicycle

2. a dog

3. a truckload of concrete blocks

4. a block of cheese

▶ PRACTICE

Write *more* or *fewer* for each statement.

5. When I change tons to pounds, I expect to have __?__ pounds.

6. When I change ounces to pounds, I expect to have __?__ pounds.

7. When I change pounds to ounces, I expect to have __?__ ounces.

8. When I change pounds to tons, I expect to have __?__ tons.

Write *multiply* or *divide*. Change the unit. You may use a calculator.

9. 32 oz = __?__ lb **10.** 40 lb = __?__ oz **11.** 2 T = __?__ lb **12.** 8,000 lb = __?__ T

13. 6,000 lb = __?__ T **14.** 15 lb = __?__ oz **15.** 10 T = __?__ lb **16.** 10,000 lb = __?__ T

Write which one is heavier.

17. 46 oz or 3 lb **18.** 2 T or 5,000 lb **19.** $\frac{1}{2}$ T or 500 lb **20.** 100 lb or 1,000 oz

Problem Solving • Mixed Applications

Special Apple Sale!
Golden Delicious, 2 apples for $1
Gala apples, $0.79 a pound

21. Analyzing Data Each apple in this display weighs 4 ounces. Which apple is the better bargain?

22. Consumer A 28-ounce box of granola sells for $3.29. Granola also is sold for $1.50 a pound. Which granola is the better buy?

23. **Write a problem** comparing two items for sale in the food store. One is sold by the pound and the other is sold by the ounce.

Mixed Review and Test Prep

Rename each fraction as a mixed number. **(pages 272–273)**

24. $\frac{15}{7}$ **25.** $\frac{11}{2}$ **26.** $\frac{12}{5}$ **27.** $\frac{13}{3}$ **28.** $\frac{11}{4}$

Choose the correct sum or difference in simplest form. **(pages 342–343)**

29. $\frac{1}{9} + \frac{1}{3} = n$ **A** $\frac{4}{9}$ **B** $\frac{8}{18}$ **C** $\frac{3}{9}$ **D** $\frac{4}{12}$

30. $\frac{13}{16} - \frac{4}{8} = n$ **F** $\frac{5}{12}$ **G** $1\frac{10}{12}$ **H** $\frac{5}{16}$ **J** $\frac{7}{8}$

MORE PRACTICE page H107

Elapsed Time

Why learn this? You can use a schedule to find the time it will take to travel from one place to another.

A group of Scouts went on a hike. They started the hike at 9:00 A.M. They stopped for lunch at 12:15 P.M. How long were the Scouts hiking?

Units of Time
60 seconds (sec) = 1 minute (min)
60 minutes = 1 hour (hr)
24 hours = 1 day
7 days = 1 week
about 52 weeks = 1 year
365 days = 1 year
366 days = 1 leap year

To find how much time has elapsed, you can count forward on the clock from the starting time to the ending time.

So, the group was hiking for 3 hr and 15 min.

Suppose a hiking and camping trip starts at 7 A.M. on July 22 and finishes at 5 P.M. on July 26. How many days and hours will the trip last?

Count the whole days from 7 A.M. July 22 to 7 A.M. July 26.

July						
S	M	T	W	T	F	S
			1	2	3	4
5	6	7	8	9	10	11
12	13	14	15	16	17	18
19	20	21	22	23	24	25
26	27	28	29	30	31	

4 days

Count the hours from 7 A.M. to 5 P.M.

10 hours

So, it will take 4 days and 10 hours to make the trip.

Talk About It CRITICAL THINKING

- At what time does A.M. become P.M?
- If you know the starting time and the elapsed time, how can you find the ending time?
- If you know the elapsed time and the ending time, how can you find the starting time?

▶ CHECK

Write the time for each.

1. Start: 5:25 P.M.
   45 min elapsed time
   End: ___?___

2. Start: ___?___
   2 hr 35 min elapsed time
   End: 8:00 P.M.

3. Start: July 12, 6:00 A.M.
   ___?___ time has elapsed
   End: July 20, 8:30 A.M.

▶ PRACTICE

Write the elapsed time for each hike.

4.

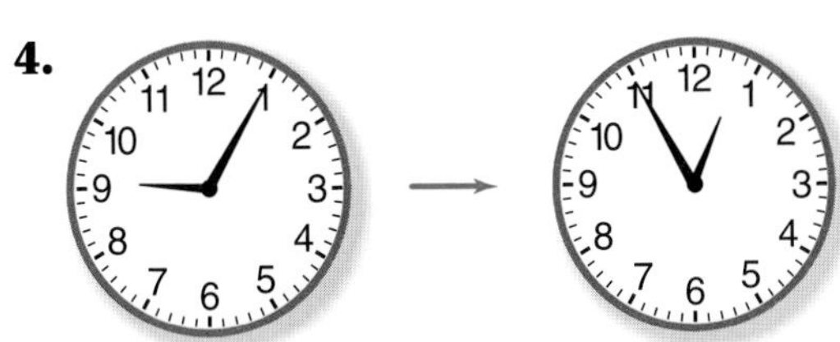

time the hike started — time the hike finished

5.

8:17

time the hike started — time the hike finished

Look at Juanita's schedule for the day and complete the table.

	Activity	Starting Time	Ending Time	Elapsed Time
6.	School	9:10 A.M.	3:25 P.M.	?
7.	Soccer Practice	3:45 P.M.	?	1 hr 55 min
8.	Dinner	?	6:40 P.M.	28 min
9.	Homework	6:45 P.M.	8:12 P.M.	?

Problem Solving • Mixed Applications

Using Data For Problems 10–13 and 15, use the following calendars.

March

S	M	T	W	Th	F	S
1	2	3	4	5	6	7
8	9	10	11	12	13	14
15	16	17	18	19	20	21
22	23	24	25	26	27	28
29	30	31				

April

S	M	T	W	Th	F	S
			1	2	3	4
5	6	7	8	9	10	11
12	13	14	15	16	17	18
19	20	21	22	23	24	25
26	27	28	29	30		

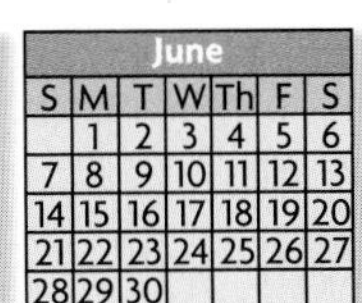

May

S	M	T	W	Th	F	S
					1	2
3	4	5	6	7	8	9
10	11	12	13	14	15	16
17	18	19	20	21	22	23
24/31	25	26	27	28	29	30

June

S	M	T	W	Th	F	S
	1	2	3	4	5	6
7	8	9	10	11	12	13
14	15	16	17	18	19	20
21	22	23	24	25	26	27
28	29	30				

July

S	M	T	W	Th	F	S
			1	2	3	4
5	6	7	8	9	10	11
12	13	14	15	16	17	18
19	20	21	22	23	24	25
26	27	28	29	30	31	

August

S	M	T	W	Th	F	S
						1
2	3	4	5	6	7	8
9	10	11	12	13	14	15
16	17	18	19	20	21	22
23/30	24/31	25	26	27	28	29

September

S	M	T	W	Th	F	S
		1	2	3	4	5
6	7	8	9	10	11	12
13	14	15	16	17	18	19
20	21	22	23	24	25	26
27	28	29	30			

10. **Time** There will be a 36-hour field trip to a historical village, starting at 8 A.M. on April 21. When will the students arrive back home?

11. **Art** The art show will be on April 11. Members want to display posters one month earlier. It takes one week to make the posters. When should they start the posters?

12. **Reasoning** June 12 is the last day of school. School starts again on September 8. Is summer vacation 100 days long? Explain.

13. The county fair is going to open here for two weeks. It will close on June 3rd. On what date will the county fair open?

14. **Time** Your lunch period starts at 11:45 A.M., and lasts 32 minutes. When will your lunch period end?

15. **Write a problem** using the calendars.

MORE PRACTICE page H108

Problem-Solving Strategy: Make a Table

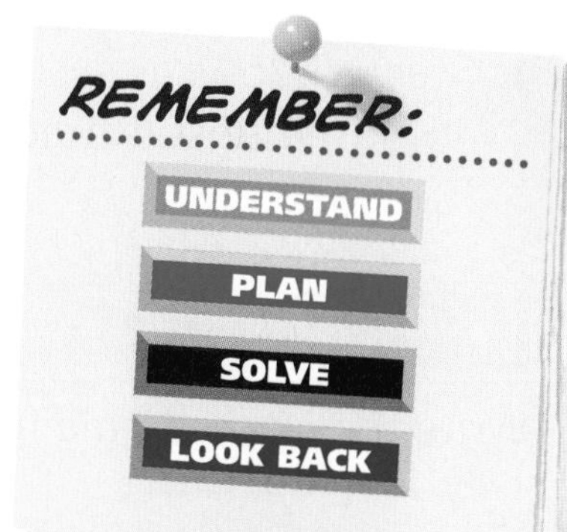

▶ **THE PROBLEM** You are helping your family plan an afternoon trip to the beach. You plan to take the earliest train out of the city and be back at 6:00 P.M. The train stops near Sandy Beach. It takes 10 minutes to walk from the train to the beach. How long can you stay at the beach?

UNDERSTAND

- What are you asked to do?
- What information will you use?
- Is there information you will not use? If so, what?

Departure	Arrival
New York City	Sandy Beach
12:10	12:55
1:30	2:15
3:00	3:45
Sandy Beach	New York City
3:45	4:15
4:30	5:15
5:30	6:15

PLAN

- What strategy can you use?

  You can use the information from the schedule to *make a table* to show the elapsed time.

SOLVE

- How can you solve the problem?

  You can make a table that shows the starting and ending time for each part of the trip. The earliest train leaves at 12:10 and arrives at 12:55. After the 10-minute walk, you arrive at the beach at 1:05.

Part of Trip	Start	End	Elapsed Time
Train From City	12:10 P.M.	12:55 P.M.	45 min
Walk To Beach	12:55 P.M.	1:05 P.M.	10 min
Stay At Beach	1:05 P.M.	4:20 P.M.	?
Walk To Train	4:20 P.M.	4:30 P.M.	10 min
Train To City	4:30 P.M.	5:15 P.M.	45 min

  The last train that will get you home before 6:00 is the one that leaves at 4:30. You must allow 10 minutes to walk from the beach to get to the train. So, you are at the beach from 1:05 to 4:20. You can count the hours and minutes to find the elapsed time.

  So, you can spend 3 hr 15 min at the beach.

LOOK BACK

- How can you decide if your answer is reasonable?
- What other strategy can you use?

▶ PRACTICE

Make a table to solve.

1. The multipurpose room is used from 11:30 until 12:45 for lunch. For the next 50 minutes, the fifth graders practice square dancing there. Then for the next 30 minutes, the fourth graders practice their play. At what time is the room free?

2. The principal plans to give each student 5 minutes to try out for the talent show starting at 3:00. The students, in order, are Ben, Callie, Denise, Edward, and Frank. At what time does Frank start?

3. The Gibb family left on July 7th for vacation. They flew to Miami and stayed 3 days. Next, they spent 5 days in Key West, 4 days in Orlando, and returned home the following day. On what date did they arrive home?

4. Tom and Joe want to see a movie on Saturday between 4:00 and 6:15. *Starship Mars* is shown daily at 1:30, 3:45, and 6:00. *The Lost Witness* is shown Monday through Friday at 4:00 and 6:45. *Ride the Wave* is shown on weekends at 2:00, 4:10, and 6:30. Which movie will they see?

Mixed Applications

Solve.

CHOOSE a strategy and a tool.

- Work Backward
- Make a Table
- Guess and Check
- Write a Number Sentence

Paper/Pencil

Calculator

Hands-On

Mental Math

5. The school assembly began at 9:10. The principal spoke for 5 minutes. For the next 1 hour 10 minutes, the students received their awards. Then there was a 10-minute break. For the next 35 minutes there was a guest speaker. At what time was the assembly over?

6. Nick and Lindsay are making shakes. The picture shows the total amount of milk needed. Nick uses 6 fluid ounces more milk than Lindsay. How many fluid ounces does each use?

7. At the school program, there were 229 students and 75 parents. The school printed 256 programs. How many more programs should the school have printed?

8. Jack is a long-distance runner. His running shoes wear out after he has run about 1,000 miles. If he runs 18 miles a week, about how long will his running shoes last?

9. Rachel arrived home at 3:30. Before that she went shopping for 2 hr 20 min. Before that she spent 30 minutes eating lunch with a friend. At what time did they begin eating lunch?

MORE PRACTICE page H108

LESSON 6

Temperature Changes

Why learn this? You can compare two temperatures of water and see which is the correct temperature to use in an aquarium.

VOCABULARY
degrees Fahrenheit (°F)
degrees Celsius (°C)

A reasonable water temperature for aquariums is about 25°C. Use a Celsius thermometer to measure the temperature of cool and warm tap water. What is the difference in aquarium water and the cool and warm tap water in Celsius degrees? Should you use cool or warm tap water to add water to an aquarium?

Degrees Celsius (°C) are metric units for measuring temperature. This is a Celsius thermometer. It shows room temperature at 20°C.

These thermometers show each mark as 5°.

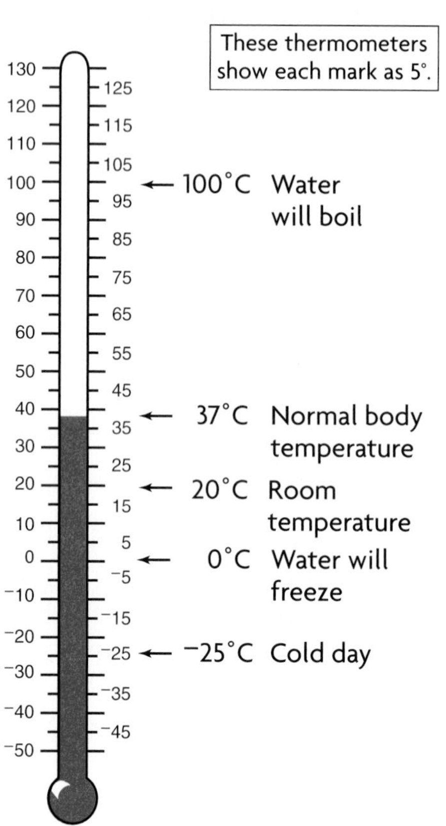

Degrees Fahrenheit (°F) are customary units for measuring temperature. This is a Fahrenheit thermometer. It shows room temperature at 68°F.

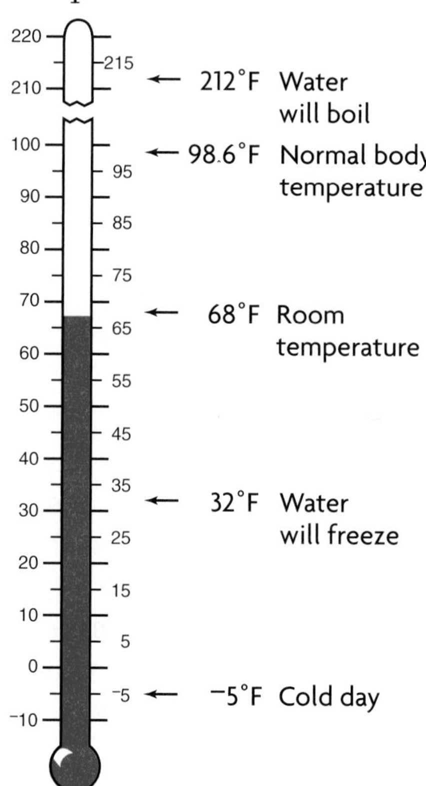

Talk About It CRITICAL THINKING

Use the thermometers.

- If the temperature was 10°C and it fell 25 degrees, what temperature is it now?
- If the low temperature was ⁻5°F and the high temperature was 22°F, by how many degrees did the temperature rise?

▶ CHECK

Find the difference in temperature.

1. 212°F and 98.6°F **2.** 100°C and $^-25$°C **3.** 68°F and $^-10$°F

▶ PRACTICE

Find the difference in temperature. Use a thermometer for Problems 4 and 7.

4. the outdoor temperature of 84°F and room temperature

5. a normal human body temperature and a fever of 104°F

6. the temperature at the top of a cumulus cloud, $^-4$°F, and the temperature on the ground at 60°F

7. the temperature in your classroom and the temperature outdoors

Copy and complete the table.

	Starting Temperature	Change in Temperature	Final Temperature
8.	12°C	rose 19°	?
9.	62°F	?	37°F
10.	9°C	fell 15°	?
11.	48°F	?	71°F

Problem Solving • Mixed Applications

12. Analyzing Data On Monday and Tuesday the temperature was 14°C. On Wednesday it was 16°C and on Thursday it was 15°C. On Friday it was 11°C. What are the mean, median, and mode temperatures for the 5 days?

13. Money Lynn bought a jacket for $38.95, gloves for $8.99, and a scarf for $9.85. How much change did she receive from $60.00?

14. Write About It Explain how to find the temperature change from 72°F to 36°F.

Mixed Review and Test Prep

Rename, using the least common multiple, and compare.
Write <, >, or = for each ●. (pages 276–277)

15. $\frac{3}{12}$ ● $\frac{1}{4}$ **16.** $\frac{5}{6}$ ● $\frac{11}{12}$ **17.** $\frac{3}{10}$ ● $\frac{3}{4}$ **18.** $\frac{3}{5}$ ● $\frac{2}{7}$

Choose the letter of the equivalent fraction. (pages 292–293)

19. $\frac{3}{4}$ **A** $\frac{8}{12}$ **B** $\frac{10}{16}$ **C** $\frac{9}{10}$ **D** $\frac{6}{8}$

20. $\frac{2}{16}$ **F** $\frac{2}{8}$ **G** $\frac{2}{32}$ **H** $\frac{1}{8}$ **J** $\frac{4}{24}$

MORE PRACTICE page H108

CHAPTER 21 Review/Test

CHECK Understanding

VOCABULARY

1. Degrees __?__ are customary units for measuring temperature. (page 382)
2. A measurement using the smaller unit is a more __?__ measurement. (page 368)
3. Degrees __?__ are metric units for measuring temperature. (page 382)

Use a customary ruler to measure these lines. (pages 368–369)

4. ______________________________
5. ______________________________
6. Draw a line that is one-half foot in length.

CHECK Skills

Change the unit. You may use a calculator. (pages 370–377)

7. 36 in. = __?__ ft
8. 72 ft = __?__ yd
9. 5 ft = __?__ in.
10. $\frac{1}{2}$ mi = __?__ ft
11. 1 pt = __?__ c
12. 2 qt = __?__ c
13. 1 gal = __?__ c
14. 1 pt = __?__ fl oz
15. 2,000 lb = __?__ T
16. 4 T = __?__ lb
17. 48 oz = __?__ lb
18. 8 oz = __?__ lb

Write the time for each. (pages 378–379)

19. Start: 2:05 P.M.
    25 min elapsed time
    End: __?__
20. Start: __?__
    2 hr 15 min elapsed time
    End: 10:45 P.M.
21. Start: May 9, 4:30 A.M.
    __?__ time has elapsed
    End: May 19, 7:40 A.M.

Find the difference in temperature. (pages 382–383)

22. high 89°F, low 62°F
23. high 14°C, low $^-3$°C
24. high 19°F, low $^-10$°F

CHECK Problem Solving

Solve. (pages 380–381)

CHOOSE a strategy and a tool.

- Draw a Diagram
- Write a Number Sentence
- Use a Table
- Make a Table

Paper/Pencil

Calculator

Hands-On

Mental Math

25. Dr. Lu does routine checkups on one day. He allows 20 min per visit. If he works from 9:00 A.M. to 4:00 P.M., and takes an hour for lunch, how many patients does he see?
26. Craig needs 2 gal of water. How many times will he need to fill an 8-oz cup to get the water he needs?

Test Prep

CUMULATIVE
CHAPTERS 1–21

Choose the best answer.

1. What is the number 7,359 rounded to the nearest hundred?

A 7,000

B 7,300

C 7,400

D 8,000

E Not Here

2. Four people each bought 6 cans of soup in different stores. Abel paid $4.20. Bethany paid $0.69 a can. Cathy's cans cost $8.64 a dozen. David paid $0.89 a can. Who got the best buy?

F Abel **G** Bethany

H Cathy **J** David

3. Which number completes the pattern?

$3{,}600 \div 12 = 300$

$360 \div 12 = 30$

$36 \div 12 = 3$

$3.6 \div 12 = \square$

A 0.03 **B** 0.3

C 3.0 **D** 30

4. Mr. Tobin had $20. He spent $6.25 on lunch. Which expression shows the amount of money that Mr. Tobin had left?

F $\$20.00 + \$6.25$

G $\$20.00 - \$6.25$

H $\$20.00 \times \$6.25$

J $\$20.00 \div \$6.25$

5. In 100 spins, which color will the pointer probably point to the most number of times?

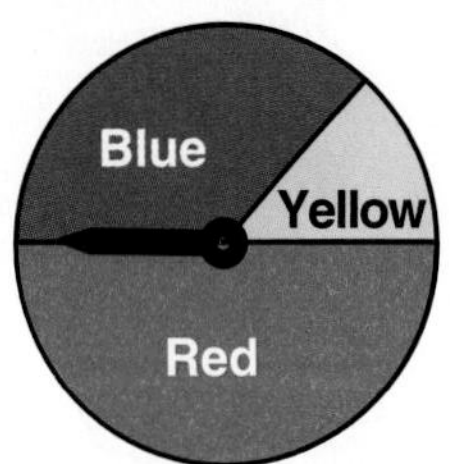

A red **B** blue

C yellow **D** green

6. Which fraction is the simplest form of $\frac{4}{6}$?

F $\frac{2}{3}$ **G** $\frac{2}{6}$

H $\frac{4}{3}$ **J** $\frac{4}{10}$

7. What is $2\frac{1}{3}$ rounded to the nearest whole number?

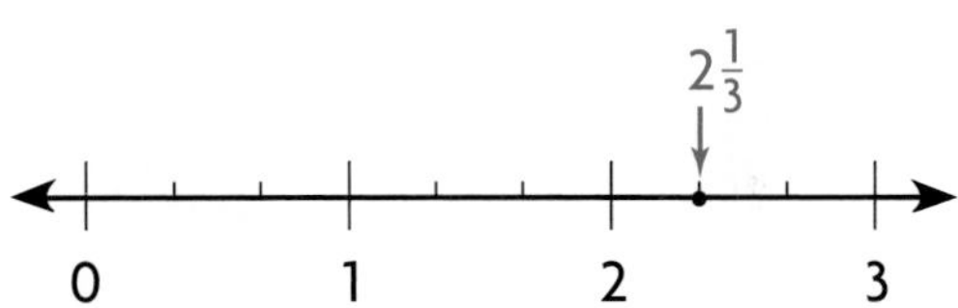

A 2 **B** $2\frac{1}{2}$

C 3 **D** $3\frac{1}{3}$

8. A group of people left on a hike at 10:15 A.M. They returned 5 hours later. What time did the hikers return?

F 5:15 A.M.

G 3:15 A.M.

H 2:15 P.M.

J 3:15 P.M.

22 MULTIPLYING FRACTIONS

SOCIAL STUDIES LINK

A *hectare* is a metric unit for measuring area. It is approximately equal to 2.47 acres.

Problem-Solving Activity

How Much Is Part of a Part?

In many communities, children inherit equal shares of their parents' farm.

Grandma and Grandpa

Child 1: 1 2 3
Child 2: 1 2 3 4
Child 3: 1 2 3 4 5 6
Child 4: 1 2

Use the family tree. Suppose Grandpa had a farm that measured 12 acres by 12 acres. He divided the farm equally among his 4 children. Then each child divided Grandpa's part of the farm equally among his children.

YOU WILL NEED: grid paper, colored markers

Draw a diagram of Grandpa's farm on grid paper.

- On the diagram, show how much land each child inherited.
- Then show how much land each grandchild inherited.
- Write each child's and grandchild's part as a fraction of the original farm.

DID YOU

- ✓ draw a diagram?
- ✓ show how much land each child and grandchild inherited?
- ✓ write each part as a fraction of the original farm?

LESSON 1

Multiplying Fractions and Whole Numbers

Why learn this? You can tell how many are in part of a group, such as the number of roses in a vase of mixed flowers.

Connie is using 16 flowers to make an arrangement. Of the 16 flowers, $\frac{3}{8}$ are roses. How many roses are in her arrangement?

$\frac{3}{8}$ of $16 = n$

MODEL

You can draw a picture to show $\frac{3}{8}$ of 16.

Step 1

Use circles to show the total number of flowers.

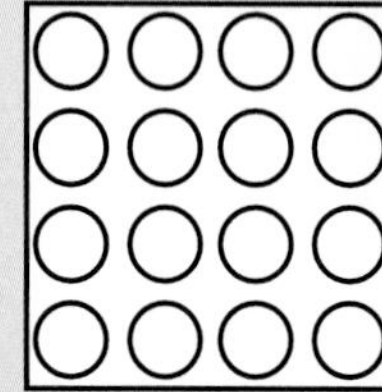

Step 2

Separate the circles into 8 equal-size groups.

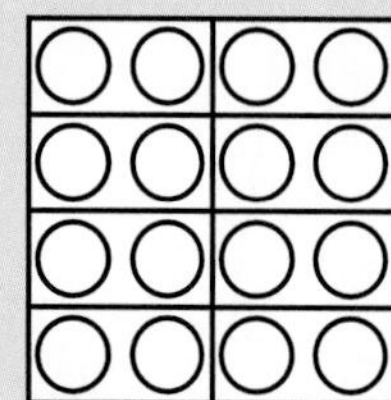

Step 3

Shade 3 of the 8 groups, or $\frac{3}{8}$ of the total.

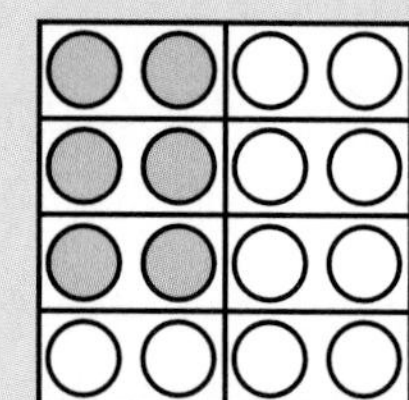

So, $n = 6$.

So, there are 6 roses in Connie's flower arrangement.

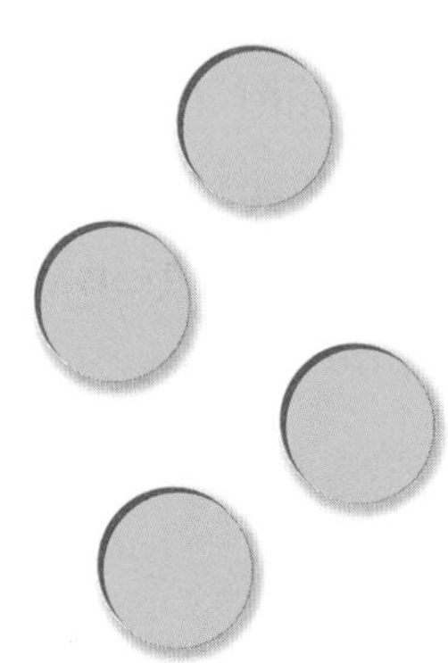

Talk About It CRITICAL THINKING

- Why were the circles separated into 8 groups?
- How can you use the picture to show $\frac{1}{8}$ of 16?

You can multiply fractions instead of drawing pictures.

MODEL

What is $\frac{1}{4} \times 16$?

Step 1

Write the whole number as a fraction.

$\frac{1}{4} \times \frac{16}{1}$ **Think:** $16 = \frac{16}{1}$

Step 2

Multiply the numerators. Multiply the denominators.

$\frac{1 \times 16}{4 \times 1} = \frac{16}{4}$

Step 3

Write the answer in simplest form.

$\frac{16 \div 4}{4 \div 4} = \frac{4}{1} = 4$

- How can you rewrite the problem to show 16 groups of $\frac{1}{4}$?

▶ CHECK

Write a number sentence for each picture.

1.  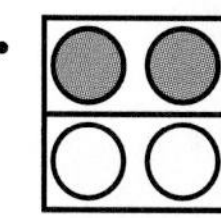

2. 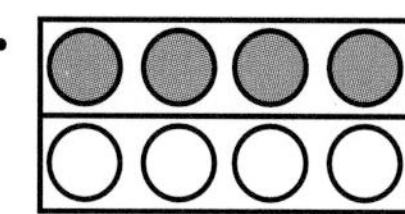

3. 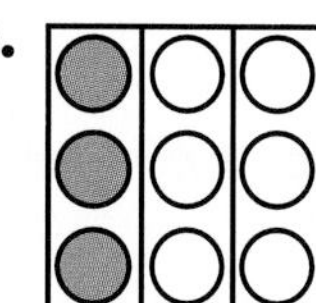

4. Draw a picture to show $\frac{1}{4}$ of 20.

5. Draw a picture to show $\frac{1}{5}$ of 15.

▶ PRACTICE

Write a number sentence for each picture.

6.  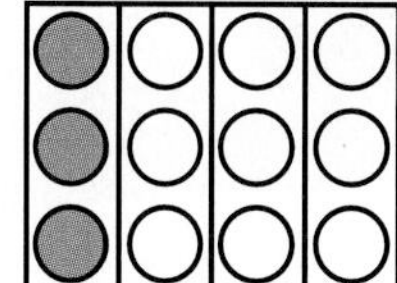

7. 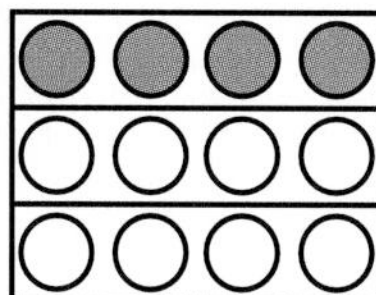

8. 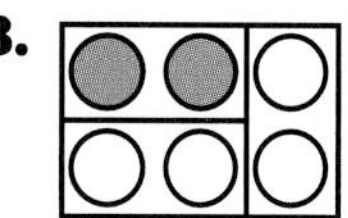

Find the product.

9. $\frac{3}{5} \times 25 = n$
10. $\frac{2}{3} \times 18 = n$
11. $\frac{2}{9} \times 18 = n$
12. $\frac{2}{3} \times 6 = n$
13. $16 \times \frac{7}{8} = n$
14. $20 \times \frac{2}{5} = n$
15. $14 \times \frac{5}{7} = n$
16. $30 \times \frac{5}{6} = n$

Technology Link

In ***Mighty Math Number Heroes***, the game *Fraction Fireworks* challenges you to multiply fractions by whole numbers.
Use Grow Slide Level V.

Problem Solving • Mixed Applications

17. Jason has 12 pairs of pants. Of the pants, $\frac{2}{3}$ are blue jeans. How many of Jason's pants are blue jeans?

18. Tod planted crops on 3 acres one year, 7 acres the next year, and 11 acres the 3rd year. What is the average number of acres planted over the 3-year period?

19. **Measurement** Ann has $\frac{5}{8}$ yard of red fabric. She needs $\frac{3}{4}$ yard to make a top. How much more fabric does she need?

20. **Write a problem** about the 30 students in Mr. Walker's class. Multiply by a fraction to find out how many are in a group.

Mixed Review and Test Prep

Rename the fractions, using the LCM as the denominator. (pages 278–279)

21. $\frac{1}{2}, \frac{1}{3}, \frac{1}{6}$
22. $\frac{2}{5}, \frac{4}{5}, \frac{2}{3}$
23. $\frac{3}{4}, \frac{2}{3}, \frac{5}{6}$

Choose the letter of the equivalent measure. (pages 374–375)

24. 10 c = __?__ **A** 5 pt **B** 2 pt **C** 4 pt **D** 3 pt

25. 1 pt = __?__ **F** 32 fl oz **G** 8 fl oz **H** 10 fl oz **J** 16 fl oz

MORE PRACTICE page H109

Multiplying a Fraction by a Fraction

You will investigate how to multiply two fractions.

Dan read $\frac{2}{3}$ of his favorite author's books.

Scott has read $\frac{1}{4}$ of the books that Dan read. What part of the author's books has Scott read?

$\frac{1}{4}$ of $\frac{2}{3} = n$

EXPLORE

Use paper folding, and color the parts to make a model of the problem. Find the product.

MATERIALS: paper, ruler, and 2 different-colored pencils or markers

MODEL

$\frac{1}{4} \times \frac{2}{3} = n$

Step 1
Fold the paper vertically into 3 equal parts. Color 2 parts to represent $\frac{2}{3}$.

Step 2
Fold the paper horizontally into fourths so that each of the thirds is divided into 4 equal parts.

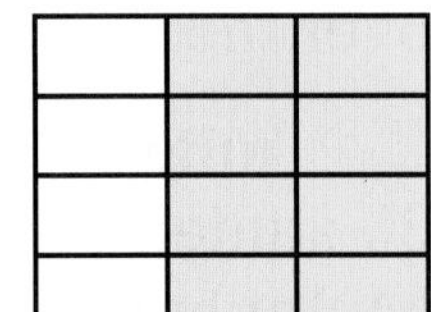

Step 3
Use the other color to shade 1 of the fourths. The area in which the shading overlaps shows the product.

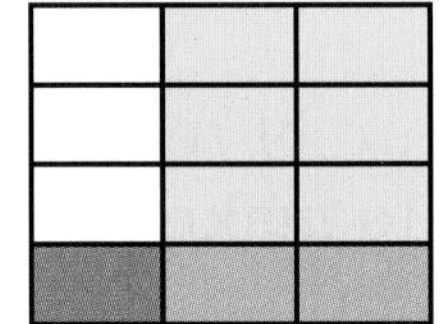

REMEMBER:

You can follow these steps when multiplying a decimal by a decimal:

Find 0.1×0.5.

Use a 10-by-10 grid and shade 5 of the columns to show 0.5. Then shade 1 row, or 0.1.

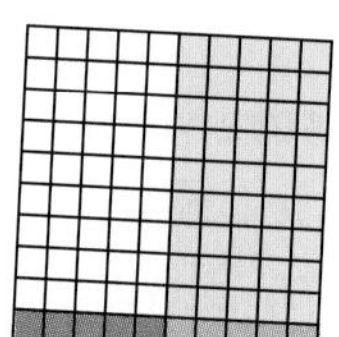

The area in which the shading overlaps shows the product, 0.05.

Record

Record the product, and answer the question in the problem above. How does your model show part of a part?

Talk About It Is the product of $\frac{1}{4}$ and $\frac{2}{3}$ greater than or less than each of the factors? Explain how you know.

▶ TRY THIS

1. Make a paper-folding model to find the product of $\frac{1}{3}$ and $\frac{3}{4}$.
2. **Write About It** How does the product of $\frac{1}{3}$ and $\frac{3}{4}$ compare with each of the factors? Why do you think this is so?

Technology Link

You can multiply fractions by using E-Lab, Activity 22. Available on CD-ROM and on the Internet at **www.hbschool.com/elab**

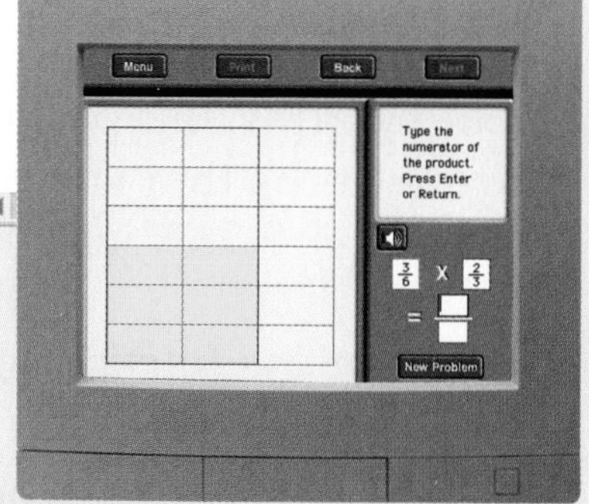

▶ PRACTICE

Make a paper-folding model to find the product.

3. $\frac{1}{5} \times \frac{1}{2} = n$ **4.** $\frac{1}{4} \times \frac{1}{3} = n$ **5.** $\frac{2}{3} \times \frac{1}{3} = n$ **6.** $\frac{2}{3} \times \frac{1}{4} = n$

Find the amount of each ingredient to cut the recipe in half.

Peanut Molasses Cookies

$\frac{1}{4}$ cup shortening	$\frac{1}{2}$ teaspoon salt
$\frac{3}{4}$ cup peanut butter	$\frac{2}{3}$ cup molasses
$\frac{1}{4}$ cup brown sugar	$\frac{1}{2}$ teaspoon vanilla
2 eggs	2 tablespoons milk
$\frac{1}{3}$ teaspoon baking soda	1 cup flour

7. shortening **8.** peanut butter **9.** brown sugar **10.** egg **11.** baking soda

12. salt **13.** molasses **14.** vanilla **15.** milk **16.** flour

Problem Solving • Mixed Applications

17. Time Richard spent $\frac{2}{3}$ hour with his dog. He spent $\frac{1}{4}$ of that time walking the dog. What part of an hour did he spend walking the dog?

18. Measurement Melissa mixed $\frac{1}{4}$ gallon of blue paint, $\frac{3}{8}$ gallon of white paint, and $\frac{1}{2}$ gallon of yellow paint. How much paint did she mix?

19. Compare Fatima bought silk fabric to make presents for her family. She used $\frac{1}{2}$ yard to make a scarf, $\frac{5}{8}$ yard to make a tie, and $\frac{1}{4}$ yard to make a hair bow. Which item required the most silk?

20. Reasoning Super Cineplex has 16 movie theaters. Each theater shows a different movie. Each movie has 7 showings per day on Saturday and Sunday. How many showings are there in one weekend?

MORE PRACTICE page H109

LESSON 3

More About Multiplying a Fraction by a Fraction

Why learn this? You can find a part of a part, such as a fraction of a part of the herb plants.

Lynn bought plants at a nursery. Of the plants, $\frac{3}{5}$ were herbs. She planted $\frac{1}{2}$ of the herbs in her backyard. What part of the plants Lynn bought were herbs that she planted in the backyard?

$\frac{1}{2} \times \frac{3}{5} = n$

You can use fraction squares to multiply fractions.

MODEL

Step 1

Show fifths of the square. Shade $\frac{3}{5}$ yellow.

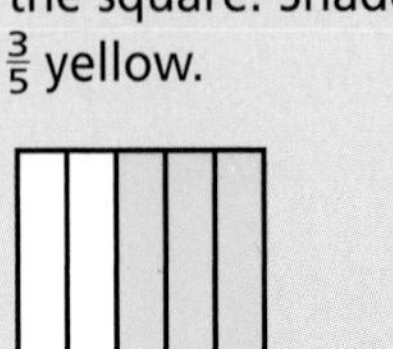

Step 2

Show halves of the square.

Step 3

Shade $\frac{1}{2}$ blue. Three of 10 parts are both yellow and blue, or green.

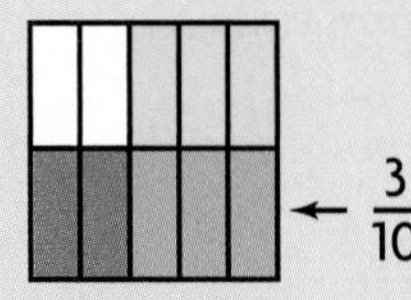

$\leftarrow \frac{3}{10}$

So, $n = \frac{3}{10}$.

So, $\frac{3}{10}$ of the plants were herbs planted in the backyard.

SCIENCE LINK

Herbs have been used for many years as medicines. Herbs have delicious flavors and aromas, but they are not vegetables. If you plant 10 herbs, $\frac{1}{2}$ spearmint and $\frac{1}{2}$ rosemary, then later you pick $\frac{1}{2}$ of the spearmint, how much of the herb garden did you pick?

Talk About It

- How much of the square is shaded by both colors?
- How does shading help you find the product?

You can also find the product of two fractions by multiplying the numerators and the denominators.

EXAMPLE

What is $\frac{1}{2}$ of $\frac{2}{3}$?

Think: $\frac{1}{2} \times \frac{2}{3} = n$

Multiply.

$\frac{1}{2} \times \frac{2}{3} = \frac{1 \times 2}{2 \times 3} = \frac{2}{6}$

Simplify.

$\frac{2 \div 2}{6 \div 2} = \frac{1}{3}$, or $n = \frac{1}{3}$.

REMEMBER:

A fraction is in *simplest form* when the GCF of the numerator and denominator is 1.

CRITICAL THINKING How does the product $\frac{1}{3}$ show that you are finding part of a part when you multiply fractions?

▶ CHECK

Write a number sentence for the picture.

1. 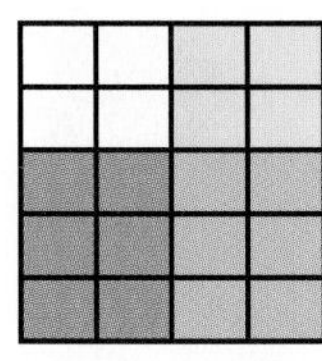

2. 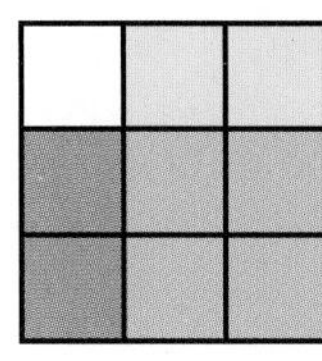

3. 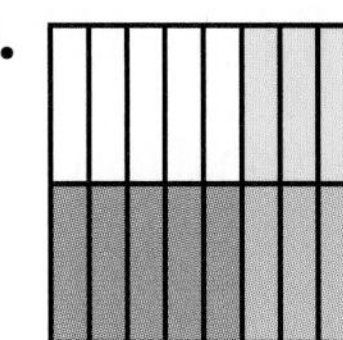

4. 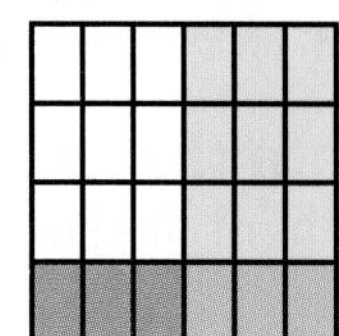

▶ PRACTICE

Draw fraction squares to find the product.

5. $\frac{1}{4} \times \frac{1}{3} = n$ **6.** $\frac{3}{4} \times \frac{2}{3} = n$ **7.** $\frac{2}{5} \times \frac{1}{2} = n$ **8.** $\frac{1}{3} \times \frac{2}{3} = n$

Multiply. Write the answer in simplest form.

9. $\frac{1}{4} \times \frac{1}{2} = n$ **10.** $\frac{4}{5} \times \frac{1}{5} = n$ **11.** $\frac{2}{5} \times \frac{3}{7} = n$ **12.** $\frac{3}{8} \times \frac{2}{3} = n$

13. $\frac{1}{8} \times \frac{2}{3} = n$ **14.** $\frac{1}{5} \times \frac{5}{12} = n$ **15.** $\frac{3}{4} \times \frac{3}{8} = n$ **16.** $\frac{3}{10} \times \frac{1}{6} = n$

17. $\frac{2}{9} \times \frac{3}{9} = n$ **18.** $\frac{2}{3} \times \frac{5}{6} = n$ **19.** $\frac{2}{15} \times \frac{3}{4} = n$ **20.** $\frac{3}{7} \times \frac{2}{9} = n$

21. $\frac{7}{10} \times \frac{2}{3} = n$ **22.** $\frac{1}{3} \times \frac{4}{9} = n$ **23.** $\frac{1}{6} \times \frac{4}{8} = n$ **24.** $\frac{5}{8} \times \frac{2}{5} = n$

Problem Solving • Mixed Applications

25. Brian has a $\frac{7}{8}$-yard-long piece of plywood. He needs to use $\frac{1}{2}$ of the plywood to make a plaque. What part of a yard will he use?

26. Time Grace worked $\frac{3}{4}$ hour on her homework. Leah worked $\frac{2}{3}$ hour on hers. Who spent more time on homework?

27. Measurement A recipe calls for 2 cups milk. Marion has 12 fluid ounces of milk. How much more milk does she need?

28. **Write a problem** in which you multiply a fraction by a fraction.

Mixed Review and Test Prep

Write each fraction in simplest form. (pages 296–297)

29. $\frac{9}{12}$ **30.** $\frac{10}{15}$ **31.** $\frac{6}{12}$ **32.** $\frac{15}{18}$

Choose the letter of the correct sum in simplest form. (pages 356–357)

33. $1\frac{1}{2} + 3\frac{5}{6} = n$ **A** $5\frac{2}{6}$ **B** $4\frac{8}{6}$ **C** $5\frac{1}{3}$ **D** $4\frac{1}{3}$

34. $5\frac{3}{5} + 2\frac{9}{10} = n$ **F** $8\frac{1}{2}$ **G** $8\frac{5}{10}$ **H** $\frac{85}{10}$ **J** $7\frac{1}{2}$

MORE PRACTICE page H109

Multiplying Fractions and Mixed Numbers

Why learn this? You can find a fractional part of recipe ingredients and lengths of material, such as flannel board or wood.

Shelly used $1\frac{1}{3}$ yards of white felt to make a flannel board. She used $\frac{1}{4}$ as much red felt to make numbers for the flannel board. How much red felt did she use?

$\frac{1}{4} \times 1\frac{1}{3} = n$

You can use fraction squares to multiply.

MODEL

Step 1

Show 2 whole squares. Divide each square into thirds. Shade 1 whole square and $\frac{1}{3}$ of the other square yellow, so that $1\frac{1}{3}$, or $\frac{4}{3}$, are shaded.

Step 2

Divide the squares into fourths.

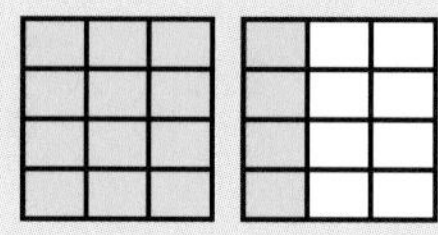

Step 3

Shade $\frac{1}{4}$ of each square blue. Each whole has 12 parts. Four of the 12 parts are both yellow and blue, or green.

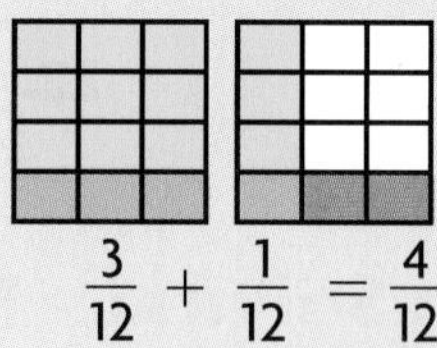

$\frac{3}{12} + \frac{1}{12} = \frac{4}{12}$

So, Shelly used $\frac{4}{12}$, or $\frac{1}{3}$ yard of red felt.

You can also find the product of a fraction and a mixed number by multiplying.

Multiply. $\frac{3}{4} \times 1\frac{1}{2} = n$

REMEMBER:

To rename a fraction greater than 1 as a *mixed number*, picture the parts. Then put them together.

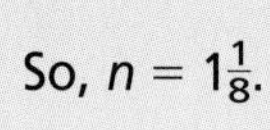

$\frac{3}{2}$ $1\frac{1}{2}$

MODEL

Step 1

Rename the mixed number as a fraction greater than 1 by multiplying the whole number by the denominator and adding the numerator. Put the result over the denominator.

$1\frac{1}{2} = \frac{(1 \times 2) + 1}{2} = \frac{2 + 1}{2} = \frac{3}{2}$

So, another name for $1\frac{1}{2}$ is $\frac{3}{2}$.

Step 2

Since $1\frac{1}{2} = \frac{3}{2}$, multiply $\frac{3}{4}$ by $\frac{3}{2}$. Multiply the numerators. Multiply the denominators.

$\frac{3}{4} \times \frac{3}{2} = \frac{3 \times 3}{4 \times 2} = \frac{9}{8}$

Step 3

Write the product as a mixed number in simplest form.

$\frac{9}{8} = 1\frac{1}{8}$

So, $n = 1\frac{1}{8}$.

▶ CHECK

Write a number sentence for the picture.

1. 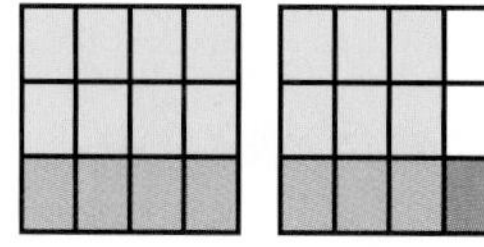

2. 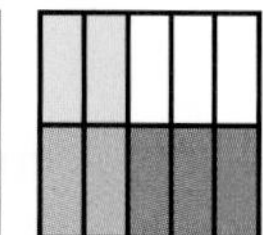

3. 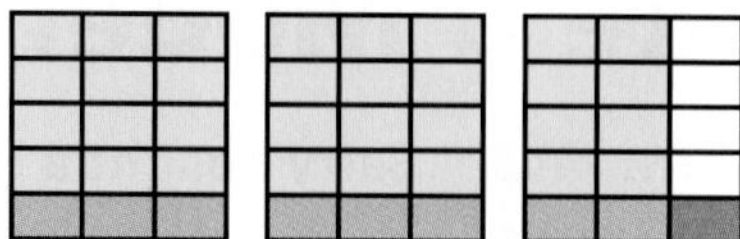

Draw fraction squares to help you find the product.

4. $\frac{1}{3} \times 1\frac{1}{5} = n$ 5. $\frac{1}{2} \times 1\frac{2}{3} = n$ 6. $\frac{1}{2} \times 3\frac{2}{5} = n$

▶ PRACTICE

Draw fraction squares to help you find the product.

7. $\frac{3}{4} \times 1\frac{1}{6} = n$ 8. $\frac{2}{5} \times 3\frac{2}{3} = n$ 9. $\frac{2}{3} \times 2\frac{2}{5} = n$

10. $\frac{1}{4} \times 2\frac{1}{4} = n$ 11. $\frac{3}{5} \times 1\frac{1}{2} = n$ 12. $\frac{1}{3} \times 3\frac{2}{5} = n$

Multiply. Write the answer in simplest form.

13. $\frac{1}{4} \times 2\frac{1}{2} = n$ 14. $\frac{1}{2} \times 1\frac{1}{4} = n$ 15. $\frac{1}{2} \times 2\frac{2}{3} = n$

16. $\frac{2}{3} \times 1\frac{1}{3} = n$ 17. $\frac{1}{4} \times 1\frac{2}{3} = n$ 18. $\frac{2}{3} \times 3\frac{1}{4} = n$

19. $\frac{5}{6} \times 1\frac{1}{4} = n$ 20. $\frac{2}{5} \times 2\frac{1}{3} = n$ 21. $\frac{3}{4} \times 2\frac{1}{4} = n$

22. $\frac{1}{6} \times 1\frac{4}{8} = n$ 23. $\frac{2}{7} \times 2\frac{4}{5} = n$ 24. $\frac{1}{4} \times 3\frac{1}{2} = n$

Problem Solving • Mixed Applications

25. **Drama** Of 24 actors who auditioned for the play, $\frac{2}{3}$ were chosen. How many actors were chosen for the play?

26. Lauren had $2\frac{1}{2}$ dozen apples. She used $\frac{1}{2}$ of them to make apple pies. How many dozen apples did she use in the pies?

27. **Consumer** Felicia has \$50.00. CDs cost \$13.99 each. How many CDs can Felicia buy?

28. **Measurement** Pang used a 3.6-meter board to make 4 shelves of equal length. How long was each shelf?

29. Cary used $1\frac{1}{2}$ yards of red ribbon, $2\frac{1}{4}$ yards of blue ribbon, and $1\frac{2}{3}$ yards of white ribbon. How many yards of ribbon did she use?

30. **Art** Lou and Leslie had $\frac{4}{5}$ package of glitter to use for their art project. They used $\frac{1}{5}$ package. How much glitter is left?

31. **Write a problem** in which you multiply a fraction by a mixed number.

LESSON CONTINUES

MORE PRACTICE page H110

Problem-Solving Strategy: Make a Model

▶ **THE PROBLEM** Barry bought a board that was $2\frac{3}{4}$ yards long to build a bookcase. He bought a board $\frac{1}{2}$ as long to build a shelf for his sports trophies. How much wood did he buy to make the shelf for his trophies?

UNDERSTAND

- What are you asked to find?
- What information will you use?
- Is there information you will not use? If so, what?

PLAN

- What strategy can you use to solve the problem?

You can *make a model* to find how much wood Barry bought to build the shelf.

SOLVE

- What model will you make to solve the problem?

You can draw fraction squares.

Draw 3 squares, and divide them into fourths. Shade 2 whole squares and $\frac{3}{4}$ of the third square yellow. Divide the squares into halves. Shade $\frac{1}{2}$ of each square blue. Now 11 parts are shaded both blue and yellow, or green. Each whole has 8 parts. So, the total is $\frac{11}{8}$, or $1\frac{3}{8}$.

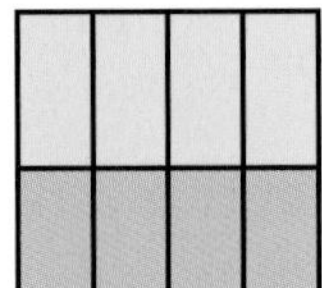 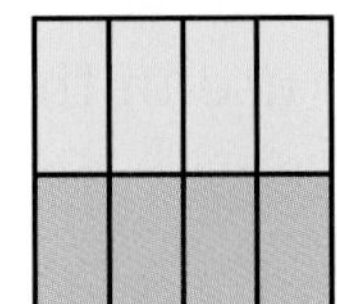 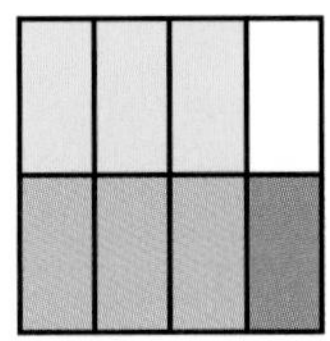

So, Barry bought $1\frac{3}{8}$ yards of wood to make the shelf.

LOOK BACK

- How can you decide if your answer is reasonable?
- What other strategy could you use?

▶ PRACTICE

Make a model to solve.

1. Cole's dresser is $5\frac{1}{4}$ feet wide. His bookcase is $\frac{2}{3}$ as wide as his dresser. How wide is his bookcase?

2. The chickens laid $6\frac{1}{4}$ dozen eggs. The farmer sold $\frac{2}{5}$ of them. How many dozen eggs were left?

3. Meg made a square design. She colored $\frac{1}{4}$ of the square blue, $\frac{1}{8}$ yellow, and $\frac{1}{8}$ green. She left $\frac{1}{2}$ of the square white. What does her design look like?

4. Carl and some friends are in line to buy tickets to the school play. Carl is next to Bill. Sam is ahead of Carl. Bill is between Carl and Lana. Angela is before Sam. Who is last in line?

Mixed Applications

Solve.

CHOOSE a strategy and a tool.

- Find a Pattern
- Guess and Check
- Make a Model
- Write a Number Sentence
- Work Backward

Paper/Pencil

Calculator

Hands-On

Mental Math

5. Mia's pencil is 11 cm long. Jim's pencil is 1.2 dm long. Whose pencil is longer? How much longer?

6. The farmer's market sells apples for $0.28 a pound. If the market sold 69.5 pounds, how much was earned?

7. Ray had $18.79 in his wallet. He bought 2 magazines for $3.95 each and a book for $6.75. A package of pens costs $1.59. How many packages of pens can Ray buy?

8. Alice and Kyle are playing a number game. Alice asks Kyle to choose a number and multiply it by 3. Then Kyle adds 6, divides by 9, and subtracts 5. The total is 4. What number did Kyle start with?

9. Write the decimal for this model.

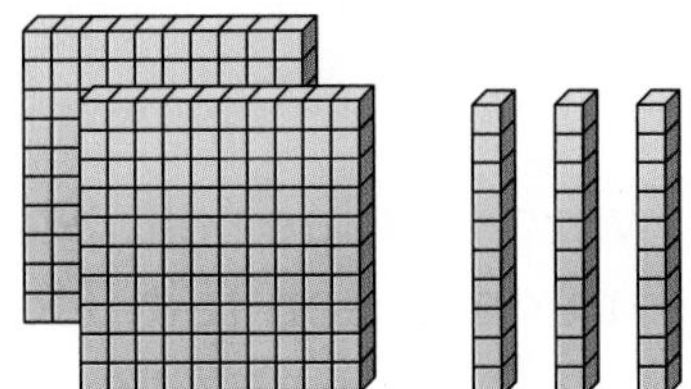

10. Holly worked in her garden 20 minutes on Monday, 30 minutes on Tuesday, 45 minutes on Wednesday, and 65 minutes on Thursday. If the pattern continues, for how many minutes will she work in her garden on Friday? on Saturday?

11. Rachel has $4.75 in coins. She has 6 dimes and twice as many quarters. The rest are nickels. How many of each coin does she have?

MORE PRACTICE page H110

CHAPTER 22 Review/Test

CHECK Understanding

Write a number sentence for the picture. (pages 388–389, 392–393)

1.

2. 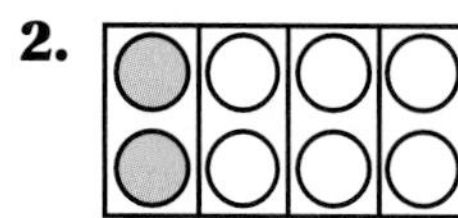

3.

4.

5. 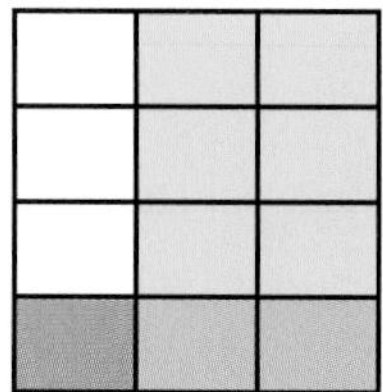

6.

7. 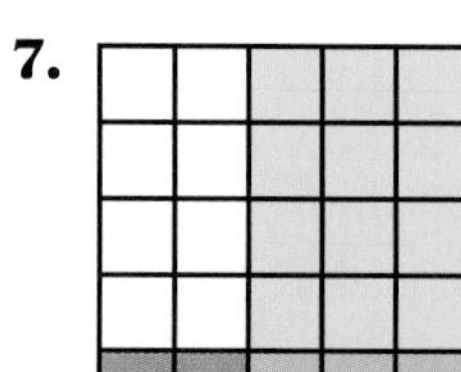

8. 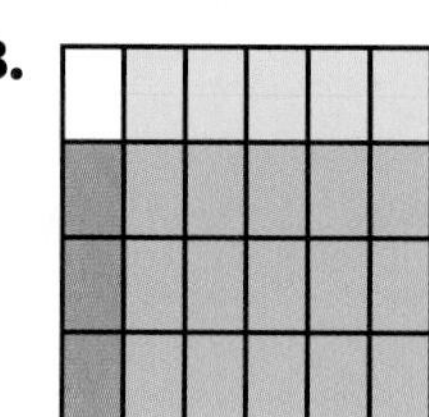

CHECK Skills

Multiply. Write the answer in simplest form. (pages 388–389, 392–393)

9. $\frac{1}{4} \times 28 = n$

10. $\frac{2}{5} \times 15 = n$

11. $21 \times \frac{2}{7} = n$

12. $16 \times \frac{5}{8} = n$

13. $\frac{1}{4} \times \frac{3}{8} = n$

14. $\frac{2}{3} \times \frac{5}{6} = n$

15. $\frac{4}{7} \times \frac{3}{8} = n$

16. $\frac{5}{9} \times \frac{4}{6} = n$

17. $\frac{1}{2} \times 1\frac{2}{3} = n$

18. $\frac{3}{4} \times 2\frac{1}{6} = n$

19. $\frac{1}{3} \times 3\frac{1}{3} = n$

20. $\frac{1}{4} \times 1\frac{1}{2} = n$

CHECK Problem Solving

Solve. (pages 396–397)

CHOOSE a strategy and a tool.

- Act It Out
- Write a Number Sentence
- Guess and Check
- Make a Model
- Find a Pattern

Paper/Pencil

Calculator

Hands-On

Mental Math

21. Paul had a board $4\frac{1}{2}$ feet long. He used $\frac{2}{3}$ of it to make a shelf. How long was the shelf?

22. Beth has $\frac{7}{8}$ yard of blue felt. She needs $\frac{2}{3}$ as much green felt. How much green felt does she need?

23. There were 70 students who wore school T-shirts on Monday. There were 75 on Tuesday and 85 on Wednesday. If this pattern continues, how many students will wear school T-shirts on Friday?

24. Buck has twice as many quarters as dimes. He has 5 fewer nickels than quarters. He has no pennies. He has 120 coins in all. How many of each coin does Buck have?

Test Prep

CUMULATIVE CHAPTERS 1–22

Choose the best answer.

1. $4 \times 3 \times 6 =$

A 12

B 18

C 60

D 74

E Not Here

2. Which fraction has the same value as the underlined digit?

$7.1\underline{3}$

F $\frac{3}{1}$ **G** $\frac{3}{10}$

H $\frac{3}{100}$ **J** $\frac{3}{1,000}$

3. The table shows the boxes of cookies sold by the Scouts.

SCOUT COOKIE SALES	
Name	Boxes Sold
Samantha	12
Shelly	20
Ashley	18
Lennie	16

Which of the following is a reasonable interval to graph the data?

A 2 **B** 10

C 15 **D** 25

4. $2.3 \times 10 =$

F 23

G 2.3

H 0.23

J 0.023

5. There were 238 girls at the first day of basketball camp. The girls will be divided into groups of 20 girls each. Which of the following is a reasonable estimate of the number of groups there will be?

A 30

B 12

C 20

D 24

6. What symbol makes the following number sentence true?

$\frac{1}{3} \bullet \frac{1}{8}$

F $<$ **G** $>$

H $=$ **J** $\approx$

7. Harry leaves for school each day at 7:35 A.M. He arrives at 8:10 A.M. How long does it take Harry to get to school?

A 10 min

B 20 min

C 30 min

D 35 min

E Not Here

8. $\frac{1}{2} \times 6 =$

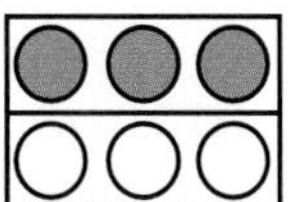

F 2 **G** 3

H 6 **J** 12

CHAPTERS 19–22

ROMAN MEASUREMENTS

PURPOSE To measure the ancient units that became customary linear measures

YOU WILL NEED ruler, yardstick, string

Compare customary units to the ancient Roman measures. With a partner, measure the length of your thumb, the length of your foot, and the distance from your nose to the tip of the middle finger of your outstretched arm. Record your measurements in customary units and in Roman measures.

The Romans used the *uncia* for the length of a thumb. The English word *inch* comes from that. Twelve uncia equals 1 foot; 3 feet made a yard. Do 12 of your uncia equal one of your feet?

Measure an adult. How can you express the measurements in Roman units?

Backpack Weight

PURPOSE To estimate—then verify—weight in pounds and ounces

YOU WILL NEED a full backpack, books, a scale that weighs in pounds

Have you ever felt weighed down by your studies? Weigh your backpack and see why.

First, estimate how much your backpack weighs. Then weigh it on a scale. How many pounds? How many ounces? How close was your estimate?

Your Joke Is How Long?

PURPOSE To change seconds to fractions of a minute

YOU WILL NEED books of jokes, timer, pencils, markers

Play this game in a small group. Each person will tell or read aloud a joke and record the time to tell it in seconds. Figure out what fraction of a minute your joke takes. With your group, add all the fractions to find how long the joke show lasts. Do the jokes add up to more than a minute? Then decide: Is the funniest joke the longest one?

HOME NOTE Ask parents or other adults if they remember any jokes from when they were kids. You might be surprised at how funny they are!

Adding and Subtracting Fractions

LaToya is carefully mixing paints for her art project. To make her favorite green color, she mixes $\frac{2}{3}$ ounce of blue and $\frac{2}{7}$ ounce of yellow. How many ounces of green paint does she make?

- Using a calculator can help you add and subtract fractions.

MATERIALS:
Casio fx 55, or another fraction calculator

Find $\frac{2}{3} + \frac{2}{7}$.

Press: **Display:**

    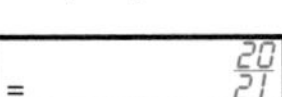 

So, LaToya makes $\frac{20}{21}$ ounce of green paint.

EXAMPLE

Eric skated $\frac{5}{6}$ mile. He took a break after $\frac{1}{3}$ mile. How far did he skate after his break?

Subtract. $\frac{5}{6} - \frac{1}{3}$

Use the SIMP key to show the difference in simplest form.

Press: **Display:**

         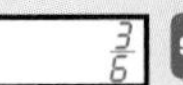  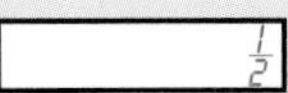

So, Eric skated $\frac{1}{2}$ mile after his break.

▶ PRACTICE

Add or subtract to solve. Write the answer in simplest form.

1. $\frac{2}{3} + \frac{1}{7}$

2. $\frac{1}{4} + \frac{1}{6} + \frac{1}{12}$

3. $\frac{7}{9} - \frac{1}{3}$

4. $\left(\frac{2}{5} - \frac{1}{4}\right) - \frac{1}{20}$

Using a Calculator

5. Linda walks 1 mile to school. She passes one stoplight after $\frac{1}{3}$ mile and another, $\frac{2}{5}$ mile after that. How much farther does she have to walk after her second stoplight?

6. There are 25 students in Mabel's class. Of the students, $\frac{1}{5}$ take French class, $\frac{2}{5}$ take Italian, and the rest take Spanish. How many students take Spanish?

CHAPTERS 19–22

Study Guide and Review

Vocabulary Check

Choose a term from the box to complete each sentence.

VOCABULARY
Celsius
Fahrenheit
precise

1. If you measure an object's length to the nearest sixteenth of an inch, you have made a _?_ measurement. (page 368)

2. Customary units for measuring temperature are called degrees _?_. (page 382)

3. Metric units for measuring temperature are called degrees _?_. (page 382)

Study and Solve

CHAPTER 19

EXAMPLE

$\frac{5}{6} - \frac{1}{3} = n$ — Use the LCD of $\frac{5}{6}$ and $\frac{1}{3}$ (sixths) to change the fractions to like fractions.

$\frac{1}{3} \times \frac{2}{2} = \frac{2}{6}$ — Multiply by $\frac{2}{2}$.

$\frac{5}{6} - \frac{2}{6} = \frac{3}{6}$ — Subtract.

$n = \frac{3}{6} \div \frac{3}{3} = \frac{1}{2}$ — To write the answer in simplest form, divide the numerator and denominator by their GCF, 3.

Estimate the sum or difference. (pages 338–339)

4. $\frac{4}{5} + \frac{2}{9}$
5. $\frac{9}{10} - \frac{3}{5}$

Find the sum or difference. Write the answer in simplest form. (pages 340–345)

6. $\frac{3}{4} + \frac{3}{4} = n$
7. $\frac{7}{8} - \frac{5}{8} = n$
8. $\frac{5}{8} + \frac{7}{12} = n$
9. $\frac{5}{6} + \frac{2}{3} = n$
10. $\frac{9}{10} - \frac{2}{5} = n$
11. $\frac{4}{5} - \frac{1}{3} = n$

Tell whether you would add or subtract to solve the problem. Solve. (pages 346–347)

12. One recipe calls for $\frac{3}{4}$ cup of flour. Another calls for $\frac{2}{3}$ cup of flour. How much more flour is needed for the first recipe?

CHAPTER 20

EXAMPLE

$6\frac{2}{3} + 1\frac{5}{6} = n$ — The fractions are unlike. Use their LCD (sixths) to change them to like fractions.

$\frac{2}{3} + \frac{5}{6} = \frac{4}{6} + \frac{5}{6}$

$\frac{4}{6} + \frac{5}{6} = \frac{9}{6}$ — Add the fractions.

$6 + 1 = 7$ — Add the whole numbers.

$7\frac{9}{6} = 8\frac{3}{6} = 8\frac{1}{2}$ — Write the answer in simplest form.

$n = 8\frac{1}{2}$

Estimate the sum or difference. (pages 354–355)

13. $2\frac{3}{7} + 3\frac{11}{12} = n$ **14.** $4\frac{1}{9} - 1\frac{7}{8} = n$

Find the sum or difference. Write the answer in simplest form. (pages 356–363)

15. $2\frac{1}{4} + 2\frac{1}{2} = n$ **16.** $2\frac{1}{3} + 3\frac{1}{6} = n$

17. $7\frac{3}{4} - 5\frac{1}{2} = n$ **18.** $4\frac{2}{3} - 3\frac{1}{6} = n$

Work backward to solve.

19. Amy's school day is 7 hours long. She spends 5 hours in class. Her lunch break is $1\frac{1}{4}$ hours long. How much time is left for other breaks?

CHAPTER 21

EXAMPLE

Change the unit.

36 in. = __?__ ft

When you change smaller units to larger units, you divide.

Think: 12 in. = 1 ft
Divide 36 by 12.

36 in. = 3 ft

Use a customary ruler to measure the line. (pages 368–369)

20. ______________________________

21. ____________________

Change the unit. (pages 370–377)

22. 12 ft = __?__ yd **23.** 3 qt = __?__ c

24. 2 gal = __?__ qt **25.** 3 lb = __?__ oz

26. 1 mi = __?__ ft **27.** 1 T = __?__ lb

Find the sum or difference. (pages 372–373)

28. 7 ft 4 in. + 3 ft 10 in. **29.** 6 yd 1 ft − 4 yd 2 ft

Write the time for each. (pages 378–379)

30. Start: 7:30 A.M.
2 hr 15 min elapsed time
End: __?__

31. Start: June 4, 5:00 P.M.
__?__ elapsed time
End: June 11, 6:30 P.M.

Find the difference in temperature. (pages 382–383)

32. high 75°F, low 56°F

33. high 12°C, low ⁻4°C

CHAPTER 22

EXAMPLE

$\frac{1}{3} \times 3\frac{1}{3}$ Rename the mixed number as a fraction greater than 1.

$\frac{1}{3} \times \frac{10}{3} = \frac{10}{9}$ Multiply the numerators and denominators.

$\frac{10}{9} = 1\frac{1}{9}$ Write the answer as a mixed number in simplest form.

Multiply. Write the answer in simplest form. (pages 388–395)

34. $16 \times \frac{3}{8} = n$ **35.** $\frac{4}{5} \times \frac{2}{3} = n$

36. $\frac{3}{4} \times \frac{8}{9} = n$ **37.** $\frac{1}{9} \times 6\frac{3}{4} = n$

Solve. (pages 396–397)

38. Ira had $5\frac{1}{2}$ pages of math homework to make up. He did $\frac{1}{2}$ of the work today. How many pages are left?

39. Sue's desk is $2\frac{1}{4}$ feet long. Her little sister's desk is $\frac{5}{6}$ as long as Sue's desk. How long is Sue's little sister's desk?

CHAPTERS 19–22

Performance Assessment

Tasks: Show What You Know

1. Estimate the sum or difference. Explain your methods. (pages 338–339)

$\frac{1}{8} + \frac{5}{9}$ $\frac{9}{10} - \frac{7}{8}$

2. Show and explain each step as you find the sum. Write the answer in simplest form. (pages 356–357)

$2\frac{3}{4} + 4\frac{1}{2}$

3. Determine the elapsed time from 10:30 A.M. to 2:45 P.M. Explain your method. (pages 378–379)

4. Use fraction squares or multiply to find the product. Explain the method you use. Write the answer in simplest form. (pages 394–395)

$\frac{1}{3} \times 3\frac{1}{4}$

Problem Solving

Solve. Explain your method.

CHOOSE a strategy and a tool.

- Draw a Diagram
- Make a Table
- Make a Model
- Work Backward

Paper/Pencil

Calculator

Hands-On

Mental Math

5. In the book club, $\frac{1}{2}$ of the students read sports books, $\frac{1}{4}$ read mysteries, $\frac{1}{8}$ read nature books, and $\frac{1}{8}$ read poetry. If 4 students read nature books, how many students are in the club? (pages 348–349)

6. David spent a total of $2\frac{1}{2}$ hours working in the yard. After raking the leaves, he spent $1\frac{1}{4}$ hours mowing, $\frac{1}{20}$ hour watering, and $\frac{1}{4}$ hour cleaning up. How much time did he spend raking? (pages 360–361)

7. Al gets home at 5:00. He plays for 45 minutes, reads for 60 minutes, helps his father cook dinner for 15 minutes, and eats dinner with his family for 30 minutes. Then he watches TV for 1 hour 30 minutes before going to bed. What time does he go to bed? (pages 380–381)

8. Todd picked $5\frac{1}{2}$ baskets of strawberries. His younger brother, Bo, picked $\frac{2}{3}$ as much as Todd. How many baskets did Bo pick? (pages 396–397)

Cumulative Review

CHAPTERS 1–22

Solve the problem. Then write the letter of the correct answer.

1. Compare. 209,897 ● 210,001

A. $<$ **B.** $>$
C. $=$ **D.** $-$

(pages 12–13)

2. 417×306

A. 2,502
B. 15,012
C. 127,602
D. 1,276,020

(pages 98–101)

3. What is the best interval for this set of data?

10, 14, 8, 12, 18

A. 1 **B.** 2
C. 5 **D.** 10

(pages 158–161)

4. 6 cm = __?__ dm

A. 0.06 **B.** 0.6
C. 60 **D.** 600

(pages 254–257)

5. __?__ mL = 6 L

A. 0.006 **B.** 0.06
C. 600 **D.** 6,000

(pages 254–257)

6. Rename $\frac{23}{7}$ as a mixed number.

A. $\frac{7}{23}$ **B.** $1\frac{2}{7}$

C. 3 **D.** $3\frac{2}{7}$

(pages 272–273)

7. What is the greatest common factor of 16 and 24?

A. 2 **B.** 4
C. 8 **D.** 12

(pages 288–291)

8. What is the least common denominator for $\frac{2}{3}$ and $\frac{3}{4}$?

A. thirds **B.** fourths
C. sevenths **D.** twelfths

(pages 322–323)

For Problems 9–10, choose the correct answer that is in simplest form.

9. $\frac{1}{6} + \frac{1}{2} = n$

A. $n = \frac{1}{8}$ **B.** $n = \frac{1}{4}$

C. $n = \frac{2}{3}$ **D.** $n = \frac{4}{6}$

(pages 342–345)

10. $8\frac{7}{12} - 2\frac{1}{3} = n$

A. $n = 6\frac{1}{4}$ **B.** $n = 6\frac{3}{12}$

C. $n = \frac{75}{12}$ **D.** $n = 6\frac{2}{3}$

(pages 358–359)

11. 5 ft 6 in. − 3 ft 8 in.

A. 1 ft 4 in.
B. 1 ft 8 in.
C. 1 ft 10 in.
D. 2 ft 2 in.

(pages 372–373)

12. Choose the correct answer that is in simplest form.

$\frac{2}{9} \times \frac{3}{9} = n$

A. $n = \frac{2}{27}$

B. $n = \frac{6}{81}$

C. $n = \frac{2}{3}$

D. $n = \frac{81}{6}$

(pages 390–393)

23 PLANE FIGURES AND POLYGONS

HISTORY **LINK**

Ancient Egyptian geometers had to solve problems like accurately measuring fields after a flood. Odd-shaped fields were marked into triangles to make them easier to measure. Our word *geometry* comes from the Greek and means to "measure the earth."

Problem-Solving Activity

Design a Geometry Game

Geometry is all about shapes and how you see them. You will design a game of Geometry Concentration. Use your observation skills to make picture cards and clue cards.

Play Geometry Concentration to test your visual memory.

YOU WILL NEED: 16 index cards, cut in half; triangle dot paper; scissors; glue.

- Draw 16 geometric figures using triangle dot paper.
- Cut out each figure and glue it to a card.
- On another set of cards, write attributes that would give someone clues about your figures.
- Try out your game using the game rules, "How to Play Geometry Concentration."
- Revise your game cards if you like.
- Trade card sets with a classmate and play again.

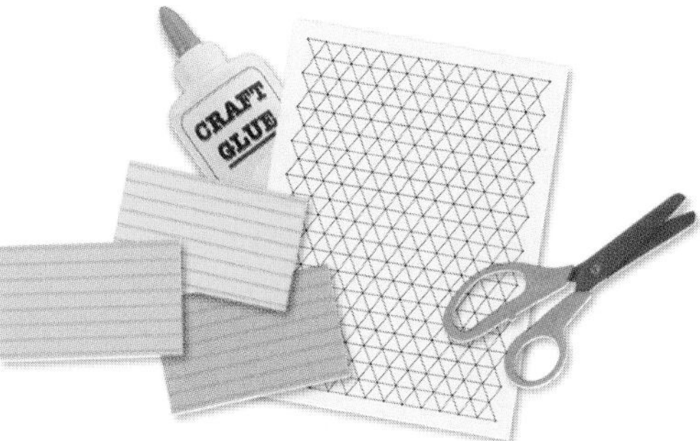

DID YOU

- ✓ make a set of picture cards?
- ✓ make a set of clue cards?
- ✓ try out your game and revise it as needed?
- ✓ trade game cards and play again?

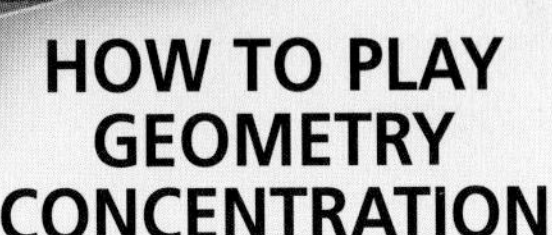

HOW TO PLAY GEOMETRY CONCENTRATION

Shuffle the picture cards and place them face down in a 4 by 4 array.

Shuffle the clue cards and lay them face down in a stack where all the players can reach them.

Play in groups of four. Take turns.

Each player picks a clue card. Turn up a picture card to see if it matches.

If the picture card is a match, you earn a point.

Return the picture card to its place but remember what it showed. You may want to choose it again later in the game.

The player with the most points after all cards are matched wins the game.

I am a quadrilateral.

I have opposite sides that are parallel.

I have at least one right angle.

LESSON 1

Line Relationships

Why learn this? You can identify points and line segments on maps, such as those used by airline navigators, sailors, and astronauts.

VOCABULARY
point
line
line segment
plane
intersecting
perpendicular
parallel

When astronauts explore space, they use geometric ideas. If they want to describe an exact location in space, they identify a geometric point. In the space around you, there are many geometric points.

A **point** identifies a location on an object and in space. It is named by a letter.	B	**point *B***
A **line** is a straight path in a plane. It has no end. It can be named by any two points on the line.	A B	**line *AB*, $\overleftrightarrow{AB}$ or line *BA*, $\overleftrightarrow{BA}$**
A **line segment** is part of a line between two endpoints.	A C	**line segment *CA*, $\overline{CA}$ or line segment *AC*, $\overline{AC}$**
A **plane** is a flat surface with no end. Planes are named by any three points in the plane.	A B C D	**plane *ABC***

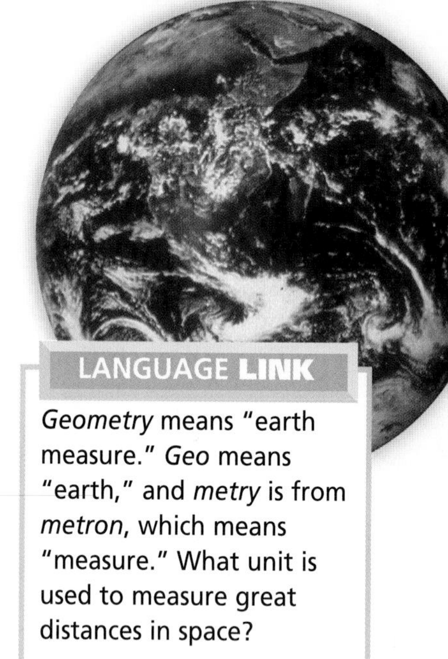

LANGUAGE LINK

Geometry means "earth measure." *Geo* means "earth," and *metry* is from *metron*, which means "measure." What unit is used to measure great distances in space?

Within a plane, lines can have different relationships.

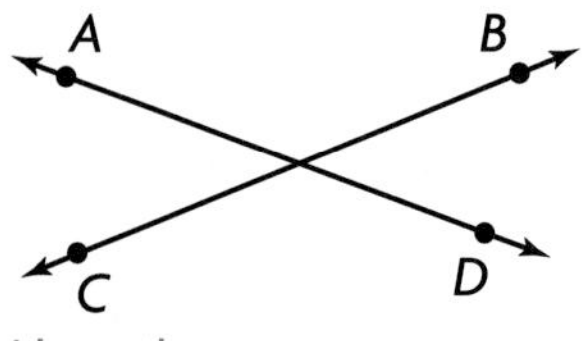

Lines that cross at one point are **intersecting** lines.

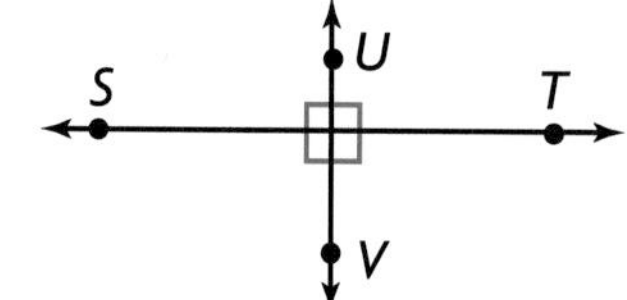

Lines that intersect to form four right angles are **perpendicular** lines.

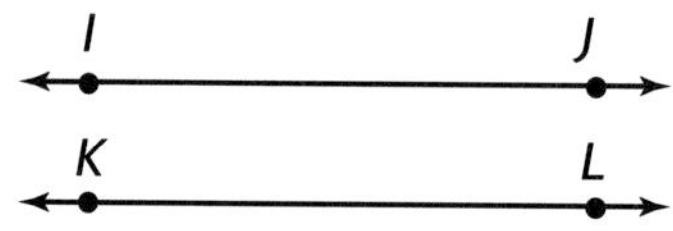

Lines in a plane that never intersect and are the same distance apart at every point are **parallel** lines.

▶ CHECK

1. Are all intersecting lines perpendicular? Explain.
2. How do you know that parallel lines will never intersect?
3. What other line segments can you name that are in the plane *ABC* pictured above but are not drawn?

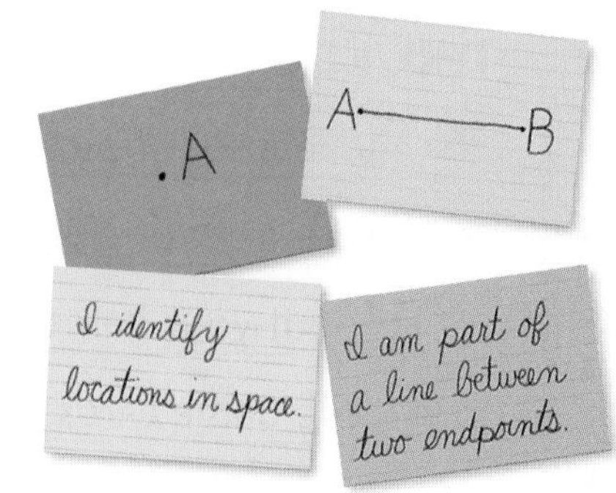

▶ PRACTICE

For Exercises 4–7, use the figure.

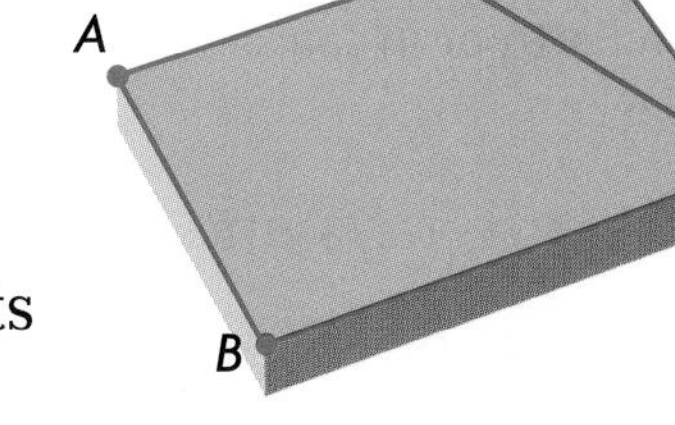

4. Name the point where $\overline{AD}$ and $\overline{CD}$ intersect.

5. Name a line segment on plane ABC that is perpendicular to $\overline{DC}$.

6. Name a line segment on the plane that intersects but is not perpendicular to $\overline{AD}$.

7. Name the line segment that is parallel to $\overline{AD}$.

Identify each line relationship. Write *parallel, perpendicular,* or *intersecting*. Some figures may have more than one answer.

8.

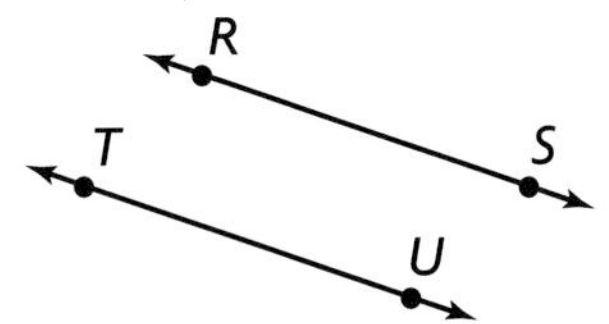

9.

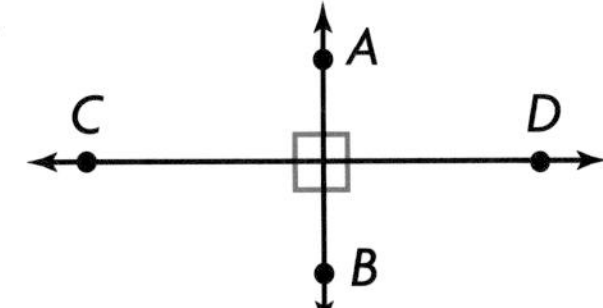

10.

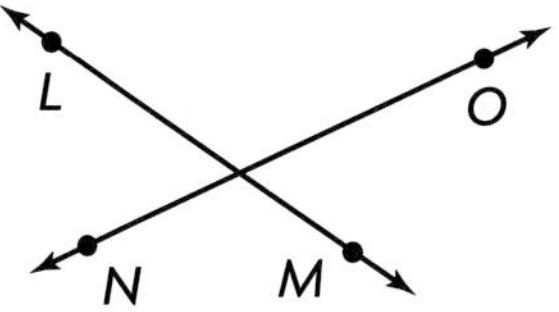

Problem Solving • Mixed Applications

Using Data For Problems 11–12, use the flight navigation chart.

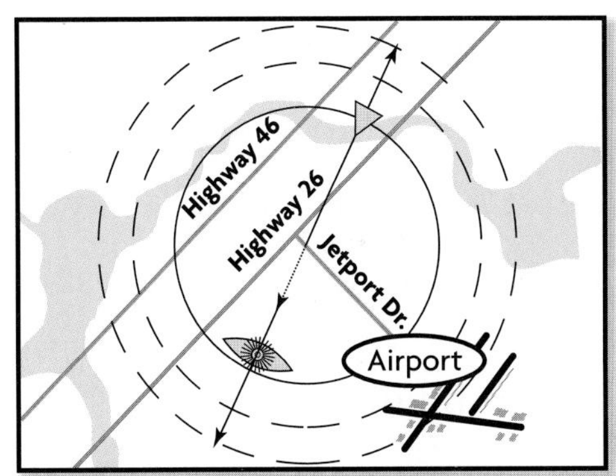

11. Visual Thinking A pilot notices Highway 46 and Highway 26 near the airport. Describe the relationship of these two highways.

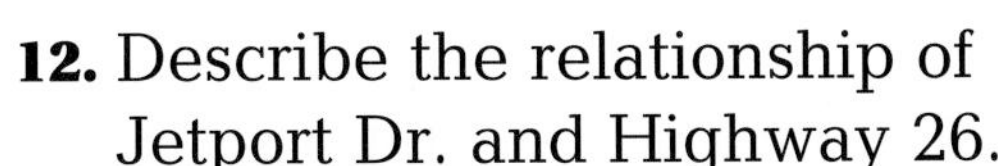

12. Describe the relationship of Jetport Dr. and Highway 26.

13. Measurement Kimberly is on a 320-mile flight. How many miles has she flown after $\frac{1}{4}$ of the trip?

14. Write About It Explain what happens to two lines in the same plane that are not parallel.

Mixed Review and Test Prep

Change the unit. (pages 370–371)

15. 9 ft = __?__ yd **16.** 2 ft = __?__ in. **17.** 2 mi = __?__ yd

Choose the letter for the correct product. (pages 390–393)

18. $\frac{3}{8} \times \frac{2}{3} = n$ **A** $\frac{5}{24}$ **B** $\frac{3}{12}$ **C** $\frac{5}{11}$ **D** $\frac{1}{4}$

19. $\frac{3}{5} \times \frac{1}{5} = n$ **F** $\frac{4}{5}$ **G** $\frac{3}{25}$ **H** $\frac{3}{10}$ **J** $\frac{1}{8}$

Rays and Angles

VOCABULARY
ray
angle

Why learn this? You can use lines and angles when locating a point on Earth or in space.

Scientists use rays and angles to locate points in space.

A **ray** is part of a line that has one endpoint and goes on forever in one direction. A ray is named by its endpoint and one other point on the ray.

Read: Ray *BC*
Write: $\overrightarrow{BC}$

When two rays have the same endpoint, they form an **angle**. An angle can be named by the vertex and one point on each ray, or by just the vertex.

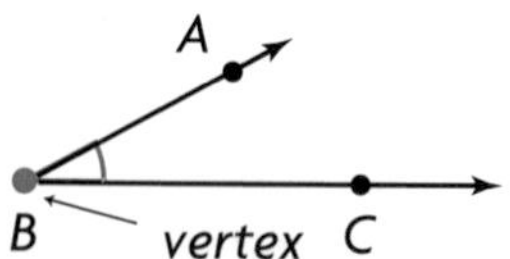

Read: angle *ABC*, or *CBA*,
or angle *B* *(the vertex must be the middle letter.)*
Write: $\angle ABC$, $\angle CBA$, or $\angle B$

Talk About It

- Name the two rays that form angle *ABC*.
- Is a line segment part of a ray? Explain.
- Name some real things that suggest a ray.

SCIENCE LINK

The National Radio Astronomy Observatory listens for sounds from outer space. The sound from an explosion that occurs in outer space reaches Earth as radio waves. Scientists use rays and angles to help them point their telescopes in the direction of the sound. How is the radio wave coming from an explosion in space like a ray?

Angles can be different sizes.

A *right* angle forms a square corner.

An *acute* angle is less than a right angle.

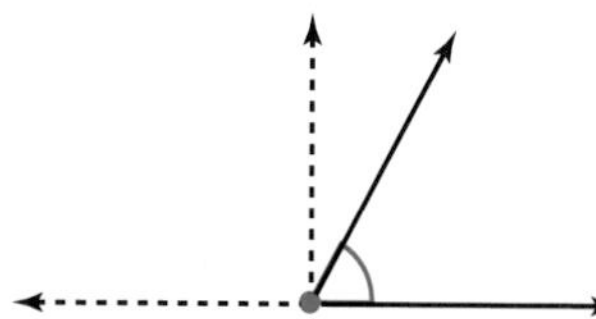

An *obtuse* angle is greater than a right angle.

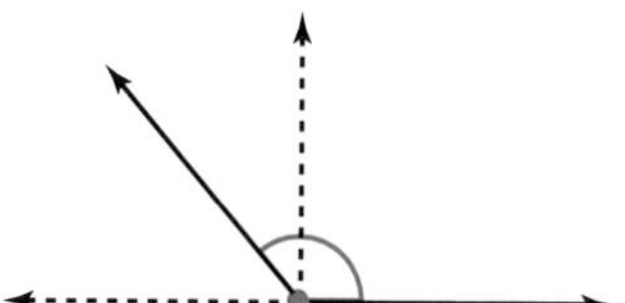

Can an acute angle fit inside a right angle? Explain.

▶ CHECK

For Exercises 1–4, use the figure.

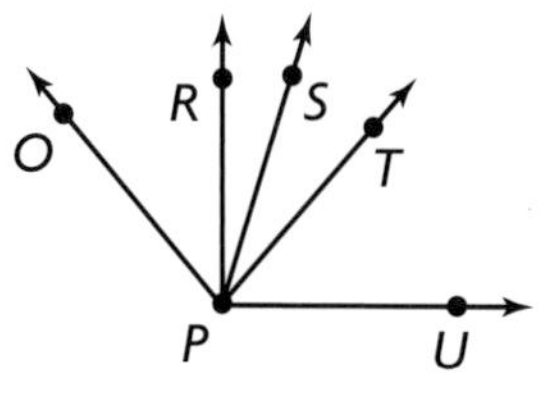

1. Name the rays.
2. Name two acute angles.
3. Name a right angle.
4. Name an obtuse angle.

▶ PRACTICE

Identify the angle. Write *right, acute,* or *obtuse.*

5. 

6. 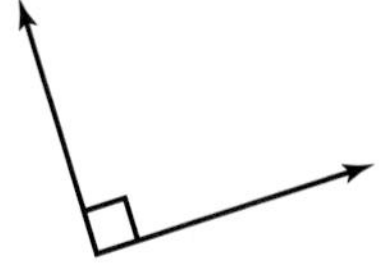

7. 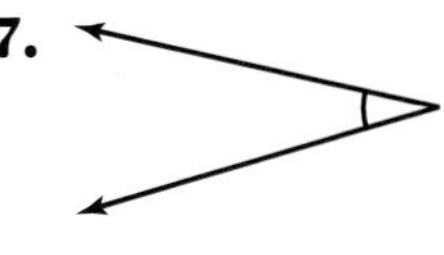

8. 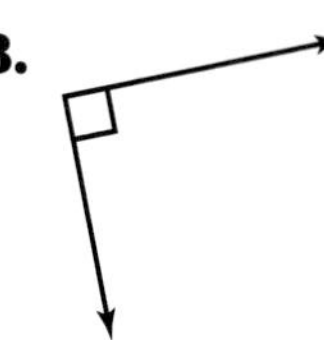

9. 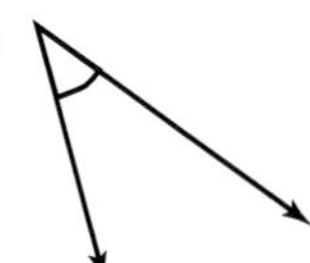

10. 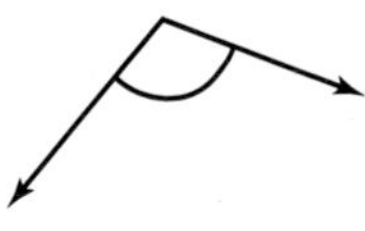

11. 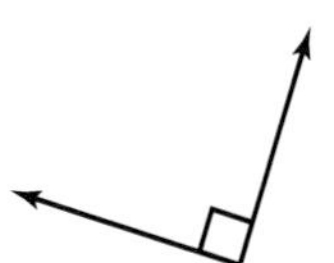

12. 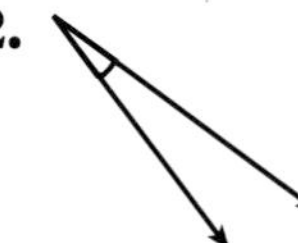

For Exercises 13–20, use the figure. Identify the angle. Write *right, acute,* or *obtuse.*

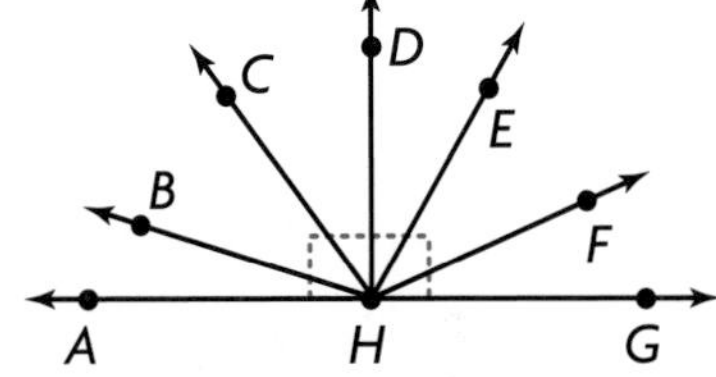

13. $\angle BHE$

14. $\angle AHF$

15. $\angle DHE$

16. $\angle EHG$

17. $\angle DHA$

18. $\angle CHF$

19. $\angle CHA$

20. $\angle DHG$

Problem Solving • Mixed Applications

Using Data For Problems 21–22 and 24, use the drawing.

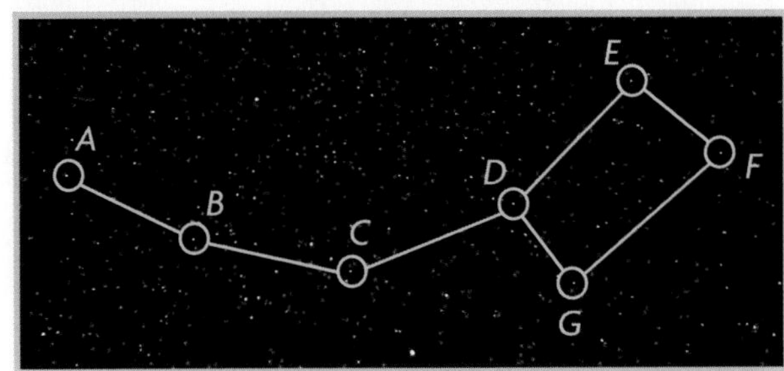

21. If the stars that make up the Little Dipper were labeled as shown, describe angle *BCD*.

22. Visual Thinking Name an acute angle in the Little Dipper.

23. Science Astronomers have named 88 constellations. Kim can identify 11 of them. What fraction of all constellations can she identify?

24. **Write a problem** using the information in the drawing of the Little Dipper.

Mixed Review and Test Prep

Write the measurements in order from shortest to longest. (pages 248–249)

25. 10 m, 10 cm, 10 km

26. 4 dm, 4 cm, 4 mm

27. 3 km, 3 dm, 3 cm

Choose the correct sum in simplest form. (pages 340–341)

28. $\frac{3}{5} + \frac{1}{5} = n$ **A** $\frac{4}{10}$ **B** $\frac{4}{5}$ **C** $\frac{2}{5}$ **D** $\frac{8}{10}$

29. $\frac{2}{9} + \frac{4}{9} = n$ **F** $\frac{6}{9}$ **G** $\frac{8}{18}$ **H** $\frac{2}{3}$ **J** $\frac{8}{9}$

MORE PRACTICE page H111

LESSON 3 • PART 1 • HANDS-ON LESSON

Measuring Angles

You will investigate how to use a protractor to measure angles.

VOCABULARY
degree
protractor

The unit used to measure an angle is called a **degree** (°). A circle is divided into 360 degrees (360°). A **protractor** is a tool for measuring the size of the opening of an angle. Its scale is marked from 0° to 180°. You can use a protractor to measure angle *ABC*.

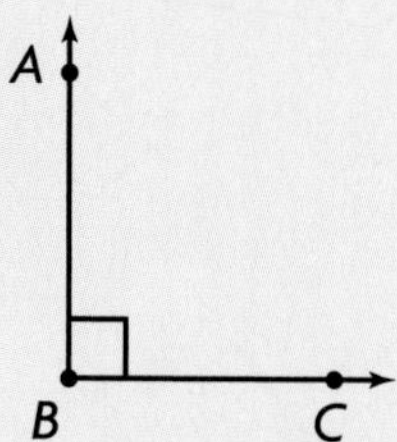

MODEL

Step 1

Place the center of the protractor on the vertex of the angle.

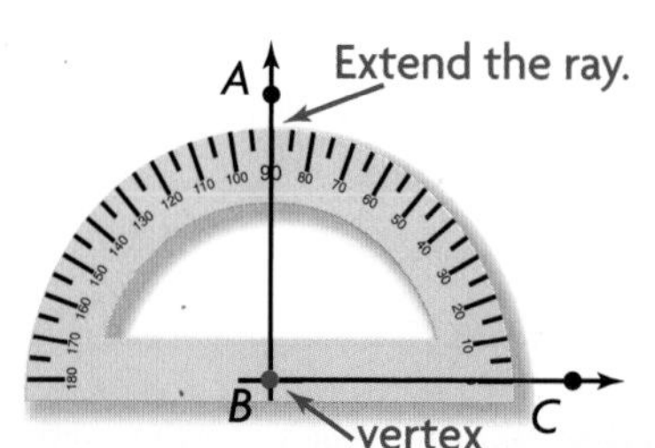

Step 2

Line up the center point and the 0° mark on the protractor with one ray of the angle.

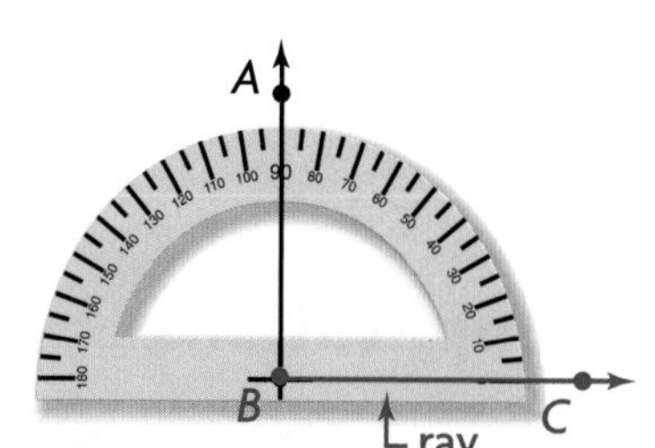

Step 3

Read the measure of the angle where the other ray passes through the scale.

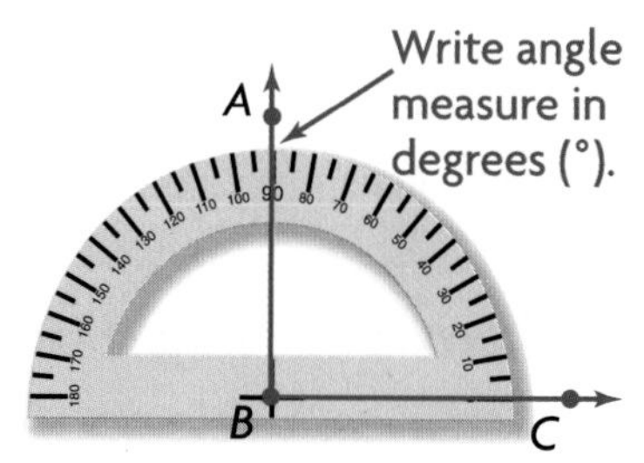

- If the rays are extended, will the angle measure change? Explain.

▶ EXPLORE

Use a protractor to measure angles *DEF* and *GHI*.

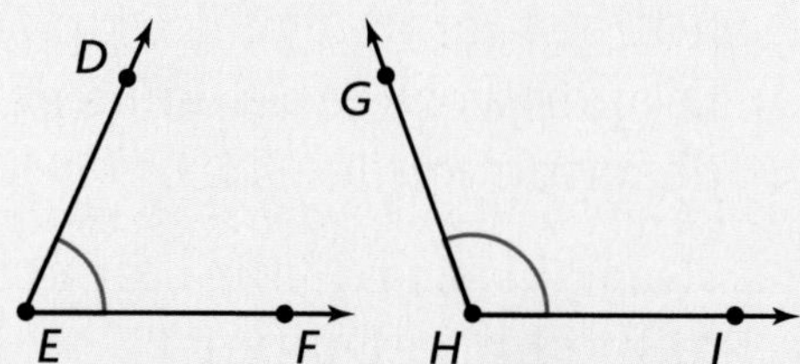

MATERIALS: protractor

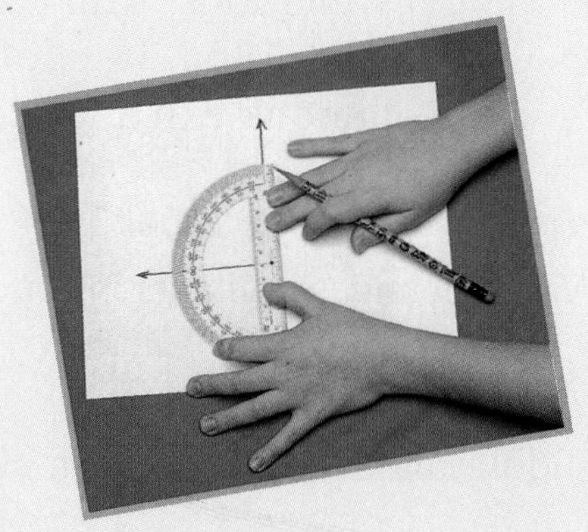

Record

Trace the angles on a sheet of paper. Write the angle measurements in degrees (°). Explain how you found the measure of each angle.

Talk About It

- How many degrees are in a right angle?
- Does an acute angle measure less than or greater than 90°? an obtuse angle? Explain.

▶ TRY THIS

Trace the angles below. Use a protractor to measure each angle. Record the angle measurement in degrees (°).

1. E, F, G

2. 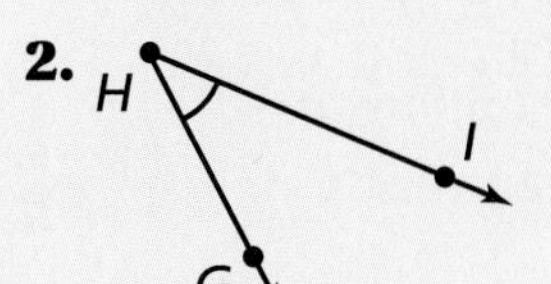

3. 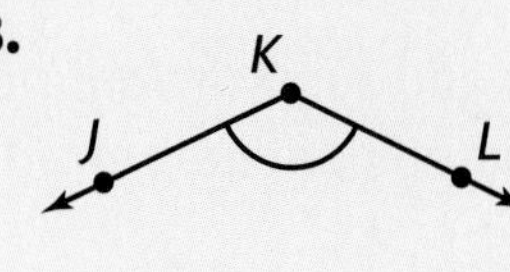

4. How many degrees are in straight angle MON? Why is this angle called a straight angle?

M O N

5. **Write About It** Explain how measuring the angles above is different from measuring the angles on page 412.

Technology Link

You can visualize angles in a pattern by using E-Lab, Activity 23. Available on CD-ROM and on the Internet at **www.hbschool.com/elab**

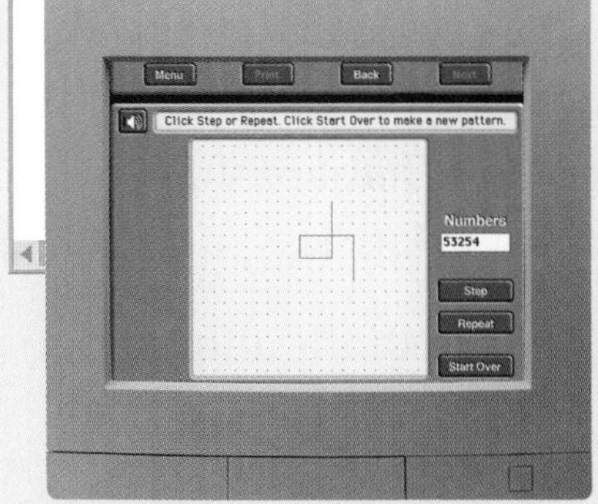

▶ PRACTICE

Trace each figure. Use a protractor to measure the angle.

6. 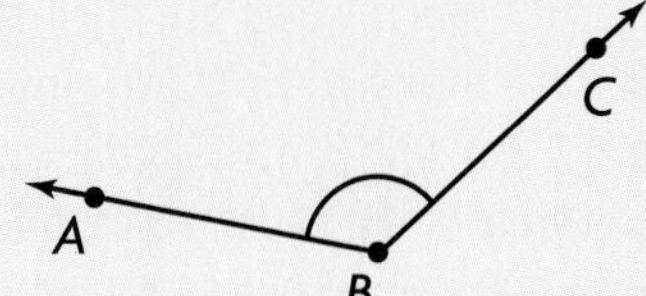

7. 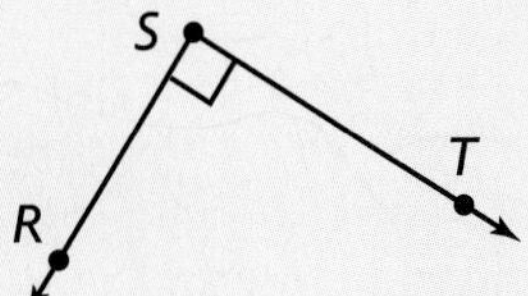

8. 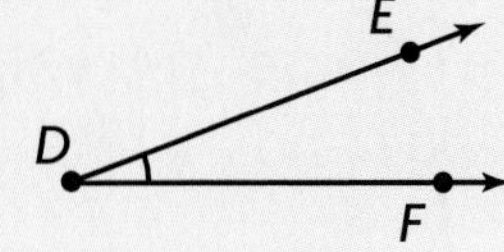

Problem Solving • Mixed Applications

Using Data For Problems 9–11, use the airline map.

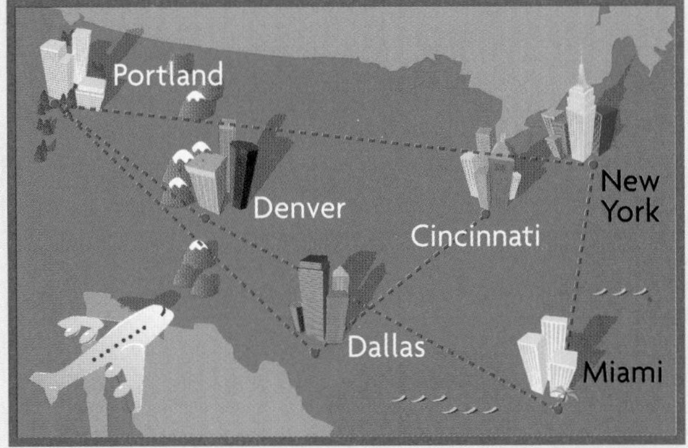

9. Measurement What is the measure of the angle formed by the airline routes with Dallas at the vertex?

10. Visual Thinking Name the city at the vertex of an obtuse angle formed by the airline routes.

11. What is the measure of the angle from Portland to Denver to Miami?

12. Measurement Andrew flew 1,238 miles from Denver to Portland. He returned to Denver, and one week later he made the same round-trip flight. How many miles did he travel on the two trips?

13. Patterns Karen started a paper route. The first week she got 1 new customer; the second week, 4; the third week, 7; the fourth week, 10. If the pattern continues, during which week will she have 40 new customers?

LESSON CONTINUES

MORE PRACTICE page H111

LESSON 3 • PART 2

Problem-Solving Strategy: Draw a Diagram

▶ **THE PROBLEM** Aunt Claire called to invite Sonia's family to her new home for the weekend. Sonia made a map from her aunt's directions. How did the map look?

REMEMBER:

UNDERSTAND

PLAN

SOLVE

LOOK BACK

UNDERSTAND

- What are you asked to do?
- What information will you use?
- Is there information you will not use? If so, what?

PLAN

- How can you solve the problem?

You can *draw a diagram* to make a map that will show the way to Aunt Claire's house. You will need a straightedge and a protractor.

From your house, drive 3 blocks east. Make a 90° turn north onto Oak St. Drive 4 blocks north, and make a 90° turn west onto Elm St. Drive 1 block, and make a 45° turn onto the interstate ramp. Take the interstate north to Exit 83, and make a 45° turn onto the exit ramp. Then make a 135° turn to the west onto Ivy Lane. Drive 2 blocks to my new house.

SOLVE

Draw the diagram on grid paper. Mark the top of the paper as *north*, the bottom as *south*, the left as *west*, and the right as *east*. Start by drawing Sonia's house at the intersection of two lines. Follow the directions to Aunt Claire's house. At each turn, use a protractor to find the angle measure of the turn. Label the street names.

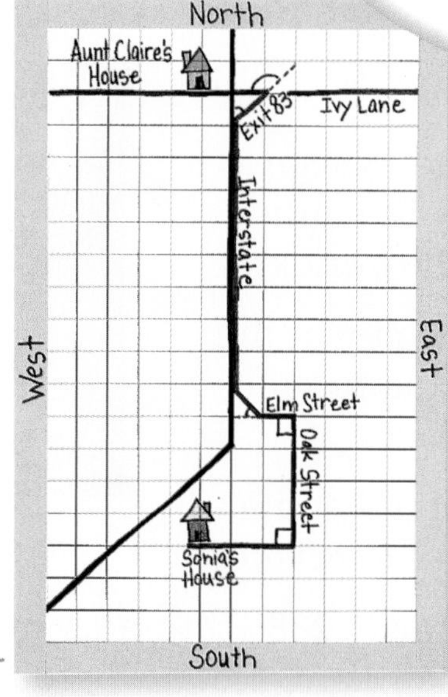

LOOK BACK

- How does drawing a diagram help you solve the problem?
- What other strategy could you use?

▶ PRACTICE

Draw a diagram to solve.

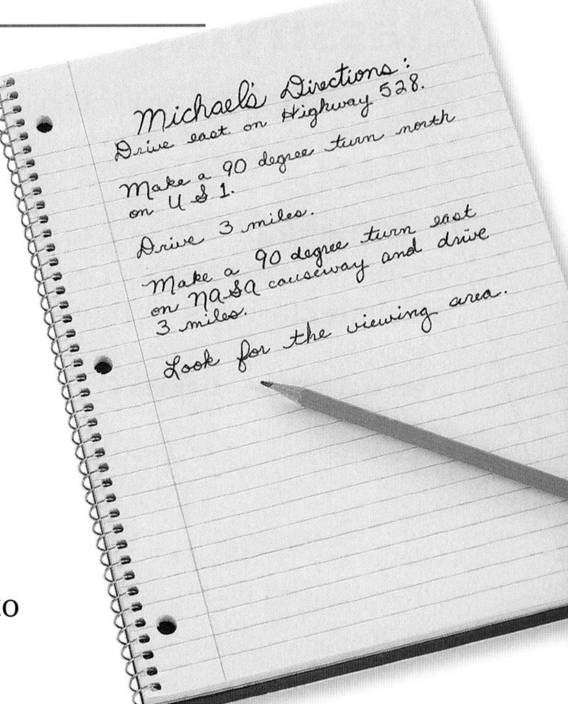

1. Michael and Chris are making plans to watch the shuttle launch. Michael gives Chris the directions to the viewing area. Make a map of Michael's directions.
2. Donald is making a coat rack, using a piece of wood that is 3 feet long. He hammers a nail into the wood every 3 inches. He does not put nails on the ends. Use grid paper. Allow 1 space to equal 1 inch. How many nails does Donald use?
3. Michelle dug 12 holes to plant trees in a circle. If she skips 2 holes after each tree she plants, will she plant all 12 trees before coming back to the first one?

Mixed Applications

Solve.

CHOOSE a strategy and a tool.

- Write a Number Sentence
- Make a Model
- Use a Schedule
- Draw a Diagram

Paper/Pencil

Calculator

Hands-On

Mental Math

4. Mr. Levy's class went on a field trip. How long was Mr. Levy's class away from school? How much time was spent at the science center?

DAY AT THE SCIENCE CENTER		
Activity	Starting Time	Ending Time
Travel to center	8:40	9:10
Exhibits	9:10	11:00
Planetarium	11:00	11:45
Lunch	11:45	12:30
Travel to school	12:30	1:00

5. Calculate the time that Mr. Levy's class spent traveling from school to the science center, and from the science center back to school. What was the total travel time?
6. Charmaine bought $\frac{1}{2}$ yard of red fabric, $\frac{3}{4}$ yard of white fabric, and $\frac{1}{8}$ yard of blue fabric. How much fabric did she buy?
7. Nathan, Holly, and Darrell live on different floors of a 3-story apartment building. Nathan does not live on the second or third floor. Holly does not live on the first or second floor. Who lives on each floor?
8. Karl sold newspapers. He collected $4.20 in coins. He had only nickels, dimes, and quarters. He had 4 nickels and 5 times as many dimes as nickels. How many quarters did he have?

MORE PRACTICE page H111

LESSON 4

Classifying Quadrilaterals

Why learn this? You can identify quadrilaterals in everyday objects, such as floor tiles and window panes.

VOCABULARY
quadrilaterals
trapezoid
parallelogram
rhombus

Quadrilaterals are polygons with 4 sides and 4 angles. Quadrilaterals can be grouped and named by the characteristics of their sides and angles.

general quadrilateral	trapezoid	parallelogram	rectangle	rhombus	square
4 sides of any length	1 pair of parallel sides	2 pairs of congruent sides	2 pairs of congruent sides	4 congruent sides	4 congruent sides
4 angles of any size		2 pairs of parallel sides	4 right angles	2 pairs of congruent angles	4 right angles

Talk About It

- Which quadrilaterals have 4 right angles?
- Which quadrilaterals have all sides congruent?
- How are a square and a rectangle alike? How are they different?

▶ CHECK

You can use a tangram to make quadrilaterals. A tangram is an ancient Chinese puzzle.

1. Trace the seven pieces of the tangram. Cut out the pieces. Rearrange all seven pieces to form as many different quadrilaterals as you can. Name them.

▶ PRACTICE

Draw and name the quadrilateral.

2. opposite sides are parallel; 2 pairs of congruent sides; 2 pairs of congruent angles

3. one pair of parallel sides

4. four sides congruent and four right angles

5. four sides congruent; 2 pairs of congruent angles

Write *true* or *false*.

6. A trapezoid has 4 sides congruent.

7. A rhombus has 4 sides congruent.

8. A square has 2 acute and 2 obtuse angles.

9. A parallelogram has 2 pairs of parallel sides.

10. A general quadrilateral can have sides of any length.

11. All 4-sided polygons are quadrilaterals.

Problem Solving • Mixed Applications

12. **Sports** The line between the bases on a softball field measures 60 feet. Rebecca hit 3 home runs. She ran from home plate to each of the 3 bases and back home for each home run. What is the total number of feet she ran?

13. **Patterns** Patricia is making a quilt. She cut fabric into 540 squares and rectangles. There are 120 more squares than rectangles. How many squares and rectangles are in the quilt?

14. **Visual Thinking** Matt ran the perimeter of a field. He ran 175 feet to the west, turned 90° north, and ran 140 feet. He then turned east and ran 175 feet. He turned 90° south and ran 140 feet. How many feet did he run? What shape was the field?

15. **Write a problem** using the information that Jon's swimming pool is 30 feet long and 16 feet wide.

Mixed Review and Test Prep

Write *multiply* or *divide*. Then write the equivalent measurement. (pages 256–257)

16. 80 mm = __?__ cm

17. 2.25 m = __?__ cm

18. 4,000 mg = __?__ g

Choose the letter for the correct sum. (pages 308–309)

19. $\frac{1}{4} + \frac{2}{3} = n$ **A** $\frac{3}{12}$ **B** $\frac{11}{12}$ **C** $\frac{2}{7}$ **D** $\frac{10}{12}$

20. $\frac{1}{5} + \frac{1}{3} = n$ **F** $\frac{8}{15}$ **G** $\frac{1}{12}$ **H** 1 **J** $\frac{1}{2}$

LESSON 5 • PART 1

Classifying Triangles

VOCABULARY
isosceles
scalene
equilateral

Why learn this? You can recognize different triangular shapes, such as road signs, by comparing the lengths of their sides.

Triangles can be classified according to the lengths of their sides.

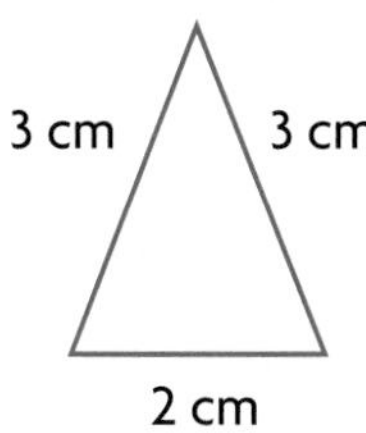

A triangle with two congruent sides is an **isosceles** triangle.

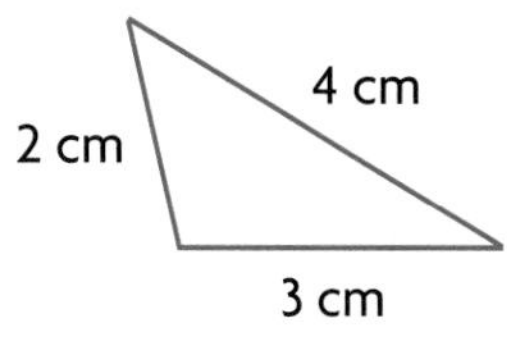

A triangle in which each side is a different length is a **scalene** triangle.

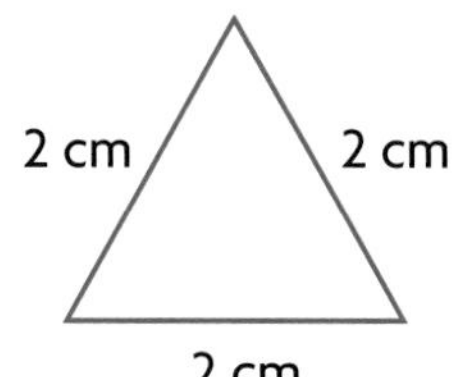

A triangle with all congruent sides is an **equilateral** triangle.

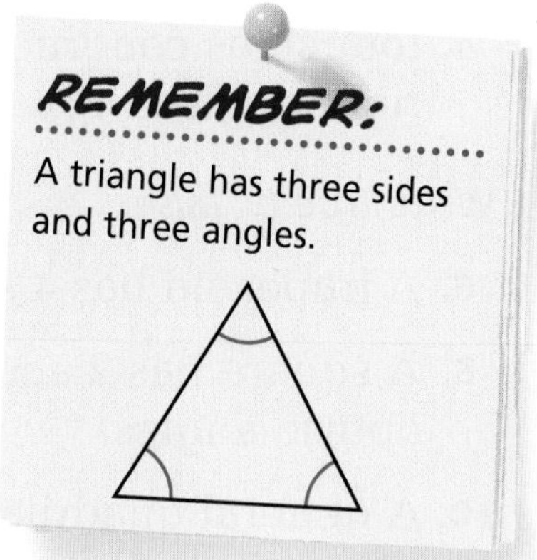

Talk About It CRITICAL THINKING

- A regular polygon has congruent sides and angles. Which triangle is a regular polygon?
- Which of the three triangles is seen most often in everyday life? Why?

▶ CHECK

Name each triangle. Write *isosceles, scalene*, or *equilateral*.

1. 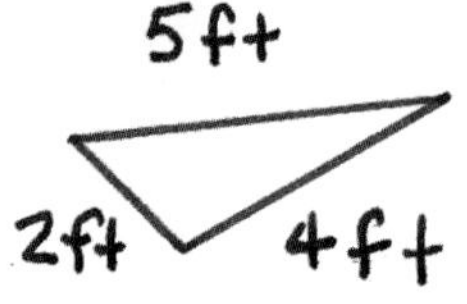

2. 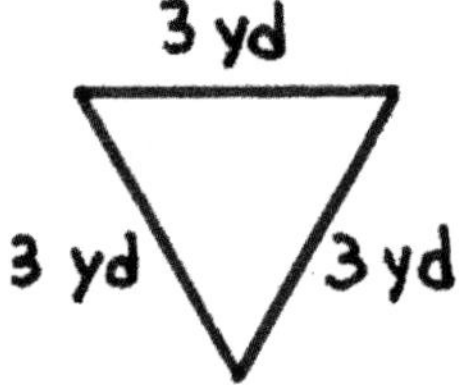

3. 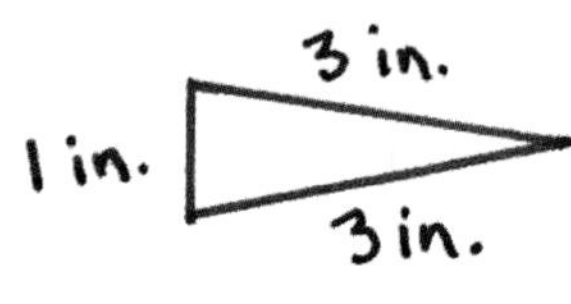

4. 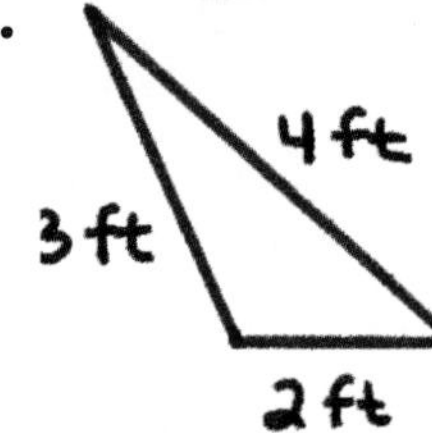

Measure the sides. Classify each triangle. Write *isosceles, scalene*, or *equilateral.*

5. 

6. 

7. 

▶ PRACTICE

Name each triangle. Write *isosceles, scalene*, or *equilateral*.

8. 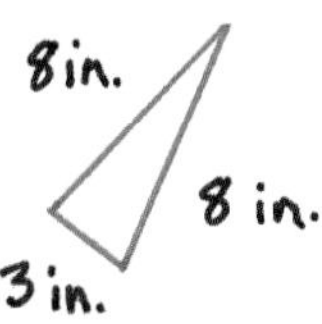

9. 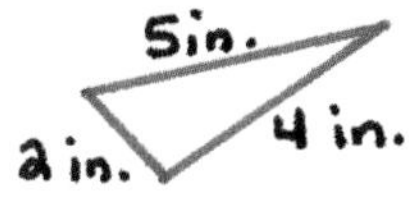

10. 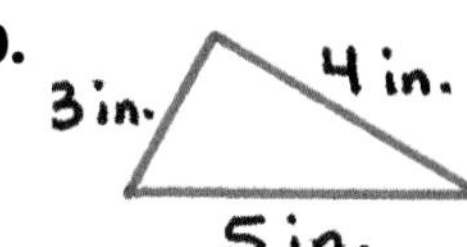

11. 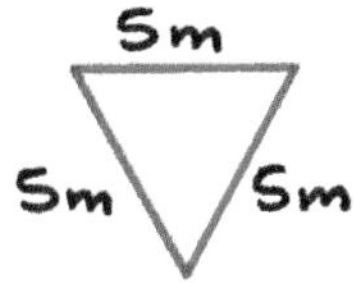

12. 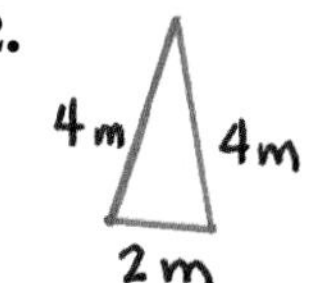

13. 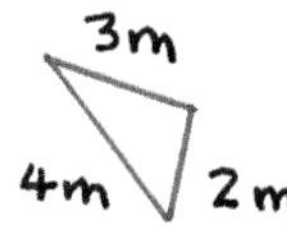

14. 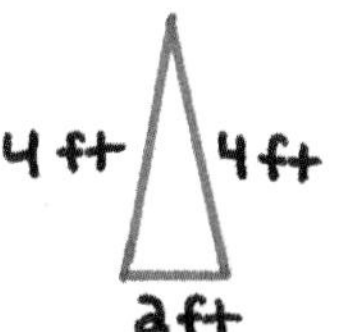

15. 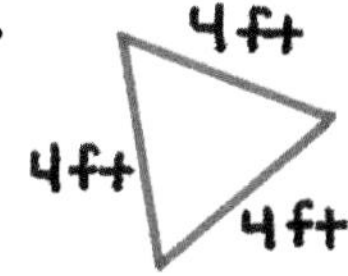

16. 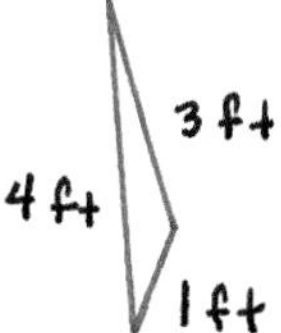

Measure the sides. Classify each triangle. Write *isosceles, scalene*, or *equilateral*.

17. 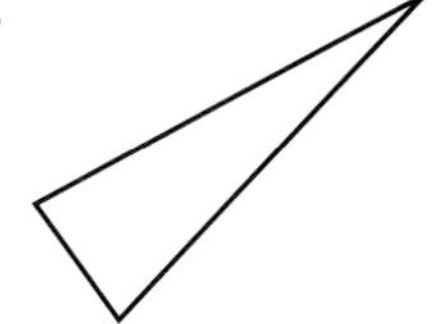

18. 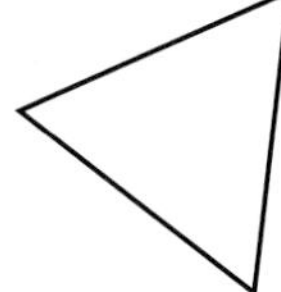

19. 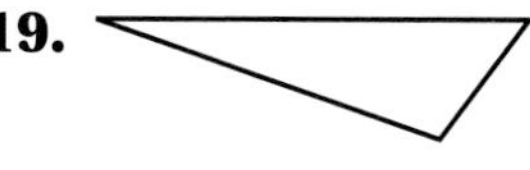

Problem Solving • Mixed Applications

20. Margaret was tiling a kitchen wall. She counted 150 pieces in the tile design. She said $\frac{1}{2}$ of the tiles were triangles, $\frac{1}{3}$ were squares, and the rest were rectangles. How many tiles were rectangles?

21. **Measurement** A spacecraft 200 miles high travels at a speed of 17,000 miles per hour. At 22,000 miles high, it travels at 6,900 miles per hour. What is the difference in the speeds?

22. **Measurement** Gwen rode her bike 1 mile north, $1\frac{1}{2}$ miles southeast, and $1\frac{1}{8}$ miles to where she started. How far did Gwen ride her bike? What shape triangle did she make?

23. **Consumer** Kim bought a radio that regularly sells for $129.95. She got an employee discount of $12.99. How much did Kim pay for the radio?

24. **Visual Thinking** Keith drew an equilateral triangle. By drawing one more line, how can he divide the triangle into two smaller triangles that each have a right angle?

25. **Write a problem** in which you have to classify a triangle. Give the dimensions of the triangle.

MORE PRACTICE page H112

LESSON 5 • PART 2

More About Classifying Triangles

VOCABULARY
right triangle
acute triangle
obtuse triangle

Triangles can be classified according to the measure of their angles.

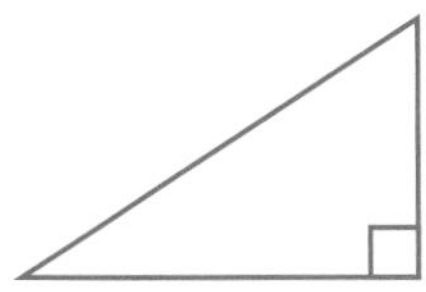

A triangle that has a right angle is a **right triangle**.

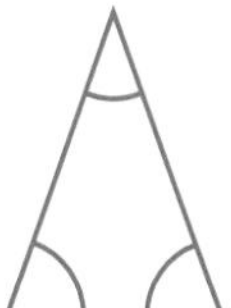

A triangle that has three acute angles is an **acute triangle**.

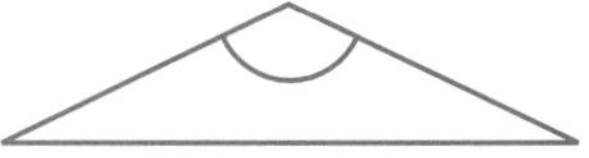

A triangle that has one obtuse angle is an **obtuse triangle**.

Talk About It CRITICAL THINKING

- How can you classify a triangle as acute or obtuse without measuring the angles?
- Can a right triangle have more than 1 right angle?
- Can an obtuse triangle have more than 1 obtuse angle?
- Can an acute triangle have more than 1 acute angle?
- Why can a right triangle never be equilateral?

Technology Link

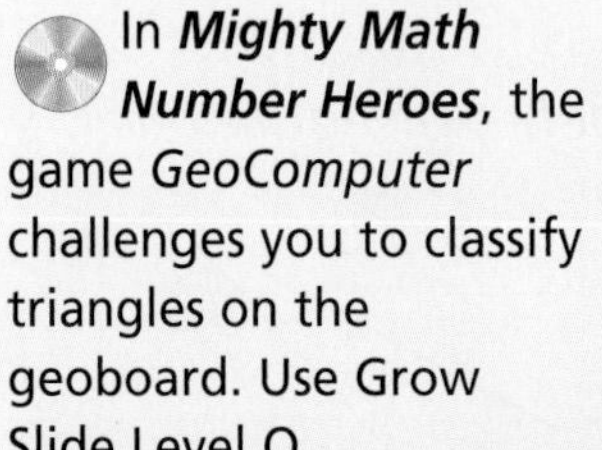

In ***Mighty Math Number Heroes***, the game *GeoComputer* challenges you to classify triangles on the geoboard. Use Grow Slide Level Q.

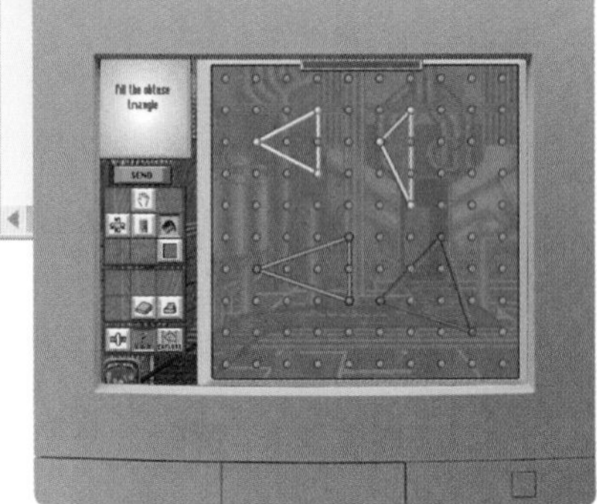

Measure the angles to determine the sum of the angles in any triangle.

Trace the triangle shown at the right. Label each vertex. Cut out the triangle. Tear the corners as shown. Place the angles together at a point on a straight line. What is the sum of the angle measures?

- How can you check the angle measures?

▶ CHECK

1. Trace the 3 triangles at the top of the page. Use a protractor to measure the angles in each triangle, and find the sum of the angles.
2. If you did not know the measure of angle *C*, how could you find it?
3. **Write About It** What rule can you write about the sum of the angle measures in a triangle?

▶ PRACTICE

Name each triangle. Write *right, acute,* or *obtuse.*

4. 

5. 

6. 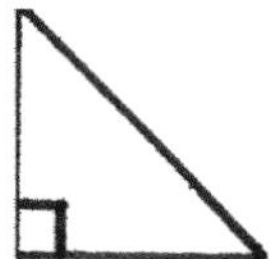

7. 

8. 

9. 

Find the measure of the unknown angle in each triangle.

10. 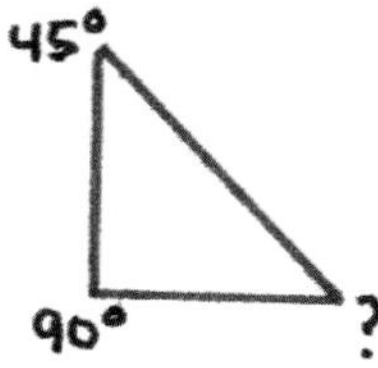

11. 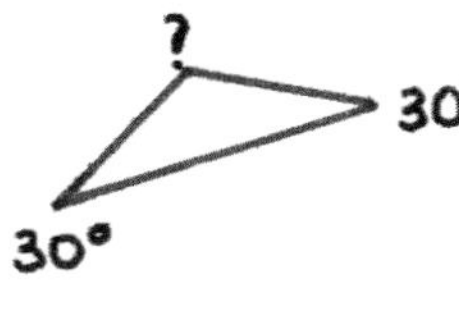

12. 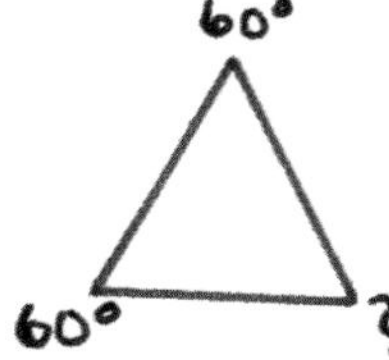

13. 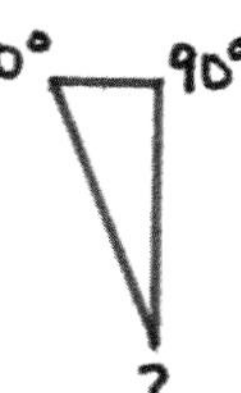

14. 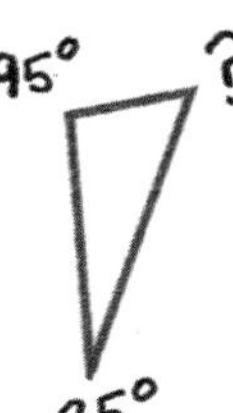

15. 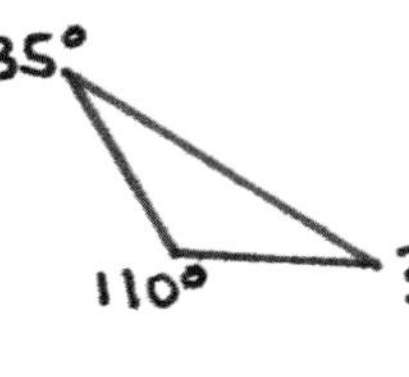

SCIENCE LINK

The shape of an airplane's wing helps determine how much "lift" is needed to get the plane off the ground.

What kind of triangle do the wings of this plane suggest?

Problem Solving • Mixed Applications

16. Time Isabel began working on her drawing at 9:00. She worked for 2 hours 35 minutes. Then she spent 30 minutes eating lunch and 45 minutes visiting a friend. She then spent 1 hour 15 minutes completing her drawing. At what time was she done?

17. **Write About It** Explain the difference between the three types of triangles—right triangle, acute triangle, and obtuse triangle.

Mixed Review and Test Prep

Copy and complete each pattern. (pages 230–231)

18. $200 \div 5 = n$	**19.** $800 \div 4 = n$	**20.** $1{,}500 \div 6 = n$
$20 \div 5 = n$	$80 \div 4 = n$	$150 \div 6 = n$
$2 \div 5 = n$	$8 \div 4 = n$	$15 \div 6 = n$

Choose the letter of the most reasonable unit of measure. (pages 250–251)

21. a bag of potatoes	**A** cg	**B** kg	**C** g	**D** mg
22. a feather	**F** kg	**G** cg	**H** mg	**J** g

MORE PRACTICE pages H112–H113

CHAPTER 23 Review/Test

▶ CHECK Understanding

VOCABULARY

1. The unit used to measure an angle is a(n) _?_. (page 412)

2. The tool for measuring the size of an angle is a(n) _?_. (page 412)

3. A triangle with all congruent sides is a(n) _?_ triangle. (page 418)

4. A triangle with two congruent sides is a(n) _?_ triangle. (page 418)

For Exercises 5–7, use the figure. (pages 408–413)

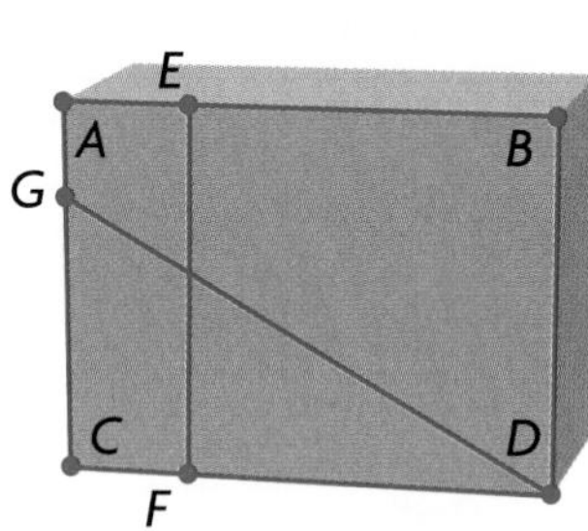

5. Name the point where $\overline{AC}$ and $\overline{AB}$ intersect.

6. Name the line segment that is parallel to $\overline{CD}$.

7. Name a line segment that intersects but is not perpendicular or parallel to $\overline{GD}$.

8. How many degrees are in the three angles of a triangle?

▶ CHECK Skills

Classify each figure. (pages 410–411 and 420–421)

9.  _?_ angle

10.  _?_ angle

11.  _?_ angle

12. 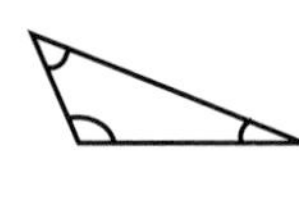 _?_ triangle

13. 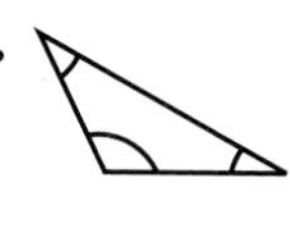 _?_ triangle

14. _?_ triangle

Name the quadrilateral. Write *trapezoid, parallelogram, rectangle, rhombus*, or *square*. (pages 416–417)

15. 

16. 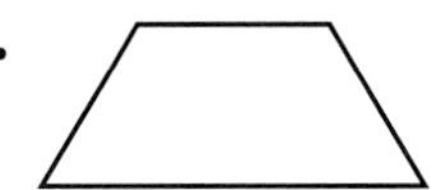

17. 

18. 

▶ CHECK Problem Solving

Solve. (pages 414–415)

CHOOSE a strategy and a tool.

- Write a Number Sentence
- Make a Model
- Work Backward
- Draw a Diagram

Paper/Pencil

Calculator

Hands-On

Mental Math

19. Eric said, "Go 3 blocks east from school and make a 90° turn north. Go 4 blocks and make a 45° turn west." Draw a map to Eric's house.

20. For 24 years, Mike has eaten 3 meals a day. About how many meals has he eaten in that time?

Test Prep

Choose the best answer.

1. Nolan bought 3 bags of birdseed. One weighed 2.2 kilograms, one weighed 4.5 kilograms, and one weighed 3.8 kilograms. Which of the following is a reasonable estimate for the total weight of the birdseed?

A 9 kg

B 6 kg

C 11 kg

D 14 kg

2. Which of the following groups of numbers is in order from *least* to *greatest*?

F 1.02, 1.15, 2.01, 2.10

G 1.15, 2.01, 2.10, 1.02

H 1.02, 2.01, 1.15, 2.10

J 2.01, 2.10, 1.02, 1.15

3. The graph shows the time Tara spent on homework for a week.

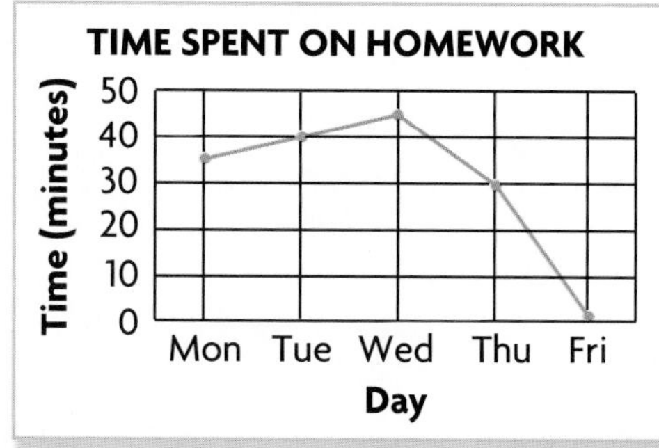

What was the difference between the day Tara spent the most time on homework and the day she spent the least time?

A 15 min **B** 25 min

C 30 min **D** 45 min

4. $47 \div 10 =$

F 0.047 **G** 0.47

H 4.7 **J** 47

5. Jacob ran 9 kilometers. How far is this in meters?

A 9 m

B 90 m

C 900 m

D 9,000 m

6. $\frac{3}{10} + \frac{2}{10} =$

F $\frac{1}{10}$ **G** $\frac{2}{10}$, or $\frac{1}{5}$

H $\frac{4}{10}$, or $\frac{2}{5}$ **J** $\frac{5}{10}$, or $\frac{1}{2}$

7. $\frac{2}{5} \times 5 =$

A 1 **B** 2

C 5 **D** 10

8. Which quadrilateral is shown?

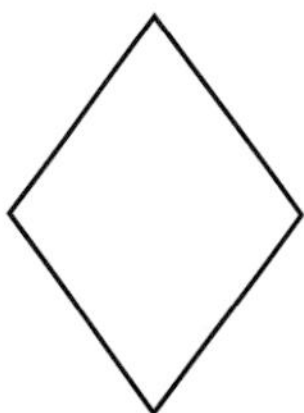

F Rectangle

G Rhombus

H Square

J Trapezoid

K Not Here

24 TRANSFORMATIONS, CONGRUENCE, AND SYMMETRY

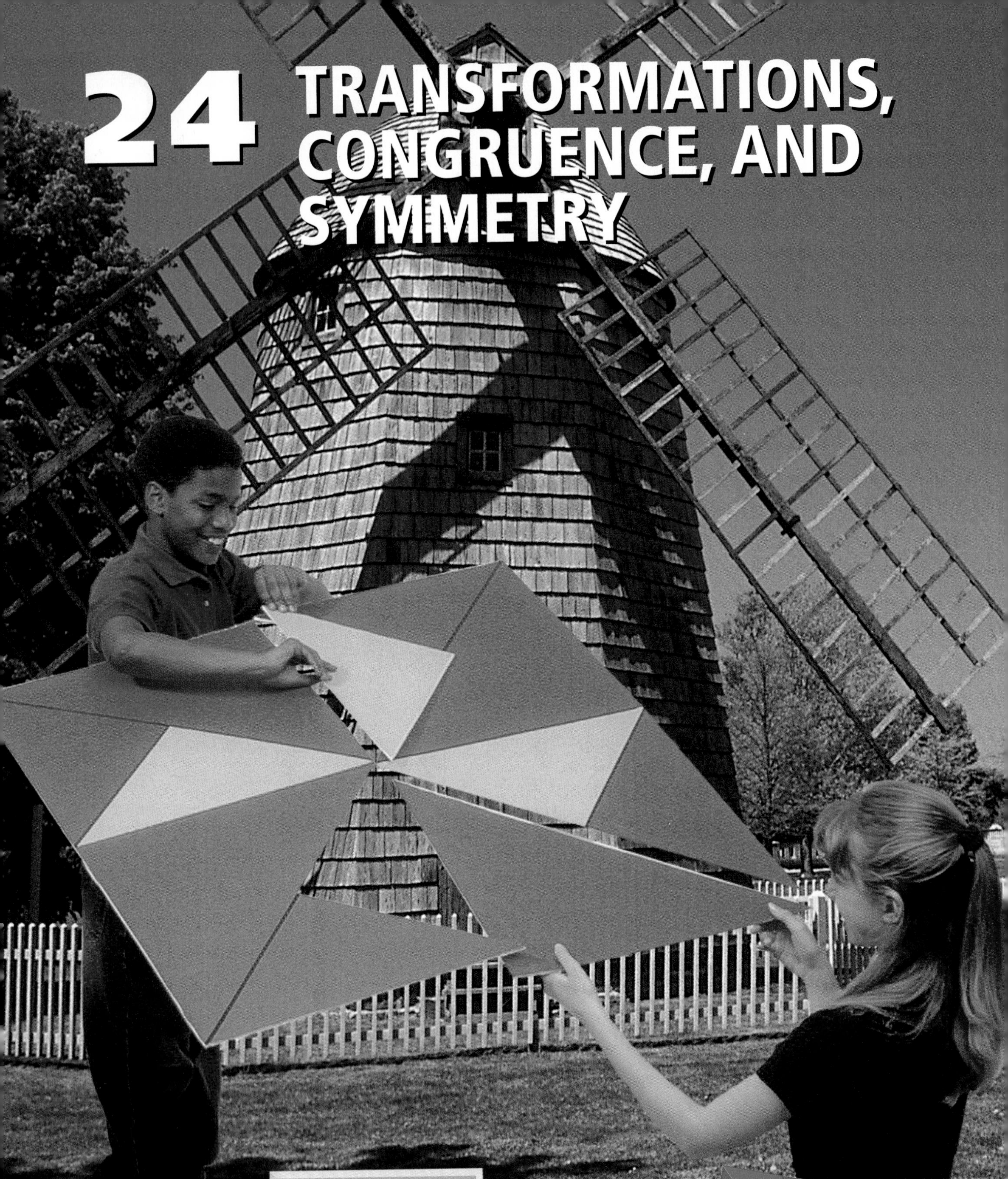

SOCIAL STUDIES **LINK**

Many of the names given to quilt patterns reflect the ways families lived 150 years ago. Pioneers heading west might have made a "Windmill" or "Mow the Lawn" quilt.

Problem-Solving Activity

A Transformation Quilt

If you made a quilt to reflect a detail of your life, what would you call it? Quilt squares can be exciting geometric designs. They also can tell a story.

Design a quilt square, and create three more squares by flipping, sliding, and turning the original square.

YOU WILL NEED: grid paper, ruler, markers or colored pencils, scissors, glue

- Analyze one of the designs shown. Find a line of symmetry. Look for a flip, a slide, and a turn.
- Design one fourth of a quilt square on grid paper, and make three copies.
- Put the four pieces together, using flips, slides, or turns.

HOW TO ORGANIZE A SQUARE

Quilt squares are organized in a 2 x 2 grid. Each square in the grid is filled with squares, rectangles, or triangles.

1.

2.

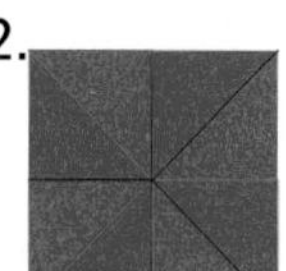

3.

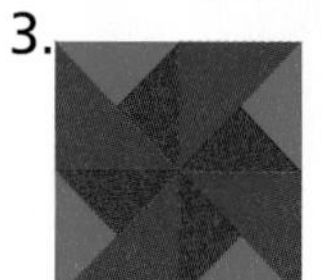

DID YOU

- ✓ analyze designs for flips, slides, and turns?
- ✓ design a quilt square of your own?
- ✓ identify flips, slides, and turns in your quilt square?

LESSON 1

Testing for Congruence

Why learn this? You can be sure quilt pieces or pieces of a model you are building are congruent.

Mr. Wade makes birdhouses. When he cuts out the pieces of wood, he makes sure they match his plans exactly. For example, the sides and angles of each front piece must be congruent to the sides and angles of *all* front pieces. Mr. Wade tests the pieces that he cuts out to see if they are congruent.

Here are two methods he can use to test for congruency.

REMEMBER:

Figures that have the same size and shape are *congruent*.

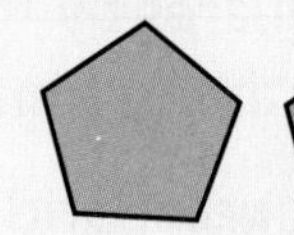
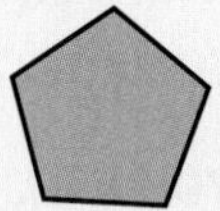

Method 1	Method 2
Place the same kind of pieces on top of one another. Make sure each piece is turned the same way. 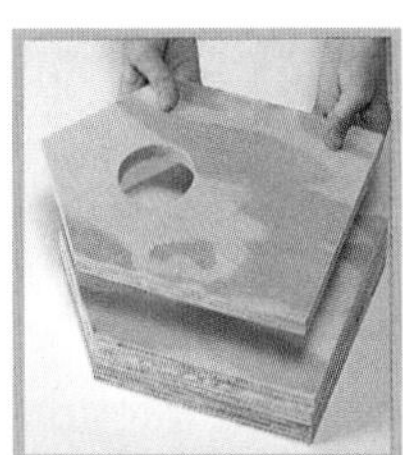	Use a ruler to measure the lengths of each side and a protractor to measure the size of each angle. 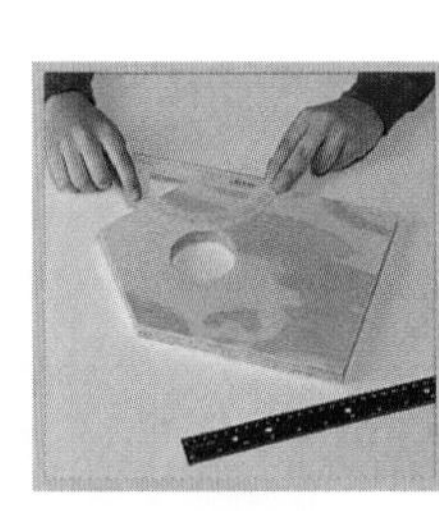

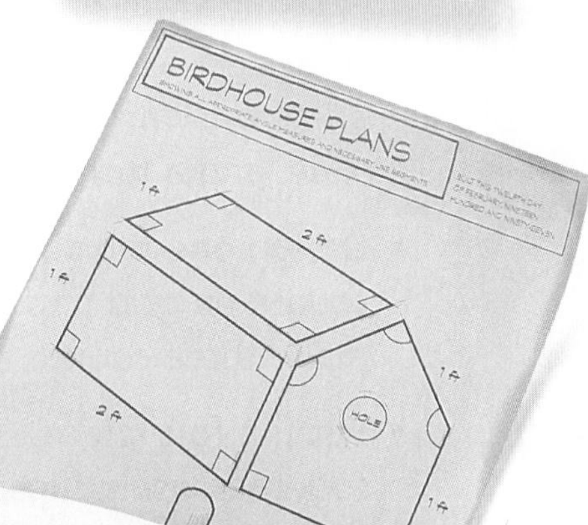

CRITICAL THINKING When might Method 2 be used instead of Method 1? Why?

EXAMPLES

A Congruent line segments

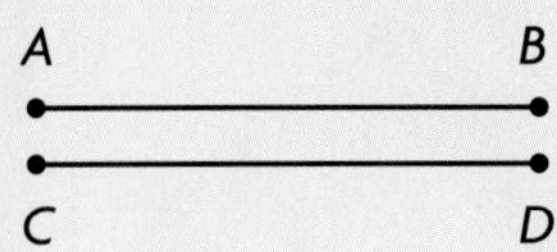

B Congruent angles

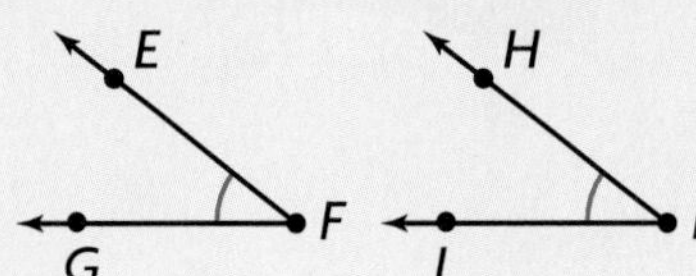

C Congruent figures

▶ CHECK

Use a ruler and a protractor to test each pair of figures for congruency. Write *congruent* or *not congruent*.

1.

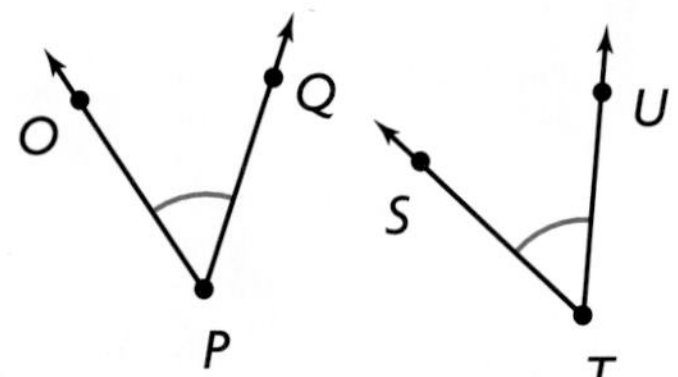

2.

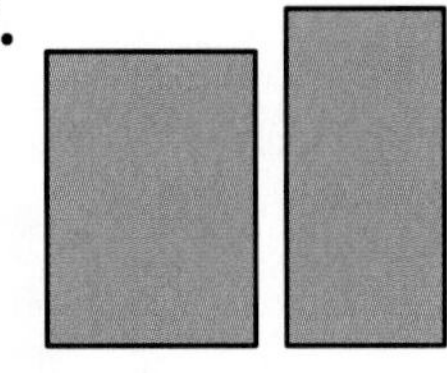

3.

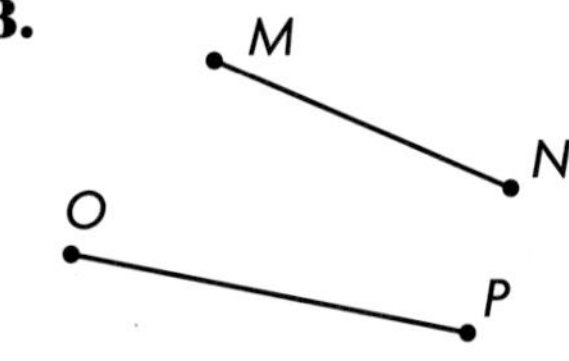

▶ PRACTICE

Write *congruent* or *not congruent*.

4. 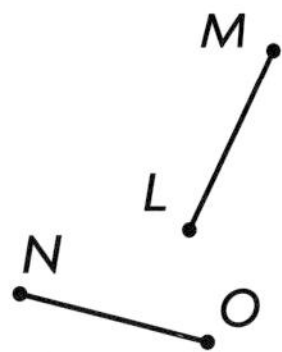

5. 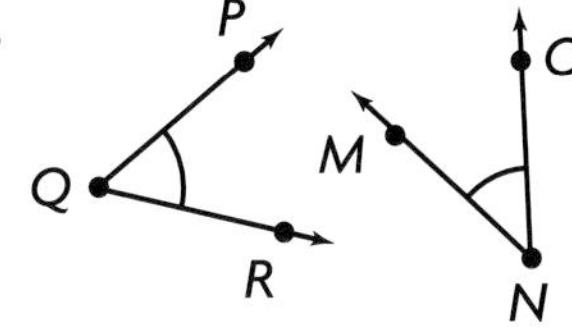

6. 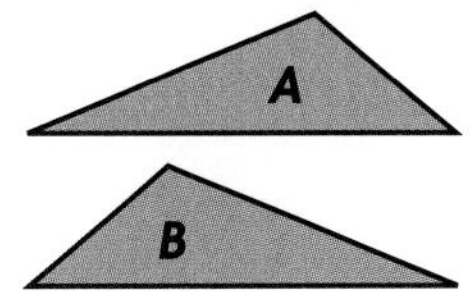

Write the letters of the two figures that are congruent.

7. a. 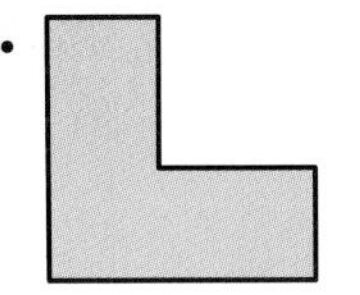

b. 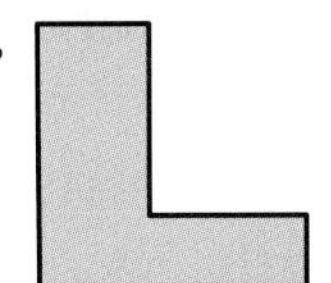

c. 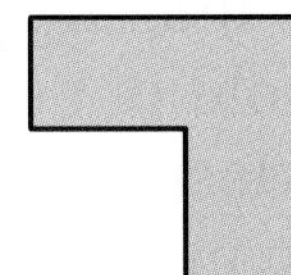

8. a. 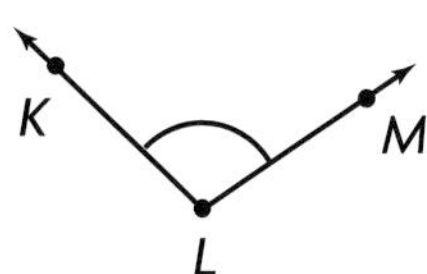

b. 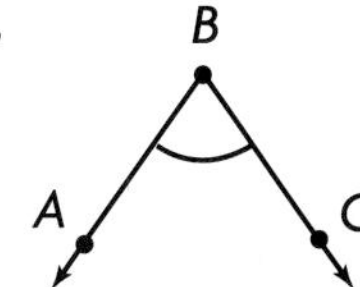

c. 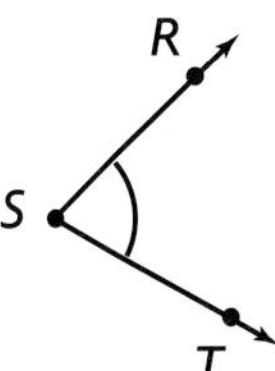

9. a. 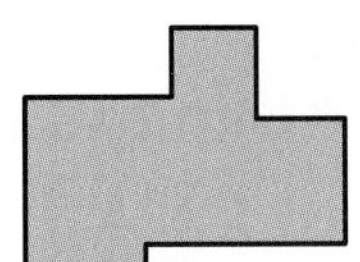

b. 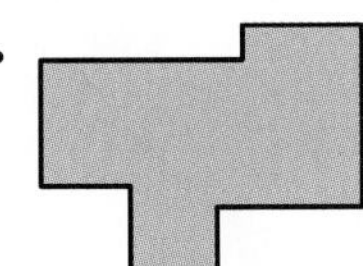

c. 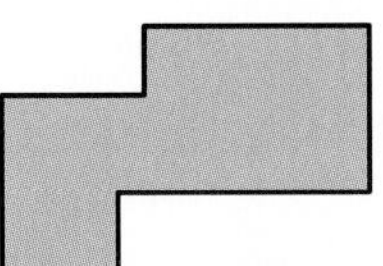

Problem Solving • Mixed Applications

Using Data For Problems 10–13, use the drawing.

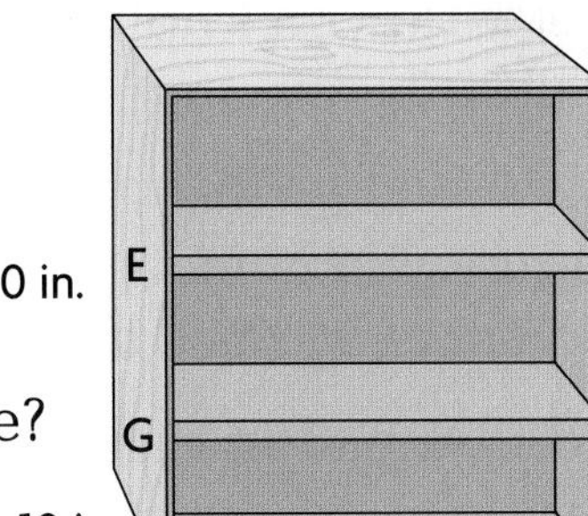

10. Reasoning Mr. Dean is building a bookcase. He cut out seven pieces of wood. Name the pairs of pieces that are congruent.

11. Visual Thinking What kind of angle is angle *EGH*?

12. Measurement What is the perimeter of the bottom piece?

13. **Write a problem** about the relationship of line segment *EF* to line segment *GH*.

Mixed Review and Test Prep

Write *true* or *false*. **(pages 416–417)**

14. A rectangle has 2 acute angles and 2 obtuse angles.

15. A parallelogram has 2 pairs of parallel sides.

Choose the letter for the correct quotient. **(pages 236–239)**

16. $3.09 \div 3 = ■$ **A** 0.103 **B** 103 **C** 10.3 **D** 1.03

17. $2.48 \div 8 = ■$ **F** 3.1 **G** 31 **H** 0.31 **J** 3.01

LESSON 2

Congruence and Symmetry

Why learn this? You can recognize symmetry in nature and in designs on art, wallpaper, and fabrics.

A *line of symmetry* divides a figure so that two parts of the figure are congruent.

Cindy's class is making T-shirt designs. Patterns are placed on the fold of decal paper, traced, and cut out. Then the new design is ironed onto the T-shirt. How many lines of symmetry does the butterfly have?

Place the pattern on the fold of the paper. Trace the pattern and cut it out.	Unfold the paper. Color the design.
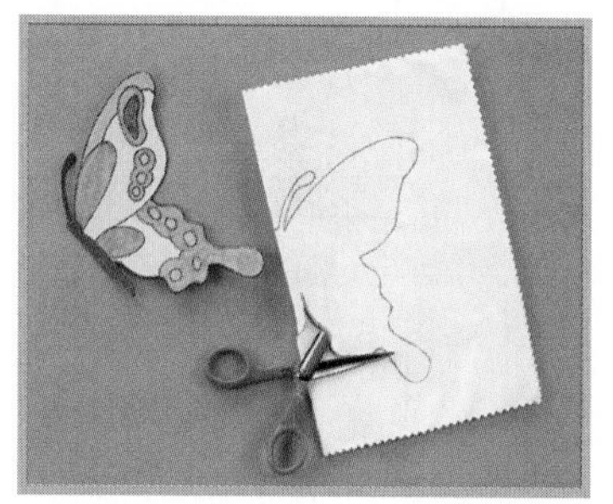	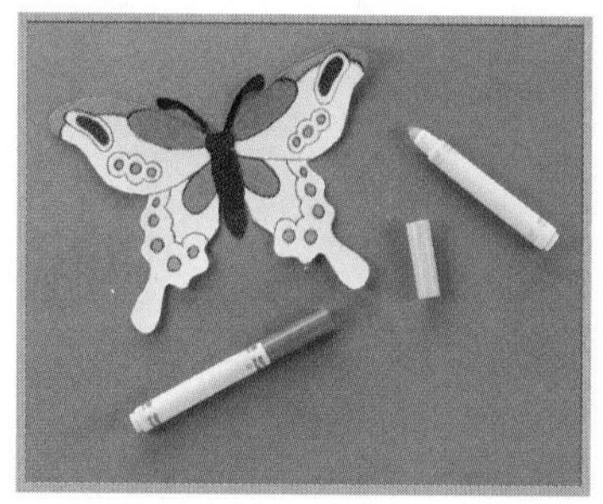

REMEMBER:

A figure has *point symmetry* if it can be turned about a central point and still look the same.

A figure has *line symmetry* if it can be folded on a line so that its two parts are congruent.

So, the butterfly has one line of symmetry.

- How do you know that the two halves of the butterfly are congruent?

A figure can have more than one line of symmetry. Find as many lines of symmetry for a square as you can.

Fold it in half in different ways so that the two halves are congruent.

- How many lines of symmetry did you find?

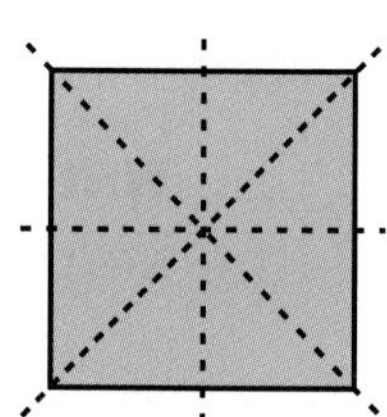

▶ CHECK

Trace each figure. Draw the lines of symmetry. How many lines of symmetry does each figure have?

1. 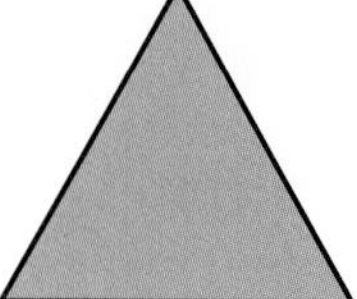

2. 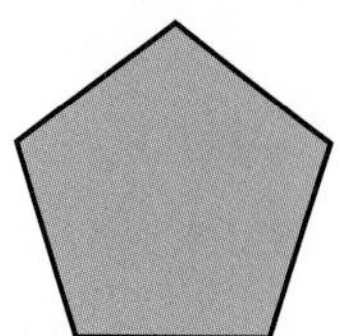

3. 

4. 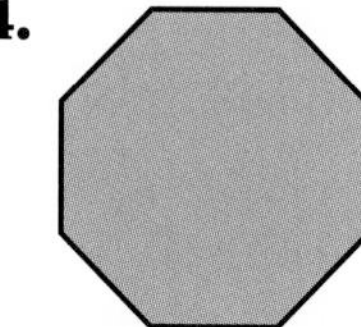

▶ PRACTICE

Tell whether the two halves of each drawing are congruent. Write *yes* or *no*.

5. 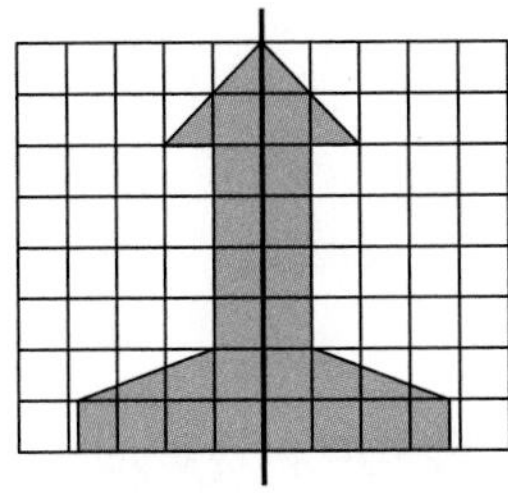

6. 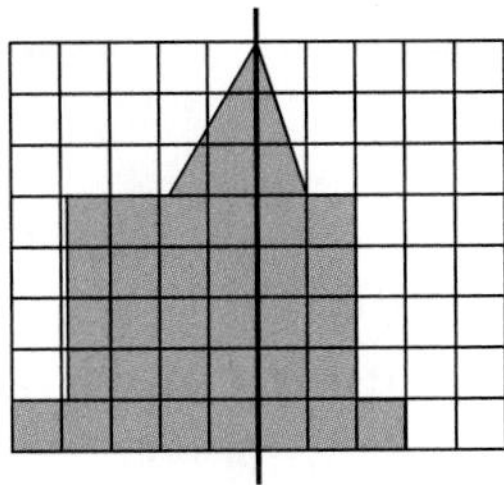

7. 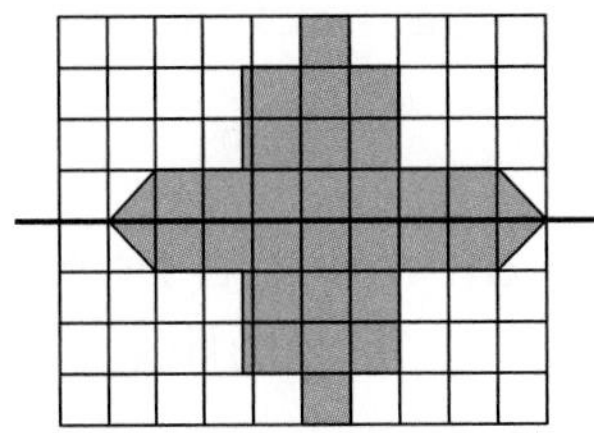

Trace each figure. Draw the lines of symmetry for each figure.

8. 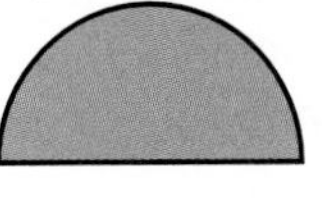

9. 

10. 

11. 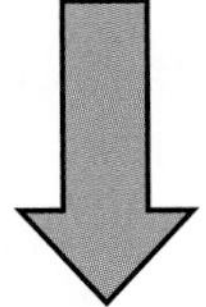

Problem Solving • Mixed Applications

Using Data For Problems 12–14, use the sign at the right.

12. Elianne likes the quilt design that has both point and line symmetry. Which design does she like?

13. Visual Thinking John likes the star design better. How many lines of symmetry are in the star design? the basket design?

14. Money Betsy has $\frac{1}{5}$ of the money she needs to buy her favorite quilt. She has $18. Which quilt is she planning to buy?

15. Write About It How do you find out if a figure has symmetry?

Mixed Review and Test Prep

Name each triangle. Write *right, acute,* or *obtuse*. (pages 420–421)

16. 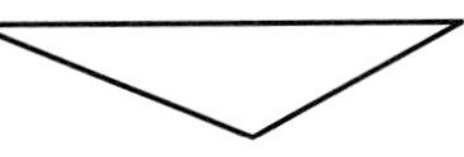

17. 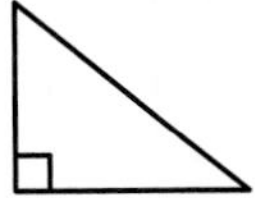

18. 

Choose the letter of the correct sum in simplest form. (pages 340–341)

19. $\frac{5}{12} + \frac{3}{12} = ■$ **A** $\frac{8}{12}$ **B** $\frac{3}{4}$ **C** $\frac{2}{3}$ **D** $\frac{7}{12}$

20. $\frac{4}{9} + \frac{2}{9} = ■$ **F** $\frac{2}{3}$ **G** $\frac{5}{6}$ **H** $\frac{9}{6}$ **J** $\frac{6}{9}$

LESSON 3 • HANDS-ON LESSON

Transformations on the Coordinate Grid

VOCABULARY
axis
transformation

You will investigate how to transform a figure on the coordinate grid.

When you move a figure to show a translation, reflection, or rotation, it is called a **transformation**. You can transform a figure on a coordinate grid.

▶ EXPLORE

Use the ordered pairs (1,2), (2,5), and (5,2) as the vertices to draw this triangle. Move the triangle to show a *translation*, a *reflection*, and a *rotation*. Name the ordered pairs that give the new location for the triangle.

MATERIALS: coordinate grids

A. Translation

Slide the figure 3 spaces to the right on the horizontal **axis** and 3 spaces up on the vertical axis.

New ordered pairs:
(4,5), (5,8), (?,?)

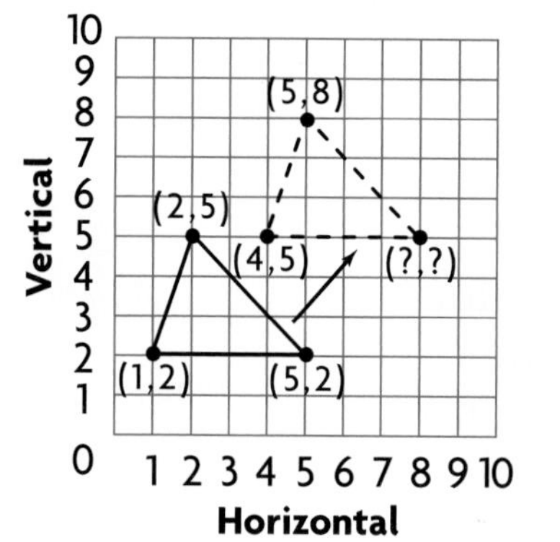

B. Reflection

Flip the figure across the line.

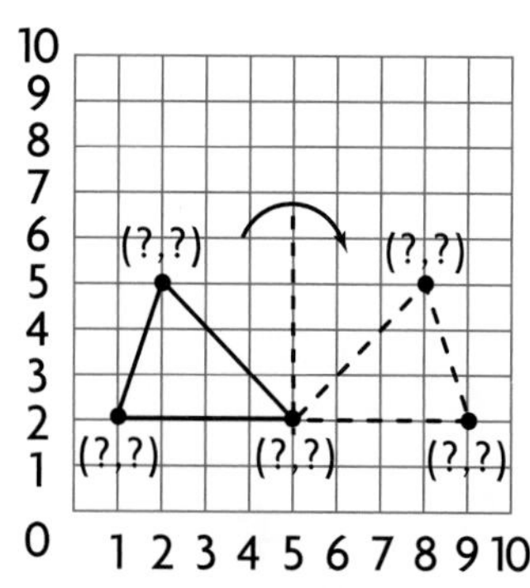

C. Rotation

Turn a figure around a point or vertex. Make the point at (1,2) end at (5,6).

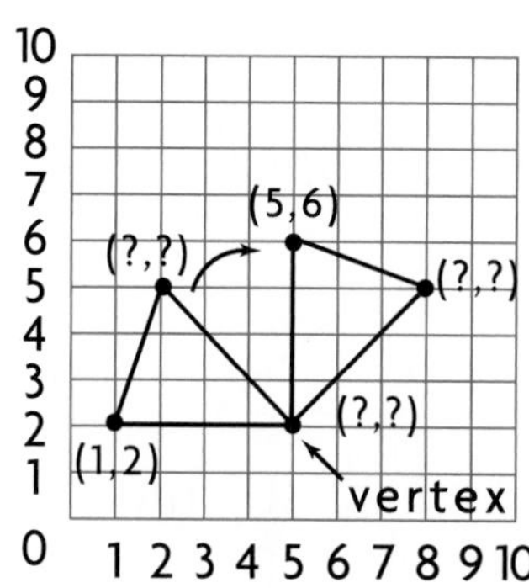

REMEMBER:

You can use two numbers to locate points on a grid. The two numbers are called an *ordered pair*.

EXAMPLE: (1,2) represents 1 space to the right of zero and 2 spaces up.

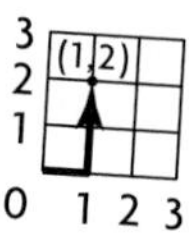

When you slide a figure, it is a *translation*.

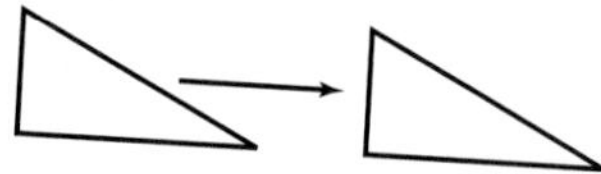

When you flip a figure over a line, it is a *reflection*.

When you turn a figure around a point, or vertex, it is a *rotation*.

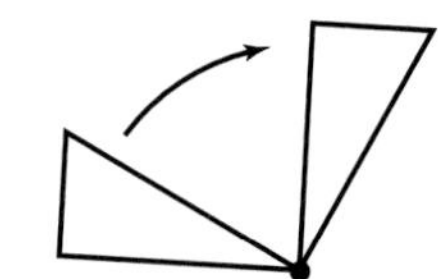

Record

Draw the original triangle and label the ordered pairs for each point. Then draw each new figure to show a *translation*, a *reflection*, and a *rotation*. Write the new ordered pairs.

▶ TRY THIS

1. Use a coordinate grid to draw the figure at the right. Label the ordered pair for each point.
2. Draw new figures to show a *translation*, a *reflection*, and a *rotation*. Label the drawings. Record the new ordered pairs.
3. How did you move the figure to show a translation? a reflection? a rotation?
4. **Write About It** Explain how you found the new ordered pairs for the rotation.

8 7 6 5 4 3 2 1 0 1 2 3 4 5 6 7 8

Technology Link

In ***Mighty Math Number Heroes***, the game *GeoComputer* challenges you to make transformations on the geoboard. Use Grow Slide Levels N and U.

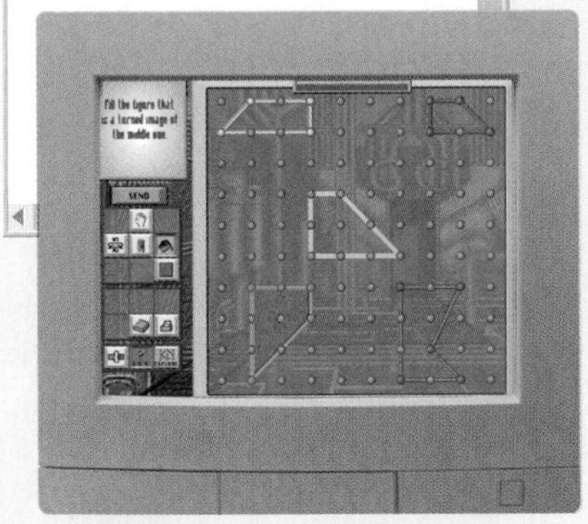

▶ PRACTICE

Copy each figure on a coordinate grid. Translate, reflect, and rotate each figure. Draw the new figure. Name the ordered pairs.

5. 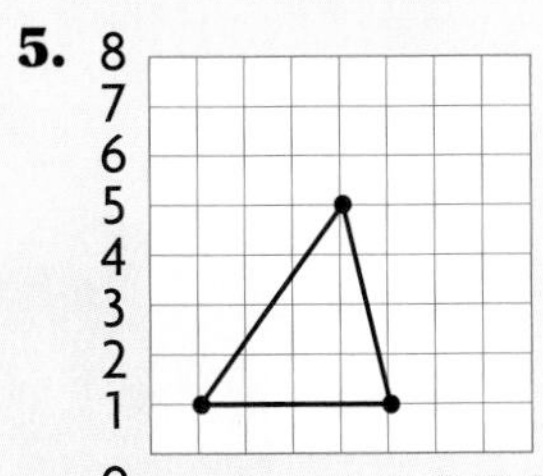

6. 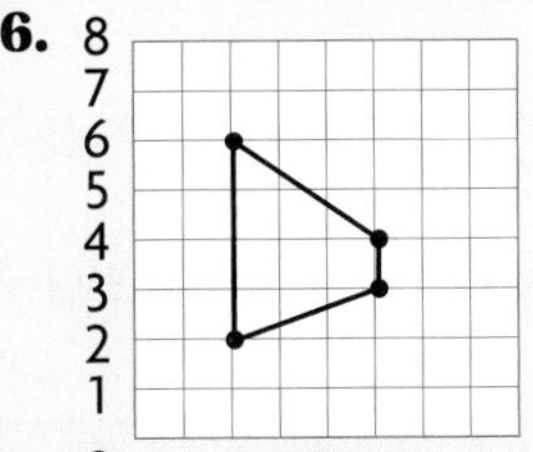

7. 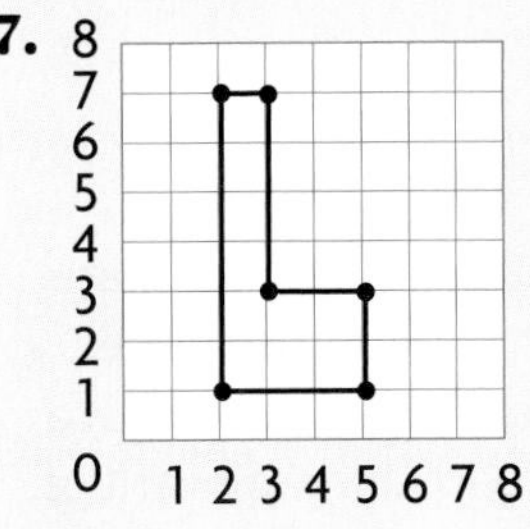

Technology Link

You can make transformations on a coordinate grid by using E-Lab, Activity 24. Available on CD-ROM and on the Internet at **www.hbschool.com/elab**

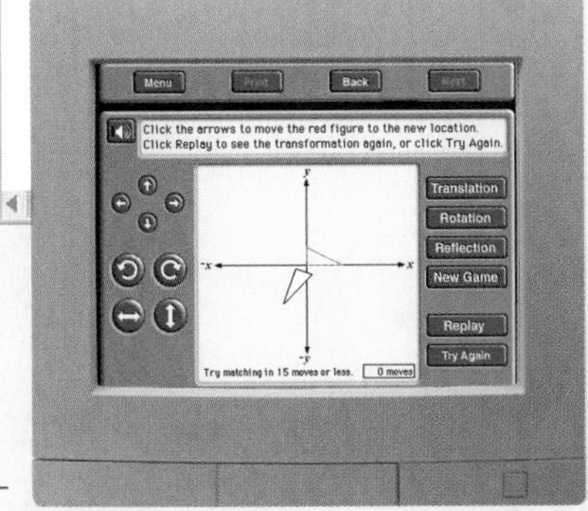

Problem Solving • Mixed Applications

8. **Visual Thinking** Ann is rearranging her furniture. The new ordered pairs for the location of the couch are (6,5), (2,5), (2,6), and (6,6). Use a coordinate grid to draw the figure showing the couch in its new location. Explain how the figure was moved.

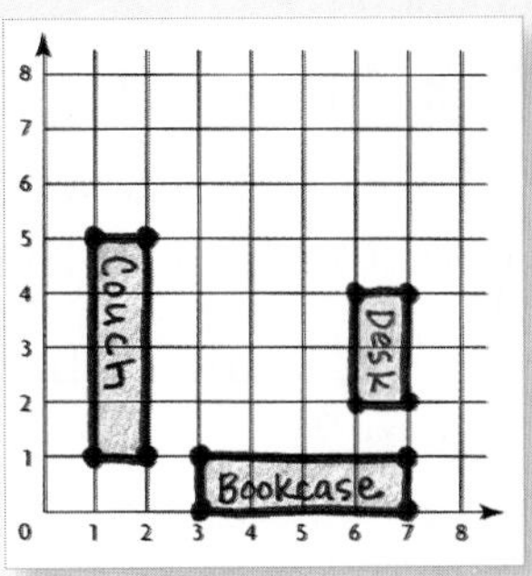

9. **Time** Jesse began studying at 10:45 A.M. He took a 25-minute break for lunch. He finished at 2:20 P.M. How long was Jesse studying?

MORE PRACTICE page H114

Tessellations

VOCABULARY
tessellation

Why learn this? You can use tessellations to make designs, such as those used on walls, floors, and fabrics.

When closed figures are arranged in a repeating pattern to cover a surface that has no gaps and no overlaps, the pattern is called a **tessellation**. Look at the examples below and name the figures.

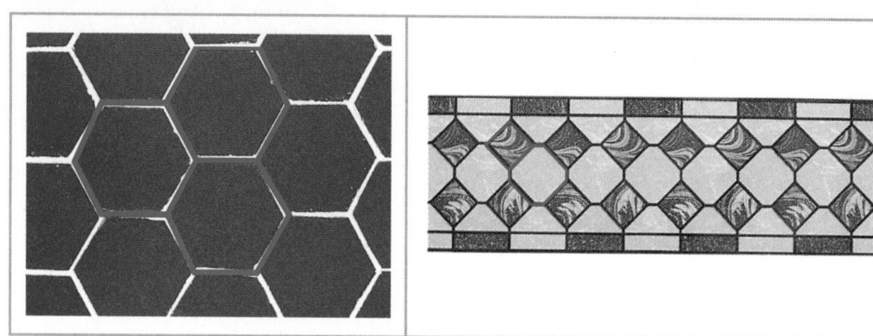

REMEMBER:

This figure tessellates.

This figure does not tessellate.

gaps

- How do you know that the figures in each example make a tessellation?

____

You can make a tessellation by transforming a figure. Follow these steps to make your own tessellation.

MODEL

Step 1
Draw these figures.

Step 2
Cut out the figures. Translate, reflect, or rotate the figures. Trace them to cover a surface with no gaps and no overlaps.

Step 3
Color or draw on your tessellation.

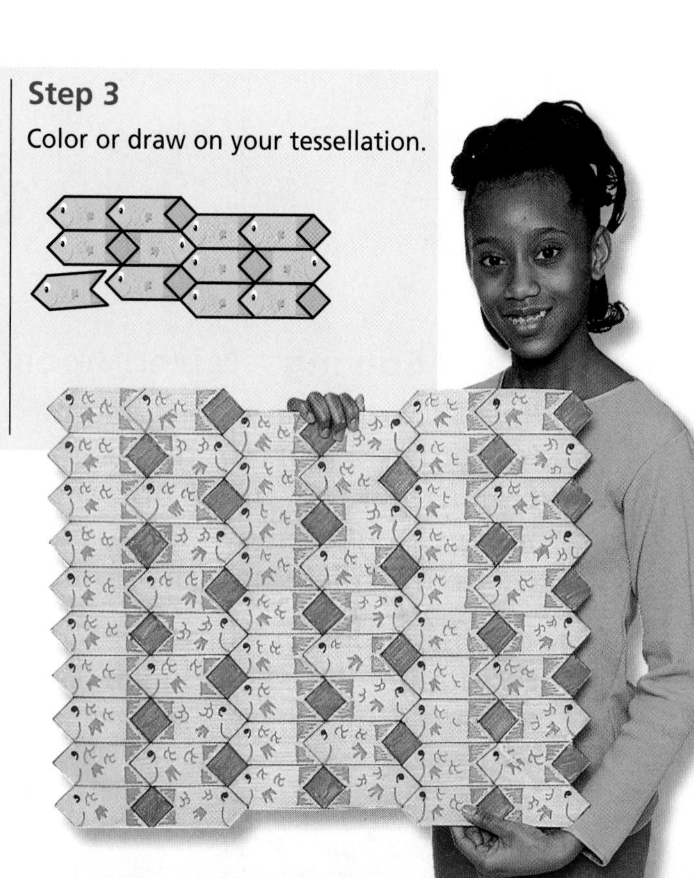

Talk About It

- What figures were used to begin the tessellation in Step 1?
- What transformations were used in Step 2?

▶ CHECK

Copy each figure. Write *yes* or *no* to tell whether each figure can be arranged to tessellate.

1. 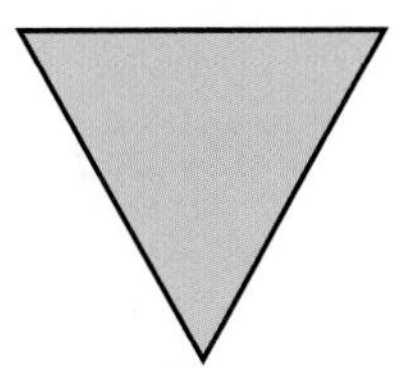

2. 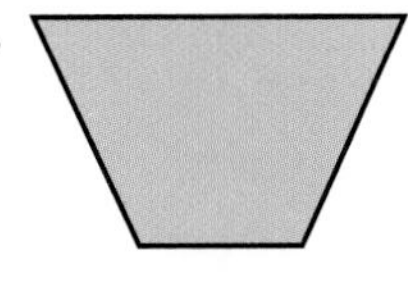

3. 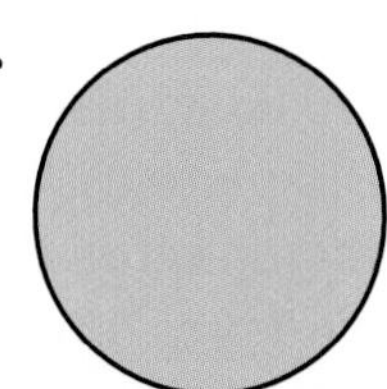

4. 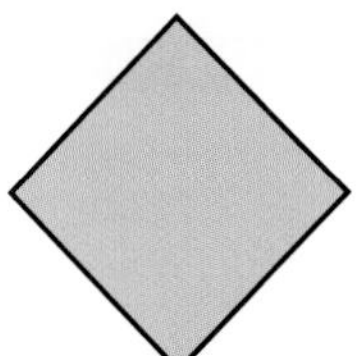

5. 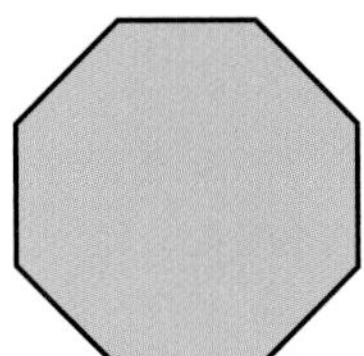

6. 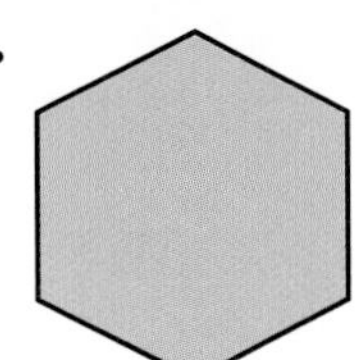

▶ PRACTICE

Copy each figure and translate, reflect, or rotate it to make a design that tessellates.

7. 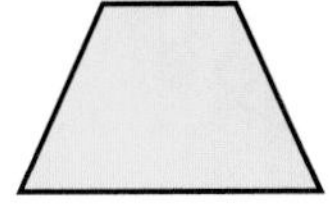

8. 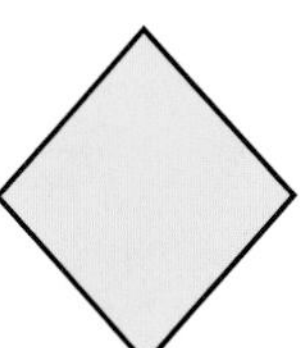

9. 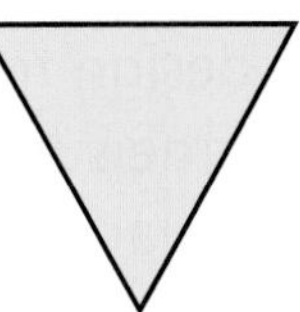

10. 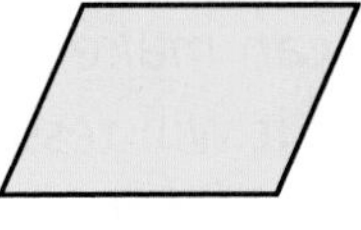

Copy the tiles and make a design that tessellates. Repeat the design 4 times to make a tessellation.

11. 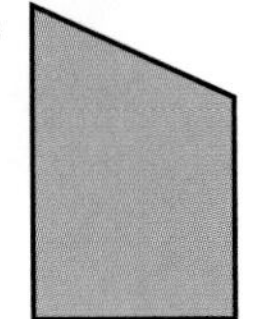 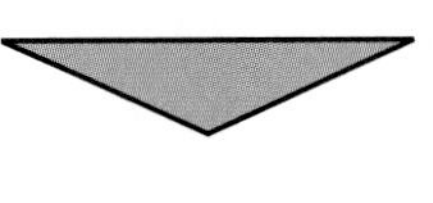

12. 

Problem Solving • Mixed Applications

13. Consumer Devon is buying 12-inch square tiles for $2.35 each. He wants to cover a floor that is 10 ft long and 8 ft wide. How many tiles will he need? What will they cost?

14. Quan bought 72 tiles. When he finished tiling the floor, $\frac{1}{6}$ of the tiles were not used. How many tiles did he have left?

15. Visual Thinking Mandy is using square and octagonal tiles to cover her kitchen floor. Draw the design that Mandy will have on her kitchen floor.

16. Write About It Describe the ways that you can move a figure to make a tessellation.

LESSON CONTINUES

MORE PRACTICE page H114

Problem–Solving Strategy: Make a Model

▶ THE PROBLEM Matt's art class is making place mats for the Student-Parent Association Dinner. The place mats must have a mosaic design using two or more polygons. The design must cover the place mat. How can Matt determine which polygons will tessellate in order to make his design?

REMEMBER:

UNDERSTAND
PLAN
SOLVE
LOOK BACK

UNDERSTAND

- What are you asked to do?
- What information will you use?
- Is there information you will not use? If so, what?

PLAN

- How can you solve the problem?

  You can *make a model* of the design to see if it will tessellate, or cover the surface. Then trace the design onto the place mat.

SOLVE

- How can you use the strategy to solve the problem?

  Use pattern blocks to make designs until you find one that tessellates. Trace the design onto the place mat. Color and decorate the design.

LOOK BACK

- How does making a model help you solve the problem?
- What other strategy could you use?

▶ PRACTICE

Make a model to solve.

1. Miguel is making a tile tray with a mosaic design. He can use two or more polygons. The polygons need to tessellate in order to cover the tray. Using pattern blocks, make a design that tessellates. Draw the design.

2. Rebecca has pattern blocks that are small equilateral triangles, small squares, and hexagons. Which two of these blocks will tessellate when arranged in a design? Draw the design.

3. The Harpers want to fence a rectangular area of their yard. They have 60 meters of fence to use. What dimensions should the fence be to give the greatest possible area?

4. Of the art projects on display, $\frac{1}{4}$ were made by third-graders, $\frac{1}{2}$ were made by fourth-graders, and $\frac{1}{4}$ were made by fifth-graders. There were 16 projects made by fourth-graders. How many projects were made by fifth-graders?

Mixed Applications

Solve.

CHOOSE a strategy and a tool.

- Make a Graph
- Work Backward
- Use a Formula
- Draw a Diagram
- Make a Model

Paper/Pencil

Calculator

Hands-On

Mental Math

5. Peggy needs a new design for a quilt she is making. She wants it to include 2 or more polygons. Use pattern blocks to make a design that tessellates for Peggy's quilt. Draw your design.

6. Mr. Jackson gave us directions to the hardware store. He said to drive 5 blocks east from our house and make a 90° turn north. Then drive 6 blocks north, and make a 45° turn east onto Clay Street. Go 3 blocks east, and the store is on the right. Make a map of these directions.

7. Erin spent half of her money for a pair of jeans. Then she spent half of what was left for a shirt. After that, she had \$8.50 left. How much did she have at the start?

8. Lana's afghan is 4 ft $1\frac{1}{2}$ in. wide and 5 ft $3\frac{1}{2}$ in. long. What is the perimeter of the afghan?

9. Jerry kept a chart of the high temperatures each day for five days. Show a different way to display the information that is in the table. Explain your choice of display.

High Temperatures	
Jan. 5	54°
Jan. 6	62°
Jan. 7	64°
Jan. 8	50°
Jan. 9	48°

MORE PRACTICE page H114

CHAPTER 24 Review/Test

▶ CHECK Understanding

VOCABULARY

1. When you move a figure to show a translation, reflection, or rotation, it is called a __?__. (page 430)

2. When closed figures are arranged to cover a surface with no gaps and no overlaps, it is called a __?__. (page 432)

Write *congruent* or *not congruent*. (pages 426–427)

3. 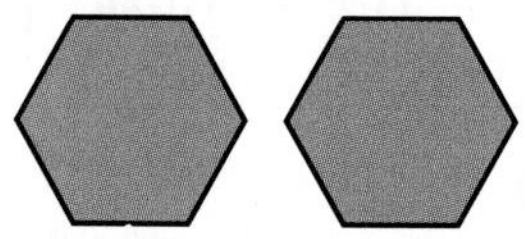

4. 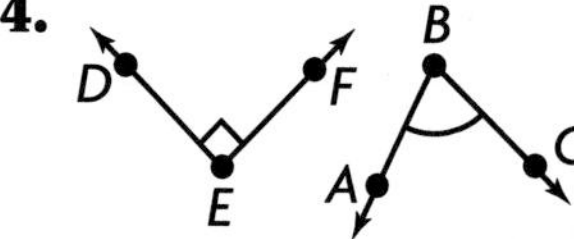

5. 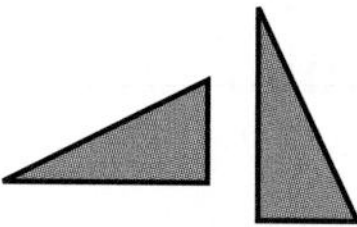

Copy each figure on a coordinate grid. Then show a translation for 6, a reflection for 7, and a rotation for 8. Name the new ordered pairs. (pages 430–431)

6. 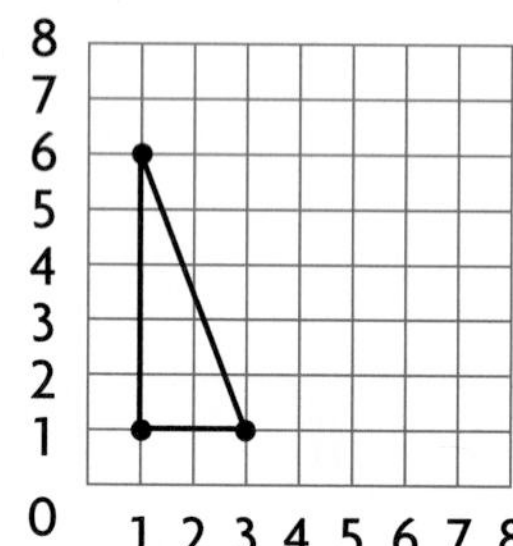

7. 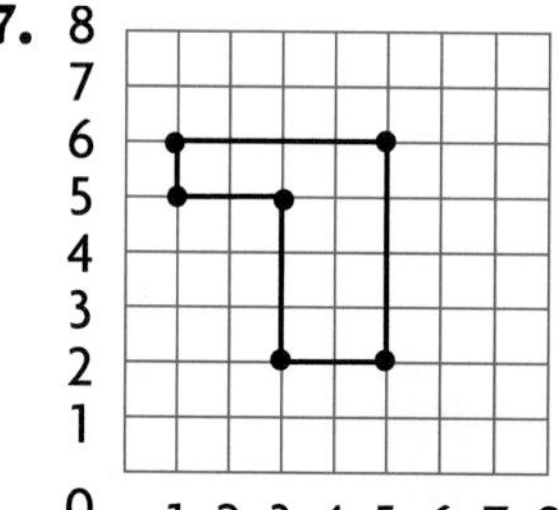

8. 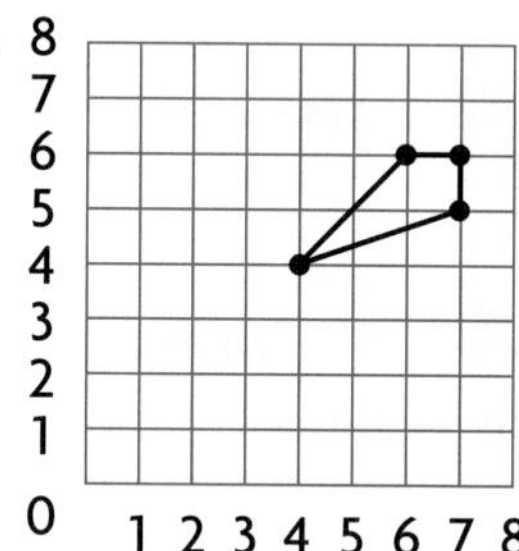

▶ CHECK Skills

Trace each figure. Draw the lines of symmetry for each figure. (pages 428–429)

9. 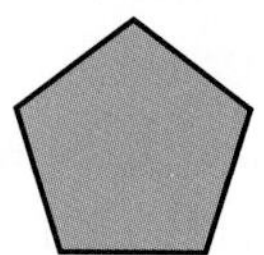

10. 

Copy each figure. Write *yes* or *no* to tell whether each figure tessellates. (pages 432–433)

11. 

12. 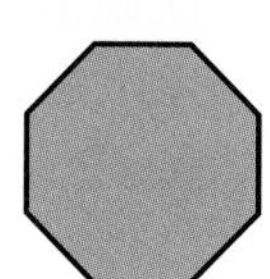

▶ CHECK Problem Solving

Solve. (pages 434–435)

CHOOSE a strategy and a tool.

- Write a Number Sentence
- Make a Model
- Work Backward
- Draw a Diagram

Paper/Pencil

Calculator

Hands-On

Mental Math

13. Kathy is making a quilt with hexagons and triangles. Trace pattern blocks to show how her design might look.

14. Mr. Cox paid $28.95 for wood and $2.03 tax. How much change did he receive if he gave the clerk two $20 bills?

Test Prep

CUMULATIVE
CHAPTERS 1–24

Choose the best answer.

1. Pat bought 11 bags of balloons for a party. Each bag has about 14 balloons. Which of the following is a reasonable estimate for the total number of balloons?

   A 50 **B** 300
   C 150 **D** 200

2. Aki bought 50 marbles. She plans to give marbles to 7 friends. What is the greatest number of marbles she can give each friend?

   F 5 **G** 6
   H 7 **J** 8

3. Reuben biked the following miles last week.

DISTANCE REUBEN BIKED	
Day	**Number of Miles**
Mon	3
Tue	5
Wed	6
Thu	8
Fri	3

   What was the mean for the mileage Reuben biked per day?

   A 3 mi **B** 5 mi
   C 6 mi **D** 8 mi

4. A floor measures 8 ft by 12 ft. What is its area?

   F 20 sq ft
   G 40 sq ft
   H 84 sq ft
   J 96 sq ft
   K Not Here

5. Bay has one white shirt, one yellow shirt, one green shirt, one pair of blue pants, and one pair of black pants. How many possible outfits can he make?

   A 4 **B** 5
   C 6 **D** 8

6. What are the factors of 16?

   F 1, 2, 8, 16 **G** 1, 2, 3, 8
   H 1, 2, 4, 12, 16 **J** 1, 2, 4, 8, 16

7. Which of the following triangles is shown?

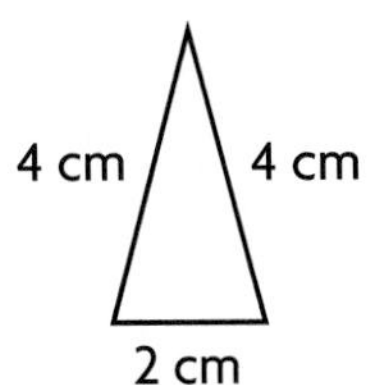

   A equilateral **B** isosceles
   C right **D** scalene

8. Which two letters are congruent?

   F T T
   G T t
   H T L
   J T ⊣

9. Which figure has 3 lines of symmetry?

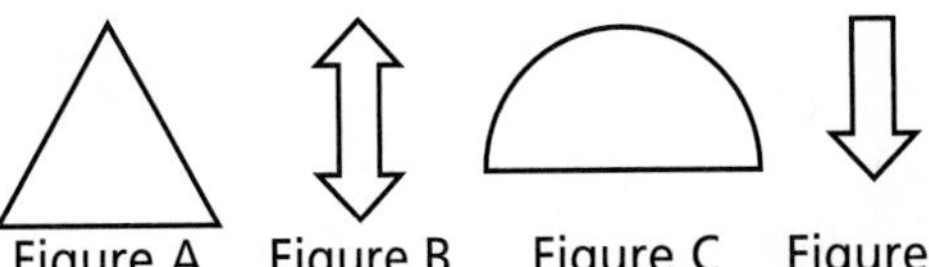

   A Figure A
   B Figure B
   C Figure C
   D Figure D

25 CIRCLES

HISTORY **LINK**

Sections of tree trunks were once used as wheels. Heavy loads could be carried using tree-trunk wheels. By 3,500 B.C., the Sumerians in the Tigris-Euphrates Valley were using carts with wheels attached to axles.

Problem-Solving Activity

The Wondrous Wheel

Can you imagine a world without the wheel? For centuries, people have put these special cylinders to work. Learn some interesting facts about wheels.

YOU WILL NEED: reference books, poster board, markers

- Choose a focus area. Look at the list to the right for ideas.
- Do your research. Find, and record, several interesting facts about wheels.
- Decide how to present these facts to the class. Will you make a model? a poster? act it out?
- Present your findings to the class.

The Wheel in Arts and Crafts
potter's wheel
carpenter's lathe

The Wheel to Navigate
gyroscope
compass
steering wheels on ships, cars

Wheels in High-Tech
disk drives
CD players
knobs and dials

DID YOU

- ✓ choose a topic?
- ✓ find and record facts about wheels?
- ✓ choose a way to present your facts?
- ✓ present your facts to the class?

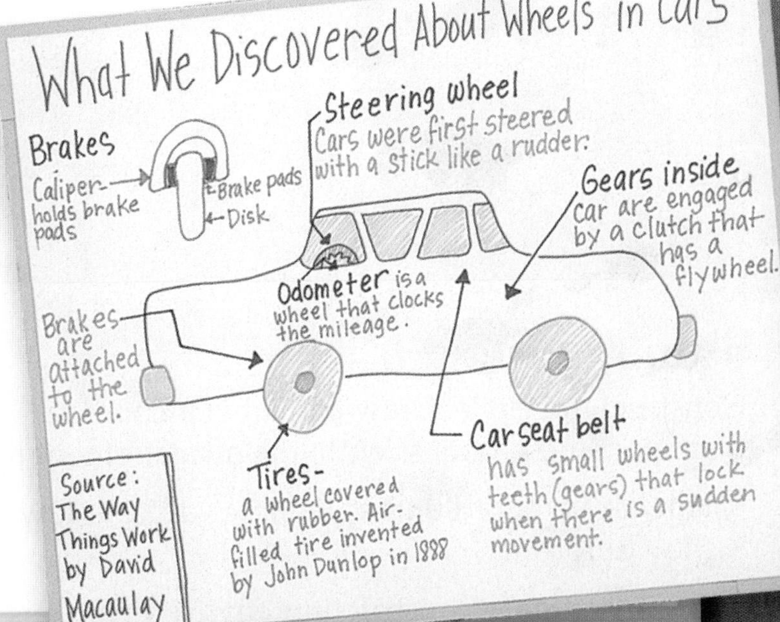

Construct a Circle

You will investigate how to construct a circle and name its parts.

VOCABULARY
circle
chord
diameter
radius
compass

A **circle** is a closed figure with all points on the figure the same distance from the center point. It has no beginning point and no ending point.

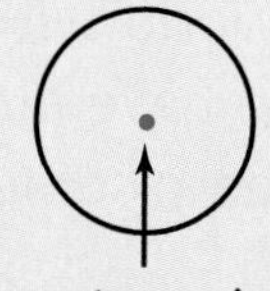

Notice that

- A line segment that connects any two points on the circle is called a **chord**.
- A chord that passes through the center of the circle is called a **diameter**.
- A line segment that connects the center with a point on the circle is called a **radius** (plural radii).

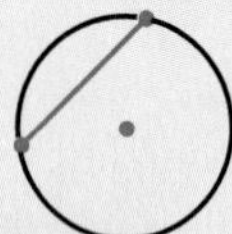

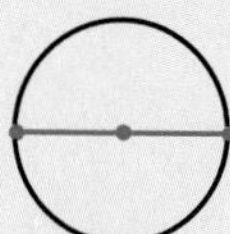

EXPLORE

A **compass** is a tool for constructing circles. Use a compass to construct a circle with a radius of 3 cm.

MATERIALS: compass, centimeter ruler

Draw a point. Place the center of the red circle of the compass over the point.	Set the compass to the length of the radius.	Hold the compass still at the center point, and move the compass to make the circle.
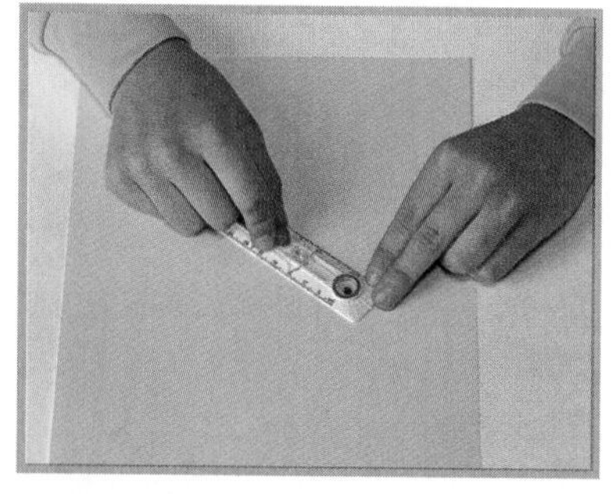	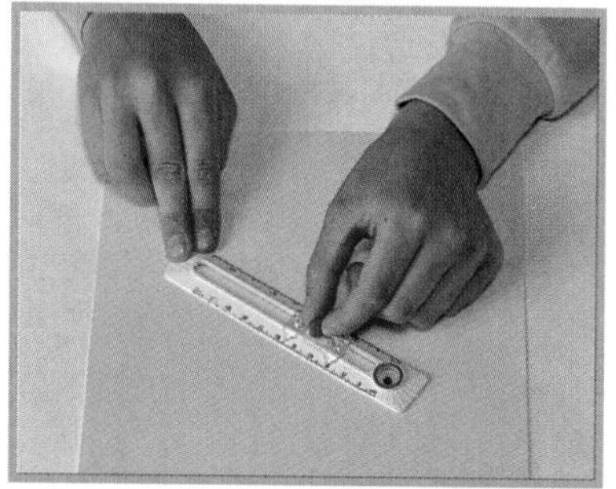	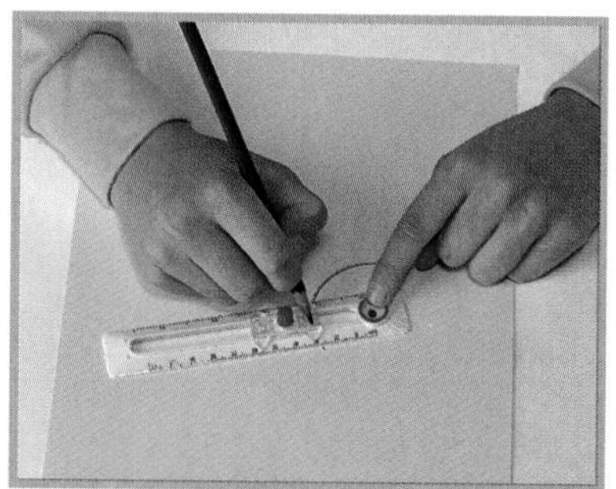

Record

Construct the circle. Draw and label a chord, a diameter, and a radius. Write the measurement of each.

- How are a chord and a diameter alike? How are they different?

Now, investigate constructing circles of various sizes.

▶ TRY THIS

Use each radius to construct a circle. For each circle, draw line segments to show a chord, a diameter, and a radius. Write the measurements.

1. 2 cm **2.** 5 cm **3.** 1 cm

4. Can the length of a chord be greater than a diameter? Explain.

5. What relationship do you notice between a radius and a diameter of a circle?

6. **Write About It** Explain how to construct a circle with a diameter of 4 cm.

SCIENCE LINK

A navigational compass is used on ships and other seagoing vessels. It has a needle that detects magnetic changes in the earth. The needle moves to show directional changes. What is the name of the line segment that crosses the circular face of the compass from east to west?

▶ PRACTICE

Use a compass to construct the circles. Find the measurements.

7. Construct a circle with a radius of 4 cm. Label and measure a diameter and a chord.

8. Construct a circle with a diameter of 6 cm. Label and measure a radius and a chord.

Write *chord, diameter*, or *radius* for each line segment.

9. 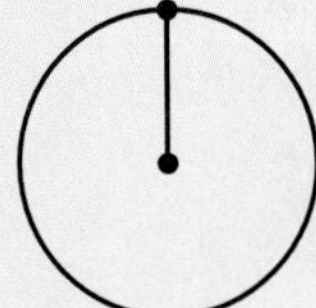

10. 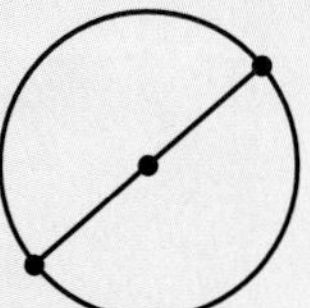

11. 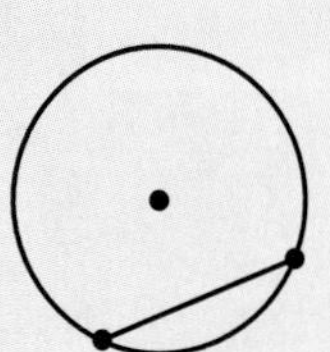

12. 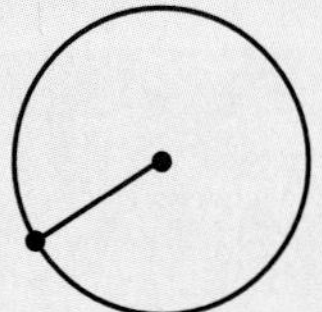

Problem Solving • Mixed Applications

For Problems 13–16, use the drawing.

13. Measurement Fernando knows that the diameters of the bicycles' tires are 20 in. and 24 in. What is the radius of each bicycle's tires?

14. Money Becky can pay for the 20-in. bike in 3 equal monthly payments. How much will each payment be?

15. Consumer If the difference in price of the two bikes is less than $20.00, Tom will buy the 24-in. bike. Which bike will Tom buy?

16. **Write About It** Explain how you could draw a diagram of a bike.

MORE PRACTICE page H115

Finding Circumference

VOCABULARY
circumference

You will investigate how to find the circumference of a circle.

REMEMBER:

Perimeter is the distance around a figure. To find the perimeter of a polygon, find the total of the lengths of the sides.

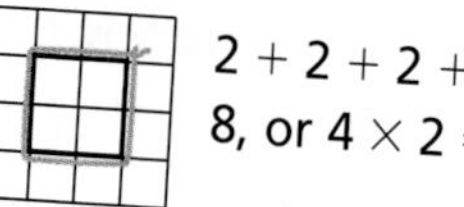

$2 + 2 + 2 + 2 = 8$, or $4 \times 2 = 8$

perimeter = 8 units

The perimeter of a circle is the **circumference**. Circles do not have sides, so you need to use a different method to find the distance around a circle.

▶ EXPLORE

Find the circumference and diameter of a circular object such as a cup or a lid.

MATERIALS: compass, cm ruler, string, circular objects

MODEL

Step 1
Wrap string around a circular object.

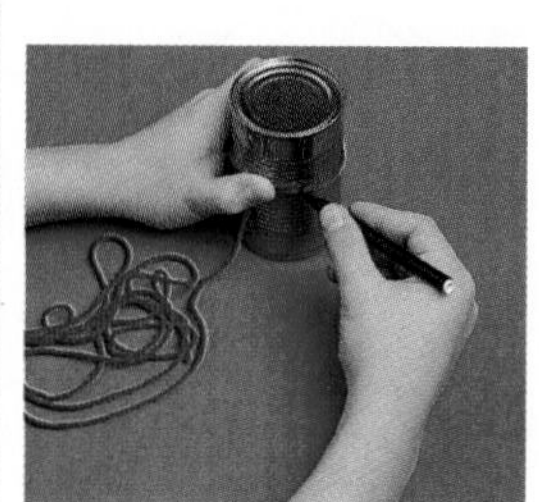

Step 2
Use a ruler to measure the length of the string.

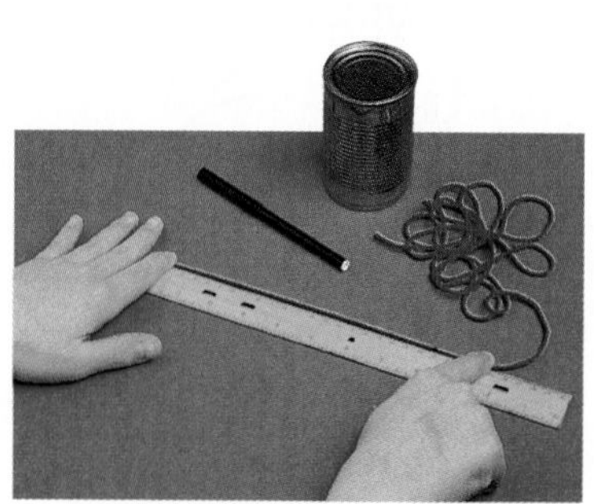

Step 3
Trace the circle and measure the diameter. (HINT: Measure the greatest distance across the circle.)

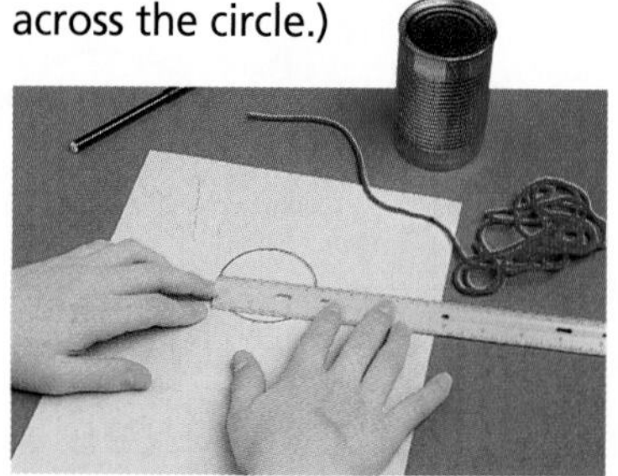

Record

Trace the circle and label it *A*. Record the circumference and the diameter to the nearest tenth of a centimeter.

Circle	Circumference (c)	Diameter (d)	c÷d
Example	15.7 cm	5 cm	
A			
B			

Now, investigate the relationship of the diameter to the circumference of a circle.

You may wish to use a calculator. $15.7 \div 5 = n$

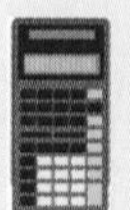

Press:

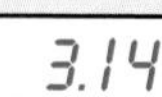

Display: 3.14

So, $n = 3.14$ cm.

▶ TRY THIS

1–3. Use the cm ruler and string to find the circumference and diameter of three other circular objects. Record both measurements in the table. Divide to find out how many times longer the circumference is than the diameter. Round each quotient to the nearest hundredth.

4. How many times longer is the circumference than the diameter of a circle?

5. **Write About It** Explain how you could find the circumference of a circle without using the string method if you know the diameter.

The relationship of the diameter to the circumference of a circle, $C \div d$, is 3.14 and is called *pi* (π).

Technology Link

You can make circles of different diameters by using E-Lab, Activity 25. Available on CD-ROM and on the Internet at **www.hbschool.com/elab**

▶ PRACTICE

6. Use a centimeter ruler and string to find the circumference of a pen or marker.

Using a calculator, divide the circumference of each object by its diameter. Complete the table by rounding to the nearest hundredth.

	Object	Circumference (C)	Diameter (*d*)	$\frac{C}{d}$
7.	Spool	9.4 cm	3 cm	?
8.	Lid	12.6 cm	4 cm	?
9.	Mug	28.3 cm	9 cm	?

Problem Solving • Mixed Applications

For Problems 10–13, use the menu.

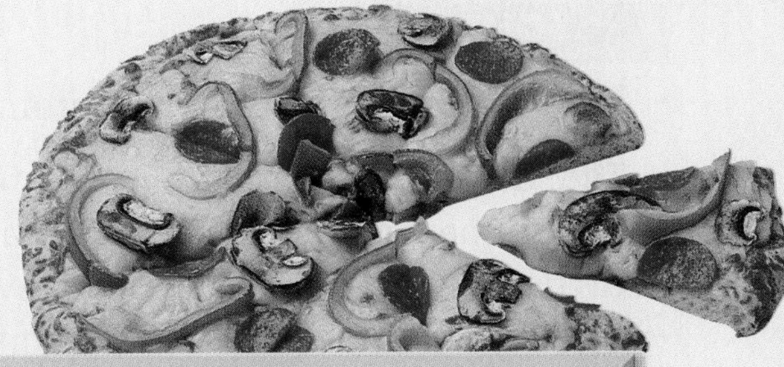

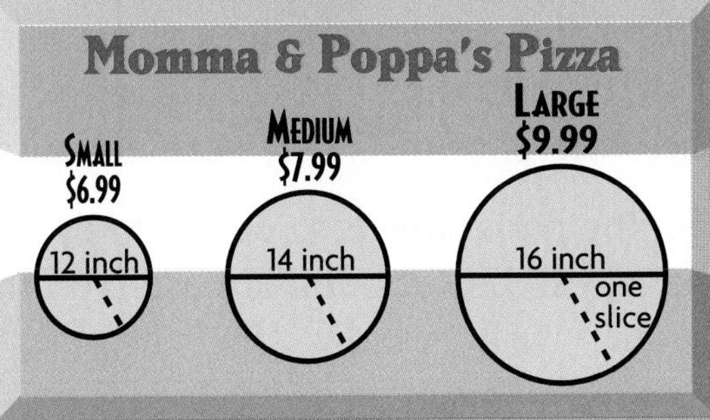

10. What is the perimeter of the smallest box that each pizza can fit into?

11. **Consumer** How much more will it cost Rosalinda to buy 3 small pizzas than to buy 2 large pizzas?

12. **Money** How much change will Darius receive from $20.00 if he buys 2 medium pizzas?

13. What is the difference in the radius of a slice from the large pizza and a slice from the medium pizza?

14. **Write About It** How would you describe to a fourth-grade student how to find the circumference of a circular object?

LESSON CONTINUES

MORE PRACTICE page H115

Problem-Solving Strategy: Act It Out

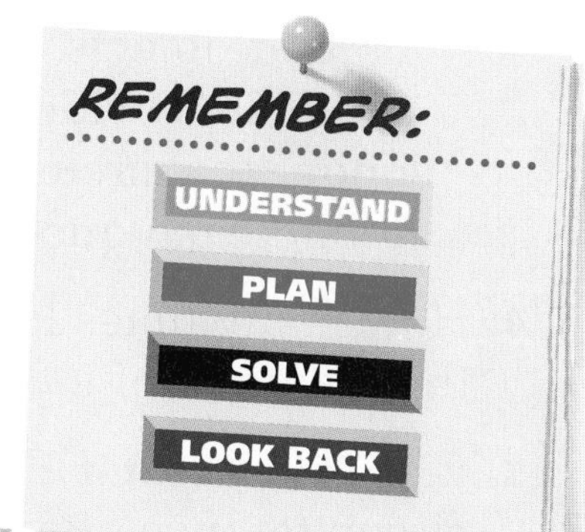

▶ **THE PROBLEM** Christy's class is making pencil holders for the crafts booth at the school fair. Everyone is bringing in cans of different sizes to be covered in brightly patterned paper. The paper must be cut to the exact size so it will fit around each can. How can Christy find out the size of the paper she needs to cover a can that is 12 cm in height?

UNDERSTAND

- What are you asked to do?
- What information will you use?
- Is there information you will not use? If so, what?

PLAN

- What strategy can you use to solve the problem?

  You can *act it out* by using string and a ruler to measure the can.

SOLVE

- How can you solve the problem?

  The surface to be covered forms a rectangle when flat, so the measurements needed are the height and circumference of the can. You know the height of the can is 12 cm. To find the circumference, wrap the string around the can and use the ruler to measure the string to the nearest tenth of a centimeter. The circumference of Christy's can measures 37.7 centimeters.

  So, the paper needs to be 12 cm by 37.7 cm. Now the paper can be cut out and pasted on the can.

LOOK BACK

- How does acting it out help you solve the problem?
- How else could you solve this problem?

▶ PRACTICE

Act it out to solve.

1. Justin is making a model of a rocket for science class. He wants to cover the cylindrical part of the rocket with foil. The cylinder is 16 cm in height, and its diameter is 9 cm. What is the circumference of the cylinder? What size should Justin cut the foil to fit the cylinder exactly?

2. Melinda wants to wrap a gift that is in a cylinder container. The cylinder is 10 in. high. The diameter of the cylinder is 3 in. She has a sheet of gift-wrap paper that is 14 in. by $9\frac{1}{2}$ in. Does Melinda have enough paper? Explain.

3. Melanie, Ashley, Jenny, Sammy, and Brooke are waiting in line to buy tickets. Ashley is in front of Sammy and after Jenny. Melanie is between Jenny and Ashley. Brooke is after Sammy. Who is first in line?

4. Corey had one $20 bill, two $10 bills, two $1 bills, one quarter, two dimes, and three pennies. He spent $16 on a CD, loaned $10.25 to his sister, and saved the rest. What bills and coins does Corey have left?

Mixed Applications

Solve.

CHOOSE a strategy and a tool.

- Write a Number Sentence
- Draw a Diagram
- Work Backward
- Make a Model
- Act It Out

Paper/Pencil  Calculator  Hands-On  Mental Math

5. Abby is wrapping a cylindrical box in gift-wrap paper. It is 18 in. tall and has a diameter of 6 in. What is the circumference of the cylinder? What size paper will Abby need?

6. The diameter of Sara's white watch is $\frac{7}{8}$ in. The diameter of her brown watch is $\frac{1}{4}$ in. What is the difference in the diameters of the watches?

7. Chris withdrew $100 from his savings account to buy clothes. He bought 2 pairs of jeans, a shirt for $18.50, and a belt for $9.50. He had $23.40 when he got home. How much was each pair of jeans?

8. Ms. Ramsey's students are doing a research report. Of the students, $\frac{1}{2}$ chose to research space exploration, $\frac{1}{3}$ chose planets, and $\frac{1}{6}$ chose the sun. If 5 of the students chose to research the sun, how many students are in the class?

9. Rod wants to take the fastest train trip to New York City. Which train should he take?

TRAIN SCHEDULE

Leave White Plains	Arrive New York City
7:15 A.M.	8:38 A.M.
9:36 A.M.	10:04 A.M.
11:16 A.M.	12:27 P.M.

MORE PRACTICE page H115

LESSON 3

Angles in a Circle

Why learn this? Builders need to know angle measures when constructing buildings and roads.

Angles are measured in degrees (°). A circle has 360°. Angles in a circle can measure from 0° to 360°.

One whole circle = 360°.	One-half circle = 180°.	One-quarter circle = 90°.
A. 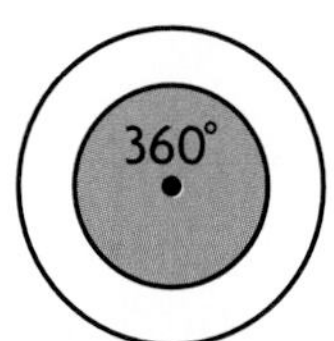	**B.** 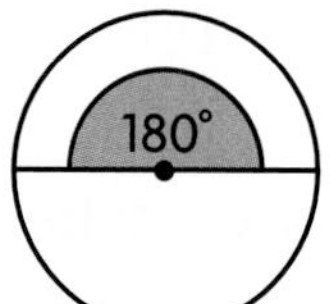	**C.** 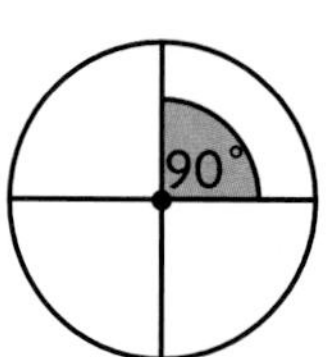

Talk About It

- In Example B, how many 180° angles are formed by the diameter?
- In Example C, how many 90° angles are formed by the two diameters?

REMEMBER:

A *right angle* forms a square corner.

An *acute angle* is less than a right angle.

An *obtuse angle* is greater than a right angle.

If you know the measure of all but one of the angles in a circle, you can find a missing angle measure.

Find the sum of the angles that you know and subtract the sum from 360°.

$90° + 45° + 60° = 195°$

$360° - 195° = n \quad n = 165°$

So, the missing angle measure is 165°.

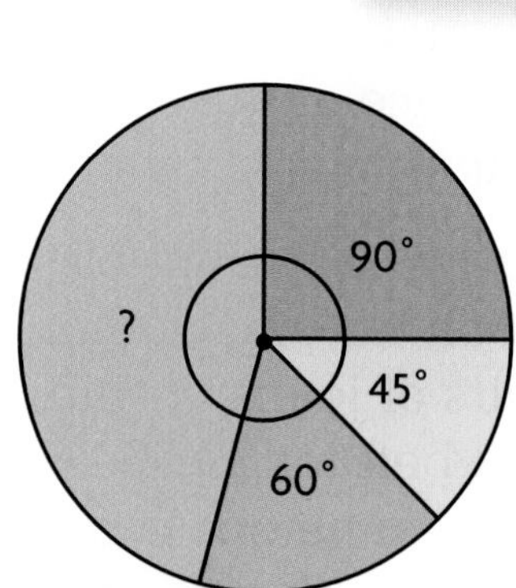

- Is the missing angle in the circle a right angle, an acute angle, or an obtuse angle?

▶ CHECK

Find the missing angle.

1. 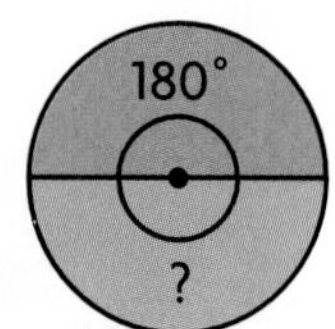

2. 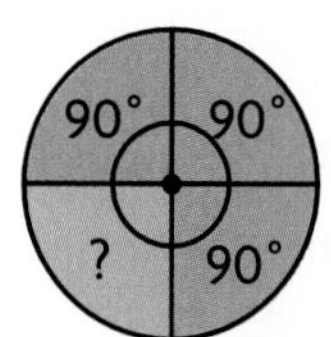

3. 

4. 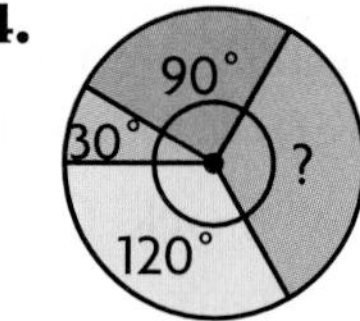

▶ PRACTICE

Write *true* or *false* to describe each statement.

5. In a circle, one diameter forms two 180° angles.

6. In a circle with two radii, one angle could measure 180°.

7. If four radii form three 90° angles in a circle, the 4th angle is acute.

8. If six radii form five 60° angles in a circle, the sixth angle is obtuse.

Find the missing angle.

9.

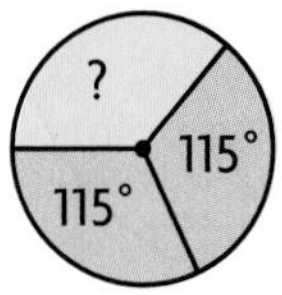

10.

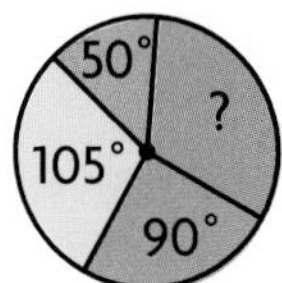

11.

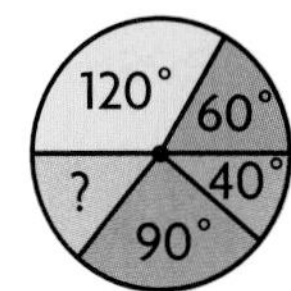

Problem Solving • Mixed Applications

Using Data For Problems 12–14, use the clocks.

SCHOOL BEGINS

12. Time Not including the 30 minutes Nancy spends eating lunch, how much time does she spend in school?

13. Visual Thinking Which clock shows an acute angle?

14. How many degrees are in the angle formed by the hands of a clock at 8:20?

15. How many degrees are in a right angle? a straight angle?

16. How many degrees are in the angle formed by the hands on a clock at 9:00?

17. **Write a problem** about the number of degrees in the angles of a sliced pie.

Mixed Review and Test Prep

Write *congruent* or *not congruent*. (pages 426–427)

18.

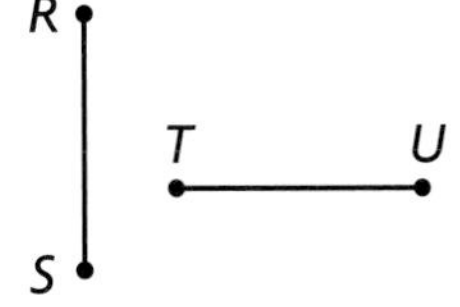

19.

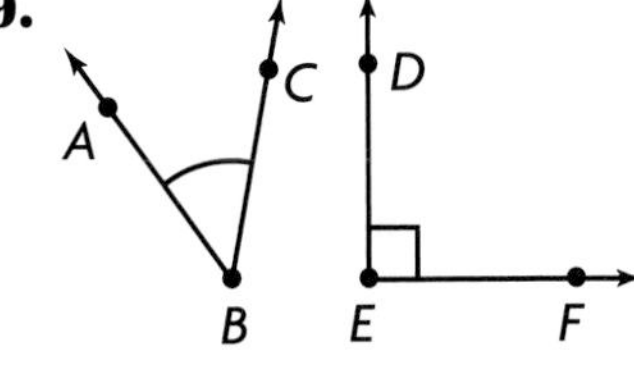

20.

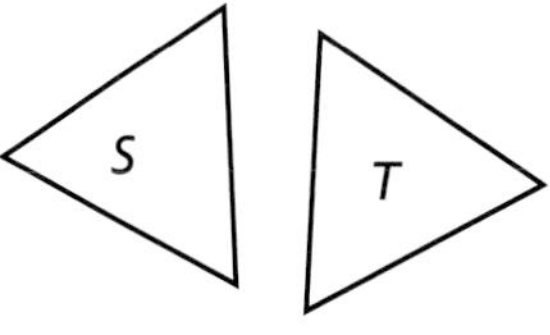

Choose the correct product in simplest form. (pages 392–393)

21. $\frac{1}{8} \times \frac{2}{3} = n$ **A** $\frac{2}{24}$ **B** $\frac{1}{12}$ **C** $\frac{3}{16}$ **D** $\frac{19}{24}$

22. $\frac{3}{4} \times \frac{3}{8} = n$ **F** $\frac{9}{8}$ **G** $\frac{8}{9}$ **H** $\frac{6}{12}$ **J** $\frac{9}{32}$

Measuring Angles in a Circle

Why learn this? You can find the number of degrees in the angle of a circle, such as an air traffic controller would use to direct a landing airplane.

The angles around the center point of a circle can be measured. You can use a protractor to find the number of degrees in each angle.

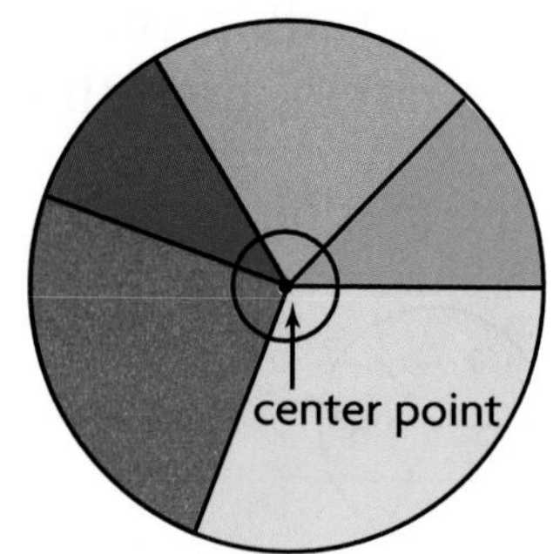

How many degrees are in each angle of the circle to the right?

MODEL

Step 1

Place the center of the protractor on the center point of the circle. Line up the protractor with one side of the angle. Read the angle where the other side crosses the protractor.

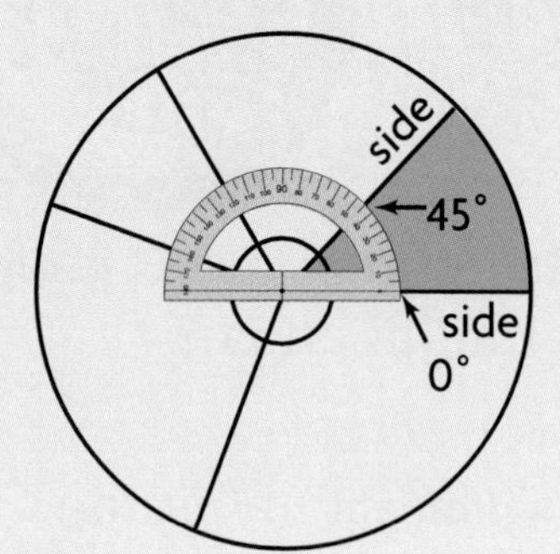

Step 2

To measure the second angle, rotate the protractor until it is lined up with the next side. Measure the remaining angles.

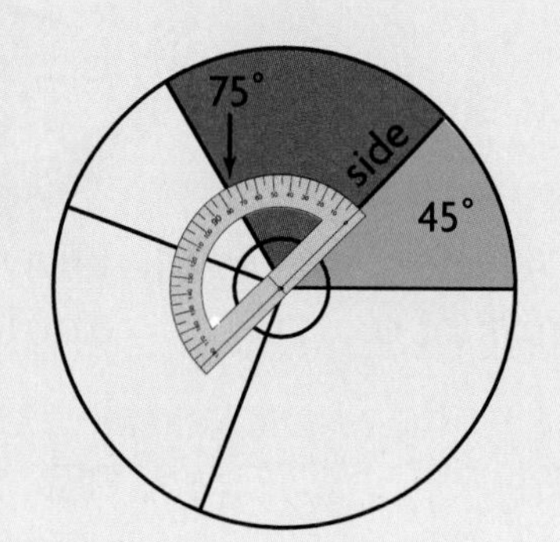

So, the angles in the circle measure 45°, 110°, 90°, 40°, and 75°.

Technology Link

With ***Graph Links Plus*** computer software, you can make circle graphs that show a measure of angles in a circle.

CRITICAL THINKING How many degrees are in the sum of the angle measures of the circle? How can you find out?

▶ CHECK

Use a protractor to find how many degrees are in each angle.

1.

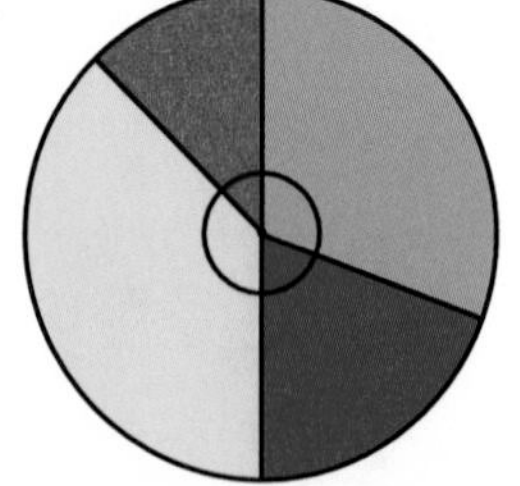

2.

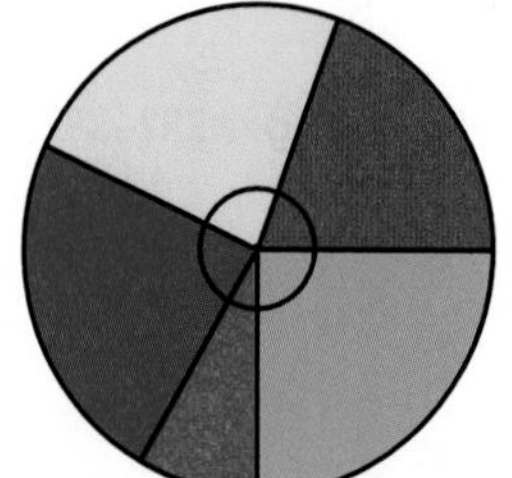

3.

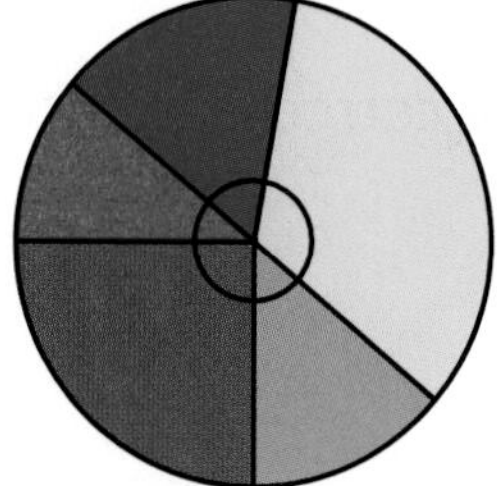

▶ PRACTICE

Use a protractor to find the number of degrees in the angles of the circle.

4. How many degrees are in the green angle?

5. How many degrees are in the blue angle?

6. How many degrees are in the red and the yellow angles?

7. How many degrees are the sum of the angles?

Use a compass and a protractor to draw a circle with the following angles.

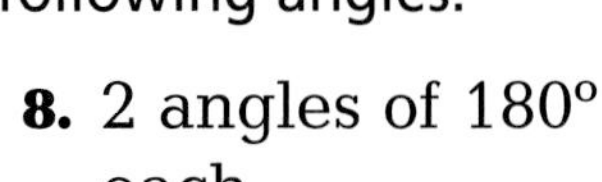

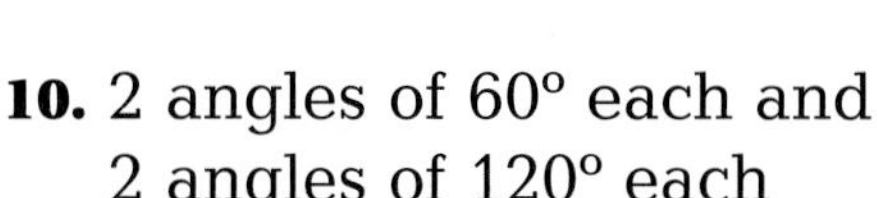

8. 2 angles of 180° each

9. 2 angles of 40° each and 2 angles of 140° each

10. 2 angles of 60° each and 2 angles of 120° each

11. 3 angles of 120° each

12. 3 angles of 100° each and 1 angle of 60°

13. 4 angles of 50° each and 1 angle of 160°

Problem Solving • Mixed Applications

14. Visual Thinking The pizza restaurant will deliver to a house only within a 3-mile radius. To get to Lani's house from the pizza restaurant, you drive 3 miles north, make a 90° turn, and drive 3 miles east. Is her house within the 3-mile radius? Why or why not?

15. Write About It Dean read the time on the clock at 6:00. He said there were no angles formed by the hands on the clock. Was he correct? Explain.

Mixed Review and Test Prep

Trace each figure. Draw the line(s) of symmetry for each figure.
(pages 428–429)

16.

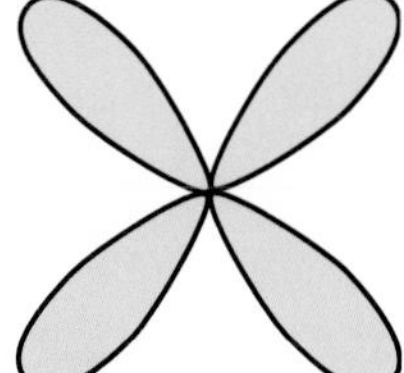

17.

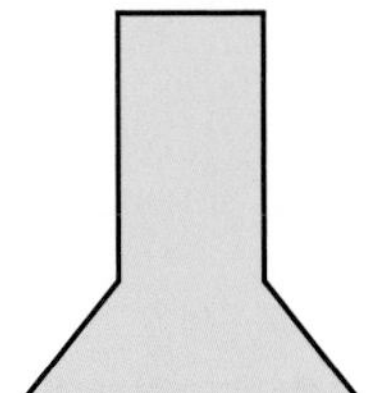

18.

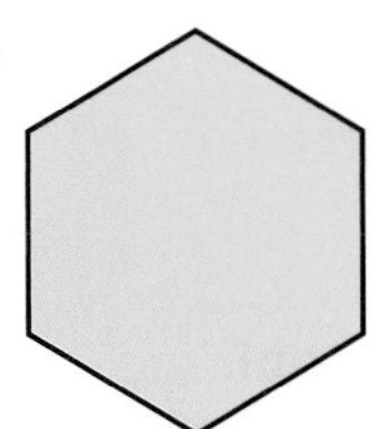

19.

Choose the unit of measure that is not equivalent. (pages 374–375)

20. 3 gal
A 12 qt
B 24 pt
C 15 qt
D 48 c

21. 2 pt
F 1 qt
G 4 c
H 1 gal
J 32 oz

22. 4 qt
A 1 gal
B 8 pt
C 40 c
D 128 oz

CHAPTER 25 Review/Test

CHECK Understanding

VOCABULARY

1. A _?_ is a closed figure with all points on the figure the same distance from the center point. (page 440)

2. A line segment that connects any two points on the circle is called a _?_. (page 440)

3. A _?_ is a tool for constructing circles. (page 440)

4. The perimeter of a circle is the _?_. (page 442)

Construct a circle with the given radius. Label and measure a radius, a diameter, and a chord. (pages 440–441)

5. 2 cm **6.** 4 cm **7.** 3 cm **8.** 5 cm

CHECK Skills

Write *true* or *false* to describe each statement. (pages 446–447)

9. There are five 60° angles in a circle.

10. There are four 90° angles in a circle.

11. A circle can have more than one obtuse angle.

12. If two of three angles in a circle each measure 120°, the third angle would be a right angle.

Find the missing angle. (pages 446–447)

13.

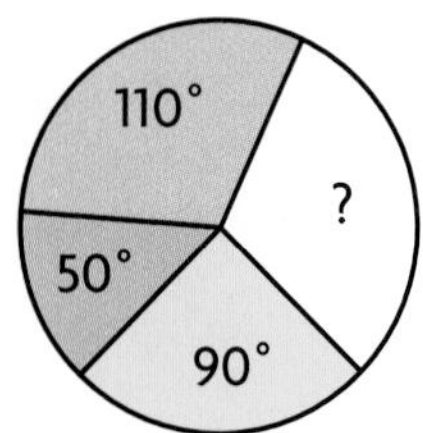

Find the number of degrees in each angle. (pages 448–449)

14.

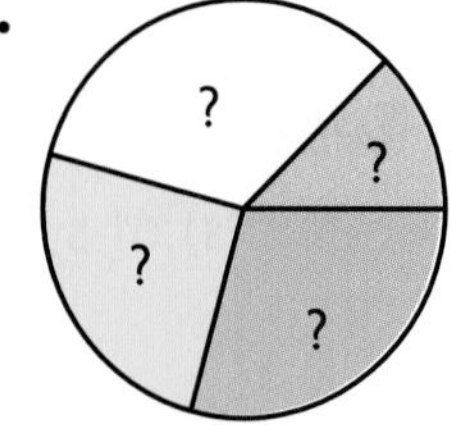

CHECK Problem Solving

Solve. (pages 444–445)

CHOOSE a strategy and a tool.

- Write a Number Sentence
- Make a Model
- Guess and Check
- Act It Out

Paper/Pencil

Calculator

Hands-On

Mental Math

15. Heather is wrapping a cylindrical box to hold her posters. It is 20 in. tall and has a diameter of 5 in. What size paper will Heather need?

16. The sum of two numbers is 64. One of the numbers is 3 times the other number. What are the two numbers?

Test Prep

CUMULATIVE
CHAPTERS 1–25

Choose the best answer.

1. A teacher bought 6 packs of paper. Each pack of paper contained 50 sheets. How many sheets of paper did the teacher buy?

A 5

B 50

C 200

D 300

E Not Here

2. 7,200 ÷ 80 =

F 70 **G** 80

H 90 **J** 95

3. Jenna has the following coins in her pocket.

2 quarters
1 dime
2 nickels

If she pulls out 1 coin, what is the probability she will pull a quarter?

A $\frac{2}{3}$ **B** $\frac{1}{2}$

C $\frac{2}{5}$ **D** $\frac{1}{3}$

4. Which expression is equivalent to (3 × 5) × 2?

F 3 × (5 × 2)

G (3 × 5) × (5 × 2)

H (3 × 5) + (5 × 2)

J (3 + 5) + 2

5. What temperature does the thermometer show?

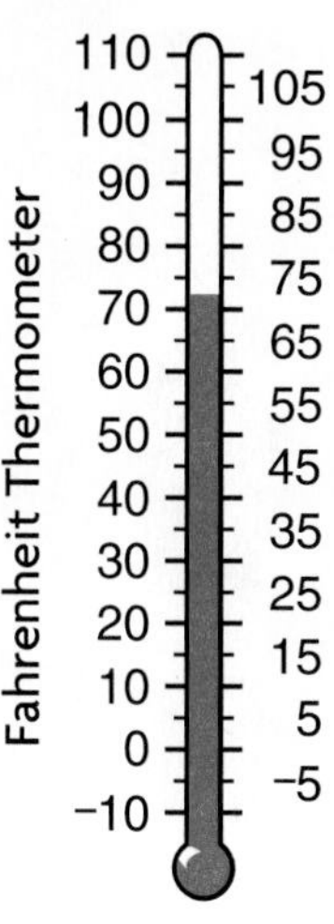

A 60°F

B 72°F

C 70°F

D 82°F

6. Chad went for a walk from his house to the store. He walked 3 blocks south, 2 blocks west, and 5 blocks north. How many blocks was his walk to the store?

F 5 **G** 10

H 12 **J** 16

7. Which letter does *not* have a line of symmetry?

A E **B** O

C J **D** V

8. A pizza measures 8 inches in diameter. What is the perimeter of the smallest box that the pizza can fit into?

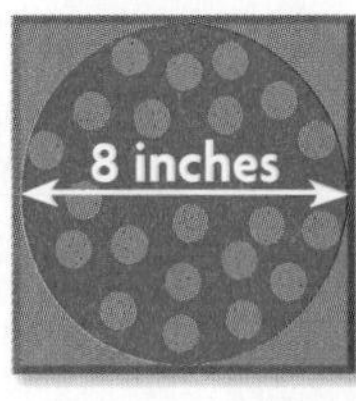

F 8 in.

G 16 in.

H 24 in.

J 32 in.

26 SOLID FIGURES

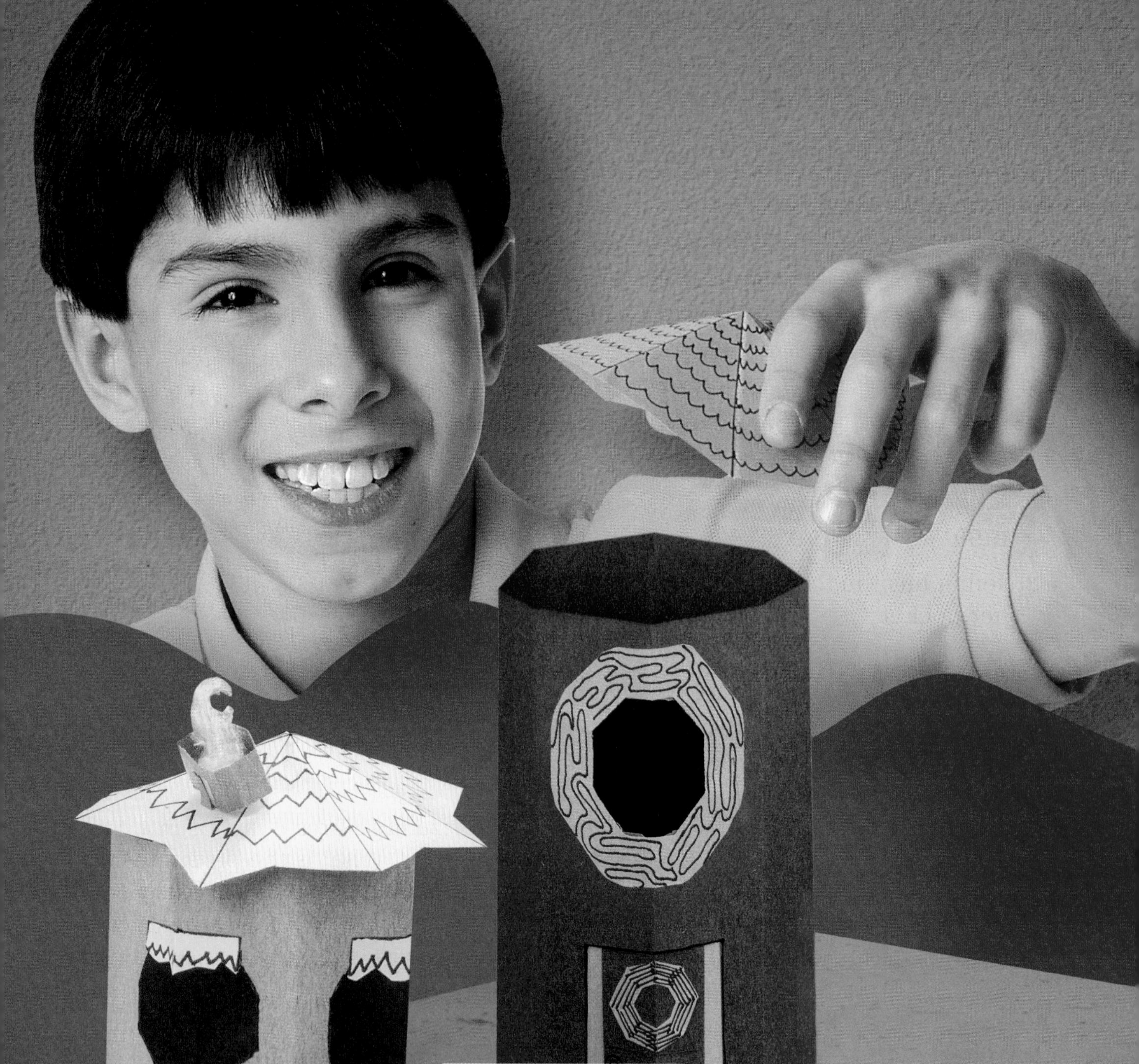

HISTORY LINK

During the 1850's and 1860's, eight-sided buildings were a popular design. If your part of the country still has very old buildings, you might see some that are octagonal.

Problem-Solving Activity

Your Octagonal Village

When people wanted to build octagonal houses, builders had to put on their thinking caps.

Make a model of an octagonal house. Then write a list of ideas to help other builders make a model of a house with more than four walls.

YOU WILL NEED: construction paper, a compass, pencil, ruler, markers, tape

- Make a model of an octagonal house.
- Make a roof that will fit over an octagon.
- Make a list of problems and how you solved them.
- Create a class village of model octagonal houses.

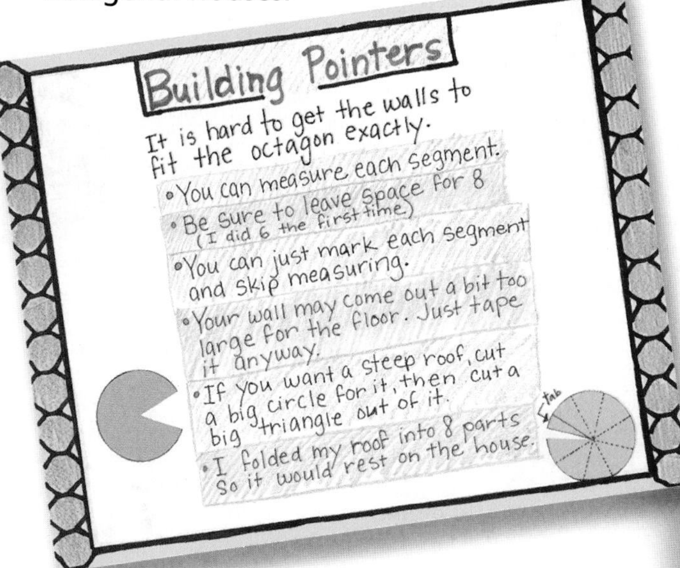

HOW TO MAKE AN OCTAGONAL HOUSE

Draw a circle with a diameter of 5 in. or less

Fold the circle in half, three times. It will be divided into eighths. Use a ruler to draw the edges of the octagon.

Start with an octagon for a base. Figure out how to plan the walls. How many will you need?

After you cut and fold the walls, decorate them. You need doors and windows! Then tape them to the base.

If you want a pointed roof, draw a circle bigger than the house. Cut out a wedge shaped like a piece of pizza. The rest is up to you.

DID YOU

- ✓ make a model of an octagonal house?
- ✓ make a list of problems and how you solved them?
- ✓ create a class octagonal village?

Prisms and Pyramids

Why learn this? You can recognize solid figures in the shapes of buildings in the world around you.

VOCABULARY
prism
base
pyramid

A **prism** is a solid figure that has two congruent faces called bases. The two **bases** of a prism are congruent polygons. A prism is named by the polygons that form its bases. All other faces are rectangles.

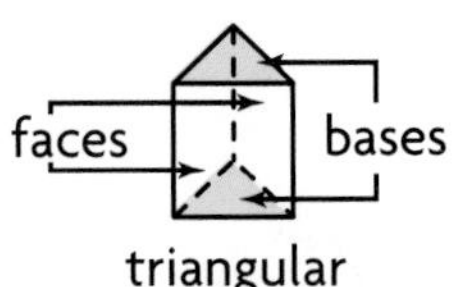

triangular prism

rectangular prism

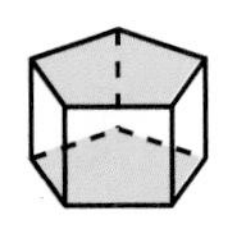
pentagonal prism

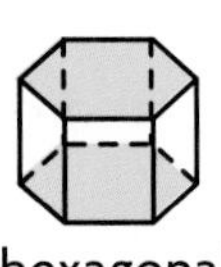
hexagonal prism

REMEMBER:

Perpendicular lines intersect to form right angles. *Parallel* lines never intersect.

Example: $\overline{AE}$ is perpendicular to $\overline{AB}$ and $\overline{AB}$ is parallel to $\overline{DC}$

Talk About It CRITICAL THINKING

- What parts of each of the prisms above are parallel? perpendicular?
- All the faces of this prism are squares. Name the prism. How is it different from other kinds of prisms?

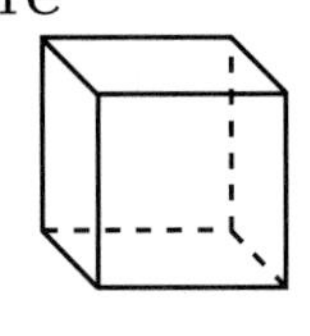

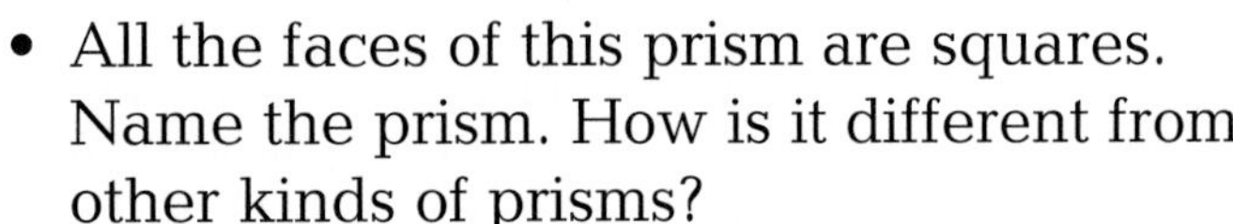

A **pyramid** is a solid figure with one base that is a polygon and three or more other faces that are triangles with a common vertex. A pyramid is named by the polygon that forms its base.

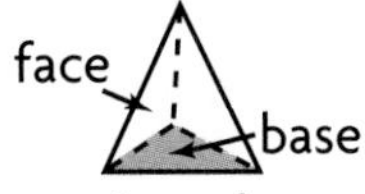

triangular pyramid

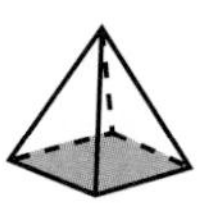
square pyramid

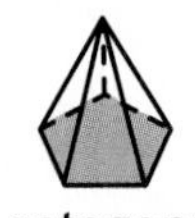
pentagonal pyramid

hexagonal pyramid

octagonal pyramid

- How are a prism and a pyramid different? How are they alike?

▶ CHECK

Write *prism* or *pyramid*. Write the polygon that names the base. Identify the solid figure.

1. 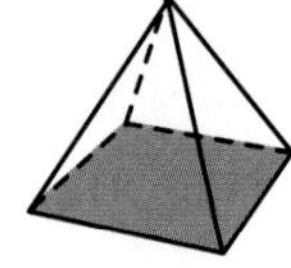

2. 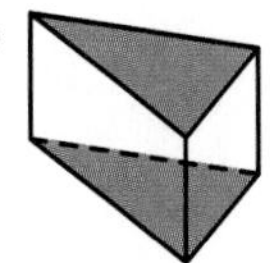

3. 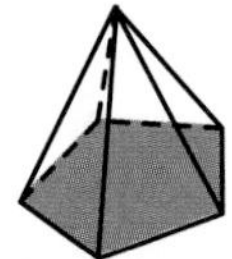

4. 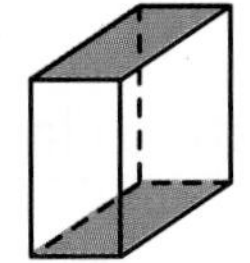

▶ PRACTICE

Write *prism* or *pyramid*. Write the polygon that names the base. Identify the solid figure.

5. 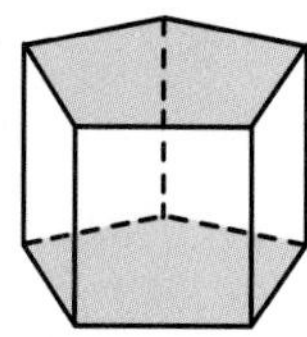

6. 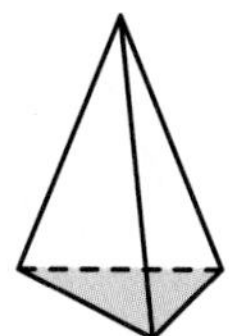

7. 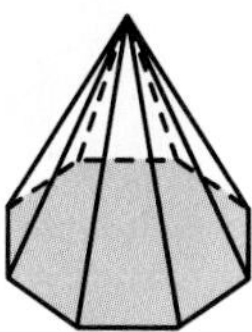

8. 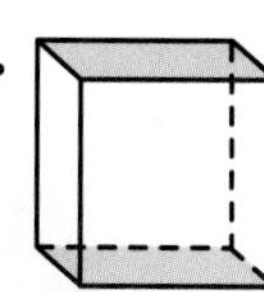

CULTURAL LINK

This building in Florence, Italy, is an *octagonal prism*. Its roof is an *octagonal pyramid*. Construction on this building was started nearly 1,000 years ago. What kind of angle does a corner of the building form?

Write the name of the solid figure. Make a drawing of each.

9. I have a base with 4 equal sides. My faces are 4 triangles.

10. All 6 of my faces are rectangles.

11. I have 2 congruent triangles for bases. I have 3 rectangular faces.

12. I have 4 congruent triangles.

Problem Solving • Mixed Applications

13. Measurement April walked around the perimeter of a rectangular building. The length of the building was 118 ft and the width was 65 ft. How many yards did April walk?

14. Visual Thinking Don bought this tent for camping. What solid figure does the tent look like?

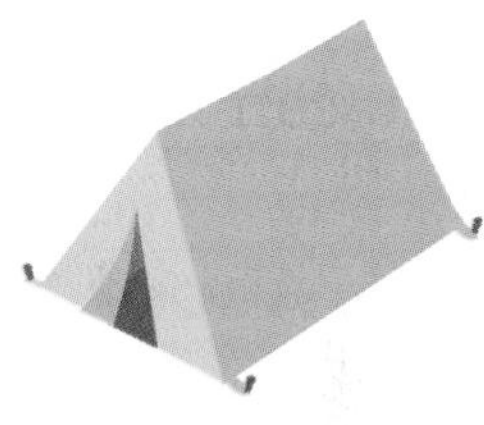

15. Time A Girl Scout troop spent 48 hours on a camping trip. They spent $\frac{1}{6}$ of the time hiking. How many hours did they spend hiking?

16. **Write a problem** in which you identify a solid figure.

Mixed Review and Test Prep

Copy each figure. Write *yes* or *no* to tell whether each figure tessellates. (pages 432–433)

17. 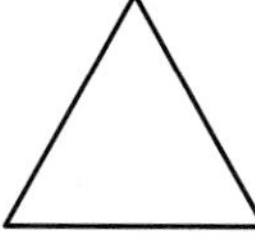

18. 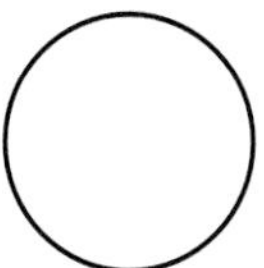

19. 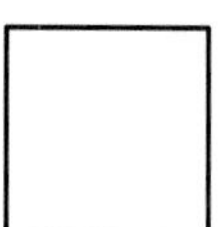

20. 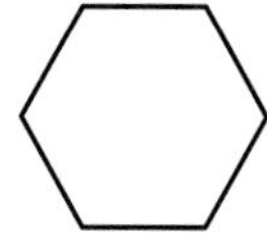

Choose the letter of the equivalent measurement. (pages 376–377)

21. 3,000 lb = __?__ **A** 1 T **B** $\frac{1}{2}$ T **C** $1\frac{1}{2}$ T **D** $\frac{1}{4}$ T

22. 10 T = __?__ **F** 1,000 lb **G** 100 lb **H** 20,000 lb **J** 200 lb

MORE PRACTICE page H117

LESSON 2

Nets for Solid Figures

VOCABULARY
net

Why learn this? You can make your own box or pyramid from a pattern.

A **net** is a two-dimensional pattern for a three-dimensional solid. Use what you know about prisms and pyramids to identify nets for solid figures.

Look at the net. Analyze ways you can fold it to make a solid figure.

Talk About It

- How many faces does this net have?
- What shape is the base? What shape are the other faces?
- What solid figure can you make by folding the net?

You can make other solid figures from patterns.

Talk About It

- What solid figure can you make by folding each pattern shown at the right?
- What shape is the base of each figure?

A.

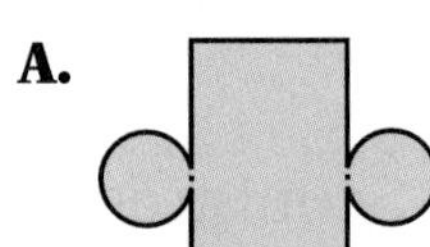

B.

▶ CHECK

Match each solid figure with its net. Write *a, b, c,* or *d*.

1.

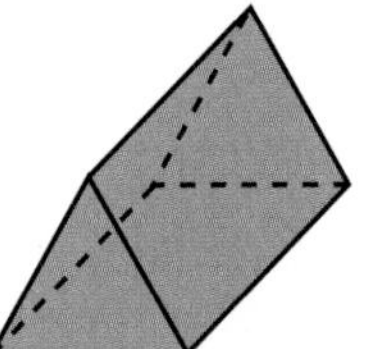

2.

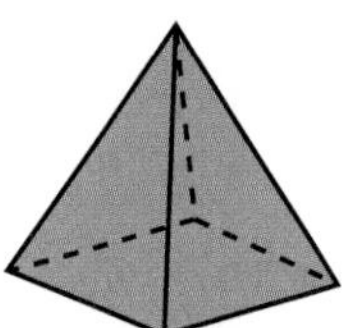

3.

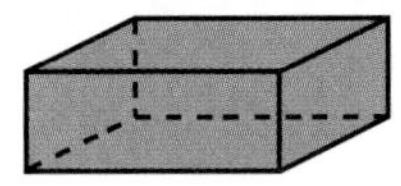

4.

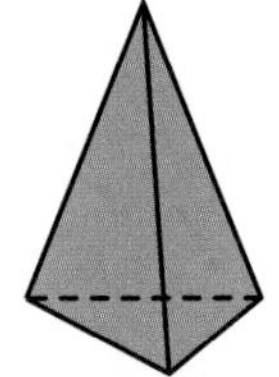

a.

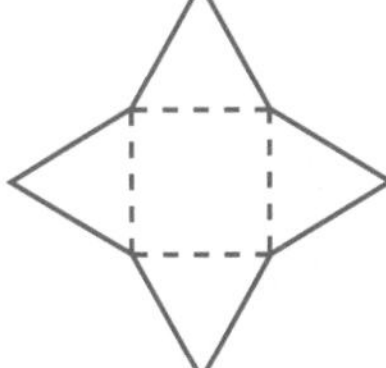

b.

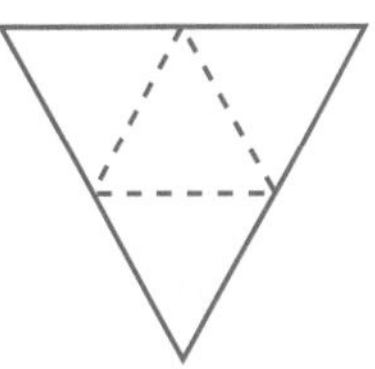

c.

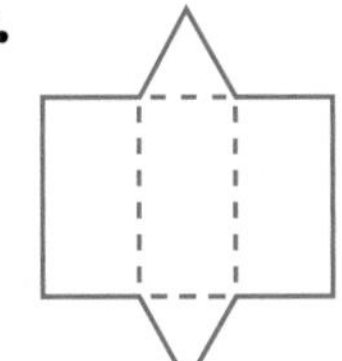

d.

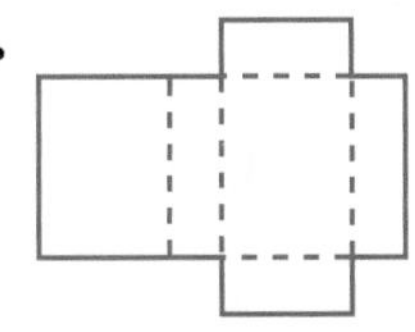

▶ PRACTICE

Match each solid figure with its net. Write *a, b, c,* or *d*.

5. 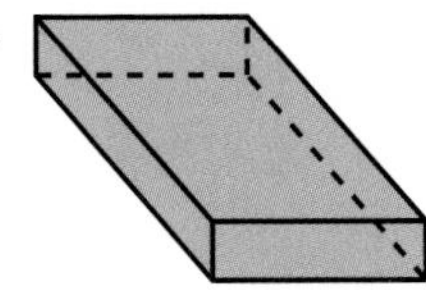

6. 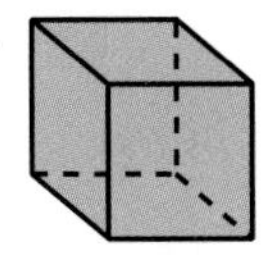

7. 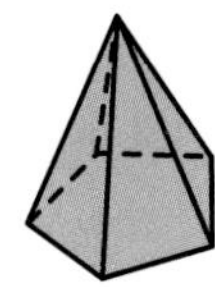

8. 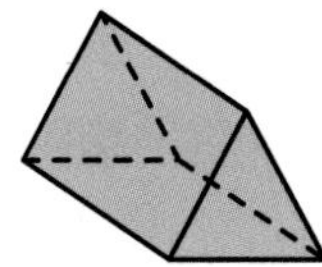

a. 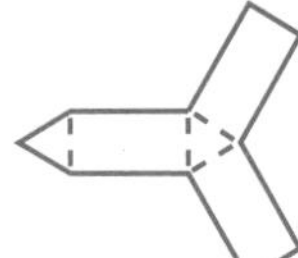

b. 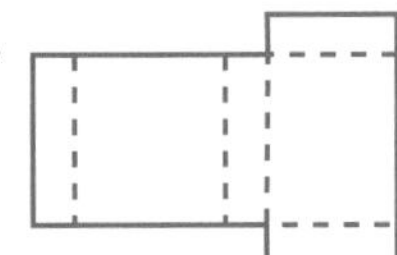

c. 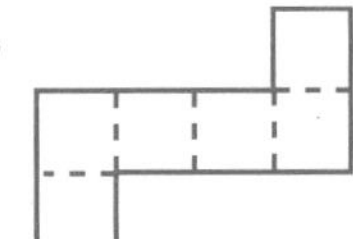

d. 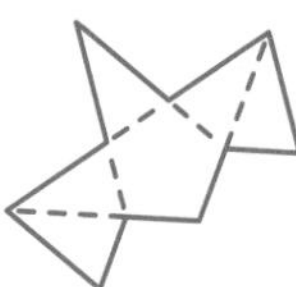

Write the letter of the pattern that can be folded to make the figure.

9. 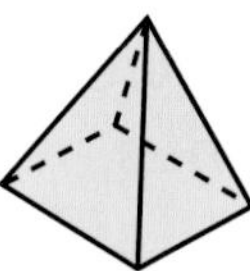

a. 

b. 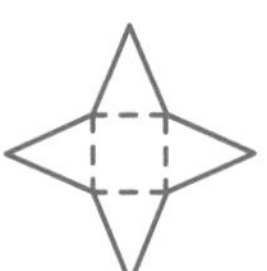

c. 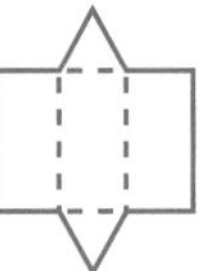

10. 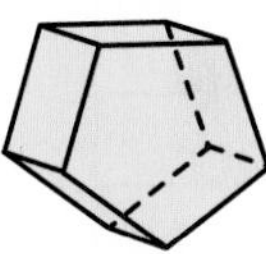

a. 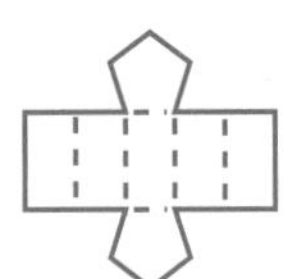

b. 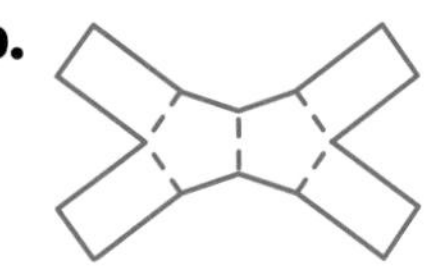

c. 

11. 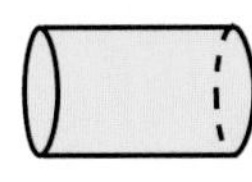

a. 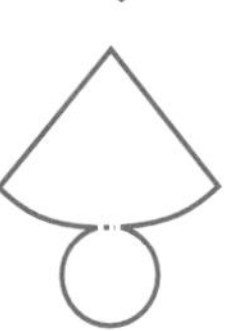

b. 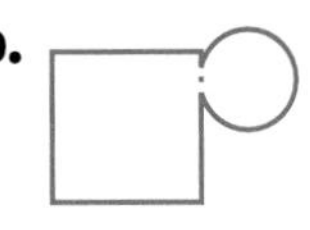

c. 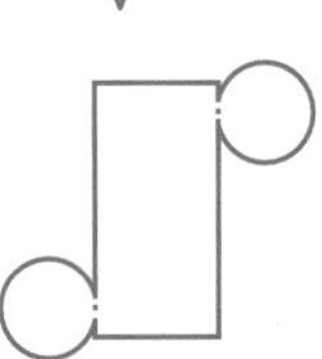

12. 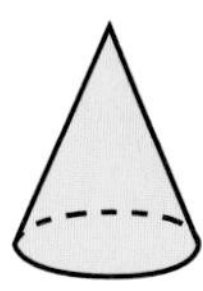

a. 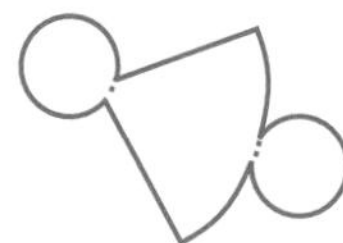

b. 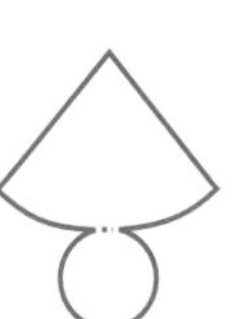

c. 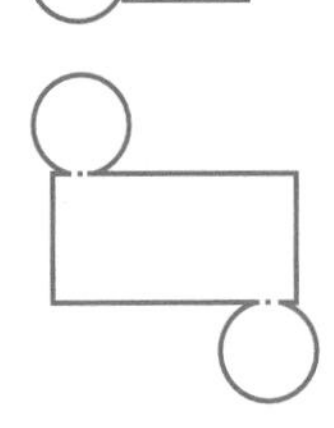

Problem Solving • Mixed Applications

13. Visual Thinking Shelly is making six cubes for a project. How many faces will she draw?

14. **Write About It** Explain how you would make a net for a square pyramid.

Mixed Review and Test Prep

Estimate each sum or difference. (pages 338–339)

15. $\frac{1}{10} + \frac{7}{8}$ **16.** $\frac{5}{8} - \frac{1}{9}$ **17.** $\frac{11}{12} + \frac{4}{10}$ **18.** $\frac{9}{10} - \frac{5}{6}$

Choose the equivalent fraction in simplest form. (pages 298–299)

19. $\frac{4}{12}$ **A** $\frac{12}{4}$ **B** $\frac{8}{24}$ **C** $\frac{2}{3}$ **D** $\frac{1}{3}$

20. $\frac{16}{18}$ **F** $\frac{9}{8}$ **G** $\frac{6}{8}$ **H** $\frac{3}{4}$ **J** $\frac{8}{9}$

21. $\frac{14}{21}$ **A** $\frac{2}{3}$ **B** $\frac{2}{7}$ **C** $\frac{3}{7}$ **D** $\frac{7}{3}$

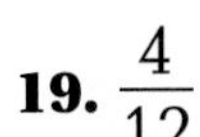
MORE PRACTICE page H117

Solid Figures from Different Views

You will investigate how to identify solid figures from different views.

A solid figure looks different when it is viewed from different positions.

Look at this figure.

Notice that

- this is a drawing of the figure viewed from the *top*.
- this is a drawing of the figure viewed from the *side*.

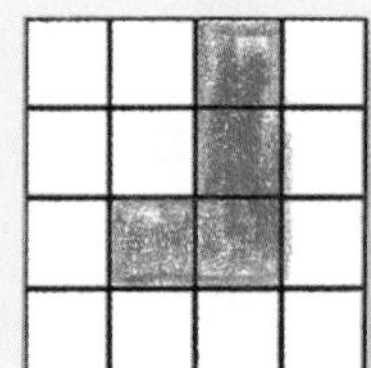

- this is a drawing of the figure viewed from the *front*.

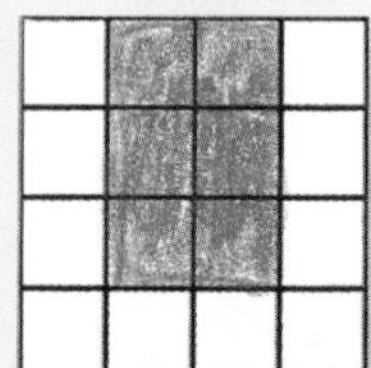

▶ EXPLORE

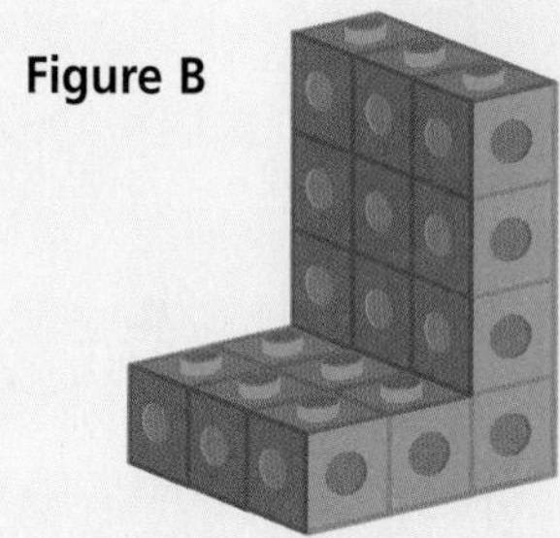

Figure B

Use 18 connecting cubes to build Figure B. Move the figure to look at it from different views.

MATERIALS: connecting cubes, centimeter grid paper

Record

Draw three pictures on grid paper to show how Figure B looks from the top, from the side, and from the front.

Now, investigate building another solid figure.

▶ TRY THIS

1. Build another figure using 24 connecting cubes. Then draw the figure on grid paper as it looks from the top, from the side, and from the front.
2. How does looking at a solid figure from different views help you identify the figure?

3. **Write About It** Suppose someone drew these views of a solid figure. Draw how you think the figure would look. Explain.

From the top **From the side** **From the front**

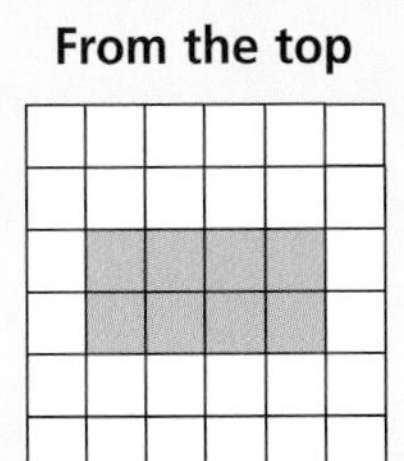
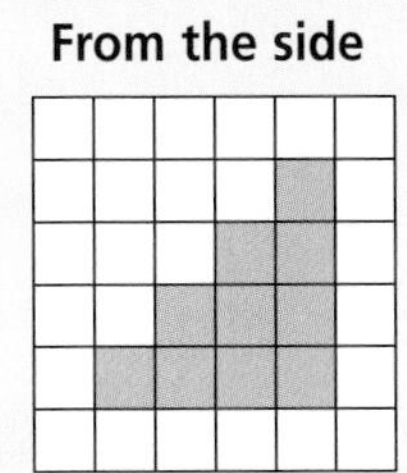
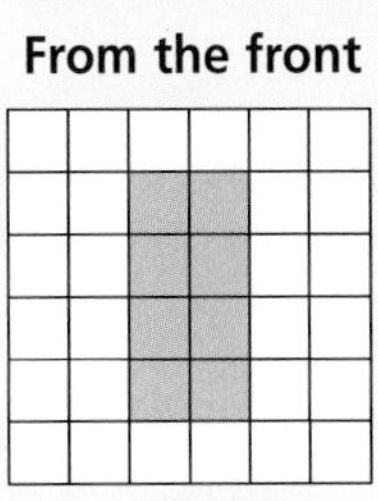

▶ PRACTICE

Use grid paper to draw each figure from the top, the side, and the front.

4.  5. 6. 

Choose the figure that is represented by each set of three drawings.

From the top **From the side** **From the front**

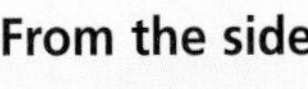

7. 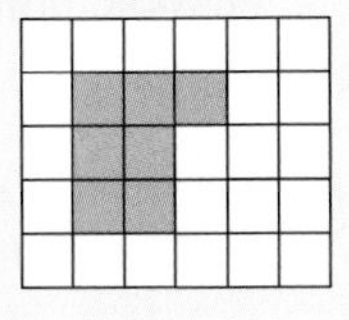 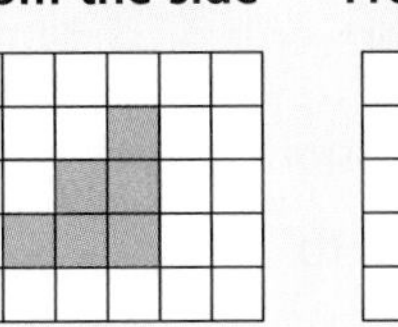 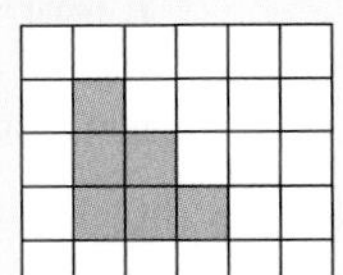 a.

8. 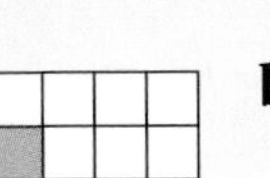 b.

9. 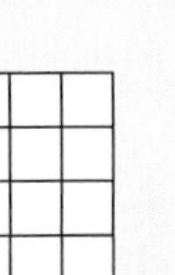 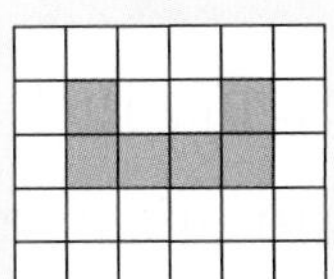 c. 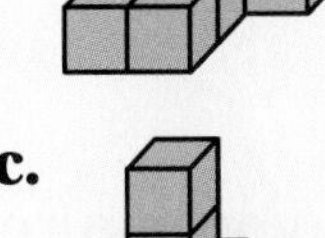

Technology Link

In ***Mighty Math Calculating Crew***, the game *Dr. Gee's 3-D Lab* challenges you to look at solid figures from different perspectives. Use Grow Slide Level N.

Technology Link

You can look at slices of solids by using E-Lab, Activity 26. Available on CD-ROM and on the Internet at **www.hbschool.com/elab**

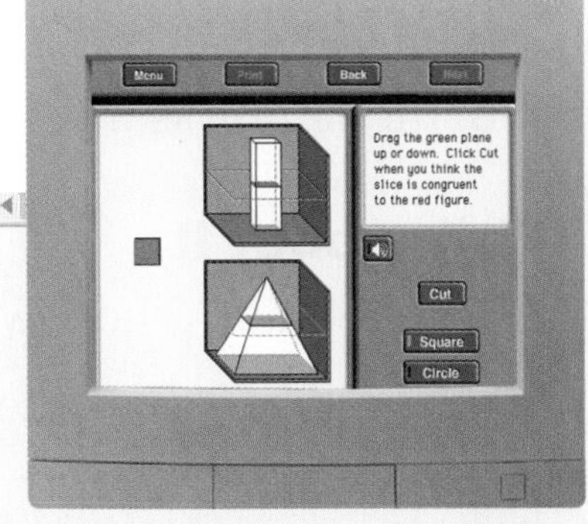

Problem Solving • Mixed Applications

10. **Visual Thinking** A shoe box is completely filled with blocks. There are 6 rows with 4 blocks in each row, and 3 layers of blocks. How many blocks are in the shoe box?

11. **Write About It** Name a solid figure and describe it from two views.

MORE PRACTICE page H117

Algebraic Thinking: Volume

Why learn this? You can find out if a box is tall enough to hold something you are packing when you know its length and width and how much it can hold.

Volume is the measure of the space a three-dimensional figure occupies. You can find the volume of a rectangular prism by using its length, width, and height. If you know the length, width, and volume, how can you find the height of the figure?

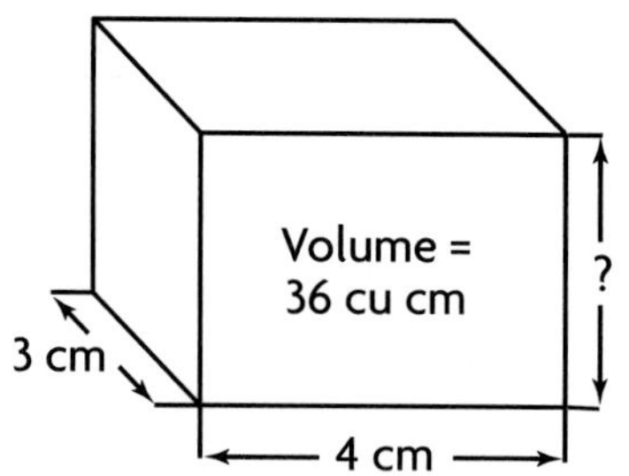

Here are two methods for solving the problem.

Method A	Method B
Use centimeter cubes to build a model that would fill the box. Then count the layers of cubes to find the height. 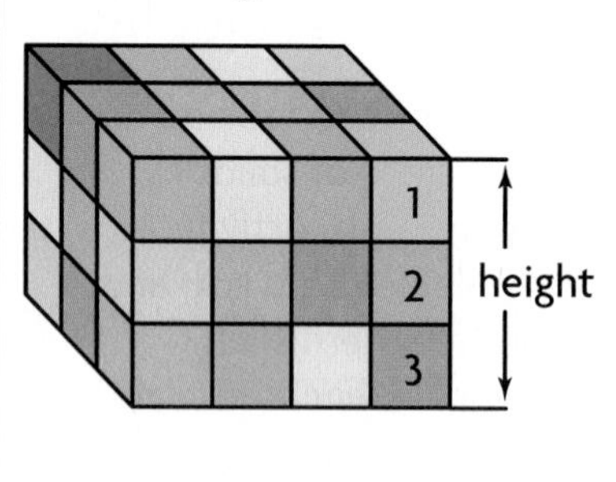	Use the mathematical formula for volume to find the height. $V = l \times w \times h$ **Think:** I know the volume is 36 cu cm, the length is 4 cm, and the width is 3 cm. So, $36 = 4 \times 3 \times h$. ← *h* represents the missing dimension. Since $36 = 12 \times h$, use division to find a missing factor. $36 \div 12 = 3$, or $h = 3$.

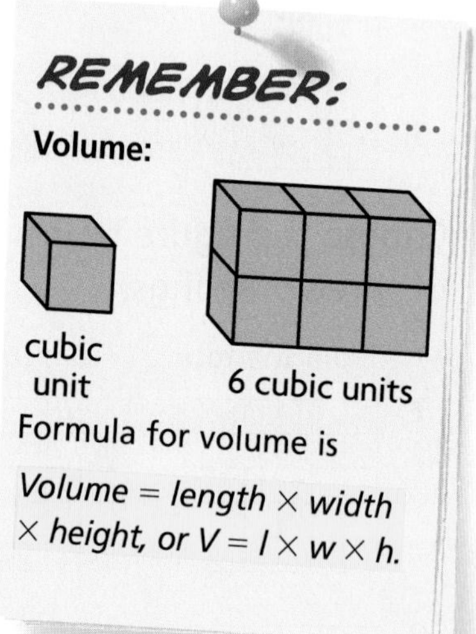

So, the height is 3 cm.

Talk About It

- In Method A, how would you make the model?
- How did you use the formula to find the missing dimension?

You can use a calculator to find the missing dimension in a formula. $V = l \times w \times h$

So, $240 = 8 \times w \times 10$.

Volume = 240 cubic inches
10 in.
?
8 in.

So, the width of the figure is 3 inches.

Calculator Activities page H60

▶ CHECK

Find the missing dimension. You may use a calculator.

1.

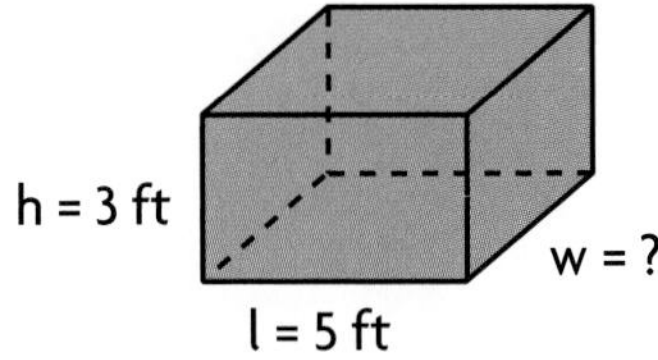

volume = 60 cu ft

2.

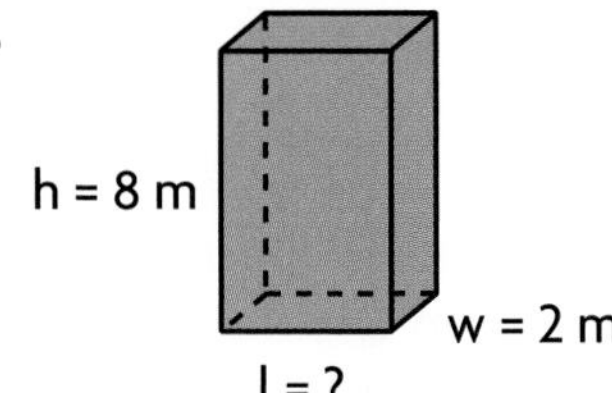

volume = 64 cu m

3.

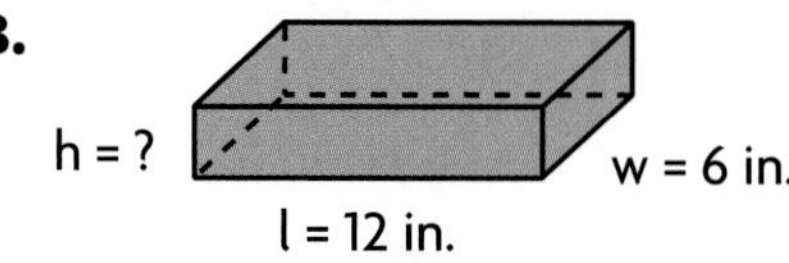

volume = 144 cu in.

▶ PRACTICE

Find the missing dimension. You may use a calculator.

4. length = 6 yd
width = 4 yd
height = ___?___
volume = 48 cu yd

5. length = 12 ft
width = 8 ft
height = 2 ft
volume = ___?___

6. length = ___?___
width = 7 m
height = 5 m
volume = 350 cu m

Complete the table. You may use a calculator.

	Length	Width	Height	Volume
7.	12 cm	?	5 cm	600 cu cm
8.	?	8 in.	5 in.	560 cu in.
9.	14 ft	9 ft	3 ft	?
10.	10 yd	7 yd	6 yd	?
11.	15 m	12 m	?	720 cu m

Shopping for a new refrigerator

Problem Solving • Mixed Applications

For Problems 12–14, use the drawings.

12. Measurement How much area will each refrigerator cover?

13. Money Lynn has $\frac{1}{3}$ of the money needed to buy the refrigerator that is 20 in. high. How much more money does she need?

14. Consumer Alan bought 2 small refrigerators. How many more cubic inches of volume do 2 small refrigerators have than one large one?

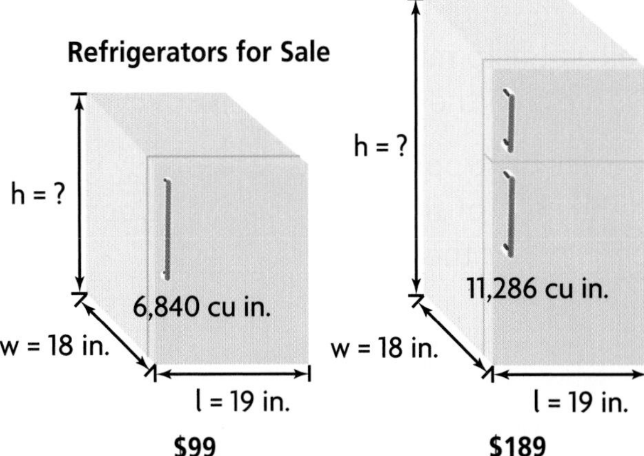

15. Write About It Explain how to find the height of a solid figure when you know the length, width, and volume.

LESSON CONTINUES

LESSON 4 • PART 2

Problem-Solving Strategy: Use a Formula

THE PROBLEM Amanda found a box at the grocery store that she wants to use to pack her sports trophies. She knows the box is 18 inches long and 12 inches wide. A label on the box says that it once contained tissues and can hold 4,320 cubic inches. Her tallest trophy measures 1 ft $7\frac{1}{2}$ in. Is the box tall enough for this trophy?

UNDERSTAND

- What are you asked to do?
- What information will you use?
- Is there information you will not use? If so, what?

PLAN

- What strategy can you use to solve the problem?

You can *use a formula* for volume and find the missing dimension.

SOLVE

- How can you use the strategy to solve the problem?

You can use the formula for volume. You know that V = 4,320 cu in., l = 18 in., and w = 12 in. The height *(h)* is the missing dimension in the equation. You can use a calculator to multiply 18×12, and then divide 4,320 by 216 to find the missing factor. So, h = 20 in.

The tallest trophy is 1 ft $7\frac{1}{2}$in., or $19\frac{1}{2}$ in. Since the height of the box is 20 in., the box is tall enough for the tallest trophy.

Problem 1
$V = l \times w \times h$
$4{,}320 = 18 \times 12 \times h$
$4{,}320 = 216 \times h$
$4{,}320 \div 216 = 20$
$h = 20$

Problem 2
1 ft $7\frac{1}{2}$ in. = ? in. (1 ft = 12 in.)
12 in.
+ $7\frac{1}{2}$ in.
$19\frac{1}{2}$ in.

LOOK BACK

- How does using a formula help you solve the problem?
- What other strategy could you use?

▶ PRACTICE

Use a formula to solve.

1. Yolanda is packing a suitcase that is 70 cm long and 40 cm wide and has a volume of 56,000 cu cm. She has a gift box to pack that is 60 cm long, 30 cm wide, and 25 cm in height. Will the gift box fit in the suitcase? Explain.

2. A toolbox is 18 in. long and 14 in. wide with a volume of 3,024 cu in. Would a cube with a volume of 1 cubic foot fit in the toolbox? Explain.

3. A playground area that is 66 ft long and 42 ft wide needs to be fenced. Will 75 yards of fencing be enough? Explain.

4. Rochelle's bedroom is 15 ft long and 12 ft wide. She is having wall-to-wall carpet installed. How many sq yd of carpet does she need?

Mixed Applications

Solve.

CHOOSE a strategy and a tool.

- Draw a Diagram
- Make a Table
- Use a Formula
- Work Backward

Paper/Pencil

Calculator

Hands-On

Mental Math

5. A swimming pool is 45 ft long and 20 ft wide. How many cubic feet of water will be enough to fill the pool to a depth of 6 ft?

6. Classes begin at 8:35. Each class is 55 min long and there is a 10-min break after each class. At what time is the third class over?

7. The Lopez family left on vacation on June 3. They drove for 4 days and spent 7 days with relatives. They drove 3 more days and spent 2 days visiting attractions. It took them 2 days to drive home. On what date did they arrive home?

8. Jon gave directions to his house. "From the school, go 4 blocks west and make a 90° turn south. Go 3 blocks south, make a 45° turn west, and go 2 blocks. My house is the second one on the left." Draw a map to Jon's house.

9. The thermometer shows the temperature at 6:00 P.M. The temperature has fallen 9 degrees since 3:00 P.M. The temperature had risen 12° from 9:00 A.M. to 3:00 P.M. What was the temperature at 9:00 A.M.?

10. Katie's book shelf is $4\frac{2}{3}$ ft tall. Her desk is $\frac{3}{4}$ as high as the book shelf. How high is Katie's desk?

11. Of the 32 students in Andy's class, $\frac{3}{8}$ prefer football to other sports. How many students prefer football?

Estimating Volume

Why learn this? You can estimate the number of items in a box, such as oranges or candy bars, without counting them.

Fresh oranges being shipped to the grocery store

Oranges are shipped in a variety of boxes. Compare these two boxes to determine which can hold more oranges.

You can use a benchmark to estimate volume in cubic units. Use 1 cubic foot as a benchmark to estimate the volume of the boxes.

A. **B.**

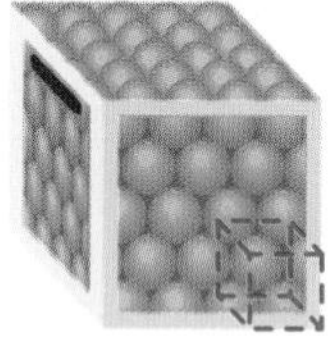
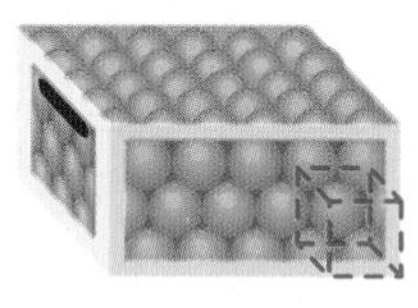
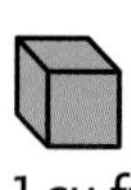

- What is the estimated volume of Box A? Box B?

So, based on your estimate, Box A can hold more oranges.

REMEMBER:

A *benchmark* is a point of reference and can help you determine whether an estimate is reasonable without counting.

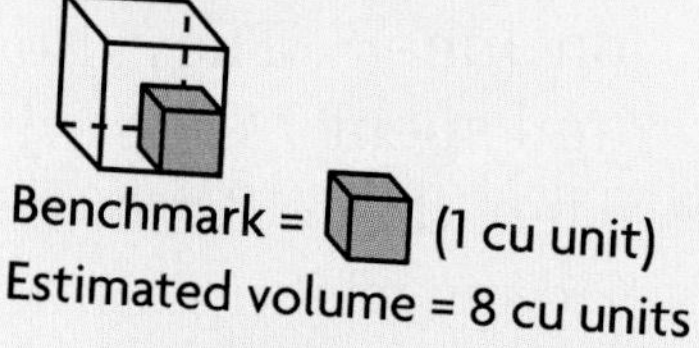

Talk About It CRITICAL THINKING

- How did you estimate the volume of the boxes?
- How many times greater than a cubic foot is a cubic yard?

▶ CHECK

Use the benchmarks at the right to name the more reasonable unit for measuring the volume of each box. Estimate the volume.

Benchmarks:

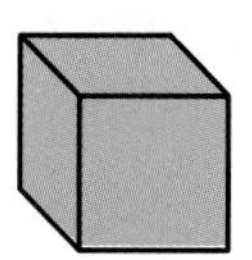

1 cubic centimeter (cu cm)

1 cubic decimeter (cu dm)

1. 

2. 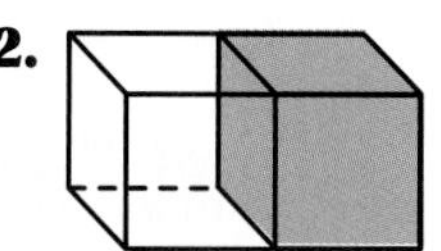

3. 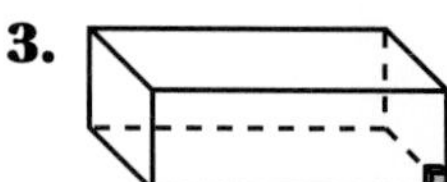

4. 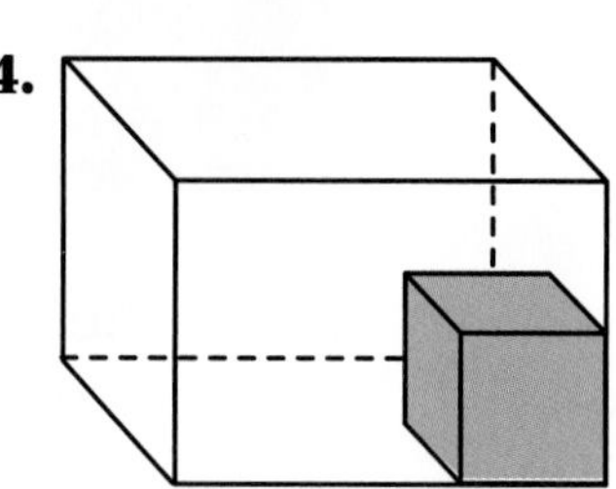

▶ PRACTICE

Use the benchmarks at the right to name the more reasonable unit for measuring the volume of each box. Estimate the volume.

5. 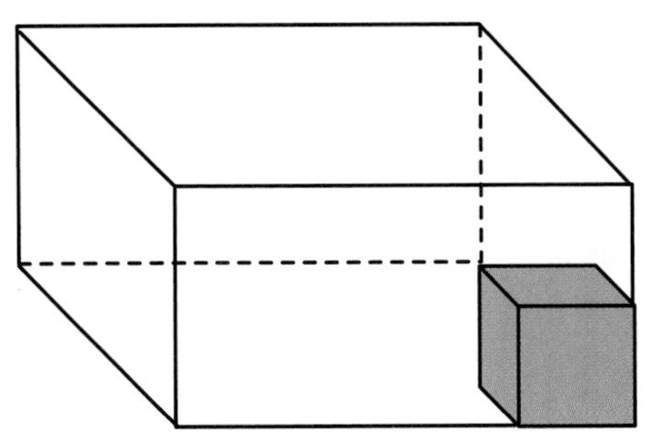

Benchmarks:

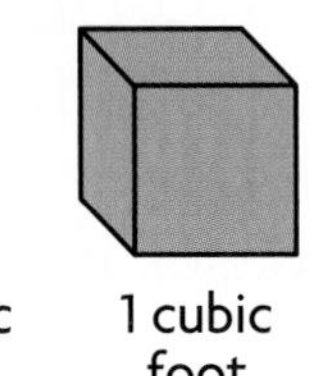

1 cubic inch   1 cubic foot

6. 

7. 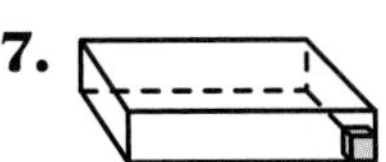

Choose the most reasonable measure. Write *a*, *b*, or *c*.

8. a tissue box **a.** 90 cu in. **b.** 90 cu ft **c.** 90 cu yd

9. a dresser **a.** 10 cu in. **b.** 10 cu ft **c.** 10 cu yd

10. a truckload of mulch **a.** 20 cu in. **b.** 20 cu ft **c.** 20 cu yd

Problem Solving • Mixed Applications

11. Reasoning Erika and Karem want to make a box large enough to hold a basketball. Karem's box has a volume of 1 cubic yard. Erika's box has a volume of 1 cubic foot. Which size is more reasonable for a basketball?

12. Estimation Marcia's lunchbox is 10 in. long, 7 in. wide. She estimates the volume as 210 cu in. Larry estimates the volume as 2,100 cu in. Which estimate is more reasonable?

13. Visual Thinking Mr. Beale is unpacking some books from a box. There are 4 layers of books. Each layer has 3 rows of books with 3 books in each row. How many books are in the box?

14. Write About It Explain how to estimate volume.

Mixed Review and Test Prep

Write *multiply* or *divide*. Change the unit. (pages 376–377)

15. 48 oz = ? lb **16.** 50 lb = ? oz **17.** 4 T = ? lb **18.** 16,000 lb = ? T

Choose the letter for the correct quotient. (pages 236–239)

19. $34.4 \div 8 = ?$ **A** 43 **B** 4.3 **C** 0.43 **D** 43.4

20. $6.86 \div 7 = ?$ **F** 9.8 **G** 98 **H** 0.98 **J** 980

CHAPTER 26 Review/Test

CHECK Understanding

VOCABULARY

1. A solid figure that has two congruent, parallel faces called bases is a __?__. (page 454)

2. A two-dimensional pattern for a three-dimensional solid is a __?__. (page 456)

3. A solid figure with one base that is a polygon and three or more faces that are triangles with a common vertex is called a __?__. (page 454)

Write *prism* or *pyramid*. Write the polygon that names the base for each. Identify the solid figure. (pages 454–455)

4. 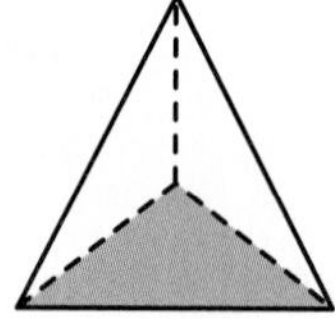

5. 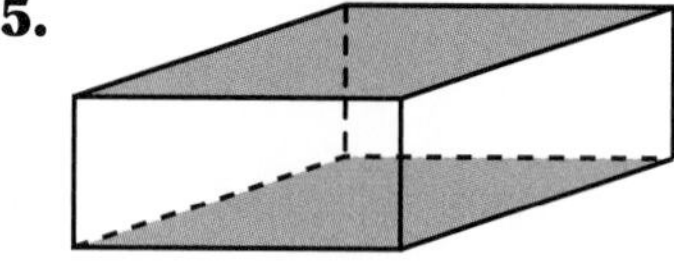

6. 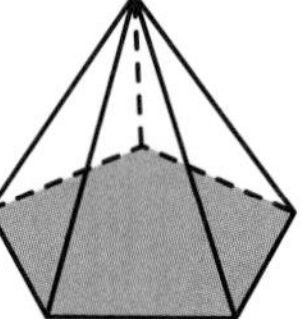

CHECK Skills

Use grid paper to draw the figure from the top, the side, and the front. (pages 458–459)

7. 

8. 

Find the missing dimension. (pages 460–461)

9. 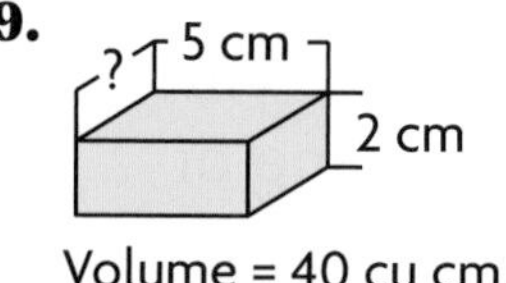

10. 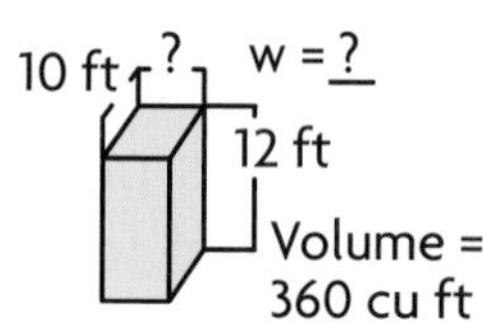

Choose the most reasonable measure. Write *a*, *b*, or *c*. (pages 464–465)

11. cereal box — **a.** 300 cu ft **b.** 300 cu in. **c.** 300 cu yd

12. washing machine — **a.** 30 cu in. **b.** 30 cu yd **c.** 30 cu ft

CHECK Problem Solving

Solve. (pages 462–463)

CHOOSE a strategy and a tool.

- Write a Number Sentence
- Make a Model
- Guess and Check
- Use a Formula

Paper/Pencil

Calculator

Hands-On

Mental Math

13. Sue's gift is 2 in. by 3 in. by 10 in. The box is 4 in. by 2 in. and has a volume of 88 cu in. Will the gift fit into the box? Explain.

14. Jeff is building a pen for his dog. He has 56 ft of fencing. What dimensions would give the greatest area possible?

Test Prep

CUMULATIVE
CHAPTERS 1–26

Choose the best answer.

1. What is the number 6,432 rounded to the nearest hundred?

A 6,000 **B** 6,400

C 6,500 **D** 7,000

2. Mrs. Davis plans to spread grass seed over her entire lawn. The lawn measures 32 feet by 71 feet. Which of the following is a reasonable estimate of the lawn's area?

F 21 sq ft

G 2,100 sq ft

H 200 sq ft

J 2,400 sq ft

K Not Here

3. Shada's frog hopped 12 feet at the Frog-Hopping Contest. How many yards did her frog hop?

A $2\frac{1}{2}$ yd **B** 3 yd

C $3\frac{1}{2}$ yd **D** 4 yd

4. Which number completes the pattern?

$2{,}400 \div 6 = 400$
$240 \div 6 = 40$
$24 \div 6 = 4$
$2.4 \div 6 = \square$

F 0.4 **G** 4.0

H 40 **J** 400

5. The table shows the estimated hiking times on three trails.

HIKING TIMES	
Trail	Time
Blue	20 min
Red	35 min
Yellow	1 hr 15 min

How long would it take to hike both the Blue and the Yellow Trails?

A 20 min **B** 55 min

C 1 hr 15 min **D** 1 hr 35 min

6. The following is an example of which kind of transformation?

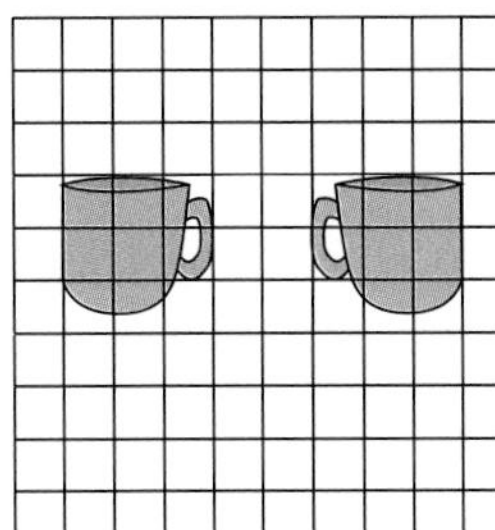

F reflection **G** rotation

H slide **J** translation

7. Which of the expressions explains how the value of *pi* is found?

A $r \div C$ **B** $d \div C$

C $C \div d$ **D** $d \div r$

8. How many faces does a triangular pyramid have?

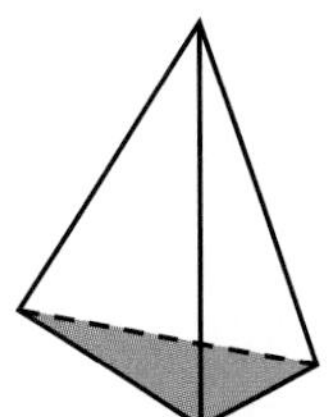

F 2 **G** 3

H 4 **J** 5

CHAPTERS 23–26

GEOMETRY SCAVENGER HUNT

PURPOSE To practice classifying polygons and other plane figures

YOU WILL NEED paper and pencil

Find examples of the figures on page H26. Look around your classroom and school. Draw the figure and describe where you found it. Is it one face of a solid object? See if you can find all of the figures.

Look for geometric shapes in furniture, buildings, and cars. What shape do you see most frequently?

Ladders for Safe Carpenters

PURPOSE To measure the angles on a triangle

YOU WILL NEED centimeter grid paper, centimeter ruler, protractor

Did you ever notice that a ladder leaning against a wall makes a triangle? A safe ladder must be placed so that the horizontal distance at the bottom is at least one fourth the length of the ladder. Make a model of an 8-ft ladder that is 8 cm long. Place this model on cm grid paper. Draw triangles showing a safe ladder and an unsafe ladder.

What angle does this ladder form with the ground? Is this ladder a safe ladder?

AMAZING CIRCLES

PURPOSE To draw a maze in a circle

YOU WILL NEED compass, paper and pencil

You can make amazing puzzles for your classmates to solve by using circles and polygons.

Draw a large circle. Within that circle, draw smaller circles and some polygons such as triangles, squares, hexagons and so on.

Make a pathway to the picture by making openings and drawing lines. Make several false pathways.

Smiley's Treasure

Place a picture at the end of the maze. Name your maze.

Anyone who solves your "Amazing Maze" keeps the picture.

Transformations

Steve is making a design for the cover of his book. He is using a paint program on the computer to design a tessellation for the cover.

MATERIALS
ALDUS® SuperPaint® or other paint program

REMEMBER:
When you move a figure to show a slide, flip, or turn, it is called a *transformation*.

MODEL

Toolbar

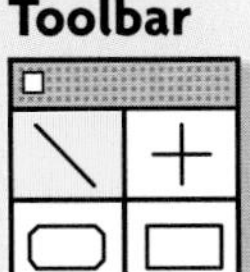

Step 1

Steve used the line tool from the toolbar to draw the two figures.

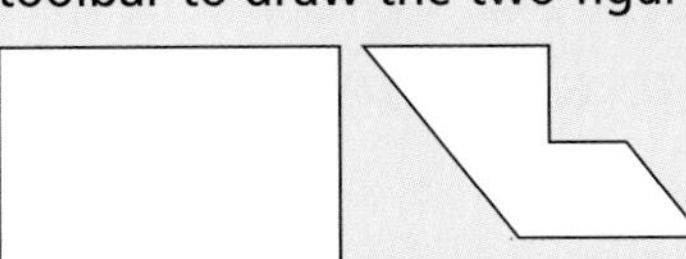

Toolbar

Step 2

Then he used the lasso 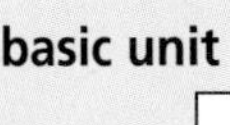 tool to highlight and move them together to make the basic unit for the tessellation.

basic unit

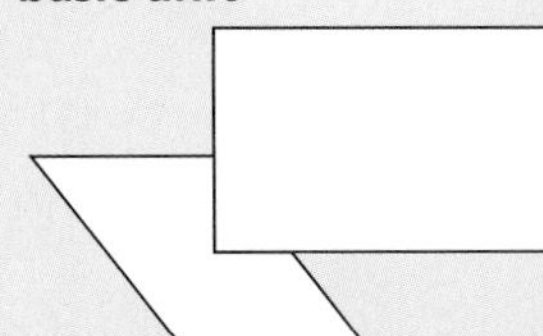

Transform
Scale Selection . . . .
Rotate Selection . . .
Flip Horizontally
Flip Vertically
Rotate Left
Rotate Right

Step 3

Next, he selected **Transform** from the menu bar. He flipped the figure horizontally and then vertically, which transformed it to make the tessellation.

▶ PRACTICE

1. Trace and cut out this figure. Transform it to draw a tessellation.

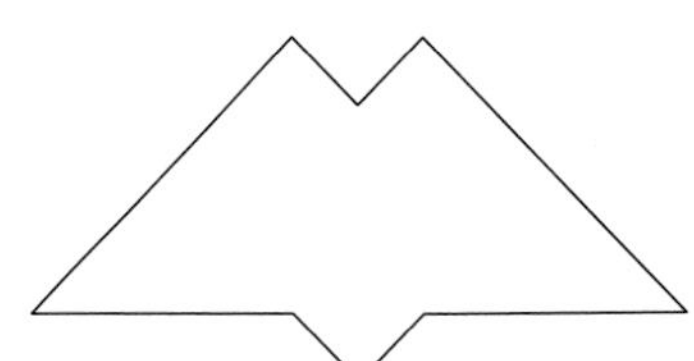

2. Draw a triangle. Transform the triangle to make a tessellation.
3. **Using a Paint Program** Draw two figures to make a basic unit for a design. Transform the basic unit to make a tessellation.

CHAPTERS 23–26

Study Guide and Review

Vocabulary Check

Choose a term from the box to complete each sentence.

VOCABULARY
prism
parallel
radius
transformation

1. Lines in a plane that never intersect and are the same distance from each other are _?_. (page 408)
2. When you move a figure to show a translation, reflection, or rotation, it is called a _?_. (page 430)
3. A line segment that connects a circle's center with a point on that circle is called a _?_. (page 440)
4. A solid figure with two bases that are congruent polygons is called a _?_. (page 454)

Study and Solve

CHAPTER 23

EXAMPLE

Identify the figure.

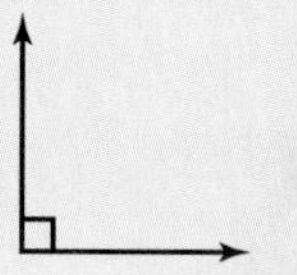

This is an angle because it is made up of two rays with the same endpoint. It is a right angle because it measures 90 degrees.

right angle

Identify the figure. Write *acute, obtuse*, or *right*. (pages 410–411, 420–421)

5. 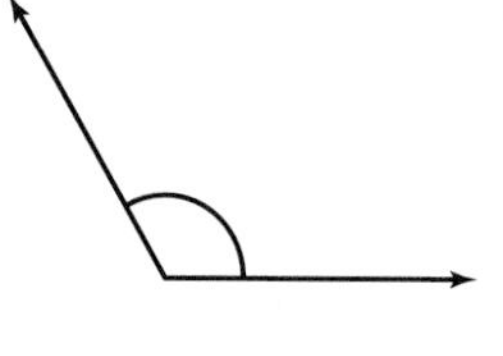

_?_ angle

6. 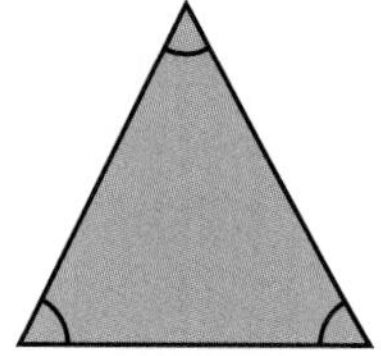

_?_ triangle

For Problems 7–8, use the figure. (pages 408–409)

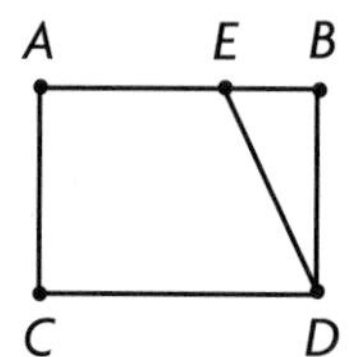

7. Name a line segment that intersects AB, but is not perpendicular to AB.

8. Name a line segment that is parallel to AB.

Identify the figure. Write *trapezoid, parallelogram, rectangle, rhombus*, or *square*. (pages 416–417)

9. 

10. 

CHAPTER 24

EXAMPLE

Tell how many lines of symmetry the figure has. (pages 428–429)

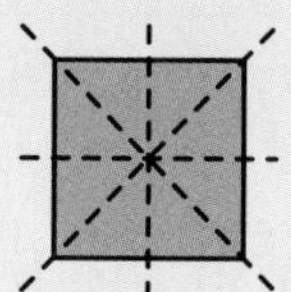

If you folded the square along any of the dotted lines, the halves would match exactly.

A square has 4 lines of symmetry.

Tell how many lines of symmetry. (pages 428–429)

11. 

12. 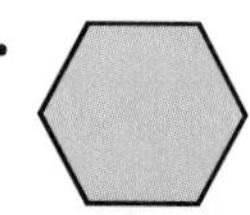

Copy the figure on a coordinate grid. Translate, reflect, and rotate the figure. Name the new ordered pairs. (pages 430–431)

13. 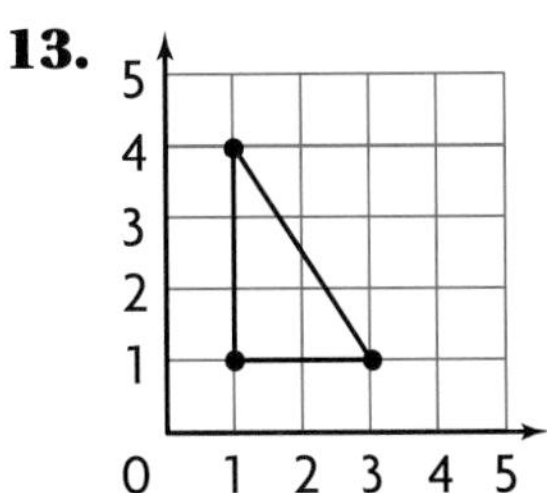

Write *yes* or *no* to tell whether the figure tessellates. (pages 432–433)

14. 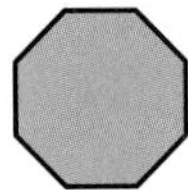

15.

Use pattern blocks to solve. (pages 434–435)

16. Ken is using tiles with these figures: hexagons and triangles. Can he make a mosaic that tessellates?

CHAPTER 25

EXAMPLE

Find the missing measurement.

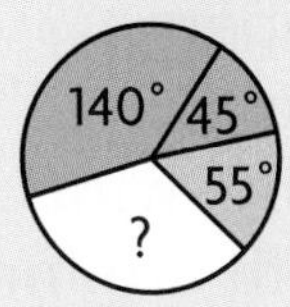

A circle has a total of 360°. Find the sum of the angles you know. Subtract the sum from 360°.

The missing measurement is 120°.

Construct a circle with the given radius. Label and measure a radius, a diameter, and a chord. (pages 440–441)

17. 2 cm

18. 3 cm

Find the missing measurement. (pages 446–447)

19. 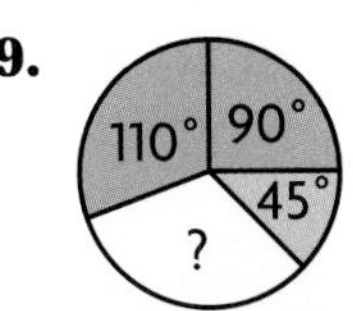

Solve. (pages 444–445)

20. Dan wants to wrap a jar in gift paper. The jar is 6 in. high. Its diameter is 5 in. Dan has a sheet of paper that is 10 in. by 10 in. Can he use it to wrap the jar? Explain.

CHAPTER 26

EXAMPLE

Choose the most reasonable measure.

a cake-mix box

a. 100 cu in. **b.** 100 cu ft

c. 100 cu yd

Think: A cake-mix box is about 8 in. by 6 in. by 2 in. wide. 8 in. × 6 in. × 2 in. = 96 cu in., or about 100 cu in.

Write *prism* or *pyramid*. Write the polygon that names the base. Identify the solid figure. (pages 454–455)

21. 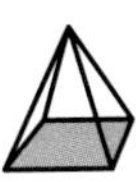

22. 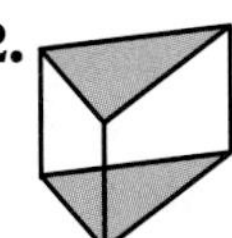

Use grid paper to draw the figure from the top, the side, and the front. (pages 458–459)

23. 

Choose the most reasonable measure. (pages 464–465)

24. a clothes dryer

a. 30 cu in. **b.** 30 cu ft **c.** 30 cu yd

Solve. (pages 462–463)

25. Kim is packing a 3-in. by 5-in. by 8-in. toy. The box is 4 in. by 6 in. and has a volume of 168 cu in. Will the toy fit in the box? Explain.

CHAPTERS 23–26

Performance Assessment

Tasks: Show What You Know

1. Explain your choices as you name classroom objects that remind you of intersecting lines, perpendicular lines, parallel lines, and a ray; and a right angle, an acute angle, and an obtuse angle. (pages 408–411)

2. Use a square piece of paper. Fold the paper to show as many lines of symmetry as you can. Draw a diagram to show the lines of symmetry you found. (pages 428–429)

3. Draw a pie sliced in half. Then slice one of the halves in half. Explain how to find the number of degrees in the angles of the sliced pie. (pages 446–447)

4. Use a 1-cm cube as a benchmark to estimate the volume of a paper clip box that measures 7 cm long, 5 cm wide, and 2 cm high. Explain your method. (pages 464–465)

Problem Solving

Solve. Explain your method.

CHOOSE a strategy and a tool.

- Use a Formula
- Make a Model
- Write a Number Sentence
- Act It Out
- Draw a Diagram

Paper/Pencil

Calculator

Hands-On

Mental Math

5. A parking lot is 50 yd by 30 yd. Light poles are placed 10 yd apart. No light poles are on the edges of the lot. How many light poles are in the lot, and where they are placed? (pages 414–415)

6. Bob is designing place mats for craft class. He can use only one shape. He is trying to decide between a hexagon and an octagon. Which shape will tessellate when arranged in a design? Make a design that Bob could use. (pages 434–435)

7. Banks roll coins in wrappers. Suppose you are making a wrapper for quarters. How wide must the wrapper be to fit around the quarters with $\frac{1}{4}$-inch extra so the sides can be glued together? How did you find out? (pages 444–445)

8. Ellen found a box that is 12 in. long and 6 in. wide. The box holds 504 cubic in. Ellen wants to store her CDs in the box. The CDs are 5 in. high. Is the box big enough for Ellen's CDs? (pages 462–463)

Cumulative Review

Solve the problem. Then write the letter of the correct answer.

1. $\begin{array}{r} 5{,}000 \\ -3{,}364 \\ \hline \end{array}$

A. 1,636
B. 1,746
C. 2,635
D. 8,364

(pages 24–25)

2. $67 \div 8 = n$

A. $n = 7$ r7 **B.** $n = 8$ r3
C. $n = 708$ r7 **D.** $n = 4{,}536$

(pages 118–119)

3. $1{,}000 \div 99 = n$

A. $n = 1$ r10 **B.** $n = 10$ r10
C. $n = 101$ r10 **D.** $n = 1{,}010$

(pages 136–139)

4. $2\overline{)8.06}$

A. 0.43 **B.** 4.03
C. 4.3 **D.** 40.3

(pages 234–239)

5. Compare. Order the numbers from least to greatest. $\frac{3}{4}, \frac{1}{6}, \frac{7}{12}$

A. $\frac{1}{6}, \frac{3}{4}, \frac{7}{12}$ **B.** $\frac{3}{4}, \frac{1}{6}, \frac{7}{12}$
C. $\frac{1}{6}, \frac{7}{12}, \frac{3}{4}$ **D.** $\frac{3}{4}, \frac{7}{12}, \frac{1}{6}$

(pages 278–279)

For Problems 6–7, choose the correct answer in simplest form.

6. $\frac{5}{6} + \frac{5}{6} = n$

A. $n = \frac{10}{12}$ **B.** $n = \frac{10}{6}$
C. $n = 1\frac{4}{6}$ **D.** $n = 1\frac{2}{3}$

(pages 304–305)

7. $\frac{5}{12} - \frac{1}{6} = n$

A. $n = \frac{1}{4}$ **B.** $n = \frac{3}{12}$
C. $n = \frac{4}{12}$ **D.** $n = \frac{2}{3}$

(pages 342–345)

8. 4 gal = __?__ qt

A. 1 **B.** 2
C. 8 **D.** 16

(pages 374–375)

9. A triangle with all congruent sides is __?__.

A. equilateral **B.** isosceles
C. scalene **D.** right

(pages 428–429)

For Problems 10–11, identify the figure.

10.

A. parallelogram
B. rectangle
C. rhombus
D. trapezoid

(pages 416–417)

11.

A. acute triangle
B. congruent triangle
C. obtuse triangle
D. right triangle

(pages 420–421)

27 FRACTIONS AS RATIOS

LANGUAGE **LINK**

Some letters have small strokes, called *serifs*, at the beginning and end. Letters without these strokes are known as *sans serif*.

Problem-Solving Activity

Double Your Initial

Have you ever wondered how to make an enlargement of a drawing? You are going to draw one of your initials. Then you will enlarge the initial to twice as tall and twice as wide.

YOU WILL NEED: centimeter grid paper, pencil, markers

Draw your initial, enlarge it, and analyze its measurements.

- Draw on centimeter grid paper one initial, no larger than 7 cm wide and 12 cm tall.
- Enlarge your initial on another piece of centimeter grid paper. Make the enlargement twice as wide and twice as high.
- Find the height, width, and area of the initial.
- Make a chart that shows the ratio between measures in the small initial and the enlargement.

1. Draw a letter on grid paper. Count the number of squares across and down.

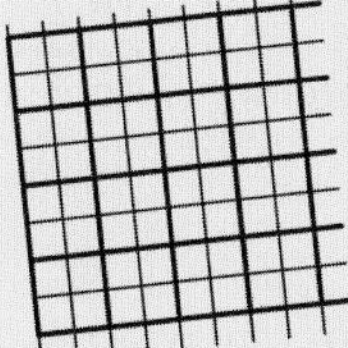

2. Darken every other grid line for the enlargement.

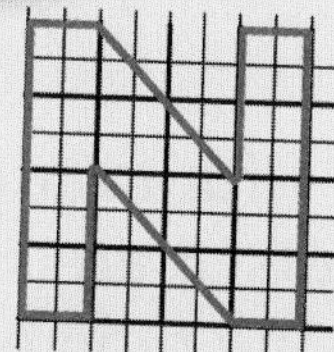

3. Use the dark grid lines to guide you as you draw the letter. Use pencil at first and do one big square at a time.

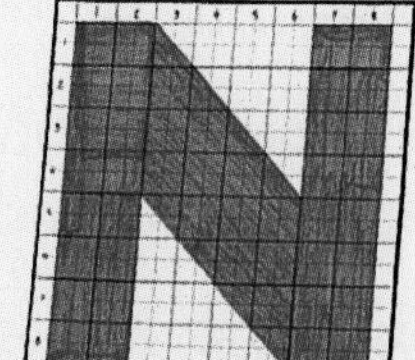

DID YOU

- ✓ make one small and one large drawing?
- ✓ find and record the height, width, and area of each drawing?
- ✓ make a chart that shows the ratio between the measures?

Understanding Ratio

VOCABULARY
ratio

You will investigate using two-color counters to show a relationship between two quantities.

You can use a **ratio** to compare two numbers in three ways. The kind of ratio you use depends on the problem situation.

EXAMPLE:   

Compare	Ratio	Type of Ratio
red counters to all counters	2 to 5	part to whole
all counters to red counters	5 to 2	whole to part
red counters to yellow counters	2 to 3	part to part

▶ EXPLORE

You can use two-color counters to help you understand ratio.

MATERIALS: two-color counters

There are 10 fifth-grade students in the school play. Of the students, 3 are singers and 7 are dancers. How can you find the ratio of the number of singers to the number of dancers?

Step 1

Use the yellow side of two-color counters to represent all 10 students in the school play. Each counter represents one student.

Step 2

Turn the red side of the counters up to represent the number of students who are singers.

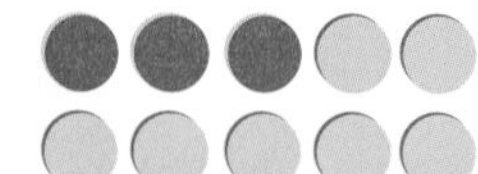

Record

Record the type of ratio the model represents.

Talk About It What do the yellow counters in Step 2 of the model represent?

Now, investigate finding other types of ratios.

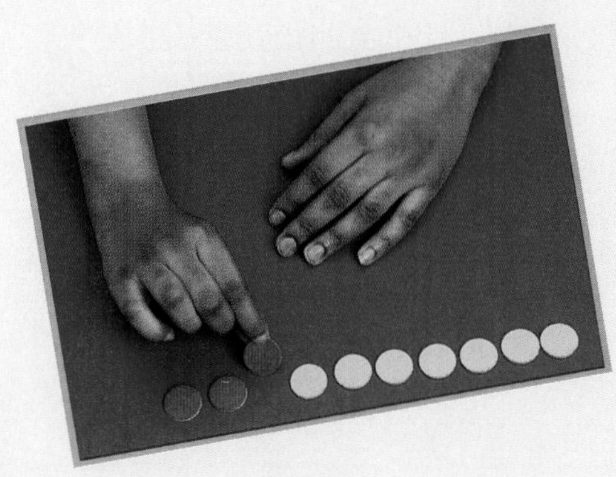

▶ TRY THIS

1. Use two-color counters. Show the ratio of the number of singers to the number of students in the play, and of the number of students in the play to the number of dancers. Draw a picture of each model. Write each ratio.
2. Which types of ratios did you model for Problem 1? How are they alike? How are they different?
3. **Write About It** Explain in your own words how to write each type of ratio.

SCIENCE LINK

From its fossil remains, scientists estimate the dinosaur *Seismosaurus* was 150 feet long. Compare the length of this dinosaur to a 6-foot human.

Think: 150 feet to 6 feet

How many times longer was *Seismosaurus* than a human?

▶ PRACTICE

Name the type of ratio and show with counters.

4. Soccer was played by 4 out of 6 students.
5. There were 3 rainy days and 7 sunny days.

Use the picture to make the comparison.

6.

_?_ wheels to _?_ skate

7.

_?_ baseballs to _?_ players

8.

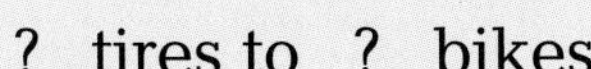

_?_ tires to _?_ bikes

9.

_?_ tennis balls to _?_ rackets

Technology Link

You can analyze ratios by using E-Lab, Activity 27. Available on CD-ROM and on the Internet at **www.hbschool.com/elab**

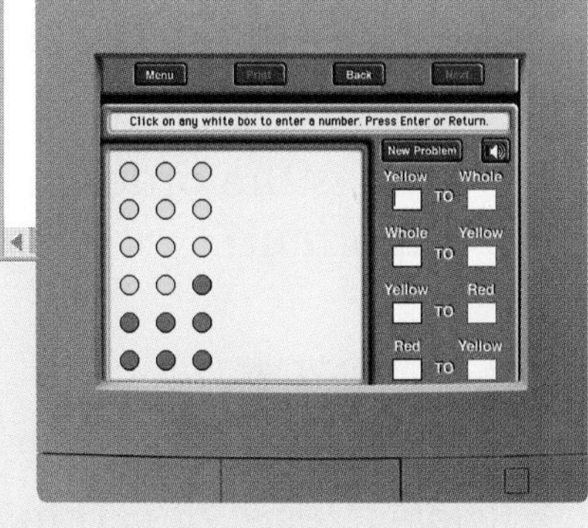

Problem Solving • Mixed Applications

10. **Language** What is the ratio of vowels to consonants in the word *MATHEMATICS*? What kind of ratio is this?
11. **Art** There are 32 students in the art club. Of the students, $\frac{3}{4}$ are in fifth grade. How many fifth-grade students are in the art club?
12. **Visual Thinking** What ratio would you write to compare the sides in an octagon to the sides in a triangle?
13. **Consumer** Sancho is buying milk. He can buy 1 gallon for \$2.69 or 1 quart for \$0.75. Which is the better buy?

MORE PRACTICE page H119

LESSON 2

Expressing Ratios

Why learn this? You can tell what part of a group you are getting when you choose your favorite color or flavor of candy or ice cream.

Lauren told her brother he could have all the red gummy bears in her hand. What part of her handful is red bears compared to the whole?

You can write the ratio of red bears to the whole handful of bears in three ways.

3 to 8 3:8 $\frac{3}{8}$

Read each ratio "three to eight."
Find other ratios by looking at Lauren's yellow gummy bears.

part:whole	whole:part	part:part
yellow bears:all bears	all bears:yellow bears	yellow bears:red bears
5:8	8:5	5:3

Talk About It CRITICAL THINKING

- Is the ratio 3 to 8 the same as 8 to 3? Explain.
- Lauren ate a yellow gummy bear from her handful. Now, what is the ratio of yellow bears to the whole handful? Explain.
- Why is the order in which you write a ratio important?

HEALTH LINK

The average 10-year-old needs between 9 and 12 hours of sleep each night. How many hours do you sleep at night? What is the ratio of your sleeping hours to the total hours in a day? What is the ratio between the hours spent awake and the hours spent asleep?

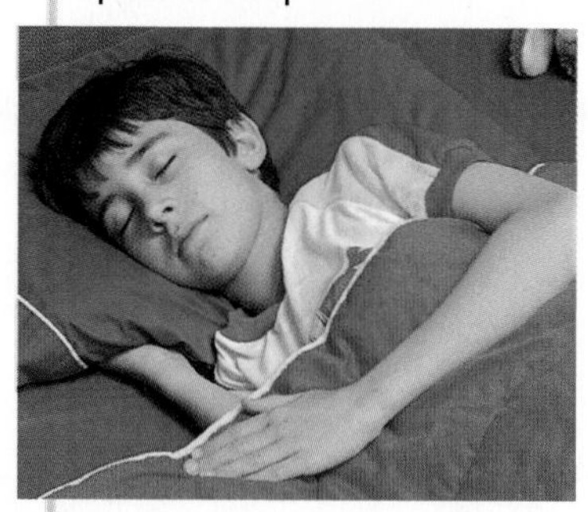

▶ CHECK

Write each ratio in three ways. Then write *part to whole, whole to part*, or *part to part* to describe the ratio.

1. circles to squares
2. all colors to red
3. circles to all figures
4. blue to red
5. all figures to squares
6. green to all colors
7. squares to stars
8. red to green
9. stars to all figures
10. circles to stars

▶ PRACTICE

Write *a* or *b* to show which fraction represents the ratio.

11. 5 to 2 a. $\frac{2}{5}$ b. $\frac{5}{2}$

12. 5:9 a. $\frac{9}{5}$ b. $\frac{5}{9}$

13. 8 to 4 a. $\frac{8}{4}$ b. $\frac{4}{8}$

14. 1:20 a. $\frac{1}{20}$ b. $\frac{20}{1}$

For Exercises 15–17, use the table. Write each ratio in three ways.

15. What is the ratio of rock CDs to country CDs?

16. What is the ratio of all CDs to show tunes?

17. What is the ratio of country CDs to all CDs?

FRANK'S CD COLLECTION

Number of CDs	Type
3	Rock
4	Country
1	Show Tunes

Problem Solving • Mixed Applications

18. Sports All 9 players showed up for baseball practice with a mitt. What was the ratio of players to mitts?

19. Lynetta found that one-fifth of the 20 M & M® candies were green. What was the ratio of green candies to the whole?

20. Visual Thinking Erika got a jewelry case for her birthday. The top and bottom of the case are five-sided, congruent figures. What solid figure can you name that describes the shape of the jewelry case?

21. Measurement Kurt made a circle graph that was divided into 4 sections. The angles in three of the sections measured 100°, 85°, and 65°. How many degrees were in the angle formed in the fourth section of the graph?

22. Using Data There are 25 students in the fifth-grade class. Of the 25 students, 5 stayed home sick. What was the ratio of sick students to healthy students?

23. Write About It How does each type of ratio help you understand the relationship between the two numbers being compared?

Mixed Review and Test Prep

Identify the angle. Write *right, acute,* or *obtuse.* (pages 410–411)

24.

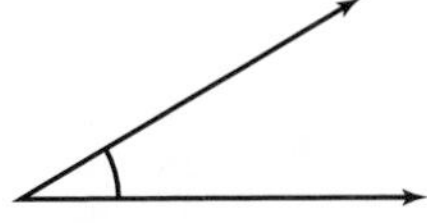

25.

26.

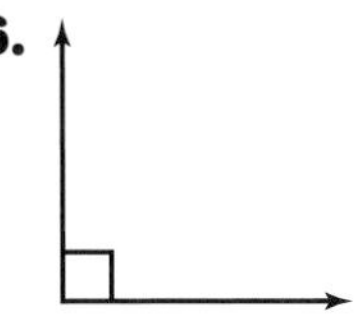

Choose the letter of the missing dimension. (pages 460–461)

27. length = 4 in.
width = 3 in.
height = 2 in.
volume = ▢

A 8 cu in.
B 24 cu in.
C 6 cu in.
D 12 cu in.

28. length = 7 ft
width = ▢
height = 6 ft
volume = 336 cu ft

F 14,112 ft
G 56 ft
H 8 ft
J 42 ft

MORE PRACTICE page H119

LESSON 3

Equivalent Ratios

VOCABULARY
equivalent ratios

Why learn this? When you need to know the ratio between large numbers, such as the ratio of girls to the total number of students in your school, you can simplify the ratio to smaller numbers.

Fernando is building a kennel for his dog. His dog is 33 inches long from its nose to the tip of its tail. How long should the kennel for Fernando's dog be?

The ratio table below is given as a guide to show the relationship of dog length to kennel length.

Length of Dog from Nose to Tip of Tail (inches)	20	25	30	36	44	51
Length of Dog Kennel (inches)	40	50	60	72	88	102

You can divide or multiply both numbers of a ratio by the same number.

$$\frac{20}{40} \xrightarrow{\div 20} = \frac{1}{2} \qquad \frac{1}{2} \xrightarrow{\times 25} = \frac{25}{50}$$

- Simplify the other ratios in the table. What is the equivalent ratio?

The ratios in the table are **equivalent ratios** because they show the same relationship. No matter what size the dog is, the ratio of the length of the dog to the length of the kennel is 1 to 2.

$$\frac{1}{2} \xrightarrow{\times 33} = \frac{33}{66} \quad \begin{matrix}\text{length of dog}\\ \text{length of kennel}\end{matrix}$$

So, the kennel for Fernando's dog should be 66 inches long.

▶ CHECK

1. Are the ratios $\frac{5}{6}$ and $\frac{15}{18}$ equivalent? Explain.
2. How can you use division to find a ratio equivalent to 25:35?
3. How are equivalent ratios like equivalent fractions?

Technology Link

With *Graph Links Plus* computer software, you can show data on a double-bar graph.

REMEMBER:

Equivalent fractions name the same amount.

Examples

$\frac{2}{3} = \frac{4}{6}$ $\frac{5}{10} = \frac{1}{2}$

A fraction is in *simplest form* when the GCF of the numerator and denominator is 1.

Example $\frac{3}{7}$

Scruffy and her kennel

▶ PRACTICE

Tell whether the ratios are equivalent. Write *yes* or *no*.

4. $\frac{2}{4}$ and $\frac{6}{12}$ **5.** 2:5 and 5:10 **6.** 4 to 12 and 1 to 3

7. $\frac{3}{4}$ and $\frac{12}{20}$ **8.** 5:10 and 1:2 **9.** 1 to 4 and 25 to 100

10. Complete the table.

Number of Apples to Make Cider	3	?	?	?
Cups of Cider	1	2	3	4

Write three ratios that are equivalent to the given ratio.

11. 3:1 **12.** 3:5 **13.** 1 to 4 **14.** 10 to 1

15. $\frac{2}{3}$ **16.** $\frac{1}{4}$ **17.** $\frac{1}{5}$ **18.** $\frac{2}{2}$

19. 9 to 3 **20.** 50:100 **21.** 26:36 **22.** 100 to 1

Problem Solving • Mixed Applications

23. Money Mary's brother earns $35 for 5 hours of work. How much does he earn for 3 hours of work?

24. Sports A soccer team has 120 toes. How many players are there?

25. Of 28 canoes on the park rack, 21 are metal. What is the ratio, in simplest form, of metal canoes to all the canoes?

26. Ann mixed a can of lemonade concentrate with 3 cans of water. What is the ratio of concentrate to water?

27. Geometry Emily baked quiche in a round pan with a diameter of 9 inches. She sliced the quiche into 6 equal pieces. How long is each piece from the center to the edge?

28. Write About It Explain how you can tell whether two ratios are equivalent.

Mixed Review and Test Prep

Write *prism* or *pyramid*. Write the polygon that names the base. Identify the solid figure. (pages 454–455)

29. 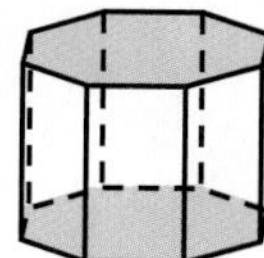

30. 

31. 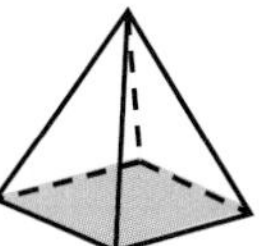

Choose the correct product in simplest form. (pages 394–395)

32. $\frac{1}{2} \times 1\frac{2}{3} = n$

A $\frac{5}{6}$ B $\frac{6}{5}$ C $\frac{10}{3}$ D $1\frac{1}{6}$

33. $\frac{1}{4} \times 1\frac{1}{2} = n$

F $\frac{12}{2}$ G 6 H $\frac{3}{8}$ J $\frac{8}{3}$

MORE PRACTICE page H119

LESSON 4

More About Equivalent Ratios

VOCABULARY
map scale

Why learn this? You can find the actual distance between two cities.

Susan lives in Dallas, Texas. She and her family are looking at a map of Texas to help them decide where to go for the weekend. How far is it from Dallas to El Paso?

Maps show great distances in a small space. A ratio that compares the distance on a map with the actual distance is a **map scale**. You can use the scale to compute the distance from Dallas to El Paso.

Dallas
El Paso
TEXAS
Houston
Corpus Christi
Mission
Gulf of Mexico
cm 0 1 2 3
mi 0 100 200 300

The distance on the map from Dallas to El Paso is 5.6 cm. The ratio of centimeters to miles is 1:100.

$$\frac{1 \times 5.6}{100 \times 5.6} = \frac{5.6}{560} \quad \begin{matrix}\text{map distance} \\ \text{actual distance}\end{matrix}$$

So, it is 560 miles from Dallas to El Paso.

CRITICAL THINKING Explain how equivalent ratios are used to compute actual distance on a map.

▶ CHECK

Use the map and the map scale above.
Copy and complete the ratio table.

	DISTANCE FROM DALLAS		
	City	Distance on Map	Actual Distance
1.	Corpus Christi	?	?
	El Paso	5.6 cm	560 mi
2.	Houston	?	?
3.	Mission	?	?

Use the map scale to complete the ratio table.

4.	**Map Distance** (cm)	1	?	2.6	?	7.8
5.	**Actual Distance** (mi)	100	150	?	680	?

▶ PRACTICE

Copy and complete each ratio table.

6.	Gallons of Gas Used	1	2	?	6	?
7.	Miles Traveled	22	44	88	?	220

8.	Number of Canoes	3	6	9	?	?
9.	Number of Passengers	9	18	?	108	270

For Problems 10–14, use the drawing of the clubhouse.

10. What is the width of the porch in units?

11. What is the actual width of the porch?

12. What is the actual area of the meeting room? (HINT: 1 sq unit = 9 sq ft)

13. What is the perimeter of the kitchen in units? in feet?

14. What is the ratio of linear units to feet?

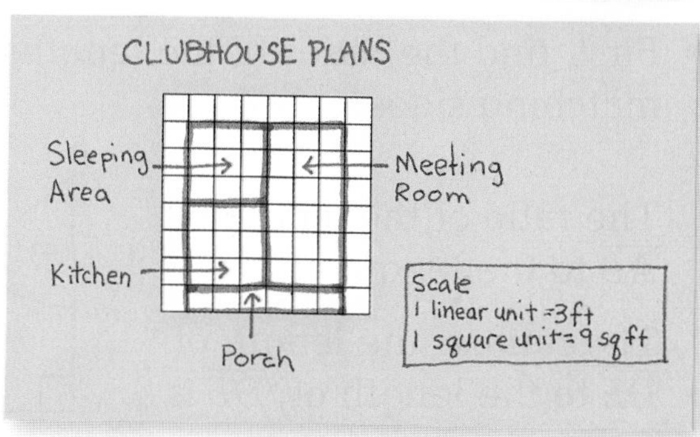

Problem Solving • Mixed Applications

15. Career An architect plans to use a scale of 1 in. = 3 ft in her plan for a new playground for the school. What length will the lines be that represent 3 ft, 6 ft, 12 ft, 18 ft, and 24 ft?

16. Geometry The playground will be 48 ft long and 42 ft wide. The principal wants a fence built around the playground. Fencing costs $12 per foot. How much will it cost to fence in the playground?

17. There are 15 girls and 30 boys at Little Hands Preschool. What is the ratio of girls to boys?

18. Write About It Explain why scale drawings are useful when making maps.

Mixed Review and Test Prep

Find the missing angle. (pages 446–447)

19.

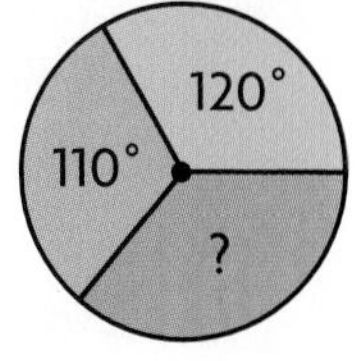

20.

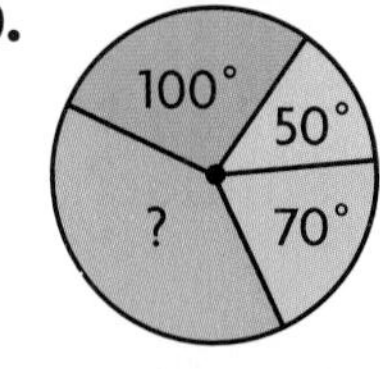

21.

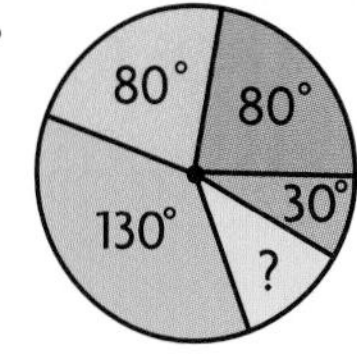

Choose the letter of the correct sum in simplest form. (pages 356–357)

22. $2\frac{1}{5} + 1\frac{1}{3} = \blacksquare$

A $1\frac{7}{8}$ B $\frac{53}{15}$ C $3\frac{8}{15}$ D $\frac{15}{33}$

23. $6\frac{1}{8} + 4\frac{5}{6} = \blacksquare$

F $10\frac{23}{24}$ G $\frac{263}{24}$ H $10\frac{3}{4}$ J $10\frac{36}{48}$

Ratios in Similar Figures

VOCABULARY
similar

Why learn this? You can enlarge or shrink a picture.

In **similar** figures, the matching angles are congruent and the sides have equivalent ratios. Similar figures do not have to be the same size.

How can you check whether the shapes of the two triangles shown are similar?

- First, find the ratios of the lengths of the matching sides.

The ratio of the length of $\overline{AB}$ to the length of $\overline{AC}$ is $\frac{6}{8}$.

The ratio of the length of $\overline{DE}$ to the length of $\overline{DF}$ is $\frac{3}{4}$.

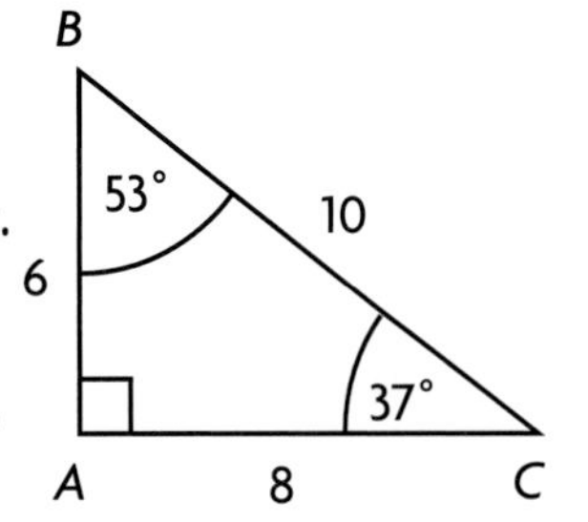

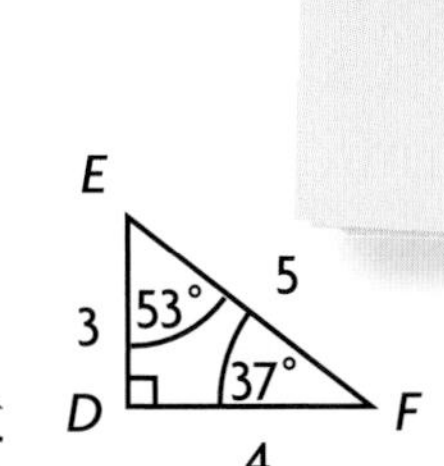

➩ Since $\frac{6}{8}\frac{\div 2}{\div 2} = \frac{3}{4}$, the ratios of the lengths of the matching sides are equivalent.

- Then, measure the matching angles.

$\angle ABC$ measures 53°; $\angle DEF$ measures 53°.

$\angle BCA$ measures 37°; $\angle EFD$ measures 37°.

$\angle CAB$ measures 90°; $\angle FDE$ measures 90°.

➩ The matching angles are congruent.

So, triangle ABC and triangle DEF are similar.

▶ CHECK

1. If you rotated triangle DEF, would it still be similar to triangle ABC? Explain.
2. If two figures are congruent, are they similar? Explain.
3. In the example above, how does the ratio of the length of $\overline{AB}$ to $\overline{BC}$ compare with the ratio of the length of $\overline{DE}$ to $\overline{EF}$?

When two rays have the same *vertex*, they form an *angle*.

Example

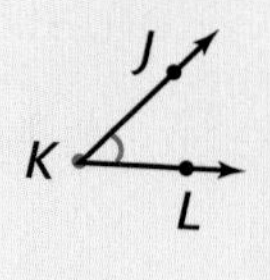

Read: angle *JKL*, or *LKJ*, or angle *K*
Write: $\angle JKL$, $\angle LKJ$, or $\angle K$

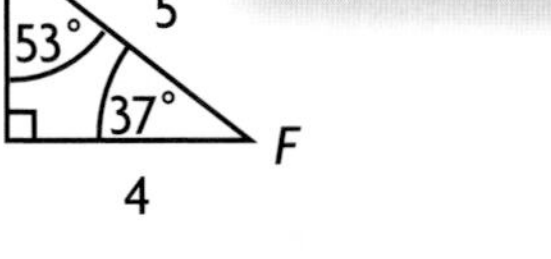

Technology Link

In ***Mighty Math Number Heroes***, the game *GeoComputer* challenges you to identify figures that are similar to a given figure. Use Grow Slide Levels L and S.

▶ PRACTICE

Write *yes* or *no* to tell whether the figures are similar.

4.

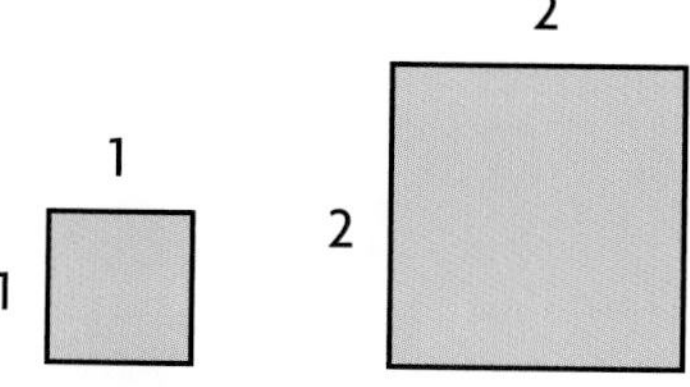

5.

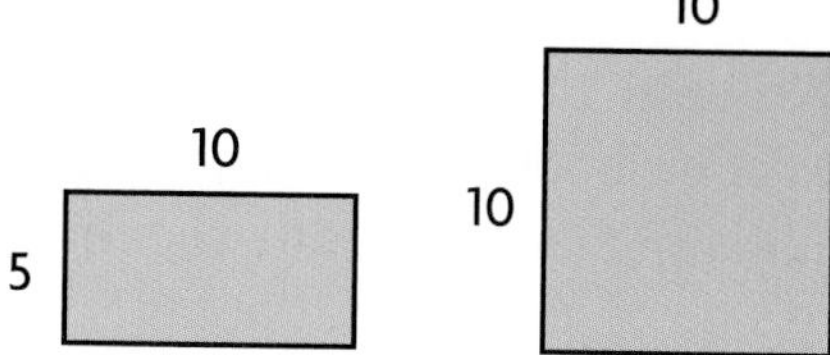

6.

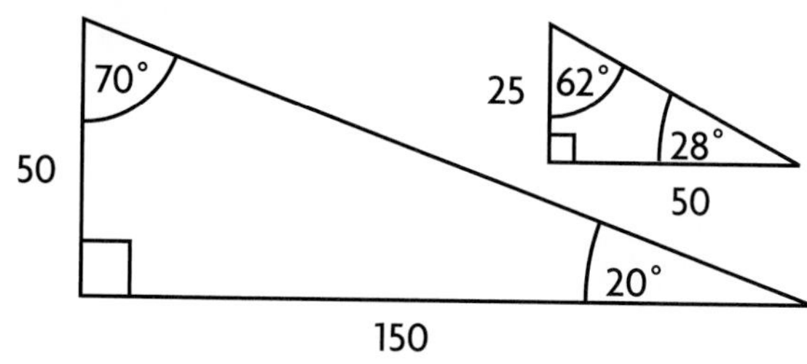

7.

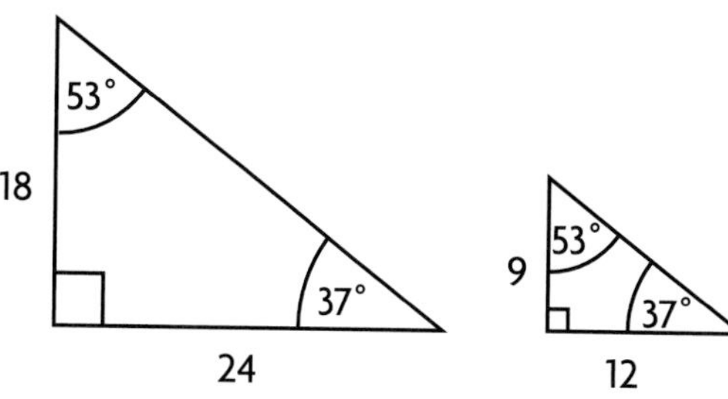

Find the length of the missing side in the similar figures.

8.

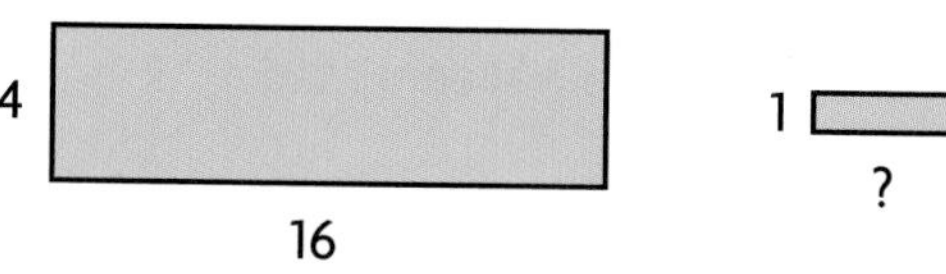

9.

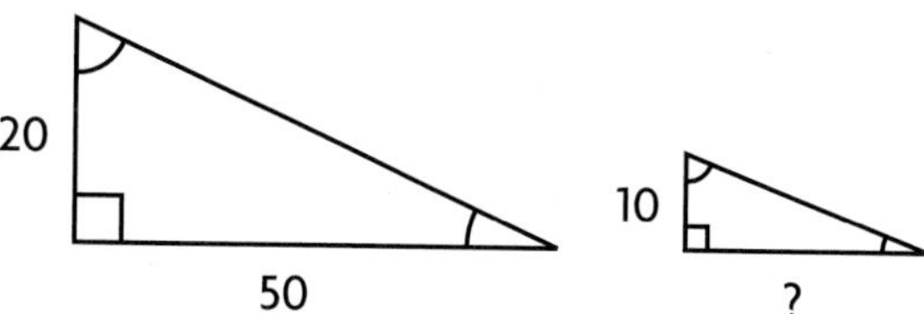

10.

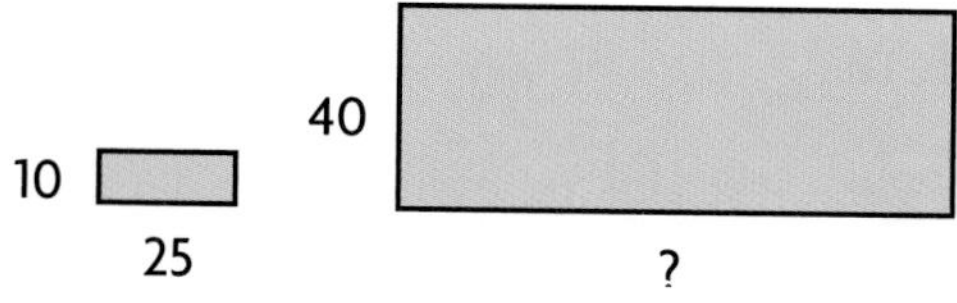

11.

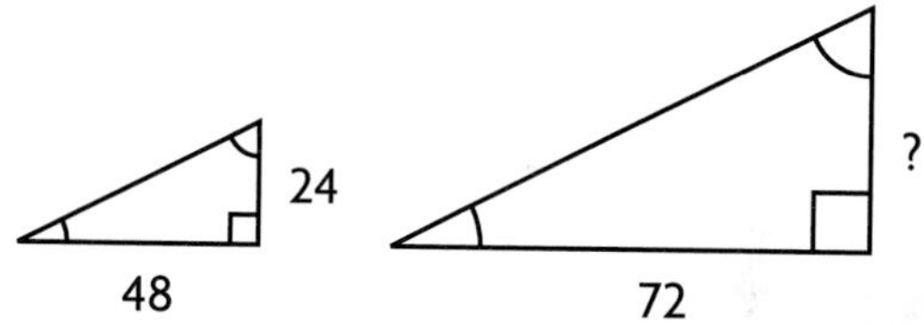

Problem Solving • Mixed Applications

12. Time Laura arrived at the dance studio at 3:25. Her first class began 15 min later. She spent 1 hr 30 min in her first class and 45 min in her second class. She had a 10-min break between classes. At what time did Laura's second class end?

13. Science The ratio of the width of a pot to the width of an African violet should be 1 to 3. What width pot should you use for a 6-inch-wide plant?

14. Measurement If 1 pound of wax makes eight 8-inch candles, how many 4-inch candles will it make?

15. Time If it takes 1 minute to read 15 lines of news, how long does it take to read 1 line of news? (HINT: 1 min = 60 sec)

16. Write About It Are a 4×4 square and an 8×12 rectangle similar? Explain why or why not.

MORE PRACTICE page H120

Problem-Solving Strategy: Write a Number Sentence

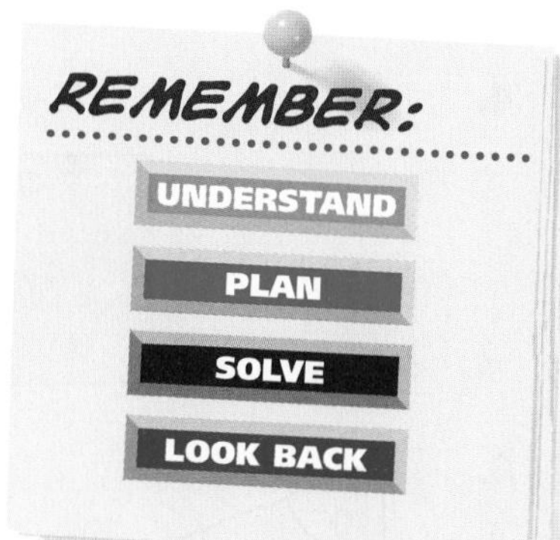

▶ **THE PROBLEM** Hakeem made a sundial for his science project. In the instruction book for making the sundial it said, "Make a triangle that is similar to the one shown." What is the length of the missing side of Hakeem's triangle?

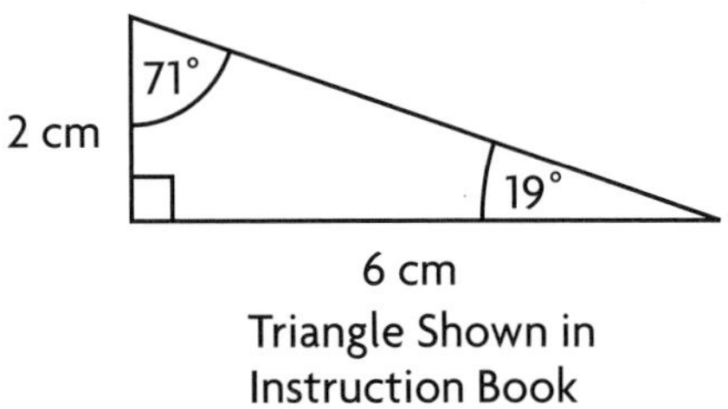

Triangle Shown in Instruction Book

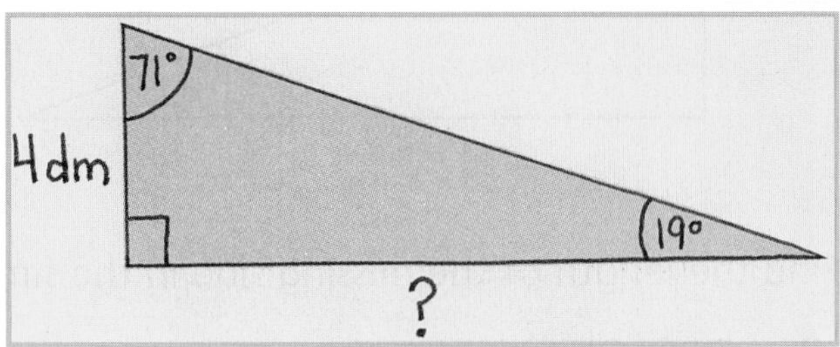

Triangle Hakeem Made

UNDERSTAND

- What are you asked to do?
- What information will you use?
- Is there information you will not use? If so, what?

PLAN

- What strategy can you use to solve the problem?

You can *write a number sentence*.

SOLVE

- How can you use the strategy to solve the problem?

First, find the ratios of the lengths of the sides of the triangle shown in the instruction book.

The ratio is $\frac{2}{6}$, or $\frac{1}{3}$.

Since Hakeem made a triangle that was similar to the one shown, write a number sentence to form an equivalent ratio and find the missing side.

$\frac{1 \times 4}{3 \times 4} = \frac{4}{12}$ So, the length of the missing side is 12 dm.

LOOK BACK

- How can you decide if your answer is reasonable?
- What other strategy could you use?

▶ PRACTICE

Write a number sentence to solve.

1. Roland made a rectangular design. Then he made a similar rectangle to frame the design. Using the rectangle shown, what is the length of the missing side of the frame?

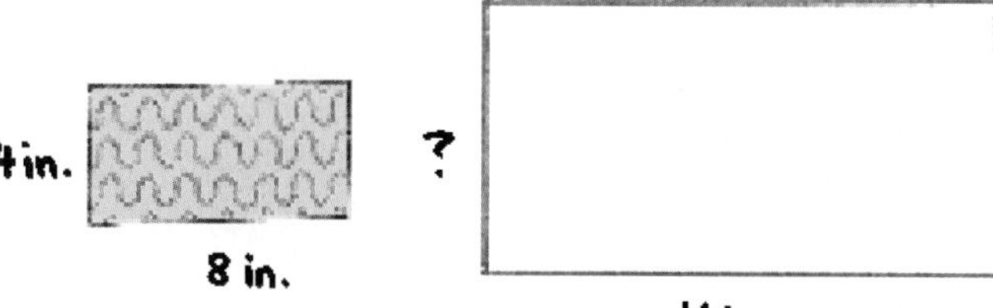

2. Rochelle covered an $8\frac{1}{2}$-in.-tall cylinder with an $8\frac{1}{2}$ in. × 11 in. paper rectangle. What is the diameter of the base of the cylinder to the nearest half inch?

3. Chad and his team started at the 1-yard line. They moved forward $3\frac{1}{2}$ yards, back $1\frac{1}{2}$ yards, and then forward 7 yards. On what yard line is Chad's team now?

Mixed Applications

Solve.

CHOOSE a strategy and a tool.

- Write a Number Sentence
- Work Backward
- Solve a Simpler Problem
- Act It Out
- Draw a Diagram

Paper/Pencil

Calculator

Hands-On

Mental Math

4. Today the mileage display on Mosi's bicycle shows 132.2 km. Yesterday he rode his bike 7.7 km. The day before yesterday he rode 5.9 km. The day before that was Friday. He rode 4.8 km. What did the mileage display show Friday morning?

5. José gave directions to get from the garage to the library. He said, "When you leave the garage, make a 90° turn east onto Elm. Walk 3 blocks, and make a 90° turn north onto Main. Walk 2 blocks and make a 90° turn east onto Magnolia. Walk 1 block to the library." Make a map of José's directions.

6. Linda poured 7.5 liters of hot water into the kitchen sink. She added 5 milliliters of liquid dishwashing soap to the hot water. How much liquid was in the sink?

7. Mr. Linnard swam 45 laps each day from Monday through Friday. He swam 66 laps each day on Saturday and Sunday. What is the mean for the number of laps he swam?

8. Eric went to a state park on Saturday. He spent $\frac{3}{5}$ of the time hiking, $\frac{1}{5}$ of the time in the park museum, and $\frac{1}{5}$ of the time taking photos. Eric hiked for 1 hour 30 minutes. How long did he spend at the park?

9. Mrs. Chung has a rectangular dining room table. She bought a rectangular tablecloth for it. Are the rectangles similar?

3 ft
6 ft
4 ft
18 ft

CHAPTER 27 Review/Test

CHECK Understanding

VOCABULARY

1. You can use a _?_ to compare two numbers. **(page 476)**

2. _?_ show the same relationship. **(page 480)**

3. In _?_ figures, the matching angles are congruent and the sides have equivalent ratios. **(page 484)**

4. A ratio that compares the distance on a map with the actual distance is a _?_. **(page 482)**

Write *a* or *b* to show which fraction represents the ratio. **(pages 478–479)**

5. 50:1 **a.** $\frac{50}{1}$ **b.** $\frac{1}{50}$

6. 9 to 5 **a.** $\frac{5}{9}$ **b.** $\frac{9}{5}$

7. 12:36 **a.** $\frac{36}{12}$ **b.** $\frac{12}{36}$

8. 25 to 100 **a.** $\frac{25}{100}$ **b.** $\frac{100}{25}$

Write *yes* or *no* to tell whether the shapes are similar. **(pages 484–485)**

9.

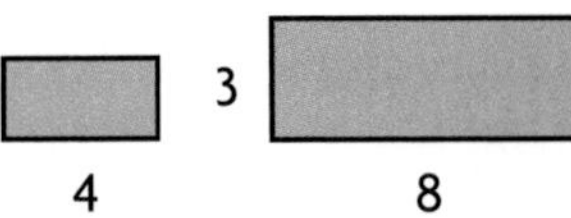

10.

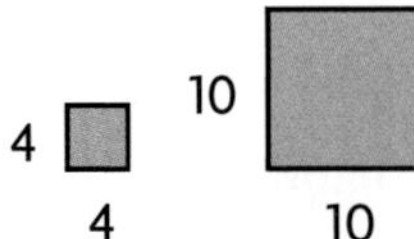

11.

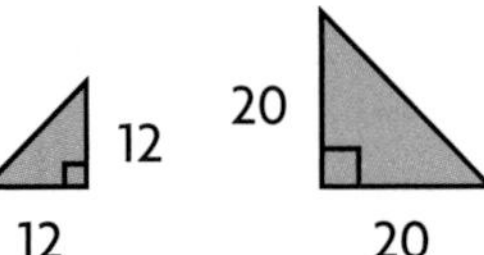

CHECK Skills

Write three ratios that are equivalent to the given ratio. **(pages 480–481)**

12. 8 to 10 **13.** 3:7 **14.** 75:100 **15.** 12 to 6

For Problems 16 and 17, use the drawing of the garden. **(pages 482–483)**

16. What is the actual perimeter of the tomato section?

17. What is the actual area of the green-bean section?

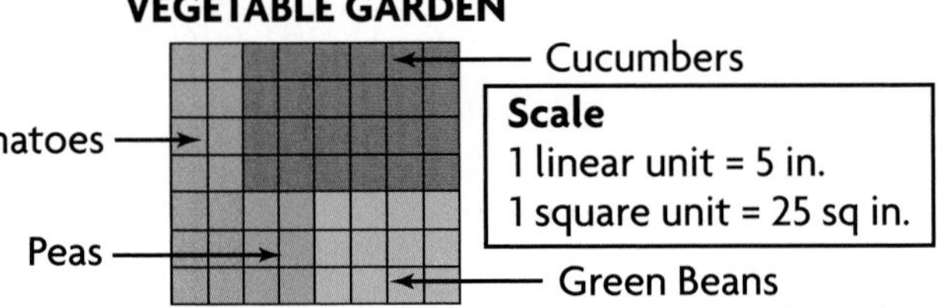

CHECK Problem Solving

Solve. **(pages 486–487)**

CHOOSE a strategy and a tool.

- Write a Number Sentence
- Work Backward
- Act It Out
- Draw a Diagram

Paper/Pencil

Calculator

Hands-On

Mental Math

18. Fred puts a rectangular note card in an envelope that is a similar rectangle. What is the length of the missing side of the envelope?

8 in.
?
3 in.
4 in.

Test Prep

Choose the best answer.

1. Mr. Kreibel had \$289.72 in his checking account. He wrote a check for \$95.89. Which of the following expressions can be used to find the amount he has left in his account?

A \$289.72 + \$95.89

B \$289.72 − \$95.89

C \$289.72 × \$95.89

D \$289.72 ÷ \$95.89

2. Sam's Deli menu includes tuna, turkey, or meatball subs on a choice of wheat, rye, or white rolls. How many choices of subs are on the menu?

F 3 **G** 5

H 6 **J** 9

3. Which of the following groups of fractions is in order from *greatest* to *least*?

A $\frac{1}{8}, \frac{1}{4}, \frac{1}{2}$

B $\frac{1}{4}, \frac{1}{8}, \frac{1}{10}$

C $\frac{1}{4}, \frac{1}{10}, \frac{1}{2}$

D $\frac{1}{10}, \frac{1}{8}, \frac{1}{2}$

4. A pack of juice has 4 cartons. Sondra drank 2 cartons of juice yesterday. Which fraction shows how much of the pack she drank?

F $\frac{1}{8}$ **G** $\frac{1}{4}$

H $\frac{1}{2}$ **J** $\frac{3}{4}$

5. 1 inch − $\frac{1}{4}$ inch =

A $\frac{1}{4}$ in. **B** $\frac{1}{2}$ in.

C $\frac{3}{4}$ in. **D** $1\frac{1}{4}$ in.

6. Which triangle is congruent to triangle *ABC*?

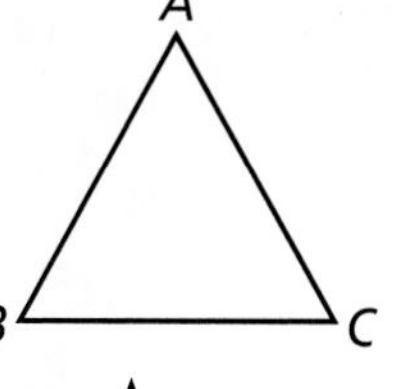

F

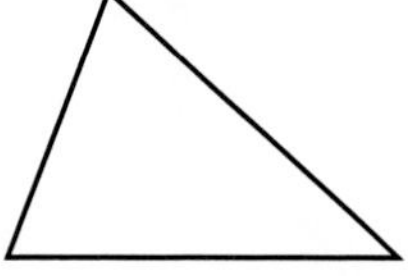

G

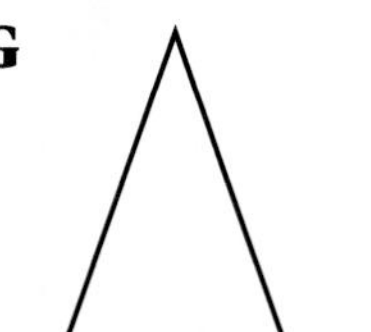

H

J

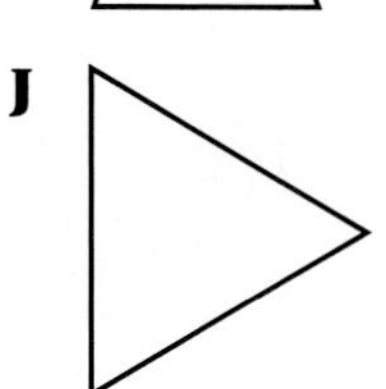

7. Which polygon is the base of the prism shown?

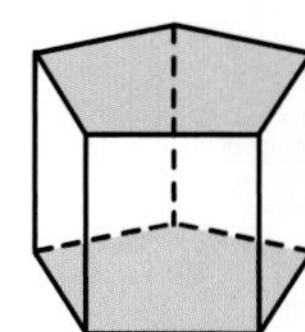

A Pentagon

B Square

C Triangle

D Hexagon

8. There are 11 girls on a basketball team. Only 5 girls can play at a time. What is the ratio of girls playing to girls on the team?

F 5 to 6

G 5 to 11

H 6 to 11

J 5 to 16

K Not Here

28 PERCENT

DATA LINK

The Mars company in Hackettstown, New Jersey makes M&M® candies. According to the company, this is the color assortment: brown 30%, red 20%, yellow 20%, green 10%, orange 10%, blue 10%.

Problem-Solving Activity

Design a Colorful Party Product

Have you ever noticed that fun products like markers, balloons, confetti, and birthday candles are made in new colors all the time?

If you were designing a fun product for a party, like balloons or candles, what colors would you choose? How many of each color would you put in a package of 100?

YOU WILL NEED: decimal grid paper, ruler, markers or colored pencils

- Decide on a party product and create a catchy name.
- Decide on colors for your product. You should have at least three different colors in a package.
- Decide how many out of 100 will be made in each color and make a model to show the percent of each color.

A FEW IDEAS FOR COLOR SETS

- everyday colors
- birthday colors
- back-to-school colors
- seasonal colors
- holiday colors

Some Flavorful Ideas

- lime - green
- kiwi fruit - green
- mango - orange
- watermelon - pink
- bubble gum - pink
- blueberry - blue

DID YOU

- ✓ decide on a party product and name it?
- ✓ choose a set of at least three colors?
- ✓ decide how many out of 100 will be made in each color, and make a model to show the percent?

Understanding Percent

VOCABULARY
percent

You will investigate how to represent percent as part of a hundred.

Did you know that "50% off" means you can buy an item for half price? **Percent** means "per hundred." The symbol for *percent* is %. 1 percent is the same as 1 out of 100.

LANGUAGE LINK

The *cent* in *percent* means "100." Use a dictionary. What other words can you find in which *cent* relates to 100?

Example
A *century* is 100 years.

▶ EXPLORE

MATERIALS: 1-inch grid paper, counters, scissors, tape

Kyle has 7 pennies. He wants to find out what percent of a dollar he has.

Use a 10×10 grid to represent the number of pennies in a dollar. Then use counters to show Kyle's pennies.

Record

Draw a picture of your 7 counters on the grid paper.

Write the percent of a dollar the model shows. Explain how you can use grid paper to show percent.

Talk About It

- How many pennies are in a dollar?
- How many squares do Kyle's pennies take up?
- What percent of a dollar does Kyle have in pennies?

Now, investigate showing other percent amounts on grid paper.

▶ TRY THIS

Place counters on the grid to show the following amounts. Draw a picture and write the percent of each.

1. 23 campers out of 100 campers
2. 42 ducks out of 100 birds
3. 16 cents out of a dollar
4. 17 kittens out of 100 pets
5. 4 dimes out of a dollar
6. 56 boys out of 100 students

7. Which is more, 23 percent or 42 percent?

8. What does 100 percent mean?

9. How is a percent like a ratio?

10. **Write About It** How could you show 100 percent on a decimal square?

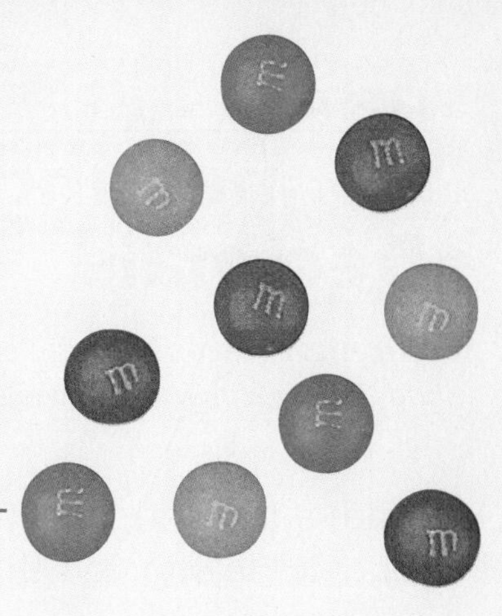

▶ PRACTICE

Use counters to show the following on your 10 × 10 grid. Draw a picture and write the percent.

11. 55 dollars out of 100 dollars

12. 65 children out of 100 people

13. 25 blue balloons out of 100 balloons

14. 20 red M&M's® out of a bag of 100

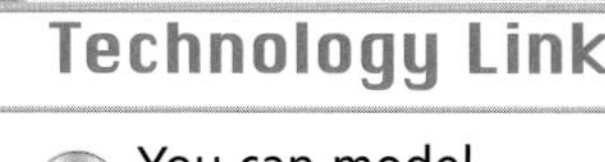

Technology Link

You can model percentages by using E-Lab, Activity 28. Available on CD-ROM and on the Internet at **www.hbschool.com/elab**

Look at the picture. Write the percent.

15. 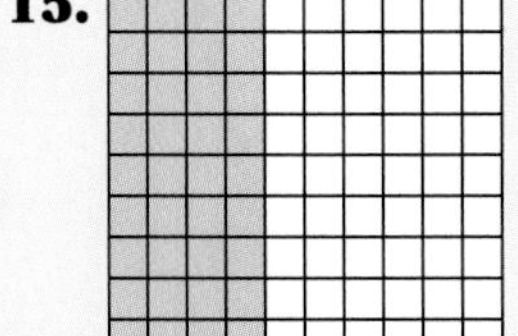

16. 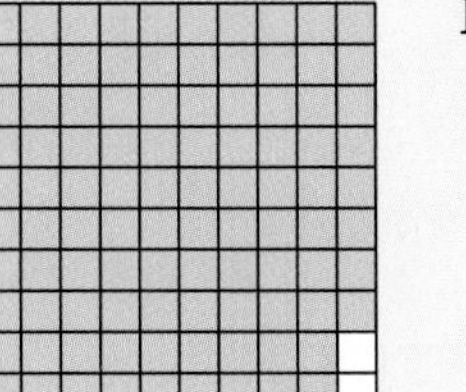

17. 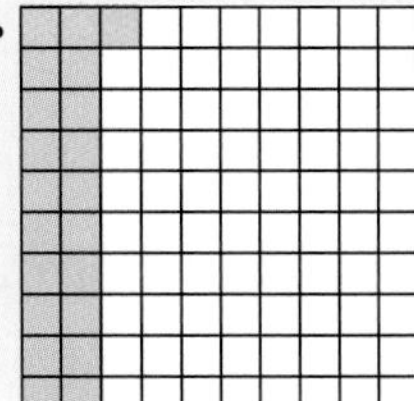

For Exercises 18–19, choose the more reasonable percent. Write *a* or *b*.

18. "Almost everyone passed the test," Miss Jones exclaimed with a big smile.

a. 99% passed **b.** 12% passed

19. "Very few children like spicy food. Out of 100 children, fewer than 5 like it," said the chef.

a. 55% **b.** 4%

Problem Solving • Mixed Applications

20. **Time** A few months ago, Hannah had 100 days to wait until her birthday. Now her wait is 90 percent over. How many days has she waited?

21. **Measurement** Rochelle bought $5\frac{1}{2}$ yards of fabric to make a new comforter for her bed. She used $\frac{3}{4}$ of the fabric she bought. How much fabric does she have left?

22. **Money** Jim gave the ice-cream vendor $1.00 for an ice-cream sandwich. He received $0.29 in change. What percent of his dollar did he spend?

23. **Write a problem** about percent. Mention part of 100 in your problem.

MORE PRACTICE page H121

Connecting Percents and Decimals

Why learn this? You can express a percent with a decimal, the same way you would write dollars and cents.

Mike surveyed 100 students on how they get to school. He showed the results on a decimal square.

Talk About It

- How many students out of 100 take the bus? What percent take the bus?
- How many students out of 100 ride bikes? What percent ride bikes?
- How many students out of 100 walk? What percent walk?

You can also write a percent as a decimal.

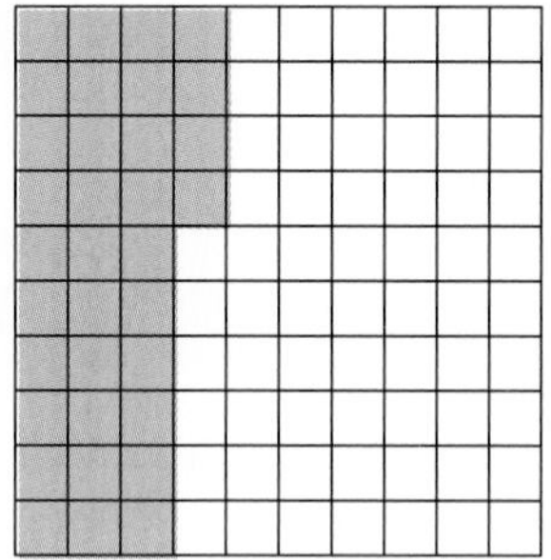

34 percent

Read: thirty-four hundredths

Write: 0.34

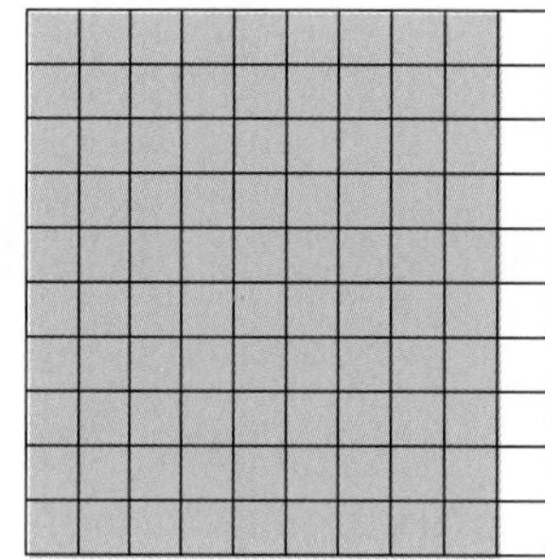

90 percent

Read: ninety hundredths

Write: 0.90

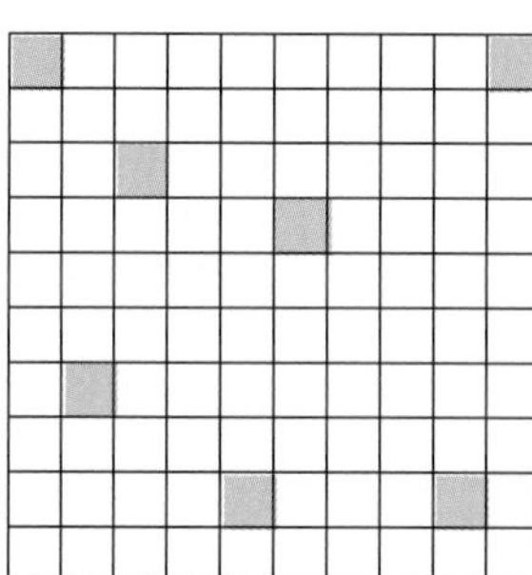

7 percent

Read: seven hundredths

Write: 0.07

Talk About It

- Do 0.90 and 0.09 represent the same number?
- What percent does 0.90 represent? What percent does 0.09 represent?
- Using what you know about percent as a decimal, how could you enter 78 percent into a calculator?

CRITICAL THINKING Explain how you know that a percent can be expressed as a decimal.

CONSUMER LINK

The United States dollar is based on a decimal system. It is easy to find percents with such a system, since one dollar has 100 parts, or cents. What are the coins that represent 10% of a dollar, 25% of a dollar, 1% of a dollar, and 5% of a dollar?

▶ CHECK

For Exercises 1–3, study the shaded parts of the grid.

1. What percent of the squares are purple?
2. What percent of the squares are red?
3. Add all the colors. What percent is the total?

▶ PRACTICE

Write the number as a percent and as a decimal.

4. fifty-one hundredths
5. eighty hundredths
6. three hundredths
7. fourteen hundredths

Write the decimal as a percent.

8. 0.75
9. 0.31
10. 0.08
11. 0.80
12. 0.15

Write the percent as a decimal.

13. 56%
14. 99%
15. 40%
16. 12%
17. 2%

Problem Solving • Mixed Applications

For Problems 18 and 20, write the answer as a percent and as a decimal.

18. **Language** The school had a spelling bee. Out of 100 contestants, 44 misspelled *aardvark*. What percent misspelled this word?

19. **Time** During the last 24 hours, Jeremy watched 2 hours of TV. Compare his hours of watching TV to his hours of doing other things.

20. **Science** Mary planted 100 marigold seeds. She had 77 sprouts. What percent of the seeds did not sprout?

21. **Write About It** How does knowing about decimals help you understand percent? Give an example.

Mixed Review and Test Prep

Name each triangle. Write *isosceles, scalene,* or *equilateral.* (pages 418–419)

22. 5 ft, 5 ft, 5 ft

23. 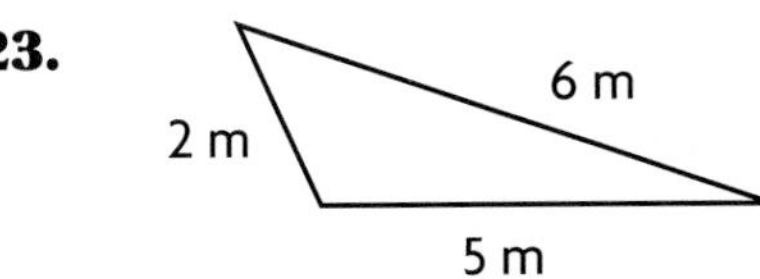

24. 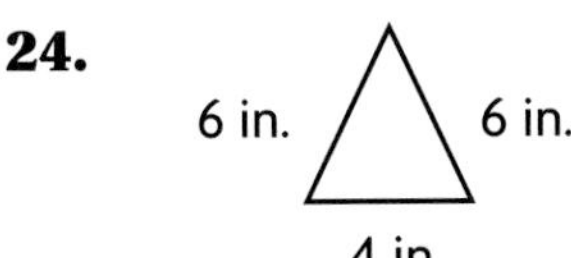

Choose the letter of the fraction that represents the ratio. (pages 478–479)

25. 6 to 2 **A** $\frac{2}{6}$ **B** $\frac{3}{2}$ **C** $\frac{6}{2}$ **D** $\frac{1}{6}$

26. 4:8 **F** $\frac{4}{6}$ **G** $\frac{8}{4}$ **H** $\frac{8}{2}$ **J** $\frac{4}{8}$

27. 9 to 3 **A** $\frac{3}{9}$ **B** $\frac{9}{3}$ **C** $\frac{1}{3}$ **D** $\frac{9}{6}$

MORE PRACTICE page H121

Connecting Percents and Fractions

Why learn this? You will know that if 20% of the students are fifth graders, 20 out of every 100, or $\frac{1}{5}$, are in fifth grade.

The Church Street Dance Club was having a square dance. There were 100 dancers. The dance did not go as planned. It turned out that 75 percent of the dancers did not know how to do-si-do! What fraction of the dancers did not know how to do-si-do?

To do-si-do, dancers pass each other right shoulder to right shoulder and circle each other back to back.

There were 75 out of 100 dancers who did not know how to do-si-do. You can show this number on a decimal square.

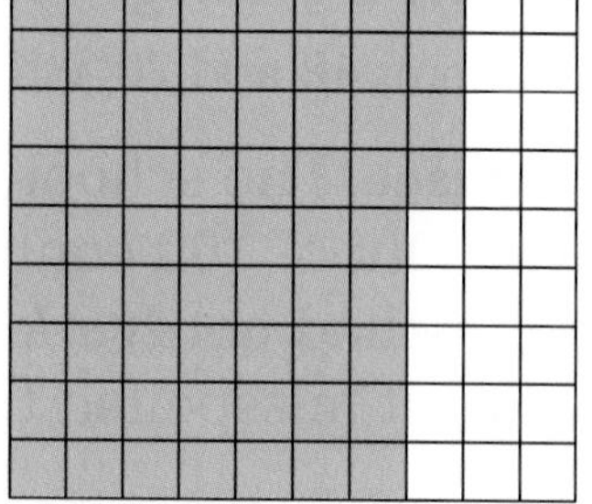

You can write it as a ratio, or a fraction: $\frac{75}{100}$.

$\frac{75}{100} = \frac{75 \div 25}{100 \div 25} = \frac{3}{4}$ Write the fraction in simplest form.

So, $\frac{3}{4}$ of the dancers did not know how to do-si-do.

- Suppose one quarter of the square dancers were wearing western outfits. What percent is that? How would you write it as a fraction?

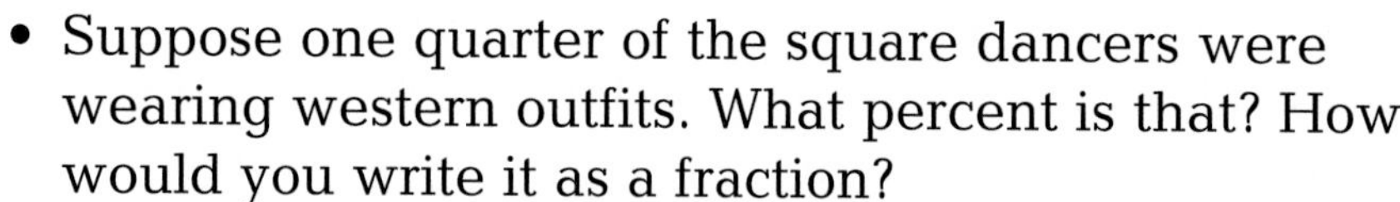

A fraction with 100 as the denominator can be written as a percent.

$\frac{1}{100} = 1\%$ $\frac{25}{100} = 25\%$ $\frac{99}{100} = 99\%$

You can use a calculator to change a fraction to a percent. First, change it to a decimal.

EXAMPLE

Change $\frac{1}{100}$ to a decimal and then to a percent.

Enter the numerator first. Divide it by the denominator.

Write 0.01 as a percent: 1%.

Technology Link

In ***Mighty Math Number Heroes,*** the game *Fraction Fireworks* challenges you to change fractions to decimals. Use Grow Slide Level Y.

Calculator Activities page H69

▶ CHECK

Write the percent as a fraction in simplest form.

1. 20% **2.** 35% **3.** 50% **4.** 48%

5. 4 percent **6.** fifteen per hundred **7.** thirty-seven per hundred

▶ PRACTICE

Write the fraction as a percent.

8. $\frac{7}{100}$ **9.** $\frac{7}{10}$ **10.** $\frac{1}{1}$ **11.** $\frac{6}{10}$

12. $\frac{2}{25}$ **13.** $\frac{3}{25}$ **14.** $\frac{16}{25}$ **15.** $\frac{6}{100}$

Write as a decimal and as a fraction in simplest form.

16. 18 percent **17.** 25 percent **18.** 33 percent

19. 3 percent **20.** 30 percent **21.** 55 percent

Problem Solving • Mixed Applications

22. Time A cruise ship went on a 100-day trip. The passengers were ashore 25 days; the rest of the time they were at sea. What percent of time were they at sea?

23. Music At the spring concert, 100 fifth graders performed. Out of that group, 35 percent played the flute. How many students played the flute?

24. A cheese pizza was cut into 8 parts and an equal-size veggie pizza into 12 parts. Ann ate 2 pieces of cheese pizza. Josh ate 3 pieces of veggie pizza. Who ate more?

25. Music Of the fifth graders, $\frac{3}{5}$ sing in the chorus and $\frac{2}{5}$ play a band instrument. Out of the 100 fifth graders, how many sing? play a band instrument?

26. The ratio of teachers to students is 1 to 20. There are 8 teachers. How many students are there?

27. Write About It Explain how you can change a percent to a fraction and a fraction to a percent.

Mixed Review and Test Prep

Tell whether the ratios are equivalent. Write *yes* or *no*. (pages 480–481)

28. $\frac{1}{4}$ and $\frac{2}{8}$ **29.** 6:12 and 1:2 **30.** 4 to 12 and 1 to 4

Choose the correct sum in simplest form. (pages 342–343)

31. $\frac{3}{4} + \frac{1}{3} = n$

A 1 **B** $\frac{13}{12}$ **C** $1\frac{1}{12}$ **D** $1\frac{1}{6}$

32. $\frac{5}{8} - \frac{1}{3} = n$

F $\frac{14}{24}$ **G** $\frac{7}{24}$ **H** $1\frac{1}{6}$ **J** $\frac{8}{12}$

MORE PRACTICE page H121

Benchmark Percents

VOCABULARY
benchmark percent

Why learn this? You can use a benchmark percent when estimating part of a whole, such as pennies in a jar.

Sean's grandma has four grandchildren. She bought a jar for each of her grandchildren. Every time the children find a penny, they place it in their jar. They want to estimate how full each jar is.

You can use percents to make an estimate. A **benchmark percent** is a commonly used percent that is close to the amount you are estimating.

25% is a good benchmark for amounts close to one fourth.
50% is a good benchmark for amounts close to one half.
10%, 75%, and 100% are other common benchmark percents.

REMEMBER:

A *benchmark* is a point of reference you can use to make a reasonable estimate.

Examples
10; 100; 1,000

Talk About It

- What benchmark percent can you use to estimate each amount in the jars above?
- What benchmark percent would you use to estimate 27 pennies as a percent of a dollar? 52 pennies? 79 pennies?

Using benchmark percents can help you estimate the percent of a total other than 100.

EXAMPLE

Of the 80 students Michael surveyed, 13% said they like to cook. What is a reasonable estimate of this percent of students?

Think: 13% is close to the benchmark percent 10%.

Since 13% is a little more than 10%, a reasonable estimate would be that about 10% of the students Michael surveyed said they like to cook.

CULTURAL LINK

Quilts were popular in 18th- and 19th-century America. Pioneer women often made quilts to record their family history. An African American influence is evident in the quilt shown in the picture. If a quilt had 25 squares and 5 of them were blue, what percent of the squares would be blue?

▶ CHECK

For Exercises 1–4, choose from the following benchmarks: 10%, 25%, 50%, 75%, or 100%.

1. 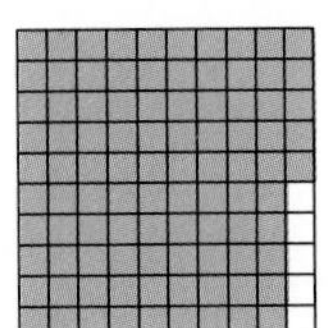 **2.** 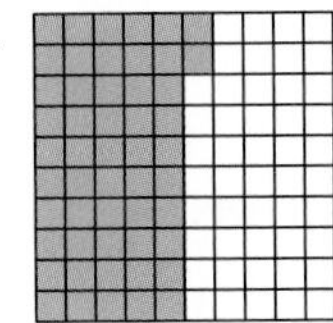 **3.** 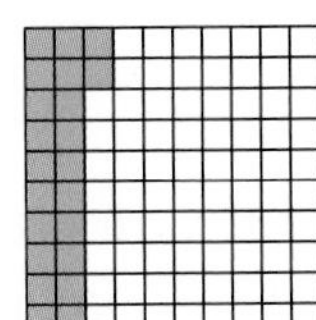 **4.** 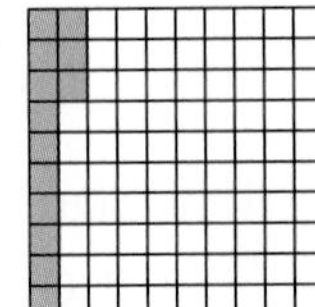

▶ PRACTICE

Tell what benchmark percent you would use to estimate each percent.

5. 72% **6.** 11% **7.** 46% **8.** 30% **9.** 97%

For Exercises 10–13, choose the more reasonable benchmark. Write *a* or *b*.

10. Three quarters of the class earned an A on the test.

a. 25% **b.** 75%

11. Very few of the children live in a house without a television.

a. 25% **b.** 10%

12. A quarter of the football team must lose weight.

a. 25% **b.** 50%

13. All of the puppies have been vaccinated.

a. 100% **b.** 50%

Problem Solving • Mixed Applications

14. Reading Mark has finished 7 out of 13 chapters of his new book. What benchmark would you use to estimate the percent of the book he has finished?

15. Geometry Lee made a scale model of his house, using a scale of 1 in. = 4 ft. The model has a 1-inch-tall fireplace. What is the height of the actual fireplace?

16. Visual Thinking How many angles will you find in 3 triangles and 4 quadrilaterals?

17. Write a problem that includes a percent that can be estimated by using a benchmark percent.

Mixed Review and Test Prep

Write *chord, diameter,* or *radius* for each line segment. (pages 440–441)

18.  **19.**  **20.** 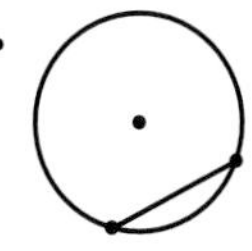 **21.** 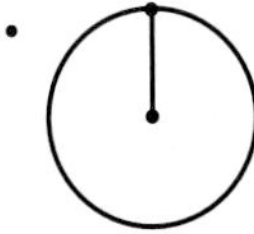

Choose the correct sum or difference in simplest form. (pages 356–359)

22. $3\frac{2}{3} - 1\frac{1}{6} = n$

A $2\frac{1}{2}$ **B** $2\frac{3}{6}$ **C** $4\frac{5}{6}$ **D** $2\frac{1}{3}$

23. $4\frac{1}{8} + 2\frac{1}{4} = n$

F $6\frac{1}{2}$ **G** $6\frac{1}{3}$ **H** $6\frac{3}{4}$ **J** $6\frac{3}{8}$

MORE PRACTICE page H122

Percents in Circle Graphs

Why learn this? You can understand the circle graphs you see in newspapers and magazines.

The fifth grade held several car washes. They made $400. They decided to go to a game of their favorite baseball team.

This circle graph shows the percentage of money they spent in each category. They spent 40% of the money on the cost of a bus, 20% on tickets, 30% on food, and 10% on programs.

Talk About It CRITICAL THINKING

- What decimal represents each section of the circle graph? What fraction?
- What is the sum of the percents that represent the whole, or the $400 the fifth grade made?
- If the fifth grade spent $40 on programs, how much did they spend on the cost of a bus? on tickets? on food?

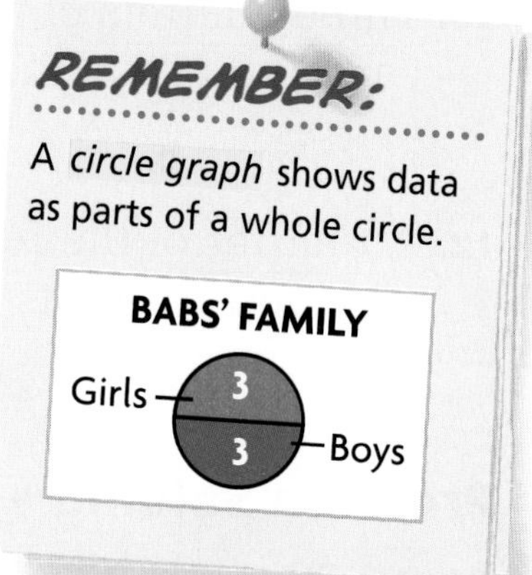

▶ CHECK

For Problems 1–3, use the circle graph.

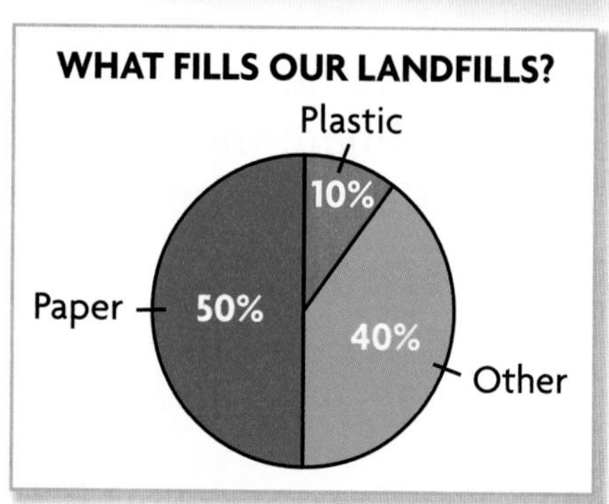

1. According to this circle graph, what fills one half of our landfills?
2. What fills one tenth of our landfills?
3. Ted saw an old toaster in the landfill. In this circle graph, under what category would it fall?

For Problems 4–6, use the circle graph.

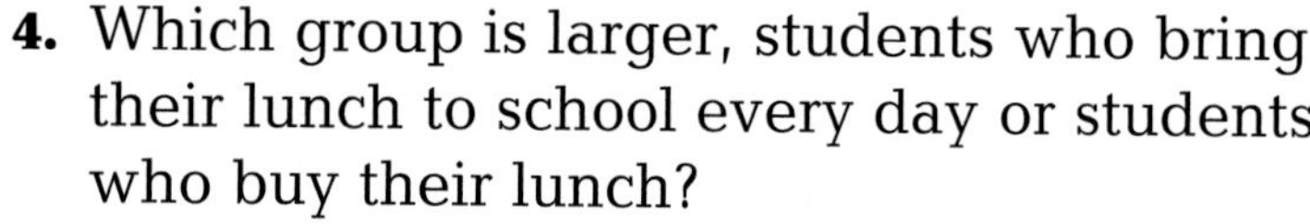

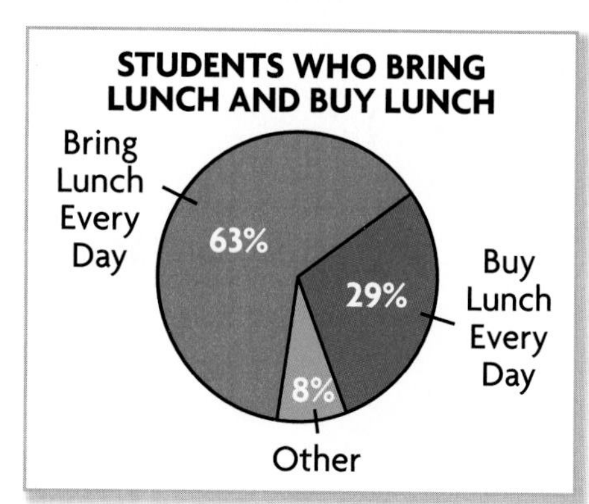

4. Which group is larger, students who bring their lunch to school every day or students who buy their lunch?
5. What does the category labeled *Other* probably represent?
6. What decimal and fraction represent each section of the circle graph?

▶ PRACTICE

For Problems 7–8, use the first circle graph.

7. Do more than half or less than half of the students surveyed get an allowance?

8. What decimal represents the students who get an allowance?

For Problems 9–12, use the second circle graph.

9. Do more students get less than \$6 a week or more than \$6 a week?

10. What percent of students get less than \$6 a week?

11. Which groups in this circle graph are the same size?

12. Which two categories cover one half of the circle graph?

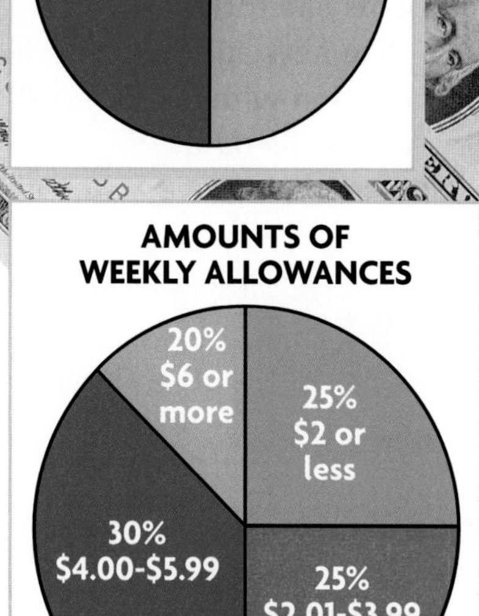

Problem Solving • Mixed Applications

Using Data For Problems 13–19, use the table.

Favorite Wheels	
In-line skates	30 votes
Bikes	10 votes
Skateboards	10 votes

13. What decimal and percent represent the students who chose in-line skates?

14. What decimal and percent represent the students who chose skateboards?

15. **Graphing** If you were to make a circle graph of these data, what would the largest section show?

16. **Compare** How many times larger would the section for in-line skates be than the section for bikes?

17. **Sports** Did more than half or less than half of the students choose in-line skates? bikes? skateboards?

18. **Number Sense** What decimal represents the students who chose bikes? What percent of the students chose bikes? (HINT: 10 out of 50 chose bikes.)

19. **Write About It** Suppose you are making a circle graph for the Favorite Wheels data, using a circle divided into ten equal sections. Explain how to represent each part of the graph using percent.

LESSON CONTINUES

Problem-Solving Strategy: Make a Graph

▶ **THE PROBLEM** Glen surveyed 200 fifth-grade students in his school to find out their favorite music. He found that 30% of the students like rock music the most, 30% like pop, 20% like country, 10% like new age, and 10% like classical. Glen wants to share this information with his class. What would be the best way for Glen to display the data?

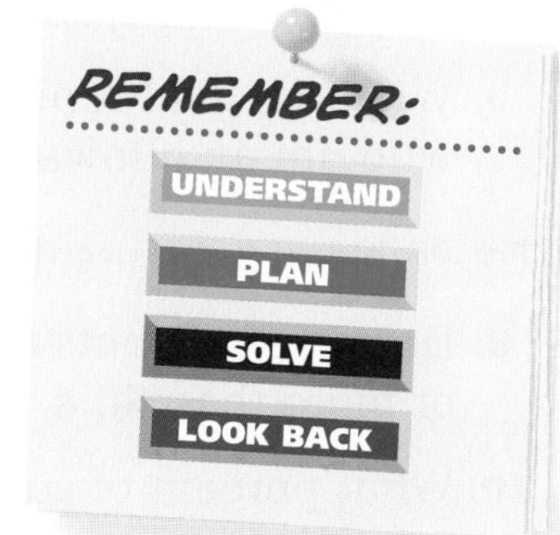

UNDERSTAND

- What are you asked to find?
- What information will you use?
- Is there information you will not use? If so, what?

What is your favorite kind of music?

PLAN

- What strategy can you use to solve the problem?

  You can *make a graph* to display the data, showing the percentage of students who prefer each kind of music.

SOLVE

- What graph would be the best to make?

  Since Glen wants to show the relationship of the parts to the whole, a circle graph would be best. Use a circle divided into ten equal parts. Shade 3 sections to represent rock music, 3 sections to represent pop music, and 2 sections to represent country music. Shade 1 section to represent new age music and 1 section to represent classical music. Label and title the circle graph.

So, rock music and pop music are the two favorite kinds of music.

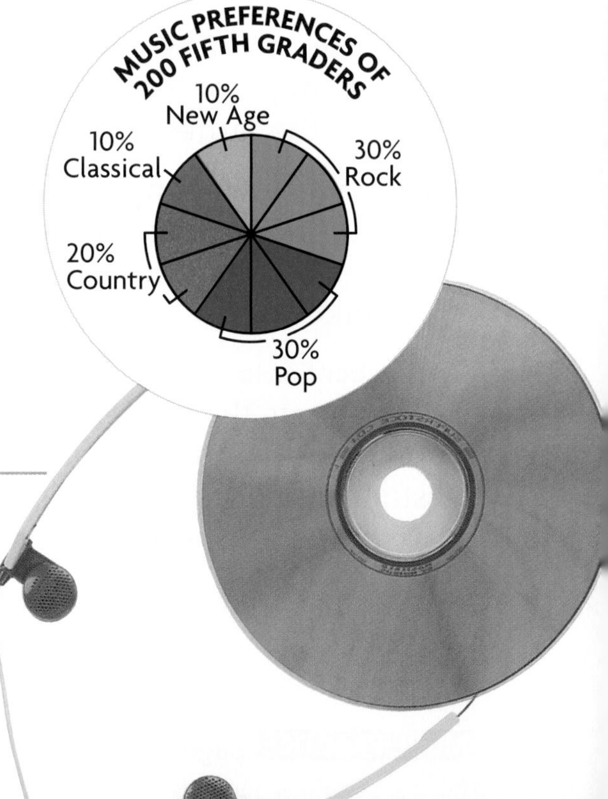

LOOK BACK

- Why is this the best way to display the data?
- What other strategy could you use?

▶ PRACTICE

Make a graph to solve.

END-OF-YEAR FIELD TRIP	
Place	**Percent of Votes**
Planetarium	20%
Theater	10%
Water Park	40%
Museum	10%
Zoo	20%

1. Randy surveyed the fifth-grade students to find out where to go for the end-of-the-year field trip. He organized the data in the table. How can he show which two choices received 50% of the votes? What graph should he make to display these data?

MORGAN'S SAVINGS	
Month	**Amount Saved**
January	$10
February	$20
March	$20
April	$30
May	$20

2. Morgan has $100 that she saved from January through May. She made a table showing the amount saved each month. How can she show two months in which she saved 50% of $100? What graph could she make to display these data?

Mixed Applications

Solve.

CHOOSE a strategy and a tool.

- Make a Graph
- Guess and Check
- Make a Model
- Write a Number Sentence
- Work Backward

Paper/Pencil

Calculator

Hands-On

Mental Math

3. Daniel surveyed 40 men and women. Of the men, 5 like to read, 7 like to do yard work, and 8 like to exercise. Of the women, 7 like to read, 5 like to do yard work, and 8 like to exercise. Which activity did both men and women prefer? How can you show this?

4. Popcorn in a movie theater costs $2.55. The same amount costs $0.35 to pop at home. A movie ticket is $3.75. It costs $2.50 to rent a video. How much do you save by renting a video and popping popcorn at home?

5. What fraction multiplication sentence does this model represent? What is the product?

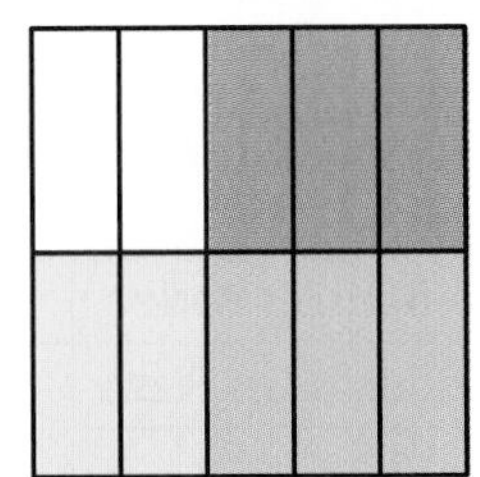

6. Mrs. Price made a long-distance phone call that cost $2.25 for the first minute and $0.30 for each additional minute. The call lasted for 18 minutes. How much did it cost?

7. There are 56 teachers at Sunridge Elementary. Of the teachers, $\frac{1}{4}$ have no children. Some teachers have 1 child, and twice as many have 2 or more children. How many have 2 or more children?

8. The Lions are ranked number 1. Since the season began they have moved up 6 places, down 2 places, down 1 place, and up 4 places. What rank were they at the beginning of the season?

MORE PRACTICE page H122

CHAPTER 28 Review/Test

▶ CHECK Understanding

VOCABULARY

1. _?_ means "per hundred." (page 492)

2. A _?_ is a commonly used percent, such as 10%, 25%, 50%, 75%, or 100%. (page 498)

Look at the picture. Write the percent. (pages 492–493)

3. 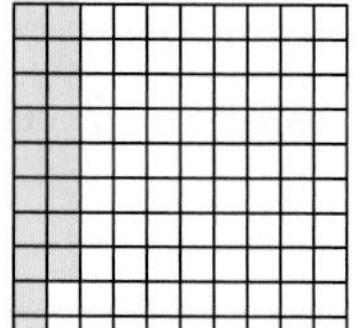

4. 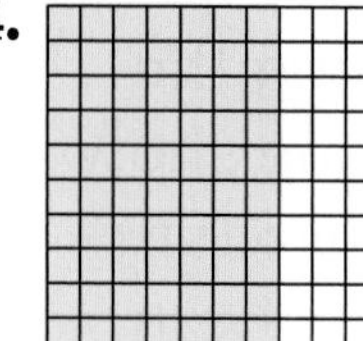

5. 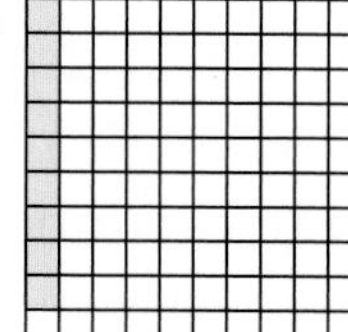

▶ CHECK Skills

Write the number as a percent and as a decimal. (pages 494–495)

6. eighty hundredths
7. fifteen hundredths
8. six hundredths

Write as a decimal and as a fraction in simplest form. (pages 496–497)

9. 4 percent
10. 75 percent
11. 20 percent

Tell what benchmark percent you would use to estimate each percent. (pages 498–499)

12. 27%
13. 12%
14. 53%
15. 98%
16. 74%

▶ CHECK Problem Solving

Solve. (pages 502–503)

CHOOSE a strategy and a tool.

- Make a Model
- Make a Graph
- Guess and Check
- Draw a Picture

Paper/Pencil

Calculator

Hands-On

Mental Math

17. Nancy surveyed the fifth-grade students to find out their favorite local pizzeria. The table at the right shows the results of her survey. How can she show the class which two pizzerias received 50% of the votes?

FAVORITE PIZZERIAS	
Pizzeria	**Percent of Votes**
Benny's Parlor	10%
Surf's Up Pizza	40%
Pizza Palace	30%
Lotsa Pizza	20%

18. Val had 100 stickers. She gave away 22 percent of her stickers. How many stickers did she give away?

19. Jared just got a raise of $1 per week in his allowance. How much more allowance did he earn in one year?

Test Prep

CUMULATIVE
CHAPTERS 1–28

Choose the best answer.

1. Which of the following groups of decimals is in order from *least* to *greatest*?

A 3.12, 3.14, 3.42, 3.89

B 3.12, 3.14, 3.89, 3.42

C 3.89, 3.12, 3.14, 3.42

D 3.14, 3.89, 3.42, 3.12

2. $5.42 - 3.86 =$

F 1.56 **G** 1.66

H 1.76 **J** 2.56

3. The graph shows magazines sold during a school fundraiser.

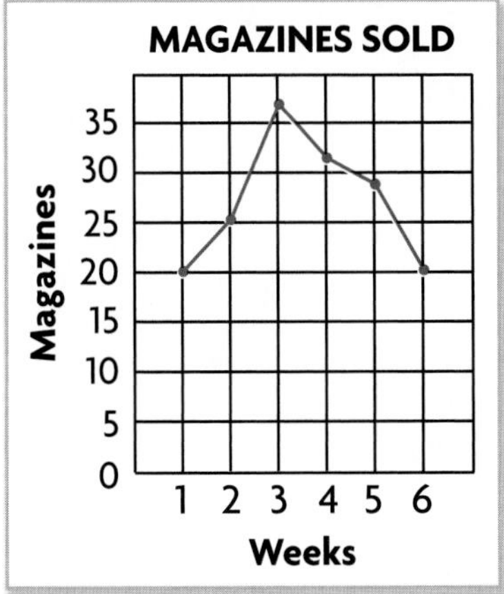

During which two weeks were more than 30 magazines sold?

A Weeks 1 and 5

B Weeks 3 and 5

C Weeks 2 and 4

D Weeks 3 and 4

4. 39 meters = __?__ centimeters

F 3.9 **G** 39

H 390 **J** 3,900

5. Cher left the house at 1:15 P.M. She arrived home 3 hours later. What time did Cher arrive home?

A 2:15 P.M.

B 5:15 P.M.

C 6:15 P.M.

D 4:15 A.M.

E Not Here

6. Point *A* of triangle *ABC* is located at which ordered pair?

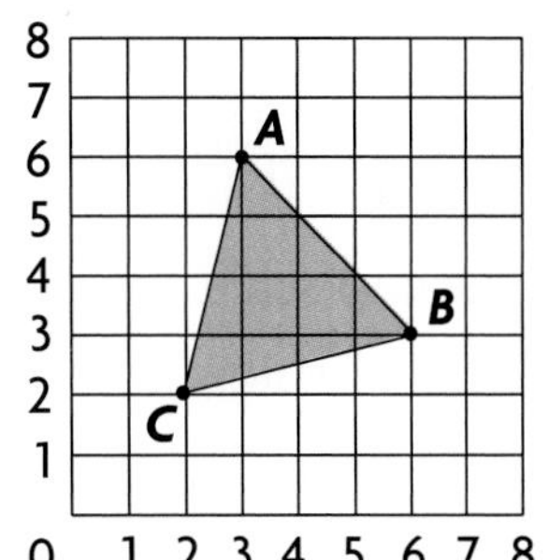

F (2,2)

G (3,5)

H (3,6)

J (6,3)

7. A map scale shows that the ratio of inches to miles is 1:10. DeShaun measures the distance between two cities and finds that it is about 6 inches. About how many miles apart are the two cities?

A 10 mi **B** 12 mi

C 50 mi **D** 60 mi

8. Lucas has completed 6 out of 25 pages in his math workbook. Which of the following is a reasonable estimate of the pages Lucas has completed?

F 25% **G** 50%

H 75% **J** 100%

Are You a Square or a Rectangle?

PURPOSE To analyze two pieces of data by using a ratio

YOU WILL NEED measuring tape or yardstick, paper and pencil, calculator

Stand with your arms stretched out so that you make a T. Have a friend measure your height and your armspan, from fingertip to fingertip, in inches. Find the ratio of your height to your armspan. If the ratio is equivalent to 1, then you are a square. If the ratio is not equivalent to 1, you are a rectangle.

Do this activity with your family. Who is a square? a rectangle?

Plan a Trip

PURPOSE To use a map scale

YOU WILL NEED map, ruler, pencil

Use your knowledge of map scales to plan a trip. Find a map for a place you would like to visit. Plan a trip there. You can travel by car at 50 miles an hour or by airplane at 500 miles an hour.

Find a place on the map. Choose a way to travel there. Decide the date and time that you will leave, how many hours you want to travel, and where you will be when it's time to go to bed.

Plan the next day of your trip. Where will you be by the end of the second day?

MAP IT!

PURPOSE To make a scale drawing

YOU WILL NEED grid paper, ruler, pencil

Make a scale drawing of your classroom. Use grid paper and a ruler. Be sure to include the scale you used. What percent of the classroom in the picture has furniture?

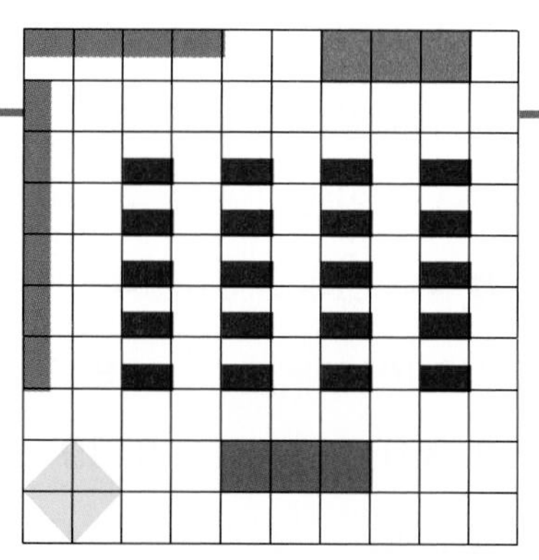

Showing Data on Double-Bar Graphs

MATERIALS: *Graph Links Plus* or other graphing software

Each day Lynn runs and rides her bicycle. She records the distance of each exercise in a table. She wants to keep the same ratio of miles run to miles biked.

LYNN'S EXERCISE SCHEDULE			
Exercise	Saturday	Sunday	Monday
Running	3 miles	4 miles	2 miles
Biking	9 miles	12 miles	6 miles

Make a double-bar graph of Lynn's distances to show a visual comparison. Look for a ratio of running to biking by comparing the height of each set of bars.

- What is the ratio of miles run to miles biked each day?

So, Lynn is keeping the same ratio of $\frac{1}{3}$ of miles run to miles biked.

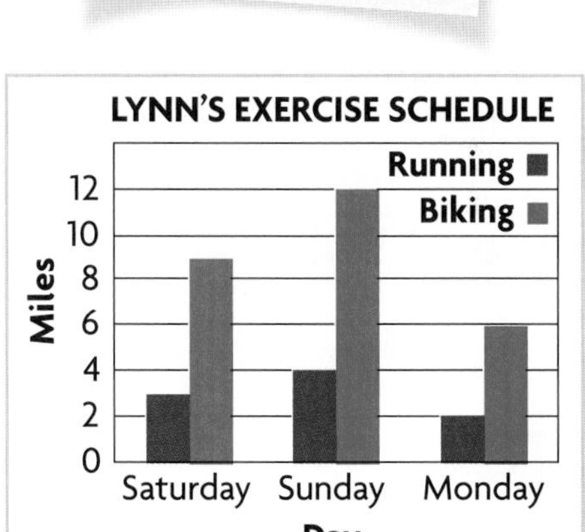

▶ PRACTICE

1. How does a double-bar graph show a ratio of Lynn's running and biking?

2. Scott says the ratio of players to basketballs at practice was the same on each day. Make a graph to show the ratio.

BASKETBALL PLAYERS			
Day	Mon	Wed	Fri
Players	8	12	?
Balls	2	?	4

3. **Using the Computer** David spends the same ratio of time exercising to the time reading on four different days. Complete the table and make a double-bar graph to show how David spends this time. What is the ratio of minutes spent exercising to minutes spent reading?

DAVID'S SCHEDULE (in min)				
Day	Mon	Wed	Fri	Sat
Exercising	40	50	?	60
Reading	20	?	15	?

CHAPTERS 27–28

Study Guide and Review

Vocabulary Check

VOCABULARY
benchmark
equivalent
percent
ratio
map scale
similar

Choose a term from the box to complete each sentence.

1. To compare two numbers, such as 3 to 1 or 5 to 7, you can use a _?_. (page 476)
2. Ratios such as 2 to 1 and 50 to 25 show the same relationship. They are _?_ ratios. (page 480)
3. A ratio that compares the distance on a map with the actual distance is a _?_. (page 482)
4. Figures that have matching, congruent angles and sides with equivalent ratios are called _?_ figures. (page 484)
5. "Per hundred" is another way to say the word _?_. (page 492)
6. A commonly used percent, such as 10%, 50%, or 100%, is called a _?_ percent. (page 498)

Study and Solve

CHAPTER 27

EXAMPLE

Write ratios that are equivalent to the given ratio.

8 to 10	Multiply or divide both numbers by the same number to find equivalent ratios.
$8 \div 2 = 4$	Divide 8 by 2, and divide 10 by 2.
$10 \div 2 = 5$	So, 4 to 5 is equivalent to 8 to 10.
$8 \times 2 = 16$	Multiply 8 by 2, and multiply 10 by 2.
$10 \times 2 = 20$	So, 16 to 20 is equivalent to 8 to 10.

Write three ratios that are equivalent to the given ratio. (pages 480–481)

7. 6 to 10 **8.** 15:5

9. 25:100 **10.** 3 to 1

For Problems 11–13, use the diagram. Find the actual measurements. (pages 482–483)

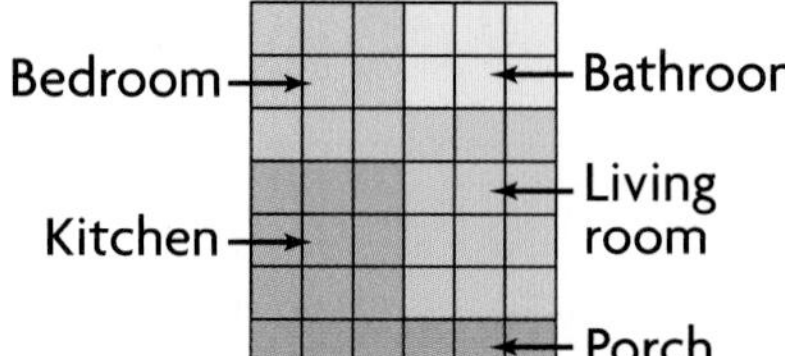

Scale:
1 linear unit = 4 ft
1 square unit = 16 sq ft

11. the perimeter of John's apartment, including the porch
12. the area of John's living room
13. the area of John's apartment, not counting the porch

Write *a* or *b* to show which fraction represents the ratio. (pages 478–479)

14. 25 to 1

a. $\frac{25}{1}$

b. $\frac{1}{25}$

15. 10:5

a. $\frac{5}{10}$

b. $\frac{10}{5}$

Write *yes* or *no* to tell whether the figures are similar. (pages 484–485)

16.

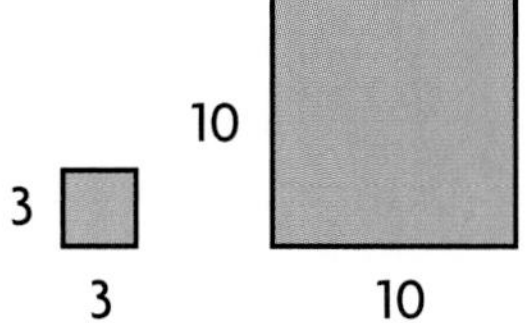

17.

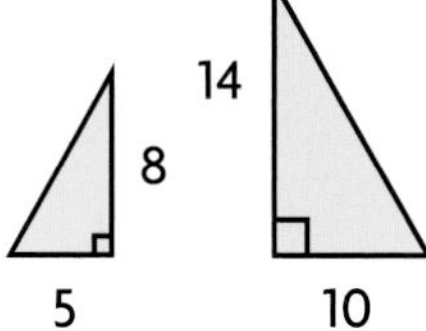

18.

Solve. (pages 486–487)

19. Rebecca enlarged a 4-inch by 5-inch photograph. The enlarged photo is a similar rectangle 8 inches wide. How long is the enlarged photo?

CHAPTER 28

EXAMPLE

Write as a decimal and as a fraction in simplest form.

75 percent

fraction: $\frac{75}{100}$, or $\frac{3}{4}$ in simplest form

decimal: 0.75

Write 75 percent as a fraction.
75 hundredths, or $\frac{75}{100}$
To find the simplest form of $\frac{75}{100}$, divide by the GCF. The GCF of 75 and 100 is 25. $\frac{75}{100} \div \frac{25}{25} = \frac{3}{4}$
You can use a calculator to change a fraction to a decimal.
$\frac{75}{100} = 75 \div 100 = 0.75$

Write as a decimal and as a fraction in simplest form. (pages 496–497)

20. 50 percent **21.** 42%

22. 8 percent **23.** 15%

24. 40 percent **25.** 5%

Look at the picture. Write the percent. (pages 492–493)

26.

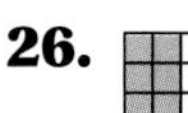

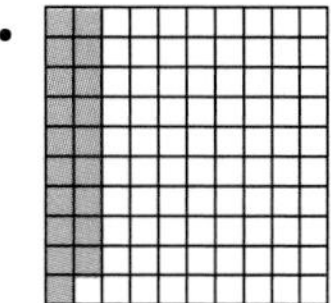

27.

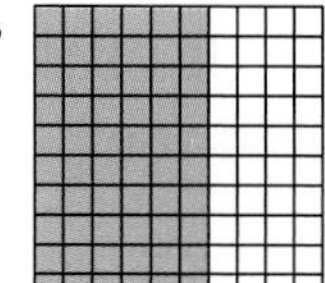

Write the number as a percent and as a decimal. (pages 494–495)

28. thirty-two hundredths

29. seventy hundredths

30. eight hundredths

Tell what benchmark percent you would use to estimate each percent. (pages 498–499)

31. 9% **32.** 54%

33. 28% **34.** 97%

Choose the more reasonable benchmark. Write *a* or *b*. (pages 498–499)

35. All the kittens are tabbies.

a. 100% **b.** 75%

36. Very few of us have red hair.

a. 25% **b.** 10%

Choose a strategy and solve. (pages 502–503)

37. Rob earned \$100. He paid 15 percent in taxes. How much money did he receive after taxes were taken out?

CHAPTERS 27–28

Performance Assessment

Tasks: Show What You Know

1. Toss a handful of two-color counters. Write the ratio of red counters to yellow counters in three different ways. Explain and write other ratios for the counters. (pages 478–479)

2. Use a circle divided into 10 equal parts to make a circle graph to show the favorite school lunch choices of the fifth-grade students. Explain how you can tell from looking at the graph which lunch one half of the students liked best. (pages 500–501)

Favorite Lunch	
Pizza	30%
Hamburger	10%
Salad Bar	50%
Tacos	10%

Problem Solving

Solve. Explain your method.

CHOOSE a strategy and a tool.

- Find a Pattern
- Make a Model
- Write a Number Sentence
- Act It Out
- Make a Table

Paper/Pencil

Calculator

Hands-On

Mental Math

3. Vince has a picture that is 4 in. wide and 6 in. long. He wants to put it in a larger frame that is a rectangle similar to the picture. He is considering a frame that is 8 in. wide. How long is the frame? (pages 486–487)

4. Rob surveyed 40 students to find out their favorite football teams. He found 20% liked the Cowboys, 30% the Jaguars, 30% the Bears, 10% the Panthers, and 10% the Falcons. Which two teams received 50%? (pages 502–503)

Cumulative Review

Solve the problem. Then write the letter of the correct answer. (pages 54–55)

1. $3.26 + 2.069 = n$

A. $n = 1.191$ **B.** $n = 4.329$
C. $n = 5.229$ **D.** $n = 5.329$

2. 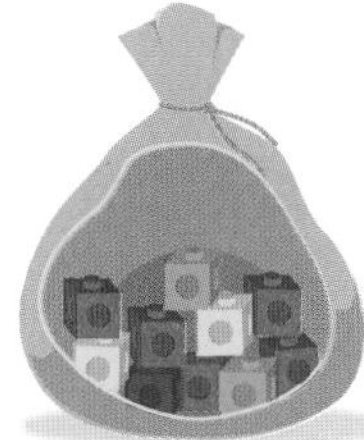

What is the probability of pulling a green or yellow cube? (pages 196–199)

A. $\frac{1}{10}$ **B.** $\frac{2}{10}$, or $\frac{1}{5}$
C. $\frac{4}{10}$, or $\frac{2}{5}$ **D.** $\frac{5}{10}$, or $\frac{1}{2}$

3. 2.99×0.5

A. 1.045
B. 1.495
C. 14.95
D. 149.5 (pages 218–223)

For Problems 4–6, choose the correct answer that is in simplest form.

4. $\frac{5}{6} - \frac{1}{3} = n$

A. $n = \frac{3}{6}$ **B.** $n = \frac{1}{2}$
C. $n = 1\frac{1}{6}$ **D.** $n = \frac{4}{3}$ (pages 320–323)

5. $5\frac{2}{3} + 2\frac{5}{6} = n$

A. $n = 7\frac{7}{9}$ **B.** $n = \frac{51}{6}$
C. $n = 8\frac{1}{2}$ **D.** $n = 8\frac{3}{6}$ (pages 356–357)

6. $\frac{2}{3} \times 3\frac{1}{4} = n$

A. $n = \frac{26}{12}$ **B.** $n = 2\frac{1}{6}$
C. $n = 2\frac{2}{12}$ **D.** $n = 2\frac{2}{3}$ (pages 394–395)

7. Find the missing measurement.

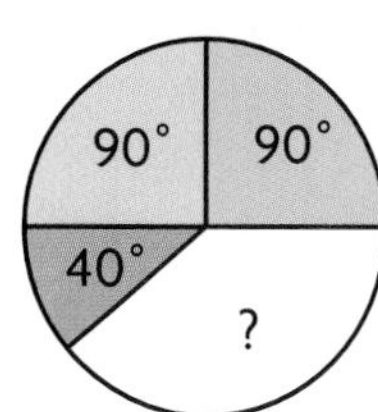

A. 45°
B. 140°
C. 180°
D. 360° (pages 446–447)

8. Identify the solid figure.

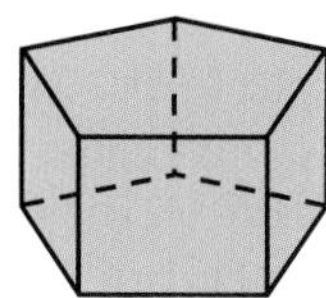

A. triangular prism
B. rectangular pyramid
C. hexagonal pyramid
D. pentagonal prism (pages 454–455)

9. Which ratio is equivalent to 2:50?

A. 1:25 **B.** 10:500
C. 14:400 **D.** 25:1 (pages 480–481)

10. How do you write five hundredths as a percent?

A. 0.5% **B.** 5%
C. 50% **D.** 500% (pages 494–495)

11. How do you write 4% as a decimal?

A. 0.04 **B.** 0.40
C. 4.0 **D.** 40.0 (pages 494–497)

1 Troubleshooting Lessons H2

Before you begin a new topic, it often helps to review things that you learned earlier. These lessons will help you get ready to learn new topics in math.

2 Extension Lessons H32

You can challenge yourself to learn new and interesting things when you try these Extension lessons.

Regrouping Across Zeros

Why learn this? Subtracting with regrouping across zeros can help you compute how much money will be left after making a purchase.

While on a field trip, Horace and his class had lunch at a restaurant. Horace ordered a turkey sandwich and milk. His check was for $3.24. He gave the clerk $5.00. How much change will Horace receive?

You can subtract to find how much change Horace will receive.

MODEL

Step 1	Step 2	Step 3
Subtract. $5.00 − $3.24 = *n* Look at the ones. Since 4 > 0, regroup. There are 0 tens, so regroup 5 hundreds as 4 hundreds 10 tens.	Regroup 10 tens as 9 tens 10 ones. Subtract the ones. Subtract the tens.	Subtract the hundreds.
4 10 ~~5~~ ~~0~~ 0 −3 2 4	9 4 ~~10~~ 10 ~~5~~ ~~0~~ ~~0~~ −3 2 4 7 6	9 4 ~~10~~ 10 ~~5~~ ~~0~~ ~~0~~ −3 2 4 1 7 6 → $1.76 Place a dollar sign and decimal point in the answer.

So, Horace received $1.76 in change.

EXAMPLES

A

$$\begin{array}{r} \overset{2\,10}{\cancel{3}\cancel{0}0} \\ -270 \\ \hline 30 \end{array}$$

B

$$\begin{array}{r} \overset{3\,\overset{9}{\cancel{10}}10}{\cancel{4}\cancel{0}\cancel{0}} \\ -\ \ 98 \\ \hline 302 \end{array}$$

C

$$\begin{array}{r} \overset{4\,\overset{9}{\cancel{10}}\overset{9}{\cancel{10}}10}{\cancel{5},\cancel{0}\cancel{0}\cancel{0}} \\ -\ \ 683 \\ \hline 4,317 \end{array}$$

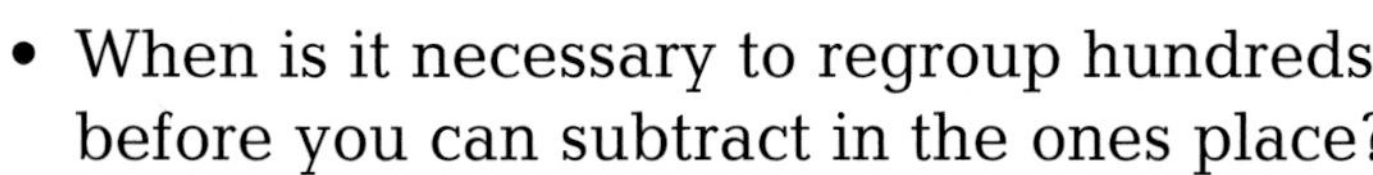

- When is it necessary to regroup hundreds before you can subtract in the ones place?

▶ CHECK

Find the difference.

1. 470 − 124
2. 300 − 79
3. 700 − 595
4. 800 − 437
5. 1,300 − 906
6. 500 − 193
7. 600 − 487
8. 700 − 78
9. 2,000 − 586
10. 4,000 − 2,074

▶ PRACTICE

Find the difference.

11. $200 - 87$

12. $450 - 145$

13. $\$6.00 - 3.21$

14. $\$5.00 - 2.18$

15. $850 - 546$

16. $900 - 785$

17. $7,050 - 2,936$

18. $\$20.00 - 12.45$

19. $\$10.00 - 5.28$

20. $8,005 - 4,752$

21. $7,400 - 2,196$

22. $\$30.05 - 18.99$

23. $600 - 259 = n$

24. $\$8.00 - \$4.51 = n$

25. $900 - 574 = n$

26. $\$20.00 - \$12.98 = n$

27. $4,700 - 1,982 = n$

28. $7,003 - 436 = n$

29. $\$52.00 - \$16.98 = n$

30. $11,000 - 687 = n$

HEALTH LINK

Protein is an important part of our diet. Our bodies use protein to make and repair skin and other body parts. Protein helps us fight disease, and it sometimes gives us extra energy. A fifth-grader needs about 55 grams of protein each day. About how many more grams of protein will Horace need after he eats lunch?

FOOD	GRAMS OF PROTEIN
turkey sandwich	about 21
glass of milk	about 8
carrot sticks	about 1

Problem Solving • Mixed Applications

31. Money Alma bought a book for \$5.95. She gave the clerk a \$10.00 bill. How much change will Alma receive?

32. Money Larry owed his friend \$7.89. Since Larry did not have the correct amount, he gave his friend a \$20.00 bill. How much change will Larry receive?

33. Number Sense Jenny had 200 sheets of paper. Ralph borrowed 18 sheets. How many sheets of paper does Jenny have left?

34. Randy read 317 pages of his book the first week and 239 pages the second week. How many pages did Randy read in all?

35. During a concert 389 seats were filled in an auditorium. At a pep rally 467 of the seats were filled. How many more seats were filled for the pep rally?

36. Consumer One television show was viewed in about sixty million homes. Write two different forms of the number that is one million less than sixty million.

37. Using Data In a recent year, 50,241,840 homes had cable television. If 7 million more homes were added to this number, what would be the total number of homes with cable television?

38. **Write a problem** about 600 students in a school. Use subtraction.

What Is a Decimal?

Why learn this? You can use a decimal to name an amount of money or record a sports score.

A *decimal* is a number that uses place value and a decimal point to show a value less than one, such as tenths and hundredths.

At basketball practice, Kate made 7 out of 10 of her free throws. How can you express as a decimal the number of free throws Kate made?

You can use decimal squares to model decimals.

Model	Fraction	Decimal
	Write: $\frac{7}{10}$ **Read:** seven tenths	**Write:** 0.7 **Read:** seven tenths

So, Kate made $\frac{7}{10}$, or 0.7, of her free throws.

At the basketball game, the team made 34 out of the 100 shots they attempted. How can you express that number as a decimal?

Model	Fraction	Decimal
	Write: $\frac{34}{100}$ **Read:** thirty-four hundredths	**Write:** 0.34 **Read:** thirty-four hundredths

So, the team made $\frac{34}{100}$, or 0.34, of their shots.

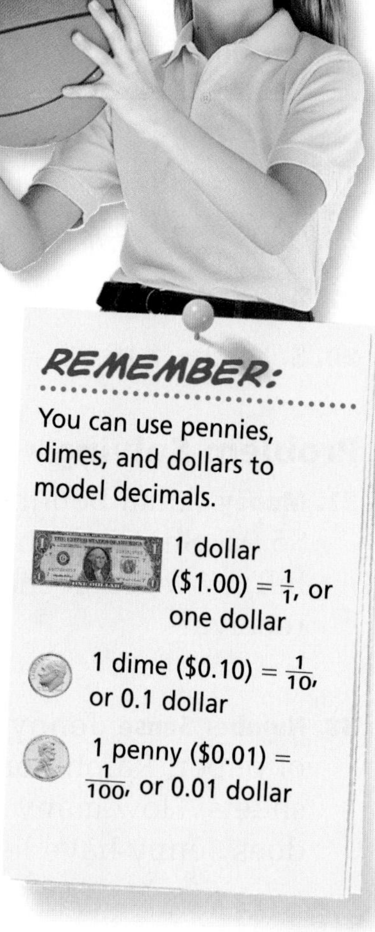

REMEMBER:

You can use pennies, dimes, and dollars to model decimals.

1 dollar ($1.00) = $\frac{1}{1}$, or one dollar

1 dime ($0.10) = $\frac{1}{10}$, or 0.1 dollar

1 penny ($0.01) = $\frac{1}{100}$, or 0.01 dollar

▶ CHECK

Write the decimal for the part that is shaded.

1. 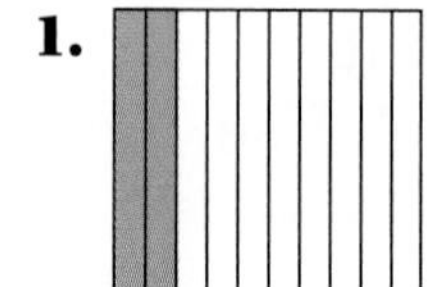

2. 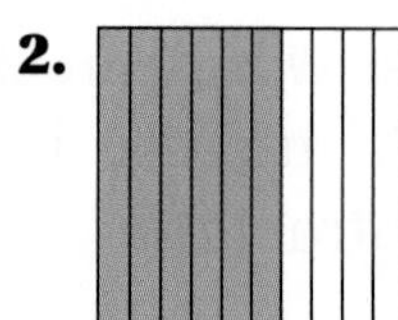

3. 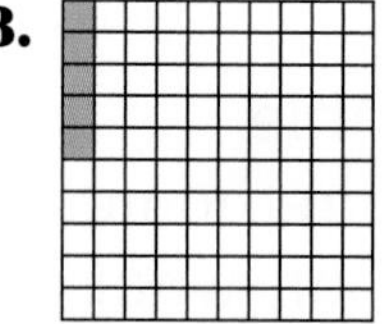

4. 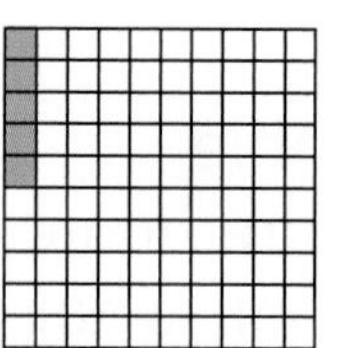

▶ PRACTICE

Complete the table.

	Model	Fraction	Decimal
5.		$\frac{3}{10}$	?
6.		?	0.8
7.		$\frac{53}{100}$	?
8.		?	0.01

SCIENCE LINK

A botanist analyzes soil mixtures to see which one will grow the healthiest plants. A mixture being studied is $\frac{4}{10}$ sand, $\frac{3}{10}$ clay, and $\frac{3}{10}$ peat. Write the decimals for the sand, clay, and peat in the mixture.

Write each amount as a decimal.

9. 6 tenths **10.** 14 hundredths **11.** 8 tenths **12.** 3 hundredths

Write each fraction as a decimal.

13. $\frac{1}{10}$ **14.** $\frac{1}{100}$ **15.** $\frac{5}{10}$ **16.** $\frac{51}{100}$ **17.** $\frac{99}{100}$

Problem Solving • Mixed Applications

18. Number Sense Joshua practiced serving a tennis ball. Out of 10 serves, 3 serves hit the net. Write as a decimal the number of serves that did not hit the net.

19. Money Felicia has 16 pennies in her wallet and 38 pennies in her drawer. Write the amount of money Felicia needs to have $1.00. Express the amount as a decimal.

20. Sports There are about 100 nations that compete in the World Cup soccer tournament. The top 24 teams play in a three-week tournament. Express as a decimal the number of top teams.

21. Write a problem using the information in the table.

BASEBALL PRACTICE		
	Number of Pitches	Number of Hits
Nick	10	7
Kyle	10	8

Rounding Decimals

Why learn this? You can estimate distances by rounding to the nearest mile.

Jerel made a map of his community. He labeled some distances on his map. To the nearest mile, how far is it from his house to school?

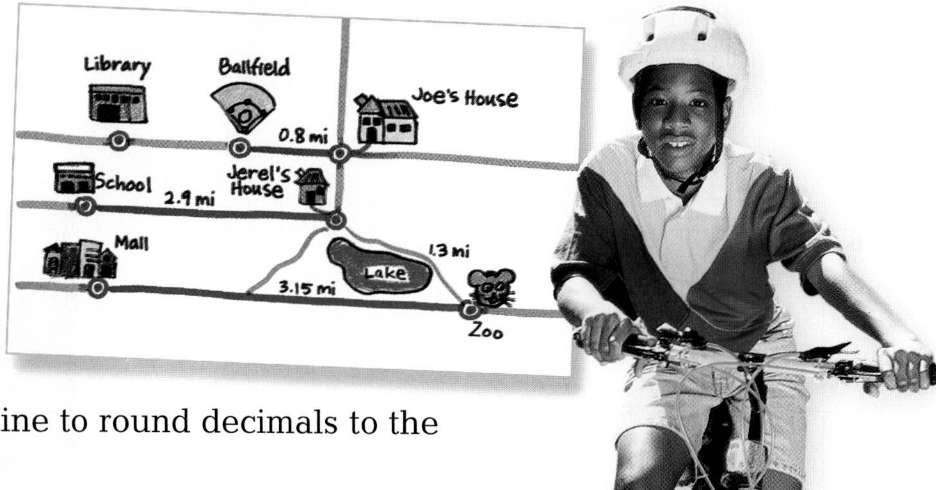

You can use a number line to round decimals to the nearest whole number.

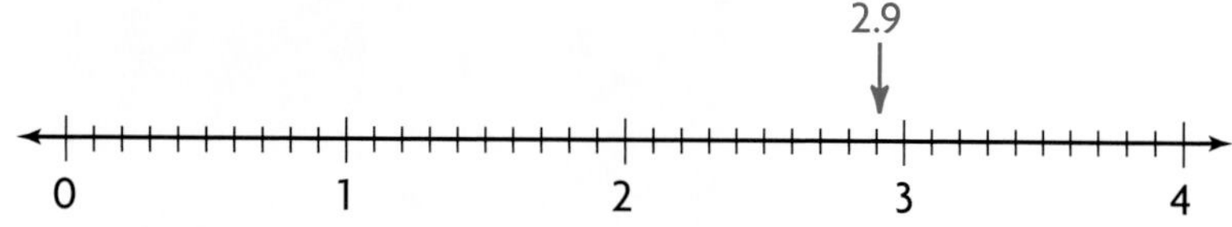

On the number line, 2.9 is between 2 and 3 but is closer to 3. So, the school is about 3 miles from Jerel's house.

To the nearest tenth of a mile, how far is it from the mall to the zoo?

You can use a number line to round to the nearest tenth.

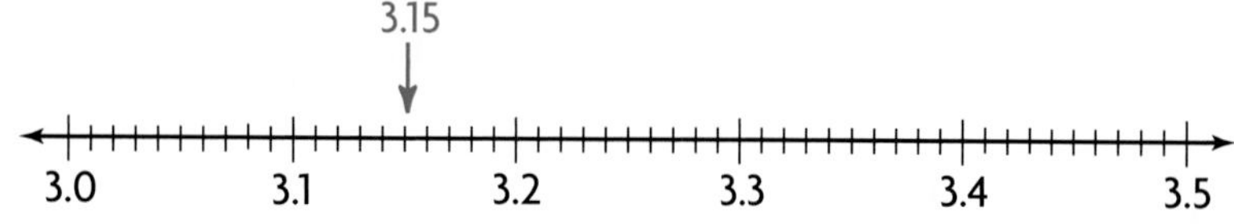

On the number line, 3.15 is between 3.1 and 3.2.

Round to the next highest tenth. So, the zoo is about 3.2 miles from the mall.

CRITICAL THINKING How is rounding decimals like rounding whole numbers?

REMEMBER:

Rounding Whole Numbers

- If the digit to the right of the digit being rounded is 5 or more, round to the next-higher digit.
- If the digit to the right of the digit being rounded is less than 5, the digit being rounded stays the same.

12 → 10   25 → 30

43 → 40   68 → 70

▶ CHECK

Round to the nearest whole number.

1. 2.1   **2.** 0.9   **3.** 1.6

Round to the nearest tenth.

4. 0.28   **5.** 1.45   **6.** 2.07

▶ PRACTICE

7. Use the number line to choose the numbers from the box that round to 5.0.

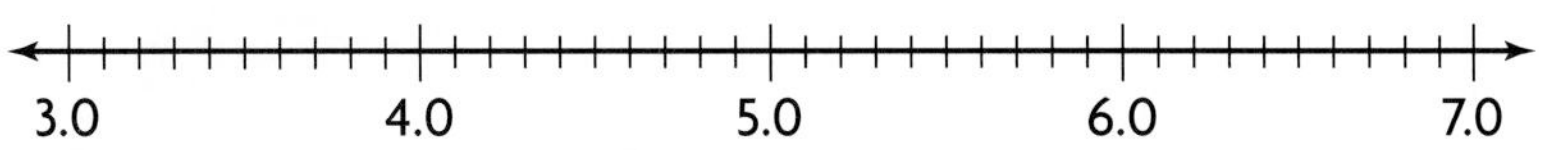

6.1	4.8	5.5	7.0
5.2	5.7	4.4	4.9

Round to the nearest whole number.

8. 2.4 **9.** 3.7 **10.** 5.5 **11.** 9.3 **12.** 8.7

13. 6.5 **14.** 7.2 **15.** 4.6 **16.** 1.8 **17.** 3.5

Round to the nearest tenth.

18. 6.49 **19.** 14.63 **20.** 35.66 **21.** 24.51 **22.** 85.50

23. 11.09 **24.** 5.97 **25.** 36.75 **26.** 19.96 **27.** 118.62

For Problems 28–32, use the table.

28. To the nearest tenth, what was Michael's score on vault?

29. To the nearest tenth, what was the highest score on floor exercise? Which gymnast received that score?

30. To the nearest tenth, in which event did Ivan score higher? How much higher?

31. To the nearest tenth, write the vault scores in order from the highest to the lowest.

32. To the nearest whole number, who scored highest in vault?

MEN'S GYMNASTICS SCORES

	Vault	Floor Exercise
Ivan	9.17	9.28
Michael	9.37	9.57
Drake	8.82	9.86
Thomas	9.87	8.88
Hugh	9.76	9.12

Problem Solving • Mixed Applications

33. Estimation Jan swam the 50-meter freestyle race in 28.25 seconds, and Sue swam the race in 27.91 seconds. To the nearest tenth of a second, what were their times?

34. Geometry Each side of a square patio is 8 feet long. Starting at one corner, there is a fence post every 2 feet. How many fence posts are around the perimeter of the patio?

35. Sports The baseball team plays 47 games in a season. They have already played 13 games. How many games are left in the season?

36. **Write a problem** about gymnastics scores using rounding.

Multiplying by One Digit

Why learn this? You can figure out how many items you need in all, such as ingredients for a recipe.

The fifth-grade students are giving a spaghetti dinner. Each student brings 3 boxes of spaghetti. There are 124 fifth-grade students. How many boxes of spaghetti are there in all?

MODEL

What is 3×124?

Step 1

Multiply the ones.
3×4 ones = 12 ones

$$\begin{array}{r} {}^{1} \\ 124 \\ \times\ \ 3 \\ \hline 2 \end{array}$$

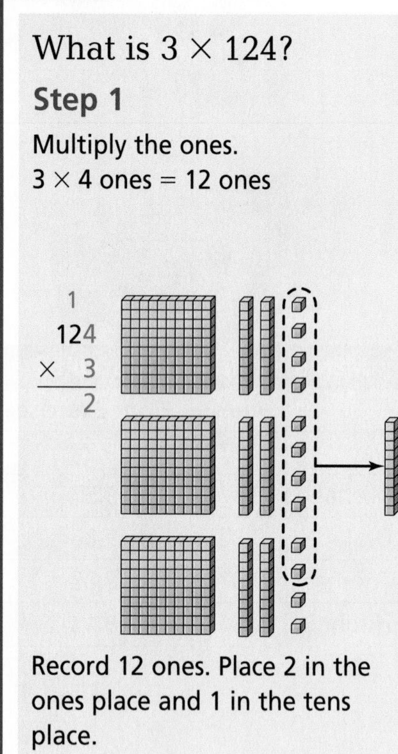

Record 12 ones. Place 2 in the ones place and 1 in the tens place.

Step 2

Multiply the tens.
3×2 tens = 6 tens
Add the regrouped ten.
6 tens + 1 ten = 7 tens

$$\begin{array}{r} {}^{1} \\ 124 \\ \times\ \ 3 \\ \hline 72 \end{array}$$

Record 7 tens.

Step 3

Multiply the hundreds.
3×1 hundred = 3 hundreds

$$\begin{array}{r} {}^{1} \\ 124 \\ \times\ \ 3 \\ \hline 372 \end{array}$$

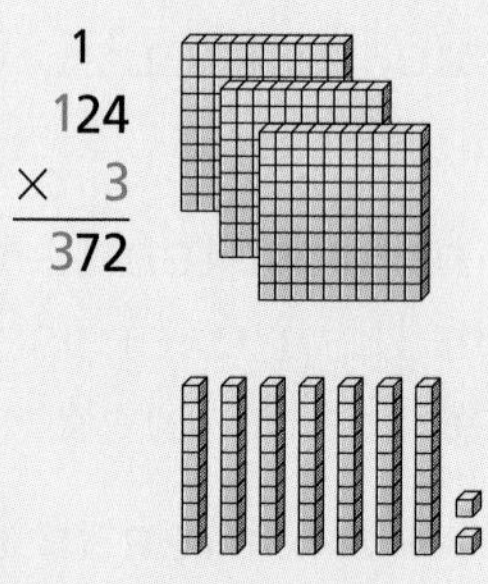

Record 3 in the hundreds place.

So, there are 372 boxes of spaghetti in all.

- In which place-value position did you need to regroup? Explain.

EXAMPLES

A
$$\begin{array}{r} {}^{1} \\ 164 \\ \times\ \ 2 \\ \hline 328 \end{array}$$

B
$$\begin{array}{r} {}^{2} \\ 209 \\ \times\ \ 3 \\ \hline 627 \end{array}$$

C
$$\begin{array}{r} {}^{3} \\ 361 \\ \times\ \ 5 \\ \hline 1{,}805 \end{array}$$

- What is the greatest number of digits that will be in the product of a 1-digit number and a 3-digit number?

▶ CHECK

Tell which place-value position must be regrouped. Find the product.

1. 314 × 3

2. 119 × 5

3. 146 × 5

4. 181 × 3

▶ PRACTICE

Find the product.

5. 112 × 3

6. 207 × 4

7. 138 × 5

8. 126 × 3

9. 127 × 4

10. 154 × 3

11. 167 × 5

12. 183 × 3

13. 272 × 4

14. 291 × 3

15. 167 × 8

16. 265 × 5

17. 223 × 4

18. 269 × 4

19. 308 × 5

20. 365 × 6

Problem Solving • Mixed Applications

For Problems 23–25, use the table.

21. Career Last month the veterinarian treated 58 dogs, 32 cats, and 10 hamsters. This month she treated 3 times as many dogs, 2 times as many cats, but no hamsters. How many more animals did she treat this month than last month?

22. Logic There are five houses on the block. Tim lives at one end of the block. Kris lives at the other end, two houses away from Scott. Will lives next to Tim, and two houses away from Ben. What is the order of the houses?

23. Consumer Mr. Goldberg wants to buy a volleyball and a basketball for Kevin. He wants to buy a volleyball and a football for Tammy. How much money does he need?

24. Money Jamal has $100.00. He wants to save half the money and spend the other half. If he buys a leather football, what else can he buy?

SPORTS EQUIPMENT PRICE LIST	
Outdoor Basketball	$15.99
Leather Football	$35.59
Hockey Stick	$13.39
Beach Volleyball	$35.99

25. **Write a problem** using the price list.

Estimating Products

Why learn this? You can estimate the total cost when you go shopping or the amount of supplies you need to take on a trip.

There are 56 Boy Scouts going on an overnight camp-out. Each Scout will take a half-gallon container filled with water. There are 64 ounces in a half gallon. About how many ounces will the Boy Scouts take?

Camping is an adventure!

MODEL

How can you estimate 56 × 64?

Step 1

Estimate. Round each factor to the nearest ten.

$$\begin{array}{r} 64 \\ \times 56 \\ \hline \end{array} \begin{array}{c} \rightarrow \\ \rightarrow \end{array} \begin{array}{r} 60 \\ \times 60 \\ \hline \end{array}$$

Step 2

Multiply.

$$\begin{array}{r} 60 \\ \times 60 \\ \hline 3,600 \end{array}$$

So, the Boy Scouts will take about 3,600 ounces of water.

REMEMBER:

To round a number:

- Find the digit in the place to be rounded.
- Look at the digit to its right.
- If that digit is *less than* 5, the digit being rounded remains the same.
- If the digit is *5 or greater*, the digit being rounded increases by 1.

Talk About It

- How were basic facts used to estimate the product?
- When might you want to estimate a product?

EXAMPLES

A
$$\begin{array}{r} 91 \\ \times 16 \\ \hline \end{array} \begin{array}{c} \rightarrow \\ \rightarrow \end{array} \begin{array}{r} 90 \\ \times 20 \\ \hline 1,800 \end{array}$$

B
$$\begin{array}{r} 67 \\ \times 33 \\ \hline \end{array} \begin{array}{c} \rightarrow \\ \rightarrow \end{array} \begin{array}{r} 70 \\ \times 30 \\ \hline 2,100 \end{array}$$

- Why are there 2 zeros in each of the products in the examples?

▶ CHECK

Round each factor to the nearest ten. Estimate the product.

1. $\begin{array}{r} 75 \\ \times 25 \\ \hline \end{array}$ **2.** $\begin{array}{r} 47 \\ \times 34 \\ \hline \end{array}$ **3.** $\begin{array}{r} 82 \\ \times 65 \\ \hline \end{array}$ **4.** $\begin{array}{r} 35 \\ \times 44 \\ \hline \end{array}$ **5.** $\begin{array}{r} 62 \\ \times 73 \\ \hline \end{array}$

▶ PRACTICE

Round each factor to the nearest ten. Estimate the product.

6. 14×12 **7.** 21×13 **8.** 25×23

9. 24×22 **10.** 28×13 **11.** 32×29

12. 36×29 **13.** 59×54 **14.** 63×24

15. 71×47 **16.** 84×79 **17.** 85×83

18. 27×33 **19.** 46×41 **20.** 58×34

21. $63 \times 82 = n$ **22.** $69 \times 75 = n$ **23.** $79 \times 84 = n$

24. $73 \times 86 = n$ **25.** $81 \times 88 = n$ **26.** $86 \times 92 = n$

27. $49 \times 63 = n$ **28.** $52 \times 67 = n$ **29.** $54 \times 81 = n$

HEALTH LINK

About half the water we lose each day can be replaced by the water content in our food, especially fruits and vegetables. Our bodies need clean drinking water to replace the remaining half. On average, a person needs about 64 ounces of water each day. About how many ounces of water does a person need in one month?

Problem Solving • Mixed Applications

30. Dario and Mark are counting the number of seats for the band concert. Dario counted 10 rows of 14 seats. Mark counted another 16 rows of 23 seats. How many seats did they count in all?

31. **Reasoning** Jasmine is 1 year younger than Hope. The sum of their ages is 17 years. Selena is twice as old as Jasmine. How old are Jasmine, Hope, and Selena?

32. **Patterns** It took Denequa 10 minutes to read 7 pages of her book. It took her 20 minutes to read the next 14 pages and 30 minutes to read the next 21 pages. If this pattern continues, how long will it take her to read the remaining 35 pages?

33. **Number Sense** Uri wrote a 4-digit number. The number of thousands is 3 times the number of tens. There are 6 ones, and the number of ones is 2 times the number of tens. The number of hundreds is 5 more than the number of tens. What number did he write?

34. Ms. Montoya's 21 students collected leaves for a science project. She challenged each student to collect at least 37 leaves. How many leaves will they collect in all?

35. **Write a problem** in which you estimate the product of 2 two-digit numbers.

Recording Division

Why learn this? Using base-ten blocks will help you better understand what happens when you divide using paper and pencil.

Ms. Pearson asked 3 students to carry some books back to the library. There were 56 books to return. Each student carried the same number of books. How many books did each carry?

Divide. $56 \div 3 = n$ $\quad 3\overline{)56}$

Use base-ten blocks to model the problem. Record the numbers as you complete each step.

MODEL

What is $56 \div 3$?

Step 1

Draw 3 rings. Show 56 as 5 tens and 6 ones.

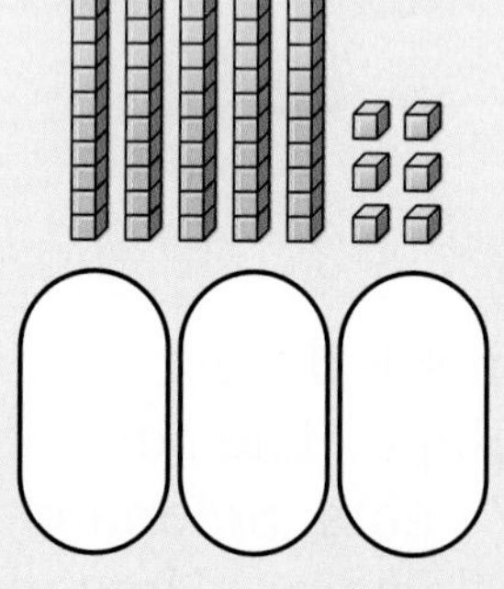

Record:

$3\overline{)56}$

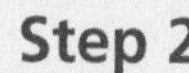

Step 2

Place an equal number of tens into each ring.

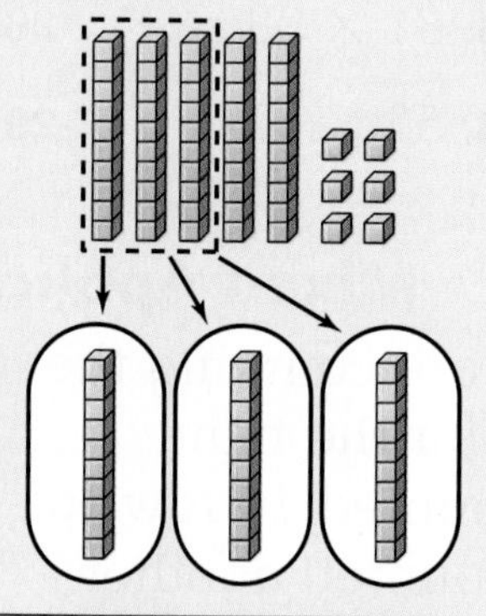

Record:

```
   1   ← 1 ten in
 3)56     each group
 – 3   ← 3 tens used
   2   ← 2 tens left
```

Step 3

Regroup the 2 tens left over into ones.

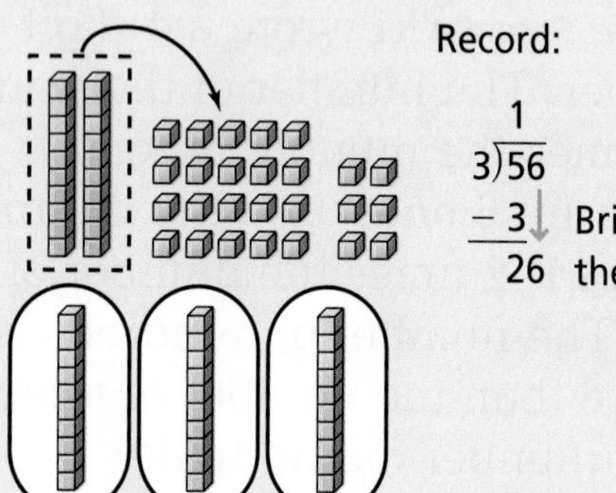

Record:

```
   1
 3)56
 – 3↓  Bring down
   26  the ones.
```

Step 4

Place an equal number of ones into each ring.

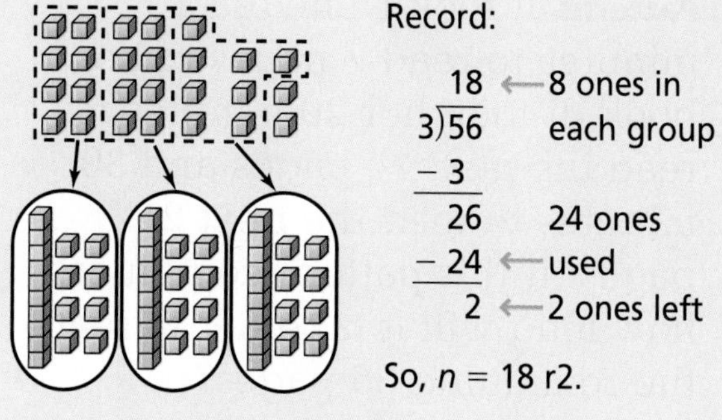

Record:

```
   18  ← 8 ones in
 3)56     each group
 – 3
   26     24 ones
 – 24  ← used
    2  ← 2 ones left
```

So, $n = 18$ r2.

So, each student carried 18 books. There were 2 books left over.

- In Step 3, why did you have to regroup the 2 tens into ones?

▶ CHECK

Match each division model with the correct division number sentence.

1. 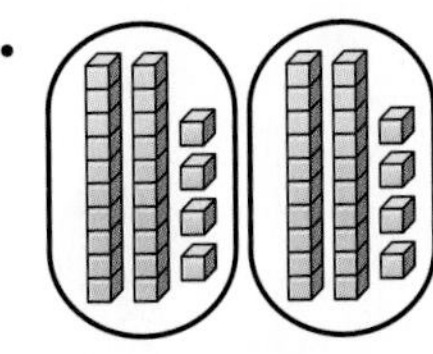

2. 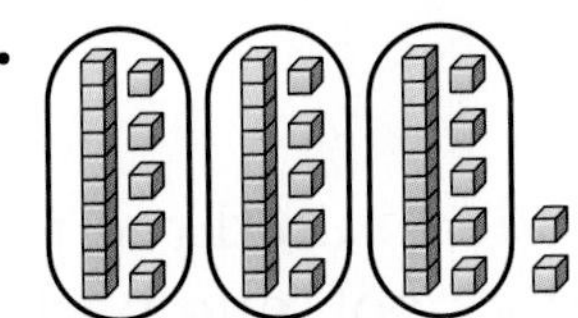

3. 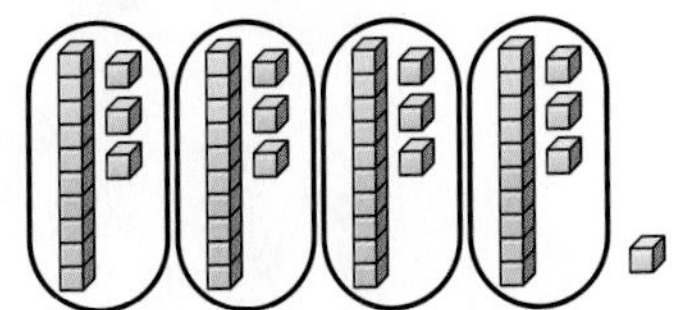

4. 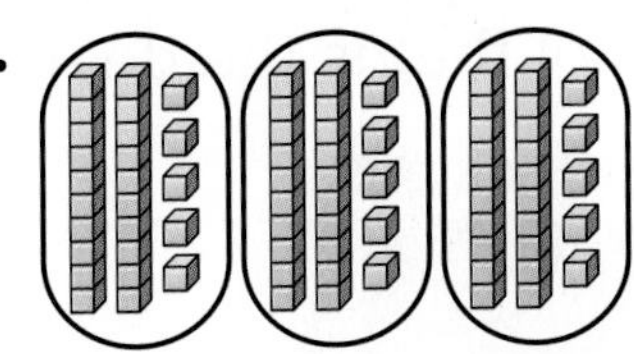

5. 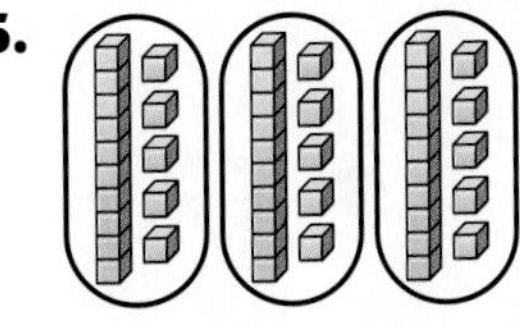

6. 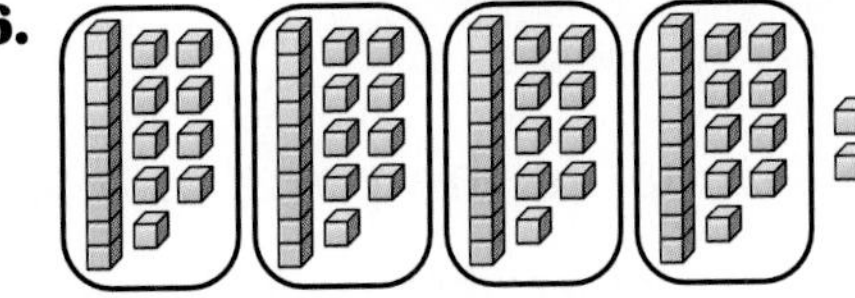

a. $45 \div 3 = 15$ **b.** $47 \div 3 = 15$ r2 **c.** $48 \div 2 = 24$

d. $78 \div 4 = 19$ r2 **e.** $53 \div 4 = 13$ r1 **f.** $75 \div 3 = 25$

▶ PRACTICE

Use base-ten blocks to model the problem. Record the numbers as you complete each step.

7. $3\overline{)69}$ **8.** $2\overline{)27}$ **9.** $4\overline{)82}$ **10.** $2\overline{)36}$ **11.** $3\overline{)43}$

12. $2\overline{)31}$ **13.** $4\overline{)55}$ **14.** $5\overline{)52}$ **15.** $2\overline{)54}$ **16.** $3\overline{)74}$

Problem Solving • Mixed Applications

17. Consumer Mrs. Swan bought 6 packages of colored pencils. She bought 96 colored pencils in all. How many colored pencils were in each package?

18. Suzanne guessed there were 3,100 marbles in the jar. Paul guessed there were 2,500 marbles. There were actually 2,995 marbles. Whose guess was closer?

19. Money Bill and Eric went to a hockey game. They each paid $10.95 for a ticket and $4.25 for snacks. How much money did they both spend?

20. Brandy made 57 cupcakes for 2 fifth-grade classes of the same size. How many cupcakes did each class get? Were any cupcakes left over?

21. Geometry A box is 8 feet long, 5 feet wide, and 4 feet high. What is the volume of the box?

22. **Write a problem** about 48 videotapes. Use division.

Fractions: Parts of a Whole

Why learn this? You can share parts of a whole amount equally with friends.

The Norwalk town pool is divided into three parts of equal size. One part is the baby pool, one part is the lap area, and one part is the deep end. What fraction represents the part of the pool that is the deep end?

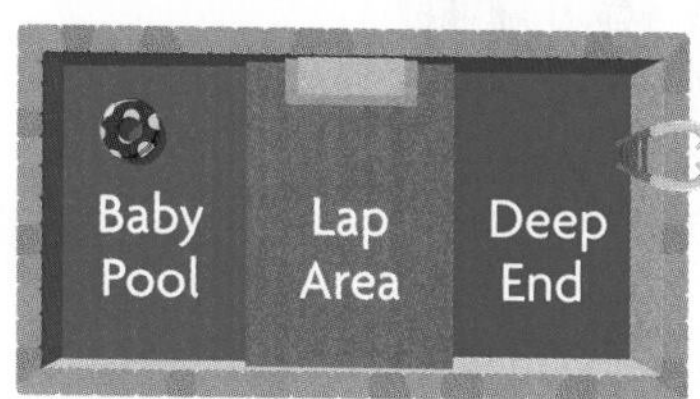

You can use a fraction to name the parts of a whole.

numerator → 1 ← number of sections named
denominator → 3 ← total number of sections

Read: one third
one out of three
one divided by three

Write: $\frac{1}{3}$

So, the deep end is $\frac{1}{3}$ of the whole pool.

- What fraction represents the part of the pool that is *not* the deep end?

EXAMPLES

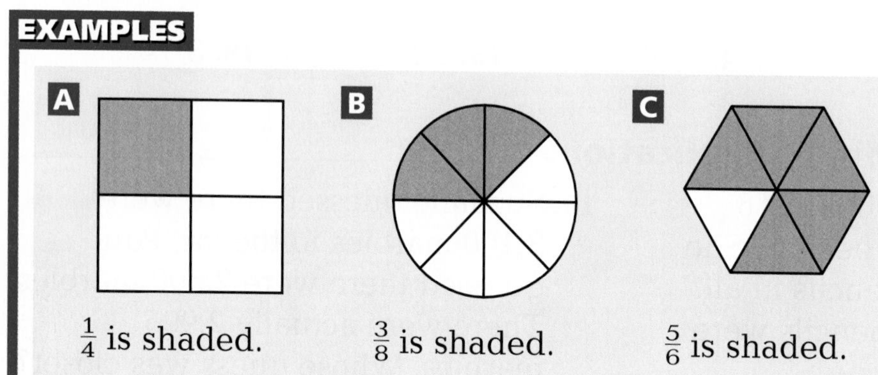

A: $\frac{1}{4}$ is shaded.

B: $\frac{3}{8}$ is shaded.

C: $\frac{5}{6}$ is shaded.

ART LINK

Artists use color wheels to help them understand how colors are related to one another. This basic color wheel shows the three primary colors (red, yellow, and blue) and mixtures of these colors. What fraction of the color wheel is mixtures of blue and yellow?

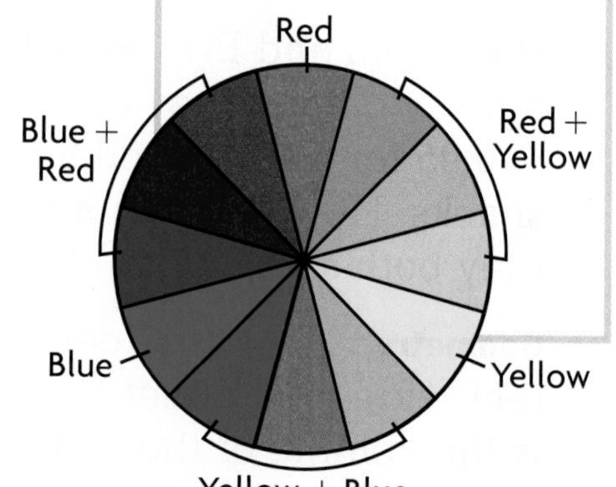

▶ CHECK

1. For Examples A, B, and C, what fraction of the whole is *not* shaded?
2. What fraction names the whole for each example?
3. What would the figure in Example C look like if only $\frac{1}{2}$ were shaded?

▶ PRACTICE

Write the fraction for the part that is shaded.

4. 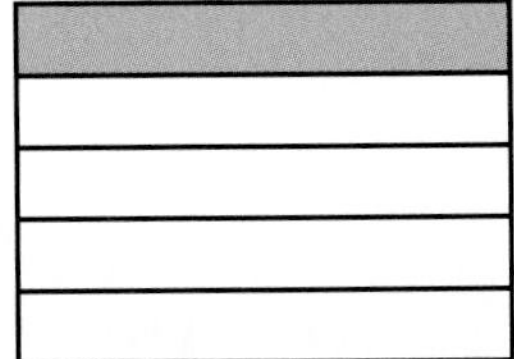

5. 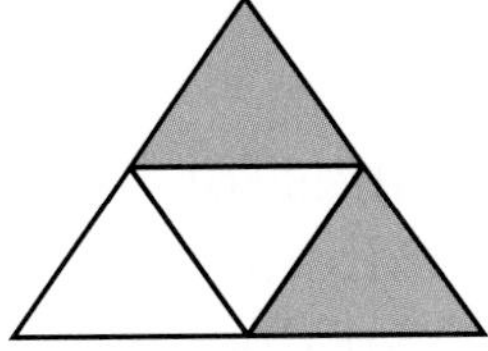

6. 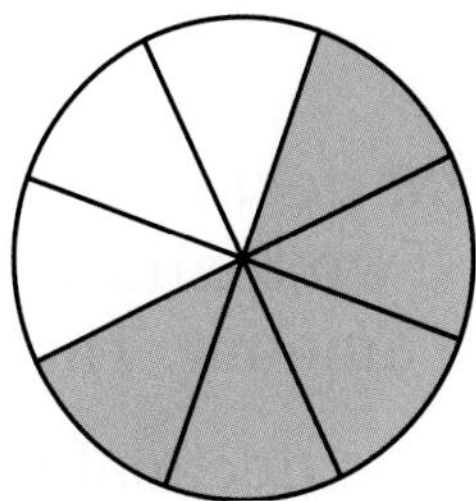

Write the fraction for the part that is not shaded.

7. 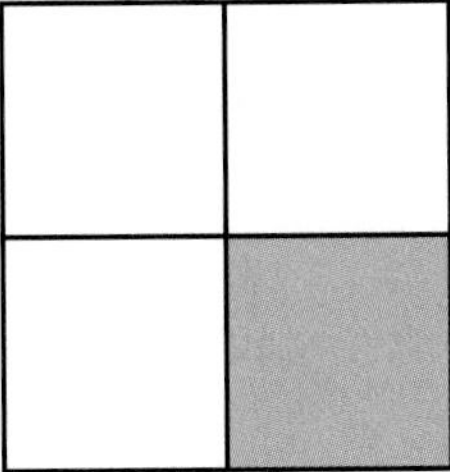

8. 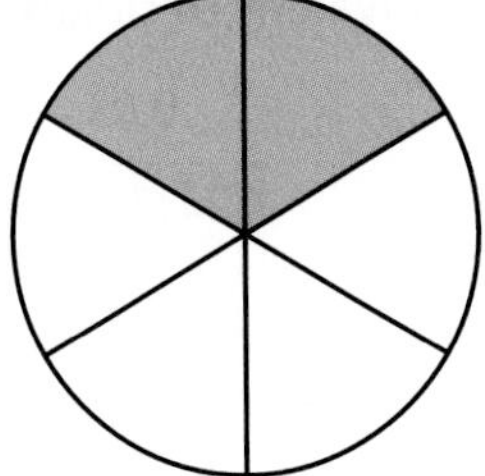

9. 

For each fraction named, give the written form.

10. one third **11.** five sixths **12.** two fifths **13.** three eighths

Problem Solving • Mixed Applications

14. Preston, Joel, and Alexis shared a pizza that was divided into 8 slices. Preston ate 3 slices, Joel ate 3 slices, and Alexis ate 2 slices. Write the fraction that shows the part of the pizza that each person ate.

15. Number Sense Patrick ate the first piece of his grandmother's apple pie. The pie had been cut into 6 pieces. What fraction names the amount of pie that is left?

Using Data For Problem 16, use the menu.

16. Money At the snack bar, Brittany ordered one slice of pizza and a small drink. How much change did she receive from $5.00?

17. Number Sense There are 230 swimmers traveling on buses to the district meet. Each bus can hold 36 people. How many buses are there?

SNACK BAR MENU

Pizza	$1.25/slice
Hamburger	$1.35
Hot Dog	$0.95
Frozen Yogurt	$0.80
Drinks	$0.85/small
	$0.95/large

18. Write a problem about a fraction, using this information: There are 24 swimmers on the Cobb Swim Team. Of the swimmers, 4 are on the relay team.

Equivalent Decimals

Why learn this? You can use equivalent decimals when you are making change for a dollar.

Equivalent decimals are different names for the same amount. Two tenths and twenty hundredths name the same amount. They are equivalent decimals.

You can use decimal squares to model equivalent decimals.

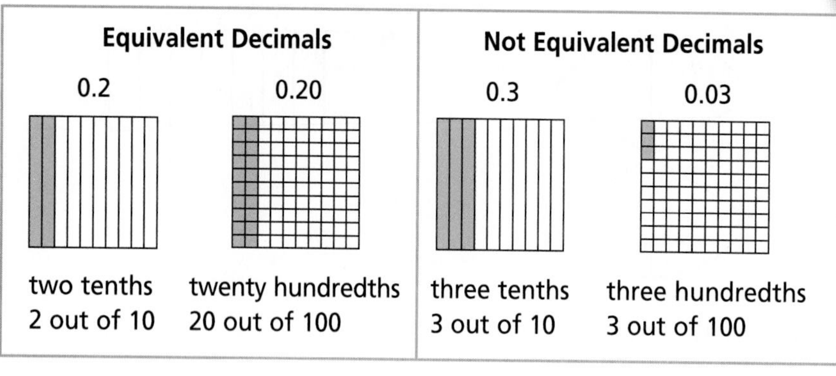

Talk About It

- How do the models for 0.2 and 0.20 show that the decimals are equivalent decimals?
- How do the models for 0.3 and 0.03 show that the decimals are not equivalent decimals?

Study these models.

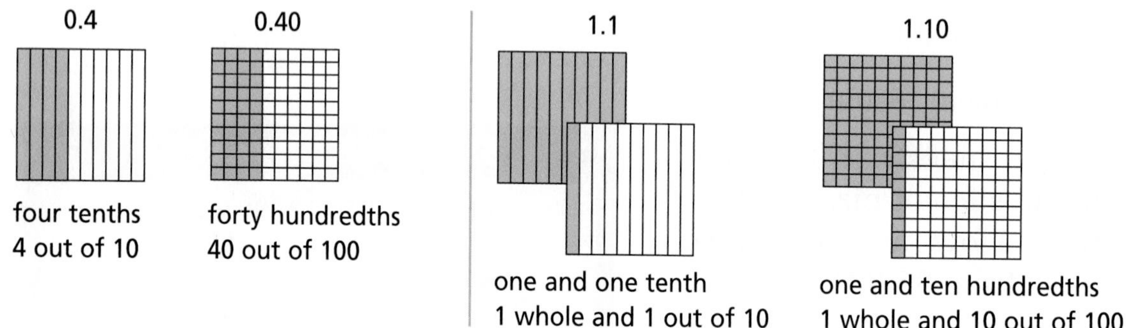

Talk About It

- Explain how you know that 0.4 and 0.40 are equivalent.
- Explain how you know that 1.1 and 1.10 are equivalent.
- Are 0.05 and 0.50 equivalent? Explain.

▶ CHECK

Write two equivalent decimals for the shaded part of each model.

1. 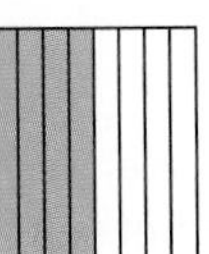

2. 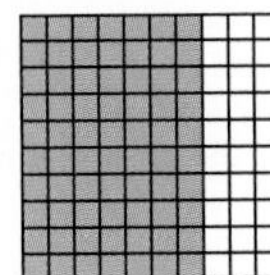

3. 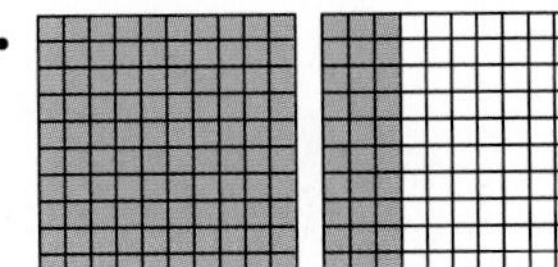

4. 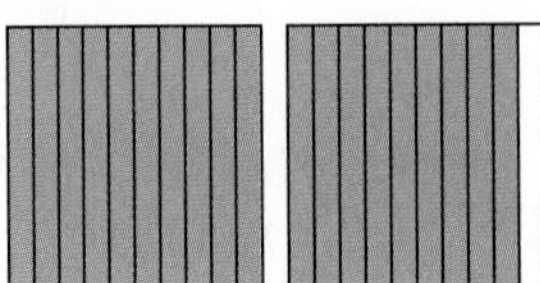

▶ PRACTICE

Tell whether the decimals are equivalent. Write *yes* or *no*.

5. 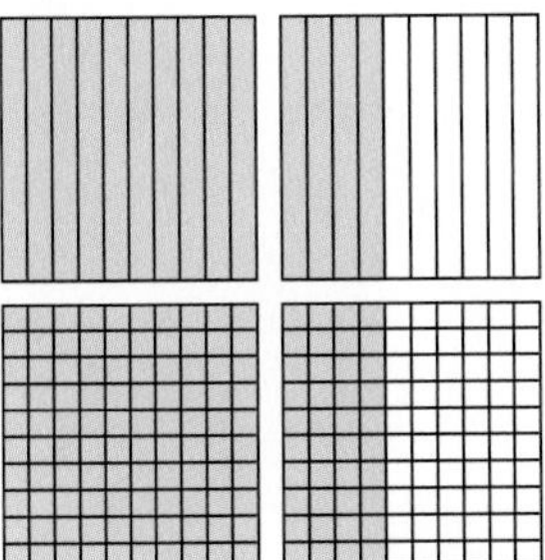

6. 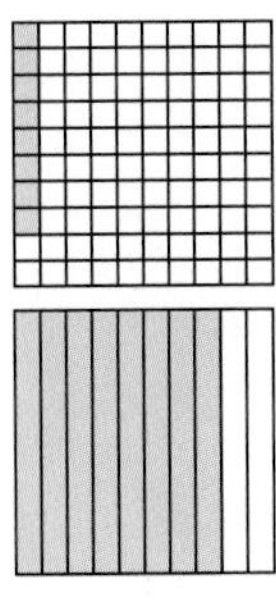

7. 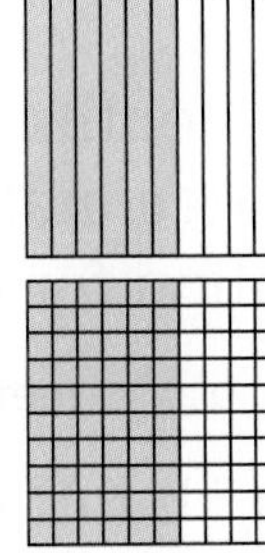

8. 15.3 and 15.03 **9.** 5.9 and 5.90 **10.** 6.20 and 6.2 **11.** 3.13 and 3.31

Write an equivalent decimal for each.

12. 0.80 **13.** 9.7 **14.** 5.60 **15.** 0.3 **16.** 2.14 **17.** 10.6

Look at the decimal squares. Write the letter of the picture that shows a decimal that is equivalent to the one shown.

18. 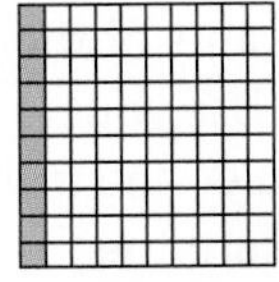 **a.** 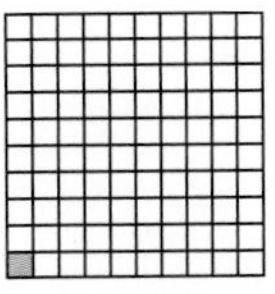 **b.** 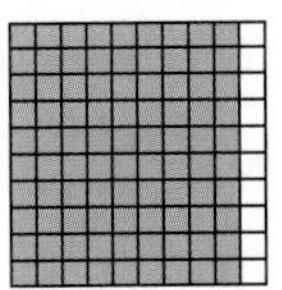 **c.** 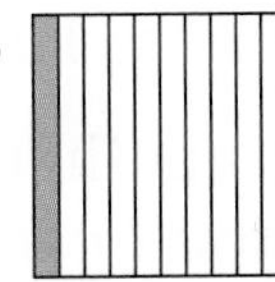

19. 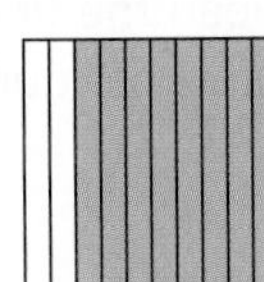 **a.** 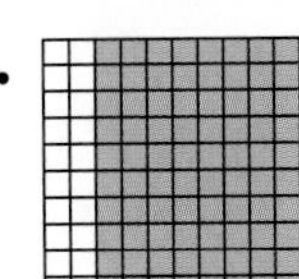 **b.** 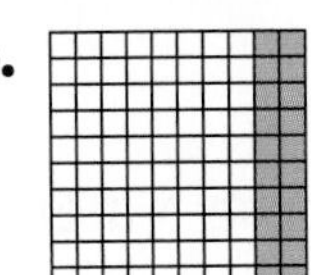 **c.** 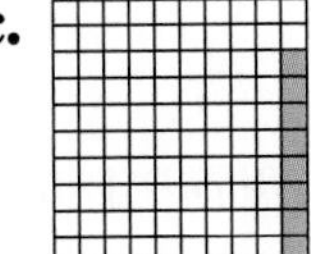

Problem Solving • Mixed Applications

20. Money Marion said that $0.50 is 50 hundredths of a dollar. Seth said that $0.50 is 5 tenths of a dollar. Why are both statements correct?

21. Number Sense Write all the four-digit whole numbers that have only 0 and 1 as digits.

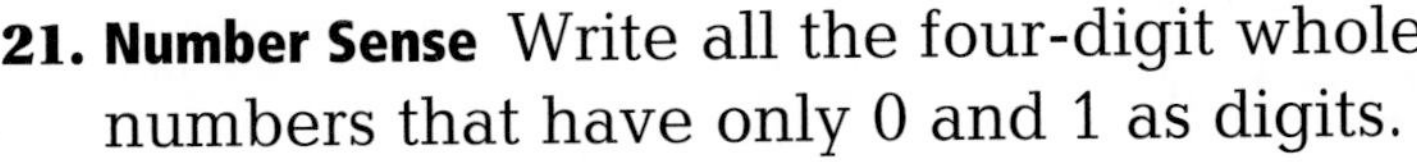

22. Compare Use models to show how you know 1.6 and 1.60 are equivalent decimals.

CONSUMER LINK

When you make change for a dollar, you use equivalent decimals. What amount is equivalent to three dimes?

Decimals and Metric Measures

Why learn this? You can use the marks on a meterstick to measure objects.

You can use a meterstick to model decimal numbers.

meter
(100 centimeters)

1.0 meter

decimeter
(10 centimeters)

0.1 meter

centimeter

0.01 meter

The *meter* is the basic unit of linear measurement in the metric system. The abbreviation for meter is *m*.

Deci- means "tenths."
There are 10 *decimeters* in a meter.
The abbreviation for decimeter is *dm*.

1 decimeter = 0.1, or $\frac{1}{10}$, meter

Centi- means "hundredths."
There are 100 *centimeters* in a meter.
The abbreviation for centimeter is *cm*.

1 centimeter = 0.01, or $\frac{1}{100}$, meter

Talk About It CRITICAL THINKING

- What part of a meter equals 1 dm? 1 cm?
- How can you write 0.5 m by using decimeters? centimeters? Hint: Use a meterstick to help you.
- What is another way to name 0.02 m by using decimeters? centimeters?

▶ CHECK

Write the missing unit. You may use a meterstick.

1. 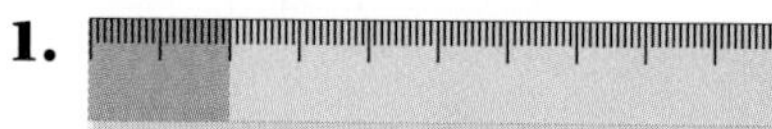

2 dm = __?__ m

2. 

0.5 m = __?__ cm

3. 5 __?__ = 50 dm

4. 5 m = 500 __?__

5. 20 __?__ = 200 dm

6. 0.3 m = 30 __?__

7. 0.07 m = 7 __?__

8. 0.6 m = 6 __?__

9. 100 cm = __?__ m

10. 10 __?__ = 1 m

SOCIAL STUDIES LINK

The French created the metric system in the 1790s. The English system of measurement is an older system, and it is based on odd measurements. For example, the inch was the distance between the first and second joints of the index finger. Use your centimeter ruler and inch ruler to measure the distance between the first and second joints of your index finger.

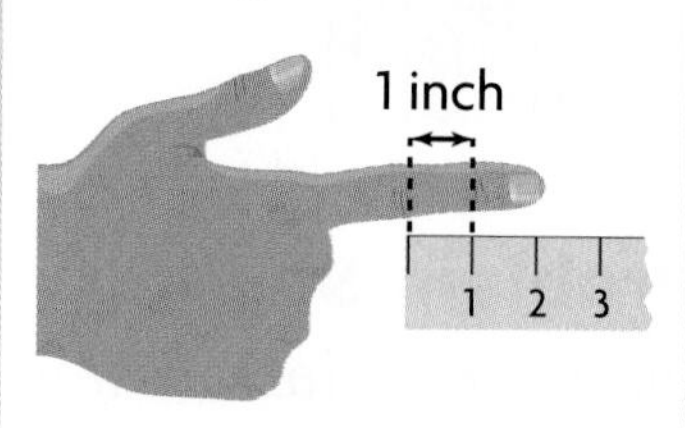

▶ PRACTICE

Copy the table. Fill in the missing measures. You may use a meterstick.

	Meter	Decimeter	Centimeter
11.	?	30	?
12.	7	?	?
13.	?	?	800
14.	0.9	?	?
15.	?	4	?
16.	?	?	2
17.	?	0.9	?
18.	0.08	?	?

Write the number. You may use a meterstick.

19. 2 m = ? dm

20. 6 m = ? cm

21. 60 dm = ? m

22. 30 m = ? dm

23. 0.7 m = ? dm

24. 0.8 m = ? cm

25. 400 cm = ? m

26. 50 cm = ? m

27. 80 cm = ? m

28. 40 dm = ? m

29. 9 cm = ? m

30. 6 dm = ? m

31. 0.53 m = ? cm

32. 8 cm = ? m

Problem Solving • Mixed Applications

33. Reasoning Kelli needs 7.5 dm of string for her art project. She has a piece of string that is 35 cm long and another piece that is 40 cm long. Does she have enough string? Explain.

34. Number Sense Marian and Tom are making banners for the school play. Tom's banner is 2 times as long as Marian's banner. Marian's banner is 245 cm long. How much shorter than 5 m is Tom's banner?

35. Estimation Jack's belt measures 39 cm in length. Is his belt longer or shorter than 4 dm? What is his belt's measurement in decimeters?

36. Compare Scott cut 2 pieces of wood that are each 46 cm long. Bill cut a piece of wood that is 8 dm long. Who cut more wood?

37. Ashley cut 4 strips of colored paper for her graph. The strips were 23 cm, 16 cm, 14 cm, and 7 cm in length. How many dm of paper did she use?

38. Write About It Explain how to change a measurement from meters to centimeters and from decimeters to meters.

Fractions as Part of a Whole or Part of a Group

Why learn this? You can use fractions to describe parts of a whole when you share food with someone.

Kira, Robbie, Micah, and Carmen shared a pizza and a basket of strawberries equally. What fraction of the pizza and strawberries did each person eat?

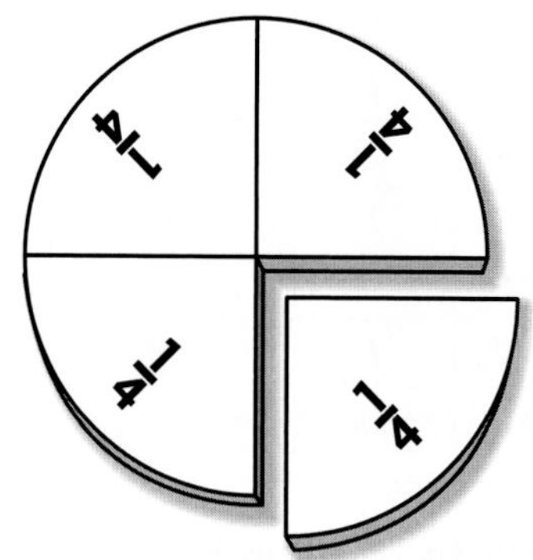

A *fraction* is a number that names a part of a whole or a part of a group.

The pizza represents 1 whole. Use fraction-circle pieces to show how 1 whole can be divided into 4 equal parts.

each person's part ⟶ 1 ⟵ numerator
total equal parts ⟶ 4 ⟵ denominator

So, each person ate $\frac{1}{4}$ of the pizza.

The basket of 12 strawberries represents 1 group. The picture shows how 1 group can be divided into 4 equal parts.

groups circled ⟶ 1 ⟵ numerator
number of equal groups ⟶ 4 ⟵ denominator

Read: one fourth
one out of four
one divided by four

Write: $\frac{1}{4}$

So, each person ate $\frac{1}{4}$ of the strawberries.

EXAMPLES

A

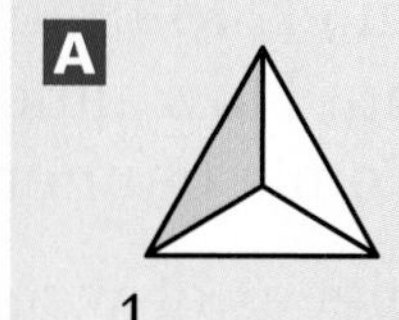

$\frac{1}{3}$ is shaded.

B

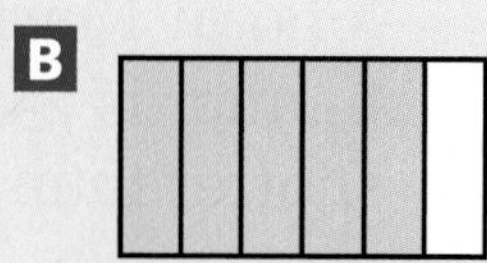

$\frac{5}{6}$ is shaded.

C

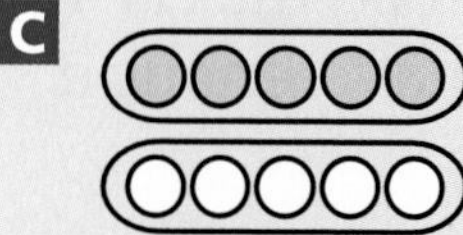

$\frac{1}{2}$ is shaded.

D

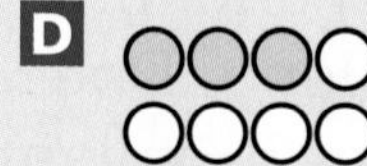

$\frac{3}{8}$ is shaded.

▶ CHECK

1. For each example, tell what fraction is not shaded.
2. How is part of a group different from part of a whole? Explain.

▶ PRACTICE

Copy and complete the table.

	Model	Write	Read
		$\frac{3}{4}$	three fourths; three out of four; three divided by four
3.		?	?
4.	?	?	four fifths; four out of five; four divided by five
5.	?	$\frac{6}{6}$	?
6.		?	?
7.		?	?
8.		?	?

Problem Solving • Mixed Applications

9. Mrs. Chang has 20 students in her class. Of the students, 5 play basketball and 5 sing in the chorus. Write a fraction to describe the number of students in Mrs. Chang's class who play basketball.

10. Reasoning There are 180 animals in the zoo. Each exhibit on the west side of the zoo has 8 animals. There are 15 exhibits on the west side of the zoo. Each exhibit on the east side of the zoo has 5 animals. How many exhibits are on the east side of the zoo?

11. Lyle has a box of 10 cookies, 8 of which are oatmeal. Write a fraction to describe the fraction of oatmeal cookies in the box.

12. Money Mr. Green traveled 5 days. Each day he spent $50 for a hotel, $30 for gas, and $25 for food. How much did Mr. Green spend in all?

13. Consumer Al bought 4 posters for $3.99 each. He also wants to buy a sign for $4.89. He had $20.50 to start with. Does Al have enough money to buy the sign? Explain.

14. Write About It When is it possible for $\frac{1}{2}$ of your age to be less than $\frac{1}{2}$ of your friend's age?

Equivalent Fractions

Why learn this? You can decide whether different fractional parts of an object name the same amount.

Martin, Rita, and Evelyn want the same amount of granola bars. Martin has $\frac{1}{3}$ of a bar, Rita has $\frac{2}{6}$, and Evelyn has $\frac{4}{12}$. Did they all receive the same amount?

Use fraction strips to model the problem.

$$\frac{1}{3} = \frac{2}{6} = \frac{4}{12}$$

Each fraction names the same amount. They are *equivalent fractions.*

So, Martin, Rita, and Evelyn all received the same amount of a granola bar.

Talk About It

- What pattern do you see in the fractions that are the same amount as one third?
- How many sixths are equivalent to two thirds? How do you know?
- How many twelfths are equivalent to four sixths?

EXAMPLES

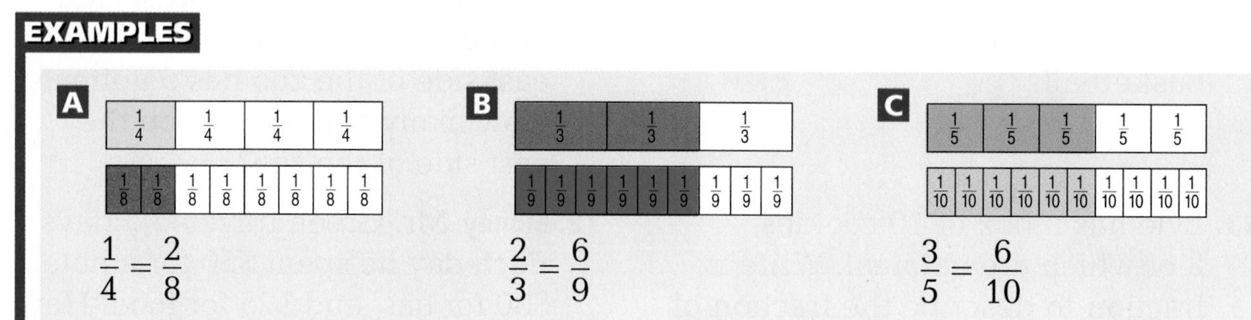

CRITICAL THINKING Explain how to use fraction strips to show whether $\frac{2}{5}$ and $\frac{3}{10}$ are equivalent.

▶ PRACTICE

Write the equivalent fractions shown by the fraction strips.

1. $\frac{1}{9}$ $\frac{1}{9}$ $\frac{1}{9}$ $\frac{1}{9}$ $\frac{1}{9}$ $\frac{1}{9}$ $\frac{1}{9}$ $\frac{1}{9}$ $\frac{1}{9}$
$\frac{1}{3}$ $\frac{1}{3}$ $\frac{1}{3}$

2. 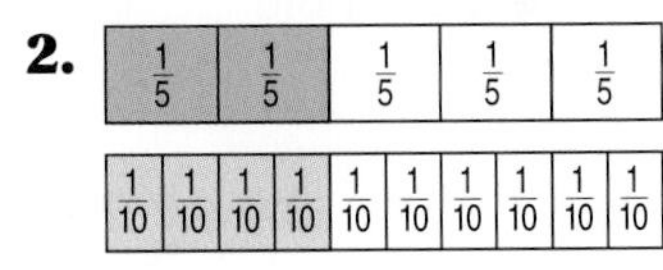

3. $\frac{1}{4}$ $\frac{1}{4}$ $\frac{1}{4}$ $\frac{1}{4}$
$\frac{1}{8}$ $\frac{1}{8}$ $\frac{1}{8}$ $\frac{1}{8}$ $\frac{1}{8}$ $\frac{1}{8}$ $\frac{1}{8}$ $\frac{1}{8}$

Use paper fraction strips to model an equivalent fraction for each. Shade part of each strip and record the fractions.

4. $\frac{1}{5}$ $\frac{1}{5}$ $\frac{1}{5}$ $\frac{1}{5}$ $\frac{1}{5}$

5. $\frac{1}{6}$ $\frac{1}{6}$ $\frac{1}{6}$ $\frac{1}{6}$ $\frac{1}{6}$ $\frac{1}{6}$

6. $\frac{1}{12}$ $\frac{1}{12}$ $\frac{1}{12}$ $\frac{1}{12}$ $\frac{1}{12}$ $\frac{1}{12}$ $\frac{1}{12}$ $\frac{1}{12}$ $\frac{1}{12}$ $\frac{1}{12}$ $\frac{1}{12}$ $\frac{1}{12}$

Find an equivalent fraction. Use fraction strips.

7. $\frac{1}{3}$ **8.** $\frac{3}{4}$ **9.** $\frac{1}{6}$ **10.** $\frac{4}{4}$ **11.** $\frac{1}{6}$ **12.** $\frac{2}{4}$

13. $\frac{3}{6}$ **14.** $\frac{2}{8}$ **15.** $\frac{3}{9}$ **16.** $\frac{5}{5}$ **17.** $\frac{4}{12}$ **18.** $\frac{7}{8}$

19. $\frac{1}{4}$ **20.** $\frac{6}{9}$ **21.** $\frac{2}{5}$ **22.** $\frac{6}{6}$ **23.** $\frac{6}{12}$ **24.** $\frac{1}{7}$

Problem Solving • Mixed Applications

25. Reasoning Quinn and his brother had lunch with 2 friends. They split the bill evenly. What fraction of the bill did Quinn and his brother pay?

26. Visual Thinking Brenda folded a paper into 4 equal sections. Britton folded a paper the same size into 8 equal sections. How many sections on Britton's paper are equal to 2 sections on Brenda's paper?

27. Money Mrs. Blanca's class is raising money to go to the circus. They need \$290.00 to pay for the bus, the tickets, and lunches. They raised \$84.95 at a car wash and \$63.25 at a bake sale. The P.T.O. donated \$116.00. How much more money does the class need to be able to go to the circus?

28. Number Sense Mike baked 12 more raisin cookies than oatmeal cookies. He baked 36 cookies altogether. What fraction of the cookies were raisin?

29. Write a problem about 4 friends who shared a pizza. Use equivalent fractions in your problem.

Customary Units

Why learn this? You can measure a package to find out how big or heavy it is, or measure a jar to see how much juice it can hold.

Linear Customary Units
12 inches (in.) = 1 foot (ft)
3 feet = 1 yard (yd)
5,280 feet = 1 mile (mi)
1,760 yards = 1 mile

In the United States, many use the customary system of measurement.

Linear units measure in one direction, such as length, width, height, or distance.

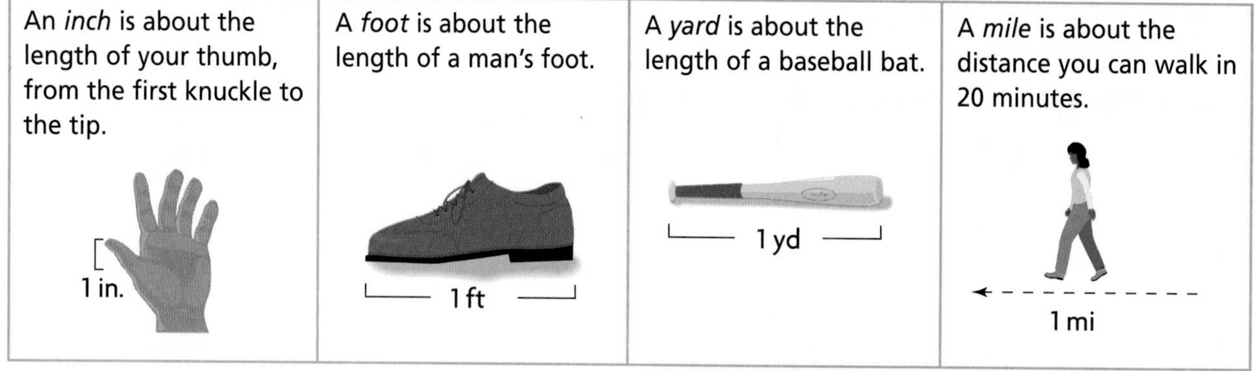

An *inch* is about the length of your thumb, from the first knuckle to the tip.

A *foot* is about the length of a man's foot.

A *yard* is about the length of a baseball bat.

A *mile* is about the distance you can walk in 20 minutes.

Units of *capacity* are used to measure the amount a container can hold when filled. Units of *weight* are used to measure how heavy an object is.

Customary Units for Measuring Liquids
2 cups (c) = 1 pint (pt)
2 pints = 1 quart (qt)
4 quarts = 1 gallon (gal)

Customary Units for Measuring Weight
16 ounces (oz) = 1 pound (lb)
2,000 pounds = 1 ton (T)

EXAMPLES

A A can of soda holds a little more than a *cup*.

B A large container of milk is a *gallon*.

C A slice of bread weighs about an *ounce*.

D A loaf of bread weighs about a *pound*.

- If you were describing the distance from home to school, would you use a linear unit, a unit of capacity, or a unit of weight? Which unit would you use?

▶ CHECK

Choose the more reasonable estimate.

1. 

2 oz or 2 lb

2. 

2 ft or 2 yd

3. 

1 gal or 1 cup

▶ PRACTICE

Write *length, capacity,* or *weight* for each given unit.

4. pint
5. foot
6. ounce
7. yard
8. gallon
9. mile
10. inch
11. pound
12. cup

For Problems 13–16, choose the more reasonable estimate.

13. Teresa's brother Tommy is 2 years old. How tall is he?

32 in. or 32 ft

14. He likes to drink juice. How much might he drink at one time?

1 gal or 1 cup

15. Tommy's mom carries him from the car seat to the house. How heavy is he?

25 T or 25 lb

16. Jimmy eats about half of a hamburger. How heavy is that?

2 oz or 2 lb

Problem Solving • Mixed Applications

17. Measurement Ralph is measuring a board to use as the base for his model plane. The model is $14\frac{1}{4}$ inches long and 13 inches wide. Ralph wants the base to be $1\frac{1}{2}$ inches longer than the plane. How long will it be?

18. Erin had a 48-ounce pitcher of lemonade. She poured 4 equal glasses of lemonade and had 8 ounces of lemonade left in the pitcher. How many ounces were in each glass?

19. Logic The medals to be awarded at the field day events each weigh 2 oz. There are 72 medals in a box. The empty box weighs 12 oz. How much does the box weigh with the medals inside?

20. Write About It Explain the differences in a linear unit, a unit of capacity, and a unit of weight.

Classifying Polygons

Why learn this? You can identify the shapes of polygons in many objects, such as a computer screen and road signs.

A *polygon* is a closed plane figure with straight sides called line segments.

Study these polygons. Name the number of sides and angles in each.

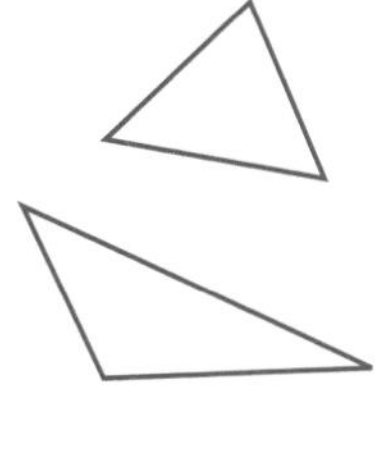

triangles

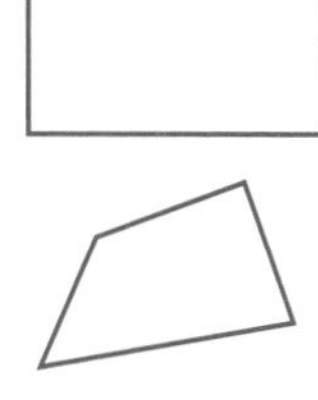

quadrilaterals

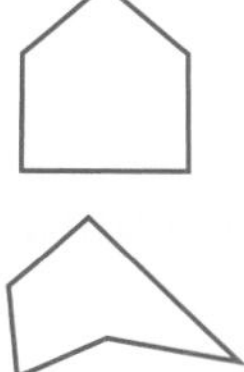

pentagons

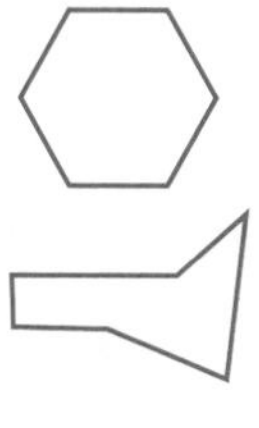

hexagons

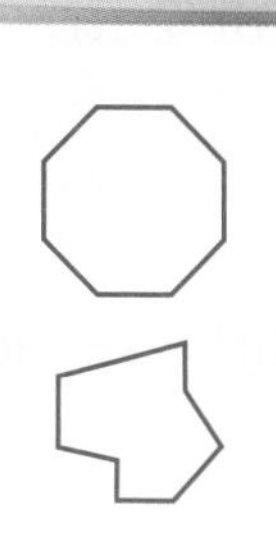

octagons

Talk About It CRITICAL THINKING

- What relationship do you see between the number of sides and the number of angles?
- How is a polygon different from other plane figures?
- Is a circle a polygon? Explain.

▶ CHECK

Name the polygon suggested by each road sign.

1. 

2. 

3. 

4. 

5. 

Name each figure.

6. 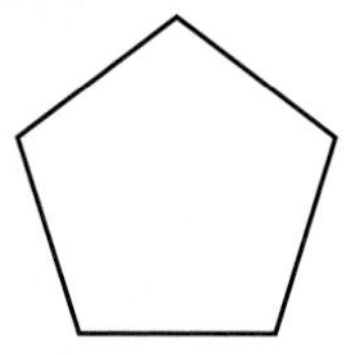

7. 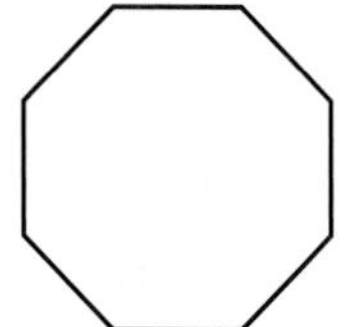

8. 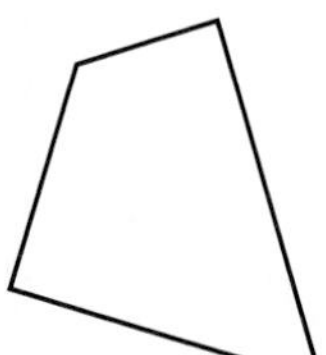

9. 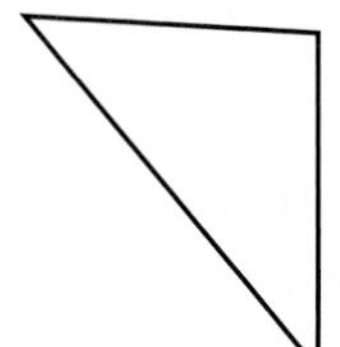

10. 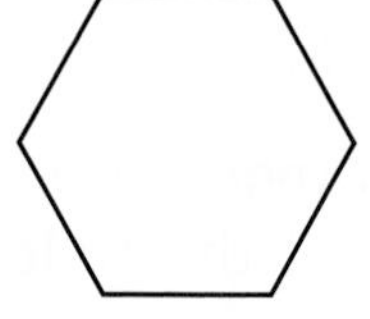

▶ PRACTICE

Copy and complete the table.

	Polygon	Number of Sides	Number of Angles	Picture
11.	Triangle	?	?	△
12.	Quadrilateral	4	?	?
13.	Pentagon	?	5	?
14.	Hexagon	?	?	⬡
15.	Octagon	8	?	?

Write the letter of the figure that is a polygon.

16. a.

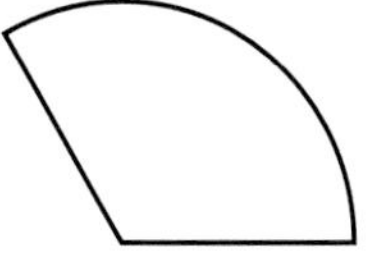

b.

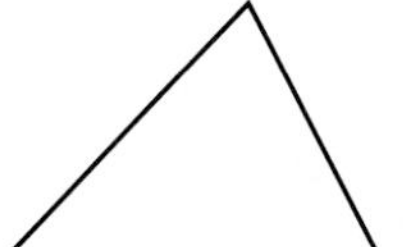

c.

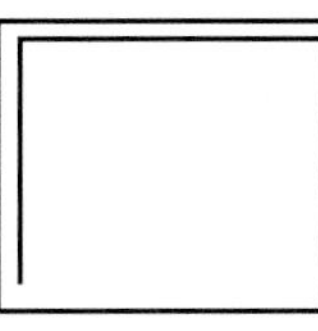

17. a.

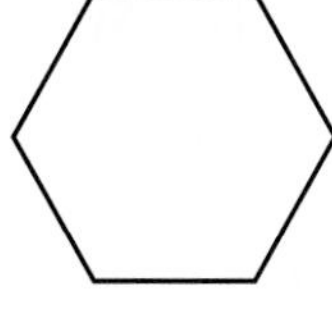

b.

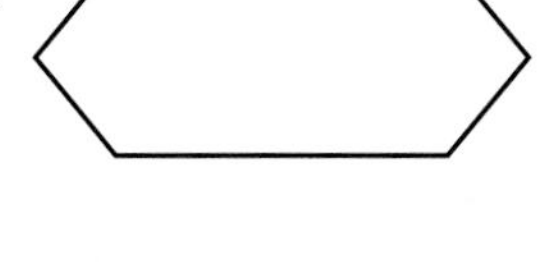

c.

18. a.

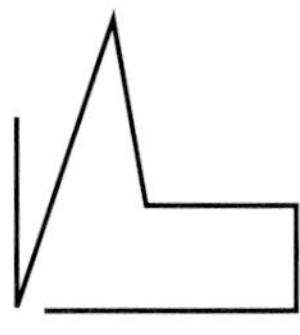

b.

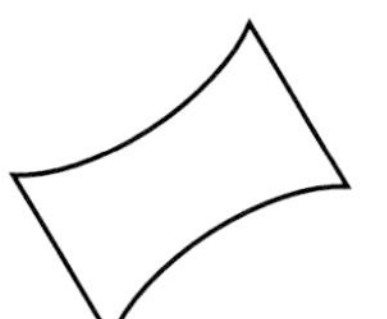

c.

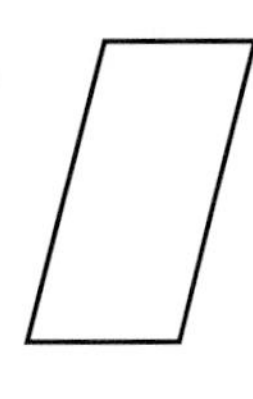

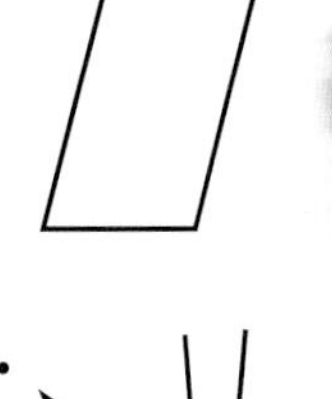

19. a. **b.** **c.**

Problem Solving • Mixed Applications

20. Geometry Rafael went to see a shuttle launch. He arrived at 2:00 P.M. Describe the angle formed by the hands on a clock for this time.

21. Measurement Preston's family drove 4 hours to reach the launch site. If they drove 55 miles each hour, how many miles did they drive?

22. Money Stephanie spent $8.35 for supplies at the craft store. How much change did she receive from $20.00?

23. **Write a problem** about a polygon you have noticed while on a car trip.

Point and Line Symmetry

Why learn this? You can see point symmetry and line symmetry in designs and paintings.

© Copyright The Andy Warhol Foundation for the Visual Arts/ARS, N.Y.

A figure has *point symmetry* if it can be turned about a central point and still look the same with each turn.

Shaded to show the turns

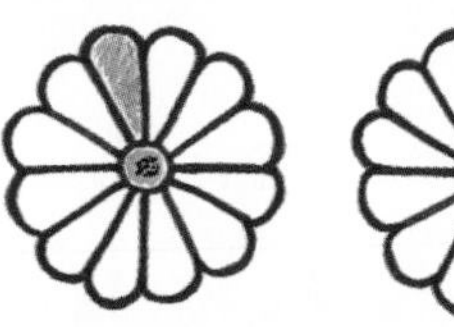    

- How could you test a square to see if it has point symmetry?

A figure has *line symmetry* when it can be folded on a line so that its two parts are identical. When the figure is unfolded, one side is a reflection of the other.

Point Symmetry 	**Line Symmetry** 	**Both Point and Line Symmetry**
	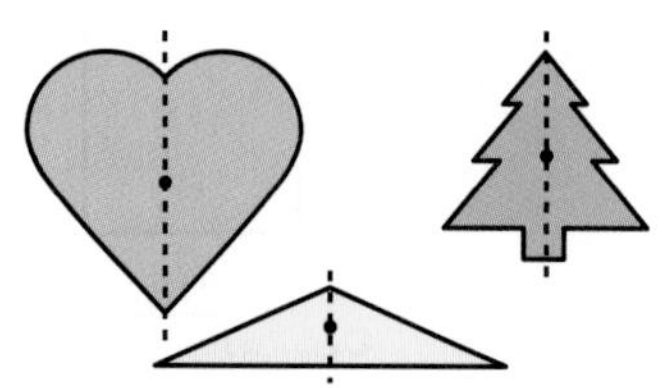	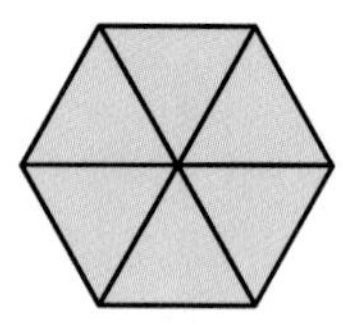 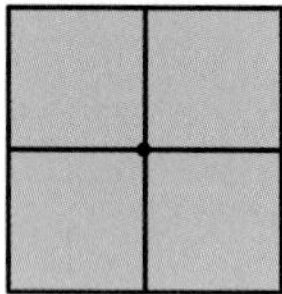

Talk About It CRITICAL THINKING

- How can you test a figure to see if it has line symmetry?
- Name something in everyday life with point symmetry, something with line symmetry, and something with both.

▶ CHECK

Write *point, line*, or *both* to tell which kind of symmetry each figure represents.

1. 

2. 

3. 

4. 

▶ PRACTICE

Write the letter of the figures with point symmetry.

5. a. 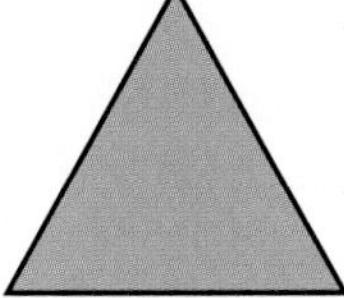 **b.** 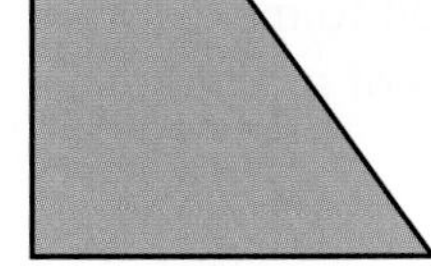 **c.**  **d.** 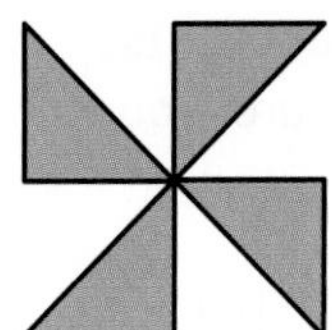

Write the letter of the figures with both point and line symmetry.

6. a. 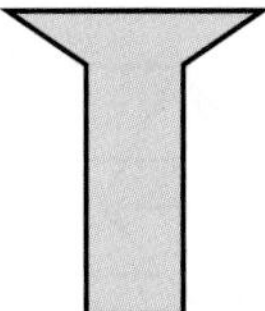 **b.**  **c.**  **d.** 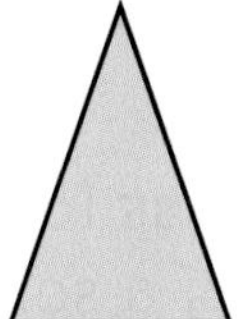

Copy each drawing on grid paper. Then draw the other half of the figure to show that it has line symmetry.

7. 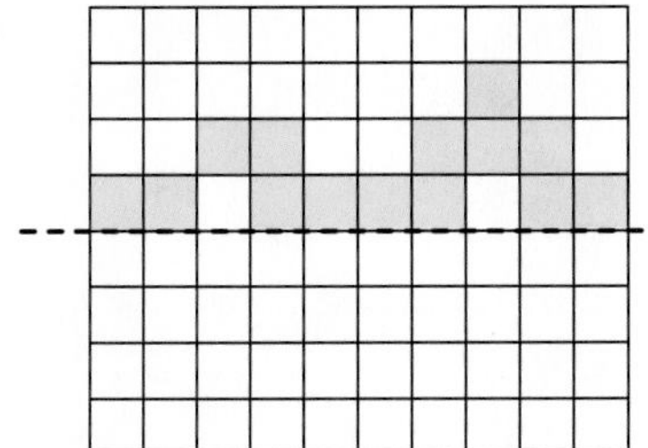 **8.** 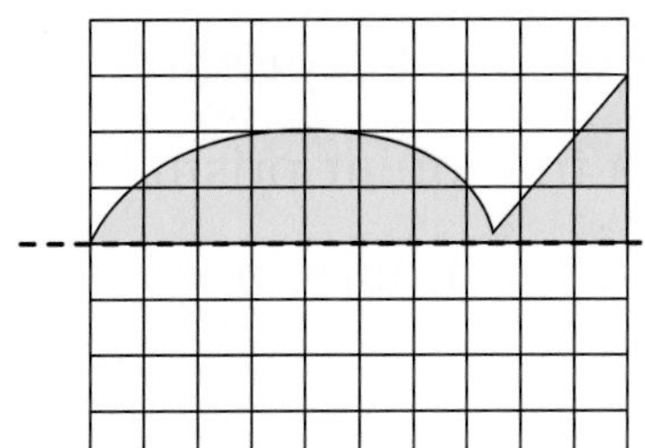 **9.** 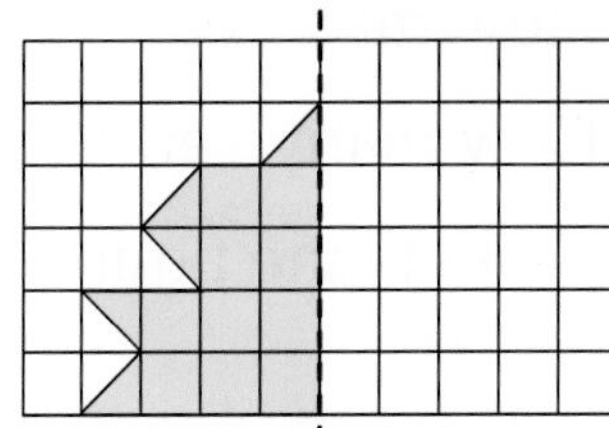

Problem Solving • Mixed Applications

Using Data For Problems 10-11, use the pictures.

10. Which of the flowers have only line symmetry?

11. Which of the flowers have point and line symmetry?

12. Compare Kimberly has two flower gardens. One flower garden is 8 ft wide and the other is 6 ft 6 in. wide. What is the difference in inches in their widths?

13. Measurement Mervin measured the height of a plant. It was $2\frac{5}{8}$ in. high. Two weeks later, the plant measured $4\frac{1}{2}$ in. high. How much did the plant grow?

14. Write About It Does the figure have line symmetry, point symmetry, or both? How do you know?

Faces, Edges, and Vertices of Solid Figures

Why learn this? You can identify the plane figures used to make a solid figure. You will see that the lid of a box is the face of a cube.

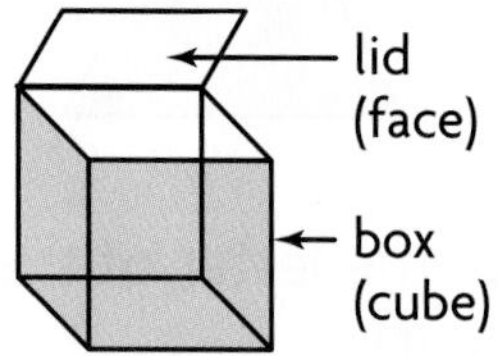

Some solid figures have faces, edges, and vertices.

Notice that

- a *face* is a flat surface of a solid figure.
- an *edge* is formed where two faces of a solid figure meet.
- a *vertex* is formed at the point where three or more edges of a solid figure meet.

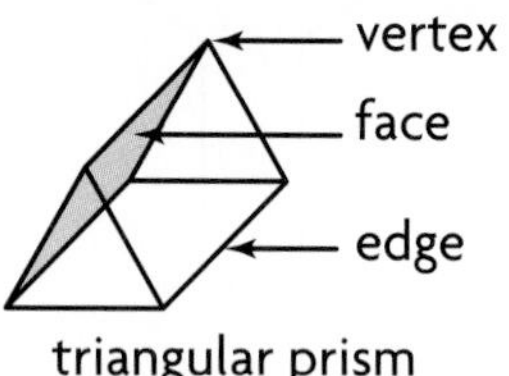

triangular prism

Talk About It

- How many faces does a triangular prism have?
- How many edges does a triangular prism have?
- How many vertices does a triangular prism have?
- What plane figures make up a triangular prism?

The pyramids of Egypt

▶ CHECK

Copy the figure. Circle each vertex in red, outline each edge in blue, and shade one face in yellow.

1. 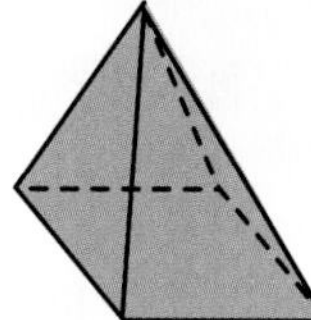

2. 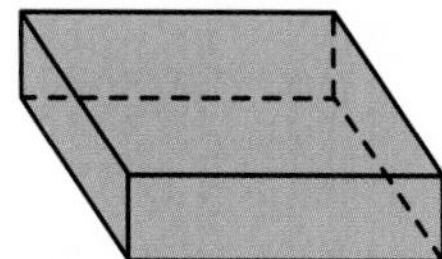

3. 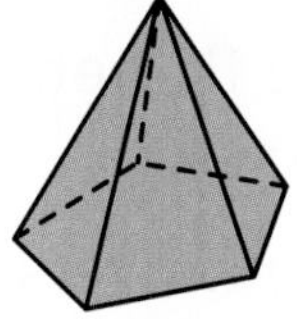

Write the names of the faces and the number of each face of the solid figure.

4. 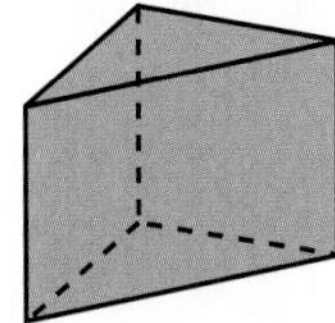

5. 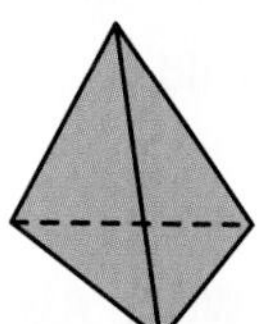

6. 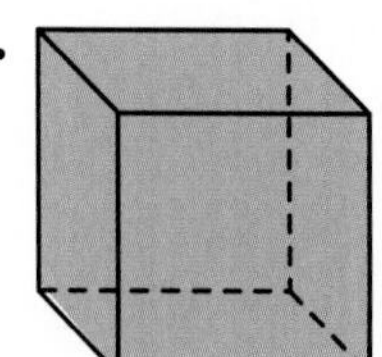

7. 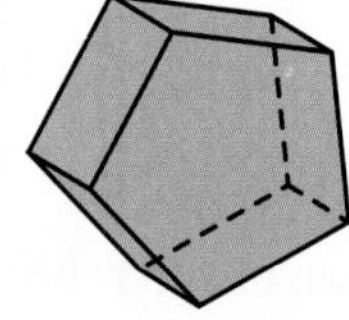

▶ PRACTICE

Copy and complete the table.

	Figure	Name of Figure	Number of Faces	Number of Edges	Number of Vertices
8.		?	?	?	?
9.		?	?	?	?
10.		?	?	?	?
11.		?	?	?	?
12.		?	?	?	?

Look at the pictures in the table to answer the following. Write *a* or *b*.

13. Which figure has more faces?

a. cube
b. triangular pyramid

14. Which figure has more triangles as faces?

a. triangular prism
b. triangular pyramid

15. Which figure has more vertices?

a. square pyramid
b. cube

16. Which figure has more square faces?

a. cube
b. square pyramid

17. Which figure has fewer vertices?

a. triangular prism
b. square pyramid

18. Which figure has more edges?

a. triangular prism
b. square pyramid

Problem Solving • Mixed Applications

19. Visual Thinking I am a plane figure. Every pyramid has at least 3 of me. What am I?

20. Visual Thinking I am a solid figure. I have 4 faces. What am I?

21. Visual Thinking I am a part of some solids. You can find me where edges meet. What am I?

22. Visual Thinking I am a solid figure. All my faces are congruent. What am I?

23. Each of 18 students will be making a model of one cube, one triangular prism, and one triangular pyramid. What is the total number of faces that will be used for the models?

24. Write About It Explain the difference between a triangular prism and a square pyramid.

Powers of Ten

Why learn this? Expressing numbers as powers of ten makes it easier to work with large numbers.

Use the chart to see the value of 1 in different place-value positions.

THOUSANDS			ONES			
Hundreds	Tens	Ones ,	Hundreds	Tens	Ones	
					1	
				1	0	= 10 × 1
			1	0	0	= 10 × 10
		1 ,	0	0	0	= 10 × 10 × 10
	1	0 ,	0	0	0	= 10 × 10 × 10 × 10
1	0	0 ,	0	0	0	= 10 × 10 × 10 × 10 × 10

$\$\ 0.10 = 10^1$
$\$\ 1.00 = 10^2$
$\$\ 10.00 = 10^3$

- What relationship do you see between place-value positions?

____

You can use exponents to express numbers. An *exponent* tells how many times the *base* number is used as a factor.

$$10{,}000 = 10 \times 10 \times 10 \times 10 = 10^4$$

exponent ↓ 4 is the exponent. It shows how many times the base is a factor.

base ↑ 10 is the base

Read: Ten to the fourth power

CRITICAL THINKING How is the number of zeros in a number related to the exponent for its power of ten?

REMEMBER:

Base-ten blocks help you visualize the size relationship of the digit 1 in different place-value positions.

Thousands	Hundreds	Tens	Ones

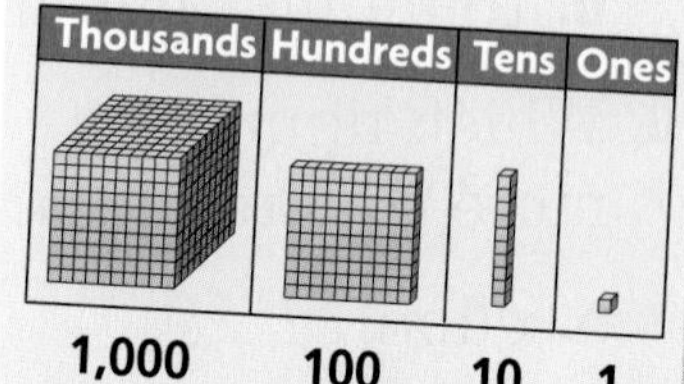

1,000 100 10 1

How many times as large as the tens block is the thousands block?

▶ CHECK

Complete.

1. $10 \times \underline{?} = 100$ **2.** $10^2 = \underline{?}$ **3.** $10^{\underline{?}} = 100{,}000$

	Place Value	Number	Multiplication	Power of Ten
4.	tens	?	10 × 1	10^1
5.	hundreds	100	10 × 10	?
6.	thousands	1,000	?	10^3
7.	?	10,000	10 × 10 × 10 × 10	10^4
8.	hundred thousands	100,000	10 × 10 × 10 × 10 × 10	?

▶ PRACTICE

Write the base and exponent for each number.

9. 10^4 **10.** 10^2 **11.** 10^5 **12.** 10^1 **13.** 10^3

Write the exponent form for each.

14. $10 \times 10 \times 10$ **15.** $10 \times 10 \times 10 \times 10 \times 10 \times 10$

16. 10×10

Express as a power of 10, using an exponent.

17. 100,000 **18.** 1,000 **19.** 10,000 **20.** 100

Answer each question.

21. What is the exponent in 10^7?

22. What is the base in 10^6?

23. The number represented by 10^4 has how many zeros?

24. What is the number represented by 10^4?

25. What is the exponent in 10^8?

26. What is the number represented by 10^5?

Complete.

27. $10^{\underline{?}} = 10 \times 10 \times 10$

28. $10^1 = \underline{\ ?\ }$

29. $10^2 = \underline{\ ?\ }$

30. $10 \times 10 \times 10 \times 10 = \underline{\ ?\ }$

31. $10 \times \underline{\ ?\ } = 10^2$

32. $10^5 = \underline{\ ?\ }$

SCIENCE LINK

Scientists use the Richter scale to describe the strength of earthquakes. The Richter scale increases by powers of ten. An earthquake registering 2.0 is 10 times stronger than a quake registering 1.0, and a quake registering 3.0 is 10×10, or 100 times stronger. How many times stronger would a quake registering 4.0 be than one registering 1.0?

Problem Solving Applications

33. There were 10 fifth graders who each volunteered 10 hours of their time to work in the library. What is the total number of hours the students volunteered?

34. Money Selena earned $10 each week for 10 weeks of baby-sitting. Ricardo earned $10 each week for 10 weeks of mowing lawns. How much did they earn altogether?

35. Number Sense Marshall is counting the number of people in the assembly. So far he has counted 10 rows, with 10 people in each row, in 10 different sections. How many people has he counted so far?

36. Write About It How would you explain to a classmate that 10^5 is the same as 100,000?

Using the Calculator to Divide

Why learn this? You can use the memory keys on a calculator to divide larger numbers more quickly.

A calculator is useful when you want to divide large numbers quickly.

Divide. 19,295 ÷ 37 $37\overline{)19{,}295}$

Estimate. $19{,}295 \div 37 \approx n$ **Think:** $\overset{500}{40\overline{)20{,}000}}$ or $\overset{600}{30\overline{)18{,}000}}$

So, $n = 500$ or 600.

Enter the problem on a calculator. Enter the dividend first.

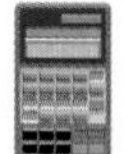

Press:

Display: = 521.48649

Talk About It

- What is the whole-number part of the display?
- What does the decimal part represent?
- What is one way you could find the whole-number remainder this decimal represents?

Here's another way to find the whole-number remainder represented by the decimal. Use the calculator's memory keys.

MR M+

M+ stores the product

MR recalls the product from memory

Some calculators use MRC for memory recall.

MODEL

Step 1
Multiply the quotient, the whole-number part of the display, by the divisor.

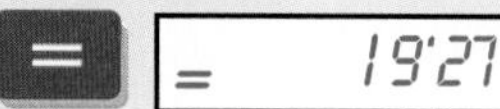

= 19'277

Step 2
Press the M+ key.

M 19'277.

Step 3
Using the MR key, subtract the product from the dividend.

M = 18.

So, the whole-number remainder is 18.

▶ CHECK

1. What happened when you pressed the M+ key?

2. What does the *M* on the display represent?

3. What happened when you pressed the MR key?

4. How can you check that a remainder of 18 is correct?

5. What happens when you press MC AC ?

▶ PRACTICE

Use the calculator to divide. Then find the whole-number remainder.

6. $13\overline{)14{,}368}$	7. $34\overline{)52{,}747}$	8. $46\overline{)24{,}391}$	9. $58\overline{)12{,}813}$
10. $27\overline{)60{,}824}$	11. $73\overline{)84{,}088}$	12. $67\overline{)53{,}094}$	13. $78\overline{)55{,}649}$
14. $91\overline{)98{,}301}$	15. $83\overline{)17{,}659}$	16. $14\overline{)40{,}687}$	17. $65\overline{)32{,}758}$

Problem Solving Applications

Use a calculator. For Problems 18–21, use the table.

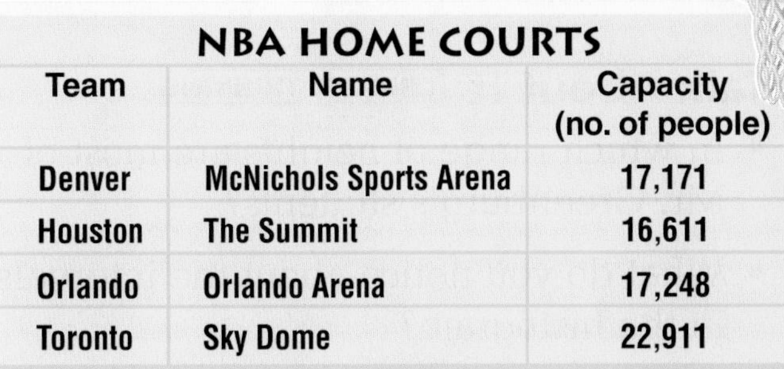

NBA HOME COURTS

Team	Name	Capacity (no. of people)
Denver	McNichols Sports Arena	17,171
Houston	The Summit	16,611
Orlando	Orlando Arena	17,248
Toronto	Sky Dome	22,911

18. **Sports** There were 15,980 fans divided into 4 equal-size cheering sections when the Magic played the Bulls at the Orlando Arena. Of the 4 sections, 3 were filled with Magic fans. How many Magic fans were there?

19. **Number Sense** On opening night the Sky Dome was filled to capacity. If everyone drove to the game in groups of 3, how many cars were in the parking lot?

20. **Number Sense** On the night Zoe went to The Summit, it was filled to capacity. T-shirts were given to every seventy-fifth person who entered. How many people got T-shirts?

21. **Consumer** On the night Alfonse went to McNichols Sports Arena, it was filled to capacity. The snack vendors sold 1 whole pizza for every 15 people there. How many whole pizzas did they sell?

22. **Reasoning** Ariana has 13,574 pennies. She has been saving pennies for 11 years. Suppose Ariana saved the same number of pennies each year. How many pennies per year did she save?

23. **Money** There were $80,350 worth of tickets sold for the winter ice-skating show. Tickets cost $25 each. How many tickets were sold?

24. **Write a problem** in which you divide using a calculator. Use the numbers 63,935 and 19.

Interpreting Histograms

Why learn this? By interpreting a histogram you can compare data that are grouped within a range, such as ages.

A *histogram* is a bar graph that shows the number of times data occur within a certain range or interval.

Mr. Greenburg surveyed his class to find out the students' heights. Then he made a histogram.

Heights of Mr. Greenburg's Students	
Range of Heights	Number of Students
48 in. - 51 in.	2
52 in. - 55 in.	5
56 in. - 59 in.	12
60 in. - 63 in.	7
64 in - 67 in.	1

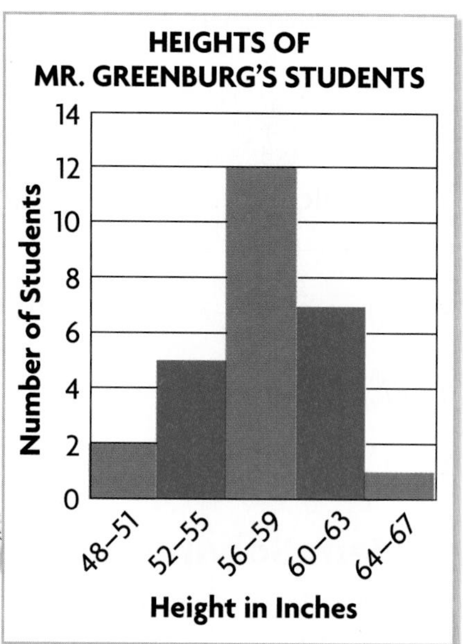

Talk About It CRITICAL THINKING

- In which range of heights are most of Mr. Greenburg's students?
- What do you notice about the intervals for each bar in the histogram?
- How are the bars in a histogram different from the bars in a bar graph?
- How are the labels along the bottom of a histogram different from those along the bottom of a bar graph?

▶ CHECK

For Problems 1–3, use the histogram.

1. During which range of months are the most cheerleaders' birthdays?

2. During which range of months do only 3 cheerleaders have birthdays?

3. How many members are there on the cheerleading squad?

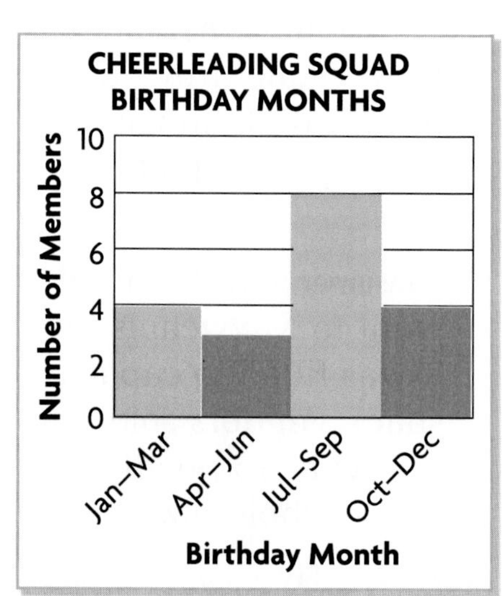

▶ PRACTICE

For Problems 4–7, use the histogram.

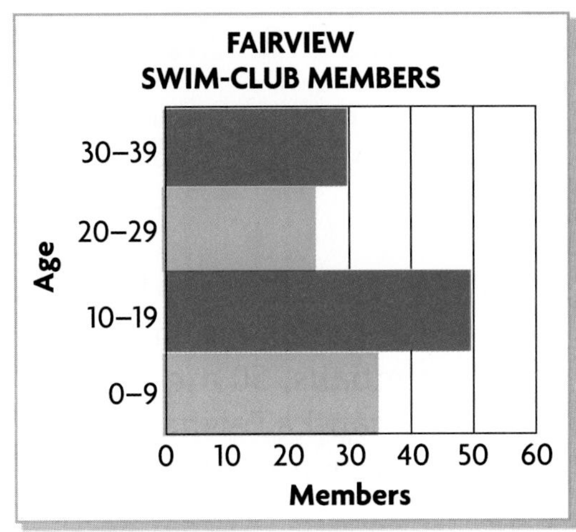

4. Between which ages are the greatest number of swim-club members? the least number?
5. How many swim-club members are under the age of 20?
6. How many more members are there between the ages 0–9 than between the ages 20–29?
7. How many swim-club members are there from the ages 0–39?

Problem Solving Applications

Using Data For Problems 8–16, use the histograms.

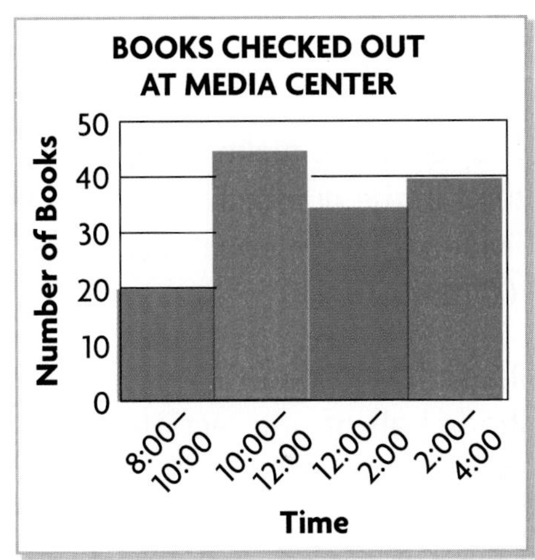

8. Between which times were the most books checked out of the media center?
9. Between which times were the fewest books checked out of the media center?
10. **Time** How many more books were checked out between 10:00 and 12:00 than between 8:00 and 10:00?
11. **Time** How many books were checked out between 8:00 and 4:00?

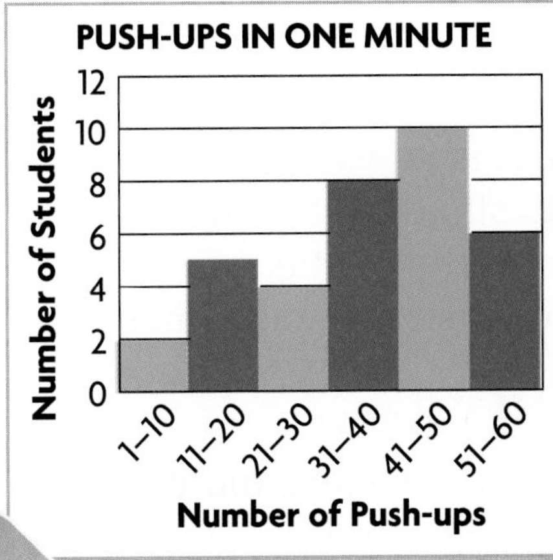

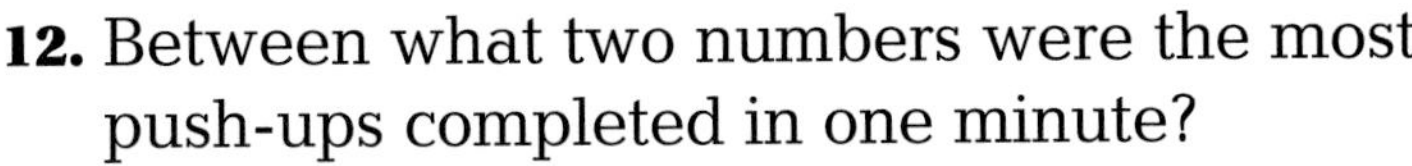

12. Between what two numbers were the most push-ups completed in one minute?
13. Between what two numbers were the fewest push-ups completed in one minute?

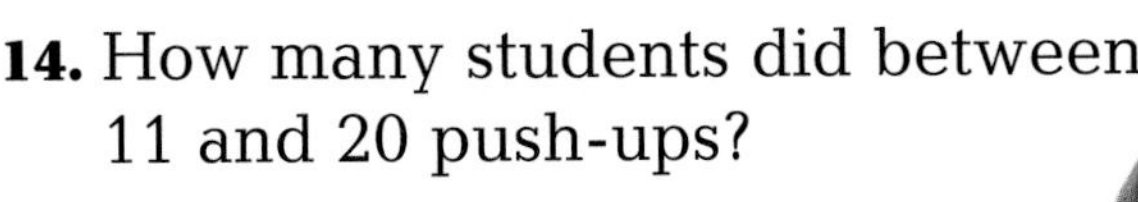

14. How many students did between 11 and 20 push-ups?
15. How many students in all did push-ups?
16. **Write a problem** using the information in one of the histograms.

Conduct a Simulation

Why learn this? You can save time and money by conducting a simulation of probability experiments.

Suppose LaTeisha wants to get a ring from a gumball machine. Of the 500 items in the gumball machine, 400 are gumballs, 50 are bouncing balls, and 50 are rings. How can LaTeisha design a simulation and see how many tries it might take before she gets a ring?

To conduct a *simulation* means to do something in a way that is easier than the actual experiment. The possible outcomes of the simulation have to match the possible outcomes of the real event.

You can use a spinner to simulate getting items from a gumball machine.

1. Decide how to make the spinner. Since there are 500 items in the gumball machine, you can make a spinner divided into five equal sections. Each section represents 100 items.
2. Shade four sections to represent the 400 gumballs. Shade half of one section to represent the 50 bouncing balls and the other half to represent the 50 rings.
3. Spin the pointer as many times as you want to simulate getting items from the gumball machine. Record the frequency of each outcome.

So, LaTeisha used green to stand for gumballs, blue to stand for bouncing balls, and red to stand for rings. She spun the pointer 10 times and recorded her outcomes in a table.

GUMBALL-MACHINE SIMULATION

Spin Number	Color	Item
1	green	gumball
2	blue	ball
3	green	gumball
4	green	gumball
5	green	gumball
6	green	gumball
7	blue	ball
8	red	ring
9	green	gumball
10	green	gumball

▶ CHECK

1. How many spins did it take for the pointer to land on red?
2. If LaTeisha spends $0.25 for each try at the gumball machine, how much money might she expect to spend to get a ring?
3. If this simulation is repeated, will the results be the same? Explain.

▶ PRACTICE

Design a simulation for each situation.

4. Taylor wants to buy a concert ticket. He can't choose his seat when he buys his ticket. Of the 1,000 seats available for the concert, 200 are in Section A, 300 are in Section B, 300 are in Section C, and 200 are in Section D. What simulation can Taylor design to determine what section his ticket might be for?

5. Melissa will be assigned a band instrument to use this year. Of the 100 instruments available, 50 are clarinets, 20 are flutes, 10 are trumpets, 10 are tubas, and 10 are saxophones. What simulation can Melissa design to determine the instrument she might be assigned?

For Problem 6, design and conduct a simulation. Copy the table for recording the results of your simulation.

6. Of the 600 prizes at a carnival booth, there are 100 teddy bears, 100 games, 100 toys, and 300 goldfish. What simulation can Jenny design to determine which prize she might win?

CARNIVAL PRIZE SIMULATION			
Teddy Bear	Game	Toy	Goldfish

Which prize might Jenny win?

Problem Solving Applications

7. **Number Sense** Randy is being assigned his school locker. There are 1,000 lockers. He wants to know his chances of getting a locker number from 1 through 100. What simulation can Randy design to determine what locker number he might get?

8. **Reasoning** At Dover Elementary, there are 5 classes in each grade, kindergarten through fifth. One class will be chosen to go on a special field trip. What simulation can you design to determine the grade level of the class that will go on the trip?

9. Misty gets to choose a pencil as a prize. Of the 300 pencils in the box, 150 are red, 60 are green, and 90 are blue. What simulation can Misty design to determine which color pencil she might get?

10. **Write About It** Do the results of a simulation tell you the exact results you would get if you conducted the actual experiment? Explain.

Estimating Quotients

Why learn this? You can estimate quotients to decide if your answers make sense.

Nell's basketball team is selling carnations. Each package of 8 carnations costs \$5.95. About how much does each carnation cost?

Since an exact answer is not needed, estimate the quotient.

Choose a compatible number that can be divided evenly by the divisor.

\$5.95 ÷ 8 **Think:** 8, 16, 24, 32, 40, 48, 56, or 64

Use a dividend of \$5.60 for a compatible number.

\$5.60 ÷ 8 = \$0.70

So, one estimate for the cost of each carnation is \$0.70.

Sometimes you can use more than one pair of compatible numbers. Since \$6.40 is also close to \$5.95 and is compatible with 8, another way to estimate the quotient is to find \$6.40 ÷ 8.

\$6.40 ÷ 8 = \$0.80 **Think:** 8 × \$0.80 = \$6.40

So, another estimate for the cost of each carnation is \$0.80.

Talk About It

- Are these both good estimates? Why or why not?
- Is \$0.70 per carnation greater than or less than the actual quotient? How can you tell?
- Is \$0.80 per carnation greater than or less than the actual quotient? How can you tell?
- If each package of 6 carnations costs \$4.69, about how much does each carnation cost?

CRITICAL THINKING Can \$1.20 be the exact cost per carnation for Nell's team? Why or why not?

SCIENCE LINK

About 250,000 kinds of plants produce seeds. The seeds vary in size, shape, and color. Begonia flower seeds are so small that about 16 million seeds weigh about one pound. Estimate how many begonia seeds would weigh about one ounce. (**HINT:** 1 lb = 16 oz)

▶ CHECK

Choose the letter of the best estimate.

1. $2\overline{)1.34}$ **a.** 0.50 **b.** 0.30 **c.** 0.60 **d.** 0.70

2. $6\overline{)5.9}$ **a.** 1.0 **b.** 10 **c.** 100 **d.** 0.1

3. $2\overline{)\$1.81}$ **a.** $0.70 **b.** $0.80 **c.** $0.90 **d.** $1.00

4. $5\overline{)\$2.63}$ **a.** $0.50 **b.** $5.00 **c.** $0.05 **d.** $50.00

5. $6\overline{)4.11}$ **a.** 0.60 **b.** 0.70 **c.** 0.80 **d.** 0.90

▶ PRACTICE

Estimate the quotient.

6. $3\overline{)3.6}$ **7.** $5\overline{)\$2.07}$ **8.** $8\overline{)4.90}$ **9.** $3\overline{)1.33}$

10. $4\overline{)4.03}$ **11.** $4\overline{)\$1.97}$ **12.** $8\overline{)2.50}$ **13.** $3\overline{)4.18}$

14. $3\overline{)\$6.76}$ **15.** $8\overline{)8.89}$ **16.** $6\overline{)4.9}$ **17.** $9\overline{)3.5}$

18. $7\overline{)3.6}$ **19.** $2\overline{)1.84}$ **20.** $6\overline{)3.58}$ **21.** $8\overline{)5.69}$

22. $31.8 \div 8 = n$ **23.** $\$27.75 \div 7 = n$ **24.** $16.2 \div 5 = n$

25. $\$82.20 \div 9 = n$ **26.** $35.8 \div 5 = n$ **27.** $4.21 \div 7 = n$

28. $27.9 \div 9 = n$ **29.** $0.45 \div 7 = n$ **30.** $17.5 \div 2 = n$

Problem Solving Applications

31. Technology Val is transferring 237 files to diskettes. She can put 8 files on each diskette. About how many diskettes will she use?

32. Number Sense A 117-minute film is recorded and divided equally onto 2 large reels. About how many minutes of film does each reel contain?

33. Science Tommy is writing a science report on his computer. He wants to explain 4 topics on one page. A page has 54 lines. About how many lines should he write on each topic?

34. The 7 teacher's aides were assigned 227 tests to grade. About how many tests did each teacher's aide have to grade?

35. A group of 168 students have signed up for computer classes. If there are 8 teachers, about how many students will be with each teacher?

36. A theater has 240 seats. The seats are arranged in 3 sections of the same size. How many seats are in each section?

Fractions as Missing Addends

Why learn this? You can find the missing amount when you know the sum and one addend.

Yesterday Josh had $\frac{1}{3}$ pound of jelly beans. Then his friend gave him some more jelly beans. Now Josh has $\frac{3}{4}$ pound of jelly beans. How many pounds of jelly beans did his friend give him?

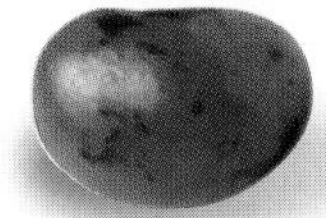

Think: $\frac{1}{3} + \underline{\ ?\ } = \frac{3}{4}$

You can use fraction bars to find the missing addend.

Find the missing addend for $\frac{1}{3} + \underline{\ ?\ } = \frac{3}{4}$.

Step 1

Use fraction bars to model the sum.

$\frac{1}{4}$ | $\frac{1}{4}$ | $\frac{1}{4}$

Use fraction bars to model the given addend.

Step 2

Compare the sum and the given addend to find the missing addend.

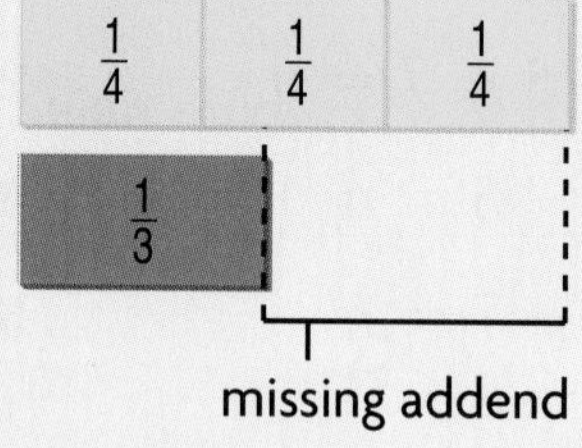

Step 3

Since the LCM of 4 and 3 is 12, the LCD is twelfths. Use fraction bars to see how many twelfths are needed for the missing addend.

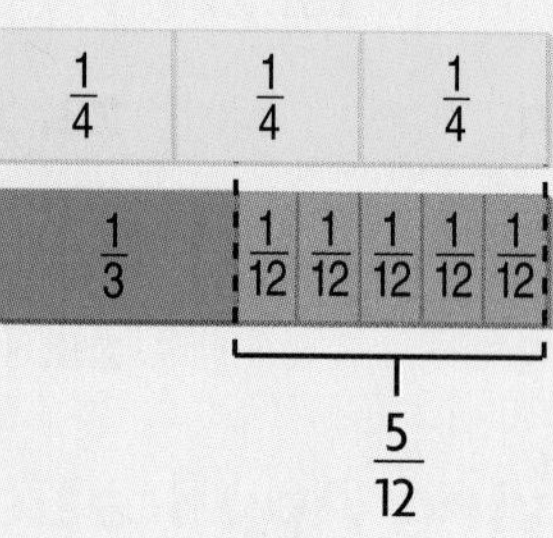

So, the missing addend is $\frac{5}{12}$.

So, Josh's friend gave him $\frac{5}{12}$ pound of jelly beans.

EXAMPLE

Find the missing addend for $\frac{3}{4} + \underline{\ ?\ } = 1\frac{1}{4}$.

Model and compare.

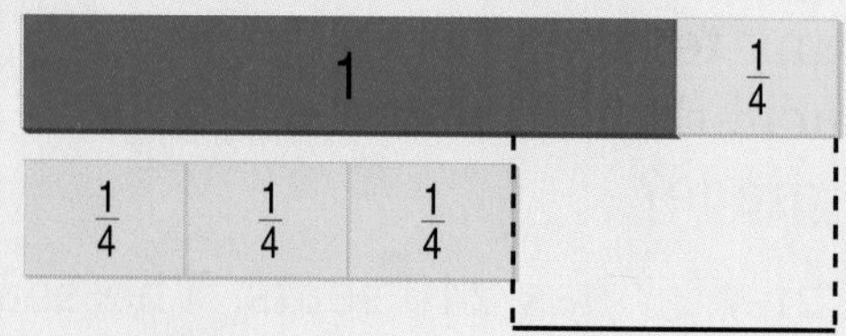

Since the LCM of 4 and 4 is 4, the LCD is fourths. Use fraction bars to see how many fourths are needed for the missing addend.

1 | $\frac{1}{4}$

$\frac{1}{4}$ | $\frac{1}{4}$ | $\frac{1}{4}$ | $\frac{1}{4}$ | $\frac{1}{4}$

So, the missing addend is $\frac{2}{4}$, or $\frac{1}{2}$.

CRITICAL THINKING What other operation can you use to find a missing addend?

▶ CHECK

Name the missing addend. You may wish to use fraction strips.

1. $\frac{1}{3} + \underline{\ ?\ } = \frac{5}{6}$

2. $\frac{1}{2} + \underline{\ ?\ } = \frac{3}{4}$

3. $\frac{5}{6} + \underline{\ ?\ } = \frac{11}{12}$

▶ PRACTICE

4. $\frac{3}{10} + \underline{\ ?\ } = \frac{4}{5}$

5. $\frac{1}{8} + \underline{\ ?\ } = \frac{3}{4}$

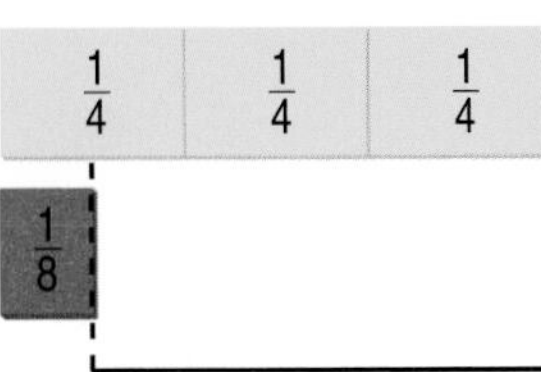

6. $\frac{1}{4} + \underline{\ ?\ } = \frac{5}{6}$

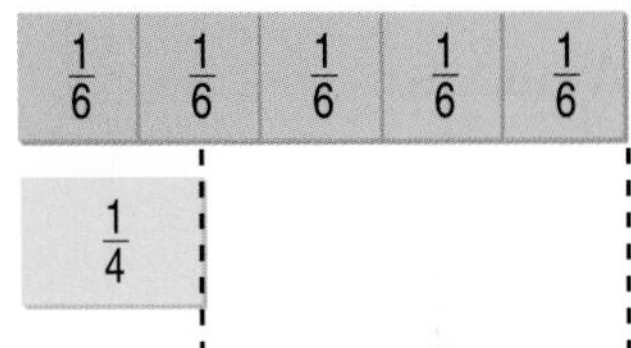

Use fraction strips to find the missing addend.

7. $\frac{1}{4} + \underline{\ ?\ } = \frac{1}{3}$

8. $\frac{7}{10} + \underline{\ ?\ } = \frac{4}{5}$

9. $\frac{1}{6} + \underline{\ ?\ } = \frac{3}{4}$

10. $\frac{1}{2} + \underline{\ ?\ } = \frac{2}{3}$

11. $\frac{1}{3} + \underline{\ ?\ } = \frac{4}{9}$

12. $\frac{1}{2} + \underline{\ ?\ } = \frac{7}{8}$

13. $\frac{4}{5} + \underline{\ ?\ } = 1\frac{3}{5}$

14. $\frac{5}{6} + \underline{\ ?\ } = 1\frac{1}{6}$

15. $\frac{5}{8} + \underline{\ ?\ } = 1\frac{3}{8}$

Problem Solving Applications

16. **Measurement** Jamie had $\frac{1}{4}$ pound peanuts. His brother gave him more peanuts. Now Jamie has $\frac{2}{3}$ pound peanuts. How many pounds of peanuts did his brother give him?

17. **Measurement** Paula measured the growth of her flower. On the first day, the flower grew $\frac{1}{6}$ inch. The plant grew some more on the second day. By the third day, the plant had grown $\frac{2}{3}$ inch. How much did the plant grow the second day?

18. Zach was baking a cake. The cake rose $\frac{1}{8}$ inch the first minute. The cake rose more the second minute. Now the cake has risen $\frac{3}{4}$ inch in all. How much did the cake rise during the second minute?

19. **Write About It** Explain how you can use fraction bars to find the missing addend.

Using Fraction Circles to Subtract

Why learn this? You can subtract to compare amounts such as those on a circle graph.

Martin surveyed his classmates to find out their favorite kind of book. Of the students, $\frac{3}{4}$ said fiction, $\frac{1}{8}$ said nonfiction, and $\frac{1}{8}$ said poetry. What is the difference between the fraction of the students who said fiction and the fraction who said poetry?

You can use fraction-circle pieces to subtract.

MODEL

What is $\frac{3}{4} - \frac{1}{8}$?

Step 1

Model with fraction-circle pieces.

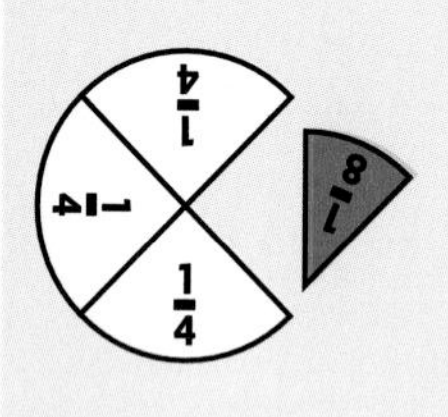

Step 2

Stack the piece for $\frac{1}{8}$ directly on top of the pieces for $\frac{3}{4}$.

Step 3

Find the least common denominator, or LCD.

The LCM of 4 and 8 is 8. So, the LCD of $\frac{3}{4}$ and $\frac{1}{8}$ is eighths.

Step 4

Use like fraction-circle pieces to see how many eighths fit exactly around. This is the difference.

So, $\frac{3}{4} - \frac{1}{8} = \frac{5}{8}$.

So, $\frac{5}{8}$ more students said fiction than poetry.

MODEL

What is $\frac{2}{3} - \frac{1}{6}$?

Step 1

Stack the piece for $\frac{1}{6}$ directly on top of the pieces for $\frac{2}{3}$.

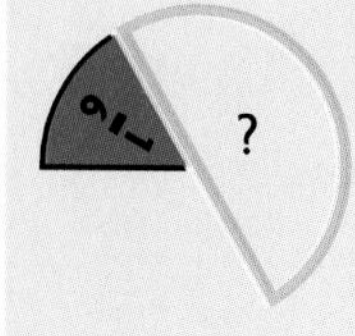

Step 2

Find the LCD.

The LCM of 3 and 6 is 6. So, the LCD of $\frac{2}{3}$ and $\frac{1}{6}$ is sixths.

Step 3

Find the difference.

$\frac{2}{3} - \frac{1}{6} = \frac{3}{6}$

Step 4

Find the largest fraction-circle piece or pieces to write the answer in simplest form.

=

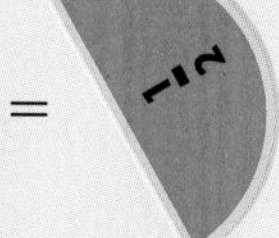

So, $\frac{2}{3} - \frac{1}{6} = \frac{1}{2}$.

CRITICAL THINKING How is using fraction-circle pieces to subtract the same as using fraction bars? How is it different?

▶ CHECK

Name the least common denominator, or LCD, for each pair of fractions.

1. $\frac{1}{2} - \frac{1}{3} = n$

2. $\frac{1}{2} - \frac{1}{4} = n$

3. $\frac{1}{2} - \frac{1}{8} = n$

4. $\frac{1}{3} - \frac{1}{6} = n$

5. $\frac{1}{4} - \frac{1}{8} = n$

6. $\frac{2}{3} - \frac{1}{2} = n$

▶ PRACTICE

Use fraction-circle pieces to find the difference. Write the answer in simplest form.

7. $\frac{1}{3} - \frac{1}{6} = n$

8. $\frac{1}{4} - \frac{1}{8} = n$

9. $\frac{2}{3} - \frac{1}{2} = n$

10. $\frac{3}{4} - \frac{1}{2} = n$

11. $\frac{7}{8} - \frac{1}{2} = n$

12. $\frac{5}{6} - \frac{1}{3} = n$

13. $\frac{3}{4} - \frac{3}{8} = n$

14. $\frac{1}{2} - \frac{3}{8} = n$

15. $\frac{2}{3} - \frac{2}{6} = n$

16. $\frac{6}{8} - \frac{1}{4} = n$

17. $\frac{6}{8} - \frac{1}{2} = n$

18. $\frac{4}{6} - \frac{1}{3} = n$

Problem Solving Applications

Use fraction-circle pieces to solve.

19. Compare Kori and Jeananne have equal-size bags of pretzels. Kori's bag is $\frac{1}{2}$ full. Jeananne's is $\frac{1}{3}$ full. How much fuller is Kori's pretzel bag than Jeananne's?

20. Compare Chen and Ruben collect stamps. Chen's stamp album is $\frac{7}{8}$ full. Ruben's is $\frac{1}{2}$ full. How much more of a stamp album has Chen filled?

21. Art The pins on Jamie's string-art design are $\frac{6}{8}$ inch apart. The pins on Nomary's design are $\frac{1}{2}$ inch apart. How much farther apart are the pins on Jamie's design?

22. Compare Lionel has a carton of eggs that is $\frac{5}{6}$ full. Kenny has a carton of eggs that is $\frac{1}{3}$ full. How much more of a carton of eggs does Lionel have?

23. Of the students, $\frac{1}{2}$ take the bus home, $\frac{1}{4}$ ride bikes, $\frac{1}{8}$ walk, and $\frac{1}{8}$ get picked up by a parent. What is the difference between the part of the students who take the bus and the part who walk?

24. Write About It When subtracting with fraction-circle pieces, why is it important to stack the pieces directly on top of one another?

Fractions in Music Notation

Why learn this? You can understand the notes used to write music.

MUSICAL NOTES (in $\frac{4}{4}$ time)	
Notes	Number of beats
whole note	4
half note	2
quarter note	1
eighth note	$\frac{1}{2}$

Composers use fractions when they write music. Each musical note represents a certain number of counts, or beats.

The time signature in this musical composition is $\frac{4}{4}$. The top number of the time signature means there are 4 beats per measure. The bottom number means a quarter note gets 1 beat.

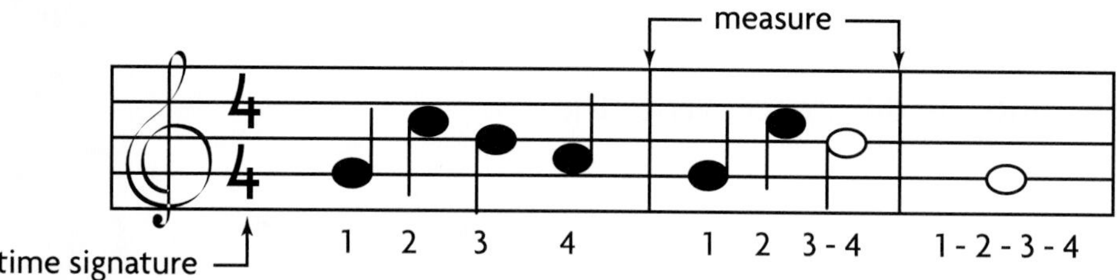

- Describe the notes and beats in each measure.

A composer must know the fractional relationship between notes.

1 whole note = 2 half notes	So, a half note is held $\frac{1}{2}$ the time of a whole note.
1 whole note = 4 quarter notes	So, a quarter note is held $\frac{1}{4}$ the time of a whole note.
1 whole note = 8 eighth notes	So, an eighth note is held $\frac{1}{8}$ the time of a whole note.

▶ CHECK

1. How many quarter notes equal a half note?
2. How many eighth notes equal a half note?
3. Describe the relationship between a quarter note and a half note.

When a dot is added to a musical note, the note is held half again as long as the original note.

half note (2 beats)	+	dot ($\frac{1}{2}$ of 2 = 1)	=	dotted half note (3 beats)
2	+	1	=	3

4. How many beats does a dotted quarter note have? a dotted eighth note?

CULTURAL LINK

In many parts of Africa, music plays an active role in daily life. Children begin playing musical instruments by the age of three or four. If they spend 10 years playing instruments before they are adults, at what age are African children considered to be adults?

▶ PRACTICE

If the time signature is $\frac{4}{4}$, tell how many of each kind of note you can put in a measure. Then write each note as a fraction in an addition number sentence, so that the sum of each number sentence is 1.

EXAMPLES

A half notes 2 half notes: $\frac{1}{2} + \frac{1}{2} = 1$

B quarter notes 4 quarter notes: $\frac{1}{4} + \frac{1}{4} + \frac{1}{4} + \frac{1}{4} = 1$

5. quarter notes and half notes
6. eighth notes and half notes
7. eighth notes and quarter notes
8. eighth notes, quarter notes, and half notes

Problem Solving Applications

Using Data For Problems 9–10, use the music at the right.

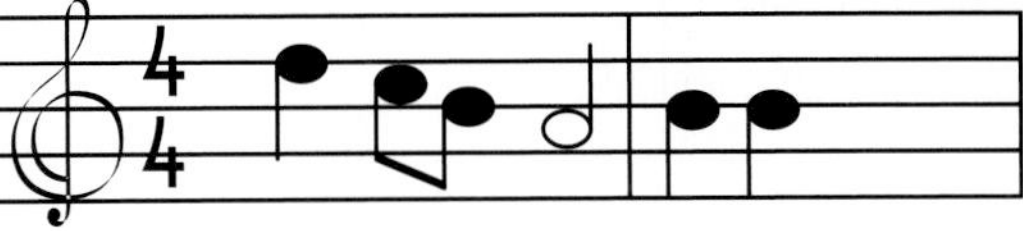

9. How many more beats are needed in the second measure?
10. What combination of notes could you use to complete the second measure?
11. The time signature of a piece of music is $\frac{2}{4}$. How many beats are there per measure?
12. **Music** Write a short musical composition with 3 measures. Use a time signature of $\frac{4}{4}$. Write the counts for each note below each note.
13. **Analyzing Data** What is the time signature of this composition?

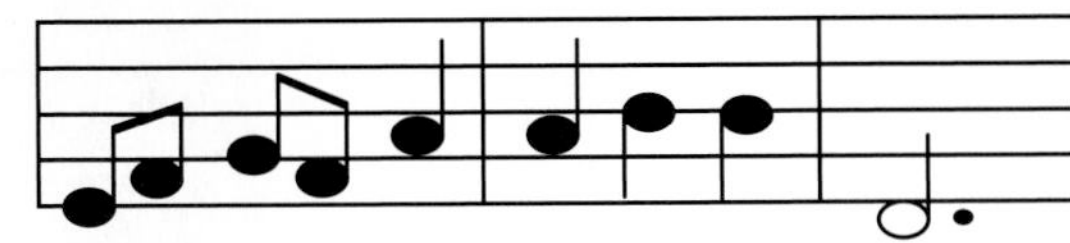

14. **Write About It** Explain how musical notation and fractions are related.

Renaming Mixed Numbers

Why learn this? You can subtract measurements that are expressed as mixed numbers.

The steel-manufacturing plant had $4\frac{3}{10}$ tons of steel. They sold $2\frac{4}{5}$ tons of the steel to a car-manufacturing plant. How much steel is left?

Subtract $4\frac{3}{10}$ and $2\frac{4}{5}$. Estimate. $4\frac{1}{2} - 3 = 1\frac{1}{2}$

MODEL

What is $4\frac{3}{10} - 2\frac{4}{5}$?

Step 1

Rename the fractions. Since the LCD is tenths, change $\frac{4}{5}$ to tenths.

$$\begin{aligned} 4\tfrac{3}{10} &= 4\tfrac{3}{10} \\ -\,2\tfrac{4}{5} &= 2\tfrac{8}{10} \end{aligned}$$

Step 2

Model the mixed number from which you are subtracting. Decide if you can subtract.

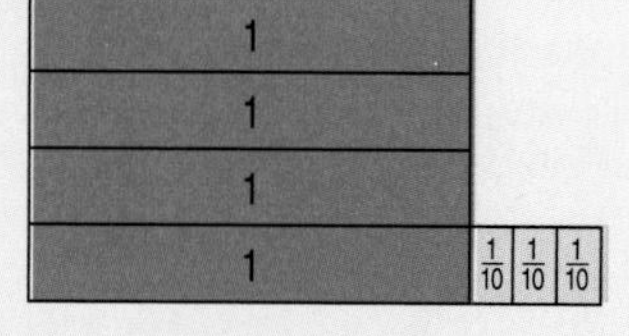

$$\begin{array}{r} 4\frac{3}{10} \\ -2\frac{8}{10} \\ \hline \end{array}$$

Step 3

Before you can subtract $\frac{8}{10}$ from $\frac{3}{10}$, you have to rename $4\frac{3}{10}$ as $3\frac{13}{10}$.

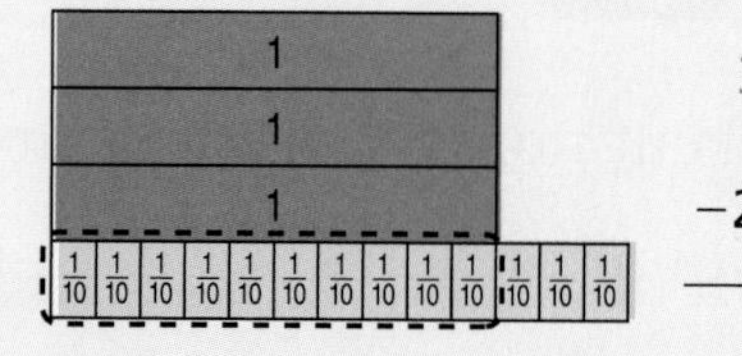

$$\begin{array}{r} 3\frac{13}{10} \\ -2\frac{8}{10} \\ \hline \end{array}$$

Step 4

Subtract the fractions. Take $\frac{8}{10}$ away from $\frac{13}{10}$.

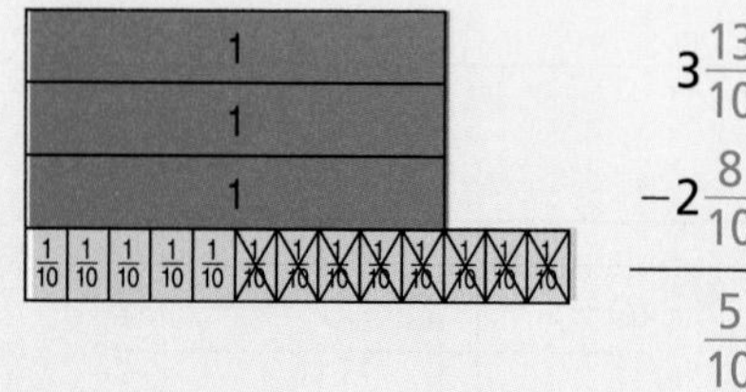

$$\begin{array}{r} 3\frac{13}{10} \\ -2\frac{8}{10} \\ \hline \frac{5}{10} \end{array}$$

Step 5

Subtract the whole numbers. Write the answer in simplest form.

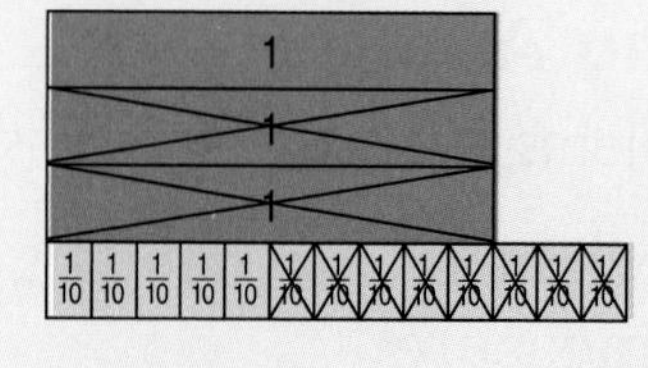

$$\begin{array}{r} 3\frac{13}{10} \\ -2\frac{8}{10} \\ \hline 1\frac{5}{10} = 1\frac{1}{2} \end{array}$$

So, there are $1\frac{1}{2}$ tons of steel left.

Talk About It

- Is the answer reasonable? Explain how you know.
- In Step 3, why did $4\frac{3}{10}$ have to be renamed as $3\frac{13}{10}$?

CRITICAL THINKING Look at Steps 1 and 3. Why must you rename twice before you can subtract mixed numbers?

SCIENCE LINK

There are 2,000 pounds in 1 ton. About how many pounds are equal to $4\frac{3}{10}$ tons?

CHECK

Decide if you need to rename. Write *yes* or *no*.

1. $2\frac{1}{2} - 1\frac{3}{4}$

2. $4\frac{1}{3} - 2\frac{5}{6}$

3. $10\frac{5}{6} - 6\frac{2}{12}$

4. $7\frac{4}{9} - 2\frac{1}{3}$

5. $12\frac{2}{3} - 3\frac{2}{9}$

6. $9\frac{3}{8} - 5\frac{3}{4}$

7. $6\frac{5}{12} - 5\frac{1}{2}$

8. $13\frac{4}{5} - 8\frac{7}{10}$

PRACTICE

Match the mixed number with the fraction bars.

9. $5\frac{1}{5}$

10. $5\frac{1}{3}$

11. $4\frac{4}{5}$

a. 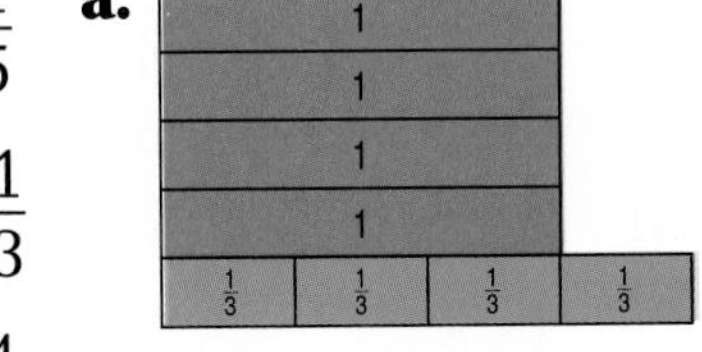

b. 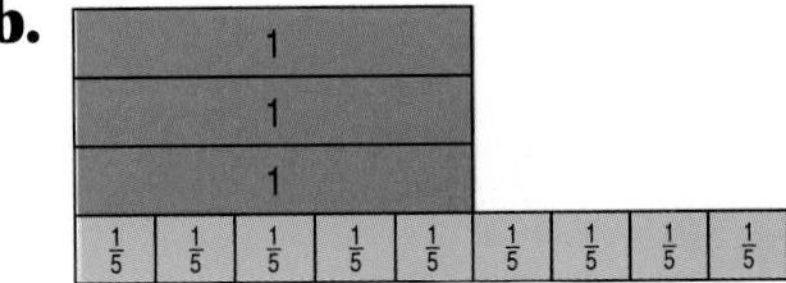

c. 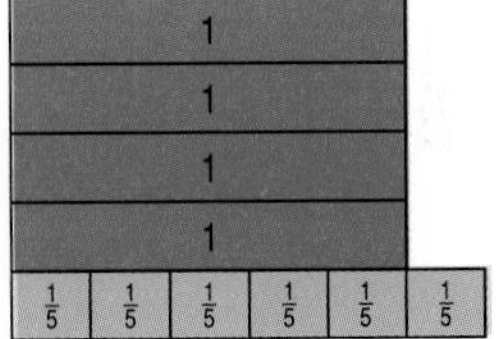

Use fraction strips to find the difference. Write the answer in simplest form.

12. $5\frac{2}{5} - 1\frac{4}{5}$

13. $2\frac{1}{4} - 1\frac{3}{4}$

14. $4\frac{1}{6} - 2\frac{5}{6}$

15. $7\frac{1}{10} - 2\frac{9}{10}$

16. $5\frac{1}{12} - 2\frac{3}{4}$

17. $7\frac{3}{8} - 1\frac{3}{4}$

18. $8\frac{1}{6} - 3\frac{2}{3}$

19. $6\frac{2}{3} - 3\frac{3}{4}$

Problem Solving Applications

20. Andrew had $6\frac{1}{4}$ feet of fencing. He used $3\frac{3}{4}$ feet to finish fencing in his yard. How many feet of fencing does Andrew have left over?

21. Mr. Alonzo bought $10\frac{1}{2}$ pounds of dirt to fill in around his bushes. He used $5\frac{3}{4}$ pounds of the dirt. How much dirt is left over?

22. **Measurement** Vivian had 2 quarts of water in a container. Today she has used $1\frac{1}{3}$ quarts. How much water is left in the container?

23. **Write About It** Explain how to rename a mixed number.

Exploring Division of Fractions

Why learn this? You will better understand division of fractions by asking the question, "How many equal parts are there?"

Sandy has a $\frac{6}{8}$-yard length of ribbon for a craft project. She must cut the ribbon into pieces that are each $\frac{2}{8}$ yard long. How many pieces of ribbon will Sandy have?

You can use fraction bars to divide fractions.

MODEL

What is $\frac{6}{8} \div \frac{2}{8}$?

Step 1

Model $\frac{6}{8}$ and $\frac{2}{8}$ with fraction bars.

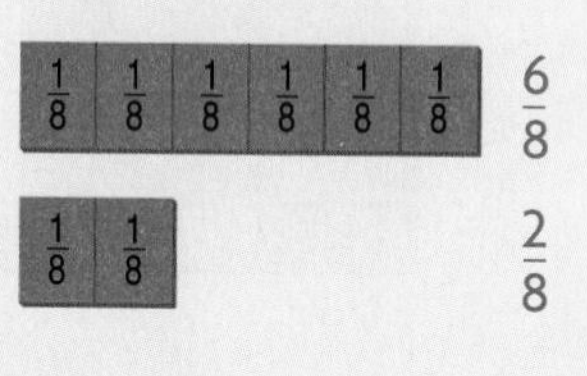

Step 2

See how many groups of $\frac{2}{8}$ are equal in length to $\frac{6}{8}$.

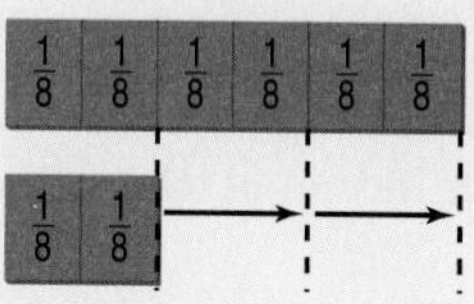

So, 3 groups of $\frac{2}{8}$ are equal in length to $\frac{6}{8}$.

Step 3

Record a number sentence for the model. Divide the numerators. Divide the denominators. Write the answer in simplest form.

$\frac{6 \div 2}{8 \div 8} = \frac{3}{1}$, or 3

So, Sandy will have 3 pieces of ribbon.

- In Step 3, what do you notice about the numerator of the quotient? the denominator?

You can also use fraction circles to divide fractions.

MODEL

What is $3 \div \frac{2}{6}$?

Step 1

Rename so the denominators are the same.

$3 \div \frac{2}{6} = \frac{18 \div 2}{6 \div 6}$

Step 2

Model $\frac{18}{6}$ with fraction-circle pieces.

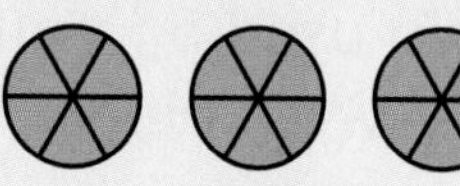

$\frac{6}{6} + \frac{6}{6} + \frac{6}{6} = \frac{18}{6}$, or 3

Step 3

See how many groups of $\frac{2}{6}$ are equal to $\frac{18}{6}$.

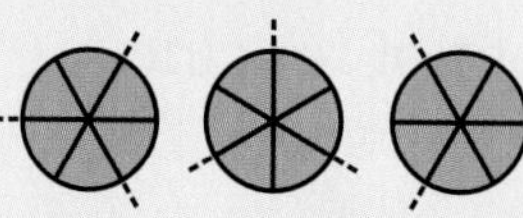

So, 9 groups of $\frac{2}{6}$ are equal to $\frac{18}{6}$.

Step 4

Record a number sentence for the model. Divide.

Simplify.

$\frac{18 \div 2}{6 \div 6} = \frac{9}{1}$, or

$3 \div \frac{2}{6} = 9$

CRITICAL THINKING What rule can you write for dividing fractions with like denominators?

▶ CHECK

Record a number sentence for the picture.

1. 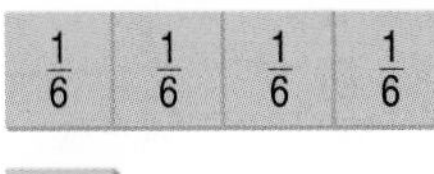

2.

$\frac{1}{8}$ $\frac{1}{8}$ $\frac{1}{8}$ $\frac{1}{8}$ $\frac{1}{8}$ $\frac{1}{8}$ $\frac{1}{8}$ $\frac{1}{8}$

$\frac{1}{8}$ $\frac{1}{8}$

3.

$\frac{1}{10}$ $\frac{1}{10}$ $\frac{1}{10}$ $\frac{1}{10}$ $\frac{1}{10}$ $\frac{1}{10}$ $\frac{1}{10}$ $\frac{1}{10}$

$\frac{1}{10}$ $\frac{1}{10}$ $\frac{1}{10}$ $\frac{1}{10}$

▶ PRACTICE

4. 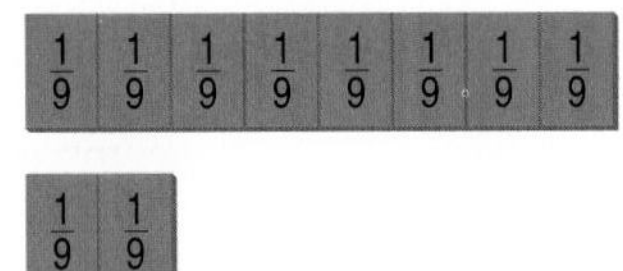

5. 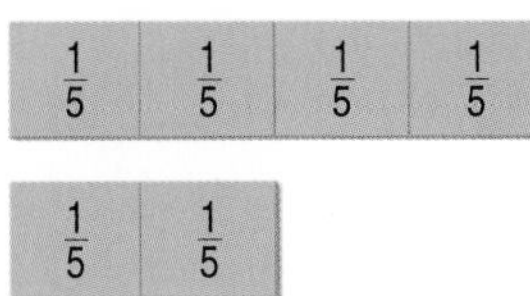

6. 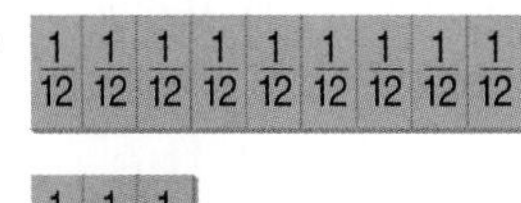

7. 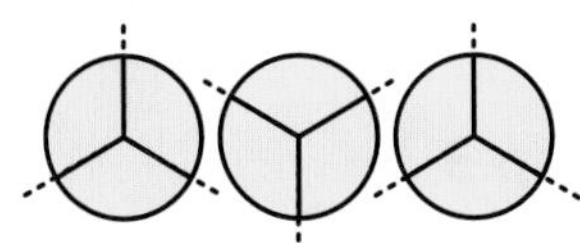

8. 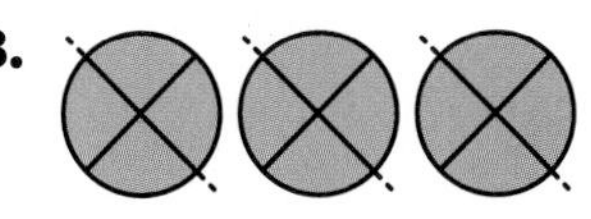

9. 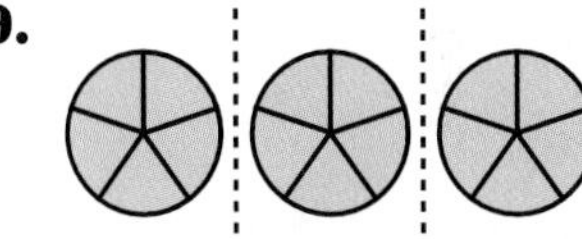

Find the quotient.

10. $\frac{3}{4} \div \frac{1}{4} = n$

11. $\frac{9}{10} \div \frac{3}{10} = n$

12. $\frac{24}{8} \div \frac{2}{8} = n$

13. $\frac{6}{9} \div \frac{2}{9} = n$

14. $\frac{6}{12} \div \frac{3}{12} = n$

15. $\frac{18}{6} \div \frac{3}{6} = n$

16. $\frac{20}{4} \div \frac{2}{4} = n$

17. $\frac{10}{2} \div \frac{1}{2} = n$

18. $\frac{16}{8} \div \frac{4}{8} = n$

Problem Solving Applications

19. Measurement Diane has a piece of paper that is $\frac{9}{10}$ meter long. She is going to divide the paper into sections that are $\frac{3}{10}$ meter long. Into how many sections will the paper be divided?

20. Choose one of the equations from Exercises 10–18. Draw either a fraction-bar or a fraction-circle model to show the division problem.

21. Measurement Louis has a piece of wood that is $\frac{10}{12}$ yard long. He is going to cut it into pieces that are each $\frac{2}{12}$ yard long. How many pieces will he have?

22. Number Sense The quotient of two fractions is 8. What are two possible division sentences for that quotient?

23. Reasoning A line segment is $\frac{6}{8}$ in. long. How many $\frac{1}{8}$-in. units are there in $\frac{6}{8}$ in.?

24. Write About It Explain how dividing fractions is like dividing whole numbers.

Angles in Circle Graphs

Why learn this? You can organize and display data on a whole circle graph, divided to show fractional parts.

Bradley is planting a vegetable garden. The table tells how much of the garden he will plant with each vegetable. Make a circle graph to display these data.

Bradley's Vegetable Garden	
Vegetable	Fraction of the Garden
Corn	$\frac{1}{2}$
Beans	$\frac{1}{4}$
Squash	$\frac{1}{8}$
Carrots	$\frac{1}{8}$

To make a circle graph, you need to find the number of degrees represented by each part. Since there are 360° about the center of a circle, multiply the fraction for each part by 360°.

MODEL

Step 1

Multiply each fraction by 360°.

$\frac{1}{2} \times 360° = 180°$ (corn)

$\frac{1}{4} \times 360° = 90°$ (beans)

$\frac{1}{8} \times 360° = 45°$ (squash)

$\frac{1}{8} \times 360° = 45°$ (carrots)

Step 2

Use a compass to draw a circle and a protractor to draw the angles.

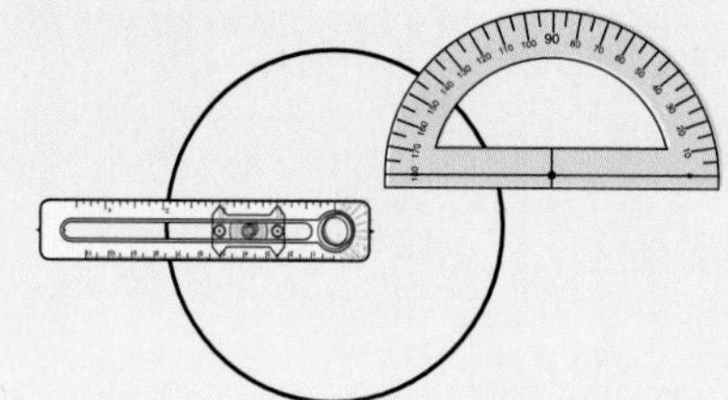

Step 3

Complete and label the graph.

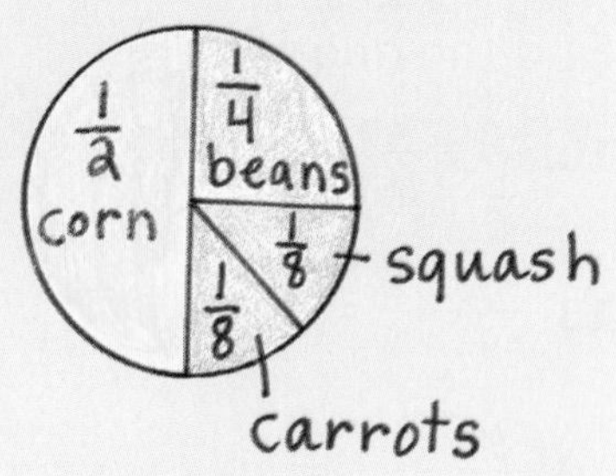

Talk About It

- Add the degrees for each part. What is the total number of degrees?

CRITICAL THINKING Explain how the circle graph shows the data differently than the table.

▶ CHECK

Find the number of degrees for the fractions in each set.

1. $\frac{1}{8}, \frac{1}{2}, \frac{1}{8}, \frac{1}{4}$

2. $\frac{1}{2}, \frac{1}{3}, \frac{1}{6}$

3. $\frac{2}{10}, \frac{3}{5}, \frac{1}{10}, \frac{1}{10}$

4. What is the sum of the fractions in each set of Exercises 1–3?

5. What is the sum of the angles in each set of Exercises 1–3?

▶ PRACTICE

Find the number of degrees for the fractions in each set.
Find the sum of the angles in each set.

6. $\frac{1}{2}, \frac{1}{5}, \frac{3}{10}$

7. $\frac{1}{4}, \frac{2}{12}, \frac{1}{3}, \frac{3}{12}$

8. $\frac{1}{3}, \frac{1}{6}, \frac{1}{2}$

For Exercises 9–12, find the number of degrees for the fractions in each table. Make a circle graph to display the data.

9.

MR. FOLEY'S WORK SCHEDULE	
Activity	**Fraction of Time Spent**
Meetings	$\frac{3}{8}$
Telephone calls	$\frac{1}{8}$
Office work	$\frac{1}{2}$

10.

CHOICE OF FOOD FOR CLASS PARTY	
Food	**Fraction of Class**
Cupcakes	$\frac{1}{3}$
Cookies	$\frac{1}{3}$
Popcorn	$\frac{1}{6}$
Fruit	$\frac{1}{6}$

11.

FAVORITE BOOKS	
Books	**Fraction of Class**
Mystery	$\frac{4}{12}$
Humor	$\frac{1}{2}$
Biography	$\frac{1}{6}$

12.

CLASS HAIR COLORS	
Color	**Fraction of Class**
Brown	$\frac{2}{5}$
Red	$\frac{1}{10}$
Blond	$\frac{1}{5}$
Black	$\frac{3}{10}$

Problem Solving Applications

Using Data For Problems 13–17, use the circle graph.

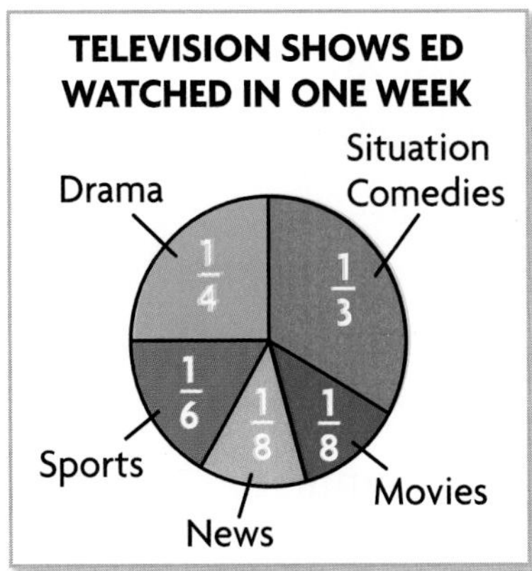

13. Ed watched 24 television shows during the week. How many drama shows did he watch?

14. Geometry How many degrees are in the angle that represents the amount of time Ed watched drama shows?

15. Write another fraction that represents the number of sports shows that Ed watched during the week.

16. Compare Which two angles are equal? How many degrees are in each angle?

17. **Write a problem** using the information in the circle graph.

Probability as a Ratio

Why learn this? You can analyze a game and figure out your chances of winning.

Eugene and Donna are playing a game, with the spinner shown below.

Eugene earns a point if the pointer lands on blue. Donna earns a point if the pointer lands on green. What is the probability that Eugene will earn a point when he spins?

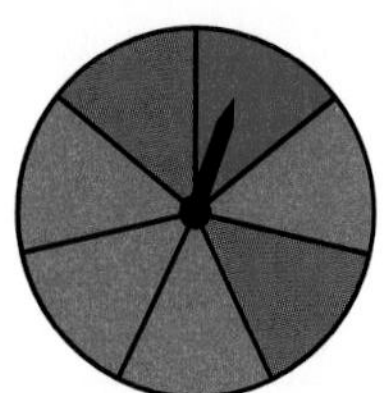

Probability of Eugene earning a point $= \frac{\text{blue sections}}{\text{all sections}}$

You can write probability as a part-to-whole ratio.

The probability that Eugene will earn a point is the ratio of the number of blue sections to the total number of sections.

So, the probability that Eugene will earn a point is 2 to 7, 2:7, or $\frac{2}{7}$.

Talk About It CRITICAL THINKING

- How would you write as a ratio the probability that Donna will not win a point when she spins?
- How is writing probability as a ratio the same as writing it as a fraction? How is it different?

▶ CHECK

For Exercises 1–6, use the spinner. Write each probability as a ratio in three ways.

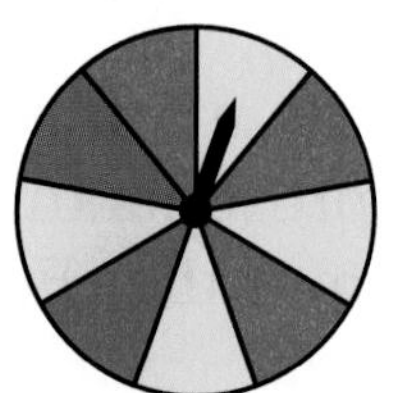

1. The pointer will land on red.

2. The pointer will land on yellow.

3. The pointer will not land on green.

4. The pointer will not land on blue.

5. The pointer will land on green or red.

6. The pointer will land on blue or yellow.

▶ PRACTICE

Write the probability of each outcome as a ratio in three ways.

7. Toss a number cube and get 5.

8. Toss a coin and get tails.

9. Spin the pointer and land on the number 4.

10. Spin the pointer and land on the number 3 or higher.

11. Toss a number cube and get an odd number.

12. Spin the pointer and land on a number less than 1.

Problem Solving Applications

Using Data For Problems 13–16, use the spinner.

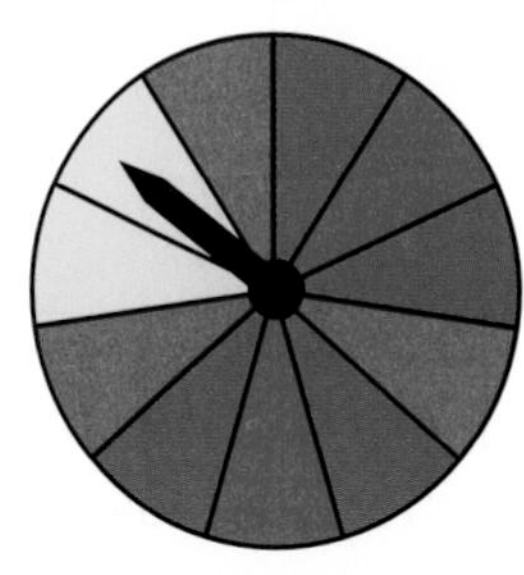

13. Franco earns a point if the pointer lands on red. Write as a ratio the probability that Franco will earn a point.

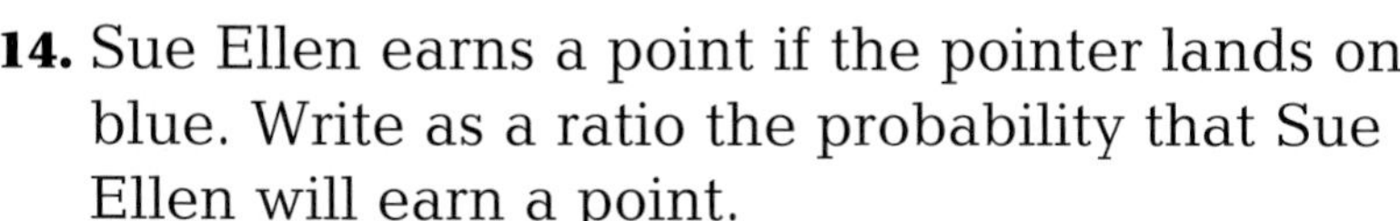

14. Sue Ellen earns a point if the pointer lands on blue. Write as a ratio the probability that Sue Ellen will earn a point.

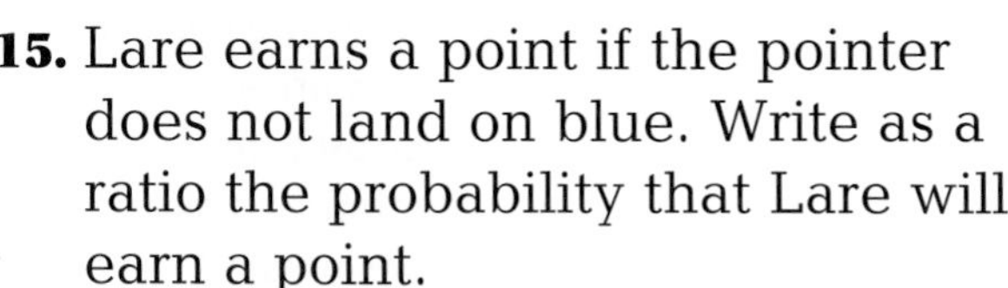

15. Lare earns a point if the pointer does not land on blue. Write as a ratio the probability that Lare will earn a point.

16. Eda earns a point if the pointer lands on either green, yellow, or blue. Write as a ratio the probability that Eda will earn a point.

17. If you put the names of all your classmates in a hat, what is the probability that you will draw a boy's name? Write the probability as a ratio in three ways.

18. Lily rolls a number cube labeled 2, 4, 6, 8, 10, and 12. What is the probability of the cube landing on 12? Write the probability as a ratio in three ways.

19. Randy pulls a marble from a bag of 1 blue, 4 green, 3 red, and 2 yellow marbles. What is the probability as a ratio that Randy will pull a green marble?

20. **Write a problem** using the spinner above in which you find the probability and write it as a ratio.

Finding Percent of a Number

Why learn this? You can find out the price of something on sale.

You can find a percent of any number, not just 100.

Kanesha likes to find bargains. She found a \$20 shirt marked "25 percent off." How much does it cost now?

What is 25 percent of \$20?
25% of \$20 = n

Here are two ways to find the percent of a number.

Use decimals.	OR	Use fractions.
Write 25% as a decimal: 0.25.		Write 25% as a fraction: $\frac{25}{100} = \frac{1}{4}$.
To find 0.25 of \$20, multiply:		To find $\frac{1}{4}$ of \$20, multiply:
$\begin{array}{r} \$20 \\ \times 0.25 \\ \hline \$5.00 \end{array}$ So, n = \$5.00.		$\frac{1}{4} \times \frac{20}{1} = \frac{20}{4} = \$5$ So, n = \$5.00

The shirt is \$5 off the regular price. \$20 − \$5 = \$15
So, the shirt now costs \$15.

You can use a calculator to find a percent of a number.

A \$60 jacket is on sale for 55 percent off.
55% of \$60 = n

Method 1      

Method 2         

So, n = \$33.
\$60 − \$33 = \$27
So, the sale price is \$27.

- Describe each method for finding the sale price.

CONSUMER LINK

How much will people pay for an item at a certain time? We all know that purchases can be affected by bargain prices. A sales manager uses this information to make the most sales possible over a period of time.

Which is the better sale price on a \$110 pair of in-line skates, \$20 off or 20 percent off?

▶ CHECK

Write the percent as a decimal and as a fraction in simplest form.

1. 37% **2.** 98% **3.** 10% **4.** 6%

5. 50% **6.** 25% **7.** 33% **8.** 100%

▶ PRACTICE

Use a decimal to find the percent.

9. 37% of 150 **10.** 98% of 50 **11.** 10% of 30 **12.** 12% of 33

13. 16% of 175 **14.** 20% of 500 **15.** 9% of 180 **16.** 90% of 350

Use a fraction to find the percent.

17. 50% of 200 **18.** 25% of 40 **19.** 10% of 260 **20.** 75% of 180

21. 40% of 280 **22.** 60% of 450 **23.** 16% of 600 **24.** 30% of 280

Use a calculator. Find the value of both numbers. Which is the greater value? Write *a* or *b*.

25. a. 40% of 25
b. 25% of 50

26. a. 50% of 32
b. 50% of 30

27. a. 90% of 150
b. 80% of 155

28. a. 50% of 400
b. 30% of 500

29. a. 7% of $650.00
b. 10% of $600.00

30. a. 75% of 53
b. 53% of 85

Problem Solving Applications

31. Consumer Ted wanted to buy a $100 bat at the sporting goods sale. He waited until Wednesday to buy it. How much did he pay?

32. Money Nick decided to buy a $22.00 basketball. He bought it on Tuesday. How much did he pay?

33. Money Jamie saw a mitt that cost $39.00. She bought it on Monday. How much did she pay?

34. Money Tonya is stocking up on $4.50 baseballs. She bought 3 on Wednesday. What was her bill?

35. Kyle bought a belt for his baseball uniform. The regular price of it was $4.95. How much was it on Tuesday?

36. **Write a problem** about something Jody bought at the sporting goods sale.

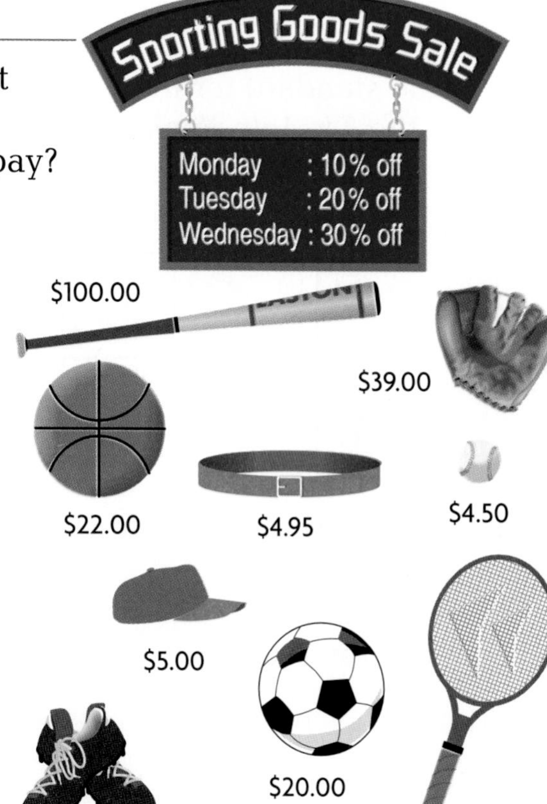

CALCULATOR Activities

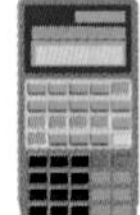

ASTRONOMICAL NUMBERS!

Powers of 10, Exponents, and Scientific Notation

A number written in scientific notation is expressed as a product of two factors. The first factor is equal to or greater than 1, but less than 10. The second factor is a power of 10.

The 10ⁿ and 10ˣ keys show how many times 10 is multiplied by itself. (HINT: 10^2 means 10×10, or 100.)

Standard form		Scientific notation
700,000	=	7.0×10^5
6,210,000	=	6.21×10^6

REMEMBER:

Expanded form is a way to write numbers by showing the sum of the value of each digit.

432 = 400 + 30 + 2
↑
standard form

Our galaxy, the Milky Way, contains at least 9.9×10^7 stars. How can you write this number in standard form?

Using the Calculator

To find the standard form of 9.9×10^7 by using the *TI Math Explorer*, enter the following:

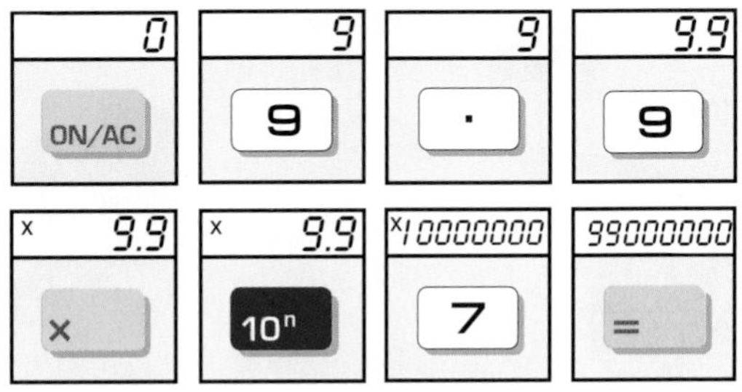

To find the standard form of 9.9×10^7 by using the *Casio fx-55*, enter the following:

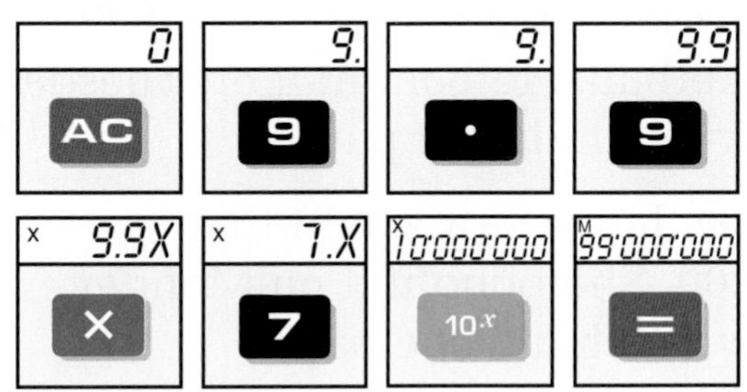

So, 9.9×10^7 written in standard form is 99,000,000.

▶ PRACTICE

Use your calculator to solve.

1. Write 3.42×10^6 in standard form.
2. Write 2.0×10^3 in standard form.
3. Write 528,000 in scientific notation.
4. Write 37,000,000 in scientific notation.

SUPER BOWL MADNESS!

Repeated Operations

It was the halftime of the Super Bowl. The Green Bay Packers were trailing the Denver Broncos by a score of 21–10. In a comeback, the Packers won the game 22–21, scoring only 3-point field goals. How many field goals did they make in the second half of the game?

REMEMBER:

Calculators are very useful tools for performing constant operations such as adding, subtracting, multiplying, or dividing the same number many times. Some calculators have a special Cons key. Other calculators use the = key.

Using the Calculator

To find the answer by using the *TI Math Explorer*, enter the following:

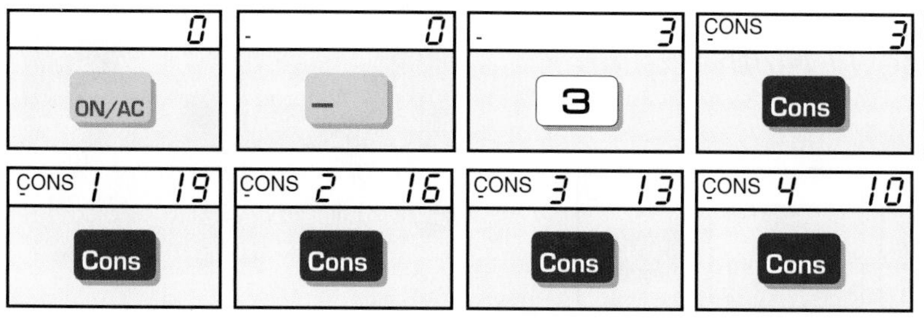

To find the answer by using the *Casio fx-55*, enter the following:

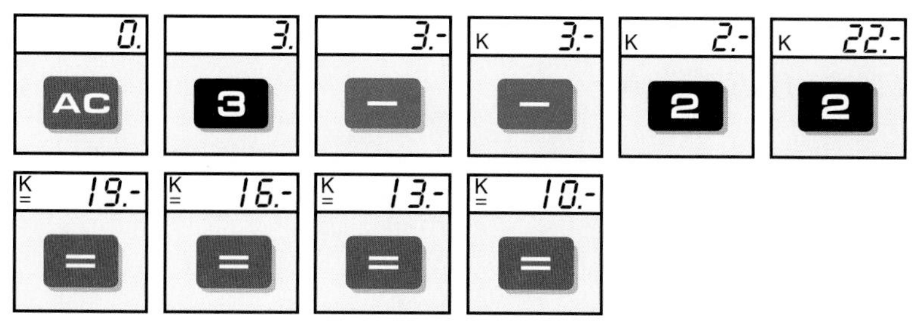

So, the Packers made 4 field goals in the second half.

▶ PRACTICE

Use your calculator to solve.

1. Two teams were tied 21–21 going into the third quarter. If one team won with a total of 49 points, how many touchdowns, at 7 points each including the "point after," did they score?
2. The New York Giants scored only field goals in their 21–18 loss to the Chicago Bears. How many field goals did they score?

Solve by using a constant operation.

3. Start with 12. Add the same number 6 times.
4. Start with 25. Multiply the same number 3 times.

GOODNESS GROCERIES!

Multistep Problems

The memory keys are used to store numbers. The M+ key stores the product. The MR key recalls the product from memory. The MC key on the *Casio fx-55* clears the number stored.

Lucy bought 4 two-pound bags of apples. The pears she bought weighed 5 pounds. She also bought some oranges. The total weight of the fruit Lucy bought was 17 pounds. How much did the oranges weigh?

Using the Calculator

To find the answer by using the *TI Math Explorer*, enter the following:

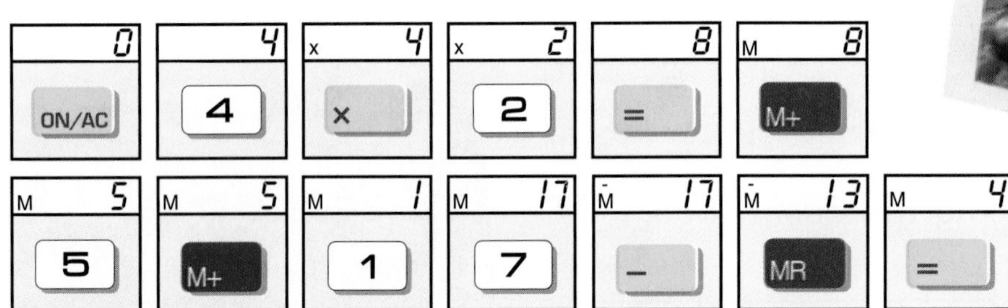

To find the answer by using the *Casio fx-55*, enter the following:

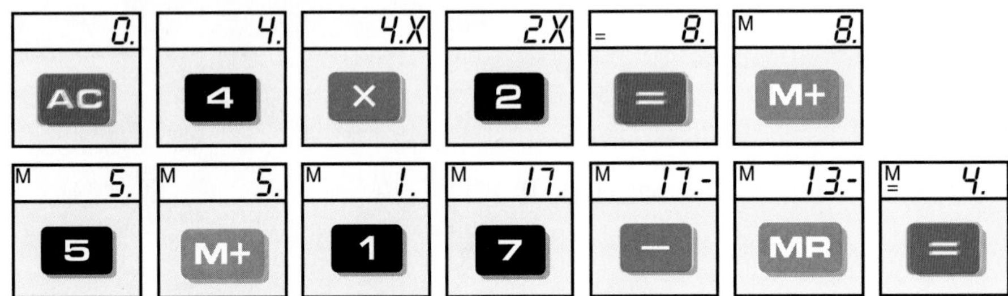

So, the oranges weighed 4 pounds.

▶ PRACTICE

Use your calculator to solve.

1. There are 6 dozen blueberry muffins on the top shelf of the store. On the next shelf, there are 9 trays of banana muffins with 8 muffins in each tray. How many muffins are there in all?

2. A carton of apple juice holds 6 juice packs. A carton of grape juice holds 8 juice packs. There are 24 cartons of grape juice. There are 12 more cartons of apple juice than of grape juice. How many juice packs are there in all?

A BREAKFAST BONANZA!

Multiplication Properties, Order of Operations

Do the operation in the parentheses first when computing the answer.

$4 + (5 \times 7) - (4 \times 3) = \underline{\ ?\ }$

$4 + 35 - 12 = 27$

Ernesto has 10 math cards from a box of cereal. To win a prize, he must order the cards in such a way that the answer is 12. Ernesto used his calculator to help him. This is the order of Ernesto's cards. Use your calculator to check whether the answer really is 12.

$36 \div (3 + 3) \times 2$

Using the Calculator

To check the answer by using the *TI Math Explorer*, enter the following:

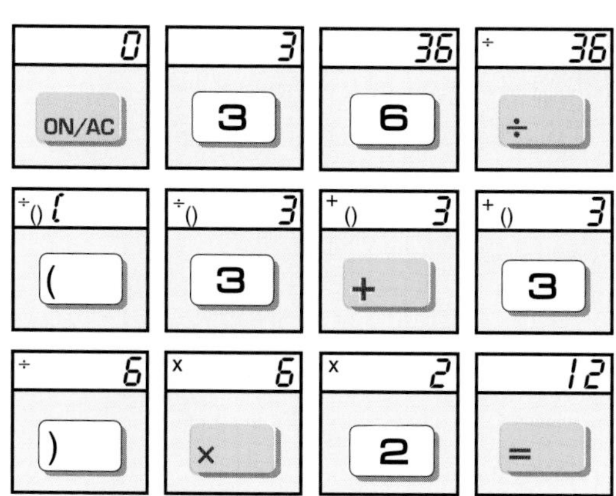

To check the answer by using the *Casio fx-55*, enter the following:

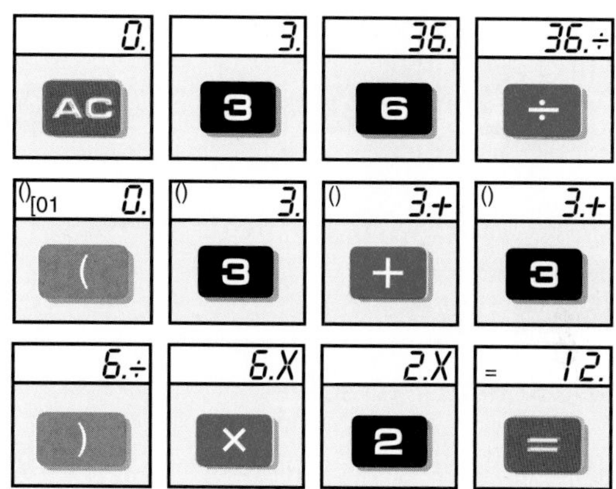

Yes, Ernesto's card arrangement results in an answer of 12.

▶ PRACTICE

Use your calculator to solve. Check each statement. Write *true* or *false*.

1. $(16 - 2) - 8 \div 2 = 10$

2. $62 - (12 - 10) \times 18.3 = 36.6$

Write parentheses to make the statement true.

3. $28 - 8 \div 7 - 3 = 5$

4. $4 \times 9 - 5 \div 8 = 2$

5. $6 \times 3 \div 12 + 6 = 1$

6. $3 \times 13 - 7 - 11 = 7$

7. $5 \times 6 - 3 \div 3 = 5$

8. $32 \div 2 + 2 \times 3 = 24$

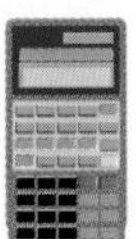

VAN-TASTIC VOYAGE!
Divide with Remainders

The integer keys, INT÷ and ÷R, allow you to show a quotient and a remainder separately.

Ms. Diaz's chess club traveled in a van for 64 days to cities hosting chess tournaments last summer. About how many weeks is that?

Using the Calculator

To find the answer by using the *TI Math Explorer*, enter the following:

To find the answer by using the *Casio fx-55*, enter the following:

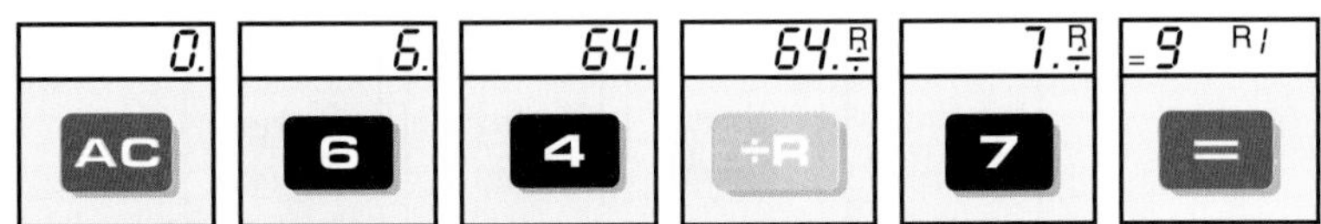

So, they traveled for about 9 weeks.

To check the answer of a division problem, multiply the quotient by the divisor, and then add the remainder. The answer is the dividend.

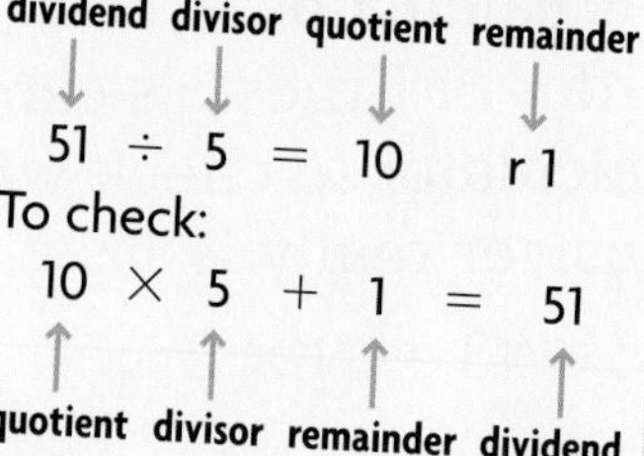

▶ PRACTICE

Use your calculator to solve.

1. Magellan's ship returned to Spain after sailing for 155 weeks. About how many years is that? (HINT: There are about 52 weeks in a year.)
2. A hot-air balloon crossed the Atlantic Ocean in 98 hours. About how many days is that?
3. The chess tournament lasted 118 hours. About how many days is that?

Use your calculator to estimate the quotient.

4. $58 \div 6 = n$
5. $126 \div 16 = n$
6. $408 \div 32 = n$

HAVE YOUR CAKE AND EAT IT TOO!

Equivalent Fractions

Jeffrey ate 4 pieces of his birthday cake. The cake was cut into 8 equal pieces. So, Jeffrey ate $\frac{4}{8}$ of the cake. Is $\frac{4}{8}$ in simplest form, or can $\frac{4}{8}$ be renamed as an equivalent fraction? You can use your calculator to check.

REMEMBER:

Equivalent fractions are fractions that name the same amount.

$\frac{16}{24} = \frac{8}{12} = \frac{4}{6} = \frac{2}{3}$

Note that $\frac{2}{3}$ cannot be simplified further. So, $\frac{16}{24}$ written in simplest form is $\frac{2}{3}$.

Using the Calculator

To find the equivalent fraction written in simplest form by using the *TI Math Explorer*, enter the following:

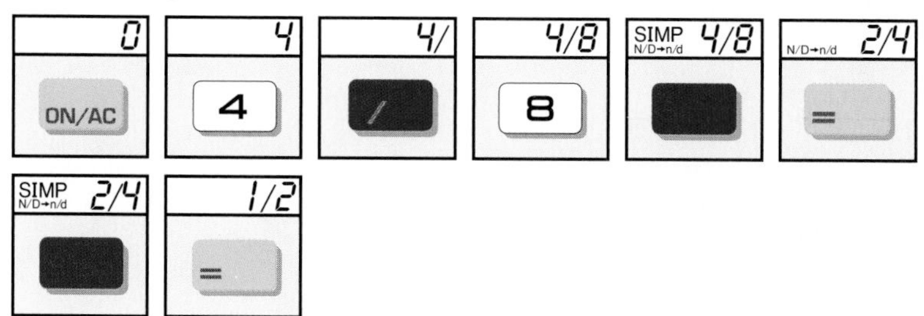

To find the equivalent fraction in simplest form by using the *Casio fx-55*, enter the following:

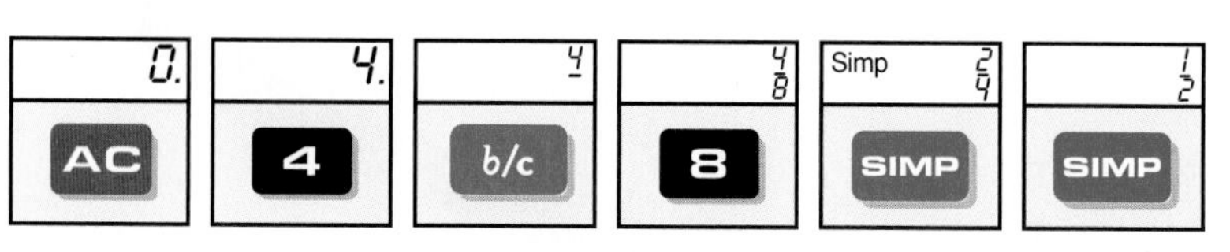

So, $\frac{4}{8}$ in simplest form is $\frac{1}{2}$.

▶ PRACTICE

Use your calculator.

1. Juan was also at Jeffrey's birthday party. He ate $\frac{6}{16}$ of the cake. What is $\frac{6}{16}$ in simplest form?

2. Who ate more cake, Jeffrey or Juan?

Write the fraction in simplest form.

3. $\frac{5}{25}$ **4.** $\frac{12}{48}$ **5.** $\frac{26}{39}$

6. $\frac{4}{16}$ **7.** $\frac{16}{32}$ **8.** $\frac{28}{49}$

9. $\frac{45}{55}$ **10.** $\frac{27}{36}$ **11.** $\frac{10}{35}$

ALL ABOARD!

Mixed Numbers

REMEMBER:

A fraction can have a numerator that is greater than or equal to its denominator.

$\frac{10}{7}$ ← numerator
← denominator

Jim has tracks for a train set. He has 35 parts that are each $\frac{1}{4}$ of a circle. How many complete circles can he make? How many parts will be left?

Using the Calculator

To find the answer by using the *TI Math Explorer*, enter the following:

To find the answer by using the *Casio fx-55*, enter the following:

So, Jim can make 8 complete circles with 3 parts left.

▶ PRACTICE

Use your calculator to solve.

1. If Jim buys double the amount of parts so that he has 70 parts, will the number of circles double too?

2. How many circles can Jim make if he has 70 parts?

Change these fractions to mixed numbers.

3. $\frac{23}{11} = n$ **4.** $\frac{307}{3} = n$

5. $\frac{73}{7} = n$ **6.** $\frac{50}{3} = n$

7. $\frac{87}{12} = n$ **8.** $\frac{746}{6} = n$

9. $\frac{124}{8} = n$ **10.** $\frac{29}{9} = n$

WORKING IN A WOOD-WORKING WONDERLAND!

Adding and Subtracting Mixed Numbers

Larry is helping his dad build shelves. He has a board that measures $11\frac{7}{12}$ ft. It is to be used in a spot that will be $9\frac{3}{4}$ ft. How much of the board must be cut off?

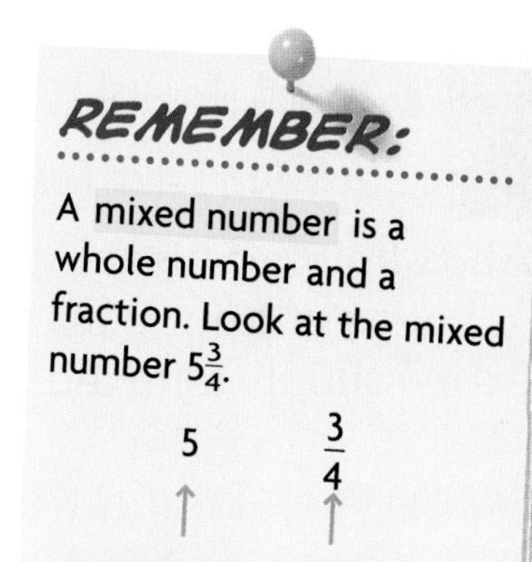

Using the Calculator

To find the answer by using the *TI Math Explorer*, enter the following:

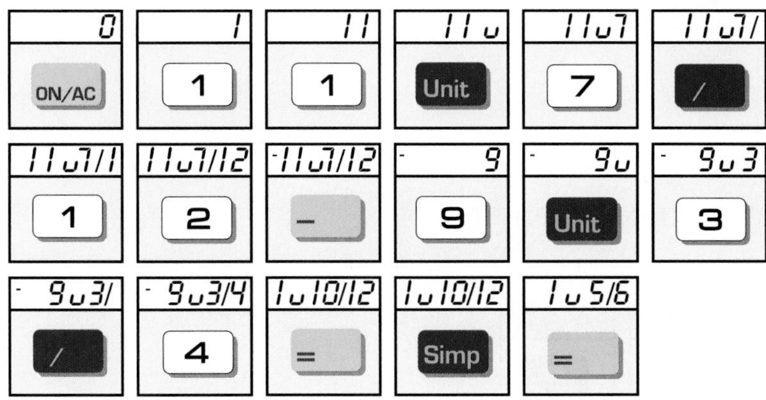

To find the answer by using the *Casio fx-55*, enter the following:

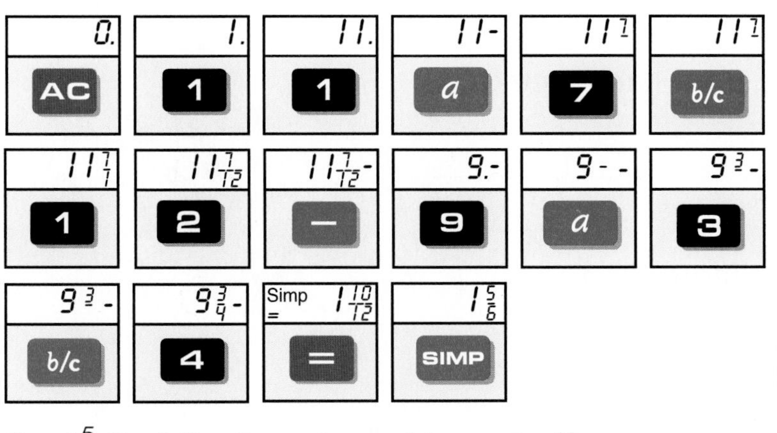

So, $1\frac{5}{6}$ ft of the board must be cut off.

▶ PRACTICE

Use your calculator to solve.

1. $16\frac{4}{11} + 17\frac{1}{6}$

2. $19\frac{2}{3} + 39\frac{3}{4} + 67\frac{4}{9}$

BABA'S BAKERY

Changing to Mixed Numbers

Ali is helping his father in his bakery. His father uses $\frac{110}{4}$ bags of flour each week. How many bags is that expressed as a mixed number?

REMEMBER:

To change a fraction to a mixed number, divide the numerator by the denominator. The quotient is the whole number, the remainder is the new numerator, and the denominator remains the same.

quotient

$\frac{15}{4} = 3\frac{3}{4}$ **remainder**

denominator

Using the Calculator

To find the answer by using the *TI Math Explorer*, enter the following:

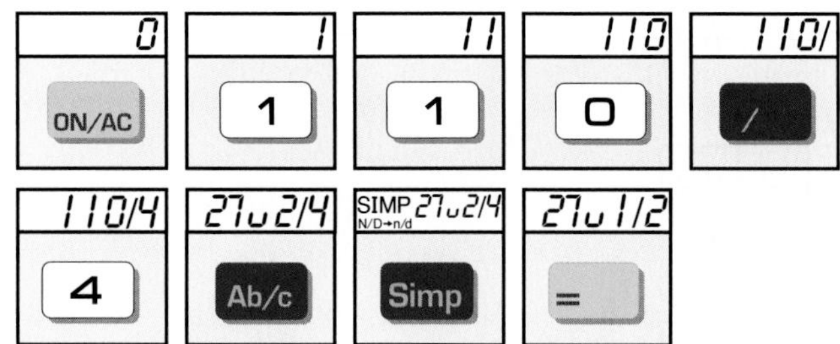

To find the answer by using the *Casio fx-55*, enter the following:

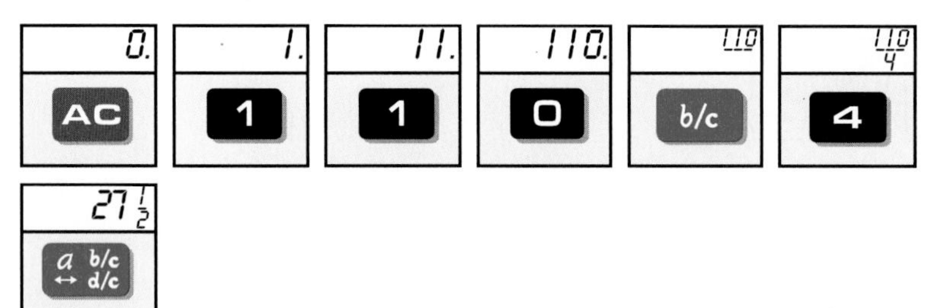

So, Ali's father uses $27\frac{1}{2}$ bags of flour each week.

▶ PRACTICE

Use your calculator to solve.

1. If Ali needed $\frac{180}{8}$ bags, is that more than or less than $27\frac{1}{2}$ bags?

2. Express $\frac{180}{8}$ as a mixed number.

Change the fractions to mixed numbers.

3. $\frac{155}{12}$ **4.** $\frac{203}{24}$

5. $\frac{300}{69}$ **6.** $\frac{155}{45}$

TO THE POINT!
Decimal Operations

Terminating decimals, such as 0.56 and 11.358, have a definite number of decimal places.

Repeating decimals, such as 0.3333... and 0.363636..., have a pattern that continues indefinitely. Repeating decimals can be written with a bar over the digit or digits that repeat.

$0.333... = 0.\overline{3}$ $\quad$ $0.13636... = 0.1\overline{36}$

Ed and Fred divided the number 0.4 by 9.9 on their calculators. Then they used a shortcut to write the quotient. What quotient did the calculators display? What is the shortcut that Ed and Fred used to write the quotient?

Using the Calculator

To find the quotient for 0.4 ÷ 9.9, enter the following on the *TI Math Explorer:*

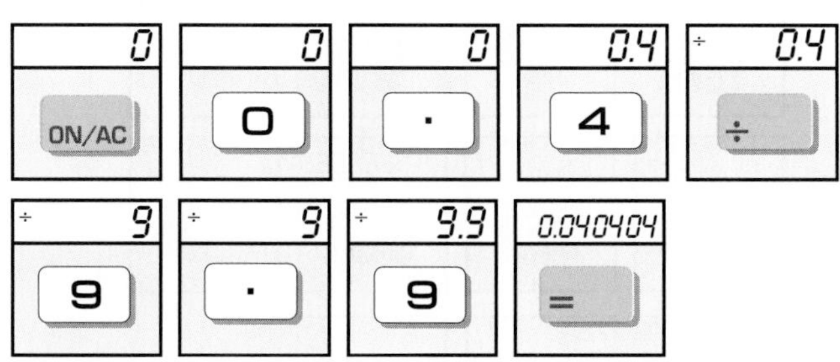

To find the quotient for 0.4 ÷ 9.9, enter the following on the *Casio fx-55*:

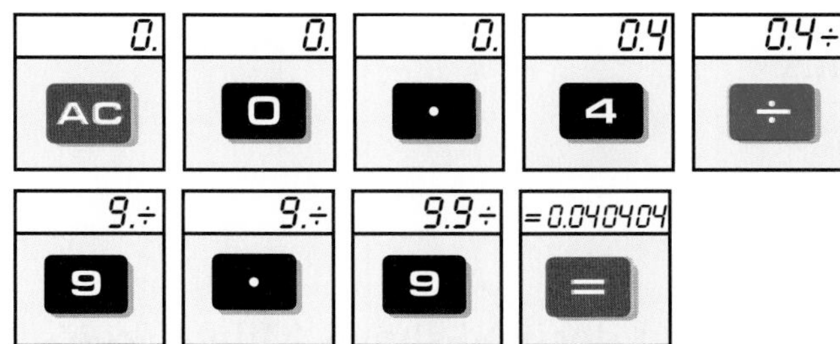

So, the calculators displayed 0.040404. Ed and Fred wrote $0.\overline{04}$.

▶ PRACTICE

Use your calculator to solve. If the answer is a repeating decimal, write your answer with a bar over the repeating digit or digits.

1. 0.6 ÷ 9.9 **2.** \$30.55 − \$25.88 **3.** 7.8 × 6.1

4. \$5.17 + \$4.33 **5.** 6.3 ÷ 9.9 **6.** 23.8 ÷ 0.99

SHOOTING HOOPS!

Decimal Estimation

By using the fix key FIX, you can tell the calculator how many decimal places you want to see in the answer.

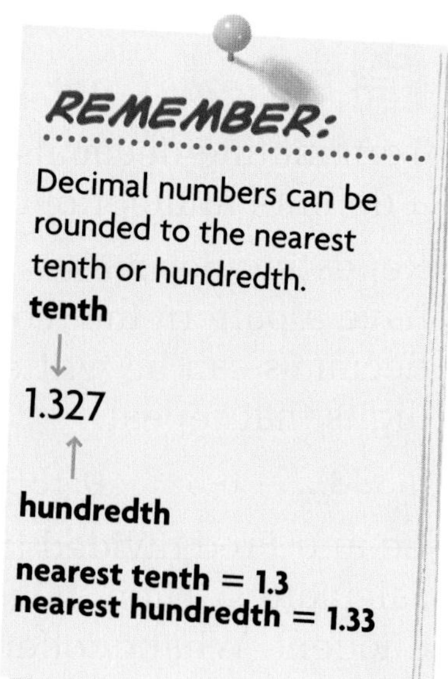

After the first 30 games of the season, the standings look like this. Since Chicago has won 29 games, what decimal number shows their wins to the nearest thousandth?

Team	W	L	
1 - Chicago	29	1	
1 - Detroit	25	5	
1 - Indiana			0.800
1 - Milwaukee	16	14	
1 - Atlanta			0.400

Using the Calculator

To find the answer by using the *TI Math Explorer*, enter the following:

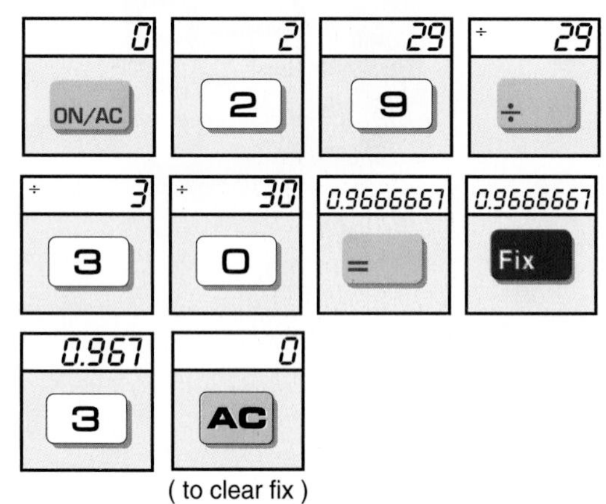

(to clear fix)

To find the answer by using the *Casio fx-55*, enter the following:

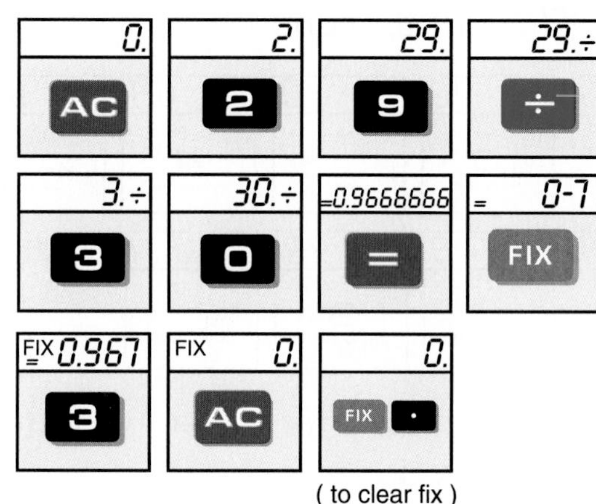

(to clear fix)

So, 0.967 shows Chicago's number of wins.

▶ PRACTICE

Use the standings and your calculator to solve.

1. What decimal shows Detroit's wins to the nearest thousandth?

2. What decimal shows Milwaukee's wins to the nearest thousandth?

3. How many games has Indiana won so far? (HINT: Multiply by the number of games.)

4. How many games has Atlanta won so far?

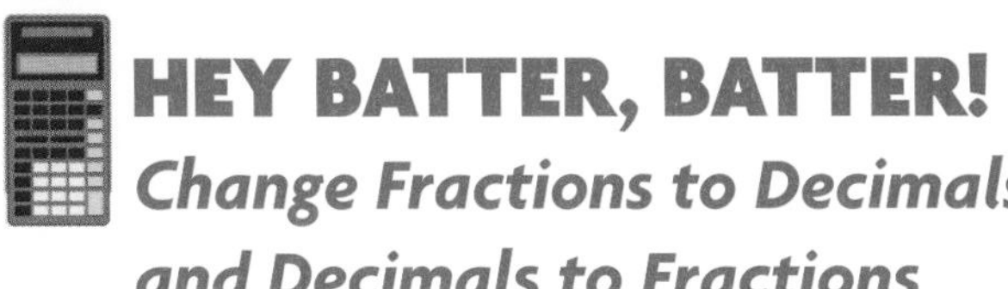

HEY BATTER, BATTER!

Change Fractions to Decimals and Decimals to Fractions

Tracy has a 0.250 batting average. What fraction of her times at bat does she get a hit?

REMEMBER:

Fractions and decimals that are equal are different ways of expressing the same number.

$0.4 = \frac{4}{10}$

$0.79 = \frac{79}{100}$

Using the Calculator

To find the answer by using the *TI Math Explorer*, enter the following:

To find the answer by using the *Casio fx-55*, enter the following:

So, Tracy hits the ball $\frac{1}{4}$ of the times she is at bat.

▶ PRACTICE

Use your calculator to solve.

1. Last year Tracy got a hit 2 out of every 5 times she batted. What decimal can you write that shows her number of hits to the nearest thousandth?

2. Her friend Joe got 1 hit out of every 3 times he batted. What decimal can you write that shows his number of hits to the nearest thousandth?

Change the following decimals to fractions.

3. 0.75 **4.** 0.80 **5.** 0.625

6. 0.45 **7.** 0.35 **8.** 0.40

9. 0.375 **10.** 0.25 **11.** 0.875

More Practice

Chapter 1

Lesson 1.1 (pages 2–3)

Tell whether the number in each picture is expressed as *cardinal, ordinal,* or *nominal.*

1. 

2. 

5 Students

3. 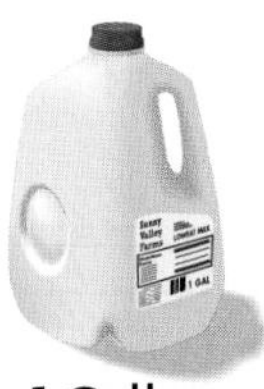

1 Gallon

4. 

Tell whether each number is expressed as *cardinal, ordinal,* or *nominal.*

5. Matthew is 1st in line.

6. Today the temperature is 56°F.

7. got home at 5 o'clock.

8. There are 33 cookies in the jar.

9. Donald is 6 feet tall.

10. I live in the 5th house on the left.

11. My address is 951 Southside Avenue.

12. There are 842 students in our school.

Lesson 1.2 (pages 4–5)

Use the benchmark number to choose the more reasonable estimate.

1. jelly beans in a jar
35 or 135

2. pretzels in a bag
20 or 200

3. marbles in a jar
50 or 250

Write *yes* or *no* to tell whether the estimate is reasonable. Explain.

4. • 12 rolls of pennies
• 50 pennies in a roll
Estimate: There is about $60.00.

5. • 90 safety pins
• 20 boxes in the store
Estimate: There are about 2,000 safety pins in the store.

6. • 30 students in a class
• 5 fifth-grade classrooms
Estimate: There are about 1,000 students in the fifth grade.

7. • 8 muffins in a box
• 20 boxes in the bakery
Estimate: There are about 200 muffins in the bakery.

Lesson 1.3 (pages 6–7)

Write the value of the blue digit.

1. 967,522 **2.** 876,534 **3.** 523,792 **4.** 117,964

5. 356,178 **6.** 692,042 **7.** 474,392 **8.** 296,574

Write the expanded numbers in standard form.

9. 90,000 + 2,000 + 0 + 40 + 6

10. 100,000 + 70,000 + 6,000 + 300 + 90 + 6

11. 200,000 + 90,000 + 9,000 + 400 + 0 + 4

12. 900,000 + 0 + 0 + 0 + 40 + 6

13. 300,000 + 40,000 + 9,000 + 0 + 30 + 7

14. 200,000 + 90,000 + 6,000 + 100 + 40 + 0

Lesson 1.4 (pages 8–11)

Write the value of the blue digit.

1. 38,107,692 **2.** 57,192,411 **3.** 192,096,422 **4.** 872,429,792

5. 296,172,045 **6.** 517,429,691 **7.** 4,723,806,125 **8.** 1,264,511,366

Write two other forms for each number.

9. 75,192,026

10. 529,100,845

11. 600,000,000 + 0 + 7,000,000 + 200,000 + 10,000 + 0 + 0 + 0 + 8

12. eight hundred thirty-six million, seven hundred nine thousand, ten

Lesson 1.5 Part 1 (pages 12–13)

Write $<$, $>$, or $=$ for each ●.

1. 526 ● 562 **2.** 7,320 ● 7,302 **3.** 8,912 ● 8,912

4. 4,919 ● 4,119 **5.** 192,113 ● 192,113 **6.** 18,095 ● 18,950

Order from greatest to least.

7. 356; 536; 365 **8.** 5,912; 5,129; 9,512 **9.** 8,460; 8,406; 8,640

Order from least to greatest.

10. 17,562; 15,652; 17,265 **11.** 11,509; 11,905; 11,095 **12.** 312,962; 319,962; 312,692

Lesson 1.5 Part 2 (pages 14–15)

Use a table to solve.

ELEMENTARY SCHOOL POPULATIONS	
Elementary School	**Populations**
Sunnyside	1,020
Oakwood	900
Greenview	850
Palm	920
Greyfield	1,300
West Creek	1,100

1. This table shows some elementary schools and their student populations. Which elementary school has the greatest population? the least population?

2. What is the population difference in the school with the greatest population and the school with the least population?

Chapter 2

Lesson 2.1 (pages 20–21)

For Exercises 1–5, use the data in the table.

LION'S FOOTBALL GAME SCORES 1998-99	
Game	**Score**
1	21
2	14
3	6
4	31
5	28

1. How many points were scored by the end of Games 1–4?

2. How many points were scored in Games 1 and 2 combined?

3. How many more points were scored in Game 4 than in Game 2?

4. How many points in all were scored during the 1998-99 season?

5. How many more points were scored in the 1998–99 season than the 79 points scored in 1997–98?

Write the related number sentence. Find the sum or difference.

6. $76 - 35 = n$ **7.** $131 - 69 = n$ **8.** $145 - 56 = n$

9. $38 + n = 79$ **10.** $46 + n = 97$ **11.** $63 + n = 165$

Solve. Use the inverse operation to check each problem.

12. $\begin{array}{r} 18 \\ +34 \\ \hline \end{array}$ **13.** $\begin{array}{r} 53 \\ -32 \\ \hline \end{array}$ **14.** $\begin{array}{r} 56 \\ +26 \\ \hline \end{array}$ **15.** $\begin{array}{r} 149 \\ -\ 58 \\ \hline \end{array}$

Lesson 2.2 (pages 22–23)

Find the difference. You may use counters.

1. $\begin{array}{r} 394 \\ -145 \\ \hline \end{array}$ **2.** $\begin{array}{r} 566 \\ -217 \\ \hline \end{array}$ **3.** $\begin{array}{r} 721 \\ -386 \\ \hline \end{array}$ **4.** $\begin{array}{r} 419 \\ -198 \\ \hline \end{array}$ **5.** $\begin{array}{r} 682 \\ -591 \\ \hline \end{array}$ **6.** $\begin{array}{r} 5,626 \\ -3,533 \\ \hline \end{array}$ **7.** $\begin{array}{r} 7,963 \\ -4,576 \\ \hline \end{array}$

Lesson 2.3 (pages 24–25)

Find the difference.

1. 100 − 72	**2.** 360 −219	**3.** $7.00 − 4.17	**4.** 900 −681	**5.** 750 −192
6. $8.00 − 3.16	**7.** $20.00 − 13.95	**8.** $40.08 − 17.76	**9.** 400 −264	**10.** $10.00 − 5.62
11. 6,007 − 434	**12.** 40,000 −24,916	**13.** 17,000 −11,326	**14.** 8,000 − 965	**15.** 70,000 −49,566
16. 3,020 −1,492	**17.** 54,000 −32,782	**18.** 27,546 − 8,493	**19.** 13,009 − 9,148	**20.** 15,120 − 6,299

Lesson 2.4 (pages 26–27)

Choose and name the operation. Solve.

1. Natalie has 48 books and Holly has 39 books. How many books do the two friends have together?

2. There were 11,561 fans at Game 1 and 15,907 fans at Game 2. How many more fans attended Game 2?

3. Charles traveled 360 miles from Springfield to Roxboro, and 576 miles from Roxboro to Brookstown. How many miles did Charles travel in all?

4. Felicia bought in-line skates for $36.50 and knee pads for 11.95. How much did Felicia spend for the two items?

Lesson 2.5 Part 1 (pages 28–29)

Choose a method and estimate each sum.

1. 15 18 25 +42	**2.** 36 41 84 +86	**3.** 26 92 41 +36	**4.** 42 39 62 +71	**5.** 29 35 56 +23
6. 15 263 198 +107	**7.** 342 407 569 +186	**8.** 198 206 476 +338	**9.** 426 396 707 +299	**10.** 945 862 787 +806
11. 103 268 214 +327	**12.** 116 110 133 +192	**13.** 205 122 540 +616	**14.** 411 912 502 +416	**15.** 134 205 897 +343

Lesson 2.5 Part 2 (pages 30–31)

Decide whether you need to estimate, find the exact answer, or both. Solve.

1. Ron had $15.00 to spend at the movies. He spent $6.50 on the ticket, $3.79 on popcorn, and $2.35 on a drink. Does he have enough left over to spend $5.00 in the game room after the movie?

2. Sabrina had $15.00. She bought a binder for $3.15, a box of pencils for $2.75, and a pack of notebooks for $5.99. How much did she spend on the items? How much change did she receive?

Chapter 3

Lesson 3.1 (pages 36–37)

Write the letter of the decimal that matches each model.

1. 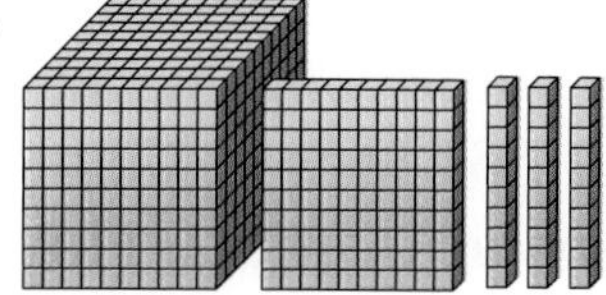

2. 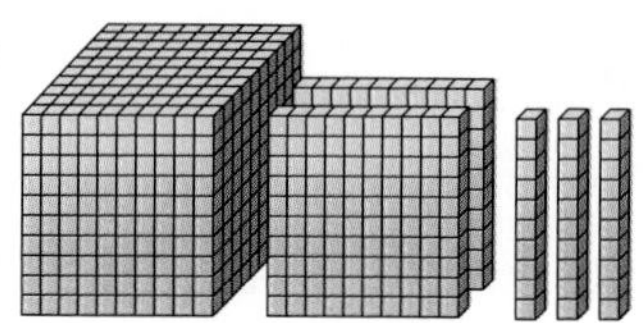

3. 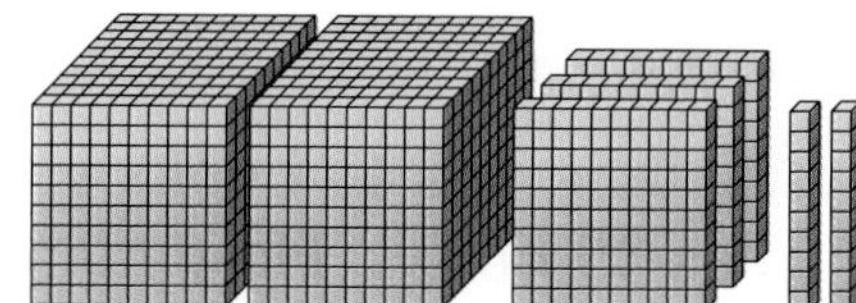

a. 2.32 **b.** 1.13 **c.** 1.23

Write the decimal.

4. one and seven tenths

5. fifteen hundredths

6. two and three hundredths

7. four hundredths

8. seven and twenty-one hundredths

9. five and five hundredths

10. one and eight tenths

11. three and four hundredths

12. sixty-eight hundredths

Lesson 3.2 (pages 38–39)

Write in standard form.

1. six thousandths

2. four and nine thousandths

3. one and twelve thousandths

4. forty-five thousandths

5. two hundred six thousandths

6. three and seventy-seven thousandths

7. one and one thousandth

8. nine and one hundred twenty-two thousandths

Write in written form.

9. 0.008

10. 0.063

11. 0.367

12. 2.019

Lesson 3.3 (pages 40–41)

Write in standard form.

1. 3,000 + 100 + 90 + 2 + 0.3 + 0.09 + 0.002
2. five thousand, two hundred sixty-four and two hundred nine thousandths
3. 1,000 + 600 + 20 + 3 + 0.1 + 0.01 + 0.007
4. four thousand, three hundred three and thirty thousandths
5. 1,000 + 700 + 20 + 0 + 0.3 + 0 + 0.002
6. two thousand, three hundred six and forty-six thousandths

Write the value of the digit 5 in each number.

7. 2,356.019
8. 1,303.056
9. 2,163.516
10. 4,928.165

Lesson 3.4 (pages 42–43)

Write an equivalent decimal for each.

1. 0.08
2. 0.30
3. 0.42
4. 1.7
5. 7.650
6. 3.64
7. 0.090
8. 0.400
9. 6.30
10. 0.8
11. 7.9
12. 0.830
13. 1.09
14. 0.51
15. 4.07

Lesson 3.5 Part 1 (pages 44–45)

Write $<$, $>$, or $=$ for each ●.

1. 0.72 ● 0.73
2. 5.31 ● 5.13
3. 6.19 ● 6.190
4. 1.41 ● 14.1
5. 7.09 ● 7.090
6. 67.19 ● 67.019
7. 3.17 ● 3.170
8. 21.86 ● 2.186
9. 696.131 ● 696.113

Order from least to greatest.

10. 3.19, 3.09, 3.11
11. 14.36, 14.63, 14.29
12. 5.01, 5.011, 5.10

Lesson 3.5 Part 2 (pages 46–47)

Make a table to solve.

1. Alisha, Sandra, and Donald went to the school nurse. Alisha's temperature was 98.9° F, and Sandra's temperature was 98.6°F, and Donald's temperature was 99.1°F. Put the temperatures in order from highest to lowest.
2. Jeff ran the race in 5.39 minutes, Kevin ran in 5.37 minutes, and Darren ran in 5.49 minutes. The lowest time wins the race. Who won the race? Who came in second? third?

Chapter 4

Lesson 4.1 (pages 52–53)

Use base-ten blocks to model. Record the sum on a place-value chart.

1. $\begin{array}{r} 0.2 \\ +0.6 \\ \hline \end{array}$ **2.** $\begin{array}{r} 0.5 \\ +0.5 \\ \hline \end{array}$ **3.** $\begin{array}{r} 1.32 \\ +0.53 \\ \hline \end{array}$ **4.** $\begin{array}{r} 0.42 \\ +1.08 \\ \hline \end{array}$ **5.** $\begin{array}{r} 1.342 \\ +0.657 \\ \hline \end{array}$

Find the sum.

6. $\begin{array}{r} 3.2 \\ +1.3 \\ \hline \end{array}$ **7.** $\begin{array}{r} 4.9 \\ +5.6 \\ \hline \end{array}$ **8.** $\begin{array}{r} 2.75 \\ +0.56 \\ \hline \end{array}$ **9.** $\begin{array}{r} 5.17 \\ +4.09 \\ \hline \end{array}$ **10.** $\begin{array}{r} 1.36 \\ +1.42 \\ \hline \end{array}$

11. $\begin{array}{r} 6.18 \\ +3.76 \\ \hline \end{array}$ **12.** $\begin{array}{r} 1.726 \\ +0.192 \\ \hline \end{array}$ **13.** $\begin{array}{r} 3.092 \\ +1.563 \\ \hline \end{array}$ **14.** $\begin{array}{r} 7.136 \\ +2.468 \\ \hline \end{array}$ **15.** $\begin{array}{r} 2.306 \\ +1.434 \\ \hline \end{array}$

Lesson 4.2 (pages 54–55)

Use an equivalent decimal to find the sum.

1. $3.17 + 0.326 = n$ **2.** $1.094 + 3.2 = n$ **3.** $8 + 4.29 = n$

4. $7.42 + 2.163 = n$ **5.** $24.7 + 16.172 = n$ **6.** $13.92 + 4.396 = n$

7. $\begin{array}{r} 6 \\ +0.7 \\ \hline \end{array}$ **8.** $\begin{array}{r} 3.5 \\ +1.36 \\ \hline \end{array}$ **9.** $\begin{array}{r} 4.09 \\ +0.328 \\ \hline \end{array}$ **10.** $\begin{array}{r} 6 \\ +2.88 \\ \hline \end{array}$ **11.** $\begin{array}{r} 4.291 \\ +0.34 \\ \hline \end{array}$

12. $\begin{array}{r} 4.9 \\ +3.16 \\ \hline \end{array}$ **13.** $\begin{array}{r} 7.96 \\ +4.012 \\ \hline \end{array}$ **14.** $\begin{array}{r} 9.1 \\ +0.756 \\ \hline \end{array}$ **15.** $\begin{array}{r} 4.372 \\ +2.4 \\ \hline \end{array}$ **16.** $\begin{array}{r} 13.2 \\ +\ 6.07 \\ \hline \end{array}$

Lesson 4.3 (pages 56–57)

Find the difference.

1. $\begin{array}{r} 1.7 \\ -0.6 \\ \hline \end{array}$ **2.** $\begin{array}{r} 3.9 \\ -3.3 \\ \hline \end{array}$ **3.** $\begin{array}{r} 3.06 \\ -2.4 \\ \hline \end{array}$ **4.** $\begin{array}{r} 6.5 \\ -5.8 \\ \hline \end{array}$ **5.** $\begin{array}{r} 6.7 \\ -3.05 \\ \hline \end{array}$

6. $\begin{array}{r} 6.26 \\ -4.13 \\ \hline \end{array}$ **7.** $\begin{array}{r} 3.2 \\ -2.345 \\ \hline \end{array}$ **8.** $\begin{array}{r} 9.463 \\ -4.96 \\ \hline \end{array}$ **9.** $\begin{array}{r} 11.179 \\ -8.186 \\ \hline \end{array}$ **10.** $\begin{array}{r} 17.492 \\ -11.36 \\ \hline \end{array}$

11. $2.96 - 1.78 = n$ **12.** $4.9 - 1.326 = n$ **13.** $6.92 - 4.176 = n$

Lesson 4.4 (pages 58–59)

Estimate the sum or difference to the nearest tenth.

1. $\begin{array}{r} 6.78 \\ +2.83 \\ \hline \end{array}$ **2.** $\begin{array}{r} 7.82 \\ +3.79 \\ \hline \end{array}$ **3.** $\begin{array}{r} 5.69 \\ -4.25 \\ \hline \end{array}$ **4.** $\begin{array}{r} 9.67 \\ +3.85 \\ \hline \end{array}$ **5.** $\begin{array}{r} 26.39 \\ -15.46 \\ \hline \end{array}$

Estimate the sum or difference to the nearest hundredth.

6. $\begin{array}{r} 3.456 \\ -2.921 \\ \hline \end{array}$

7. $\begin{array}{r} 6.866 \\ -5.732 \\ \hline \end{array}$

8. $\begin{array}{r} 1.791 \\ +3.249 \\ \hline \end{array}$

9. $\begin{array}{r} 7.893 \\ +4.869 \\ \hline \end{array}$

10. $\begin{array}{r} 5.625 \\ -2.711 \\ \hline \end{array}$

Estimate the sum or difference and compare. Write < or > for each ●.

11. 7.24 + 6.29 ● 10.31 + 3.42

12. 12.19 − 6.36 ● 10.91 − 4.13

13. 9.62 − 3.59 ● 12.21 − 6.67

14. 37.82 + 29.63 ● 39.46 + 31.49

15. 6.54 + 3.92 ● 5.45 + 4.62

16. 44.92 − 23.02 ● 66.70 − 42.85

Lesson 4.5 Part 1 (pages 60–61)

Choose and name the operation. Solve.

1. Rob bought a CD for $15.45. He gave the cashier $20.00. How much change did he receive?

2. Nina jogged 3.25 miles on Saturday, 2.70 miles on Sunday, and 3.5 miles on Monday. How many miles did she jog on all 3 days?

3. Barbara drives 36.3 miles to get to the beach and Rick drives 25.9 miles to get to the beach. How many more miles is Barbara's trip?

4. Cassandra bought a shirt for $19.75, shorts for $16.50, and shoes for $29.25. How much did Cassandra spend on her new outfit?

Lesson 4.5 Part 2 (pages 62–63)

Write a number sentence to solve.

1. Greg's bank statement shows a starting balance of $57.95. The statement also shows he made deposits of $109.62 and $72.56. He wrote checks for $13.99 and $50.75. What is Greg's current balance?

2. At basketball practice Jeremy made 29 baskets, Josh made 35 baskets, and Austin made 25 fewer baskets than Jeremy and Josh combined. How many baskets did Austin make?

Chapter 5

Lesson 5.1 (pages 74–75)

Write the name of the multiplication property used in each number sentence.

1. $7 \times 1 = 7$

2. $6 \times 2 = 2 \times 6$

3. $(4 \times 2) \times 3 = 4 \times (2 \times 3)$

4. $9 \times 3 = 3 \times 9$

5. $2 \times 1 = 2$

6. $8 \times 0 = 0$

7. $(8 \times 3) \times 6 = 8 \times (3 \times 6)$

8. $2 \times 0 = 0$

9. $5 \times 4 = 4 \times 5$

Copy and complete the equation. Identify the property used.

10 $9 \times 8 = \blacksquare \times 9$

11. $7 \times (3 \times 2) = (7 \times \blacksquare) \times 2$

12. $5 \times 0 = \blacksquare$

13. $(2 \times 4) \times 6 = 2 \times (\blacksquare \times 6)$

14. $8 \times \blacksquare = 8$

15. $5 \times 3 = 3 \times \blacksquare$

Show two ways to group by using parentheses. Find the product.

16. $4 \times 3 \times 2 = n$

17. $5 \times 9 \times 3 = n$

18. $6 \times 5 \times 8 = n$

19. $5 \times 4 \times 4 = n$

20. $7 \times 2 \times 6 = n$

21. $8 \times 5 \times 4 = n$

Lesson 5.2 (pages 76–77)

Explain how you would model with colored counters.
Use the colored counters shown on page 76.

1. 600×6

2. 629×3

3. 427×5

4. 632×7

Solve by using colored counters.

5. $4 \times 156 = n$

6. $5 \times 329 = n$

7. $2 \times 421 = n$

8. $9 \times 219 = n$

9. $7 \times 624 = n$

10. $3 \times 783 = n$

11. $6 \times 427 = n$

12. $8 \times 418 = n$

Lesson 5.3 (pages 78–81)

Find the product or area.

1. 159×5

2. 217×3

3. 162×4

4. width: 3 ft
length: 132 ft

5. width: 5 mi
length: 241 mi

6. $362 \times 4 = n$

7. $526 \times 7 = n$

8. $424 \times 4 = n$

9. $842 \times 6 = n$

Lesson 5.4 (pages 82–83)

Use unit cubes to build each rectangular prism. Find the volume.

1. 3 cubes long
5 cubes wide
4 layers high

2. 4 cubes long
9 cubes wide
3 layers high

3. 6 cubes long
2 cubes wide
5 layers high

4. 8 cubes long
6 cubes wide
3 layers high

5. 3 cubes long
6 cubes wide
9 layers high

6. 6 cubes long
2 cubes wide
4 layers high

7. 5 cubes long
7 cubes wide
2 layers high

8. 7 cubes long
3 cubes wide
4 layers high

9. 8 cubes long
5 cubes wide
10 layers high

Use unit cubes to build each prism. Copy and complete the table.

	Length of Base	Width of Base	Height	Volume
10.	7 cubes	4 cubes	2 cubes	?
11.	?	2 cubes	5 cubes	50 cu units
12.	4 cubes	?	6 cubes	72 cu units
13.	6 cubes	5 cubes	?	120 cu units

Lesson 5.5 Part 1 (pages 84–85)

Find the area.

1. 15 in., 4 in.

2. 31 yd, 4 yd

3. 25 in., 7 in.

4. 34 yd, 6 yd

5. $l = 17$ in.
$w = 5$ in.
$A = \blacksquare$ sq in.

6. $l = 23$ m
$w = 7$ m
$A = \blacksquare$ sq m

7. $l = 32$ cm
$w = 4$ cm
$A = \blacksquare$ sq cm

8. $l = 36$ ft
$w = 8$ ft
$A = \blacksquare$ sq ft

Find the volume.

9. 7 in., 8 in., 3 in.

10. 8 ft, 5 ft, 8 ft

11. 6 yd, 5 yd, 3 yd

12.

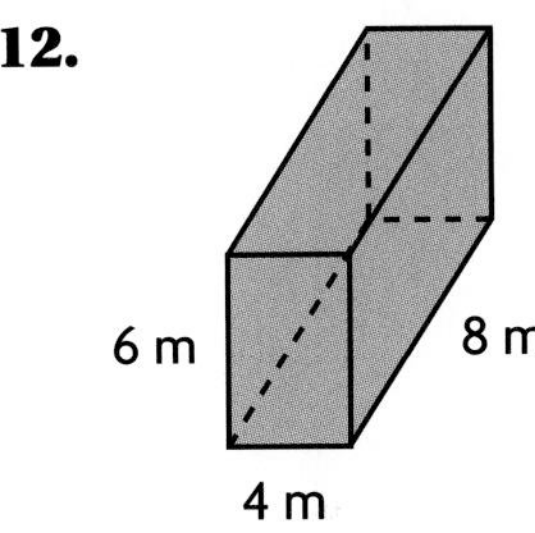

13. $l = 4$ ft
$w = 7$ ft
$h = 7$ ft
$V = \blacksquare$ cu ft

14. $l = 6$ ft
$w = 3$ ft
$h = 3$ ft
$V = \blacksquare$ cu ft

15. $l = 2$ ft
$w = 6$ ft
$h = 8$ ft
$V = \blacksquare$ cu ft

16. $l = 8$ ft
$w = 6$ ft
$h = 3$ ft
$V = \blacksquare$ cu ft

Lesson 5.5 Part 2 (pages 86–87)

Use a formula to solve.

1. Jade is tiling her kitchen floor. The floor is 15 feet long and 12 feet wide. How many square feet does Jade need to tile?

2. Nathan is choosing an aquarium for his iguana. One aquarium measures 5 feet × 4 feet × 3 feet and the other measures 6 feet × 3 feet × 3 feet. Which aquarium has the larger volume?

3. The Y.M.C.A. swimming pool measures 50 ft by 25 ft by 8 ft. What is the volume of the pool?

4. Marsha bought a new carpet that measures 9 ft by 12 ft. The carpet costs $25 per sq yard. How much did Marsha pay for the carpet?

Chapter 6

Lesson 6.1 (pages 92–93)

Use grid paper to model. Find the product.

1. $20 \times 32 = n$ **2.** $40 \times 21 = n$ **3.** $30 \times 14 = n$

Use the Distributive Property to rewrite each equation. Find the product.

4. $17 \times 34 = n$ **5.** $30 \times 27 = n$ **6.** $11 \times 34 = n$

Lesson 6.2 (pages 94–95)

Find the product.

1. $\begin{array}{r} 17 \\ \times 12 \\ \hline \end{array}$ **2.** $\begin{array}{r} 14 \\ \times 14 \\ \hline \end{array}$ **3.** $\begin{array}{r} 23 \\ \times 18 \\ \hline \end{array}$ **4.** $\begin{array}{r} 34 \\ \times 25 \\ \hline \end{array}$

5. $\begin{array}{r} 43 \\ \times 26 \\ \hline \end{array}$ **6.** $\begin{array}{r} 137 \\ \times\ 34 \\ \hline \end{array}$ **7.** $\begin{array}{r} 67 \\ \times 43 \\ \hline \end{array}$ **8.** $\begin{array}{r} 73 \\ \times 36 \\ \hline \end{array}$

9. $82 \times 41 = n$ **10.** $109 \times 38 = n$ **11.** $76 \times 35 = n$

12. $113 \times 42 = n$ **13.** $65 \times 42 = n$ **14.** $68 \times 24 = n$

Lesson 6.3 (pages 96–97)

Estimate the product by rounding each factor to its greatest place-value position.

1. $\begin{array}{r} 175 \\ \times\ 22 \\ \hline \end{array}$ **2.** $\begin{array}{r} 142 \\ \times\ 36 \\ \hline \end{array}$ **3.** $\begin{array}{r} 209 \\ \times\ 66 \\ \hline \end{array}$ **4.** $\begin{array}{r} 159 \\ \times\ 92 \\ \hline \end{array}$

5. $46 \times 423 = n$ **6.** $45 \times 509 = n$ **7.** $86 \times 362 = n$ **8.** $72 \times 166 = n$

Lesson 6.4 (pages 98–101)

Estimate to the greatest place-value position. Then find the product.

1. $\begin{array}{r} 123 \\ \times 116 \\ \hline \end{array}$ **2.** $\begin{array}{r} 162 \\ \times 126 \\ \hline \end{array}$ **3.** $\begin{array}{r} 216 \\ \times 153 \\ \hline \end{array}$

4. $\begin{array}{r} 324 \\ \times 276 \\ \hline \end{array}$ **5.** $\begin{array}{r} 159 \\ \times\ 92 \\ \hline \end{array}$ **6.** $\begin{array}{r} 488 \\ \times 319 \\ \hline \end{array}$

7. $346 \times 172 = n$ **8.** $526 \times 955 = n$ **9.** $421 \times 965 = n$

10. $645 \times 319 = n$ **11.** $751 \times 863 = n$ **12.** $839 \times 572 = n$

Lesson 6.5 Part 1 (pages 102–103)

Find the perimeter and area for each figure.

1. 143 in. by 82 in.

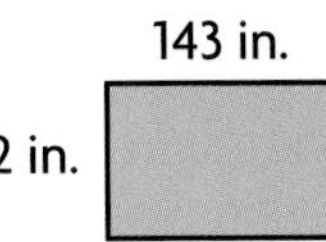

2. 96 ft by 117 ft

3. 194 yd by 65 yd

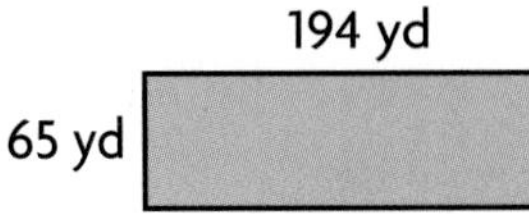

4. 139 cm by 316 cm

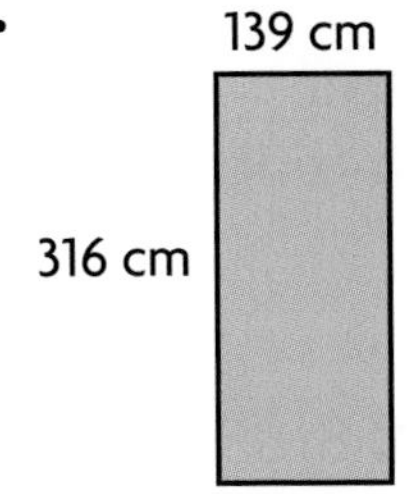

5. 157 m by 227 m

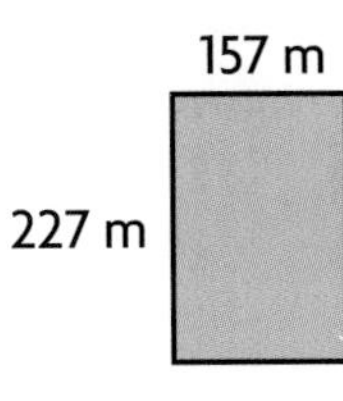

6. 253 in. by 198 in.

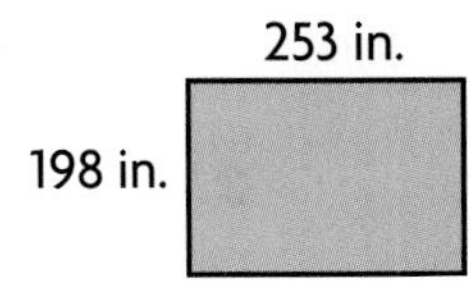

Lesson 6.5 Part 2 (pages 104–105)

Draw a diagram to solve.

1. Stephanie wants to fence in a rectangular section of her yard. She has 76 yards of fencing to use. What dimensions will give the greatest possible area?
2. Lydia has 104 feet of border to go around a flower bed. What dimensions should the flower bed have so it has the greatest area?

Chapter 7

Lesson 7.1 (pages 110–111)

Use mental math and a calculator. Test each number for divisibility by 2, 3, 4, 5, 6, 9, and 10. List the numbers that work.

1. 30 **2.** 48 **3.** 65 **4.** 114 **5.** 140

6. 210 **7.** 300 **8.** 426 **9.** 1,368 **10.** 2,728

11. 360 **12.** 73 **13.** 526 **14.** 2,000 **15.** 5,115

Lesson 7.2 (pages 112–115)

Copy each problem. Draw a box where the first digit in the quotient should be placed.

1. $4\overline{)421}$ **2.** $5\overline{)132}$ **3.** $3\overline{)417}$ **4.** $4\overline{)611}$ **5.** $7\overline{)620}$

Estimate the quotient.

6. $239 \div 6 \approx n$ **7.** $364 \div 6 \approx n$ **8.** $823 \div 4 \approx n$ **9.** $734 \div 8 \approx n$

10. $127 \div 4 \approx n$ **11.** $342 \div 5 \approx n$ **12.** $583 \div 6 \approx n$ **13.** $418 \div 5 \approx n$

Find the quotient.

14. $3\overline{)137}$ **15.** $5\overline{)258}$ **16.** $4\overline{)172}$ **17.** $6\overline{)193}$ **18.** $4\overline{)955}$

19. $2\overline{)762}$ **20.** $7\overline{)439}$ **21.** $8\overline{)353}$ **22.** $3\overline{)724}$ **23.** $9\overline{)642}$

Lesson 7.3 (pages 116–117)

Estimate the quotient.

1. $4\overline{)388}$ **2.** $3\overline{)879}$ **3.** $2\overline{)813}$ **4.** $7\overline{)215}$ **5.** $6\overline{)364}$

Find the quotient.

6. $4\overline{)163}$ **7.** $6\overline{)842}$ **8.** $2\overline{)617}$ **9.** $5\overline{)407}$ **10.** $8\overline{)857}$

11. $735 \div 7 = n$ **12.** $722 \div 3 = n$ **13.** $323 \div 4 = n$ **14.** $972 \div 9 = n$

Lesson 7.4 (pages 118–119)

Use divisibility rules to predict if there will be a remainder.

1. $4\overline{)142}$ **2.** $5\overline{)295}$ **3.** $9\overline{)296}$ **4.** $3\overline{)192}$ **5.** $6\overline{)329}$

Find the quotient. Check by multiplying.

6. $5\overline{)523}$ **7.** $2\overline{)628}$ **8.** $7\overline{)819}$ **9.** $9\overline{)326}$ **10.** $4\overline{)591}$

11. $723 \div 8 = n$ **12.** $486 \div 3 = n$ **13.** $721 \div 6 = n$ **14.** $438 \div 7 = n$

15. $542 \div 3 = n$ **16.** $681 \div 7 = n$ **17.** $765 \div 5 = n$ **18.** $286 \div 6 = n$

Lesson 7.5 Part 1 (pages 120–121)

Solve. Explain how you interpreted the remainder.

1. A group of 130 fifth-grade students went on a field trip to the zoo. They were put into 8 groups. How many students were in most of the groups?

2. The candy shop is selling a box of truffles for $14.75. They have 305 truffles already made. Can they fill 12 boxes of 25 truffles to sell?

Lesson 7.5 Part 2 (pages 122–123)

Guess and check to solve.

1. Sydney is 5 years old. Her cousin is 3 times as old. How old will Sydney be when she is half as old as her cousin?

2. The sum of two numbers is 29. Their product is 190. What are the two numbers?

Chapter 8

Lesson 8.1 (pages 128–129)

Complete the pattern.

1. $240 \div 60 = n$
$2{,}400 \div 60 = 40$
$24{,}000 \div 60 = 400$

2. $160 \div 40 = 4$
$1{,}600 \div 40 = n$
$16{,}000 \div 40 = 400$

3. $140 \div 20 = 7$
$1{,}400 \div 20 = 70$
$14{,}000 \div 20 = n$

Find the quotient.

4. $810 \div 90 = n$ **5.** $1{,}500 \div 50 = n$ **6.** $270 \div 30 = n$ **7.** $4{,}500 \div 50 = n$

8. $24{,}000 \div 80 = n$ **9.** $180 \div 20 = n$ **10.** $21{,}000 \div 70 = n$ **11.** $63{,}000 \div 90 = n$

12. $3{,}600 \div 40 = n$ **13.** $2{,}400 \div 60 = n$ **14.** $2{,}000 \div 40 = n$ **15.** $32{,}000 \div 80 = n$

16. $93{,}000 \div 30 = n$ **17.** $37{,}000 \div 20 = n$ **18.** $56{,}000 \div 70 = n$ **19.** $920 \div 10 = n$

Lesson 8.2 (pages 130–131)

Estimate the quotient.

1. $49\overline{)296}$ **2.** $63\overline{)431}$ **3.** $24\overline{)789}$ **4.** $62\overline{)3{,}592}$ **5.** $49\overline{)3{,}492}$

6. $147 \div 23 \approx n$ **7.** $209 \div 71 \approx n$ **8.** $8{,}211 \div 93 \approx n$ **9.** $242 \div 33 \approx n$

10. $3{,}569 \div 41 \approx n$ **11.** $1{,}499 \div 47 \approx n$ **12.** $8{,}569 \div 79 \approx n$ **13.** $2{,}991 \div 76 \approx n$

14. $2{,}482 \div 53 \approx n$ **15.** $7{,}205 \div 76 \approx n$ **16.** $4{,}539 \div 89 \approx n$ **17.** $5{,}592 \div 68 \approx n$

Lesson 8.3 (pages 132–133)

Copy each problem. Draw a box where the first digit in the quotient should be placed.

1. $8\overline{)2{,}461}$ **2.** $23\overline{)3{,}907}$ **3.** $49\overline{)3{,}149}$ **4.** $26\overline{)4{,}971}$ **5.** $63\overline{)4{,}629}$

Find the quotient.

6. $18\overline{)2{,}461}$ **7.** $23\overline{)3{,}907}$ **8.** $49\overline{)3{,}149}$ **9.** $26\overline{)3{,}971}$ **10.** $63\overline{)4{,}629}$

11. $24\overline{)2{,}342}$ **12.** $36\overline{)4{,}956}$ **13.** $48\overline{)1{,}973}$ **14.** $31\overline{)2{,}697}$ **15.** $64\overline{)9{,}107}$

Lesson 8.4 (pages 134–135)

Write *too high, too low,* or *just right* for each estimate.

1. $\begin{array}{r} 1 \\ 34\overline{)81} \end{array}$ **2.** $\begin{array}{r} 1 \\ 29\overline{)49} \end{array}$ **3.** $\begin{array}{r} 2 \\ 36\overline{)132} \end{array}$ **4.** $\begin{array}{r} 6 \\ 41\overline{)219} \end{array}$ **5.** $\begin{array}{r} 7 \\ 67\overline{)422} \end{array}$

6. $\begin{array}{r} 4 \\ 21\overline{)109} \end{array}$ **7.** $\begin{array}{r} 4 \\ 18\overline{)43} \end{array}$ **8.** $\begin{array}{r} 2 \\ 59\overline{)120} \end{array}$ **9.** $\begin{array}{r} 1 \\ 42\overline{)89} \end{array}$ **10.** $\begin{array}{r} 7 \\ 32\overline{)221} \end{array}$

Choose the better estimate to use for the quotient. Write *a* or *b*.

11. $23\overline{)163}$ **a.** 7 **b.** 8 **12.** $46\overline{)286}$ **a.** 5 **b.** 6

Find the quotient.

13. $23\overline{)192}$ **14.** $41\overline{)547}$ **15.** $17\overline{)396}$ **16.** $36\overline{)408}$ **17.** $48\overline{)636}$

18. $54\overline{)6{,}491}$ **19.** $82\overline{)6{,}091}$ **20.** $66\overline{)7{,}276}$ **21.** $34\overline{)4{,}217}$ **22.** $65\overline{)7{,}293}$

23. $27\overline{)8{,}954}$ **24.** $22\overline{)1{,}631}$ **25.** $62\overline{)5{,}420}$ **26.** $31\overline{)1{,}742}$ **27.** $21\overline{)1{,}327}$

Lesson 8.5 (pages 136–139)

Divide. Check by multiplying.

1. $16\overline{)52}$ **2.** $42\overline{)255}$ **3.** $26\overline{)397}$ **4.** $31\overline{)779}$ **5.** $53\overline{)3{,}721}$

6. $29\overline{)1{,}511}$ **7.** $37\overline{)2{,}153}$ **8.** $64\overline{)3{,}078}$ **9.** $36\overline{)\$52.92}$ **10.** $11\overline{)\$32.12}$

11. $2{,}679 \div 33 = n$ **12.** $2{,}763 \div 51 = n$ **13.** $1{,}061 \div 27 = n$ **14.** $4{,}742 \div 64 = n$

15. $14{,}261 \div 14 = n$ **16.** $79{,}216 \div 58 = n$ **17.** $46{,}987 \div 89 = n$ **18.** $53{,}845 \div 52 = n$

Lesson 8.6 Part 1 (pages 140–141)

Tell what operation should be used to solve each problem. Then solve.

1. Jack was given 156 game tokens for his birthday party. He and 12 friends shared the tokens evenly. How many tokens did each person get?

2. Jack's mom ordered 6 large pizzas for $7.32 each. How much did she spend on the pizzas?

Lesson 8.6 Part 2 (pages 142–143)

Write a number sentence to solve.

1. Anne Marie bought a new stereo system for $1,265. She put down $185 and will pay off the rest in 12 months. What are her monthly payments?

2. Marcus sold 36 magazine subscriptions for his school's fund-raiser. Each subscription is $22 for one year. How much money did Marcus raise?

3. Kathy and Kevin went to baseball practice. Kathy hit 47 out of 60 pitches. Kevin hit 35 out of 60 pitches. How many more hits did Kathy get?

4. Jeff buys 2 pair of tennis shoes for $47 a pair. He has a discount coupon for $10 off the price of one pair when you buy two pairs. How much will both pairs of shoes cost?

Chapter 9

Lesson 9.1 (pages 154–155)

Use index cards to find the median and mode for each set of data.

1.

SEA SHELL COLLECTION					
Name	Tom	Kay	Jim	June	Rick
Shells	198	250	284	250	190

2.

SIT-UPS					
Name	Joe	Kim	Roy	Meg	Jill
Number of Sit-ups	39	43	51	43	46

3.

NEWSPAPERS SOLD					
Week	1	2	3	4	5
Number	32	40	31	32	61

4.

BOOKS READ					
Name	B.J.	Pete	Kris	Sid	Carl
Number of Books	11	13	17	11	15

Lesson 9.2 (pages 156–157)

Find the mean, median, and mode for each set of data.

1. 4, 6, 9, 10, 6

2. 20, 32, 34, 52, 32

3. 14, 18, 12, 22, 14

4. 3, 9, 14, 3, 16

5. 34, 19, 21, 19, 32

6. 17, 11, 21, 15, 11

7. 41, 19, 64, 15, 41

8. 20, 43, 26, 31, 20

9. 171, 136, 171, 132, 135

10. 107, 119, 134, 119, 106

11. 99, 78, 39, 65, 39

12. 109, 141, 148, 131, 141

Lesson 9.3 (pages 158–161)

Choose the most reasonable interval for each set of data.

1. 50, 100, 75, 60, 25

2. 15, 20, 37, 35, 40

3. 3, 5, 1, 4, 7

4. 20, 40, 60, 45, 50

a. 1	**b.** 10
c. 5	**d.** 25

Choose the more reasonable scale for the set of data.

5.

FIFTH-GRADE SURVEY	
Favorite Animal	**Number of Students**
Cat	20
Dog	40
Horse	30
Bird	10
Rabbit	9

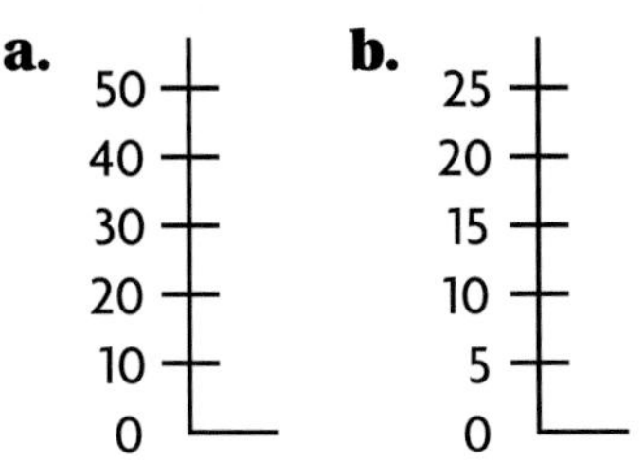

6.

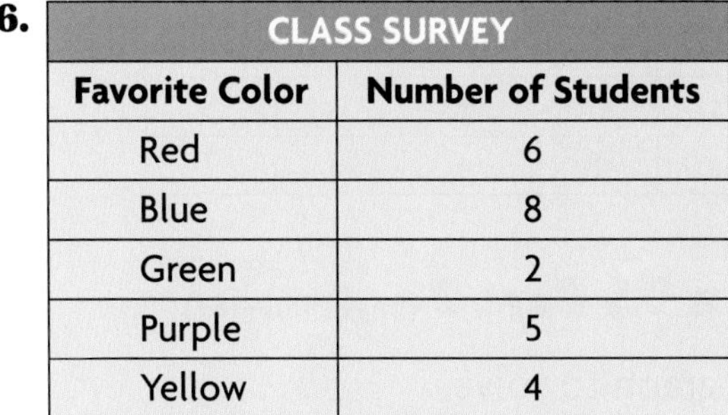

CLASS SURVEY	
Favorite Color	**Number of Students**
Red	6
Blue	8
Green	2
Purple	5
Yellow	4

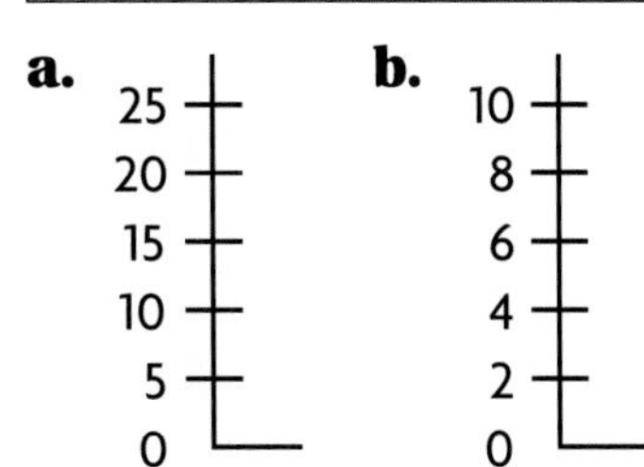

Lesson 9.4 (pages 162–163)

Make a line graph for each set of data.

1.

AVERAGE TEMPERATURE					
Month	Aug	Sep	Oct	Nov	Dec
Temperature	92	85	80	75	70

2.

INCHES OF SNOW				
Month	Dec	Jan	Feb	Mar
Inches	4	5	6	2

3.

THE ROGER'S FAMILY ELECTRIC BILL					
Month	Jan	Feb	Mar	Apr	May
Bill	$120	$125	$115	$100	$92

4.

BOWLING ALLEY ATTENDANCE					
Week	1	2	3	4	5
People	140	90	130	100	150

Lesson 9.5 Part 1 (pages 164–165)

For Problems 1–4, choose a type of graph or plot. Explain your choice.

1. money Jenny earned baby-sitting from June to August
2. books collected from 2 schools for book drive
3. comparing boys' and girls' favorite ice cream flavors
4. Tammy's math scores for this grading period

Draw the graph or plot that best displays each set of data.

5.

FAVORITE SPORT					
Sport	Hockey	Tennis	Basketball	Golf	Soccer
Boys	5	14	22	4	12
Girls	4	20	18	2	8

6.

NUMBER OF ROCKS IN A COLLECTION								
Number of Rocks	5	6	7	8	9	10	11	12
Frequency	1	3	6	3	5	4	7	5

7.

FAVORITE COLORS				
Color	Red	Blue	Yellow	Green
Boys	11	9	0	5
Girls	8	4	6	7

8.

SOCCER TICKETS SOLD					
Day	1	2	3	4	5
Number	32	20	45	13	7

Lesson 9.5 Part 2 (pages 166–167)

Make a graph to solve.

1. Mr. Lynch surveyed his class to find out their favorite activities for Fun Friday. He organized the data in the table. What graph or plot should he use to display the data?

FUN FRIDAY ACTIVITIES				
	Board Games	Playground	Movie	Classroom Games
Boys	9	7	3	4
Girls	4	6	4	3

2. Ms. Jacob's class collected pennies for 5 weeks to raise money for the school. She organized the data in a table. What graph or plot should she use to display the data? Make the graph or plot.

PENNY COLLECTION					
Week	1	2	3	4	5
Number of Pennies	185	180	200	190	315

Chapter 10

Lesson 10.1 (pages 172–173)

For Problems 1–3, use the circle graph.

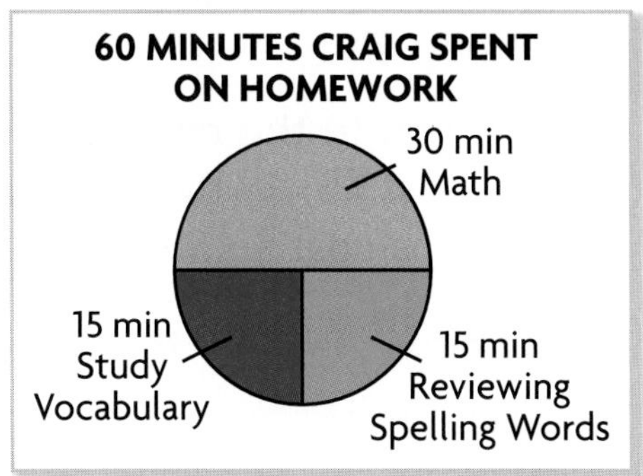

1. What does the whole circle represent?
2. What fraction of the time Craig spent doing homework was spent studying vocabulary?
3. How many minutes did Craig spend on math and reviewing spelling words?

Describe how the circle graph would change for the data.

4. Craig spends 30 minutes on math and 30 minutes reviewing spelling words.
5. Craig spends 20 minutes on math, 20 minutes on vocabulary, and 20 minutes reviewing spelling words.

Lesson 10.2 (pages 174–175)

Use fraction-circle pieces to make a circle graph. Then draw the circle graph.

1.

RYAN'S BOOK COLLECTION		
Book	**Number**	**Fraction**
Fiction	25	$\frac{1}{2}$
Nonfiction	10	$\frac{1}{5}$
Humor	5	$\frac{1}{10}$
Mysteries	10	$\frac{1}{5}$

2.

MRS. POTTER'S HERBS	
Type of Herb Plant	**Fraction of Plants**
3 basil plants	$\frac{1}{3}$
3 oregano plants	$\frac{1}{3}$
3 dill plants	$\frac{1}{3}$

3.

TROPICAL FRUIT	
Fruit	**Fraction**
Strawberries	$\frac{1}{3}$
Blueberries	$\frac{1}{4}$
Pineapple	$\frac{5}{12}$

4.

8-DAY VACATION	
Activity	**Fraction**
Everglades	$\frac{1}{4}$
Beach	$\frac{1}{2}$
Fishing	$\frac{1}{8}$
Shopping	$\frac{1}{8}$

Lesson 10.3 (pages 176–177)

For Exercises 1–3, use the circle graph.

$1.00 STEPHEN SPENT AT THE CANDY STORE

$0.50 Candy Bar

$0.30 Lollipops

$0.20 Gumballs

1. Stephen spent $1.00 at the candy store. What part of $1.00 did he spend for a candy bar and gumballs?

2. What fraction represents the part of the $1.00 Stephen spent for a candy bar? gumballs? lollipops?

3. How would the circle graph change if the candy bars cost $0.40, the gumballs cost $0.10, and the lollipops cost $0.50?

Make a circle graph for the data in each table.

4.

$1.00 SPENT IN A HARDWARE STORE		
Item	Amount Spent	Decimal Point
Nail	$0.10	0.1
Hook	$0.10	0.1
Screw	$0.30	0.3
Bolt	$0.20	0.2
Wire	$0.30	0.3

5.

$10.00 SPENT AT THE MALL		
Item	Amount Spent	Decimal Point
Book	$3.00	0.3
Card	$2.00	0.2
Soda	$1.00	0.1
Pen	$3.00	0.3
Gum	$1.00	0.1

Lesson 10.4 (pages 178–179)

Explain why each graph does not correctly show the data.

1.

Duncan's Video Collection	
Animated	3
Comedy	4
Drama	1
Action	2

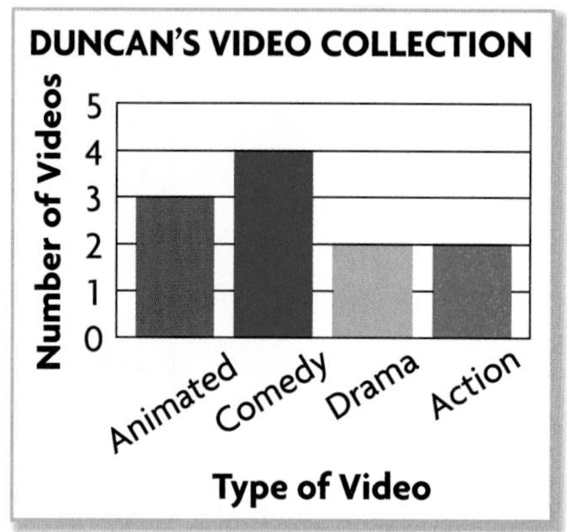

2.

Growth of Duncan's Video Collection	
Jan	1
Feb	2
Mar	4
Apr	6

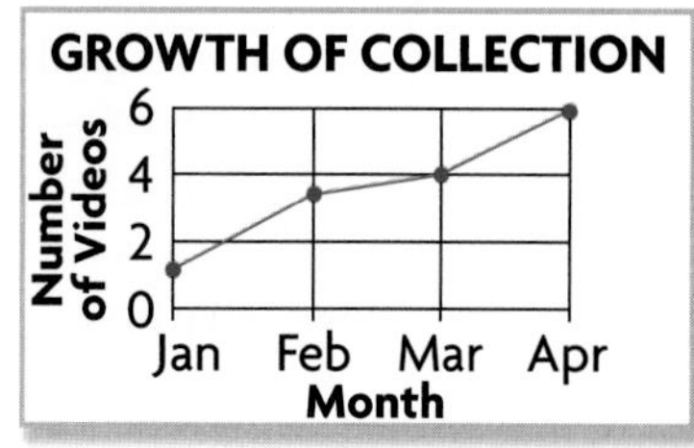

3.

Duncan's Video Collection	
Animated	0.3
Comedy	0.4
Drama	0.1
Action	0.2

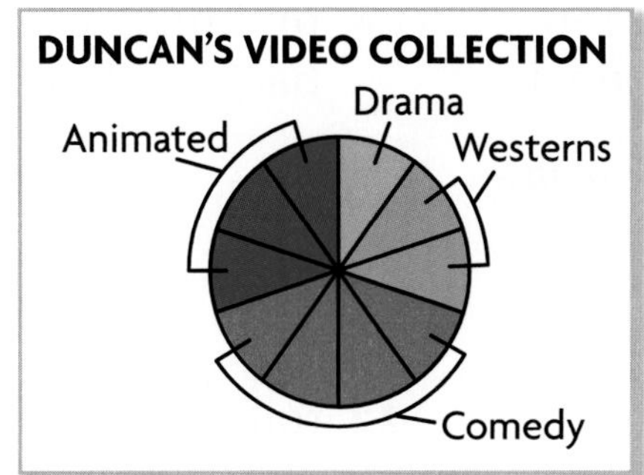

Lesson 10.5 Part 1 (pages 180–181)

Choose the best kind of graph to display the data. Explain your choice.

1. the amount of rainfall in your city each day for a month
2. the number of students' birthdays in each month
3. how you spent two hours on the Internet
4. book sales during May
5. population of 5 different cities
6. how your allowance is spent

Lesson 10.5 Part 2 (pages 182–183)

Choose the best kind of graph to display the data. Then make the graph.

1. Mr. Green's class is signing up for projects to display book reports. There are 8 students making mobiles, 16 making dioramas, and 6 making book jackets. What graph could you use to display these data?
2. On Friday Joey had baseball practice for 80 minutes. He spent $\frac{1}{8}$ of his time doing warm-up exercises, $\frac{1}{2}$ of his time running, $\frac{3}{8}$ of his time working on ball handling. What graph could you use to display the data?

Chapter 11

Lesson 11.1 (pages 188–189)

Write *certain* or *impossible* for each event.

1. that there are 60 seconds in 1 minute
2. pulling a purple counter out of a bag containing only red counters
3. rolling one cube numbered 1-6 and getting a number from 1 to 6
4. that there are 12 hours in a day
5. that there are 7 days in a week
6. pulling 1 dollar out of your pocket containing only 3 quarters

7. rolling two cubes numbered 1–6 and getting a number less than 1

8. pulling a yellow marble from a bag of all yellow marbles

Write whether each event is *likely* or *unlikely*.

9. getting a good grade on a test if you study hard

10. 80° weather in Alaska in January

11. spinning an even number on a spinner that is numbered 1, 2, 4, 6, 8

12. rolling a 6 every time you roll a number cube

Lesson 11.2 (pages 190–191)

For Problems 1–4, use the bag of marbles.

1. Make a table of possible outcomes.
2. Predict and record the number of times you think each outcome will occur if you pull from the bag 10 times.
3. Pull from the bag 10 times, replacing the marble after each time. Record the results in the table.
4. Explain how your predictions compared with the results.

For Problems 5–6, use the table and spinner.

Spinner Experiment				
Outcome	Green	Blue	Yellow	Red
Frequency	||	||	𝍸	|

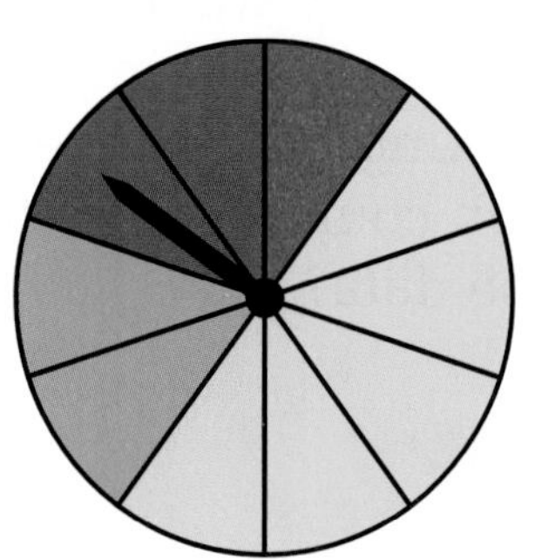

5. Why do you think yellow was spun most often?
6. Why do you think red was spun the least?

Lesson 11.3 Part 1 (pages 192–193)

Copy and complete the tree diagram. Tell the number of choices.

Sport	Day	Choices
1. Swimming	Tues	Swimming on Tues
	?	Swimming on Thurs
2.	Fri	?
3.	Mon	?
4. Basketball	?	Basketball on Wed
5.	Fri	?

Find the number of choices by making a tree diagram.

6. **Outfit Choices**
   Top: White, Brown, Black, Green
   Pants: Blue, White, Black

7. **Sandwich Choices**
   Bread: White, Wheat, Rye
   Type: Roast Beef, Turkey, Chicken

8. **Bicycle Choices**
   Color: Red, Black, Purple
   Speed: 10-speed, 12-speed

Lesson 11.3 Part 2 (pages 194–195)

Make an organized list to solve.

1. Roland is conducting a probability experiment with a coin and a number cube numbered 1-6. How many possible outcomes are there for this experiment? What are they?

2. Use the digits 4, 5, and 6. List all the two-digit numbers you can make without repeating any digits in the same number.

Lesson 11.4 (pages 196–197)

Write a fraction for the probability of pulling each color marble.

1. blue **2.** yellow **3.** red **4.** orange

Write a fraction for the probability of spinning each color.

5. blue
6. green
7. yellow or blue
8. green or red

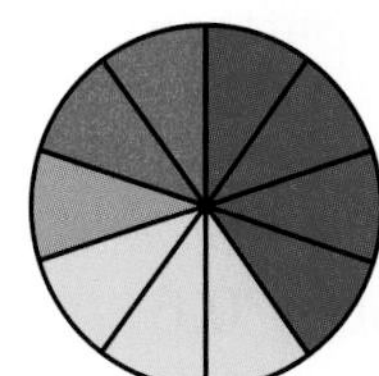

Write the probability of spinning red.

9.

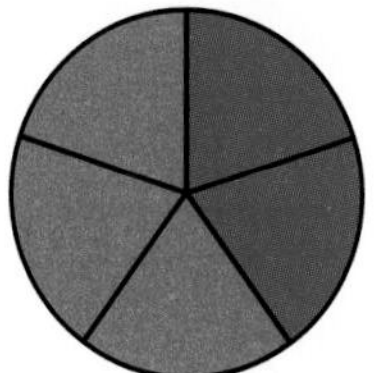

10.

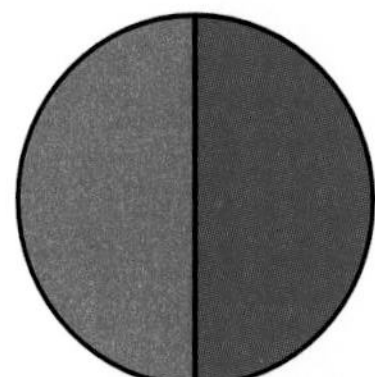

11.

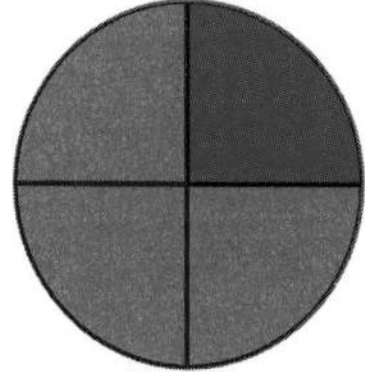

Lesson 11.5 (pages 198–199)

For Problems 1–6, use the spinner. Write each probability as a fraction. Tell which outcome is more likely.

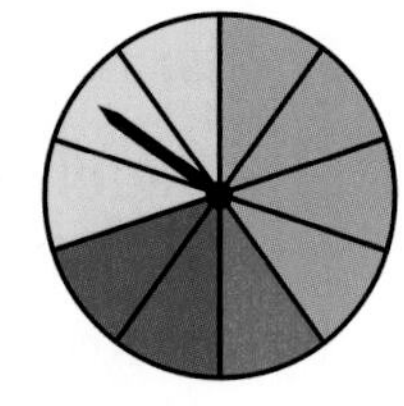

1. You spin green; you spin blue.

2. You spin red; you spin yellow.

3. You don't spin yellow; you don't spin blue.

4. You don't spin green; you don't spin red.

5. You spin either blue or yellow; you spin either red or green.

6. You spin either blue or red; you spin either yellow or green.

Chapter 12

Lesson 12.1 (pages 210–211)

Make a model to find each product.

1. $3 \times 0.6 = n$ **2.** $4 \times 0.9 = n$ **3.** $6 \times 0.19 = n$ **4.** $5 \times 0.24 = n$

5. $2 \times 0.7 = n$ **6.** $7 \times 0.31 = n$ **7.** $4 \times 0.14 = n$ **8.** $5 \times 0.31 = n$

Lesson 12.2 (pages 212–213)

Draw models to find each product.

1. $2 \times 6 = n$
$0.2 \times 6 = n$
$0.02 \times 6 = n$

2. $3 \times 8 = n$
$0.3 \times 8 = n$
$0.03 \times 8 = n$

3. $5 \times 3 = n$
$0.5 \times 3 = n$
$0.05 \times 3 = n$

4. $1 \times 7 = n$
$0.1 \times 7 = n$
$0.01 \times 7 = n$

Use mental math to complete the pattern.

5. $1 \times 4 = 4$
$0.1 \times 4 = 0.4$
$0.01 \times 4 = n$

6. $1 \times 60 = 60$
$0.1 \times 60 = n$
$0.01 \times 60 = 0.6$

7. $1 \times 37 = 37$
$0.1 \times 37 = n$
$0.01 \times 37 = n$

8. $15 \times 1 = 15$
$15 \times 0.1 = n$
$n \times 0.01 = n$

9. $14 \times 1 = n$
$14 \times 0.1 = n$
$14 \times 0.01 = n$

10. $71 \times 1 = n$
$71 \times 0.1 = n$
$71 \times 0.01 = n$

11. $1 \times 112 = n$
$0.1 \times 112 = n$
$0.01 \times 112 = n$

12. $172 \times 1 = n$
$172 \times 0.1 = n$
$172 \times 0.01 = n$

Lesson 12.3 Part 1 (pages 214–215)

Multiply. Write each product.

1. $0.5 \times 0.9 = n$ **2.** $0.2 \times 0.9 = n$ **3.** $0.3 \times 0.3 = n$ **4.** $0.7 \times 0.4 = n$

5. $0.6 \times 0.3 = n$ **6.** $0.7 \times 0.7 = n$ **7.** $0.4 \times 0.9 = n$ **8.** $0.2 \times 0.4 = n$

9. $0.6 \times 0.6 = n$ **10.** $0.8 \times 0.5 = n$ **11.** $0.8 \times 0.9 = n$ **12.** $0.8 \times 0.7 = n$

Lesson 12.3 Part 2 (pages 216–217)

Make a model to solve.

1. Rebecca has \$3.35 in coins. She has 6 nickels and 3 times as many dimes as nickels. The rest are quarters. How many of each coin does she have?

2. Renee and Deon cut pizza into 10 equal pieces. They put pepperoni on 0.5 of the pizza. Then they put onions on 0.4 of the pepperoni pieces. What part of the pizza has pepperoni and onion?

Lesson 12.4 Part 1 (pages 218–221)

Choose the best estimate. Write *a*, *b*, or *c*.

1. $36 \times 0.6 = n$	**a.** 210	**b.** 21	**c.** 2,100
2. $42 \times 0.4 = n$	**a.** 17	**b.** 70	**c.** 170
3. \$0.73 × 8 = *n*	**a.** \$0.60	**b.** \$60.00	**c.** \$6.00
4. \$0.36 × 5 = *n*	**a.** \$0.20	**b.** \$2.00	**c.** \$20.00

Use estimation and patterns to place the decimal point in each product.

5. $3.2 \times 7 = 224$ **6.** $0.32 \times 7 = 224$ **7.** $3.2 \times 0.7 = 224$

8. $0.32 \times 0.7 = 224$ **9.** $32 \times 0.7 = 224$ **10.** $3.2 \times 0.07 = 224$

Lesson 12.4 Part 2 (pages 222–223)

Estimate each product.

1. 7×0.21 **2.** 6×0.33 **3.** 0.6×73 **4.** 36×0.5

5. 0.98×52 **6.** 49×0.04 **7.** 79×0.02 **8.** 0.17×97

Estimate to place the decimal point. Then find the product.

9. \$7.25 × 4 **10.** 2.8×6 **11.** 0.8×9.9 **12.** 3.79×68

Lesson 12.5 (pages 224–225)

Find the product.

1. $\begin{array}{r} 6.45 \\ \times\ 2.8 \\ \hline \end{array}$ **2.** $\begin{array}{r} 23.9 \\ \times\ 4.3 \\ \hline \end{array}$ **3.** $\begin{array}{r} 31.2 \\ \times\ 3.8 \\ \hline \end{array}$ **4.** $\begin{array}{r} 49.76 \\ \times\ 0.36 \\ \hline \end{array}$ **5.** $\begin{array}{r} 309.73 \\ \times\ 2.9 \\ \hline \end{array}$

6. $\begin{array}{r} 57.3 \\ \times\ 6.03 \\ \hline \end{array}$ **7.** $\begin{array}{r} 17.9 \\ \times\ 8.2 \\ \hline \end{array}$ **8.** $\begin{array}{r} 17.28 \\ \times\ 6.4 \\ \hline \end{array}$ **9.** $\begin{array}{r} 42.5 \\ \times\ 6.04 \\ \hline \end{array}$ **10.** $\begin{array}{r} 1.007 \\ \times\ 8.6 \\ \hline \end{array}$

11. $3.7 \times 1.4 = n$ **12.** $1.7 \times 1.6 = n$ **13.** $4.5 \times 3.9 = n$

14. $2.3 \times 2.6 = n$ **15.** $1.5 \times 1.1 = n$ **16.** $3.7 \times 4.2 = n$

Chapter 13

Lesson 13.1 Part 1 (pages 230–231)

Copy and complete each pattern.

1. $3{,}000 \div 6 = n$
$300 \div 6 = n$
$30 \div 6 = n$
$3 \div 6 = n$

2. $4{,}000 \div 8 = n$
$400 \div 8 = n$
$40 \div 8 = n$
$4 \div 8 = n$

3. $24{,}000 \div 5 = n$
$2{,}400 \div 5 = n$
$240 \div 5 = n$
$24 \div 5 = n$

4. $5{,}000 \div 2 = n$
$500 \div 2 = n$
$50 \div 2 = n$
$5 \div 2 = n$

5. $12{,}000 \div 8 = n$
$1{,}200 \div 8 = n$
$120 \div 8 = n$
$12 \div 8 = n$

6. $7{,}000 \div 4 = n$
$700 \div 4 = n$
$70 \div 4 = n$
$7 \div 4 = n$

Lesson 13.1 Part 2 (pages 232–233)

Write a number sentence to solve.

1. Courtney and 4 friends went to lunch. The bill was $35. They shared the bill equally. How much did each pay?

2. Stewart saves $14.95 from mowing lawns each week. In 9 weeks, how much will he have saved?

Lesson 13.2 (pages 234–235)

Make a model and find the quotient.

1. $800 \div 5 = \underline{?}$ **2.** $0.21 \div 7 = \underline{?}$ **3.** $4.5 \div 9 = \underline{?}$

4. $3.6 \div 6 = \underline{?}$ **5.** $0.18 \div 9 = \underline{?}$ **6.** $0.8 \div 4 = \underline{?}$

Lesson 13.3 (pages 236–239)

Find the quotient. Check by multiplying.

1. $8\overline{)4.8}$ **2.** $5\overline{)13.5}$ **3.** $3\overline{)6.06}$ **4.** $4\overline{)4.16}$

5. $7\overline{)7.28}$ **6.** $2\overline{)4.96}$ **7.** $9\overline{)27.9}$ **8.** $6\overline{)42.6}$

9. $6.39 \div 3 = \underline{?}$ **10.** $20.8 \div 4 = \underline{?}$ **11.** $18.6 \div 6 = \underline{?}$ **12.** $15.4 \div 2 = \underline{?}$

Lesson 13.4 (pages 240–241)

Use estimation or patterns to place the decimal point.
Then find the quotient.

1. $3\overline{)1.5}$ **2.** $3\overline{)12.15}$ **3.** $6\overline{)0.36}$ **4.** $2\overline{)15.28}$

5. $4\overline{)24.8}$ **6.** $5\overline{)0.45}$ **7.** $5\overline{)17.45}$ **8.** $7\overline{)21.14}$

Lesson 13.5 (pages 242–243)

For Problems 1-4, use the table on page 242. Choose the operation and solve.

1. How much salmon will Mr. Regan have after sharing with 5 neighbors?
2. How many more pounds of salmon than haddock did Mr. Regan buy?
3. How many pounds of seafood did Mr. Regan buy in all?
4. Mr. Regan bought the same amount of shrimp 5 weeks in a row. How many pounds of shrimp did Mr. Regan buy?

Chapter 14

Lesson 14.1 (pages 248–249)

Choose the most reasonable unit of measure.
Write *mm, cm, dm, m,* or *km*.

1. height of a classmate
2. distance to the North Pole
3. length of a chalkboard
4. width of a paperback book
5. thickness of a dollar bill
6. distance of a marathon

Write the measurements in order from shortest to longest.

7. 9 dm 9 mm 9 cm
8. 2 km 2 dm 2 cm
9. 7 cm 7 m 7 mm
10. 13 m 13 dm 13 mm
11. 8 mm 8 cm 8 m
12. 10 cm 10 km 10 m

Lesson 14.2 (pages 250–251)

Choose the most reasonable unit. Write *kg, g,* or *mg*.

1. 

2. 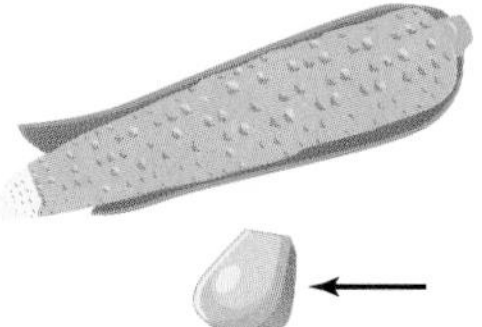

3. 

Choose the more reasonable measurement.

4. 
5 g or 5 kg

5. 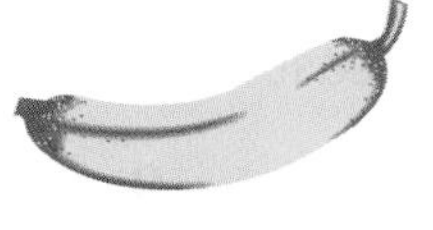
300 g or 300 kg

6. 
1 g or 1 kg

7. 
7 kg or 7 mg

Lesson 14.3 (pages 252–253)

Choose the reasonable unit. Write *mL, L,* or *kL.*

1. 

2. 

3. 

4. 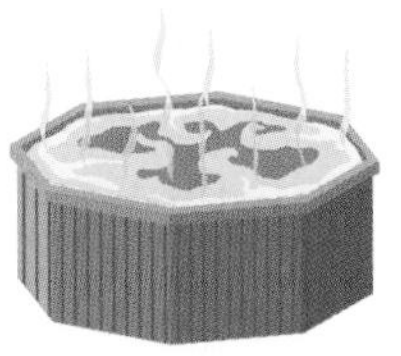

Choose the more reasonable measurement.

5. 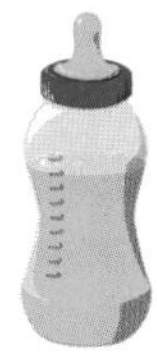
240 L or 240 mL

6. 
2 L or 2 mL

7. 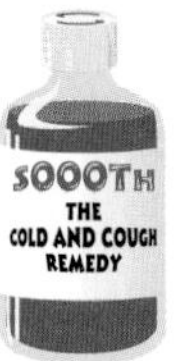

120 mL or 120 L

8. 

18 mL or 18 L

Lesson 14.4 (pages 254–255)

Choose the smaller unit of measure. Write *a* or *b*. Use the prefix to help you.

1. a. millimeter
b. centimeter

2. a. liter
b. kiloliter

3. a. kilogram
b. gram

Choose the larger unit of measure. Write *a* or *b*. Use the prefix to help you.

4. a. decimeter
b. meter

5. a. liter
b. milliliter

6. a. centimeter
b. kilometer

Write the equivalent measurement.

7. 6 centimeters = __?__ meter

8. 9 kilograms = __?__ grams

9. 2 milligrams = __?__ gram

10. 7 grams = __?__ milligrams

11. 3 decimeters = __?__ meter

12. 5 milliliters = __?__ liter

Lesson 14.5 Part 1 (pages 256–257)

Write the missing unit.

1. 40 km = 40,000 __?__

2. 3 kg = 3,000 __?__

3. 7 m = 700 __?__

4. 3.7 m = 370 __?__

5. 5 km = 5,000 __?__

6. 9.462 L = 9,462 __?__

Write *multiply* or *divide*. Then write the equivalent measurement.

7. 4.21 g = __?__ mg

8. 2.4 m = __?__ cm

9. 50 cm = __?__ dm

10. 6,500 ml = __?__ L

11. 2,000 mg = __?__ g

12. 3,400 mm = __?__ m

13. 5.9 L = __?__ mL

14. 3,000 g = __?__ kg

15. 4,200 mL = __?__ L

Lesson 14.5 Part 2 (pages 258–259)

Draw a diagram to solve.

1. Eileen's book has a mass of 0.525 kg. Jeanne's book has a mass of 0.640 kg. What is the total mass in grams of the two books?

2. Kim has 1.9 L of lemonade in a pitcher. How many milliliters of lemonade are in the pitcher?

Chapter 15

Lesson 15.1 (pages 270–271)

Write the fraction shown.

1. 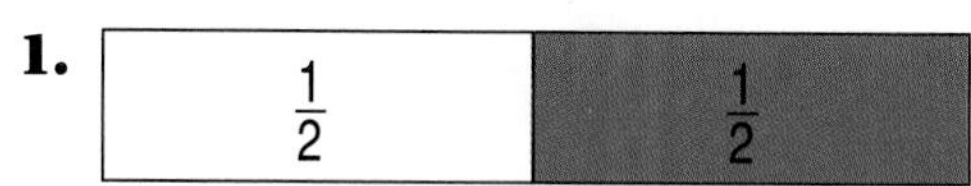

2. $\frac{1}{8}$ $\frac{1}{8}$ $\frac{1}{8}$ $\frac{1}{8}$ $\frac{1}{8}$ $\frac{1}{8}$ $\frac{1}{8}$ $\frac{1}{8}$

3. 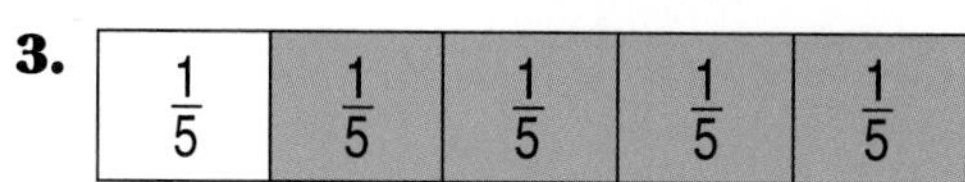

4. $\frac{1}{4}$ $\frac{1}{4}$ $\frac{1}{4}$ $\frac{1}{4}$

Shade a fraction strip to show the fraction.

5. $\frac{1}{10}$ **6.** $\frac{1}{3}$ **7.** $\frac{2}{5}$ **8.** $\frac{7}{8}$ **9.** $\frac{3}{10}$

Draw a number line. Locate the fraction.

10. $\frac{7}{10}$ **11.** $\frac{2}{6}$ **12.** $\frac{5}{8}$ **13.** $\frac{5}{6}$ **14.** $\frac{2}{3}$

Lesson 15.2 (pages 272–273)

Rename each fraction as a mixed number.

1. $\frac{23}{7}$ **2.** $\frac{19}{4}$ **3.** $\frac{8}{3}$ **4.** $\frac{9}{5}$ **5.** $\frac{16}{5}$

Rename each mixed number as a fraction.

6. $3\frac{1}{9}$ **7.** $4\frac{2}{5}$ **8.** $1\frac{3}{4}$ **9.** $6\frac{2}{3}$ **10.** $2\frac{3}{5}$

11. $5\frac{1}{4}$ **12.** $7\frac{3}{8}$ **13.** $2\frac{9}{10}$ **14.** $9\frac{4}{5}$ **15.** $8\frac{3}{8}$

16. $4\frac{3}{5}$ **17.** $6\frac{2}{9}$ **18.** $2\frac{5}{12}$ **19.** $13\frac{3}{4}$ **20.** $3\frac{9}{10}$

Lesson 15.3 (pages 274–275)

Use counters to name the least common multiple for each.

1. 2 and 6 **2.** 5 and 3 **3.** 7 and 2 **4.** 3 and 2 **5.** 4 and 5

6. 4 and 3 **7.** 8 and 4 **8.** 3 and 9 **9.** 4 and 6 **10.** 8 and 16

Rename each pair of fractions so they have the same denominator. Use fraction strips and the LCM's from Exercises 1–4.

11. $\frac{1}{2} + \frac{1}{6}$ **12.** $\frac{1}{3} + \frac{2}{5}$ **13.** $\frac{2}{7} + \frac{1}{2}$ **14.** $\frac{2}{3} + \frac{1}{2}$

Lesson 15.4 (pages 276–277)

Rename, using the least common multiple, and compare. Write $<$, $>$, or $=$ for each ●.

1. $\frac{1}{3}$ ● $\frac{2}{9}$ **2.** $\frac{3}{4}$ ● $\frac{5}{8}$ **3.** $\frac{1}{3}$ ● $\frac{5}{24}$ **4.** $\frac{3}{4}$ ● $\frac{11}{12}$

5. $\frac{1}{2}$ ● $\frac{5}{6}$ **6.** $\frac{1}{5}$ ● $\frac{3}{4}$ **7.** $\frac{4}{5}$ ● $\frac{2}{3}$ **8.** $\frac{3}{15}$ ● $\frac{1}{5}$

9. $\frac{2}{3}$ ● $\frac{1}{4}$ **10.** $\frac{5}{6}$ ● $\frac{4}{9}$ **11.** $\frac{1}{6}$ ● $\frac{3}{8}$ **12.** $\frac{1}{4}$ ● $\frac{5}{6}$

Lesson 15.5 Part 1 (pages 278–279)

Rename the fractions, using the LCM as the denominator.

1. $\frac{2}{3}, \frac{3}{4}, \frac{1}{2}$ **2.** $\frac{2}{3}, \frac{4}{15}, \frac{1}{5}$ **3.** $\frac{5}{6}, \frac{3}{8}, \frac{1}{4}$

Write in order from least to greatest.

4. $\frac{1}{2}, \frac{3}{4}, \frac{11}{16}$ **5.** $\frac{3}{4}, \frac{5}{6}, \frac{2}{3}$ **6.** $\frac{4}{9}, \frac{1}{3}, \frac{5}{6}$

Write in order from greatest to least.

7. $\frac{3}{4}, \frac{4}{5}, \frac{1}{2}$ **8.** $\frac{7}{12}, \frac{1}{4}, \frac{3}{8}$ **9.** $\frac{1}{2}, \frac{4}{5}, \frac{7}{10}$

10. $\frac{3}{8}, \frac{4}{16}, \frac{2}{4}$ **11.** $\frac{2}{3}, \frac{5}{9}, \frac{5}{6}$ **12.** $\frac{1}{3}, \frac{10}{15}, \frac{2}{5}$

Lesson 15.5 Part 2 (pages 280–281)

Draw a diagram to solve.

1. Lauren is making soup. She adds $\frac{2}{3}$ cup carrots, $\frac{3}{4}$ cup potatoes and $\frac{1}{2}$ cup of celery. List the ingredients in order from the least amount to the greatest amount.

2. Bert made cookies. He put in $\frac{2}{3}$ teaspoon baking soda, $\frac{1}{4}$ teaspoon salt, and $\frac{1}{3}$ teaspoon cinnamon. What is the order of ingredients from greatest to least?

3. Larry planted $\frac{1}{3}$ of his garden with carrots, $\frac{1}{4}$ with potatoes, and $\frac{5}{12}$ with radishes. List the plants in order from the one with the least area to the one with the greatest area.

4. Susan made a fruit sauce for her waffles. She used $\frac{1}{4}$ cup strawberries, and $\frac{3}{8}$ cup blueberries. Did she use more strawberries or blueberries?

Chapter 16

Lesson 16.1 (pages 286–287)

Use square tiles to show all the rectangles that can be made using each number.

1. 29 **2.** 25 **3.** 16 **4.** 7

Write *prime* or *composite* for each number. Identify the square number.

5. 24 **6.** 36 **7.** 22 **8.** 17

9. 32 **10.** 41 **11.** 2 **12.** 37

Lesson 16.2 (pages 288–291)

List the factors of each number.

1. 12 **2.** 25 **3.** 14 **4.** 36 **5.** 16

6. 20 **7.** 15 **8.** 42 **9.** 56 **10.** 32

List the factors of each number. Write the greatest common factor for each pair of numbers.

11. 10, 35 **12.** 4, 32 **13.** 6, 16 **14.** 9, 27 **15.** 8, 20

16. 16, 20 **17.** 9, 12 **18.** 7, 28 **19.** 4, 20 **20.** 12, 30

21. 14, 21 **22.** 12, 18 **23.** 18, 36 **24.** 20, 30 **25.** 8, 24

Lesson 16.3 Part 1 (pages 292–293)

Find an equivalent fraction. Use multiplication or division.

1. $\frac{5}{15}$ **2.** $\frac{2}{3}$ **3.** $\frac{4}{12}$ **4.** $\frac{1}{5}$ **5.** $\frac{6}{30}$

6. $\frac{2}{12}$ **7.** $\frac{1}{9}$ **8.** $\frac{7}{28}$ **9.** $\frac{3}{9}$ **10.** $\frac{2}{11}$

Which fraction is *not* equivalent to the given fraction. Write *a, b,* or *c.*

11. $\frac{2}{7}$ **a.** $\frac{4}{14}$ **b.** $\frac{5}{14}$ **c.** $\frac{6}{21}$

12. $\frac{3}{15}$ **a.** $\frac{6}{30}$ **b.** $\frac{1}{5}$ **c.** $\frac{1}{3}$

13. $\frac{1}{3}$ **a.** $\frac{3}{9}$ **b.** $\frac{3}{6}$ **c.** $\frac{2}{6}$

14. $\frac{8}{12}$ **a.** $\frac{7}{10}$ **b.** $\frac{2}{3}$ **c.** $\frac{6}{9}$

15. $\frac{2}{4}$ **a.** $\frac{4}{9}$ **b.** $\frac{5}{10}$ **c.** $\frac{4}{8}$

Lesson 16.3 Part 2 (pages 294–295)

Draw a diagram to solve.

1. Juan has 24 sports cards, of which 6 are basketball cards. He says $\frac{1}{4}$ of his cards are basketball cards. Is he correct? Explain.

2. At the grocery store Mrs. Jewel spent $\frac{3}{8}$ of her money on fruits and $\frac{1}{4}$ of her money on meat. On which item did Mrs. Jewel spend more money? Explain how you know.

Lesson 16.4 (pages 296–297)

Write each fraction in simplest form. Use fraction bars.

1. $\frac{2}{12}$
2. $\frac{7}{9}$
3. $\frac{4}{14}$
4. $\frac{6}{22}$
5. $\frac{2}{5}$
6. $\frac{3}{18}$
7. $\frac{6}{14}$
8. $\frac{9}{21}$
9. $\frac{3}{4}$
10. $\frac{11}{88}$
11. $\frac{7}{49}$
12. $\frac{8}{20}$
13. $\frac{12}{15}$
14. $\frac{14}{28}$
15. $\frac{16}{28}$

Lesson 16.5 (pages 298–299)

Write each fraction in simplest form.

1. $\frac{2}{32}$
2. $\frac{8}{44}$
3. $\frac{12}{33}$
4. $\frac{5}{45}$
5. $\frac{2}{17}$
6. $\frac{15}{30}$
7. $\frac{18}{39}$
8. $\frac{42}{49}$
9. $\frac{20}{50}$
10. $\frac{9}{30}$
11. $\frac{27}{63}$
12. $\frac{12}{56}$
13. $\frac{21}{51}$
14. $\frac{36}{45}$
15. $\frac{16}{40}$

Chapter 17

Lesson 17.1 (pages 304–305)

Write an addition sentence for each drawing.

1. 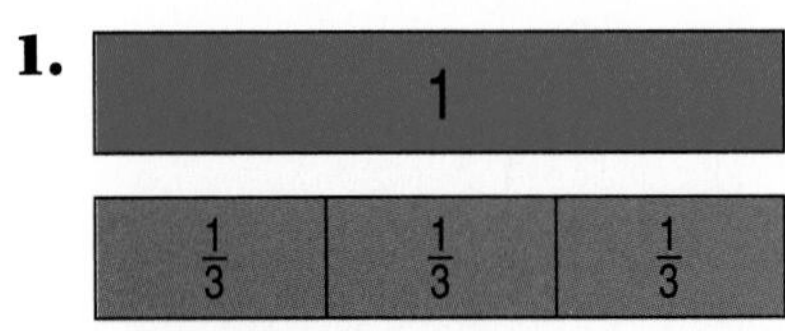

2. 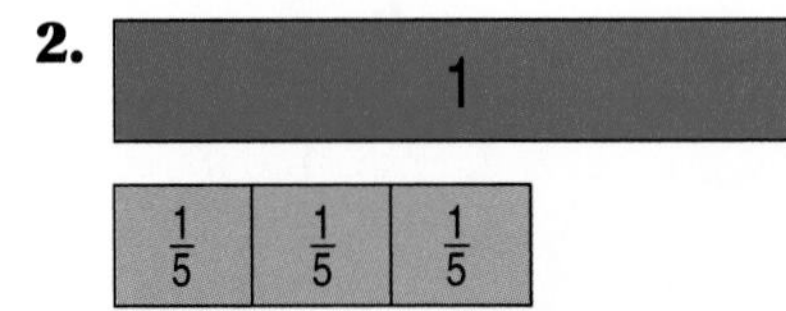

3. 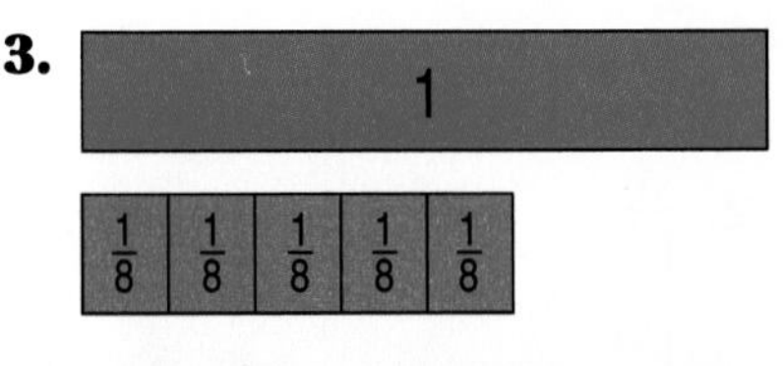

4. 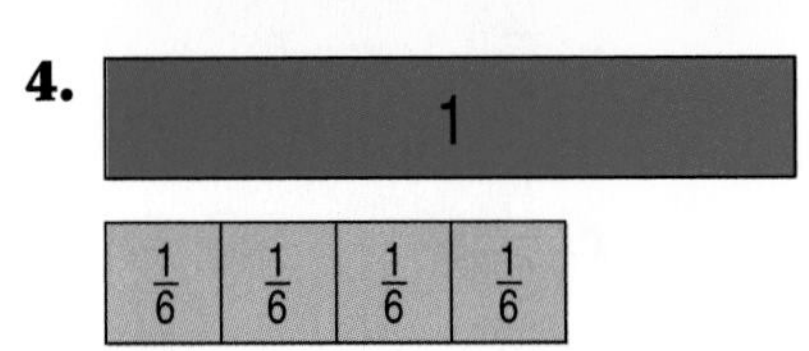

5. 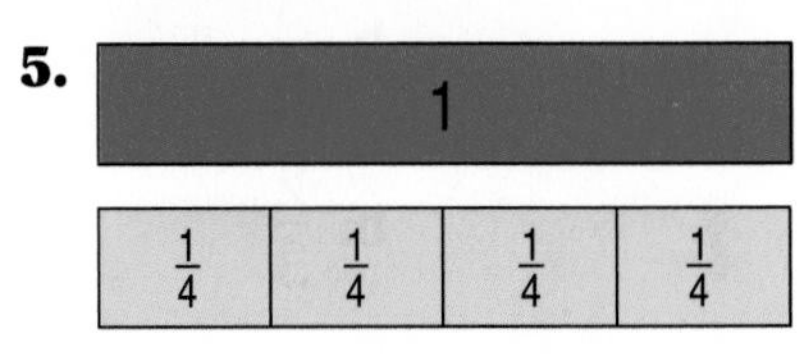

6. 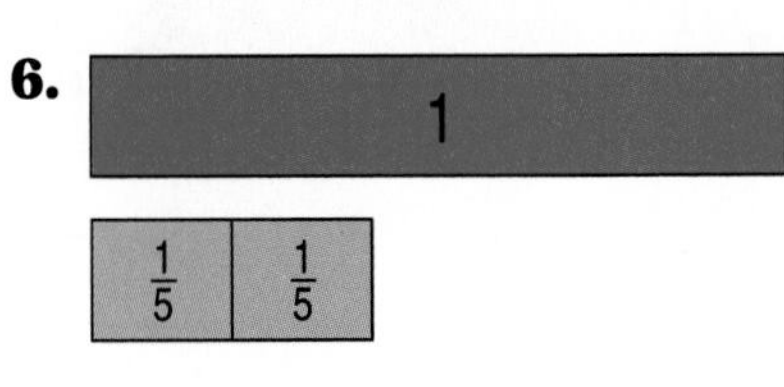

Use fraction strips to find the sum. Write the answer in simplest form.

7. $\frac{2}{6} + \frac{3}{6} = n$ **8.** $\frac{1}{9} + \frac{4}{9} = n$ **9.** $\frac{1}{8} + \frac{6}{8} = n$

10. $\frac{1}{4} + \frac{1}{4} = n$ **11.** $\frac{3}{5} + \frac{4}{5} = n$ **12.** $\frac{2}{3} + \frac{2}{3} = n$

13. $\frac{3}{8} + \frac{4}{8} = n$ **14.** $\frac{2}{9} + \frac{8}{9} = n$ **15.** $\frac{9}{10} + \frac{3}{10} = n$

Lesson 17.2 (pages 306–307)

Use fraction bars to find the sum.

1. $\frac{2}{3} + \frac{1}{4} = n$ **2.** $\frac{1}{2} + \frac{5}{8} = n$ **3.** $\frac{1}{6} + \frac{2}{3} = n$

4. $\frac{1}{2} + \frac{7}{10} = n$ **5.** $\frac{1}{3} + \frac{7}{12} = n$ **6.** $\frac{1}{2} + \frac{5}{6} = n$

7. $\frac{3}{4} + \frac{3}{8} = n$ **8.** $\frac{1}{6} + \frac{1}{3} = n$ **9.** $\frac{4}{5} + \frac{1}{2} = n$

Lesson 17.3 (pages 308–309)

Use the LCM to name the least common denominator, or LCD, for each pair of fractions.

1. $\frac{1}{2}$ and $\frac{1}{6}$ **2.** $\frac{1}{5}$ and $\frac{1}{3}$ **3.** $\frac{1}{8}$ and $\frac{1}{4}$ **4.** $\frac{1}{2}$ and $\frac{1}{10}$

Use fraction strips to find the sum. Write the answer in simplest form.

5. $\frac{1}{2} + \frac{5}{12} = n$ **6.** $\frac{3}{4} + \frac{1}{8} = n$ **7.** $\frac{1}{6} + \frac{3}{4} = n$ **8.** $\frac{5}{6} + \frac{1}{2} = n$

9. $\frac{1}{4} + \frac{3}{8} = n$ **10.** $\frac{1}{6} + \frac{2}{3} = n$ **11.** $\frac{2}{5} + \frac{1}{2} = n$ **12.** $\frac{1}{3} + \frac{4}{9} = n$

Lesson 17.4 Part 1 (pages 310–311)

Use the LCM to name the least common denominator, or LCD, for each group of fractions.

1. $\frac{1}{8}, \frac{1}{2},$ and $\frac{1}{4}$ **2.** $\frac{1}{3}, \frac{1}{12},$ and $\frac{1}{4}$ **3.** $\frac{1}{2}, \frac{1}{6},$ and $\frac{1}{3}$

4. $\frac{1}{3}, \frac{1}{6},$ and $\frac{1}{2}$ **5.** $\frac{1}{5}, \frac{1}{3},$ and $\frac{2}{15}$ **6.** $\frac{2}{3}, \frac{1}{12},$ and $\frac{1}{6}$

7. $\frac{1}{4}, \frac{1}{2},$ and $\frac{3}{16}$ **8.** $\frac{2}{3}, \frac{1}{9},$ and $\frac{1}{3}$ **9.** $\frac{1}{2}, \frac{1}{10},$ and $\frac{1}{5}$

Use fraction strips to find the sum. Write the answer in simplest form.

10. $\frac{2}{3} + \frac{1}{4} + \frac{5}{12} = n$ **11.** $\frac{1}{3} + \frac{4}{9} + \frac{2}{3} = n$ **12.** $\frac{1}{2} + \frac{3}{4} + \frac{2}{3} = n$

13. $\frac{1}{10} + \frac{2}{5} + \frac{3}{10} = n$

14. $\frac{1}{4} + \frac{1}{2} + \frac{5}{6} = n$

15. $\frac{5}{6} + \frac{1}{2} + \frac{1}{3} = n$

16. $\frac{1}{2} + \frac{3}{8} + \frac{3}{4} = n$

17. $\frac{1}{2} + \frac{1}{2} + \frac{1}{5} = n$

18. $\frac{5}{8} + \frac{1}{4} + \frac{1}{2} = n$

Lesson 17.4 Part 2 (pages 312–313)

Make a model to solve.

1. Greg plants $\frac{1}{3}$ of his garden with tomatoes, $\frac{1}{2}$ with herbs, and $\frac{1}{6}$ with jalapenos. What part of Greg's garden is planted?

2. Jill does aerobics for $\frac{1}{2}$ hour 5 times a week. How long does Jill do aerobics each week?

Chapter 18

Lesson 18.1 (pages 318–319)

Use fraction strips to find the difference. Write the answer in simplest form.

1. $\frac{2}{4} - \frac{1}{4} = n$

2. $\frac{6}{8} - \frac{3}{8} = n$

3. $\frac{7}{10} - \frac{2}{10} = n$

4. $\frac{9}{12} - \frac{7}{12} = n$

5. $\frac{7}{9} - \frac{4}{9} = n$

6. $\frac{4}{5} - \frac{1}{5} = n$

7. $\frac{5}{6} - \frac{4}{6} = n$

8. $\frac{11}{12} - \frac{5}{12} = n$

9. $\frac{7}{8} - \frac{3}{8} = n$

Lesson 18.2 (pages 320–321)

Use fraction bars to find the difference.

1. $\frac{6}{8} - \frac{1}{2} = n$

2. $\frac{3}{8} - \frac{1}{4} = n$

3. $\frac{1}{3} - \frac{1}{6} = n$

4. $\frac{1}{2} - \frac{3}{10} = n$

5. $\frac{2}{4} - \frac{1}{8} = n$

6. $\frac{5}{6} - \frac{2}{3} = n$

Lesson 18.3 (pages 322–323)

Name the least common denominator, or LCD, for each pair of fractions.

1. $\frac{1}{2}$ and $\frac{1}{8}$

2. $\frac{1}{3}$ and $\frac{1}{12}$

3. $\frac{1}{2}$ and $\frac{1}{6}$

Use fraction strips to find the difference. Write the answer in simplest form.

4. $\frac{1}{2} - \frac{3}{10} = n$

5. $\frac{4}{8} - \frac{1}{4} = n$

6. $\frac{1}{3} - \frac{1}{9} = n$

7. $\frac{3}{4} - \frac{1}{8} = n$

8. $\frac{9}{12} - \frac{3}{12} = n$

9. $\frac{6}{9} - \frac{1}{3} = n$

Lesson 18.4 Part 1 (pages 324–325)

Use a ruler to find the difference.

1. $\frac{3}{8}$ in. $-$ $\frac{3}{16}$ in. $= n$ **2.** $\frac{1}{2}$ in. $-$ $\frac{5}{16}$ in. $= n$ **3.** $\frac{3}{4}$ in. $-$ $\frac{5}{8}$ in. $= n$

4. $\frac{11}{16}$ in. $-$ $\frac{5}{8}$ in. $= n$ **5.** $\frac{3}{4}$ in. $-$ $\frac{1}{16}$ in. $= n$ **6.** 1 in. $-$ $\frac{3}{4}$ in. $= n$

Lesson 18.4 Part 2 (pages 326–327)

Work backward to solve.

1. Derrick's sprout is $\frac{11}{16}$ inch tall. It had grown $\frac{3}{8}$ inch from Wednesday to Friday. It had grown $\frac{1}{4}$ inch from Monday to Wednesday. How tall was Derrick's sprout on Monday?

2. Matthew's leaf is $\frac{3}{4}$ inch wide. It had grown $\frac{5}{16}$ inch from Sunday to Tuesday. How wide was Matthew's leaf on Sunday?

Chapter 19

Lesson 19.1 (pages 338–339)

Write whether the fraction is closer to 0, $\frac{1}{2}$, or 1. You may use a number line.

1. $\frac{7}{8}$ **2.** $\frac{1}{9}$ **3.** $\frac{4}{11}$ **4.** $\frac{2}{12}$ **5.** $\frac{5}{9}$ **6.** $\frac{6}{10}$

Estimate each sum or difference.

7. $\frac{2}{5} + \frac{4}{9}$ **8.** $\frac{1}{10} + \frac{5}{8}$ **9.** $\frac{8}{9} - \frac{3}{7}$

10. $\frac{7}{9} + \frac{1}{5}$ **11.** $\frac{7}{10} - \frac{1}{12}$ **12.** $\frac{2}{10} - \frac{1}{12}$

Lesson 19.2 (pages 340–341)

Find the sum. Write the answer in simplest form.

1. $\frac{3}{4} + \frac{1}{4} = n$ **2.** $\frac{2}{5} + \frac{2}{5} = n$ **3.** $\frac{3}{8} + \frac{3}{8} = n$

4. $\frac{4}{7} + \frac{1}{7} = n$ **5.** $\frac{2}{6} + \frac{3}{6} = n$ **6.** $\frac{3}{12} + \frac{4}{12} = n$

Find the difference. Write the answer in simplest form.

7. $\frac{5}{8} - \frac{2}{8} = n$ **8.** $\frac{4}{7} - \frac{3}{7} = n$ **9.** $\frac{9}{11} - \frac{7}{11} = n$

10. $\frac{4}{5} - \frac{2}{5} = n$ **11.** $\frac{9}{10} - \frac{1}{10} = n$ **12.** $\frac{7}{8} - \frac{3}{8} = n$

Lesson 19.3 (pages 342–343)

Find the sum or difference. Write the answer in simplest form.

1. $\frac{3}{4} - \frac{1}{4} = n$
2. $\frac{1}{3} + \frac{4}{9} = n$
3. $\frac{5}{7} - \frac{3}{7} = n$
4. $\frac{2}{3} + \frac{3}{4} = n$
5. $\frac{2}{3} - \frac{5}{12} = n$
6. $\frac{5}{8} - \frac{1}{3} = n$
7. $\frac{5}{9} + \frac{4}{9} = n$
8. $\frac{5}{6} + \frac{1}{2} = n$
9. $\frac{11}{15} - \frac{2}{5} = n$
10. $\frac{1}{2} + \frac{2}{3} = n$
11. $\frac{3}{5} - \frac{1}{4} = n$
12. $\frac{2}{3} + \frac{3}{5} = n$

Lesson 19.4 (pages 344–345)

Find the sum or difference. Write each answer in simplest form.

1. $\frac{3}{10} + \frac{1}{2} = n$
2. $\frac{1}{4} + \frac{5}{6} = n$
3. $\frac{7}{9} - \frac{4}{9} = n$
4. $\frac{2}{8} + \frac{2}{8} = n$
5. $\frac{1}{2} - \frac{3}{7} = n$
6. $\frac{1}{2} - \frac{2}{9} = n$
7. $\frac{1}{3} + \frac{1}{4} = n$
8. $\frac{3}{4} - \frac{5}{9} = n$
9. $\frac{7}{10} + \frac{5}{10} = n$
10. $\frac{2}{3} - \frac{8}{18} = n$
11. $\frac{5}{7} - \frac{2}{3} = n$
12. $\frac{6}{7} + \frac{1}{2} = n$

Lesson 19.5 Part 1 (pages 346–347)

Tell whether you would add or subtract to solve the problem. Solve.

1. Madison practiced piano for $\frac{3}{4}$ hour on Monday and $\frac{1}{3}$ hour on Tuesday. How long did she practice on both days?
2. The Cohens had $\frac{1}{2}$ gallon of milk. They used $\frac{1}{4}$ gallon. How much milk do they have left?

Lesson 19.5 Part 2 (pages 348–349)

Draw a diagram to solve.

1. Some fifth graders took a survey asking students whether they liked mysteries, comedies, or dramas best. The survey showed that $\frac{2}{5}$ liked mysteries best, $\frac{1}{2}$ preferred comedies, and $\frac{1}{10}$ liked dramas. There were 5 students who preferred dramas. How many students took the survey?
2. Ginger, Rebecca, and Alvin are comparing the number of pages they read. Ginger read 18 pages, Rebecca read 6 pages fewer than Ginger. Alvin read 7 pages more than Rebecca. How many pages did Alvin read?

Chapter 20

Lesson 20.1 (pages 354–355)

Round the mixed number to the nearest $\frac{1}{2}$ or whole number. You may use a number line or a ruler.

1. $6\frac{1}{6}$ **2.** $1\frac{7}{8}$ **3.** $3\frac{2}{5}$ **4.** $9\frac{5}{12}$ **5.** $4\frac{1}{3}$ **6.** $7\frac{3}{4}$

Estimate the sum or difference.

7. $2\frac{1}{8} + 3\frac{3}{4}$ **8.** $4\frac{2}{9} - 1\frac{1}{5}$ **9.** $3\frac{5}{8} + 3\frac{9}{16}$

10. $7\frac{6}{7} - 6\frac{11}{12}$ **11.** $1\frac{1}{9} + 9\frac{2}{12}$ **12.** $7\frac{1}{8} - 4\frac{4}{9}$

Lesson 20.2 (pages 356–357)

Find the sum. You may wish to draw a picture. Write the answer in simplest form.

1. $2\frac{2}{7} + 4\frac{3}{7}$ **2.** $4\frac{1}{2} + 1\frac{1}{4}$ **3.** $7\frac{1}{6} + 2\frac{2}{3}$ **4.** $5\frac{1}{3} + 3\frac{2}{12}$

5. $7\frac{2}{7} + 2\frac{1}{2} = n$ **6.** $4\frac{1}{2} + 4\frac{1}{4} = n$ **7.** $8\frac{2}{3} + 1\frac{1}{4} = n$

8. $3\frac{4}{9} + 5\frac{2}{3} = n$ **9.** $6\frac{3}{4} + 2\frac{4}{16} = n$ **10.** $5\frac{5}{6} + 1\frac{1}{3} = n$

11. $4\frac{1}{12} + 3\frac{3}{4} = n$ **12.** $5\frac{7}{15} + 3\frac{3}{5} = n$ **13.** $6\frac{4}{9} + 7\frac{1}{3} = n$

Lesson 20.3 Part 1 (pages 358–359)

Subtract. Write the answer in simplest form.

1. $3\frac{2}{5} = 3\frac{6}{15}$, $-1\frac{1}{3} = 1\frac{5}{15}$

2. $6\frac{7}{12} = 6\frac{7}{12}$, $-3\frac{1}{4} = 3\frac{3}{12}$

3. $9\frac{3}{4} = 9\frac{3}{4}$, $-5\frac{1}{2} = 5\frac{2}{4}$

4. $7\frac{7}{9} - 5\frac{2}{3} = n$ **5.** $8\frac{9}{10} - 4\frac{3}{5} = n$ **6.** $4\frac{1}{2} - 3\frac{3}{8} = n$

7. $3\frac{7}{12} - \frac{2}{6} = n$ **8.** $9\frac{7}{10} - 3\frac{1}{2} = n$ **9.** $6\frac{13}{14} - 2\frac{2}{7} = n$

10. $4\frac{3}{8} - 2\frac{1}{4} = n$ **11.** $7\frac{3}{4} - \frac{8}{16} = n$ **12.** $9\frac{3}{5} - \frac{1}{10} = n$

Lesson 20.3 Part 2 (pages 360–361)

Work backward to solve.

1. Elizabeth spent \$69 on a new outfit. She spent \$23 on a skirt and \$18 on a blouse. How much did she spend on the new shoes?

2. Jerry worked on his homework for $1\frac{1}{2}$ hours. During that time he spent $\frac{3}{4}$ hour doing math and $\frac{1}{2}$ hour reading a science chapter. How much time did he spend reviewing vocabulary words?

Lesson 20.4 (pages 362–363)

Use fraction bars to find the difference.

1. $7\frac{1}{2} - 2\frac{1}{4}$

2. $4\frac{2}{3} - \frac{1}{6}$

3. $9\frac{2}{3} - 3\frac{1}{6}$

4. $5\frac{1}{2} - \frac{1}{8}$

5. $7\frac{1}{6} - 3\frac{2}{3} = n$

6. $3\frac{5}{6} - 1\frac{2}{3} = n$

7. $6\frac{2}{5} - \frac{1}{10} = n$

8. $9\frac{1}{4} - 5\frac{1}{8} = n$

9. $2\frac{1}{3} - 1\frac{8}{12} = n$

10. $4\frac{3}{8} - \frac{3}{4} = n$

Chapter 21

Lesson 21.1 (pages 368–369)

Draw a line segment to the given length.

1. $3\frac{3}{4}$ inches

2. $2\frac{1}{16}$ inches

3. $4\frac{9}{16}$ inches

4. $1\frac{1}{4}$ inches

Use a ruler to compare the measurements. Write $<$, $>$, or $=$ for each ●.

5. $4\frac{3}{16}$ ● $3\frac{3}{4}$

6. $5\frac{1}{16}$ ● $5\frac{3}{16}$

7. $6\frac{3}{4}$ ● $6\frac{1}{8}$

8. $1\frac{4}{16}$ ● $1\frac{1}{4}$

9. $1\frac{5}{8}$ ● $1\frac{3}{4}$

10. $2\frac{7}{8}$ ● $3\frac{1}{8}$

11. $2\frac{7}{16}$ ● $2\frac{1}{2}$

12. $4\frac{5}{16}$ ● $4\frac{1}{4}$

Lesson 21.2 Part 1 (pages 370–371)

Change the unit. You may use a calculator.

1. 15 ft = __?__ yd

2. 60 ft = __?__ yd

3. 62 yd = __?__ ft

4. 156 in. = __?__ ft

5. 8 ft = __?__ in.

6. 17 yd = __?__ ft

7. 3 mi = __?__ ft

8. 3,520 yd = __?__ mi

9. 252 in. = __?__ ft

Write *multiply* or *divide*. Solve.

10. How many feet are in 60 inches?

11. How many inches are in 4 feet?

12. How many yards are in 7 miles

13. How many feet are in 2 miles?

14. How many feet are in 7 yards?

15. How many inches are in 6 yards?

Lesson 21.2 Part 2 (pages 372–373)

Rename the measurements.

1. 39 in. = _?_ ft _?_ in.

2. 17 ft = _?_ yd _?_ ft

3. 64 in. = _?_ ft _?_ in.

4. 6 ft 7 in. = 5 ft _?_ in.

5. 9 ft 14 in. = 10 ft _?_ in.

6. 7 yd 1 ft = 6 yd _?_ ft

Find the sum or difference.

7. 7 ft 5 in.
+3 ft 9 in.

8. 4 yd 3 ft
+7 yd 2 ft

9. 13 ft 8 in.
− 9 ft 3 in.

10. 12 yd 1 ft
− 7 yd 2 ft

Lesson 21.3 (pages 374–375)

Change the unit.

1. 10 c = _?_ pt

2. 7 pt = _?_ c

3. 2 pt = _?_ fl oz

4. 4 gal = _?_ qt

5. 40 fl oz = _?_ c

6. 7 gal = _?_ qt

7. 3 pt = _?_ c

8. 12 c = _?_ fl oz

Write <, >, or = for each ●.

9. 2 gal ● 10 qt

10. 4 c ● 2 pt

11. 1 c ● 16 fl oz

12. 4 pt ● 6 c

Lesson 21.4 (pages 376–377)

What unit would you use to describe the weight of these objects?
Write *tons, pounds,* or *ounces*.

1. a child

2. an elephant

3. a book

4. a box of cereal

Write *multiply* or *divide*. Change the unit. You may use a calculator.

5. 8 T = _?_ lb

6. 12,000 lb = _?_ T

7. 80 oz = _?_ lb

8. 50 lb = _?_ oz

Write which one is heavier.

9. 5 lb or 84 oz

10. 4 T or 6,000 lb

11. 130 oz or 9 lb

12. 10 lb or 30 oz

Lesson 21.5 Part 1 (pages 378–379)

Write the elapsed time for each hike.

1.

Time the hike started

Time the hike finished

2.

Time the hike started

Time the hike finished

Look at Roberto's schedule for the day and complete the table.

	Activity	Starting Time	Ending Time	Elapsed Time
3.	School	8:30 A.M.	2:50 P.M.	?
4.	Swim Practice	3:35 P.M.	?	1 hr 30 min
5.	Dinner	?	6:30 P.M.	40 min
6.	Homework	7:05 P.M.	8:14 P.M.	?

Lesson 21.5 Part 2 (pages 380–381)

Make a table to solve.

1. Mrs. Winter's class members are making 5 minute presentations starting at 12:35. The students, in order, are Clara, Bobby, Renee, Pam, and Paul. At what time does Pam start her presentation?

2. Three classes are scheduled for 45 minute research time. Ms. Hodson's class begins at 9:05 and Mrs. Atwood's class begins at 9:50. What time is Mr. Bower's class scheduled?

Lesson 21.6 (pages 382–383)

Find the difference in temperature.

1. room temperature of 79°F and the outside temperature of 88°F

2. a fever of 101°F and normal human body temperature

Copy and complete the table.

	Starting Temperature	Change in Temperature	Final Temperature
3.	78°F	?	87°F
4.	13°C	rose 11°	?
5.	63°F	?	45°F
6.	7°F	fell 2°	?

Chapter 22

Lesson 22.1 (pages 388–389)

Write a number sentence for the picture.

1. **2.** 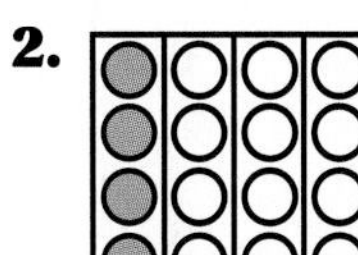 **3.** **4.**

5. 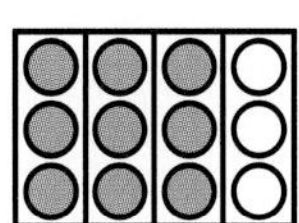 **6.** **7.** **8.**

Find the product.

9. $\frac{2}{3} \times 12 = n$ **10.** $\frac{1}{4} \times 28 = n$ **11.** $\frac{3}{4} \times 12 = n$ **12.** $\frac{5}{6} \times 12 = n$

13. $15 \times \frac{2}{5} = n$ **14.** $14 \times \frac{2}{7} = n$ **15.** $24 \times \frac{3}{8} = n$ **16.** $18 \times \frac{1}{9} = n$

17. $\frac{1}{6} \times 12 = n$ **18.** $20 \times \frac{2}{5} = n$ **19.** $10 \times \frac{1}{5} = n$ **20.** $27 \times \frac{2}{3} = n$

Lesson 22.2 (pages 390–391)

Make a paper-folding model to find the product.

1. $\frac{1}{3} \times \frac{1}{3} = n$ **2.** $\frac{1}{2} \times \frac{2}{3} = n$ **3.** $\frac{2}{3} \times \frac{2}{9} = n$

4. $\frac{1}{4} \times \frac{3}{4} = n$ **5.** $\frac{3}{4} \times \frac{2}{5} = n$ **6.** $\frac{1}{5} \times \frac{2}{3} = n$

Lesson 22.3 (pages 392–393)

Multiply. Write the answer in simplest form.

1. $\frac{1}{6} \times \frac{1}{3} = n$ **2.** $\frac{3}{5} \times \frac{1}{3} = n$ **3.** $\frac{2}{3} \times \frac{4}{9} = n$ **4.** $\frac{3}{8} \times \frac{2}{5} = n$

5. $\frac{1}{7} \times \frac{1}{6} = n$ **6.** $\frac{3}{4} \times \frac{4}{5} = n$ **7.** $\frac{6}{7} \times \frac{1}{3} = n$ **8.** $\frac{5}{9} \times \frac{3}{4} = n$

9. $\frac{7}{8} \times \frac{3}{7} = n$ **10.** $\frac{4}{15} \times \frac{3}{8} = n$ **11.** $\frac{4}{7} \times \frac{3}{10} = n$ **12.** $\frac{7}{12} \times \frac{6}{7} = n$

13. $\frac{4}{7} \times \frac{2}{3} = n$ **14.** $\frac{3}{4} \times \frac{3}{8} = n$ **15.** $\frac{2}{3} \times \frac{5}{6} = n$ **16.** $\frac{3}{8} \times \frac{2}{3} = n$

17. $\frac{5}{8} \times \frac{3}{4} = n$ **18.** $\frac{2}{5} \times \frac{3}{10} = n$ **19.** $\frac{4}{7} \times \frac{1}{4} = n$ **20.** $\frac{2}{16} \times \frac{2}{2} = n$

21. $\frac{2}{3} \times \frac{6}{7} = n$ **22.** $\frac{2}{9} \times \frac{1}{3} = n$ **23.** $\frac{9}{10} \times \frac{5}{12} = n$ **24.** $\frac{3}{4} \times \frac{2}{5} = n$

Lesson 22.4 Part 1 (pages 394–395)

Multiply. Write the answer in simplest form.

1. $\frac{1}{2} \times 2\frac{2}{3} = n$
2. $\frac{2}{3} \times 1\frac{2}{5} = n$
3. $\frac{1}{4} \times 2\frac{1}{7} = n$
4. $\frac{3}{4} \times 1\frac{2}{3} = n$
5. $\frac{2}{5} \times 1\frac{2}{3} = n$
6. $\frac{3}{5} \times 1\frac{1}{6} = n$
7. $\frac{1}{6} \times 2\frac{2}{5} = n$
8. $\frac{3}{4} \times 3\frac{1}{3} = n$
9. $\frac{1}{5} \times 1\frac{3}{4} = n$
10. $\frac{1}{3} \times 3\frac{1}{9} = n$
11. $\frac{5}{6} \times 4\frac{3}{5} = n$
12. $\frac{2}{7} \times 3\frac{2}{4} = n$

Lesson 22.4 Part 2 (pages 396–397)

Make a model to solve.

1. Samuel had $2\frac{1}{4}$ dozen markers. After awhile, $\frac{1}{3}$ of the markers dried up and he threw them away. How many dozen markers does he have left?

2. Bruce bought 3 books. He received $3.77 back in coins. He has 10 quarters, half as many dimes as quarters, 3 times as many nickels as dimes, and the rest are pennies. How many of each coin does he have?

Chapter 23

Lesson 23.1 (pages 408–409)

For Exercises 1–4, use the figure.

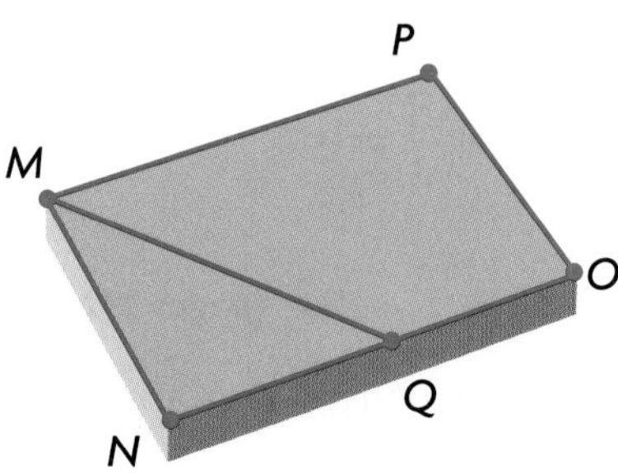

1. Name the point where *MN* and *NO* intersect.
2. Name the line segment that is parallel to *PO*.
3. Name the line segment that intersects but is not perpendicular to *NO*.
4. Name a line segment on plane *MNO* that is perpendicular to *PO*.

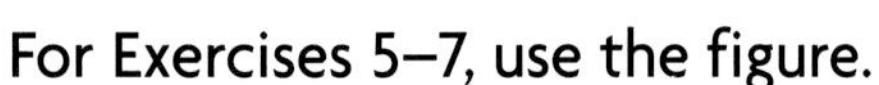

For Exercises 5–7, use the figure.

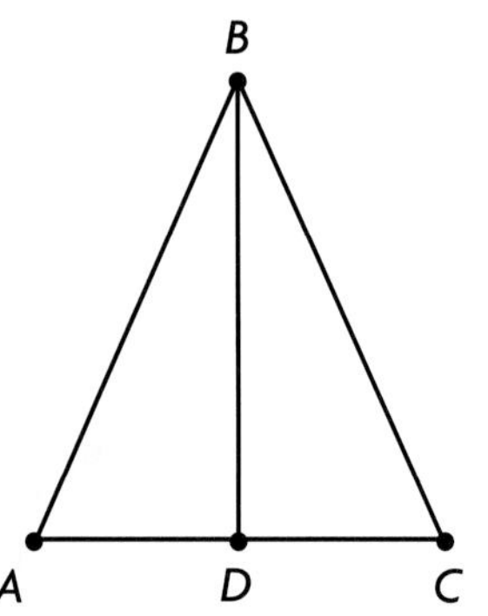

5. Name the line segment that is perpendicular to *AC*.
6. Name the point where *AC* and *BD* intersect.
7. Is line segment *AB* parallel to *BC*?

Identify each line relationship. Write *parallel, perpendicular,* or *intersecting*. Some figures may have more than one answer.

8.

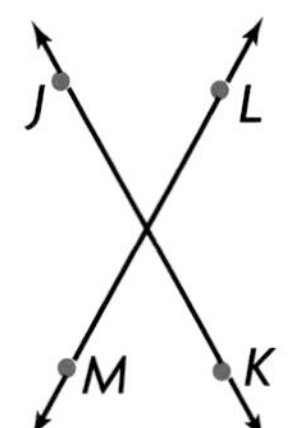

9.

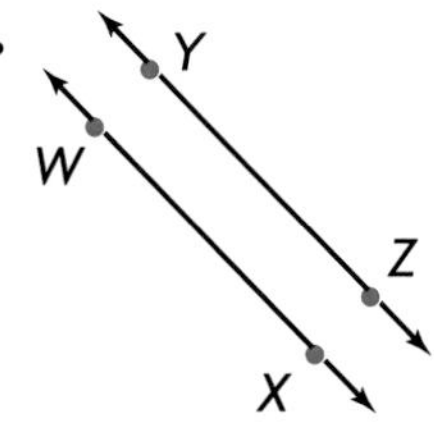

10.

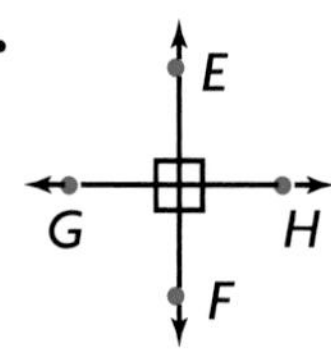

Lesson 23.2 (pages 410–411)

Identify the angle. Write *right, acute,* or *obtuse.*

1. **2.** **3.**

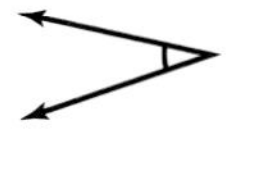

4.

For Exercises 5–12, use the figure. Identify the angle. Write *right, acute,* or *obtuse.*

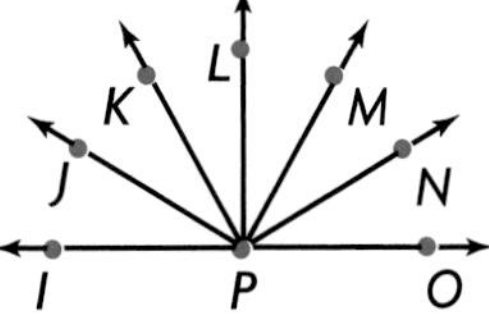

5. $\angle IPL$ **6.** $\angle KPL$

7. $\angle JPI$ **8.** $\angle IPM$

9. $\angle NPO$ **10.** $\angle LPO$

11. $\angle JPN$ **12.** $\angle NPI$

Lesson 23.3 Part 1 (pages 412–413)

Trace each figure. Use a protractor to measure the angle.

1.

2.

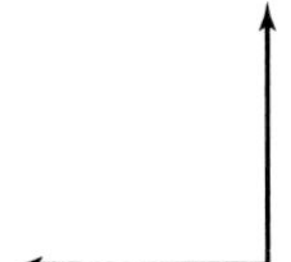

3.

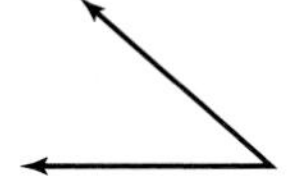

4.

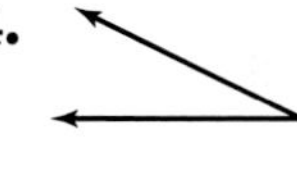

Lesson 23.3 Part 2 (pages 414–415)

Draw a diagram to solve.

1. Sandy is having a birthday party. She gave Terry directions to her house. Make a map of Sandy's directions.

2. Rex is hanging pictures in a straight line on a 6-foot wall. He hammers a nail into the wall every 9 inches. He does not put nails on the ends. How many pictures can Rex hang?

Sandy's directions:

Drive north on 34th Street. Make a 90° turn east on Riverview Blvd., and drive 2 blocks. Make a 90° turn right on Elm Street. Look for the balloons on the mailbox.

Lesson 23.4 (pages 416–417)

Draw and name the quadrilateral.

1. two pairs of congruent sides and four right angles

2. four congruent sides and 2 pairs of congruent angles

Write *true* or *false*.

3. A trapezoid has 2 pairs of parallel sides.

4. All quadrilaterals have 4 sides.

5. A square has 4 right angles.

6. A rectangle has 2 pairs of congruent sides.

Lesson 23.5 Part 1 (pages 418–419)

Name each triangle. Write *isosceles, scalene,* or *equilateral.*

1. 5 m, 5 m, 5 m

2. 8 cm, 2 cm, 7 cm

3. 5 cm, 6 cm, 4 cm

4. 3 ft, 3 ft, 1 ft

5. 7 in., 7 in., 7 in.

6. 2 m, 2 m, 2 m

7. 2 in., 3 in., 4 in.

8. 7 ft, 14 ft, 14 ft

9. 3 in., 4 in., 1 in.

10. 6 cm, 6 cm, 3 cm

11. 5 yd, 2 yd, 4 yd

12. 4 m, 4 m, 4 m

Lesson 23.5 Part 2 (pages 420–421)

Name each triangle. Write *right, acute,* or *obtuse.*

1.

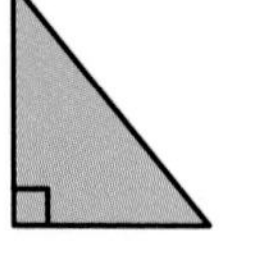

2.

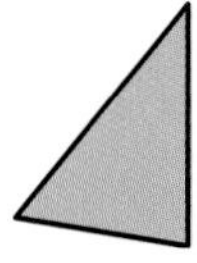

3.

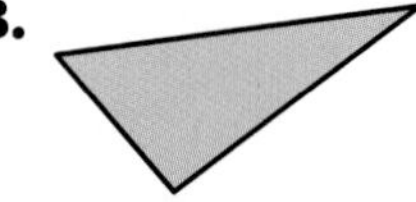

4.

5.

6.

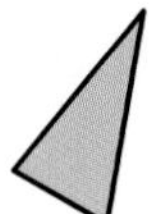

Find the measure of the unknown angle in each triangle.

7. 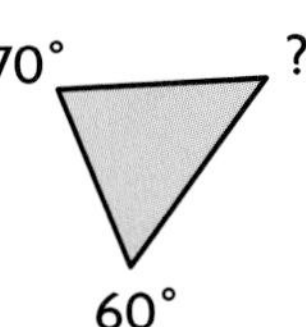

8. 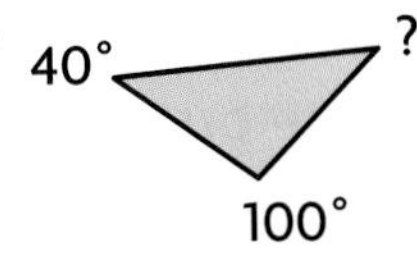

9. 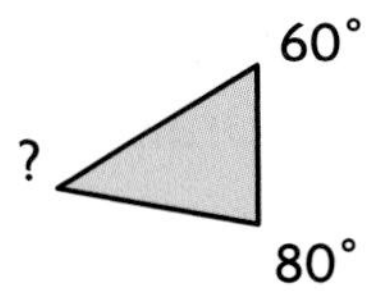

10. 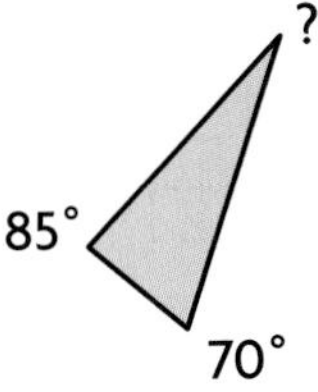

11. 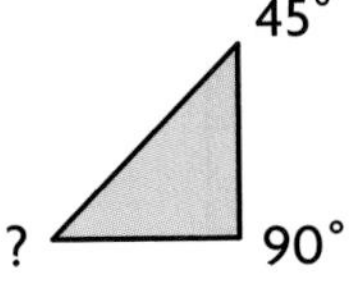

12. 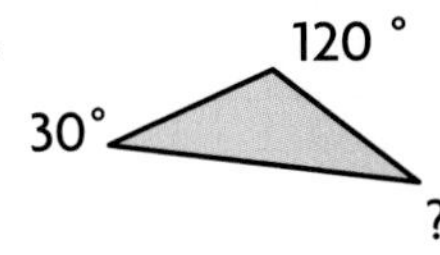

Chapter 24

Lesson 24.1 (pages 426–427)

Write *congruent* or *not congruent*.

1. 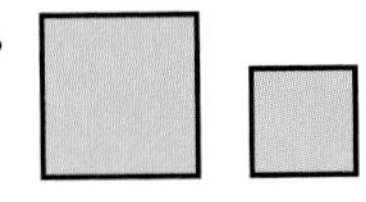

2. 

3. 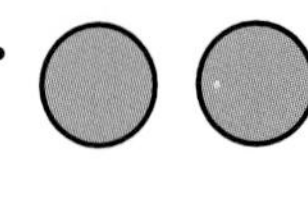

Write the letters of the two figures that are congruent.

4. a. 

b. 

c. 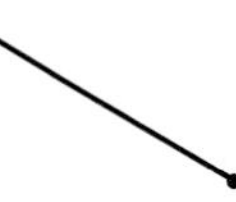

5. a. 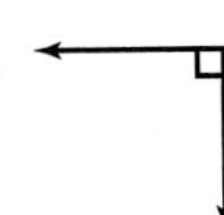

b. 

c. 

Lesson 24.2 (pages 428–429)

Tell whether the two halves of each drawing are congruent. Write *yes* or *no*.

1. 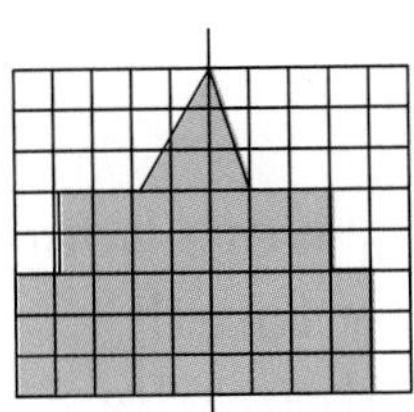

2. 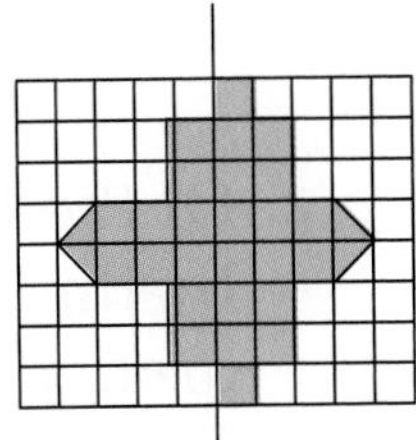

3. 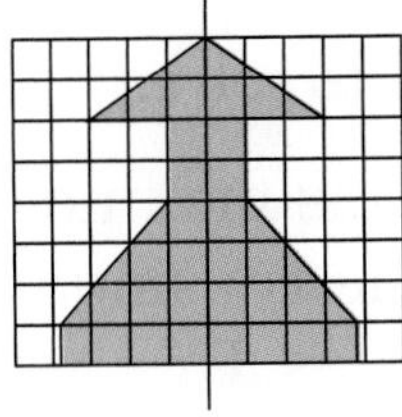

Trace each figure. Draw the lines of symmetry for each figure.

4.

5. 

6. 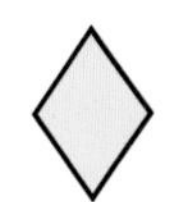

Lesson 24.3 (pages 430–431)

Copy each figure on a coordinate grid. Translate, reflect, and rotate each figure. Draw the new figure. Name the ordered pairs.

1. 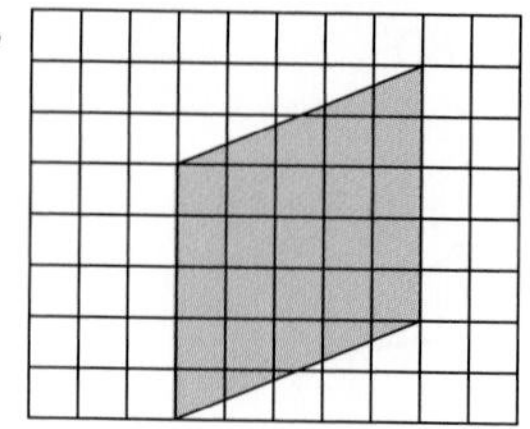

2. 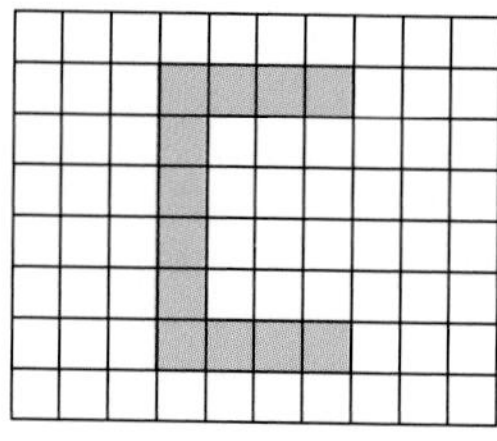

3. 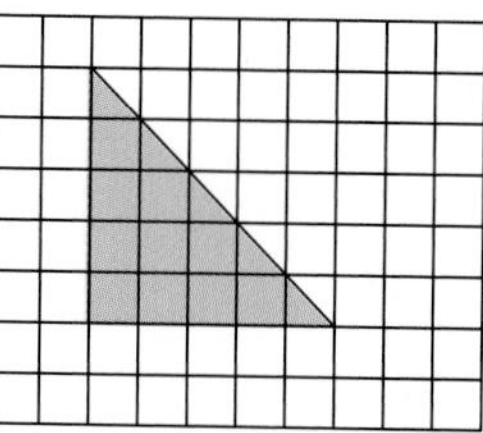

4. 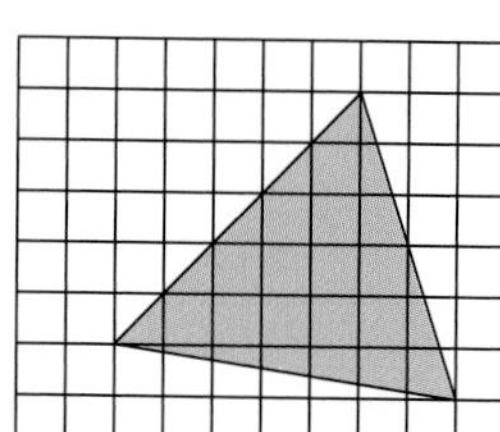

5. 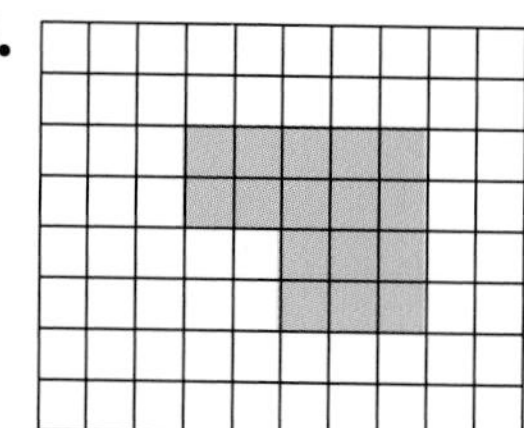

6. 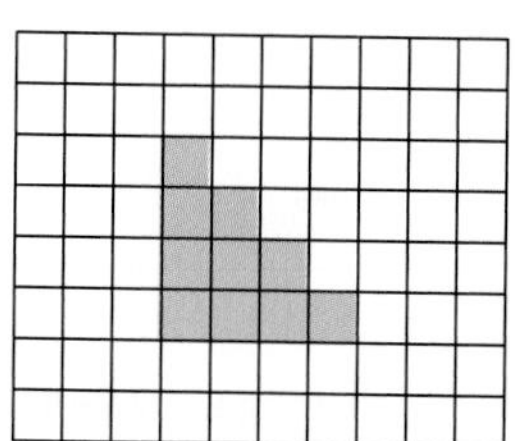

Lesson 24.4 Part 1 (pages 432–433)

Copy each figure. Write *yes* or *no* to tell whether each figure can be arranged to tessellate.

1. 

2. 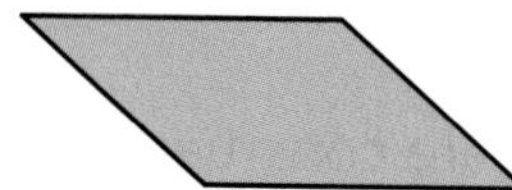

3. 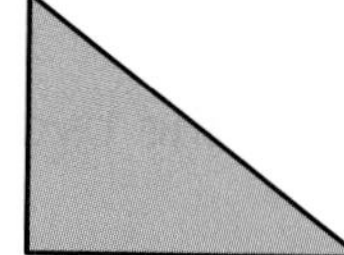

Copy each figure and translate, reflect, or rotate it to make a design that tessellates.

4. 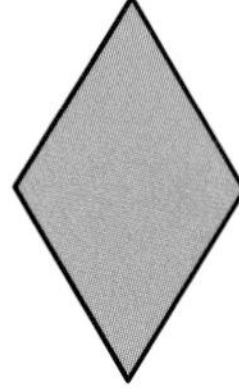

5. 

6. 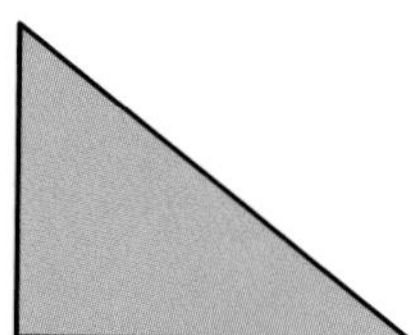

Lesson 24.4 Part 2 (pages 434–435)

Make a model to solve.

1. Cassandra is making a mosaic design. She is using trapezoids and triangles. Draw a design that may look like Cassandra's.

2. Of the hot lunches, $\frac{1}{8}$ were bought by third graders, $\frac{1}{4}$ by fourth graders, and $\frac{5}{8}$ by fifth graders. There were 30 third graders who bought hot lunches. How many fifth graders bought hot lunches?

Chapter 25

Lesson 25.1 (pages 440–441)

Use a compass to construct the circles and find the measurements.

1. Construct a circle with a radius of 5 cm. Label and measure a diameter and a chord.

2. Construct a circle with a radius of 7 cm. Label and measure a radius and a chord.

Write *chord, diameter,* or *radius* for each line segment.

3. 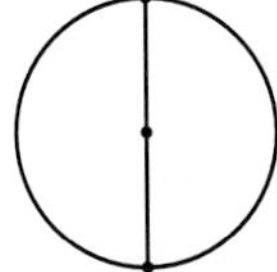

4. 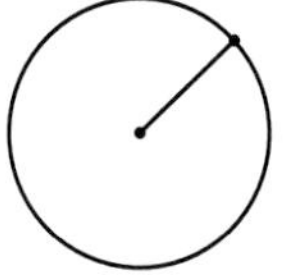

5. 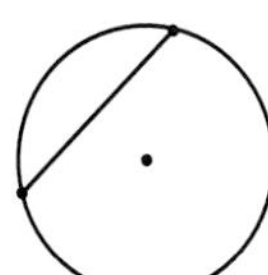

6. 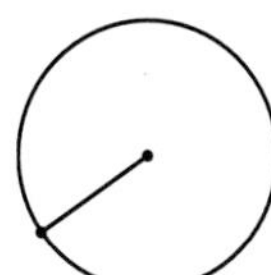

Lesson 25.2 Part 1 (pages 442–443)

Use a calculator to divide the circumference of each object by its diameter. Complete the table by rounding to the nearest hundredth.

	Object	Circumference (*C*)	Diameter (*d*)	$\frac{C}{d}$
1.	ball	12.6 cm	4 cm	?
2.	jar	15.6 cm	5 cm	?
3.	vase	28.2 cm	9 cm	?
4.	glass	25.1 cm	8 cm	?
5.	roll of tape	18.9 cm	6 cm	?
6.	stick	6.28 cm	2 cm	?

Lesson 25.2 Part 2 (pages 444–445)

Act it out to solve.

1. Liza, Ian, Wade, Max, and Audrey are waiting on a bench for the school bus. Wade is on the left end, Ian is between Liza and Wade. Max is on the far right. Who is Audrey between?

2. Lakeisha had one $20 bill, one $10 bill, two $5 bills, one $1 bill, three quarters, and two dimes. She spent $21.25 on a shirt and $15.50 on a CD. What bills and coins does Lakeisha have left?

Lesson 25.3 (pages 446–447)

Write *true* or *false* to describe each statement.

1. In a circle with three radii, each of three angles could measure 120°.

2. In a circle, one diameter forms two acute angles.

3. If in a circle, four radii form three 80° angles, the fourth angle is acute.

4. If in a circle, six radii form five 60° angles, the sixth angle is acute.

Find the missing angle.

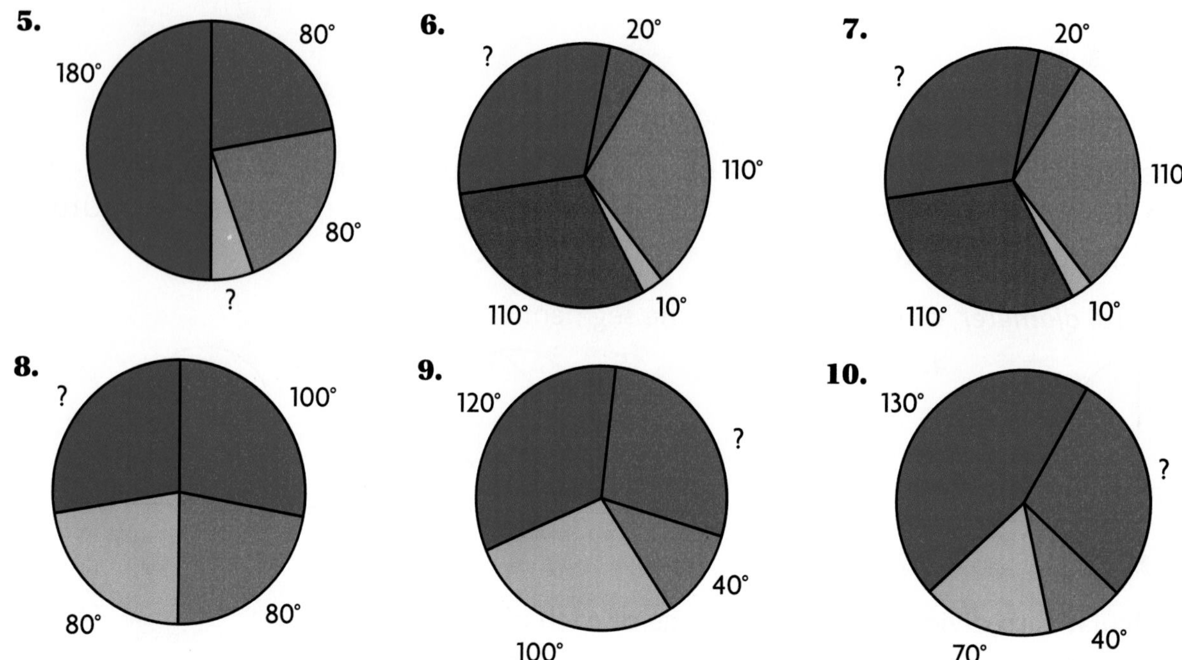

Lesson 25.4 (pages 448–449)

Use a protractor to find how many degrees are in each angle.

1.

2.

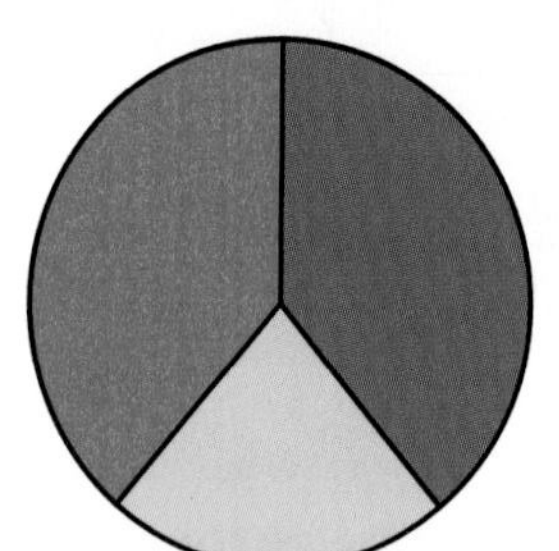

3.

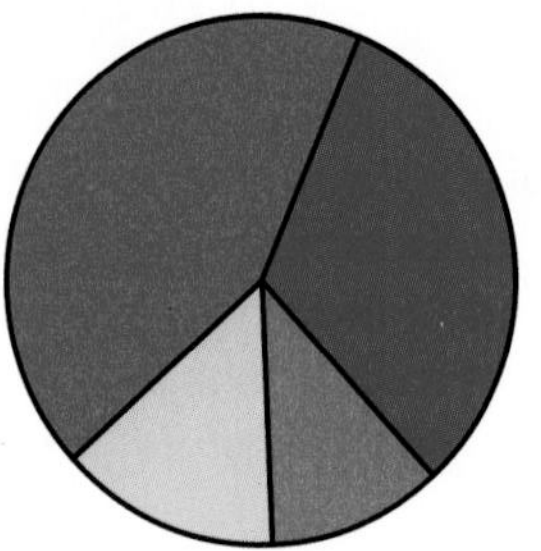

Use a compass and a protractor to draw a circle with the following angles.

4. 4 angles of 90° each
5. 2 angles of 60° each and 2 angles of 120° each
6. 6 angles of 60° each
7. 2 angles of 110° each and 1 angle of 140°
8. 3 angles of 80° each and 1 angle of 120°
9. 4 angles of 80° each and 1 angle of 40°
10. 3 angles of 60° each, 2 angles of 45° each and 1 angle of 90°
11. 2 angles of 90° each and 3 angles of 60° each
12. 3 angles of 25° each, 3 angles of 45° each, and 3 angles of 50° each

Chapter 26

Lesson 26.1 (pages 454–455)

Write *prism* or *pyramid.* Write the polygon that names the base. Identify the solid figure.

1. 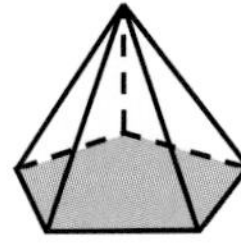

2. 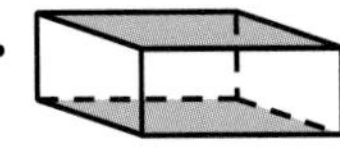

3. 

4. 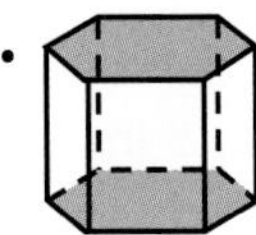

Write the name of the solid figure. Make a drawing of each.

5. I have 6 congruent squares.

6. I have a hexagonal base and 6 congruent triangles.

7. I have 6 rectangular faces.

8. I have an octagonal base and 8 congruent triangles.

9. I have 2 triangular faces and 3 congruent rectangles.

Lesson 26.2 (pages 456–457)

Match each solid figure with its net. Write *a, b, c,* or *d.*

1. 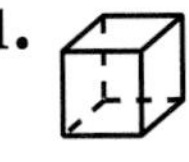

2. 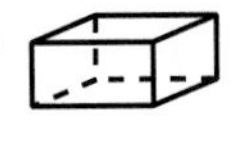

3. 

4. 

a. 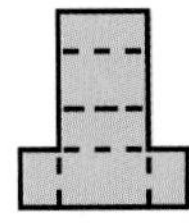

b. 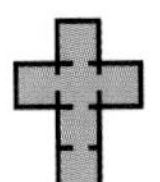

c. 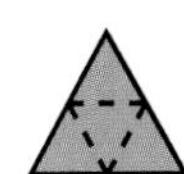

d. 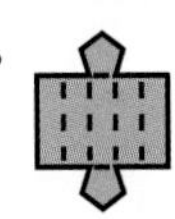

Lesson 26.3 (pages 458–459)

Use grid paper to draw each figure from the top, the side, and the front.

1. 

2. 

3. 

Lesson 26.4 Part 1 (pages 460–461)

Find the missing dimension. You may use a calculator.

1. 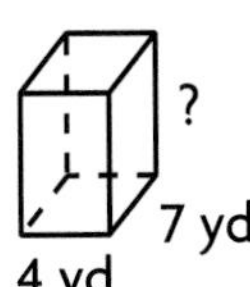

volume = 168 cu yd

2. 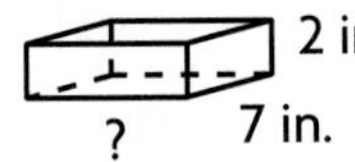

volume = 154 cu in.

3. 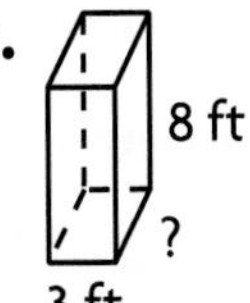

volume = 288 cu ft

4. length = 7 ft
width = ?
height = 2 ft
volume = 84 cu ft

5. length = 15 in.
width = 9 in.
height = 4 in.
volume = ?

6. length = ?
width = 11 cm
height = 8 cm
volume = 352 cu cm

Complete the table. You may use a calculator.

	Length	Width	Height	Volume
7.	9 in.	5 in.	8 in.	?
8.	9 cm	10 cm	7 cm	?
9.	12 ft	4 ft	3 ft	?
10.	6 yd	15 yd	11 yd	?

Lesson 26.4 Part 2 (pages 462–463)

Use a formula to solve.

1. A pencil box is 13 in. long and 6 in. wide. It has a volume of 234 cu in. What is the height of the pencil box?

2. Trevor is putting down linoleum in his kitchen. His kitchen is 16 ft wide and 24 ft long. How many square feet of linoleum does Trevor need?

Lesson 26.5 (pages 464–465)

Use the benchmarks at the right to name the more reasonable unit for measuring the volume of each box. Estimate the volume.

1.

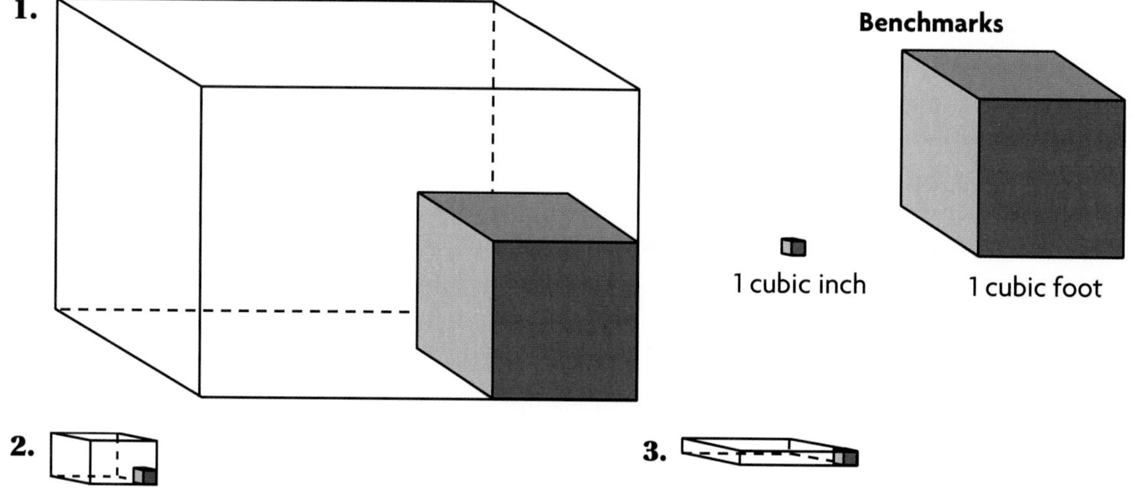

2.

3.

Choose the most reasonable measure. Write *a*, *b*, or *c*.

4. a suitcase **a.** 1 cu in. **b.** 1 cu ft **c.** 1 cu yd

5. a shoe box **a.** 110 cu in. **b.** 110 cu ft **c.** 110 cu yd

6. a refrigerator **a.** 80 cu in. **b.** 80 cu ft **c.** 80 cu yd

7. a model car **a.** 2 cu in. **b.** 2 cu ft **c.** 2 cu yd

Chapter 27

Lesson 27.1 (pages 476–477)

Name the type of ratio and show with counters.

1. Of the 8 books on a shelf, 5 are fiction.

2. There were 7 boys and 10 girls.

3. During vacation, 3 of the 7 days were rainy.

4. There are 6 roses and 7 daisies.

5. Of the 9 students, 2 are sick.

6. Homework was finished by 9 out of 11 students.

Lesson 27.2 (pages 478–479)

Write *a* or *b* to show which fraction represents the ratio.

1. 2 to 5 **a.** $\frac{2}{5}$ **b.** $\frac{5}{2}$

2. 1:10 **a.** $\frac{1}{10}$ **b.** $\frac{10}{1}$

3. 3:11 **a.** $\frac{11}{3}$ **b.** $\frac{3}{11}$

4. 6 to 5 **a.** $\frac{5}{6}$ **b.** $\frac{6}{5}$

For Exercises 5–8, use the table. Write each ratio in three ways.

5. What is the ratio of non-fiction books to fiction books?

6. What is the ratio of mystery books to non-fiction books?

7. What is the ratio of all books to comedy books?

8. What is the ratio of fiction books to all books?

SHELBY'S BOOK COLLECTION	
Number of Books	**Type**
4	Comedy
9	Fiction
7	Non-Fiction
3	Mystery

Lesson 27.3 (pages 480–481)

Tell whether the ratios are equivalent. Write *yes* or *no*.

1. 3:4 and 9:12

2. $\frac{1}{3}$ and $\frac{6}{9}$

3. 3 to 10 and 6 to 7

4. 1:2 and 2:3

5. $\frac{2}{5}$ and $\frac{4}{10}$

6. 4 to 9 and 2 to 6

Write three ratios that are equivalent to the given ratio.

7. $\frac{2}{3}$

8. $\frac{3}{5}$

9. 1 to 5

10. 6 to 1

11. 15:30

12. 20:60

13. $\frac{4}{5}$

14. 8 to 1

15. 3:21

16. 10 to 1

17. 12:36

18. $\frac{3}{4}$

Lesson 27.4 (pages 482–483)

Copy and complete the ratio table.

1.	**Number of Cars**	2	5	?	11	?
2.	**Number of Passengers**	10	25	40	?	75

3.	**Number of Buses**	1	6	12	?	?
4.	**Number of Passengers**	9	54	?	153	189

5.	**Number of Boxes**	1	4	?	8	?
6.	**Number of Cookies**	12	48	72	?	120

Lesson 27.5 Part 1 (pages 484–485)

Write *yes* or *no* to tell whether the shapes are similar.

1.

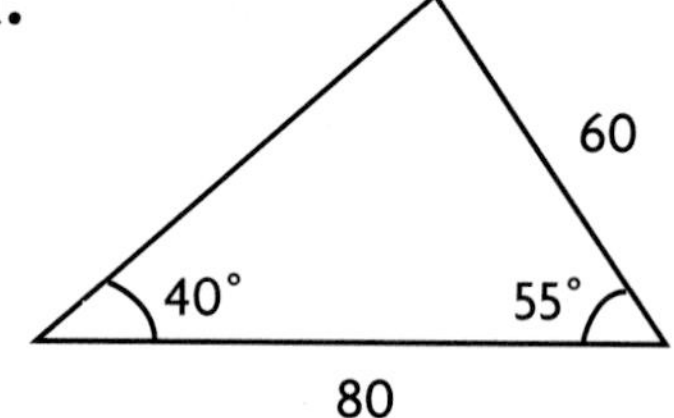

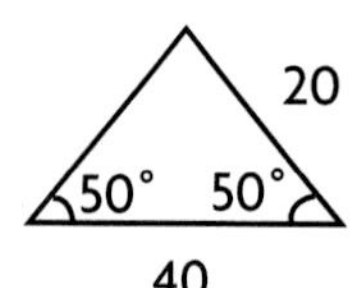

2.

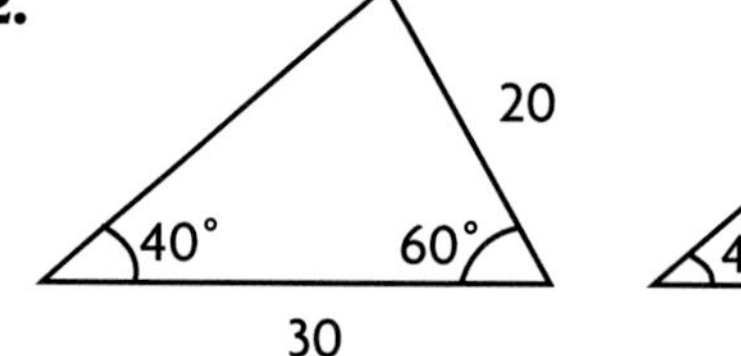

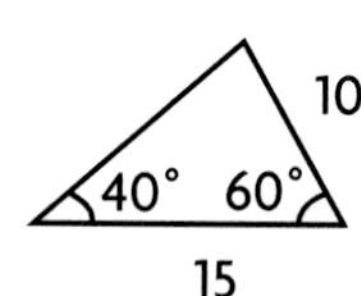

3.

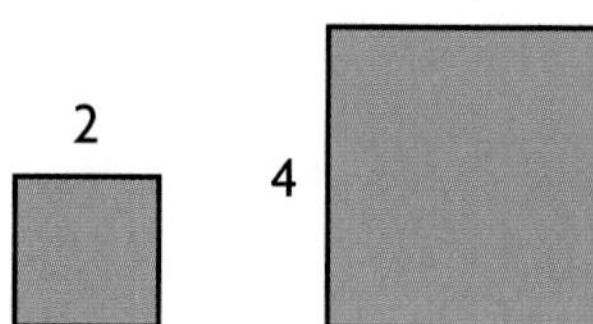

4.

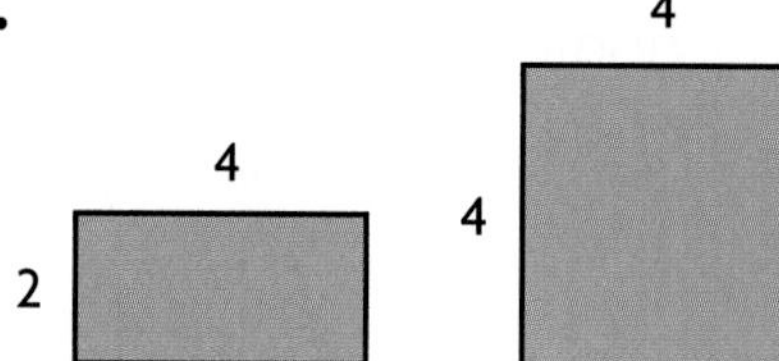

Find the length of the missing side in the similar shapes.

5.

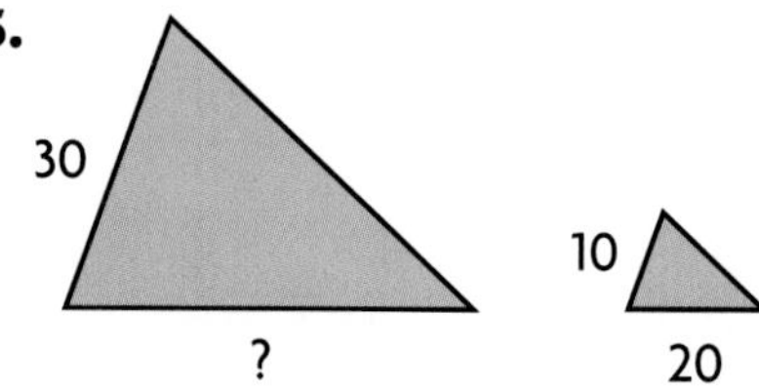

6.

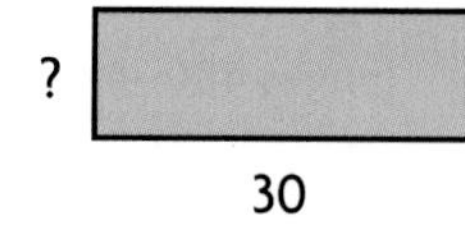

Lesson 27.5 Part 2 (pages 486–487)

Write a number sentence to solve.

1. Josie has a framed picture of her family that measures 8 in. by 10 in. She has a similar framed picture of her best friend that measures 4 in. on one side. What is the length of the other side of the frame?

2. Shakira has a vase with a 14-inch circumference. What is the diameter of Shakira's vase to the nearest half inch?

Chapter 28

Lesson 28.1 (pages 492–493)

Use counters to show the following on your 10-by-10 grid.
Draw a picture and write the percent.

1. 25 books out of 100 on a shelf

2. 42 women out of 100 people

3. 4 dogs out of 100 animals

4. 12 parrots out of 100 birds

Look at the picture. Write the percent.

5. 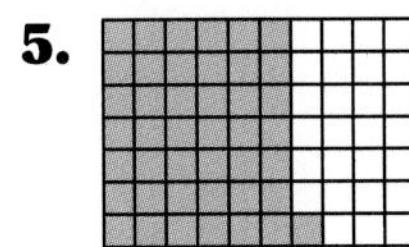

6. 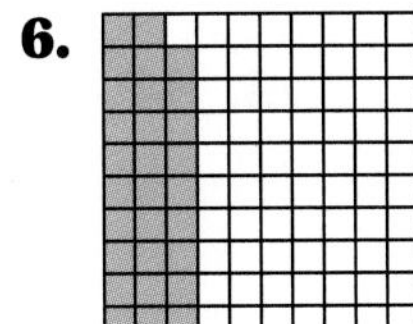

7. 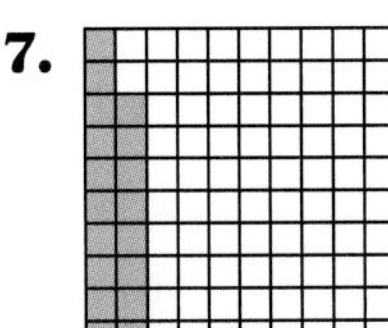

8. 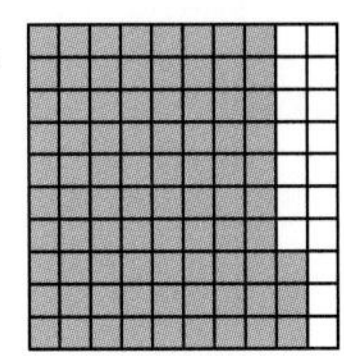

For Exercises 9–10, choose the more reasonable percent. Write *a* or *b*.

9. "Very few people like anchovies. Out of 100 people, fewer than 12 like anchovies," said the pizza man.
a. 10% **b.** 80%

10. "Almost every member of the team placed in at least one event," said the coach.
a. 15% **b.** 98%

Lesson 28.2 (pages 494–495)

Write the number as a percent and a decimal.

1. forty-six hundredths

2. eight hundredths

3. twenty-one hundredths

4. twelve hundredths

Write the decimal as a percent.

5. 0.93 **6.** 0.41 **7.** 0.06 **8.** 0.50 **9.** 0.24

Write the percent as a decimal.

10. 92% **11.** 17% **12.** 3% **13.** 70% **14.** 37%

Lesson 28.3 (pages 496–497)

Write the percent as a fraction in simplest form.

1. 65% **2.** 25% **3.** ten percent **4.** thirty per hundred

Write the fraction as a percent.

5. $\frac{9}{100}$ **6.** $\frac{8}{10}$ **7.** $\frac{3}{3}$ **8.** $\frac{4}{25}$

Write as a decimal and as a fraction in simplest form.

9. 13 percent **10.** 77 percent **11.** 40 percent **12.** 70 percent

Lesson 28.4 (pages 498–499)

For Exercises 1–4, choose from the following benchmarks: 10%, 25%, 50%, 75%, or 100%.

1. 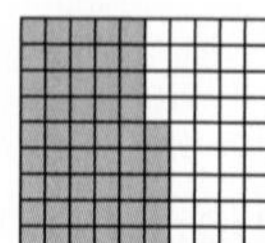 **2.** 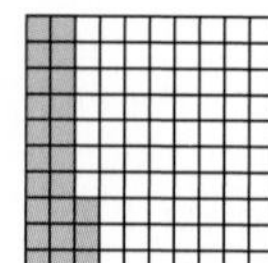 **3.** 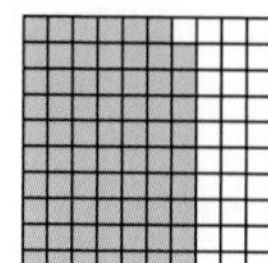 **4.** 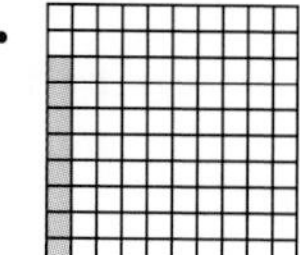

Tell what benchmark percent you would use to estimate each percent.

5. 89%	**6.** 33%	**7.** 76%	**8.** 9%	**9.** 48%
10. 66%	**11.** 53%	**12.** 13%	**13.** 94%	**14.** 19%

Lesson 28.5 Part 1 (pages 500–501)

For Problems 1-2, use the circle graph.

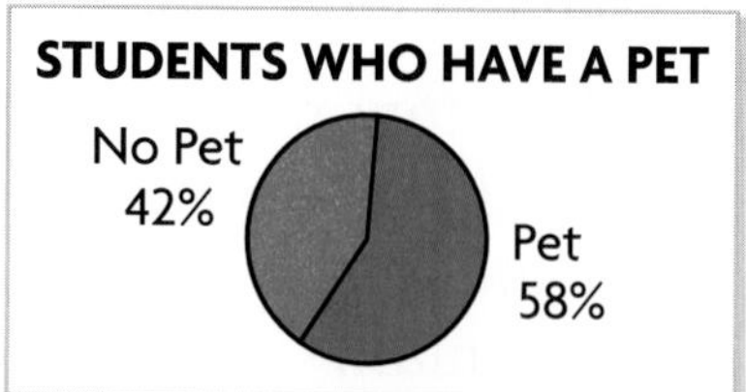

1. Do more than half or less than half of the students surveyed have a pet?
2. What decimal shows the students who have a pet? who don't have a pet?

For Problems 3–5, use the circle graph.

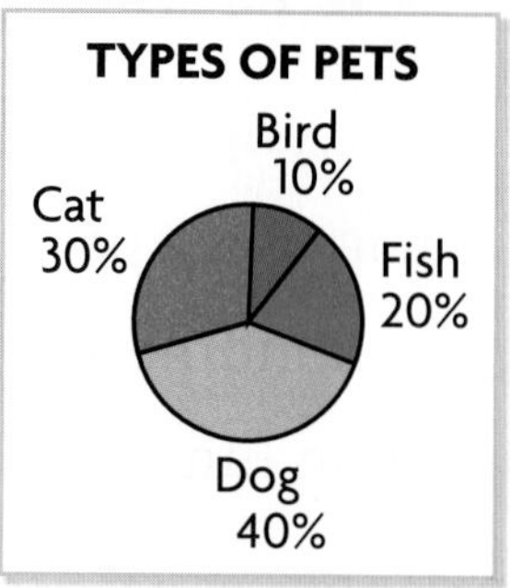

3. Do more students have a cat or a dog?
4. What decimal represents the students who have a dog? a cat? a bird? a fish?
5. Which two categories cover one half of the circle graph?

Lesson 28.5 Part 2 (pages 502–503)

Make a graph to solve.

1. The fifth graders voted for class president. They organized the data in the table. How can they show which two students received 50% of the votes? What graph should they make to display these data?

CLASS PRESIDENT ELECTION	
Student	**Percent of Votes**
Brett	20%
Carla	30%
Owen	40%
Kay	10%

2. Tina saved \$100 in 5 weeks from baby-sitting. She made a table showing the amount she saved each week. In which two weeks did she save 50% of the \$100? What graph could she make to display these data?

TINA'S SAVINGS	
Week	**Amount Saved**
1	\$30
2	\$10
3	\$20
4	\$25
5	\$15

Be a Good TEST TAKER

A test is one way you show what you have learned. Almost every day in math class you answer questions, use manipulatives, or solve problems on paper. All of these activities are not very different from the tests you will take. So, you are getting ready for tests every day.

THE TIPS ON THESE PAGES WILL HELP YOU BECOME A BETTER TEST TAKER.

GETTING READY FOR A TEST

What you do at home the night before the test and the morning of the test is very important. Studying hard at the last minute can make you so tired on the day of the test, that you will not be able to do your best. But spending some time thinking over the topics and reminding yourself of what you have learned are important. Follow these tips:

- GET A GOOD NIGHT'S SLEEP.
- EAT A GOOD BREAKFAST.
- DO NOT WORRY AND GET UPSET.
- DO THE VERY BEST YOU CAN DURING THE TEST.

TAKING THE TEST

Understand the Directions

Listen carefully to the teacher when the directions are given. Read the directions printed on the test carefully. Ask yourself these questions:

- Do I have pencils and a good eraser?
- Can I write on the test itself?
- Do I have to mark an answer sheet?
- How many questions are on the test?
- How long can I work on the test?

Ask your teacher for help if you do not understand the directions.
Follow all test directions carefully.

Test Answer Sheet

Test Title

MATH

Answer the Questions

On some tests you are asked to explain your thinking. The questions require that you write an explanation of how you got an answer or why your answer is reasonable. Organize your thoughts before you write!

"Explain how to find the perimeter of the cover of your math book. Find the perimeter."

9 inches

11 inches

Math Book

11 x 2 = 22 inches
9 x 2 = 18 inches
22 + 18 = 40 inches

I can find the perimeter of my math book by using a ruler to measure the length and the width. I multiplied the length by 2 and the width by 2 and added the 2 products together. The perimeter of my book is 40 inches.

Multiple-choice questions have answer choices. First, solve the problem. If you are not sure your solution is correct or you do not find an answer choice that matches your solution, follow these tips:

- Skip the choices that look wrong to you. Sometimes estimating can help you eliminate unreasonable choices.
- Then concentrate on the choices that look like reasonable answers.
- Skip the question if all the choices seem right to you.

9. Peter has 424 baseball cards. Maria has 266 cards. How many cards do they have in all?

A 188 cards **B** 610 cards
C 20 cards **D** 690 cards

Answer choices A and C are not reasonable because each is less than one of the addends. Choice B is not correct because if you round each addend to the nearest hundred, the estimated sum is closer to 700, not 600. So, Choice D is the correct one.

Mark Your Answers

Sometimes you will do all your work and show your answers on a piece of notebook paper. At other times you will use a separate answer sheet. This answer sheet may be scored by a machine. Since a machine can't tell the difference between your answers and stray marks, mark your answers carefully.

Study the answer sheet. Find out which way the numbers go. Sometimes the numbers go down a column. Sometimes the numbers go across the answer sheet. On some answer sheets you only have to mark the letter of the answer you choose. On other answer sheets you might have to make a mark for each digit of your answer in the right order.

Keep your place on the answer sheet. Make sure you mark the answer for each question on a choice for the right question number.

Erase an answer cleanly if you want to change it.

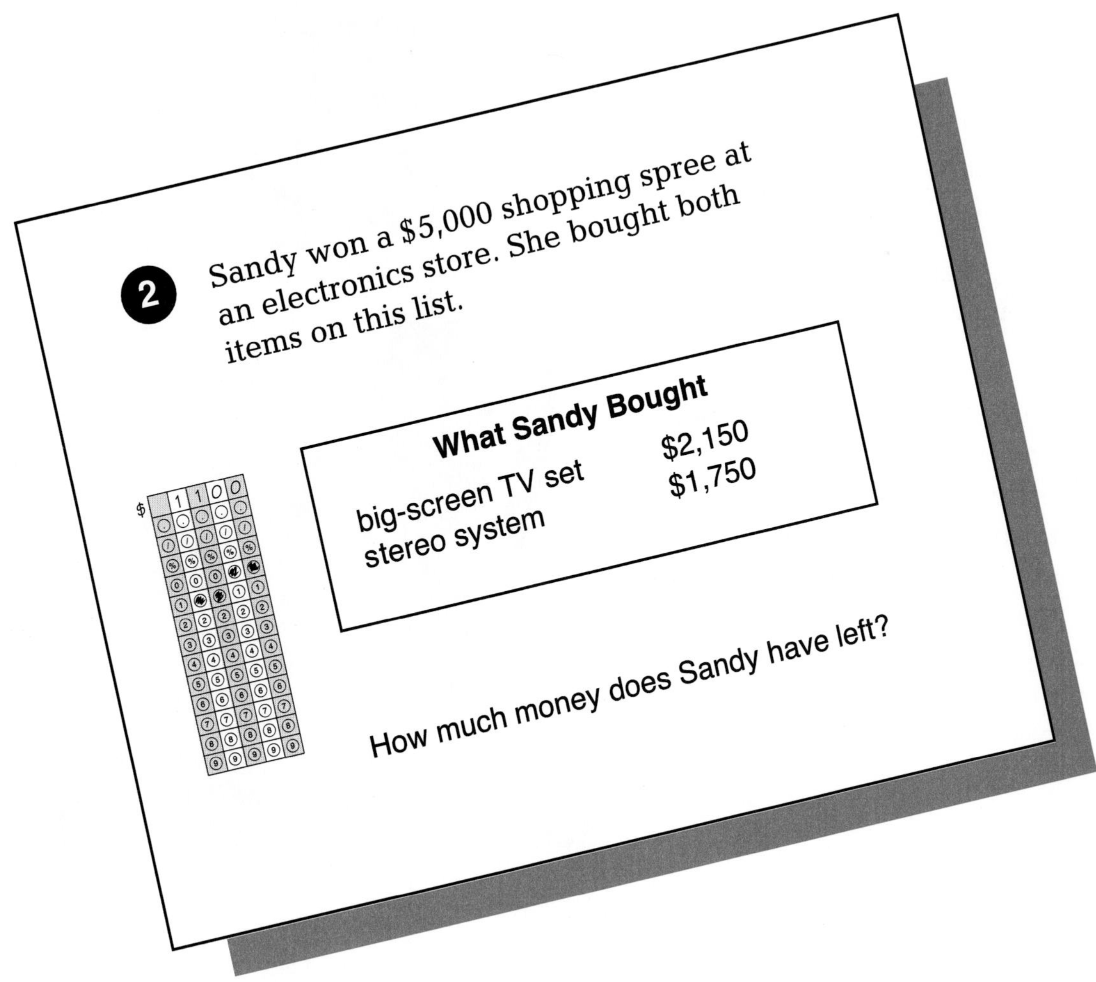

Keep Track of Time

If you have a set amount of time to complete a test or a section of a test, look at the clock to find out how much time you have left. Sometimes your teacher will write on the chalkboard the number of minutes remaining. Glance quickly at the clock or the chalkboard to keep track of the time.

If you don't have many minutes left, try to work faster. But don't work so fast that you make careless mistakes.

If you know that you can't answer all the questions that are left, look at them to find the easiest ones. Answer those and skip the rest.

REVIEWING YOUR RESULTS

If you finish before the time is up, look over your answer sheet. Erase any stray marks you see. Use any time you have left to check your answers.

Be sure that you have marked each answer in the correct place on the answer sheet.

If your graded test is returned to you, look carefully at the questions you missed. Try to determine what errors you made. Rework the problems if you can. Don't hesitate to ask your teacher for help in understanding what errors you made.

YOU CAN BE A **GOOD TEST TAKER.** REMEMBER THESE TIPS. THEY WILL HELP YOU DO WELL ON EVERY TEST!

ADDITION FACTS TEST

	K	L	M	N	O	P	Q	R
A	3 + 8	2 + 9	6 + 4	8 + 7	3 + 4	7 + 7	1 + 8	4 + 5
B	4 + 9	9 + 2	7 + 5	6 + 0	9 + 3	5 + 4	6 + 3	9 + 7
C	8 + 8	1 + 9	6 + 2	5 + 8	8 + 0	7 + 6	7 + 1	6 + 9
D	5 + 5	4 + 3	9 + 4	8 + 6	6 + 5	0 + 9	5 + 6	7 + 9
E	4 + 7	9 + 1	8 + 5	7 + 0	7 + 2	8 + 3	4 + 8	7 + 3
F	5 + 2	6 + 8	1 + 7	2 + 3	4 + 4	5 + 3	9 + 9	3 + 6
G	0 + 8	7 + 4	8 + 2	1 + 6	8 + 4	5 + 1	3 + 3	2 + 7
H	9 + 8	2 + 6	9 + 5	8 + 1	3 + 9	5 + 7	4 + 2	6 + 6
I	3 + 7	7 + 8	9 + 0	4 + 6	2 + 8	6 + 7	9 + 6	3 + 5
J	0 + 7	8 + 9	2 + 5	6 + 1	5 + 9	2 + 4	0 + 6	3 + 2

SUBTRACTION FACTS TEST

	K	L	M	N	O	P	Q	R
A	16 − 7	9 − 0	14 − 8	8 − 3	12 − 5	5 − 5	17 − 8	12 − 7
B	13 − 8	8 − 6	9 − 4	6 − 2	12 − 6	14 − 7	10 − 6	7 − 4
C	8 − 2	13 − 7	9 − 8	15 − 9	5 − 4	14 − 5	9 − 3	11 − 6
D	10 − 8	5 − 3	11 − 4	8 − 0	14 − 6	6 − 6	10 − 7	12 − 4
E	11 − 3	14 − 9	10 − 5	12 − 9	13 − 5	7 − 6	12 − 3	11 − 2
F	7 − 5	13 − 6	8 − 4	15 − 7	11 − 8	9 − 6	6 − 0	17 − 9
G	10 − 9	7 − 3	11 − 9	16 − 9	8 − 5	10 − 3	7 − 7	9 − 2
H	18 − 9	15 − 8	8 − 1	12 − 8	9 − 5	11 − 7	8 − 7	15 − 6
I	6 − 5	16 − 8	8 − 8	10 − 2	6 − 3	9 − 7	11 − 5	7 − 1
J	13 − 4	9 − 9	7 − 0	13 − 9	7 − 2	6 − 4	10 − 4	9 − 1

MULTIPLICATION FACTS TEST

	K	L	M	N	O	P	Q	R
A	6 × 2	6 × 5	8 × 7	9 × 0	5 × 8	2 × 8	9 × 9	6 × 7
B	8 × 8	9 × 1	4 × 9	5 × 6	5 × 2	8 × 4	0 × 5	5 × 4
C	9 × 5	4 × 8	2 × 6	8 × 9	8 × 0	9 × 6	3 × 3	5 × 7
D	5 × 5	6 × 4	8 × 5	4 × 2	7 × 3	0 × 8	3 × 4	8 × 6
E	4 × 7	7 × 8	2 × 4	3 × 7	7 × 2	7 × 4	3 × 9	3 × 6
F	3 × 8	7 × 1	1 × 5	5 × 3	6 × 0	2 × 9	7 × 6	1 × 9
G	6 × 9	4 × 3	7 × 9	2 × 5	9 × 7	1 × 7	9 × 4	0 × 7
H	4 × 4	9 × 8	1 × 6	3 × 2	4 × 6	0 × 9	3 × 5	6 × 8
I	6 × 3	7 × 0	5 × 1	4 × 5	6 × 1	2 × 3	7 × 5	2 × 2
J	5 × 9	7 × 7	9 × 3	8 × 3	9 × 2	6 × 6	0 × 6	2 × 7

DIVISION FACTS TEST

	K	L	M	N	O	P	Q	R
A	9)45	6)42	6)12	8)64	1)9	5)0	8)16	1)8
B	6)6	7)35	5)15	6)18	8)72	2)6	2)18	7)56
C	9)81	4)16	1)7	7)21	2)8	9)54	1)3	5)45
D	2)10	4)28	8)0	9)36	4)20	9)72	3)27	9)27
E	7)49	2)12	8)40	5)10	8)48	1)4	5)35	4)12
F	3)9	6)36	4)4	8)24	2)14	8)32	1)5	7)63
G	5)25	4)36	9)18	3)6	7)14	4)24	5)20	3)0
H	7)28	3)18	6)54	7)0	4)8	6)48	4)32	9)9
I	3)15	9)63	3)21	2)16	5)30	7)42	6)30	6)18
J	6)24	3)24	8)56	3)12	5)40	1)6	2)4	1)1

TABLE OF MEASURES

METRIC	CUSTOMARY
Length	
1,000 millimeters (mm) = 1 meter (m)	12 inches (in.) = 1 foot (ft)
100 centimeters (cm) = 1 meter	36 in., or 3 ft = 1 yard (yd)
10 decimeters (dm) = 1 meter	5,280 ft, or 1,760 yd = 1 mile (mi)
1 kilometer (km) = 1,000 meters	
Capacity	
1,000 milliliters (mL) = 1 liter (L)	1 tablespoon (tbsp) = 3 teaspoons (tsp)
250 milliliters = 1 metric cup	8 fluid ounces (fl oz) = 1 cup (c)
	2 c = 1 pint (pt)
	2 pt = 1 quart (qt)
	4 qt = 1 gallon (gal)
Mass/Weight	
1,000 milligrams (mg) = 1 gram (g)	16 ounces (oz) = 1 pound (lb)
1,000 grams = 1 kilogram (kg)	2,000 lb = 1 ton (T)

TIME

60 seconds (sec) = 1 minute (min)
60 minutes = 1 hour (hr)
24 hours = 1 day
7 days = 1 week (wk)
52 weeks = 1 year (yr)
12 months (mo) = 1 year
365 days = 1 year
366 days = 1 leap year

FORMULAS

Perimeter of rectangle	$P = (2 \times l) + (2 \times w)$
Perimeter of square	$P = 4 \times s$
Circumference	$C = \pi \times d$
Area of Rectangle	$A = l \times w$
Volume of prism	$V = l \times w \times h$

SYMBOLS

$=$	is equal to
$>$	is greater than
$<$	is less than
$\approx$	is approximately equal to
1:3	ratio of 1 to 3
$\overrightarrow{AB}$	ray AB
$\overleftrightarrow{AB}$	line AB
$\overline{AB}$	line segment AB
$\angle ABC$	angle ABC
$\triangle ABC$	triangle ABC
π	pi (3.14)
$^\circ$	degree
°C	degree Celsius
°F	degree Fahrenheit
(2,3)	ordered pair 2,3

GLOSSARY

A

acute angle An angle that measures less than a right angle *(pages 410, 446)*

acute triangle A triangle that has three acute angles *(page 420)*
Example:

analog clock A clock that shows 12 hours on a face with hands to indicate the hour, minute, and second *(page 378)*

angle A figure formed by two rays that meet at a common endpoint *(page 410)*

area The number of square units needed to cover a surface *(pages 79, 82, 84)*

ascending In order from least to greatest number *(page 67)*

Associative Property of Addition Addends can be grouped differently. The sum is always the same. *(page 52)*
Example: $3 + (5 + 10) = 18$
$(3 + 5) + 10 = 18$

Associative Property of Multiplication The property which states that when multiplying three or more factors, any two of the factors can be multiplied, and the remaining factors may then be multiplied without changing the total product *(page 74)*
Example: $(3 \times 4) \times 5 = 3 \times (4 \times 5)$
$12 \times 5 = 3 \times 20$
$60 = 60$

average The number found by dividing the sum of a set of numbers by the number of addends *(page 156)*

axis (of a graph) The horizontal or vertical number line used in a rectangular graph or coordinate grid (plural: axes) *(page 430)*

B

bar graph A graph that compares facts about groups *(pages 159, 180)*

base A face of a solid figure by which the figure is measured or named *(page 454)*
Example:

base
Cylinder

benchmark Numbers like 10, 25, 50, or 100 that are used to help make estimates *(pages 4, 464, 498)*

benchmark percent A commonly used percent that is close to the amount you are estimating *(page 498)*

billion 1,000 millions, written 1,000,000,000 *(page 9)*

C

capacity The amount of liquid a container can hold *(page 252)*

cardinal Numbers that tell how many *(page 2)*
Examples: 4 puppies
93 cents

centimeter (cm) A unit for measuring length in the metric system *(page 248)*
0.01 meter = 1 centimeter

century One hundred years *(page 492)*

certain Something that will always happen *(page 188)*

chord A line segment with endpoints on a circle *(page 440)*
Example:

circle A closed figure with all points on the figure the same distance from the center point *(page 440)*
Example:

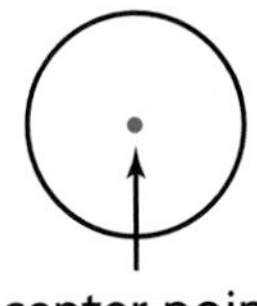

circle graph A graph in the shape of a circle that shows fractions, percents, or decimals as parts of a whole *(pages 172, 500)*

circumference The perimeter of a circle *(page 442)*
Example:

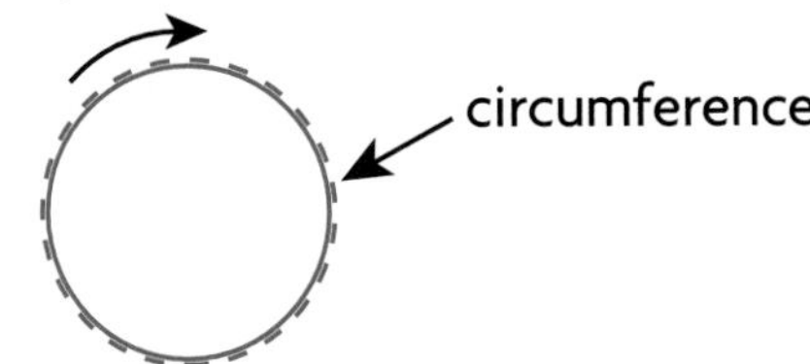

common factor A number that is a factor of two or more numbers *(page 288)*
Example: The common factors of 6 and 12 are 1, 2, 3, and 6.

common multiple A number that is a multiple of two or more numbers *(page 274)*
Example: A common multiple of 2, 3, 4, and 6 is 24.

Commutative Property of Addition Addends can be added in any order. The sum is always the same. *(page 52)*

Commutative Property of Multiplication The property which states that when the order of two factors is changed, the product is the same *(page 74)*
Example: $5 \times 7 = 7 \times 5$
$35 = 35$

compass A tool used to construct circles *(page 440)*

compatible numbers Pairs of numbers that are easy to compute mentally *(pages 28, 112, 130)*

composite numbers Numbers that have more than two factors *(page 286)*
Example: 6 is a composite number since its factors are 1, 2, 3, and 6.

cone A solid figure with a circular base and one vertex *(page 456)*
Example:

congruent figures Figures that have the same size and shape *(page 426)*
Example:

cube A solid figure with six congruent square faces *(pages 82, 454)*

cubic units The number of cubes with dimensions of 1 unit × 1 unit × 1 unit that can fit inside a solid figure, that gives the volume *(page 82)*

cylinder A solid figure with two parallel bases that are congruent circles *(page 456)*
Example:

D

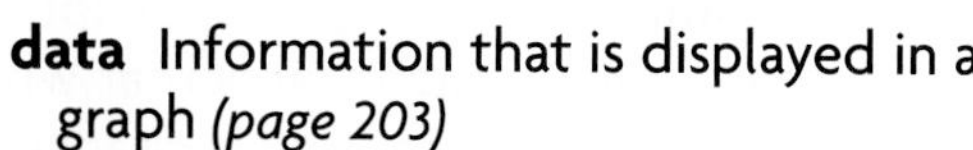

data Information that is displayed in a graph *(page 203)*

decimal A number that uses place value and a decimal point to show values less than one, such as tenths and hundredths *(pages 36, 176)*

decimal point A point that separates the whole = number places from the decimal places in decimal numbers *(page 52)*

decimal system A system of computation based on the number ten *(page 211)*

decimeter (dm) A unit for measuring length in the metric system *(page 248)*
10 centimeters = 1 decimeter

degree (°) A unit for measuring angles and for measuring temperature *(pages 382, 412)*

degree Celsius (°C) A metric unit for measuring temperature *(page 382)*

degree Fahrenheit (°F) A unit of the customary system for measuring temperature *(page 382)*

denominator The number that is below the bar in a fraction and tells the total number of equal parts *(page 276)*

descending In order from greatest to least number *(page 67)*

diameter A line segment that passes through the center of a circle and has its endpoints on the circle *(page 440)*
Example:

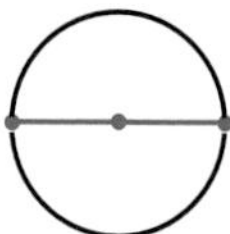

digital clock A clock that tells the time by showing the digits that change on each hour, and minute *(page 378)*

direct measure Obtaining the measure of an object by using measuring devices *(page 368)*

Distributive Property of Multiplication The property which states that multiplying a sum by a number is the same as multiplying each addend by the number and then adding the products *(page 92)*
Example:

$$3 \times (4 + 2) = (3 \times 4) + (3 \times 2)$$
$$3 \times 6 = 12 + 6$$
$$18 = 18$$

divisible A number is divisible by another number if the result of the division is a whole number and the remainder is zero *(page 110)*
Example: 18 is divisible by 3.

division Separating into equal groups *(page 234)*

double-bar graph A graph used to display two sets of data in the same graph *(page 166)*

E

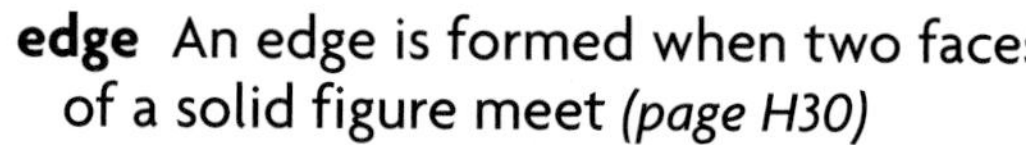

edge An edge is formed when two faces of a solid figure meet *(page H30)*

equally likely Outcomes that have the same chance of occurring *(page 196)*

equilateral triangle A triangle with three congruent sides *(page 418)*
Example:

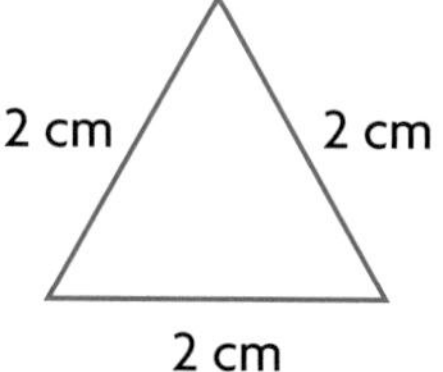

equivalent Numbers having the same value *(page 240)*

equivalent decimals Decimals that name the same number or amount *(pages 42, 54, 222)*
Example: 0.5 = 0.50 = 0.500

equivalent fractions Fractions that name the same number or amount *(pages 292, 480)*
Example: $\frac{3}{4} = \frac{6}{8}$

equivalent ratios Ratios that name the same comparisons *(page 480)*

event Something that happens in a probability experiment that results in an outcome *(page 188)*

expanded form A way to write numbers by showing the value of each digit *(page 6)*
Example: $635 = 600 + 30 + 5$

exponent A number that tells how many times the base is used as a factor *(page H32)*

exponent
↓
Example: $10^3 = 10 \times 10 \times 10$
10 is the base.

expression A collection of numbers, operation signs, and sometimes, variables that names a number *(page 147)*
Examples: $7 + 3$ $3 \times (2 + n)$

extrapolate To estimate or predict a value or quantity beyond the known range *(page 164)*

F

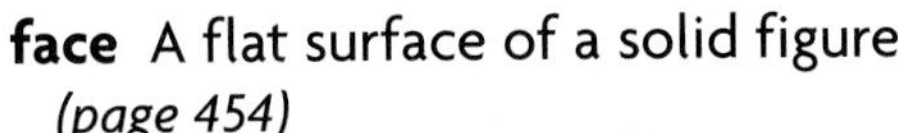

face A flat surface of a solid figure *(page 454)*
Example:

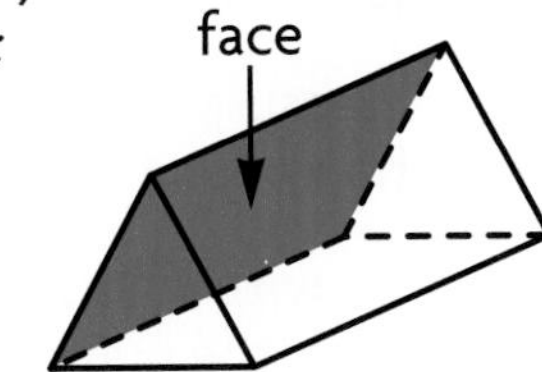

factor A number multiplied by another number to find a product *(page 286)*

formula A set of symbols that expresses a mathematical rule *(page 84)*
Example: $A = l \times w$

frequency The number of times an event occurs *(page 190)*

function The relationship between two sets *(page 480)*

G

gram (g) A unit for measuring mass in the metric system *(page 250)*
1,000 milligrams = 1 gram

greatest common factor (GCF) The greatest factor that two or more numbers have in common *(page 288)*
Example: 6 is the GCF of 18 and 30.

H

histogram A bar graph that shows the number of times data occur within a certain range or interval *(page H36)*

hundredth A decimal or fraction that names one part of 100 equal parts *(pages 36, 210)*

I

impossible Something that will never happen *(page 188)*

inequality A mathematical sentence that shows that two expressions do not represent the same quantity *(page 12)*
Example: $3 + 2 > 4 - 1$

intersecting lines Two lines that cross at exactly one point *(page 408)*
Example:

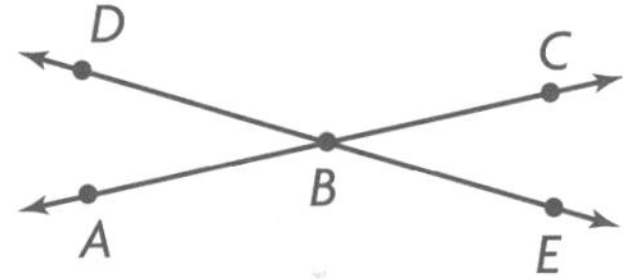

interval The distance between the numbers on the scale of a graph *(page 158)*

inverse operations Opposite operations that undo each other; addition and subtraction or multiplication and division are inverse operations. *(page 20)*

isosceles triangle A triangle with two congruent sides and two congruent angles *(page 418)*
Example:

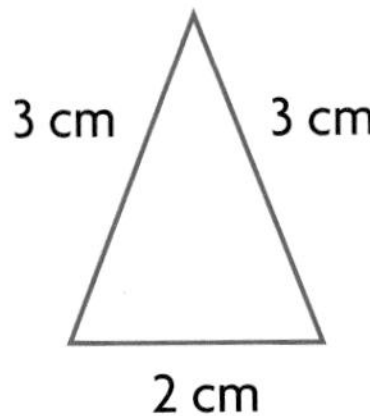

K

kilogram (kg) A unit for measuring mass in the metric system *(page 250)*
1,000 grams = 1 kilogram

kiloliter (kL) A unit for measuring capacity in the metric system *(page 252)*
1,000 L = 1 kiloliter

kilometer (km) A unit for measuring length in the metric system *(page 248)*
1,000 meters = 1 kilometer

L

least common denominator (LCD) The least common multiple of two or more denominators *(pages 308, 322, 342)*
Example:
The LCD for $\frac{1}{4}$ and $\frac{5}{6}$ is twelfths.

least common multiple (LCM) The least number other than zero that is a multiple of two or more given numbers *(pages 274, 308, 322)*
Example: The LCM of 6 and 9 is 18.

leaves The ones digits of a stem-and-leaf plot *(page 156)*

like fractions Fractions that have the same denominator *(page 304)*
Example: $\frac{1}{8}$ and $\frac{5}{8}$

likely In probability, a *high* possibility (as opposed to a *low*, or unlikely, possibility) that an event will happen *(page 188)*

line A straight path in a plane extending in both directions with no endpoints *(page 408)*
Example:

line graph A graph that shows how data change over time *(pages 164, 180)*
Example:

line of symmetry A line that divides a figure so that the two parts of the figure are congruent *(page 428)*
Example:

line plot A diagram that shows the frequency of data *(page 164)*

line segment Part of a line between two endpoints *(page 408)*
Example:

line symmetry When a figure can be folded on a line so that its two parts are congruent *(page 428)*

liter (L) A unit for measuring capacity in the metric system *(page 252)*
1,000 milliliters = 1 liter

M

map scale A ratio that compares the distance on a map with the actual distance *(page 482)*

mass The measure of the quantity of matter of an object *(page 250)*

mean One way to find a number that represents all the numbers in a set *(page 156)*

median The middle number in an ordered series of numbers *(page 154)*
Example:
The median of 1, 3, 4, 6, and 7 is 4.

memory key A key on the computer key-board that is used to store numbers *(page H60)*

meter (m) A unit for measuring length in the metric system *(page 248)*
100 centimeters = 1 meter

milligram (mg) A unit for measuring mass in the metric system *(page 250)*
1,000 milligrams = 1 gram

milliliter (mL) A unit for measuring capacity in the metric system *(page 252)*
0.001 L = 1 milliliter

millimeter (mm) A unit for measuring length in the metric system *(page 248)*
1,000 millimeters = 1 meter

million 1,000 thousands; written 1,000,000 *(pages 8–11)*

mixed decimal A number that is made up of a whole number and a decimal *(pages 40, 224)*
Example: 2.43

mixed number A number that is made up of a whole number and a fraction *(pages 272, 394)*

Examples: $2\frac{1}{2}$

mode The number that occurs most often in a list of data *(page 154)*
Example: The mode of 1, 3, 4, 4, and 6 is 4.

multiple A number that is the product of a given number and another whole number *(page 274)*

multistep problems Problems that require more than one step to solve *(page H60)*

N

net A two-dimensional pattern for a three-dimensional solid *(page 456)*

nominal A number that names a thing *(page 2)*
Examples: 337 Havana St.
Hank is number 44 on his team.

numerator The number above the bar in a fraction that tells how many parts are being considered. *(pages 276, H14, H20)*

O

obtuse angle An angle that measures greater than a right angle *(page 410)*
Example:

obtuse triangle A triangle that has one obtuse angle *(page 420)*
Example:

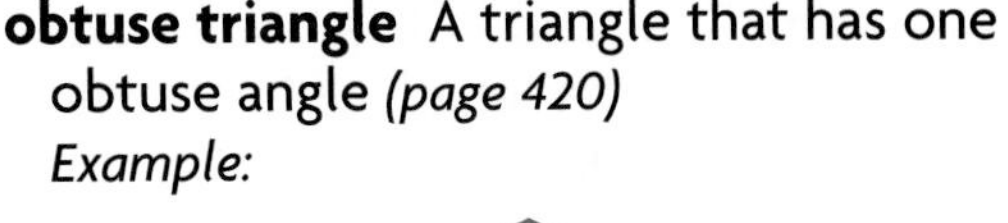

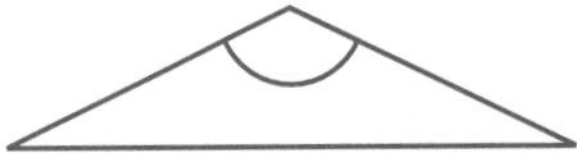

octagonal pyramid A pyramid with an octagon for a base *(page 454)*

order of operations The correct order in which operations are done within an expression *(page H61)*

ordered pair A pair of numbers used to locate a point on a grid *(page 430)*
Example: (5,3)

ordinal Numbers that tell position or order *(page 2)*
Examples: Jon won first place.
Jean is 4th in line.

P

parallel lines Lines in a plane that stay exactly the same distance apart *(page 408)*
Example:

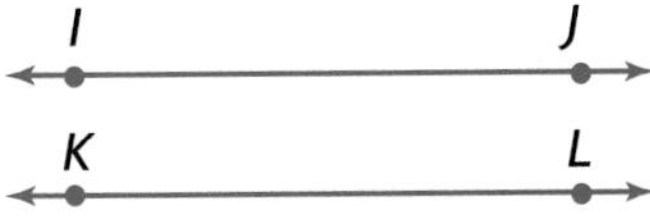

parallelogram A quadrilateral with opposite sides parallel and congruent *(page 416)*

percent A ratio of some number to 100 *(page 492)*

perimeter The distance around a figure *(pages 102, 442)*

period Each group of three digits in a number *(page 8)*

perpendicular lines Two lines that intersect to form right angles *(page 408)*
Example:

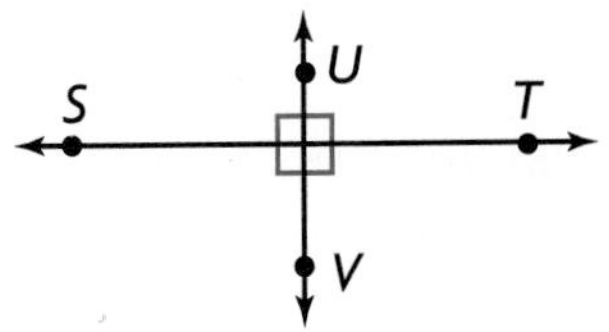

pi (π) The ratio of the circumference of a circle to the length of its diameter (π = 3.14) *(page 443)*

plane A flat surface that extends without end in all directions *(page 408)*

point Identifies a location on an object and in space *(page 408)*

point symmetry When a figure can be turned about a central point and still look the same *(page 428)*
Example:

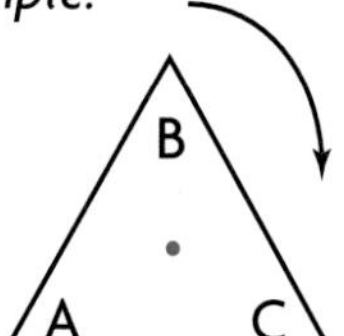

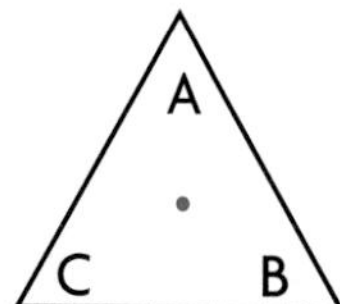

polygon A closed plane figure with straight sides that is named by the number if its sides and angles *(pages 454, H26)*

possible outcomes Something that has a chance of happening in an experiment *(page 190)*

precise Finding a unit that measures nearest to the actual length of an object *(page 368)*

prime factor A factor that has exactly two factors, itself and 1 *(page 287)*

prime numbers Numbers that have only two factors, 1 and the number itself *(page 286)*
Example: 5, 7, 11, 13, 17, and 19 are prime numbers.

prism A solid figure whose ends are congruent, parallel polygons, and whose sides are rectangles *(page 454)*
Example:

pentagonal prism

probability The chance of an event happening *(page 196)*

$$P = \frac{\text{number of ways the event occurs}}{\text{number of ways all events can occur}}$$

product The answer to a multiplication problem *(pages 286, H60)*

Property of One for Multiplication The property which states that the product of any number and 1 is that number *(pages 74, 286)*
Examples: $5 \times 1 = 5$
$16 \times 1 = 16$

protractor A tool for measuring the size of the opening of an angle *(page 412)*

pyramid A solid figure with a base that is a polygon and three or more faces that are triangles with a common vertex *(page 454)*
Example:

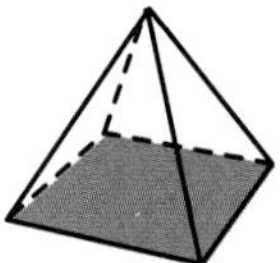

Q

quadrilateral A polygon with four angles and four sides *(page 416)*

R

radius A line segment with one endpoint at the center of a circle and the other endpoint on the circle (plural: radii) *(page 440)*
Example:

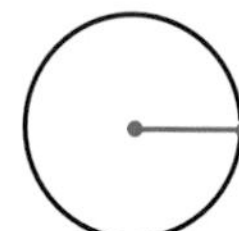

range The difference between the greatest and least numbers in a set of data *(page 162)*

ratio A comparison of two numbers *(page 476)*

ray A part of a line that begins at one endpoint and extends forever in only one direction *(page 410)*

reasonableness Appropriateness or good approximation in a number answer *(pages 96, 99)*

reflection When a figure is flipped across a line *(page 430)*

relative size The size of one number in comparison to the size of another number or numbers *(page 44)*

rhombus A parallelogram with four congruent sides whose opposite angles are congruent *(page 416)*
Example:

right angle An angle that forms a square corner and measures 90° *(pages 410, 446)*
Example:

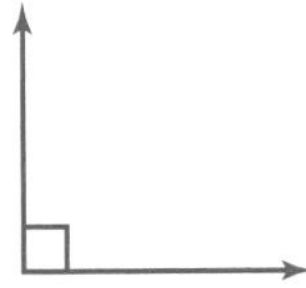

right triangle A triangle with one right angle *(page 420)*
Example:

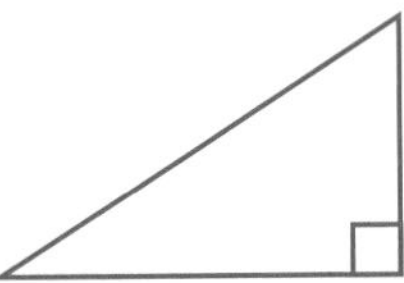

rotation When a figure is turned around a point or vertex *(page 430)*
Example:

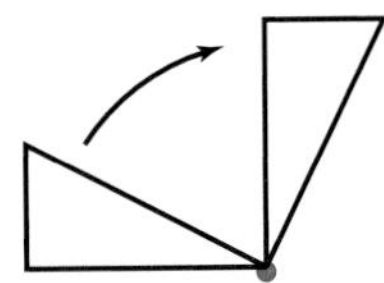

rounding Replacing a number with a number that tells about how many or how much *(pages 28, 96, 354, H10)*

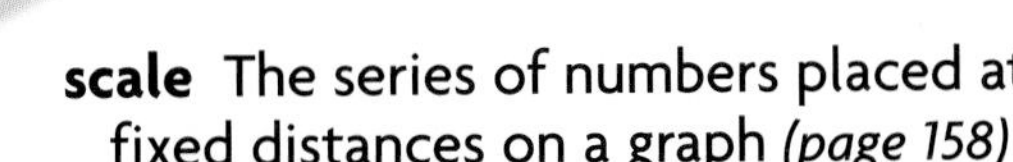

scale The series of numbers placed at fixed distances on a graph *(page 158)*

scalene triangle A triangle with three unequal angles and sides that are not congruent *(page 418)*
Example:

scientific notation A method of expressing a number between 1 and 10 as a power of 10 *(page H58)*
Example: $7.0 \times 10^5 = 700{,}000$

similar figures Figures that have the same shape but may not have the same size *(page 484)*
Example:

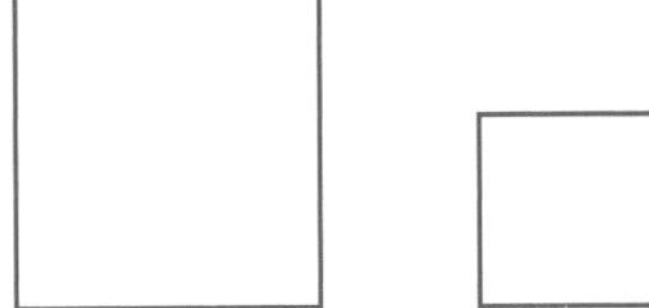

simplest form A fraction that has 1 as the greatest common factor of the numerator and denominator *(pages 296, 298, 318, 392, 480)*

simulation To do something in a way that is easier than the actual experiment, or to match possible outcomes of a real event *(page H38)*

slope The incline of a line *(page 178)*

square number A product that can be shown in a square array or model; a product of two equal numbers *(page 286)*

standard form A way to write numbers using the digits 0–9, with each digit having a place value *(page 8)*

stem The tens digit of a stem-and-leaf plot *(page 156)*

stem-and-leaf plot Shows data organized by place value *(page 156)*

survey To ask questions to find the most frequent choice of a group *(page 166)*

tenth A decimal or fraction that names one part of 10 equal parts *(pages 36, 210)*

terminating decimal A decimal that ends; a decimal for which the division operation results in a remainder of zero *(page H67)*

Example: $\frac{1}{2} = 0.5$

tessellation A repeating pattern of closed figures that covers a surface with no gaps and no overlaps *(page 432)*
Example:

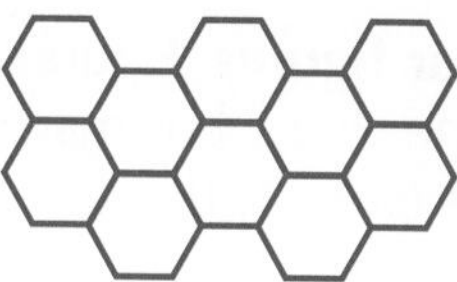

thousandth One part of 1,000 equal parts *(page 38)*

transformation The movement of a figure, either a translation, rotation, or reflection *(pages 430, 469)*

translation When a figure slides in any direction *(page 430)*
Example:

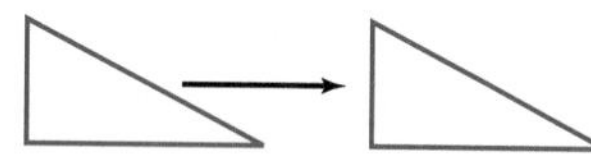

trapezoid A quadrilateral with only one pair of parallel sides *(page 416)*
Example:

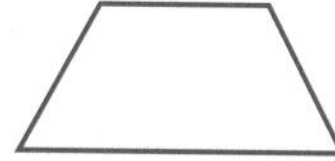

tree diagram An organized list that shows all possible outcomes of an event *(page 192)*

U

unlike fractions Fractions that have different denominators *(pages 306, 320)*

Example: $\frac{3}{4}$ and $\frac{2}{3}$

V

Venn diagram A diagram that uses geometric shapes to show relationships *(pages 298, 331)*
Example:

Numbers Divisible by Two or Three

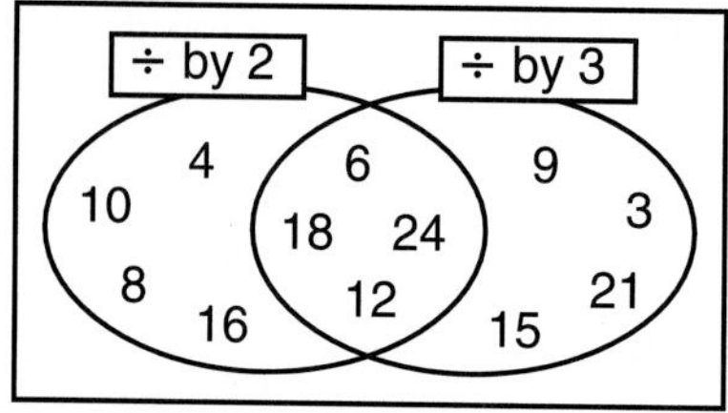

vertex The point where two rays of an angle, two sides of a polygon, or three or more edges of a solid figure meet *(pages 410, 454, 484)*
Example:

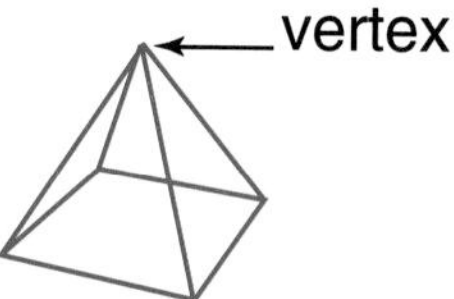

volume The measure of the space a solid figure occupies *(pages 82, 252, 460)*

Z

Zero Property for Addition When zero is added to any addend, the sum is the other addend *(page 52)*

Zero Property for Multiplication The property which states that the product of zero and any number is zero *(page 74)*
Examples: $13 \times 0 = 0$
$0 \times 7 = 0$

D

E

F

G

H

I

K

L

M

S

T

Y

Z

Photo Credits
Page Placement Key: (t)-top, (c)-center, (b) bottom, (l)-left, (r)-right, (fg)-foreground, (bg)-background, (i)inset.

Harcourt Brace & Company: 003 (tl), 003 (tc), 003 (c), H4 (cr), H08 (b), H09 (cr), H11 (tr), H23 (br), H24 (bc), H24 (br), H26 (tr), 31 (r), 38 (cr), 39 (c), H42 (r), H46 (c), H54 (tr), H59 (br), H60 (tr), 63 (c), H64 (r), H65 (br), H67 (cr), 70 (tr), 77 (tr), 78 (r), 080 (br), 86 (br), 104 (cr), 104 (br), 104 (br), 119 (br), 119 (cr), 119 (cr), 131 (tc), 131 (tr), 133 (cr), 150 (l), 150 (c), 150 (r), 157 (tr), 172 (tr), 174 (r), 178 (tr), 179 (cr), 186 (tr), 194 (tr), 194 (tr), 212 (cr), 219 (cr), 223 (tr), 224 (tr), 246 (bc), 248 (tc), 248 (tr), 251 (tr), 251 (cr), 275 (r), 276 (br), 281 (tr), 290 (bc), 294 (br), 297 (cr), 305 (cr), 309 (cr), 313 (cr), 318 (tr), 320 (r), 325 (r), 371 (tr), 380 (br), 401 (tr), 404 (tr), 434 (cr), 464 (br), 472 (cr), 478 (br), 486 (br), 490 (br), 493 (tr), 503 (cr), 506 (t), 510 (bl), 510 (br), 186-187 (bg); Allan Landau 3, 7 (r), 14 (r), 18 (c), 28 (br), 34 (c), H44 (tr), 051 (t), 53 (tr), 56 (tr), 84 (l), 86 (cr), 92 (b), 110 (t), 112 (tr), 120 (tr), 134 (b), 140 (c), 154 (cr), 154 (c), 154 (t), 174 (cr), 178 (br), 182 (r), 189 (cr), 190 (r), 190 (bg), 191 (r), 192 (r), 194 (r), 206 (bl), 208 (cr), 208 (cl), 210 (b), 214 (tr), 215 (cr), 216 (b), 222 (tr), 232 (b), 234 (bc), 236 (tr), 240 (r), 242 (t), 248 (b), 252 (c), 270 (r), 272 (tr), 274 (t), 280 (r), 285 (r), 286 (br), 288 (b), 289 (tr), 302 (c), 306 (r), 316 (bg), 316 (c), 317 (cr), 320 (cr), 336 (l), 338 (tr), 356 (tr), 362 (t), 372 (r), 374 (tr), 376 (tl), 386, 388 (tr), 394 (tr), 396 (r), 412 (br), 414 (b), 432 (br), 434 (b), 442 (cl), 442 (c), 442 (cr), 443 (cr), 444 (r), 452 (bg), 456 (tr), 458 (c), 462 (cr), 475 (c), 476 (tr), 476 (br), 478 (tr), 482 (b), 492 (r), 492 (br); ASG Sherman Graphics, Inc. (br), xviii-1 (c), xviii-1 (l), H02 (c), 003 (tr), 004 (bc), 004 (bl), 004 (tr), 017 (r), 20 (t), H20 (cr), H24 (bl), H24 (bc), 27 (br), H28 (bc), 30 (c), 34 (br), 34 (r), 35 (br), 36 (tr), H36 (c), H38 (r), H40 (tr), 046 (br), 50 (c), 50 (c), H50 (r), 55 (c), H56 (br), 58 (tr), 60 (tc), 61 (c), 63 (r), 66 (t), 068 (c), 068 (c), 068 (c), 069 (br), 72 (c), 74 (r), 75 (cr), 81 (tr), 81 (cr), 83 (tr), 084 (cr), 084 (c), 085 (br), 87 (b), 96 (tr), 100 (c), 101 (cr), 114 (cr), 116 (c), 117 (br), 120 (br), 121 (r), 126 (r), 126 (tl), 134 (cr), 136 (r), 140 (r), 146 (tc), 146 (tr), 146 (tr), 146 (r), 147 (c), 152 (c), 152 (cl), 152 (cr), 154 (tr), 158 (r), 170 (cl), 170 (tr), 170 (bc), 176 (tr), 177 (tr), 183 (tr), 188 (tr), 188 (br), 190 (br), 191 (bc), 199 (c), 202 (cr), 208 (c), 209 (br), 210 (t), 211 (cr), 217 (cr), 221 (c), 231 (b), 231 (cr), 233 (br), 238 (cr), 241 (cr), 242 (br), 243 (cr), 246 (bg), 247 (br), 249 (r), 250 (cl), 255 (r), 256 (b), 257 (r), 259 (br), 266 (r), 268 (r), 269 (br), 272 (tr), 277 (c), 277 (cr), 278 (r), 279 (tr), 284 (br), 287 (tr), 293 (br), 295 (br), 299 (cr), 302 (cl), 303 (br), 307 (br), 316 (br), 317 (bc), 323 (r), 324 (tr), 334 (bl), 336 (br), 337 (b), 339 (cr), 344 (tr), 345 (tr), 346 (tr), 347 (tr), 352 (cl), 352 (cr), 352 (c), 354 (tr), 355 (cr), 358 (t), 363 (br), 366 (cr), 366 (c), 366 (cl), 367 (tr), 369 (tl), 369 (tc), 369 (cl), 369 (c), 378 (tl), 378 (cr), 378 (cr), 383 (cr), 386 (r), 386 (c), 387 (br), 391 (c), 401 (tr), 406 (r), 406 (c), 407 (r), 415 (tr), 416 (b), 417 (cr), 424 (c), 425 (br), 426 (cr), 428 (tr), 428 (cl), 428 (c), 435 (br), 438 (tr), 438 (tl), 438 (c), 439 (br), 442 (br), 444 (cr), 449 (cr), 457 (r), 462 (br), 463 (tr), 465 (cr), 468 (tr), 475 (cr), 475 (br), 479 (tr), 481 (cr), 490 (tr), 490 (cr), 490 (c), 491 (bc), 494 (tr), 498 (cl), 502 (br), 506 (cr), 084-085 (bg), 100-101 (bg), 116-117 (bg), 154-155 (bg), 208-209 (bg), 246-347 (c), 302-303 (bg), 352-353 (bg), 352-353 (bg), 352-353 (bg), 366-367 (bg), 386-387 (c), 438-439 (c), 452-453 (bg), 490-491 (bg); Weronica Ankarorn H34 (tr), 62 (b), 82 (b), 93 (t), 94 (r), 116 (tr), 136 (tr), 193 (br), 268 (bl), 356 (cr), 361 (br), 392 (tr), 397 (br), 432 (tl), Richard A. Arnold xviii-1 (br), Victoria Bowen H05 (bc), Eric Camden 344 (cl), 344 (c), 344 (cr), RichFranco 004 (c), 004 (cr), H19 (r), H22 (cl), H37 (bc), H40 (br), 46 (cr), 100 (br), 158 (b), 166 (cr), 250 (b), 298 (b), 373 (r), 374 (br), 426 (cl), 426 (c), 429 (cr), 432 (c), 433 (bc), 433 (r), 440 (cr), 440 (bl), 440 (bc), 440 (br), 447 (c), 447 (cr), Ed McDonald 84 (br); Seri O'Neal H12 (tr), 157 (cr), 250 (cr), 312 (r), 326 (r), 368 (t), 368 (br).

Others: Front and Back Cover: Renee Lynn/Tony Stone Worldwide
Stephen Dunn/Allsport U.S.A. 27 (cr); Doug Pensinger/Allsport U.S.A. H07 (cr), 44 (tr); Anthony Neste 190-191 (bg); Art Resource, Inc. H28 (tr) Dave Bartruff/Artists International 498 (br); Bettmann Archive 95 (tr), 130 (cr); Bruce Coleman, Inc. 084-085 (bg), E. Foster/Bruce Coleman, Inc. H10 (tr), D.P. Hershkowitz/Bruce Coleman, Inc. 172 (r), James Lowenthal/Bruce Coleman, Inc. 411 (cr), David Madison/Bruce Coleman, Inc. 376 (br); Corbis Media 138 (br), 139 (cr); Cordon Art BV 230 (br); Corel Co. xviii-1 (cr), 51 (b), 115 (r), 139 (tc), 175 (tr), 175 (tr), 290 (cr), 420 (br), 421 (tr), 446 (tr), 50-51 (bg); Gilbert R. Boucher II/Daily Herald 357 (cr); Focus on Sports 37 (cr); Hershey 291 (cr); Image Bank 454 (cr); HansNeleman/Image Bank 142 (cr); Joseph Enterpises, Inc. 34 (c); Julie Bendel 112 (b), 112 (b), 112 (b); Metatools H26 (br), H26 (bc), H26 (br), H28 (bl), H29 (cr), H53 (r), 76 (b), 102 (br), 119 (br), 163 (r), 181 (l), 183 (bl), 183 (br), 220 (br), 239 (tr), 248 (tl), 303 (c), 387 (br), 438 (bg), Motion Picture & Television Photo Archive 008 (tr), 009 (tr), 9 (cr), 161 (cr), 161 (c); NASA 006 (tr), 006 (b), 008 (bc), H27 (r), H58 (cr), H58 (br), 118 (tr), 408 (cr), 406-407 (bg); Panoramic Images 474-475 (bg); Photo Researchers, Inc. 239 (tc), 441 (tr); Lawrence Migdale/Photo Researchers, Inc. 163 (cr); Richard Parker/Photo Researchers, Inc. H29 (c); Elaine Rebman/Photo Researchers, Inc. 395 (tr); David Weintraub/Photo Researchers, Inc./Photo Researchers, Inc. H33 (cr); PhotoDisc H13 (br), 18 (bc), 20 (br), 22 (tc), H26 (bl), H28 (br), H29 (br), H30 (cr), H43 (r), 45 (br), 50 (br), H62 (r), 90 (br), 90 (bc), 108 (bc), 111 (br), 113 (cr), 113 (cr), (bc)7 (bg), (bc)9 (cr), 152 (bc), 160 (tr), 160 (cr), 161 (t), 166 (tc), 212 (br), 222 (tr), 228 (bc), 235 (cr), 251 (tl), 270 (tr), 271 (cr), 284 (bg), 313 (tr), 324 (br), 327 (cr), 361 (tr), 366 (br), 418 (cr), 495 (c), 499 (cr), 154-155 (bg), 268-269 (b), 438-439 (bg); PhotoEdit H63 (tr), 507 (tr); Michelle Bridwell/PhotoEdit 340 (tr), Mary Kate Denny/PhotoEdit 225 (cr), Myrleen Ferguson/PhotoEdit 258 (cr), Tony Freeman/PhotoEdit H16 (tr), Tony Freeman/PhotoEdit 342 (br), Richard Hutchings/PhotoEdit 360 (cr), Vincent Merritt/PhotoEdit 218 (tr), Michael Newman/PhotoEdit H56 (tr), Frank Siteman/PhotoEdit 348 (tr), D. Young-Wolff/PhotoEdit 284 (c), 21 (tr), 59 (r), 212 (tr), 253 (c), 253 (tr), 390 (tr), 485 (cr), 497 (tr), 501 (cr), 502 (cr)Sears Roebuck & Co. 232 (cr), 232 (cr); David Austen/Stock•Boston 142 (br), Philip Jon Bailey/Stock•Boston H26 (bl), James Blank/Stock•Boston 75 (c), Mark Burnett/Stock•Boston 340 (r), Mark C. Burnett/Stock•Boston 253 (bl), Rob Crandall/Stock•Boston 132 (tr), Bob Daemmrich/Stock•Boston 57 (cr), 310 (tr), 461 (cr), John Elk III/Stock•Boston 464 (tr), Thomas R. Fletcher/Stock•Boston 162 (r), Kevin Horan/Stock•Boston H48 (br), Julie Houck/Stock•Boston 84 (cr), John Lei/Stock•Boston 26 (r), (bc)8 (bc), Richard Pasley/Stock•Boston 341 (tr), Frank Siteman/Stock•Boston 480 (br); Eising/StockFood America H08 (br); SuperStock, Inc xviii-1 (cr), H29 (bc), 30 (b), 068 (br), 98 (cr), 101 (tr), 115 (cr), (bc)8 (tr), 221 (tr), 346 (br), 410 (tr), 445 (br), 452 (br), 455 (tr), 483 (tr), 34-35 (bg); The Lowe Art Museum, The University of Miami 96 (br); The Stock Market (bc)8 (br), Geoffrey Clifford/The Stock Market H48 (tr), AnthonyEdgeworth, Inc./The Stock Market H04 (tr), H04 (tr), H04 (tr), Jon Feingersh/The Stock Market 58 (cr), Mark Gamba/The Stock Market 141 (cr), Dennis M. Gottlieb/The Stock Market H66 (br), Maggio Kalish/The Stock Market 424 (bg), Benjamin Rondel/The Stock Market 40 (t), Pete Saloutos/The Stock Market 343 (cr), Ben Simmons/The Stock Market 336-337 (bg), Peter Steiner/The Stock Market H28 (bc); Swarthout/The Stock Market H25 (cr); Eleanor Thompson/The Stock Market 195 (br), 321 (cr);Ward/The Stock Market 42 (r); Tony Stone Worldwide H05 (tr), 41 (c), 191 (r), 100-101 (bg); Doug Armand/Tony Stone Worldwide 254 (tr); Bob Daemmrich/Tony Stone Worldwide H39 (cr); Bruno De Hogues/Tony Stone Worldwide H47 (cr); Donovan/Tony Stone Worldwide 302 (l); ChipHenderson/Tony Stone Worldwide H06 (tr), H17 (br); Chuck Keeler/Tony Stone Worldwide 182 (b); Steve Leonard/Tony Stone Worldwide H59 (cr); Alan Levenson/Tony Stone Worldwide 76 (t); Mark Lewis/Tony Stone Worldwide 22 (tr); James Martin/Tony Stone Worldwide xviii-1 (bg); Lawrence Migdale/Tony Stone Worldwide 370 (cr); Chris Noble/Tony Stone Worldwide 13 (r),; Dennis O'Clair/Tony Stone Worldwide 38 (tr); Jim Pickerell/Tony Stone Worldwide 496 (tr); Don Smetzer/Tony Stone Worldwide H69 (cr); Thomas Styczynski/Tony Stone Worldwide 50-51 (bg); Tom Tietz/Tony Stone Worldwide 311 (br); Gary Vestal/Tony Stone Worldwide 242 (br); Stuart Westmorland/Tony Stone Worldwide 001 (tr); Art Wolfe/Tony Stone Worldwide H21 (r); Keith Wood/Tony Stone Worldwide H14 (tr); Thomas Zimmerman/Tony Stone Worldwide 41 (t); Uniphoto 010 (cr), 101 (cr), 296 (tr); Renee Comet/Uniphoto 298 (tr); Daemmrich/Uniphoto 72 (bg); Westlight 474-475 (c).

$408 \div 4 = n$, $n = 102$; $6.07 \times$

$631 \div 6 = n$, $n = 105$ r1;

$6.07 \times 17 = n$, $n = 103.19$; 26

$\div 4 = n$, $n = 102$;

$n = 105$ r1; $235 \div$

$6.07 \times 17 = n$, $n =$